THE WRITER'S HANDBOOK

The Writer's Handbook

Edited by

SYLVIA K. BURACK
Editor, The Writer

Publishers   THE WRITER, INC.   Boston

"Piquing the Reader's Curiosity," by Joan Aiken. Copyright © 1995 by Joan Aiken Enterprises Ltd.

"Writing the Feature Article." Copyright © 1993 by Rita Berman.

"Beginning" reprinted from *Writing the World,* by Kelly Cherry, by permission of the University of Missouri Press. Copyright © 1995 by the Curators of the University of Missouri.

"Tricks of the Wizard's Trade," by Susan Dexter. Copyright © 1997 by Susan Dexter.

"A Conversation with Richard Ford," by Matthew Gilbert. Reprinted courtesy of *The Boston Globe.*

"Doing It for Love," by Erica Jong. © 1997, Washington Post Book World Service, Washington Post Writers Group. Reprinted with permission.

"A Conversation with Jane Yolen," by John Koch. Reprinted courtesy of *The Boston Globe.*

"Between the Real and the Believable," by Charles McCarry. Copyright © 1994, Washington Post Book World Service/Washington Post Writers Group. Reprinted with permission.

"The Creative Power of Doing Nothing," by Colleen Mariah Rae, adapted from a chapter in *Movies in the Mind,* by Colleen Mariah Rae, published by Sherman Asher Publishing. Copyright © 1996 by Colleen Mariah Rae.

Library of Congress Catalog Card Number: 36–28596
ISBN: 0-87116-183-4

Printed in The United States of America

CONTENTS

SPECIALIZED FICTION

NONFICTION: ARTICLES AND BOOKS

WHERE TO SELL

Background
for Writers

❏ 1

DOING IT FOR LOVE

BY ERICA JONG

DESPITE ALL THE CYNICAL THINGS WRITERS HAVE SAID ABOUT WRITING for money, the truth is we write for love. That is why it is so easy to exploit us. That is also why we pretend to be hard-boiled, saying things like "No man but a blockhead ever wrote except for money" (Samuel Johnson). Not true. No one but a blockhead ever wrote except for love.

There are plenty of easier ways to make money. Almost anything is less labor-intensive and better paid than writing. Almost anything is safer. Reveal yourself on the page repeatedly, and you are likely to be rewarded with exile, prison or neglect. Ask Dante or Oscar Wilde or Emily Dickinson. Scheme and betray, and you are likely to be rewarded with wealth, publicity and homage. Tell the truth, and you are likely to be a pariah within your family, a semi-criminal to authorities and damned with faint praise by your peers. So why do we do it? Because saying what you think is the only freedom. "Liberty," said Camus, "is the right not to lie."

In a society in which everything is for sale, in which deals and auctions make the biggest news, doing it for love is the only remaining liberty. Do it for love and you cannot be censored. Do it for love and you cannot be stopped. Do it for love and the rich will envy no one more than you. In a world of tuxedos, the naked man is king. In a world of bookkeepers with spreadsheets, the one who gives it away without counting the cost is God.

I seem to have known this from my earliest years. I never remember a time when I didn't write. Notebooks, stories, journals, poems—the act of writing always made me feel centered and whole. It still does. It is my meditation, my medicine, my prayer, my solace. I was lucky enough to learn early (with my first two books of poetry and my first novel) that if you are relentlessly honest about what you feel and fear,

you can become a mouthpiece for something more than your own feelings. People are remarkably similar at the heart level—where it counts.
Writers are born to voice what we all feel. That is the gift. And we
keep it alive by giving it away.

It is a sacred calling. The writers I am most drawn to understand it
as such: Thomas Merton, Pablo Neruda, Emily Dickinson. But one
doesn't always see the calling clearly as one labors in the fields of love.
I often find myself puzzling over the choices a writer is given. When
I am most perplexed, I return to my roots: poetry. The novel is elastic:
It allows for social satire, cooking, toothbrushes, the way we live now.
Poetry, on the contrary, boils down to essences. I feel privileged to
have done both.

And I am grateful to have found my vocation early. I was also blessed
to encounter criticism early. It forced me to listen to my inner voice,
not the roar of the crowd. This is the most useful lesson a writer
can learn.

Lately, we keep hearing dire warnings about the impending death of
the novel. As one who has written frankly autobiographical fiction
(*Fear of Flying*), historical fiction (*Fanny, Serenissima* or *Shylock's
Daughter*) and memoir (*Fear of Fifty* and *The Devil at Large*), I think
I've begun to understand how the process of making fiction differs
from that of making memoir. A memoir is tethered to one's own experience in a particularly limiting way: The observing consciousness of
the book is rooted in a real person. That person may be fascinating,
but he or she can never be as rich and subtle as the characters that
grow out of aspects of the author. In the memoir, the "I" dominates.
In the novel, the "I" is made up of many "I"s. More richness is possible, more points of view, deeper imitation of life.

When I finished *Fear of Fifty*, I felt I had quite exhausted my own
life and might never write another book. What I eventually discovered
was that the process had actually liberated me. Having shed my own
autobiography, I now felt ready to invent in a new way. I wanted to
write a novel about the 20th century and how it affected the lives of
women. I wanted to write a novel about a Jewish family in the century
that nearly saw the destruction of the Jewish people.

I began by reading history and literature for a year. And when I
started to write again, it was in the voice of a woman who might have
been my great-grandmother. Liberated from my place and time, I found

myself inventing a woman's voice quite different from my own. But as I began to fashion this alternate family history, I found myself at play in the fields of my imagination. Characters sprang up like mushrooms after the rain. I couldn't wait to get to work in the morning to see what I thought and who was going to embody it.

Eventually I found I had four heroines, born in different decades, and that they were all mothers and daughters. Each had a distinctive voice and way of looking at the world. Each was me and not me.

Graham Greene once said, "The more the author knows of his own character the more he can distance himself from his invented characters and the more room they have to grow in."

That seems to me precisely right. A novelist's identity is fixed. Her character, however, can fly.

A character may even access some deep memory in the writer's brain that seemed lost forever. Fictional characters excavate real memories. Flaubert, after all, claimed to be Emma Bovary and gave her his restlessness and discontent. In some ways an author may be freer to expose himself in a character unlike himself. There is liberty behind a mask. The mask may become the condition for speaking the truth.

The line between novel and autobiography has never been as blurry as it is in our century. And this is probably a good thing. The novel endures because it mimics truth. So if we find truths in autobiography in our age, even fiction will come to mimic that genre. And genres themselves matter less and less. The most enduring books of the modern era are, like *Ulysses,* full of exposition, narrative, dramatic writing and even poetry.

As a reader, I want a book to kidnap me into its world. Its world must make my so-called real world seem flimsy. Its world must lure me to return. When I close the book, I should feel bereft.

How rare this is and how grateful I am to find it. The utter trust that exists between reader and author is like the trust between lovers. If I feel betrayed by the author, I will never surrender to him or her again.

That trust is why it is so hard to start a new book. You must find the right voice (or voices) for the timbre that can convince the reader to give himself up to you. Sometimes it takes years to find the tone of voice that unlocks the story.

The books we love best kidnap us with the first line. "Whether I shall turn out to be the hero of my own life, or whether that station will be held by anybody else, these pages must show" (*David Copperfield*). "You don't know about me, without you have read a book by the name of *The Adventures of Tom Sawyer,* but that ain't no matter" (*Huckleberry Finn*). It's not only the question of an arresting opening—the writer's best trick—but of letting the main character's quirks show, too. I tried it myself in *Fear of Flying:* "There were 117 analysts on the Pan Am flight to Vienna, and I'd been treated by at least six of them." And it's easier to do in the first person than in the third.

But as I said in the beginning, you must do it for love. If you do it for money, no money will ever be enough, and eventually you will start imitating your first successes, straining hot water through the same old teabag. It doesn't work with tea, and it doesn't work with writing. You must give all you have and never count the cost. ("Sit down at the typewriter and open a vein," as Red Smith said.)

Every book I have written has subsumed all the struggles of the years in which I wrote it. I don't know how to hold back. Editing comes only after the rush of initial feeling. I end up cutting hundreds of pages sometimes. But in the writing process, I let it all hang out. Later I and my editor chop.

Generosity is the soul of writing. You write to give something. To yourself. To your reader.

❑ 2

BEGINNING

BY KELLY CHERRY

I AM A WRITER. I WRITE THOSE WORDS—"I AM A WRITER"—JUST LIKE that, as if it were as easy as that, or as if it mattered. It has not, in truth, been easy, but it does matter. I *trust* that it matters *literarily,* but I *know* that it matters *literally.*

The house in which I am writing is set in the middle of an arboretum; if you don't know to look for it, you're not likely to find it. The postman refuses to deliver packages to the door: too long a hike, too many mosquitoes. I don't mind. I welcome the solitude, the temporary lull in my life.

Why do I sit here writing? What earthly purpose does my writing serve? For a moment, let's set aside the conventional answers. The conventional answers include communication (as of an idea), aesthetic gratification (the reader's, or just the writer's), even art for art's sake. Let's even set aside the work's own demand to be brought into being. All of these are true answers but do not go beyond the specific case. We're seeking something deeper, something broader on which the whole of literature is based. Well, as you can guess, it's not for money. Some few writers do earn newsworthy incomes, of course; not very many serious ones do, and hardly any innovative ones do. A few more earn sufficient incomes because they were brought along by publishers when the publishing industry was willing to think of an advance not as a down payment on subsidiary rights but as an investment in an author's career; these writers were given time to develop a steady readership. Most of us, if we depended on our writing for an income, couldn't keep body and soul together.

Not long ago, as I was feeling very tired, I decided to figure out how many words I'd written in the past ten years alone. It came to one million finished words, or minimally five to ten million draft words, or one million draft words every one to two years, not counting personal and professional correspondence and research notes. I teach full time. When I teach fiction writing, I average, per semester, three thousand pages of student manuscripts to read and mark in sentence-by-sentence detail. That is excluding non-degree students, independent study tutorials, and the odd novel in the anonymous knapsack. Like most writers, I also give readings, serve on panels, do workshops, apply for grants—a series of time-consuming steps that might be called The American Literary Soft-Shoe Shuffle.

Looking at those figures made me proud, but also tireder. I kept thinking how, if I were a different kind of writer, or perhaps Joyce Carol Oates, they would have added up to 730 books, all published, instead of 9½, of which 4 have been published and 5½ are in my desk drawer. But my case—this specific case that is mine—is no different from any other writer's; what I do and experience professionally is no different from what other writers do and experience. This is not just my life; it's a writer's life, and after all, a writer doesn't just choose it; clearly, she does anything she can to be allowed to live it, including—frequently with the secretly compelling sense of being a bit of an adventurer—throwing the rest of her life completely out of alignment.

So. The question returns. Why?

Why does anyone consent to the emotional, financial, spiritual, and even physical contortions that are necessary in order to lead the writer's life in America today? There are almost no grants. Only a few serious writers receive large advances; often, there are no advances at all. But we are blockheads, Dr. Johnson, who would write, who do write, for free! We would give our work away! Yet all too often, manuscripts filed in our desk drawers remain in our desk drawers. We write, most of us writers, without hope of publication or comprehension, happy and grateful when they come but not daring to assume either. We give our lives to our work. Even my dog, who wishes I'd stop this thing I'm doing and come play with him, puts his front paws in my lap and looks up at me, asking, Why?

The answer's as close on the question's heels as Duncan is on mine.

The answer is, *For the same reason I am telling you what my life as a writer is like.*

You had, most probably, no idea who I am; now, like it or not, you're stuck with an idea of me. Not necessarily—though possibly also—an idea of mine, but necessarily an idea of me. You now know that there exists at least one person with the inner dimensions I have described. You may or may not be interested in my life, but that's not the point; and I might have lied—but I haven't. The point is simply that you are now obliged to recognize the writer of this piece as a conscious being.

We are all of us poets and storytellers, making literature of our lives, and when we listen to one another, we learn, through that exercise of the imaginative faculty, that this planet is a reality in at least more than one mind.

A writer is someone who makes the tracks of her mind's thinking visible for anyone who wants to follow her. This doesn't mean she is limited to autobiography; far from it. She *can* imagine the imaginations of others, even the imaginations of imaginary people, called characters or personae.

Critics, we may say, are census-takers.

But the writer knows that these imaginary constructs are dependent for their being on language. Therefore she agonizes over her verbs; she frets over her nouns; she restructures her sentences, paragraphs, scenes—and still she can't help knowing that no matter what she finally decides, everything hinges on whether it's Tuesday or Wednesday, and what she ate for breakfast. The only way I can say I sit *here* writing is *by* writing. Writing locates the *here,* and by unavoidable implication, a *there.*

I stand and stretch, look out the kitchen window. With the porch light on, I can see black oak, white oak, bur oak, black cherry, and shagbark hickory. Arrowwood and elderberry bushes are clumps of shadow; flowering raspberry surrounds the house. Asleep or skittering at the edges of the lawn are possums, foxes, rabbits, woodchucks. I can hear the shy whistle of the phoebe and the evening flute concerto of the woodthrush, and in the distance, the low thrum of Beltline traffic.

I turn back to the kitchen. The lighted fish in the aquarium are living their silent lives. Do you know that the female swordtail has no tail? That, deprived of a mate, she may change her sex?

Black oak, white oak, bur oak, black cherry, and shagbark. These trees, whether or not they grow *really,* independent of perception, now grow in your brain. I've planted them there; my words are seeds. We are rooted in our language. Whether or not this world exists independ- ently of our consciousness is a question for the idealists and the empiricists still to debate; but your consciousness of my consciousness has unquestionably grown. It buds; it will leaf.

The world is populated by people who become human through their imaginative awareness of others' inner lives. It is the writer who works hardest to heighten, provoke, prod, even create, germinate and engender that awareness. What joy, what privilege!—to be so essential to existence. This is the writer's earthly purpose and her cause, which she serves gladly, in any circumstances, with a sense of its utter and transcending importance. That's why I said "matters." That's why I said "literally." In the beginning *is* the word.

❏ 3

WHAT EMILY DICKINSON KNEW

BY HELEN MARIE CASEY

IF THERE'S ONE THING EMILY DICKINSON KNEW FOR SURE, IT WAS what a good poem should do. "If I feel physically as if the top of my head were taken off, I know that is poetry," she wrote.

Dickinson was attempting to describe for her sister-in-law the power of poetry to envelop and even to devastate the reader (or listener). Her physical description was an effort to convey that successful poems are not effete passages or bookish exercises; they are chillingly annihilating. They have the power to alter us irrevocably.

Poetry, the Belle of Amherst knew, is that form of communication in which words are never simple equivalents of experience or perception. The words themselves, the words as words, have a life as sounds, as images, as the means for generating a series of associations.

Contemporary poet and critic Ann Lauterbach claims that "For poets, the world is apprehended *as* language . . . Every object in the world is simultaneously itself and its word." It is impossible to put too much weight on the importance of each individual word. Yet, paradoxically, poetry is that art form in which what is unsaid is often as important—or more important—than what is said. And, to the bewilderment of some, it is a literary genre in which the voice, the tone, the texture, and the poetic form—that is, the way of saying what the poem is saying—are also fundamental parts of what is being said.

Poets are certainly not the only writers to concern themselves with the simultaneous life of language as symbol *and* as nonreferential but it is poets who most seem to insist on seeing and hearing words as if each is a multi-faceted gem that has, in the hands of the skillful artist, the capacity to resonate and to go in multiple directions at once.

Take, for example, the lines that begin the Wallace Stevens poem, "The Course of a Particular":

> Today the leaves cry, hanging on branches swept by wind,
> Yet the nothingness of winter becomes a little less.
> It is still full of icy shades and shapen snow.

Syntactically, the lines are constructed like direct prose statements. Yet, we know that leaves do not, in fact, cry. We recognize that we are dealing with language used imaginatively, language used to do something other than simply deliver a message.

We recognize immediately that mood will be part of what we derive from the poem and that the images—*wind, winter, icy shades, snow, leaves crying*—will be part of the way the poem says what it wants to say.

We recognize in words like *still, shades,* and *shapen snow,* a recurrent "s" sound. Looking back over the first two lines we hear additional "s" sounds in the endings of the words *leaves, branches, nothingness, becomes, less,* and *shades.*

The repetition of "win" in *wind* and *winter* is the repetition of a sound that requires us to blow out as wind itself blows.

In poetry, the sounds, shadings, color, and associative values of the words are every bit as important as the specific denotative meanings. This does not mean that the language of poetry is imprecise. On the contrary, there is absolutely nothing arbitrary about a poet's choice of vocabulary or about the manner in which the poet arranges and juxtaposes the words selected. There is nothing superfluous in poems that work.

The reason many readers keep their distance from poetry is probably best captured by the observation of a student who wrote, "The trouble with poems is they start out to be about one thing, and then they end up being about something else." What the student understood is that part of the magic of poetry is its ability to sustain multiple levels of meaning, to be at once literally what it seems to be and also to exist, because of the power of suggestion, on a figurative level. What is frustrating to her is the richness and texture of a successful poem. What she thinks she would like is a straightforward description in which everything is laid out clearly.

It is the misperception that poems ought to be easy to apprehend that leads so many beginning poets to mistrust the powers of allusion and suggestion and to err by telling all. They bore readers and deny them the thrill of discovery. In addition, they often believe that ambiguity is some kind of writing sin and fail to see that, in fact, intentional ambiguity can be the source of irony, humor, foreboding, and thematic weight in a poem.

If there were a single question that might be a productive spring-board to the creation of richer poems, it might well be this: Have I wholly engaged the imagination of my readers by creating the path we shall traverse together and then purposefully stopped short on it, allowing the reader to go on without me?

There is, of course, no single solution to the question of how to write effectively, but I am inclined to trust Marianne Moore's observation in her poem, "Bowls": "Only so much colour shall be revealed as is necessary to the picture."

❏ 4

BETWEEN THE REAL AND THE BELIEVABLE

BY CHARLES McCARRY

SOME TWENTY YEARS AGO I PUBLISHED A NOVEL IN WHICH ONE OF the characters, a pathologically jealous young woman, was so obsessed with her husband, an American spy who kept his operational life secret from her, that she embarked on a series of joyless adulteries in order to accumulate secrets of her own, and so become his romantic equal.

Soon after this work appeared, I found myself at a dinner party in Northampton, Mass., seated next to an agitated feminist, who, like my unhappy character, was young and beautiful and a recent bride. Throughout dinner, she told me how much she hated the girl in the book, whose behavior she had found to be utterly unrealistic and an insult to women—"male chauvinist propaganda," she called it.

I was not surprised by the onslaught. For a writer in America, going out to dinner is like living as an American in Europe: Total strangers think they can say anything they like to you. Still, I had trouble grasping the point. Why did a 1950s fictional character have to conform to an ideological model that had not yet been invented at the period in which the novel took place?

I asked my critic to tell me in plain English why she disliked and distrusted my character so. After a moment of angry silence the woman threw half a glass of California burgundy on my best gray suit and replied, "Because I used to be just like her!"

On the way home, my wife wisely told me I should take this happening as a compliment. But there was more to it than that, as is perhaps demonstrated by the fact that I have never even considered using the wine episode as a scene in a novel. Truth in life and truth in art are not the same, and for the reader—that passive collaborator who must complete the author's work by developing it in his mind as if it were a strip of exposed film—suspension of belief is quite different from believing what one is expected to believe.

Unlike speech, which slips into the consciousness obsequiously through the ear, the written word clambers into the mind through the window of the eye. It is more likely to be welcome if it wears the mask and costume of a harmless guest at a masked ball than if it carries the blackjack and clinking tool kit of a real burglar. People do not like to be surprised, but fiction that abjures the element of surprise is mere bedtime story.

Over the years I have moved back and forth between novels and nonfiction, including collaborations on the memoirs of well-known public figures—"like a polygamist moving from bedchamber to bedchamber," as a friend, monogamous in literary matters, put it. Others have suggested that what I learn from writing about the real world must be of direct use to me in writing novels.

Not really. For one thing, writing is famously a cure: By the mystical process of transforming the invisible contents of the mind into black ink on a white page, you get rid of the damn stuff forever. For another, though reality checks are part of the process, no true novel can be made from anything but the imagination and its silent partner, experience, which is not at all the same thing as research.

Knowledge of the world of affairs does confer certain secondary benefits on the novelist: He learns for a fact that the great are only the small made large. But there is very little he can carry back and forth between the two forms, though they are much alike from a technical standpoint—he uses the technique of fiction (action proceeds from character, dialogue reveals inner meaning, surprise is the soul of narrative) to write about real people in real life, and the fundamental problem is the same in both forms: The greater the verisimilitude, the greater the will to resist it.

For a decade at the height of the Cold War, I worked abroad under cover as an intelligence agent. After I resigned, intending to spend the rest of my life writing fiction and knowing what tricks the mind can play when the gates are thrown wide open, as they are by the act of writing, between the imagination and that part of the brain in which information is stored, I took the precaution of writing a closely remembered narrative of my clandestine experiences. After correcting the manuscript, I burned it.

What I kept for my own use was the atmosphere of secret life: How it worked on the five senses and what it did to the heart and mind. All the rest went up in flames, setting me free henceforth to make it all up. In all important matters, such as the creation of characters and the invention of plots, with rare and minor exceptions, that is what I have done. And, as might be expected, when I have been weak enough to use something that really happened as an episode in a novel, it is that piece of scrap, buried in a landfill of the imaginary, readers invariably refuse to believe.

□ 5

SERENDIPITY AND THE WRITER

BY C. J. NEWTON

> **serendipity,** *n.* [coined by Horace Walpole (c. 1754) after his tale *The Three Princes of Serendip* (i.e. Ceylon), who made such discoveries.] an apparent aptitude for making fortunate discoveries accidentally.
> —*Webster's Dictionary of the English Language, Unabridged*

RECENTLY WHEN DISCUSSING MY WRITING WITH A FRIEND I sketched out my plans to finish one novel and start another, and gave specific dates for each stage. My friend was rather surprised at this "conscious control" of creativity. After we spoke, I realized that a writer must combine rational structure and method—for example, writing at a certain hour every day, or committing to write so many words per week—with the unplanned, magical side of writing that so often surprises us. We need to be open to serendipity.

The unsummoned inspirational component of writing is a subject for research by psychologists, a source of wonder for those who see it happen, and a mystery frequently to writers ourselves. I am not recommending that you dissect every creative experience. However, it can be useful to look at the circumstances that led to your inspiration, to the particular time and place at which the sudden torrent of associations, images, and dialogues opened like a cloudburst. You may find the influence of serendipity.

In my own case serendipity prompted me to visit a town, which inspired a novel, which led to another novel, which led to my first fiction sale.

For years while living in San Francisco I "intended" to visit Half Moon Bay, about 30 miles south. After eight years of intending, I drove there one evening on a twisting road through groves of eucalyptus trees. Through a clearing, I beheld the Pacific Ocean, and a rich small town. In a flash I *felt* a mystery novel—characters, settings, and plot outline—set there. I still can't explain it.

Here is the serendipitous part. Half Moon Bay has a Portuguese community that sponsors a picturesque annual parade. As I subsequently researched the town for my mystery, I became interested in Portugal's history.

And later, when I wanted to write a novel satirizing attorneys, I was able to apply my knowledge of Portuguese names, references, and culture in a convincing depiction of a fictional republic founded by Portugal in Central America. The result was *Costa Azul,* which I wrote after the mystery (but which found a publisher first). Half Moon Bay was a "fortunate discovery" indeed.

Travel

If you can afford it, travel to faraway places is very stimulating. Hearing French spoken on the busy streets of Montreal, seeing otherwise-modern people in Montevideo enjoying *maté* tea made from traditional gourds, hiking cobblestoned streets in Lisbon, passing café patrons who may be lovers, spies, or solid civil servants—all these can add fuel to your creative fire.

Adventure can be as close as your neighboring town. Like most teenagers I yearned to escape from my hometown for more exciting places. Yet I wasn't far from New Windsor, New York, the site of George Washington's last winter as Continental commander. Less famous than Valley Forge, the New Windsor Cantonment offered high drama as Washington battled his final enemies, and intrigue and boredom, as he waited to sign the Treaty of Paris that ended the war. I felt that this would be a perfect setting for a historical novel.

Take a new look at your neighboring towns. You may find rich material for historical or contemporary fiction.

Getting there

Tour Books from the American Automobile Association are great resources. Free to members, they include richly informative descriptions of overlooked gems like local museums and historical houses, complete with opening hours and admission prices.

Use public transportation. Once you accept the waiting as constructive idleness—a gift of time when you are free to let your mind wander

or compose—you may actually enjoy the journey as much as the destination. It is pleasurable to leave the driving to the bus or train driver,
and to look out the window. If public transportation is not practical,
then drive to a reasonable point and walk the rest of the way. You'll
gain many impressions exploring the site on foot. Always bring a notebook to record them.

Feeding your creativity

Here is an outline for using an excursion to feed your creativity:

1. Carefully observe the physical look of the place: the grade of
descent to a beach, or, in an urban setting, the names of streets and
the architecture.

2. As an exercise, narrate your own movements. Try a first-person
point of view, then switch to third person to describe your actions from
the outside.

3. Observe people buying, selling, fishing, talking on cell phones,
cutting hair, or unloading trucks. File them as background to your
fictional construction.

4. Sketch a fictional character and motive for his or her being there,
and walk the character through a few scenes.

5. Collect brochures and newspapers. Visit local bookstores, libraries, and museums.

6. If possible, travel home by a different route from the one you
took to get there.

By varying your routine journeys, you can stimulate that part of
your mind where inspiration visits. All roads can lead to serendipity.

❑ 6

A WRITER'S BEST FRIEND

BY JULIUS GOLDSTEIN

AFTER FORTY AND MORE YEARS OF THE PRECISE AND CONFINING work of a dentist I resolved to free myself; to go from filling teeth to fulfilling myself. I decided after much soul searching to become a writer.

I started writing in a tentative way, confronting all the problems of a beginning writer. My writing rambled, I preached too much, I explained too much, and I told too much. I attended writer's workshops where I exposed my vulnerable ego to the eyes and ears of mentors and tormentors.

My writing improved slowly, but my self-editing was weak. I plodded along, just not able to break through the quagmire of mediocrity.

While reading my latest work aloud, my dog Fred (under my desk) started scratching my shoes. I pushed him away and started to read aloud again. Again at the same sentence, Fred started scratching my shoes. I realized that I had a grammatical error at just the spot on the paper where Fred had started scratching. Just a coincidence, of course. How could a dumb mutt have any literary talent?

I continued to read aloud. A low growling arose from under my desk. I looked down at my script, and I perceived that my chief character was not credible. I made the correction. Excitement mounted in me. Did Fred have an instinctive flair for literary criticism? I dismissed the thought as being unworthy of consideration.

I began typing early in the morning. My words just klunked along. My dog started yelping without letup. I read at the point where his yelping began, and no question—the klunkiness began there. I rewrote it. Fred still yelped, but more softly. Another revision, and Fred gurgled with delight. My words soared and sang. There was no longer any doubt; my dog was a skilled editor.

At my writer's workshop session my instructor commented on the

20

vast improvement in my writing. She was proud of the influence the class had on my writing; I knew better. I felt guilty about not giving Fred some credit.

After a particularly grueling, growling writing session I became annoyed with Fred's constant barking at my story. I could no longer tolerate his criticism, so I locked him out of the room.

The following day when I returned to the final draft, there were chew marks all over it, with certain parts gnawed into illegibility. On rereading it I realized how much more smoothly the words flowed than the day before. Fred had taken it upon himself to cut all the fat out of my story. I had been chewed out by editors before, but never like this!

I now realized what a gifted editor I possessed, and I officially acknowledged his talent and dedication by dropping the first two letters from his name. I now addressed him as Ed. I purchased a remnant of an authentic oriental rug for Ed's office under my desk and hand-printed an official sign, "The Editor Is In." In gratitude he licked my shoes.

I no longer received publishers' rejections. My problem was finding time for the assignments that poured in.

About a month later I noticed that Ed was listless. When I read aloud his ears did not perk up. The vitality in his bark was gone. Was Ed suffering from "Editor's Burnout"? I could not forgive myself. In my desire for recognition, I had driven him to this state. I consulted with all the leading veterinarians, to no avail.

Ed passed away recently, a martyr to the cause of good editing. An autopsy verified the cause of death: documentitis. He had died from ingesting too many imperfect sentences.

In a shady corner of my backyard on a polished piece of black granite stands the following inscription:

To dearest Ed, who's gone away
You made me the writer I am today.

❑ 7

THE JOURNEY INWARD

BY KATHERINE PATERSON

"DO YOU KEEP A JOURNAL?" NO, I ANSWER A BIT RED-FACED, BECAUSE I know that *real* writers keep voluminous journals so fascinating that the world can hardly wait until they die to read the published versions. But it's not quite true. I do make journal-like entries in used schoolgirl spiral notebooks, on odd scraps of paper, in fairly anonymous computer files. These notations are all so embarrassing that I am hoping for at least a week's notice to hunt them down and destroy all the bits and pieces before my demise.

I write these entries, you see, only when I can't write what I want to write. If they were collected and published, the reader could logically conclude that I was not only totally inept as a writer but that I lacked integration of personality at best, and at worst, was dangerously depressed.

If I had kept a proper journal, these neurotic passages would be seen in context, but such is not the case. If my writing is going well, why would I waste time talking about it? I'd be doing it. So if these notes survive me, they will give whatever segment of posterity might happen upon them a very skewed view of my mental state.

The reason I am nattering on about this is that I have come to realize that I am not alone. As soon as my books (after years of struggle) began to be published, I started to get questions from people that I had trouble answering in any helpful way: "Do you use a pen and pad or do you write on a typewriter?" (Nowadays, "computer" is always included in this question, but I'm talking about twenty years ago.)

"Whatever works," I'd say. Which was true. Sometimes I wrote first drafts by hand, sometimes on the typewriter; often I'd switch back and forth in an attempt to keep the flow going. The questioner would thank me politely, but, looking back, I know now that I had failed her.

"Do you have a regular schedule everyday or do you just write when you feel inspired?" the person would ask earnestly. I am ashamed to say, I would often laugh at this. "If I wrote only when I was inspired," I'd say, "I'd write about three days a year. Books don't get written in three days a year."

Occasionally, the question (and now, I know, all these were the same question) would be framed more baldly. "How do you begin?" "Well," I would say, "you sit down in front of the typewriter, roll in a sheet of paper and . . ."

If I ever gave any of you one of those answers, or if any other writer has ever given you similar tripe, I would like to apologize publicly. I was asked, in whatever disguise, a truly important question, and I finessed the answer into a one-liner.

How *do* you begin? It is not an idle or trick question. It is a cry from the heart.

I know. That's what all those aborted journal notes are about. They are the cry when I simply cannot begin. When no inspiration ever comes, when neither pen, nor pencil, nor typewriter, nor state-of-the-art computer can unloose what's raging about inside me.

So what happens? Well, something must. I've begun and ended over and over again through the years. There are several novels out there with my name on the cover. Somehow I figured out how to begin. Once the book is finished, the memory of the effort dims—until you're trying to begin the next one.

Well, I'm there now. I have to begin again. What have I done those other times? How have I gotten from that feeling of stony hope-lessness? How do I break through that barrier as hard as sunbaked earth to the springs of creativity?

Sometimes, I know, I have a conversation with myself on paper:

What's the matter?
What do you mean "what's the matter?" You know perfectly well. I want to write, but I can't think of a thing to say.
Not a single thing?
Not a single thing worth saying.
You're scared what you might say won't be up to snuff? Scared people might laugh at you? Scared you might despise yourself?
Well, it is scary. How do I know there's still anything in here?
You don't. You just have to let it flow. If you start judging, you'll cut

off the flow—you've already cut off the flow from all appearances—
before it starts.

Grump.

Ah yes, we never learn, do we? Whatever happened to that wonderful idea of getting up so early in the morning that the critic in you was
still asleep?

How do I know it will work this time?

You won't know if you don't try. But then, trying is risky, and you
do seem a bit timid to me.

You don't know what it's like pouring out your guts to the world.

I don't?

Well, you don't care as much as I do.

Of course I do. I just happen to know that it is so important to my
psychic health to do this that I'm willing to take the risk. You, my
friend, seem to want all the creative juices inside you to curdle and
poison the whole system.

You're nothing but a two-bit psychologist.

Well, I've been right before.

But how do I begin?

I don't know. Why don't we just get up at five tomorrow, come to
the machine and type like fury for an hour and see what happens?
Could be fun. Critic won't be up, and we won't ever have to show
anybody what we've done.

Now you understand why I have to burn this stuff before I die.
My posthumous reputation as a sane person of more than moderate
intelligence hangs in the balance. But living writers, in order to keep
writing, have to forget about posthumous reputations. We have to become, quite literally, like little children. We have to remember our
early griefs and embarrassments. Talk aloud to ourselves. Make up
imaginary companions. We have to play.

Have you ever watched children fooling with play dough or finger-
paint? They mess around to see what will emerge, and they fiddle with
what comes out. Occasionally, you will see a sad child, one that has
decided beforehand what he wants to do. He stamps his foot because
the picture on the page or the green blob on the table falls short of the
vision in his head. But he is, thankfully, a rarity, already too concerned
with adult approval.

The unspoiled child allows herself to be surprised with what comes out of herself. She takes joy in the material, patting it and rolling it and shaping it. She is not too quick to name it. And, unless some grownup interferes, she is not a judge but a lover of whatever comes from her heart through her hands. This child knows that what she has created is marvelous simply because she has made it. No one else could make this wonderful thing because it has come out of her.

What treasures we have inside ourselves—not just joy and delight but also pain and darkness. Only I can share the treasures of the human spirit that are within me. No one else has *these* thoughts, *these* feelings, *these* relationships, *these* experiences, *these* truths.

How do I begin? You could start, as I often do, by talking to yourself. The dialogue may help you understand what is holding you back. Are you afraid that deep down inside you are really shallow? That when you take that dark voyage deep within yourself, you will find there is no treasure to share? Trust me. There is. Don't let your fear stop you. Begin early in the morning before that critical adult within wakes up. Like a child, pour out what is inside you, not listening to anything but the stream of life within you. Read Dorothea Brande's classic *On Becoming a Writer,* in which she suggests that you put off for several days reading what you have written in the wee hours. Then when you do read it you may discern a repeated theme pointing you to what you want to begin writing about.

Begin, Anne Lamott suggests in her wonderful book *Bird by Bird,* in the form of a letter. Tell your child or a trusted friend stories from your past. Exploring childhood is almost always an effective wedge into what's inside you. And didn't you mean to share those stories with your children someday anyhow?

While I was in the midst of revising this article, my husband happened to bring home Julia Cameron's book, *The Artist's Way.* Cameron suggests three pages of longhand every morning as soon as you get up. I decided to give the "morning pages" a try and heartily recommend the practice, though these pages, too, will need to be destroyed before I die.

When I was trying to begin the book which finally became *Flip-Flop Girl* (and you should see the anguished notes along the way!), I just began writing down the name of every child I could remember from the fourth grade at Calvin H. Wiley School. Sometimes I appended a note that explained why that child's name was still in my head. Early-morning exercises explored ways the story might go, and I rejected most of them, but out of those fourth-grade names and painful betrayals a story began to grow. Judging from the notes, it was over a year in developing and many more months in the actual writing. But I did begin, and I did finish. There's a bit of courage for the next journey inward.

Now it's your turn. Bon voyage.

□ 8

"I" Is Not Me

By Margaret Maron

RECENTLY, AN IRATE READER TOOK ME TO TASK FOR MY NOVEL, *SHOOT-ing at Loons*. Offended when my first-person narrator remarked that someone was "not much taller than me," the reader acidly inquired if grammar were no longer important.

"It is clear that you don't know any better than to let your character—a judge with a law degree, for heaven's sake!—use bad grammar," he fumed, "but why didn't your editor catch it? Don't editors edit anymore?"

Fortunately for me, my editor is more astute than that particular reader. She knows the stylistic difference between an author's formal voice and a character's narrative voice and would never try to smooth away my "I" character's verbal idiosyncrasies. Nevertheless, that letter did make me stop and reconsider how, as writers, we often do use a first-person voice as a shorthand method to convey character and personality without actually having to spell them out.

The omniscient author's voice pays strict attention to the laws of grammar and punctuation; the narrative voice pays strict attention to the character of the "I" who is telling the story.

As someone who reads Fowler's *Modern English Usage* for sheer pleasure, I do know the difference between subjective and objective pronouns; and yes, I do try to use them correctly when writing third-person or formally. (Actually, Fowler prefers "Not much taller than me" over "Not much taller than I," which "strikes the reader as pedantic.") But that is neither here nor there. The truth is that when I write first-person fiction, I deliberately mimic language that will let my readers know this person's social class, present emotional status, and whether he is likeable or mean-minded, brave or timorous, a whining pessimist or a cheerful optimist.

This is especially useful in the short story form, where every word counts.

In my short story, "Deadhead Coming Down," no third-person description of an easily bored trucker can match the immediacy of his
own voice saying,

> There's not one damn thing exotic about driving a eighteen-wheeler. Next
> to standing on a assembly line and screwing Bolt A into Hole C like my no-
> 'count brother-in-law, driving a truck's got to be the dullest way under God's
> red sun to make a living. 'Specially if it's just up and down the eastern seaboard
> like me.

The trucker speaks in short blunt words and his coarse denial of his
brother-in-law's worth foreshadows his truly callous actions in the
story.

Conversely, when I wrote "On Windy Ridge," I hoped that the
slower, dreamlike pacing and choice of elegiac language would help
convey the image of a middle-aged mountain woman who possesses
both intelligence and a slightly psychic sensitivity:

> Waiting is more tiresome than doing, and I was weary. Bone weary . . . but
> my eyes lifted to the distant hills, beyond trees that burned red and gold, to
> where the ridges misted into smoky blue. The hills were real and everlasting
> and I had borrowed of their strength before.

In *Shooting at Loons,* the novel that so exercised my overly pedantic
reader, my narrator is Deborah Knott, a district court judge in her
mid-thirties. Even though she knows better, Deborah is a breezily colloquial Southerner who makes grammatical slips because she is the
daughter and sister of semiliterate dirt farmers who will use dialect,
split infinitives, double negatives, sentence fragments, dangling partici-
ples, and a host of other colorful grammatical errors till the day they
die. True, she has a law degree; true, she is a judge. Neither has turned
her into a grammarian. (I was once sent to the principal's office because I would not agree when the English teacher insisted that *it's* was
the possessive of *it.* She, too, possessed an advanced degree.)

With one foot in North Carolina's agrarian past and the other firmly
planted in its high-tech present, Deborah is never going to "get above
her raising." Not if I have anything to say about it.

After all, I have a classic precedent for claiming the right to a narrative voice that is not necessarily my own.

In a preface to one of his books many years ago, a certain writer
used his formal voice to explain the technical side of creation: "In this

book a number of dialects are used . . . . The shadings have not been done in a haphazard fashion, or by guesswork, but painstakingly, and with the trustworthy guidance and support of personal familiarity with these several forms of speech." Then switching into his first-person narrative voice, that same author wrote, "You don't know about me without you have read a book by the name of *The Adventures of Tom Sawyer,* but that ain't no matter."

Had Mark Twain written the whole book as omniscient and highly literate author, *The Adventures of Huckleberry Finn* would be a forgotten piece of 19th-century esoterica. Instead he gave us Huck's distinctly ungrammatical *"I"* voice and the book remains a living, breathing masterpiece a hundred years later.

❏ 9

THE CREATIVE POWER OF DOING NOTHING

BY COLLEEN MARIAH RAE

LET'S SAY YOU'VE BEEN WORKING ON A STORY. IT'S COMING, BUT IT'S not coming fast enough. What will speed things up? Surprisingly: *Doing nothing*. Now's the time to turn to your unconscious and to let it do the work for you.

This is often the hardest part of the writing process but an essential part of the creative process. For a week, allow the unconscious to do its work. And, paradoxically, without any conscious effort on your part, your creative product will grow.

The trick is to do nothing long enough for the work to come to fruition in your unconscious. But because this is hard, what follow are some tips for *what to do when you're doing nothing; and how to do nothing so effectively that your story will pop from you full-blown.*

So, for the first tip: *What to do when you're doing nothing.*

It's always important to know where you're going, if you have any hope of reaching your goal. Here, the goal's a finished story that pops like Athena from the head of Zeus, and the only way to achieve this is through doing things that unclutter the unconscious sufficiently to allow it to devote full-time to the job.

This is the time to cook, build a model, swim, play chess, hike, paint, play music, or repair a toaster—whatever it is that puts you into that "time out of time state," where you lose all track of time. What you're looking for are activities that allow you to *immerse* yourself in an experience without thought. Whatever takes you away from the ceaseless round of chatter unclutters the unconscious. What works for you? Include it in your day, every day, because each day takes you through the same cycle of creativity in an abbreviated way.

For me, painting is the best "immersion" activity. I can so lose myself in the process that when I stop, I discover surprisingly that hours have

30

passed. While I'm painting, I'm not thinking. But I'm not floating in a sea of no-thought: I'm doing what Aldous Huxley thought so important he had birds in his fictional country in *Island* crying "Attention, attention, attention." I am focused in on what I'm doing with a highly concentrated attention.

So that's what to do when you're doing nothing: anything that allows you to immerse yourself fully in the activity and at the same time challenges you enough, but not too much. Do anything, that is, but write. During this stage of the process, do anything but write—even one word. And, don't tell your story to anyone. Telling it will dissipate the energy. Keeping your story inside creates a pressure-cooker sensation—eventually you will feel as though you're going to explode if you can't let your story out. And that's the sensation you're aiming for.

Now for the second tip: *How to do nothing so effectively that your story will pop from you full-blown.* This is often the most fun, because it isn't so "hands-off" as immersion. You can really feel you're doing something to work with your unconscious—even though you *are* letting go and trusting the unconscious to do the work for you. I call this *active incubation,* because you're building bridges between the conscious and the unconscious mind.

One of these bridges you probably know well: How often have you said, "Let me sleep on it"? It's one of the best problem-solving tools we have. And it works for writing so well that I've come to believe that I couldn't write a darn thing worth publishing if I couldn't sleep on it. I'll go to sleep unclear of how to proceed in a story and wake in the morning with the answer.

You can also build bridges during your waking hours. Either way, it's still the same process: You have to silence your analytical mind long enough to let the unconscious speak. You have probably had a few such experiences: Names you couldn't remember an hour before come to you as soon as you get into the mind-numbing rhythm of vacuuming, or as you're washing the car, you recall what it is you forgot to buy at the store.

I make use of active incubation every day I write. I don't take a shower until I get stuck in my writing stint for the day, because invariably it's in the shower that ideas pop up. My writing journals are filled with "shower thought" notations.

Other things that shift me from that "stuck" analytical place also include water: I love to sit by a waterfall or any running water—even the fountains in shopping malls will do. Find your own. Some writers get unstuck sitting by a fire; some with candlelight; some while they meditate. Others can't write if they aren't driving. One of my students puts Grieg on the car stereo and drives across the desert, preferably during lightning storms. Any activity that stops analytical thought lets inspiration surface. And just a suggestion: Always keep a small notebook with you, so you won't forget your breakthroughs—write them down!

But there's more to active incubation than just getting out of your own way. This is the time to work actively with your unconscious. One way to do that is through what I call a "nightly recap." Lie in bed in the dark and try to visualize your story as clearly as possible; let all the details come alive for you. Summon the smells, tastes, textures, emotions, sounds. Make them as vivid as you can. You may find yourself in a state similar to Robert Louis Stevenson's, who was thrashing about in his bed one night, greatly alarming his wife. She woke him up, infuriating Stevenson, who yelled, "I was dreaming a fine bogey tale!" The nightmare from which he had been unwillingly awakened was the premise for *Dr. Jekyll and Mr. Hyde*.

When you wake in the morning after such a night, don't get out of bed. Stay there, moving only to pick up your already open notebook and uncapped pen. Write without thinking—anything about your story that comes to mind. Write for at least five minutes before you get up. Then close your notebook without reading what you've written. You'll read it later—when this period of doing nothing comes to an end. To read it too soon flips you into analytical thought.

"Silent movies" is another technique that helps build the pressure. Set a timer for ten minutes, and then sit without thinking until the timer rings. If thoughts do come, just let them move through your mind; don't hold onto them. Stay still. For the next ten minutes, see your story as a movie in your mind. Make it as vivid as you can; flesh out the details. Go back and forth, back and forth. Stop the projector, reverse the film, run it forward again. See it more and more clearly each time it reels by. Watch, but do not let yourself write—no matter how strong the urge.

Finally, for the last ten minutes, sit quietly without consciously thinking, until your urge to write is so strong that you just can't resist it. Then, and only then, pick up your pen and write.

Make these silent movies as often as you can during the days of this period of doing nothing. If you can't spend a full 30 minutes on it, cut back to five-minute segments. Remember: Don't read anything you write.

There's another aspect to this part of the creative process that's often given short shrift: solitude. Give yourself time alone each day, even if it's only to take a walk. A quiet walk alone can help your writing more than you'll ever know.

What if you do all this, and no story seems ready to pop into your head? In his autobiography, *Education of a Wandering Man,* Louis L'Amour said,

> There are so many wonderful stories to be written, and so much material to be used. When I hear people talking of writer's block, I am amazed. Start writing, no matter about what. The water does not flow until the faucet is turned on. You can sit and look at a page for a long time and nothing will happen. Start writing, and it will.

That's every writer's secret: not waiting for the muse. Give yourself a week at most to do nothing, then sit down to write.

Set yourself a schedule, and give yourself a goal. When I was writing fiction full-time, my writing hours were 7:00 a.m. till noon. My goal was to write five pages per day. Sometimes I finished the five pages *before* noon, and then I was free to stop. Sometimes I finished the five pages by noon, but even if I hadn't, I still stopped. It's a goal, not a stick.

When your writing is coming easily, it feels too good to stop. I rarely would stop if I had finished my five pages before noon, for instance. But I always remembered advice that came from a *Paris Review* interview with Ernest Hemingway. Although he wrote only in the morning, he said he would make a point of stopping before he'd written everything that was in him that day to write. It's great advice. If you know what's going to happen in the next scene, it'll prime your pump the following day.

Become aware of your own pattern. You may work best doing 16-hour-a-day stints for three weeks straight. Or you may find you can write only one hour a day without exhausting yourself. So schedule an hour and set a goal of a page a day. Even if you write only five pages a week, you'll still have produced 260 pages in one year. That's a whole book! The important thing is to find your own pattern—and then make it a habit. Good habits are just as hard to break as bad ones.

Rollo May's message in *The Courage to Create* is that for the creative person, fear never goes away. How can it? When we're working with the unconscious, as we must do in writing fiction, we walk up to the abyss every day and jump in. A very scary process! Allow yourself time to sharpen pencils or stare out the window for ten minutes or so before you start. After that, stay in your chair until your allotted hours are up, whether you've written anything or not. You'll find that the sheer boredom of doing nothing is often a catalyst to a remarkable gush of words.

❑ 10

Do the Writing Only You Can Do

By Christopher Scanlan

TWENTY YEARS AGO, WHEN ONE OF MY RELATIVES WAS IN THE MIDST of a painful divorce, I found myself wondering how children react to their parents' separation. What came to mind was one of those "What if" questions that drive many writers, in this case, "What if a little girl made an inventory of every item in her father's study the day before he moved out of the house?"

I made some notes, wrote drafts, discarded them, and tried again. The piece sat in my desk drawer, off and on, for years. I wrote other short stories, but always found myself returning to that one.

Many, many drafts later, I finally reached a point at which I was willing to send it out. A long list of publications rejected the story, including *Redbook,* and I can't say I blame them. I knew that it still wasn't good enough. But in my heart, the story never died. I kept at it: reading books about children and divorce, rewriting draft after draft. A newsroom colleague who had written award-winning fiction suggested that the story ended on page 10 of my 12-page manuscript. I made the cut and sent it around again. This time, the editors at *Redbook* liked the story.

Many people say they want to write, but they don't know what to write about. Looking back at the stories that I am proudest of, I can detect a central fact about each of them: They are pieces that only I could have written. That realization led me to a rule I try to live by: Do the writing only you can do.

Keeping the faith

How many times have you said to yourself, "That would make a great story," but then let the idea succumb to the doubts that plague most writers. Novelist Gail Godwin believes the writer must ignore the carping and criticism of the inner voice (she refers to it as "the watcher at the gates") that tells many of us that we have no talent, that our ideas are worthless, and that there is no point in trying.

My short story ends after Emily, a precocious 12-year-old, has faked an upset stomach to stay home and record every item in the den occupied by her departing father, just as I had dreamed it all those years ago:

> She imagined making a scrapbook, like the one Mrs. Markham had everyone make of their class trip. She would paste in the list of everything in his den, all the books, the pictures, the furniture. Paste in the pictures she'd taken. Write captions underneath. That way, even if her father took everything away, she would always remember what it looked like. And when he finally came home, she would surprise him. He would return, carrying all his boxes back into the den, and he would try to remember where everything went. He'd be standing there, rubbing his chin, when she walked in with the scrapbook. "Daddy, your books go here. Schoolbooks on the top shelf, paperbacks on the next one. That chair? Put that right over there. No, no, your diploma goes on that wall. Here, let me show you," Emily would say, taking charge.

A friend describes me as "sports-challenged" because I have so little interest in sports. I like to point out that I might care about the World Series or the Super Bowl "if my coach had given me a full uniform when I played Little League."

For years, hearing people laugh when I recounted my comic adventures as an uncoordinated, pint-sized athlete, I used to wonder if it might make a good story, but then the "watcher" at my gate would whisper, "no one cares" about my life on the bench. That was before I resolved to do the writing only I can do. I sat down and put the anecdotes on paper. On the day Super Bowl XXIX was played, my essay, "Stupor Bowl," appeared in *The Boston Globe Magazine*. It recalled the days three decades before when "I was small and scrawny, a clumsy flop at tennis, golf, backyard football, you name it. I lagged behind the pubescent progress of my friends, whose voices were deepening, whose chins were sprouting hairs, who really needed to wear jockstraps."

Silence the watcher at the gate to your imagination by keeping the faith in your ideas, because those are the ones that will set you, and your stories, apart.

Every writer has a territory, a unique landscape of experience and emotional history. Like any landscape, there are safe havens and dangerous places. I could easily write a light-hearted piece about being the father of three girls. But the topic that needed exploring was my darker side: my temper with my kids. The essay I wrote begins with this painful scene:

It's late at night, and I'm screaming at my kids again. Yelling at the top of my lungs at three little girls, lying still and terrified in their beds. Like a referee in a lopsided boxing match, my wife is trying to pull me away, but I am in the grip of a fury I am unwilling to relinquish. "And if you don't get to sleep right now," I shout, "there are going to be consequences you're not going to like."

First published in *The Boston Globe Magazine,* the essay has been reprinted many times. Some of my friends had cautioned me against publishing this piece; people might get the wrong idea about me. But writing it helped me understand myself and, more important, treat my family better. Judging from the letters and phone calls I've received from readers grateful to see a painful issue in their life aired publicly, it's helped others, too. Explore a dangerous region of your writer's territory by writing a piece nobody can write but you.

Letting the story speak

It was a dream assignment. *The Washington Post Magazine* assigned me to write a profile of the first Vietnamese graduate of West Point. Tam Minh Pham was a young man who marched with the long gray line of cadets in 1974, returning home just in time for the fall of his country and six years imprisonment. But his American roommate never forgot him, and twenty years later marshaled his classmates to cut through bureaucratic red tape and bring their buddy to America for a new life.

It didn't take much reporting for me to decide that this was a powerful story, worthy of the length of a cover piece. The only problem: The top editor didn't agree, and I was advised to stick to the prescribed limit. But when it came time to write, I had trouble holding back. I decided to write the first draft for myself and worry about length later. I began this way:

As usual, bribes loosened the guards' tongues. Another transfer was coming. By this time, after four years in jungle camps guarded by the North Vietnamese army, the inmates were going to a prison run by the Cong An, the security police. When he heard the rumor, Tam Minh Pham knew what to do. For years, he'd heard the stories about the cruel men in yellow uniforms who took people away in the dead of night, about the torture, the killings. He waited for the camp to quiet down and the night air to fill with the scent of cooking fires, and then he crept out of his bamboo hut to the garden.

That opening scene went on for another 500 words, much too long for the kind of story I knew the editor was expecting. Fortunately, he was willing to take a look. The next day, word came back that some changes were needed; the piece, now scheduled for the cover, needed to be longer.

The quickest way to lose editor's interest is to give them something different from what they expected. At the same time, writers need to let the story speak if they are going to produce stories that break barriers for themselves and their readers.

Tapping your private stock

We were on our honeymoon in Europe, a month-long trip that had already taken us to Germany, Holland and Paris. Now with a week left before we headed home, we were making good on a promise to a friend: to visit the grave of a man we had never met, who had died in a war fought before my wife and I were born. Pfc. John Juba, the half-brother of our friend back home, had died in the 1944 Normandy invasion, but no one in his family had ever seen his grave. Finding it took two train trips, four cab rides, and visits to three cemeteries, before we finally stood in front of the marble tombstone in the Brittany countryside where the soldier was buried. In my hand was a bouquet of white roses that an elderly farmer had let us cut from his garden. Beside us stood a man named Donald Davis, the cemetery's superintendent. In "The Young Who Died Delivered Us," the account of our search, I described the moment this way:

> The graves at Brittany lie beyond the Wall of the Missing—4,313 white crosses and Stars of David lined up on a manicured field like a marching band at halftime. Five varieties of grass keep it green all year round. The cemetery was empty and so quiet we could hear the rain falling on the flower beds bordering the graves. . . . I laid the flowers in front of the cross and knelt to take a picture for his mother.
> "Wait." Davis bent down and turned the bouquet around so the flowers faced the camera. "Otherwise, all you'll get is a picture of the stems." Every trade has its secrets.
> "Rest in peace, John," I said under my breath.

Readers are deluged today by clichés, commonplace descriptions, and derivative plots. Search, as you write and revise, for the telling details and observations that give resonance and meaning to your story, that set it apart, and your chances of producing a piece with universal appeal are strong. Draw on your individual experiences by tapping the "private stock" of experience, memory, and feeling that is inside you. The story of that pilgrimage to a soldier's grave has paid off with publication of "The Young Who Died Delivered Us" in six different newspaper magazines, as well as a reprinting in a popular textbook. But most rewarding were the letters from readers who saw themselves in our search. Wrote one man who helped lay out the cemetery where John Juba is buried: "You seem to have caught the feelings experienced by us who were there."

Spreading the word

It was an offhand comment by an interview subject. I was reporting a story for Knight-Ridder Newspapers about guns and children, when Mary Steber of Liverpool, N.Y., told me that she and her suburban family had never worried about guns until their 14-year-old son, Michael, was shot to death while watching a football game at a classmate's house. The friend's father, a retired policeman, kept a collection of firearms in an unlocked closet.

"You warn your kids about sex and drugs and alcohol and getting in a car with a stranger," Mrs. Steber said. "Yet guns were never mentioned in our house. We never thought of it as a problem."

Now whenever Michael's siblings visit a new friend, they make a point of reassuring their parents, "Don't worry, they don't have guns."

When I heard that, I thought, "What a great message for parents." Our own daughters had just reached the age of sleep-overs and visits to their friends' homes. Before we let them pay a visit, we started asking parents of our kids' friends, "Do you have guns in your house?"

Almost every day, it seems, the news reports yet another shooting of a child with a gun left unattended. Perhaps the Steber family's common-sense approach, if heeded by enough parents and gun owners, might save a life. To spread the word, I wrote an essay I called, "It's 10 p.m.: Do You Know Where Your Guns Are?" and began sending it around to newspaper op-ed pages. So far, its child-protecting message has reached readers of *The Christian Science Monitor, St. Petersburg Times,* and *The Orlando Sentinel.*

We all have stories that only we can tell. How we dealt with the loss of a parent, coped with an out-of-control emotion, why we cheered getting fired, the time your sister nearly burned the house down, the way your children's school deals with a social problem, retracing a memorable trip, recreating a haunting memory.

List the stories only you can write. Then write them.

□ 11

RHETORICALLY SPEAKING

BY LOUANNE JOHNSON

I PEEKED IN THE WINDOW. THIRTY FRESHMAN HONOR STUDENTS SAT waiting, pens poised above their brand-new notebooks. They were ready. I wasn't sure I was, but I decided to go ahead and give my plan a shot. If they got it, fine. If they didn't, I'd think of something.

"Good morning, ladies and gentlemen!" I shouted as I marched across the floor and slammed my briefcase down on the instructor's desk. Silence. "As you know," I went on, "this is an honors level composition course. You are here because you have high grade-point averages, and your high school teachers think you are good writers. Perhaps you are. I intend to find out." One boy in the back of the room put his head down on his desk. I ignored him.

"My name is Miss Johnson. I've been a writer for the past thirty years. I am also a former officer of the United States Marine Corps. I'm not used to taking any crap, and I don't intend to take any from you. If you expect to get an A in this course, you're going to have to earn it. If you aren't ready to work, the door is open. Make your choice, and make it now."

I could tell from their expressions, and their glances toward the door, that every student in the class wanted to leave. But they were smart kids, smart enough to know that walking out of a required course on the first day of college would not be an intelligent move. They sat still. Without saying anything further, I made a quick turnabout and marched out of the room, letting the door slam behind me. Before they had a chance to recover, I swung the door open again and sashayed daintily back inside.

"Hi," I said, as I giggled and patted my hair. "My name is, like, LouAnne, and I'm, like, your instructor, and I want everything to be, like, really cool, so everybody can, like, express himself or herself without, like, being afraid of any put-downs or anything. Oka-a-ay?"

The boy who had put his head down on the desk during my drill sergeant routine sat up straight and glanced at the girl beside him. She raised her eyebrows and shrugged. A few small smiles showed me that some of the students were starting to catch on. But most of them sat, staring at me, clearly confused. I giggled again and ran out of the room.

The third time I opened the door, I walked in and smiled pleasantly. "Good morning. I am your instructor. My name is LouAnne Johnson, and I hope that we will accomplish two things in this class. Number one, we will meet the requirements for this course. Number two, you will actually learn something about writing."

I picked up a marker and drew two vertical lines, dividing the white board behind me into thirds. I labeled the sections #1, #2 and #3, then asked the class members to vote which of my three different introductions represented "the real Miss Johnson." I recorded their votes on the board. The boy in the back voted for #1, but the rest of the class voted for #3.

"Why did you pick the third one?" I asked. "Anybody? Just speak up."

"I could just tell," one young woman said.

"You seemed real," somebody added from the far corner. "Genuine."

"But why?" I insisted. "Can somebody try to explain it?"

There was such a long silence that I almost gave up. Then a young man in the front row adjusted his glasses and cleared his throat. "I believe there was some element in your voice that matched the expression on your face and the look in your eye. They all matched, so to speak. I didn't sense any incongruity."

"Thank you very much," I said, and I meant it. His explanation was even better than the one I had planned. "Just as you can sense that a person is pretending, acting insincerely, you can also sense dishonesty in writing. I'm sure you've all read pretentious prose that put you off because it tried to impress you. And it's quite likely that you've thrown down some article or essay you'd started to read that may have contained a brilliant idea, but was so poorly presented and illogically organized that it wasn't worth the effort it would have taken to read it." A few nods encouraged me to continue.

"When you write compositions for me, don't try to sound like a textbook, or your high school English teacher, or your favorite author. While I'd encourage you to use techniques and writing styles that you admire, I don't mean for you to try to copy them. Learn how to use them; make them your own. Write in your own voice. Each of you has a particular combination of vocabulary, tone of voice, facial expressions and gestures that creates a distinct, individual personality when you express your ideas during a conversation. But when you write, you can rely only on language—word choice, sentence style, punctuation—to communicate your personality."

It worked. They got it. Instead of deluging me with the standard five-paragraph essay, written entirely in passive voice, using the longest possible words, these students learned to use language either to show or hide their personalities, depending upon the assignment. To project a sense of objectivity in her research paper, for example, one young woman, Suzette, chose relatively formal language and complex sentence structure:

College campuses can be misleading, with their tree-lined walkways, stately lecture halls, and dormitories. Statistics have repeatedly demonstrated that America's colleges and universities are not the safe havens many parents believe them to be.

Later, Suzette wrote a personal essay on the same topic, but the voice was completely different.

My parents think I'm safe here at NMSU. They don't know about the date rapes and muggings. And I'm not going to tell them. They would just worry about me, because they don't realize how much the whole world has changed since they went to college.

In this essay, colloquial phrases, first-person voice, and simpler sentence structure gave a good sense of Suzette's personality and attitude: She's young and scared, but she's determined to be independent.

Although all of my students agreed that finding their own voices was necessary, some of them needed extra time and practice before they finally "got it right." One young man became frustrated when his peer critique group pronounced that he was almost, but not quite, there.

"How do they know whether it's my voice or not?" he challenged me.

"Other people can critique your writing for form and content," I said, "but no one else can know whether you have said what you wanted to say, whether the message the reader receives is the one you meant to send."

"How will I know when it's right?" he asked.

I was tempted to say, "How do you know when you're in love?" But I realized that my voice might not be the one this particular student needed to hear. So I quoted from journalist Marya Mannes's essay, "How Do You Know It's Good?" Mannes's answer? "When you begin to detect the difference between freedom and sloppiness, between serious experimentation and egotherapy, between skill and slickness, between strength and violence, you are on your way. . . ."

My student frowned for a moment, digesting this new idea, then smiled. "Why didn't you say that before?"

□ 12

KEEP YOUR WRITING ON TRACK

BY GENIE DICKERSON

"WHAT IS THE USE OF WRITING WHEN YOU ARE ON THE WRONG road?" said English writer and naturalist John Ray. A wrong turn—a seeming shortcut—may detour us and prove fatal to our writing.

Detour 1: Writers clubs, classes, and conferences. *Rationalization:* I always get fired up about writing by these groups, and I pick up pointers. *Rebuttal:* A little fire goes a long way. If social activities cut into your writing time, you have been sidetracked and may find it wise to return to the main road. As for picking up pointers from other writers, only firsthand experience will teach you which pointers are valid.

Detour 2: A book as first project. *Rationalization:* The money and satisfaction are in books. *Rebuttal:* Except for big-selling books, magazine writing offers writers more money, more readers, more contact with editors, as well as greater opportunities for developing your writing skills. For an inexperienced writer, the trap in writing a book first is procrastination. Magazine and newspaper work require all facets to be completed in a timely manner. With a book, it's easy to put off less-fun tasks.

Detour 3: Looking for an agent. *Rationalization:* A writer needs an agent to sell writing. *Rebuttal:* The search may be unnecessary. Virtually all novices start selling their writing without agents. After writers have sold work on their own, they find that agents are more receptive to them.

Detour 4: The presumption that editors have time to read every word sent to them. *Rationalization:* My piece will sell on the basis of the beautiful last paragraph. *Rebuttal:* Editors and other readers are not inclined to drag themselves through slow material. Discounting the importance of a gripping lead is a dead end.

Detour 5: Co-authoring. *Rationalization:* I'm not sure enough of my ability to write something by myself. *Rebuttal:* Unless both authors are good workers and contribute complementary skills to the project, the partnership will produce nothing but false hopes.

Detour 6: Dependence on computer spelling and grammar checkers. *Rationalization:* I don't have time to waste on boring details—the computer can do it for me. *Rebuttal:* Spelling and grammar checkers miss a lot. Spelling and grammar are what make up English. Don't let computer aids replace what you need to know. Computers can flag typographical errors, but total dependence on spelling and grammar checkers is the wrong route.

Detour 7: Asking friends to read and comment on your unpublished writing. *Rationalization:* Even if my friends aren't experts, they can make comments like ordinary readers. *Rebuttal:* Unless your friends read your type of writing, they may not be the best judges of the salability of your manuscripts. Worse, they may flatter you or shoot you down, misleading you on the quality of your work.

Detour 8: Writer's block. *Rationalization:* I sit down at the computer but can't think of anything to write. *Rebuttal:* A sure barrier to Easy Street. Ignore the block, and jot down whatever you have done or talked about or thought up in the previous 24 hours. Publications buy essays about neighborhood walks, humorous pieces about incidents at the grocery store, and how-to articles about pulling weeds. Thoughts sell, just about any thoughts that are well presented. Once you begin to write, the creative change of pace will energize you to develop your thoughts.

Detour 9: Letterhead stationery, business cards, bumper stickers, and T-shirts that say "Writer." *Rationalization:* They define me as a serious professional. *Rebuttal:* Are you hornswoggling yourself? Are the stationery, business cards, bumper stickers, and what you wear more for convenience and fun?

Detour 10: Overemphasis on creativity. *Rationalization:* The more literary and creative your writing is, the less smooth, clear and logical it needs to be. *Rebuttal:* Writing is, above all, communication. If people have to exert themselves to understand a piece of writing, they won't read (or buy) it.

Detour 11: Treasure hunt. *Rationalization:* I refuse to write for small publications. Why should I do a piece for $25 when other writers get $2,500 from glossier magazines for the same amount of work? *Rebuttal:* Everyone starts at the beginning.

Detour 12: Lost in research. *Rationalization:* I love hunting for background facts. *Rebuttal:* Research can be a form of procrastination. Once you find the information you need, you can return to the drawing board, which is more fun anyway.

Detour 13: Computer roadblock. *Rationalization:* I have to get my new word processor up and running before I can write. *Rebuttal:* Dust off your typewriter, and use it. Or do rough drafts by hand. Conquer your computer after you get at least some writing done.

Detour 14: Avoid submitting manuscript. *Rationalizations:* a) Publishers won't pay me, a beginner, enough to cover my time. b) My work isn't good enough to submit yet. c) I don't need to see my byline in print in order to be a writer. d) Researching markets takes too much time. e) Contemporary literature isn't very good, so editors wouldn't recognize or appreciate my writing. f) I submitted a few things, but they were rejected. *Rebuttal:* Despite imperfections, the best way to improve your writing and develop into a professional is to submit your manuscripts frequently to editors. By saying yes or no, and often with specific helpful comments, editors are our best teachers. Inventors work much the same way as writers do, by trial and error, and experimentation with modifications. And who knows? You just might earn that $2,500 on your first manuscript submission.

Detour 15: Not including an SASE with submissions. *Rationalization:* Stamps are expensive, and editors ought to pay for half of the cost of submissions. Why would I want my manuscript returned? If the editor doesn't buy my story, I can run off a fresh copy on my printer. *Rebuttal:* Publishers don't believe they owe free lancers anything. Most editors will not read or return a manuscript if you don't enclose a stamped return envelope. Send an SASE to make sure the editor received your piece, to show professionalism, and to invite helpful comments from the editor. To economize on manuscripts mailed flat, enclose a business-size SASE (#10) and a note saying that you don't need your manuscript returned.

To succeed as a writer, you must stay on track. Every writer needs self-discipline. Detours are paved with rationalizations, but common sense keeps writers on the main road.

❑ 13

A GUIDE TO DEALING WITH REJECTIONS

BY FRED HUNTER

ALL OF YOUR FAVORITE AUTHORS, ALL BEST-SELLING AUTHORS, AND all of the authors you love who have not yet been discovered by the general public have two things in common: Their work has at one time been rejected, and they've managed to go beyond that rejection to earn their respective places in the literary spectrum.

Rejection is an unfortunate fact of life for writers, and it's never easy to take. Although it's true that all writers suffer rejection, that fact can seem like little more than a useless bromide to a writer who's just opened his mail to find a form letter saying, "don't call us, we'll call you" (and believe it or not, I've actually received one that said that).

When I finished writing my first mystery, *Presence of Mind,* I decided that instead of using an agent I would attempt to sell the book myself. I put together cover letters and samples (the first three chapters) and sent them to ten publishers at a time until the book was accepted. I was very fortunate in that it sold to one of the first five publishers to whom it was sent, but by the time that happened I had sent out thirty samples, so for over a year afterward I was still receiving rejections for a book that was already accepted for publication. This gave me the unique luxury of being able to take an objective look at the business of rejection. Even though rejection letters are rarely personalized, from the editors who have taken the time to offer comments I've gleaned a few hints on how to handle rejection.

• Editors are people

Although writers often think of editors as unfeeling ogres, they really are basically just people with particular tastes who select books much the way any other reader would. It helps to think of how you read novels: When you're reading a book by a new author, even one that was recommended to you, you will either like or dislike the book, and your gut feeling will help you decide whether or not you will ever revisit that author's work.

Writers would like to think that editors can go beyond their personal taste and objectively recognize fine writing, and I have news for you: They do. But they will still rarely buy a book that doesn't appeal to them personally, any more than you would.

One rejection letter I received particularly illustrates this. It said, "Your writing is better than 90% of what crosses my desk . . . but I found the detective too smug (in the same way that Hercule Poirot is, and I didn't like him, either)." I hardly needed to point out to this editor how well the Poirot books have sold; she certainly knew that. The fact remained that my style just didn't appeal to that editor. It was comforting, though, to know that she wouldn't have bought Agatha Christie, either.

To give you an idea of how subjective editorial reactions are, I received one rejection letter that said, "There's too much character development in this book, and not enough plot," while another editor commenting on the same manuscript said, "The plot is very strong, but I thought the characters were a bit thin."

The fact that the responses of different editors are often so contradictory points up how important it is that you are satisfied with your own work, and that you have faith in it before submitting it. Obviously, it would be foolhardy to attempt to rewrite your manuscript based on the comments of one editor; however, if three editors tell you, "This manuscript is too wordy," I would do some heavy cutting before sending it out again.

• Rejection is part of a writer's life

Carolyn Hart, author of several award-winning mystery novels, says, "To be a writer, you have to be willing to fail. Even exceptional writers have their work rejected." Once you've completed your masterpiece, you've left the artistic part of writing and entered the business side, and it's best to approach it as you would any other business. You're a salesman, and your product is your work. As with any other product, some will buy it, some won't. It's O.K. to be disappointed when you don't make a sale to a particular editor, but you shouldn't be devastated. An editor will not buy a product that he doesn't believe he can sell to his audience. But there's always another editor and another audience.

• Always be working on something else

Start writing your next piece the minute you drop your current completed manuscript in the mailbox. Barbara D'Amato, author of the popular Cat Marsala mysteries, says, "I know many otherwise sane people who will write something, send it off, and then wait and wait and wait for it to be accepted somewhere before starting on something else. You have to start your next book right away, otherwise you're putting all your emotional stock in one thing."

Madeleine L'Engle, the highly esteemed author of both fiction and nonfiction, suffered a ten-year stretch of not being able to get her work published *after* the success of her earlier novels. She writes very candidly about that decade of rejection in her book *A Circle of Quiet*. During that period she continued to write, eventually going on to win the Newbery Medal for *A Wrinkle in Time*.

Far from finding these examples discouraging, writers should realize how large a role perseverance plays in the business of getting published. In my own work, even though I had some early success, I wasn't quite so fortunate when I tried to launch my second series. I submitted the first book in the series to publisher after publisher for almost two years before it was accepted. Even with a track record, I still had to find an editor who liked the book enough to take a chance on it. By the time the first book was sold, I'd completed the second and started the third. I found continuing to write was infinitely preferable to sitting at home developing ulcers.

But how do you go on writing without the encouragement of success? You must focus on the writing itself, not on the possible rewards. It's like the old joke about the restaurant with no prices on the menu: If you have to ask the price, you can't afford to eat there. Similarly, if your goal as a writer is anything other than the work itself, you can't afford to be one.

• Never give up

"I like to think it's a fortuitous world," says Carolyn Hart. "You can be an excellent writer and still fail, but you should never, never give up, because you never know when things will turn around—and the only way for that to happen is to keep writing."

Keep believing that things will turn around. Though it may take years, you *will* eventually find that editor who falls in love with your work . . . but that editor will never get to see your work if you allow rejections to make you give up along the road.

Disraeli said it better than anyone else: "The secret of success is constancy of purpose."

I wish I'd written that.

❏ 14

MYTHS OF THE WRITING LIFE

BY JAMES A. RITCHIE

RECENTLY I'VE FOUND THAT MANY OF THE OLD TRIED AND TRUE rules of fiction writing, and the writing life in general, have come under attack. So I think it's time to set the record straight.

Myth: You don't have to write everyday.

Fact: Well, no, you don't. You don't have to write at all. There probably isn't a soul in the world who will care if you never write another word.

And, yes it is possible to sell a few short stories, a few articles, a little of this and a pinch of that, if you write only on Saturday, or during the full moon, or whenever the mood hits. You may even legitimately call yourself a writer—small "w"—by working in this manner.

But unless you work at least five or six days a week, no excuses, you will never be able to call yourself a Professional Writer, meaning a writer who earns a living from writing fiction. And because writing, like playing the violin, requires hundreds and thousands of hours of practice to get right, you will never develop your talent to the fullest unless you write nearly everyday.

Even if you succeed financially, the first million or so words you write will screech and jangle the nerves as will a violin played by a rank beginner.

And anyone who tells you otherwise is a dilettante, a dabbler.

Myth: Procrastination is no more than your subconscious telling you the story isn't ready to be written.

Fact: No, procrastination is your way of telling the world you're too lazy and too soft to stick it out when the writing gets tough. Good writing is always difficult, always hard work. Anytime the words are flowing too easily you'd better look at your hole card.

Unless, when you're old and gray, you're certain you'll be content looking back and realizing you published only a tiny fraction of what you might have, and that most of it was mediocre at best, get over the notion that procrastination is ever a good thing.

Myth: It isn't the writing that matters, it's the act of creating, and since a writer works all the time, you're creating even when you're fishing, crocheting, or watching a football game, as long as you're *thinking* about writing.

Fact: Horse hockey. There may be some truth to the statement that a writer works all the time, but it's only at the keyboard that a writer creates anything.

At best, the work a writer does in his or her mind between stints at the keyboard is only planning to create. It's easy to justify anything, but justified or not, I can guarantee Joe Blow, that writer down the street with half your talent but twice your drive, is going to succeed much sooner that you do if you buy into this one.

Myth: It's the editor's job to fix my bad grammar (style, paragraph, plot line, etc.).

Fact: Why should he? I was once—briefly and small time—an editor. I quickly learned two things. One: many, many would-be writers expect editors to do everything, from correcting horrific spelling to transcribing handwritten manuscripts, to teaching them how to write basic English.

An editor's job is actually pretty simple when it comes to manuscripts: Keep the ones good enough to publish and reject the others. That's all there is to it.

Yes, once an editor finds a good story, one that really could see publication as is, he or she will say, "Now, let's see what we can do to make this story even better."

But, that's it. Editors should not be expected to rewrite, correct grammar or spelling (except for an occasional typo), or give writing lessons. And they do not ever read handwritten manuscripts.

I also learned that editors do not enjoy rejecting stories. Editors, in fact, love finding stories good enough to publish. So don't blame the editor if you receive a rejection slip instead of an acceptance letter.

Myth: You can't get an agent until you've been published, and you can't get published until you have an agent.

Fact: This one is nonsense. Agents are in the business of finding new, publishable writers. It's how agents, at least reputable agents, earn their money. But the key word is *publishable*. Almost all agents read queries, and so do many publishers.

Myth: Big name writers get such large advances there's no money left over for the rest of us.

Fact: There's a grain of truth in this, but there is a reason for it. Simply, big name writers get big bucks because they write big novels that sell in big numbers.

But remember that just about every big name writer out there was once an obscure, unpublished writer who earned very little or nothing. They may even have believed the same myth.

Instead of wasting energy griping about how much money somebody else makes, study what she does and how she does it. Then, one of these days, you may pull down huge advances while others gripe about you.

Myth: You must have a college education to be a professional writer.

Fact: I hope not. I dropped out of school in the eighth grade. I did take a G.E.D. test years later, but that's it. I tried college for a few months, quickly realized my time would be much better spent writing, and dropped out without taking a single writing course.

And I'm now working on my sixth novel.

Myth: A would-be fiction writer shouldn't read other people's fiction because it will unduly influence his own writing.

Fact: If you don't read other people's fiction, and lots of it, you will never, ever succeed as a writer. Period.

You *want* to be influenced. In the early stages of your career, and even when you're established, studying other writers, and imitating their style, is exactly how you learn to write well yourself. There is no other way. So read everything, and read often.

Myth: Writing fiction is an art, and rewriting only obscures the artist's spontaneous vision.

Fact: Yes, writing fiction is an art. But it's also a craft. Failure to rewrite will guarantee that the artist's vision will never be seen by anyone except those unfortunate friends and family members forced to read it.

How much rewriting is enough? Beats me. Dean Koontz claims to rewrite each page an average of 26 times. Ernest Hemingway is said to have rewritten *A Farewell to Arms* 39 times.

My own rule is to rewrite until it's either as good as I can get it, or until I'm so sick of the process I can't take it any more. As Hemingway explained in an interview, you rewrite until you get the words right, then you stop.

The competition is fierce. Getting the words "almost right" isn't going to get you anything except rejection slips to paper your office walls.

Myth: You must be certifiably insane to be a fiction writer.

Fact: All right, so this one is true.

□ 15

THE WORD POLICE

BY BETH LEVINE

IT'S SUNDAY NIGHT AND THE SMELL OF CHINESE FOOD HANGS LOW over the city. Two figures are poised outside of a neon-lit overpriced specialty food store.

"Look, Joe, here's another one: 'Gormet Pastries,'" Lisa observes.

"Don't these people have any respect for the law? Let's take him in," Joe sighs, exasperated.

Joe pulls down on his snap brim hat. He and Lisa (and that's *Lisa;* not Leesa, Lysa, or Lise), a woman with determinedly clicking high heels, enter the aforementioned "Gormet Pastries."

The owner, a member of the I-Dress-Only-In-Black-And-Not-Be-cause-It's-Slimming tribe, eyes them disdainfully. "Can I help you?" he asks faintly.

"Are you the proprietor of . . . *Gourmet* Pastries?" Lisa inquires, annoyed. This jerk can't spell and he's looking down on *her?*

"Yes. Is there a problem?"

The couple looks at each other meaningfully before whipping out their pocket-sized New Webster's Dictionaries.

"Word Police," Joe says with a penetrating stare. The owner turns pale, and his eyes start to dart around the store. Joe points to the back of the sign in the window and sure enough, there is *GORMET* in all its purple shame. The owner pales. "I . . . uh . . . guess I never noticed," he stammers.

"No, you people never do!" Joe exclaims. "Don't you ever *proof* things before shelling out your money? Day after day, you come in here and you never *noticed* a sign three feet high?"

Lisa puts her hand on his arm. "Easy, Joe," she says quietly. Turning to the owner, she asks, "What's your name, buddy?"

"Lonnee. L O N N . . ." He stops when he sees Joe and Lisa's faces turn pale. They are looking at a sign behind the counter that reads *Baking Done on Premise.*

"What is that?" Joe asks curtly. "You bake with the hope that it might come out right?" Lonnee looks confused, as Joe begins to tie two copies of *The Chicago Manual of Style* to Lonnee's wrists. The three begin to shuffle to the door, while Lisa reads him his rights.

"You have the right to remain silent—something we prefer, actually. You have the right to remain literate. In the absence of this ability, you have the right to an English professor, which the court will provide."

Lonnee raises his head in defiance. "Ha! I just catered an affair for Edwin Newman; he'll defend me! He owes me!"

"I don't think so. The man has principles—and that's *ples* not *pals*," snaps Joe. He sadly shakes his head and looks at Lisa. "Pathetic, isn't it?"

As they pass, the customers of the soon-to-be renamed Gourmet Pastries watch in open-mouthed horror. "He seemed to pay such attention to details. Who knew?" says one.

A mother looks down at her ashen-faced 10-year-old son. "See, sonny? He probably cheated his way through spelling class, too. Thought he could get away with it. See? It always catches up to you." The boy bursts into tears. (When he grows up, he will produce an Academy Award-winning documentary on his experiences, "Scared Grammatical.")

Later, Joe and Lisa emerge from the New York Public Library as the former owner of Gormet Pastries is bundled off into a library bus.

"What a dope," says Joe. "I'm glad they threw the book at him, not that he could read it. Imagine—dragging Edwin Newman's name into it!"

"Let's go get a cup of coffee," says Lisa. She takes Joe's arm, and they proceed to Bagels 'N Stuff. Joe balks when he sees the sign.

Lisa reassures him, "Well, it's a little cutesy, but I think colloquially it's correct." Joe stares at her intently as they enter the restaurant.

Ten minutes later, the two are relaxing in a booth.

"How'd you get into this crazy business, Joe?" Lisa asks meditatively.

"I started as a copy editor at a book publisher. I loved the job, but then to save money, the publisher . . ." Lisa leans over and pats his hand. Joe bravely continues, "The publisher started allowing books to go to press with *Britishisms* intact so they wouldn't have to spend money to reset type. *Colour* instead of *color,* that sort of thing. I said no. This far I will bend and no further.

"Turns out my boss used to work for McDonald's and was the one responsible for 'Over 5 billion sold,' not even knowing it should be 'More than 5 billion.' He was that sloppy. So he fired me! That's when I realized my true vocation: Cleaning up this ungrammatical city of ours."

Lisa sighs. "Sometimes I wonder if it really does matter."

Joe spills his coffee. "What? How can you possibly say that?"

"Oh, *more than, over. Gourmet* with or without a u, does it really amount to," she pauses before uttering the cliché, "a hill of beans?"

Now it's Joe's turn to reach for her hand. "Don't burn out on me now, baby. It happens to others, but not to us. It's in our blood."

Lisa's eyes well up. "I can't take it anymore. Everywhere I go—the bank, the sandwich shops, dry cleaners—there are typos everywhere. I went to buy a co-op, but when I saw the awning said 'Two Fourty,' I couldn't do it. I have no friends, because I'm always correcting them. Countermen hate me, because I'm forever pointing out that it's ice*d* tea, not *ice* tea. And don't even talk to me about apostrophes; they show up everywhere but where they are supposed to. Joe," Lisa's tears spill out, "I want to be like other people. I want to be sloppy."

Joe takes his hand away. "But we can't be like other people. We're a breed. We're . . . The Word Police. If we slip, it's the end of the civilized world, the demise of the society of Safire and Newman and Webster. It means the Lonnees and McDonald's of the world win."

Restlessly, Joe taps the end of his pencil on the tabletop. "Language defines what we can think," he continues. "I believe undisciplined, careless writing makes for undisciplined, careless thinking. How can you formulate ideas without appropriate tools—clarity, attention to detail? Without them, the world's thinking becomes muddled and uninformed. The mind is a muscle. Use it or lose it."

"We could go away, Joe," Lisa says plaintively through her sobs. "We could go to France. We don't speak French, so we'd never know when something was incorrect."

"Sorry, Lisa, I can't turn my back on murderers of the mother tongue. I need the facts, ma'am." Joe gives Lisa a despairing look, and then throws a dollar on the table. Coat collar up, hat brim pulled down, he sadly leaves Lisa and Bagels 'N Stuff behind, but not before pointing out to the amazed proprietor that *decaffeinated* has two Fs in it.

"I'll let you off with a warning this time," he says, exiting to chase a passing exterminator's truck with *MICES, TERMITES AND ROACHES* written on the side.

Back at the table, Lisa watches him go and says softly to herself, "I'll miss ya, Joe. Paris would of been swell." She shudders after mouthing the foul words of her new world. Picking up her decafeinated coffee, she drinks the bitter cup.

❏ 16

WHEN TO QUIT YOUR DAY JOB

BY BILL VOSSLER

HOW DO YOU KNOW IF IT IS TIME TO QUIT YOUR DAY JOB AND SPEND full time on magazine writing? Are there guidelines, or must you merely make a blind leap?

After 15 years of full-time magazine writing, I've distilled the following guidelines I wish I had known earlier, some of which will probably surprise you:

If you have six month's to a year's worth of funds on hand. From idea to query to article to paycheck often takes six months, or even longer, during which time you need to pay your bills and eat, so you'll need a solid backlog of money.

If you enjoy solitude. Almost every writer works alone. If you don't like to be alone for long blocks of time, you must adjust, or you won't last long in the writing game.

There is a middle ground: Make sure the types of articles you write require interviewing people. Even so, there will still be large blocks of time where you will have only yourself for company.

If you are a self-starter. When you take on your dream job, you are the boss. Make yourself daily assignments, and generally apply seat of pants to chair; no one else will do it for you. To free lance, you need to take charge of your own life, day after day after day.

If you love writing. Though this seems obvious, there are writers who don't love writing. Writing for a living can at times become a tough job, and motivating yourself is going to be very difficult. On the other hand, if you do love writing, you're in for a great and wonderful ride.

If you tend not to procrastinate. With one caveat: Everybody procrastinates a little, but the writers I know who are successful, procrastinate in an odd way: They don't do *this* writing, but they do *that* writing instead. In other words, rarely do they put off writing in exchange for, say, watching TV or reading a thriller. They put off one writing job for another. They are always forging ahead. They are always aware that writing is their job, and they always must be involved in some aspect of it.

If you understand the general concepts of article writing. In other words, you know something about query letters, slants, article beginnings and endings, magazine analysis, photos (both shooting them and where to find them), research, and of course, writing clear sentences.

It's simple: If you don't know your business, you won't get published, which means you won't be a full-time writer for long.

If you aren't devastated by rejection. Nobody is happy with rejection. I've published more than 2,100 articles, and I still get rejections, but I don't allow them to crush me and keep me from writing.

You must get inured to rejection, or you won't be able to survive as a full-time writer, because you *will* get rejected, often at the most inopportune time. You must learn what you can from the rejection, and move on. There are more ideas to pitch, more magazines to read, more articles to be written.

If you have sold at least ten articles. Not freebies, but articles that you've actually been paid for. The first time I quit my day job to free lance full time, I had sold only two articles, both to the same magazine, for $40 each. But I *did* have two dozen more articles out, and a quick bit of math told me that if I sold only a quarter of those, I'd have enough money for the next two months. *But none of them sold.* Even though I thought I was ready, reality proved I still did not know enough about writing to go full-time. If I had sold ten articles to half a dozen magazines, it would have been proof that I probably knew enough about free lancing to make a go of it, full-time. Actually, it took me four more years to learn enough to go full-time.

If you've earned at least $300 each from two of those articles you sold. Writing is going to be your business. A business needs a product that people want, and it needs cash flow. If you are selling only to lower-tier markets at $50 or less per article, you probably won't be able to make it as a full-time free lancer. You must start selling to the middle-tier ($300 and up) magazines before you can support yourself.

In the end, only you can decide whether it is time to make the break to full-time free lancing. Each individual's circumstance is different. For instance, when I went into writing full-time, I was single with no dependents, and therefore, I needed less money to survive every month.

Above all, you must be practical. Many writers with the traits and abilities to make it as full-time writers don't make it because they simply *want* to write, instead of being *capable* of writing full time. Knowing the difference is hugely important.

Of the dozens of different jobs I've held in my lifetime, from custom combiner, to theater projectionist, to coach, farm laborer, and others, not one of them came close to giving me the joy and satisfaction that I now get as a full-time, free-lance magazine writer. You can do the same, if you work hard enough to learn your craft and apply what you've learned to your writing. Then soon your day job will be just a memory, because you've set yourself up for success as a free-lance full-time writer.

❏ 17

CONFESSIONS OF A LAZY RESEARCHER

BY NANCY SPRINGER

I LOATHE RESEARCH. ALL THROUGH SCHOOL I KNEW I COULD NEVER be a writer, because writers are supposed to love research, and I detest it. I *hate* digging for picky little facts! I want to tell stories; I don't want to worry about the *details!* My aversion to research paralyzed me so badly that I didn't start writing novels until I had a brain spasm in which I thought that I wouldn't have to worry about research if I wrote fantasy. (Wrong!) Since then I have published realistic novels for children and young adults, horror, mainstream, mystery, some nonfiction. Of necessity, I've learned to handle research. Want to know how? The lazy way, that's how.

The Internet, you're thinking? Nope. I surf not, nor have I yet set foot on the Information Super-Highway. I spend quite enough of my time hunched in front of a computer screen. Anyway, all the techno-hoopla annoys me. I'm contrary by nature; this trait has served me well as a fiction writer.

So, you're thinking, she spends of lot of time in the library. Not me. The air always seems gray in a library. And the book I need is always out, or the copy is missing, or it's at another library, and anyway, you can't keep the books long enough. Once every month or two I might venture into the library for something.

So how do I research? In a sense, my whole life is research: to try to pay attention, to be observant. The kinds of information you need for fiction writing you can't find in reference books—smells, textures, color nuances, slang, dialect, jokes, bumper stickers, tattoos, the taste of fast food. . . . Most of what you need to know, you learn best in your everyday life. I keep notebooks to help me remember what I have learned. Nothing's a total waste, not even visiting Aunt Marge; you might use her flamingo lamps in a book sometime. Moreover, being a writer gives you a great excuse to do fun things: horseback camping, scuba diving in a quarry, painting your body blue—whatever. Being a writer gives you all the more reason to have a life.

To supplement real life as research, I read nonfiction for pleasure. The more I write fiction, the more I hunger for intriguing, quirky nonfiction, and my taste in pleasure reading has become so esoteric it's almost pathological. I browse and prowl, I haunt book sales and yard sales and used bookstores. (I can never find the kind of book I want in a chain bookstore.) When everybody is saying, "I just want to read *Women Who Run With the Wolves*," I won't go near it. Instead, I read a book called *Frogs: Their Wonderful Wisdom, Follies and Foibles, Mysterious Powers, Strange Encounters, Private Lives, Symbolism & Meaning*, by Gerald Donaldson, and two books with frog themes eventually result.

At the time I read my finds, I have no idea how I will use them, if ever. It doesn't matter. I am reading for fun. Other favorite finds: *The Encyclopedia of Bad Taste*, by Jane and Michael Stern; *Big Hair: A Journey into the Transformation of Self*, by Grant McCracken; and *The Book of Weird* (formerly *The Glass Harmonica*), by Barbara Ninde Byfield.

Other than this sort of goofing off, I do no research at all before I start to write a book. None.

I have my reasons for doing as little research as possible. One is financial. Time is money; I need to earn a living; I want to spend my work time writing, not researching. But the main reason I don't research before writing is simply that ideas don't stay fresh forever. When I get a book idea, I want to run with it, not diddle around gathering a lot of facts I might not even read.

When I'm ready with the idea for my next book, I sit down and write. As I write, I come up against research questions, of course. A lot of them I can finesse; over the years I've discovered that "facts" are not nearly as solid as I used to think—such as what kids wear, for instance, if I'm writing a YA. Ask ten different kids, and you'll get ten different answers, so I just ask one kid, my own, and let it go at that.

I take care of a lot of my research by yelling downstairs—my husband will tell me what model car the prospering pediatrician ought to drive this year. Other times, I might have to grab a book—over the years I have acquired a motley assortment of dictionaries and encyclopedias—or I might need to call that wonderful person, the reference librarian. Sometimes, though seldom, I have to write myself a note to verify something when I get time. Only very occasionally do I actually have to stop writing until I clear something up. Even then, the stoppage is usually only for a day, as compared to the three to six months a lot of writers spend on research before writing. In my not-so-humble opinion, there's a lot to be said for writing the book first, thereby finding out what you *really* need to find out. As a kind of fringe benefit, this method forces me to abide by that classic fiction-writing rule: Write What You Know.

After I finish the first draft, it usually takes me no more than a few days to get answers to any questions that might have come up, usually by means of that time-honored ploy of the lazy researcher: I ask somebody who is likely to know. For instance, with a question about guns, I call my brother, the ex-cop and quondam gunsmith. Chatting with him for ten minutes or so is a lot more pleasant and less time-consuming than reading a bunch of gun books. For a question about secondary sexual characteristics of turtles, I call a friend who's a naturalist. For medical questions, my sister-in-law the physician, et cetera . . . . The only drawback to this method is that sometimes it's hard to get the information you really need. Normal people don't think like writers, so even when you're asking a specific question—what color are toad guts?—they manage to give you a vague answer. For this reason, I often call fellow writers with research questions in their areas of expertise, and I find them much better than my sister-in-law at giving me the information I need.

Doing my research this way, I haven't spent an extra moment peering into a bilious computer screen. Instead, I have had an interesting conversation with a real human being.

That's how I handle my research, and I love it. I've published thirty books doing research this way. You might argue that I could write bigger books and make more money if I did more research, and you might be right. But I'm contrary: I'd rather write my books my way, and besides, I'd rather have a life.

❑ 18

THE POWER OF A BOOK

BY MARY WARREN

I ALMOST MADE THE BIGGEST MISTAKE OF MY LIFE AND ABANDONED the juvenile field . . . until a book arrived in the mail that carried me back to my childhood.

A prodigious reader, I discovered that books like *Heidi* and *The Secret Garden* and *Emily of New Moon* could carry me far away to different lands and different centuries.

My favorite books were Laura Ingalls Wilder's Little House series. Each year a new one appeared under the Christmas tree with my name on the gift tag. There came an autumn, however, when it looked as if no further Wilder book would be there. *The Little Town on the Prairie* seemed to finish off the story of Laura and Mary's childhood years. Surely Laura would marry Almanzo Wilder because that was the author's name, wasn't it?

One stormy November day, I sat down at my desk to write to my favorite author, telling her how much I enjoyed each book, and how I wished she could write one more to end the series with Almanzo's courtship. I already knew that I wanted to be a writer when I grew up, but I was far too shy to admit that to Mrs. Wilder.

Instead, I asked her how to make sourdough. Back came a letter from the Wilder farm in Missouri, written in Laura's handwriting on lined stationery. In addition to telling me exactly how to make sourdough, she assured me that the book I'd requested, *These Happy Golden Years,* was going to be on the bookstore shelves in time for Christmas.

Although Laura Wilder never lived to see my work in print, she has always remained my role model. When I teach or lead workshops, I use her carefully detailed descriptions of prairies, blizzards, and warm family life as examples. I have read her books countless times, as I struggle over my own depictions of characters and scenes.

When Laura needed a long sentence, she crafted one. When a short one worked best, that is what she used. At least one of her sentences in *The Long Winter* is 42 words long. Another is only three: "Pa's nose purpled." Those were the only words necessary to show how cold it was.

One day, a 12-year-old boy growing up on a midwestern farm wrote to me, telling me why he liked my books. He wrote about his pets, the farm animals, and his hobbies. At last he got around to what he *really* wanted to say. "P.S. I want to be a writter." (The spelling is his.)

That farm lad reminds me of the little girl growing up in Brooklyn many years ago. But at least he set *his* shyness aside long enough to confide: "I want to be a writter." I am glad he liked my books. I hope his dream of being a published author has come true.

What about the book that arrived in the mail the other day and stirred me to take another look at the direction I wish to take? *Dear Laura* (compiled by HarperCollins editor, Alix Reid) is a charming collection of over 100 letters written to Laura Ingalls Wilder from the 1930's into the early 1950's. A copy of my letter to Laura Wilder is on page 44, and her return letter to me, with directions on how to make sourdough, is on the very next page!

I had forgotten about the warm way youngsters respond to books that touch them until I sat down and laughed and wept over every page of *Dear Laura*. It reminded me of the meaning books can bring to children's lives, how a special book may act as a rudder to steer them, fostering hope and understanding.

Not long ago, I went to my files and leafed through the letters and the crayoned illustrations of scenes from my books that children had sent to *me*. Many of them begged me to write more books.

Yes, I've changed my mind. I want to begin writing for a young audience once again.

How To Write—
Techniques

❑ GENERAL FICTION

❑ 19

Writing What You Feel

By Eileen Goudge

It's the oldest advice in the business: Write what you know. But what does it mean exactly? Years ago, when I was teaching a writing class, many of my students handed in short stories that for one reason or another didn't work—but no matter what my criticism, the response I most often heard was: "That's the way it happened!" Yes, I'd patiently point out, but a story about an insurance agent in Dayton attending his grandmother's funeral isn't likely to set the publishing world on fire. "Aren't we supposed to write what we know?" the puzzled student would ask. To which I would reply, "If you wrote what you *felt* about your grandmother's death, you might have something worth reading."

Is the success of *Presumed Innocent* due in part to its author's having actually committed murder? No . . . not that we know of, anyway. What we *do* know is that Scott Turow is an attorney, and his experience in that field is part of what makes the novel such a vivid and compelling read. More important, though, is that as readers we're made privy to many of the frustrations Mr. Turow himself must have felt while navigating the shoals of the District Attorney's office, with its rampant egos and unsavory dealings. What makes *Presumed Innocent* work, ultimately, is Mr. Turow's honesty in sharing with us his deepest, darkest emotions. And who among us *hasn't* experienced feelings about our jobs, marriages, families that might not be suitable for a *Dick and Jane* reader?

Simple, huh? Don't just write about what happened; write how you *feel* about what happened? Well, not quite. Because what happens in a novel is either imaginary, or a fragment of something that has occurred in real life—then magnified times a hundred. How the heck, you might ask, do I know how I would feel about being shipwrecked, or having my wife leave me for my best friend, or being sentenced to life in prison?

73

The short answer is, you don't. The trick is to write about people and situations that carry at least an echo of your own experience, enough of an echo for you to be able to put yourself in your characters' moccasins and to walk a mile in them while you're at it. And along the way, if you're lucky, you might even discover a few things in your own North Forty that you hadn't really looked at, or weren't quite ready to dig up. At the end, your short story or novel will be the richer for it, and you'll most certainly be the wiser.

When I was writing my first novel, *Garden of Lies,* this lesson was brought home to me in a particularly dramatic way. Rachel, an OB/Gyn intern at a Catholic hospital, discovers unexpectedly that she's pregnant—a plot contrivance that mirrored a similar situation in my life. My own pregnancy—fortunately, in this case—ended in miscarriage, but not before I'd suffered a moral crisis of epic proportions. What I took away from that experience was that believing absolutely in a woman's right to choose is one thing, but that actually *making* that choice is something else altogether.

Faced with the same choice, my heroine, Rachel, must also cope with the disenchantment of realizing that her lover, David Sloane, the hospital's chief OB/Gyn resident, isn't the caring, sensitive man she thought he was. Quite the opposite, in fact. Having the baby is out of the question, David scoffs. He'll arrange for an abortion. What's the big deal? It's no worse than having a tooth pulled.

Rachel rebels in a way that's both unexpected and unsettling. After a period of agonizing, she agrees to have an abortion, but only if *he* performs it. No unmarked grave for their child, she says. He must fully understand what he's asking her to do, and that what they'll be destroying is a *life,* their baby's life.

David is horrified. He accuses her of being sick, crazy, demented. But Rachel stands firm, and he's left with no choice in the end but to give in to her demand. On a stormy night, in a colleague's borrowed office, the dark deed is done—an act with unforeseen consequences that resonates throughout the rest of the novel.

Over the years, many readers have told me that this scene is among the most powerful and disturbing in all my novels. What makes it so compelling? Well, for one thing, life and death matters usually are. But what if it had been told from David Sloane's point of view? His stake in the action is much smaller than Rachel's; his main fear is of being trapped into parenthood. Not only that: His conflict revolves mainly around whether or not he can convince Rachel to undergo an abortion (at hands other than his, of course). He's experiencing none of the emotional see-sawing of his lover; hence his angst is of little interest to us.

But look what happens when we meet David again, in a later chapter. Years have passed, and the full impact of what he'd been forced to do has come home to roost. He's impotent, and it's eating him alive. It's payback time in the not-so-O.K. corral, and when he exacts his revenge on Rachel, it'll be more than blood that gets spilled.

Now we're cooking with gas. Ask any man who's suffered from impotence, and you'll no doubt understand what David is feeling. By switching to his point of view, we're taken right to the very vortex of his torment. And his dilemma, though arguably self-inflicted and certainly less than sympathetic, becomes as wrenching in its way as was Rachel's.

To sum it up, the best kind of writing—the *heartfelt* kind—is at its core comprised of two absolutely essential ingredients:

1) Creating scenes in which the emotional stakes are high.

2) Writing the scene from the point of view of the character with the most to gain, or, as the case may be, to lose.

Another strong example of a scene in which the emotional stakes are high—one that was alchemized from my own real-life experience—can be found in *Such Devoted Sisters.* Angered by her selfish older sister's betrayal, Dolly commits an act of vengeance so heinous that its fallout continues into the next generation. The year is 1954, and Dolly mails a damning document to the House Unamerican Activities Committee that ultimately costs her movie-star sister, Eve, both her career and her life.

What sparked this dramatic scene was an incident in which my own sister wrote a letter to the San Francisco *Chronicle,* accusing me of having lied in an interview I'd given about having been on welfare for a brief time when I was a young, single mom in the early Seventies. I understand now what her motives were: She was "protecting" my parents, who (though I didn't hold them responsible then and don't now) must have felt guilty that they'd somehow let me down. But at the time, it was extremely hurtful.

In using it as the nucleus for my scene, however, I was not only able to bring more than one shade of gray to a character many might have perceived as a villainess; I was also able to spin straw into "literary gold." Loving my sister as I do (and knowing she loves me), I tried hard to put myself into her mind, to imagine what she must have been feeling as she dropped that letter into the mailbox. And this gave me the added dimension I needed to bring home to the reader the horror that strikes Dolly the moment her letter slips from *her* fingers, and the mailbox clangs shut.

Which brings me to my second point: Which of these two characters has the most to gain or lose? Eve might seem the obvious choice. She loses *everything,* including her mind. But what hell is blacker than the ones we create for ourselves? In the years following her sister's suicide, Dolly is tormented with guilt. She yearns to somehow right the terrible wrong she's committed. How can she make amends to her sister, who's now dead? Through Eve's children, it turns out, two young runaways with whom Dolly is eventually reunited. The novel, in the end, becomes one of heartwarming redemption rather than of revenge (a dish, as the late Dorothy Parker once wrote, best eaten cold).

In *Blessing in Disguise* I used my own struggle as a new stepmom in creating the conflict between my heroine, Grace, and Hannah, her sixteen-year-old stepdaughter. My own stepdaughter, then eleven, was on a guerilla mission, it seemed to me at the time. And the target was easy: me. I didn't even know enough to duck, until it was too late. What I learned the hard way was that for a blended marriage to work, parents must also be partisans. They must stand united, or be divided. For children, step and otherwise, if allowed to run rampant, will eventually cause the walls to crumble.

Though my own marriage ended unhappily, I took what I'd learned from the experience and applied it to Grace's conflict. Frustrated with her boyfriend's blindness where his bratty daughter is concerned, Grace gives him an ultimatum: Fish or cut bait. Either wise up about Hannah, or lose her, Grace. If only I'd done the same!

A note of caution: Life has an eerie habit of imitating art. While deep in the throes of writing *Trail of Secrets,* which features a love affair between a champion show-jumper and New York City mounted policeman, I became quite caught up in the romance of horses, and in the mounted police in particular. In the course of my research I rode on patrol with the commanding officer, a dynamic woman in her forties.

Even more thrilling, I fell in love with my hero—literally! Tony Salvatore, a composite of several officers I had the good fortune to get to know, became so real to me that if he had existed, I'd have jumped onto the back of his horse and ridden off into the sunset with him. In a heartbeat.

What I came to realize was that my "love affair" with Tony had more to do with my failing marriage than the novel I was writing. In the midst of all this, it dawned on me that what I needed more than a mid-life-crisis *affaire de coeur* was a change of lifestyle. My blue-blooded heroine, Skyler, resists falling in love with Tony (with whom she had a one-night stand that left her pregnant). Hers is a life of privilege and white-shoe social connections. Would marriage to Tony mean giving all that up? After years of poverty, I, too, was enjoying a life of privilege, but, as Skyler learns, that lifestyle can be like a too-tight corset at times. While she chooses marriage and motherhood, I chose freedom.

But my own tale has a happy ending as well. Shortly after leaving my marriage, I met a wonderful man who is everything I'd ever imagined in a hero. Sandy Kenyon is a talk-show host who interviewed me over the radio while I was promoting the paperback publication of *Blessing in Disguise*. We had such a good time talking, we just kept at it, and a year and a half later we were married!

My newest novel, which I'm currently in the process of writing, is a sequel to *Garden of Lies,* and among its many highly dramatic plot strands, there's a love affair between my widowed heroine, Rose, and a dynamic radio talk-show host. She's not quite ready to fall in love . . . but he's so perfect for her that, one by one, her reservations begin to melt.

By now, you may be asking yourself a similar question: Where do I start? Which of my many life experiences should I draw from? And how do I go about tapping into the emotional core of these experiences?

There are no easy answers. Knowing what to write about is almost as difficult as knowing how to write it. But a good place to start, I've found, is by paying attention to that "small, still voice" in the back of your head. The things that matter most to us are what we remember best, and the daydreams we think of as harmless indulgences often have deeper significance. Anyone who has kept a journal knows that what you *intend* to write isn't always what ends up on paper. Learning to tune in to those feelings and observations is the key to successful writing in general.

At the risk of sounding somewhat New Age, I've found that my Muse speaks loudest during my quietest moments. While I can't always predict when she'll make an appearance, or what pearls she'll throw my way, what I *have* learned to do is to listen. She's almost never wrong, and has yet to lead me astray. All she asks is that I remain loyal in return.

Years ago, I attended a lecture given by a well-known novelist who offered a priceless gem of wisdom: You can court many muses, but marry only one. What's important is to maintain a *focus,* to keep the channels free of static so that the signal always comes in loud and clear. How you achieve that only *you* can determine. If you're staring at a blank page (or screen), waiting for inspiration, don't hold your breath. Inspiration is fickle; like love, it pounces when you least expect it.

Inspiration *can* be cultivated, however. I formed the habit early on of carrying a notebook with me wherever I went, so I can jot down thoughts and ideas as they come. Over time, I've come to see that these flashes of inspiration, while seemingly random, have a circadian rhythm all their own. The most brilliant flashes usually come a) just before I fall asleep; b) just as I'm waking up; or c) anywhere in, or near, running water. I've concluded that for me the best way to coax an idea out of its cave is either to close my eyes and let my mind drift—or to take a bath. Usually, the combination of the two works like a charm.

Our minds are scavengers that pick up anything and everything, but during periods of rest and reflection only certain things rise to the surface. These idea/memories are usually the ones deemed by our unconscious most useful or in some way noteworthy. An example of how and why I chose to apply such "flotsam" to a particular scene can be found in *Trail of Secrets.* In creating the conflict between Kate and her husband, Will, I'd been wrestling over the question of what makes a good marriage go bad. Will is unfailingly kind to Kate, and despite financial setbacks is a wonderful provider. They were once very much in love and still share much affection for one another. What went wrong?

I was stuck . . . until I recalled something my ex-husband had said in a joint therapy session not long before we separated. "That's not the way it happened!" he'd bellowed at one point. And therein lay the tale. What he could have said was, "That's not how I *remember* it." But instead, he chose to believe that his version of certain events was the *only* version.

Suddenly, the path to understanding was clear. My character, Will, isn't a bad husband or even a bad man. He simply lacks the ability to see past the end of his nose. His opinion is the only one that counts, and if he doesn't want to look at something, he convinces himself it simply isn't there. No wonder Kate is frustrated!

To recall the grandaddy of all aphorisms: Nothing worth having is achieved without a struggle. Telling a story off the top of your head is the simplest way to go about it, but what will you have to show for it in the end? On the other hand, writing from the deepest part of you, reaching into dark cupboards you'd just as soon remained shut, is enormously challenging, often scary—yet always the most rewarding. For the best fiction—like the most convincing lie—is usually built upon a grain of truth.

❑ 20

SEVEN KEYS TO EFFECTIVE DIALOGUE

BY MARTIN NAPARSTECK

GOOD DIALOGUE MAKES CHARACTERS IN A STORY SOUND LIKE REAL people talking, yet no one I know talks like a character, even in the best novels. This seeming contradiction can be explained by examining the seven attributes of good dialogue.

1. **Every voice is unique.**
In my novel *A Hero's Welcome,* Culver and Mabel talk:

"Hi," she said softly.
"Hi."
"You feeling better?"
"Yeah."
"You had too much to drink."
"I know."
"Maybe you should go back to your room and sleep it off."
"I would miss the party."
"It's not much fun anyway."
"Maybe I should have some coffee?"

Although both characters are products of middle-class, Eastern America, they are individuals, and I tried to keep that in mind. I tried to reflect Mabel's caring for Culver's condition and to capture Culver's condition—near-drunkenness—and a desire to continue the conversation. She speaks in longer sentences and controls the subject; he often speaks in incomplete sentences and only in response to her verbal initiatives. The differences may be subtle, but readers are unlikely to confuse who is speaking, despite the lack of attribution. Any time you have two or more characters speaking, make their rhythms differ. Some can speak staccato, some can speak with flow, some can use profanity, others can use big and fancy words. Assign a different voice to each character.

2. **Don't make speeches.**
Unless your character is running for president or teaching a litera-

ture class or is pompous, don't let him rant on for more than three or four sentences without being interrupted by another character. In my novel *War Song,* Fernandez says,

"In case you never heard, war is hell. War is hell. Some people got to get killed so others can live in freedom. I know that might sound corny to you, but if enough people believed it this world would be a lot better off."

Then he's cut off by a character who finds his little speech pompous.

In real life we don't usually tolerate being lectured at. Sitting in a classroom or in a church, we might have to, but not always even then. We prefer a chance to respond. In a bar or a living room, we're likely to respond with our own opinion before the speaker gets too carried away. Your characters should display the same intolerance.

3. Authors are not tape recorders.

In "Deep in the Hole," a short story published in *Aethlon,* I have Mickey, a member of his college's baseball team, say to his literature professor, "I have a game on Wednesday and I wonder if it would be all right if I skipped the class. I can read all the. . . ." Because it's a highly autobiographical story, and because I was tremendously awkward in speech in the late 60's, I feel certain the real-life dialogue this bit of fiction is based upon went something like this: "Eh, I have, eh, you know, a game on Wednesday and I, eh, wonder, would it be, eh, all right. . . ." All those "ehs" and that "you know" may be O.K. for a sentence or two, but for a whole story it would not only annoy most readers, but would distract them to the point of losing them. A fiction writer is not a journalist, and he has no obligation to act like a stenographer or a tape recorder. The idea is to capture both the essence and the underlying emotion of what's said, not to reproduce a transcript.

4. People tell more little lies than big ones.

Probably most people who commit a murder will tell the police they didn't do it. Big lies are part of life and should be part of stories. But most of us don't get that much opportunity to tell big lies (most of us will never be asked by the police if we committed a murder). But smaller lies are part of our everyday conversations. In my *Ellery Queen* short story, "The 9:13," two men are alone in a train station, and one tells the other his name is Thunder, but two pages later he says:

"My name ain't Thunder."
"What?"
"My name ain't Thunder."
"No?"
"No, it ain't."
"Oh."
"Ain't you curious what it is?"
Joe stammered a bit.
"It's Eddie."
"I—I see."
"Ain't you curious why I told ya it was Thunder?"
"Yes, I suppose so. Why?"
"Why what?"
"Why did you tell me your name was Thunder?"
"I ain't gonna tell ya."

Eddie's lie has no real purpose, but the fact that he chose to tell this particular lie in this particular manner reveals something about his character. Not everyone's playfulness is malevolent. Have your characters lie about small things in a manner that reveals who they are.

5. Dialogue is made up of monologues.

When someone is speaking to you, consider how you typically devote part of your attention to what she's saying, but you are also focused on what you're going to say when it's your turn to speak. In "Getting Shot," a short story of mine published in *Mississippi Review,* a soldier who has been wounded in Vietnam is told by his lieutenant:

"You're gonna get a Purple Heart out of this. What do you think about that?"
"Not much." I'm smiling like a teenage kid just got his first lay, and the Louey, he knows it.
He pats my right shoulder. "Sure, sure." He adds, "Sure."

Although the narrator responds to what the lieutenant has said, he clearly has something else on his mind, part of which reflects the false bravado he assumes the situation requires. The lieutenant, while detecting that and playing along, uses a bit of staccato speech to end that portion of the conversation so he can move on to other things.

6. Every word in dialogue represents a choice.

Every word you ever spoke in your life represented a choice. You could have chosen to be silent. You could have used another word. Consider this bit of dialogue (from *War Song*): "Don't you wanna go home?" It could have been, "Do you not desire to return to your home?" Or, "Have you no desire to go home again?" The choice is based on who the character is. One test that works for me is to write the same bit of dialogue a dozen or more times, at least in my mind, sometimes on my computer screen, and then, only then, to decide which is most appropriate for a particular character under this particular circumstance. Chances are the first words you choose are not the ones that best reflect the character. As with all other writing, nothing improves dialogue like rewriting.

7. All dialogue should reveal character and/or advance plot.

I have never included a piece of dialogue like this in any story I've ever written (thank the great muse):

He told me how to get to Salt Lake City from Logan.
"Take Valley West Highway until you come to the Interstate 15 interchange and proceed on to the interstate, going south, for about 90 miles, and when you come to the exit marked 600 north, get off and follow the signs to downtown." Thanks to his accurate and detailed directions I found my way to Salt Lake City safely.

Any dialogue that simply exchanges information between characters (who was the 26th president of the U.S., what does antidisestablishment mean) is static. Stories need to move forward. Just as you never need to say the character walked to the other side of the room (unless it's the first time this guy has walked in 10 years), you never need to reveal how someone learned the directions from here to there. Just assume, as your readers will, that there are some bits of conversation we know take place in real life but which are far too boring to include in a story.

But do let a character say, "You're fired," even though it reveals a bit of information the listener didn't know, because it changes the life of the poor guy. If the dialogue doesn't change the listener's life, no matter how slightly, or help us better understand who the speaker is, leave it out.

Each of the first six examples I've given help make the speakers sound like real people. But only the seventh one is likely to reflect accurately a real bit of conversation. And that's the one you should never use.

□ 21

The Novel—You Do It Your Way, I'll Do It Mine

By Dorothy Uhnak

I ADMIT TO BEING AN ECCENTRIC WRITER. I'VE YET TO MEET ANOTHER writer who works as I do, so don't consider this an instructional article. But do take from it whatever methods will serve you best. And don't permit *anyone* to tell you that *your method* of working is wrong. It is the work itself that counts.

Years ago, as a fairly accomplished knitter, I undertook to copy a very complicated Irish-fisherman quilt. It contained at least seven different patterns: twists and cables and popcorns and secret family weaves. Looking at the picture of the quilt in question, I stopped cold. Never, not in a million years, could I do this. It then occurred to me, you don't knit a whole quilt all at once. One stitch at a time; one line at a time; one pattern at a time.

Maybe this isn't a very good analogy for writing a novel, but after all, we do write one word at a time, one line at a time, one paragraph and one page at a time. The unifying force of all the pieces, in the novel as in the quilt, draws the whole thing together.

The unifying force in my novels has always been the characters. I care about their growth or regression, about the circumstances that change them and move them through the story, much as life molds and shapes each of us.

What I must know, absolutely, before I start a novel is who each character is at the beginning and who he will be at the end. I'm never really sure how the characters will get from the first place to the last, but I am positive where they will end up.

The Ryer Avenue Story (St. Martin's Press, 1993) had six characters not of equal importance but essential, since the story belonged to all of them. We meet them as children, 11- and 12-year-olds. What I knew about them was simple. They lived and played together on the Avenue in the Bronx where I grew up. In middle age, all five boys and one girl were successful, accomplished people, some more than others. They moved in life from when we meet them on the street of a cold snowy night until they are confronted in mid-life with a problem set in motion when they were kids.

The first thing I had to know about these people was what they looked and sounded like. My characters have to be named absolutely on target. Megan Magee could not be Mary Reardon; Danny DeAngelo could not be Bobby Russelli. They become as real to me as people I actually know and speak to day after day. (You wouldn't want to address your best friend Sally as Luanne, would you?)

Here is my first eccentricity: I work on a standard Hermes 45 typewriter. I have three machines carefully stored away—don't ask how one gets ribbons—you remember ribbons? No? Well, anyway—I don't go near my heavy, trusty machine for quite a while.

First, I research as meticulously as possible in order to know the world in which my people live. For Ryer Avenue, I used the neighborhood where I was born and raised. But I never did go to their Catholic school (St. Simon Stock in the Bronx). Some of my friends did, and I absorbed their stories, peeked through their school windows and stole into their church when I was a child. I didn't know why I did these things until years later: It was material I would need to draw on one day.

To describe accurately a scene in the death camps of WWII, I read almost more than my mind could hold of horror stories. There is no way I could write substantially about any of this. But I had the good fortune of talking with an older friend who told me he had been one of the young American lieutenants in the advanced group entering the death camps and opening them up for our troops. He lent me that part of his life in one long, dark, horrible conversation, during which we left our cake uneaten and the coffee cold. He gave me this part of himself to use in my novel, and later when he read the book, he said I had made him nicer than he really was, but I don't think so.

In my Ryer Avenue story, one of my characters becomes a big shot in the movie industry; one a leading light of the church; one a promising, rising politician; the woman becomes a psychiatrist. Each area had to be researched. If Gene O'Brien was to work in the Vatican, I needed to be very sure I knew what his physical surroundings would be and what his daily routines would encompass. I consult my research notes until I'm thoroughly familiar with the material and can place my people in an environment formerly alien to me.

Before setting one word on paper, I had to visualize scenes that would define each character as a child: Megan in the classroom; Dante in his father's shoe repair shop; Eugene at church; Willie losing himself in the world of movies. Since the novel begins in the childhood of my characters, I walked around with each kid in my head, one at a time. I needed to know how the characters looked, sounded, acted, reacted, what they showed of themselves and what they hid. Only then did I sit, fingers on the trusty faithful noisy Hermes 45 keys, and pound out the chapters, one at a time.

I have the whole scene completely worked out before I begin to work: no notes (except for background research), just a scene that comes as I walk, rest, stare blankly at TV, even as I read a book by another writer. When I place the character in the scene, he or she knows how to move, what to think, what to say. By this time, I can hear each individual voice. No character sounds exactly like any other. They may all use certain phrases, expressions, and expletives, but each voice belongs only to the speaker.

Sometimes the scene I'm describing leads directly to the next scene, sometimes not. There are times when I get a whole chapter down on paper; other times, only two or three pages. And then I walk away. I've been known to work for fifteen minutes at a stretch or for ten hours. It is the story going on in my head that dictates my working hours. No nine-to-five for me!

The creative work for me is not done at the typewriter. It's done through all the long hours of listening, imagining, getting to know and trust my characters as they move through their lives toward the resolutions I know they must reach. Sometimes, I am surprised by the routes they take, the diversions they encounter.

One time when I was working on a television script, my producer called to ask about Act Five. I told him it was terrific; worked out exactly right. He asked me to send it to him. One problem—I hadn't typed it. I buckled down and did the annoying job of putting words to paper.

I don't wait for "inspiration," unless inspiration can be described as continuous, uninterrupted thinking, living with the story, and the fictional people who are taking on their own lives. With this strange method of working, I accomplish more than if I sat down at a given hour and stayed put for four or five hours, without knowing what I was going to write. I usually wait until the scene, chapter, or event is practically bursting from my head—then I form the scene into words on paper.

This process occurs during the first draft. I do go over every page before beginning a new session. I make my notations; slash things out and cram things in. I usually try to stop work when I have a strong feeling about what will come next; save it, walk it, think it, let it have free flow until the pictures, words, and actions must absolutely be on paper.

My working habits on the second draft are more typical of other writers', and I work long hours. I change, rewrite, or leave untouched pages and pages of the manuscript. I see where a character has taken over and where he or she shouldn't have; where I have interfered when I shouldn't have.

In the second draft, sometimes incredible moments happen when I find myself reworking something I hadn't intended to, and the descriptions and conversations soar. I feel myself to be the medium by which the story is told. I just write what I feel I'm supposed to write. Magic. Sometimes it's absolutely wonderful. (Sometimes it isn't!)

In my novel, *Codes of Betrayal,* a very strange thing happened. My heroine, Laura Santangelo, comes into her apartment, stunned and angry to find one Richie Ventura sitting on her couch, his feet up on her coffee table. The chapter ends with Laura saying, "Richie, what the hell are *you* doing here?"

I didn't know what he was doing there. I hadn't a clue. I just instinctively felt his presence was absolutely necessary. I had to let my mind flow to find the logic for the scene. I would not invent some fraudulent reason just because I liked the slam-bang last sentence in that chapter. I skipped ahead, did a few chapters, and suddenly it came to me: Richie was in her apartment for a very specific reason, and he had a very valid excuse to offer Laura. I backtracked and let them work it out.

One thing my publisher asked me to do with that novel was to give him an outline of the last half of the book. I told him it was impossible; the work would proceed step by step from what came before. He insisted; I wrote an outline. It was cold, bloodless, meaningless. The characters were sticks with wooden personalities. If I had followed it, my book would have sunk. My publisher returned the outline and said, "I guess you don't do outlines."

A very strange thing happens when I finish a book. I send it off to a woman who puts it on her computer to get it into wonderful-looking condition. It goes to the publisher who loves it and makes a few suggestions here and there. Then I handle the three-hundred-plus-page manuscript, all neatly and professionally typed, and have the eerie feeling that I didn't write this book, that I didn't put in any *real* time. I didn't work hours and days in my little workroom. I feel that I started at the sea down the hill from our house; I walked the dogs and the cats; I stared at the television; I knitted; I read books. When and how did that book get written?

At that point, I have to just let the whole thing go. It's out of my hands. It belongs to others now. I need to get free of all emotion about it. Yes, I did write it; yes, I did work hard on it; yes, I did agonize and complain and question myself and my talent and the worth of the story itself. Yes, I did actually write it, if in my own particularly eccentric way.

I've knitted only one Irish quilt, but I have written ten novels, so I guess I just keep at it, one word at a time, one line at a time, one paragraph, one page and chapter at a time.

The big problem now is the very beginning of the search for the next group of people, floating around, trying to get my attention. Or rather, trying to take over my life, body, and soul. You do it your way, I'll do it mine.

❏ 22

TURNING YOUR EXPERIENCE INTO FICTION

BY EDWARD HOWER

"THAT WOULD MAKE A GOOD STORY—YOU OUGHT TO WRITE IT!" How many times have you heard people say this, after you've told them about some interesting experience?

But if you're like me, you may not *want* to write directly about yourself, except perhaps in your private journal. This doesn't mean, however, that your own life can't be used as material for fiction. Using your own experiences as starting places for stories or novels gives your work an authenticity that made-up adventures may lack. A great many fiction writers have mined their own pasts—some of them over and over throughout their careers.

Advantages of starting with yourself

Writing stories that are similar to real-life occurrences allows you to relive and to re-examine your life. In fiction, you can explore all the might-have-beens of your past. You can experience the loves that didn't quite happen but that might have proved blissful or (more interestingly) disastrous in tragic or amusing ways. You can delve into your worst fears, describing what might have happened if you hadn't been so careful about trusting strangers or about avoiding life's dark alleys.

And by creating characters similar to yourself and to people you've known, you can get a perspective on your past that couldn't come from direct, analytic examination. One of the most gratifying experiences I had in writing my last novel was getting to know my family all over again in ways I'd never previously considered. Some anger resurfaced, but so did a lot of compassion. And I finally got a kind of closure on my sometimes painful childhood that had eluded me before.

I've emphasized writing about the past here rather than about the present. This is because I think it's a lot more productive to deal with material from which you have psychic distance.

Selective memory can produce interesting, emotionally charged material for fiction. Recent events, however, are hard to deal with creatively. Immediate reality intrudes, and issues unresolved in life resist resolution in fiction.

Searching your life

Here's an exercise I used while I was writing my semi-autobiographical novel, *Night Train Blues.* I've frequently given the exercise to students in my creative writing workshops, too. It's designed to help retrieve buried memories and then transform them into usable images, characters, and episodes for stories or longer fiction.

First, decide on a period in your life you'd like to write about. A year in your past in which emotionally intense experiences happened is often the best one. This doesn't mean that the events need to be melodramatic. Small traumas and triumphs often make the best material for fiction, especially if they involve people you've had strong feelings about. Events that caused you to change your attitude toward yourself and other people are especially good. For this reason, many writers choose a period from childhood or adolescence—the times of many emotional changes.

Start the exercise in a quiet place, alone. Get comfortable, close your eyes, and take slow deep breaths. Now imagine yourself going home during the time period you've chosen. Picture yourself approaching the place where you lived. Imagine entering it. What do you see . . . hear . . . smell? Go into the next room. What's there? Now go into the room in which you kept your personal possessions. Stand in the middle of the floor and look around. What do you see . . . hear . . . smell? Now go to some object that was especially precious to you. Hold it. Feel it. Turn it around. Get to know it again with as many senses as possible. Then ask yourself: Why did I choose this object?

As soon as you're ready, open your eyes and start writing as fast as you can. First describe the object in great detail. If you want to discuss people and events associated with it, that's fine, too. Finally, write about the object's importance to you. You might give yourself ten to fifteen minutes for the entire exercise. Don't edit what you write. Don't even pause to look back over it—fill as much paper as you can. If you write fast, you'll fill at least a page, probably more.

When I did this exercise, the object I found was an old wooden radio with a cloth dial and an orange light that glowed behind it. I mentally ran my fingers over its smooth, rounded surfaces. I put my nose up to it and smelled the dusty cloth warmed by the pale bulb behind it. I twisted the dial, and listened to my favorite childhood stations.

Thinking about the radio's meaning for me, I remembered the warm relationship I'd had with the person who gave it to me. The radio also re-acquainted me with country songs I later came to associate with an important character in my novel, my young hero's wandering older brother. So I gave my fictional narrator a radio similar to the one I'd had, and I let him find solace in its music, too.

My students have also come up with radios given to them by important people in their lives. Dolls and stuffed animals, sports equipment, pictures, china figurines, tools, articles of clothing—all have been highly evocative objects that eventually radiated emotions not only for the writers but for their fictional characters as well. Cars, records, and clothes were important items for people returning to adolescence. Each freshly-recalled object resonated with feelings about rebellion, first love, and newfound freedoms.

Transforming truth into fiction

Now it's time to turn this object into the central image of a story or novel chapter. Write "If this were fiction . . ." at the top of a page. Give yourself a different name. You are now a fictional character, one who resembles you but who will gradually develop his or her own personality as you continue working.

Then jot down some answers to these questions:

Character development

1. What does the choice of this object tell about the character (A—"you") who chose it?
   - Who is A? Describe this person quickly.

2. Imagine that another character (B) gave A the object.
   - Who is B? Describe B quickly.
   - What is B's relationship to A?

3. Imagine that yet another character (C) wants the object.
   - Who is C? Describe C quickly.
   - What is C's relationship to B and A?

When trying to imagine B and C, you might choose people from your own life or people like them who might have given you the object or might have coveted it. Characters often come from composites of several people you knew—the physical attributes of one person, the voice of another, the sense of humor or the mannerisms of another.

One way to get to know characters not modeled after yourself is to start the visualization exercise again, this time treating someone you knew as you did the object in the previous exercise. Follow the person around in your visualization, observing and listening closely. Then write a fast page or two about what you discovered.

Another good way to understand a character is to make lists of his or her attributes and preferences. Jot down his or her favorite clothes, food, TV show, brand of car, breed of dog, film hero, period in history, childhood memory, and so forth. Say what religious, political, and ethical beliefs the character has. Expand the list until you feel you know as much about this fictional person as you do about your best friend. You may not use much of this material in the actual story, but it gives you the background of the character that you need in order to write with authority.

Plot development

The treasured object can give you some ideas about what storyline to follow. Try answering these questions:

1. **A and the object**
   - Why does A treasure it? What will A do with it?
   - What problems might result from his having it?
2. **B and the object**
   - Where did B get the object? Why did B give it to A?
   - What problems might result from B giving it to A?
3. **C and the object**
   - Why does C want the object?
   - What problems might result from C trying to get it?

All plots involve conflicts—thus the emphasis on problems. Once you've listed some conflicts, choose one that interests you and try answering some more questions:

1. What events might foreshadow this conflict?
2. What dramatic action might result from this conflict?
3. How might the conflict be resolved?

By this time, you've probably discovered that although the story has ostensibly been about an object, it's really about people. One is a central character who probably resembles you in some ways, and one or more other characters are based—closely or loosely, it doesn't matter—on people you've known.

Deciding on a setting

To become familiar with your fictional locale, try closing your eyes and visualizing the place where you found the object in the original exercise. Observe the details of the room, the sounds you hear from the other rooms, and the view from the windows. Then, as if you were a bird, fly out a window to observe the neighborhood, the town or city, the county or region. Pay attention to details—the clothes people are wearing, the kinds of cars in the streets, the signs in shop windows. Smell the smells. Listen to the sounds of life. Feel the energy given off by ball parks, bars, beaches, playgrounds, political rallies. After you've flown around for a while, return to your region . . . neighborhood . . . dwelling . . . and room—for a last look-around.

Then start writing as fast as you can about things you've discovered on your journey. You might want to draw a quick map with concentric circles radiating out from your own small world. You don't need to include everything you found—this isn't a memory test. But do go into detail about discoveries that stand out sharply. Be aware that the best details of a setting give off strong emotions, providing atmosphere for your characters to move around in. The way they respond to their environment will help define who they are and what they do.

Development of a theme

To get a grip on the story's meaning, it will be helpful to go back to the treasured object at least one more time and answer these questions:

1. How does the object resemble
   - you
   - character A
   - character B and/or C

2. What effect does the object have on the relationship
   - between A and B
   - between B and C
   - between A and C

Again, you'll probably discover that whatever your story means, it has to do with people developing relationships with each other, entering into conflicts, and trying to find resolutions to them. The treasured object may fade in importance by the time you've finished the story's last draft. But it will have served its purpose.

Truth and invention

What if the characters and plot of your fiction closely resemble real people and/or events that have actually occurred? Does it matter?

I don't think it does. If you use the *techniques* of fiction-writing—characterization, plot, conflict, dialogue, description, and so on—then what you'll have at the end will be fiction, regardless of its source.

But you may still find that similarities between your life and your fiction inhibit your creative writing. You might also worry that readers who know you could be disturbed by what you write. In this case, you can do what a great many authors have done throughout history (sometimes on the advice of their attorneys)—make alterations in their fiction to avoid resemblances to actual people, places, and events.

• With characters, change one or more of these attributes: size, shape, hair color, accent, nationality, clothes
• Change the story's setting to a different region
• Move the story backward or forward in time

Having made these changes, you'll probably have to change other details of the fictional work in order to fit in the new material. This in itself can become part of the creative process, helping you to imagine more and remember less. At the end, even those who know you best may not be clear about what you've recalled and what you've made up. And you may not be sure, yourself.

If this happens, you may be certain you've moved from autobiography to fiction—one of the most interesting and satisfying ways in which your writing can develop.

□ 23

DIALOGUE AND CHARACTERIZATION

By Maya Kaathryn Bohnhoff

"SHOW, DON'T TELL" IS ONE OF THE FIRST RULES OF THE FICTIONAL road, yet one of the hardest to master. How do you show the reader your protagonist is strong-minded to the point of being argumentative or that your heroine tends to bite off more than she can chew? Yes, you could just *say* it: "Justin was strong-minded to the point of being argumentative." "Matilda had a tendency to bite off more than she could chew." But these statements are meaningless if Justin doesn't insist on his own way of doing things or Matilda doesn't constantly try to overreach her abilities.

Before you can either tell or show the reader anything about your characters, you must know them yourself: their history, their educational level, their loves and hates and foibles. You must know how they feel about life, the universe, everything.

The puppet master

Knowing these things, you must be able to portray your characters as individuals, which means that they should be distinctive. Further, the reader should never see the "strings" by which you, the writer, are manipulating the characters. Your heroine is strong-willed, savvy self-assured . . . until a scene requires her to whine and grovel. So she whines and grovels. You are playing (evil laughter) the puppet master.

Like a real human being, a fictional character must seem to be the product of both nature and nurture. Some of the best moments of high drama, in real life and in literature, occur when flawed human beings do incredible things. By having a character's flaws imposed from *outside* the story by the (evil laughter) puppet master, you rob yourself and your reader of this drama.

If you really *need* this character to whine and grovel at this point, let the weakness come from *inside,* and show the reader the genesis of

95

that weakness. Perhaps you can have your strong-willed, savvy young protagonist be weakened by grief over the loss of a loved one. This weakness is contrary to her self-image, which in turn makes her angry at herself and the universe, and results in guilt. These forces can make a normally rock-solid personality resemble gelatin. This character's greatest struggle may be to rediscover herself, and she may be less than consistent as she goes about it.

"I'm wounded!" she said lightly.

Dialogue is, at once, one of the most essential tools of characterization and one of the easiest ways to undermine it.

The title line of this section was in a manuscript I was given at a writer's conference some years back. In the context of this story, the coupling of this exclamation with an inappropriate modifier suggested that the speaker had ceased to have a human appreciation of pain. Since this was not the case, it made the narrative voice (and hence the writer) seem unreliable.

"You're so smart!" he snorted wryly.

They call it "said-book-ism": People *snort* and *exhort* when perhaps they ought to just *say* something. Snorts are fine once in a while, but unwatched, they proliferate like March hares.

A close companion of said-book-ism is "adverbitis," which can affect both dialogue and action. Mark Twain is supposed to have said, "If you see an adverb, kill it." Extreme, but some stories have led me to suggest that if the writer cut about three-quarters of the adverbs, the manuscript would improve dramatically.

> In the kitchen, he found Constance preparing their meal. He watched her QUIETLY. He found that he was still anxious and closed his eyes TIGHTLY and sighed LOUDLY.
> Constance jumped. "Jerrod!" she cried ANXIOUSLY.
> "I'm sorry, Constance." Jerrod smiled NERVOUSLY.

The adverbs here disrupt the dialogue and produce shallow characterization. We know these people are nervous or anxious, but couched in weak adverbs instead of strong verbs their anxiety is barely felt.

Here's the same passage, reworded:

> Constance was in the kitchen preparing a simple meal. He watched her in silence for a moment, anxiety digging pitons into the wall of his stomach. What he meant as a cleansing breath came out as a melodramatic sigh.

Constance jumped and turned to face him. "Jerrod!"
His smile dried and set on his lips. "I'm sorry, Constance."

Using mountain-climbing gear to evoke a mental image of anxiety for the reader conveys much more than "he said anxiously." It's through dialogue, thought, and action that your reader knows your characters and gauges their feelings. If these essentials are not fully formed, your characters will not be fully formed. If your dialogue lacks emotional depth, so will your characters. Strong verbs are better tools for building depth into dialogue than are weak verbs qualified by adverbs.

I challenge thee to a duel (of words).

Poorly constructed dialogue can reduce reader comprehension, hamper pacing, and make characters seem like bad high school actors flogging their way through scenes in which no one understands his lines or motivation. Worse, it may seem as if the lines have been forgotten altogether and the characters have resorted to ad-libbing without listening to each other.

Here's an example:

JERROD: "Constance, I'd like you to meet my friend, Peter Harrar."
CONSTANCE: "I'm glad to meet you."
PETER: "The pleasure is all mine, my lady. (*He tries to read her mind.*) Oh, that was dumb!"
JERROD: "I agree!"
PETER: "I apologize, my lady."
CONSTANCE: "No need, sir."
JERROD: "What's the matter, Peter? Forget that she's a level five Psi?"
PETER: "One of these days, friend! Would it be too rude just to bow?"
CONSTANCE: "No . . . no. I don't think so."
JERROD: "Don't you think you're overdoing it a bit?"
PETER: "No, I don't think so."
CONSTANCE: "I don't think so either. Leave him alone, Jerrod. At least he knows the meaning of the word respect."
JERROD: "Him???"
PETER: "Yeah, me."

What's wrong with this conversation? Simply that it's not a conversation—it's a duel (or the three-participant equivalent). It's also repetitive, trivial, and long.

The original scene staggered under the weight of stage business that seemed to exist only to give the characters something to do with their bodies. When I stripped away all the aimless movement that accompanied this dialogue, what was left was a barrage of small talk that took up several pages and failed either to advance the story or reveal character.

"It is a matter of life and death!"

Avoiding the use of contractions in an academic paper or essay may be a good idea, but in fictional dialogue it is a bad idea simply because real people generally do use contractions in their speech.

> "I have to talk to Matilda." Justin tried not to let his desperation show.
> "She is not receiving visitors," the guard told him.
> Justin balled his fists against the desire to use them. "This cannot wait. I have got to speak to her. I am telling you-it is a matter of life and death."

The lack of contractions here stiffens the prose and removes any urgency from the scene. Ultimately, poor Justin does not come across as a man desperate to see his beloved. The narration—his suppressed desperation, his desire to manhandle the guard—is at odds with the preciseness of the dialogue. Desperate people are not precise in their speech. They're, well, desperate.

Will the real Dinsdale please speak up?

Speech and thoughts should reveal character, show strength or weakness; truth, falsehood or ambiguity. They must seem like thoughts the readers have or, at the very least, thoughts they can imagine others could have. Also, the words a writer uses should be those that readers imagine a particular character would use.

If a character is supposed to be callous, then the words he uses should reveal his callousness.

> Ariel followed Dinsdale down the long, dark flight of stairs. At the top of the third landing, she slipped and fell.
> Below her, Dinsdale stopped and glanced back over his shoulder. "What's the matter?" he asked callously. Good God, she might have broken her neck!

Dinsdale's dialogue could just as easily have read: *"What's the matter?" he asked fearfully.*

The only difference between Dinsdale's being a rogue or a gentleman is in the adverb chosen to modify "asked." This should raise a few red flags.

Let's try a different approach:

Ariel followed Dinsdale down the long, dark flight of stairs. At the top of the third landing she slipped and fell.

Below her, Dinsdale stopped and glanced back over his shoulder. Hell, he thought, she might have broken her neck and stuck him with having to dispose of the body. "Trying to reach the bottom more quickly, my lady?" he asked.

I don't have to tell you that Dinsdale spoke callously; his thoughts and words are snide and uncaring. They make even a simple glance over the shoulder seem heartless. An acid test for dialogue, then, might be to ask: If I strip away all modifiers, what do these words tell me about the character?

Get real!

You have to develop an ear for dialogue. You can do several things when you write dialogue to make it sound real:

• *Strip away all stage business and action.* Try to write dialogue as if you were eavesdropping in the dark. No movement, just people talking.

• *Read your dialogue aloud to see what it sounds like if spoken by a real person.* Imagine your characters in a real-life situation, saying these words.

• *Ask if everything you've written is necessary.* Does it advance the plot or reveal character? Real people "um" and "uh" and "y'know" their way through life, and they indulge in conversations that wander. Fictional characters can't afford those luxuries.

• *"Run the scene" in your mind and put in the action and atmosphere only after you're satisfied that the words work.* If necessary, modify the pacing of the dialogue to work with the action.

Obviously, there are other ways to make your dialogue realistic. Here are a few of them:

Get your plot straight. If you don't know where your characters are going or where they've been, it will be reflected in what they say. Don't contradict yourself or your characters. Make sure the plot is convincing, that the elements are clear and flow logically. Then, cut any elements that don't advance the plot, develop or reveal character, or give the reader necessary information. A single plot flaw can make your entire story unravel.

Establish a definite point of view. You may wish to write dialogue from one character's viewpoint, allowing the viewpoint character's thoughts to reveal to the reader who he is.

Watch the pace. If the pacing of a scene is off, the gist of conversations can be lost, and important clues about character missed. Don't let "stage business" get in the way of dialogue. We don't need to know whether a character brandished his revolver in his left or right hand. Nor, once informed of a fact, do we need to be reminded of it every time he speaks.

Tighten your prose. Good dialogue can be the very embodiment of the phrase "elegant in its simplicity." Unless you've created a character who is known by his very penchant for tangled phrases, keep the dialogue as direct as possible. The purpose of speech is communication: Characters communicate with each other and through your characters, *you* communicate with your reader.

Know your characters. Learn who they are, then introduce them to the reader. Put words in their mouths that will make us like or dislike them (depending on their roles in your story), but their words must, above all, make us *care* what happens to them for better or worse. Above all, don't pull their strings. Give them distinctive personalities and motivation, put them in a situation, then stand back and watch what they do and listen to what they say.

There's a story in that.

□ 24

Whose Viewpoint?

By Gail Radley

ONE OF THE FIRST DECISIONS YOU'LL HAVE TO MAKE WHEN WRITING a story may seem like the simplest: in whose viewpoint to tell it. Many writers grab instinctively at "I" or "he" or "she" without giving the matter much thought. There is a variety of viewpoints from which to choose. You may even, with care, use more than one viewpoint. Each choice casts the story in a different light, offering distinct advantages and disadvantages. While your instinctive choice may be the best one, it should be backed by knowledge.

The once-popular omniscient viewpoint gives all-seeing writers the chance to drop at will into the minds and hearts of any character. The advantage of omniscience is that readers can see the big picture, with its web of conflicting emotions and goals. But, like most big pictures, it has to be seen from a distance, and readers may not have focused anywhere long enough to care. When reader empathy is missing, the story goes out the window.

Some viewpoints are rarely used—second person, for example, which seems quirky and may annoy the reader:

You phone your mother. She starts nagging again, and suddenly you don't care if you ever see her again. You slam down the receiver.

"Wait a minute," the reader protests. "I *love* my mother. We get along fine." And then, if the reader continues reading, there may be a battle of assertions on your part and protests on the reader's for the rest of the story.

The objective viewpoints—first and third—in which the viewpoint character acts as observer and reporter, are used more often. With the objective approach, the only feelings and thoughts revealed are the narrator's. A first-person objective narrator might say:

101

I sat nearby as George phoned his mother.

"How are you?" he asked. There was a stretch of silence in which George grimaced. He slammed down the receiver. "Nagging as usual," he told me. "I don't care if I ever see her again."

Here George reveals his feelings and thoughts to the narrator, who relays them to the reader. Though readers are a step removed from the hero, they get some insights into George's make-up from the narrator's "report."

The first-person objective narrator—who is observing the hero—may not only speculate about George's feelings, but offer his own opinions:

George's stomach is probably churning uncomfortably, I thought. I couldn't count the times I'd seen him reach for the antacids after a conversation with his mother. I'd often thought George took her too seriously. What he considered nagging, I'd have taken as expressions of concern. I wished I'd had a mother who'd taken as much interest . . .

Now the narrator is in danger of wresting the story away from George; suddenly readers are more concerned about the sort of mother the poor narrator had! Within limitations, the objective first-person can give a fairly intimate view of the hero. You may have a problem, however, if George decides to storm off, leaving the narrator alone in an empty room to speculate.

This problem can be resolved by using the third-person objective viewpoint. As with the first-person objective, the style is that of observer/reporter:

George phoned his mother. "How are you?" he inquired.

"I wish you'd call earlier," she complained. "I've been sitting here all morning wondering what you're doing. I've told you time and again . . ."

George listened a moment, his face contorting. Then he clapped down the receiver. "Nagging as usual," he mumbled to Rover.

Not knowing George's innermost thoughts and feelings may help build suspense; it's hard to know what he'll do next. On the other hand, knowing George only through observation may hold the reader at a distance.

For this reason, most writers settle on a *subjective* point of view, either first or third. In first-person subjective, the hero tells his own story. Readers know exactly what he thinks and feels moment by moment. It's a sure way for the writer to build reader identification and give the story authenticity. Of course, there are drawbacks. Readers may tire of the incessant "I," and the story may be overly melodramatic, particularly when the hero or the situation is very emotional. It is hard to present a picture of the protagonist without the clichéd device of having him gaze into a mirror, a puddle, or a store window! Also, when the writer uses a first-person narrator, shifting to another viewpoint can be very awkward.

All of these problems can be resolved with the third-person subjective viewpoint. Here, the writer "becomes" the viewpoint character, relating his thoughts and feelings, but no one else's. The degree of limitation the writer accepts, however, is flexible. The character may not be able to see himself, but the writer can choose to step back to allow description and commentary on the character. Additionally, when writing in third person, it is much easier to change viewpoints from one character to another.

But changing viewpoints must be done with care. Early versions of my juvenile novel, *Odd Man Out* (Macmillan 1995), were met with skepticism. The story is about eleven-year-old twins, Kit and Jordy, who befriend Oakley Duster, a mentally challenged man in their rural community. Eventually, they are called upon to make a public stand in support of this man, a decision each twin finds difficult, but for different reasons. The story belonged to both of them, and though it would have been simpler to tell it in *one* twin's viewpoint, I felt strongly that showing the perspectives of both twins would help reveal the complexity of their problem and allow me to develop their changing relationship more fully, without casting either twin as the bad guy. Just when readers might be annoyed with Kit for blowing up at Jordy, I'd take them into *her* mind to help them understand *her* struggles. In addition, telling the story from both male and female viewpoints is likely to attract more readers.

How could I keep the readers' empathy? I'd have to spend sufficient time in each twin's viewpoint for readers to get to know them both. Then, when I wanted to change viewpoint, I'd do it at chapter breaks, a point when readers are ready for change. (A shift of viewpoint within a chapter could be indicated by leaving an extra space between passages.) I mentioned the viewpoint character's name within the first two or three sentences to orient the reader. Thus, one chapter begins:

Awkwardly, Kit set the overstuffed laundry basket on the basement floor. She pulled the chain that lit the bulb dangling above the washing machine and glanced around the basement. Its gloom suited her.

A "Jordy" chapter begins:

Kit was quiet as they walked home from the bus stop Tuesday, Jordy noticed. He himself felt restless and discontented.

I also took care to divide the number of chapters equally between the twins, for the most part alternating, giving each character equal time for development.

Paul Zindel used a similar technique in *The Pigman,* in which classmates John and Lorraine alternately tell the story of their encounters with Mr. Pignati. Using the first-person for each, Zindel was able to develop truly distinctive voices. Chapter 1, with John as the viewpoint character, begins:

Now I don't like school which you might say is one of the factors that got us involved with this old guy we nicknamed the Pigman. Actually, I hate school, but then again most of the time I hate everything.

Chapter 2 shifts to Lorraine's viewpoint:

I should never have let John write the first chapter because he always has to twist things subliminally.

These two characters not only have different problems and personalities, but different vocabularies, as well. Notice, too, how Lorraine's mentioning John's name helps orient readers. In the first-person, shifts in viewpoints are rarely used. Zindel handles it here by giving the characters the task of writing their story jointly.

It is possible to shift viewpoints successfully, but proceed with caution! Avoid bouncing from character to character; change viewpoints only when necessary, and allow each viewpoint character uninterrupted time. Develop characters fully, so that readers perceive their individuality. Signal the shifts through chapter or line breaks, use of the characters' names, and distinctive vocabularies and manners of speech.

When selecting the viewpoint for your stories, don't gloss over the choices. First, understand the differences; then trust you instincts. The result will be a richer, more complex and memorable story.

❏ 25

How to Write a Novel: Questions and Answers

By Sidney Sheldon

Q. *What are some of the devices you have found most successful in keeping your readers turning the pages?*

A. The most successful device in keeping readers turning pages is to end each chapter on a note of suspense. Mickey Spillane wisely said that the first page of a novel will determine whether someone buys the book, and the last page determines whether that person will buy your next book.

Q. *Inexperienced writers tend to have difficulty establishing a voice in their fiction. How can they go about finding their voices?*

A. The way to find a voice is to make your characters real. I once planned to write a novel using only dialogue and no description. The readers would know who was speaking purely from the character's way of talking. The only reason I didn't go ahead with it was that I found out that a French writer had gotten there first.

Q. *Given that writers are always studying people they meet or observe for character ideas, do you think a fiction writer is a better judge of character than a non-writer?*

A. Fiction writers are better judges of character than anyone else. They are also more intelligent and purer in heart.

Q. *How, if at all, do your experiences and relationships with people reveal themselves in your novels?*

A. Some wise person once said that writers paper their walls with themselves. Everything that a writer sees or hears usually winds up in some form in his or her work. Many novels are autobiographical to a large extent. I've used incidents in my life in many of my books.

Q. *How concrete is your outline when you start out writing; how thoroughly developed is your story?*

A. When I begin a novel, I start with a character. I have no idea what the plot is going to be. Incidentally, this method of working is not one that I would recommend to an inexperienced writer because there are too many pitfalls along the way. I dictate the first draft of my novels and as I talk, the characters come to life and the plot begins to take shape. When I have finished the first draft, which can run to 1,500 pages, I take the typed pages and begin to rewrite, to polish and cut and shape. I do a dozen complete rewrites and spend two years on each book.

Q. *Do you have favorite themes or types of characters to write about, and why?*

A. I like to write about themes that are larger than life—people in desperate trouble, headline events that take place around the world. It's fun for me, and I think it's fun for my readers.

Q. *It seems that lengthy descriptions are less acceptable in today's novels than they have been in the past. Given that, how can a writer create a good setting without overdoing it?*

A. Lengthy descriptions are not less acceptable today if they are done well. Any good writing is appreciated, whether it's the description, the characterization, or dialogue.

Q. *Do you think it's absolutely necessary for readers to genuinely care about the major characters and what happens to him or her?*

A. I don't believe it is important for the reader to necessarily like every character, but it is important for the reader to understand and empathize—even with the villains—so that they at least have an understanding of their motivations.

Q. *Is it a good idea for writers to read novels by other authors while working on their own?*

A. I don't read other novels while I'm working on my own books. I'm too immersed in the world of my own characters. When I'm not working on a novel, I read a great deal.

Q. *Are there any "pre-writing" methods you use? For example, do you keep journals? Scribble down notes on scraps of paper? Record your dreams?*

A. Throughout my life I have jotted down ideas as they come to me for future consideration. The only "pre-writing" I do involves research for the book. Once I begin writing the novel, the characters direct the story.

Q. *Do you become so involved, so absorbed with a character you're working on that you actually take on some of that character's attributes?*

A. The characters in my novels are very real to me while I'm writing their story, but life goes on, and I meet new characters every few years. I've had a few murderers in my books, so if I took on their personality, I'd be in real trouble!

Q. *When you're working on a novel, do you try to remain solely "the creator" or do you also assume the role of critic?*

A. While I'm writing the first draft of a novel, it's very important to let the creator take over and to keep the critic away. Once the first draft is finished, the critic should go to work. Being a critic of your work initially as you go along is much too inhibiting.

Q. *Your protagonists are morally strong individuals, and likewise, the endings of your novels leave the reader with the sense of justice having been served. How essential to modern storytelling is the element of good vs. evil?*

A. I think the element of good vs. evil goes back to the most ancient storytellers. I believe that if evil triumphs, the reader is left with a feeling of disappointment. It's like a sonata where the last chord is dissonant.

Q. *Do you think it's helpful for beginning writers to try to emulate another author's style?*

A. I think every writer should develop his or her own style, and not emulate any other author. As a beginning exercise, it might be interesting to read a story by a famous author and then try to retell the story in your own words as though you had created it. But it is very important to find your own voice.

Q. *Why do so many successful first novelists have difficulties writing their second novels?*

A. One of the reasons that some successful first novelists have problems writing their second novel is that they are intimidated, afraid that they can't live up to their first success. Some writers seem to have only one novel in them, especially if that novel is autobiographical. Carl Reiner wrote a wonderful play called *Exit Laughing,* about a playwright who wrote a smash hit and had trouble writing a second play until he moved back into the poverty-stricken life he was living when he wrote his hit play.

Q. *How do you react to advice and criticism from your editor?*

A. Since I do up to a dozen complete rewrites before my publisher even sees a manuscript, by then, it's pretty much ready for publication. The suggestions made are usually minor, and if they are helpful, I'm happy to adopt them.

Q. *Every now and then, one reads a novel with "lasting" qualities, and that novel is remembered for years afterwards. What can a writer do to make his characters and plot memorable?*

A. The characters should be honestly drawn, and the plot exciting.

□ 26

MAKING EVERY WORD COUNT IN YOUR STORY

BY DIANE LEFER

YEARS AGO, WHEN MY STORIES STARTED COMING BACK IN THE MAIL with written comments instead of form rejection slips, I was both elated and frustrated. "Needs tightening," I read again and again. I pictured a screwdriver and hadn't the slightest idea what these editors wanted me to do.

I didn't see anything wrong with a sentence like, *She squeezed the trigger and fired a shot from the gun held in her hand.* These days, I can't stop myself from thinking, "Well, gosh, I didn't think she fired it by licking the trigger with her tongue." But even as I now laugh at the sentence, I'm not making fun of the writer. From experience with my own writing, from reading manuscripts in slush piles, and from working with students at various stages of development, I'm convinced we pick up the habit of being long-winded because we've often won praise for it. I've isolated some of these habits to keep my students and myself alert.

The getting A's in high school English habit

George Bernard Shaw said you're not a writer till you know five synonyms for every word. That may be true, but I suggest that a writer who knows five synonyms should also know enough not to use them, because there are very few true synonyms. I can't tell you how many stories I've read in magazine slush piles in which a character makes herself a cup of coffee and then—I'm already cringing in anticipation of the language that all too often follows—*she brings the cup of hot brown liquid to her lips and savors the aromatic beverage.* Personally, I often crave a cup of coffee. I do not crave a cup of hot brown liquid!

Why do we do it? In part, because we've been taught that word repetition is bad, but in creative writing, word repetition is often good.

Repetition may create an incantatory effect. When the same word shifts its meaning slightly in the text, it may add depth to a story. There are much worse sins than using a word twice. The only caution I would advise is: if you see a word repeated again and again in a paragraph, you may be dragging out the scene, and this is place where your manuscript can be tightened or condensed. For example, when the character drinks her morning coffee, you probably don't need the details of her making it, pouring it, inhaling the aroma, and finally drinking it. Unless there's something very unusual about her coffee routine, this is a conventional scene that does not require details.

We also stretch out our sentences to show off our extensive vocabularies because substitution, euphemism, and indirect statement are stylistic features of much of the writing of earlier times. Novels considered classics have admirable features, but the language and style come from a world very different from our own. Many writers, trying to model their own writing on work they've been taught is great, end up writing in old-fashioned language that isn't natural or comfortable for them—or for their characters.

So why did your English teachers love it? Why did you get A's for writing that way? In part, because your teachers studied and respected classics, in part because such writing indicates a fascination with language that should be encouraged in a young writer. They often praised you for writing that later, as literary writers, you learned to drop or use with caution.

The creative writing rules habit

One problem I often see in manuscripts is a description of ordinary actions, such as leaving or entering rooms, presented in excruciating detail:

His thigh muscles contracted as he rose from his chair. He approached the door, placed his hand on the doorknob, the smooth surface against his right palm as his fingers grasped. He turned the knob, pushed against the wood, opening the door, and paused a moment on the threshold before walking out, turning, closing and locking the door behind him by inserting and turning the key he had at the appropriate moment removed from his pocket.

When I read such a passage, I know the writer has heard the rule, "Show, Don't Tell" so many times, she or he is afraid to summarize anything and is thinking of the rule rather than its effect. I think the show-don't-tell rule is overapplied most often in portrayals of emotion. Think of the opening sentence to Ford Maddox Ford's novel, *The Good Soldier:* "This is the saddest story I have ever heard."

The story the narrator goes on to tell certainly isn't the saddest *I* have ever heard, but I found that stark assertion irresistible as an opening. I would not have read on if the narrator had begun with a conventional show-don't-tell portrayal of sadness: *When I heard the story I'm about to tell you, my eyes clouded with tears, my throat constricted, muffled sobs and a deep sigh rose from somewhere within me, and I shuddered with the chill of the saddest feeling I had ever known.*

Obviously, this example is exaggerated, but many writers do feel they're not allowed to say, *He cried,* or *He felt sad,* but must illustrate the emotion with the wetness of tears and tightness in the throat. I'm not suggesting that emotion must always be presented through a direct statement.

One of my favorite sentences of all time comes from "The Johnstown Polka," a short story by Sharon Sheehe Stark (from *The Dealer's Yard and Other Stories,* (Morrow, 1985). It's about Francine, who years earlier lost her husband and children in the Johnstown flood and whose continuing emotional wound is invisible to those around her:

> But what they perceive as tranquility, Francine experiences as a sort of unpleasant limpness, her heart a slack muscle, as if after having delivered an outsized grief, it never quite snapped back and stubbornly holds, if not sorrow itself, then the soft shape of it.

That's the kind of line that makes me stop short. I have to put down the book. Pick it up again and reread the sentence. Which is one great advantage a story has over a movie: If you're overwhelmed, you can stop and catch your breath. The written story can't go on without you.

This sentence illustrates why I love literary fiction. Looking at this sentence, I know I can't duplicate it. But maybe I can say something else. Everyone has thoughts, feelings, ideas that truly matter. If, as writers, we're going to have something as a standard, something to strive toward, Stark's sentence is an example of what language can do. But no one, not even a literary genius, has something profound to say all the time. When you don't, spare the reader the carefully crafted restatement of what everyone already knows (e.g, tears are wet); you're better off writing, "I felt sad."

The speech and presentation habit

Many of us have experience in lecturing, giving speeches, making presentations. In this context, we learn to *Tell them what you're going to tell them, then tell them, then tell them what you've told them.*

The technique of redundancy is reinforced by TV news. The anchorperson says:

> An early morning fire destroyed three buildings and left twenty families homeless in Mayberry. And now we go to Mary Jones, live on the scene. . . . Mary?
> "I'm here in Mayberry, at the scene of an early morning fire that destroyed three buildings and left twenty families homeless."

Then Mary briefly interviews a man who says,

> "We lost everything and we're homeless, but we're alive and that's what counts."

Then back to the anchor, who says,

> "Terrible situation, all those people homeless after the fire. But they're alive, and that's what counts."

I see this pattern again and again in short stories. The writer explains in the first paragraph what the story's going to be about and what's going to happen. The last paragraph sums up the material and repeats the meaning to be drawn from it. Not only does this kill suspense, but it detracts from the meaning. A wonderful short story can't be summarized in a paragraph. There is no one single meaning or lesson readers should take from it. Of course, this problem can be easily solved by cutting the first and last paragraphs, but I find that many writers also fall into this pattern throughout the development of the story. They will often begin a scene by telling what is about to happen. Then, after presenting the interaction between characters, they won't let the moment speak for itself but will summarize it. For example:

> On Sunday morning, Glenn and Linda had a fight about how much he'd had to drink at the party.
> "Why did you have to get drunk at that party?" Linda asked.
> "I had two drinks. Big deal. Just two drinks," Glenn said.
> Linda threw up her hands in despair. She was upset over Glenn's drinking and that they were fighting about it.

Editing can solve this problem, but when there's an overall effect of redundancy, the manuscript may become tedious, and it's less likely that an editor will want to bother.

Most important, you're tightening your prose not only to improve your chances of publication; you're also doing it for your reader. Sentences that develop obvious information encourage the reader to skim. Wouldn't you rather have your readers pay attention because every word counts?

❏ 27

PEOPLE, NOT PUPPETS

BY CAROLYN VEITENHEIMER

EXCEPT FOR PINOCCHIO, PUPPETS DOOM A STORY, BECAUSE READERS don't love them or worry about them or even hate them. Characterization is work—harder than setting, harder than conflict, harder than plot. But you already have the tools to create viable characters: your everyday dealings with people.

A full cast of characters moves across the stage of your own life: the grocery store cashier, mailman, bank teller—these and dozens more remain one-dimensional characters. You recognize them: They're an integral part of your world, but you don't know too much about them. Your association with any cashier or postman or banker would be about the same.

Because people encounter them daily, one-dimensional characters belong in fiction, adding to the realism and providing clues about setting and the main character's world. These one-dimensional characters—puppets that an author can manipulate to suit the plot—are not difficult to portray.

Three-dimensional characters, on the other hand, are not plot puppets; they drive the plot. In your own life, three-dimensional characters are people you know a lot about: your family, your friends, some of your co-workers. They charm and frustrate, confront and console you. Your encounters with them force you to adjust your behavior and moods.

Whether you are presenting one-dimensional or three-dimensional characters, you must involve your readers—including editors—letting them learn about characters just as they would learn about real people. How do people get to know strangers? A new woman, Estelle, joins an office staff. After hiring her, the personnel manager states that this new employee is a "cracker-jack," that she'll "stir up the office with her ideas." This is the manager's direct characterization, telling *about* a person.

Different people respond to labels in different ways. Some, bored with the "same old" office routine, welcome a dynamic employee. Others, immune to office politics, concentrate on their work. Julia, insecure about her position in the office hierarchy, fears this interloper.

On Estelle's first day, Julia watches her tour the office with the personnel manager. She notices details about her new co-worker: tailored suit (stiff creased, new), tan wool (pale for her complexion), low-heeled shoes (sturdy), short hair (severe). About 35, a ready smile.

Julia processes these snapshot observations in subtle ways. The suit is more formal than the typical clothes worn to this office. Is Estelle ambitious? A clothes horse? Still, Estelle is not showy—the neutral color and low heels prove that. She's about Julia's age, so they might share similar interests. Their kids might be about the same age, for instance. Her haircut shows that she's not vain—she seems to be all business. Will she compete for the next promotion? Her smile is warm, though, not an ingratiating grin.

Although Julia hasn't heard Estelle speak yet, she's started to characterize her.

In the staff lounge, Julia hears people talk about the new employee. "Estelle's super qualified: a master's degree, six years' experience running her own company."

"She's going places! I guess she won't hang out with us drones."

"I'll bet her closet's stuffed with designer suits."

Julia reflects on her own hopes for promotion—the years of extension courses and volunteering to work overtime. She smooths out the skirt of her clearance-rack dress—purchased three years ago—and wonders how much an executive suit would cost.

The initial perceptions, Julia's and others', are the first phase of indirect characterization: *reaction.* With indirect characterization, the observer reacts to a person. Direct characterization—with labels like "perceptive" or "sneaky"—pigeon-holes a person, but real people have many facets. Besides, the labeler may be wrong.

The second phase of indirect characterization is *action:* how the person behaves in different situations. As in the reaction stage, the observers collect data to add to an overall impression: Estelle borrows a mug in the staff lounge without asking permission; she doesn't add a quarter to the collection jar with its huge sign "Coffee, 25¢"; she kicks her shoes off during the morning break.

Combined with Julia's first impressions, Estelle's actions in the staff lounge indicate that she's an opportunist, behaving professionally in front of managers, sloppily around peers.

But Julia still views Estelle as a cardboard silhouette; she will not know her in-depth until she enters the third phase of indirect characterization: *interaction.* Conversation is the primary way to interact with people, with its corollaries of body language and tone of voice.

"How do you like it here?" Julia asks Estelle, expecting bravado. After all, Estelle is ambitious, well-qualified and assertive.

Instead of bravado, Estelle shows hesitancy.

"This place is a dream come true, but I'm not sure I'll fit in. I tried to buy the right clothes, but I feel like someone else."

"I noticed your suit. It's classy."

"Good, because I have to wear it every other day. I spent three-quarters of my clothes budget on it. The clerk at Filene's insisted that I buy a 'power suit' as an investment. I chose this blah color hoping people wouldn't recognize it three times a week."

"What did you wear for your last job?"

"My bathrobe and slippers. I worked at home, over the computer. This whole office scene terrifies me."

Later, Julia observes another form of interaction, Estelle's connecting with other people. She flirts with male employees and laughs at rude jokes. Is this her way of trying to fit into the office, or is this her lifestyle? When she talks to the receptionist, Estelle finishes the receptionist's sentences. Is she impatient or receptive?

The direct characterization pegged Estelle as a visionary mover-and-shaker, a stereotype transcended by Julia's observations. The layers of indirect characterization—reaction, action, and interaction—transform Estelle into a multidimensional woman with hopes and fears. Nervous about Estelle's role in the office, Julia at least sees her as a complex woman.

To develop characters, follow the same processes you use to get to know people. In *The Kitchen God's Wife,* Amy Tan introduces Helen using all these approaches. Winnie describes Helen, a woman she has known for over fifty years: "Helen thinks all her decisions are always right, but really, she is only lucky." This direct characterization by Winnie sets up a contrast between Winnie and Helen that appears in incidents throughout the narrative.

When Winnie first meets Helen, they are young brides of second-class pilots rooming in a monastery. The reader pictures Helen, then called Hulan, through Winnie's reactions: "Really, she had the manners of a village servant. . . . Hulan could not be called pretty, even if you judged her with an old-fashioned eye. . . . Her plumpness was round and overflowing in uneven spots, more like a steamed dumpling with too much filling leaking out the sides." With her background and delicate appearance, Winnie feels superior to Hulan.

Hulan dominates their initial conversations with her active imagination: "'The water from this spring,' she said, 'is heavy as gold, sweet as honey, but clear as glass. . . . I heard you can fill a cup with this water, then drop the black rocks into the cup to try to make the water overflow. But not a drop will spill out, it is that thick!'" When they visit the spring, "Hulan drank that tea and said it was truly magic. It ran through her blood, immediately entered her heart and liver, then made her feel completely peaceful." In contrast, Winnie finds a teahouse that charges too much for tea.

Hulan's exuberant actions contrast to Winnie's behavior when their husbands fly off to battle: "Hulan waved harder and harder, tears streaming. The planes raced down the runway. And then she was waving furiously, crazily, like a wounded bird, as if this effort and all her wishes and hopes could lift them up safely. . . ." Winnie struggles to hide her fear.

Later, when Japanese planes drop pamphlets over a village, Hulan and Winnie are caught up in a panic and separated. Hulan rescues Winnie from the confused mob by stealing a pedicab:

> I didn't even think. I just ran over and pushed him off the seat as hard as I could. When he fell, I jumped on and pedaled away to get you. I saw your green coat, saw you were looking for me as well. But right before I called out to you, at that same moment, someone ran up to me. . . . When he swung, I grabbed the stick, then used it to beat him away.

Hulan's actions add to Winnie's understanding, transforming Hulan from an awkward peasant into a resourceful friend. Tan presents Helen through Winnie's first-person narrative.

In *The Accidental Tourist,* Anne Tyler portrays Muriel Pritchett from a limited omniscient point of view. The first time Muriel appears, she stands behind the counter of the Meow-Bow Animal Hospital. "She had aggressively frizzy black hair that burgeoned to her shoulders like an Arab headdress." This portrait carries a hint of direct characterization with the qualifier "aggressively," underscored by her initial interaction with Macon, the main character.

> "Can't you leave him home with your wife?" she asked.
> He wondered how on earth her mind worked.
> "If I could do that," he said, "why would I be standing here?" . . .
> "I'm a divorsy myself," she said. "I know what you're going through."

Later Muriel tells Macon, "I'm not scared of a thing in this world." Her actions in training his dog, Edward, prove her strength, yet alarm Macon.

> "Down," Muriel said levelly.
> With a bellow, Edward sprang straight at her face. Every tooth was bare and gleaming. . . . Muriel instantly raised the leash. She jerked it upward with both fists and lifted Edward completely off the floor. . . .
> Edward's throat gave an odd sort of click.
> "Stop it. It's enough! You're choking him!"
> Still, she let him hang. . . . Muriel lowered Edward to the floor. He landed in a boneless heap. . . .
> Edward raised his head and feebly licked his lips.
> "See that? When they lick their lips, it's a sure sign they're giving in," Muriel said cheerfully. . . .

Tyler lets the reader shape opinions of Muriel through direct and indirect characterization, through reaction, action, and interaction.

In your pre-writing period, brainstorm about the character in different situations. Describe the character: home in on details, including work clothes, casual clothes, physical appearance, habits and gestures, hobbies, tastes in entertainment. You probably will not use all these details in your story, but they breathe life into your character. List adjectives that describe her. As an occasional bit of direct characterization, these might speed up your story. These tags also individualize her, shape her beyond the confines of the story's plot.

Description alone does not develop character: A dressed-up doll is still a doll. Put your character in a situation where other people react to her. Engage her in different types of conversation, from trivial to confessional to angry. To add substance to your character, follow her thoughts. Key in on her unspoken thoughts during her conversations. For a parallel strategy, trace the backstory, the path she followed to arrive at this scene. Through dialogue or snatches of exposition, you might add texture to your story with some of the backstory.

Characterization does not follow a rigid order. You might present interaction followed by action, with direct characterization near the end of the story. You may eliminate one or more elements. For a one-dimensional character, you could present expected actions and interactions, such as a waiter spieling off specials and toting the food. Some fiction—such as mysteries and Westerns—emphasize action and reaction over interaction.

Work on characterization; human beings do not laugh or cry on cue. Cut the marionette strings that manipulate your fictional people. Remember Pinocchio. As a puppet, he made us care about Geppetto. As a child, Pinocchio made us care about him.

❏ 28

EMOTION: THE DRIVING FORCE IN YOUR STORY

BY MADELEINE COSTIGAN

STORY IDEAS CAN COME FROM ANYWHERE—A SNATCH OF CONVERSA-tion, an intriguing character, a pivotal event in a person's life. But what makes these ideas come alive on the page is the emotion they generate in the mind of the reader—not the writer. The writer may need to feel deeply to communicate emotion, so deeply that Tennessee Williams felt it necessary to warn, "Don't let anybody see you at your typewriter." Yet in fiction it's what's on the page that counts.

Norman Mailer tells of the young writer who came home from an evening in which he had met the most wonderful woman in the world. He was so transformed by the experience that he decided to write a story about it and immediately sat down at his desk. "I love you," he wrote. "I love you." The words recreated the entire evening in his mind, and he spent hours reliving every moment. His reader, however, was left with nothing—except perhaps a vague suspicion that he had interrupted the start of a love letter.

So how is it done? Why is it that one writer can graphically describe a character's blood, sweat, and tears, yet leave the reader unmoved, while a writer such as John Galsworthy can deliver in one sentence an emotional punch that leaves the reader reeling?

After publishing short stories in major magazines for several years, it became clear to me that just when I thought I'd made a breakthrough, I'd soon discover that what I'd actually come up with was at best an efficient, perhaps even powerful way to evoke a particular emotional response—germane to one story.

Later, as assistant fiction editor at *McCall's,* I added a new dimension to my understanding of fiction and had a unique opportunity to work with many fine writers and editors. But I can't claim to have ferreted out any trade secrets or magical clues that simplify the com-

121

plex process of fiction writing. I did, however, make a few interesting discoveries: Every writer struggles. Even those who constantly improve their skills don't find writing easier. And the quality of a story is usually in direct proportion to the number of drafts it has been put through.

Before a story is accepted by any magazine, it must pass muster with several editors. Because editors endure the same pressures and traumas as anyone else, a story that is written close to the bone has a better chance of acceptance, particularly when it happens to connect with the editors' perception of human experience. To be effective, the story will deeply involve the reader with the characters and what is happening to them. The writer sustains this involvement through emotion. Emotion must drive every element of the story: characterization, plot, theme, and setting. Each scene must further the plot, disclose significant aspects of the characters, contribute to the theme and be anchored in such a way that the reader has a sense of place.

In everyday life, most people mask their emotions a good bit of the time. In fiction, your characters may conceal themselves from one another but not from the writer. The writer sees beyond the mask. To reveal a character in crisis, the writer has to be more than the fly on the wall. It's fine to see what the character does and hear what the character says, but the reader wants to know how the character feels in this particular life crisis. And why. The writer must draw the reader not just into the story, but so deeply into the characters that the reader is likely to speculate about what the characters would or would not do, even after the story ends.

Now back to writing full time, I am once again engaged in unraveling the mystery that is fiction writing from yet another vantage point. How does the writer communicate authentic emotion? Each story is new territory, and there are no easy answers that will guarantee a story's success. Yet, having read numerous manuscripts from new and established writers, there are a few commonplace snares I caution you to avoid:

1. *Don't play it safe.*

The writer can't skate on the surface of a problem and hope to portray genuine emotion. Go to a character's deepest level, reveal the character intimately. There's a catch to this. In revealing the character, the writer also gets revealed, even though the material is in no way

autobiographical. When you write fiction, you tell more abou
than about any character. There's no place to hide. So, i̇ ᵧₑₑ
yourself shying away from a scene, or attempting to gloss over a crucial
event, stop where you are and work it through. In doing so, you'll come
to a greater, more thorough knowledge of your characters and their
situation, which will lead you to the compelling truth at the heart of
your characters' fear, love, anger, grief, or joy. Thus enlightened, you
can rewrite the scene drawing from the landscape of your own psyche.
But don't expect to be comfortable; if you are, you probably won't
be convincing. Or, as an editor once wrote to me when returning a
manuscript—"Nice writing, but it didn't get me in the heart, which is
where I like to be got."

Before sending a story out, ask yourself this question: Will it get the
reader in the heart? If it doesn't, revise.

2. *Beware of sentimentality.*

If playing it safe is one extreme, mawkish sentimentality is the other.
Early on, the fiction writer is wise to relegate sentimentality to Valentine's Day. How do you know if you're getting maudlin? If you find
yourself describing choking sobs, churning stomachs, pounding hearts,
pulsating bodies, and other clichés, you're mired in sentimentality.
Readers will reject such off-the-top-of-the-head writing. Go back and
concentrate on more relevant details. Impact comes from images that
conjure up appropriate feelings in the reader.

Real emotion is simple, but there is nothing simple about creating
emotional response in the reader. To avoid having a strongly emotional
scene turn saccharine, I find it helpful to inject a note of humor, or a
tangential thought to cut tension.

In my story, "The Second Son" (*Good Housekeeping*), the emotion
I was working with was grief and the way different members of a family
deal with it. Joanna's fourteen-year-old son, Jamie, has died of an aneu-
rysm. While grieving for Jamie, Joanna relives the time shortly after
her brother Charles's death when he was two years old and Joanna
was four. Unless handled with care, such a scene can get very sloppy.
I rewrote it several times before I decided on the following paragraphs:

She remembers the sprays of white flowers, her father crying on the way to
the cemetery. Was it all right to notice? Or was it like reminding Uncle Rob
that he always told the same jokes? Grown-ups didn't cry, especially fathers.
Her sister, Emily, caught her father's fingers and said, "I'll give you all my
pennies if you'll just stop crying."

What a silly thing to say! But the next minute her father stopped crying and put his arm around Emily, leaving Joanna wishing she'd thought to say it.

Sometimes, knowing what to play down or leave between the lines is as important as knowing what to emphasize. Which details most affected the character? Was the character's thinking process logical or disjointed?

Space is so limited in a short story that I find it best to spend little time on physical description and concentrate on what's inside. Try to brush in enough of the concrete and specific to illuminate your character; yet leave enough space for your reader's imagination to operate. Waste no words on the banal; search out the detail that is unique, telling.

In "The Second Son," I needed to portray Emily, Joanna's sister, without having her appear in the story. My way of handling this was to give a brief glimpse of Emily in Joanna's thoughts.

Emily, with her penchant for taking people in hand! Joanna imagined herself becoming one of Emily's projects—doing laps in the pool at the Y, volunteering.

3. *Never trivialize real problems with unreal solutions.*

Nothing is more discouraging to an editor than seeing a promising story fall apart at the end. If the ending is predictable, unbelievable, ambiguous, contrived, or out of sync with the actual story, the reader will feel cheated, no matter how fine the writing.

A real conflict doesn't just disappear or get resolved by a fortunate turn of events. As the story unfolds, characters and plot progress toward a realistic resolution that is both inevitable and unanticipated.

Sometimes it's a matter of focus. Should your focus be from a wide angle? Or quite narrow? It makes a difference. And only you can decide. The short story has been called "the art of the glimpse." But there are no absolutes.

How to stay focused, yet keep the reader off center at the same time? Arturo Vivante has said that a little inconsistency in a character can help to make the character more interesting.

In the above-mentioned story, Joanna longs to talk about Jamie. Elizabeth, her mother, can't bear to and resorts to silence or to changing the subject whenever Jamie is mentioned. Then Mark, Joanna's younger son, is accidentally confronted with a pipe and package of tobacco Jamie had hidden. Joanna is speechless. Mark has practically canonized Jamie and isn't prepared to deal with such hard evidence of his brother's frailty. With effort, his grandmother finds the words to tell Mark of an incident involving Joanna's deceased brother Charles and reminds him of the importance of remembering the actual person, not just the idealistic fragments that memory conveniently selects.

Much moved, Joanna tells her mother how much her response has helped Mark:

"Mm," her mother says. "Do you think there's enough celery in the potato salad?"

What did she expect? Joanna asks herself. That her mother would start organizing support groups for bereaved parents? Talking about Charles seems to have exhausted her. *Living requires enough energy, never mind reliving,* Joanna thinks. Still, she knows her mother's words will come back to her.

For now she does what Emily would do, the sensible practical thing that will erase that unfamiliar gray tinge from her mother's face. She pronounces the potato salad to have just the right amount of celery.

"Good," her mother says. "I was hoping you'd say that."

The intensity of the moment forces Elizabeth to step somewhat out of character during her conversation with Mark. Yet, it is clear that at the end of the story she is the same reticent person she was at the beginning. What has changed is Joanna's perception of her. And it is this change in perception that deepens the relationship between mother and daughter and resolves their conflict.

Fiction writing remains an elusive process that demands a fusing of disparate elements. Exploring the chemistry of these elements when filtered through the writer's imagination yields infinite possibilities. Sometimes this pursuit can seem as futile as the alchemists' quest. But when the elements converge in a story that portrays truth, the experience can be most satisfying.

❏ 29

PITCH-PERFECT DIALOGUE

BY SHELBY HEARON

I'M AN INVETERATE EAVESDROPPER. NOTHING IS MORE FUN THAN GO-ing out for an early-morning muffin or a late-night plate of fried eggs and listening to the couple or the family in the booth behind you. A few lines of conversation, scraps of talk, and you know at once what the relationship between the people is, what the problem is, where they're coming from. All without even turning your head.

Achieving the same instant sense of "knowing all about" fictional people is more difficult. For one thing, you don't have the tone of voice, which is so revealing. In real life, the transaction—"I think I'll have the pancakes" and "I'm looking at the waffles"—can be heard with several different undertones, inflections, nuances. But on the page it's hard to convey what the listener knows is the subtext. Yet, the secret of pitch-perfect dialogue begins there: with trying to figure out what you know and how you know it when you're listening in on other lives.

Private eyes and spies provide unbeatable "eavesdropping" opportunities on the printed page. Who could confuse a character from P. D. James saying, "That was preternaturally slow," with one from Elmore Leonard asking, "Wha' took you so long?"

But in addition to these obvious clues in vocabulary and syntax, I always start on a new character by asking myself what I want to tell the reader first about the person. How to tell something is not nearly as difficult as deciding what is the crucial trait to reveal. But, say you decide to show right at the start how your character (let's take a father-type of guy) feels about his body and how he feels about authority: If you're dealing with men, you know they spend a lot of time wishing their bodies were different, and a lot of emotion on their relation to the guy in charge.

So you decide—two birds with one stone—to have your father-type in the hospital about to have his gallbladder out. He's prepped, waiting on that tight, white-sheeted bed, and in comes John Archer, abdominal surgeon.

Your man says:

"Hey, Arch, watch out when you're messing around down there below the belt you don't remove anything I may need. Ha ha."

Or he says:

"Jeez, Dr. Archer, I'm scared blue. I can't help it, look at me, I'm cold as a fish. My old man, he flat out died from this same trouble. Younger than me."

Or he says:

"Morning, John. I guess I'm as ready as I'll ever be. Maybe taking some of my gall out will make me easier to live with. I know a few who'd agree with that."

Or he says:

"Well, Doc, don't take this as lack of confidence, but my law partners, malpractice litigators par excellence, will be looking over your shoulder when you pick up that knife."

Let's take another example. Say you want to show that the way a young woman feels about her man goes right back to how she feels about her mom. So maybe you start with her having lunch with him in a public place.

She says:

"The pastrami was O.K., I don't care all that much, the corned beef probably isn't any better, but just once I'd like to order for myself. Just once I'd like to open my mouth and say exactly what I want."

Or she says:

"You're sure? Gosh, you're always paying for everything. Lunch, the trip to Cancun, that totally gorgeous pink sweater. Really, I mean it, you make me feel really special."

Or she says:

"Here, I'll read it for you. I think you left your glasses on the dashboard. You like that soup, remember? The sort of borsch. It agrees with you, you said last time."

From here, it's just a matter of a phone call to Mom, in which we overhear a few snippets of conversation, to make your point that history, at least in our love life, always repeats.

An aid to writing convincing dialogue, and one you'll unconsciously pick up when you're listening in, is to give your character her or his own special metaphors. I often do this, as an exercise, just to get new voices clearly in my head: Have each character say, "It's hot as ———," "I'm mad as ———," "It's time to ———," "No point in ———." And I always have my ear out for phrases I have never heard before. One I picked up when I moved to Vermont (writers love to move around to new places for this reason!) and I'm sure to put to use soon is: "He may not be the sharpest knife in the drawer, but ———." And almost anything can follow—"he's a true friend," "steady as night and day," "somebody you can trust," etc. I jot down every sentence like that I overhear.

Another choice the writer can make in deciding how to reveal character through dialogue is selecting who gets to say what lines. My own preference is to "cast against type," to use a film term. For example, listen to a couple fighting: One of them wants to get married, the other doesn't. One of them has been hurt to the quick by the cavalier attitude of the other. Readers will be more apt to hear the fight and really feel they have come to know these two people, if you do the unexpected. *He* wants to get married; *she* wants to play around. He's been wounded by her; she has grown tired of all the talk about commitment.

"I want marriage. I want the whole baggage. The dirty socks and pink toothbrush and recycle bins."

"Place an ad."

"Do you know how comments like that hurt? Do you have a clue how words can bruise?"

Read them with *she said* and then *he said,* then reverse it and read *he said* and *she said,* and you hear the impasse between them in a new way.

Or try a parent and child.

"I never know where you are or when you're coming home."

"Lighten up. What are my options in this burg, anyways?"

Spoken by a parent to a child, the reader doesn't really hear the words, because expected scenarios get in the way. But spoken by a twelve-year-old boy to his forty-five-year-old mother, the two lines seem fresh, and a new situation is suggested. The reader is drawn into the story.

A lot of times, real life suggests these switches on the expected. I can recall when I was a young mother, driving to the trailhead in the

Rockies to pick up my backpacking son, gone sometimes for days at a time. Then, three years ago, I went back to Aspen after a long absence, to see if I could do the day hikes I'd done years before. (To prove that if I wasn't the sharpest knife in the drawer, at least I wasn't rusty.) And there my son was, grown, driving me to the trailhead, setting a time when I had to return, checking to be sure I had a windbreaker in case of a summer storm, and proper gear. And I'm sure our conversation mirrored the ones we'd had in the past, with the roles reversed.

Go back to the thrillers I mentioned earlier. What if Elmore Leonard's guy on the lam in Florida says, "That was preternaturally slow," and P. D. James's man in London asks, "Wha' took you so long?" There would be a sense of having met someone unexpected and the surprise would engage the reader.

In my current novel, *Footprints,* I have a couple whose daughter died in a car wreck, and her heart is transplanted into a southern preacher's chest. The father (a brain scientist) is devastated; he clings to the belief his daughter is still alive, and becomes very mystical about the transplant. His wife, in turn, becomes quite scientific in her handling of loss, exploring in a cool, investigative manner the theories of what life is, what the mind or self really is, considering the transplant almost akin to Frankenstein's borrowed life.

But why not imagine you are listening to them talk over coffee in the booth behind you. What does she say to him? What does he say to her? What does the reader overhear?

❏ 30

TITLES

BY BARNABY CONRAD

ASIDE FROM MAKING YOUR LITERARY PRODUCT UNIQUE AND SERVING as sort of a trademark, the primary function of a title is to lure unsuspecting readers into your story. Although titling is one of the most imprecise, capricious, and subjective components of a story, most people have definite ideas of what a good title is or should be.

In hindsight, and after millions of copies of a book have been sold, it is easy to say that *The Catcher in the Rye,* for example, is a great title. But suppose you were the first person to hear J.D. Salinger propose, as the title for his first novel, that peculiar juxtaposition of words. Would you rush out to buy a book called *Pansy?* That was one of the many titles Margaret Mitchell came up with for *Gone With the Wind* before it was published by Macmillan. Other suggested titles included *Tote the Weary Load, Tomorrow Is Another Day, Milestones, Ba! Ba! Black Sheep,* and *Jettison.* It has been said that eighteen titles in all were considered before the author came up with *Gone With the Wind* from Ernest Dowson's poem "Cynara." Would we even now think the phrase "gone with the wind" so memorable a title if the novel had sold, say, only hundreds of books instead of multimillions?

As Somerset Maugham said so accurately: "A good title is the title of a book that's successful." The title of one of Maugham's many successful novels, based loosely on Paul Gauguin, was *The Moon and Sixpence.* "People tell me it's a good title, but they don't know what it means. It means reaching for the moon and missing the sixpence at one's feet."

To be good, it's not always necessary for a title to be understood.

Maugham had originally titled his masterpiece, *Of Human Bondage, Beauty and Ashes,* but ultimately discovered it had been previously used.

Walker Percy said that a good title "should intrigue without being too baffling or too obvious." Some titles baffle us until we have read the book—and sometimes even afterward: *A Clockwork Orange, Catch 22, Kaputt, Shibumi, The Milagro Beanfield War, Like Water for Chocolate, The Unbearable Lightness of Being,* et cetera. Their very unfamiliarity and strangeness are calculated to lure readers into finding out what the story is about.

Just where do titles come from—and when?

"The title comes last," said Tennessee Williams.

Hemingway said: "I make a list of titles *after* I've finished the story or book—sometimes as many as a hundred. Then I start eliminating them, sometimes all of them."

It is often startling to hear of the terrible first choices of famous novels. Charles Dickens originally wanted to call the classic novel that ended up as *Bleak House, Tom-All-Alone's The Ruined House.* His *Hard Times* started out as *Two and Two Are Four.*

When Charles Dickens planned to write an exciting serial, he immediately encountered title trouble. His first titles were:

Time!, The Leaves of the Forest, Scattered Leaves, The Great Wheel, Round and Round, Old Leaves, Long Ago, Far Apart, Fallen Leaves, Five and Twenty Years, Years and Years, Day After Day, Felled Trees, Memory Carton, Rolling Stones, Two Generations. Later he jotted down other possibilities: *One of These Days, Buried Alive, The Thread of Gold, The Doctor of Beauvais.*

And then, on March 11, 1859, he wrote a friend: "I have got exactly the name for the story that is wanted; exactly what will fit the opening to a T: *A Tale of Two Cities.*"

Where does the imagination for a great title come from?

Many writers find their titles in the body of the work itself, perhaps in the dialogue. Margaret Mitchell's title idea *Tomorrow Is Another Day* was a cliché taken from Scarlett's thoughts.

Many titles have come from nursery rhymes, such as *When the Bough Breaks, The Cradle Will Fall,* and so forth. Ed McBain has written a dozen crime books with titles like *Cinderella; Mary, Mary; Jack and the Beanstalk.*

Over the years, Shakespeare has been one of the most tapped, and seemingly inexhaustible, sources of titles. For example, *Something Wicked This Way Comes, Cakes and Ale, Remembrance of Things Past, The Sound and the Fury, The Dogs of War, The Winter of Our Discontent, To Thine Own Self Be True.*

Thomas Wolfe's title *Look Homeward, Angel* came from a line in Milton's "Lycidas," but only after such titles as *They Are Strange, They Are Lost,* and *The Exile's Story* were rejected by his renowned editor, Maxwell Perkins. (Wolfe's wonderful title *You Can't Go Home Again* came not from a poem but a chance remark by a friend.)

Lines from songs have provided many good titles, such as: *Blue Skies, From Here to Eternity, Body and Soul.*

The Bible, of course, has been a gold mine, especially Ecclesiastes (*The Sun Also Rises*) and The Song of Solomon (*The Sound of the Turtle*), and many more.

Common phrases can make good titles:

I Can Get It for You Wholesale; They Shoot Horses, Don't They; You Could Look It Up; Born Yesterday; Fun While It Lasted. Simply using the hero's or heroine's name as a title was more common in the past than it is today; for example: *Pamela, Tom Jones, Emma, Madame Bovary, Jane Eyre, David Copperfield, Nana, Tom Sawyer, Ivanhoe, Ethan Frome, Jude the Obscure, Anna Karenina.*

Nor have single-name titles gone totally out of fashion in more modern novels: *Rebecca, Laura, Lolita, Mrs. Bridge, Elmer Gantry, Youngblood Hawke,* and *Forrest Gump.*

More common are variations using a name, such as:

The Prime of Miss Jean Brodie, Sophie's Choice, Henderson the Rain King, Portnoy's Complaint, and *What Makes Sammy Run?*

Place names are frequently used in titles either alone—*USA, Middlemarch, Wuthering Heights, Winesburg, Ohio, The Cruel Sea, The Big Sky, The Secret Garden*—or in conjunction with other words—*Babylon Revisited, Manhattan Transfer, Barchester Towers, Brideshead Revisited.*

Appomattox would be an adequate title; Bruce Catton's *A Stillness at Appomattox* is a great one.

So when all is said and done, we see that the art of titling is a curious and mercurial and mysterious one.

To show the disparity between some original titles and the ones ultimately published, here is a list of well-known works:

Previous Titles	Published Titles
With Due Respect	A Moveable Feast
The Sentimental Education of Frederick Henry	A Farewell to Arms
Catch 19	Catch 22
Twilight	The Sound and the Fury
Blanche's Chair in the Moon	A Streetcar Named Desire
Finnerty's Ball	The Man With the Golden Arm
They Don't Build Statues to Businessmen	Valley of the Dolls
Tenderness	Lady Chatterley's Lover
All's Well That Ends Well	War and Peace
Four and a Half Years of Struggle Against Lies, Stupidity, and Cowardice	Mein Kampf
Pumphrey	Babbitt
The Last Man in Europe	1984
The Mute	The Heart Is a Lonely Hunter
Before This Anger	Roots
The Birds and the Bees	Everything You Always Wanted to Know About Sex (But Were Afraid to Ask)
The Kingdom by the Sea	Lolita
No Safe Harbor	Ship of Fools
To Climb the Wall	The Blackboard Jungle
The Whale	Moby Dick
Too Late, Beloved!	Tess of the D'Urbervilles
Private Fleming, His Various Battles	The Red Badge of Courage
Something That Happened	Of Mice and Men
The Sea-Cook	Treasure Island
The Man That Was a Thing	Uncle Tom's Cabin
Bar-b-que	The Postman Always Rings Twice
A Day of Fear	Matador

□ 31

BUILDING A CHARACTER'S PAST

BY MICHELLE RAE

SOMEONE'S PAST, WHETHER THAT SOMEONE IS A REAL PERSON OR A fictional character, affects everything he says, does, and thinks. Past choices lead to present decisions. This is the most important thing to remember when planning the life your character led before you decided to put him into a story.

To write a credible story with characters who create their own destinies and live their own lives within the framework of your story, you must design people with reasons to say, act, and think the way they do; you must give them pasts that deeply affect the present.

You do this by developing a *backstory* for each character. Behind the actual story line is a "shadow" story that motivates the character to do what he does—the shadow of his past. Stories without a well-designed backstory confuse readers and often leave them wondering why a certain character acted a certain way or did a certain thing.

For this reason, you must develop the backstory as rigorously as you do the main story, even though the reader will never be aware of most of the work you do. Its only purpose is to reveal motivation, not for the character to give long monologues on his life and how he feels about it.

Allow the backstory to grow naturally out of the main story. Don't bog it down with unnecessary information. If it isn't absolutely *vital* to the main story, cut it. Your story won't suffer from a lack of character development; it will benefit from more action in the present, which is what really matters. The past is only a stepping stone to the present.

Begin by writing a character biography for each main character. Include everything that could be important in your story, but if, while you're writing, you run across something that is missing, don't be afraid to add to your biography. The following is a good start: hair and eye color, age, gender, anything noteworthy in the character's appearance, family, religion, hobbies, education, job, morals, values, opinions, love life, likes and dislikes, ambitions, goals, attitudes, temperament, IQ, personality, skills, and abilities.

Ask your character the same things you'd ask a real person you just met. You'll want to know about his job, family, hobbies, and everything else that makes him a unique person. It's almost like going on a first date. For your character biography, you have to move on to the second and third dates, learn all about him or her, and think about the future.

Minor characters need only to be sketchy, but make sure you add something memorable about each one. It may be a unique way of walking, an oft-repeated phrase, or a strange type of clothing, but make it something that won't overshadow your main characters and give the minors an importance they don't have in the story. That would cheat your readers and confuse them.

Use the biography only as a reference tool; don't allow it to rule the character's life. You must let him evolve during the course of the story just as the real person would evolve if put into the same situation. People are always in a state of flux, and characters must be even more willing to change. If all your character does is sit on a bar stool all day, or do nothing but watch television, what kind of story will result? Most certainly a boring one.

Concentrate on feelings and sensations when creating the backstory, as well as the main story. People remember the way they *felt* more than what they *did,* and this is what most affects them in the present and in the future. Think back to a time when you were thoroughly embarrassed. Do you remember exactly what happened, or do you remember only how it *felt* to be embarrassed? Emotions are what life is all about, and they must be as well developed as the rest of your character's life, or he won't ring true.

Emotion is associated with every experience a person has during the course of his life, and you must make the emotion true for every scene of your story. A cop who had to arrest his own brother experiences an emotion during and after the bust, even if it isn't described in detail. How would he feel if his brother called him two years later asking for help? How would he handle it? That might be the plot of your story.

Story problems also create the backstory. If you don't know how one of your characters will act in a certain situation, or if one of them surprises you by stealing the show, you'll have to go back to your character biography to find out why.

Say that your story is about a superstar pitcher who loses his confidence when he injures his throwing arm, but in his mind, he keeps returning to the way his father pushed him to become a pitcher in the first place. Do you continue with your inspirational story of his return to the major leagues, or do you follow the father angle?

It's entirely up to you, but your character must be the person you're trying to create. Maybe this particular pitcher doesn't want to do the therapy necessary for him to return to pitching; maybe the story is really about his journey to forgiving the father, who'd forced him into something he didn't want to do; maybe he'd always wanted to be a computer programmer, so he starts taking classes. You have to make that choice, according to the past you've created for your character.

Use the past to highlight the present, to determine what is in the character's past to motivate him to do what he does in the present, which *must* be the focus if you are trying to create a realistic, believable story. Let the backstory show through the main story, but not in long monologues, description, or flashbacks. Backstory works best as short dialogue, subtly worked into the basic story because it adds layering to the characters, making them more authentic.

Fit backstory into the main story: It makes everything happen, but the readers don't see it. The past isn't dramatic until it has some context in the present, so if you include only those elements of a character's past that affect the present, your story will be fascinating and believable.

PIQUING THE READER'S CURIOSITY

BY JOAN AIKEN

ONCE WHEN I WAS SITTING IN A PACKED LONDON UNDERGROUND train, I heard the following snatch of conversation between two men who were standing close by me, but I never saw their faces among the crowd of rush-hour passengers. The first voice, the sort that alerts you at once to listen, asked, "Did I ever tell you the story of the mushroom?"

"No, what was it?" the other voice asked.

"Well, there were only two officers in charge. A couple of days before this happened they had vacuumed the parade ground. Lord, those Germans are thorough! You could have rolled out pastry on that parade ground."

"But what about the mushroom?"

"I was coming to that. There was this white flagpole in the middle of the parade ground. . . . Ah, Charing Cross, here we are."

The train stopped, the two men got out, taking with them forever the secret of what happened to the mushroom. That was about thirty years ago, but I still wake sometimes in the small hours and occupy myself with speculations as to where and in what circumstances the mushroom turned up.

Curiosity is the main characteristic that divides human beings from other animals. Of course some animals are inquisitive, too, but not to the ruinous degree that has brought the human race to its present precarious clutch on atomic development and other undesirable areas of knowledge. If only our earliest ancestor had not rubbed two sticks together and discovered how to light a campfire. . . . But here we are, congenitally inquisitive, and there is no going back. We long to find out what began it all, and what happened in the end. Ancient myths and folk tales give warnings about the perils incurred from prying into other people's business: Prometheus stealing fire from the gods; Psyche spilling hot oil from the lamp on Cupid in her eagerness to discover the identity of her nightly visitor; the terrible revelations of Bluebeard's chamber.

Magic—a dangerous force, like electricity, like radiation—is unleashed by attempts to discover what lies ahead, to divine the future, to skip all the tedious intervening chapters and turn on to the very last page. Why do we read stories? Because we long to find out what happened next. Any writer who can evoke this curiosity is sure of an audience. But how is it done? How can you keep your readers atwitter with suspense? Some authors can relate the most wonderful, hair-raising events in such a flat, disinterested manner that they might just as well be recounting the annals of the local archaeological society, while others make the most trifling event full of entertainment and surprise. The important factors are who is telling and who is listening.

One way to arouse curiosity, and a very good one, is to imply that there is a secret waiting to be revealed. What kind of secret? Well, it must be an important, a crucial one, or it would not have been kept secret in the first place. The revelation must then be postponed for as long as possible. This is a matter of judgment, for if you delay the revelation *too* long, the reader may become impatient, and close the book, or turn on to the end; or, even worse, when the disclosure comes, it comes as an anti-climax and the disappointed reader may feel that it was not worth waiting for.

Dickens was a very shrewd hand at delayed-action disclosure: A main part of his technique was to provide half a dozen subplots, each with its own mystery, so that, in *Our Mutual Friend,* for instance, there is the mystery of the dead man found in the Thames, the mystery of Silas Wegg's evil hold over Mr. Boffin, and Mr. Boffin's peculiar behavior, the involved goings-on of the Lammles and Veneerings and their financial dealings, the paranoid behavior of Bradley Headstone, and the very odd, inscrutable relationship of Fledgeby and Riah—and a wealth of other oddities. The reader is given continual short glimpses of all these strange connections, enough to whet curiosity. But it is not until well after the halfway mark of the book that any explanations are forthcoming, and, as fast as one mystery is unravelled, another is brought back, to keep the reader turning the pages until the very end. Dickens's work had to be planned in installments for serial publication, so there was an obligation to provide a cliffhanger for the end of each part.

Fiction writing in Dickens's day had undergone a total change from the tranquil pace of the eighteenth century, before the Industrial Revolution, when readers, living mostly in the country, had unlimited reading time and were prepared for a novel to begin in a leisurely manner.

Writers then had all the time in the world to convey their message, and readers could settle down comfortably for a nice peaceful three-volume reading orgy in the long lamplit winter evenings.

All this came to an abrupt end in 1859 with the publication of Wilkie Collins's *The Woman in White,* which appeared serially in *All the Year Round.* A mass audience of middle-class readers had arrived. They wanted action. Stories had to begin with a bang: the Dover coach on a foggy night brought to a halt by a lone horseman; an escaped convict confronting a terrified boy in a lonely churchyard; wills, legacies, deathbed dramas. Wilkie Collins was a master hand at a gripping beginning. The protagonist in *The Woman in White* is first seen fleeing from her persecutors across Hampstead Heath. *The Moonstone* (not actually a moonstone, but a yellow diamond) opens with the storming of Seringapatam and the theft of the jewel from the forehead of the Brahmin god.

The only problem with such a rousing start is that not every writer has the ability to maintain the tension at this pitch for the rest of the story. Wilkie Collins at his best could do so, but he was not always *at* his best, and sometimes the tension began to sag as the plot became almost too formidably complicated.

How can this kind of lapse be avoided—apart from having a simpler plot? Keep your tale peppered with odd, unexplained episodes. You can have characters behave seemingly out of character, turn nasty, be seen in unexpected places in unlikely company. Your hero, for instance, meets an old friend who greets him with a blank stare, with no sign of recognition; a faithful hound growls at his master of ten years; two old women are seen in a village street looking at photographs, and one of them suddenly shrieks in astonishment.

To keep the reader's attention focused on your hero (who is engaged in a struggle against apparently insuperable odds), it can be useful to endow him with an unexpected minor attribute that will stand him in good stead in confronting a vital crisis. He is a qualified tea-taster; or she has perfect musical pitch; he speaks ten different African languages; she is an expert on the kind of paint Velasquez used. The reader must, of course, have been previously informed of this specialized knowledge or skill, but in a passing, offhand way. If it comes as a complete surprise to the reader at the moment of crisis (he was the only man in England who could undo a particular knot), the reader could be justifiably annoyed. "Author's convenience" must be avoided at all costs. The author's real skill lies in creating the type of situation that would require the hero or heroine's unique expertise to be brought into play. There is a folk-tale model based on exactly this pattern: The hero is sent into the world on a seemingly hopeless quest, accompanied by six friends. One can run faster than anyone in the world; another is a champion archer . . . and so on. Here, of course, the pleasure for the reader lies in anticipating the triumph of the hero and his friends.

I had a good time writing my children's book, *The Whispering Mountain,* in which the hero, a short-sighted, delicate, unathletic boy, has to contend with a gang of local bullies and with a couple of London criminals. He always carries with him a tiny *Book of Knowledge,* which invariably provides him with the precise bit of know-how to meet each emergency. I happen to own such a book, and so was able to tailor the emergencies in the story to fit the information it provided. The idea, of course, is not new: I adopted it from *The Swiss Family Robinson,* in which the calmly competent mother of the family is always able to produce from her reticule the necessary ball of string, pair of pliers, or sticking plaster to deal with a problem.

Naturally, a story need not be presented on such a simplistic physical level to keep the reader's curiosity stimulated. Jane Austen arouses and maintains interest easily and spontaneously with her basic problem situations. How will the Bennets ever manage to marry off all those five daughters? How will Anne Elliot manage to endure the painful ordeal of encountering her lost lover again after eight years of heartbreak? What is the mystery attached to Jane Fairfax? Why wouldn't she go to Ireland? How will poor little Fanny Price make out when she is sent to live among those rich scornful relatives?

A tremendously important element of readability is the solid basis of the plot. A well-balanced, strong story generally has one or perhaps two crucial events in it. One, fairly early on, is to give you a foretaste of what the writer is able to provide. Charlotte Brontë whets your appetite by telling about Jane Eyre's incarceration in the Red Room and the consequent ghostly terrors. Then the story settles down to sober reality until the second explosion with the mad Mrs. Rochester in the attic. Mystery novelist Reginald Hill, in one of his Detective Dalziel mysteries, teases the aghast reader early on with a wild description of a crazed gunman and mayhem in a village street; then he rewinds the story to an earlier point of time, and so keeps readers on tenterhooks, waiting while he leads up again to the moment when all hell is going to break loose. And then he deals the expectant reader another shattering surprise.

Readers today are much more sophisticated than they used to be. They are accustomed to fictional trickery, guessing games, speeding up and slowing down of action, even unresolved questions and crises. They have only to walk along the street or into a supermarket or bookstore to see racks and racks of paperbacks and hardbacks, all screaming their messages of drama and sensationalism. But it is still possible to find a simple straight-forward story that will keep the reader breathless, attentive, and compulsively turning the pages. The novels of Sara Paretsky, Tony Hillerman, Reginald Hill, Dick Francis, and Rosamund Pilcher are good examples.

Fiction today has to compete with television, videotapes, films, rock music, virtual reality; and the horrors and crises in world news, exciting discoveries and inventions, and human deeds and misdeeds.

Sometimes a story depends for its momentum on a single character, or on the relationship between two characters. We love Character A and would like to see him on good terms with Character B, but they have always been at odds. How can an agreement between them be brought about? The relationship between Beatrice and Benedict in Shakespeare's *Much Ado About Nothing* is a fine example of such a story.

In *Little Lord Fauntleroy,* Frances Hodgson Burnett accomplishes this in a domestic setting. Character A won't love B, but B wins him over. The crusty old Earl of Dorincourt is unwillingly obliged by law to accept his unknown American grandson as his heir; how long will it take the gallant little fellow and his gentle gracious American mother to win their rightful places in the old aristocrat's rugged heart? Of course, it does not take very long, but the course of the story is pure pleasure for the reader all the way, even with the end so clearly in view.

Another heroine who achieves her end by possessing startlingly unexpected attributes and winning hearts all the way is Dorothy Gilman's

Mrs. Pollifax, a senior citizen spy. Often teamed with tough male colleagues who at first deeply mistrust and resent her, she breaches their
defenses by candor, practical good sense, humor, courage, and a touch
of mysticism that is irresistible. We all love to read about good tri-
umphing over evil, and to be given the certainty that it will do so, with
a touch of humor thrown in, is an unbeatable combination.

Unrecognized love must always command the fascinated attention
of readers, and Rebecca West makes tantalizing use of this knowledge
in her magnificent novel, *The Birds Fall Down.* In this story, the clever
but repulsive double agent Kamensky is infatuated by the teenage
heroine Laura, but she is wholly unaware of this from first to last,
believing that he intends to assassinate her. The unacknowledged duel
between them builds up to an almost intolerably suspenseful climax,
heightened by the fact that most of the other characters, Russians,
are given to immense, loquacious, red-herring monologues on every
conceivable topic, always just at the moment when some catastrophe
seems imminent, or a train is about to leave.

Virginia Woolf had an idea for a play, never actually written: "I'm
going to have a man and a woman . . . never meeting, not knowing
each other, but all the time you'll feel them coming nearer and nearer.
This will be the really exciting part, but when they *almost* meet—only
a door between—you see how they just miss." Perhaps not surprisingly, she never did put the idea into a play or story. But Mary Wesley,
in her novel, *An Imaginative Experience,* used a similar plot, except
that she does finally permit her couple to meet. This kind of scheme
for a story clearly displays that fiction is a kind of teasing game carried
on between writer and reader, a game like Grandmother's Footsteps,
in which I, the writer, try to steal up on you, the reader, without
allowing you to find out beforehand what I intend to do.

And the theme of *curiosity,* dangerous, misplaced, unwarrantable
curiosity, takes us, by way of myth and folklore, to ghost stories and
the supernatural. "A Warning to the Curious" is the title of one of
M.R. James's best-known ghost stories, and a very terrifying story it
is, yet entirely convincing. Who could resist the possibility of discovering one of the legendary three royal crowns, buried somewhere,
long ago, on the Suffolk coast "to keep off the Danes or the French or
the Germans." But the surviving crown has a ghostly guardian, and
the fate of the inquisitive rabbity young man who goes after it is very

awful indeed. All the details in this story are exactly right: the foggy, sandy countryside, and the character of Paxton, the silly young man who has dug up the crown and now wishes he hadn't. The narrator and his friend try to help, but "all the same the snares of death overtook him," James states, but then proceeds to describe a harrowing chase through the fog, poor Paxton pursued by a creature "with more bones than flesh" and a "lungless laugh." Paxton is finally found with his mouth full of sand, his teeth and jaws broken to bits. . . .

Operas have overtures, in which snatches of all the best arias are beguilingly introduced, giving the audience a taste of the pleasures to come. In the same way, the shrewd writer will, by an opening sentence, sound the *voice* of his story, suggest what is likely to happen, and so whet the reader's appetite: "The marriage wasn't going well and I decided to leave my husband," says Anne Tyler at the start of *Earthly Possessions;* "I went to the bank to get cash for the trip." And so she set the style and tempo for a wildly free-wheeling and funny plot.

Your voice can be humorous or terrifying, sad, wild, or romantic; only *you* can give it utterance, only you can lead your reader by a cobweb thread through the windings of your own particular story. What did happen to the mushroom? Each of us has his own theory as to that.

□ 33

Making the Reader Care

By Marjorie Franco

EMOTION, OR A STATE OF FEELING, IS SOMETHING WE ALL EXPERI-ence, and for most of us our persistent memories are of situations or happenings that aroused a powerful emotion. When writing a story, the author uses a variety of emotions, trusting the reader to experience them along with the character. The character needs to be convincing enough to cause the reader to recall his or her own emotions, though not necessarily the specific experience that aroused them.

A friend once told me that her brother's favorite memory of childhood was of a summer night when he and the other members of his family stood around in the kitchen eating ice cream cones. Happiness, no doubt, was the emotion he connected to the scene, and this simple emotion resulted from many factors, including the summer night, the kitchen, the cold sweetness of the ice cream on his tongue, and above all, the sharing of pleasure with a loving family.

Although this memory from real life is different from the world of fiction, it is an example of how we remember moments that affect us. Our storehouse of memory continues to grow from childhood on, providing us with ideas for characters, setting, and conflicts, which, with the help of imagination, craft, and an appropriate tone, we weave together to create a story we hope will make the reader care.

Not an easy task, and one that beginning writers sometimes sidestep by having emotion occur off scene, or by simply stating it in narrative.

In *Lectures on Literature,* Vladimir Nabokov writes that memory causes the perfect fusion of past and present; that inspiration adds a third ingredient, the future. The writer, he believes, see the world as the potentiality of fiction.

An observant writer once saw a woman getting off a bus, and was so struck by something about her appearance and manner, she became the inspiration for a character in his story.

Henry James, sitting next to a woman at a dinner party, listening to her describe an event that actually took place, began thinking along fictional lines, sowing the seeds for what would become his novella *The Aspern Papers*. Once the idea had formed in his mind, he didn't want to hear the woman's entire story, for he was already creating his own.

We may begin creating a fictional character with a real person in mind, but the end result is never a duplicate of that person, because it's impossible to get inside another person's head, no matter how well we may know him or her. But it is necessary to get inside our characters, to know their personalities, strengths and weakness, what will make them feel love, hate, joy, anger, fear and pain; what experiences will affect their lives, and how they will deal with their problems. Much of this is revealed by showing them interacting with other characters in particular situations; with scene and dialogue; and with conflict.

The idea for my story "Between Friends" (*Good Housekeeping*) began with a real person in mind, but the character of Janet quickly took on her own personality and became fictional. The protagonist, Alison, welcomes new arrival, Janet, to the neighborhood, and they become friends. The conflict begins with Janet's casual criticism of Benny, Alison's son. Gradually, it escalates to the point where Janet says, "Maybe you've put your job before the interests of your child. Maybe if you'd stayed home more things would have been better." Words are exchanged, and the friendship ends with bitter feelings on both sides.

I believe the reader can relate to this confrontation, for we have all experienced criticism, as well as the hurt and feeling of rejection that accompany it. And when the critic is a friend, we may feel doubly rejected. Alison, who has gone out of her way for Janet, feels she's been treated unfairly, just as the reader may have felt at some time, even though the situation might have been different. Here, again, I trust the reader to tap into emotions that may be latent and experience them vicariously with the character.

The climax of the story occurs when a desperate Janet comes to Alison for help. Alison is about to leave for an important job interview, but when Janet says, "It's Andy, he ate a whole bottle of aspirin," she is horrified, and putting aside their differences (as well as her interview), she immediately drives Janet and Andy to the hospital.

Here, Alison has to make a quick decision, and the one she chooses says something about her character, her sense of right and wrong. Another person, unwilling to sacrifice an important interview for someone who has treated her badly, might have called an ambulance and left Janet and her son to wait for its arrival.

In addition to trying to show insight into the main character, I was also trying to establish empathy for Janet, the antagonist. Janet has her own problems. Perhaps she regrets having given up her job to stay home with her children; perhaps her criticism of Alison is grounded in envy; and, most important of all, perhaps she feels responsible for placing her son in danger, guilty of an act of negligence, the same kind of negligence of which she had accused Alison's son. Anger, envy, and guilt are emotions that have touched us all.

In our attempt to make the reader care, I believe we must keep in mind the difference between identifying with and relating to characters. The definition of identify is "to be, or become the same." Writers who create unique characters shouldn't expect the reader to identify with them. I take the view that though there is a universality in human beings, still each of us is different in a unique way. In contrast, the definition of relate is "to have a relationship or connection," a better goal, I think, for making the reader care.

As important as characters are to a story, they would not hold the reader's attention without some form of conflict. Conflict moves the story and keeps the reader interested while waiting to discover what happens next. Conflict generates emotion and requires the character either to solve the problem or to deal with it in a satisfactory way.

In my story "Midnight Caller" (*Good Housekeeping*) Dianne, a teacher and recently divorced mother of an infant son, is receiving anonymous phone calls, usually at midnight. She lives on the second floor of a three-story building; her friend Greta lives upstairs with her teenaged son, and another friend, Hank, lives on the first floor. Safety is of great importance to Dianne: On her own, and responsible for her infant son as well as for herself, she has tried to protect herself by choosing to live near friends. When the phone calls begin, she persuades herself that her name was picked at random from the phone book; still, they represent a threat to her feeling of safety and cause her a sense of unease. Then one snowy night, with all the roads blocked, all feelings of safety vanish and unease gives way to outright fear.

"What are you wearing?" the voice on the phone says. "Is it the yellow nightgown with the ruffles, or the white one with the lace?" Slowly, as if in a dream, she touches the neck of her nightgown and runs her fingers over the yellow ruffles. She hangs up, heart pounding, wide awake after being startled out of a sound sleep, and goes to her son's room.

The setting contributes to the tension—the apartment building surrounded by snow "thick on the rooftops and the bare trees, high where it had drifted against fences in backyards"—and so does the detail: the nightgown with the ruffles, her son's room "small, shadowy and warm, smelling of baby powder and freshly washed blankets. Clean."

Dianne's desire for safety is in conflict with the outside threat, the fact that she is interacting with an unknown person. By using certain words, abstractions are made concrete: "pounding" and "startled" contrast with "warm," "baby powder," and "clean."

In the end, Dianne discovers the identity of the midnight caller. It is not Hank, her neighbor, or one of her students at school, possibilities she had considered. It is Greta's son, who has often baby-sat for her. Like Alison in the first story I mentioned, Dianne is faced with a difficult and very important decision.

In these two stories, I've tried to show how characters, conflicts, and settings can generate emotion in the reader. But the emotion expressed through the character must first be felt by the writer who uses memory, experience and observations together with creative imagination to write the story and present it with clarity so the reader will understand.

Readers don't need to have conscious memory of events in their lives that aroused certain feelings in order to imagine a fictional situation and relate to it either positively or negatively. But those feelings can be touched by the characters in a story and the events in their lives, and when that happens, readers begin to care.

□ 34

STRATEGIES FOR REVISING SHORT STORIES

BY GEOFFREY BECKER

"REVISION IS GOOD. ON THE OTHER HAND, YOU CAN ALWAYS TRY TO write it right the first time." This provocative statement from a professor I had in graduate school seemed obvious. We all knew that the initial writing of a story was only about twenty percent of the ultimate effort involved. After that came the hours of cutting and pasting, crossing out paragraphs, scribbling in the margins.

But those words kept me thinking for years. While I still believe he oversimplified things, I've also come to understand the truth of what he said. Do things "right"—or close to "right"—the first time and revision is easy and a pleasure. Write a story that has problems at some basic level, and no amount of cosmetic surgery is likely to save it.

Paradoxically, in order to reach the level where one does things "right" the first time, it's usually necessary to do things "wrong" quite a lot. Experienced (or unusually gifted) writers are already at a place where they don't make beginner's mistakes.

In my own teaching experience, I've been amazed at different people's notions of what constitutes a revision. I've had students tell me they've done seven drafts of a piece, only to discover that each rewriting involved making a few changes to a hard copy, entering those on the computer, then printing the story out again. Version seven isn't noticeably different from version one. Perhaps the problem is with the word "draft," since in the computer age, the old meaning—a new, completely retyped set of pages that involved some human being fingering each keystroke—is completely dead. We need to be careful about confusing the two: One involves interaction with a manuscript, the other pressing a button. Truman Capote joked about Jack Kerouac, "That's not writing, that's typing." But it's not a joke that some people actually confuse rewriting with printing out a new copy.

To revise a first-draft short story, it's important, first, to recognize how close you are to having achieved what you want. If you are very close, great; you can set about the business of fine-tuning and editing. But if you don't know what you've got, it may be a good idea to view the piece as an experiment. Consider beginning again from scratch, using the same materials, but this time with the benefit of experience that comes from having told the story once before. Perhaps you chose the wrong point of view. Perhaps you chose the wrong scenes to dramatize. This is the most drastic kind of rewriting, but it can also be the most rewarding. Too many beginning writers approach their fiction as finished once an initial draft exists. It has a beginning, an ending, a middle—it must be a story. They are unwilling—understandably, considering the work that was involved in the writing—to start over. Instead, they change a little dialogue here, remove an adverb there. The story changes, but doesn't improve.

If only we knew the rules, we wouldn't make mistakes! We *would* write it right the first time. But there are no rules. The best writers are constantly violating, with gleeful impunity, what they think *might* be the rules. They play around with the point of view, shift tenses all over the place, and they *still get published.*

The only real rule is this: Anything that works is O.K. It's not that the goalposts keep getting moved; they aren't even there. A good story succeeds on its own terms.

All of which can be, well, frustrating. The following suggestions may help you avoid some common writing traps, and also guide you toward ways of looking at your finished story and seeing it in a new light. Most new writers working on short stories have difficulty with revision. We'd rather be potters: Throw a pot, glaze and fire it, sell it. But it's a rare first-draft short story that is strong enough to be sent out into the world without further attention.

Try to avoid writing a story that:

• *Begins in a static place with a character staring at something (often a photograph), then remembering something that took place in a different time and place.* This is the classic "frame" device, but unless something is going to happen in the frame itself, why not look in on the story at a more compelling moment?

• *Is all dialogue.* This can certainly be done, and has been. But in stories by beginners, it's often a sign that the author hasn't done the extra work necessary to imagine an interior life for the characters and is simply observing them. Another story to avoid is the one that takes place entirely over the phone. This is not particularly dramatic, since phone conversations usually recount things that happened elsewhere. Essentially, what you'd be giving the reader is a person alone in a room holding a receiver. Yes, there are two characters, but they are miles apart. (Point-of-view shifts can seem really odd in these stories.)

• *Has a narrator so vile and unpleasant that there is no reason for readers to want to spend time in his or her company.* We read because we want to learn about other people, even ugly ones. If you're going to give readers a mass-murderer-serial-rapist (every college-level creative writing instructor gets two or three of these stories a semester), you'd better have really imagined an interior life for him and not have shown him simply as the sum of his actions.

• *Hangs together only by virtue of some huge metaphor.* A married couple has a garden they enjoy working in. As the years go by, it goes to weed. One night, they have a terrible fight. It looks as if they may divorce. In the morning, the two of them go out and start putting the garden back in shape. This ends up being more about the garden than about the people (not to mention that it's terribly obvious and cliché).

• *Gains all its momentum through gradually revealing to the reader information that the main character had access to all along.* Play fair: If you're writing a third-person story from the point of view of Tom, who is home from college and acting distant and strange and can't relate to anyone, but you don't let us know until page fifteen that it's because he figured out two weeks ago that he's gay, you've cheated.

• *Simply follows the decline of a character with a serious illness and ends with his or her death.* The most emotional thing that can happen to us in real life can be predictable and unengaging on the page.

You've got a completed draft, with a title. It's got the shape of a story, but you know it's not finished. How do you take it further?

Try asking these questions:

Where does the story really start? Go back and look at your opening. Have you done significant "pre-writing"? I've learned that the first drafts of my own stories rarely begin until somewhere around the middle of page two. What seemed like a beginning (and was, in the sense that it got me going) is not always the place that the story kicks into gear. You may be able to cut more than you thought possible. Look for those places. Remember, cutting is *good*. To paraphrase Jay Leno in those old Doritos ads: "Cut all you want—you can always write more."

Are there too many characters? Can you justify them? Are there people given stage time who have no bearing on the story at all?

Have you included more than is necessary? While you create, you're figuring out for yourself what's going on as well as explaining it to the reader, which is why things don't just get neatly onto the page in perfect order. Paring down to the essential comes later, and, if you were writing well to begin with, such tightening can be a real pleasure. Which scenes are doing nothing (except perhaps showing off how good you are with language)?

Is your dialogue doing something? Does it develop character? Move the plot? Ideally, it should do both. Dialogue gives fiction transparency and breaks things up rhythmically, too. Watch out for dialogue that exists solely to give the reader information, or is merely chitchat. Also, look out for "Ping-Pong" dialogue, with the speakers constantly referring to each other by name. Try to avoid unnecessary "tagging" of dialogue with adverbs, or elaborate ways of getting around the word "said."

Do you know what the story is about? Now that the story exists, you can read it with a critical eye. Writing is a process of discovery, and your story is certain to have grown in ways you hadn't planned. Where can it be developed to explore further what you've so far only touched on? Have you shown the crucial moments of decision and discovery? The crisis action? Is what you've written original, or have you fallen into some cliché? Don't have your characters and situations develop in a way you think they *ought* to; let them surprise you. Life is, after all, surprising.

Have you paid attention to the most simple details? Sometimes, in their attempts to achieve loftier, more literary goals, writers overlook the mundane, everyday things that help make fiction believable. Have you committed technical errors? Sent someone to a Vikings game in May? Had them put a pot of water on to boil, then go off to pick up the kids after school? A lot of fiction writing is about keeping track of the little things, moving people across rooms, etc. What time is it? What's the weather like?

Have you really cut all you can? You've worked and worked and you still hate what you've done. Circle *everything* that strikes you as boring or nonessential. Cut until you can cut no more. See what's left. For instance, scenes that do nothing more than transport a character from one place to another can often be dispensed with. Does your character spend pages three and four on a bus?

When you think there's nothing else to be done, put the story away. Don't send it out. It will change (well, you will, anyway) over time. Wait two weeks. Then reread it, and see what you did.

Finally, cultivate a couple of people in your life to show your work to. It's good to have someone who loves and accepts everything you write as brilliant, but in addition, see if you can find someone a little tougher, whose opinion you trust, and bounce your story off that person, too. In the end, the best thing you can do is develop two sides of yourself: one that's experimental, risk-taking and imaginative, another that is tough, no-nonsense and ruthless. Trust them both, but not at the same time.

□ 35

FIVE BEGINNERS' PROBLEMS AND HOW TO SOLVE THEM

BY MONICA WOOD

FIRST, THE BAD NEWS: DESPITE A DAZZLING VARIETY IN THE STORIES they choose to tell, beginning fiction writers are easy to spot. Their efforts are thwarted by the same problems: inconsistent point of view; wooden dialogue; too many modifiers; autobiography masquerading as fiction; and trick endings. The good news is that once they recognize these problems and learn to solve them, their writing leaps almost instantly to another level. Nothing is more satisfying to any writer, beginning or otherwise, than learning to use new fiction-writing techniques.

One: Inconsistent point of view

Many beginning writers make the wise choice of first person for telling their first stories. The "I" narrator helps to keep a story focused and the narrative consistent. Not all stories work best with an "I" narrator, however, and this is where third person comes in.

Most beginners don't discover the complications of point of view until they begin writing in the third person. When writing in the third person, you have two choices: *omniscient point of view* and *third-person limited consciousness point of view.* Understanding the differences between these points of view will help you gain control over your own writing in a way you never thought possible.

The omniscient narrator is usually all-knowing, letting the reader in on the thoughts and feelings of any or all of the characters. (Look to any fairy tale or nineteenth-century novel for an example.) The omniscient narrator can see what the characters can't see and hear what the characters can't hear:

Irritated, Larry stood on the corner wondering what had become of Iris. He adjusted the cuffs of his shirt, as he listened to the gonging of the town

153

clock. Across town, in the confines of her drawing room, the object of Larry's irritation was petting her Siamese cat and humming an aria whose rhythm exactly matched Larry's fretful pacing.

Here we have two characters as seen by one narrator. The omniscient narrator has the authority to set us down on a street corner to look at Larry, and then whisk us uptown to see Iris, all in the space of a paragraph. This is not as easy as it looks. Unless your prose has the pristine consistency of tone that comes with years of writing experience, the omniscient narrative quickly deteriorates into a muddle of shifting viewpoints:

> Larry stood on the corner, wondering what was keeping that dratted Iris. Ten minutes late already, but of course she wouldn't bat an eye over a measly ten minutes. Across town, in the confines of her drawing room, the object of Larry's irritation was petting her Siamese cat and humming an aria whose rhythm exactly matched Larry's fretful pacing.
> Darn that Iris, Larry thought. Isn't this just like her . . .

In this example, a colloquial tone ("dratted," "bat an eye," "Darn that Iris") jars against a more formal, genteel tone ("In the confines," "object of irritation," "fretful pacing"). This is not an omniscient narrative; this is a narrative that shifts abruptly from Larry's viewpoint to Iris's and back again. In short order, the story will begin to unravel and the hapless reader will be left to wonder who the main character is supposed to be.

One effective technique for avoiding the shifting point of view syndrome is to write the story in a *third person, limited consciousness* point of view. With this technique, the reader is privy to the thoughts and feelings, or consciousness, of only *one* character:

> Irritated, Larry stood on the corner, wondering what was keeping Iris. The town clock gonged ten times. Perhaps she had forgotten him—again. Perhaps at this very moment she was ensconced in her drawing room, running an idle hand over the pampered pelt of her Siamese cat.

In this version, we are allowed inside only one character—Larry— which gives the story a consistency that the earlier, shifting version lacked. We see Iris as Larry imagines her, not the way she really is. As a result, the reader will feel more anchored to one character, and the story will seem more focused and polished. At first you might resist the limitations of this technique, but with practice you'll discover its capacity for unifying your narrative and deepening your characterizations. Sticking to one character's viewpoint offers you ample opportunity to explore the complications of his personality, because everything that happens in the story is filtered through his experience.

If you *must* give another character a viewpoint, try alternating point of view in sections—write two or three pages in Larry's viewpoint, leave a couple of blank lines, then start a new section in Iris's viewpoint. You can go back and forth like this if the story is long enough. Most short stories run nine to fifteen pages, however, which doesn't leave much room for two characters' viewpoints.

Two: Wooden dialogue

Writing dialogue is a tricky business, but there are several techniques you may use to avoid having your dialogue sound like a beginner's.

Avoid hellos and goodbyes. Beginners often waste precious pages with the beginnings and endings of conversations. "Hello." "Jack, is that you?" "Yeah, it's me." "Well, what do you want?" This kind of ambling paralyzes the story's forward motion. When the phone rings, skip the pleasantries and get to the point:

Jack picked up the phone. It was Jill, with a song and dance about why she couldn't make it to the ball game.
"You know how Mother is," she said. "I can't leave her for one second."

And when it's time to hang up, dispense with the farewells:

"Mother was fine when you wanted to go to the auction last Saturday," Jack said.
"Are you going to start on me? Don't start on me, Jack."
They went on like this for twenty minutes before hanging up. Jack hauled on his coat and started up the hill.

Similarly, when characters are meeting one another, skip the introductions and get to the real conversation:

Felix ushered me into the room and made some introductions. "You're a *philanthropist*?" a woman in green said to me. "I've never met a philanthropist who was still living."

Use contractions. Nothing ruins a line of dialogue like an uncontracted verb. "I *do not* want you to come" sounds stilted, whereas "I *don't* want you to come" sounds natural. Can'ts, don'ts, won'ts, and couldn'ts almost always read better than cannots, do nots, will nots, or could nots.

Don't use dialogue to fill in the plot. Beginners' dialogue often seems staged for the reader's benefit:

> "Rachel," Bob called, running to her. "I haven't seen you since your father's computer-graphics company burned down three months ago."

In this line of dialogue, *computer-graphics company* sticks out as unnatural, as does *three months ago.* Rachel already knows what happened, so Bob has no reason to state the obvious. (Besides, he's out of breath from running and couldn't get all those words out in one take anyway!) If you must convey information about the plot, use a combination of dialogue and narrative:

> "I haven't seen you since the fire," Bob said. Three months had passed, but he could hear it still, that magnificent popping and sparking, and finally the handmade sign—SINCLAIR COMPUTER GRAPHICS—crashing into a flaming heap on the sidewalk. "How's your father, anyway?"
> "You've heard of a man without a country?" Rachel said. "Sometimes I think a man without a company is worse."

Avoid dialogue tags like "he chortled" or "she sneered." Elaborate dialogue tags mark a beginner. A simple "he said" or "she asked" should suffice in most cases.

These techniques take the wooden quality out of dialogue. You might try reading dialogue aloud, to yourself or to a friend, in order to catch trouble spots. If it doesn't sound right, it isn't going to read right.

Three: Autobiography disguised as fiction

Most of us write to share something of ourselves—our outlook, our family history, a personal trauma or triumph, a turning-point event that altered our lives. Sharing and recording our lives is a worthy purpose, and that's what autobiography is for. Unfortunately, many beginners write fiction that is only thinly disguised autobiography. Their "fiction" suffers from the constrictions of real life—if the real character had a Caddy with blue pinstripes and whitewalls, then the car takes up space in the story, whether it's relevant or not. The result is a story that takes forever to begin, because the author spends too much time being accurate.

Good stories require something more than the truth. Real life doesn't have the urgent shape of fiction; it has far too many detours and irrelevancies to make a story by itself. You must alter the truth, often dramatically, in order to make stories. If your storyteller is an "I" narrator who looks like you, thinks like you, and acts like you, then your story is headed for trouble. Narrators are characters, not authors. If you, the author, are skinny, make the narrator stout. If you have a pet dog, give the narrator a pet llama. Once you separate yourself from the narrator, you are free to invent in ways that the "real" story, no matter how interesting in itself, would never allow. This is no time to be faithful! Cheat on the truth; that's how stories are born.

Four: Too many modifiers

Test yourself by going through one of your stories and circling all the adjectives and adverbs (especially those ending in "ly"). You may be surprised at how many there are. Adverbs and adjectives can add luster to your prose, but their overuse can be deadly. Many beginning writers, unsure of their storytelling powers, rely too heavily on modifiers to set a scene or create a character. Ironically, too many modifiers serve to muddy rather than clarify description, as in the following story excerpt:

Alice deftly sprayed the antique mahogany table and fiercely wiped it down, her first meaningless chore of the muggy August day. The other chores, dashed onto a scrap of bright white monogrammed paper in Mrs. Delano's self-consciously elegant hand, would have to wait. Mrs. Delano liked this handsome table to shine brilliantly. Alice rubbed and rubbed, stopping just short of meeting her own meekly subservient reflection. Wincing, she stood up, put a hand to her permanently aching back and arched like an old, arthritic cat. Her simple blue cotton uniform with the starched white collar had once fit so neatly, but now it pulled slightly at the waist, a sign that she had been in Mrs. Delano's beautiful Tudor-style house much too long.

The author wants to convey a sense of Alice's hopelessness, but the barrage of modifiers is not much help. The most important and telling detail—the too-small uniform—is all but lost in the clutter. Look how much more poignantly you can convey Alice's plight by removing the modifiers and letting the detail shine through:

Alice sprayed the table and wiped it down, her first chore of the day. The other chores, dashed onto a scrap of paper in Mrs. Delano's elegant hand, would have to wait. Mrs. Delano liked this table to shine. Alice rubbed and rubbed, stopping just short of meeting her own reflection. Wincing, she stood up, put a hand to her back and arched like a cat. Her uniform strained at the waist, a sign she had been here too long.

Removing modifiers can help you find the story you want to tell. Beginners tend to rely on adjectives and adverbs to do the hard work of description. Don't fall into that trap. Using modifiers is not a short-cut to characterization. Don't be content to tell us that Character A speaks "airily"—give us some airy dialogue instead.

Five: Trick endings

Beginning writers somehow have the idea that a story's ending must be a grand surprise. Stories of the supernatural rely on the element of surprise, of course, as do mystery and suspense stories, but in contemporary, literary fiction, the "trick" or "surprise" ending is a sure mark of a beginner. For example, the narrator turns out to be a pig or a car; the main character puts a gun to his head and fires; the real-estate agent turns out to be the homebuyer's long-lost daughter. Variations on these last-minute strategies occur dismayingly often in first fictions.

One way to test the integrity of an ending is to ask yourself if the resolution comes from within the character or from an outside element. A character who changes his mind, or "comes to realize" or takes Path A over Path B should do so as a result of his own actions, not someone else's. Never allow someone to come in at the last minute to get the character out of a jam. Take the gun from the character's head—now what does he do? He has to solve his problem in some way, doesn't he? If the real-estate agent and the homebuyer are not long-lost mother and daughter, then something else (something more interesting) must be binding them. Surprise or trick endings let the writer off far too easily. Stories that come to rest as a result of the characters' own motivations and behavior are the hardest to write but the most sat-isfying to read.

If you recognize your own writing in some or all of these examples, do not despair. Addressing yourself to the task of solving these com-mon problems means you are no longer a beginner!

❏ 36

WHAT EVERY GOOD STORY NEEDS: URGENCY

BY SHERRI SZEMAN

IF I HADN'T FALLEN OFF THE MOUNTAIN, I NEVER WOULD HAVE BElieved it. Actually, I did believe it before I fell off the mountain, but the first sentence of this article is an example of what writers need to have in their fiction in order to have vibrant, intriguing, publishable work: URGENCY. When a piece of fiction has urgency, the reader can't wait to keep reading. He doesn't want to eat dinner or do the dishes or even go to sleep! All he wants to do is read! All writers can learn to put urgency in their work, improving it and making it more publishable.

Before the twentieth century, not many writers worried about keeping their readers' attention, so urgency was not a question writers necessarily had to deal with. Now, however, writers are competing with television, videos, and movies for their audiences, so their task is more challenging than their predecessors'. Urgency cannot be "pasted on" or simply attached to the piece of writing. It must be an integral part of it, inseparable from the plot or the characters. It is urgency that will keep the readers clamoring for more, so it must be honest urgency, that is, it must evolve naturally from the characters, the plot, and the circumstances of the short story or the novel you are writing.

Take, for example, the first paragraph of my novel *The Kommandant's Mistress,* the story of a Nazi commander of a concentration camp who forces a Jewish inmate to be his mistress during the war. Part One of the novel is narrated by the Kommandant, while Part Two is narrated by the girl, Rachel. Not only does the opening sentence present urgency, but other sentences of that paragraph reinforce that initial urgency. I've italicized these sentences for emphasis:

Then I saw her. There she stood, in the village store, her hair in a long braid down the center of her back, her skin white in the sunlight, and *my hand went*

159

to my hip, seeking the weight of my gun. As the girl spoke, I stumbled back against one of the shelves, my fingers tightening at the leather around my waist. While the shopkeeper arranged the food in the bag, the morning sun glinted on the storefront windows, illuminating the girl. The wooden shelves pressed into my shoulder and back. *Sweat dampened my forehead and ribs.* Another shopper spoke, frowned, pushed aside my arm to reach a jar on the shelf behind me, *but I didn't move. My hand slid down over my hip and leg. No, I'd forgotten that I no longer wore my gun.*

The reader now wonders: Who is this girl, and why is this man looking for her? Why did he have a gun, and why does he want to shoot her? What's happened between them that he seems afraid to confront her? And, finally, what happened that he no longer wears his gun?

Urgency must be maintained throughout the piece of fiction to be effective, however. It doesn't keep your readers' attention if you present them with urgency in the opening sentence and paragraph, but then lapse into long-winded, overblown scenic descriptions. If it takes your readers 50 pages before they come to the next instance of urgency, you'll lose them before they get to it. For urgency to be effectively maintained, it must be integral to the plot or to the character. In *The Kommandant's Mistress,* for example, after the war, the Kommandant is intent on finding the girl (for reasons which he does not reveal) before he is arrested and tried for war crimes. Though at various times he spots the girl for whom he searches, he is not courageous enough or physically near enough to confront her, while at the same time being pursued and sometimes ambushed by the men who are chasing him so that they can bring him to trial. Thus, the Kommandant is desperate to find the girl before his pursuers find him, so that he can give his version of what happened before he is executed for his war crimes. These two levels of urgency keep the reader turning pages. (In fact, when I was on tour and met some of my readers, they "complained" to me that my book kept them awake all night because they "couldn't put it down.")

In Part Two of *The Kommandant's Mistress,* when Rachel gives her version of the events, the urgency is different, though related to the urgency in Part One. Rachel constantly thinks she sees the Kommandant, and, naturally fearing him, she keeps moving in order to avoid him. Her husband David has had enough of this constant moving and is threatening divorce, unless she becomes less "obsessed" with the Kommandant. Rachel, therefore, needs to deal with her experience in the camps before it destroys her relationship with her husband and, some might say, before it destroys her own sanity. Here is a passage from her version which illustrates the urgency (once again, I have italicized the pertinent passages):

Now it was quiet, and *I didn't hear the noise that had woken me.* I went to the front door; yes, it was locked. I moved the curtains.
The car was there again.
I raced upstairs, my heart pounding. I yanked open the bottom dresser drawer and *grabbed the pistol.* It was already loaded. *It was always loaded.* I readied it for firing as I rushed back down the stairs, to the window beside the front door. Breathing heavily, I pushed the curtains aside.
The car was gone.
After an hour I went upstairs, pulled a blanket from the cupboard, and *returned to my post* by the front door. I sat there, my face next to the glass, my hands tense around the gun.
The car did not come back that night.
The gun and I did not sleep.

Urgency moves the Kommandant and Rachel through their respective stories. It gives them a "reason" for telling their stories; it also gives the reader a reason for reading them.

I didn't always use urgency in my writing, and I don't think it's a coincidence that before *The Kommandant's Mistress,* which was when I first became aware of the concept of urgency, my fiction was constantly rejected, sometimes with the criticism to eliminate the "dry descriptive passages" and to "get on with the story." After I realized that these criticized passages didn't contain urgency, I eliminated them. Now I use this technique in all my fiction, and whether or not they call it "urgency," so do other successful writers. Here are some opening lines from some of my stories to give you an idea of the different ways you can impart urgency. Notice that your titles can also be used to develop urgency effectively:

In the beginning, God created Nebraska, and boy, did he make a mistake. ("Dismal, Nebraska")

The day I learned to fly, I was three years old. ("Learning to Fly")

When I was seven years old, the rock on which the Church had stood for almost two thousand years trembled, collapsed, and crumbled into dust. ("Dancing for the Blind")

We weren't always living in the Ice Age, Eddie and me. ("Love in the Time of Dinosaurs")

It's true, I admit it: I'm a freak. ("Hunchback of the Midwest")

This is how the plan to kill your husband could begin. ("Naked, With Glasses")

Open any book of award-winning short stories, and you'll find the same thing: urgency in the opening sentence that compels the reader to continue reading:

I'm not trying to flatter myself, but I was the first colored woman he ever seriously considered loving. (Kathleen Collins' "Stepping Back")

I am not a lucky traveler. (C. W. Guswelle's "Horst Wessel")

Later we will tell how we happen to be here in the first class lounge of the *United States,* but for the time being: there are three of us, and we are, incredibly, the only persons seated in a space that is at least fifteen meters wide and perhaps twenty-five meters long. (Robley Wilson, Jr.'s "The United States")

The woman who can't dance moves in with the Arthur Murray Studios dance instructor. (Mary Peterson's "To Dance")

As to Caesar's health, there seems to me no cause for alarm. (John Gardner's "Julius Caesar and the Werewolf")

She had kept the bottle stuck down inside a basket of clothes that needed ironing, and throughout the course of the day whenever she had a chance to walk through the back room where the basket was kept, she would stop for the odd sip or two. (Gerald Duff's "Fire Ants")

The examples of urgency in quality published fiction are endless. Some writers call it by different names; John Jakes, for example, calls this element "intrigue," but the concept is the same. As you write, you should ask yourself questions such as these: "Where's the urgency in this chapter?" "Why does this character have to tell his story now?" or "When's the last time I put some urgency in here?" Last year, just as an experiment, I gave my freshman composition students the traditional first-person story assignment, but told them they had to include urgency. I simply told them that the first sentence, the first paragraph, and various sentences or paragraphs throughout the narrative had to make me keep reading. In class, I made them all write the first sentence of a proposed story, which, of course, they were allowed to change when they wrote their real stories. Most of the sentences were similar, but all showed a grasp of the concept:

By the time the gun went off, it was too late.

He tried to warn his brother, but he'd already grabbed the gun and headed out the door.

When I saw Stephen with that girl, I knew exactly what I had to do.

I might have spent the rest of my life in jail if it hadn't been for that one night.

For the actual assignment, the students not only turned their practice sentences into real opening sentences with wonderful urgency, they managed to keep the urgency through their entire narratives.

If beginners can so easily impart urgency to their narratives, then it should be an even simpler task for creative writers, published or not. Urgency is one of the most vital things new writers need to learn. Without it, your fiction is likely to put readers to sleep; even worse, after reading the first sentence, readers may never even buy your novel. Notice how many people browsing in a bookstore pick up a book and read the opening before they decide to buy it, and how many of those books get put back on the shelves. It's a good exercise for writers at all levels: Go to the bookstore and spend an hour or so reading the opening lines in novels. How many of them impart urgency? How many keep you turning pages, right there in the bookstore? How many do you buy so that you can finish reading? If a work of fiction can't pass the urgency test, it isn't very likely to have either a large or an enthusiastic audience. Never assume you have a captive audience: You don't. As a writer, you have to earn your audience. Whether you want to write bestsellers or masterpieces (or both), the best way to attract an audience and to keep it is through urgency.

☐ SPECIALIZED FICTION

❏ 37

TWILIGHT FOR HIGH NOON: TODAY'S WESTERN

BY LOREN D. ESTLEMAN

PARDON ME WHILE I INDULGE IN SOME SELF-CONGRATULATION: I WAS right. In 1981, when TV sitcoms and big-screen space operas had all but crowded out the traditional western, and Louis L'Amour's career was drawing to a close with Tom Clancy's ascendant, I went out on a limb in an article for *The Writer* Magazine and predicted the triumphant return of frontier fiction.

Only four years later, Larry McMurtry's monumental tale of a cattle drive, *Lonesome Dove,* swept to the top of *The New York Times* bestseller list and captured the Pulitzer Prize. The subsequent TV adaptation gunned down the ratings competition, saved the endangered television miniseries from extinction, and spawned three successful sequels and a regular series. In the meantime, *Dances with Wolves,* Kevin Costner's epic motion picture based on Michael Blake's acclaimed novel about a white man living with Indians, recovered its investment ten times over and took seven Academy Awards. Next in the chute was Clint Eastwood's *Unforgiven,* a grittily realistic movie about an Old West assassin, and the big winner at the Academy Awards in 1993.

The effect on Hollywood was as sudden and startling as the Gunfight at the O.K. Corral. Immediately, every major studio gave the green light to western productions that had been languishing in its story department for years. By the middle of the 1990s, more westerns were opening in the nation's theaters than at any time since the 1950s.

The pundits who had smugly announced the permanent closing of the frontier were stumped for an explanation. Writers of westerns were not.

What *Lonesome Dove, Dances with Wolves,* and *Unforgiven* have in common that set them apart from the long stream of *High Noon* imitations of decades past was a regard for authentic history. The flawed, emotionally repressed cattlemen of *Lonesome Dove* had as little in common with the heroic cowboys of 1946's *Red River* as Kevin Costner's flesh-and-blood Sioux had with the cardboard savages of the old B western; and there was certainly little of John Wayne's swagger or Gary Cooper's stoic self-sacrifice in Clint Eastwood's gunfighter, a drunken, whoring killer. They presented raw, unflinching portraits of imperfect humanity that audiences the world over recognized as genuine.

Not every entry in this spate of big-screen westerns was successful. Those that failed were dismal attempts to revive the old mythology of fast-draw contests and heroic loners with no visible means of support, dedicating their lives to the eradication of evil. Time was when these stereotypes were fresh and popular. But an increasingly sophisticated public, made cynical by real-life assassinations and corruption in high places, demands realistic characters in plausible situations.

TV documentaries such as Ken Burns's *The West,* and exhaustive revisionist histories such as Dee Brown's *Bury My Heart at Wounded Knee,* Paula Mitchell Marks's *And Die in the West,* and Evan S. Connell's *Son of the Morning Star,* have all reached wide audiences who can no longer be expected to embrace tall tales directed at readers who never ventured west of Chicago. Responding to a growing appetite for historical accuracy, a new breed of western writer is mining primary resources for people and facts that require no dramatization to attract reader interest.

Fortunately, there is no shortage of such raw material. The historical James Butler Hickok and Martha Jane Cannary were far more complex and interesting than the Wild Bill and Calamity Jane of fiction, and the thousands of less noted participants in the Westward Expansion all loom larger than life in our pampered time. Consider the haunted, burned-out expressions on the faces of those long-dead prairie wives photographed in front of their mean soddies. Yes, there were women out West; and theirs is but one of the many hundreds of tales that have yet to be told.

The traditional western is dying out, along with the readership that made it popular. Today's publishers have jettisoned the very word "western," substituting the labels "frontier fiction" and "American historical." Books herded into these categories are immediately distinguishable from their predecessors, first, by their length—100,000 words plus, as opposed to the 60,000-word horse operas of old—second, by their covers, which feature great sweeps of land and ethnically diverse casts instead of WASPish gunslingers facing off on a dusty street— third, by their reviews. *Publishers Weekly, The New York Times,* and the *Bloomsbury Review* take serious notice of these books as often now as they ignored the work of Luke Short and Ernest Haycox in the past. Today's western writers demonstrate a deeper understanding of the role of the American West in the shaping of a nation, and consequently of that nation's place in the history of the world.

As a writer, I welcome the larger canvas. In the past, I often felt constrained by the need to tell a grand story in a narrow space, and once ran afoul of an editor at Doubleday when an early entry in my Page Murdock series ran more than 300 pages in manuscript. Compare that with the freedom I felt to include this passage in Murdock's latest adventure, *City of Widows* (Forge, 1994):

Desert heat doesn't follow any of the standard rules. You'd expect it to be worst when the sun is straight up, but a hat will protect you from it then. When the only shade for miles is on the wrong side of the shrubbery you're using for cover, there is no hiding from that afternoon slant. I turned up my collar and unfastened my cuffs and pulled them down over the backs of my hands, but I could feel my skin turning red and shrinking under the fabric. Pinheads of sweat marched along the edge of my leather hatband and tracked down into my eyes, stinging like fire ants. The water in the canteen tasted like hot metal. I wanted the Montana snow, blue as the veins in Colleen Bower's throat with the mountain runoff coursing through it carrying shards of white ice . . .

That editor would probably have insisted I make do with the bare statement "It was hot," and get to the shooting. The end of space restrictions allows me to enlist the climate and topography of the West as characters in the plot.

One of the most significant—and progressive—developments of the new western has been the increase in women writers. Their ability to empathize with the courageous women who left behind the security of civilization to build a new life in the wilderness is largely responsible for the western's acceptance in the literary mainstream. In the past, the few women who ventured into the genre, including Dorothy M. Johnson ("The Man Who Shot Liberty Valance," "A Man Called Horse") and Willa Cather (*My Antonia, Death Comes for the Arch-*

bishop) were obliged to write from the male point of view. Successors such as Lucia St. Clair Robson, author of *Ride the Wind,* told from the perspective of Comanche captive Cynthia Ann Parker, have changed all that—to everyone's benefit.

Consider this frontier fiction staple—the showing of a notorious outlaw's corpse for profit—as transformed by Deborah Morgan in her short story "Mrs. Crawford's Odyssey" (*How the West Was Read,* Durkin Hayes, 1996), simply by adopting the point of view of the dead man's mother:

> This could not be her twenty-two-year-old son. Matthew had golden features, sunlit hair, a strong, square-set jaw. Laid out before her was an old man, bald, with flesh of a blue-white translucency, like watered-down milk. The heavily rouged cheekbones emphasized vast, dark hollows that should have been a jawline.
> Someone had made a terrible mistake, she was sure of it. She grabbed at that thread of hope, caught it, held it taut. This eased her, and she approached the deceased like any slight acquaintance might—respectfully, but thankful it's not one of your own. Only when she was leaning over the body did she discover death's ruse and see, unmistakably, her child.
> She clasped her hand over her mouth, a futile attempt to contain her emotions. Tears flowed until she believed that she would never be able to cry again.
> "My dear, precious boy," she said at last, "what have they done to you?"

Few male writers could write so poignantly and convincingly about a woman regarding the lifeless body of the boy to whom she gave birth.

Publishers are actively seeking women interested in tapping the rich vein of material concerning women out West. The market has rarely been so open to newcomers.

The West was settled by many different kinds of people: whites, blacks, Indians, immigrants, consumptives, heroes, and scoundrels. Bill Hotchkiss's *The Medicine Calf* and *Ammahabas* absorbingly follow the life of Jim Beckwourth, the black trapper and fur trader who became a Crow chief, and Cherokee writer Robert J. Conley (*The Dark Island, Crazy Snake*) stands at the summit of an impressive career built upon the Native American experience. In the heyday of the traditional western, such characters were regulated to secondary roles, either as villains or as comic foils.

When in my *Writer* article I first echoed Horace Greeley's advice "Go West," the necessary reference material resided only in libraries, bookstores, and county courthouses. Today, the writer with access to a computer can tap into a wealth of information on the geography, living conditions, and history of the West through the Internet. Rounding up the facts has never been so easy, but be warned: There is no longer an excuse for getting them wrong. Today's readers have the same access, and if you err, you will hear from them.

The timespan embraced by the new western is limitless. Once restricted to the bare quarter-century between the end of the Civil War in 1865 and the closing of the frontier in 1890, it now encompasses prehistoric Indian life as exemplified by the "People" series written by anthropologists W. Michael and Kathleen O'Neal Gear (*People of the Fire, People of the Silence,* and many more), and the struggles of modern westerners to come to terms with their heritage, as recounted by John L. Moore in *The Breaking of Ezra Riley.*

Freed from the tyranny of "acceptable" timeframes, I took advantage of all I had learned about the West in twenty years of researching and writing westerns to tell a fictional story based on the mysterious life of the musician who wrote the famous ballad "Jesse James." History knows nothing of this individual beyond the name he signed to his composition, so I co-opted him as representative of the itinerant modern minstrels whose music brought romance to the frontier and preserved its legend. My novel *Billy Gashade* (Forge, 1997) follows its narrator from his fateful role in the New York draft riots of 1863 to his final stint as a ghostwriter of songs for Gene Autry musicals in 1935 Hollywood:

. . . I don't regret much. I've known some of the best and worst men of my time, survived events that sent better men than I to their graves more than half a century ago and as I was told by one of the strong, intelligent women who have charted the course of my life, I have my gift. Unlike its composer, the song I wrote fifty-three years ago grows stronger each year. A month hardly passes that I don't hear it on the radio or in a supper place with a live performer, usually at the request of one of the patrons, even if whoever sings it usually leaves out the last verse:

> *This song was made by Billy Gashade*
> *Just as soon as the news did arrive.*
> *He said there was no man with the law in his hand*
> *That could take Jesse James alive.*

The "best and worst men"—and women—of Billy's time include Jesse James, Boss Tweed, Edith Wharton, Allan Pinkerton, Oscar Wilde, George Armstrong Custer, and Greta Garbo. The liberty offered by the new western permitted me to include people and places not commonly associated with the "western," and thus to help stretch the limits; for the history of what was once dismissed as the Great American Desert is the history of America.

The mystique of the frontier has always been freedom: from restrictions, from convention, from one's past. Today, at long last, the western itself offers that same freedom, as well as the opportunity for the writer—any writer—to slap his or her brand on an exciting, expanding market. So saddle up.

□ 38

PARTNERS IN CRIME

BY MARCIA MULLER

LIKE MANY CRIME WRITERS, I CAME TO THE GENRE THROUGH MY love of reading, and the novels that most appealed to me were those featuring private investigators. Possibly because I don't respond well to any type of authority, I was fascinated by detectives who, unhampered by regulations and procedure, would set off down the mean streets to right wrongs, strong and unafraid. As one who had always wanted to write, I'd then dream of creating my own character who would walk those streets, strong and unafraid.

Unfortunately, almost all the fictional models at that time were male, and while I could empathize with men and understand them on an individual basis, of course I didn't know the slightest thing about actually *being* male. Thus, the character I'd dream of creating was always a woman.

By the time I'd seriously begun to consider writing a novel featuring a private investigator of my own, I'd discovered several authors who were doing excellent characterization within the framework of the crime novel. Bill Pronzini (whom I did not know at the time, but to whom I'm now married) wrote about a detective who had no name, yet I knew intimate details about him that made him more real to me than many characters *with* names. Lillian O'Donnell had created New York City policewoman Norah Mulcahaney who, in addition to a lively professional life, found time to marry; her family life provided a rich backdrop to the cases she solved.

When I sat down to write my first (never published, and quite horrible) Sharon McCone novel, I was well aware that I could create a woman who would conform to the stereotype of the hard-bitten loner with the whiskey bottle in the desk drawer. Or I could make her a camera who observed the world around her without fully reacting or interacting. Or, at the far end of the spectrum, I could create a woman who would be a fully developed individual.

Sharon McCone, I decided, was to be as close to a real person as possible. Like real people she would age, grow, change; experience joy and sorrow, love and hatred—in short, the full range of human emotions. In addition, McCone was to live within the same framework most of us do, complete with family, friends, coworkers, and lovers; each of her cases would constitute one more major event in an ongoing biography. This choice also had a practical basis. In writing crime fiction, the author frequently asks the reader to suspend disbelief in situations that are not likely to occur in real life. Private investigators do not, as a rule, solve dozens of murder cases over the course of their careers. And what few criminals they do encounter do not tend to be as clever and intelligent as their fictional counterparts. To make the story convincing to the reader, the character and day-to-day details of her life had to be firmly grounded in reality.

The choice made, I realized I hadn't a clue as to how to go about creating such an individual. I had a name: Sharon, for my college roommate; McCone, for the late John McCone, former head of the CIA (a joke, since politically Sharon is as far from any CIA employee as one can get). I also had a location, San Francisco, my adopted home city. But as for the rest . . . ?

Should I make my character like me in back-ground, lifestyle, appearance, and spirit? Certainly not! At the time I had no job, no recognizable skills, no prospects, a failing marriage, and was afraid of my own shadow. I longed to be three or four inches taller, to be fifteen to twenty pounds lighter, to be able to eat all the ice cream I wanted and never gain an ounce. And I was vehemently opposed to making Sharon's background similar to mine, lest I fall into the trap of undisciplined autobiographical writing.

I therefore began building McCone's character by giving her a background as different from mine as I could make it. She is a native Californian; I am not. She comes from a large blue-collar family; I do not. She put herself through the University of California at Berkeley by working as a security guard; I was supported by my parents during my six years at the University of Michigan. And Sharon has exotic Native American features and long black hair, is enviably tall and slender, and can eat whatever she likes without gaining weight. Since I don't possess such qualities, I wanted to spend time with a character who did.

At the time I was developing McCone, I was participating in an informal writers' workshop that met every week; fear of having nothing to read aloud at the sessions drove me daily to the typewriter. I chose to take the suggestion of the group leader (a published author) to work up a biographical sheet on McCone, in which I fine-tuned the other details of her life: names of parents and siblings; likes and dislikes; religious and political attitudes; talents and weaknesses; even the circumstances of her first sexual experience.

By the time I'd completed the biographical sheet, McCone finally emerged as real to me. Still, it was in a form that was more like a questionnaire than a work of fiction. At this point I was forced to face the fact that the only way to develop a character fully is to write her. And write her, and write her. . . .

Anyone who claims that first manuscripts aren't simply learning exercises is either exceptionally gifted or completely deluded. My early efforts were stiff and wooden and—with the exception of McCone's narrative voice, which was the same from the very first—totally different from what eventually saw publication.

I was insecure as to how to go about constructing a mystery, and in spite of my resolve to let the events flow from character, I found the stories becoming very plot-driven. I manipulated secondary characters and their actions to fit the plot; kept elaborate charts showing what every person was doing at every moment during the story; wrote long accounts of the back story (the events that set the crime in motion). I wasted paper, time, and energy concocting cryptic clues, red herrings, and unnecessary complications. Even after my third novel manuscript was accepted for publication, I continued to fall back on stock scenes and situations: ongoing antagonism between private investigator and police; the standard body-finding scene; the obligatory talk about the case in the office of Sharon's boss.

Fortunately, through all of this, McCone came into her own as a person and also became my full partner in fictional crime. I take little credit for this; it simply happened. Writers constantly talk about how their characters "just take over," and when I hear myself doing the same, I feel vaguely embarrassed, but it *does* happen, and is vitally important to any long-running series.

My theory about this phenomenon is that knowing one's character intimately allows the writer to tap into her subconscious, which usually works far ahead of the conscious mind. The fictional character's actions and reactions often have little to do with the writer's original intention. In this area, McCone has served me well.

I first experienced her determination to be her own person while writing the second book in the series, *Ask the Cards a Question* (1982). In my previous efforts, Sharon had many analytical conversations about her cases with her boss, Hank Zahn, and they inevitably took place in his office at All Souls Legal Cooperative, the poverty law firm where she worked. A third of the way through *Cards,* it seemed time for one of these talks, so I had Sharon leave her office for Hank's. But contrary to my intentions, she detoured down the hall to the desk of the co-op's secretary, Ted, to ask him where Hank was, and in doing so, she—and I—took a look around the big Victorian that housed All Souls. What I saw was a goldmine in terms of places to set scenes and characters to play in them: There were rooms, lots of them; there were attorneys and paralegal workers and other support staff, some of whom lived there communally, and often had potlucks and parties and poker games. As in any situation where people live and work at close quarters, there was the opportunity for conflict and resolution.

Where Hank Zahn had once been the only partner who had an identity, I now began to flesh out others. A number of them became important in McCone's life. They began to demand more important roles, and soon I realized that they—as well as McCone—would determine the direction that the series as a whole would take.

The development of fully realized characters is essential to creating a strong series. Without them, the author is simply manipulating cardboard people aimed at a specific—and usually contrived—end. Eventually the writer will become bored with the artificiality of the story and lose all sense of identification with the characters. And if the writer is bored, imagine the poor reader!

Over the twenty years I've been writing the McCone series, I've made a number of choices and changes, and each of these came from within Sharon's character and her reactions and interactions with others. This involves a firm commitment on my part to remain flexible, willing to switch directions mid-stream. Initially, this was a rather frightening process, but the rewards have proved considerable.

Different facets of McCone's character have been revealed to me by her interactions with other characters. A violent confrontation with a man she considered the most evil person she'd ever encountered, and the choice she made in dealing with him, affirmed that she was unable to step over the line into pointless violence. Another confrontation, this time when the lives of people she cared about were at stake, demonstrated that she could take violent action when the circumstances justified it.

During the past four years, McCone has revealed feelings and attitudes that have dictated radical changes in the overall direction of the series—long before I considered making any. When the All Souls partners threatened to confine Sharon to a desk job (*Wolf in the Shadows*, 1993), I'd originally intended for them to work out some sort of compromise, coupled with expanding the scope of her responsibilities. At the end of the novel, I was still undecided as to the nature of that compromise. But at the beginning of the next novel in the series, *Till the Butchers Cut Him Down* (1994), McCone made the decision for me: She decided to leave the co-op and establish her own agency, while retaining offices in the house—thus permitting her to continue her association with people for whom she cared.

But only months after her new office furniture was delivered, McCone began to doubt the wisdom of her decision. As I was writing a scene in *A Wild and Lonely Place* (1995), I found her saying, "No wonder I avoided having clients come to the office. . . . Actually, a lot of things about All Souls were beginning to pale for me." Her doubts mirrored my own, which I'd scarcely confronted until that point. She decided for me that the time had come to leave All Souls; time, in fact, for All Souls to become defunct. With roots in the 1970s, it was an outmoded institution; my attempts to bring it into the 1990s with its virtues intact had failed.

But in what direction to go? And where? Certainly not a stereotypical seedy office where McCone would keep a bottle in her desk drawer. And certainly not a suite in a high-rent building; she is too frugal for that.

The answer came to me while I was walking on the Embarcadero, San Francisco's waterfront boulevard, with a friend who was talking about some people she knew who had offices in a renovated pier. I looked around, spotted the San Francisco fireboat station, and noted a space between it and Pier 24 that was almost large enough for a fictional Pier 24½. The surrounding area was an exciting one, undergoing a renaissance; artists' lofts, lively clubs, trendy restaurants, and unusual sorts of enterprises abounded. And there was also San Francisco's rich maritime history, which offered many possibilities. Immediately, Sharon McCone made the decision to move her offices to Pier 24½.

But would I be forced to abandon Hank Zahn, his wife Anne-Marie Altman, Rae Kelleher, and Ted Smalley? Of course not. The co-op had paled for Anne-Marie several books before; it would now do the same for Hank, and they would decide to form their own law firm, then ask McCone to share a suite of offices with them. As for Rae and Ted, they would need jobs when All Souls went under, so Ted would come along as office manager, Rae as the first of what McCone hoped would be many operatives. Without delay, Sharon, Hank, and Anne-Marie signed a lease for space at Pier 24½.

A long and intimate association with well-rounded characters can not only enrich a series, but also an author's life. Over the years, I've found myself moving closer to McCone in spirit. Where she was once the independent, strong, brave half of the partnership, I've now become more independent, strong, and brave myself.

It's strange but gratifying to know that my own creation has empowered me. That's what the series is all about: to entertain and inspire the reader; perhaps to make some readers think more seriously about an issue that's important to McCone and me; and to give escape and pleasure to those who buy our books.

❑ 39

TRICKS OF THE WIZARD'S TRADE

BY SUSAN DEXTER

FANTASY IS THE OLDEST FORM OF LITERATURE—THE GREAT UMbrella that arches over *all* fiction. Fantasy is also a marketing category, shelved and intermingled with science fiction, wearing scaly dragons on its covers in place of shiny spaceships. Fantasy's themes spring from the collective unconscious. Fantasy is populated by archetypes and demons common to us all. Our dreams and our nightmares. Fairy tales.

It's *hard* to be original in this genre. But limits are illusions. Consider: We have but 26 letters in our alphabet. And they'd best be used in combinations readers will recognize as *words*. Now, *there's* a limit. Music? Even worse, but composers don't seem to mind that there are only so many notes to go around.

"Never been done before" may truly be impossible. But "Never been done like *that* before"? That sounds like a goal to me. *Star Wars* didn't wow the world because it was a *new* idea; it resonates with audiences because it's a very *old* story: a fairy tale, right down to the princess. Retell an old tale—do it in a fresh way, and your readers will gasp in wonder. Do it well, and you'll have editors drooling.

The first trick in a wizard's bag is this: Look at your sources of inspiration. Be a *reader,* before you begin to write. Read new fantasies. Keep up with the field. Read the classics. Comic books aren't forbidden fruit—just don't make them an exclusive diet. Read fairy tales. Read folklore. Study the magic and mythologies of many cultures. If you feed your subconscious properly, it will supply your storytelling needs.

Go to your public library. Breathe in the fresh air and book dust. Surf the Net later. No need to memorize the Dewey System to graze the shelves productively. The 200's are philosophy and religion—*all* religions. Folklore lives in the 398.2's—right next to the prettified fairy tales "retold for children." You'll find original folk tales that will make your hair stand on end and get your juices flowing. Arrowsmith's *Field Guide to the Little People* will convince you that elves are neither Disney critters nor the fantasy analogue of Vulcans, but beings far more ancient and interesting. *The Golden Bough*, Frazer's study of myth and religion, supplied the magical system my wizard Tristan used in *The Ring of Allaire* and its two sequels. I doubt that a thousand authors mining day and night could exhaust that book's possibilities.

Remember the hero has a *thousand* faces. If you confine your reading to role-playing manuals, the stirring high fantasy you hope to craft will be a pale, weak thing, a fifth-generation videotape. Recycled characters stuck in a plot that's a copy of an imitation of Tolkien won't excite an editor these days. Read to understand what the classic themes are. Tolkien based *The Lord of the Rings* solidly on the northern European mythic tradition. It's not a copy of anything, but we respond to it as something familiar.

Fantastic elements work only if you make *reality* real. If I carelessly give my horses "paws," will you believe what I tell you about dragons? So think about the nuts and bolts, and don't trust Hollywood to do it for you. Castles—where did people *live* in them? Surely everyone wasn't born a princess. Who grows the food, does the laundry, cleans up after the knights' horses? When you research actual medieval cultures, you'll turn up truths far stranger than anything you could *invent*. Your characters should have real lives, with routines, habits, responsibilities. Most of us have to work for a living, and while being a princess may be a full-time job, being an elf is not. My title character in *The Wind-Witch* stands out from the pack of fantasy heroines: Not only is she *not* a princess, but she has a job—two jobs: She's a farmer and a weaver. Getting her sheep through lambing season matters just as much to Druyan as warding off a barbarian invasion or discovering her magical talents. That makes her *real*, for all that she can literally whistle up a storm. Readers can identify with her.

Magic was the science of its day. Science is of fairly recent origin. Both science and magic seek to explain and control the natural world, usually for a man's benefit. Study belief systems. Decide what suits your story, and stick to that. Don't throw in random demons just because they sound cool. Plan your world, if you want it to work for you.

Maps are more than endpaper decorations, and you should start drawing one before you ever start writing your fantasy. Never mind your quest-bound characters: A map will keep *you*, the author, from getting lost. If the desperate ride from Castle A to Castle B takes three days, then the trip back from B to A can take *longer* once the pressure's off; but if the journey takes *less* time, you have major explaining to do. Maps can spare you such *faux pas*.

Maps can suggest plot solutions. In the real world, things are where they are for good reasons. Castles protect and are not built where there's nothing worth contesting. Towns are tied to trade; they grow where roads cross, beside safe harbors. As I began to write *The Wind-Witch*, I had established in an earlier book that my Esdragon had a cliffy coast and treacherous seas. Now I needed it to suffer an invasion—by sea. Where could the invaders strike? Well, the Eral are after plunder, so they want towns. And Esdragon's towns—as in the real-world town of Cornwall, on which I based my fictional duchy—are mostly at the mouths of the rivers that drain the upland moors and reach the sea as broad estuaries. I put rivers on my map, decided which were navigable for any distance—and *presto!* I had many places for my raiders to plunder, distant from one another, spots for Druyan to try to protect from the back of her magic-bred horse.

A primitive map has charm—perhaps one of your characters drew it—but there are tricks to convincing cartography. You can't draw a straight line without a ruler? Relax! Nobody can, and there are rather few straight lines in nature anyway. Now get yourself a real map. Any continent or bit of one will do. Put tracing paper over your selection. Pencil some outlines, imagining how the coast changes as the sea level rises—or falls. Hills become islands, islands change into peninsulas. Valleys become arms of the sea. The combination of wind and wave nibbles cliffs, isolating outcrops. It's your pick.

Change the scale. Use an island to make a continent, or vice versa. Turn your map upside down. When I designed Esdragon and Calandra, I basically used Europe—but I stood it on end, balanced on the tip of Portugal. Copy the shape of the water spot on your ceiling or the last patch of snow lingering on your sidewalk.

Study actual maps. Where do rivers flow? How do they look? Mountain ranges trap rain and alter climate. So where will your forest be? Your dry grasslands? Your band of unicorn hunters needs to cross the Dragonspike Mountains. Where are the passes? Are they open year-round or only seasonally? The threat of being trapped by an early winter can add drama. A map will remind you of that.

God, as Mies van der Rohe said, is in the details. As the creator of your paper world, you have responsibilities. *You* must concern yourself with the details, for there is no *Fodor's Guide to Middle Earth,* or Esdragon, or your elfin kingdom. Which brings us to the Rule of Names.

Basic rules for name use apply to all fiction. Just as you vary your sentence lengths, so you should choose names with differing lengths and sounds. Your names must not all begin with the same letter of the alphabet. Characters and countries must not be easily confused with one another. A name that brings to mind an over-the-counter remedy will not work for your hero.

World-makers need to name *everything.* Adam got off easy doing just the animals! I need to name kingdoms, heroes, continents, castles, islands, mountains, rivers, lakes, gods, horses, magic swords and cats. Unlike the author of the police procedural, I can't get my names by stabbing a random finger into the phone book.

Names in fantasy present special pleasures and certain problems. Names must always be apt, but you can toss off grand heroic names without the twinge of conscience you'd feel about giving such names to real children who'd be attending real-world schools. Remember, though, that names are tools. They make your invented world convincing and solid, but they must evoke the feel of *your* world. You can't just put the *Encyclopedia of Mythology* into a blender. In folkloric tradition, names have serious power: To know a creature's true name is to control it. That power carries over into fiction. Poorly chosen names can strain your reader's willing suspension of disbelief until it snaps. And then where are you?

You will be wise not to leave your naming to chance, or to the last minute. Under the pressure of mid-paragraph, you will either heave up a melange of x's, q's, and z's, or you'll clutch and settle for names as bland as tapioca. Planning ahead avoids both extremes. Compile a list of useful names.

You can keep that list in your PC or on the backs of old envelopes, but a small notebook is the handiest. I use an address book—durably hardbound, alphabetized pages, large enough not to be easily mislaid. I list names down the left margins, circling those I use and noting where. I may reuse a name from time to time, certain names being as common in Esdragon as John is in this world.

I glean and gather from sources readily available to all. Start with baby-name books. The older thebetter; you aren't after the trendy and popular. Copy whatever catches your eye. Histories of popular names offer archaic forms and less common variants. Rhisiart, in *The Wizard's Shadow*, is a name that is simply a Welsh version of Richard. The Welsh struggle to represent with their alphabet the sounds of a name they got from Norman French gives the name an exotic look.

Invent your own names. Dickens did it. Lord Dunsany was a master at it. Tolkien invented whole *languages* and took his names from them. You may enjoy playing with sounds. When I wrote *The Ring of Allaire*, I struggled for a week for a proper name for Valadan, my immortal warhorse. Wanting a proud, noble, brave name, I began with *val*, from valiant, and went on from there. Whereas Kessallia in *The Prince of Ill Luck* just popped out of my subconscious one day. Learn to spot a "keeper" like that.

Use the phone book. Use the newspaper—all those lists of engagements, weddings, obituaries. Chop off the front half of a name, or use just the ending. Stick a syllable of one name onto part of another. Minor changes yield fresh names. Switching just one letter made Robert into *Robart,* and gave Druyan's brother a familiar yet not ordinary name.

Watch movie credits. Watch the Olympics—you'll hear scads of less usual names, like Oksana, and they're *spelled* for you, right on the screen. What could be easier?

Once you have your names, use them wisely. Pick those that fit your story and its cultures. Save the rest for your next project.

The true test of imagination may be to name a cat, as Samuel Butler said. I doubt that correctly naming a dragon is far down the difficulty scale, though. World-making and myth-making are not for the fainthearted, nor the short attention span. The good news: No license is required! Only the will to do the job right—which is the *real* power behind *any* wizard's spell.

❏ 40

WRITING THE DISASTER NOVEL

BY RICHARD MARTIN STERN

DISASTERS, MAN-MADE OR OCCURRING IN NATURE, ARE OBVIOUS SUB-jects for fiction. I refer to such events as wars, hurricanes, floods, fires, avalanches, earthquakes and the like, all of which are the stuff out of which memorable fiction can be fashioned.

They offer scope for heroics, self-sacrifice, crisis, love, hate, all of the conflicts and emotions of which men and women are capable.

But in writing them there is one danger that must at all costs be avoided if a successful story is to be achieved: allowing the disaster itself to overwhelm your tale, instead of remaining in the background as it should. Let me illustrate.

A Tale of Two Cities is set against the backdrop of the French Revolution and the reign of terror and could have been set in no other time or place. But it is not *about* the Revolution; it is about the characters Dickens invented and the story he contrived for them.

The single scene in which the woman does not even drop a stitch in her knitting as she watches the severed heads fall from the guillotine is the only scene I can remember that actually shows the reign of terror in action, but the strain and horror of the times permeate the entire novel through the thoughts and actions of Dickens's characters. It is this concentration on the characters and *their* story that makes the tale as memorable as it is.

In a like manner, *Gone With The Wind,* a story of our own Civil War, is not about the war, the battles, the ebb and flow of the huge forces involved, but about the characters Margaret Mitchell depicted and how they are affected by the war and react to it and to one another. The war is the background, the setting against which the tale is told, and the emphasis is on the characters alone.

The truism, of course, is that there is no substitute for characterization, the invention and presentation of people the readers can identify with, and with whom they can suffer, or fear, or love, or despair, whether the action takes place in a drawing room or in temporary shelter from a blizzard out on the frozen tundra.

A novel of mine called *Snowbound Six* is about winter Search & Rescue in the mountains of New Mexico. In the book, the snow is always there, and the cold, hypothermia which can kill, an avalanche, struggle for survival in an ancient cave and the S&R team's attempts to reach the victims. But the emphasis is on the individuals, victims, rescuers, and interested bystanders alike, and the effects of the disaster on them, how under great strain they react and how in various ways their lives are affected. The disaster, in short, is the background; the people are the story, which is as it must be.

In writing about disasters, it is easy to forget this basic fact and to be carried away by the fascinating complexities or the factual dangers of the situation, to invent ingenious mechanisms for survival and concentrate on them, to get lost in the sheer magnitude of whatever disaster you are dealing with and make all this the central body of your tale. Not madness, but failure lies in that direction.

During World War II, the British were successful in stealing German coding machines called collectively Enigma, and with them they were able to intercept and decode German messages, orders, and actual battle plans.

All this was done in the greatest of secrecy by an isolated group of cryptographers and mathematicians. At times it even became essential that lives be sacrificed because saving them might let the enemy know that their codes had been broken.

All of this is a tremendous story that can now be told, and it has been written—as nonfiction. The writer of a successful *fictionalized* tale against this setting would have to ignore the actual workings of Enigma, however fascinating the details might be, to concentrate instead on the men and women involved and show the *effects* of Enigma—its successes and failures—on them, as for almost the entire duration of the war they dwelt under enormous strain and in such secrecy that the existence of the organization was never known except in top governmental circles.

There would be ample scope for jealousy, love, agonizing decisions, the pressures of day-and-night labor in order to keep up with events, and internal conflicts inevitably arising under such clandestine and painstaking demands.

The machines would always be there, and the war itself would be ever-present as the messages were intercepted and their meanings laboriously extracted. But, to repeat, the story would be about the people, the characters.

Too much of today's disaster and action fiction tends to ignore this basic principle and concentrates instead on gunfire or explosions or careful, detailed descriptions of avalanches or buildings collapsing in earthquakes—in short, special effects that may be ingenious, but are scarcely satisfying to the reader. The writers forget that what the reader identifies with are the characters.

When I set out to write *The Tower,* one of the two books on which the film *The Towering Inferno* was based, I had only the basic idea of people trapped by fire on the top floor of a gigantic skyscraper.

The possibilities for disaster were almost endless, and the material I managed to assemble was both vast and fascinating. The World Trade Center in New York was then under construction, and I managed to get a schematic wiring diagram of the entire complex, including the electric substation that was built solely to provide electricity to the Trade Center. There were numerous magazine articles about the complexities and difficulties the builders were encountering. I had accounts of skyscraper fires that had actually taken place both here and abroad, and accounts of elevator failures in them (the basis for signs now in every hotel telling guests to use only the stairs in case of fire). I had geologic studies of the bedrock upon which the twin towers would rest seven stories beneath the surface, along with studies on the near impossibility of evacuating modern high-rise buildings if disaster struck, and so on.

I could, and did, use almost all of the material in the book, but neither it nor the fire was paramount. The story was, as it had to be, about the people involved—who they were; how they came to be on the scene, either trapped inside or outside trying to help; how they reacted during the crisis, some growing in stature, some diminishing in panic.

The temptation to describe the design and structure of the building in detail, or the intricacies of the wiring, the way the elevators worked and how because of smoke they could become inoperable—in short, the temptation to include the physical makeup of the disaster—was enormous, but it had to be resisted. Page after page went into the wastebasket because the description was not germane to the story.

Readers do not identify with concrete and steel or with wiring and ingenious mechanisms. Readers identify only with people, their personal problems, their loves and dislikes, their heroism or the lack of it, their speech and mannerisms, their fears and their strengths, and above all, with their interactions with one another. This is the basic fact that must be kept in mind in writing a disaster novel or indeed, any fictional tale.

Your goal should be that long after the facts of the story have faded in memory, at least some of your characters in the tale will remain in the readers' minds, and if you have done your job well and made the story powerful enough, you can hope that the readers may find themselves wondering how they might have behaved under similar circumstances.

Then, and only then, will you have succeeded in what you set out to do.

❏ 41

PLOTTING A MYSTERY NOVEL

BY CAROLYN HART

HOW DO YOU PLOT YOUR NOVELS? THIS MAY BE THE QUESTION WRITers hear most often.

It's as if, after enjoying a particularly succulent dish, I ask a cook, "May I have that recipe?" The cook smiles, nods, offers a list of ingredients. But if I try that recipe in my own kitchen, somehow the finished dish won't be the same.

The cook's answer is quite similar to those of authors when asked how to plot. We launch into quick answers that make plotting sound, if not easy, at least quite reasonable and straightforward.

We lie. Oh, not intentionally, of course. But our answers simply don't capture the reality of plotting a novel. Plotting is never easy, rarely straightforward, and cannot be reduced to a formula.

I'm especially attuned to the deficiency of our rote answer—outline, outline, outline—because I'm presently engaged in plotting a new mystery. It should be easy, right? No. No. No!

It is terribly difficult, as all novelists know. And every novelist has an individual way of responding to the challenge. Some novelists pose that wonderful, familiar question, "What if?" Some do detailed character sketches and carefully outline every chapter. Others write a one- or two-page synopsis. We all struggle, but I truly believe there is no easy route to writing a novel. But perhaps the imperfect, tantalizing suggestions of how I forge a story will help you discover your own process.

These are the facts I must know in order to start a mystery novel:

1. The protagonist
2. The victim
3. The murderer
4. The title

The most important decision to make is who will be the main protagonist. In my Death on Demand series, it is Annie Laurance Darling, who is aided and abetted by her husband, Max. In my Henrie O series, the protagonist is retired newswoman Henrietta O'Dwyer (Henrie O) Collins. There is a world of difference between the two series, and all the differences can be traced to the personalities of the protagonists.

Annie and Max are young and enthusiastic. Annie is quite serious and intense, but she loves to laugh. She owns a mystery bookstore, and her vocation and avocation are mysteries. Max is sexy, fun and handsome, rich, easy-going and loving. He is, in fact, the kind of man women adore.

So, what do we have in the Death on Demand series? A young, eager bookstore owner who in various novels in the series falls in love, plans a murder mystery weekend, participates in a community play, gets married, teaches a class on the three great ladies of the mystery, learns about the many faces of love, celebrates the brilliance of Agatha Christie, and serves as the author liaison at a book fair. These novels also have sub-plots featuring subsidiary characters, avid reader Henny Brawley, curmudgeonly Miss Dora Brevard, and Annie's mother-in-law, unflappable, ethereal, unpredictable Laurel Darling Roethke.

In sharp contrast, Henrie O is a sixty-something, savvy, sardonic woman who has seen good and bad in a long life, has few illusions, a passion for truth, and a determination to do what she feels she must. In the first book in the series, Henri O refuses to be vanquished by either an old lover or a hurricane, and in the process of solving a murder decides that silence best serves those she loves. In the second, Henrie O saves a man unjustly accused despite the power and money arrayed against her. In my newest novel, *Death in Lovers' Lane*, Henrie O faces a hard personal decision. In discovering the murderer of a student reporter, she brings a resolution to three old unsolved crimes.

Who these people are and what they do determine the structure, tone, and objective of the books.

The Death on Demand novels are written in the third person, which makes it easy to switch viewpoints and offer the reader insights. Each book opens with a series of vignettes that give the reader an instant slice of the life of a character who will be important to the book. The recurring minor characters offer another way to entertain the reader, and that is the objective of the Death on Demand books—to entertain. Everything about their creation—the mystery bookstore, the young lovers, the subsidiary characters—is calculated to result in a good-humored novel that provides mystery lore, entertaining characters, and, hopefully, an intricate mystery.

The Henrie O mysteries are another pot of soup entirely. They are written in the first person to engage the reader totally in Henrie O's life, thoughts, and actions. I chose for her to be an older woman because I want to celebrate age and experience. In *Dead Man's Island,* Henrie O waits for an elevator . . . .

I saw my own reflection: dark hair silvered at the temples, dark eyes that have seen much and remembered much, a Roman-coin profile, a lean and angular body with an appearance of forward motion even when at rest—and the angry light in my eyes. I can't abide meanness.

The Henrie O novels are sparsely written, with quick, short, vivid sentences of a newspaper article. Henrie O wryly comments on life as she has lived and observed it, but these are not light, entertaining novels.

The differences between the two series clearly illustrate the importance of the protagonist. A book mirrors its protagonist. The choice of protagonist provides the tone, background, pace, taste, and scope of your novel.

Who will your protagonist be? A cop, a midwife, a divorcee, a lawyer? Each would make a different story out of the same facts. Is the story set in San Diego, Des Moines, Chicago, Paris, Birmingham? That depends upon the protagonist, too.

Everything else in the novel flows from the choice of the protagonist. Choose a cop, and you can have a serial killer, domestic violence, a drive-by shooting. But if you decide to create an amateur sleuth, that sleuth's vocation or avocation will determine who might be a likely murder victim.

Annie, a bookstore owner who lives on a resort island off the coast of South Carolina, is most unlikely to have contact with a murdered drug dealer. In *Death on Demand,* the victim was a mean-spirited mystery author murdered at a gathering of mystery writers in Annie's store. Victims in my other novels range from a well-to-do club woman to a love-hungry wife, to a cold, hard judge, to a crabby voyeur who snooped on the wrong night. But all of my victims grew out of Annie's world. Their existence was dictated by Annie's milieu.

Henrie O plays on a much larger stage. In *Dead Man's Island,* the story grows out of her background as a reporter, but that background can have inhabitants from diverse places. *Death in Lovers' Lane* revolves around personal responsibility and how much information is owed to society. Henrie O makes some difficult judgments, but, as she emphasizes in that book, judgments never come easy.

So, you begin to see how stories flow. The choice of a protagonist determines the background. The choice of the background determines the victim. The choice of the victim determines the murderer, because the persons involved in the victim's life make up the circle of suspects. One of the suspects will be the villain.

Villains can be flawed, likable people, or they can be horribly selfish and mean. Your choice, but this choice is once again the result of earlier choices.

In *Design for Murder,* Corinne, the victim, is the wealthy, selfish, egocentric society matron who tries to control the lives of those around her. Her circle included:

• Leighton, the charming, handsome, not-so-grieved widower
• Gail, the emotional, love-struck, frightened niece
• Bobby, the abrasive, tough, self-serving reporter
• Roscoe, the self-contained but passionate lawyer
• John, the ambitious, determined, aloof doctor
• Sybil, the lusty, willful, spoiled sybarite
• Tim, the gifted, immature, self-centered artist
• Edith, the nervous, sensitive, hardworking club woman
• Miss Dora, the eccentric, unpredictable, waspish old woman
• Lucy, Corinne's childhood friend who once loved Corinne's brother
Each person in Corinne's life—and death—evolved from Corinne's personality.

In *Death in Lovers' Lane,* the victim is a bright, beautiful student reporter, and Henrie O is her journalism professor, who insists the student find fresh facts if she intends to write about three unsolved crimes in the university town. When I was plotting the book, I knew the milieu—a university town, a campus. What kind of unsolved crimes might there be? I came up with three: the double murder of a student couple in Lovers' Lane; the shooting of a respected businessman; and the disappearance some years earlier of the dean of students.

I then had four victims: the student reporter, the lovers, the businessman, and the dean. Whom did they know? Who loved them—or hated them?

Now that you've seen how to create the characters in your novel, you may reasonably complain that this isn't a plot. No, it isn't, but you are on your way. The plot does not arrive full blown, at least, not for most writers. Some writers outline an entire novel. I am in awe of them, but most of us do not have that kind of linear skill. We begin with people. We decide the general theme. In the novel I'm plotting now, Henny Brawley is putting on a Fourth of July celebration in honor of South Carolina history, from a woman's perspective. Lt. Gen. (ret.) Charlton (Bud) Hatch insists on changing the focus to men, which puts him at cross purposes with a good portion of island society.

I know who the protagonist is: Annie.

I know who the victim is: Bud Hatch.

I know who the murderer is: (Of course, I won't tell you!)

I know who the suspects are: Henny Brawley, Bud's mistress, his next-door neighbor, an alienated stepdaughter, the director of the library, the director's lover, a librarian, a handyman.

I know the title: *Yankee Doodle Dead.* I have to have a working title when I begin a novel. It gives me a sense of reality, and it also defines the ultimate story. In *Yankee Doodle Dead,* a Yankee (Bud Hatch) comes to town and ends up dead.

So, I have a great deal, but where is the plot?

Darned if I know, and I'm not being flippant or dismissive or coy. This truthful admission is perhaps the best help I can ever offer to a new or struggling writer: All the planning in the world won't create a novel. That takes magic, and the magic happens when you write. If you figure out all the elements I've listed, you won't know how the story ends, or what's going to happen in Chapter 9, but you have enough to begin.

That's how I do it: I begin writing, and the people come to life—or death—and events occur, and I will have the great adventure of finding out who these characters are, what they are going to do, and ultimately, with them, I will—haphazardly, surprisingly, unexpectedly—reach the final chapter.

Yes, I get stuck. Sometimes everything I've written seems dull and boring, and I can't figure out how to move ahead. But if I keep on thinking about those characters, and if I sit at my computer and write, things will begin to happen. And finally I'll know that the novel exists, that it's out there, all I have to do is find it.

It isn't a straightforward process. I can't diagram it, but this is how I plot—and write—a novel. It's scary, but it's a great adventure.

❑ 42

WRITING THE SUPERNATURAL NOVEL

BY ELIZABETH HAND

I'VE ALWAYS THOUGHT THAT THE OLDEST PROFESSION WAS THAT OF storyteller—in particular, the teller of supernatural tales. A look at the cave paintings in France or Spain will show you how far back our hunger for the fantastic goes: men with the heads of beasts, figures crouching in the darkness, skulls and shadows and unblinking eyes. Take a glance at the current bestseller list, and you'll see that we haven't moved that far in the last twenty thousand years. Books by Anne Rice, Stephen King, Joyce Carol Oates, and Clive Barker, among many others, continue to feed our taste for dark wine and the perils of walking after midnight. But how to join the ranks of those whose novels explore the sinister side of town?

First, let me distinguish between supernatural fiction and its tough (and very successful) younger cousin, the horror novel. Horror novels depend heavily upon the mechanics of plot, less-than-subtle characterizations, and shock value—what Stephen King calls "going for the gross-out." In spirit and execution, they aren't that different from the "penny dreadfuls" of a century ago, crude but effective entertainments that tend to have a short shelf life. Unlike more stylized works such as *Dracula, The Turn of the Screw* or *The Shining,* most horror novels lose their ability to chill the second time around—they just don't stand up to rereading. As Edmund Wilson put it, "The only horror in these fictions is the horror of bad taste and bad art."

In the wake of Stephen King's success, the 1980's was a boom decade for horror fiction. But the market was flooded with so many books—and so many second-rate Stephen King imitators—that publishers and readers alike grew wary. With the dwindling reading public, it's far more difficult today to get a supernatural novel into print.

But the readers *are* there. And they're quite a sophisticated audience, which makes it both more challenging, and more fun, to write the sort of novel that will appeal to someone who prefers *The Vampire Lestat* to the *The Creeping Bore*.

More than other genres, supernatural fiction is defined by *atmosphere* and *characterization*. By atmosphere, I mean the author's ability to evoke a mood or place viscerally by the use of original and elegant, almost *seductive* language. Science fiction and fantasy also rely heavily upon unusual settings and wordplay, often against a backdrop of other, imagined, worlds. But the most successful supernatural novels are set in *our* world. Their narrative tension, their very ability to frighten and transport us, derives from a conflict between the macabre and the mundane, between everyday reality and the threatening *other*— whether revenant, werewolf, or demonic godling—that seeks to destroy it.

The roots of supernatural fiction lie in the gothic romances of the eighteenth and nineteenth centuries with their gloomy settings, imperiled narrators and ghostly visitations. Even today these remain potent elements. Witness Anne Rice's vampire Lestat during a perambulation about prerevolutionary Paris:

> The cold seemed worse in Paris. It wasn't as clean as it had been in the mountains. The poor hovered in doorways, shivering and hungry, the crooked unpaved streets were thick with filthy slush. I saw barefoot children suffering before my very eyes, and more neglected corpses lying about than ever before. I was never so glad of the fur-lined cape as I was then. . . .

Much of the pleasure in Rice's work comes from her detailed evocations of real, yet highly romanticized, places: New Orleans, Paris, San Francisco. It pays to have firsthand knowledge of some desirable piece of occult real estate: Readers love the thrill of an offbeat setting, but they also like recognizing familiar landmarks. So, Stephen King has staked out rural Maine as his fictional backyard. The incomparable Shirley Jackson (whose classic "The Lottery" has chilled generations of readers) also turns to New England for the horrific doings in *The Haunting of Hill House*, *The Bird's Nest* and *We Have Always Lived in the Castle*. Daphne du Maurier's novella "Don't Look Now" gives us a tourist couple lost amidst the winding alleys of Venice, a notion creepy enough to have inspired Ian McEwan's nightmarish *The Comfort of Strangers*. Just about any setting will do, if you can imbue it with an aura of beauty and menace. My neo-gothic novel *Waking the*

Moon takes place in that most pedestrian and bureaucratic of cities, Washington, D.C. But by counterpointing the city's workaday drabness with exotic descriptions of its lesser-known corners, I was able to suggest that an ancient evil might lurk near Capitol Hill:

> From the Shrine's bell tower came the first deep tones of the carillon calling the hour. I turned, and saw in the distance the domes and columns of the Capitol glimmering in the twilight, bone-colored, ghostly; and behind it still more ghostly buildings, their columned porticoes and marble arches all seeming to melt into the haze of green and violet darkness that descended upon them like sleep.

Style, of course, is a matter of taste and technique, and as with all writing, your most important tools should be a good thesaurus and dictionary. (Good taste in reading helps, but is probably not necessary.) A thesaurus can transform even the oldest and most unpalatable of chestnuts. "It was a dark and stormy night" becomes "Somber and tenebrous, the vespertine hour approached."

The danger, of course, is that such elevated diction easily falls into self-parody. But when well-done, it can quickly seduce the reader into believing in—well, in any number of marvelous things:

> Last night I dreamt that I woke to hear some strange, barely audible sound from downstairs—a kind of thin tintinnabulation, like those coloured-glass bird scarers which in my childhood were still sold for hanging up to glitter and tinkle in the garden breeze. I thought I went downstairs to the drawing room. The doors of the china cabinets were standing open, but all the figures were in their places—the Bow Liberty and Matrimony, the Four Seasons of Neale earthenware, the Reinecke girl on her cow; yes, and she herself—the Girl in a Swing. It was from these that the sound came, for they were weeping.

This is from Richard Adams's superb *The Girl in a Swing,* to my mind the best supernatural novel I've ever read. One of the problems in writing supernatural fiction stems from the fact that "ghost stories" are nearly always better when they are really *stories,* rather than full-length novels. Indeed, many of the classic works of dark fantasy—*The Turn of the Screw,* Charlotte Gilman's "The Yellow Wallpaper," Oliver Onions's "The Beckoning Fair One"—are novellas, a form that particularly suits the supernatural, but which is a hard sell: too short for publishers looking for meaty bestsellers, too long for a magazine market that thrives on the 5,000- to 7,000-word story. It is very difficult to sustain a high level of suspense for several hundred pages. Chapter

after chapter of awful doings too often just become awful, with the
"cliffhanger" effect ultimately boring the reader.

Characterization is one way of avoiding this pitfall. If your central
characters are intriguing, you don't need a constant stream of ghoulish
doings to hold a reader's attention. Think of Anne Rice's Lestat, whose
melancholy persona has seen him through several sequels. Or the callow student narrator of Donna Tartt's *The Secret History,* a novel
which has only a hint of the supernatural about it, but which is more
terrifying than any number of haunted houses:

> Does such a thing as "the fatal flaw," that showy dark crack running down
> the middle of a life, exist outside literature? I used to think it didn't. Now I
> think it does. And I think that mine is this: a morbid longing for the picturesque
> at all costs.

The Secret History is told in the first person, as are *The Girl in a
Swing,* Rice's *Vampire Chronicles,* and *Waking the Moon.* In supernatural fiction, it is not enough that the protagonist compel our interest.
Readers must also be able to truly *identify* with him, to experience his
growing sense of unease as his familiar world gradually crumbles in
the face of some dark intruder, be it spirit or succubus. That is why
the first-person narrator is so prevalent in supernatural tales. It is also
why most uncanny novels feature individuals whose very *normalcy* is
what sets them apart from others. Like us, they do not believe in
ghosts, which makes it all the worse when a ghost actually does appear.

But "normal" does not necessarily mean "dull." Richard Papen, the
narrator of *The Secret History,* is drawn into a murderous conspiracy
when his college friends seek to evoke Dionysos one drunken winter
night. In *The Girl in a Swing,* Alan Desland is a middle-aged bachelor
whose most distinguishing characteristic is his extraordinary *nice-
ness*—until he becomes obsessed with the beautiful Kathe, who may
be the incarnation of a goddess—or of a woman who murdered her
own children. And in C. S. Lewis's classic *That Hideous Strength,* an
entire peaceful English village is besieged by the forces of darkness.

As with all good fiction, it is important that the central characters
are *changed* by their experiences, whether for good or ill. Lazy writers
often use mere physical transformations to effect this change: The
heroine becomes a vampire. Or the heroine is prevented from becoming a vampire. Or the heroine is killed. Far more eerie is the plight of
the eponymous hero of Peter Ackroyd's terrifying *Hawksmoor,* a po-

lice detective who finds himself drawn into a series of cult murders that took place in London churches two hundred years before:

> Hawksmoor looked for relief from the darkness of wood, stone and metal but he could find none; and the silence of the church had once again descended as he sat down upon a small chair and covered his face. And he allowed it to grow dark.

While he is very much a twentieth-century man, Nicholas Hawksmoor's unwanted clairvoyance gives him a glimpse of horrors he is unable to forget, and forever alters his perception of the power of good and evil in the world and in his work.

In many ways, the intricacies of *plot* are less central to supernatural fiction than is *pacing* (another reason why short stories usually work better than novels). A careful balance must be achieved between scenes of the ordinary and the otherworldly. Usually, a writer alternates the two, with the balance gradually tipping in favor of the unreal: Think of Dracula moving from Transylvania to London, and bringing with him a miasma of palpable evil that slowly infects all around him. In *Waking the Moon,* my heroine's involvement with the supernatural parallels her love affair in the real world. However you choose to do it, don't let the magical elements overwhelm your story completely.

Especially, don't let the Big Supernatural Payoff come too *soon.* (The only thing worse that killing off all your werewolves fifty pages before the end is penning these dreadful words: IT WAS ALL A DREAM.) Think of your novel in musical terms: You wouldn't really want to listen to one Wagnerian aria after another, would you? Well, neither would you want to read page after page of mysterious knockings, stakes through the heart, and screams at midnight.

Finally, dare to be different. Does the world really need another vampire novel? How about a lamia instead? Or an evil tree? As always, it's a good idea to be well-read in your chosen genre, so that you don't waste time and ink reinventing Frankenstein's monster. In addition to the works mentioned above, there is a wealth of terrific short supernatural fiction that can teach as well as chill you. *Great Tales of Terror and the Supernatural* (edited by Herbert A. Wise and Phyllis Fraser) is perhaps the indispensable anthology. There are also collections by great writers such as Poe, Robert Aickman, John Collier, Edith Wharton, Isak Dinesen, Sheridan Le Fanu, M. R. James, and many, many others. Jack Sullivan has written two books that I refer to constantly:

Elegant Nightmares and *Lost Souls*, classic studies of English ghost stories that can serve as a crash course on how to write elegant horror. These, along with Stephen King's nonfiction *Danse Macabre*, should put you well on your way to creating your own eldritch novel. Happy haunting!

❑ 43

WRITING HISTORICAL FICTION

BY WILLIAM MARTIN

"NEVER LET THE FACTS GET IN THE WAY OF A GOOD STORY."

I can't remember where I heard that remark for the first time, but it's my favorite wiseguy answer whenever anyone asks me what the most important rule is for the historical novelist. And it's true.

No matter how many interesting facts you may have collected about, say, the battle of Midway, no matter how many fabulous events cry out for dramatization when you decide to write your Civil War epic, remember this: Character and plot are master and mistress of the historical novel, just as they are of any genre of mainstream fiction. *And you have to do all that research.*

But if you write a historical novel, you'll have a good chance of catching a publisher's eye, because there's always an audience for historical fiction. And you'll find that historical fiction has built-in advantages for any writer:

(1) There's no such thing as writer's block when you write historical fiction, because you always have your research to keep you working. *Blocked? Me? No way. So what if I've been reading old diaries for a week. I may read them for another week, too, and well, yeah . . . eventually I'll have to write, but . . .*

(2) History gives you character. History books and primary sources—old newspapers, diaries, ship's logs, and the like—are filled not only with details, but with the power of personality, and personality breathes life into fiction. And after you've spent time looking at an era through the eyes of those who lived it, you realize that beliefs, manners, and human trappings may change, but human nature doesn't.

(3) History gives you structure. It's always offering you another set of beginnings, middles, and ends, whether you're talking about something as specific as a single battle or as expansive as a century. This means you always have structure. And structure means story.

And the hard facts of life in mainstream popular fiction is that readers want story.

Interesting characters inhabiting a world that has no suspense, no drama, and no payoff, will not pay your bills. But there are plenty of stick figures walking through best sellers, simply because the authors knew how to pack their tales with conflict, movement, and climax.

The ideal, of course, is to create characters driven by strong personalities and motivated by strongly-held beliefs, then test the personalities and challenge the beliefs, so that conflict, movement, and climax rise inevitably from the decisions the characters make. This is true whether your fiction is set in the present or past. But it never hurts to have a single strong plot element to keep your characters focused.

When I wrote my first novel, I looked to the past, to the history-soaked turf of Boston, where I found the facts from which to fashion a good story: In the nineteenth century, Boston was a peninsula surrounded by tideflats; the tideflats were filled with trash and gravel, and the twentieth-century city took shape. In the upscale Back Bay neighborhood, you can still dig down through the basement floors and into the muck below to find artifacts tossed into the landfill a century ago. What if there was buried treasure down there, too?

And what would the treasure be? How about something that itself was rooted in Boston history, something made from gold and silver, perhaps? And who was Boston's most famous silversmith? Once you start asking yourself the right questions, the answers can flow with the logic of a good story.

A tea set crafted by Paul Revere would have been valuable when it was made and is priceless today, especially if it had passed through famous hands before disappearing into the Back Bay. The most famous hands in America during Revere's time? George Washington's.

Initially, I planned to write a short historical prologue following the tea set's journey from Revere to the President's mansion to the Back Bay, then get on with my treasure hunt—modern characters digging through the modern city. But my opening scenes changed all of that.

I had decided to begin with a historical event—a banquet held in Boston in 1789, when the gentlemen of the city honored the new President. It would be a perfect place for Revere to give America's greatest hero a gift. But a banquet can make for a boring scene, even if the guest list includes Washington and Revere. I knew the facts. I had to give them a good story.

That was when the character of Horace Taylor Pratt took shape—a Yankee shipper modeled after several hard-headed shippers I had read about. He watched the far horizons for the return of his ships, but always kept one eye on the pennies in his pocket and would see a ceremonial tea set as a grand waste of money.

Here is the first paragraph:

Horace Taylor Pratt pulled a silver snuffbox from his waistcoat pocket and placed it on the table in front of him. He hated snuffboxes. They were small, delicate, and nearly impossible for a man with one arm to open. Whenever he fumbled for snuff, Pratt cursed the two-armed world that conspired against him, but when he wanted a clear head, he had to have snuff. This evening, he wanted wits as sharp as a glasscutter.

The opening tells us a lot about Pratt in a small space: He is short-tempered, self-pitying, and about to cause trouble. Perhaps the most telling phrase in the paragraph is *wanted wits as sharp as a glasscutter.*

Every scene you write should create conflict. And the best conflict flows from the character. In every scene, no matter what genre you're exploring, always ask yourself: *What does the main character in this scene want, and who's in his way?* When you find the answer, you'll understand your scene. Keep asking, and eventually, you'll understand your novel.

After introducing Pratt, I reveal the room and the historical giants who fill it, but my focus remains on Pratt and his young son, who is mortified to see his father taking snuff in the presence of George Washington. We are, as I like to say, looking at history from ground level, focused as much on details like the snuffbox and the emotions of Pratt's son as on the new President.

Readers of historical fiction love to come into the company of historical giants, to imagine what they would do in the presence of a George Washington. Your characters, in scenes like this, are the stand-ins for your readers. You must always try to see the giants of history, or grand historical events, through your characters' eyes, colored by your characters' emotions and brought to life by the tactile details of their surroundings.

And always look for the conflicts within the conflict. In that opening scene, Pratt wants to make his opinions known: He thinks the tea set is a hypocritical waste of money, commissioned by the gentlemen of Boston to curry favor with the new President. That's the main conflict.

But a scene that has smaller conflicts popping off within it will be richer and more textured, especially if the conflicts are built around details specific to the era in which the book is set. So, Pratt wants snuff, but he lost an arm at Bunker Hill, so he has to fumble with the snuffbox. *Conflict.* He takes his snuff and sneezes boorishly, angering the gentlemen around him. *Conflict.* His son is embarrassed. *Conflict.* Pratt tells the boy he'll curry favor with no man and take snuff in front of any, even the President. Then Revere brings in the tea set and all hell breaks loose.

Cut to the present. A history graduate student named Peter Fallon is studying Pratt's old ledgers and finds a strange note, written to Pratt from the White House on the night in 1814 that the British burned Washington. It mentions a tea set, arriving in the Back Bay "ten to fifteen days hence." It's signed by someone named DL. Fallon ends the scene wondering, who is DL?

I decided to answer that question in the next scene, and that decision made *Back Bay* a best seller. I cut back to the White House in 1814 and the character of DL, Dexter Lovell, a Pratt agent who engineers the theft of the tea set from under Dolly Madison's nose. With that scene, history became more than a mere set-up for the modern treasure hunt. The movement of the tea set through history *became the story.*

By alternating chapters throughout the book, I was able to propel the story along on converging tracks, past and present, that finally meet. Writing *Back Bay* became like writing a serial, with a cliffhanger at the end of every chapter. I would leave my characters twisting in 1814, jump forward and move on to characters twisting in the present, then jump back, and do it again. The reader who might want to skip chapters wouldn't dare, because every chapter was focused on that tea set—stealing it, losing it, hunting for it, finding it, and losing it again.

There is a term in screenwriting called the *through-line*: the idea that keeps the story moving. What does the character want and how is he drawn along?

Think of your novel as a journey. Your readers want to be taken along with your characters through time, across space, toward a conclusion that satisfies them—and may teach them something, too. A plot element like that tea set can cut through your story like the white line down the middle of the road, whether you're traveling across a thousand years of history or a few weeks.

With *Cape Cod,* I attempted a novel that was broader in scope than anything I'd written before. I decided once more to set historical and modern stories on converging tracks, and even though *Cape Cod* is thirty percent longer than *Back Bay,* covering ten centuries instead of two, I found a plot element to hold it together—the lost log of the *Mayflower.* The log—and the knowledge it may contain—gives every chapter and every character a focus, past and present.

In my new novel, *Annapolis,* I have written another multi-generational saga. This one follows an American naval family from the early eighteenth century to the present, while telling the story of the U.S. Navy from the Revolution to Vietnam. It's not a buried treasure story, but I find that the things I learned in *Back Bay* and refined with *Cape Cod* still help me to organize great spans of time.

Annapolis is ninety percent history (compared with fifty percent in *Back Bay* and seventy-five in *Cape Cod*), but I still employ that past-and-present converging-track structure, because in a book like this, modern characters provide an important perspective. As they attempt to understand the mysteries of the past, they demonstrate for the reader how directly past affects present, whether we're discussing grand political movements or the misguided decisions of ancestors who lived two hundred years ago.

But in order for their perspective to have dramatic meaning, the modern characters need that plot element to tie them directly to the historical characters. In *Annapolis,* I've built an old Annapolis mansion, so all the characters will have something to fight over when they're not sailing off to war. But the book is really unified by a thematic element rather than a physical object.

I know that starting with a theme and tacking on a story is going back-end-first. Still, a little thematic control may be the best way to find a through-line in a book that covers nine historical eras, eight wars, six battles, about two hundred characters, *and* is a book-within-a-book, to boot.

A modern character, Jack Stafford, is writing the story of his family in the Navy. His theme is the evolution of honor. But he cannot confront the last, most painful chapter, in which honor is sacrificed in Vietnam. So he asks another character to read his book from the beginning. Through the nine interconnected stories, each sustaining suspense and providing a climax of its own, his characters wrestle with their visions of honor, and the story travels inexorably back to the Mekong Delta, a dark night in 1968, and a final clash between honor and chaos.

Jack Stafford never worries about facts getting in the way of *The Stafford Story*, his book within the book, because he knows that the facts of history provide some of the best stories. And he learns, as he confronts Vietnam, that sometimes it is as important to be true to the spirit of history as to the letter.

And that's something I've been learning since I wrote about that 1789 banquet. Know the facts, use them because they bring the past to life, but remember why your readers are there. They want to see history before it became history, when nobody knew what was going to happen next.

In my *Annapolis* research, I read a riveting war patrol report by the commander of the submarine *Nautilus*, the first U.S. vessel to find the Japanese fleet at the battle of Midway:

0824: The picture presented on raising the periscope was one never experienced in peacetime practices. Ships were on all sides moving across the field at high speeds and circling away to avoid the submarine's position . . .

There is a sense of awe in that passage that you can almost feel, a sense of fear that you can almost smell, because you know that some of those Japanese ships are going to come after the *Nautilus*. Do the commander and the fictional lieutenant that I put aboard fight or run? Live or die? We know who won the battle of Midway, but for the reader who goes aboard that cramped little submarine, the only question is, what happens next?

Even in a submarine, I look for the ground-level perspective on history. I ask myself, what does it feel like in my characters' shoes? How are they changed by their confrontation with history? How do they change history as they go through it? To a reader of fiction, the answers to these questions are as important as the facts of history . . . maybe more so, because they tell the human story embedded in history.

□ 44

THE CRAFT OF THE ESPIONAGE THRILLER

BY JOSEPH FINDER

WHEN I WAS IN MY MID-TWENTIES AND STRUGGLING TO WRITE MY first novel, *The Moscow Club,* I got to know another aspiring writer, a cynical and embittered (but very funny) man, and told him I was immersed in the research for a spy thriller I hadn't begun to write. He shook his head slowly and scowled. "That's a sign of desperation," he intoned ominously. "Research is an excuse for not writing."

This ex-friend has given up trying to write and is working at some job he despises, while I'm making a living writing novels, so I think there may be a moral here. That old dictum writers are always accosted by—"Write what you know"—is, in the espionage-thriller genre, at least, a fallacy.

Obviously, research is no substitute for good writing, good storytelling, or the ability to create flesh-and-blood characters. But even the masters of the spy novel plunge into research for the worlds they create. John le Carré (the pen name for David Cornwell) was for a short while a spy for the British secret service, but nevertheless, he assiduously researches his spy tales. In the extensive acknowledgements at the end of *The Night Manager,* he thanks numerous sources in the U.S. Drug Enforcement Agency and the U.S. Treasury, mercenary soldiers, antiques dealers, and the "arms dealers who opened their doors to me." The novel only *reads* effortlessly.

I suppose you can just make it up, but it will always show, if you do, and the spy thriller must always evoke an authentic, fully realized world. Readers want to believe that the author is an authority, an expert, an insider who's willing to let them in on a shattering secret or two.

But no one can be expert in everything. My first novel was about a CIA analyst who learns of an impending coup attempt in Moscow and is drawn into the conspiracy. In the first draft, however, the hero, Charles Stone, was instead a ghostwriter for a legendary American statesman. Luckily, my agent persuaded me that no one wants to read about the exploits of a ghostwriter.

Transforming Charlie into a CIA officer took a lot of rethinking, but fortunately, I had sources: While a student at Yale, I'd been recruited by the CIA (but decided against it), and I had some friends in the intelligence community. They helped me make Charlie Stone a far more interesting, more appealing and believable character.

The best ideas, I believe, spring from real-life events, from reading newspapers and books, and from conducting interviews. Frederick Forsyth came up with the idea for his classic thriller, *The Day of the Jackal* (a fictional plot on the life of Charles de Gaulle), from his experience working as a Reuters correspondent in Paris in the early 1960s, when rumors kept circulating about assassination attempts on de Gaulle. Robert Ludlum was watching TV news in a Paris hotel when he happened to catch a report about an international terrorist named Carlos; this became the seed for one of his best novels, *The Bourne Identity*.

When I first began thinking about writing the novel that later became *The Moscow Club,* I was a graduate student at the Harvard Russian Research Center, studying the politics of the Soviet Union. I remember reading Forsyth's *The Devil's Alternative,* which concerns intrigue in the Kremlin. Why not try my hand at this? I thought. After Mikhail Gorbachev became head of the Soviet Union and began the slow-motion revolution that would eventually lead to the collapse of that empire, I began to hear bizarre rumors about attempts in Moscow to unseat Gorbachev. The rumors didn't seem so far-fetched to me. But when *The Moscow Club* came out at the beginning of 1991, I was chided for my overly active imagination. Then, in August of that year, the real thing happened: The KGB and the military banded together to try to overthrow the Gorbachev government—and suddenly, I was a prophet!

My second novel, however, was a significant departure from this political background. *Extraordinary Powers* concerns Ben Ellison, an attorney for a prestigious Boston law firm (and former clandestine operative for the CIA). He is lured into a top-secret government experiment and emerges with a limited ability to "hear" the thoughts of others. This sprang from a reference I'd come across in a study of the KGB to some highly secret programs in the U.S. and Soviet governments that attempted to locate people with telepathic ability to serve in various espionage undertakings. Whether or not one believes in ESP, the fact that such projects really do exist was irresistible to me. I sent *Extraordinary Powers* to a friend who does contract work for the CIA; he confided in me that he'd received a call from a highly placed person in a government agency who actually runs such a project and had used psychics during the Gulf War. He wanted to know whether I'd been the recipient of a leak.

With this seemingly fantastic premise at the center of my novel, it was crucially important that the world in which this plot takes place be a very real, very well-grounded one. Because I wanted the telepathy project to hew as closely to reality as possible, I spent a great deal of time talking to patent lawyers, helicopter pilots, gold experts, and even neurologists. I was relieved to get letters from a world-famous neurobiologist and from the editor of *The New England Journal of Medicine* saying that they were persuaded that such an experiment was within the realm of possibility.

In one crucial scene in *The Moscow Club,* Charlie had to smuggle a gun through airport security, but I had no idea how this might actually work, so I tracked a knowledgeable gun dealer, and after I'd convinced him I was a writer, not a criminal, he became intrigued by the scenario and agreed to help. It turned out that this fellow had a friend who used to be in the Secret Service and had actually taken a Glock pistol and got it past the metal detectors and X-ray machines in security at Washington's National Airport and onto a plane to Boston. He then showed me exactly how he'd done it, so I could write about it accurately. (I left out a few key details to foil any potential hijacker.)

Can readers tell when a scene or a detail is authentic? I believe so. I'm convinced that painstaking research can yield a texture, an atmosphere of authenticity, that average readers can feel and smell. (There will always be a few experts waiting to pounce. In *Extraordinary Powers,* I mistakenly described a Glock 19 as having a safety, and I continue to get angry letters about it.)

The longer I write, it seems, the more research I do. For my forthcoming novel, *Prince of Darkness,* whose hero is a female FBI counter-terrorism specialist, I managed to wangle official cooperation from the FBI, and I spent a lot of time talking to several FBI Special Agents. I also interviewed past and present terrorism experts for the CIA, asking them such questions as, would they really be able to catch a skilled professional terrorist—as well as some seemingly trivial ones.

Since the other main character in *Prince of Darkness* is a professional terrorist-for-hire, I thought it was important to talk to someone who's actually been a terrorist. This was not easy. In fact, it took me months to locate an ex-terrorist (through a friend of a friend) who was willing to talk. But it was worth the time and effort: My fictional terrorist is now, I think, far more credible than he'd have been if I'd simply invented him.

I've done interviews with a convicted forger for details on how to falsify a U.S. passport; with a bomb disposal expert about how to construct bombs; with an expert in satellite surveillance to help me describe authentically how the U.S. government is able to listen in on telephone conversations. I've often called upon the expertise of police homicide detectives, retired FBI agents, helicopter pilots, pathologists, even experts in embalming (or "applied arts," as they are called).

Since an important character in *Prince of Darkness* is a high-priced call girl, I spent a lot of time interviewing prostitutes, expensive call girls, and madams. As a result of this groundwork, I think this particular character is more sympathetic, more believable, than I'd have drawn her otherwise.

Because international settings are often integral parts of spy novels, I strongly believe that travel—really being there in Paris, say, or Rome, or wherever—not only can help you create plausible settings, make them look and smell and feel real, but can suggest scenes and ideas that would otherwise never occur to you. But not everyone can afford to travel (or likes to; ironically, Robert Ludlum, whose plots traverse the globe, abhors traveling). No doubt you can get by tolerably well consulting a good guidebook or two.

Gathering research material is a strange obsession, but it's by far the best part of writing thrillers. I will admit, however, that this passion can go too far. In Rome, I was pickpocketed while standing in a *gelato* shop. When I realized that my passport and all my cash and travelers checks were gone, I panicked. I searched for the perpetrator and came upon a man who looked somewhat shifty. I approached him and pleaded, in my pathetic Italian, *"Per favore, signore! Per favore!* My passport! *Per piacere!*" When the man responded by unzipping his travel bag to prove he didn't have my belongings, that he was innocent, I knew I'd found my man. I told him quietly: "Look, I'm on my honeymoon. If you give me back my passport and my money, I promise I won't turn you in."

He looked around and furtively put my passport and wallet back in my bag.

At this point any sane tourist would flee, but, I went on, "One more thing. If you'll agree to be interviewed, I won't call the police."

He looked at me as if I were out of my mind. "I'm quite serious," I said. "Let me buy you an espresso."

He sat down at a table with me as I explained that I was doing research for a novel partly set in Rome. Flattered that a writer would take an interest in his life, he began to tell me all about how he got into this line of work, about his childhood in Palermo spent snatching purses, about how he travels around Europe frequenting international gatherings of the rich and famous, how he lives in hotels and is often lonely. He explained how he spots an easy mark, how he fences passports, which travelers checks he has no interest in. He demonstrated how he picks pockets and handbags, and taught me how to make sure it never happened to me again.

Much of the information I gleaned from this pickpocket later turned up in the Italy sequence in *Extraordinary Powers.*

I'm certainly not suggesting that a committed espionage novelist must go out of his way to get his pockets picked in Rome, or consort with convicted forgers, assassins, or terrorists. But the longer I write espionage fiction, the more strongly I'm convinced that if you're going to write about unusual people and circumstances in a compelling and plausible way, there's really no substitute for firsthand experience.

❑ 45

DISCOVERING A STORY
IN HISTORY

BY SONIA LEVITIN

"I'M WRITING A HISTORICAL NOVEL ABOUT THE RECONSTRUCTION PE-riod," a student told me. "I'm using my great-grandmother's Civil War diaries."

"Wonderful," I said. "Now, what's your story?"

The student was baffled and a little insulted. Story? Hadn't she just told me?

What she had told me was simply that she was delving into a certain period in American history—a time filled with drama and conflict, and she had resources at her command. What I needed to know is exactly what any editor and every reader wants to know: What happens in this story to make readers identify with the characters? What dangers do they face? How do they apply courage, ingenuity, and risk to their personal challenges? What are the stakes?

I have written various historical novels set in different periods. My most recent, *Escape from Egypt,* is set in Biblical times and deals with the Israelites' enslavement, exodus, and the wilderness sojourn. Dramatic events all, but the story had to come from specific charac-ters, all drawn boldly and vividly, to convince the reader that these long-ago events happened to real people. Only in that way do we in-volve readers, make them care.

Some say that history is dry, while the novel is juicy. There is the difference. Most writers of pure history remember the facts and forget the people. For the novelist, the facts are the foundation, the people are everything else.

To breathe life into history, writers must ask two questions: First, what aspects of human endeavor never change? Second, how have things changed since the distant past in the story?

What doesn't change is the need for people to survive, to be loved, to win the approbation of their peers, and to reach some personal/ spiritual conclusion. What do change are manners, customs, ways of thinking about the world and one's place in it. Some things go in cycles. Society moves from repression to permissiveness, back to strict control. Individuals continually battle the restrictions, which becomes the basis for many a story.

The historical novel, like any other, needs a protagonist who must battle the status quo. In my novel, *Roanoke,* protagonist William Wythers is a pauper wrongly accused of a crime. He sails for the New World to clear his name and to win fame and fortune, thus battling the status quo that relegated paupers to prison. William does not meet his goal in the ordinary sense; instead, he discovers a terrifying and captivating land. When war breaks out with the local Native Americans and most of the colonists are murdered, William survives. Why? Because he has been able to adapt to the new land, to accept change, and also (not incidentally) because he has fallen in love with a Native American girl. In a historical novel, or any novel, love can be the element that keeps the hero on course; it is the one ingredient that remains constant in a world of turmoil and change. We know the hero by what or by whom he loves, and often it is this very love (commitment) that saves him.

The hero in a historical novel must often leave his old world of conflict and conformity. Every patriot, pilgrim, and adventurer begins by stepping out of the old world and finding not only new worlds "out there" but new attitudes within. This is the universal lesson of history. Without change there is no growth.

Against this universal background, the novelist must prepare something unique and challenging, new characters with fresh faces, characters who behave boldly but in conformity with all that we know of psychology. Motivation must be clear.

In planning the plot for *Escape from Egypt,* I realized that the two primary characters, Jesse, the Israelite slave, and Jennat, the young Egyptian-Syrian concubine, must be given different lives and different motives for needing to escape from Egypt. For Jesse, it was enough that he was an Israelite whose people were ultimately released through Moses' leadership. For Jennat, however, an entirely different scenario had to be created, and it was this that became part of the plot.

Jennat and Jesse have shared a mutual attraction—forbidden love, of course. The Bible gave me the bare bones of the action: Ten plagues are unleashed upon stubborn Pharaoh. His innocent subjects suffer, too. Jennat is one of them. The final plague, the death of all the first-born of Pharaoh's subjects, gave me the perfect plot point I needed. Instead of seeing it only as part of the retribution against Pharaoh, I made this plague very personal. It provides the impetus for Jennat to leave Egypt and join the Israelites in their exodus. What happens is that Jennat's mistress loses her beloved son to the plague. Because of Jennat's association with Jesse, an Israelite, Jennat's mistress blames *her* for the death of the child and, insane with grief, tries to kill her. Jennat flees and joins the Israelites in their exodus and the wilderness adventures. Similarly, other historical events are brought into the lives of the various characters, influencing their actions, propelling the story.

Momentous events—a migration, invasion, invention, or a major ca-tastrophe—can be the foundation for your novel. But the nuts and bolts, the action that keeps the reader turning the page, has to come from within the characters themselves, their personal struggles as they are swept away by major forces that seem to be controlling their lives.

For characters to be real, they must be in conflict. That is where the action comes in. The novelist creates conflict from every premise. The Israelites are slaves and want to escape. Or do they? In my novel, Jesse's father, a renegade and an opportunist, doesn't want to leave Egypt at all! Jesse's mother, on the other hand, is passionate about wanting to flee. Thus, Jesse is immediately plunged into conflict be-tween the two.

Remember, the unfolding of historical events is never smooth, never easy. Among this country's westward migrants there were those who came unwillingly, resentfully. There was conflict with natives, with recalcitrant beasts, with fellow travelers, and most of all, there was conflict within.

In *The No-Return Trail,* my heroine, Nancy Kelsey, is faced with numerous conflicts, some recorded, some invented. It is the novelist's privilege to invent, as long as the facts are not overlooked. For Nancy, I invented a bossy sister-in-law and a blunt, stubborn husband, as well as a mother who grieved over her departure. None of these seems too farfetched, considering the situation. Even a few known facts can provide the seeds of conflict. For example, Nancy was the youngest in her family. As such, she would very likely be intimidated by an older in-law. Her husband was an uneducated woodsman and in later years an itinerant preacher. Certainly, he would have had a fiercely independent nature, and like other men of his day, probably spent little time romancing or sweet-talking a young wife. Thus, we can assume that Nancy longed for talk and tenderness and the companionship of other women. It is these personal reflections that make Nancy real and empathic. This personal background provides the necessary drama for the story, as Nancy sets out to be with other women but ends up the only female among thirty men who made it to California. History provides the facts; the novelist seeks out the dramatic irony that brings a story to an emotional high. For everything gained there is something lost: This is the premise of the historical novel, which, even more than the "regular" novel, imitates life.

How do we create new characters in a historical setting? My own method is, first, to immerse myself completely in the period, until I know almost instinctively what my protagonist eats for breakfast, what he hears outside the window, what smells greet him upon arising, what kind of song springs to his lips, what curses, what endearments. Because everything we say and do and think is anchored in the time and place we find ourselves.

For my *Journey to America* trilogy, I researched what was playing at the movies in the late forties, what songs were popular, the actual names of the restaurants we frequented, and even the price of an egg sandwich. On my extended calendar, I always look up the date and the day of the week, and I consult almanacs to check the weather. Why go to all that trouble? Because I know that the background I provide is as accurate as it can be, and lends veracity to the whole.

I particularly enjoy researching and using medical information in my historical novels. Everyone is interested in health and remedies. I find it amusing to note some of the outrageous "cures" that were perpetrated upon innocent patients, and also to note their abiding faith in their physicians. Probably every writer favors certain details; my personal favorites are the domestic details of housekeeping, clothing, and personal care.

In *Escape from Egypt,* the opening scene between Jennat and her mistress takes place while the latter is having her hair done. Her washstand, mirror, tiny cosmetic cups, and trays are straight out of a museum, prototypes of the things we still use today. The hairdresser inserts several hair pieces, as much tricks of the trade then as now!

Why does it matter what powders, scents, and colors women used back then? Because it makes people seem more real, more like us, engrossed in minutiae of living even while major historical events are exploding all around them. This is what makes the historical novel exciting, for while empires rise and fall, epochs emerge or end, everyday life goes on *just as if nothing were changing*.

Actual historical events are the "wall" or the structural foundation of the historical novel. Between these "walls" the characters come and go, live out the desires, compulsions, or regrets that you, the novelist, create. One character hates his father. Another is haunted by an evil memory or a damaging secret. If a character is hell-bent on proving his courage, it's a sure bet that he was once a coward, and that secret becomes a compelling part of the plot.

Of course, the outcome of actual historical events is already known. The cataclysm inevitably must occur. This creates a sense of tension in the historical novel, the inevitability of crisis known to the reader, pitted against the ignorance, complacency or apparent helplessness of the characters. Eventually the characters are forced to see and to act.

If the characters are provocative, complex, and *real,* the outcome doesn't matter as much as the journey to that outcome, because the novelist is more concerned with "how" than with "what." How do people survive tough challenges? How do they find the courage to make the right decisions? How can they go against the current of overpowering events and still come out victorious?

This is the task and the pleasure of writing the historical novel, to ponder the past, to find its truths, and then to invent new lives that will speak these truths to the reader.

❑ 46

Why Horror?

By Graham Masterton

Few people understand that writers are writing all the time.

To think that a writer is writing only when he or she is actually hammering a keyboard is like believing that a police officer's job is "arresting people."

Even while they're not sitting down at the word processor, writers are writing in their heads. Inventing stories. Playing with words. Thinking up jokes and riddles and metaphors and similes. These days, I write both historical sagas and horror novels. Most people relish historical sagas, but I'm often asked, "Why do people like horror?"

I think they like horror novels because they depict ordinary people dealing with extraordinary threats. They like to imagine, what would *I* do if a dark shadow with glowing red eyes appeared in my bedroom at night? What would *I* do if I heard a sinister scratching inside the walls of my house? What would *I* do if my husband's head turned around 360 degrees?

I've found my inspiration for horror stories in legends from ancient cultures, and my research into how these demons came to be created by ordinary men and women is fascinating. Each of them represents a very real fear that people once felt, and often still do.

There are beguiling men who turn into evil demons. There are monsters that suck your breath when you're asleep. There are gremlins that steal children. There are horrible gorgons that make you go blind just to look at them, and vampires that drain all of the energy out of you. There are zombies who come back from the dead and torment you.

My favorite Scottish demons were the glaistigs, hideous hags who were supposed to be the ghosts of women haunting their former homes. They were frequently accompanied by a child who was called "the

little plug" or "the whimperer." If you didn't leave out a bowl of milk
for the glaistigs, they would suck your cows dry or drain their blood.
Sometimes a glaistig would carry her little whimperer into the house,
and bathe it in the blood of the youngest infant in the house, and the
victim would be found dead and white in the morning.

Now, this is a legend, but you can understand what genuine fears it
expresses. A woman's fear of other women intruding into her home,
as in the film, *Fatal Attraction*; a man's fear of losing his livelihood;
parents' fear of losing their children to malevolent and inexplicable
illnesses, such as crib death. What I do is take these ancient demons,
which are vivid and expressive manifestations of basic and genuine
fears, and write about them in an up-to-date setting, with modern characters.

The very first horror novel I wrote was called *The Manitou*. A manitou is a Native American demon, and in this novel a 300-year-old
medicine man was reborn in the present day to take his revenge on
the white man. I was inspired to write that by *The Buffalo Bill Annual, 1956*.

Since then I have written books based on Mexican demons, Balinese
demons, French demons and Biblical demons, two dozen in all, and
I'm working on another one about the Glasgow woman who makes
a pact with Satan so that her house disappears every time the rent
collector calls.

I started writing horror novels at school, when I was 11. I used to
read them to my friends during recess. Reading your work out loud is
always invaluable training. When I met one of my old school friends
only recently, he said, "I'll never forget the story you wrote about the
woman with no head who kept singing 'Tiptoe Through the Tulips.' It
gave me nine years of sleepless nights, and I still can't have tulips in
the house."

Horror books seem to sell well all over the world, with some notable
exceptions, like Germany. The French love horror, and the Poles adore
it. In France, *Le Figaro* called me "Le Roi du Mal," the King of Evil.
I was the first Western horror novelist to be published in Romania,
home of Dracula. I received a letter from a reader this week saying,
"I have to write to congratulate you on a wonderful book, rich with
ideas and shining with great metaphors. Also very good printing, and
excellent paper, which is appreciated here because of bathroom tis-
sue shortage."

How extreme can you be when you write horror? As extreme, I think, as your talent and your taste permit, although gruesomeness is no substitute for skillful writing. I had several complaints about a scene in my book *Picture of Evil,* in which the hero kills two young girls with a poker. People protested my graphic description of blood spattering everywhere. In fact, I never once mentioned blood. All I said was, "He clubbed them to death like two baby seals." The reader's imagination was left to do the rest.

It is catching the mood and feel of a moment that makes your writing come to life. Most of the time you can dispense with whole realms of description if you catch one vivid image; catching those images requires thought and research. When I write historical novels, I frequently rent period costumes which my wife and I try on so I can better understand how my characters would have moved and behaved when wearing them. How do you rush to meet your lover when wearing a hobble skirt? How do you sit down with a bustle?

We also prepare food and drink from old recipes, using cookbooks by Fannie Farmer, Mrs. Beeton, and Escoffier. One of the least successful period drinks we prepared was the King's Death, drunk by King Alfonso of Spain in the Men's Bar of the Paris Ritz. The King's Death is made with wild strawberries marinated in Napoleon brandy, then topped up with half a bottle of champagne—each! We served it to some dinner party guests, and they became incoherent and had to go home.

Whether you're writing history or horror, thrillers or love stories, the most important technique is to live inside the book instead of viewing it from the outside. Your word processor or typewriter is nothing more than a key that opens the door to another world. When I'm writing, I step into that world, so that it surrounds me. So many writers as they write look only forward at the page, or screen, forgetting what's all around them.

Think of the rain on the side of your face and the wind against your back. Think of what you can hear in the distance. Think of the fragrances you can smell. Most of all, *be* all your characters: Act out their lives, act out their movements and their facial expressions, and speak their dialogue out loud. Get up from your keyboard sometimes, and do what you've imagined; then sit down and write it. The Disney artist Ward Kimball used to draw Donald Duck by making faces in the mirror. You can do the same when you're writing about the way your characters act and react.

Your best research is watching real live people living out their real lives. Watch every gesture, every nuance, listen to people's conversations and accents. Try to propel your story along at the pace that *you* would like to read it. Avoid showing off in your writing; all that does is slow down your story and break the spell you have been working so hard to conjure up. How many times has your suspension of disbelief been broken by ridiculous similes, like "her bosoms swelled like two panfuls of overboiling milk."

Two similes that really caught my attention and which I later used in novels were an old Afrikaner's description of lions roaring "like coal being delivered," and the hideous description by an Australian prisoner of war of two of his fellow prisoners being beheaded: "the blood spurted out of their necks like red walking-sticks."

To my mind, the greatest achievement in writing is to create a vivid, spectacular novel without readers being aware that they are reading at all. My ideal novel would be one that readers put down, and discover that they're still in it, that it's actually come to life.

The other day I was reading *Secrets of the Great Chefs of China*, and apart from the eel recipe, where you throw live eels into boiling water and have to clamp the lid down quickly to stop them from jumping out of the pot, the most memorable advice the book gave was, "A great chef prepares his food so that it is ready for the mouths of his guests; it is both a courtesy and a measure of his professionalism." That goes for writing, too.

❏ 47

TELL THE READER WHERE IT HURTS

BY GEORGE C. CHESBRO

DOES YOUR HERO OR HEROINE HAVE A PROBLEM? NO PROBLEM. LIKE a grain of sand in an oyster, something out of place in a fictional character—a constant irritation, a character flaw, inconsolable sorrow, a physical disability—can often result in something gleaming, rare, and of great worth. For an author, this means the creation of a fictional character who is three-dimensional and, well, "rounded," who moves around on the pages and through the plot instead of just sitting there; also a person whose welfare the reader may come to care about as much as the resolution of whatever game is afoot, and perhaps even more. This burden borne by the character may be an essential part of the plot, but not necessarily—unless, of course, the theme is revenge, where pain and rage are the driving forces. The point of the "problem" is that it gives the heroine or hero a unique perspective on life and events, which can then be shared with the reader. People who know serious suffering often feel empathy with the underdog, and pain compels them to swim naturally—and believably—in ever deeper and darker waters that more balanced and less haunted people would certainly avoid.

Literature, especially mystery fiction, abounds with examples: alcoholics, compulsive thieves, the lame, lonely, paralyzed and blind. However, for the purposes of this discussion, I will limit my observations to my fictional creation, one Dr. Robert Frederickson, aka Mongo the Magnificent, who is an achondroplastic dwarf.

When the notion of a dwarf as private investigator first occurred to me, I vigorously opposed the idea. I was searching for a "different" kind of series character, but this was ridiculous. I couldn't see how anybody would take him seriously—not prospective clients, and, even more dreadful to contemplate, not editors, who would scoff at the exploits of such an unlikely character and reject my efforts. I would be wasting my time.

This constant specter of rejection and humiliation was, of course, precisely the point, and is at the core of what makes Mongo such a rich human being. But it took me a while to realize this.

Fortunately for me, Mongo is tough, and he would not be denied. Try as I might to conjure up a more "suitable" candidate who would be easier for me to work with, the damn dwarf just kept tapping at the back doors of my mind, insisting that I give him a chance to live, grow, and show me what he could do. Well, what was I to do?

I still didn't believe I could sell this guy, but in order to get him off my mind's back porch, I let him in, looked him over a bit more carefully, sat down at my typewriter, and sent this wounded but incredibly resilient man out into the world. Almost immediately Mongo began to touch me in a myriad of odd and mysterious ways. Regardless of how he was treated by prospective clients and editors, *I,* at least, would afford him the dignity and respect he deserved. I could feel his pain to a level matched only by his brother, Garth, who had abruptly materialized at his side.

The observation is frequently made that Mongo does not in any way consider himself handicapped, and the fact that he is a dwarf is irrelevant. This is true for Mongo and (one hopes) the reader. But Mongo's dwarfism is never irrelevant to the author, nor to Garth, whose bottomless love for and ferocious devotion to his brother, whom he nurtured and protected in childhood, has led him into those same dark and dangerous waters, where he has been permanently damaged, albeit in a radically different manner. Their strong bonding dates back to a time when Mongo's dwarfism *was* a problem, and it's important for me as the writer to know that, and also that a key to Mongo's character is that he has always been driven to overcompensate for his slight stature, to excel at every challenge he undertakes. This he has done, as a circus headliner, martial arts expert, criminologist, college professor, and, finally, as a private investigator.

Ordinary people do not lead extraordinary lives. If Mongo had not been born a dwarf, it's quite possible that he and Garth would have ended up as dairy farmers on their family's ranch in Nebraska. Then where would *I* be?

Let me give some concrete examples of how Mongo's "problem" has been invaluable to me as an author in both characterization and plotting.

In his debut, we met a man who was determined to achieve the same measure of success in the private arena as he had in the worlds of the circus and academia. Then, Mongo's problem was not that he was a dwarf, but, rather, who was going to *hire* a dwarf private investigator. No Maltese Falcons for Mongo. Only the people who knew Mongo *personally,* who appreciated just how effective he could be, would seek out his help. *I* knew that Mongo's being a dwarf was going to cause him problems, and so the plots of both *Shadow of A Broken Man* and *City of Whispering Stone* have their roots in academia. In *City of Whispering Stone,* Mongo is hired by his former boss in the circus. Being a dwarf did not define what Mongo could do, but it did define the manner in which I could initially unleash him against his foes.

See how useful this "problem" business can be, and how it works? It focuses the minds of both the author and reader.

Then came *The Beasts of Valhalla*. Here, in the first book of what I would come to think of—after the fact—as an epic trilogy (including *Two Songs This Archangel Sings* and *The Cold Smell of Sacred Stone,* with *Second Horseman Out of Eden* as a kind of coda), the lives of the brothers undergo sea changes. As Mongo returns home to Nebraska after an absence of many years to attend the funeral of a favorite nephew, he is haunted by memories of his childhood. There, the reader finally gets an insight into just how tortured those early years were for a dwarf growing up in a rural community in the heartland of America. Mongo had to battle not only evil forces that literally threaten to destroy humankind, but also personal ghosts and demons that threaten to drain his resolve, resources, and courage by once again making him feel small.

The brothers emerge victorious from this great adventure. Garth, however, has been seriously damaged psychologically; now their childhood roles have been reversed, and it is Mongo who must keep a cautious eye on Garth, who, in certain situations, can turn into an avenging angel who takes no prisoners. Again, while Mongo's dwarfism plays only a marginal role in the plots of these books, the *pain* of his past is very evident, and permeates the atmosphere of all the novels. One hopes it has deepened the character and enriched the plots.

And now *Garth* has a "problem," multiplying the possibilities for characterization, new perils, plot twists and turns. While Mongo's

"problem" was the heart of *The Beasts of Valhalla,* it is Garth's spiritual pain that throbs at the center of *Second Horseman Out of Eden.*

By the end of the trilogy and coda, the brothers have become world-
famous, retained by Fortune 500 companies and government agencies.
They are wealthy and comfortable. The devices that launched the plots
of my early books are no longer required, indeed, they would not work.
Mongo, who has taken his brother, once a cop with the NYPD, on as
a partner, has more work than he can handle. His cases can come from
anywhere. The fact that he is a dwarf is now even less relevant to plot,
but not to *character.* And surely not to the reader who has been following Mongo's exploits, for they understand how the dwarf became father
to the giant.

All of this information about Mongo and my insight into what makes
him tick did not come to me full-blown. In the beginning I knew only
that he was a dwarf. Fiction writing is a spooky business, truly a dark
art. Novels, like mushrooms, grow in dark places. There is an absolutely marvelous and magical process I call "discovery" that is a gift
to the author when character and story become organic, living things.
First you start, and then you find out things as you go along, sometimes
in one book, other times over the course of many books. Mongo and
Garth are very real to me, *alive,* and so they keep growing and changing
in ways that often surprise and delight me. (Fiction writing can be
thought of as dreams becoming words, a kind of controlled madness.)

I believe that any success enjoyed by the series is a result not so
much of the plots (which have been accurately described as ranging
from the bizarre to the very bizarre), as of the character of Mongo.
The very first discovery I made about him, apart from his dwarfism,
was that *everything* he did was part of a quest for dignity and a desire
to be taken seriously—just as every one of us, at one time or another,
has felt very small in a world of giants that threatens to crush us.
Voilà: Reader identification and a willingness to trek with Mongo into
some very strange worlds. In exchange for my granting Mongo's request for dignity and to be taken seriously, he has given me a number
of rich rewards, including a modicum of success that allows me to
make a living doing exactly what I want to do—dream. And it all began
with my reflection on one man's pain, and where it might take him.

Telling the reader where a character hurts can often lead to considerable pleasure, satisfaction, and success for an author.

❑ 48

CLUES TO WRITING
A MYSTERY NOVEL

BY T. JEFFERSON PARKER

BEFORE STARTING A NEW BOOK, I MAKE A DEAL WITH MYSELF. IT doesn't involve character, atmosphere, structure, or setting. Rather, it's an agreement I make with my reader, something to keep me honest over the long haul of writing a novel.

Here are my rules when I begin.

One: Write as well as you can, never down, always up to your readers; do not pander; do not cheat; do not be dishonest. If something rings false to me, it will surely ring false to my reader, too. Treat that reader with the same respect with which you treat yourself.

Two: Make sure that what you're offering your readers is worth the several hours of reading it will take. You can make a thousand promises to your readers in the opening pages of a book, and you will have to make good on every one in a surprising, satisfying, and believable way. Deliver. After all, your pact implies that your readers will leave the novel somehow richer. Give your readers the bargain of a lifetime.

Three: Don't be afraid to entertain: You are writing popular fiction, not an instruction manual, a position paper, or an essay.

Four: Leave your readers with a feeling of something experienced, not just something read. Give them an emotional reality. Make it impossible for them simply to chuck your book into the wastebasket when they've finished reading it and grab the next one. Make your novel linger, haunt, last.

These are the self-imposed commandments I try to follow when I work. I forget them sometimes, ignore them others, amend them often. I never achieve them all perfectly.

Before I come to the point of writing, though, there is the odd fallow period during which I'm sniffing for the trail of the new book. At those times—and they may be as brief as days or as long as months—none of the above rules is relevant yet. I'm a bloodhound then, or a detective, maybe, trying to pick up the scene or the clues that will lead me to the new book. This gestation period can be brief or long, but it is generally an anxious and troubling time. When I was young and frenzied with ambition, I finished up the final draft of *Laguna Heat* on a Friday, ending roughly five years' work. The following Monday I began writing my next novel. (It was never published and probably should not have been.) Conversely, after *Summer of Fear* was finished, I took off almost half a year before finding it again.

And what is "it"? A certain scent, a smell, an emotional aroma is what you're searching for. Like many good things in life, you don't really know what it is until you find it. When you do find it—or more accurately, when it finds you—it is immediately recognizable. It's something outside you that sparks something inside you. The spark starts a fire. The fire burns for two or three years, during which time you write the book. The novel is an attempt to see what the fire leaves. It is an attempt to find something new, something born of the union between what you believed you might find, and what was actually there. If all that sounds vague, maybe I can explain.

Here's an example: After I'd finished writing *Laguna Heat,* I was sniffing around for something new. The scent hit me loud and clear one day when I was in a liquor store off Harbor Boulevard in Costa Mesa. I stood in the checkout line and there was something about the man in front of me that made me think he must be an American Vietnam War veteran. I also noticed that the clerk was a young Vietnamese woman. I stood waiting, wondering what might be going through their respective minds. What did she think of him? He of her? Could their paths possibly have crossed many years ago, in her war-torn country? Could he have fought alongside her father or brother? Against them? Could these two have actually met?

Eavesdropping shamelessly, I moved to the side just a little to watch their transaction. He stepped up to the counter, and before he could say one word, the young woman reached up to the cigarette rack above her and took out a pack of Pall Malls—soft-pack, regulars. She set them on the counter in front of him. He looked at them, then at her, then said his first words to her: "How did you know that's what I wanted?"

She smiled shyly. "Some things," she said, "I just know."

He paid and left.

Well, that's the kind of moment a novelist lives for, a moment loaded with intrigue, expectation, surprise. It connected directly with some of the things I'd been thinking about for most of my adult life—the war, what it meant to us and to them, how it changed the psyche of the republic and the face of the globe. I did not serve in Vietnam, so such questions were large, complex abstractions to me. Suddenly, they were made real, the "something" outside directly colliding with the "something" inside. I had just gotten my first whiff of the new book.

What did this tiny moment in the history of the Vietnam War have to connect with inside me? Well, all that I was. All the hours of newsreel footage of dead soldiers and body counts I had watched. All the newsprint I'd read. All the stories from friends and acquaintances who'd gone to 'Nam. All the hours of reports, synopses, analyses. All the feature films, from *Coming Home* to *Apocalypse Now* and beyond. All of the 20 years I'd been wondering about this pivotal thing in my own history. All of this fuel rushed out to meet that moment of spark— the American vet having his mind read by a young Vietnamese refugee.

Leaving that liquor store on Harbor, I knew certainly that my next book would be an attempt to deal with those things and that I would set that book in Orange County, California. Why? Because there we have a place called Little Saigon that was and is the largest enclave of Vietnamese on earth, outside of Vietnam itself. I can remember my first forays into the clubs and bars of Little Saigon, notepad in pocket, mind literally reeling at all the "material" I was discovering. It was the discovery of a large part of myself that I had known was there but had no access to before. The mystery of that encounter, the tonnage of things left unsaid in that brief moment, stayed with me for the three years of writing *Little Saigon,* and beyond.

I had another similar moment, though it was less dramatic, as I was preparing to write my fourth novel. I was sitting on a patio chair on my deck, which overlooks Laguna Canyon. It was late afternoon, then it was evening, then it was night. My wife, suffering a brain tumor, was beside me. Our dogs were sprawled around us. We had watched the light fade into sunset, experiencing each increment of the growing night. We said hardly a word. Watching anything fade was a painful correlative to what we both knew was happening to her.

As we sat there and looked out to the hillsides, Catherine noted the odd way the hills formed what looked like a supine female (torso and legs) at night, and the way the distant lights of Laguna illuminated up from her middle. Cat named her "Lady of the Canyon." For a brief moment, I was filled with a new love for this suffering young woman, and for the house in which we lived, and for the hillsides that cradled us. It was an overwhelmingly powerful love, and almost unbearably sad. And I knew that my next book would be an attempt to celebrate that love somehow. The book became *Summer of Fear,* in which crime writer Russell Monroe tries to help heal his ill wife while a murderer stalks the city around him. It is a gut-wrenching, chaotic book—confessional, tortured, and dark. But it ends in hope and redemption. In some ways, that book is a fictionalized accounting of things that we wanted to come true. Cat never got to read the ending. But the Lady of the Canyon that she had noticed is in that novel, in fact, she plays an important part.

I offer these moments to demonstrate how strangely a book can begin. The emotions that draw one to the blank page are often vague, poorly understood, ephemeral. The writing then becomes a journey of discovery rather than a mission of execution. The fire burns and what it leaves behind is the book.

❑ 49

FINDING THE ALIEN VOICE

BY DEAN WHITLOCK

EVERYONE SPEAKS WITH AN ACCENT. OFTEN, WE'RE NOT AWARE OF it, because we're usually talking with family and friends who have the same accent we do. It's not till we strike up a conversation with someone from Boston, Bombay, or, for that matter, Betelgeuse that we hear the strangely inflected English we call an accent. Of course, it's not just the place of birth and upbringing that determine our accent. Social class, level of education, and favorite movie heroes all have an effect on how we sound when we speak. Instead of accent, think of the word *dialect*. It's a broader term that includes pronunciation, word choice, word order, rhythm, idioms, contractions, and consistent breaking of the rules of grammar. These are the factors that give each of us our distinctive voice.

Every character in your story should also have a unique voice. When you remove the "said Harry," you should still be able to tell it's Harry speaking. Unfortunately, there's a tendency in science fiction and mystery (my two favorite genres) to adopt a flippant, bantering tone for the main characters. Science fiction heroes often sound like Han Solo; mystery sleuths often sound like Sam Spade or Kinsey Millhone. These characters work, they're successful and popular, so of course they get copied. Unfortunately, all the heroes begin to sound alike. What's really unfortunate is when all the characters in a single book sound alike.

We run into a different problem when a character is an obvious alien—a Russian in a spy novel, for example, or an extra-terrestrial from Bernard's star. We have to make the character understandable to the reader, so the character must speak English. In science fiction, the usual convention is to assume that everyone speaks some sort of intergalactic Esperanto (Federated or Galactic Standard or some such). Then the aliens also begin to sound like Han Solo. Or they go the other way and speak like Oxford Dons. In the spy novel, the Russian is given a pseudo accent that reads suspiciously like Boris Badenov confronting Bullwinkle.

Even worse, beginning writers sometimes try to *show* what the language sounds like through the use of what I call creative phonetics; for example, "Zis eggplahnt, eet ez burned—how you say? Ouver doan." They even do it with native English speakers: "Pahk the cah in Hahvahd Yahd, dahling." At best, this is shallow stereotyping; at worst, unreadable.

How then do you find—and portray—your character's voice? Here are a few techniques that can help:

1. Listen carefully.
2. Learn the language.
3. Act the part.
4. Write out loud.
5. Break the rules.
6. Tell, don't show.

1. Listening is the only way you can hear how people speak. Most of the time, we listen in order to discover the meaning in a person's speech. We don't really pay attention to the word order, rhythm, and other characteristics of the speaker's voice. In order to write a believable character, however, you must listen closely to people who are like your character. Depending on upbringing and region, people make sometimes very subtle choices of phrasing that give their speech a characteristic syntax and rhythm; for example:

"You can't mean it," which to me sounds British, as opposed to "You're pulling my leg," which is very American, as is "You've got to be kidding." Or even this inversion, which I would put in the mouth of a city dweller, "Are you kidding me?"

Similar differences occur in every aspect of a spoken voice; only by listening will you hear them.

2. If you don't speak your character's language, at least learn *about* it. Find a teacher of that language who can describe how it differs from English and can give you examples of exactly literal translations. Human languages seem to have a universal basic grammar, but there are lots of differences nonetheless. Consider word order again. If your character is a native-born French woman, she will not arrange her

words in the same order that a native English speaker would. Differences in syntax between French and English would make her tend to say, "There is the house of my uncle," rather than, "There is my uncle's house."

That's an example of a fairly superficial difference, one that a French person would quickly overcome when learning to speak English. There are other differences, however, that are not so easy to unlearn. Russian, for instance, doesn't have articles, and it doesn't use pronouns the same way English does. That's one reason Boris Badenov says things like, "Is nice day, yes?" If you must have Russians or Chinese or Mexicans speak English, listen first to a native speaker of their language or read informal texts.

If you can't listen to or read works by someone like your character (because your character is not of this planet, for example), then you must use your imagination. But first listen to earthly aliens and contemplate their languages. Think about why they speak the way they do and how their languages differ from ours. Consider how you can use those differences to help your alien speak a realistically foreign English. Consider, too, that the structure of the language will reveal a great deal about the alien's culture. Imagine, for example, a culture that had no word for "please." Or no active verbs. Or no future tense.

3. When actors prepare their roles, they study and listen to people like their characters (see point 1). They often write biographies of their characters. They write down the characters' favorite foods, colors, hobbies, sports, all the likes and dislikes that make the character interesting and three-dimensional. Writers often do this, too, of course, but actors go on to practice moving as their characters would move. And when they practice their lines, they speak in their characters' voices. You must know your own characters just as well, particularly the leads, and so you must rehearse their parts. Not necessarily the action; you can let that play out in your mind. But do get into the roles and act, and then put what you say down on paper. You are all the actors in your story; you must portray all the characters, and all differently.

4. When you sit down to write, speak the lines out loud. Make sure you listen carefully to how you sound. Do you sound like the models you've been listening to? Do you sound like the characters you've been rehearsing? Listen to the rhythm of your words as you say each

character's lines. Listen to the word choice, the grammar, the accent. Make sure your characters sound real, and don't all sound the same.

5. When people speak, they break the rules of written grammar, and people from different regions break different rules. When you write dialogue, you have to break the rules in the same way your characters do. Grammar for expository writing must be more formal than spoken grammar, to make up for the lack of context—the expressions, gestures, and ability to interrupt and correct that are all part of a conversation. In written fiction, however, characters must speak in realistic voices, or their dialogue will seem stilted and unnatural. The expressions and gestures are written into the narrative between the spoken lines. By listening to the models for your characters, you will hear how they bend grammar. Write the grammar you hear; no one is grading you on it.

6. Dialect is one case where the old adage, "Show, don't tell," does not hold true. Do not try to write exactly what your characters sound like. Don't try to create phonetic spellings for the mispronunciations that people make. I once started reading a novel about the Scottish clearances, in which every character spoke in a hideous caricature of Robert Burns's poetry:

"Ah dinna ken why the laird's goon awa', lassie. 'A's nicht sich a braw mon, hissel'."

And so on through an entire book. Or so I assume. I put it down before the end of the first chapter. It was just too much work translating the dialogue into English. However, you can always enliven a character's voice with a few odd contractions and misspellings. Just make sure it's only a few and that they are obvious and appropriate. You can get away with "gonna" and "kinda" and "ain't." A character from the South can say "y'all" if it fits. A laconic New Englander can say "yup" (though you risk offending those readers who are sure it's pronounced "ayup" or "ayuh").

Instead of creating phonetics, set up your readers' expectations—prepare them to hear what you want them to hear—with a few choice words of description about how the character speaks. For example:

Bill was a cranky old bastard with a slow way of drawing out his words that turned his Maine accent into self parody.

She had a high voice made even more shrill by the precise, almost British, way she enunciated every word.

He had a thick Texas drawl peppered with folksy expressions that he'd picked up from his mother . . . or, more likely, his mother's maid. [When you make a promise like this, however, you'd better deliver the folksy expressions in the ensuing dialogue.]

Now here is a sample of dialogue with an extra-terrestrial from my short story "Iridescence." The alien (a Lyrin) and the human narrator are introducing themselves. The human has been delirious from a poisonous sting, and the Lyrin has been caring for him, but this is their first chance actually to converse. The Lyrin speaks first:

"This one is Ayer," he said solemnly.

"Ayer," I repeated, trying to voice the y and roll the r as he had. He bowed again, then waited.

"Jensin Lord," I said. I realized this was a ceremony for him, this trading of names. I kept my voice grave and bowed.

"Jensin Lord," he repeated. He softened the j, but it sounded fine. "This one is Jensin Lord. . . . It is a long name."

Notice that I characterize the alien's accent through the human's ears: the voiced y, the rolled r, and the softened j. Notice also the alien's passive phrasing, and the way he refers to himself and the human as "this one." He speaks English very well, but his native language does not have the pronouns "I" or "you," nor does it have any verb tenses for that type of direct address. Individuals are always referred to as "this one" or "this Ayer," as in, "this one, he is thirsty," instead of "I am thirsty" or "I thirst." This reflects behavior patterns in the Lyrin culture: No individual ever puts himself or another individual forward. The individual is always secondary to the group, and that is reflected in the language.

Here is another sample, closer to home. The speakers are native-born Vermonters with, at most, high school educations. They're "woodchucks," local slang for rednecks, and they'd be the first to admit it. The excerpt is from my story "Roadkill":

"That's a pretty funny notion, Bun," I said when I had it straight. "You telling me that fox is helping the other animals cross the road?"

"Yeah."

"You mean, like skunks and squirrels?"

"Yeah."

"Foxes eat squirrels, Bun."

"Not this one."

I had to sit a minute on that one, too. Then I asked him, "You seen this?"

"What do you think? I'm making it up?"

"Well, I don't know. It's a pretty damn strange idea, that's all."

"You're telling me?"

Notice how the speakers drop the leading "are" and "have" from compound verbs in the questions "You telling me . . ." and "You seen this?" Notice, also, that one of them uses "pretty" twice, in "a pretty funny notion" and "pretty damn strange." These are common usages among my neighbors. I also threw in the local idiom, "I had to sit a minute on that one." Notice, though, that I used "yeah" instead of "ayuh" or some other pseudo-phonetic spelling. There is no way to reproduce realistically on paper the way these men would say that word. So I used "yeah," which is more or less universally accepted as American slang for "yes" and fits any accent.

"Roadkill," by the way, is first-person, the narrator being one of the men in the conversation above. Naturally, the narration has to be in his voice. Here are a couple of paragraphs:

Bun was already backing out of the dooryard, but I grabbed the handle and yanked the door open and jumped in. He swung it around and fired it out of there with me flapping in the breeze. The door slammed on my leg and left a bruise, but I got myself pulled in finally.

I asked him, "You want me to drive?"

He didn't even answer, just floored it down the road. So we cruised nowhere for an hour or so. Didn't see any fur neither, flat or walking. Bun was tensed up like a dog before a thunderstorm, speeding up and slowing down and looking out into the fields more than he watched the road. I decided it'd be a good idea to use my seat belt.

The narrator's voice is consistent, in the narration and in the dialogue. And though it's subtle—and therefore unobtrusive—the accent is there in the word choice, phrasing, local grammar, and idioms. He may be from Vermont, but he speaks with his own alien voice.

❑ 50

WHAT MAKES A GOOD SPY THRILLER?

BY MAYNARD ALLINGTON

I RECENTLY HEARD A JOURNALIST WHO SHOULD KNOW BETTER GIVE some bad advice to a group of aspiring writers who wanted to know how to write a novel. Pounding his fist on the podium, he replied, "Put a sheet of paper into your typewriter and start writing!" That's a bit like telling someone interested in bullfighting to grab a cape and go into the ring. The bull, of course, has his own theory about what will ensue.

Writing a novel is not so different from going into battle. You are facing a long campaign. Before you mount your first offensive, certain logistics have to be in place.

Amateur writers generally ignore this. In their eagerness to write, they lay down a barrage of words on the computer screen the moment an idea strikes. You may produce four or five good chapters before the screen goes blank from writer's block—the battle fatigue of amateur novelists.

What essentials must be in place before you begin writing? The three most important are premise, plot, and character.

The critical first step common to all novels has to be the selection of a *premise*. Not just any premise, but one strong enough to carry a story line through three or four hundred manuscript pages. Don't confuse premise with theme. The theme of *The Caine Mutiny* (perhaps the most *technically* perfect novel in 20th century literature) is of a young man coming of age in war. The premise is far more sweeping. A naval crew at sea finds itself under the command of a paranoid captain whose instability leads to a mutiny during a typhoon, and to the subsequent court martial of the officer who relieved him of his post.

Novels that bore the reader invariably lack a strong premise, and they end up as rejects, so choose your premise carefully. Ask yourself two questions: Is your premise *big* enough to carry a novel, and is it *believable*?

The premise of my novel *The Grey Wolf* builds out of an abortive military coup by a cadre of senior Soviet officers against Stalin in 1942. What would be the consequences if British Intelligence were secretly involved in the conspiracy?

Clearly, this premise is big enough to support a multitude of chapters and a large cast of characters. But is it credible? A strip search of history isn't required, only a simple frisk. It yields some relevant facts: There was, indeed, a failed assassination attempt on Stalin in 1942 in Moscow; the fact that political commissars could, and often did, countermand orders in the field caused deep discontent in the Soviet officer corps; and finally, it is known that Churchill was an outspoken and bitter enemy of communism from the time of the Bolshevik Revolution.

All of this evidence is enough to validate our premise. Time to move on to the next step in the process: plot.

I am often asked, "Do you start out with characters, or with a plot?" The truth is, these generally develop at the same time. A plot in its purest form is a story line choreographed along what Truman Capote has called that "great demanding arc" of beginning, middle, and end. Obviously, you must have some idea of your key characters before you can construct your plot.

At this juncture in *The Grey Wolf,* I knew the lead character would be a British Intelligence officer. Waiting for him in Moscow would be his Soviet NKVD counterpart. I had a vague idea for a heroine who would play a role in the assassination attempt on Stalin. I knew the assassin would be a staff briefing officer who would have routine access to the Soviet leader inside the Kremlin. I had no idea what these characters looked like. They were only mock-ups standing in for the real characters who had not yet reported to the set.

The plot, too, was still unformed. I had yet to figure out how to get Churchill and the British SIS (Special Intelligence Service) involved in the conspiracy. The action, I knew, would move from London to Murmansk, then on to Moscow by rail. The coup would, of course, fail. At that point the Churchill government would abandon its agent, who would be captured, interrogated in Lubyanka prison, and would later escape. The last long section of the novel would involve a chase north to Archangel where the climax would take place after a German air raid.

Now there is a certain form to what I have just described—the shadow of a beginning, middle, and end—but it is far from a plot. It resembles more the sequences of a film script, which must be broken down into scenes, or in the case of a novel, into chapters.

The next step, then, is to develop a chapter outline showing exactly how and where your events will unfold. Having an outline doesn't mean you won't encounter small diversions that force you to improvise on your plan, but it embodies your strategic vision.

As you work on a chapter outline, never forget that conflict is the fuel of a novel. It may be physical conflict, goal-oriented conflict, sexual conflict, or even self-conflict, but it *has* to be there in some form. Even in the planning stage you must measure every chapter against that standard. If conflict is not evident, eliminate the chapter.

Now that you've finished your chapter outline, you're ready to start writing, right? Wrong. Your characters aren't in place. Remember those cardboard characters we left stranded in the plot? Time to summon the real cast for a dress rehearsal.

Inept spy novelists have a tendency to draw their heroes and villains from a roster of clichés. How many CIA and KGB agents in fiction are duplicates of each other? In a setting where the focus is on action, it's easy to lose track of the human factor.

This brings us to a classic model of spy fiction—Graham Greene's *The Ministry of Fear,* set in London during the blitz. After half a century in print, it's still a prototype to be studied for all the elements I have mentioned so far, especially character.

Chapter One finds Arthur Rowe drawn to a small street fair in Bloomsbury. Rowe is a troubled man. The *fête* holds comfortable childhood associations for him, so as dusk approaches, he lingers among the stalls and bunting. Some women have baked a chocolate cake with real eggs and butter (a rarity in wartime Britain) to raise money for war relief. It will go to the person who can give the closest estimate of its weight. A guess costs sixpence. What we don't yet know is that the cake contains a capsule of microfilm.

Rowe enters a fortuneteller's booth to have his palm read. In the course of their talk, he innocently blurts out a phrase that is, in fact, a coded response. The fortuneteller informs him it is the cake that he wants, and gives him the weight. Rowe acquires the cake about the time the real spy is rushing into the fortuneteller's booth. Rowe has walked off with microfilm in a cake meant for a German spy.

An ordinary novelist would have let the action take over from there. But Greene is no ordinary novelist. Now we learn why Arthur Rowe is a troubled man. He has killed his terminally ill wife, whom he loved, and has never come to grips with his own actions. This is his *psychological* characterization, an element many writers overlook. It is what sets Arthur Rowe apart from the standard hero in the standard thriller. He is a complex figure who could have stepped out of a literary novel.

Another model worth examining is *The Spy Who Came in From the Cold,* arguably John Le Carré's best novel. The opening sentence jerks us to attention. Alec Leamas is waiting at a West German checkpoint in Berlin for an East German defector to come across. It's a dark, icy October night, the zone lit by arc-lamps. Finally, the defector, Karl, appears, walking his bicycle across the no-man's-land between the checkpoints. Midway, sirens peal and powerful searchlights come on. Karl tries to run but is cut down as Leamas watches. Leamas knows that his man has been betrayed by an East German agent named Mundt. Karl is the last agent in Leamas's network, all of whom have been eliminated by Mundt. Leamas is through, and realizes it.

Chapter Two opens with Leamas on a plane bound for London. Le Carré now gives us a physical description of Leamas and tells us a great deal about him, this in third-person narrative from the novelist's point of view. It's the technique an amateur might use, but Le Carré makes it work. How? Because of the selectivity of the information. He uses no clichés. Then, through Leamas's own self-reflection, we get a picture of a tough, embittered, burnt-out spy who is all but finished. Finally, we see him through the eyes of a stewardess serving him a drink. Three views of Alec Leamas—each different, but giving the reader a three-dimensional character.

I have used these two examples because they illustrate such opposite approaches to characterization. Arthur Rowe's physical description is deliberately vague. His character is projected through his psychological frame of mind. So are the background description and action. Greene forces the reader to experience everything through the eyes of a man tortured by his own role in the mercy killing of his wife. Premise, plot, and character were never more masterfully entwined.

The facets of character I have discussed here so far must be set in your mind before you write the first sentence of your novel. Until you have absorbed your characters totally, you can't make them act and speak credibly. Don't forget that dialogue, apart from moving a story forward, can also serve to *develop* the character you have created in your mind. For example, an early scene in *The Grey Wolf* has an SIS officer named Rosewall trying to recruit the lead, Antony Ryder, into British Intelligence. The scene takes place in a London Pub:

"That's the problem," Rosewall went on. "Your file doesn't tell me anything. A chronology of events, that's all it is. I don't really know much about you at all. Nobody does. I find that rather curious . . ."

"How?"

"Because most people leave clues behind in their relationships with other people. You appear to have had no relationships. Would it interest you to know that most of your instructors at university didn't remember you?"

"It wouldn't matter to me one way or the other."

"What does matter to you?"

"Nothing in particular."

"I rather imagined you were a bit young to be that cynical."

"It's not cynicism."

"Then what would you call it?"

"I wouldn't call it anything."

This is only a small excerpt of dialogue, but it illustrates how well this device can work. Rosewall is telling us a great deal about Antony Ryder. And in the *tone* of his responses, Ryder is telling us a great deal about himself.

Premise, plot, and character. Once you have them in position, you're ready to begin your novel. You may still have problems to solve as you write, but you will have launched a successful plan of attack.

But wait! I almost forgot. I wanted to tell you how a spy thriller differs from a literary novel. Answer: It doesn't. Every great thriller has the architecture of a literary novel. The best of these works transcend category. They soar away from a specific genre into that mysterious landscape of great literature where books never die.

□ 51

SERIES CHARACTERS: LOVE 'EM OR LEAVE 'EM

BY ELIZABETH PETERS

CONAN DOYLE LEARNED TO LOATHE HOLMES SO INTENSELY, HE TRIED to murder him. At the opposite end of the spectrum are such writers as Dorothy Sayers, whose affection for Lord Peter Wimsey has prompted a certain amount of rude speculation. What is it about series characters? Is there a happy medium between loving and loathing them? Do the advantage of series characters outweigh the disadvantages? Should you, if you haven't done so already, consider starting a series?

In addition to the non-series Barbara Michaels novels, I write three different series, featuring Jacqueline Kirby, librarian; Vicky Bliss, art historian; and the notorious Amelia Peabody, Victorian gentlewoman Egyptologist.

None of the novels in which these three characters first appeared was intended to be the beginning of a series. The reason the series developed is simple and crass: There was a demand. I don't know why publishers suddenly decided that series characters were "in." They had always been popular, as witness Holmes, Poirot, Wimsey, et al., but it was not until ten or fifteen years ago that interest resurfaced. Now, many mystery writers have a series character, and those who do not are being pressured to create one.

The demand of the market is important. If publishers aren't buying a particular type of book, there is not much point in writing it, except for your own satisfaction. However, it is a big mistake to write only for the market, and a bigger mistake to do something you detest simply for the sake of sales.

There are certain disadvantages to a series. It does limit the author to some extent; a given plot may not be suitable for your character. Another disadvantage is that you have to reintroduce the character in every book, and it requires some skill to tell a new reader what he needs to know without boring those who have read earlier books and without slowing the action. Publishers want series, but they also insist that each book stand on its own. This may not be literally oxymoronic, but it's darned hard to do.

However, this last problem is simply one of craftsmanship, and I find that the advantages of a series character far outweigh the disadvantages. Over the space of several books, you can develop the character far more richly and convincingly than is possible in one book, and I believe character has become increasingly important in the mystery novel. Readers are no longer satisfied with stereotypical robots—the Young Lovers, the Detective, the Sinister Lawyer, and so on. The most successful writers of the New Golden Age have succeeded in large part, not so much because of the ingenuity of their plots, but because readers like their characters and want to know more about them.

And, in my opinion, the author should feel the same way about the characters. If, as you hope, the series is a success, you are going to live with these characters for a long time. If you don't like them, they will get on your nerves, and you will either loathe them or become horribly bored by them. (Readers are less likely to become bored than you are. If they do lose interest in your characters, you will know about it; they will stop buying the books.) But there's no reason for you to take on a task you despise when, with a few relatively simple tricks, you can learn to enjoy your characters and look forward to the next visit with them. After writing seven books in the Amelia Peabody series, I am finding her and her family more fascinating every time around.

The most important thing is to begin by creating realistic characters. This may sound paradoxical when applied to Amelia, but in fact she is far less of a caricature than some readers believe. I had read an enormous number of contemporary novels, biographies, social histories, and travel books before I began writing the series, and there are many real-life parallels to Amelia's career, opinions, and behavior, as well as those of her eccentric husband, Emerson. Even Ramses, their catastrophically precocious son, is based to some extent on actual Victorian children, and, to an even greater extent, on normal boys of all eras who exhibit similar tendencies.

If the protagonists of the novel are properly conceived, they will behave consistently and comprehensibly. Of course this requirement is true of character development in general, but it is particularly important with series characters, whom the reader comes to know well. One useful result of consistently drawn characters is that you will find their personalities often determine the way the plot is going to develop. By now I am so familiar with the behavioral patterns of the Emersons that I have only to set up a situation and describe how they will inevitably react.

Just because a character is consistent, however, doesn't mean his behavior should always be predictable. In fact, seemingly irrational behavior makes a character more realistic; real people don't always behave sensibly either. Yet, if we examine the true motives that govern their behavior, we find it is not inconsistent, that we ought to have anticipated it. It is the author's task to establish this. The reaction you want from a reader is a shock of surprise, followed immediately by a shock of recognition: "Oh, yes, of course. I ought to have realized . . ." that despite her constant criticism of her son, Amelia would kill to protect him; that though Emerson complains about his wife's recklessness, he is secretly amused by and appreciative of her courage; that while Ramses sounds like a pompous little snob, he is as insecure as are most young children.

The best way of establishing character is through actions rather than words. This is particularly true if you are writing in the first person. Amelia describes herself as hard-headed and unsentimental, but it should be apparent by page ten of the first book in the series that she is a soft touch who acts on impulse, and then has to scramble desperately to find logical reasons for her actions.

But the smartest thing I did with the Amelia series wasn't done deliberately; it was pure serendipity, or luck, or as I would like to believe, "a writer's instinct."

Crocodile on the Sandbank, the first book in the series, ended like any conventional romantic mystery novel, with Amelia happily married to the hero. This should have been the end of the story; conventional literary wisdom maintains that the protagonist of a series should remain single and therefore open to further adventures, amatory and otherwise. But when I decided to resurrect Amelia, I had to resurrect Emerson as well. I mean, there he was. Worse—he and I had got Amelia pregnant. Emerson may have done it on purpose, but I certainly didn't. The demands of a husband interfere considerably with a heroine's activities as a detective; the demands of a baby are almost impossible to dismiss.

If I had intended *Crocodile* to be the first in a series, I wouldn't have been as specific about dates. Not only did Amelia inform the reader of her age (curse her!), but historical events mentioned in the book tied it to a particular year. As the series continued, there was no way I could get around this, or fudge the date of Ramses' birth, or keep him and his parents from aging a year every twelve months.

I decided to regard these developments not as limitations but as challenges. Could a spouse and a baby be advantages to a heroine, instead of the reverse?

There are two ways of dealing with a detective's spouse. The first and perhaps most common method is to make the spouse a minor character (babies are particularly useful in keeping wives in the background). I chose the second alternative: husband and wife operating as equal, active partners in a genuine team. Note that word *equal.* I wanted my readers to feel that it would be inconceivable for either Amelia or Emerson to function independently of the other.

Insofar as the romantic element was concerned. . . . Well, that was another challenge. I couldn't see any reason husband and wife shouldn't be enthusiastic lovers as well as affectionate, supportive mates, but in order to maintain the "sexual tension" editors are always demanding, the marriage had to be questioned, even threatened, periodically. Rivals who crop up from time to time keep both Amelia and Emerson on their toes (so to speak). In the Amelia novel *The Snake, the Crocodile and the Dog,* I resorted to an even more drastic expedient, which resulted in a severe, potentially destructive strain on their relationship. However, the real conflict stems from the personalities of the major characters themselves. Amelia's air of smug self-confidence conceals a painful inferiority complex, particularly with regard to her personal appearance. She'll always be jealous of more beautiful women, and Emerson will never stop wondering what *really* happened when his wife was in the clutches of her devoted admirer the Master Criminal. Their marriage will never be boring and neither of them will ever take the other for granted.

The birth of Ramses presented even greater difficulties, and more provocative possibilities. In the second book of the series, I hadn't quite come to grips with the difficulties, so I did what most writers do with inconvenient babies: I left Ramses at home and allowed his parents to continue their activities without him. By the third book, *The Mummy Case,* I was ready to cope not only with Ramses, but with the tripartite relationship.

During this novel, Ramses developed into one of the most perniciously obnoxious children in all of mystery fiction—or so I have been told. I'm rather fond of the poor little devil myself, and I do not respond politely to readers who want me to drown him. However, by the fifth book I decided he was getting a little out of hand, so I copied a device by another writer, and introduced two children who were so awful they made Ramses look sympathetic by comparison. They also forced Amelia to reevaluate her feelings for her son. He becomes a full and active participant in his parents' adventures, supplying both comic relief and much-needed assistance in critical situations. His participation stems naturally and inevitably from his own character traits, which are the result not only of heredity but of upbringing; as he matures he will undoubtedly play a larger and quite different part. His relationship with his parents will change as well; a young adult can't (or shouldn't!) be treated like a child.

So the baby, who might have been a liability, is developing into an individual with considerable future potential. Ramses is about to enter adolescence, and I await this development with much interest.

The minor characters who populate a series are almost as important as the protagonists, and this, I think, is another way in which the New Golden Age mysteries differ from those of the first Golden Age. Instead of a single sidekick or bumbling foil from Scotland Yard, the Emersons have acquired a group of friends, enemies, and hangers-on who form a pool from which I can draw: Gargery, the cudgel-wielding butler; Kevin O'Connor, the brash young reporter; Abdullah, the loyal foreman; Evelyn, Amelia's sister-in-law; Nefret, the golden-haired beauty who has won Ramses' adolescent heart; and above all, Emerson's hated rival, the Master Criminal. The utility of a cast of supporting characters should be obvious. Like the major characters, they have changed and developed during the course of the books, and their occasional reappearances add to the reader's feeling that these are real people with decided personalities and distinctive foibles.

This is why I do not anticipate ever becoming bored with my series characters. Like real people, they change. Like real people, they are not always predictable. I have a rough idea of what is going to happen to them, but I could not emulate Agatha Christie and write the last book in the series now. I don't know what the Emersons are going to do until they do it—but when they do it, I am not really surprised. "Of course. I should have known. . . ."

From a purely practical viewpoint, there is one simple way to avoid being bored by your series characters: Don't confine yourself to a single series. Some writers can do this; I don't believe I could. The Barbara Michaels novels give me the opportunity to use plot ideas that don't fit any of the series characters, and the two other series I write as Elizabeth Peters allow me to employ themes and interests unsuited to Amelia and company.

To a lesser extent—probably because I have written less about them—Vicky and Jacqueline are also maturing and changing. Jacqueline has become a best-selling writer of romances, a development she regards with a distinctly jaundiced eye, and somewhere in her background there is a Mr. Kirby. Who is he and what happened to him? Some day I may find out.

As for Vicky, she's not getting any younger, and when I began *Night Train to Memphis,* I decided it was time for Vicky to sort out her feelings, not only for the dashing Sir John Smythe, but for her exasperating but engaging boss, Herr Direktor Schmidt. By the time I finished the book, I was a trifle surprised, and decidedly intrigued, to discover how Vicky, as well as John and Schmidt, have changed since they first appeared on the literary scene.

And that, dear Reader (to quote Amelia), is the real trick. Let your characters grow; allow them to mature and develop; put them into situations that will force them to exhibit hitherto unsuspected aspects of their personalities. The other day I was talking with a friend who inquired interestedly, "Is Vicky going to get pregnant in this book?" My reaction was instantaneous, spontaneous, and, I am afraid, typical of the generation in which I was raised. "Pregnant?" I squawked indignantly. "She isn't even married!"

I am fairly sure Vicky's reaction would be, if not identical, equally indignant. But one never knows. At least *I* never know, and that's why I like writing about my series characters.

If you don't like yours and can't make them into people whose company you enjoy, be brutal. No, not that brutal; I do not recommend killing off major characters, no matter how much you detest them. You can be sure some of your readers have become attached to them and will resent you for bumping them off. Just ignore them for a while. Shrug and smile politely when readers ask when you are going to return to Harry or Jennifer or whoever. Start another series, with characters who do appeal to you. You may find, after enough time has elapsed, that Harry and Jennifer aren't as repellent as you thought. If they still don't appeal to you, let them languish in the limbo of forgotten literary figures. The bottom line is simple: Enjoy your characters or leave them alone.

❑ 52

SCIENCE FICTION THAT SELLS

BY MICHAEL A. BURSTEIN

SCIENCE FICTION DIFFERS FROM ALMOST EVERY OTHER FORM OF LIT-
erature in that the writer cannot make any assumptions about the
reader's expectations. When you begin to write a mainstream story
set in contemporary times, or a story set in a known historical period,
you can safely assume that the reader has some familiarity with the
background of the world, and you can build your story on that background.

But as a writer of science fiction, you have no such luxury. Almost
by definition, you can set your story anywhere or "anywhen." Even if
you set the story in "the future," different readers will have different
ideas as to what the future will hold. How, then, can a writer create
such a world? What kind of characters can be placed in that world,
and how can we possibly write stories that will seem authentic to
our readers?

I am a relatively new science fiction writer, with only two published
stories and two more sales to my credit. But I turned a critical eye to
my first published story, "TeleAbsence," to try to discern exactly what
made it a contender. What I discovered were some nearly universal
principles for constructing good science fiction.

"TeleAbsence" is about an inner-city child named Tony who sneaks
into a telepresence school using a pair of Virtual Reality glasses—or
"spex," as I call them—that he's stolen from another student. When
Tony puts on the spex, he takes on that student's image and persona
as far as the rest of the class is concerned. The school is heavenly,
compared to the dilapidated school Tony attends in New York City.
Students can "jack in" from all over the country and experience a
classroom environment that can be manipulated almost by pure
thought. Textbooks automatically adjust themselves to a student's
reading level, and the teacher can shake up the classroom to simulate

an earthquake. Tony is desperate to stay, but knows that it is only a matter of time before the teacher and the other students discover the truth.

From this description, you may already have ascertained what I consider the first and most important step in constructing good science fiction, and that is to start with a good *idea*. Science fiction is more idea-based than anything else. The idea for this story came from a comment I heard at a science fiction convention, that by the year 2000 everyone would have an electronic mail address. I wanted to point out that the recent explosion of the Internet into many people's daily lives did not mean free access to information for everyone. But, the basic concept I was interested in, the Internet, was no longer science fiction; it was real science.

So I extrapolated. Instead of the Internet, I created a system of Virtual Reality schools, which had originally been designed as a solution for violence in schools. Instead, the public money to fund them never materialized, and the technology was adopted by private school systems that could afford them. The analogy was solid, but subtle enough for the reader not to feel beaten over the head with my message.

Once I had my idea, I needed to develop the *characters* and *plot* that worked best for this idea. I tend to feel that plot and characters must always be developed together, and in science fiction they must be thought of in the context of the scientific or technological advance your story is about. As a general rule, when writing science fiction, you can get the characters out of your idea by asking the question, *Whom does this hurt?* No one cares to read about someone whose life is made happy by scientific advances; good science fiction comes from stories of everyday people dealing with technological developments being thrust upon them.

To illustrate the power of asking the question posed above, let me tell you about my original idea for character and plot. I briefly considered writing about a scientist who has a friend, a teacher, who is killed because of school violence. The scientist then goes on to develop the technology for telepresence schools, and all ends happily. I abandoned this idea after less than a page of writing, not only because it says the opposite of the message I wanted to get across, but because the story of a scientist solving a problem is a very old tradition in science fiction, bordering on cliché. Instead, I asked myself who would be hurt by the technological development of VR schools and realized that it would be those same students who were supposed to benefit from it. Not only did I have a better story, but I had dramatic irony and the ability to show the reader what these schools would be like—all by asking one simple question about character.

Also, in a good science fiction story, the characters should always be comfortable in their world, accepting situations that seem fantastic to the reader. The classic example is from the opening sentence of a Robert Heinlein novel: "The door dilated." None of the characters in this world of the future is surprised at the thought of a "dilating" door. Such doors are as commonplace in that world as hinged swinging doors are in ours. When we turn on a television set, we don't react by saying, "My God! Moving pictures and words are coming out of that little box!" Nor should your science fiction characters react to the everyday technology of their world.

In the same way, Tony in "TeleAbsence" understands exactly what the telepresence school is all about. Yes, he does have the thrill of discovering new things when he sneaks into the school, since he's never been to one before, but he is familiar with the concept. When the story begins, he is completely cognizant of the existence of the telepresence schools. He has heard about them all his life; they are as ubiquitous in his world as a jet airplane is in ours.

The overriding principle in creating a plot is that it must be based on the science fictional extrapolation of the story. In true science fiction, the story would fall apart if the science were removed.

There is no way that "TeleAbsence" could be about a child who sneaks into a regular school.

Beginning writers often commit this plot error in writing what is sometimes called a "space western." In such a story, a space patroller (sheriff) rides his spaceship (horse) around the galaxy (town), having shootouts with space pirates (outlaws), firing his laser pistol (six-shooter). *If a story does not need to be science fiction to work, then it is not science fiction and should not be written as such.*

Although the same should not be said about the way one works *conflict* into a science fiction story, putting elements of science fiction into it can make the conflict much more powerful. In "TeleAbsence," Tony is scared of being found out, but imagines he is safe because the

student whose spex he is using can't jack in without them. Then Tony
is confronted in a manner very suitable to science fiction, as is seen
in the following:

Tony was interrupted by a sharp buzz, and he looked up. At the front of
the classroom appeared an older man with thick grey hair. He headed straight
for Tony, a scowl on his face, and Tony looked down again, in fear.
  He heard Miss Ellis speak. "Mr. Drummond, what are you doing here?"
  The man didn't answer Miss Ellis. He went right up to Tony and said, "Give
them back! They're mine!"
  Tony shivered. It had been too good to last; now he was going to be found
out. This man was obviously Andrew's father, come to get the spex back.
  "Mr. Drummond!" said Miss Ellis, with an angry tone that was familiar to
Tony. "I would appreciate it if you would not interrupt my class to talk with
your son! Can't this wait until later?"
  "This is not me—I mean, this is not my son!" Mr. Drummond shouted.
  There was silence for a moment. Tony felt Miss Ellis move next to him and
Mr. Drummond. "What's going on?" she asked.
  "This kid stole my—I mean, my son's spex!"
  Tony looked up at Miss Ellis and saw her smile. Facing Mr. Drummond, she
said, "That's you, isn't it, Andrew?"
  For the first time since he appeared, "Mr. Drummond" looked uncomfort-
able. "Ummm, yeah, Miss Ellis. I had to use Dad's spex to jack in. Whoever
this is—" he pointed at Tony—"stole my own spex."
  "Ah-ha. Andrew, go home. I'll take care of this."
  "Ummm. You won't tell my Dad, will you? I don't want him to know that
I've been careless."
  "No. I won't tell him. Now go. I'll contact you later."
  The image of Andrew's father vanished, and Miss Ellis turned to Tony. He
was on the verge of tears.

We've seen how to develop the idea, plot, and characters for a science fiction story, but how do you explain the background of your
world so readers will understand and appreciate it? Above all, *avoid
the infodump,* an expository lump that does nothing but provide information. When contemporary characters make phone calls or fire guns
in a mainstream story, they don't stop to contemplate and explain the
technology to the reader. When characters avoid taking the subway or
walking through certain neighborhoods, they don't stop to deliver a
treatise on the sociological development of their hometown.
  But what about a science fiction story? I like to call the technique
painting tiny brushstrokes. I must admit that I cheated a little, as "Tele-
Absence" is set in a classroom, and therefore I can have the teacher
explain things to her students; that's a lot more logical than having a
22nd-century police officer deliver an interior monologue on the me-

chanics of his laser pistol while in hot pursuit. And even in the classroom, I tried to keep such explanations to a minimum. For example, here is an excerpt from a scene where the students are discussing their hometowns in class:

Since he knew Los Alamos better than East Lansing, Brian chose to talk about his original hometown instead of where he was now. Tony barely paid attention as Brian talked about the joys of small-town life and then displayed some pictures from a family photo album that he was able to pull up using his computer. Miss Ellis then discussed the arid mountainous area where the town was located, and how there had been a scientific laboratory there until the year 2010.

Janice went next, and again Tony was too scared to pay attention. Janice described San Francisco, and, possibly still thinking about lunch, mentioned the delicious seafood and sourdough bread. Miss Ellis talked about other things, such as the earthquakes that San Francisco had experienced, and the Golden Gate Bridge, which she said had been one of the longest suspension bridges in the country until the earthquake just last year that destroyed it. She showed three-dimensional video images of the earthquake, and even made the classroom shake up a bit, so the students could experience a bit of what an earthquake was like.

Notice the details that are merely implied. What kind of future has the closing of a major scientific laboratory? Why hasn't Miss Ellis mentioned an attempt to repair the bridge? These little details can make the world more realistic. Here's another example, later in the story:

The following Monday afternoon, Tony took the subway down to Greenwich Village. He had to show a pass at 96th Street in order to continue under the fence, but Miss Ellis had arranged everything.

That's all that's mentioned. Tony doesn't ruminate over recent history, nor does he explain to the reader why the fence is there and why he needs a pass to go downtown. But the frequent reader of science fiction can draw the appropriate conclusions.

There are two more important points for writing good science fiction. First, make sure you puzzle out all the consequences of the idea you are extrapolating before you sit down to write, or else some astute reader will wonder why, if there is a cure for death in your story, no one seems to mention the overpopulation problem. This is a major problem in TV science fiction such as *Star Trek*: If replicators can create anything people might need, why does there still seem to be a capitalist-based economy? Don't be guilty of this error.

Finally, if you want to write publishable science fiction, try to end on a positive note without losing sight of the story you're trying to tell. I wanted Tony to end up in the telepresence school, which would have been a happy ending, but that wouldn't have made my point. And the obvious, unhappy ending was for him to return to his old school. Instead, Miss Ellis takes him on as a private student in the afternoons. They don't have the advantages that the technology might give them, but the reader feels hopeful for the future. And that's the best way for a science fiction story to end.

❏ 53

BUILDING CONFLICT IN THE HISTORICAL ROMANCE

BY PATRICIA WERNER

CONFLICT, SET IN A COLORFUL BACKGROUND, IS WHAT DRIVES THE historical romance. Here are some of the techniques for weaving threads of conflict into a complex tapestry that will appeal to readers.

Plotting opposites

History itself offers barriers an author can use to create obstacles between lovers. One popular technique is having the hero and heroine on opposite sides of two warring factions (such as the North and South during the Civil War or the British and the Colonists during the American Revolution).

Another possible choice could be to make the main characters members of feuding families. Or they might be from different social classes or ethnic backgrounds. By using incidents in the story to show the characters' personal goals, you can bring them into conflict with each other. Such incidents move the plot forward.

For example, a railroad baron may want to buy a widow's land to lay track through the mountains. But the widow wants to hold on to her land because it's her son's birthright, and she promised her father she would never sell it. Or perhaps the land offers her a chance to prove that she can be a successful rancher.

In this plot, the railroad baron and the widow have different ideas for proper use of the land. But if, in spite of this conflict, the baron and the widow are attracted to each other, you have the set-up for a valid historical romance plot. Your challenge as the author is to let those two characters work out their conflicts and acknowledge their love by the end of the book.

Motivation and purpose

Motivation provides the reason your characters take certain actions.

Although in life people sometimes seem to do things for no apparent reason, your characters must act *with* reason, and their actions must be consistent with their personalities. Plant these reasons, or motives, either in the thoughts of the character, or in dialogue in which the character confides hopes, dreams, and secrets to another character. This will reveal your characters' motives and show the reader how and why the hero's and heroine's purposes are truly in conflict.

For example, in my historical romance *The Falcon and the Sword*, set in the early barbarian kingdoms of what later became known as France, the heroine, Judith, has attached herself to her childhood friend, a princess who has just married the king of Neustria. (Neustria, Austrasia, and Burgundy were Frankish territories in 567 A.D.) Judith's purpose is to protect the newly married princess from an evil, jealous concubine. Thus Judith's friendship with the princess *motivates* her to keep watch over her friend.

The hero, Marcus, is an envoy from the kingdom of Austrasia and his political purpose is to serve *his* king. The two kings are warring brothers. Judith finds herself in a position to act as a spy for Marcus. It would have been easy to end the book there and have him take her back to Austrasia. But being people bound by the moral code of the Franks called for a blood feud. Hence, when the princess is murdered, Judith's moral code *motivates* her to avenge her friend's death, keeping her apart from Marcus, whose purpose is to wage a war for his king.

Your characters' motives must be believable, and to achieve this credibility, you must put yourself into your characters' thoughts and get to know them. Try to live the scene as you write it, so you will know which motives are logical for each character. Ask yourself, does this character have a reason for his or her actions? Don't write anything that seems vague to you, or it will certainly seem even vaguer to your readers.

Emotional conflicts

Let emotional conflicts provide an undercurrent for the larger historical issues. Emotions draw the reader into a story. The characters react emotionally to the need to meet the social or political challenges of the plot, and this advances the story.

Here is how I showed social conflicts arousing emotions in *Velvet Dreams*: The impoverished Duke of Sunderland goes to America to seek an American heiress to pay his bills. He doesn't intend to marry for love. Socialite Amanda Whitney wants to marry only for love, so from the start their actions are at cross-purposes. Amanda's mother threatens to kill herself if Amanda marries the ne'er-do-well American whom Amanda is secretly pledged to, thus putting her under emotional pressure.

But Amanda has misjudged her American suitor, who jilts her. Her anger at the Duke's overt desire to marry her for money and her desire to prove her mother wrong motivate her to rebel and turn to a French scholar for solace. She is in conflict with the Duke, with her mother, and with the societal values with which she was raised. All of these conflicts provide excitement, danger, and action, which hold the readers' interest.

One man, one woman

When your hero and heroine fall in love with each other, they must be free of all ties. The one woman-one man historical romance is standard for the genre, which has well-defined conventions when it comes to love—though both hero and heroine may have had previous relationships or even marriages. They must not, however, indulge in romantic dalliances with anyone else *while their relationship is developing,* especially not after they have gone to bed together. Timing here is the key to emotional entanglement.

In some circumstances, it is permissible for the heroine to become romantically and physically involved with another man before falling in love with or consummating her relationship with the hero. This adds to the original conflict and makes the reader turn the pages to find out which man will win. But this should always be very carefully done and well motivated, or it will offend readers.

In *The Falcon and the Sword,* Judith takes a barbarian lover for protection. Though she cares for him, according to the conventions of historical romance, he has to leave or die before she can form a relationship with Marcus. Her barbarian lover is killed in battle; Judith grieves; Marcus rescues her from the Saxons. Only then, after a slow, emotional build-up, does their love take root, and they finally consummate their relationship.

Setting

Setting can provide another wedge between characters. Perhaps the heroine is in a place she despises, but she has to be there to carry out her mission. Or the place represents something from her past that must be avenged or purged. Her resentment of the hero may stem from the fact that he is so much a part of that place that he could never think of leaving. Or perhaps he cannot leave because he has responsibilities there.

In a historical romance, the characters may be sent on journeys, thus separating the hero and heroine for several chapters. In a novel this long, there is room for adventures. It is a convention of this genre that when hero and heroine are apart, they should continue to think of one another.

Complications

Complicate the conflicts wherever possible. Carefully weave together the historical, romantic, and goal-oriented conflicts. Every step the heroine takes toward *her* goal should inadvertently antagonize the hero or frustrate *his* goal. This action and reaction will advance the plot, but at the same time, you must draw the hero and the heroine deeper and deeper into their relationship. In spite of all their conflicts, make them care about what will happen to the other person if their own goal is met.

Push your heroine into such a tight corner that she has few choices that would help to get her out. Use motives that make for difficult choices. And the result of each choice should throw her back into the path, or arms, of the hero.

Secrets

Give either the hero or heroine a secret: One can wear a disguise to obtain information or to hide something. Here the conflict stems from the fact that the disguised character must pretend to be another person, at the same time wishing deeply to reveal the truth.

In my novel, *Cimarron Seductress,* Roslyn Dwayne, an ex-outlaw named Cimarron Rose, decides to leave the outlaw life. She goes to live in Indian territory with distant relatives who know nothing of her past. There, she is attracted to Marshal Luke McBride. But she learns to her horror that he is looking for Cimarron Rose, a woman he believes can lead him to the Doolin gang, who accidently killed his sister in a shootout during a bank robbery at Southwest City.

Can Roslyn admit that she is Cimarron Rose? No. Because by this point in the story, her uncle, who's lost his wife, has come to depend on her to take care of his sons, her cousins. If she tells the truth, she'll not only lose Luke but will also disappoint her new family. But she cannot live the lie forever. When an old crony of Doolin's shows up, saying that Doolin's been hurt, is nearby, and needs help, the old loyalty tears at her. The Doolin gang took her in when she was small—orphaned when her parents died in a train wreck. Bill Doolin taught her how to survive in a tough situation. Surely she owes him something, too.

Build the conflicts one on the other. You are not simply retelling a well-known historical event; you must entangle the central characters deeper and deeper into multiple plot conflicts. It must appear as if they cannot escape but of course they must. How does the author achieve this without jarring the reader or making one of the characters do such a sudden about-face that it appears ridiculous?

Make your characters undergo change. Plant the seed early on that the character actually wants to change, so that when it occurs, the change will be motivated. For example, Roslyn had already decided to become a law-abiding citizen *before* she met Marshal McBride. He had already decided to give up his badge and turn to ranching once the culprits were caught. So their resolution at the end seems convincing.

At the resolution of the story, self-revelation brings hero and heroine to accept their mutual love in spite of the difficult conflicts. Luke realizes that Roslyn really is no longer a woman on the wrong side of the law, that she acted as she did because of loyalty, not cowardice. He would want her to be no less loyal to him. Love conquers all? Yes, but it must do so in a believable and well-motivated way.

What about sex?

Make the passion sizzle while the conflicts grow. These two characters burn for each other, but they are in conflict with one another because of their opposing goals. Their inner conflict keeps them from acknowledging their love at first. Their passion for each other should be followed by denial, or a feeling of guilt, or anger. Sexual encounters as well as their arguments must ring true.

Most editors leave the number of love scenes and the degree of explicit sex up to the author. Historical romances are categorized by editors as sweet, spicy, or sensual. Sweet romances do not lack in sexual attraction that leads to passionate embraces; the characters may even go to bed together near the end of the novel—but the curtains are drawn.

Spicy romances take time out from plot developments and other adventures to present a few steamy scenes. Sensual romances have many explicit love scenes, but even so, they should be well integrated into the story line; each love scene—justified and well motivated—should intensify the conflict.

Length

Most historical romances run from 100,000 to 135,000 words. The novel must have a happy ending, otherwise it will be classified as a saga or mainstream historical novel. Your manuscript will be from 400 to 550 typewritten double-spaced pages, producing a book that will run from about 364 to 474 printed pages.

Do enough research to make the setting and story come alive in your mind, and to write a salable book, keep the conflict going till THE END.

❑ Nonfiction: Articles and Books

□ 54

Do's and Don'ts of Magazine Article Writing

By Donald M. Murray

THERE ARE EXCEPTIONS TO EVERY RULE IN WRITING: THE BEST WRITing often occurs when the experienced writer cuts across the grain of tradition. Most of us, however, have to know the "rules" and traditions to bend or break them. Here are some of the basics of magazine article writing that should be mastered *before* you bend them or break them.

Point of view

Your magazine article should have a strong point of view, express a vigorous opinion, important news, a revelation, an argument, an edge that answers the readers' questions: "Why should I bother to read this?" In writing magazine articles—unlike writing news stories—you shouldn't try to be on all sides of the subject, but should make clear to the reader what side you're on. Everything in your article should reflect that view.

The lead

A good magazine article doesn't need an introduction, so don't begin with the background of your subject, how you happened to get interested in it, why the reader should read it, or how you obtained the basic information for it. Begin your article with conflict that produces tension, often revealed by including a brief example or anecdote and problem that will be resolved at the end. It's a good rule to start as near the end as possible and then plunge your reader into the central tension. When you've involved your reader in this way, weave in background facts or information as you think the reader needs it to understand the purpose and point of your piece.

Authority

Early in your article, you should—briefly—establish your authority by revealing your connection with the theme of your article, including some specific, accurate information that will persuade your reader that you know your subject and have the right to be heard and trusted. A calm, confident voice will help you achieve this and will make the connection with the readers so they will say, "Yes, that's the way it is."

Voice

The voice of your article should be conversational: It's not a lecture, a sermon, or an attack, but rather, the voice of a friend discussing an issue you want to share with the readers. The intensity and tone of your voice is tuned to the subject and to your readers.

Selection and development

Don't include all the facts you've gathered in the course of your research, but make a careful—and ruthless—selection of the details that will fulfill the promise of your lead. Then develop your lead fully so your readers will recognize its significance. You can't get away with writing "it was a disturbing experience," but must explain in detail what disturbed you, how and why and what it means in the context of your article. You have to do more than summarize: You must show why and how it was disturbing and what is the importance of the shock or surprise.

Exposition and pace

Keep readers moving forward so they won't lose interest, but slow the pace when you feel that the readers need time to absorb and reflect on what has been written. You can achieve this variety of pace by weaving necessary exposition into the text, tucking factual sentences into your paragraphs. But don't ladle the facts or information you think necessary onto the readers in huge servings; dole it out in spoon-sized portions.

Sequence

Through your narrative, take your reader on a journey from lead to ending. The sequence or order of your narrative depends on your knowing how to make the article most effective. This will not necessarily follow the order in which you experienced the events or story you are relating. Magazine articles distort time for effect. If you are using chronological order, you should not record what you say evenly—sixty minutes to the hour, twenty-four hours to the day. Sometimes you have to recount the events of a war, for example, describing weeks of boredom, punctuated by seconds of terror. As an article writer, you should skip over the boredom—unless *that* is the subject—and develop and expand the moments of terror.

Transitions

Use as few transitions as possible. Give readers the information you think they need when you think they need to know it. Anticipate and answer the readers' questions when you feel they would be raised. I used to write articles one paragraph to a page, and later rearrange them in the order the reader would need to know them. I never had to write a transition like, "Meanwhile, back at the ranch. . . ."

Faces

Readers like to read about people who express ideas, theories, concepts, issues. They walk on the page, talk, confront each other, engage in dialogue; they reveal themselves through physical actions—not "he was fat," but "the floor sagged when he stepped into the room," and vocally through direct quotes: Not, "he talked about the problems of school funding," but, "I was learned by chalk and blackboard. I don't need no computer to help my kid graduate from high school."

Sources

Use live as well as written sources. When you bring those authorities on the page, they speak directly to your readers and help convince them of the validity of your article's theme.

Endings

Don't end your article with a formal conclusion that tells readers what you've said, what the article means and how they should react. It's too late at this point to explain the significance of your article, too late to command readers to think or feel a particular way. The most effective ending gives readers information—a quotation, a statistic, a fact, a scene, an anecdote—that will make them think and feel.

❏ 55

WRITING AND SELLING PERSONAL EXPERIENCE ARTICLES

BY MOIRA ALLEN

PERSONAL EXPERIENCE ARTICLES OFTEN MAKE UP 75% OR MORE OF A typical magazine's unsolicited submissions, yet they are the least likely to be accepted.

The reason is that typical personal experience pieces are "articles about *me,* the author." What editors are looking for, however, is "articles about *you,* the reader."

Look at the table of contents of any information-oriented magazine, and you'll see what I mean. Note how many titles include phrases like "how to" or "how you can." Editors are looking for articles that will help readers improve their lives, relationships, skills, or knowledge. For most magazines, such "service" pieces make up 80% to 90% of the editorial content.

That can create some pretty tough odds. For example, if an editor could purchase only ten articles per month out of 100 submissions, a personal experience piece might have a 1-in-75 chance of acceptance— while a service article's chances could be as high as 9-in-25. (Of course, the reality is far worse: Editors receive far more than 100 articles per month, and may purchase fewer than 10.)

But you can beat those odds. You can lift your personal experience article out of the slush pile by offering an editor the best of both worlds: A personalized service piece. To do this, you must ask yourself how your experience relates to the reader. For example:

• Is this an experience the reader may wish to share or enjoy?
• Is this an experience from which the reader can learn or benefit?
• Is this an experience the reader might wish to avoid?
• Is this an experience that will help the reader cope with a difficult problem or situation?

Experiences to share

Perhaps you've achieved a success or a goal, or simply had a good time. Would others want to do the same? If so, you can tell them how!

For example, perhaps you've just come back from a great vacation. So tell your readers about it: Most travel articles are basically personal experience pieces. But they must be written in a way to become the reader's experience as well—either vicariously, or by enabling the reader to duplicate the experience.

If you spent your vacation at a fascinating destination, tell readers how to get there, what to see, where to find the best lodging, or what to expect from the culture or environment. Tailor your account to the audience you're trying to reach: Your readers will want to know about the most challenging hiking trails, the best restaurants, or how to get a bargain in the shops or bazaars. Or you could focus your article on little-known details of an exotic culture, or the nuts and bolts of making travel and hotel arrangements.

Describing the service aspects broadens the market dramatically. A piece on your "best camping trip ever" can discuss equipment and supplies for one magazine, the "ten best campgrounds" in a particular region for another, or how to get the kids unplugged from their computer games and into the great outdoors. In short, you should be asking yourself not only how the reader can benefit from your experience, but how many different types of readers might be able to benefit.

Your experience should be one that a reader would like to share in the future. Readers are interested in new experiences, in things they might want to do—and you should try to show them how!

Experiences that enrich

If any single focus dominates the article market, it is "how to improve your life." Self-improvement themes pervade magazines of every description: How to improve your health, well-being, inner self, relationships, careers, skills, homes, hobbies. Nothing attracts a reader like the promise that an article will make life *better.*

To tap into this market, explore areas in your life that you have made better or have made you better. Topics may range from the deeply personal (overcoming a fear, meeting a challenge) to the seemingly trivial (brightening your work area with potted plants). Any improvement that you've made in your own life could be one that others would like to emulate.

Suppose, for example, that you've recently quit the corporate rat-race to become a full-time free-lance writer. Presumably, that was a quality-of-life decision (I've never read an article about someone joining the *corporate* world to improve his quality of life!). Your article could discuss not only why you did it, but how—including the advantages and disadvantages of such a decision.

On the positive side, has your decision led to more quality time with family, more freedom to control your life and destiny, more opportunities to enjoy the "little things" like gardens and sunsets and the freedom to linger over your morning coffee? On the down side, how do you cope with the difficulties involved in developing good work habits without the incentive of external deadlines, the lack of social interaction and office lunches, the anxiety of having no secure paycheck or benefits? Such an article could serve the needs not only of other writers but anyone who is self-employed or a telecommuter.

Self-improvement articles don't necessarily have to be based on life-changing experiences. In many cases, an area of your life that *hasn't* changed can also be the basis of an excellent article. For example, is your relationship with your spouse running smoothly, with few hassles or arguments? Are your children well-behaved, getting good grades and staying off drugs? How do you account for it?

It's easy to overlook aspects of our lives that are going well, because these don't call attention to themselves. If something is going well in your life, however, keep in mind that thousands of potential readers wish they could say the same. They'd love to know your secrets for a successful relationship, or your tips on how to raise happy and well-adjusted children. If you've learned from an experience, show readers how they can learn from it.

Experiences to avoid

Sometimes the experiences from which we learn the most are the negative ones. Writers don't simply learn from their mistakes; they write about them. At least, they should! Experiences that you wish you could have avoided, that taught you a valuable (or painful) lesson, make wonderful service articles. What would you have done differently, if only you had known then what you know now? What steps would you take, what preparations would you make, to avoid the consequences of your experience?

Readers willingly pay to listen to your good advice. Through personal experience articles, you give advice by the page, colored by your own vivid account of what can happen if that advice is not heeded. While it's too late for you to avoid the difficulties you encountered, it's never too late to help others do so.

Unpleasant experiences don't necessarily lead to unpleasant articles. Someone once said that comedy equals tragedy plus time: The best time to write about your experience is when you're finally able to look back on it and laugh. The resulting article will be both helpful and entertaining.

Remember that disastrous family hiking trip you took in the Mega-Bugga Woods, when your dog broke its leash and tangled with a skunk, when you got the worst sunburn of your life, and your child became a hands-on expert at identifying poison ivy? By the end of the day, you might have sworn never to set foot on another hiking trail again. By the time your sunburn began to fade, however, you knew you had an article.

Readers will laugh at your horrified reaction as your "beskunked" dog returns to frolic with you—and will learn about hiking safety for pets (including the equipment every hiker needs when taking pets on the trail). They may wince at the description of your sunburn, but they'll be glad to know what sort of protective clothing a hiker should wear, as well as the types of first-aid supplies to bring along. Add a sidebar on how to identify toxic plants, and you'll have an article that could find a market in family magazines, travel publications, even pet magazines.

Of course, not every unpleasant experience lends itself to such light-hearted treatment. Some are more serious and should be handled carefully and with sensitivity. Yet even potentially devastating experiences can often be avoided with the proper precautions. If you've suffered through such an occurrence, you will be providing a valuable service to others by putting those precautions on paper.

Some painful or traumatic experiences cannot be avoided; they can only be endured. When someone faces a tragedy or loss, he or she will want to hear from someone who has been through a similar experience, how it feels, what can provide comfort. That's the big difference between a "coping" article written by an expert, and one written by an ordinary person (like you) who has been there, endured, and somehow managed to pull your life together again. Experts have good advice (which you may be able to incorporate into your article), but your personal experience "humanizes" that advice and makes it meaningful to the reader.

Writers will never run out of markets for articles on how to cope with grief, trauma, or loss, because people will never cease to experience these things. And because traumatic events affect different people in different ways, even within a single family unit, an effective article can reach many different markets. For example, suppose you are writing about the trauma of losing a job. You might choose to focus on how this experience affected you, the family provider who is suddenly unemployed. You might write an article on how you coped with your feelings of anger, loss, helplessness, and frustration, or about the steps you took to find a new job. Or you might deal with issues of financial adjustments, or how to find support—financial or emotional—during your job hunt.

Your article options don't end there, however. Unless you have no one to support but yourself and your cat, the loss of your job will affect others as well. How did it affect your spouse—and how did your spouse's response help (or hinder) your own recovery? How did it affect your children, not only emotionally but in terms of the change in financial status? What could a reader do to help other family members cope, and how can family members themselves help?

Any type of loss, large or small, raises issues and emotions that must be dealt with, either as an individual or as a family. By using your own experience as the basis for a service article, you send the message that resolution and recovery are possible: One *can* take steps to work through the event and rebuild one's life, because you've done it and told how.

Using experiences wisely

Once you've decided what experiences you want to write about, another question you must answer is how to present the problem and solution. While there are many ways to use one's experiences effectively in an article, these four are perhaps the most common:

• **As a framework** to support the factual information. Use your experience as a vehicle for the information you've gathered from expert sources, such as interviews or research. Show how that information affected, or is reflected in, your own experience. Use phrases like "we learned" or "we discovered" instead of "experts say."

• **As anecdotal material** to support and illustrate the factual information. Use the factual information as your framework and highlight each point with an example or illustration from your experience.

• **As an anecdotal lead and conclusion.** Some articles begin and end with an anecdote (e.g., "When Mary's house burned down, she had no idea that her troubles were just beginning. . . ."). The body of the article, however, may be purely factual and include few personal details. Writers often invent this sort of anecdotal material, but such inventions generally feel "faked." Editors largely prefer the real thing.

• **As a sidebar.** You may prefer to restrict your primary article to the facts, and use the personal experience elements as a sidebar to illustrate and enhance those facts. Another approach is to use the factual material as a sidebar to the personal story. (This works particularly well when your material lends itself to a list format.)

Some final tips

Besides asking yourself how the experience relates to the reader, you must also ask yourself how *you* relate to the experience. For example:

• **The experience must be over.** If you don't know how the story ends, you're not ready to write about it. If an event is painful, you need sufficient time and distance to gain some "closure" before you're ready to write about it for others. Wait until you've reached a point of resolution; then you can help readers reach it as well.

• **Provide a solution.** Readers want to know how to change things, fix things, make things better. If your conclusion is that life will never get better, choose another subject.

• **Offer the reader an attainable goal.** If your idea of the perfect vacation is to climb Mt. Everest, that's fine—but the experience may find a rather limited readership. Offer readers an experience they can attain, and offer specific steps to help them attain it.

• **Present evidence that your suggestions work.** If, for example, you're describing "Ten Ways to Get Your Novel Published," you'd better have published a novel! Either describe steps that worked for you, or the advice of experts that has been shown to work for others.

Whatever approach you choose, it's the "been there, done that" element that will bring your article to life. Editors are eager for articles that combine useful, factual information with the warm, human touch of experience. Turning your story of "what I did" into an article on "how you can do it" is one of the best ways to save your material from the slush pile.

❑ 56

WRITING HUMAN
INTEREST ARTICLES

BY JANET FABYANKOVIC
AND CATHERINE PIGORA

WRITING HUMAN INTEREST ARTICLES REQUIRES HAVING A PASSION FOR people and their unique stories. You are not only giving readers factual information, such as a person's lifestyle, tragedies, or secrets, but allowing them to see what goes on through the eyes of others. Numerous women's and religious magazines are excellent publications to target with queries of real life dramas or people narratives.

Media professionals often look to other communication sources for ideas, or draw on personal human interest stories in local or national newspapers or magazines. Recently, both print and visual media have been saturated with true-life dramas in which women or children are abused, kidnapped, acquire rare diseases or are betrayed by society, the legal system, or by men.

Many first-time writers became published when they presented accounts of how they faced and overcame adversity in columns such as "Drama in Real Life," featured in *Reader's Digest*. Mothers often become published authors when they write about their personal experiences raising a physically challenged child, surviving a marital storm, or coping with a cancer diagnosis.

It's important to find and write a chronicle that most readers can relate to, even if they haven't encountered the same situation. Although a reader may not be a grandmother who lost a grandchild when her son was divorced, she can relate to the loneliness, despair, and other similar emotions a person deals with during separation or loss.

Disaster stories provide another outlet for tales of ordinary people who become empowered with strength and courage by an extraordinary experience. If you write about a father who saved a child in an airplane crash, or a dog who rescued a baby during a fire, try to find a slant that is unique, especially if the story was covered numerous times in print and on television.

Because of their busy schedules, reporters often don't do a follow-up on original stories. Many times, incidents that occur after a heroic event have as much impact as the original piece. Or the subject may present a new perspective on the event after having time to digest it.

One teenager who risked his life saving a friend from gang violence later becomes a police dispatcher to assist with crime cases; a couple adopted a five-year-old girl whom they saved from a fire after discovering that her whole family was killed in the tragedy.

Many article writers study national trends and issues, then find a local angle that has universal appeal. With child abuse a current topic, well-written pieces that focus on a nearby shelter for battered children or a profile of an outstanding counselor may appeal to editors.

A writer may decide to collaborate with another writer, especially if both authors have a different specialty or flair that enhances an otherwise ordinary manuscript. When you face writer's block, enlisting another writer may be a good solution and add a new point of view to your piece. At an interview, two writers may have different observations or one writer may ask questions that the other might have missed or not thought of at the time.

Make sure to have a few questions jotted down for reference, but once the interview begins, don't be afraid to be spontaneous and ask spin-off questions from comments that surface in discussions. No one knows exactly what will take place during the interview. Being flexible yet professional will put the interviewee at ease. Always be considerate if a person responds with tears, anger, or a request for privacy on certain issues.

Where do you find ideas for a human interest story? Fortunately, they are easy to spot, since most people have a personal story to tell. Scan newspapers, television segments, journals, magazines, videos, or computer systems for a start. Or contact local schools, government stations, organizations, and other institutions and ask to be placed on their mailing list for releases, newsletters, and bulletins.

By perusing such publications, you may come across a story idea that could be pitched to a national magazine or journal using a different slant. For example, a feature from a hospital newsletter about a blind lady who saved a suicide victim's life on the internet was reworked and submitted to a national journal seeking accounts of emergency rescues. Written from a crisis perspective, it was immediately accepted and published.

Many writers get story ideas at bus stops, from visits to social agencies, and chats with friends or relatives. If your specialty is medical or social issues, it's imperative to develop a link with a physician or attorney. Specialized writers, such as entertainment critics, often use human interest stories as sidebars to a related article, especially when local children or adults have been involved.

After coming up with an idea, appropriate research is imperative for background, proper spellings of names and places, and additional information that will enhance your article. If your topic (such as a rare disease) is unusual and many readers may be unfamiliar with it, you should include a description of symptoms and diagnosis for its characteristics to allow medical perspective.

Once you select your subject, write an article lead that will attract the reader's attention. For example, if the story is based on an abused woman, try to create an intense, active scene as your beginning. ("As she came out of unconsciousness with blood dripping down her face, Jessica couldn't believe that the man she married only two months ago did this to her.")

Let the story unfold naturally. Remember to be patient and sensitive to the people you interview, allowing them to reveal what happened in their own way and time. Try to imagine yourself in the subject's place, and don't ask any questions that might be too upsetting, unless the person being interviewed brings up the delicate topic (or welcomes any questions.) Several writers give their interviewees the option of answering only the questions that they may feel comfortable with. Although these journalists are respected, occasionally their articles are rejected by publications that prefer a more probing approach for greater emotional impact. Obtain publication guidelines before submitting queries or articles, to determine exact editorial focus.

Capturing the mood of the story can make your article more compelling. As you describe an athlete who wins a tournament while battling the effects of leukemia, make the words active to set the pace of the event. However, if you're describing a daughter's last goodbye to her mother in a hospice, sensitivity is a must.

By spending a little extra time with the person after the interview, a writer can obtain quotes and facts that will add the extra human touch to the article. The main character must be someone whom the readers will care about and can identify with. It isn't a fast-paced, "just the facts, ma'am" piece.

Treat your subject with respect so that in revealing the story you don't offend the person who trusted you with his or her personal life. An article on suicide can be serious and poignant without being depressing. Often people grant interviews in hope of helping others prevent or cope with a similar situation. Celebrities and officials sometimes risk revealing their own or their family's weaknesses as a stepping stone to their own recovery, as in the case of Betty Ford, who helped thousands recover from addictions. Assure those you interview that you will write an inspirational, informative piece, not an exposé.

Writers who are determined to make a literary mark or spotlight a social issue may disguise themselves as a homeless lady, elderly person, or prisoner to illustrate what it's really like to "walk in their shoes." They're able to add suggestions and present possible solutions to problems that their subjects face.

Not all human interest stories are traumatic. In fact, some writers recognize that tragic stories are often too complicated or emotional for their tastes, so they concentrate on writing upbeat narratives and profiles. Their writing repertoire might include a four-year-old child who charms the audience with her singing and dancing, a farmer who makes friends with a wild pheasant, or the story behind a circus, regatta, or concert. Occasionally they may tour with symphonies, bands, police, or paramedics so they can include first-hand accounts and relevant quotes.

When you write a human interest story, a sincere concern for people combined with curiosity, good writing skills, effective research, and editing are essential to bring your views to life and intrigue an editor.

□ 57

Six Steps to Salable Articles

By Michelle Howell

Has a magazine ever rejected your article, then published one on the same subject shortly afterward? This happened to me, not once, but three times. The first time, I was filled with righteous indignation, convinced that someone stole my idea. By the third, I took time to read the competition. Color me embarrassed—it was much better than mine.

I knew that the magazines I queried had liked my ideas, but my execution fell short. What did these pieces have that mine didn't? I pulled out the articles I had written and compared them with those published. I didn't find one thing that made the articles stand out from mine; I found six.

Include or improve these six elements in your articles and watch your sales increase!

Your lead

Mickey Spillane once said, "Your first page sells your book, the last sells your next book." The same principle applies to an article's opening and conclusion.

With stacks of unread manuscripts littering an editor's desk, your lead must reach out and grab his or her attention. Your opening must also make readers keep reading. With this goal in mind, pull out the stops—question, tease, entice, anger—but make them read on!

Many techniques exist for writing leads. Here are a few:

1) Open with a question: "If you and your husband both died tomorrow, who would be awarded custody of your children?" You've immediately involved the reader. The situation is personal. The lead emphasizes the importance of choosing a guardian for the children by forcing the reader to think the unthinkable. Make sure that if you open

with a question, your article eventually answers that question. In this case, the answer is that unless you name a guardian for your children in your will, the courts decide.

2) Set a scene: "Ten feet under, the water is so muddy you can't see your nose on your face. Maybe, if your intention is to catch an 80-pound catfish by hand, it's better that way." This was my lead for "Hand-Grabbling for Cat," which appeared in *Heartland USA*. Note that it involves readers again, this time by placing them at the scene. Make them see it. Make them feel it. Make them *have* to know how it ends.

3) Funnel: Another piece of mine, this one for *The Mother Earth News*, began with a funnel lead: "Almost everyone lives on the verge of bankruptcy." The funnel lead opens with a broad statement to engage the reader, then narrows the focus. This particular article discusses credit ratings and how they affect our finances. It needs a strong lead to make a reader sit up, take notice, and ask, Am I that close to the edge? Do credit ratings have an impact my finances?

4) Quote: By associating the subject of your article with a quote that many have heard or can understand, you make the reader a partner in your article. Marlys Harris does this in the lead for her piece, "Insurance That Will Serve Your Needs," which appeared in *New Choices:* "'God is in the details,' as they say, and so is a good insurance policy."

5) Statistics: "Men may be the spice of life, yet no man stands between a woman and her chocolate. Americans consume 2.8 billion pounds of chocolate each year. That's more than 11 pounds of melt-in-your-mouth goodness for every man, woman, and child." This was my lead for "Chocolate Passion," which appeared in *Complete Woman*. The statistics convince the reader that chocolate craving is not unique (and yes, those mini Hershey bars do add up).

6) Bait and switch: Make a statement that many readers will agree with, then contradict it. The second paragraph of my chocolate article reads: "Chocolate is the most universally liked flavor in the world. So why are we forced to deny ourselves what we crave the most? Chocolate clogs our arteries, rots our teeth, and sends us to the anti-acne aisle in the drug store. Or does it? Chocolate may not be the villain that we've always believed." Here I listed the health hazards of chocolate, then planted a seed of doubt.

Many good leads use a combination of these approaches. Notice that the first two paragraphs of my article, "Chocolate Passion," contain statistics, questions, and bait and switch.

Don't promise what you can't deliver. "You too can be a billionaire!" may get their attention, but for an article on simple money management, it may also leave the readers with moneymaking ideas of their own—like suing the author for false claims. Always back up your leads with solid, well-researched articles.

Anecdotes

Anecdotes are a key ingredient in your article. They enable the reader to feel, to see what you see. Suddenly, a hypothetical situation becomes a real story involving people like you and me. Use details to give your anecdotes life.

Anecdotes also help set the tone of your article, as in the following:

We arrived in Rome the day before my husband's week-long business conference, and took a walk along a street near our hotel. Concerned that I would be on my own in a foreign country while he attended lectures, Steve busily plotted my days. After chattering on for several minutes, he stopped in front of a laundry. "Or," he said teasingly, "you could follow their advice." He pointed to the laundry window where a sign read "Ladies—leave your clothes here and spend the afternoon having a good time."

This anecdote signals a light, humorous approach. If you are writing an article on the perils of travel, then by all means find someone who has had a life-threatening situation and recount his story.

Where do you find anecdotes? Often, you'll get an article idea from an incident that happened to you or someone you know. For instance, my article on hand-grabbling for catfish began with a bizarre story I overheard. This age-old method of fishing had escaped my notice for some forty-odd years. Yet, when I mentioned it to others, I was amazed at the number of people who had heard it, seen it, done it. I got all the stories I needed.

The internet is another excellent source. Searches include e-mail messages. What? You thought e-mail was private? Think again. You'll get all the anecdotes you need, and more. Change the names and locations—you don't have to identify the source for an effective anecdote—

or, open up conversations with your web sources and pump them for more information.

Quotes

For authority and color, let the experts make your point for you. Try to quote two or three experts for each article. If you're writing for regional markets, local people serve admirably as experts. If you write for a national magazine, choose experts from a geographical spread. Don't use, say, three experts from the University of Florida. Use only one from the university, one from the northeast, and another from the west.

Identify your experts by name, title, and location the first time you refer to or quote them. This proves these people really exist. If possible, use a few words of personal identification—appearances or mannerisms. For instance, the harried public defender or the limp in the walk of a retired NFL linebacker. Identify where you got the quote, if not in person. A book? A newspaper article?

Sometimes, you may come across an expert who does not want to be identified. Honor his or her request; you can still use the quote by applying a broad label. I once labeled my expert a former Miss Teen USA and got the credibility I wanted, but by omitting her name, her state, and the year she was crowned, she kept her anonymity.

What if your expert is a brilliant scientist, but a poor speaker? You can edit quotes as long as you don't change the tone or meaning; most sources will thank you for this. I have deleted words when my subject rambled, corrected improper English, and combined sentences for a tighter, more decisive sound, but I have never altered the intent or meaning to suit my purposes.

Description

Description should be a natural part of your writing, but don't stop the pace of an article to throw in a paragraph or two of description. Weave it into your writing. Use all five senses—sight, touch, hearing, taste, smell. If you are writing an article on a jungle safari, your readers should smell the damp, lush vegetation, feel the moist heat radiating from the thick jungle floor, and jump as the scream of an Amazon parrot shatters the stillness.

Technically challenged, I thought that an article on the Pentium® processor would tax my descriptive skills. I found that, by using metaphors and similes, I could make comparisons to something the reader knows. You can, too.

Transition

Move the reader smoothly through your article. Here are three effective techniques:

1) 1, 2, 3 transition. The how-to article is a perfect example.

2) Time transition. Keep the reader chronologically oriented. In other words, if you are writing a true crime article, start with the background of the victim or perpetrator (depending on your viewpoint), then move on to what led up to the crime, the crime itself, and the aftermath.

3) Echo transition. You can jump-cut from one area or scene to another. Here's an example from my article, "Boiled Peanuts and the Labor of Love," which appeared in *Mississippi Magazine:*

It was the summer of '72, the last stop in a trek that had lasted four years. There had been whispers of home in the occasional songs I heard over rare multi-band radios carried by fellow travelers. But nothing in those four years ever reminded me as much of my home and youth as when I smelled the musty odor of boiling peanuts over an open fire in the streets of Thailand.

Here, the smell of boiling peanuts triggered the switch. Another way to use echo transitions is to repeat a word or phrase from the end of one part of your article to the beginning of another.

Conclusion

An article should come full circle. In your conclusion, reiterate or refer back to your lead. This is what readers will take away with them. Make them feel that they are better for having read your article. This is your chance to leave the reader feeling enlightened, or wanting to take action.

Used correctly, these six elements all involve the reader. An article that makes readers first feel, then understand, is an article that makes an impact. By including and strengthening these elements, your articles will be read, published, and remembered.

❏ 58

PICKING A VICTIM:
A BIOGRAPHER'S CHOICE

BY CARL ROLLYSON

ONE OF MY READERS RECENTLY WROTE TO ME THAT SHE HAD NOT "picked a victim" yet, but she was giving serious thought to writing a biography. How did one go about it? she wanted to know. I relish the idea—I must admit—of thinking of the biographee as a victim. The biographer, after all, has enormous power, picking and choosing what aspects of a life to emphasize, what parts to leave out. Like a novel, a biography is a story in which characters are manipulated and moved about to suit the biographer's point of view. My attraction to the form derives from this urge to reconstitute a life within the covers of a book. I don't blame anyone for feeling victimized by the "biografiend." In miniature, a biography is rather like having to sit still for a photograph that you do not want taken of yourself. You're robbed in some way of your substance. And you are probably not consoled by the "biografriend's" insistence that he or she admires you and must have a picture. At the same time, in my role as biographer I am like a reporter or a novelist who has few, if any, scruples about getting the story.

I subscribe, in other words, to a conflict of interest theory of biography. There is my interest in writing a book about, say, Susan Sontag. And then there is Susan Sontag's interest in herself. These interests are mutually exclusive. Susan Sontag is the subject of my book, whereas Susan Sontag is the subject of *her* life. Biographers often ignore this fundamental point or won't admit it—at least they won't own up to it when they are writing about writing biographies. If you've read biographers on biography, you know they sound like a very noble lot—especially Leon Edel. You'd never guess he was a snoop just like the rest of us, trying to get the low-down on Henry James. Do you think Henry James would have given Leon Edel permission to write a biography about him?

I like the feeling of working against my subject, of trying to find out things that he or she has tried to bury or to obfuscate. I have learned to be wary of my subjects. I find them enormously entertaining. I learn a great deal from them, but I don't trust them. Not because they're all liars, but because they want to have it their way.

It may sound as though I take a hostile attitude toward my subjects. No, I'm just skeptical, and I like to turn over their lives from many different angles to see what I can shake loose for my narrative. Without this sense of resistance, of friction, I wonder whether biography would be quite so appealing. As much as most kids growing up, I liked digging for buried treasure, and when there was no buried treasure to be found, I buried some myself for later discovery. I think of my subjects the same way: They like hiding things, and they may even have a sneaking admiration for the one who finds them out. I know I have conducted more than one interview in which the interviewee was not forthcoming until it was made clear that I had already done some digging and had turned up some pretty tantalizing items.

I think the biographer is ultimately his or her own authority. I borrow that phrase from R. G. Collingwood. He has in mind the fact that any genuine work of history is more than the sum of its evidence; it depends, in fact, on the interpreting mind of the historian, who must bring together disparate materials and insights—rather like a detective—into a unified, organic whole. That whole is, essentially, a story, a narrative of meaning. Otherwise, Collingwood argues, there is only scissors-and-paste history, in which the historian slaps together fragments of evidence and testimony from his sources or authorities. This quilt of fact and speculation might make a rather gaudy design, but it would not be a work of history.

The biographer, I would argue, does much the same thing. For example, for my biography of Lillian Hellman (published in 1988), I assembled the following raw material for Chapter 17: a letter from Walter Jackson Bate (at one time chairman of Harvard's English department); a journal kept by Ken Stuart (a student in Lillian Hellman's Harvard writing class); interviews with faculty members who knew Hellman during her Harvard stay; an interview with her physician; and a few newspaper articles. All of these materials would not have added up to Chapter 17. First of all, I didn't use all of the evidence; some was redundant. Though some was fascinating, there was too much to fit into my narrative, already burdened with significant detail. I knew that readers would stand for only so much on this phase of Hellman's career. To relate all of it would have seriously damaged the shape of my book; it would have placed too much emphasis on that period of Hellman's life.

Considerations of this kind I call esthetic. I wanted to write a good book and knew I would have to be selective. Just as important, however, were the selections I had already made in previous chapters, where I emphasized Hellman's contentiousness, her pride in her work, her attraction to young people, her generosity, and her tendency to be highhanded. All of these qualities I found in my evidence for Chapter 17—although as individual bits of evidence, these sources contradicted each other. Bate, for example, was offended by an incredibly demanding and insensitive bitch, while Ken Stuart was charmed by her shrewd and patient handling of young writers, including himself. In the chapter as published, I hope these seeming contradictions are resolved—that is, that they are understandable, given the different contexts Hellman found herself in. With students she would never behave the way she behaved with Bate. He was supposed to be the red carpet man, the one who should have fawned over her. With Ken Stuart, it was just the opposite: Hellman knew she was there to give him something. Nowhere in Chapter 17 do I make this comparison between Hellman's treatment of Bate and Stuart, but I believe it is there in the configuration of my narrative, and that it can be found by readers who have been following the whole story of my book.

While I was writing the biography of Hellman, I often had a sense of her struggling for possession of my book. There was no doubt in my mind that she did not want me to write it my way. Not just because I would find out things—like her Communist Party membership—but because, like a dramatist, I was setting her up in scenes that were not of her own making. I was questioning her memoirs and producing an alternative version of her life.

Biographers worry when they are cut off from some of the evidence. When I began my research on Hellman, I did not know that she had restricted her archive. That piece of shocking news was announced by Richard Wilbur during an interview. "I hope the unavailability of the Texas material does not pose too great a problem for you," he remarked in his characteristically understated way. "What?" I gulped.

"Oh, I hear that Lillian restricted everything for the use of her author-
ized biographer," Wilbur casually noted. "Oh, yes," I said, with as
much of a knowing air as I could assume. I had a good sweat over this
setback. I remember announcing it to a colleague in the street—my
way of admitting the worst and taking it as a challenge. Somehow I
forced myself to feel good that Lillian Hellman was going to make
things hard for me. I wanted to write about her so badly, it may not
have made a difference if I had gotten the word about Texas earlier.
Still, I am grateful for having begun in ignorance of this fundamental
fact.

I knew I had to reconstruct the Texas archive. I reasoned that
through a long career, Hellman would have left papers, letters, and
various traces all over the country—especially in New York and Hollywood—and I was not wrong. Not only was I able to locate nearly
everything that was in Texas in the Academy of Motion Picture Arts
and Sciences, the University of Southern California Library, Boston
University Library, the Wisconsin Center for Film and Theatre Research, and in the hands of her friends all over the country, I found
new material—hundreds of letters, a screenplay Hellman never acknowledged, her husband's diary, and many, many other items that
were not in the Texas archive. I also consulted half a dozen excellent
dissertations written during the years the Texas archive was open, and
this doctoral work proved invaluable in reconstructing my understanding of Hellman's working papers.

For me, the most important thing is the overwhelming desire to write
about a particular figure. That usually means I already have—even if
I can't articulate it yet—a vision of my subject. I have already decided
I'm right for the biography. Everything else, then, will have to fall in
line, no matter what obstacles I encounter. To prospective biographers
I recommend that you know why you want to write about so-and-
so. When you have convinced yourself—or as I like to say, deluded
yourself—that you are the best person for the job, then it is time to
take on all the other troubles you will surely face. I'm reminded of
Brenda Maddox, who has written a splendid biography of Nora Joyce.
She went to Richard Ellmann, generally acknowledged to be *the* Joyce
biographer. "A biography of Nora?" Ellmann asked incredulously.
"What for?" There was no new material worth writing about. Besides,
hadn't he, *the* Richard Ellmann, done the definitive biography of James

Joyce? There was nothing left to be done. And Maddox, the Joyce scholar apparently observed, was only a journalist. Thank heavens Brenda Maddox went ahead—discovering, by the way, much new material and no doubt changing the way James and Nora Joyce will now be viewed.

Speaking only for myself, I hope to tell a good story. Because it is a story, I have to deal with everything—not just my subject's public face. I want the gossip, the intimacies, everything that I can find out that made that person what she or he is.

Writing biography is a shameless profession, an exercise in bad taste, a rude inquiry. Most biographers I have met prefer not to say so in public. We are journalists and sometimes scholars who try very hard to be accurate. But is it any wonder that the biographer's choice gets expressed as the picking of a victim?

❑ 59

WRITING MEDICAL ARTICLES

BY JAN ROADARMEL LEDFORD

GOOD NEWS, WRITERS! THERE'S A TOPIC THAT'S ALWAYS HOT. EVERY-one wants to read about it. It's time-honored, yet on the leading edge of technology. It's medicine!

The surprising news is that you don't need a medical degree to write many types of medical articles. Naturally, it helps to be working in the medical field in some capacity. But any writer who is interested enough to do careful research can turn out good, solid articles on medical topics. Your best investments are a medical terminology class at your local vocational-technical school, an illustrated medical dictionary, a drug reference book, and a basic text on medicine, such as *The Merck Manual.*

The two cardinal rules for writing medical articles are the same for any type of writing: Know your audience and know your target publication. There are basically two types of audiences: the lay and the professional. The markets, however, are vast.

Writing for the lay audience

The usual purpose of lay-oriented medical writing is to inform. An-swering questions is what this type of material is all about. To organize your thinking, ask yourself: What does the patient (reader) need/want to know? What do care-givers want the patient to know? What action do we want the reader to take?

With answers in hand, you can formulate an outline that includes an introduction (scenarios and statistics work very well here), a definition of the problem, cause(s) of the problem, treatment options, and the expected outcome. This outline will fit almost any medical condition that you care to write about. Depending on your slant, you may want to concentrate more on one area than another. For example, an exposé on the side effects of a specific treatment would dwell more heavily on the "expected outcome."

As always, you must write on a level appropriate for your audience. If you are approaching a newspaper, you will use a simpler vocabulary and shorter sentences than when writing for a trade journal. In any case, be sure to define medical terms or replace them with common lay terms. (For example, say "gum" instead of "gingiva.") An anatomical drawing is often helpful in introducing terms and in orienting your readers.

While you do not need medical credentials to write for the average reader, you may need someone with medical credentials to add credibility to your article. This might be accomplished by interviewing, then quoting, a person in the field. Or, you might consider writing as a coauthor or ghost author for a medical professional. You know the writer's admonition to "write what you know." Your reader (and editor) is going to ask, "*How* do you know?" Associating your work with someone who has medical credentials will answer that question.

If you understand medical terms and statistics, you can search through medical journals and "translate" technical research into lay-oriented articles. Find someone (well-known, if possible) who has a stake in the research to add human drama and interest to your story. Be sure to get your numbers right. Case studies in such journals make for interesting reading as well. (Wouldn't your readers be fascinated to learn about a procedure in which a surgeon used a piece of donor sclera [white of the eye] as a framework on which to rebuild someone's external *ear?*)

Your local newspaper and health magazines are not the only markets for your lay-oriented medical articles. Many general-interest magazines have a health-related column or use medical information. Parenting magazines are a good market because parents are extremely concerned about their children's health. Scientific magazines are interested in new technology. There are support groups or foundations for many diseases, widening your market to newsletters. Or, you could turn your article into a brochure and offer the copy to physicians or interested organizations. The American Academy of Ophthalmology, for example, has patient education brochures on all types of eye disorders. (Note: this might be a one-time sale or a work-for-hire situation.)

Depending on your topic, you may want to market the piece to appropriate non-medical trade journals. Suppose you've written a great article on carpal tunnel syndrome (CTS). Who would be interested? Any professional whose work involves the wrist motion that aggravates the problem: athletes, mechanics, typists. The same goes for any other type of medical condition. Ask yourself: Who is affected by this condition? Every answer identifies a potential market.

Writing for medical professionals

The same approach can be used to write for professional medical trade journals. Before you start, consider the education level of your audience, and adjust your language and terminology appropriately. For example, a medical assistant may be trained at a vocational school or on the job. A physician's assistant has at least a four-year college degree. You must do meticulous research when writing for medical professionals, regardless of their education level. If you say something wrong, they'll know it!

Suggesting that you start out by writing for medical professionals with "lower" levels of credentials is like suggesting that a fiction writer start out by writing for children. Writing for children is *not* easier: It's different. But it *is* true that the higher the level of medical professional that you're writing for, the greater your need for medical credentials personally, or for an association with someone who has the credentials. This "associate" may agree to pay you for your work if his or her name is given as the primary or sole author. However, your payment will probably come in the form of copies. It is considered an obligation and a privilege to share medical knowledge with your colleagues; hence, monetary reimbursements are not usually offered.

The trades, however, may offer regular pay or an honorarium. And don't limit your market or your slant. You might sell your article on carpal tunnel syndrome to *RDH* (a trade journal for dental hygienists), but by changing your slant a little, you might place the piece in the *Professional Medical Assistant* (a journal of the American Association of Medical Assistants). *PMA* has a feature called "The Two-Minute Clinic" and might be interested in an informational article that would help readers learn more about CTS.

If you move into writing for regular medical journals, you'll receive one of a writer's greatest rewards: editorial feedback. In journals that select articles by peer review, the reviewer is required to give the reason(s) that an article is rejected. What a wonderful way to learn the craft! A physician-client hired me to write an article on a unique surgical procedure he'd used. I told him from the outset that because the technique was controversial, we might have trouble placing it. He wanted me to go ahead, so I wrote the piece and then made a list of medical journals that published related surgical cases. I sent the article to the first (and most prestigious) journal on the list. As I feared, the article came back. But with it came the reviewer's comments and suggestions I used to make the article stronger and sent it to journal Number Two. This journal also rejected it . . . but also sent comments, which I again utilized. Journal Number Three published the twice-improved piece. Not only was the physician happy, but I had learned and grown as a writer. This type of feedback doesn't often come in fiction writing. Or in most types of nonfiction writing, for that matter.

Additional research sources

Besides using a good medical dictionary and general medical text as part of your research, don't overlook your local physicians and other health care workers as references. Not only can you interview them, but you also may be able to use their extensive personal libraries. In addition, you can ask them for patient education brochures. Virtually every practice in all branches of medicine uses handouts to inform their patients.

Earlier I mentioned organizations that deal exclusively with certain diseases and conditions. Check your local library's reference shelf for the *Encyclopedia of Organizations* published by Gale Research, Inc. Not only are these organizations good potential markets, but they can also supply a wealth of information. Some of these organizations run local support groups. These, in turn, may be able to put you in touch with individuals who are experts on the condition or who actually have the disorder themselves.

The National Library of Medicine offers on-line information via MedLine. Using appropriate key words, you can search the NLM computer banks for journal articles related to your topic. You must specify if you want to search back prior to the last several years. But in medical writing, you usually won't want to use a reference over five years old, anyway, unless you are doing a historical piece. The program can retrieve the abstracts for you. Often the abstract alone gives enough information for a lay-oriented article. Or, you can order the full article on-line or through your library. The reference list at the end of any medical article may supply further resources to check into.

Medical writing is challenging and extremely rewarding. You have the potential to reassure, to encourage, and to offer hope through your words. For more information about this branch of writing, contact the American Medical Writers Association, 9650 Rockville Pike, Bethesda, MD 20814–3998.

□ 60

How to Avoid
Transition Trauma

By Bharti Kirchner

TO BE EFFECTIVE, AN ARTICLE MUST BE CLEAR AND HAVE A CONTINU-
ous flow. Sentences, paragraphs, and sections must be linked together
logically to provide information as the reader needs it. As a writer,
you may have to skip over time periods, bounce between locations,
present contrasting ideas and still be able to make sense if you use
suitable transitions. This may be a bridging word, phrase, or sentence—*yet, however,* or *furthermore*—that allows readers to shift
smoothly, from idea to idea, from one time, place, or thought to another. Transitions smooth the passage from the beginning of an article
through the body and on to the end. The more effective your transition,
the better your piece will read. Here's an example:

I was cocooned in the luxury of my four-star hotel. The police were questioning suspects.

The reader will be lost unless you supply a transition between the
sentences, such as:

I was cocooned in the luxury of my four-star hotel, while *just outside* the
police were questioning the suspects.

The English language is full of transitional words or phrases, such
as *besides, granted that, speaking of, in addition,* and the oft-quoted
meanwhile, back at the ranch. But using them may not be enough to
carry the reader forward, as you would like.

Transitional devices
You must establish a real connection between the ideas so that one
topic naturally follows another. Ultimately, it's the logical link that

creates the real transition, not the transitional words themselves. Present your material so your ideas progress in the order in which the reader needs to know them. You may, for example, follow a chronological sequence, by giving a minute-by-minute detailed account of a fire or bombing incident. Or, you may organize spatially by taking a reader on a tour of an area by going north to south. You may go from general points to specific facts.

Where transitions go

Transition words or phrases can go between paragraphs, between sentences, or within a sentence, wherever there is a shift. For example:

Tea cozies come in various shapes and designs. *Nevertheless,* unless they are padded, they are mere decorations.
Bright nail polish may have its place, *but* it's not in the office.

Think of an article as a series of paragraphs, with transitions the glue that holds them together sequentially. Generally speaking, each paragraph in an article deals with different aspects of the central topic. To move on to a new point, to another paragraph, you must flag a "watch your step" signal to your reader. There are several techniques that you may use to do this effectively.

Start a new paragraph with a different time frame. This technique is most effective when the passage of time is long or when a specific date is mentioned.

Eventually, he quit the company and sued the owner.
In April 1997, she moved back to her native England.

Another device is to ask a question in the last sentence of a paragraph—"Why is cholesterol so important?"—then answer it in the following paragraph saying, "The link between cholesterol and heart disease has become accepted."

You might give an illustration or explanation of the point made in the previous paragraph, sometimes by going from the general to the specific. Stated opinions or facts can be supplemented with quotes from experts in a new paragraph, effecting a transition.

A short sentence can begin a new subtopic in a new paragraph. For example, after describing a political candidate's academic background, you might insert another trait in the paragraph that follows: "He is a religious man."

Another useful technique is to shift the action to a different location. For instance, describe a foreign dignitary's attendance at a church service, then in a new paragraph focus on another aspect of his visit that takes place in a different site.

Across the street, demonstrators gathered.

Often at the end of an article, you can summarize your findings in a separate paragraph with a transition such as:

What all this shows is that the presidential contest is wide open.

To make a paragraph coherent, all the sentences must deal with the same topic and should relate to one another. You can achieve this with a transition word or phrase, or with the use of pronouns. For example, you can start a sentence with the words "senior citizens" as the subject, then change to the pronoun "they" in the next sentence, thereby connecting them. You can bridge similar ideas in a sentence by using a simple *and,* which also will eliminate too many short choppy sentences. Instead of similarity, you might make a difference with "but, of course."

You can tie together different sights and sounds in a scene, all within a paragraph, with appropriate transition phrases to help orient the reader.

On my left was a rose bush. *Straight ahead* was the patio where the music came from.

Too many instances of *indeed, accordingly,* and *therefore,* etc. can, however, be distracting. See if you can cut some out and still make the meaning clear.

Subheads, bullets, numbers, and sidebars

Though not transitions in themselves, these devices divide an article into readable blocks and provide visual clues that a change is occurring. A reader can skip over a subhead without losing the meaning of the entire article.

Occasionally a piece can be best presented through a series of bulleted or numbered paragraphs, each discussing a separate fact, thus obviating the need for transition.

If you can't come up with a transition, chances are that either the paragraph is in the wrong place, or, though related, it doesn't connect to the central topic. Before discarding the paragraph, consider using sidebars. They usually include such information as resources, with names and addresses; an interview with an expert; a set of tips; even a quiz.

The lack of a connector can cause vagueness or confusion, but the wrong one can alter the meaning.

The price of single-family dwellings fell nationwide to the lowest in ten years. *Consequently,* an average San Francisco home sold for $250,000.

You might be scratching your head to recall the time when $250,000 was considered a low price. Now, plug in your suggestion for a good transition in the above. Here's *one* solution:

The price of single-family dwellings fell nationwide to its lowest in ten years. *Nevertheless,* an average San Francisco home is now selling for $250,000.

Lack of awareness or of structuring often causes writers to misuse or omit transitions. One way to solve the problem is to read your piece aloud to detect any awkward jumps.

In summary, deal with one thought thoroughly before you proceed to the next, adding transitions as needed. This will help you write the kind of article that editors find easy to accept.

□ 61

SHARING MEMORIES WITH YOUR READER

BY EILEEN HERBERT JORDAN

THE HARDEST PART ABOUT WRITING A PERSONAL ESSAY IS HAVING something happen to prompt it. You can't make it up—it has to be real. At the same time, it should move the reader in a way that many feel only fiction can. And it almost always has to be about you, often only you, while reaching out to people you will never know, have never thought about, and cannot even imagine. That's the second hardest part.

As an editor and a writer, I have known this for a long time—but I guess you never stop learning. Not long ago I was working on an essay with a magazine editor, doing a telephone revision. Using her computer, she would cut a line, a phrase, switch a sentence (people who use computers love to switch sentences), and read it back to me. Something was wrong. And it was getting wronger. Wait, I said to her at last. You're losing *me*. It isn't *me* any more. And I was right. In a personal essay, for better or worse, you must never lose the *me* in the writing—I can't think of a better way to put it. This doesn't mean that you don't need editorial guidance; you probably do, as I do. It does mean, however, that in whatever you write, whether of losses or gains, of births or deaths, of meetings or farewells, you must tell it the way it was *for you*—and let the reader make his own connection.

So there are two problems. Now, what can you do about them? Let's start with the first: having something happen. Obviously, the working writer does not simply hang around waiting for tender moments. They don't come like rockets out of the sky; they sneak up when no one is looking. Sometimes they even come and go, and you don't realize they were there. But once they have come and gone, what you have on your side, and what you must hold on to, is Time. Time is a wonderful conductor of memories. Watch it work: It is wonderfully efficient, stripping excess baggage from the moments you are trying to recall and making them stand alone. After you have tried your hand at a few pieces and feel more comfortable about writing them, you will find that you are growing more skillful at isolating moments in time. All of us have an inner eye that we may not even realize—or use. Once trained, it will operate thereafter on automatic pilot, recognizing incidents that bear repeating or cry out for interpretation. You'll see why, and you'll find a way to mold them.

It might be helpful if you take notes, though personally I don't find it helpful, as I am an inefficient note taker. I have a blank notebook and a pen on my coffee table, and another in my pocketbook, and I do use them. But sometimes when I reread what I have written, I have no idea what I had in mind at the time. Music works much better for me: A snatch of song can often pinpoint an interlude. But I like my inner eye best. See what works for you.

At times, I use the second person in writing an essay. The French always considered this *intime,* and, when it works, it *does* add a degree of intimacy you would not otherwise have. I used it in a piece for *Modern Maturity.* In fact, the piece itself is possibly a good example of the way an essay evolves.

Some time before, my five-year-old grandson had presented me with a gift—one of his prized stuffed animals. Maybe as you read this, you're saying, who cares? Maybe you are thinking it's too trivial to ask, Why did he do it? What did it mean to me? Well, you're wrong. Call it loneliness. Loneliness is a road with a lot of paths branching off from it, going in different directions—you can frequently see one from another. As a widow, I was on one of them (which my grandson, of course, knew), and he was just starting off on another, the beginning of growing up. He had a brand-new brother, so he no longer was the baby of the family. I saw his pain, and he saw mine; the gift made both of us feel better. Judging from the mail I received, I guess it made a lot of readers feel better, too. They seemed to recognize that no matter what path of loneliness they were on, they weren't on it alone.

I've saved the best for last: Help is not just on the way for you—it is here. For you have a built-in audience. You see, we are an inarticulate lot, all of us. (Psychiatrists have made fortunes on this fact alone.) We don't or we won't or we can't express the emotions we feel; we bury them so deep that no laser beam could reach them. We take antidepressants and tranquilizers and stomach soothers and say nothing. Then, if we are lucky, someone writes something and evokes a lost memory, a long-ago joy, a sorrow we had once, a time in our lives . . . *the last day of college . . . the night you met him . . . the birth of the baby . . . the letter lost in the mail . . .*

We know that what has happened to us happens to other people, but it's more persuasive to read it for ourselves and be sure.

❏ 62

WRITING ARTICLES THE PROFESSIONAL WAY

BY RUTH DUSKIN FELDMAN

THERE ARE THREE KINDS OF WRITERS: THOSE WHO WRITE SOLELY FOR self-expression, those who are published occasionally, and those who make writing a career. Many aspiring writers think you begin in the first category and gradually move into the second and then the third. But my observation and experience tell me that people in the third category—those who strive to make a living as writers—approach their work very differently from those who don't.

Many would-be writers separate the process of writing from the process of marketing what they write. They struggle to perfect their craft, to say what they want to say as well as it can be said. That's certainly a worthwhile goal. But if you want to sell what you write, you must play by the rules of the marketplace. Your writing—from the start—must be aimed toward publication.

Professionals who write for magazines normally write on assignment. Writing on assignment means that all of your writing time is spent in remunerative activity. Equally important, it means that you know exactly who your audience is and how to focus your article. Unfortunately, it's hard to get an assignment without credits (previously published work), and you can't get credits without writing on speculation. But whether you're writing on assignment or "on spec," the same marketing principles apply. You need to sell an editor on your idea and your ability to carry it out. The best way to do that is to write a query.

A query is a letter intended to find out whether an editor wants to see your article. The response you're seeking is a go-ahead to submit the full article. The query should include salient information about the subject, succinctly and provocatively stated. Within one single-spaced page (or, at most, two), your query must show that your topic is timely, that it will "turn on" the magazine's readers, and that you can deliver what you promise: a well-researched, well-written, publishable article.

A query can be written before or after the article. A query written in advance can help you shape the finished piece; often the lead paragraphs are almost identical. More important, in constructing a query you force yourself to think through the form the article should take: what information to include and what main points to cover in what order. When you sit down to write the article, instead of staring at a blank sheet of paper, you have a blueprint to follow.

Here's how I led off one query (and later, the published article in *Chicago Parent*):

Dear (Editor's Name):

Let's Bring Back Grandma-Care

Everybody talks about the day care crisis, but hardly anybody mentions one solution that can be beneficial for the child and the entire family: part-time care by a grandparent.

As a busy professional writer, I never expected to be minding my baby grandson two days a week while my lawyer daughter works; but I've been doing just that for the past year, and loving it. My daughter and I call our arrangement "shared parenting," and we've uncovered several other families that are doing the same.

My query continued with some facts that appeared in expanded form further down in the body of the article:

"Grandma-care" is an old idea whose time may have come again. With more than half the mothers of babies and preschoolers in the work force, nearly one out of four of their young children, if not supervised by the father, are spending the day with Grandma, and another 10 percent with other relatives. And a recent Harris poll shows that the average working parent would prefer to have a family member mind the kids.

I went on to mention the length I had in mind (a fairly standard 2,000 words), sources I planned to tap (studies on the importance of the grandparent-grandchild relationship, as well as interviews with families engaging in "grandparent-care"), and a brief summary of my relevant professional experience. I enclosed a few clips of published work. (But don't let a lack of credits and clips deter you: A recent survey of 32 national magazine editors, conducted by Lee Jolliffe of the University of Missouri, found that the writer's experience carried less than three percent weight in editors' judgments of queries. The most important criteria were writing skill and the merits of the idea itself.)

Both the query and the article should be targeted at a specific magazine and its audience. The topic, the choice of words, the suggested length, all must be appropriate. Does that mean if one editor rejects a query you have to start from scratch? Of course not. I often recycle queries among magazines with similar audiences—for example, *Woman's Day* and *Family Circle*—or adapt a query to a magazine with a different audience.

Some writers find it easiest to write for a few magazines they read regularly and know well. I prefer to be more eclectic. I've sold articles to a wide variety of national, regional, local, women's, in-flight, and travel magazines. First, I decide on a topic I want to write about. Then I look for one or more markets it's likely to fit. Sometimes I've sold an article two or three times, each time revising and refocusing it with a different audience in mind.

Tailoring your writing to different audiences is not as difficult as it may seem. Do you speak to a child the same way as to an adult? Of course not. Successful oral communicators adjust their speech to the person they are communicating with. Successful writers do, too.

I began my adult career as a teacher. I've never forgotten the advice given to beginning instructors: Start where your students are; don't assume knowledge they don't have. For writers, that advice translates into: Get inside the reader's head. Make sure you're talking his or her language.

Often all that's required is a slight shift of viewpoint. For example, after my article on grandparent-care appeared in *Chicago Parent,* I sold a somewhat different version to *New Choices for the Best Years,* (now called *New Choices: Living Even Better After 50*), a national magazine for the 50-plus age group. *New Choices* pitched it toward grandparents rather than parents by reversing the opening paragraphs—emphasizing the experience of a grandparent-caregiver more than the need for good day care.

It's a good idea to study several issues of the magazine you intend to approach and send for its editorial guidelines (enclosing an SASE). The more familiar you are with the publication, the more readily you can put yourself in the place of its readers. Are they predominantly men or women? How old and how educated? What are their occupations and interests? What are their problems? What do they want and need to know?

My article on rafting Utah's Green River first appeared (after many rejections) in *Utah Holiday*. I later recast it (and cut it almost in half) for the *Chicago Sun-Times* travel section. Still later, *Going Places,* a magazine of the Montgomery Ward Travel Club, bought a third, even trimmer version.

The "hook," or focus, of the original *Utah Holiday* piece—what sold the editors on running yet another article on whitewater rafting in a state where that activity is practically de rigueur—was gender. The article, "Nine Women on a Raft," ran in a special section called "Summer and Self." It was a reflective reminiscence of an adventurous bonding experience among the all-female participants, several of whom had left nervous husbands at home, and of the interplay between the women and our strapping young male guide. It was also a story about age and the fulfillment of dreams. I began with a quotation from the philosopher Søren Kierkegaard:

> "It is very dangerous to go into eternity with possibilities which one has oneself prevented from becoming realities. A possibility is a hint from God. One must follow it."

The first few paragraphs briefly recounted how, ten years earlier, I had begun writing for brochures from rafting companies, only to be discouraged by my acrophobic spouse. Then I wrote:

> Reaching the half-century mark forces the realization that possibilities are not forever. So, the August after my fiftieth birthday and my daughter Laurie's law school graduation, we kissed her still-dubious father goodbye and set out on a ninety-six-mile journey down Utah's Green River with Adventure Bound, Inc., an outfitter that has run river excursions for nearly a quarter-century in Utah and Colorado.
>
> Our route lay through Desolation and Gray canyons, which stretch end to end on the site of an ancient lake. The rapids increase gradually in turbulence— numerous and rough enough to challenge novices, yet not too dangerous to paddle.

Next came a paragraph about the region's discovery and about the fur traders, beaver trappers, gold miners, cattle ranchers, and dam promoters who had "failed to tame that wilderness." Then I launched into a selective chronological narrative of our journey (including my being thrown from the raft by the force of a particularly nasty rapid) and the women's varied reactions. In the final paragraphs, I returned to the opening theme:

> While my comrades headed for a washroom and a change of clothes, I stripped off my pedal pushers and wet sneakers and swam into the current until my strength was spent, then sank onto a wooden float, breathing heavily and contemplating the brilliant blue sky. My arm was bruised from my baptismal spill, and my coccyx bone was saddle-sore, but I never had been more content.
>
> I recalled the correspondent in Stephen Crane's "The Open Boat," who, cast adrift with three shipmates, knew at the time that it was the best experience of his life. Our situation had been far less perilous, the finish unmarred by tragedy. But we too had escaped a certain danger and experienced exhilaration in following our possibilities down river.

In the *Going Places* version, which was aimed at men *and* women considering rafting for the first time, I dropped the literary references, played down the feminine angle, and wrote shorter, declarative sentences. In the opening paragraphs, I pared down the introductory explanation and the historical material and added this:

> I was in good physical shape, yet by no means an athlete. But there was no need to be. Adventure Bound has taken first-time rafters ranging in age from 10 to 83 on river trips.
>
> . . . . The canyon walls—more than 5,000 feet deep at one point—guard a near-virgin wilderness. Since we would be far from civilization for four days, it was reassuring to know that the raft would be inspected by park rangers, that guides were Red Cross trained, and that no passenger had ever been seriously injured.

I included more specifics about how rivers are rated for difficulty and about clothing and equipment, and eliminated the final paragraph, ending with "I had never been more content."

Did these changes cramp my writing style? Although I prefer the *Utah Holiday* version, the *Going Places* piece retains much of the feeling of the original. Making the changes was the necessary price for presenting my message to a wider audience.

A market-oriented approach to article writing can make it more likely that *your* words will reach an audience. In my book, that is what writing is about.

❏ 63

CREATIVE NONFICTION: WHERE JOURNALISM AND STORYTELLING MEET

BY MARK H. MASSÉ

A DEDICATED FIFTH-GRADE TEACHER GIVES HER STRUGGLING STU-dents hope in a depressed New England mill town (*Among School-children,* by Tracy Kidder). A power-hungry Southern sheriff clashes with a proud African-American community leader in rural Georgia (*Praying for Sheetrock,* by Melissa F. Greene). Innovative crisis work-ers in Oregon help clients battle mental illness as they heal their own emotional pain in my book, *FRONTLINE.*

These may sound like fictional narratives, but they are factual ac-counts—products of extensive research and reportage, combined with dramatic storytelling techniques. Welcome to the exciting world of creative nonfiction. In the 1960s and 1970s, when Truman Capote *(In Cold Blood),* Gay Talese *(Honor Thy Father),* and Tom Wolfe *(The Right Stuff)* were melding in-depth reporting with literary writing, their work was called New Journalism. Currently, the term "creative nonfiction" is increasingly popular. The good news for today's writers is that this genre offers new, expanding opportunities to craft distinc-tive, evocative stories using a combination of fiction and nonfiction techniques.

To produce successful creative nonfiction, you must have a credible and compelling story to tell. It should inform and enlighten the reader and be based on verifiable facts. Yet, a good creative nonfiction writer will transcend the conventions of fact-based journalism by portraying characters with psychological depth, providing riveting details and de-scriptions, and presenting a true story that uses dramatic scenes to engage the reader's interest and emotions.

A telling comparison

Compare the following two treatments of a scene from a 24-hour crisis hotline. First, a straight news approach:

Pat, a veteran crisis worker, sits in one of the clinic's cluttered offices and answers another call.

"I got a .45 here on my lap, and I've spent the last week convincing myself that I shouldn't pull the trigger," the man on the line says. "But I've run out of reasons. I'll give you five minutes to convince me that I shouldn't kill myself."

"That's not going to work," Pat says firmly. "You could give me five minutes or five years, and I still might not have an answer that I could give you. What I can do is help you to find you own reasons to go on living—if that's what you want to do."

The same scene in creative nonfiction style (from *FRONTLINE*):

A dozen steps away in the cluttered buckstopper office, which overlooks the wide, sagging front porch, Pat instinctively takes a deep breath and plants his bare feet firmly on the scruffy brown carpet before answering the phone.

"I got a .45 here on my lap, and I've spent the last week convincing myself that I shouldn't pull the trigger. But I've run out of reasons." The voice on the other end is deep and gruff-sounding, the craggy voice of a longtime pack-a-day man. His words are flat, emotionless. "I'll give you five minutes to convince me that I shouldn't kill myself."

The first thing that pops into Pat's mind is the one-liner that he told the crisis team at last Monday's group debriefing session: "Suicide is our way of telling God—you can't fire me, I quit!" But Pat isn't smiling. The familiar queasy feeling of fear is welling up inside him.

"That's not going to work," he tells the caller. "You could give me five minutes or five years, and I still might not have an answer that I could give you." He pauses, not knowing if he'll hear the click of a receiver. "What I can do is help you to find your own reasons to go on living—if that's what you want to do."

By including concrete details and sensory imagery to describe the scene (e.g., bare feet on a scruffy carpet; craggy voice of a longtime pack-a-day man), I tried to evoke a mood and make an impact on the reader. The use of extended dialogue and internal monologue—other techniques of creative nonfiction—heightened the tension in this life-and-death drama. Through numerous interviews, oral histories, and months of "participant observation," I learned firsthand about the demanding life of a crisis worker. Tom Wolfe calls this approach "saturation reporting," getting to know people, settings, and story background in sufficient detail to craft a literary journalistic tale.

Extensive research into the inner world of crisis intervention enabled me to write the kind of dramatic scene typically found in fiction. In the excerpt from *FRONTLINE,* I was able to "get inside the head" of the crisis worker and share his thoughts, feelings, and fears with the reader. Ultimately, this scene worked because of the same dynamic that drives successful short stories and novels: a sympathetic protagonist confronted with a complicated problem, conflict, and crisis in which the outcome is uncertain.

To write creative nonfiction successfully, focus on these fundamentals:

1) An appropriate subject
2) Research
3) A dramatic story

Choosing an appropriate subject

The first consideration in approaching a creative nonfiction project is the author's interest in and connection to a given subject. An appropriate topic is one that can be presented with sufficient scope to achieve the intimacy, insight, and drama required of a well-written work of creative nonfiction. In my study of the Eugene, Oregon, crisis intervention team, access to crisis workers' personal and professional lives over several months gave me the opportunity to compile detailed material that I would later rely on when writing my nonfiction narrative.

There is a wide range of subjects suitable for creative nonfiction treatment. Here is a list of possible categories for your consideration:

- Adventure
- Biography
- Business
- Communities
- Crime stories
- Family sagas
- Government & politics

- History
- Institutions
- Personal experience
- Popular culture
- Science & technology
- Sports
- Travel

Before embarking on a work of creative nonfiction, ask yourself: What is this story going to be about? What are the broader themes and/or ramifications of this subject? How can I marshal the facts, the emotions, and the deeper meanings of this story?

For example, in telling his story of friendships in a Massachusetts nursing home (*Old Friends*), Pulitzer Prize-winning creative nonfiction writer Tracy Kidder examined a much larger landscape: aging in America. My tale of Oregon crisis workers on the "front line of pain" isn't merely about mental illness; ultimately, it is a universal story of heroism in everyday life—how "ordinary" people (caregivers) are capable of extraordinary achievements in serving others in need. This theme is appropriate for any good story, whether fiction or nonfiction.

Research

Maybe you don't fancy yourself as brilliant a chronicler of popular culture and the American scene as Tom Wolfe. Perhaps you aren't as renowned for your powers of observation and reporting as John McPhee. Do Joan Didion's remarkable insights into the seemingly ordinary events of everyday life intimidate you? Don't despair. In deciding whether to tackle a work of creative nonfiction, go back to the basics of what makes a writer in the first place.

Are you a good people watcher? Observe the particulars of how a person dresses, walks, eats, gestures. Train your ear to hear the subtleties of a conversation—the trace of an accent, the tone of a voice, an inflection. By putting gestures and conversation together, try to detect any underlying meaning to the dialogue. Concentrate on the recurring details of the environment you are studying, such as "official or unofficial" norms, customs, and rituals.

As a careful and sensitive observer of individuals and groups, you may be able to conduct the saturation reporting that is the foundation of creative nonfiction. Excellent interviewing skills will be vital to your research. In studying people over an extended period of time, you must be adept at gaining their confidence and cooperation. This is achieved by your personal credibility and persuasiveness, combined with sensitive, creative interviewing techniques. Your ability to converse with rather than interrogate your sources will determine how successful you will be in portraying your characters accurately and with the detail required of a fully developed, complex story.

Creative nonfiction has been called the "literature of fact" for good reason: Writers in this field depend on information to generate a story. In addition to observing and conducting interviews, you must immerse yourself in your subject by reading voraciously, using electronic information retrieval services (computerized databases) and contacting experts. When collecting facts, you must "sweat the details."

Creative nonfiction writers must not violate the rules of accuracy and honesty. In the words of Gay Talese, "All that we write should be verifiable." Before you write a single line of internal monologue for a character, make sure you have in your interview notes the actual words from the person about what he or she was thinking at a given time.

A dramatic story

The years I have spent as a fiction writer—honing my narrative skills, structuring dramatic scenes, developing complex characters, drafting realistic dialogue—gave me the confidence to write creative nonfiction. Before you attempt a work of creative nonfiction, you must know the difference between such basics as narration, description, and exposition. Once you have mastered these storytelling techniques and acquired research and reporting skills, you may have the tools to produce vivid, innovative nonfiction narratives.

A creative nonfiction story begins with sound research. Cull your notes for scenes with dramatic potential (e.g., arguments, crises, confrontations, discoveries), including names of the characters involved, a description of the complication, and the resolution—if there was one. Also, list your scenes chronologically—a valuable aid when it comes time to plot your story.

Selecting the appropriate narrative structure is just as essential for a work of creative nonfiction as it is for a novel. Review your material carefully, and remember that form should follow function. How can you best present this story in a way that informs, enlightens, and engages the reader? If there is a natural progression to the story, then a chronological structure may be appropriate. But even with a chronological structure, you may choose to begin the story *in medias res* (in the middle of the action) with a dramatic opening, before flashing back or forward to resume the story.

When chronicling the accounts of several individuals in a creative nonfiction story, you may find it helpful to use parallel narratives that converge at a climactic point in the "plot." Another tried-and-true method is the quest or journey story, in which characters pursue a dream, destination, or goal and the plot develops accordingly.

Like the fiction writer, the author of creative nonfiction must decide on the proper point of view of his or her story. The best approach is to let the strength of your material determine whether you use first- or third-person viewpoint or a combination of the two. Another key decision you must make is how much of a role (if any) you will play in the story: Remember, the presence of the writer as a character may detract from the story's dramatic action.

Although a creative nonfiction story uses a mixture of narrative techniques, it remains a fact-driven literary form, emphasizing concrete, verifiable details about characters, events, settings, and dialogue. Unlike the fiction writer, who can rely solely on his or her imagination to weave a story, the creative nonfiction writer is bound by facts, opinions, observations, and other information collected during the research phase. But, the imagination of the dramatic nonfiction author plays an important role in the creative and persuasive "telling" of a true story.

❑ 64

WRITING OPPORTUNITIES IN THE GREAT OUTDOORS

BY BRIAN McCOMBIE

WITH OVER 120 MILLION AMERICANS PARTICIPATING IN OUTDOOR AC-tivities each year, it's no wonder that there are dozens of national and regional magazines serving this market. Add the scores of tabloids, hundreds of newspaper features and columns, plus the many general-interest magazines that publish outdoor-related pieces, and there are significant opportunities for the writer with outdoor experiences.

My first success with outdoor writing came about eight years ago, when a small hunting and fishing magazine published my humorous essay about a canoe/camping trip gone awry. Since then, I've written how-to pieces, essays, interviews, and book reviews for a variety of outdoor publications.

Am I a specialist in any of the areas in which I write? No, though I have broad knowledge in a number of areas—conservation, natural history, various wildlife issues, hunting, and fishing. When I get an idea for a query or receive an assignment, I immerse myself in the activity and record my experiences as they happen. If the piece is issue-oriented, I do the necessary research at a library or interview experts in the field. Only after I feel fully comfortable with my level of knowledge is it time to write.

Hooks and bullets?

With approximately 75 million people hunting and fishing every year, magazines devoted to these sports activities represent over 60% of the outdoor writing market. The backbone of these publications is the how-to article that provides useful information for the practicing hunter and fisherman, but there are also openings for many more types of writing than the standard "hook-and-bullet" piece (as insiders refer to how-to fishing and hunting articles). Study this market's Big Three—

Sports Afield, Outdoor Life, and *Field & Stream*—and you will discover articles and essays on conservation, wildlife laws and regulations, history, camping, backpacking, and emergency outdoor medicine. The mid-sized and smaller magazines don't have this range of coverage, but they still publish humor, interviews, personal essays, and breaking news.

Then there are the dozens of outdoor magazines devoted to a specific non-hunting or non-fishing activity. *American Hiker, Backpacker Magazine,* and *Canoe & Kayak Magazine* are good examples. Some cover a range of outdoor activities, like *Silent Sports,* which uses articles on cross-country skiing, backpacking, camping, and cycling. A number focus on outdoor sports within a specific region. Articles that inform, share experiences, and give practical advice are the editorial focus of these publications. New product reviews are becoming increasingly popular, as are "destination" articles about places where outdoor activities take place, opinion pieces, essays, and interviews.

Finding your niche

Outdoor writing is a market of niches, and you'll need to find yours. Start by making a list of your outdoor experiences, noting how many times a year you participate in the activities; where and with whom you participate in them; and events that may have occurred.

Next, read a number of magazines in your field of interest, and make a note of the following:

How many of the feature articles fall into the how-to category? What other types of writing does the magazine publish?

Is the focus of articles first-person (writer's personal experience) or third-party (experts in the field)? A mixture of the two?

What columns are open to free lancers? To determine this, see if they are written by the same person each issue; if not, they are probably open to free-lance contributions.

Pay special attention to the back page—often a place for short, first-person essays by a variety of writers.

Read the letters to the editor, too. There's no better place to discover the concerns and interests of the readership. And, as always, request and study writer's guidelines, if available.

Now, review your list of outdoor experiences. What types of articles and essays are you reasonably qualified to write? For instance, if you have canoed a number of times, but not regularly and always with your much more experienced friend as guide, you aren't ready to write for an audience of seasoned canoeists. Don't be discouraged. You can always become more familiar with an activity; but your present knowledge may be enough for certain types of articles. Remember that every form of recreation has many more novices than masters; perhaps you can write a short do's and don'ts piece for the first-time canoeist; interview three canoeing instructors on the basic ways to use a paddle; or write a humorous essay (as I did) from a beginner's point of view.

Even if you are fairly experienced, increase your knowledge with some more research before you query a magazine. The more you know, the easier it is to make your first sale.

High-impact queries

It's not enough to become well-versed in an activity or subject before you query the editor of an outdoor magazine; you also have to find a new twist to the material. As an example, bass fishing is a very popular topic in many outdoor magazines, with literally hundreds of articles published every year. This strong demand, however, produces an endless recycling of the same article ideas. If an editor needs yet another 2,000 words on "The Secrets of Summer Bass," he is likely to use regular contributors.

The good news for writers is that editors and their readers become bored with the same old material. How to get an editor's attention? Break out of the rut. Query for an article or essay centered on a new technique; a unique method; a way to solve a common problem; a novel use for a product; or a way to do something less expensively.

As you participate in the activity and do research, you'll discover what is already standard practice and knowledge. Then, improve upon what is known. Experiment (when it's safe to do so, of course). Ask others what approach or technique they have used successfully. Find out what tactics or methods were popular ten years ago, and see how they can be revived and updated.

Present your great new idea in the first sentence of the first paragraph of your query. Follow up with a few specifics. Now that you've piqued the editor's interest, explain why you're the person to write the article. With a little luck, you'll be well on your way to making a sale.

Photos

Most outdoor publications insist that photos accompany articles (and sometimes essays, too). Though the magazine may actually use only a few (usually 2 to 6 per article), editors like 15 to 20 to choose from. Some prefer all color or black-and-white; others a combination of the two. Many magazines include photo payment in the total fee; others pay extra for the photos they print, ranging from $10 and up for a single black-and-white shot, $30 to $250 for color, and $200 to $700 for a color photo that appears on the cover.

You don't have to be a professional photographer to sell your work. But you do have to take clear, well-lighted shots that reinforce some element of your text. Best advice: Have people doing something in your photos, because magazine editors hate static shots. For example, don't take a picture of an empty bike trail; instead, show two or three bicyclists peddling. Similarly, rather than telling readers how to set up a tent, include a series of step-by-step photos.

A 35-mm camera is standard equipment. New models do just about everything automatically, from focusing to selecting the correct lens opening for the right lighting. Most magazines have photo guidelines that will tell you not only the types of photos desired and how much they pay, but other important information, such as the preferred type and speed of film.

Take many photos, especially when you're starting out. Film is relatively cheap, and more photos mean you have more of a chance of taking publishable ones. You will also need to provide captions and get permission from the people in the photos to use their likeness.

Solid knowledge, a compelling twist, and strong photographic support: These are the elements for success in outdoor writing.

□ 65

TRAVEL WRITING IN FACT AND FICTION

BY JANE EDWARDS

LOOKING BACK, I SEE MY CHILDHOOD AS A KALEIDOSCOPE OF BURMA-Shave signs and boxcars bearing the mountain goat logo of the Great Northern Railway huffing and puffing across the Rockies; of being tucked into an upper berth, clothes swaying in a little hammock above my head, and spending the night in tiny roadside cabins resembling houses from a Monopoly set; of moving out, moving away, moving on with parents who searched for work all through the Depression.

By the time I was nine, my family had crisscrossed the Western states at least twenty times; sometimes by rail, more often in an elderly automobile, while my brother and I played endless games of War and Chinese checkers in the back seat. I remember train wrecks, two of them, and having to be let out of the car every few miles to be sick by the side of the road.

Some people might assume that after such a nomadic start I would have had enough traveling to last me a lifetime. Who, me? And miss seeing the rest of the world? No way!

Having by age nineteen finally conquered motion sickness (being too terrified to throw up when a violent electrical storm struck the DC-3 in which I was flying across the mountains from Acapulco to Mexico City), I've been going places ever since. And enjoying encores of every trip by using spots visited as settings for my novels and short stories.

Sometimes, the narrative was imposed upon a background. My first book, *What Happened to Amy?*, concerned a mystery novelist who unwittingly devised a fictional plot bearing an uncomfortable resemblance to some actual skulduggery being perpetrated in her neighborhood. Convinced that she was wise to them, the bad guys kidnapped her secretary, then attempted to burn down her house to destroy the manuscript.

My placid hometown didn't seem a believable site for such dirty deeds. But two hours down the road, the Monterey Peninsula was just remote enough and sufficiently tinged with glamour to make spine-tingling events seem at least within the realm of possibility.

On other occasions, it was a setting that suggested the plot. "Mystery on the High Seas," my first short story (published in *Calling All Girls*), owed its existence to our trip to Hawaii aboard the *Lurline*. Noticing the valuable gems worn by some of our fellow passengers, I began to wonder how a jewel thief might go about smuggling a stolen necklace ashore. The on-board kennel suggested a possibility for my young heroine to investigate.

Most of our trips weren't immediately recycled into fiction. Ancient lands I visited during a Mediterranean cruise in 1978 became the locale for *Dangerous Odyssey,* which I wrote a dozen years later. Mythology and the history of Greece both played a part in this contemporary tale of the quest for a priceless treasure. Guidebooks purchased for a few *drachmas,* maps detailing the old section of Athens, souvenir post-cards and museum brochures, all helped me plot the adventure. Resources such as these, available only on the spot, are absolutely priceless when attempting to evoke the atmosphere of a place after the first sharp memories have blurred. On every trip I gather up as much printed material as I can stuff into my suitcase. Sooner or later, it will come in handy when I attempt to conjure up images and describe them so vividly that readers can see that place in their mind's eye.

Written notes, scribbled along the way, are invaluable in evoking atmosphere. Into a shorthand book (lightweight with pages that lie flat) go hundreds of disjointed jottings: what local people wear, how they get around, what kind of money they spend, how their children react to strangers. Before the impact of an experience has a chance to fade, I struggle to describe sunlight striking a timeworn marble column; the scorching heat in a glass-blower's shop; the staccato click of worry beads being fingered by Turkish men in business suits. Someday—I hope—each of those fragments of experience will help me call to mind a scene and reproduce it accurately.

Other more prosaic notes record events as they take place. A journal page proved a lifesaver in plotting *Dangerous Odyssey.* This novel of romantic suspense is set in part on the island of Mykonos. Having trapped my heroine aboard a yacht owned by the rich villain, I ran into problems devising a logical way for her to escape. Fortunately, I ran across a few handwritten paragraphs describing how our ship had anchored out past the breakwater at that particular port-of-call. Because of Mykonos' shallow harbor, cruise passengers are routinely ferried ashore by launch.

This solved the dilemma. I simply wrote the *Golden Odyssey* into the scene and had Kelsey outwit her adversaries by slipping ashore via launch. The episode gave me a chance to draw a word-picture of Mykonos' square whitewashed houses and conical windmills shimmering across a sapphire blue sea. Better yet, the chase seemed believable because it *could* have happened exactly that way.

References to ethnic foods can help you conjure up a particular spot. The mention of *baklava* or *moussaka* guarantees instant images of Greece. Jerk chicken and Blue Mountain coffee? No worries, mon; that's Jamaica! Soda bread and tea? Irish fare on a "soft" day—drizzly, that is.

A few foreign words sprinkled through a narrative are like herbs in the stew. Used sparingly, they add zest and authenticity to your narrative. But since relatively few American readers understand Gaelic, German, or Greek, I try to find an offhand way to translate foreign phrases:

"Cead mille failté," Rory muttered.
"A 'hundred thousand welcomes' indeed!" Tara thought in annoyance. (*The Ghost of Castle Kilgarrom*)

"Güten tag"—"Good day," Wendy said. ("The Case of the Musical Ghost")

Kelsey replied, *"Ohi, efharisto"*—"No, thank you"—but with such a pleasant smile that no one took offense. (*Dangerous Odyssey*)

Instead of sprinkling my pages with foreign words, I prefer to characterize people of different cultures by the rhythm of their speech:

"It's back to Dublin he's gone," Brigid said. (*The Ghost of Castle Kilgarrom*)

Anton Jablonsky nodded. "That is so. Afraid I have been for thirty years. Then, this morning, I decide. Out the truth must come!" ("Demolition Dolly and the Professor's Secret")

The hotel manager's round black eyes glowed with admiration. "The *kyria*'s so-beautiful hair caught his attention, understandably." (*Dangerous Odyssey*)

A tape recorder can be a tremendous help to the traveling writer. The push of a button will take you back to a corner of the world you visited years earlier and reproduce for you the crisply accented lecture of a guide at the Tower of London; the rhythmic click of castanets in Sonora; the gondolier's rendition of "Santa Lucia." Using this method to evoke memories is almost as effective as paying a return visit to a given locale. Carry extra tapes and extra batteries as a safeguard against disaster.

I enjoy digging up entertaining facts about the places we visit, then using them in my stories. To avoid sounding like a guidebook, I try to work these tidbits into conversations between my characters:

"Amsterdam means 'dam on the River Amstel,'" Jan said. "Come along and look at the houses. Each one is different because until the time of Napoleon no house had a number." ("The Dutch Diamond Mystery")

"My mom told me the Acropolis is called the Sacred Rock," Zoe said, noticing the rapt expression on Kelsey's face. (*Dangerous Odyssey*)

"During the Troubles," Aileen explained, "the Irish people were not even allowed to refer to their homeland by name. So poets made up a special alias for Ireland. They called it 'Cathleen O'Houlihan.' Whenever they wrote about 'Cathleen O'Houlihan,' their Irish readers knew exactly what they meant." ("The Theft of The O'Houlihan")

Doing your homework before packing for a trip can ease your introduction to unfamiliar territory. If your destination is within the U.S. or Canada, contact the local Chamber of Commerce several weeks in advance. Explain that you intend to visit their area, and ask them to send you a packet of tourist information. They'll be delighted to oblige.

Addresses and 800 numbers for all state and provincial visitors' bureaus as well as for many large cities are listed in the annual *Rand McNally Road Atlas*. Travel clubs like AAA provide detailed tour books to members. A few publications also list sources of information for foreign countries. Packets from overseas can take a long time to arrive, so do some backup research in the meantime. Before relying on guidebooks, check to see whether they were updated or if their copyright was issued some time back.

Along with current resources, I delve into every article I can find about a place I'm about to visit. Geography doesn't change, and now and then you'll come across a fascinating item in some old magazine that can be used to add drama and color to your tale.

I knew very little about Oregon at the time I decided this state would make an ideal setting for my book, *Yellow Ribbons*. Searching for background material before visiting in person, I turned up a decade-old issue of *National Geographic* that proved to be a goldmine of information about the dunes that stretch for fifty miles along the coast. Learning about the "mushers," their teams of Siberian huskies, and their use of the sandy wastes to practice for sled races inspired a memorable scene I'd otherwise never have included in the book.

Last summer, when I decided to try writing nonfiction as a change of pace, it seemed logical to start with travel articles. I had visited all fifty states, after all, besides dozens of countries on five continents. Most of my fiction used settings drawn from those experiences.

I soon found that free-lancing destination pieces for the Sunday travel pages of a regional newspaper was considerably different from tossing a cast of imaginary characters into a strange place and relating their adventures. Novels allow space for a rich variety of detail. Even short stories give their authors scope to expand a bit on topics they believe will interest their readers. Conversely, a destination *article* must provide an overview of an entire travel experience. *Facts* lie at its core: how to get there, where to stay, which attractions merit a visit, what dinner for two at a decent restaurant will cost.

All this (not to mention comments on scenery, climate, recreational facilities and the best buys in local shops) needs to be packed into about 750 tightly written words, leaving room for photos and a short sidebar or two. Newspaper editors always want people in those photos, preferably families who look as if they're having a good time. Prints or negatives are usually acceptable. Magazines, on the other hand, generally require slides for illustrations. *Learn their requirements before leaving home, and load your camera accordingly.*

Authors of travel articles should hook the reader's interest with their very first sentence—just as they do in writing fiction. A feature I wrote describing a Panama Canal transit began: "One month ago we stood on the deck of the *Sky Princess* and watched the sun rise in the west. Yes, *west. . . .*"

In the past several months, I have sold "spin-offs" from my newspaper features to almost a dozen magazines. And I have two nonfiction travel books in the planning stages. All this was the result of my refusing to stay home.

How about you? Do you have a story to tell? Go someplace!

❏ 66

From Food Processor to Word Processor

By Susan Kelly

I BEGAN WRITING ABOUT FOOD FOR TWO REASONS: FIRST, I LIKE TO cook as much as I like to eat; second, I wanted a break from what I usually write about, which is crime. (Let me note here that many mystery authors manage to combine corpses and cuisine, à la Katherine Hall Page and Robert B. Parker. For myself, I'd just as soon keep the two separate.)

The first thing I noticed when I began researching the field is the enormous editorial appetite (first awful but irresistible pun) for articles about food and cooking. I was staggered by the number of journals devoted to the culinary arts. On my local grocery store's magazine rack, which is by no means either huge or comprehensive, I counted three publications devoted just to Italian cuisine. I couldn't begin to count the other special interest journals: vegetarian, light, country, ethnic, heart-safe, etc., or the large number of general magazines that publish articles on food.

Newspapers, daily or weekly, big city or small town, print vast numbers of articles on food and cooking. (The larger papers devote whole sections to the subject.) Most newspapers will consider free-lance work. Rates vary widely. You may not get paid much—or indeed anything by a very small publication—but you will have garnered a byline and a clip to add to your store of credentials.

The market for articles on food is a thriving one. And why not? Aside from sex and death, I can't think of a greater human interest subject than food.

Here is my own personal recipe for writing about food and cooking, one that I have checked in my test kitchen. The ingredients are given in order of assembly, but feel free to rearrange them or make substitutions—as any innovative cook would do.

1. **Go with your particular interest and expertise.** This is especially important for the beginner. After you've established yourself, you can branch out into other areas. But for the time being, if you have the world's best recipe for gefilte fish, or *caldo verde,* or cassoulet, or pot roast, or linguine with clam sauce, or if your grandmother was the best German cook in recent history, the world wants to hear about it.

2. **Decide the focus of your piece and then pare (second awful but irresistible pun) that down as much as possible.** It's no good trying to dash off a 2,000-word piece on "Italian Food." There are thousands of *books* on this subject already, and many others to come. Editors need articles with narrowly focused topics and with fresh slants.

To provide focus as well as originality, it helps to think in terms of categories. The following lists are by no means all-inclusive, but may be extensive enough to inspire you to create your own:

Ethnic: Thai, French, Italian, Jewish, Polish, Irish, Creole, African, Portuguese, Caribbean, Mexican, Swedish, Chinese

Provincial/Regional: Southern, New England, Southwestern, Pacific Rim, Tuscan, Provençal, Mediterranean, Iberian, Cantonese

Holiday: Thanksgiving, Passover, Easter, Christmas, Asian New Year, Chanukah, Kwanzaa

Seasonal: spring, summer, fall, winter (or by month)

Occasional: wedding, birthday, anniversary, graduation, bar mitzvah/ bas mitzvah, christening, bridal or baby shower, cocktail party

Meal Type: breakfast, brunch, lunch, tea, dinner, late supper

Health/Vegetarian: Low fat/low cholesterol, low salt, low sugar or sugar-free, meatless, non-dairy

Food Types: appetizers, soups, main courses, salads, desserts

Clearly, you don't have to consider all those categories. A choice of three is a good start. To illustrate my point: If you want to write about Italian cooking, why not do a piece on an Italian Christmas Eve dinner? Or, since the traditional Italian Christmas Eve dinner involves twelve fish dishes, refine the topic further by considering a fourth category, that of the food group. If your interest—or expertise—is Jewish cooking, think of writing an article about a seder dinner. There you have ethnicity, holiday, and meal type established for you. Once your imagination starts rolling, the possibilities are endless. A vegetarian Thai summer luncheon; a Scottish brunch for New Year's Day; a Provençal birthday picnic for two; a low-fat Mexican dinner.

3. **Write *articles* about food and cooking, not recipe files.** Your articles should offer helpful practical information beyond lists of ingredients and cooking times. Editors and their readers want serving suggestions, menu plans, and whatever other instruction and guidance you can offer. Tips about table decoration are always welcome, as are suggestions about wine appropriate to the food.

4. **Articles about food and cooking benefit from background.** In addition to giving instructions, include anecdotes. These can be personal— how *you* became interested in cooking such and such; first time you cooked it; your guests' reactions to it.

If you have no personal anecdotes, historical and cultural ones will do fine. If you are writing about veal Marengo, for instance, you might want to mention that the dish was invented to celebrate Napoleon's victory over Austria in the Italian town of Marengo. If you are writing about champagne, you might recount the legend that the bowl-shaped champagne glass (from which, incidentally, one should never drink) was formed from the mold of the breast of the mistress of the French king. Or that *puttanesca* sauce is alleged to have been the invention of Italian prostitutes seeking to whip up a quick snack for their clients. Such stories add real spice (third awful but irresistible pun) to a piece.

5. **Bear in mind that food and travel overlap.** Think of the Korean produce markets of New York. And the Polish sausage-makers of the Pioneer Valley in Massachusetts. Or the chowder specialists of coastal Maine. Or the Italian immigrant fishermen of San Francisco, who invented *cioppino*. Readers enjoy local color along with a recipe.

6. **Always get exact quantities of ingredients for recipes—and then test them yourself.** Make sure the instructions you give your readers are as clear and exact as possible. Be precise—even though anyone

who cooks knows that exact times and measurements are absolutely essential only in certain kinds of baking. I suppose everyone's heard the story about the published recipe that called for a can of condensed milk to be placed in a crockpot along with the rest of the ingredients. Now, common sense would dictate that one would *pour* the condensed milk from the can *into* the crockpot. Unfortunately, some readers, not explicitly *told* to do so, *didn't*. The results of that omission were . . . explosive!

If you offer recipes with variations or substitutions for ingredients, be sure to check out all those as well. Fat-free unflavored yogurt seems like a perfectly acceptable replacement for sour cream, and many times it is. In other cases—ugh. You can't predict with assurance. Don't take someone else's word. Perform your own taste-test.

7. **If you are writing about a professional chef, be sure to interview him or her.** This means going beyond accumulating the basic biographical and career data. Get permission to watch the chef in action. Request (no, insist on) written copies of any recipes the chef is willing to share. Ask for the chef's own personal serving and wine suggestions. Get the menu, whether the chef is an independent caterer or the employee/owner of a restaurant, so you can refer to it while you write. Talk to the chef's colleagues and competitors.

A real bonus of a thorough interview is that you will probably be invited to sample the chef's art.

8. **Time your article appropriately.** This is of special importance to a free lancer. Allow a lead time of a month for a small newspaper, two months for bigger ones, and up to a year for magazines. Publishers plan each issue well in advance for a number of reasons—the tightness of printing schedules is the foremost. No publisher is willing to incur the expense involved to disrupt the deadlines except for a drastic reason. Don't submit an article on fourteenth-century English Valentine's Day treats to a magazine in December and expect to see it in print in February. A year from that February is more like it.

9. **Finally, read at least a year's back issues of the magazine you're interested in querying about an article idea.** This will give you a clear sense of what particular publications seek and the tone and style in which your article should be written.

Some magazines look for pieces with a light or humorous touch. Others demand a more serious, almost scientific, approach. Still others want a definite historical, cultural, regional, or social orientation. Also, bear in mind a magazine's audience. A journal whose typical reader is a college graduate, a resident of an upscale city neighborhood or affluent suburb, and a professional earning in excess of $150,000 a year will not be interested in an article on the manifold culinary uses of Fritos.

Do not worry if the publication you've targeted for your article on "low-fat pasta salads for an informal June wedding" published a similar-sounding piece five years ago. Yours, because it's yours, will be different. And in any case, such ideas are always recycled.

❏ 67

WHEN YOU WRITE A PERSONAL EXPERIENCE ARTICLE

BY JUDY BODMER

SOMETHING HAS HAPPENED TO YOU AND YOU WANT TO WRITE ABOUT it. Does that mean it's marketable? Not necessarily. Many people who take my creative writing class do so because they've been through a divorce, had a child die, experienced a life-threatening illness, or have come to a place in their lives at which they want to pass on what they've learned to another generation and would like to write about their experiences.

Some of them get published. Others don't. Those who do have learned the basic principles of writing a marketable personal experience article: They slant their idea to a specific audience, choose one of the three types of articles that will tell their story best, use all four of the basic elements of a personal experience article, and target the right market. The secret to getting a personal experience article published is to use your experience as a stepping-stone to help others who have faced similar situations. Writing about a tragic event, such as the death of a child, probably won't sell until the writer understands what he or she learned while going through the experience. A couple of angles one could use are: 1) how to cope with the death of a child or 2) how to help a friend grieve.

The experience you write about doesn't have to be tragic. It can be as simple as baking cookies with your grandchildren, watching your son play baseball, or writing thank-you notes. It may take you quite a while to process and find the right slant. Keep asking yourself, what did I learn that will help someone else? When you've finally found the message in your experience, describe it in one sentence or phrase; it will keep your article on track. You won't be tempted to go off on interesting but irrelevant sidetracks that may have really happened but have nothing to do with the theme. Your phrase should read something like this:

- Six steps that helped me forgive.
- Ways to cope with an empty nest.
- How to handle stress.

Don't skimp on taking this step. One of the main reasons articles are rejected is that they aren't focused.

Three Kinds of Personal Experience Articles

Once you know the theme, you are ready to choose the type of article you want to write. Basically there are three: *straight narration, partial frame,* and *full frame.*

Straight narration

This type of article reads like a short story: It has a beginning, a middle, and an end. You set scenes, use dialogue, and action. As in a good short story, the tension should mount until it is resolved. The message woven throughout the piece is driven home with a powerful ending. The straight narration approach is best used to describe a dramatic event: a daring rescue off a mountaintop; surviving an airplane crash; or having a baby in the middle of a snowstorm. This is where you should let your personality and the personality of the people involved shine through. Use strong nouns and active verbs. Show the action. Don't just say you and your husband had a fight, show it.

Partial frame

This type of article is used most frequently. It usually opens with an anecdote and then makes a transition into the body of the article. For example, a taxi driver picks up a fare in New York City. In the body of the article you show how that fateful day changed the taxi driver's life forever. Or you open with a description of taking your three young children grocery shopping. The body of the article then discusses the simple trick you learned that helped turn a sometimes frustrating chore into a game your children all love.

Full frame

Here you first set a scene of your article using description, dialogue, and action. You then move into the body and list the points you plan to cover; for instance, the five things your mother never told you about sex. Each point is then expanded, sometimes quoting experts, statistics, or anecdotes. In the end, you shift back to the opening scene to wrap up your discussion.

An article I wrote for a parenting magazine on why I watch my son play baseball opens as I sit in the stands. I describe being cold, burning my mouth on hot coffee, and seeing my son strike out. In the body of the article I discuss the reasons parents put themselves through this often painful experience. For the ending, I returned to my opening scene describing my son asking for money to buy a hamburger and the coach coming up and talking to me. Through action and dialogue I answer the question that I presented in my opening.

The Four Elements of a Personal Experience Article

Before you begin to write, make a rough outline using the following four elements of a personal experience article.

1. *The opening.* Choose an aspect of your story that will catch the reader's attention. It can be an anecdote, a quotation, an intriguing situation or a question that must be answered. One of my articles opened with an anecdote about a minister who counseled a couple. The wife wanted to leave her husband because she couldn't take the black book any more. The black book turned out to be a list that the husband was keeping of everything she'd done wrong since the day they married.

2. *The transition.* Transition statements that are pretty straightforward and sound almost trite tell the reader where you are going.

In "Helping Friends Who Grieve," which appeared in *Reader's Digest,* Lois Duncan describes the fatal shooting of her daughter. After opening with the tragic event, she uses the following transition statement: "Here is some advice I wish I'd been given when heartbreak was a stranger." The transition for my black book article was, "If you are keeping a similar list, what I learned may help you."

Writing a good transition statement is probably the most important step in writing personal experience articles. If you've processed your theme, it should be easy to write. It will also help you focus your article to a specific audience.

3. *The body.* In the body, you discuss what you learned from your

experience. You can use bullets, numbers, headings (remember readers and editors love white space), or just develop the idea in narrative form. Each point can be enhanced with more details, examples from other people, quotes from experts, statistics, or another example from your life. In my black book article, I talked about the steps needed to achieve forgiveness.

4. *The ending.* In the end, drive home your message. Here you can summarize the points you've made, quote an expert or someone famous, challenge your reader, or project the future. Whenever I'm stuck, I look back at my opening. Is there some element there that you can draw on to help you wrap up your article? In the transition statement of my baseball article, I asked, "Why do I do this?" For the ending I answer with the question, "Where else can I watch my son grow into a man?"

THE MARKET

Many magazines are looking for personal experience pieces; the trick is to match your theme with the right magazine. Once you've found a promising market, study a couple of issues. (The library is a good source for periodicals, or write for a sample copy.) Look at the cover, the table of contents, and the ads. Read the articles. Try to get a feel for the reader.

An author I know sold an article on her Hawaiian camping trip to the *Seattle Times* and then rewrote her camping experience from a different angle and sold it to *Seattle's Child.* One of my students wrote a piece about the ways she has made her long commute fun. She sold it to a newspaper in Seattle, which has a terrible traffic problem. Another young author sold a piece to *Seventeen* about how to make the most of being grounded—something she had experienced a lot of growing up.

Timeliness is also a factor. Seasonal material should be submitted six to twelve months ahead of the holiday or special celebration. (Check your market list for individual magazine requirements.) During the Christmas season, collect ideas and write about them while you're still under the influence of the season. Then starting in January send them out. If the idea hasn't sold by June, put it away, rework it if necessary, and try again the following year.

Magazines receive lots of submissions for the major holidays, but they are constantly looking for articles about some of the lesser known ones such as Arbor Day, St. Patrick's Day, or Martin Luther King's Birthday. They want stories about swimming for summer, skiing in winter. My baseball article was set in May and was just right for the next Mother's Day.

After choosing a market, you will save time by querying magazines to see if they'd be interested in your idea. Most magazines reply to queries within two weeks to a month. (Again, check your market lists. Some magazines want to see only the completed article.)

Once you receive a positive response to your query, try to picture a typical reader sitting across from you at lunch and write to him or her. This will help give your reader a truly personal experience.

With planning and persistence, personal experience articles can be a good way to break into publishing. They take little research, are in great demand, and pay anywhere from $15 to $2,000. Another benefit of these articles: There's nothing more rewarding than touching someone's heart.

❏ 68

WHEN A BIOGRAPHER'S SUBJECT IS LESS THAN PERFECT

BY DAVID ROBERTSON

RECENTLY, I HAD THE PLEASURE OF READING IN A NATIONAL NEWS-paper a favorable, front-page review of my first biography. The book's subject is James F. Byrnes, a former U.S. Secretary of State, who was an unrepentant segregationist, a firm advocate of the atomic bombings in Japan, and the architect of the Republican "southern strategy" that has given us such leaders as Newt Gingrich. Stating that I had chosen a "sometimes wholly unsympathetic subject," the reviewer praised the book as a "balanced, deeply researched and sympathetic history of the man."

My first reaction to the review was like that of a boy who had learned how to aim a pellet gun, but who then shot and killed a songbird: I felt pride in my skills, but was appalled at the results. What had I done by raising in public memory the life of such an apparently unsympathetic figure? And if I, as the biographer, had been found sympathetic to such a life, what did that say about me, and the uses to which I had put my life and literary work?

Upon reflection, however, I decided to accept the praise for what it is. Even unsympathetic subjects deserve an accurate accounting of their minor virtues, as well as their major vices. If nothing else, such a biographical account can help explain to the reader how the subject failed to achieve a good, or at least decent, life by choices taken or not taken. And, frankly, for a biographer searching for a modern subject, twentieth-century history offers far more major figures whose lives will provide shock and disapproval than admiration and self-identification. Think, for example, of the number of twentieth-century leaders who were "great" in the sense that Stalin was great, rather than that Eleanor Roosevelt was a great leader.

Whether in dealing with a public or a private figure, with a sympa-

thetic or unsympathetic subject, the writing of all biographies is, I
believe, a deliberate grappling with the "other," an entity different from
us, a person whose life we cannot fully comprehend or approve. The
first biographer to learn this hard lesson was the biblical Jacob, who
spent all night wrestling with an angel in an attempt to learn the other
being's true name. (Jacob got his hip broken for his trouble.) But the
resulting struggles, particularly with an unsympathetic subject, can
strengthen a biographer's skills, just as I feel mine were strengthened
by my struggles to determine whether Secretary Byrnes led an admirable or unadmirable life.

Currently, I am grappling with my own dark angel; I am writing a
second biography of a man who, unlike Byrnes, is largely an admirable
figure, but whose personality and actions are disturbing to me. The
subject is Denmark Vesey (1767?–1822), a former slave who purchased
his own freedom and then attempted the largest slave insurrection in
the history of the United States at Charleston, South Carolina. In many
ways, we are similar: Vesey, like me, was in his late forties when
he attempted his uprising; we could have spoken in several foreign
languages; we both spent much of our free time as manual laborers,
and have no illusions about the horrors of American slavery. But as I
walk the nineteenth-century streets of Charleston at night, passing
Vesey's carpentry shop where he had planned his revolution, one
thought is inescapable to me: I am a white southerner. Had Vesey's
plot succeeded, his followers were under his strict orders to kill *every*
white person at Charleston, including men, women, and small children,
before burning the city and seizing ships at harbor to sail for Africa.
Hence, although I am Vesey's biographer and intend to write sympathetically of his life, there is no doubt that, had we chanced to meet,
Denmark Vesey would have cut David Robertson's throat.

My experience in writing and researching lives of subjects whose
actions appear malevolent or whose historical image resists a biographer's self-identification has led me to adopt certain techniques. I offer
these techniques to other biographers struggling with a less-than-
sympathetic subject.

Write the life your subject lived. Some subjects, as disparate and
attractive as Alice James or Adlai Stevenson, engage a biographer's
admiration for what they could not or did not do. But frequently in
writing of public or famous figures, the biographer is tempted to scold

or rebuke the subject for not living the life the biographer expected. This can be great fun at the expense of the dead, of course, as Lytton Strachey demonstrated in *Eminent Victorians*. But recent biographies of John Kennedy and Lyndon Johnson have been marred, in my opinion, by the biographers' refusal to consider the historical and political limits to their subjects' actions and their personal failings. Byrnes, for example, as a Supreme Court Justice, U.S. Senator, and the "Assistant President" during World War II, did far less than he should have to protect civil liberties for blacks and the rights of organized labor. But in researching the careers of other prominent southern politicians—including Justice Hugo Black of Alabama, who served with Byrnes on the Supreme Court—I discovered that Byrnes often did more than his contemporaries expected of him, and sometimes did so to his personal disadvantage. Justice Black chose to remove himself from electoral politics and try to do what was right; Jimmy Byrnes chose to remain in politics and to do what was possible. I chose to write the life of the politician, not the jurist.

Such a decision means that the biographer must emphasize historical context as well as personality. Expect to do far more research in history and social sciences if you choose to write on an unsympathetic subject. (My bibliography and endnotes to the Byrnes biography ran to 69 small-type pages.) That research helped me comprehend—if not fully approve—the planned ferocity of Denmark Vesey's attempted revolt. I discovered that during Denmark Vesey's lifetime, South Carolina contained more African-born people in bondage than any other slave-holding state at the time. These proud men and women considered themselves to be *African,* not African-American, and in a type of "ethnic cleansing," their masters were attempting to destroy their ties to marriage, parenthood, their religion, and their nations. Vesey, who probably had traveled to Africa, preached to these first-generation slaves that he was attempting to liberate not only them, but also their right as a people to exist unmolested in their own homeland. Considered historically as an armed struggle against physical and cultural genocide, Vesey's actions appear more expedient. Do we blame the Cheyenne for taking no prisoners at Little Big Horn?

Don't be surprised by surprises. In writing a biography of an unredeemably selfish or cruel individual, don't be surprised by occasional acts of generosity or sentimentality. Include them, not as unaccountable surprises, but as further evidence for your case. Sentimentality is the weakling brother of brutality. Even human monsters will occasionally show pity or indulgence as if to convince themselves, if not the reader of their biographies, that they really *aren't* monsters. Hitler, an acquaintance told me, was very fond of lighthearted movies and large, friendly dogs. Stalin, with his baggy-seat trousers, his beloved pipe tobacco, and his crinkly brown eyes, could appear as Uncle Joe from the Old Country. The contiguous existence of pity and brutality within one uneasy individual is a concept as twentieth-century as Freud, who warned us that inside each sadist is a powerless child terrified of becoming a victim, and as ancient as Tacitus, who wrote of one cruel Caesar that if we could see his soul at night, we would see a face self-lacerated in fear.

Occasionally, a subject acting against type can illuminate the larger personality the biographer wishes he had been. Byrnes, who after his retirement from the Department of State spent much of his life frustrating efforts to put civil rights legislation into effect in the South, was outraged when a black friend of his was denied the use of a public restroom in South Carolina in the 1960s. Byrnes wrote angry letters, and considered all sorts of political retribution, in an effort to convince a white segregationist that Byrnes' black friend was "special," and therefore deserving of all the civil liberties and rights of any U.S. citizen. Yet Byrnes seemed never to have considered that, legally and morally, all individuals are special, regardless of their skin color. Byrnes' failure to make an intuitive and ethical leap toward all U.S. citizens, regardless of his good intentions in this single episode, illuminates both his possibilities and his limitations as a national leader.

Shake hands with your dark side. "If Hitler could have had any friends, I would certainly have been among his close friends," Albert Speer tells us in his memoirs of the Third Reich. Speer's account of how he became Hitler's chief architect and armaments minister is in many ways also the "best" biography of Hitler, but it is in no way an *apologia* for the madness and unadulterated evil of Adolf Hitler. Speer's book is, rather, a disturbing account of how a possibly decent individual came in his writing to identify with such an evil person. Speer's account is plainly self-serving. But it offers a statement *in extremis* of the final temptations and difficulties besetting the biographer of an unsympathetic subject.

Leon Edel has warned us of what he called "transference," whereby a biographer's subject becomes an idealized self-portrait of the biographer. Transference occurs most commonly when the subject is considered admirable. Conversely, when writing of an unsympathetic subject, the biographer is in danger of being unnerved by recognizing his own baser impulses in the actions of the subject. I began to be concerned with my own past untruthfulness, for example, after years of seeing in Jimmy Byrnes' life how easily a lie can advance a career. Similarly, I have never felt the lash of slavery; but what if I had? And what if I had then met Denmark Vesey, a man of biblical presence and authority, who secretly handed me a weapon and told me, as he told his other followers at Charleston, "And they shall utterly destroy all that was in the city, with the edge of the sword"?

In recognizing the parts of our personality we wish to deny, we can to a degree control them or change them. In writing about an unsympathetic subject, you must expect to learn as much about your own darker side as about your subject's. When the subject's baser motives hit too close to home, the biographer can be tempted to write an overlong justification of the subject's actions, or be cowed into an embarrassed silence. But if a biographer is honest about his or her own strengths and weaknesses, then that biographer can write about an unsympathetic subject with uncommon honesty and strength.

All of which brings us back to Jacob struggling with his angel at night. Jacob, you will recall, never learned the angel's true name. But in acknowledgement of Jacob's struggles, and the wound he received, the angel told Jacob *his* true name. Jacob became a better, and different, person for knowing it. Similarly, the struggles and personal wounds a biographer sustains in writing about an unsympathetic subject can, at the end of the subject's life, leave the biographer with a different and better identity: as a researcher, biographer, and as literary artist.

□ 69

CREATING GREETING CARDS

BY WENDY DAGER

HAVE YOU EVER RECEIVED A GREETING CARD THAT WAS SO "YOU," IT could have been written by you? Have you ever had a brief, funny thought that would make a great T-shirt slogan, or perhaps composed a poem that brought tears to the eyes of a reader?

Using one or all of these criteria can help you break into greeting card writing, an industry that boasted $6.3 *billion* in sales last year, representing 7.4 billion greeting cards sold.

There are now approximately 1,500 greeting card companies. Although the majority of them do not accept submissions from free lancers, many are eager for writers who can provide them with fresh ideas. Just follow these simple rules, and you'll find yourself hooked on creating one-liners, poems, and words of wisdom specifically for the greeting card market.

1. Always send for guidelines. Get addresses of greeting card companies, either from *The Writer* Magazine or from the *Greeting Card Industry Directory*. (The directory is expensive, and I wouldn't advise your buying it unless you have made a few sales first.) The Greeting Card Association (1200 G Street N.W., Suite 760, Washington, D.C. 20005), which publishes the directory, is very receptive to inquiries and will send a price list of all the books, tapes, and related industry information they publish. In addition, some greeting card companies have their addresses on the backs of their cards, or the name of their city and state (so a writer can call information and get a phone number, then call the company and see if they will provide an address for freelance submissions).

If a company does accept work from free lancers, the guidelines will tell you the required format for submissions, the style they are looking for (some even give examples of published cards), and the occasions and holidays for which they need ideas. For example, some companies may produce cards for Christmas, but not Chanukah.

2. Brainstorm! Keep pads of paper around the house so you can scribble down thoughts while you are doing chores, or invest in a voice-activated tape recorder (about $35 at discount stores) to record ideas. Make up your own worksheets. For example, for Christmas ideas (usually, a company accepts seasonal ideas for the following year right *after* the holiday), write down the many things associated with it—Santa, tree, tinsel, presents, reindeer, etc.—then try to think of them in a funny or sentimental scenario. This method can be applied to any holiday or occasion. Recall situations you've been in or things your friends or relatives have said. Are they quirky, funny, silly, romantic? Can you tighten them to create a greeting card?

3. Most companies prefer submissions on 3"x5" cards, using the following format: O indicates what's to appear on the *outside* of the card; I is for the *inside*. You can put the holiday or occasion on the topmost line of the card, as follows:

Christmas
O: What has a red suit, white beard and flies?
I: A Santa who never bathes! Merry Christmas!

Girlfriends
O: He got me an iron for my birthday, which I used right away . . .
I: He should be coming out of the coma soon.

You can also put a description of the artwork you visualize on the top line, or in parentheses after O:

Birthday
O: (photo or picture of a gorilla)
I: Happy Birthday! You're in the primate of your life!

There is no need to send a mock-up of the card, unless it is a puzzle, maze, or game. Check greeting card counters in stores for examples; these types of cards are usually directed at children.

Other greeting card companies accept submissions on 8 1/2"x11" sheets of paper (indicated in their guidelines). They might also be willing to consider faxed or E-mailed submissions, but you must first clear this with the editor. On the back of each card, put your name, address, and phone number. I recommend purchasing a self-inking stamp with this information (about $15 or less), to save time. Do *not* send simultaneous submissions. If a company rejects your ideas, then you can feel free to send them somewhere else. As a rule, do not send fewer than six or more than twenty ideas. Some companies will specify in their guidelines how many ideas (called a "batch") they will consider at one time.

Put a code number on the lower right hand corner of each submission (Birthday ideas can be B1, B2, B3, etc.; Christmas can be C1, C2, etc.), and keep track of what ideas correspond to which code numbers. Keep copies of all your submissions and the names of the companies to which you send them. A company may decide to purchase your idea C2, but, if you don't know which one they're buying, you're in trouble!

4. Expect to wait at least one month for a response, sometimes longer. After two months, send a polite follow-up letter inquiring about your submission. Enclose a self-addressed stamped envelope for their reply.

5. Greeting card companies receive hundreds of ideas a year and buy only a select few, so if you submit twenty ideas and sell one, you have beaten the odds. The company will send you a contract, indicating that they would like to purchase your idea and are buying all rights to it, which of course, means that it becomes their property. You must also attest to the fact that it is, indeed, *your* idea to sell. Read the contract carefully before signing it, then return it. Don't forget to make a copy for yourself. Generally, payment arrives thirty days or so after publication of the card, along with several samples of the finished card. It is rare, though not unheard of, for a writer to receive writing credit on the back of the card.

6. How much can you expect to be paid? Anywhere from $25 to $150 for each idea purchased, with $100 the average for a one- or two-line gag. Although not the norm, royalties are sometimes negotiable (a company's guidelines will indicate if they pay royalties). Payment for a poem is more, about $200 on the average, for all rights.

Because greeting card companies are as individual as the people who run them, payment varies. The companies that give royalties are indeed a minority, and flat-fee is the norm, on acceptance or on publication, for all rights. While most companies do not allow the writer to retain rights to his work, there are a few that do. Your contract will tell you if you are selling all rights to an idea.

7. Some companies will indicate that they wish to hold an idea for further consideration. This generally means it must pass a review board

before they decide to accept or reject it. In this case, do not submit
the idea elsewhere until the company has made its final decision. Sometimes they will hold an idea up to six months; after sixty days, however,
you may send a polite letter with SASE, inquiring about its status. If
they decide not to purchase your idea, you are then free to submit it
to another company.

8. I'm often asked, "How can I keep a company from 'stealing' my
ideas?" You must keep in mind the old saying, "There is nothing new
under the sun." Maybe someone, somewhere, has already come up
with your idea and has beaten you to the punch. Editors have reputations to maintain, and it is highly unlikely that they will steal your
idea. You may submit your idea anywhere you choose (following guidelines, of course). If your work is rejected, it is because an editor simply
cannot use it or may already have something similar; if it is rejected
a number of times, consider discarding or reworking it. Editors want
to accept new ideas; that's their job.

Some other tips:

• Always enclose a self-addressed stamped envelope with the proper
postage with any correspondence to a greeting card company.

• Always be polite when you write to an editor. I once sent a thank-
you note to an editor for purchasing an idea, and she remembered me
the next time she needed a one-liner for a card. Now she regularly
faxes me cartoon cards that need inside gags.

• Diversify. Some companies may want punchy one-liners or thoughtful poetry for plaques, magnets, buttons, mugs, key chains, and "soft-
line" items like T-shirts and aprons. Keep in mind that "brevity is the
soul of wit." It's a tiny space you're trying to fill, so conserve your
words, but pack them with wit.

• There's always a market for humor of various types: risqué, studio,
juvenile, cute, silly, contemporary, or laugh-out-loud.

• Keep in mind that women purchase 85% to 90% of all greeting cards.

• Do not telephone an editor. Mail or fax is preferable.

• Don't take rejections personally. Relax, have fun, and fine-tune your
rejected work, especially if editors offer encouragement and tell you
to keep at it.

Some of the larger greeting card companies, like Hallmark (and some
of the small ones just starting out), do not accept work from free lancers and use only staff writers. Do not let this deter you. Keep sending
to other companies for guidelines and you may find one that likes your
writing style.

□ 70

CONDUCTING THE "SENSITIVE" INTERVIEW

BY KATHLEEN WINKLER

A DAUGHTER WHO WAS STALKED AND KILLED BY A FORMER LOVER. Surgery that left impotence in its wake. An abortion kept secret for years. A past that includes painful abuse.

Occasionally in your writing career you may find yourself interviewing people about topics that are very hard to talk about. Sometimes it's because they are physically unpleasant or embarrassing. Sometimes it's because they are emotionally wrenching. In either case, you as the writer have a great challenge: to make your subjects feel comfortable enough to share sensitive, intimate experiences with you so your readers can benefit from them.

An awkward interviewer, trampling on the subject's sensibilities, will not only not get a good story, but can also do great damage to the subject, who may never again trust anyone enough to open up.

A skilled and sympathetic interviewer, on the other hand, will not only elicit a moving story from the subject, but may actually help him or her come to terms with an experience kept hidden or repressed for years.

It all depends on how you go about it.

As a medical writer for fifteen years, I've interviewed people on such intimate topics as sexual function, emotional responses to physical scars from surgery, and life-threatening illness. In the course of writing *When the Crying Stops: Abortion, the Pain and the Healing* (Northwestern Publishing House), I interviewed twenty women about their abortion experiences and subsequent reactions. Some of these women had never told their stories to anyone before the interview.

As a result of these often painful interviews, I've developed an approach to sensitive interviewing and some helpful ways to make such interviews easier for me and for the subject, and more productive.

I believe that the number one rule for interviewing on any topic, especially a sensitive one, is respect for the person sitting across from you. Always keep in mind that he or she doesn't *owe* you anything. In most cases your subject is telling his or her story out of a simple desire to help others cope with the same or a similar problem, with no expectation of any kind of reward. The subject, therefore, has the right to decide how much to share. While as the interviewer you can encourage the sharing and make it as free of stress as possible, you must not try to force the person to reveal more than he or she is willing to. The subject has the right to end the interview at any point, or to say, "I don't want to talk about that"—and you must respect that decision.

There are some things you can do to make a sensitive interview as tension-free as possible for the subject, and, at the same time, get the information you need to write an honest and moving piece.

• Since it's absolutely essential to use a tape recorder during the interview—especially if there are likely to be any legal aspects to the project—ask the subject for permission to do so, explaining that you want to be sure your quotes are accurate. But get the permission on tape before you begin.

• Preparation is important. Never try to "wing" an interview. Learn as much as you can about the person in advance. If the story is likely to have a psychological or medical slant, do your research: Familiarize yourself with the problem and the various treatments and side effects. In dealing with a social problem—child abuse, spouse battering, etc.— read current background material on all aspects of it.

• Prepare your questions carefully ahead of time. Start with the general, less threatening questions and move on to those dealing with the more difficult, personal aspects of the experience. Begin by asking about the subject's childhood and the events that led up to the traumatic experience. This will help relax your subject and get the dialogue flowing.

• When you arrive at the interview, the subject is likely to be nervous. A warm smile, a handshake, and a friendly comment—"I'm so happy to meet you; I think it's wonderful that you are willing to share your experience with others"—will go a long way toward putting the subject at ease.

• If your subject is especially nervous, confront that fact—don't ignore it—saying, "I know this may be difficult for you. That's understandable. Many people are uneasy at first, but it won't be as hard as you may think."

• Start with a disclaimer, if you think it will help. Say, frankly, "I hope you will want to share your thoughts and feelings, but I won't pressure you to say any more than you want to." If you have agreed to anonymity for the subject, emphasize at the outset that you will not, under any circumstances, break that promise.

• Use broad, general questions at first, asking such non-threatening questions as, "Tell me a little about yourself: Where are you from? What was it like growing up in your family? How did you get along with your siblings? Parents?" If this leads to an appropriate opening, you might follow the answer with, "Can you tell me a little more about that?" Obviously avoid questions that can be answered with "yes" or "no." Have a summary question ready for the end—"What's the most important effect this experience has had on you? What is the most helpful thing you would like to share with the readers?"

• Move gradually, in chronological order, through the part of the person's life that is relevant to the story. If the subject wanders and gets off track, bring the interview back to the main topic by saying something like, "We're going to get to that in a minute, but right now I'd like to hear more about—." A little humor never hurts: "Hold on a bit; we're getting way ahead of ourselves."

• When you are ready to deal with the sensitive topic, warn the person by saying, "We've come to the point where I need to ask you some more specific questions about what happened." If the subject becomes emotional, confront that directly, saying, "Go ahead and cry if you feel like it. I certainly understand. I would have cried, too, in that situation." Don't try to hide your emotional reaction; if you actually do respond with tears, that's O.K. I've never done a sensitive interview in which the subject cried and I didn't shed a few tears, too.

• Give your subject plenty of time to respond to your questions. If she or he stops at a critical point, pause, too, and then make a casual comment to start the conversation flowing again: "That must have been very hard for you. What happened next?" Keep your voice warm and sympathetic.

• Never make a judgmental comment. Obviously, remarks like, "How could you have done that!" are taboo, but so are even subtle gestures or verbal responses, no matter how repellent you may find what the subject says.

• Get on tape the subject's wishes about using real names in your feature.

• When you have finished the interview, thank the person warmly, and leave your card so she or he can reach you if she wishes to give you some additional information. Don't be reluctant to call her back for clarification or more details. Store the tapes in a fireproof safe. It is not advisable to show the subject a transcript of the tape recording or the manuscript prior to its publication.

Though telephone interviews on sensitive subjects can be done, they do present a different challenge. Sometimes the anonymity of the phone allows a nervous subject to talk more freely, but it can, in some instances, be inhibiting.

• Always tell the person that the phone interview is being tape recorded. I usually say, "I'm taping this, so you don't have to worry about talking slowly enough for me to take notes."

• As in a face-to-face interview, you must establish a personal relationship over the telephone, which presents some difficulties. Chat casually at first, in a warm, friendly tone, asking about the weather, how the person likes living in his or her hometown, how he or she spent the weekend. Get to know the subject a bit before jumping into the interview.

• Schedule your phone interview at a time when you are not likely to be interrupted. Disconnect your call-waiting! Late night often works best for me. There's something about quiet houses and low lights that encourages the flow of conversation.

Talking to people about their most intimate, personal problems and experiences can be exhausting and emotionally draining, for you as well as for your subject. Don't schedule too many such interviews back to back or you may find yourself on overload. Allow time for a break between interviews.

Some of your subjects may well be in need of professional counseling and may try to put you into the role of therapist. Remember that your job is only to ask the questions and listen—which may in itself be therapeutic for the subject. Never offer advice. It may in some instances be appropriate to ask, "Have you ever had professional help in dealing with this problem? You might find it helpful."

Sharing the darker side of pain often helps the teller and the reader to know that they are not alone, that other human beings have had similar experiences and survived.

As writers, we have a tremendous responsibility in doing sensitive interviews. We have a responsibility to our subjects not to betray their trust. And, in addition, we have a responsibility to our readers to present these stories as honestly and with as much empathy as we can. Conducting ourselves with the utmost professionalism is the only way to live up to it.

❑ 71

MAKE YOUR OPINIONS COUNT

BY RON BEATHARD

THE RESPECTED NEWSPAPER TRADITION OF PROVIDING AN OPEN FO-
rum for ideas, opinions, and commentaries can mean a sale for you.
For the op-ed page, which runs opposite a newspaper's editorial page,
editors are looking for serious, fact-filled opinion pieces on local, national, and world issues, and informal, even humorous, personal essays. It's a writing opportunity with few constraints: No editor stands
over your shoulder, red pencil in hand, deleting with the remark,
"That's editorializing!" Of course it is; that's why you are writing it.
Your op-ed piece is your letter to the world.

There is strong competition from syndicated columnists and recognized authorities who cover the Big Topics of the Week—health care,
foreign relations, Supreme Court decisions, and scientific and technical
subjects (the ozone layer, space exploration, and economics)—but
there is a niche for you.

Op-ed writing is a stimulating challenge. Within a short space you
have to grab and hold the reader's attention, make your arguments
cogent, your writing style forceful, and leave the reader thinking—not
an effortless task, but certainly a rewarding one. In addition, writing
op-eds is an efficient use of your writing time. Articles are short, aver-
aging 600 to 900 words. (Every word counts; no puffery here.) Although all your facts and quotes must be carefully documented, lengthy
research is not required, interviews are usually not needed, and the
editor provides whatever artwork is necessary to accompany your article.

Choosing subjects to write about is difficult, not because there are
few, but because there are so many. From heavy and serious questions
of global significance to warm and friendly themes, the field is limited
only by your imagination.

Make a list of all the areas in which you are knowledgeable or experienced. (You'll be surprised how many there are.) Determine what the reader wants and needs to know about the subject—facts, details, opinions, and experiences—then add your perspective and viewpoint. Use the writing style that best fits the tone and subject of your piece: formal or informal, journalistic or descriptive.

Write about the local angle of a national issue. What will be the consequences of a Congressional bill on your school district? How do government health policies influence the economics of your community? Should a military installation near your town be closed?

Describe your thoughts and observations about a season or holiday, the first day of school, or vacation recollections—everyday topics to which you can add a special touch. Your personal essay can be warm and entertaining, light and humorous, or serious and provocative. Editors are looking for material that is different from traditional syndicated columns.

One advantage you have over national columnists is that you can write on subjects of local interest and history. What is the impact of a local factory closing? Does the community need that new bond issue? Why is it important for your town to preserve its historical heritage, and what is the most desirable and feasible way to bring it about?

Use your personal experience. You are a scout leader; how does scouting have to change to meet the problems and needs of today's youth? If trees and flowers are among your interests, how do they affect the environment? If you do volunteer work at the hospital, how has the role of volunteers changed as a result of new medical practices?

Draw on your professional experience. As an English teacher, state your views on why Americans can't spell. As a pharmacist, write about your role and relation to the consumer, or your thoughts on the health care crisis. As a librarian, discuss the impact of illiteracy in the United States, and the effect of new technologies on Americans' reading habits.

Use a spinoff as a start-up. Perhaps you have written a major magazine article, so your interviews, research, and notes are completed. Take this background information, condense the facts and details, add your thoughts and observations, and you'll have an op-ed piece.

In general, editors believe strongly in and have a deep commitment to the First Amendment. They want to provide opportunities for discussion of controversial subjects on their op-ed pages, with solid opinion and viewpoints based on clear reason—not the "I've-got-something-to-get-off-my-chest" approach. (That's for the letters column.) Because many controversial subjects—abortion, gun control, health reform—are popular with both readers and writers, an editor may be overstocked, so query first.

Choose a subject that is timely, yet has a long shelf life. Today's front-page story may be old news by the time your article hits the editor's desk. Because many editors publish op-ed pieces on a space-available basis, it may be weeks or even months before your article is published.

As you read newspapers and magazines, be alert for both light and serious short items and news anecdotes that could spark an idea for an op-ed article. Start a file.

There are more than 9,000 daily and weekly newspapers in the United States, and marketing your articles to the right paper requires a little research. Read the op-ed pages of as many papers as you can. Many editors outline their free-lance or guest-column policies on the op-ed page and are anxious to publish well-written, thought-provoking articles.

Unless you have a specific question for the editor—subject matter, payment, rights, etc.—a query letter is not necessary. A cover letter should accompany your article, stating your qualifications if the subject is scholarly or technical, citing sources if appropriate, and listing your previous credits.

Payment varies—small local papers may pay nothing; major city dailies, $100 or more—and is usually made on publication.

Some editors prefer that a writer live in the paper's circulation area; others may want to buy exclusive rights, or will allow you to resell your article outside the paper's circulation area. Since editorial policies differ, query first if you have any questions or concerns.

Writing op-ed articles requires clarity, brevity, and succinctness—qualities that can improve *any* of your writing.

❑ 72

THE BUSINESS OF WRITING ABOUT BUSINESS

BY CHRISTINE M. GOLDBECK

WALL STREET REPORTERS AREN'T THE ONLY WRITERS MAKING MONEY from the business community. Most business journals and regional weekly or monthly publications dealing with issues and information important to business people depend on free-lance writers, and pay well for the articles they receive or assign.

Step one to breaking into this market is to tell yourself that business is not intimidating or boring. That you aren't an M. B. A., that you flunked high school economics, that you don't know the difference between a mutual fund and a certificate of deposit—none of this really matters. The business community is not an ogre, and all business people are not stuffed shirts who are too busy with the bottom line to talk about their industry or their enterprise. Nor is business writing non-creative and rigidly routine.

In fact, many business owners and operators like to share their expertise and experiences. So, not only will you get bylines and make money writing about business, you will learn a lot.

Call the local Chamber of Commerce or any other business support agency to inquire whether there is a business journal published in your area, and check your newspaper to see whether it has a business page. Bigger daily papers usually run such a page in each issue. Smaller dailies often publish a business page on a weekly basis.

Business story subjects run the gamut: new businesses, profiles of business people, the grand opening of a business, a store reopening a year after it was destroyed by fire, trends in an industry, affirmative action contracts, a bankrupt bagel shop, a new product sold in the area, college bookstores selling quarts of milk for continuing education students . . . as long as it relates to doing business and you can write it for business people, you're in.

343

A newspaper editor will want samples of your published works in order to assess your ability to write interesting business copy. Business journals usually have writer's guidelines and on request, will mail them to you, along with a sample issue. Therefore, that byline might be but a telephone call to an editor away.

Let's say you've received a go-ahead from a business editor on an article about a business in your community. Now what?

You will of course want to set up an appointment to interview the owner, and to be prepared for that interview by learning something about him or her, the company, and the industry. Your local community library, as well as area university libraries, are great places to obtain information on the businesses and types of industries in the area. Take time to familiarize yourself with all the information that is available.

These are some of the references you should consult for background information on a company or a business executive:

• **Annual reports.** A public company's annual report contains helpful information (in addition to the stuff they write for stockholders). Look for statistics that reveal financial information about the company.

• **Trade journals** (magazines and newspapers devoted to a specific industry).

• **Local chambers of commerce and business associations.** Staffs at such agencies are usually good about giving you some information about their member companies, many of which are small- to medium-size private enterprises. So, if you need to know the identity of the president of Aunt Mabel's Meatballs, call the Chamber of Commerce nearest to the location of the business.

• **Commercial on-line services, the Internet, and the World Wide Web.** Here you'll find a wealth of information about industry trends and specific companies and business leaders. (For a recent piece on how high paper prices are affecting profit in a number of industries, I went to an on-line newsstand, searched under the key words "paper," "costs," and "paper prices," and got more information than I was able to use. But, it certainly gave me a lot of background, which I used to formulate questions for my interviews.) Dun & Bradstreet and other business references can also be contacted via the Internet.

Like a typical newspaper or magazine article, a business feature is built on the five Ws (*who, what, where, when,* and *why*—and don't forget *how*), answering such questions as:

What is the business: What does it make or what services does it provide for sale? Where is it located? How long has the company been in business? How does it market its product or service?

Once you have that vital information, you will need to focus on the people who run the business, asking every interviewee from whom you need information the following kinds of questions:

- What is your business strategy?
- How are you marketing your product?
- How much did you invest to start the business? Did you get loans, and if so, what kind?
- Who is your competition and how do you try to stay ahead of them?
- How much do you charge for your product?
- Is this a sole proprietorship, a privately held company, or a public operation?
- What are your annual sales?
- How many employees do you have?

Let's say you're going to write about your neighbor who makes meatballs and sells them to local supermarkets. If your piece is for a mainstream newspaper, the editor will probably instruct you to take what is called a "general assignment approach," which simply means you will have to use a style the average newspaper reader will understand and find satisfying. You won't use business lingo, and you will find something interesting, even homey, about your subject or topic and center your story on that specific point.

You will ask your subject how, when, and where she got started, why she wanted to sell her meatballs, and what made her think this business could be profitable. What did she do before making meatballs? Your lead might read:

Up to her elbows in ground beef, Susan Tucker fondly recalls the times she and her Aunt Mabel made meatballs for the Saint Mary's Church socials. A year ago, Tucker gave up her 7-to-3 job sewing collars on coats to sell "Aunt Mabel's Meatballs." "Too bad Mabel isn't here to see how good business has been," she says.

This type of human interest piece, extolling personal success, the local church, and good old Aunt Mabel, sells mainstream newspapers.

If your piece is for a business journal, you'll need to handle it a little differently, since you are writing for a different audience—business people.

Something like this might work:

An Olive County businesswoman last year used a recipe for homemade meatballs to launch a business that currently employs ten people. Susan Tucker, the owner of Aunt Mabel's Meatballs, started the business in the kitchen of her Brownsville home. Within six months, she had made enough money to purchase and renovate an old restaurant located in Brownsville's commercial district, where she and her employees now make meatballs for wholesale and retail sales. They package and ship their product to a number of supermarkets and restaurants in the region and sell hot meatball hoagies to downtown shoppers, as well.

"I started out making and selling meatballs wholesale to places like Acme Market and Joe's Spaghetti House," Tucker says. "After we moved into this building, I thought it would be a good idea to sell the product retail, so I started selling sandwiches and fresh meatballs from here. That proved to be a good decision, too."

Tucker invested no capital when she launched the business. She says there was little overhead cost, and she quickly recouped what she paid for beef, eggs, and the other ingredients by selling the meatballs for $2.99 per pound.

See the difference? It's the same story, but tailored for a different readership.

This method of getting the information and writing a business journal piece can be used for any type of business or industry. Here's another example, using a service industry executive as the source:

The president of Bridgetown Health Services Inc. says his company now sells medical insurance to small businesses that have fewer than five employees. Owen Johnson says that the small business health plan was created in order to stay competitive in the ever-evolving health industry. The new policy was put on the market October 1, and within two months, the company had signed up 500 small businesses.

"There are major competitors trying to break into this marketplace. We wanted to get a jump on them. By selling our 'Small Business Health Plan,' we believe we have entrenched ourselves in the Northeast Pennsylvania medical insurance field," Johnson said. "It proved to be a good business decision."

Reporting on business is not difficult when you know your subject, get the vital information, then ask those extra questions specific to doing business in a particular field. If you were writing a piece about a fire, a murder, a local church yard sale, a visit from the Pope, you would ask questions specific to that event or person. This is really all you will do in business writing: You will write the story so that your readers—business people—will be informed and entertained. Also, you'll build up your publication credits, make new contacts, and learn interesting things about the people in your area.

Reference materials I recommend and which you may want to have on hand include *The Associated Press Stylebook and Libel Manual,* which contains a section on business writing, and *BusinessSpeak,* compiled by Dick Schaaf and Margaret Kaeter (Warner Books). Both should be available through a local bookstore or in a good public or business library.

Trade groups with information about business journals include the Association of Area Business Publications, 5820 Wilshire Blvd., Suite 500, Los Angeles, CA 90036, (213) 937-5514, and The Network of City Business Journals, 128 S. Tryon St., Suite 2350, Charlotte, NC 28202, (800) 433-4565.

There are also professional societies for business writers. Write the Society of American Business Editors and Writers, Missouri School of Journalism, 120 Neff Hall, Columbia, MO 65211, or the American Business Press, 675 Third Ave., Suite 415, New York, NY 10017.

❑ 73

TRUE CRIME WRITING: A DYNAMIC FIELD

BY PETER A. DEPREE

FEW GENRES IN JOURNALISM TODAY ARE AS EXCITING AND PROFITable as true crime, whether article or book. Although this piece focuses on the true crime article, many of the techniques and methods discussed in the following six steps are readily applicable to the true crime book.

STEP ONE: *Researching the field.* Buy several true crime magazines and spend a rainy afternoon getting a feel for the slant and depth of the articles. Jot down what you liked and didn't like about them. Then, dash off a request to the editorial office of one or two of the magazines for the writers guidelines (include the requisite SASE).

STEP TWO: *Finding a crime.* Visit your local library and look in the index of the biggest newspaper in your area under the heading Murder/ Manslaughter, going back about four years, and photocopy those index pages. (Most crimes more than four or five years old are too stale to fit the slant of true detective magazines.) Highlight the crimes that seem most likely to make interesting true crime pieces. The few sentences describing each article will give you a good feel for the highlights of the case. Select about half a dozen cases that look promising. As you peruse them, you will whittle down the group for one reason or another until you're left with one or two that have all the elements you need for an effective true crime piece. Most detective magazine guidelines will help you narrow them down: The crime is always murder; the "perp" (police parlance for perpetrator) has been convicted; there was a substantial investigation leading to the arrest; the crime took place reasonably near your area (important, since you'll have to go to the court to gather research); and photos are available for illustration.

STEP THREE: *Doing the research.* First, with the index as a guide, collect all available newspaper articles on the crime you've selected so you can make an outline before reading the trial transcript. Your library should have either back issues or microfilm (provided you followed Step One and picked a case no more than four years old). If there are two or more newspapers in your area that covered the crime, get copies of all of them. Often, pertinent details were printed by one paper but not the other.

STEP FOUR: *Reading the trial transcript.* Call the clerk's office of the court where the trial took place and ask for the case number on the crime and whether the transcript is available to the public (it usually is). By now you should have a three- or four-page outline based on all the articles you've read. Take your outline and a lot of paper and pens to the courthouse, and be prepared to spend a whole day reading the trial record; even a trial that lasted only three or four days can fill several bound volumes. (When I was doing research for a book on the Nightstalker serial killer case in Los Angeles, the court record was 100,000 pages long and filled three shopping carts!) Skim and make notes of the quotes and material you'll need; this will be a lot easier if you've prepared your outline carefully, since you'll already know the key names to watch for—the lead detective, prosecutor, defense attorney, victim, witnesses, responding officer, and so forth. You'll need to look for material on several different levels simultaneously: details for accuracy, dramatic quotes, colorful background, etc. There will usually be far more of these elements than you could possibly pack into an article, so you have the luxury of choosing only the very best. You may discover a brand-new form of writing frustration when you have to slash all those dramatic prosecutorial summations and subplots down to the required word count.

Use whatever form of research you're comfortable with. I find a combination of scribbling notes in my own pseudo-shorthand and dictating into a hand-held recorder suits me. (Pack enough spare batteries and tapes!) I can mumble into my recorder faster than I can write. Having photocopies made at the court is usually prohibitively expensive, so copy very selectively. As a rule of thumb, the parts of a transcript that yield the most important factual information are the opening remarks of both attorneys; the questioning of the lead detective; the testimony of expert witnesses such as forensic technicians; and the summing up of both attorneys. A couple of tips: Dates are especially important, and so are names.

Almost as important as the transcript is the court file. Specify to the court clerk that you would like that as well as the transcript.

STEP FIVE: *Writing the article.* Reread the writers guidelines for the magazine to which you're submitting your piece, then write the kind of article *you* would find exciting and surprising (or shocking) to read. Chances are that if a particular detail, scene, or quote piques your interest, it belongs in your piece. Don't get lost in boring minutiae, but do remember that sprinkling in telling details seasons the piece and sharpens the focus.

If your detective used a K9 dog to search for evidence, you might mention that it was a Rottweiler named Butch, with a mangled ear. If the ballistics expert test-fired the gun, you could throw in that detail, noting that he fired it into a slab of gel, then retrieved the bullet and viewed it under a comparison microscope for tell-tale striations, and so on. The trial transcript is packed with details like these that make your article stand out from a "made-up" detective story.

As you're writing, watch your length. Editors are not impressed with articles that run a few thousand words over their suggested length.

STEP SIX: *Secondary wrap-up research.* True crime editors are picky about certain details, especially names (check those writers guidelines again!). If you mention "Mr. Gordon," you should specify that he is Commissioner John Gordon of the Gotham City Police Department. Change the names of witnesses or family members, for obvious reasons. Go back to the library to check the details that will give your writing authority. For instance, if the crime was committed with a shotgun and you don't know a pump-action from an over-&-under, you need to do some minor research to find out. If your crime involves DNA fingerprinting, you'll need to spend no more than an hour in the library to find enough useful facts to give your article a little snap. I recently wrote an article on a killer who was suffering from paranoid schizophrenia. In just four pages in two college psych textbooks—twenty minutes' investment of my time—I came up with more than enough facts for my piece.

What to watch out for

There are at least four articles in my computer that are almost completely written, but went nowhere. Why? Because I made stupid, unnecessary mistakes—mistakes that *you* would never make if you follow a few simple rules. The following three are non-negotiable:

1) *Never start on an article without querying the magazine first.* Nothing is quite as frustrating as writing twenty detailed pages on the Longbow rapist, only to discover that Joe Bland already sold that piece to your target magazine a year ago. You now have a pile of perfectly good kindling.

2) *Always make doubly sure the trial transcript is available.* You should never have to invest more than one or two full days in researching the transcript and court file, but that doesn't help when on the day you need it you learn that the whole file was shipped five hundred miles away so the appeals judges could study it at their leisure. (We're talking *months* here.)

3) *Never start an article without making sure photos are available.* Etch this in stone. No true crime magazine will run an article without *at least* three photos. The minimum basics are a photo of the perp; one of the victim; one of the crime scene. These can be what I call "documentary-grade"; sometimes, even a particularly sharp photo clipped from a newspaper will suffice. But query your target magazine first, and always make sure the picture is in the public domain (i.e., a high school yearbook photo of the killer, a photo of the victim distributed to all the papers, a snapshot of the bank building where an armed robbery took place).

True crime writing might be called entry-level journalism. If you can write a tightly researched and entertaining piece following these suggestions, you'll have a better chance of success.

❏ 74

WRITING THE FEATURE ARTICLE

BY RITA BERMAN

THERE IS A GOOD STEADY MARKET FOR FEATURE ARTICLES. READERS are always looking for ways to improve themselves. Pick up any magazine at the newsstands. What do you see? Articles on how to cope with a teenager or a baby, make tasty meals in 30 minutes, take off ten pounds. How to live longer, happier, wealthier, understand and buy art, learn word processing, or—how to write. All of these feature articles are aimed directly at the reader.

The content of a feature article is more important than the author's name, so the unknown writer has as good an opportunity as the well-known one to have an article accepted, provided that the manuscript is well done and meets the editor's needs.

"Find facts that are new and known by few," an editor told me when I began my writing career. Sounds gimmicky, but it's good advice. Remember that a feature article focuses on the human-interest angle of facts, but this is not a hard and fast rule. Many feature articles are instructive or informational: how-to, how-I, or how-you. The principles of these how-tos (also known as service articles) are that you state the problem, offer a solution, and end with a result. Your advice must guide the readers through the steps taken so that they, too, can recreate your success. Other features are based on interviewing an expert or recognized authority in the field you wish to write about, then in your article, sharing their experiences and knowledge with the reader.

You must do a lot of thinking and planning, as well as gathering and organizing facts. You need to consider the subject of the article; how much readers will be interested in that subject; possible markets; sources that could provide ideas and facts; who might be interviewed for the article; and whether illustrations or photographs may be needed.

By the time you have collected notes, material, photographs, or illustrations, the article may be taking shape in your mind. Before writing your feature, organize your thoughts and material. Know what you want to put into your article, but don't try to keep it all in your head. *Use an outline to get started and stay on track.*

1. On your worksheet, write the working title, which could change after you've written the piece, or as you go along.

Titles are the bait you use to attract editors and readers. Most magazine titles rarely exceed six to eight words. A good title should suggest the contents and tone of the story. Titles cannot be copyrighted, but avoid using one that might be confused with a previously published piece.

2. Jot down a list of words, phrases, or sentences to remind you of all the items and points you wish to cover in your feature.

3. Decide what kind of lead to use to attract the reader:

The question lead: What can you do to get a million dollars?
The controversial statement: It's easy to get a million dollars.
The case history or anecdotal lead: I made my first million—the easy way.
A *statement of fact:* There are more millionaires than ever.
A *descriptive lead:* A million dollars in gold lay gleaming in the vault.

A strong lead is crucial in feature writing because this is what draws the reader into the article, and immediately after the lead, you proceed in a way that will sustain that reader's interest and provide the reason or justification for your lead.

This transition from the lead to the text is sometimes referred to as the bridge, hook, angle, or peg of the story.

Example: For one feature, "How We Sold Our Home" (published in *Army, Navy, Air Force Times*), I used a grabber lead about military families being familiar with change-of-station orders, and how we had led a nomadic existence for 12 years.

4. After your lead, what kind of bridge will you use to hold readers' interest?

In my feature, a paragraph stating that about 7 million homes change hands each year provided the bridge; the rest of the piece was my personal story. I involved the readers by informing them that selling our house without using a real estate broker saved us thousands of dollars. That was my response to the reader's natural "what's in it for me?" question. No matter what the subject—going on a cruise, or trying to avoid paying more taxes—readers always ask, "What's in it for me?"

5. The body of your piece. What anecdotes, examples, or facts will you use to prove the point you want to make? For a how-to piece this is where you will describe the pitfalls, things that didn't work, as well as tips that will lead to a satisfactory conclusion.

I continued my home sale feature by describing a few simple steps that should be followed when selling without an agent. Then I was off into the body of the story, repeating and expanding the reasons for selling the house ourselves, and describing how we did it: preparing the house and grounds; pricing the house realistically; and how we saved time and money when we conducted the sale.

6. The conclusion. A final strong paragraph should wrap it all up effectively for the reader.

My last paragraph for "How We Sold Our Home" echoed my lead by referring to military families and their nomadic way of life. This helped reinforce the message to the military readers of *Army, Navy, Air Force Times* that they too might be moving and selling a house sometime in the future.

Do not try to write any of the sections in final form at this stage. The outline should be used as a guide to prompt the flow of thoughts and to keep you moving in the right direction. It will be particularly helpful if for any reason you have to put the article aside.

Writing the rough draft

With the outline to guide you, you will be ready to begin writing your feature. Write directly and simply, as if talking to your readers. Short paragraphs. Write to be understood, not to impress. As your piece begins to take shape, you will have to consider what transitions are needed to take the reader from example to example, and how you will tie the whole thing together. Keep the feature story flowing toward a strong closing paragraph to balance the hard-hitting lead.

Use subheads and a blurb so that readers can grasp the main idea quickly. A blurb is a summary of what the article is about. You need to know this yourself in order to write the feature. If you are unable to compress the scope of the feature into a sentence or two, perhaps you need to think about it some more.

For informational articles, sidebars and boxes keep the article tight and give it impact. In "How We Sold Our Home" I included a box headed "What do real estate terms mean?" listing key words and definitions such as *appraisal, closing costs, earnest money.*

Tell the reader how and where to get more information on the topic, including addresses and phone numbers, if available. If the how-to was based on interviews, give your sources credit for their remarks.

Accuracy is essential in how-to articles, so recheck your facts before you send out the manuscript.

Revision

You should spend almost as much time on revising and rewriting as you spent on thinking, planning, and writing your rough draft. Are the points in good logical order? The best possible words? It's fun to cross out words you have written and substitute new ones that are clearer and give sharper meaning to your story.

If a sentence sounds awkward on rereading, rephrase it. Chop a long sentence into two. Write in simple sentences rather than long, compound or complex ones.

Allow some time to elapse between the first and second draft. If I wait for a day or two, sentences or sections that need reworking seem to leap off the page. Try to read the article aloud, or better still, tape it. Listening to your words will uncover writing weaknesses.

Write to space

The only way you can cut a feature, if it ends up being too long, is to prune throughout. An alternative is to write to space from the outset. Do this by assigning a specific number of words to each section of your outline. As a guide, for a 1,500-word piece you might allot 50 words for the introduction, 150 words for the bridge, 1,200 words for the body of the piece, and 100 words for the conclusion. An average page of typing contains 250 words (25 lines of 10 words), so 1,500 words should run approximately six pages.

Getting the feature published

The usual publication outlet for features is in the monthly or quarterly magazines, thousands of which are published in all regions of the country. New magazines hit the newsstands every month, and the old ones change their formats. In addition, magazines sold by subscription only also have a constant need for steady, reliable writers who can write interesting features. Names and addresses of consumer, special interest, trade, and a host of other magazines can be found in the back of this book; select the best possible markets for your feature.

Many listings request that writers query instead of submitting a completed manuscript. By querying, you find out if—and where—there is interest in your piece. Make a list of markets to query, and send for writers guidelines before you write your query letter. Guidelines provide information on topics that are wanted, word length, preferred submission format, whether photographs are needed, the rights bought, pay scale, and other useful information about editorial needs.

Select one publication and submit a query letter. If you draw a negative response, revise the letter and work your way through the market list. After you get a go-ahead from an editor, you can prepare the article to meet the magazine's editorial needs, and thus increase your chances of being published.

❑ 75

BIOGRAPHER AT WORK

BY GALE E. CHRISTIANSON

THE BIOGRAPHER BONDS HIMSELF TO HIS SUBJECT IN A UNION MORE symbiotic than matrimony. Almost never are the two separated during the long months and years of their association, for dreams and nightmares are as much the stuff of writing lives as the countless hours passed in airless archives or mornings wrestling with the blank page.

Thus your subject must be a companion whose character faults, which magnify in the glare of intense scrutiny, are offset by accomplishments sufficiently redeeming to override skepticism and assuage doubt. Such was the case for me with the great Isaac Newton, the subject of my first biography. Though mean-spirited and given to withering tirades against those who challenged his scientific ideas, the inventor of calculus, the mortal who flung gravity across the void, is forever woven into my tapestry of the blessed.

My feelings for Loren Eiseley, the anthropologist, literary naturalist, and author of some of this century's most elegant and evocative essays, are rather more ambivalent. While writing Eiseley's life, I was gradually overwhelmed by his tendency to cast events in conspiratorial hues and to blame everyone but himself for his sufferings. To put it simply: Had I known what I was getting into with Eiseley, I think I would have passed.

Yet the biographer should also be cautious when his prospective subject seems too companionable. Identifying too closely with the subject violates the constraints essential to writing biography. Psychoanalysts term this process "co-creation" or the "commingling of consciousness." Setting out to write the life of another, the biographer is actually carrying on an interior dialogue with himself, while plying his own emotional terrain.

After choosing a subject, the real work begins. Almost every serious biographer (we are not here concerned with so-called celebrity biographies or what I call tabloidism) must face the daunting prospect of burrowing deep into one or more archives. But it is well to complete as much background reading as possible before immersing yourself in the primary sources. Since it is not only unwise but impossible to attempt to include everything about a life, however important, the researcher must be selective. The late Barbara Tuchman characterized biography as a prism of history, while others have likened it to fine portraiture. Leon Edel, best known for his multivolume life of Henry James, speaks of "the figure under the carpet," whose true identity can be resolved only by carefully scrutinizing the tea leaves of research. Whatever the method or the metaphor, the biographer must create a unique angle of vision by fitting keys to locks that yield only to the right questions.

Some biographers enter archives armed with little more than a pencil and a generous supply of 3" by 5" cards; others carry laptop computers whose clicking keyboards serve as a constant distraction to those with a sensitive ear. My preference is the portable archives made available via photocopying. With photocopies at one's fingertips, dates, quotations, and myriad other details can be rechecked as often as need be, thus minimizing the number of inadvertent errors that steal into a manuscript.

Moreover, the biographer's perspective is subject to change. This is especially true when dealing with letters, diaries, and notebooks, which may require several readings. Notes are inevitably incomplete and have a way of growing cold during the months or possibly years that may pass before the author returns to them.

But most important to me is that an exact copy recharges the atmosphere as the original did when I first viewed it in the archives. Photocopies are the catalysts of inspiration and of musing, and serve as a constant reminder of the responsibility one bears to one's subject.

Finally, the more quickly material is gathered the sooner one can return home. The costs of photocopying are but a fraction of what it takes to hole up in major cities, where archives tend to be found.

To my continual surprise, I am often asked if I research the *whole* life before I begin to write it. The answer is an emphatic "yes," for, to paraphrase Kierkegaard, a life must be lived forward but it can only be understood backward.

No writer can tell another when enough research is enough, when science must yield to art. This is a personal matter based on a hidden clock whose ticking is as individual as the human thumbprint. But one thing is certain: There will never be a book without writing, and without self-imposed deadlines, the writing will never begin.

To biographers of people who have only recently died, primary sources constitute more than words and images captured on paper. These include the house in which one's subject came into the world, and perhaps left it; the church in which he attended Sunday school; the neighborhood streets along which he bashfully walked hand in hand with his first love; and, if one is very lucky, the living memories of those who grew up with him and took his measure "way back when."

Interviewing friends, relatives, and colleagues of your subject is a tricky albeit rewarding business, best left until you are conversant with the archives. It is only at this point that the right questions can be asked. The web of memory is often very delicate, and responds most sympathetically when probed by a gentle and informed petitioner. And the more you address the same questions to various individuals, the sounder the process. Above all, listen. It is often the seemingly little things these people say that turn out to be the most important.

And what about writing the life of a living person? Having never done so, I can only say, *caveat emptor!* Since the life is not a finished thing, its telling will be superceded by future works based on a sounder perspective. Access to information may also be a problem, even if the subject is cooperative in the beginning. What is gladly given with one hand can be angrily snatched away by the other, especially if the subject's views and those of the biographer clash. With so many other wonderful subjects to choose from, why run the risk?

In her often cited account of Shakespeare's imagined sister, Virginia Woolf asserted that the writer must have "a room of one's own." What is true of the novelist and the poet is no less true of the biographer. "You must have a room, or a certain hour or so a day," wrote the mythographer Joseph Campbell, "where you don't know what was in the newspapers that morning, you don't know who your friends are, you don't know what you owe anybody, you don't know what anybody owes you." This is the place of creation where the writer brings forth what he or she is—and is to be.

Saturated with facts and documents, the writer confronts a ream of blank pages. Do not be surprised or dispirited if nothing happens right away, for obviously a book never writes itself. Someone, presumably the author, must shape the narrative while deciding which details to retain or to cut, which gestures to play up or to play down, which lines to quote or to omit.

A biography can begin at any point in a subject's life, from birth to the deathbed, from the moment when lightning struck, to the transforming pain caused by the loss of a loved one. The tale begins by fitting one of those precious keys into a lock, turning it, and bidding the reader to enter. During my research on Loren Eiseley, for example, it became clear that he had idealized his father, an itinerant hardware salesman who reminded me of no one so much as Willy Loman. Thus the book begins with three-year-old Loren in the arms of Clyde Edwin Eiseley, gazing into the midnight sky of a chill and leafless Nebraska spring in 1910, an incident Loren recounted in an essay penned many years later. The two are transfixed by Halley's comet.

"If you live to be an old man," his father whispered, "you will see it again. It will come back in seventy-five years."

"Yes, Papa," the boy replied dutifully. Tightening his hold on his father's neck, he promised that when he grew old, he would gaze on the comet a second time and remember the person he would always care for more than any other.

Once you begin, set yourself a challenging yet reachable goal. Mine is some 1,000 words a day, the equivalent of about three typed pages. When the gods are kind, as happens on occasion, the total may double, but more often than not I fall a few paragraphs short. I also try to finish a day's writing at a point which will stimulate the creative flow the next morning, the psychological equivalent of priming the pump.

There is much to be gained by reading fine literature while trying to approximate it oneself. The genre does not matter: Novels and essays, short stories and narrative histories, poetry and plays all serve to deepen one's sensibilities.

Your actual voice can also help to locate your literary voice. At day's end, or night's if you are an owl, read your edited work back to yourself aloud. You will not find it easy to ignore dissonant sound waves. Take pleasure in selecting chapter titles as well as epigraphs, if you plan to use them. A copy of *Bartlett's Familiar Quotations* interleaved with scores of ragged markers is a positive sign that you are well on your way. As for the biography itself, keep in mind the fact that Hemingway had thirty titles in reserve, should his editor veto *For Whom the Bell Tolls.*

In time—if you have the determination and the talent—something will happen. You will experience one of those very special days when the narrative voice and the mind become one. It will not last; the days of the storm petrel must inevitably follow. Yet you will also find, when rereading your manuscript for the twentieth time, that you were not appreciably better on your best days than on your worst. Your mind has been operating at two levels, the one conscious but illusory, the other subconscious but real. You have subtly programmed yourself to remain within certain boundaries, both scholarly and aesthetic. You have found your own way of identifying with your subject, and mutual suspicion has yielded to trust. The pages, so pitifully few in the beginning, are piling up with satisfying regularity. You are a biographer.

□ 76

WRITING FOR THE TRADES

BY MARY E. MAURER

THERE ARE THOUSANDS OF OPPORTUNITIES FOR WRITERS IN TRADE, technical, and professional journals. I stumbled upon the trade field quite by accident, when I agreed to write a profile about the business of a friend. Now half of my income is derived from trade magazines. These publications serve a readership united by occupation or industry, avocation or education. There are also many "trades" serving members of associations or unions.

Trade magazines typically carry business-related news of new products and trends, features on successful businesses and their owners or managers, and service pieces on solving management, employee, and/or customer problems. Within major occupations and industries, there are often magazines for specific aspects, such as marketing, buying, selling, design, production, and training.

Why write for the trades? It's an excellent way for you to hone your craft and be published regularly, thus building up your clip files. Writing for the trades also enables you to strengthen a relationship with an editor, since many have small staffs and are eager to find hardworking serious writers. Regular sales to the trades can provide you with a steady income; pay for trade articles averages $50 to $200 for 1,200 to 1,800 words.

Do you have what it takes? That depends on two things:

1. How serious are you about writing? Articles written for the trades are informative, instructional, technical; they are rarely just entertaining. That means your writing must be clear and focused for a specific purpose and audience.

2. Are you willing to become an "industry expert"? Writers wishing to break into the trade market need to have or develop a strong understanding of the occupation or industry. You *must* know your subject thoroughly.

To become a trade expert, first, examine your own profession or hobbies. What do you know? What skills do you have? What intrigues you? Next, look into the careers of friends or family members. Does anyone have an occupation you find fascinating? Consider your community. Is it rural or urban? Is your town or region famous for a particular product?

Next, review your current writing interests. Very often your *general* interests can be focused and developed so you can write for a trade publication in the same field. Interested in gardening? Become an expert in commercial gardening, and try to write for *GrowerTalks,* a publication catering to commercial greenhouse growers. Do you often write about health topics? Increase your knowledge of physical fitness, and aim a piece at *Fitness Management,* the magazine for commercial, corporate, and community fitness centers.

You may also want to specialize in a particular type of article: **profiles** (of successful owners, managers, businesses); **how to** (cut costs, increase production, stop shoplifters); **forecast** (technical trends, industry changes); **product reports** (what's new, what it does, and who is using it); **history** (profiles of those who helped shape the industry); and **health and safety** (tips on increasing worker productivity through healthy habits and accident prevention).

Once you decide on the area you wish to develop, you have several options. Of course, you'll do the kind of reading and research required for any article. However, for the trades you'll also need to follow those steps to become an "expert":

1. Develop contacts within the industry. Talk to people who are working in the trade. See how they work and ask them about their problems. Develop a list of technical people you can call on for information.

2. In addition to reading general magazines and books, read technical reports, manuals, and trade journals to determine where your knowledge fits into the "big picture" of the industry.

3. Attend trade shows and conferences related to your specialized field. You'll pick up useful information, see new products, meet new people.

4. Visit stores, manufacturing plants, farms, whatever is connected to your specialty.

Now you're ready to write, but you have to study the market. You *must* know and understand the trade journal readership: You can't fake it. Readers of trade publications have very specific expectations. A good list of selected trade magazines is included in this book, but you'll find the most extensive list in *Encyclopedia of Associations* (published by Gale Research), available in the reference department of most large public libraries. It lists trade, business, and commercial organizations, educational organizations, hobby and avocational organizations, and others. You'll find the name of the publication, address, year founded, circulation, size of staff, and other interesting bits of information.

You can sometimes find copies of trade publications at the library, as well as on large newsstands; if not, you can order sample copies. Study at least six different publications in your area of interest; read as many issues as you can. Begin by examining the contents. What is the purpose of the magazine? Study the style and format. Does the magazine use second or third person, active or passive voice? How is technical information offered? What about buzz words, jargon? Every occupation uses some "industry-specific" vocabulary. How does the magazine use graphics, photos? Read the advertising. What is being sold? Who is the target customer?

Write a brief letter of introduction to each editor, detailing your knowledge and background in the industry. Include your resumé and published clips, if they are pertinent. Ask for a copy of their writers guidelines and an editorial calendar if one is available.

Study the guidelines, and *follow* them. Write clearly, with your readers' needs in mind. The best way to be successful in the trades is to find your niche and be knowledgeable and dependable.

Your work, and your chances of being published regularly, will be enhanced by photos, charts, sidebars, and so forth. Editors of trade magazines are always pleased to find writers who are competent with a camera, though you need not be a professional photographer. Add to your article's visual impact by breaking it into clearly defined sections with bullets and headings.

Ready to write for the trades? Remember: Become an expert and know your readers, and your dreams of a byline will be fulfilled.

❑ **POETRY**

❑ 77

WHAT MAKES GOOD POETRY?

BY PETER MEINKE

WHAT MAKES GOOD POETRY? IS ONE OF THOSE SUBJECTS THAT MAKES me (and most poets) groan: It's amorphous, subjective, and potentially endless. But like many vague questions, it *does* force you to think and take a stand; in fact several stands, as the ankle bone's connected to the foot bone. In a recent discussion, here's the stand I wound up on, for you to look at and consider from wherever *you're* standing. It's an important question, after all, one that we're constantly deciding as we pick up and put down poems, choose which books to buy out of the unlimited choices, and tell our friends, "You have to read *this!*"

A serious and talented young writer asked, "How can you tell when a poem is *really* good?," the unspoken corollary question being, "How can we make our own poems better?"

Although everyone has thought about this, many people tend to answer along the lines of "I know it when I see it." This is unhelpful because intelligent and sophisticated people like different poems and different poets: Many readers admire John Ashbery, Howard Nemerov, Gwendolyn Brooks, Charles Simic, language poets, new formalists (make any random list)—but these are seldom the same people. So, unless we simply believe that good poetry is the kind we write ourselves, it could be helpful for us to use whatever definition we come up with as a way to measure the poems we're working on.

Our tastes are probably "set" when we're very young, by the first poems that moved us, by our first real teachers (academic or not). Nevertheless, it seems to me that there are some useful things to say on this subject, even though there's no agreement on how to apply them; so I've broken my definition into six intertwining parts, as follows.

We've all had the experience of being bowled over (goosebumps, tears, laughter, gasps) from reading or hearing a poem. But a truly good poem is as good or better upon rereading. Unlike novels or even short stories, our favorite poems tend to be those we read over and over again. "Age cannot wither her, nor custom stale / Her infinite variety." This suggests something about the nature of poetry: 1) *It withholds something from us at first,* yielding its secrets slowly, like a lover. In our poems, it's almost always a mistake to tell too much, to supply "answers." A poem isn't a sermon or a lecture. "Let us go then, you and I," is the (English) beginning of "The Love Song of J. Alfred Prufrock." Who is "you"? Who is "I"? After all this time, scholars still disagree.

I think a good poem performs two opposite functions at once: 2) *It surprises and satisfies.* Without both of these qualities, a poem either doesn't work, or doesn't work *for long.* (I take for granted that one aspect of good poems is that they *repay* this rereading.)

A poem can surprise in lots of different ways. It can surprise by vocabulary: "Buffalo Bill's / defunct / who used to / ride a watersmooth-silver / stallion" (E. E. Cummings). Or by image: "Dumb / As old medallions to the thumb" (Archibald MacLeish). Or by idea: "My little horse must think it queer / To stop without a farmhouse near / Between the woods and frozen lake / The darkest evening of the year" (Robert Frost).

But after the surprise, a good poem also seems *inevitable*. A typical reaction to a good poem, expressed in various ways, is, "I knew that, but didn't know I knew it." You don't learn things from poetry the way you do from geography (the capital of Costa Rica is San José) or history (the battle of Blenheim was in 1704). Rather, poetry satisfies an inner sensibility (linked to that early-formed "taste") which, though varying from reader to reader, is real and particular.

This feeling of inevitability is connected to the poem's music, its interesting sounds. 3) *A good poem sounds special,* either melodious like T. S. Eliot, homespun like Robert Frost, jumpy like William Carlos Williams, etc. A poem sets up a rhythm: the insouciant in-your-face tone of "Buffalo Bill's / defunct" is matched perfectly by its ending: "how do you like your blueeyed boy / Mister Death." The hint of formal rhythms in the beginning of "Prufrock" culminates in the iambic pentameter of its last lines:

> We have lingered in the chambers of the sea
> By sea-girls wreathed with seaweed red and brown
> Till human voices wake us, and we drown.

And the problem of how to end his stanzas of triple rhymes, with one unrhymed line, in Frost's "Stopping by Woods" is solved by his repeating his last line: "And miles to go before I sleep, / And miles to go before I sleep," making a quadruple rhyme and a perfect stop.

As writers, we have to learn to follow the poem's music, and hope that the sense follows along. When Wallace Stevens begins, "Chieftain Iffucan of Azcan in caftan / of tan with henna hackles, halt!" we know he's drunk on the delights of sound, not sense (though it *does* make sense, sort of). "Follow the music and not the meaning" is generally good advice when you're rewriting your poems. It will hardly ever be your idea that's original: If anything, it will be your voice. Sonnets by Shakespeare, Donne, Wordsworth, Frost, Millay, Wilbur, Dove don't sound at all alike, even though they might have the exact same rhyme schemes and number of syllables.

4) *A good poem is memorable.* It becomes part of our mental/emotional landscape: Every line we remember changes us as every leaf changes the skyline. The key word here is *line:* Looking through our own poems, we should try to make each line memorable. Why should anyone read this? Why should anyone read this *twice?* I remember that John Donne was the first one to affect me that way: "Come live with me, and be my love," "She, she is dead; she's dead," "For God's sake hold your tongue, and let me love." I wanted to memorize (and did) line after line. This, by the way, is one advantage of formal poetry—it's easier to memorize—but that's another topic!

5) *Poems speak to the unanswerable questions.* By moving primarily through images rather than logical constructions, poems address the essentially mysterious aspects of life: Why are we here, who am I, what's true or false, what is the good life? These are the important questions, and the very act of asking them is as close to a definitive answer as we're likely to get. This is why even people who dislike poetry embrace it at the major turnings of their lives: birth, death, love, celebration and mourning.

This doesn't mean a poem has to be murky or unfathomable. Rather it means, like that rare thing, a clear and pure lake, a good poem has depth. The strange thing about "clear" poems like "Stopping by Woods on a Snowy Evening" or "A Red Wheelbarrow" is that they are less clear on rereading, i.e., they can go in many directions, all kinds of "meanings" are suggested. (To say a poem has many meanings is far from saying that it's meaningless.) Even a simple love poem means something different to a high school girl, a farm boy, a widow, a grandfather. Your idea of what dire event Yeats is predicting in "The Second Coming" will depend on your religion, personality, and life experience. But that poem is plenty clear enough!

My last definition is this: 6) *A good poem fulfills its promises.* What it sets out to do—musically, visually, emotionally—it accomplishes. At the end of a poem, we feel we have arrived. "A poem should not mean / but be," "And Richard Cory, one calm summer night, / Went home and put a bullet through his head," "Without a tighter breathing / And Zero at the Bone—," "And the heaviest nuns walk in a pure floating / Of dark habits, / keeping their difficult balance." These last lines, whether formal or free, are set up by what has gone before, and click into place like the last piece of a puzzle. They seem in retrospect, as I said before, inevitable.

In some ways, these are vague descriptions—but if you apply these to your own poems, they can become quite specific. I hope they help. In the end, of course, good poems resist definition and explication: Like the natural things of this world, they are what they are.

I'll conclude here with a short poem of my own. Normally I'd just read or print this poem without elaborating on it—but this is a poem in which I've tried to capture what it feels like to want and/or need to write poetry, and what elements are necessary for its creation. I think, with careful and friendly rereadings, these elements will make themselves clear. But it's also a love poem. It is the nature of poetry, and of the world, to be more than one thing at once.

The Shells of Bermuda

First the wind through the window lifting
this room with breath tugging the curtains waking
the flowers turning one by one slowly
the pages of old books Then the sun
through the windows glinting in corners
warming the tops of tables The cicadas'
shrill vibrations the woodpecker's percussion
even the high whine of Mrs. Rheinhold
as she scolds her children *Pamela! Paul!*
All necessary: but the window most of all

There are moments in every day
when a hunger seizes and the hands

tremble and a wall turns transparent
or a cup speaks   Suddenly
bright as the shells of Bermuda
the combs for your long hair blaze on the desk
(from *Night Watch on the Chesapeake* by Peter Meinke, U. of
Pittsburgh Press, 1987)

□ 78

A Serious Look at Light Verse

By Rosemarie Williamson

I HAVE BEEN WRITING AND SELLING LIGHT VERSE FOR NEARLY THIRTY years. As an art school graduate (who had always enjoyed humorous writing), I had been undecided about my career choice until I enrolled in a creative writing course at a then-nearby New Jersey university. When my professor, who was both knowledgeable and enthusiastic, happened to spot a few of my verses lying around on the table beside my assignment pad, she got very excited. "These are great," she said. "Send them out—flood the market!"

I will never forget her words. I did indeed send my light verse out, to two of the markets she had suggested. To my utter amazement, within a week I received an acceptance from both *Good Housekeeping* magazine and *The Saturday Evening Post*. Hallelujah—I was hooked!

An early acceptance by *The Saturday Evening Post* was "Cost Plus":

> She sells
> Sea shells
> By the sea shore.
> Sam sells
> Clam shells
> For a bit more.

A sale to *Good Housekeeping* from the same period was "Mob Psychology":

> You join the bargain-hunting group,
> Grabbing and unfolding—
> Then find the only thing you want
> Is what some stranger's holding.

This is all well and good, you may be thinking, but how does the verse itself come about? Surely it doesn't evolve full-blown? Not at all. There are a few simple rules to remember, and within these confines, your creativity can run wild. First, you must have a funny idea. (If you find something amusing, chances are others will, too.) Everyday events provide one of the richest sources for humor; the office, supermarket, church, sporting events, shopping mall—all can produce laughable situations.

Possibly the easiest and most common poetic form for humor is the four-line verse, called the quatrain. The quatrain is a neat little package whose length makes it ideal for use as a magazine filler, or for other spots where space is limited. Its brevity is particularly suited to telling a "joke in rhyme," which essentially defines light verse. Making each word count, the first three lines build up to the fourth line, the all-important punch line.

Second in importance is the title, which can serve one or more functions. Titles can provide background material, act as lead-ins, or simply be relevant wordplay. Remember that a clever title is your first chance to catch an editor's eye.

Following are two favorite titles of mine—which may have been instrumental in selling the verses:

Of All the Gauls!

Caesar's legions, so we're told,
Were famous for their marches.
Which may account for Rome today
Being full of fallen arches.

(*The Wall Street Journal*)

Handwriting on the Cave

A caveman's life was fraught with fear,
His world was full of predators,
And it's much the same for modern man,
Except we call them creditors.

(*The American Legion Magazine*)

A word about meter

In a humorous poem the meter (or rhythm or beat) should be regular and simple, to make sure that readers' (or listeners') attention will focus on the words and not be distracted by unexpected changes in rhythm. Otherwise, double entendres and other forms of wordplay could easily be missed. Irregular and even innovative meter certainly has a place in the poetic scheme of things. Long, rambling epics, elegiac stanzas, and free verse are all perfectly acceptable forms, but they're *not* light verse—whose format is quite different.

Two examples of uncomplicated metric lines come to mind. Familiar to most of us, the first line is from a nursery rhyme, and the second from a Christmas carol:

MAry, MAry, QUITE conTRAry

and its inverse

it CAME upON a MIDnight CLEAR

You will notice that I have capitalized the accented or "stressed" syllables; the unaccented or "unstressed" syllables are in lower case. The first line starts with a stressed syllable, the second with an unstressed one. Either would be a splendid vehicle for light verse. (No need, here, to go into the intricacies of "iambic tetrameter," etc. Life is complicated enough! I just remembered that years ago I wrote a short verse called "They Trod on My Trochee"—which remains unsold!)

So far we have a boffo title and a knee-slapping punch line, but what about the other lines? Not to mention the rhyme scheme—what is appropriate for light verse? The first three lines of a humorous quatrain should provide fodder for the grand finale in the fourth line. If the last line concerns a dog, the build-up lines could be full of canine humor— "Dry Bones," old sayings, puppy puns, etc. When my children were growing up, we had a family dog. Kids-plus-dog inspired the following poem, which ran in *The Saturday Evening Post*:

Dog Days

School is out, the weather's nippy—
They forecast snow; the kids yell "Yippee!"
And greet the flakes with eager glance,
But Fido views the scene askance—
"Although for kids it has its assets,
It's enough to BURY us poor bassets!"

I had more to say about the subject than usual, so I extended it into a set of three couplets.

The most common rhyme scheme for a quatrain is to have the second and fourth lines rhyme. Frequently, the first and third lines also rhyme (but with a different end-rhyme sound from lines #2 and #4). The following verse (which I sold to *The Wall Street Journal*) demonstrates the most common rhyme scheme:

Gag Rule

While dental work for some is painful,
And frequently induces squawking,
My complaint is somewhat different—
It means I have to give up talking!

While you'll be aware of the second/fourth line rhyme in this poem (a copy of which hangs in my dentist's office!), there are other things going on as well. You'll note the dentist-related wordplay of the title. The word "squawking" is funny-sounding—even more so when associated with supposedly mature adults. The last line, however, is the real clincher, with its surprise ending.

Endowed with a good sense of humor, you're already halfway there, and the rest of the trip is fun.

Markets

An investment that's sure to pay long-term dividends is the purchase of a few books: an introduction to poetry that explains basic terms and concepts, as well as that perennial poet's pal, a rhyming dictionary. Public libraries are virtual wellsprings of information about and examples of light verse by well-known humor writers—from the amiable Robert Benchley to the tart-tongued Dorothy Parker.

Several of the so-called slick magazines are good markets for light verse. This can be an off again-on again situation, however, so it's best to check recent issues to determine their current editorial policy.

Literary and college magazines can be good markets for beginning as well as established verse writers. *Cimarron Review,* a publication of Oklahoma State University, bought two of my verses, one of which follows:

From "A" to Zebra

Our kids described their zoo trip to us,
Excitedly, at home that night:
"We saw most animals in color—
But the striped one was in black and white."

A real plus in writing light verse is the fact that the entire process can be just plain FUN! Not many professions can offer such an enticing "perk." With practice, you can learn to view life's little annoyances as raw material for humor—it becomes positively addictive. After writing—and selling—light verse for nearly thirty years, I find the challenge just as exciting today as when I started out, and that's saying quite a bit.

❏ 79

SETTING FREE THE POEMS

BY T. ALAN BROUGHTON

A FEW YEARS AGO, I FOUND MYSELF WRITING A LETTER TO MY thirty-five-year-old daughter reprimanding her for the messy condition of her house when my wife and I had visited it briefly on a fall afternoon. I won't go into the complicated reasons for taking exception to the piles of magazines, the clothes tossed here and there, the dishes stacked not just in the sink but wherever any space was left. I wrote the letter, she wrote back (in more temperate terms than I deserved), and I was left a week later with astonishment at my own behavior. Are we always doomed to be parents to our children? I remember saying firmly to my parents when I was in my thirties, "At a certain point, we have to decide whether we can get over the fact that you made me and helped to bring me up. Either you let go and we make a friendship, or we freeze in the past, struggling to be polite." That fall day I had been standing again at the doorway to my daughter's disheveled bedroom in her teenage years. But a few weeks after I had written that letter, I felt an immense relief. We were too old for that. She was on her own. I didn't have to burden myself any more with thinking that I knew who she was or what she ought to be. I thought I knew her because I had been in on the making of her existence. Now I could see her as a stranger whom I loved. The attachment was still there, but the freedom was far greater.

Poems aren't really the poet's children, of course. If we take that analogy too far, the writer in us may retreat too fully from the far less controllable and more surprising world of wordless reality. Art should never be a substitute for living. But we sometimes form relationships with what we write that are as fatally flawed as the pattern I've described above. The questions, then, are when do we need to cut loose from the poem we've made? How do we do that? Why is it necessary? My experience in some thirty-five years of teaching writing is that very

377

few writers are at a loss for ways to begin poems. We all have something to say, even if we make that beginning difficult by being overly self-critical. The difficulty is in letting the poem grow beyond its origins, in not limiting it to that impulsive moment when we began, a moment that tried to convince us that it must be honored and cherished, that *it* was the poem and ever will be. The hard part comes in setting the poem free to become what it needs to be, which is rarely what we first thought it had to be.

Here are two examples by poets whose accomplishments are sufficient to have earned our trust: Ezra Pound and William Carlos Williams.

In a Station of the Metro

The apparition of these faces in the crowd;
Petals on a wet, black bough.

Think of these as three lines because, even if the first is the title, it serves the function of a line in the poem as a whole. It is Pound's haiku—deft, suggestive, intense, full of a resonant silence. No time here to go into its layers of emotion and perception. I only want to glimpse its past to demonstrate how far this final version is from its origins. In a discussion of the poem, Pound says he stepped out of a subway train in Paris "and saw suddenly a beautiful face, and then another and another, and then a beautiful child's face, and then another beautiful woman, and I tried all that day to find words for what this had meant to me, and I could not find any words that seemed to me worthy, or as lovely as that sudden emotion. . . . I wrote a thirty-line poem, and destroyed it because it was what we call work 'of second intensity.' Six months later, I made a poem half that length; a year later I made the following hokku*-like sentence."

Of course, we've never seen a copy of that original version, because he destroyed it, but I'm sure I know what it suffered from. I've kept reams of my own worksheets, which I rarely look at again. But I keep them because they give me a certain sense of security; after all, I can always go back to an earlier version if I really mess up. Any of you who suffer from the same slightly timorous approach to revisions might

---

*Alternate spelling of *haiku*.

want to try that method. What Pound must have discarded were many lines, exploratory images, associations from times and places not immediately present in the experience itself—in short, all the detritus the mind spews out as it attempts to find its way, like the chips of marble gathering around the jut of stone that soon becomes a knee, a tensed thigh. The poem begins to insist on what it must become, whether we knew it or not when we began. At a certain point the poem stops being a collection of words that are serving the maker's needs and becomes a work the poet must serve with everything she or he has learned.

Note the insistence in Pound's statement on the beautiful faces, but in particular how it closes in on the phrase "another beautiful *woman*." If there is one thing that this poem is *not* about, it's the faces of beautiful *women* in the setting of a subway station—one which we know Pound could do very well, with that extraordinary mixture of irony and sensuality. He waits six months and tries again. I suspect he did not destroy the next version. Perhaps his interest in Fenellosa and Chinese poetry intervenes. Often what a poet needs in the search to distance a work sufficiently from himself or herself is that objective fascination with matters of syllables, line lengths, sounds, images, even the simple appearance of the shape on a page. Now he is ready for the "hokku-like sentence." Thirty lines have become three. What has happened is that the essence of the experience has insisted on being the poem. The passage of time is one of the poet's keenest instruments in the toil of revision. By the end, the poet's relationship to the work is *radically* different from what it was in the beginning, if that word can be taken to mean that the poet has found a way back to the deepest roots of the poem, something he did not know he knew when he began. The child becomes the father of the man?

Or try this equally famous poem by Williams:

> so much depends
> upon
> a red wheel
> barrow
> glazed with rain
> water
> beside the white
> chickens

This poem has been discussed, analyzed, anatomized, and chased around every classroom so often that it is miraculous how well it still survives. But even though many critics are aware that a personal experience is "behind" the poem, very rarely does this enter into discussions of the poem. Why? Primarily because that personal experience has been excluded from the finished poem. If it were essential, you can be certain Williams would have included it somehow.

For instance, what if the title of the poem were: *View from the Window of a Dying Child's Bedroom*. It could have been—if Williams were a much lesser poet. Apparently, the poem is derived from Williams's experience as the attending physician at the house where one of his patients, a child, was close to dying. In some pause while everyone was waiting, Williams gazed out the window. What else he saw in addition to the shiny, wet wheelbarrow and the chickens, we don't know. Any backyard contains more junk—to say nothing of trees, bushes, maybe a visible street, etc. I have no proof, but I can well imagine Williams beginning with the elegiac and intense combination of the child's toy, the indifferent chickens, the beauty of everything shining and renewed after a rainfall, the poignant awareness of death hovering in the room where he stands. Somewhere along the way, Williams jettisons the possible tones of bathos, the pathetic extensions of his own emotions into the images of the child's world, and gives us in their place a honed, clear combination of images that are focused outward into an immensely suggestive area that can never be filled with the words of our explanations—*so much depends upon*. Four words that have only the hint of image in the etymology of the word *de-pends*. The poem has been set free from its limiting circumstances.

These poems have served as good advisors to me over the years. I gladly take the beginnings of my poems from whatever source announces itself. Full of anxiety and a kind of joy, I watch those words start to mar the page or screen. I don't say it consciously, but even as they continue down the page, I can't help sensing that they are only the first cries of a poem that will grow into something quite different, growing away from me but taking me with it—finally to become something quite separate from me and what I thought the poem was, but blessed for the journey it has let me take in its presence.

□ 80

IN PRAISE OF RHYME

BY JENNIFER SHEPHERD

AFTER MY LACK OF SUCCESS IN RECEIVING PUBLICATION FOR RHYMED poetry, I decided to test the "audience" of real people out in the world, not just higher-ups in the literary community. Where I live, we have a lot of coffeehouses where there are regular poetry readings.

I read some of my work for an audience of about 100 people, and I found their response to be very warm. They didn't treat my poems as if they were less important or more superficial because they were in rhyme form. In fact, listeners that evening said that the rhyme actually helped them focus on the various pieces they heard, allowing them to analyze and retain the poems better.

This got me thinking about the exclusionary nature of many poetry editors, how rhyming is just not considered "cool" these days. I can't help wondering if, in the universal rebellion against rhyme, the literary community has been missing out on a heck of a lot of fun.

Ideas that pour forth naturally from a poet's brain in rhyme form do so for reasons of their own. Should rhyming poetry automatically be categorized as less profound, less worthy of consideration, than the non-rhyming kind? To do so excludes a large number of thoughtful rhymers from even receiving attention from both audience and peers.

Poetry used to be romantic and playful entertainment, conveyed primarily via storytellers' presentations. Anecdotes, songs, and tall tales anchored themselves more easily in the listener's mind when they were expressed through rhyme. Rhyme allowed people to carry the poet's sentiments home with them, because the words became fixed in their brains.

We now live in a much more literate age, and almost anyone can pick up a volume of poetry and begin to read. But we also live in an era of information and entertainment overload. Commercial jingles, news report sound bites, and the latest overplayed hit song on the radio flood us with far too much stimuli. Time seems to be speeding up, while our memories and attention spans get shorter. Most people remember very little of what they hear or see these days. And poetry, foremost among all artistic forms, is getting lost in the shuffle.

Meanwhile, poets from all over the world do their best to raise their voices above this cacophony. They continue to express ideas that they feel have value to an audience consisting of 1) themselves; 2) a hand-picked "worthy" few; or 3) as many people of the general public as possible.

All of them want essentially the same thing. The greatest poets of both past and present have sought to create doorways through which others can enter into a thought-provoking, reality-shifting experience.

Rhyme need not detract from creating this experience. Quite often, rhyme can actually enhance the balance and impact of a poem. Rhyme serves as a framing device for the poet's thoughts—the wooden beams, if you will, of a writer's doorway to reality. If the linguistic carpenter is at all skilled, rhyme can perform its task well.

Shakespeare's most affecting work still stimulates and captivates us, "in spite of" its iambic pentameter. And his work remains portable, readily available to the average memory, not just because of its age, but because it is structured in rhyme.

Yes, it's true—clumsy young poets sometimes fasten upon rhyme with a death grip, refusing to let go until they have created poetry destined to make readers (and listeners) scream with terror. But just because the occasional poem has imprinted itself indelibly upon your memory doesn't mean that you should greet each new rhymed poem with a visceral gasp, its very appearance causing you distress.

Don't berate rhyme. It has no power to harm you, in spite of the rumors circulating among many contemporary poets. Content that is vague or vacuous deserves blame; the rhyme form in itself does not.

So try stepping beyond the current literary norms. Be open to creating and enjoying poetry of all kinds. And the next time you encounter a rhyme, let it linger and possibly carve out a few neural pathways. That way, the piece might remain locked in your memory box and filed under "fun."

And who among us couldn't use a bit more fun?

❑ 81

THE WISDOM OF
A WISHY-WASHY POET

BY RACHEL HADAS

IN THINKING ABOUT WHAT I WOULD WRITE THAT WOULD BE HELPFUL
to aspiring authors, I thought I'd steer a middle course between the
Scylla and Charybdis of too grand and too pedestrian. I will, therefore,
not attempt to inspire the reader with transcendent words of wisdom
about the beauty of poetry (I'm principally a poet and have more
confidence in my wisdom regarding poetry than, say, fiction); neither
will I remind readers to keep copies of all their work, be sure to have
their name on every page, and enclose self-addressed envelopes with
their submissions, sound as such reminders would be.

Instead, I'm offering a list. Not DO's and DON'TS, but rather, something closer to the way my own zig-zaggy mind and wishy-washy temperament seem to operate. People often find themselves teetering
dizzily between opposing instincts and options; certainly, writers, and
perhaps especially beginning writers, do. Very often there is something
to be said for both sides, even if the two seem in blatant contradiction.
Finally you have to decide; but for the dedicated writer, there's always
another chance, another way to tackle the problem, another way to go
about getting this particular poem or manuscript done.

I am not guaranteeing success or even enlightenment, but I hope to
provide some food for thought and perhaps spark some recognition
along the way. Writers need to remember that they are not alone. And
finally, I append to my list of ON THE ONE HAND/ON THE OTHER HAND
a small dessert tray of quotes I've come across recently, from writers
I admire, which are (I hope) both entertaining and enlightening.

• Autonomy
On the one hand—You can't help learning from the work of other writers, and you should do just that. Read all you can; you can't be a good

writer unless you are familiar with literature. Furthermore, ask the advice of other writers/readers regarding your own work.

On the other hand—You need to make sure that what you are writing comes from you and is not just an imitation of or a homage to some other writer. Reading too much may even interfere with the development of your own voice. You are alone in this business and need to make your own decisions; don't depend on the advice of others, which is fallible anyway.

• Consistency

On the one hand—Develop your own individual style, tone, or voice and stick to it! Your work will be more distinctive and recognizable that way.

On the other hand—Don't lock yourself into a single mode because it has worked for you once or because you're afraid to stray from one style. Be wily, restless, experimental, dialogic. Have the courage of your own wishy-washiness.

• Scale: universality

On the one hand—Don't be afraid to tackle immense topics: love, death, the meaning of life, what's wrong with the world today.

On the other hand—Don't be afraid of what may seem very limited, even miniature topics.

• Obscurity

On the one hand—Avoid pretension and obscurity. If you don't know what you're saying, how can anyone else be expected to? And even if you do know, since people can't read your mind, they may well be puzzled by sudden allusions, leaps, or discontinuities.

On the other hand—Poetry is better at flying than any other literary form, so don't be afraid to leap, glide, and skip steps. Also, it's all right not to understand everything one writes or reads; like dreams, poems can be both enigmas and solutions.

• Poetry

On the one hand—Poetry can do anything from exhort, pray, sing, lament, insult, or narrate to telling a joke, cursing an enemy, or depicting a scene. What you attempt to do in poetry shouldn't be limited by a narrow sense of the limits of genre.

On the other hand—Poetry is better at some things than others. Are you sure that what you're writing isn't really a story or article, a cartoon or editorial, a personal letter, photo, or painting? There's also the historical aspect to be aware of; at certain times in the past, treatises on farming or astronomy or philosophy were often in verse. Nowadays, they rarely are. Do you want to buck this trend? Can or should you? Maybe. . . .

• Your audience

On the one hand—Be aware of your audience. Who are you writing for? Who are they likely to be? Who do you want them to be?

On the other hand—All you can do is write as well as you can, be persistent, be adaptable within your aesthetic limits, and get published; the audience will take care of itself. Furthermore, certain poets we now think of as great—Emily Dickinson and Cavafy are two who come to mind—published little or no work during their lifetimes.

• Writer

On the one hand—Remember to ask yourself such questions as what gives you the right to be called an author? Why do you want to be an author in the first place? Why do you want to publish?

On the other hand—If you are writing, then you're a writer, and naturally you want to publish.

• Perfectionism

On the one hand—Poems (this is true for all writing, of course, but even more so of poetry) are made of words, and every word counts. Revise, revise, cut, polish, expand, move things around, until the poem is as good as you can possibly make it. One good poem is worth a thousand sloppy ones.

On the other hand—Endless fussing over details can undermine your confidence in your own work and leave you unable to finish anything, whether it's a poem or a manuscript, so you can move on to the next thing.

• Inspiration

On the one hand—Try to have a regular schedule for writing, at the same time every day if possible, whether or not you feel inspired on a given day. Waiting for the Muse to descend is a romantic holdover, childish and self-defeating more often than not.

On the other hand—Grinding away at your writing whether you feel like it or not is a recipe for boredom—the reader's as well as yours. Writing on a regular schedule is, at least for poets, obsessive and unnecessary. Be free, spontaneous, untrammeled.

• Teaching

On the one hand—You can learn to be a better poet in all sorts of ways: courses, workshops, conferences, writing groups, and, of course, reading.

On the other hand—Writing cannot be taught.

* * *

To anchor you after that dose of dialectics, here are a few wise words I've turned up in my magpie-like pokings:

"All objects await human sympathy. It is only the human that can humanize." (Louise Bogan)

"The subconscious, when dredged up without skill or imagination, can be every bit as tiresome as the conscious." (Louise Bogan)

"How can a person not personify?" (James Merrill)

"There is nothing in the human predicament that is truly sectarian, parochial, narrow, foreign, of 'special' or 'limited' or 'minority' interest; all subjects are universal." (Cynthia Ozick)

"Precocious adolescents make do with whatever odd conglomerate of wave-worn diction the world washes up at their feet. Language at this stage uses them; years must pass before the tables turn, if they ever do." (James Merrill)

"Last year's writers are routinely replaced by this year's; the baby carriages are brimming over with poets and novelists." (Cynthia Ozick)

❑ 82

CREATE YOUR OWN POET'S LIBRARY

BY DAVID KIRBY

MOST WRITERS I KNOW HAVE A COLLECTION OF TOTEMS ON OR NEAR their desks: a photo of Whitman, a strand of heather from the Brontës' parsonage, a fortune-cookie slip promising great success. These are our power objects, the ritual devices we gaze at, touch, even talk to as we prepare to shoulder the mantle of authorship. Where would we be without them?

Well, we'd probably be right there at our desks anyway, doing the best we can. But good writing comes more easily when it takes place within a rich, familiar environment that not only locates us in a sympathetic time and space but also reminds us of a larger context, that realm where the immortals dwell. A friendly physical setting is a point of departure for a writer as well as a source of continuous encouragement during that long journey we make every day through an often-strange landscape of fresh feelings and new ideas.

I've got my gadgets and gizmos—postcards, mementoes, strange things I've put on my desk unthinkingly but for some reason never removed—yet books are the things that help me the most with my own writing. I always use the same coffee cup, a chipped, badly stained object that my sons gave me years ago, though in a pinch I suppose I could drink my morning jolt of "rocket fuel" from some other vessel. But there are certain books I find indispensable. One person's lifesaver is another's dust trap, of course, so I trust you'll edit this list to meet your own requirements as you compile or revise your poet's bookshelf. Some of these items are available on CD-ROM or come already included in a computer's hard drive. However, even the most computer-centric writers I know still surround themselves with their favorite books.

Personally, I couldn't get along without:

(1) A dictionary, probably two. Almost any dictionary will do for

daily use as long as it is comprehensive enough to be useful and small enough so that you can handle it comfortably. After that, it's nice to have *Webster's Third New International Dictionary* (Merriam-Webster), or, even better, the *Oxford English Dictionary* (Oxford University Press), which comes in a compact (i.e., small-print version). Mark Twain said that the difference between the right word and the one that is almost right is the difference between "lightning" and "lightning bug," and certainly the dictionary's principal purpose is to steer the writer toward the most precise expression. But it can also be used as a aid to inspiration. The poet Carolyn Knox writes a poetry that is so lush and word-drunk that I once asked her, "Do you just look through the dictionary sometimes for interesting words?" Her answer was, "Of course. Don't you?" I didn't then, but I do now.

(2) The Bible. The Judeo-Christian tradition permeates the whole of Western culture. But our ordinary lives are shaped by religious language as well; just listen to what a self-described atheist says when he pounds his thumb with a hammer and you'll see what I mean. The Garden of Eden, the Flood, the Marriage of Cana: these are timeless stories of innocence, righteousness, and love, chapters in a rich anthology that addresses our deepest sorrows and our highest hopes. From Dante to Dickinson, writers have always borrowed from the Bible and always will.

As with the dictionary, any standard version will do, though an index is essential. The Bible is a big book in more ways than one, and if you're looking for the story of Abraham and Isaac, you won't want to spend hours wandering in the desert with Moses and the Chosen People.

(3) A real thesaurus. I say "real" because these days, every computer comes equipped with a thesaurus of sorts, but to date there is no substitute for *Roget's International Thesaurus* (HarperCollins). For instance, if I want to consider synonyms for "totem," which occurs in the first sentence of this article, I can hit the Alt-F1 keys on my keyboard, but then the screen tells me "Word Not Found" in my computer thesaurus. On the other hand, if I look up "totem" in *Roget's,* I can choose from "earmark," "emblem," "token," and "badge" as well as "genius," "demon," "good angel," and a dozen other choices. This is one more case of the computer being faster but not better than the book.

Besides, computer tools don't really encourage serendipity. Again, imagine you're looking up "totem." Your computer may tell you there's no such word, but on the way to looking it up in *Roget's,* you may (as I just did) stumble across "stiacciato," which can be used in place of "mask," "plague," "medallion," "cameo," etc. A real thesaurus reminds us of the richness of our language in a way that the more efficient if single-minded computer cannot.

(4) A one-volume encyclopedia. Of course a multi–volume set would be ideal, but something along the lines of *The Columbia Encyclopedia* (Columbia University Press) is ideal for most purposes, especially when you take shelf space into account as well as cost.

(5) *Bartlett's Familiar Quotations* (Little, Brown). Did Samuel Johnson say "A little knowledge is a dangerous thing" or "A little learning is a dangerous thing"? You often hear the former, but the latter is correct. And by the way, Alexander Pope said it, not Johnson.

(6) A current edition of an almanac, such as the *World Almanac* (World Almanac). Recently I was writing a poem about rhythm and blues and I needed to find out when Fats Domino was born, and that's not the kind of thing you're going to find in the encyclopedia. (Answer: February 26, 1928.)

(7) Langford Reed's *The Writer's Rhyming Dictionary,* with an introduction by John Holmes (The Writer, Inc.). Even a free-verse poet will from time to time want to find a word with a very particular sound, and this or a similar book will lead you to the right one. It will also surprise you: how else would you learn that the rhymes for "Christmas" include "anabasse," "contrabass," "octobass," "Boreas," "isinglass," and "galloglass," as well as a bunch of words you already know?

Yes, the version of Windows on my computer has a rhymer, but I value it more for its speed than for its usefulness. For as with the dictionary and the thesaurus, the rhyming dictionary permits the kind of happy accident of which wonderful poems are made. Speaking of which . . .

(8) Jack Elster's *There's a Word for It!* (Pocket Books) is an engrossing guide to all those words you know exist even if you don't know what they are. Thanks to Elster, I found out that I am a "cruciver-

balist." No, not someone who nails grammar books to boards—a cruci-verbalist is a devotee of crossword puzzles.

More seriously, suppose you want to describe someone who hates men. Everyone knows that a woman hater is a "misogynist." "Misan-thrope" isn't the word you want, because a misanthrope hates every-one. But a "misandrist" is someone who hates men only.

(9) *The Oxford Companion to American Literature* and *The Oxford Companion to English Literature* (Oxford University Press). These two books, like the next item on this list, keep me out of trouble because through them I stay connected with the great tradition out of which all writing flows. After all, you can't do something new unless you have an idea of what has already been done.

Right now I'm working on a poem about my recent trip to Venice, so before I began to write I reminded myself of what Shakespeare said about that city in *The Merchant of Venice* and *Othello*. I don't plan to outdo Shakespeare, of course, but I do want to say something different from what he said.

(10) At least one anthology of classic poetry. This can range from such manageable volumes as Oscar Williams' *Immortal Poems* (Pocket Books) or William Harmon's *The Concise Columbia Book of Poetry* (Columbia University Press), which contains the 100 poems included most often in more than 400 anthologies, to the thousand-plus-page textbook you kept from your college days. Again, the point is to be able to connect with the best of the past and use it in the best way.

(11) Half a dozen current poetry collections. Obviously a poet's connection with the past is essential, but it is equally clear that poets need to learn from their contemporaries. Right now I'm looking at the spines of recent books by Primo Levi, Marilyn Hacker, Reginald Shepherd, and Dorothy Barresi; I also see two anthologies, the *Coffee-house Poetry Anthology* edited by June King and Larry Smith (Bottom Dog Press), which emphasizes the oral tradition, and *The Party Train: A Collection of North American Prose Poetry,* edited by Robert Alex-ander, Mark Vinz, and C. W. Truesdale (New Rivers Press). A sumptu-ous feast is served 24 hours a day within the modest space these books occupy, and whenever I pick up one of these collections, I am certain of getting my Recommended Daily Allowance of Vitamin P.

As with the older poetry, this new writing is not something I want either to duplicate or deny. What I seek in these pages is inspiration, an inkling of what has been done and what remains for me to do. This is the part of my poet's bookshelf that changes most frequently, and it is the part least likely to be cloned by any other poet. Vitamin P takes many different forms, and you know which poets are best for you.

(12) A book from The Wild Card Category. You have a further chance to personalize your poet's bookshelf by including something so outlandish that only you would find it useful. One of my favorite books in this category is *The Romance Writers' Phrase Book* by Jean Kent and Candace Shelton (Berkley Publishing Group). This is a book of over 3,000 "tags" or one-line descriptions used to convey emotion— or passion, actually, since romance heroes and heroines seem never to do anything halfway.

In the "Eyes" chapter, for example, you will find such headings as "Expression," "Color," "Movement," and so on, with dozens of tags under each, such as (from "Expression") "her wide-eyed innocence was merely a smoke screen," "his eyes were cold and proud," and "his eyes glowed with a savage inner fire." I love to dip into this book whenever I think I'm being too stiff or pedantic. Then my own eyes begin to glow with a savage inner fire as I return—no, swagger—to my task.

Are these the books you need to make your own poetry the best it can be? Many of them are, no doubt, whereas others may strike you as unimportant. The idea is to create your own poet's bookshelf and stock it with works that will, like old friends, gaze down upon you and murmur silent encouragement as you pursue your craft.

❏ 83

YESTERDAY'S NOISE: THE POETRY OF CHILDHOOD MEMORY

BY LINDA PASTAN

How sweet the past is, no matter how wrong, or how sad.
How sweet is yesterday's noise.
  —Charles Wright, "The Southern Cross"

I WROTE AN ESSAY TEN YEARS AGO CALLED "MEMORY AS MUSE," AND looking back at it today I am struck by the fact that in the poems I write about childhood now the mood has changed from one of a rather happy nostalgia ("Memory as Muse") to a more realistic, or at least a gloomier, assessment of my own childhood and how it affects me as a writer ("Yesterday's Noise"). Let me illustrate with a poem called "An Old Song," from my most recent book.

An Old Song*

How loyal our childhood demons are,
growing old with us in the same house
like servants who season the meat
with bitterness, like jailers
who rattle the keys
that lock us in or lock us out.

Though we go on with our lives,
though the years pile up
like snow against the door,
still our demons stare at us
from the depths of mirrors
or from the new faces across a table.

And no matter what voice they choose,
what language they speak,
the message is always the same.
They ask "Why can't you do
anything right?" They say
"We just don't love you anymore."

392

As A. S. Byatt said about herself in an interview: "I was no good at being a child." My mother told me that even as a baby I would lie screaming in the crib, clearly terrified of the dust motes that could be seen circling in the sun, as if they were a cloud of insects that were about to swarm and bite me. By the time I was five or six, I had a series of facial tics so virulent that I still can't do the mouth exercises my dentist recommends for fear I won't be able to stop doing them. I'm afraid they'll take hold like the compulsive habits of childhood that led my second-grade teacher to send me from the room until I could, as she put it, control my own face. There was the isolating year (sixth grade) of being the one child nobody would play with, the appointed victim, and there was the even more isolating year (fourth grade) of being, alas, one of the victimizers. There was my shadowy room at bedtime, at the end of a dark hallway, and, until some worried psychologist intervened, no night light allowed.

I thought about calling my last book *Only Child* because something about that condition seemed to define not only me, but possibly writers in general who sit at their desks, necessarily alone, for much of the time. In some ways, of course, it defines all of us, born alone, dying alone, alone in our skins no matter how close we seem to be to others. I tried to capture my particular loneliness as a child, my difficulty in making friends, my search for approval, in what I thought would be the title poem of that book:

Only Child*

Sister to no one,
I watched
the children next door
quarrel and make up
in a code
I never learned
to break.

Go Play!
my mother told me.
Play! said the aunts,
their heads all nodding
on their stems,
a family of rampant
flowers

and I a single shoot.
At night I dreamed
I was a twin
the way my two hands,
my eyes,
my feet were twinned.
I married young.

In the fractured light
of memory—that place
of blinding sun or shade,
I stand waiting
on the concrete stoop
for my own children
to find me.

At a reading I gave before a group of Maryland PEN women, someone who had clearly not read beyond the tables of contents of my
books introduced me as a writer of light verse. I remember thinking
in a panic that I hardly had a single light poem to read to those expectant faces, waiting to be amused. Did I have such an unhappy life,
then—wife, mother, grandmother, with woods to walk in, books to
read, good friends, even a supportive editor?

I am, in fact, a more or less happy adult, suffering, thank God, from
no more than the usual griefs age brings. But I think my poems are
colored not only by a possibly somber genetic temperament, but also
by my failure at childhood, even when I am not writing about childhood
per se. And more and more, as I grow older, those memories themselves insist upon inserting themselves into my work. Perhaps it is the
very way our childhoods change in what I called "the fractured light
of memory" that make them such an inexhaustible source of poetry.
For me, it is like the inexhaustible subject of the seasons that can be
seen in the changeable light of the sun, or the versatile light of the
imagination, as benign or malevolent or indifferent, depending upon a
particular poet's vision at a particular moment.

I want to reflect a little then on those poems we fish up from the
depths of our childhoods. And for any teachers reading this, I want to
suggest that assigning poems to student writers that grow out of their
childhoods can produce unusually good results, opening up those frozen ponds with what Kafka called the axe of poetry.

Baudelaire says that "genius is childhood recalled at will." I had a
19-year-old student once who was not a genius but who complained
that he couldn't write about anything except his childhood. Unfortu-

nately, his memory was short, and as a result, all of his poems were set in junior high school. He had taken my course, he told me, in order to find new subjects. I admit that at first glance junior high doesn't seem the most fertile territory for poems to grow in. On the other hand, insecurity, awakening sexuality, fear of failure—many of the great subjects do exist there. It occurred to me that when I was 19, what I usually wrote about were old age and death. Only in my middle years did I start looking back into my own past for the subjects of poems. This started me wondering about the poetry of memory in general. Did other poets, unlike my young students, come to this subject relatively late, as I had? As I looked rather casually and unscientifically through the books on my shelves, it did seem to me that when poets in their twenties and thirties wrote about children, it was usually their own children that concerned them, but when they were in their late forties or fifties or sixties, the children they wrote about tended to be themselves.

Donald Justice, in an interview with *The Missouri Review,* gave as good an explanation of this as anyone. He said, "In the poems I have been thinking of and writing the last few years, I have grown aware that childhood is a subject somehow available to me all over again. The perspective of time and distance alter substance somewhat, and so it is possible to think freshly of things that were once familiar and ordinary, as if they had become strange again. I don't know whether this is true of everybody's experience, but at a certain point childhood seems mythical once more. It did to start with, and it does suddenly again."

There are, first of all, what I call "Poems of the Happy Childhood," Donald Justice's own poem "The Poet At Seven" among them. But for poets less skilled than Justice, there is a danger to such poems, for they can stray across the unmarked but mined border into sentimentality and become dishonest, wishful sort of recollections. When they are working well, however, these "Poems of the Happy Childhood" reflect the Wordsworthian idea that we are born "trailing clouds of glory" and that as we grow older we are progressively despiritualized. Even earlier than Wordsworth, in the mid-17th century, Henry Vaughan anticipated these ideas in his poem, "The Retreat."

I mention Wordsworth and Vaughan because in looking back over the centuries at the work of earlier poets, I find more rarely than I expected poems that deal with childhood at all. Their poems are the exceptions, as are Shakespeare's 30th Sonnet and Tennyson's "Tears, Idle Tears." Perhaps it wasn't until Freud that people started to delve routinely into their own pasts. But nostalgia per se was not so rare, and in a book called *The Uses of Nostalgia: Studies in Pastoral Poetry,* the English critic Laurence Lerner comes up with an interesting theory. After examining pastoral poetry from classical antiquity on, he concludes that pastoral poems express the longing of the poets to return to a childhood arcadia, and that in fact what they longed to return to was childhood itself. He then takes his theory a step further and postulates that the reason poets longed for childhood is simply that they had lost it. He writes, "The list is varied of those who learned to sing of what they loved by losing it. . . . Is that what singing is? Is nostalgia the basis not only of pastoral but of other art too?" Or as Bob Hass puts it in his poem "Meditation at Lagunitas," "All the new thinking is about loss./ In this it resembles all the old thinking."

But though there are some left who think of childhood as a lost arcadia, for the most part Freud changed all of that.

We have in more recent times the idea of poetry as a revelation of the self to the self, or as Marge Perloff put it when describing the poems of Seamus Heaney, "Poetry as a dig."

The sort of poems this kind of digging often provides are almost the opposite of "Poems of the Happy Childhood," and they reflect a viewpoint that is closer to the childhood poems I seem to be writing lately. In fact, a poem like "Autobiographia Literaria" by Frank O'Hara actually consoles the adult by making him remember, albeit with irony in O'Hara's case, how much more unpleasant it was to be a child. If the poetry of memory can console, it can also expiate. In his well-known poem, "Those Winter Sundays," Robert Hayden not only recreates the past but reexamines his behavior there and finds it wanting. The poem itself becomes an apology for his behavior as a boy, and the act of writing becomes an act of repentance.

If you can't expiate the past, however, you can always revise it—and in various and occasionally unorthodox, ways. Donald Justice in the poem "Childhood" runs a list of footnotes opposite his poem, explaining and clarifying. Mark Strand in "The Untelling" reenters the childhood scene as an adult and warns the participants of what is to occur in the future.

Probably the most ambitious thing a poem of childhood memory can accomplish is the Proustian task of somehow freeing us from time itself. Proust is perfectly happy to use random, seemingly unimportant memory sensations as long as they have the power to transport him backwards. When he tastes his madeleine, moments of the past come rushing back, and he is transported to a plane of being on which a kind of immortality is granted. We can grasp for a moment what we can never normally get hold of—a bit of time in its pure state. It is not just that this somehow lasts forever, the way we hope the printed word will last, but that it can free us from the fear of death. To quote Proust: "A minute emancipated from the temporal order had recreated in us for its apprehension the man emancipated from the temporal order." Proust accomplished his journey to the past via the sense or taste, but any sense or combination of senses will do. In my poem "PM/AM," I used the sense of hearing in the first stanza and a combination of sight and touch in the second. Here is the second:

AM**

The child gets up
on the wrong side of the bed.
There are splinters
of cold light on the floor,
and when she frowns
the frown freezes on her face
as her mother has warned her it would.
When she puts her elbows roughly
on the table her father says:
you got up on the wrong side of the bed;
and there is suddenly
a cold river
of spilled milk.
These gestures are merely formal,
small stitches in the tapestry
of a childhood she will remember
as nearly happy. Outside
the snow begins again,
ordinary weather
blurring the landscape
between that time and this,
as she swings her cold legs
over the side of the bed.

But did I really say: "A childhood she will remember as nearly happy"? Whom are you to believe, the poet who wrote that poem years ago or the poet who wrote "An Old Song"? As you see, the past can be reinterpreted, the past can be revised, and the past can also be invented. Sometimes, in fact, one invents memories without even meaning to. In a poem of mine called "The One-Way Mirror Back," I acknowledge this by admitting: "What I remember hardly happened; what they say happened I hardly remember." Or as Bill Matthews put it in his poem "Our Strange and Lovable Weather"—

> . . . any place lies about its weather,
> just as we lie about our childhoods,
> and for the same reason: we can't
> say surely what we've undergone
> and need to know, and need to know.

This "need to know" runs very deep and is one of the things that fuels the poems we write about our childhoods.

But the simplest, the most basic thing such poems provide are the memories themselves, the memories for their own sakes. Here is the third stanza of Charles Simic's poem "Ballad": "Screendoor screeching in the wind/ Mother hobble-gobble baking apples/ Wooden spoons dancing, ah the idyllic life of wooden spoons/ I need a table to spread these memories on." The poem itself, then, can become such a table, a table to simply spread our memories on.

Looking back at some of my own memories, I sometimes think I was never a child at all, but a lonely woman camouflaged in a child's body. I am probably more childlike now. At least I hope so.

---

*"An Old Song" and "Only Child" appear in *Heroes In Disguise,* Norton, 1991.
**"AM" is from *PM/AM:New and Selected Poems,* Norton, 1982.

❏ 84

WRITING POETRY FOR CHILDREN AND YOUNG ADULTS

BY PAT LOWERY COLLINS

FOR YOUNG CHILDREN, A POEM IS A DEEPLY SATISFYING WAY OF LOOK-ing at the world. Fascinated at first by rhyme for its own sake, they soon begin to appreciate poetry that deals with simple concepts. They love slapstick, the wildly impossible, the ridiculous, word play, fanciful questions, clever and unexpected conclusions, twists and turns. They dote on repetition, used to great effect in *A Fine Fat Pig,* by Mary Anne Hoberman, in which the word abracadabra, used as an exclamation, precedes each line describing a zebra.

They revel in the action rhymes, finger play, and later, jump rope games, that depend on onomatopoeia, hyperbole and alliteration, as well as in such farcical verse as *Merry Merry FIBruary,* by Doris Orgel. Using these last two devices and the fun of a deliberate fib, the claim is made that "On the first of FIBruary/Setting out from Hackensack/ My Aunt Selma, in a seashell/ Sailed to Samarkand and back."

Poetry books for this age group are heavily illustrated, not only to complement the words, but also sometimes to explain them. And since poets are usually very visual writers, they will often provide the artist with exciting possibilities for illustrations without really trying.

The combined *Hector Protector* and *As I Went Over the Water* by Maurice Sendak is an unusual case in which poems and illustrations are all of one piece. Words emphasizing the text pepper the illustrations, and much of the action is in the pictures instead of the words. But in most cases, poems, even for the very young, rhymed or un-rhymed, should be able to stand on their own.

Sometimes a single poem is used as the entire text for a picture book, illustrated so as to enhance or help to develop a concept or story. The text of my nonfiction book, *I Am an Artist*, is actually one long poem conveying the concept, through the finely detailed paintings of Robin Brickman, that art is a process which begins with our experiences in the natural world.

It's been my observation that children in the middle grades (ages 9–12) are no longer as fascinated by rhyme. To some degree they want a poem to be as profound as what they are experiencing in life, something that takes them seriously. Yet, they still look for poetry that is simple and unlabored. *Haiku,* three unrhymed lines (in Japanese they must consist of 17 syllables) offering an unusual perspective on a spark of reality, is a perfect vehicle. Writing in this form is not as easy as it sounds. To provide an example, I struggled to produce: "Evening/is quietly stitching/the seam of night."

Children of this age are intrigued by the subtlety of haiku, and its shortness is irresistible to those just learning to put their own thoughts on paper.

But humorous, silly verse, either in such traditional forms as the limerick or in new and inventive ways, still holds great appeal. Thus the information that "Oysters/are creatures/without/any features," provided by John Ciardi in *Zoo Doings,* may be better remembered than the multiplication tables.

It is also a good time for books such as *Alice Yazzie's Year,* by Ramona Maher, in which unrhymed poems, each one complete in itself, taken together tell a story of a year in the life of a Navajo girl, a year that holds such mysteries as the birth of a lamb. We are told that "The new lamb sucks/The pinyon burns low/The lamb goes to sleep/ His nose is a black star."

Poems about parents quarrelling or grandparents dying are often interspersed with poetry in a lighter vein in collections for this age group. One that does this effectively is *Knock at A Star,* collected by X. J. Kennedy and Dorothy M. Kennedy.

Language for its own sake becomes the focus again for readers about eleven to twelve, when communication with peers, intrigue, and secrets are important. Poetry is then a vehicle to express feelings without exposing them. Tools for this are found in nonsense sounds, obscure meanings, double meanings, rhyme, and, of course, humor. The mystery of nonsense—even an entire made-up language—seems to hold the same allure as it had for the four-year-old. Young readers are all too willing to accept the special logic of Lewis Carroll's "Jabberwocky" and will have no trouble figuring out that when the Jabberwock "came whiffling through the tulgey wood/And burbled as it came," the "beam-ish boy" slays him as his "vorpal blade went snicker-snack!"

But these same children are also looking for poets able to look at life in the ways that they do. The poetry of Walter de la Mare has a timeless appeal because he affirms feelings that are universal. His book *Peacock Pie* was first published in 1913 and has been in print ever since. I'm currently illustrating a collection for Atheneum called *Sports, Power and Dreams of Glory, Poems Starring Girls,* edited by Isabel Joshlin Glaser, that affirms the dreams and aspirations of young women in such poems as "Abigail," by Kaye Starbird*, which ends by saying, "And while her mother said, 'Fix your looks,'/ Her father added, 'Or else write books.'/ And Abigail asked, 'Is that a dare?' And wrote a book that would curl your hair."

Teenagers may establish a passionate identification with one particular poet as they look for role models, a sense of history, a way to understand the world as it changes in and around them. By this time, they have probably been made aware of the mechanics and craft of poetry and are intrigued by experimentation. They can appreciate any poet whose vision is not too obscure. Because of the need of adolescents to deal with strong feelings and disturbing issues such as death and suicide, they are often attracted to poets with dysfunctional lives, for example, Sylvia Plath and Anne Sexton.

Most poetry for this age group appears in anthologies related to a single theme, to a city or to some historical period.

My own feeling is that even though the poetry you are compelled to write may turn out to have a special appeal for this age group, you will be competing with Shakespeare, T. S. Eliot, Walt Whitman, Emily Dickinson, and a cast of thousands. Of course, there is a lot of wonderful poetry out there for young children too, but not enough of it. And here I think the masters of today are a good match for those of yesterday and have an edge because they speak to the familiar.

But knowing your audience is only a beginning. There are a number of other things you should bear in mind in writing poetry for young people.

Don't fall victim to the mistaken notion that writing poetry for children of any age is easier than writing for adults. Your perspectives and

---

*Excerpted from "Abigail," in *The Pheasant on Route Seven,* by Kaye Starbird. Copyright ©1968 by Kaye Starbird. Reprinted by permission of Marian Reiner for the author.

topics may be different, but the skills you must bring to task are the same, skills honed through years of reading good poetry and working to develop your craft. Your most important assets will be a good memory and a strong awareness of the child within you.

It is a common misconception that almost anyone can write poetry for children. It's true we can get away with serving them peanut butter sandwiches for dinner, but it better be creamy peanut butter or the kind with just the right amount of nuts. Just so, the quality of poetry we give our children should be the best available, from the very beginning of their awareness of language.

Another misconception is that almost any idea for a children's book should be written in rhymed verse. Quite the opposite is true. Although there are exceptions, even reasonably good verse will not necessarily make for a more compelling text, and bad verse can, in fact, be deadly. So many "first" manuscripts in verse are submitted to editors that there is almost a universal resistance to them. Here I must admit to being an offender myself with my first book for children, *My Friend Andrew*. Looking back, I realize that any advantage I may have had was somehow knowing enough to keep it simple.

Things I personally object to, not under the control of the poet, are anthologies that include bad poems simply because they're by "good" poets, and minor poems by major poets because they're short; uneven collections by one poet or many; and anthologists who completely overlook contemporary poems and poets. The inability of some editors to recognize good poetry or to appreciate a child's ability to understand abstract concepts is a real problem.

Besides being as meticulous when writing poetry for children as you would be in writing for adults, you should, under penalty of a one-way trip down the rabbit hole, avoid all of the following:

• Poetry that talks down to the reader or is used as a vehicle to deliver a moral or message, unless it is written with good humor, as when Shel Silverstein, in his *Where the Sidewalk Ends*, admonishes readers to "Listen to the Mustn'ts."

• Near rhymes. They stop children in their tracks and detract from the flow of the poem. An example would be "lion's" rhymed with "defiance" and "cat" with "hate" in the poem "My Old Cat," by Hal Summers. (*Knock at A Star*)

• Rhymes that are too cute, convenient, or overused. "Rain" rhymed with "Spain" comes to mind.

• Lazy images. Even well-known poets sometimes do this, settling for the most obvious image, metaphor, or simile as in "wide as the sky."

• Rhyme for rhyme's sake, not because it will assist in saying what you want to say in the most interesting way. If, as with the book, *Madeline,* by Ludwig Bemelmans, it would be hard to imagine your own story being told in any other way, then, by all means, go for it. (I felt this way about *Andrew.*)

• Subject matter inappropriate for the intended age group, sometimes directed more to the parent than the child, or dealing with subjects outside the child's experience.

• Distorted rhyme that's hard to read aloud. Always read your own work aloud to avoid this.

• Poetry that is florid and old-fashioned, written in the accepted style of an earlier period.

• Poetry that is too complex or obscure. Young readers won't want to struggle to understand what may be very personal imagery.

• Writing presented in the form of a poem that isn't poetry by any stretch of the imagination and isn't even good prose.

• Writers who believe they must write like another poet in order to be published.

There was only one Dr. Seuss. If he had insisted on being another Edward Lear, we would have missed his unique vision and voice. If you aren't sure enough of your own voice, keep studying the work of poets you admire—their pace, rhyme schemes and structure—and keep writing until you find how to say what you want to in ways uniquely yours.

Like Valerie Worth, in her *All the Small Poems,* you may have wonderful, quiet perceptions to express about everyday objects and happenings. Borrow her microscope if you must, but wear your prescription lenses and present the world through your observations and special talents, having in mind that building a poem is much like building a block tower: You will be balancing one word or line against another; arranging and rearranging; dropping one word, adding another, until the poem begins to say what you had in mind all along or what may never before have occurred to you. When a poem really comes together, really "happens," it is a moment like no other. You will feel like the child whose tower at long last has reached the sky.

Today, the market for children's poetry is quite different from what it was in the inhospitable 1980s. Then, there were a few poets who had cracked the barrier somewhat earlier and continued to be published, but a limited number of new names came on the scene. Thanks to the firmer financial footing of most book departments for young readers, to some editors who realize that poetry rounds out a list, and to the demand by teachers and librarians, there is currently greater opportunity for new poets. A number of publishing houses are actively seeking poetry for children, but they are highly selective and still apt to overlook a talented newcomer in favor of a poet more likely to turn a profit.

But the field of poetry has never been considered a lucrative one. There are exceptions, as with any art form, and for some poets, who continue to put their words down on paper napkins and laundry lists, there is really no escape.

❏ 85

ALL LINES LEAD TO RHYME

BY ADDIE ADAM

LIGHT VERSE IS POETRY WRITTEN IN THE SPIRIT OF FUN. WHEN WELL done, the poem appears to have been written effortlessly by a poet enjoying himself. Don't be deceived. Its art is subtly buried in the poet's playful approach. Writing light verse often demands more attention to technique than that needed for more serious poetry.

In studying the writings of Richard Armour, Ogden Nash, and Dorothy Parker, among others, I discovered tricks of meter, rhyme, and subject matter used to enhance their verse. In this article, I will use my own verses as examples: not that I feel they are as well-written as those of the masters, but because I know how and why I wrote them.

Getting ideas for light verse

Light verse is usually written in first person with the writers poking fun at faults and frustrations they have in common with their readers. For subjects, you as a writer need only to look around at your job, the boss, coffee breaks, paychecks, office parties, raising children, washing windows, a visit to the dentist.

Drill Master

When my mind is being logical
I'd never think him diabolical,
But when my dentist starts to drill me,
I'm quite convinced he's out to kill me.

It helps to keep an on-going list of ideas, so that when you sit down to write, you have a decent starting point. Your list might include the woman ahead of you at the grocery check-out line, clutching a fistful of coupons; the guy who swings around your car to beat you to a parking space; and other typical shopping frustrations.

405

Christmas Shopping

Christmas list in hand, I spend
The time from morn 'til dark,
Up and down the tinseled streets
Looking for a place to park.

Study people. Fortunately for the light verse writer, people are delightfully impractical, contradictory, and impulsive. Also remember that each age group has its own jargon.

Favorite Jeans

My nerdy sister patched my jeans:
She's going to be dead meat.
I've lacy ruffles 'round my legs,
Pink daisies on my seat.

A matter of meter

Light verse writers do not need to master intricate meter forms, but they should be able to count off the meters in a line of verse to make sure it works with another line. The simplest meter is iambic, an unaccented syllable followed by an accented one:

Growing Like a Weed

They say with hydroponics
We'll be growing plants in space.
I watch the sky for roots of weeds
To dangle in my face.

The couplet and the quatrain are adequate for light verse. The couplet consists of two rhymed lines, but usually, two couplets are combined to make a four-lined poem:

Copy Boy

This grimy stranger at my door,
I swear I've seen somewhere before.
And then I find that mud has done
A carbon copy of my son.

The quatrain can rhyme the first and third lines, and the second and fourth. But, if you are as lazy as I am, just rhyme the second and fourth, as in the following:

Statistics

Women drive as well as men—
So says research and such—
But when it comes to bottom lines,
That isn't saying much.

Tricks and gimmicks

1. The funniest part of a poem, like the punch line, should be in the last line . . . and often in the last word.

Do You Like My Hair-Do?

I asked you for your honest thoughts.
Your frankness, dear, was brutal.
Would I prefer sweet-coated words?
My answer: Absolutal!

2. Use contrasting words, such as "beneath" and "beyond," "outlaw" and "in-law," "overplay" and "underpay":

Clean Sweep

Most housewives handle chores, but I
Can't look on housework fondly.
The work is not beneath me, though,
I find it's just beyond me.

3. Link a strong word with a weak one, as in the last line of "Chaos":

Chaos

Through drought, tornado, earthquake, flood,
We learn to cope, it's written,
But did that writer ever own
A Kamikaze kitten?

4. Titles can be tricky, but a title is as much a part of the poem as the punch line. Because of the brevity of the verse, in many instances, vital information cannot be supplied in the body of the poem. For example, in my poem, "Do You Like My Hair-Do?," without the title, the poem would be meaningless. The title should be tightly linked to the poem but must never give away the funny ending. Titles can be

puns, coined words, clichés, rhymed words, or words with a double meaning. The following title is an example of a double-meaning:

Switcheroo

My kids would never turn out lights,
I couldn't teach them to.
But now that they are in their teens,
I wonder why they do.

5. Light verse is probably the only type of poetry in which you can scatter clichés to your heart's content. You can use a humorous twist on a word to suggest several interpretations.

Such a Close Couple

Our thinking and working and loving alike
To others may seem rather odd,
But even in arguments, we come across
Alike as two peeves in a pod.

6. You can use interesting dialect:

Unisex Clothes

In summer, shapely front and stern,
Her figure shows which outfit's her'n.
When winter snow and winds are whizzin'
It's tough to tell twixt her'n and his'n.

7. Often words, new or coined, catch people's fancy.

Flop Crop

My family taunts my gardening skills
With squash, beans and tomatoes.
But this I know, I'm sure a pro
At raising couch potatoes.

As in the third line of "Flop Crop," inner rhyme (know/pro) is a plus.

8. Be a creator of words. On the surface, your coined words may seem a clumsy attempt to force a rhyme, but its surprise appearance

is a source of humor. The word should closely resemble the actual word it is replacing.

Granddaughter's Bedtime

At sack-time I'm the guy she picks
To be her story-teller.
She likes my monster-pirate plots
In place of Cindereller.

You will always find a receptive audience for light verse. To a busy person, a short funny poem brings a moment of laughter and relaxation.

Light verse can be any length. Four-liners often sell best because editors can tack them onto columns that run short. But you can write light verse any way you choose: long or short, inside out, or upside down. There is only one strict rule: Have fun!

❏ PLAYWRITING

❏ 86

BLAH, BLAH, BLAH—THEN THE CURTAIN FALLS

BY KENT R. BROWN

I'VE JUST ELBOWED THE LITTLE OLD LADY TO MY LEFT. "OOPS, sorry," I say as I fold my coat in my lap. "These seats are so narrow, aren't they?" "Not for me!" she retorts, freezing me with that classic little-old-lady look that little old ladies have when they've just been elbowed in the ribs. A moment later the lights start to dim. A few muffled coughs here and there, then silence. The curtain begins to rise. The expectation is palpable!

We are members of tonight's audience, my feisty companion and I, and we haven't come to listen to blah, blah, blah! We have gathered around the theatrical campfire to reaffirm our existence in the universe—"I walk this earth," we each say to ourselves as the curtain goes up, "and I want someone to acknowledge the struggle of living. My struggle!"

What theatrical campfires? I know you just want ten quick steps to successful playwriting. Well, not yet. If you're going to write plays, it's essential for you to understand the emotional core of the theatrical experience.

In its most skeletal state, your play must focus primarily on a central character who makes a conscious decision to journey—psychologically and emotionally—from point "A" to point "B" in order to achieve an objective. This journey must then be impeded by an obstacle—usually another character or your central character's psychological imperfections—thus forcing your central character to make further choices and initiate actions to overcome the obstacle. The vast majority of plays are constructed around this dramatic equation.

Now here's the heart of the issue: It must not be easy for your characters to achieve their objectives. They must claw, fight, lie, cheat, plead, love, withhold, release, bargain, sacrifice themselves, or barter with the enemy, anything to reach point "B."

After all, it's not easy for those of us in the audience to get through our lives; why should your characters have it any better?

Only difficult choices made under pressure, choices that carry important consequences, will be respected by the audience. If you trivialize your characters or what they want, we won't care what happens to them. If the struggle is genuine, based on stakes worth fighting over, then we'll join you on the journey. And in going the distance with your characters, we might find some answers to questions we've been asking for centuries: Who are we and what is our role in this universe? How do we handle the chaos of living? We look to choices and behaviors of others—even those dramatized on a stage—to live a better life.

In short, then: No conflict—no interest; no interest—no audience— and all of this within two hours for a long play, and forty minutes or so for the shorter one-act. No easy task.

"Stop," you say. "No more lectures. I've got it. No pain, no gain! I'm gonna cram a few depressed people into a stuffy room, have them scream at each other and knock down a case of booze—maybe even pull out a gun and wave it around a bit. Drop in a few gut-wrenching harangues about how sex, power, and big government are killing us— all very now—and hit 'em with the death of my goldfish when I was six! Lots of pain there. That'll keep 'em in their seats!"

No! That'll just make them wish they'd stayed home to watch *Seinfeld*. Don't use both barrels at a live theater audience. Leave that for Quentin Tarrantino and the big screen. Live theater is about seduction, not about blatancy. Drama requires the slow revealing of key pieces of information, which allows your audience to play detective and discover the clues to your characters' behavior.

Refrain from telling the audience the significance of your characters' actions. The audience can determine the life-likeness of your work, much as a jury of peers evaluates evidence presented in court. The audience will take the measure of your characters' moral fiber and extract meaning from the way they behave.

A Walk in the Woods, by Lee Blessing, ostensibly examines the tense professional relationship between an American and a Soviet diplomat as they negotiate arms reduction agreements. The stakes are obviously high, but the play is really about how two strangers representing opposing ideologies come to respect and even to love one another as individuals. Perhaps, then, implies Blessing, the enemy is as essentially human as we are, and by killing the enemy we are killing ourselves. World annihilation, then, is global suicide. In writing a play about two solitary individuals discovering their own commonality, Blessing invites his audience to apply this idea to greater issues with greater consequences.

Let's strip away the specter of a nuclear holocaust for a moment and focus on a single father working in his den late after dinner, ledgers spread out before him. Rusty, his teenage son, steps in the doorway, pauses a moment watching his father, then knocks tentatively. "Dad?" The father puts his hand up in the air and continues working. In the awkward silence that follows, Rusty tucks in his shirt. After a moment, the father lowers his hand and turns toward his son.

"What is it, Rusty? I'm very busy." "Can I have the—" "Finish your homework?" "Uh, yeah. Finished all of it. So, could I have the car keys?" "For what? It's late." "The guys are going over to—" "No. I don't like you hanging out with—" "I'll be home by—" "I don't think so." "Look, Dad, I said I finished my homework, so what's the big—" "Don't use that 'Look,-Dad,-I've-finished-my-homework' tone with me!"

Is this a play about car keys and a bunch of grungy friends? I don't think so. It's a play about territorial control, about negotiating freedom from a constricting environment. It's a play about a father who senses his son's life is getting further away from his influence and control.

Also—as a sidebar—the language suggests an undercurrent of tension. Several lines are unfinished; both characters are trying to achieve their objectives. Each character serves as the impediment to the other. Who in the audience has not been in the same or a similar situation?

Enough of this death-and-doom stuff, you say. You want to write comedies. Great, but the same essential rule applies—the audience still wants a struggle with high stakes. Take *The Odd Couple,* a very funny play about two wacky, foible-ridden, mismatched, middle-aged men, who have a hard time rooming together in a New York apartment. Right? Yes and no. It's really about the near destruction of a genuine friendship. The stakes are high here: Real friends are, quirks and all, difficult to find and hold onto. Besides, is there anyone in the audience who is flawless? Don't we all fear rejection and want to seek validation from others?

All drama, comic or serious, examines worlds that are upended,

social states that are in flux. The journey is intended to put the world
on an even keel again, if only for a moment. In comedy, the audience
says, "Whew, that was close, but we survived." Laughter helps keep
the tigers at the gate. In drama, however, a few tigers have to wreak a
little havoc inside our emotional compound before the point is made.

So much for theory and metaphor and tigers and car keys! What
about a few quick tips to tide you over until you write the big one?
Well, try these:

• Avoid characters who whine and moan about their lives. Who cares!
Yes, the past informs the present, but avoid meandering memory walks.
We want to learn what the characters are going to do about their lives
now, in the present tense.

• Regardless of whether point "B" is ever reached, someone in the
play must be altered in some fashion. In *Death of a Salesman,* Willy
Loman never comes to an awareness of himself, but his son, Biff, does.
And so, too, of course, does the audience.

• Make sure you give your obstacle some substance. You will actually
weaken the respect and encouragement you want the audience to feel
for your central character if the "bad guy" is trite.

• Keep your dialogue short. The energy generated by a quickened
interchange creates a sense of immediacy, that something is happening
in front of the audience. Playwrights love to write scathing or heart-
wrenching monologues delivered by actors silhouetted against the balcony window. But you take your chances: Most audiences don't have
the patience for extended indulgence.

• Stay away from overt exposition, like "Hey, Margie, you look better
than you did six months ago when I visited you in the wacko ward
the day after you dove off the third-floor balcony after learning your
boyfriend, Bob, was seeing your best friend, Cindy Lou." Your characters already know that. Have them move on from there. The audience
will catch up.

• Vary the age and gender of your characters. We all have distinctive
and unique interpretations of the world. You'll find your audience will
often care about the "fabric" of your world if the diversity recognized
within their own lives can be identified on stage. A cautionary note:
Few plays feature prominent roles for children. They are often difficult
to cast and direct.

• Let your characters interact in the world you've created for them.
Experienced playwrights often admit, "I didn't know Martha was going

to do such and so until she did it. So I decided to stay with her for a while to see where she was taking me." Don't be so quick to control every moment. See what happens. You can always press "delete."

• Keep your central characters in the room! Playwrights often send central characters out to get a pizza when the tension mounts, so others can talk about them in their absence. By leaving your main characters on stage to respond to the comments of others, tension increases.

• Read plays! It's startling how many playwrights try to approach a form they know little about. Read just two plays a week and you'll have read over a hundred in less than a year. Read two plays by the same author to get a feel for the author's dramatic technique. Read the Greeks and Shakespeare, as well as David Mamet and Terence McNally; Sheridan and Molière, as well as Tennessee Williams and Wendy Wasserstein. Toss in the Wilsons—Lanford, August, and Robert! Analyze how the heavy hitters have attempted to solve the very same problems you're trying to solve.

• Now that you're reading more plays, attend more performances. The prices of big-city shows are a bit steep, granted, but you're investing in your talent. Playwrights must understand how other dramatists bring their talents to bear on a script. Always remember that your play is what the audience is there to see: live people locked in a present tense struggle. Learn what good actors can accomplish on the stage. To understand what the actor has to do, take an acting class!

• Attend rehearsals at the local community theater, your local high school, anywhere. Observe how the director and actors communicate with one another, how they try to make the characters reveal their motivations. Then sit in the audience on opening night and feel the energy that exists between performer and patron.

• You need to write only an hour or so five days a week. You'll be amazed at the amount of material you'll create. Write without monitoring yourself, without judging the quality of your work. You can always nip and tuck it later. If your fingers are moving across the keys, don't pull the plug!

• At the end of each week's work, ask yourself whether your characters are just spouting snappy one-liners or making those lines achieve their objective. Are the obstacles you've created turning up the heat? Are your characters behaving with a psychological logic consistent with who they are and what they want?

• If your second draft is finished, and there's no theater within miles
of you, invite people to sit in your living room and read your play. You
don't need a fully mounted production to hear and see whether your
characters have a life. Don't direct your readers by telling them your
intention and what they should feel and think about their characters.
Give them copies of your script a week before, and let them tell *you*
what they've discovered. Then ask them to respond to the play, and
don't get defensive. If there is a cluster of similar reactions to your
work, take them seriously. Then put your script away for a week or
two before examining it again. A little distance often brings structural
and character glitches to the surface.

• Get copies of *The Dramatists Sourcebook* (Theatre Communications
Group, Inc., 355 Lexington Ave., New York, NY 10017) and *The Playwright's Companion* (Feedback Theatrebooks, 305 Madison Ave.,
Suite 1146, New York, NY 10165). Both books will make you feel
connected to the playwriting community and help you shape your material for submission.

❑ 87

PLAYWRITING QUICK AND DIRTY

BY JULIE JENSEN

PLAYWRITING IS A SOCIAL ACTIVITY. IT USES THE WRITER'S PUBLIC self, the self that tells a story to a large group of people, as opposed to the one that tells an intimate tale to a lover or the one that writes a letter to a friend.

The public nature of storytelling means something very important to the writer: He is managing other people's time. One's failure as a novelist means that a reader puts down the book and does not take it up again. Failure as a playwright means incurring an audience's displeasure, maybe even anger—an audience held hostage, remember. Those two failures are very different from one another . . . and there's little question that the second is scarier.

I propose here to ease the danger of failure as a playwright.

Dialogue

It has been claimed that more people have tried to write a play than have tried to write a story, a poem, a song, or a novel. The reason given was that would-be writers found irresistible the idea of other people saying their words out loud. If this is true, we should begin with dialogue, a playwright's great friend and eternal nemesis.

The first thing to remember is that dialogue is action. That means that you want to discourage your characters from talking about what has already happened or what might happen. You might also want to forbid them from talking about how they feel about what did or might happen. But what about exposition? you'll ask.

Disguise exposition. A piece of expositional dialogue that is only exposition should be cut; all expositional dialogue should have at least one other function besides exposition. Perhaps it can further the conflict, complicate the plot, or raise the stakes. Just make sure it does something but sit there and awkwardly explain the past.

If you follow this dictum, you magically rid your play of some early-writer awkwardness. For instance, characters don't ever say the words "I remember"—and that is a blessing. Likewise, one character never has to tell another character something they both already know, such as how many children they have or where they live.

The other secret about exposition is not to off-load it all at once. Sprinkle it around. That gives you a better shot at disguising it. Risk being obscure rather than flat-footed.

Third on the list is fairly obvious: Characters should sound different from one another. That's just another way of saying no two characters are the same. They may all have the same accent or speak in the same dialect, but making them sound different is an early test for making sure each one is unique.

The next thing to keep in mind is so important that it should be first: Characters should want something from a scene, and what they want should be pretty specific and definable. What's more, their desires must be at least slightly at odds with those of others. This sounds crass, but characters are not people you take to lunch. They're more calculating than that. When they don't want something pretty specific, they just wander around. The scene they're in is a floater, as useless as dead seaweed.

Finally, make dialogue lean. Dialogue is a race horse, not a mule or a work plug. When you finish a scene, go at it with a pencil. Try to get it down to its essence. Sometimes that's too lean, and then you can allow a little more flesh, but not fat. Put dialogue on an exercise program, to keep it moving and to keep it trim.

Now a surprising reversal. Sometimes dialogue is not spoken. Try to give characters the option of occasionally *doing* something instead of speaking. There is, for example, a reason that Nora's door slam at the end of *A Doll's House* is such a memorable moment. She has nothing more to *say,* and what she *does* is infinitely stronger than anything she could say. Playwrights often get caught in the web of believing that saying is all. Well, it isn't all, not anywhere near all. It's just talk. Doing something often has greater power.

I realize that some of my so-called *dialogue* rules are *character* rules. Occasionally I confuse them, because characters are what they

say, and of course, what they do; dialogue is merely one of the convey-
ances.

Character

The most important thing about characters is that they should be
interesting—that is, interesting to you.

That puts you on the spot: You have to take responsibility for your
characters, and as a result, you're less likely to let them wander into
tedium. It's a little bit like taking your cousin to a party. You don't
want her to fail because that would hurt her feelings, and you like her.
So you ask her good questions, laugh at her jokes and, in general,
encourage her. That's about as far as the cousin metaphor goes, though,
because it's your job to get your characters in a whole lot of trouble.
But that's plot, and that comes later. Back to character.

Believable characters are off balance in some way. They're excessive
in one direction, deficient in another. And they are tenacious; they
don't easily give up their imbalance.

I used to have a test for characters that I called the "Othello test":
Could my character hold her own in a play with Othello? I mean, that
man was off balance! And he was also tenacious. He was capable of
believing big and acting big. If my characters could pass this test, I
knew they were large enough to be in a play.

Second, your characters have to want something specific. You've
heard that one before, but it's worth repeating. It's not quite enough
for Hamlet to want something big like revenge; it's also important that
he want something more immediate, like convincing his girlfriend he's
nuts. This immediate goal helps move things along and prevents the
scene from floating.

Third, characters should have a well-defined rhythm or tempo that
will help you imagine how they would move as well as how they would
tell a joke. But moving is the critical thing here: Your characters need
to be moving, perhaps working. People are, after all, very busy. They
don't sit around and carry on long conversations; they catch things in
quick takes while doing something else.

Next, characters have blind spots. This might be the same thing as
fatal flaw, except more specific. Blind spots are the habitual behavior
that results from the fatal flaw. In *Death of a Salesman*, Willy Loman
wanted to be well liked. He wanted it so much that he lied to himself
and others. Habitually. That's his blind spot. Blind spots enable a char-

acter to move from 0 to 60 in a single breath; they make characters funny and tragic.

Characters have always just come from somewhere else. And when they were there, they did something. That means that characters come to any scene with some baggage, with an attitude. Don't make them explain where they've been or what they did; that would violate the dialogue rule about exposition. But as the playwright, you have to know where they've been and what they've done. That information always affects the opening of the scene, but it also affects rhythms, tempo, attitude, patience, and innumerable other intangibles within a scene.

I also like characters who surprise me, who surprise themselves. Surprise is one of a playwright's best weapons, in my opinion far too underused. Playwrights are generally a bit too preoccupied with character consistency, thereby setting up characters and making their choices predictable, the outcome predetermined.

Remember the laughing scene in Beth Henley's *Crimes of the Heart?* That scene becomes the climax of the play because it is so surprising. Likewise, Sam Shepard's errant brother in *True West,* who steals all the toasters in the neighborhood and toasts an entire loaf of bread. The audacity, the surprise of these two scenes delights and gratifies the audience.

Now a human truth and also a character truth: Characters, like most people, almost never tell the truth. Sometimes they're protecting themselves, sometimes they're manipulating others, sometimes they've got a skewed vision of the world. And sometimes they're just polite and go along when someone else seems to know more. If you remember this dictum, your plays will also be saved from another early-writer problem: creating a character who knows everything and tells all. In other words, you will be saved from writing yourself into plays, that witty but put-upon, sensitive but all-knowing bore.

And that leads us neatly to a suggestion that characters should have a nice mix of traits. I like my characters smart about some things, funny about some things, and eloquent about some things. But heaven forbid that any character should be smart about all things, funny about all things, or worst of all, eloquent about all things!

I like characters best when they cannot help but be themselves, when I as a writer just have to relent and let them do what they will. Imagine Shakespeare's delight at having created Falstaff, then just hanging around while the old man went wild in front of him.

Finally, I need to remind you that this list applies to major characters only. If you make all your characters this complicated, you'll give your *Hamlet* away to Fortinbras. Too much complication in a minor character can be a dangerous thing.

Plot

Now we move to a consideration of plot, which these days is more important than it used to be. First, plot should answer a question. Will Godot come? No, not today. Will the guys in *American Buffalo* make a fortune from the rare nickel? No. Will Jesse in *'night, Mother* kill herself? Yes. They're simple questions; they don't involve interpretation. But they are what compel an audience to stay to the end.

Your plot also needs to be clear to the audience almost at once, at least by the time you're ten percent into the play. So if your play is ten pages long, the audience needs to know the question by the end of the first page; if your play is 100 pages long, they need to know it by page ten.

At about this same point, you'll want to accomplish something else: the inciting incident, the event that gets it all going. If your play is a football game, the inciting incident is the kick-off. It is not the coin toss or the eager expression on the faces of the players while they're listening to the national anthem. It is what gets things moving and does so strongly. After the Ghost visits Hamlet, the play has been kicked off; after the guests arrive at George and Martha's house in *Who's Afraid of Virginia Woolf?*, the play has been kicked off.

The easiest way to work on plot is to keep asking yourself, "And then what? And then what?" That keeps you and ultimately your audience focused on events and outcomes. And it keeps the story moving.

Another way to think about plot is to ask what the character wants, and what she will do to get it. This question also implies the necessary element of conflict. And no plot is possible without conflict. Even though it's against our higher moral order and runs counter to how we want to live our lives, conflict in all its myriad possibilities is absolutely essential to plot.

When I was first studying playwriting, I heard over and over again that a plot had a beginning, middle, and end. I never could understand that. Everything has a beginning, middle, and end. A flat line, a knotted thread, the deck of a ship. And yet none of those is a plot.

This metaphor is more helpful to me: A plot looks like a long slope up a hill. The climax is the peak. As you progress up the long slope, however, there are several impediments or plot points. Fences and forests, rivers and riots. Your job is to decide what the fences, forests, rivers and riots really are, and then space them out. Here's how it works: Hamlet wants revenge. He's walking the long upward slope of revenge. A lot of fences and forests: Ophelia is one, Polonius another. A lot of rivers and riots: Gertrude is one, Laertes another. There is also the truly big pinnacle, Claudius. The interruptions are called plot points. They are challenges or complications, things that impede the progress of the hero or heroine, things that cause danger. These impediments get bigger as the play goes on. Then by the end either the impediments win or the hero does. And that's the plot.

There are a couple more points to make about plot. By the halfway mark or thereabouts, I like to put a big X: That's the point of no return. After that point, the character can't go back. After he's killed Polonius, Hamlet can't go back. After Martha in *Who's Afraid of Virginia Woolf?* has gone upstairs with the biologist, she can't go back.

Finally, there is the resolution that occurs after the climax. The climax answers the question, and the resolution is a moment of quiet, a settling in, of getting used to the answer. In Hamlet the question is, "Will Hamlet get revenge?" The answer is, "Yes, but he'll die, too." So the settling in is Horatio's farewell speech and the scene in which Fortinbras takes over the kingdom.

A settling in does not need to take very long. In a shorter play, it can be a quiet line and a pause. But it can also take a whole scene.

And now here is my final advice about plots and about playwriting in general: If you sat down and told a story, you would know instinctively how to tell it. Plot structures are instinctive structures. Writing a play is the same. Go ahead and tell the story. After you've finished, think about structure.

Writing a play is like telling a story to some friends, hoping they'll respond as you did: that it was funny, that it was sad, that it was infuriating, that it was a relief, that it was a damn shame. So go ahead, write your play. Then pick up these notes and figure out if there's something you'd like to change.

❑ 88

CREATING EFFECTIVE STAGE CHARACTERS

BY DAVID COPELIN

ONE OF THE GREATEST REWARDS OF WRITING PLAYS LIES IN CRAFTING memorable characters. I love those wonderful moments in the process when characters you've invented start developing traits you never imagined for them, changing in ways that make them seem almost autonomous, creating *themselves.*

Although such moments can't be guaranteed, you can prepare for them by choosing those techniques of characterization that will help you jump-start the souls of the diverse citizens of your imagination.

How do you do this? Let's look at three areas of character creation: the *verbal,* the *non-verbal,* and the *relational.*

To dramatize the world is to unmask it. A novelist can describe characters at length, telling us who they are, what they look like, what they think and feel, and even how we should react to them. But a playwright's characters must unmask *themselves*—and quickly. Characters reveal who they are through their stage behavior: their words, their interaction with other characters, their strategic silences, their presence or absence in a particular scene. Stage characters also comment on each other. Some of that commentary is credible, some is not. Part of the role of the audience, part of their pleasure, is to figure out which part is which.

Since plays are so compressed in time and space, a little has to stand for a lot. So, to the extent that you can sketch a character's "character" with a few lines of dialogue, or through a minimal number of gestures, you will be a master of dramatic economy. In the most successful plays, such economy exposes both character and the world that surrounds that character in a theatrically involving way.

Dialogue is a primary means of communication in the theater. The first thing to remember about dialogue is that you can do quite a lot with very little. For example, take Tom Stoppard's provocative comedy *Travesties*. At one point in the play, mention is made of an imminent world-wide social revolution. A British Embassy bureaucrat inquires, "A *social* revolution? Unaccompanied women smoking at the opera, that sort of thing?"

We laugh, and we instantly understand who the character is, the nature of the society he's used to, and his utter incomprehension of a radically changing world. Stoppard tells us everything we need to know *in one line.*

Depending on who they are and what they want, characters will have different strategies of communication. In David Mamet's *Sexual Perversity in Chicago,* a young woman has just begun a love affair and has been with her new boyfriend for several days. When she returns to the apartment she shares with a woman friend, her roommate greets her laconically: "Your plants died."

In that brief moment, we learn a good deal about the roommate's personality, the women's relationship, the passage of time, domestic responsibility, jealousy, and cynicism. In performance, this moment is both funny and poignant.

Some characters don't talk much, but are devastatingly powerful. (Check out Ruth in Harold Pinter's *The Homecoming.*) Some characters chatter on and on, but are of little consequence in a play's power scheme. Such chatter can be quite useful as a source of comic relief, or it can be a convincing mannerism of disguise for a character who needs to conceal something from other characters and from the audience.

Audiences tend to believe whatever stage characters say. You can use this credulity in many ways. One of your most interesting options is to have characters *lie*—to themselves, to other characters, and to the audience. Moreover, characters who sometimes lie may also sometimes tell the truth! This is a situation ripe for dramatic exploitation.

Characters who reveal small truths win an audience's confidence; they can then conceal the larger truths you're *really* writing about until late in the play, and the audience will forgive you—and the characters—the deception.

Have you noticed that direct audience address has become quite commonplace in contemporary plays? Have you noticed how mixed the results are? If you have one of your characters confide in the audience, make sure that the character *has* to do so. Don't use this technique simply because it appears to be easier than juxtaposing characters with different agendas. Such appearances deceive the audience.

It's usually unwise to have a character state the theme of your play. Focus instead on what the characters *want* and on what actions they take to get it. The audience will then have all the information they need to perceive the theme on their own.

Try not to have your characters explain their own or each other's motivations. Plays in which every character speaks as though she or he has had years of psychotherapy tend to be dramatically inert, because they do too much of the audience's work, too little of their own.

How do you choose one mode of verbal communication over another? Think of your cast of characters as an orchestra—whether chamber, full, or jug band doesn't matter. Much of your play's "music" comes from the permutations and combinations of characters as they speak and interact, so mixing speakers with different voices and rhythms automatically creates a theatrical "score." Of course, you may be writing a play in which all the characters *need* to sound alike. If so, go ahead. But this is not a choice to be made *unconsciously*. Your choice must reveal the *interplay* between plot and character, the *tension* between individual personalities and the situations they find themselves in. That's what's important dramatically.

As a play evolves, any kind of change in a character is permissible, as long as he or she behaves consistently within the parameters that you set. Altering a character's age, class or gender can have a positive impact on both the story and the other characters in the play, especially if the change makes your character less stereotypical, more idiosyncratic—and *raises the stakes*. This criterion also applies to adding, deleting and combining characters. Each such change will force you to review your dialogue, and probably to revise and tighten it.

Once your characters are established verbally, with their conflicting personalities revealed by their particular and unique ways of speaking, remember that, on stage, they also exist visually. That raises a whole different set of challenges—the *non-verbal*. Since you're writing for performance, you need to think about *people*, not just about words on a page; about non-verbal communication; and about communication in three dimensions.

Be aware that while words are important, visual elements, silence, and non-verbal sound all must be part of your playwriting strategy. Words express only what characters need to *say*. A character's tone of voice, body language, and the like express the emotions that underlie those words more complexly. This is what actors call "subtext." What's *between* the lines may reinforce what's being said out loud, or contradict it. In either case, what isn't spoken may well be more important to the persuasiveness of your play than what *is*.

The 18th-century diarist Samuel Pepys often wrote of going to the theater "to hear a play." We don't do that anymore; nowadays, we go to *see* a play. The difference is crucial. For modern people, seeing is believing. Therefore, in the theater, where the entire visual and aural context can be manipulated for effect, lighting and non-verbal sound can contribute to an audience's understanding of character as strongly as do your words. You need to appreciate what non-verbal communication can and cannot do to help you define your characters. How do they walk? What radio station do they listen to? Should the lighting make them look innocuous or sinister? Do they belch? And so on.

You can combine verbal and non-verbal means to present character far more effectively than you can express it with either mode alone. In Marie Irene Fornes's play, *The Conduct of Life,* an overworked, exploited domestic servant in the household of a Latin American fascist talks to us as she goes about her chores. She lists a number of things she does as soon as she wakes up, adding, "Then I start the day." After another list of chores, she repeats, "Then I start the day." After a third list, she says it again. And we're exhausted!

We understand, we *feel,* the dreariness of the character's life, and the oppression of her situation, even as we see her do her chores quickly and efficiently. The playwright's words and the actress's physicality combine to create an unforgettable character and theater with a powerful political sensibility.

You must also consider the *relational* aspects of character.

What do I mean by that?

I've been talking about character as if each personality in a play were an individual, distinct from other characters and more or less independent of them. But characters in plays are even less autonomous than human beings are in the "real" world. Whatever may be the rules of the dramatic universe you've created, chances are that *relationships* between characters are more important to the play's energy and forward motion than the individual characters you create one by one can ever be.

Try thinking about your characters in pairs, in triangles, in the context of their society, as well as individually. You can create character groupings that illustrate the workings of social forces without being too obvious about it, without losing the charm of the immediate and personal. If you need to, you can alter audience expectations of time, space, blood ties, cause and effect, or anything else that they usually take for granted. It's fun, and it stops conventional thinking in its tracks—one of the reasons we have theater in the first place.

For example, look at Caryl Churchill's *Cloud 9*. This justly celebrated play subverts commonplace notions of what character is in the theater and in the world. Churchill's highly economical method, which only a truly imaginative playwright could use so effectively, explodes received ideas about gender and its immutability. By having men play female characters and women play male characters, by having them interact in highly provocative ways, Churchill dramatizes complex issues that range from patriarchy and imperialism, to domestic violence and sexual pleasure. The play is exhilarating, because Caryl Churchill has the wit and the craft to turn our expectations of character upside down—and make us like it.

You will probably not want or be able to use every technique for presenting character that you run across, but your own arsenal of ways to make the people "work" is bound to grow, whether you write kitchen-sink realism, post-neo-futurist cabaret sketches, playlets for children, or any other dramatic form that puts human beings on a stage.

Remember, the wide variety of character-revealing techniques is there to serve your purposes. If you can't find contemporary techniques that fulfill your needs, feel free to invent (or revive!) those that do. Whatever makes your characters memorable makes *you* a better playwright.

❏ 89

FINDING A THEME
FOR YOUR PLAY

BY PETER SAGAL

USUALLY WHEN PEOPLE ASK ME WHAT MY PLAYS ARE ABOUT, I HEM
and haw and squint off into the sky and then come up with something
like, "Well, there's this guy, and he has this dog . . . . and then this
army invades. . . . well, it's really kind of a love story, in the end." I
feel silly, and my questioner hasn't learned anything, which may be
right, because if he wants to know what the play is about, he should
see the thing. I mean, we write immortal works of dramatic literature,
not slogans.

But I recently wrote a play that could be summarized in a single
sentence.* This was a first for me, and because of this, and because
the sentence in question invoked some political and moral questions,
I became instantly known as a Dramatist of Serious Theme. This makes
me bristle, because like every other normal writer, I resent any praise
that is not universal. What are my comedies, chopped liver?

Nonetheless, I'm now known as a guy with something to say, and
I've been asked here to give some tips on how to say it, that is, how
to approach the problem of Theme in playwriting. (That raises the
ancillary question of how you write a play when you have *nothing* to
say, which is a problem I face daily.) Somebody—I think it was Woody
Allen quoting Samuel Goldwyn—said that people go to the theater for
entertainment; if you want to send a message, call Western Union. But
the theater has changed a lot and seems to be surviving only because
of its toehold in Meaning; i.e., movies and TV may give you cleavage
and explosions, etc., but if you want to learn something, come to the
theater. Somebody else said—and this time I know, it was the actor

---

*"A Jewish lawyer defends the First Amendment rights of a man who says the Holo-
caust did not happen." (*Denial*, Long Wharf Theater, Dec. 1995)

Simon Callow—that in this day and age, going to the theater for "entertainment" is like going to a restaurant for indigestion.

So how to approach the theme play, the political or "problem" play? First of all, it seems to me that the playwright should always begin not from a statement, but a question. It is boring to be told an opinion, but it is interesting to be asked for your own. Thus, a writer who sets off to tell us, "Racism is bad!," for example, will probably ultimately irritate the audience, because they know that racism is bad and they're sorry, but frankly they don't feel that they had to pay $20 or whatever to be told again. But a writer who asks the audience, "Why is racism bad?" or even "Is racism ever justified?" will hold the playgoers' attention, because they may never have thought about it before, and their answers may surprise or please or horrify the playwright.

Once you have framed your question in an interesting and provocative way, how do you dramatize it? Here we fall into the great Unknown, because the answer depends on your particular vision of drama and the theater, and my answer may not suit you and your purposes. For example, if you're Brecht, you'll pose your question by writing it on a banner and hanging it upstage center. What I do is try to make the Thematic Problem into a personal one.

Sometimes it's obvious how to do this, sometimes it's not. If you're writing about True Love, then clearly your play will need some lovers. If it's about racism, then a racist or two will be in order. More complicated questions require more complicated solutions, but part of your job as a dramatist (some would say your *whole* job) is to find that telling situation, that moment of crisis and decision plucked from the entire span of an infinite number of imaginary lifetimes, that perfectly distills the essence of the question you're addressing. For example, let's say you want to write about the tension between duty to self and duty to country. You want to write about a solider. But which solider, in which war? An Englishman fighting in World War I? A Jew fighting in World War II? An Asian American fighting in Vietnam? Any situation will give different emphases to different sides of your question. How do you choose?

In considering this choice, remember that the worst sin the dramatist can commit is to lie to an audience. In this context, it means putting a question out there and then making the answer easy or simple when it's not. There's a great temptation when asking an important question—"Will True Love Always Triumph?"—to go immediately for the best and most comforting answer—"Yes!"—and ignore all the evidence to the contrary that's in the world, in your heart, in your own play. Consider *King Lear*. Its answer to that particular question would be a resounding *No,* so during the 17th century, the play was rewritten by Nahum Tate to answer *Yes:* Cordelia, quite alive at the end, united with Edmund and her loving father. That rewritten version was rejected by history for, among other things, being a lie.

So if you are going to ask a tough question, and you should, you must be merciless in your search for the answer. Let the situation of the play be rife with ambiguity and doubt. Let your characters be contradictory, holding both bad and good within them. Let the most horrible opinions be held by the most pleasant and attractive people. Let good people do terrible things to one another; let them react to kindness with anger and to attacks with fear. Because that's what happens in the real world, and if by chance you do want to say, ultimately, something good—that Love will triumph, that freedom is precious and worth fighting for—it won't help your case to set your play in a fantasy world where these things come easier than they actually are.

What I've often done is to take a character I admire and like, and then either put that character in a very difficult position, or cause him or her to do something rather unpleasant and then have to deal with the results. In my play *Denial* I took a character who was very confident in her support of free speech and confronted her with another character—very charming, by the way—who made her want to scream and strike out every time he opened his mouth. In *Angels in America,* by Tony Kushner, a lead character, who is charming and sympathetic and funny, abandons his lover in time of crisis, so we are left to ask ourselves—we, who think of ourselves as charming and sympathetic and funny—if when the time came, we might do the same thing.

The second worst sin in the theater, after lying, is to be boring. In fact, it's often in the pursuit of not being boring that we end up telling our worst lies. There's a strong temptation—driven by the market and our own inclination to be cheerful—to preach to the choir. The theater of today desperately wants to say something Useful and Good about the world; it wants to condemn what needs condemning and praise what needs praising, according to the mores of the day. But the problem is that unless you do that from a deeply informed, dramatically charged, almost universally comprehending place, you're going to bore the heck out of your audience.

How do you achieve that kind of aesthetic Buddha-nature, where you comprehend everything, where all forces balance, where the true strengths and faultlines of the universe reveal themselves?

Work hard, write every day, and tell the truth. It may not work, but nothing else will.

❑ JUVENILE AND YOUNG ADULT

❑ 90

HANDS-ON RESEARCH:
FINDING A BAGPIPER

BY ELOISE McGRAW

I ENJOY RESEARCH. I LOVE FINDING OUT ALL ABOUT A PLACE AND time and the people who lived then and how they dressed and what they believed, and then recreating it all in fiction. The search for accuracy has led me into some long and arduous paper chases through interlibrary loan, but I've never minded. Sound book research can not only expand your education in all directions; it can keep you from making a fool of yourself. The local library can be a writer's best friend.

But how can you find out things no book ever tells you?

Imagine yourself standing on the roof of Notre Dame Cathedral. How much—if any—could you see of a house across the street? Now transfer yourself down to the street in front of such a house. How well—if at all—could you see a person standing on the cathedral roof? Imagination isn't going to give you those answers; there's too much you don't know. Guess at matters of hard fact, and you're sure to expose your ignorance. But how to find out more about that cathedral roof? Not one solitary guidebook provides a clue.

To many writers, the element of *place*—the setting—is not as important as other elements of the story. To some of us it is fundamental. When I write, the inner process is like watching a movie—in living color—with sound. If I have no clear mental picture of where and when everything is happening, and a reliable inner map of the landscape, I'm stymied. My characters are, too. They either stumble around in a sort of fog or just sit there, mum.

There are a number of ways to find out what you're writing about. You can go to Paris—or wherever—yourself. Frequently, this is not possible. I hadn't the leisure or the money to travel to the Nile Valley during the years I was writing three novels about Egypt. In any case, my setting was *ancient* Egypt, and no traveler can go there except via

437

the library shelves, the museum collections, and his own powers of visualization. Years later, when I finally did go to Egypt, I found that these three approaches had not let me down; in fact, the research I had done enabled me to see ancient Egypt right through the modern overlay.

Historical novels aren't the only books that require research. Twelve of my nineteen novels have contemporary settings, but there wasn't one that didn't require a little research into *something*. I've had to find out about knots, codes, World War II fighter planes, sleight-of-hand tricks, parrots, logging, old stagecoach schedules, company mergers, fox-hunting lingo, pioneer gravestones, and so-called antique stores that sell toys and ice-picks and buttonhooks just like the ones I grew up with. But first—most memorably—circuses.

I took my initial plunge into real research only because my editor gave me a shove. It was my very first book—already written, already accepted and awaiting (though I was unaware of it) the back-and-forthing between editor and author that grooms a manuscript for publication. I knew nothing about this process. I knew almost nothing about circuses or bareback riders, either—though that's what my book was about. It must have read convincingly, because when my editor inquired if I had, myself, worked in a circus, she seemed taken aback when I said no. "I've read three books about them, though," I assured her. Whereupon my education, in circuses *and* research, began, and has continued to this day.

There are times when nobody can answer your question. Faced with a well-documented historical fact—a baffling suicide, an inexplicable disappearance or usurping, a war that led nowhere—how do you discover the cause behind the effect, the powerful human motivations, that nobody has documented at all? And here's a more prosaic sort of poser: How many days would it take, by what route, to travel from Egypt to Babylon in 1500 B.C.? How many miles to walk from Hastings to Canterbury in 1067, through what sort of countryside?

To answer such questions you must use plain ingenuity, a kind of labor-intensive jigsaw puzzle technique (to gather and fit together various unrelated scraps of information), and some leaps of imagination (to fill in the picture they suggest).

I managed to solve the Hastings-to-Canterbury puzzle by such means. Other questions immediately arose, all having to do with the creation of the Bayeux Tapestry, on which my main character was going to work. How long would it take her to embroider one figure, one sail? Would the work hurt her fingers or tire her back? I wasted time asking people who didn't know. The hands-on method was the only one left.

I had to learn from a book how to do the three stitches used on the Tapestry. That done, I selected one scene and drew it on linen (using the old art school squaring-off method) to exact size, 40 by 20 inches. Using my drawing table—minus its board—as a stretcher I settled down to embroider the scene in a wool thread similar to the handspun original, keeping track of the hours and my sensations. It took me 200 hours, working two to three hours a day during one spring—writing the book in the mornings and embroidering in the afternoons. It's not your back that gets sore; it's your fingertips—but only on the outline stitch.

Now, as research this was going overboard. I know that, but I enjoyed every minute—and learned to embroider, besides.

The historical past—even the dimmest, most distant past—at least concerns the real world. What about the worlds you invent yourself?

Fantasy—dreaming them up or writing them down—seems easy and is anything but. It is a brave (or naive) beginner who tackles it. Consider Flannery O'Connor's comment: ". . . when one writes a fantasy, reality is the proper basis of it. . . . I would even go so far as to say that the person writing the fantasy has to be even more strictly attentive to the concrete detail than someone writing in a naturalistic vein—because the more convincing the properties in it have to be."

In short, fantasy must seem even more real than real. The strange landscapes, the smell and color of the dragons, the squeaky voice of the talking mouse, the details of every chair and mantle ornament in the old rabbit's living room, must be clearly visualized and sharply described.

Visualizing—that's the hard part. When I was planning *The Moorchild*—a fantasy—my first worst hurdle was getting the visual landscape in my mind. This is not a problem with a historical novel, because you've read up on your chosen place and period until you feel more solidly oriented in, say, 17th-century London than you do in your own neighborhood. Obviously, it is not a problem with a modern-day setting. But with a fantasy, where are you?

The Moorchild was based on elements of British and European folk-lore—that is, on a well-established body of *traditional* fantasy. Because of this matrix, I did not feel wholly free. I had two places to invent—one an isolated human village at the edge of a non-specific moor in a non-real time similar to the early Middle Ages. The other place, hidden under the nearby moor, would be the Mound, the parallel world of my (also invented) non-human creatures, the Moorfolk.

The landscape inside the Mound gave me very little trouble. Lodged in a far corner of my mind, just waiting, was the memory of a salt mine I visited as a child—a vast, glittering cavern where sound drifted eerily without echo, where on a slope I'd judged only a short walk away a donkey and cart looked the size of toys, where an hour flew by like an instant and yet stood still, all these years later, in vivid recollection. Once I'd thought of that salt mine my imagination took off, and I had my Mound. But a wholly fanciful setting for my human characters seemed wrong for a story based on elements of real folklore. I wanted to give my village solid, pseudo-historical reality based on the real world. Yet I didn't want to use an identifiable country because I wanted to keep this a fantasy. Deadlock.

I had to work my way out of it, using trial and error with no idea what would work. From the beginning, I had thought of a countryside and climate reminiscent of (perhaps) northwest England or the Scottish Highlands—so I started with that, and read up on the medieval use of such lands, the woods, the common fields, the "waste land," the shared plows and animals, what kind of houses, which crops. Then I mentally situated my village in such surroundings—feeling as though I were constructing a cardboard stage with a painted backdrop—and gave it the few craftsmen such a village would need: a miller, a blacksmith, a potter.

With nearly total lack of confidence, I started my characters moving through this jerry-built environment. And astonishingly—as if each character carried a magic wand—the details came alive; the place became real and substantial to me, feature by feature, as the villagers moved through it. The vaguely mentioned hillside apple orchard a child climbed past took solid root and was there for good. Once a woman hurried up the village street I could see the street—grassy and crooked, with the well halfway along, and old Fiach with his dog sitting in the sun. Soon I knew where everybody lived, and the ways to the fields and the moor and the woods, and the whole place was mine. I can't guarantee that this method will work for you, but unpromising as it feels while you're doing it, it's worth a try.

I went through a similar process to invent my Moorfolk—who are *not* elves, nor fairies, nor brownies, nor any other of those remarkably well-documented traditional beings. I drew some qualities and habits from such creatures, especially their non-human emotions and attitudes, but my Moorfolk are themselves. And this painted me into another corner; for unlike the sprites of folklore, who all play fiddles, Moorfolk play bagpipes.

So I suddenly needed to know what bagpipes look like up close, how all those tubes and tassels and straps are hung together, how you hold bagpipes when you play, which bit you blow into. Is the conglomeration heavy to carry, where do you feel the pressure, how do you work that bag when both hands are busy fingering stops, what's the hardest trick in playing it, could an undersized child of nine or ten ever manage it at all . . . ? My questions, like my ignorance, were endless, and called for some hands-on answers. But how to find a bagpiper, just like that? The nearest I'd ever come to one was in northern Scotland.

I was dwelling hopelessly on the air fare to the Highlands or even to Indianapolis, home of an old friend's ex-son-in-law, who, I thought, used to play the pipes. My daughter then reminded me of the Highland Games held annually on a nearby college campus—always accompanied by an entire—and undoubtedly local—bagpipe band. I phoned my suburban chamber of commerce and learned the name of an expert high-school-age piper who lived just a few blocks away. I got enthusiastic cooperation, all my answers, and a hands-on, ear-splitting hour I'll never forget.

In that instance, the hopeless turned out to be easy. But that doesn't always happen. You have to be prepared to go the extra mile. No matter; it's that mile that's often the most rewarding.

□ 91

FORGET THE ALAMO: WRITING HISTORY FOR CHILDREN

BY SYLVIA WHITMAN

GROWING UP, I FELT THE SAME WAY ABOUT HISTORY AS I DID ABOUT spinach: Everybody said it was good for me, and I detested it. Elections, treaties, dates, and more dates—what a bore! Luckily, I loved to read. Just as I managed to meet my minimum RDA of vitamins with frozen peas and grape juice, I got a rough sense of the past through biographies and novels like *Johnny Tremaine* (1943), Esther Forbes's award-winning story of an apprentice silversmith on the eve of the American Revolution. The last thing I ever expected, though, was that I would end up writing history books that teachers could inflict upon kids.

I first started to enjoy history in college in the early 1980s. By then "social history" had moved into the academic mainstream. Although it would seem that social historians should be poring over the guest list of the Boston Tea Party, they are more likely to be studying the propaganda of rebellion or 18th-century perceptions of Native Americans. Social historians are the "big picture" people: They tend to highlight change instead of chronology; to focus on processes rather than events; to think in terms of decades instead of weeks or months; to follow the transmutations of ideas as they trickle down from the intelligentsia and trickle up from popular culture. Also, in the 1980s, stirrings of multiculturalism were beginning to influence scholarship, and women's studies was gaining respectability. I had long taken an interest in the activities of my mother and grandmothers, my personal links to the past. At last, academia was encouraging me to place family history in a broader context.

Developments at the university level have influenced elementary and secondary school curricula. Time lines are now merely a springboard in many history classes. Teachers searching for books and periodicals to enrich textbook fare and stimulate research projects have helped feed a boom in nonfiction of all kinds for children. If you're interested in writing about the past you have a captive audience.

Fact vs. fiction

Most of the biographies I devoured as a child read like novels. I remember in particular one about Clara Barton, founder of the American Red Cross. In the opening chapter, Clara is celebrating her sixth birthday. As she divides up her cake, she forgets to leave herself a piece. Although the scene skillfully makes a point about Clara's selflessness, the author would never get away with all that embellishment today. It's historical fiction, not history.

Teachers and publishers expect authors to adhere to certain scholarly conventions. You can conjecture from the evidence; you can contrast opposing viewpoints; you can report conversations documented in journals or letters or tape recordings. But you can never invent characters or recreate dialogue. Writing "pure" history requires a sort of collage mentality. You have to search out the juiciest facts, then juxtapose them to support your points.

Going to the sources

Some authors avoid putting any of their own words into the collage by compiling anthologies of first-person quotes. This cut-and-paste approach asks young readers to extrapolate a lot. I prefer to blend primary and secondary sources—combining accounts by people who lived through or witnessed events with analysis and reports by academics or journalists. By paraphrasing, quoting, and interpreting, you can give more structure to the collage. You can also scale history down to an elementary reading level.

Before I begin a first draft, I survey the topic in the library to find out what's on the shelf, what's in print, and what might be available through interlibrary loan. My proposals always include an outline and a bibliography. Neither is considered binding, but they force me to think early about structure, about themes, and especially about the variety of my sources.

Cast your net widely. Researching *Hernando de Soto and the Explorers of the American South,* I relied on four published accounts. Luis Hernandez de Biedma described the group's wanderings. Although both de Soto's secretary and a Portuguese nobleman documented the

ruthlessness of the Spaniards, the latter also admired his leader's pa-
nache. Garcilaso de la Vega, a 16th-century mestizo historian who
nicknamed himself "the Inca," didn't travel with the expedition, but
his romantic version based on interviews with survivors stands out for
its sympathetic portrayal of Native Americans. Instead of designating
one chronicle as the "true" version, I juggled all four. I let my readers
see the seams of history—the biases of the winesses, and the "facts"
on which they disagreed.

With secondary sources, try to draw on recent work by young historians as well as classics by old masters. Essential to my book *This
Land Is Your Land: The American Conservation Movement* was William Cronon's *Changes in the Land: Indians, Colonists, and the Ecology of New England* (1983). Each generation rewrites history. It's not
coincidence that Cronon published his groundbreaking study about the
colonial deforestation and economic exploitation of the Atlantic coast
after Earth Day 1970. Even if you're writing about Pilgrims, make sure
you've skimmed titles from the past three decades.

And don't overlook related works in other disciplines—art history,
literature, anthropology, sociology, even science. To find out about
Native American trail building for *Get Up and Go! The History of
American Road Travel,* for instance, I consulted several anthropologi-
cal studies of the Iroquois. A balanced bibliography always results in
a better book.

Don't limit your search for lively details to books, either. I love
leafing through old magazines to get a feel for an era through ads,
advice columns, radio shows, and lyrics. I often use song titles as
section headings, such as "You'd Be So Nice To Come Home To"
(a WWII era hit) or "Fifteen Kisses on a Gallon of Gas" (an early
car tune).

As Studs Terkel has demonstrated in his many collections of interviews, oral history brings the past to life. I've used personal reminiscences in all of my "People's History" books. In addition to quoting
from Terkel's *The Good War* and other first-person accounts, I always
try to do some original research. Posting notes on the bulletin board
at a local senior center produced a lode of informants on WWII, including a charming saxophone player who had joined the Marines in order
to play in the band and had ended up a Japanese POW. Most newspapers list community meetings, and I added some color to *This Land*

Is Your Land by attending a local reunion of the Civilian Conservation Corps. To track down a talkative trucker, I started with a phone call to a garage listed in the Yellow Pages. If you have access to the Internet, you can easily contact people beyond your neighborhood. From a small town in New York, I arranged interviews with transportation engineers on the West Coast by posting a note in a cyberspace discussion group. Eloquent or unpolished, these voices add texture to the collage. Their conversational tone makes history more accessible to young readers.

Nothing beats photographs for pulling the past out of the mist. Much admired authors like Russell Freedman (*Franklin Delano Roosevelt*, 1990) and Jerry Stanley (*Children of the Dust Bowl*, 1992) write books that are almost photo essays. Although most publishers, like mine, handle all the layout and illustration, editors always appreciate ideas. If you come across an exciting photo, make a photocopy—with credit information—to submit with your manuscript. Because color is expensive to print and stock photo agencies often charge hefty fees, black-and-white "public domain" snapshots from libraries, historical societies, and government agencies are usually more attractive. A small publisher might expect you to round up illustrations yourself. If you don't find appropriate pictures in published material and don't have time to comb through archives, you could hire a photo researcher.

These are a few major archives:

*Library of Congress, Prints and Photographs Division, Washington, DC 20540

*National Archives and Records Administration, Still Picture Branch, 8601 Adelphi Road, College Park, MD 20740

*International Museum of Photography, George Eastman House, 900 East Avenue, Rochester, NY 14618

The three C's

Although most authors present history as a narrative, it may take other forms, too. In *Ticket to the Twenties: A Time Traveler's Guide* (1993), Mary Blocksma breaks down the decade into flashy chapters on everything from jive talk to breakfast. Did you know the first electric pop-up toaster hit the market in 1926? Instead of merely listing the presidents, consult *How the White House Really Works* (1989), George Sullivan's "upstairs, downstairs" tour of 1600 Pennsylvania

Avenue. While most titles fall into the categories of biography, survey, or "issue" book, your imagination is the only limit.

Once I begin writing, I stick to the three C's—*clarity, context,* and *cohesion.* Although the vocabulary you use may be simple, writing for children is often harder than writing for adults. Just try summarizing the causes of World War II in a paragraph or two for someone with no knowledge of European history. To the degree possible, keep background brief, points clear; write straightforward topic sentences, and leave the nuance to the details.

To aid the reader in evaluating an event or a person, try to include context about the period. This is the sort of low-key background that often appears in popular histories for adults, from Frederick Allen's *Only Yesterday: An Informal History of the 1920s* (1931) to David Brinkley's *Washington Goes To War* (1988). Whether you write about Earth Day or Ralph Nader or highway planning in the '60s and '70s, remind your readers that in those decades, Americans were beginning to "question authority." Since many children today have working moms, they may not appreciate the change in women's roles that "Rosie the Riveter" represented during the 1940s. Therefore, in *"V" Is for Victory: The American Home Front During World War II,* I discuss the public relations efforts of the government Office of War Information and the ads that defense plants ran to encourage people to apply for wartime work. Make it real. Describe the smell of Main Street in the heyday of horse-drawn wagons or the pastimes of Sunday afternoons before the advent of television and the NFL.

Finally, focus on themes. In a biography, you might want to trace the influence of a particular trait or skill over a lifetime—for instance, Rachel Carson's keen observation. Describing the World War II home front, I emphasized Americans' shared sense of purpose, despite racial and ethnic tensions. Since authors for young people face strict limits (in some cases, several centuries compressed into 60 pages of manuscript), they have to cull their research ruthlessly. The key-concept method gives you criteria for deciding what to keep and what to discard. Writing history, after all, is the art of pulling facts out of a grab bag and turning them into a story worth remembering.

❏ 92

WRITING BIOGRAPHIES FOR YOUNG PEOPLE

BY JAMES CROSS GIBLIN

THERE WAS A TIME WHEN IT WAS ACCEPTED PRACTICE FOR YOUNG people's biographies to whitewash their subjects to a certain extent. For example, juvenile biographies either ignored or gave a once-over-lightly treatment to personal failings like a drinking problem, and they scrupulously avoided any mention of complications in their subjects' sex lives.

Such whitewashing was intended to serve several different purposes. It protected the subject's reputation and made him or her a more suitable role model, one of the main goals of juvenile biographies in earlier periods. At the same time it shielded young readers from some of life's harsher realities.

All this has changed in the last twenty-five or thirty years as an increased openness in the arts and the media has spread to the field of children's literature. Young people who watch TV talk shows after school and dip into celebrity tell-all books expect more realism in the biographies that are written expressly for them. As a consequence, juvenile biographies of Franklin D. Roosevelt now acknowledge that he had a mistress, and young adult studies of John F. Kennedy frankly discuss his health problems and womanizing.

Today, the chief goal of a young people's biography is not to establish a role model but rather to provide solid, honest information about a man or woman worth knowing for one reason or another. However, a children's writer still has to make judgments about what facts to include in the biography and how much emphasis to give them. These judgments aren't always easy to arrive at, as I've discovered with the biographies I've written for young people. Each book presents its own unique problems, for which unique solutions must be found.

Much depends on the age of the intended audience. For example,

447

when I was writing a picture book biography of George Washington for ages six to nine, I felt it was important to describe Washington's changing attitude toward slavery, from easy acceptance in youth to rejection as he grew older. With that background in place, I was confident even quite young readers could grasp the significance of Washington's will, which specified that his slaves would be freed after the death of his wife, Martha.

A picture book biography of Thomas Jefferson presented a much more complex set of problems. Although Jefferson had written in the Declaration of Independence that "all men are created equal," he never rejected the concept of slavery as Washington did. How could he? The very existence of his beloved Monticello depended on slave labor. After much thought, I decided there was no way I could avoid discussing Jefferson's conflicted position. But I tried to present it as clearly and simply as possible and was careful not to let the discussion overshadow Jefferson's many accomplishments.

The role of the slave Sally Hemings proved harder to deal with. Whenever I mentioned in talks with writers that I was doing a biography of Jefferson, African-Americans in the audience invariably asked how I was going to treat Sally. I told them I intended to incorporate items from the historical record in the main text—that Sally had come into Jefferson's household as part of his wife's inheritance from her father; had accompanied Jefferson's younger daughter to Paris when Jefferson was the American ambassador to France; and had become one of the most trusted house slaves at Monticello in her later years.

In the back matter, along with other additional information, I said I'd include the story that one of Sally's sons, Madison Hemings, told an Ohio journalist in the mid-19th century. According to Madison, Jefferson had made Sally his mistress after his wife's death and had fathered her seven children, five of whom lived to adulthood and three of whom "passed" as white.

My editor felt that the latter story, aside from being controversial, would be too complicated for six-to-nine-year-olds to absorb. She urged me to leave it out, and in the end I decided she was right. If the book had been directed toward an upper elementary or young adult readership, I would have insisted on the story's retention. But I decided it was probably too involved for a younger audience.

However, the references to Sally Hemings remain in the body of the book, letting readers know that a slave by that name figured in Thomas Jefferson's life. When those same readers grow older, they can read about Sally in greater detail in other books about Jefferson. Meanwhile, my book—while not going deeply into the matter—will at least have introduced Sally to them instead of pretending she didn't exist.

Biographies for older children confront the writer with a different set of difficulties. What sort of balance do you aim for between the subject's achievements and his failings? This question was brought home to me in a particularly vivid way when I was working on a biography of Charles A. Lindbergh for ages ten to fourteen. Rarely in American history has there been such a sharp dichotomy between a subject's accomplishments—in Lindbergh's case his almost incredible solo flight to Paris in 1927, along with his other contributions to aviation—and his errors, namely his flirtation with fascism in the 1930s and his open admiration of Nazi Germany.

If I'd been writing a biography for adults, I might well have focused more intently on the part Lindbergh played in bringing about the appeasement of Adolf Hitler at Munich and his subsequent speeches urging the United States to take an isolationist stand with regard to the war in Europe. But while I went into this phase of Lindbergh's life in some detail, I decided it was my duty as a biographer for young people to "accentuate the positive," as the old song lyric goes.

An adult biographer may choose to expose or debunk his subject, assuming that readers will be able to compare his version of the person's life with other, more favorable accounts. I don't believe that option is open to the juvenile biographer, whose readers will most likely have little or no prior knowledge of the subject and thus will be unable to make comparisons. Such readers deserve a more even-handed introduction to the person.

Of course, that wouldn't be possible if one were writing about a destructive personality like Adolf Hitler, Joseph Stalin, or Senator Joseph McCarthy. But even in the portrayal of someone as reviled as these men, the juvenile biographer would have the responsibility of trying to help young readers understand how a human being could be capable of such inhuman acts. In other words, the writer wouldn't simply wallow in the person's excesses, as some adult biographers might be tempted to do, but instead would try to offer a full-scale portrait and locate the sources of the person's evil actions.

If you're thinking about writing a biography for young people, here are a few questions you would do well to ask yourself. Having the answers in hand should save you time when you're researching and writing the project.

Depending on the age group of the readers, how best can you convey an accurate, three-dimensional picture of the subject in ways that the intended audience can comprehend?

If the book is for younger children, should you discuss the seamier aspects of the subject's life, or merely hint at them and leave a fuller treatment to biographers for older children?

If you're writing for an older audience, how much space should you devote to the darker side of the subject's life and experience? In a biography of sports star Magic Johnson, for example, should you go into detail about the promiscuous behavior that, by Johnson's own account, was responsible for his becoming infected with the AIDS virus, or should you merely mention it in passing?

As you seek answers to these questions, you'll have to rely ultimately on your own good taste and judgment, combined with your knowledge of the prevailing standards in the children's book field. Perhaps the most decisive factor of all, though, will be your feeling for the subject.

Jean Fritz, the author of many award-winning biographies for young people, once said that she had to like a subject tremendously before she could write about the person. I'd amend that to say I must be *fascinated* by a subject in order to invest the time and energy needed to discover what makes the person tick.

The intensity of your fascination with your subject should be of great help as you decide how much weight to give the person's positive and negative aspects. It should also communicate itself to young people, making them want to keep on reading about the intriguing man or woman at the center of your biography.

❏ 93

WHEN YOU WRITE HUMOR FOR CHILDREN

BY JULIE ANNE PETERS

CHILDREN ARE BORN TO LAUGH. IN FACT, HUMOR IS THOUGHT TO BE the first expressive form of communication. Good writers understand the value of humor when they write for children. Not only does humor entertain and amuse them, but it lures the most reluctant reader.

When my first book, *The Stinky Sneakers Contest,* was selected by third-grade children in Greater Kansas City as their favorite book of 1995, I was delighted—and shocked. Humorous books rarely win awards. In the kingdom of exalted literature, humor is relegated to serfdom. But the award confirmed my belief that even though funny books infrequently win prestigious literary prizes, they do become children's favorites.

Writers often tell me, "I'm not a funny person. I can't write humor." Piffle! Betsy Byars, grandmistress of humorous children's books, reveals the secret. "The funniest word in the vocabulary of a second grader," she says, "is 'underwear.'" Use it liberally. "Poo poo" works for preschoolers. Or you can rise above so-called potty humor and choose one of the standard humor devices that follow.

Surprise

Writers and illustrators of picture books are guaranteed laughter or smiles by springing the unexpected on their young readers. Books are the perfect vehicle for creating humor through surprise. James Stevenson demonstrates this very effectively in his book, *Quick! Turn the Page.*

To bring about surprise, take an expected event or consequence and create the unexpected. A boy bounces a ball. He expects it to go up and come down. Page one: Ball goes up. Page two: A wild monkey in a banyan tree snatches the ball and steals off to . . . ? Next page.

Surprise can delight page after page, intermittently, or just once, with a surprise ending. Read Judith Viorst's poem, "Mother Doesn't Want a Dog," for a classic example of a surprise ending.

Exaggeration

The earliest American humor used exaggeration in its purest form: larger-than-life heroes performing superhuman feats. Remember Pecos Bill, Paul Bunyan, and John Henry? The American tall tale is still a favored form of humor for children. Anne Isaac's *Swamp Angel* moves this classic genre into the 1990s with her female superheroine. Not only does Swamp Angel fend off Thundering Tarnation, the marauding bear, she has to prove herself to taunting backwoodsmen who'd have her stay at home, quilting.

Transcendental toasters, madcap Martians, and articulate animals are all examples of truth stretching. My favorite mouthy mammal is the mutt, Martha, in Susan Meddaugh's *Martha Speaks*. After Martha dog eats a bowl of alphabet soup, she becomes quite the loquacious pooch. "You people are so bossy. COME! SIT! STAY! You never say please."

Journey beyond the bounds of possibility to create exaggerated humor. How about a plucky petunia? A daring doormat? Even preschool children can differentiate between the real and unreal as they gleefully embrace the fun in make-believe.

Word and language play

With wordplay, language is key to the rhythm, sound, and rhyme that carries your story forward. Readers become reciters. Jack Prelutsky, Shel Silverstein, and Joyce Armor are wizards of wordplay in their witty poetry. Nancy Shaw's "Sheep" books are shear joy (yes, pun intended).

If you're not a poet and you know it, try your hand at literal translation. *Amelia Bedelia* books by Peggy Parish teach you how. Amelia Bedelia, the indomitable maid, takes every order, every conversation, every suggestion literally, and sets herself up for catastrophe. Children love trying to predict the consequences of Amelia's misunderstandings.

Role reversal

Eugene Trivizas chose role reversal to retell a classic fairy tale in his *The Three Little Wolves and the Big Bad Pig*. To make the most effective use of role reversal, choose familiar characters acting out of character. Turn everyday events topsy-turvy. Harry Allard uses children's perceptions about substitute teachers (whether true or not) when he changes meek, mild Miss Nelson into bleak, vile Viola Swamp. You may choose to switch family members, as Mary Rodgers did with her mother/daughter exchange in *Freaky Friday*, or people and their pets, aliens with automobiles, princes and paupers. Stay away from twins, though. It's been done and done and done.

Nonsense

Nonsense includes incongruity and absurdity, ridiculous premises, and illogical series of events. What makes a nonsense book funny is its weirdness. *Imogene's Antlers*, by David Small, is the story of a young girl who wakes up one day to find she's grown antlers. This is a problem. Imogene has trouble getting dressed; she can't fit through narrow doorways; her antlers get caught in the chandelier. Even worse, her mother keeps fainting at the sight of her. Though children recognize the absurdity of Imogene's situation, they also see how well she copes with her sudden disability. This book speaks to children's physical differences, which is a fundamental value of humor.

Literary humor helps children grow. It offers distancing from pain, from change and insecurity, from cruelty, disaster and loss. Children are not always sophisticated or mature enough emotionally to laugh at themselves. Humorous books with subtle serious themes offer children ways to deal positively with life's inequities. They offer a magic mirror, through which children's problems—and their solutions—can be reflected back.

Slapstick

Farce and horseplay have been part of the American humor scene since vaudeville—maybe before. Who knows what Neanderthals did for fun? Physical humor appeals to the child in all of us. Hectic, frenetic chases and bumbling, stumbling characters cause chaos in the pages of children's books. Your plot will immediately pick up pace if you include a frantic fiasco or two. Check out Betsy Byars' *Golly Sisters*. May-May and Rose's calamitous capers are rip-roaring fun. Avi used slapstick masterfully in his book *Romeo and Juliet Together (And*

Alive) At Last! His high schoolers' rendition of Shakespeare's master-piece would make The Bard weep (with tears of laughter).

Satire

You can achieve humor by poking fun at human vices, human foibles or the general social order, which rarely makes sense to children, so they love to see it pulverized on paper. My favorite satirical series is "The Stupids," by Harry Allard. I swear these people lived next door to me when I was growing up. James Marshall's illustrations add hilarity to the humor.

To write effective satire for children, you must recognize the ridiculous in youngsters' lives. Make fun of uppity people's pretensions, lampoon restrictions, and spoof the silly societal mores children are expected to embrace. Create characters who teeter on the edge, who challenge the status quo—and thrive. Read Sid Fleischman's *The Whipping Boy* for a lesson in writing satire.

Adolescent angst

Family and school stories, growing up and coming-of-age novels make up the bulk of children's humorous fiction. Adolescence just seems to lend itself to humor. Laughter helps older children deal with life's larger dilemmas: death, divorce, disability, senility, loss, and unwelcome change. Reading about characters who successfully and humorously overcome obstacles provides children with painless lessons on how to handle their own problems.

For my book *B.J.'s Billion-Dollar Bet,* I started with a troublesome topic—betting. Frequently, I overhear conversations between kids who are placing bets: "Oh, sure. I bet you," or "Wanna bet? Come on, let's bet on it." And they bet away valuable items—clothing, sports card collections, lunch money. To show the consequences of betting, I created B.J. Byner, a compulsive gambler who bets and loses all of his possessions, then begins to bet away his family's belongings. When B.J. loses his mother's lottery ticket in a wager, then finds out the ticket is a fifty-million-dollar winner, he has to get that ticket back!

I hope young readers will see that the risks of gambling are considerable; the losses more than they may be willing or able to pay. Betting can result in loss of friendship, family conflict, and, as with any addiction, loss of control and self-respect. If I hadn't chosen a humorous premise for this book, it would have been too preachy.

Middle-grade and young adult novels include more urbane, cerebral humor. These young people are developing their own individual views of the world, and social relationships take on a major role.

For my middle-grade novel, *How Do You Spell Geek?*, I began with a funny, offbeat character, Lurlene Brueggemeyer, the geek, and built the story around her. The issues are serious ones—judging people by their appearance, shifting alliances between friends, peer pressure, and self-examination, but I gave my main character, Ann, a sarcastic sense of humor and a wry way of watching her world get weird, which seems to lighten the load.

Read the masters of middle-grade humor: Ellen Conford, Barbara Park, Beverly Cleary, Betsy Byars, Daniel Pinkwater, and Jerry Spinelli, among many, many others.

There are humor writers who defy classification; they relate to their audiences through rebellion, radicalism, and general outrageousness. Three young adult authors who fall into this special category are M.E. Kerr, Richard Peck, and Paul Zindel. Their books validate an emerging adult's individuality, passion, and self-expression.

If you plan to try your hand at humor, steer clear of targeting a specific age group. I've received letters from eight-year-olds who are reading my junior high novel, *Risky Friends*. And I'm sure you know high schoolers who still get a hoot out of Dr. Seuss. Even though sense of humor evolves as we grow older, we never lose appreciation for the books that made us laugh when we were younger.

Humor writing is a spontaneous act. It comes from deep within, from your own wacky way of looking at the world. One word of caution: Humor has power. What we laugh at, we make light of. What we laugh at, we legitimize and condone. Cruelty is never funny. Violence isn't funny. Torture, torment, neglect, war, hatred, and preying on others' misfortunes are not subjects for children's humor. There's a fine line between sarcasm and cynicism; between light-spirited and mean-spirited. So be aware. If you do write humor for children, observe the limits.

There's more than one way to connect with children through humor (beyond using "underwear"). In fact, with all the techniques available, and given the fact that children laugh easily, your chances of eliciting gleeful responses are excellent.

❏ 94

DYNAMIC DETAILS
MAKE A DIFFERENCE IN
CHILDREN'S FICTION

BY BEVERLY J. LETCHWORTH

Marcy edged closer to the lake, amazed at the large number of snow geese. She stood quietly, not wanting to disturb them. But despite her caution, an alarm jetted through the flock, and they rose together in a mob of blurred white, their flapping wings sounding like the clattering of a thousand clapping hands. Marcy gasped as the rising mass spewed into the air and spread quickly across the fields.

WHAT MADE THIS PARAGRAPH SO EFFECTIVE? DETAILS—DETAILS THAT worked. Specific, well-chosen details that wove in sensory perceptions, imagery, and a simile helped make the scene come alive and made the setting real, believable. Readers could see the geese, hear their wings, and feel Marcy's wonderment. They felt involved.

That's the goal of good storytelling: Involve your readers so they feel they're part of the action. Readers must feel connected to your characters, settings, even to objects, or they'll lose interest in the story. This holds true for any fiction writing, whether for adults or children.

But in writing children's fiction, you must consider more restrictions, because children are bored by long descriptions about settings or characters. Therefore, details must be limited and chosen with care. Opt for those details that convey only the most significant aspects of a setting, character, or object.

Also, keep in mind that the younger the reader, the fewer details should be used. For young children whose attention span is short, details must be strictly limited. In a description about an attic, you may choose to say only, "The attic was dim and dusty. Cobwebs hung in the corners. Bulging boxes and broken furniture lined the walls." These few details offer readers definite sensory images that bring the scene to life. Sometimes, a single detail is enough to set the tone: "An owl hooted low and loud, making her shiver."

As children mature, they can grasp more details and appreciate the many layers of a character or setting; and, indeed, they can absorb some of the subtleties.

Let's go back to the attic and add more details suitable for older readers.

The attic lay dim and dusty before her—a small room with a low ceiling that seemed a perfect size for an Alice-in-Wonderland escape. Bulging boxes overflowing with old clothes sat like curled-up sleepers, and a torn overstuffed chair seemed a fat lady at rest beside them. From all corners cobwebs hung in tattered white streamers, looking soft and gauzy in the dusky light.

More depth has been added, but you'd better stop here or the description will become tedious. Even for teenagers, don't overdo the details. The detailed style of Charles Dickens is passé today; children of the computer age with its easy access to quick information won't keep reading a book that's verbose.

You can achieve a fast-paced, stimulating style by using methods for selecting and using effective details. It takes practice, but it's worth the effort.

1. Establish what age group you're writing for to determine how many details to include.

2. Select the most telling details to describe the particular situation and connote specific aspects of the setting or character.

For physical description of a character, choose only one of two details, rather than a whole paragraph to reveal the essence of that character. For example: "Straight-backed, her head high, she strode into the room." Or, "He didn't bother to push the long, greasy hair from his eyes as he lurched down the steps."

To convey an emotional reaction without becoming wordy, you may show your character's sadness by simply saying, "Again she felt the familiar sharp sting of tears behind her eyes."

An individual object may often merit some detail. Again, choose the best detail to make it real to the reader. "The satin dress lay across the bed, as smooth and soft as melted gold." Or, "Amid the jumble of plastic glasses and shriveled plants, the silver bell glinted like a jewel on the sunny kitchen windowsill." Or, "The fern hung from the ceiling and dripped its lacy fronds onto the floor."

3. Use the five senses to bring your scene to life. Sight is vital in descriptions, but don't neglect the other senses. Bring in sound, smell, taste, and touch whenever possible, for they add depth and realism. And don't forget color.

4. Use specific details so readers can see and feel the scene. First, envision the setting you want to describe, and make a list of its specific qualities. A run-down bookstore may include details such as: water stains on the ceiling, books piled haphazardly on shelves and in corners, a cat meowing from a shelf, a crooked wood floor, cobwebs in the windows, musty smell, dust and grit on books. From this list, choose three details that would set the ambiance of the scene without becoming tiresome.

5. If you can't visualize a setting adequately, visit the type of place you have in mind. A wealth of details will present themselves, some you never expected. For example: When you envision a boat dock, you can see water, fishing boats, nets and rods, heavy ropes. What you couldn't imagine was the slap of water against the boats, the gentle sway of the dock beneath your feet, the cloying fish smell, gulls. These sensory details will add the realism needed to make readers feel they are there.

Of course, it's not always possible to visit a place. Not many of us can take a quick trip to a rainforest or go to a circus whenever we want to. If you can't visit, then read, read, read about the setting you want to use. Study pictures that will give you a better sense of the sights, sounds, maybe even the smells of the particular locale.

6. Create similes and metaphors when appropriate. Remember the satin dress and the silver bell. Figures of speech enhance details, but for young readers, use details cautiously. Young minds can't always grasp the comparisons, so use them sparingly, and keep them simple and easy to understand. For older readers, figures of speech can be used more frequently.

7. Occasionally, allow your characters to describe the details of a setting or object. This technique offers a change of pace and gives the reader the benefit of a character's feelings and opinions about a place or object.

8. Break up descriptions in order to incorporate more appropriate details as interestingly as possible. Sprinkle details throughout the scene so there are no long stretches of solid text. One of my stories for middle-grade readers, set in 1850, features Lithia Ann, a free black girl who dreams of getting an education so she can become a teacher. Her walk into town with her brother Roan needed to include many details. I tried to scatter them in between dialogue, thoughts, and action to make the following scene more appealing.

As they walked, the smell of the river wafted around them. It flowed on their right, a wide ribbon of currents, always moving, always changing. Lithia Ann felt its strength and it always revived her. Some of her worry dropped away, and she took deep breaths of the river's scent.

In the distance blared a deep mournful steamboat whistle. The *James Hawthorne,* thought Lithia Ann. She could always tell the steamboat by its deep haunting sound, just as she could identify other steamboats by their particular-sounding whistles.

As they passed shops and stores, Lithia Ann called out the names of various businesses. It was still exciting to be able to read the names and signs in the windows.

"Some day you'll be able to read too, Roan," she said enthusiastically. "Then you'll know what everything is." She remembered the first time she had realized that a group of letters spelled a word: C-A-T. . . .

Soon they reached the bustling wharf. Noises pushed aside Lithia Ann's thoughts. Grunts and yells, thuds, and bangs filled the streets as men unloaded cargo from flatboats and steamboats tied at the pier. Dogs barked, horses snorted, mules brayed. . . .

Lithia Ann and Roan rested on the wooden boardwalk in front of the hotel. A fishmonger with his cart of fresh fish called to passersby, "Fresh fish, fresh fish, fit for the pan!"

An old woman pushed a wheelbarrow filled with strawberries. "Straaaawberrrries!" she shouted. Lithia Ann's mouth watered.

Roan dashed up to the cart and held out his hand to the old woman. "No money, no berries," she said harshly, pushing past him.

"I only wanted one," Roan said sadly, when Lithia Ann took him by the hand.

I hope that these specific details help you visualize the sights, sounds, and smells of a river town in the 1850s and make you feel as if you are walking the dirt streets with the characters.

Details are vital elements of any story, for they picture the world of the characters. Like yarn in a rug, details woven throughout the plot, ever-changing in color and pattern, offer readers a way to "belong" to the story. As a writer, you must strive to bring out this involvement. Only by presenting the most effective details can you make this happen.

□ 95

CAPTURING THE YOUNG ADULT READER

BY CHERYL ZACH

TRYING TO CAPTURE THE YOUNG ADULT READER IS A BIT LIKE ALICE'S pursuit of the White Rabbit; these young people are almost as elusive and as hard to pin down. So who's really reading young adult books, and how do we write for them? There's no simple answer.

The young adult books you find on library or bookstore shelves run the gamut from innocent first-kiss stories to accounts of the much more serious consequences of an unintended pregnancy, from lighthearted running-for-class-president tales to suspenseful live-or-die mysteries.

Librarians were the first to search for young adult books that would be of interest to high school or mature junior high students. But as the concept of books aimed especially at this age group became common, bookstores stepped in to define the label "young adult." Some of the confusion may have been caused when booksellers and publishers, perhaps in an attempt to broaden the market, perhaps in recognizing that children like to "read up"—that is, read about characters slightly older than themselves—lowered the age levels of YA to include readers as young as ten or eleven.

At the same time, some editors and librarians feel that readers 16 to 22 are underserved. Many readers that age are turning to adult books, but do adult authors address their particular concerns?

Obviously, the subject matter portrayed in books for pre-teens won't be the same as in novels for older teens. To make the equation even harder to solve, the age at which teenagers and adolescents experience physical, emotional, and mental maturation varies widely.

So defining the YA reader depends partly on whom you ask. Yet despite this problem of definition, the YA novel is too important a genre to be ignored. The coming-of-age novel chronicling a young person's first experiences with romance, with death, with adult actions

461

and consequences, with personal responsibility is too significant to be considered only as a marketing ploy.

As a result, authors and publishers strive for meaningful YA books, while sometimes targeting different age groups. Junior high students often enjoy Lois Lowry's perceptive, humorous Anastasia books and also feel the tug of Lurlene McDaniel's poignant novels of critically ill adolescents.

Older teens may be drawn to the darker threads of a Lois Duncan mystery, such as *Killing Mr. Griffin,* or to Christopher Pike's or R.L. Stine's more graphic horror novels. Novels such as my own *Runaway* and *Family Secrets* also deal with more mature themes—a pregnant teen on the run; an adopted teenager seeking her birth parents and discovering a dark secret in her family's past.

Some books seem to span the age groups; historical novels like my *Carrie's Gold* or *Southern Angel,* a Civil War saga, or fantasy novels such as Lloyd Alexander's Prydain Chronicles or Anne McCaffrey's Dragonsinger books, seem to attract readers from a wide age group, sometimes including adults. These books often have significant themes, but the fact that the stories are presented in another time or place, free of the restraints of modern costume and slang and social traditions, perhaps contributes to their ageless appeal.

Although topics and treatments may vary in books for younger or older teens, fortunately other aspects will not. Readers of any age will respond to well-drawn, three-dimensional characters, a significant problem that the protagonist (not a helpful adult) will resolve or come to terms with, realistic dialogue, and a fast-paced plot with compelling scenes.

In addition, modern readers expect a quick beginning that sweeps them immediately into the story. They want to be introduced to the main character right away, to see at least a hint of the problem this young person faces, and they want to care enough about his or her character to guarantee that they will hang around to see what happens.

How does the YA author create likable, yet vulnerable characters? Go into their backgrounds; examine their families, and their position in the family (the oldest child is often expected to be more responsible; the youngest may be more indulged). Look at their relationships with their parents, with their siblings, with school friends and teachers, with the neighbor next door, the neighborhood or school bully, the part-time employer. Consider a character's earlier experiences—even a child has a past!—and see what has helped make him into the person he is today. Your characters may not be perfect, but make sure they're basically decent; you have to like your characters first, if you want your readers to like them, too.

The protagonist should have a real problem, an age-appropriate problem that young people will identify with. Try to be honest with your readers; never condescend to them. I know that to a ten-year-old, getting the wrong teacher on the first day of school can be a real disaster; that a fifteen-year-old may really be in love, no pat-on-the-head infatuation here; that a sixteen-year-old could be in a life or death situation if he defies the local gang. Keep up with what's happening in real life, and keep in mind that adolescence today is not the same as it was twenty years ago. Watch the news, read teen magazines and listen to teen music. Make sure the setting and the dialogue are up-to-date. I get some of my best ideas from newspaper or news stories. (The plot of *Runaway* evolved from a short article in the back pages of my local paper.)

Also, remember that just as the novel itself has a shape, a rise and fall and rise to an ultimate climax, scenes also have their own shape and purpose. A scene that does not move the story forward, provide more understanding of the character, create suspense or humor, or provide information about the setting has no place in your YA novel. Test every line of dialogue and every paragraph of narrative to make sure it is absolutely necessary. For today's impatient readers, you must write cleanly and succinctly, in graceful prose. Make every word count.

Finally, be sure the climax is truly the most exciting part of the book. Show how your young protagonist rises to the most difficult challenge he or she has faced, and meets it head-on in a scene that is played to its emotional, physical, and intellectual zenith, so that your readers will sit on the edge of their seats and be unable to put the book down until they know what the resolution will be. And then, we writers—along with teachers and parents—will hope that kids, no matter what their ages, will be eager to read another YA novel, and another, and another.

□ 96

WRITING FOR CHILDREN'S MAGAZINES

BY DONNA FREEDMAN

NOT EVERYONE CAN WRITE FOR CHILDREN, BUT EVERYONE SHOULD want to: Children's magazines can be a lucrative market. I've been paid as much as $350 for a 150-word article. And there are hundreds of free-lance opportunities, from Sunday-school papers to glitzy, high-tech skateboard 'zines. The market has grown markedly in recent years: In 1985, the Institute of Children's Literature identified 354 free-lance markets; today, ICL lists 582 such markets.

Writing for kids isn't easy. You have a small space in which to pack a lot of information. You have to write in language they can understand, and you need ideas that will grab the attention of youngsters who are increasingly distracted by CD-ROM, cable television, video games, and other competing entertainment.

Most important of all, you need to put aside any preconceived notions about childhood. Children are a lot more sophisticated than they were in your own childhood years, and they want articles and stories that are relevant to their world. Children's publications now call for writing that reflects the realities of modern life: latchkey kids, for example, or single-parent families.

Pastimes and hobbies may be a lot different from those you remember. Small-town kids may still go to the old swimming hole in the summer, but suburban and urban youngsters today are more likely to play soccer or spend their free time on their skateboards. Therefore, you need to familiarize yourself with what they are doing if you want to write for them. Borrow a friend's children, teach a Sunday-school class, coach a sports team, or eavesdrop at McDonald's. Do anything to get an idea of what kids are like today.

Although juvenile magazines publish a fair number of short stories, you're much more likely to sell nonfiction: articles that paint vivid pictures of historical events or use colorful, down-to-earth imagery to explain a scientific or technological phenomenon. Profiles of famous people can no longer be dry as dust: Readers want to feel the wind on Amelia Earhart's face, or hear the crash as Thomas Edison's prototype light bulb shatters on the floor.

Editors are looking for more biography, history, and hard science. Nature is a perennial favorite, but most magazines already have backlogs of articles about Really Interesting Animals or Fascinating Natural Phenomena. It's not that these ideas can't make good reading, it's that they need a new approach.

For example, *Highlights for Children* recently published an article about a tiger in an animal sanctuary. Normally, the magazine doesn't use pieces set in zoos or sanctuaries, but this piece was different because the writer used her senses to create a picture of the sleekness of the tiger's fur, the roughness of its tongue, its ever-changing moods. It worked because it was evocative. If it had been encyclopedic—"Tigers live in Asia. They are endangered."—it would have been boring, and not held the attention of young readers.

Even an article that has a lot of information needs to be written in an exciting, attention-getting style. Since slang or jargon tends to sound phony when used by adults, concentrate on unusual details and the newest research you can find. Intrigue readers and show them how much you care about the subject, whether it's tiger fur or in-line skating.

You don't need to be a rocket scientist to write about the space program, or an entomologist to write about dung beetles. All you really need is a dedication to research, an ability to write clearly and concisely, and a respect for your young audience.

One of the most common mistakes writers make is writing "down" to children—being too sweet, too jaunty, or too didactic. Children don't want to be patronized or preached at.

The worst crime of all is to try to shoehorn in some moral. If there's a lesson to be learned, you should show it, not tell it. Your average nine-year-old isn't going to have an epiphany like, "Guess I should have listened to what the Sunday-school teacher/Grandma/my dad said." If he read anything preachy or boring, he'd groan out loud: "Give me a break!" Like most of us, kids read magazines to be entertained.

Articles and stories need to fit into very small spaces in the magazines. Even if a magazine specifies 800 to 1,200 words, don't feel compelled to use up all the allotted space. Editors love tight writing, because children, particularly beginning readers, are more likely to finish a short piece than a daunting 1,200-worder.

Marketing skills are as important as writing skills. There's no sense writing a piece on the maternal instincts of wolverines only to find that there's no market for such an article. And if you're sending out ideas blindly, without the slightest bit of market research, you're not just wasting postage, you're wasting an editor's time.

A little market research would show, for instance, that *Cricket* doesn't publish horror stories; that *Highlights* steers clear of pop culture; that the editors at the Children's Better Health Institute don't like stories that feature junk food.

Also, it's not enough to know what kind of articles the editors want; you also need to know what kind of writing they prefer. It's almost impossible to get a sense of a magazine's voice from writer's guidelines. The only way to do that is to read several issues of the magazine to give you an idea of what you might be able to sell.

The stories and articles in children's publications may be slangy and colorful, or written in a graceful, literary style. Not a single word is wasted; each is carefully chosen for maximum impact.

You might consider subscribing to a few magazines, such as *Highlights, Cricket,* and *Cobblestone.* Or spend a couple of hours each month in the local library, reading as many children's magazines as possible. Go through back issues, too.

The Writer Magazine is a good place to find other outlets for your work. So are specialty publications, such as *Children's Writer* (published by the Institute of Children's Literature) or the Society of Children's Book Writers and Illustrators *Bulletin.*

Sunday-school papers and other religious periodicals are always hungry for good writing, and they publish up to 52 times a year. They tend to pay less than mainstream children's magazines, but they're a good place for beginners to hone their writing skills, learn to work with editors, and compile some clips.

It's a lot tougher to sell to a high-profile magazine. The best-known publications may get as many as 1,000 unsolicited manuscripts each month. One way to break in is through the "front of the book" sections found in many magazines. These are made up of very short items about interesting or newsworthy children's activities. Your local newspaper is a great resource for front-of-book items. Did a youngster in your town start a recycling program, climb a mountain, break a 10k record in his age group? Other kids want to know about it.

Juvenile magazines devote a lot of space to puzzles, crafts, hidden pictures, dot-to-dot, and word finds. This can be another good way to break into the market. Your experience with children might also help you sell a story or an article. For example, you might package an article on Halloween with an easy-to-do crossword puzzle using lots of spooky words. Or a story about friendship could go hand-in-hand with a craft page on how to make friendship bracelets.

Some writers believe they can get away with lazy research or substandard writing because it's "only" for kids. Nothing could be further from the truth. Editors will accept only the very best for their young readers.

❑ 97

POINT OF VIEW IN CHILDREN'S BOOKS

BY CARREL MULLER

FOLKTALES CAN TEACH WRITERS SOME TRICKS IN WRITING A SUCCESS-ful children's book, even though many of the techniques used in folk and fairy tales do not follow the standard rules for writing books for children—especially the rules on point of view.

Point of view is the unique vision of the character through whom the reader experiences the story. Rules for point of view in writing for children are: 1) There should be only one viewpoint character; 2) the viewpoint character's story should be told in the first person or the third person; 3) never use an omniscient author.

The omniscient author is the all-knowing one who can tell you what every character is thinking, seeing, and doing. Since the child reader will be confused by many characters telling the story, single point of view is essential, because these young readers are just beginning to move from self-absorption into an awareness of others. As children mature, their identification with a character's experiences helps them grow in understanding themselves and in recognizing that others think, feel, and dream as they do. Also, since the single viewpoint is the natural way of experiencing life, it is the best way to tell children's stories.

These rules are excellent when writing for children. But what about folklore? Children delight in "Hansel and Gretel," "Cinderella," "Snow White," and all the tales from the folk tradition. The techniques used by the storyteller in folk and fairy tales do not follow the above rules for point of view. The storyteller can draw from a rich oral tradition many techniques that can be used to tell not only folktales, but every-thing from fantasy to historical fiction. The use of the storyteller's techniques is the use of the *Narrative Voice*. First, let us consider the narrative voice and its techniques, then, we'll look at two variations of the narrative voice: the narrative personality and the more fully developed narrative character—techniques being used by talented authors to create outstanding books.

Narrative voice techniques include: 1) using multiple viewpoints; 2) making moral judgments of characters; 3) being intrusive; 4) using formula openings; 5) giving plot summaries in the opening or in the title; and 6) always controlling the reader/listener's vision for dramatic effect.

Narrative voice, derived from the oral tradition, defies the rules for single viewpoint character. For example, we find not one but two viewpoint characters in "Hansel and Gretel." But, since they share the same problems and experience the same adventure, their dual viewpoint is almost like a single viewpoint character, and because the storyteller directs our vision, no confusion occurs.

Two other examples from the oral tradition defy the rules. In "Snow White" and "Cinderella," a reader has no difficulty picking out the viewpoint character, even though neither one tells her own story. The storyteller informs the child what Snow White's *evil* stepmother thinks and plans, what the *compassionate* hunter does to trick the Queen, as well as what *poor, frightened* Snow White thinks and feels as she flees through the forest. The child reader is not confused because the storyteller is in control. The storyteller makes moral judgments: *evil* stepmother; *compassionate* hunter; *poor, frightened* Snow White.

Also, the storyteller moves from forest to castle and back again. The child moves from scene to scene as the storyteller directs for dramatic effect. The storyteller, not confined to mere narration, uses action and dialogue to create dramatic scenes. Just think of the wonderful mirror-mirror scenes that would be missed if the story were told only from Snow White's point of view. The drama of the poisoned apple scene would be lost if the child didn't know the apple was poisoned. The voice of the storyteller, or the narrative voice, controls the reader's vision of the story: setting scenes, making moral judgments, and directing our empathy toward the main character. The narrative voice, like the omniscient author, knows all and tells readers what they need to know to create a dramatic irony.

One technique from the storyteller's bag of tricks is the formula opening—for example, "Once upon a time . . ." or "Once there was. . . ." Skillful authors use these introductions and their variations as signals to the reader/listener. For example, after a two-paragraph description of motorcars, Ian Fleming begins *Chitty Chitty Bang Bang* with the words, "Once upon a time there was a family called Pott." He signals to the reader that the know-all storyteller, or narrative voice, will now relate the tale. In this fantasy adventure, two children, a brother and sister, like a Hansel and Gretel, share the same adventure. The use of more than one main character is not confusing because the storyteller's voice is directing the reader's vision.

Roald Dahl's strong narrative voice controls and directs the child's vision in *James and the Giant Peach*. He begins, "Here is James Henry Trotter," introducing his main/viewpoint character. He makes it clear that James is the one with whom the reader will empathize by his moral judgments of the characters. He describes James as "*poor* James," and Aunt Sponge and Aunt Spiker as "I am sorry to say that they were both really horrible people. They were selfish and lazy and cruel. . . ." Note that the "I" is not the main character James, but the intrusive voice of the narrator. In his fantasy Dahl's narrative voice controls our vision of the story by setting dramatic scenes and directing our empathy toward the main character.

Natalie Babbitt uses the narrative voice in her award-winning *Tuck Everlasting*. She begins with a description of the season and her "Ferris Wheel" image of time. This image of the wheel—the sun—the turning of time and seasons is the thread with which she sews together the events of the story. Her descriptions in connecting phrases, sentences, and paragraphs stitch together different characters and scenes as the reader moves effortlessly from chapter to chapter. Right after her opening description, her narrative voice reveals the plot structure: "Three things happened, and at first there appeared to be no connection between them." She then lists the events: 1) Tuck family members coming to the wood at Treegap; 2) Winnie Foster running away; 3) a stranger's appearance at the Fosters' home. Her all-knowing narrative voice hooks the reader and foreshadows, "No connection, you would agree. But things can come together in strange ways." She speaks directly to the reader, yet her voice is not as intrusive as Dahl's, for she does not make moral judgments of the characters. She directs our empathy to Winnie with whom the reader identifies, and she allows Winnie gradually to make moral judgments of the other characters.

Is there any difference between omniscient author and narrative voice? Yes. Consider *The Boggart,* by Susan Cooper. As omniscient author, Cooper uses multiple viewpoints: Tommy in Scotland; the Boggart; and the four members of the Volnik family. These multiple viewpoints are at first confusing to the reader, who wonders whose story it is. A strong narrative voice setting up the story at the beginning would have prepared the reader for the constant changes in viewpoint. The shifting scenes and changing viewpoints in *The Boggart* break its continuity. A strong narrative voice or even an intrusive one would have made the reading smoother with transitional phrases, sentences, or paragraphs. The strength and control of the narrative voice guides children when a story is told from more than one viewpoint. The use of the narrative voice would have made Susan Cooper's wonderful story more accessible to the many children who are not the best readers.

The technique of revealing the plot and/or stating the theme at the beginning of the story is a signal sent by the narrative voice that he knows all and will fill in the details if you stay and listen. "Why" stories reveal their plot, not in the first sentence or paragraph, but in the title, e.g., *Why the Sun and Moon Live in the Sky,* by Elphinstone Dayrell. Sid Fleischman uses revealing titles in many of his award-winning books. In his Newbery Award book *The Whipping Boy,* such chapter titles as "Revealing Jemmy's plan to trick the villains" and "In which Prince Brat lives up to his name" entice the reader to read on.

Joan Blos applies this technique to the plot in her Newbery Award work of historical fiction, *A Gathering of Days: A New England Girl's Journal, 1830–32.* It begins with a letter from the journal's elderly author, who knows all past events and reveals the main events in the plot. Does it stop the reader from reading? No. This storyteller's trick entices the reader to discover: how the girl's best friend died; whom her father married; and why she left the farm. This technique can be used in a variety of ways to arouse curiosity and hook the reader.

Sometimes the narrative voice can be more than a controlling device; it can be a narrative personality. In such stories, the narrative voice's opinions and attitudes, likes and dislikes, color the story. This device is great for telling ghost stories, and especially humorous stories. In *The Best Christmas Pageant Ever,* Barbara Robinson uses a narrative personality, the daughter of the woman in charge of the Christmas pageant. The child narrator knows the Herdman children as only a child can and voices her dislike and fear of these grammar school bullies. As she tells of her mother's dilemma—putting on a pageant taken over by the Herdmans—the child as observer/narrator knows all the characters and it is her voice that reports all the conversations. She is a personality, without being a fully developed character in the story. Readers never learn her name and are given only her own description of herself as a "medium kid" who "kept her mouth shut" for fear of the Herdmans. Her childlike vision and observations are straightforward, honest, and wonderfully humorous. She is more than a narrative voice; she is a narrative personality. The simplicity and understatement of her vision color the readers' perception of the characters and events.

The narrative voice can be taken one step further and become, not only a narrative personality, but a fully rounded character with a name, attributes, and an identity as the storyteller. Uncle Remus and Scheherazade are famous examples from children's books. Each is a character who provides a framework for the telling of old tales.

In his books *Ben and Me* and *Mr. Revere and I,* Robert Lawson created narrative characters—a mouse and a horse—who present fictional biographies. Amos the mouse places himself in Benjamin Franklin's life and takes credit for Franklin's inventions and ideas. So through action and dialogue, he is a first-person viewpoint character as well as a narrator of this humorous biography. Thus, we have come full circle through the storyteller's techniques of narrative voice to narrative personality, to fully developed narrative character, back to the viewpoint character.

From what viewpoint will you tell your children's story? You will have more choices if you consider the narrative voice and its variations within the storyteller's bag of tricks.

□ 98

WHEN YOU WRITE A BIOGRAPHY
FOR CHILDREN

BY RUTH TURK

IS WRITING A BIOGRAPHY FOR CHILDREN DIFFERENT FROM WRITING one for adults?

As a writer of seven published biographies for young readers, I must admit that while some of the basics are similar, there are enough differences to make this undertaking a challenging and rewarding experience.

From the outset it is important to keep in mind that the subject you choose must be attractive, not only to you, the writer, but to your young readers. While your primary goal is to impart authentic biographical information, you will write more convincingly if you have respect for your subject. When I researched the life of blind singer Ray Charles, I was impressed by the courage he manifested in dealing with blindness, racism, poverty, and a serious drug problem. As a result, I did not minimize these aspects of his life, but portrayed them with the clarity and honesty they deserved.

Whether the age level you are targeting is primary or middle grade, do not "talk down" to your readers. While your writing must be straightforward and uncomplicated, young readers will resent oversimplification. If you use technical terms, it makes sense to include a glossary. Equally important is the use of lively verbs and adjectives that jump from the page, maintain a brisk pace, and help create glowing visual images in the young mind. Conditioned by rock music, skateboards, television, and computers, young people today march to a different drum from those in previous generations. How to compete? The best way is to hook that juvenile with the opening paragraph, then follow through with the complete biography.

Author Lillie Patterson's young adult biography of Martin Luther King, Jr. opens with a dramatic account of the Rosa Parks incident in

Montgomery, Alabama, in 1955. When Rosa refuses to give up her seat for a white passenger, the driver stops the bus.

"Look, woman, I told you I wanted the seat. Are you going to stand up?"

"No," said Parks.

"Well, if you don't, I am going to have you arrested."

"Go on and have me arrested," said Rosa Parks.

After starting her book with the story of the Montgomery Bus Boycott, the author proceeded to introduce her subject, Martin Luther King, Jr. in chapter two, and followed through with the chronological development of his life.

If your subject is not alive, there are advantages and disadvantages. One advantage is the fact that the subject cannot object to what or how you write. Still another is that the last chapter ends with the subject's death and rarely has to be updated. Research on any subject, living or dead, starts with your reading everything written about her or him, including articles in newspapers and other periodicals, as well as history books concerning the relevant time periods. Reading the work of other biographers will help to determine your own insights and points of departure.

Reference librarians are particularly helpful in helping you find memoirs, journals, and letters of both deceased and living subjects. Browsing in secondhand bookshops and museums will often unearth nuggets of information that don't always turn up in public libraries or large bookstores. In researching the lives of Louisa May Alcott and Edith Wharton I was able to locate literary foundations in New England in areas where both women lived and wrote their timeless masterpieces. These organizations forwarded books, pamphlets, and photos that helped me create a composite portrait for each biography.

Incidentally, as you conduct your research, keep track of good photographs that you can later recommend to your publisher's photography department. An editor or publisher seriously considering a manuscript may appreciate photo sources, even though the photo staff usually tracks down their own. My experience with pictures for a juvenile biography of playwright Lillian Hellman was atypical, but rewarding.

When my editor informed me that a photograph of Hellman in her early childhood could not be located, I did a bit of detective work on my own. After learning the name of the playwright's last personal secretary, I surmised that she might still be living in the same city where she had worked years ago. I got her phone number and called to persuade her how meaningful it would be for young readers to see Lillian as a little girl. Did she know where such a picture could be found? She did. A week later the photograph was in the hands of my delighted editor. Moral of the story? Don't hesitate to go beyond authorship limits if it will enhance the quality of your work.

If your subject is alive, you may encounter a few frustrations on the road to success, such as his or her refusal to be interviewed personally. You may have to rely on friends, relatives, or possibly enemies (the third category is one I cannot recommend!). If you are fortunate enough to set up interviews, prepare a list of carefully thought-out questions, and plan to use a tape recorder. If your subject won't agree to being taped, be prepared to jot down notes you can incorporate later on. When you use quotations, be sure to cite accurate sources and dates; your publisher will require you to include these credits in the finished biography. Though it is comforting and convenient to have the subject's approval, it is not mandatory to obtain permission to write the story of someone's life.

Before you undertake comprehensive research about your subject, be certain to consult *Books in Print* to find what other books of a similar nature are available. There could be a half dozen or more authors who have chosen to write about the same subject. In that case if you are still determined to go ahead, you will need to come up with a different approach or format, or both.

For a children's biography, plan the number of chapters before you begin to write (ordinarily from six to twelve, depending on your organization of the material). As you accumulate dates, facts, and incidents, keep them in separate folders so they will be easily accessible as you develop the different chapters. Occasionally, you will come across items about the subject that appear to be unrelated, for example, an account about a friend or member of the subject's family. Don't discard these references; you may use one when you least expect it.

Scan current periodicals for mention of your subject's awards or citations for past achievements. If your accepted manuscript is already in its final publishing stage, your editor may suggest a brief epilogue to bring the biography up to date. For instance, when I learned that

Amy Carter was getting married, I was able to insert that fact on the last page of my biography of former first lady Rosalynn Carter. What happens to the family members in your subject's life will be of interest to young readers, especially when it is a famous family.

When the first draft of your manuscript is completed, try testing parts of it on a few willing listeners, preferably those at the age level for whom you're writing—but do not include close friends or relatives! Most young people will be objective and will react quickly and honestly, which is what you want. If you belong to a writer's critique group, ask for their comments and make use of those that are constructive. Most writers, particularly those who write for children, will benefit from an impartial sounding board. Sometimes when a manuscript is read aloud, nuances may be picked up more readily than when the same material is read silently. If a human sounding board is not available, read what you've written into a tape recorder, then play it several times. You will be surprised at the changes you might make as a result of listening.

Another way to receive valuable feedback is to arrange visits to elementary school classes. Many teachers will welcome a local writer willing to read her work to children and then discuss it with them. Insights and reactions from unbiased young listeners are usually constructive and gratifying.

Researching and writing a biography for children is not a quick or easy project. It takes time, dedication, and discipline. It also means always keeping in mind the young person for whom you are writing. An adult reader may struggle a bit longer with a boring biography before he gives up; ten-year-olds will continue to read only as long as the first page unless you, the author, hook them immediately and hold them for the duration.

Exciting fiction can stimulate a child's imagination, but a carefully researched and well-written biography can present accurate information, intriguing insights, historical perspective, and unforgettable role models. Children's biographies do more than record facts. As the author, you are documenting creative human goals and achievements that young people will remember long after they grow into busy and sophisticated adults.

As a biographer for children you are performing a special service for coming generations. When you complete that first biography, you might be understandably weary, but you'll also feel proud. I know.

❑ 99

Is It Good Enough for Children?

By Madeleine L'Engle

A WHILE AGO WHEN I WAS TEACHING A COURSE ON TECHNIQUES OF fiction, a young woman came up to me and said, "I do hope you're going to teach us something about writing for children, because that's why I'm taking this course."

"What have I been teaching you?" I asked her.

"Well—writing."

"Don't you write when you write for children?"

"Yes, but—isn't it different?"

No, I assured her, it isn't different. The techniques of fiction are the techniques of fiction, and they hold as true for Beatrix Potter as they do for Dostoevsky.

But the idea that writing for children isn't the same as writing for adults is prevalent indeed, and usually goes along with the conviction that it isn't quite as good. If you're a good enough writer for adults, the implication is, of course, you don't write for children. You write for children only when you can't make it in the real world, because writing for children is easier.

Wrong, wrong, wrong!

I had written several regular trade novels before a publisher asked me to write about my Swiss boarding school experiences. Nobody had told me that you write differently when you write for children, so I didn't. I just wrote the best book I possibly could; it was called *And Both Were Young*. After that I wrote *Camilla,* which has been reissued as a young adult novel, and then *Meet the Austins*. It's hard today for me to understand that this simple little book had a very hard time finding a publisher because it's about a death and how an ordinary family reacts to that death. Death at that time was taboo. Children weren't supposed to know about it. I had a couple of offers of publication if I'd take the death out. But the reaction of the family—children as well as the parents—to the death was the core of the book.

Nowadays what we offer children makes *Meet the Austins* seem pale, and on the whole, I think that's just as well, because children know a lot more than most grown-ups give them credit for. *Meet the Austins* came out of my own family's experience with several deaths. To have tried to hide those deaths from our children would have been blind stupidity. All hiding does is confuse children and add to their fears. It is not subject matter that should be taboo, but the way it is handled.

A number of years ago—the first year I was actually making reasonable money from my writing—my sister-in-law was visiting us, and when my husband told her how much I had earned that year, she was impressed and commented, "And to think most people would have had to work so hard for that!"

Well, it is work, it's most certainly work; wonderful work, but work. Revision, revision, revision. Long hours spent not only in the actual writing, but in research. I think the best thing I learned in college was how to do research, so that I could go right on studying after I had graduated.

Of course, it is not *only* work; it is work that makes the incomprehensible comprehensible. Leonard Bernstein says that for him music is cosmos in chaos. That is true for writing a story, too. Aristotle says that what is plausible and impossible is better than what is possible and implausible.

That means that story must be *true*, not necessarily *factual*, but true. This is not easy for a lot of people to understand. When I was a school child, one of my teachers accused me of telling a story. She was not complimenting me on my fertile imagination; she was accusing me of telling a lie.

Facts are fine; we need facts. But story takes us to a world that is beyond facts, out on the other side of facts. And there is considerable fear of this world.

The writer Keith Miller told me of a young woman who was determined that her three preschool children were going to grow up in the real world. She was not, she vowed, going to sully their minds with myth, fantasy, fairy tales. They were going to know the truth—and for truth, read fact—and the truth would make them free.

One Saturday, after a week of rain and sniffles, the sun came out, so she piled the children into her little red VW bug and took them to the Animal Farm. The parking lot was crowded, but a VW bug is small, and she managed to find a place for it. She and the children had a wonderful day, petting the animals, going on rides, enjoying the sunshine. Suddenly, she looked at her watch and found it was far later than she realized. She and the children ran to where the VW bug was parked, and to their horror, found the whole front end was bashed in.

Outraged, she took herself off to the ranger's office. As he saw her approach, he laughed and said, "I'll bet you're the lady with the red VW bug."

"It isn't funny," she snapped.

"Now, calm down, lady, and let me tell you what happened. You know the elephant your children had such fun riding? She's a circus-trained elephant, and she was trained to sit on a red bucket. When she saw your car, she just did what she was trained to do and sat on it. Your engine's in the back, so you can drive it home without any trouble. And don't worry. Our insurance will take care of it. Just go on home, and we'll get back to you on Monday."

Slightly mollified, she and the kids got into the car and took off. But she was later than ever, so when she saw what looked like a very minor accident on the road, she didn't stop, but drove on.

Shortly, the flashing light and the siren came along, and she was pulled over. "Lady, don't you know that in this state it's a crime to leave the scene of an accident?" the trooper asked.

"But I wasn't in an accident," she protested.

"I suppose your car came that way," she said, pointing to the bashed-in front.

"No. An elephant sat on it."

"Lady, would you mind blowing into this little balloon?"

That taught her that facts alone are not enough; that facts, indeed, do not make up the whole truth. After that she read fairy tales to her children and encouraged them in their games of Make Believe and Let's Pretend.

I learned very early that if I wanted to find out the truth, to find out why people did terrible things to each other, or sometimes wonderful things—why there was war, why children are abused—I was more likely to find the truth in story than in the encyclopedia. Again and again I read *Emily of New Moon,* by Lucy Maud Montgomery, because Emily's father was dying of diseased lungs, and so was mine. Emily had a difficult time at school, and so did I. Emily wanted to be a writer, and so did I. Emily knew that there was more to the world that provable fact, and so did I. I read fairy tales, the myths of all nations, science fiction, the fantasies and family stories of E. Nesbit. I read Jules Verne and H. G. Wells. And I read my parents' books, particularly those with lots of conversation in them. What was not in my frame of reference went right over my head.

We tend to find what we look for. If we look for dirt, we'll find dirt, whether it's there or not. A very nice letter I received from a reader said that she found *A Ring of Endless Light* very helpful to her in coming to terms with the death of a friend, but that another friend had asked her how it was that I used dirty words. I wrote back saying that I was not going to reread my book looking for dirty words, but that as far as I could remember, the only word in the book that could possibly be construed as dirty was *zuggy,* which I'd made up to avoid using dirty words. And wasn't looking for dirty words an ugly way to read a book?

One of my favorite books is Frances Hodgson Burnett's *The Secret Garden.* I read it one rainy weekend to a group of little girls, and a generation later to my granddaughters up in an old brass bed in the attic. Mary Lennox is a self-centered, spoiled-rotten little heroine, and I think we all recognize at least a little of ourselves in her. The secret garden is as much the garden of Mary's heart as it is the physical walled garden. By the end of the book, warmth and love and concern for others have come to Mary's heart, when Colin, the sick boy, is able to walk and run again. And Dickon, the gardener's boy, looks at the beauty of the restored garden and says, "It's magic!" But "magic" is one of the key words that has become taboo to today's self-appointed censors, so, with complete disregard of content, they would add *The Secret Garden* to the pyre. I shudder. This attitude is extreme. It is also dangerous.

It comes down to the old question of separate standards, separate for adults and children. The only standard to be used in judging a children's book is: *Is it a good book?* Is it good enough for me? Because if a children's book is not good enough for all of us, it is not good enough for children.

□ 100

MAKING YOUR STORY BREATHE

BY NORMA FOX MAZER

WHEN I PICK UP A BOOK IN THE LIBRARY OR THE BOOKSTORE, I ALWAYS want to know what it's about. Yet when I'm asked the same question about a story on which I'm working, I stumble anxiously over my words. I don't want to answer! I dislike taking the fascination of creating a world and characters and reducing it to a few phrases. All the same, answering this question is what I force myself to do for every book I write. Ideally, I know what the book is "about" (and can state it in a single sentence) *before* I start writing. Sometimes this actually happens.

One night years ago, while I was washing dishes, a sentence appeared in my head. I say "appeared" because it was so clear I seemed to see it: "A girl is kidnapped by her father." I knew at once that I'd been given a gift: a story in seven words. The hard work was over. All I had to do now was ask the myriad questions implicit in that sentence—and answer them by telling a good story. Those questions, beginning with *why? how? when?*, became *Taking Terri Mueller*.

More often, though, rather than a gift, what I have is a muddle. I hate to confess this, after so many years of writing. Doing it right seems simple: Decide what you're going to write about, work a story around it, and go to it. Yeeeaaah! I have written and rewritten hundreds of pages and found myself still sweating out what the story is really about. This happened with my novel, *Missing Pieces*. I began by wanting to write about a close-knit, self-sufficient female household: mother, daughter, and elderly aunt. Right away, I knew the odd house they live in (built on a hill, tiny black-and-white tiles in the hall, kitchen in the basement . . .), I knew Aunt Zis, with her pride and bony shoulders, and I knew a little about Jessie—fuzzy eyebrows and a mouth that worked overtime.

I developed Jessie, and a couple of friends for her, each with her

481

own story (racism, shyness); threw in a boy; worked up a love life for her overweight mother, Maribeth; and in an escalating series of scenes went after the main story: the terrors of aging (beloved Aunt Zis) as seen through Jessie's eyes and heart. Early on, to explain this manless family, I wrote a few sentences about Jessie's father, "the disappearing dude," as she jauntily called him, who'd taken off when she was small.

O.K. The usual rounds of writing and rewriting, and off to the editor at last. The manuscript came back with a three-page comment that boiled down to: too many stories, not enough focus. And, oh, by the way, I'm really interested in that father.

My initial reaction was a snappish, "Well, I'm not!" An attitude. It lasted overnight. But by morning the thought was, "Oh . . . actually, I'm kind of interested in the dude, myself."

I began to tell the same story, but in a new light, focusing on Jessie and her father. I threw out the old title, deleted scenes, recast others, created new ones. Still, it took at least one more major revision before I could put the story into this sentence: *A girl whose father left her years ago is tormented by her desire to know why he did it and who he really was.*

Once a premise is clear, it always seems obvious, and I'm amazed that it eluded me for so long. After it's nailed down, the story opens up for me, and I can go to work on making it breathe. That single sentence (sometimes paragraph) is the spine of the story; around it grows the flesh and blood. And this is where the tools of the trade come into play: *narrative, dialogue, characterization.*

I work to make my story live and breathe (or appear to, anyway; we are illusionists only) in a variety of ways, some hard to describe, others quite pragmatic. Let me get the hard-to-describe stuff out of the way. It has to do with getting to a place that I think of as the free place. In that place, there are no constraints. Scenes appear in my head, words appear on the screen. There is some level of truth or sight here that is exhilarating. It's like crossing a border. On this side, the usual side, I'm walking a path through a dim woods, moving along, but not seeing enough. There are shadows everywhere, and I'm anxious about getting where I'm going.

If I'm lucky and cross the border, everything changes, becomes lighter, vaster, more open. An endless meadow in which I romp and fly. How to get into that meadow, where I'd like to abide? It's not exactly sheer chance, but there's no map, either. Often enough, I'm stuck on the woodsy side, slogging along and devising little tricks and ways of doing things to keep me going forward.

Sculptors start with a lump of clay; writers, with nothing: It's all in the head. When I'm drafting, what I want is something malleable, something to work on—words, scenes, characters. My best trick is to sit in front of the computer wearing my drafting hat, a battered gray fedora, pulled down over my eyes, and type without stopping. The hat over the eyes keeps me from seeing anything but what's on the only screen that matters—the one in my mind.

The next day, before the hat goes on, I look at what I produced. A mess! My heart sinks. With a little effort, I can remember that I've done this 24 times before, and 24 times a novel emerged. But, of course, that was the past and it happened through sheer chance and good luck. This time, I can tell, it's the end of my life as a writer. I don't write stories, I make messes! Still, what are messes for, except to be cleaned up, so I might as well get to it. I start by putting in all the capitals and commas and correcting the spelling. This is soothing. I'm not doing real writing, which means I don't have to be anxious.

It never fails that while I'm doing this, ideas sprout on nearly every line, and one thing leads to another, which leads to a cheerful frame of mind and the possibility that I might still make it as a writer. I do another five or six messy pages. After several months of this routine, I come out from under the hat with a rough, but not impossible, draft.

I begin rewriting and revising. I love this part, but I can still use help. I'll do anything to give it to myself.

Here are a few of my tricks:

1. Eavesdrop. A sentence heard on the fly on a busy New York City street—"They destroyed my innocent childhood"—gave me a sudden insight into Diane, one of Jessie's friends in *Missing Pieces,* and was the basis for at least two important scenes I hadn't known I was going to write.

2. Free write, just as the kids do in school. In *After the Rain,* the letters Rachel writes her brother were never intended for the book. They began as a way for me to get to know more about her.

3. Switch from first person to third, or from third to first. If, for instance, you've written the draft in third person, rewrite your entire

manuscript in first person. This doesn't mean merely changing all the "she said"s to "I said"s. It means seeing the story in a fresh way. Third person is the storytelling voice. It has greater freedom than the first person: It's a voice that can know more than the character knows; a voice that can give the viewpoint of more than one character. Transforming a third-person narrative into first person forces a sharper concentration on the character's views, thoughts, and feelings.

How about the reverse? First person is necessarily the narrower vision, but the voice is capable of drawing in the reader more swiftly. The first-person voice rarely stops to notice the scenery (those awful long paragraphs of description I used to think I had to master to be a *real* writer). Only as much of the story can be told as the first-person character is capable of understanding, noticing, and reporting. When your characters are adolescents, this is a severe limitation. First person can also be too talky: Somebody's always in your ear saying, I, I, I, I.

When I rewrite a manuscript into the third person, I always feel grateful for the new notes that are rung, the new details observed. In the third person, things leap out that I, as author, can write into the story but the close-in, first-person viewpoint couldn't notice and still remain a true first person.

4. Take another step with the voice and rewrite the manuscript once more, from third person back to first, or from first person back again to third. Yes, this seems like a lot of work, and it is. But for me, it never fails to add something new, fresh, and vital.

The third-person characters who spent their time in the first person would emerge opened up, with a more intimate tone, while the first-person characters, as a result of their brief third-person lives, now have steadier, quieter, more mature voices.

5. Use pictures. When I was writing *Taking Terri Mueller,* I had a problem with Terri's father; I hated him. He was a great dad, relaxed, loving, and attentive, but I hated him for kidnapping his daughter, and the emotion put me into writer's gridlock. I came across a magazine picture of a man holding a baby up toward his face and smiling with ecstatic love. I ripped the picture out and taped it over my typewriter. Every day, before I did anything else, I looked at that picture and thought, "This is the way Terri's father feels about her. This was how much he loved her as an infant and has gone on loving her." Finally, I could comprehend how devastating it was for him to think he was going to lose Terri. After that I could write again.

6. Read out loud. The last thing I do is read the manuscript to someone else. The last two words in that sentence are crucial for me. I can read something out loud to myself and be quite satisfied, but when I read the same thing to my husband Harry, the blunders leap out at me. As for silent reading, it's amazing how often my eye skips over sentences on the screen that are awkward or unclear. Unheeding, I speed past the extra adjective, the unneeded adverb, but the moment I have to speak them, I stumble. Narrative holes loom bigger, too, when spoken.

7. Talk the talk. Dialogue is tricky. We all have verbal ticks, but putting them into dialogue rarely works. What do people really say when they get mad, when they're baffled, amused, amazed? I say what I would say, or what I'd like to say. (I'm not confrontational, but I love writing noisy, loud, decisive characters.) Then I write it, then I rewrite it, then I read it out loud.

8. Finally, when you think you have nothing left to do, do this: Go through each chapter as if you *must* cut it by ¼, and be merciless with anything that is repetitious, unclear, clichéd. Be on the lookout, too, for those bits that make you chuckle fondly or glow a little inwardly. Those are nearly always the ones that ought to come out, where the writer is working too hard at being a Wonderful Writer.

Did I say somewhere that when you get the premise, the hard work is over? Silly me. The most dazzling, dramatic idea to come down the pike in the last decade isn't worth much if not brought to life, if the characters don't (as one of my readers once so winningly said) walk alongside the reader. This is what I really want when I write and what all the work and revisions are about: creating a space and a place that is unique, a world the reader enters and might never want to leave.

❑ 101

LET YOUR THEME CHOOSE YOU

BY MARION DANE BAUER

SOME YEARS AGO, AFTER THE PUBLICATION OF MY FOURTH OR FIFTH novel for young people, I made a horrifying discovery: I was writing the same story . . . every time!

No matter that sometimes the main character was a girl, sometimes a boy. No matter that the settings changed with every book. No matter that the stories varied widely: one, a girl running away from home; another, a girl delivered into foster care; another, a young woman struggling with mental illness; another, a boy coming to terms with his brother's heroism—or lack of it—during service in World War II. My theme never changed. Every story began with a young person alienated from a parent or parent figure. Every story ended when my young character made a connection with that important person again.

My first thought upon facing this discovery was, "My career is over. I have nothing more to say!" Then I went on to write another book and another and another. I was still a writer, after all. Usually I wrote the kind of story that I was most comfortable with—realistic, hard-hitting family dramas. Sometimes I tried other forms—ghost stories and light fantasies. Those alienations and connections between parent and child kept right on happening.

Finally, I took the biggest step ever, a novella called *Ghost Eye*. "This will be entirely different," I told myself. The main character wasn't even a child. He was an odd-eyed white Cornish rex cat, haughty, disdainful, with no interest in connections of any kind. Yet, when he arrived at the concluding scene of the story, what happened? My haughty, independent cat turned, for the first time, to the girl who was supposed to be his mistress, the one he had been rejecting from the beginning, settled next to her, and rumbled into a contented purr. Parent-connection made, again! No matter how different my choice of genre and characters and style.

486

It was time, I decided, to accept this "truth" of mine, just as I accept the color of my eyes. And having accepted this theme, I realized that instead of trying to escape it, it was time to begin, consciously, to mine it. So in my next story, my main character was alienated from her beloved older sister. And in the next I had the mother run away instead of the child. It has been like stumbling into a gold mine. I know where to go looking for my stories now, and each one, when I find it, is totally mine.

None of us is limited to the facts of our own lives when we write our stories. Even if you've grown up on a farm, you can still gather the information and experience you need to write about a child growing up in the city. Even as an adult, by using your imagination and empathy, you can write from the point of view of a young girl . . . or for that matter, a mother raccoon. Though law-abiding, you can write a murder mystery; you can even write a murder mystery from the point of view of the murderer. The possibilities for creating characters, settings, plots are as wide as your imagination, as rich as your ability to learn. But your themes will, inevitably, emerge from your own psyche.

You don't choose your themes; they choose you. The meaning of your stories will rise out of your deepest longings, often out of longings so deep that you haven't admitted them even to yourself. Your convictions, your confusions, your most passionate dreams will be there whenever you begin a story, so you might as well learn to tap into them.

How can you do that? First, by recognizing inspiration when it comes. Inspiration is energy, pure and simple. When an idea has the ability to touch your center, it will carry a kind of excitement with it, a shimmer of vitality, of possibilities yet unexplored. The idea itself may have no discernible connection to your life, but if it has the potential to be the core of one of your stories, the excitement will be there.

To be a fiction writer is to keep your story sensors open all the time. Whether you are reading a newspaper, listening to a friend's complaints about her boss, or observing a stray dog, every piece of information you take in is sifted through your imagination for possible stories. But the stories for which you can, almost instantly, *feel* a resolution are the ones that are fully yours. They tie into your personal themes.

Every one of my stories begins with an emotion. Or perhaps it would be more accurate to say, each begins with a situation that evokes an emotion in me. A boy wanting to "show them all" with a .22 rifle draws on my own, mostly buried, rage. A girl feeling cut off from her much-loved older sister reaches into my loneliness, my longing for the sister I never had.

But if the story is mine to write, the resolution will arrive almost simultaneously with the idea. And the resolution will involve emotion, too. When I feel Michael's rage I know that when he finally turns to the stepfather he has always rejected, the rage will begin to heal. Touched by Caitlin's loneliness, I can at the same time imagine what a reconciliation with her sister will feel like. I may not yet know *how* she will arrive at that reconciliation, but I know exactly what the end of the story will be. And in knowing that, I know both why I am writing the story and what it will mean.

Understanding the emotional conflict that sets off your story and the emotional resolution that brings it to a conclusion gives you a framework; your task then is to fill in that framework with your character's struggle to resolve her conflict.

Can your themes or mine ever change? They can indeed, but only as we do, only as we discover new personal truths. I have recently written the text for a picture book called *Jason's Bears*. Actually, that small story took me five years and uncounted drafts before it was completed. The writing took that long because I had stumbled into a story problem for which my old "theme" could not provide a resolution.

Jason, who loves bears, is being tormented by a bullying older brother into thinking that the bears he loves are waiting in every corner of his house to eat him up. The solution was clearly that the little boy should not put himself further under his big brother's power; he had to find his own power before he could come to terms with those bears, and he finally did. But he found it only after I had discovered some of my own power as a writer and could believe in such an ending.

Every person has a unique set of longings, as well as a different set of resolutions to those longings. That is why no one can write *the* "story for all time." And yet the reason stories can be written at all is that nothing points more inevitably to the universal than the personal and unique. Each of us seeks another person's insights to understand our lives.

So if you find yourself repeating a single theme, or two or three themes, relax. You are in good company. Remember that Mark Twain wrote of hope and disillusion in a thousand different guises. In story after story, Jane Austen tweaked homely commonplace. Edgar Allan Poe was obsessed with evil. Your gift, your need, your longing will also be your creative fire. And it will turn up again and again, whether you ask it to or not.

❑ Editing and Marketing

❑ 102

Negotiating the Book Contract

By Sherri L. Burr

Your dream is about to be realized. Your first book contract arrives in the mail. You go directly to the advance clause. It is exactly as you agreed. You look no further, sign the contract, and return it, confident of your great deal.

You are deliriously happy, until one day you run into an experienced writing friend. She's unhappy because she has not received a single royalty from her publisher since her advance.

"How could that happen?" you ask.

"I never read the fine print that said royalties were paid on net proceeds. I thought I'd be paid on the gross sales price. Instead, the publisher is paying me a percentage based on the amount that is received from booksellers, minus a few deductions for shipping costs and other overhead charges. My current statement says I owe the publisher money."

"That's terrible," you reply, secretly wondering if the same thing could happen to you. You rush home, take out your contract, and begin to read it. You are appalled by what you find and wonder what to do.

While this may never have happened to you, it serves as a reminder to review your contract carefully before signing. It is easy to understand why writers do not read their book contracts carefully. Contracts are usually written in "legal garbage-ese" and printed in the smallest type that the best computer scientists can design. The saying, "The big print giveth and the small print taketh away," is particularly appropriate to book contracts.

But don't despair; all contracts are negotiable. You just need to invest some time in determining what rights you should keep, and what rights the publisher will want. Here are some important issues to consider when reviewing your contract:

Manuscript clause

Many book contracts begin with a standard clause dealing with the specifics of the manuscript: the title, the name of the author, the length, the due date, how many copies you must deliver in hard copy and on disk. Sometimes, in this clause the publisher reserves the right to reject the final manuscript as unacceptable or unpublishable.

A savvy negotiator may be able to get the publisher to waive this clause, but don't count on it. Instead, try to insert that the publisher's right of rejection must be "reasonably exercised," which is often implied in the contract. Publishers rarely reject a manuscript at the final stages, unless they think that it is unpublishable.

What makes a manuscript unpublishable? The final draft may not be as well written as the initial proposal. Or the subject of the book has become dated: A psychological profile of George Bush that might have sold in 1987 would not be acceptable in 1989. Or the manuscript may contain damaging information about a prominent family, and the publisher becomes worried about potential libel suits. For these and other reasons, the publisher will insist on keeping an "out" clause in the contract, permitting the return of all rights to the author.

If a publisher does exercise its "out" clause, what happens to your advance? Often, the advance is tied to the production of an acceptable manuscript. Under most contracts, if the publisher deems your manuscript unacceptable, you must refund the advance.

In Joan Collins' well-publicized dispute with Random House, however, a jury ruled that she did not have to return her advance—even though Random House found her manuscript unacceptable—and that the company had to pay her part of the additional monies due on her contract. Instead of the usual clause that the author must produce an "acceptable" manuscript, Ms. Collins' contract merely required her to produce a "completed" manuscript. Although this case has been unusual for the publicity it generated, there have been other instances where the publisher, as an act of good will, has permitted the author to keep the advance.

Copyright issues

Ideally, the contract should provide that the publisher will register the copyright *in the name of the author.* Some contracts, particularly those from university and small presses, state that the publisher will register the copyright *in the name of the publisher,* but this clause is negotiable.

The "Rights and Royalties" clauses are critical for you to understand. If your publisher has only the capacity to publish your book in English and distribute it in Canada and the United States, why grant the publisher all the rights to your book, including the right to publish it in any translation throughout the world? Instead, tell the publisher that you want to sell the rights only to the English-language edition in specific countries. Also, consider selling the publisher audio and electronic rights only if the company has these divisions. If not, retain the rights for sales at a later date.

If your publisher is a major conglomerate with movie divisions and your book has movie potential, consider granting the publisher the movie rights, but only if you are sure that you or your agent could not sell the movie rights yourselves for more profit. Ask your agent about his contacts with Hollywood and whether he has sub-agency relations with Hollywood agents.

You should also be aware that the publisher may ask to split the movie rights 50–50. Try to negotiate to a more profitable (60–40, 75–25, 85–15) split, because the publisher will be acting as your agent.

Royalty provisions

Traditional publishers typically offer a royalty fee of 10% to 15% on the retail price for hardcover books, but less for paperback. On mass market paperback books, publishers may print 500,000 copies or more, offer authors a 5% royalty, and sell the books in discount markets such as K-Mart and Wal-Mart. Writers or their agents can propose a royalty schedule. For example, after the first 10,000 or 50,000 or 100,000 or so in sales, the royalty fee increases according to an agreed-upon scale.

Some smaller presses offer payment on net proceeds because they sell fewer copies and therefore receive less money. Make sure the term "net proceeds" is concretely defined in your contract; it is important to specify that net proceeds include the money that the publisher receives from its sales. In a net profit deal, you should be able to negotiate a higher royalty percentage payment, at least 10% to 15% or more.

Accounting provisions

Accounting provisions indicate when you can expect to receive royalty checks. Most trade publishers have semiannual accountings; most academic and small presses have annual accountings. Payments are made within 30 to 90 days following the close of the accounting period.

These provisions may be difficult to negotiate because they often depend on the publisher's overall accounting practices. However, trade publishers have been known to provide shorter accounting periods for their best-selling authors who are generating a great deal of revenue. You can ask for a similar arrangement, but if you do not yet fall into this category, do not be surprised if your publisher resists setting up a different system for you.

Warranties

Almost impossible to negotiate, these clauses require the author to guarantee to the publisher that:

- the author is the sole creator and owner of the work.
- the work has not been previously published.
- the work does not violate another work's copyright.
- the work does not violate anyone's right of privacy.
- the work does not libel or defame anyone.
- the work does not violate any government regulation.

If you or your work violates the above warranties, the publisher has a right to cancel the contract.

Warranty clauses are often accompanied by an indemnity provision, requiring the author to indemnify, or repay, the publisher, should the work violate a warranty provision. If the publisher is sued because of the author's work, the author must defend the lawsuit and reimburse the publisher for any related expenses.

Expenses, permissions, and fair use

Publishers may grant authors budgets to cover certain expenses, such as those connected with travel or interviews. This is obviously a negotiable point, though it may be difficult for a first-time book author to negotiate reimbursement for such expenses.

If you plan to quote from copyrighted works, you should get the permission of the copyright holder (usually either the author or the publisher) to do so. Sometimes the publisher will grant a budget for permission fees; other times, you must cover the cost of such permissions.

In some cases, authors claim a fair-use privilege to use other people's work, such as when critiquing it, in which case permission is not needed. Determining whether the fair-use privilege applies requires authors to use their best judgment. However, you should be aware that if the copyright owner sues, you have to pay to defend both yourself and the publisher.

New editions, author's copies, out of print

The contract may also specify that the publisher has the first right to publish further editions of the work. This should be a negotiable item. Authors of a continuing series (such as mysteries) and textbook publications should beware of such clauses, because they may give the publisher the right to name other writers to produce additional editions. Obviously, the original author would want to retain this right.

The author's copies clause specifies how many free copies of your book you will receive, and the cost of any additional copies you may want to purchase. Sometimes these clauses specify that you cannot resell reduced-price copies. Try to strike this portion of the clause or spell out circumstances where resale would be permitted, such as when you sell copies at a lecture, conference, or book signing.

Also, make sure that the contract provides that when the book goes out of print, all rights revert to the author.

Assignment

A clause that has become standard in the era of mergers and acquisitions is the assignment clause, granting the publisher the right to assign the contract to another publisher. You could easily sell your book to Publisher A only to have Publisher Q purchase or merge with Publisher A soon thereafter. With an assignment clause, Publisher Q would assume the responsibility for publishing your book. You would be protected because the book would still be published.

Your contract may contain fewer clauses than those mentioned here, or it may be more extensive. Whether it's long or short, in large or small print, you should read your contract carefully! You will not only avoid royalty payment shock, but also prevent your book contract dreams from becoming nightmares should some unforeseen disaster strike. Having read your contract, you will know that the price of a magnifying glass could prove a good investment!

❑ 103

PROMOTING YOUR WRITING CAREER

BY LINDA BATT

BEST-SELLING MYSTERY NOVELIST WILLIAM BAYER RECENTLY TOLD an audience that publishers expect writers to promote themselves and their books. If prominent authors must be both creators and purveyors, it's time for the rest of us to consider promotion as a part of the writing profession. The unfortunate truth is that many writers, including me, are usually not very good at sales.

I began looking at the self-promotion techniques of successful authors as a model for my own use. What I found could benefit you, too.

First, this top-paid group of professionals had all developed some basic tools. When authors agreed to speak at the yearly college writing conference I'd organized, each one immediately sent me a resume, a bio, a photo, and clips—a procedure that makes good sense.

If you were looking for a job as a head nurse, a high school teacher, or a research biologist, you'd take certain logical steps. You'd think of all your past experiences, all your achievements, all your attributes that make you right for the job, and then you'd slave for hours over a resume that showed you at your very best. How many of you have done this for your free-lance careers?

It's time to try. Write a resume that sells your writing ability. Include work experience, education, awards—the same items you put on the resume that got you your daytime job.

Don't stop there. Next write a brief biography of about 100 words that can be shortened to 50. This comes in handy, since many magazines give some information about the author with each piece they publish. If you don't know what to include, go to your local library and read the bios at the end of articles in a variety of publications.

Have your picture taken in black and white in poses that you like, not just the usual head and shoulder shot. Keep several copies, along with copies of your published articles. File them so you can find them easily and send the most appropriate ones to editors with your submissions.

I took all those steps and developed another promotional tool that has worked well for me: I send Selected Published Works pages with submissions, listing particular types of writing with the titles of my articles and dates of publication, making sure to include the most current credits. If I'm writing an advice article, my published works page would start with other advice pieces I have sold and then include my published general articles. If I'm trying to sell a travel article, my published works page would definitely list my travel articles near the top. Sending this sales tool along with a few of my clips gives the editor a feel for my experience and may make him or her give me a go-ahead or an assignment to write the piece I've suggested in my query letter.

Volunteer to write for a local charity. Your name will go on the publication, and everyone in the organization will think of you as an author. I volunteer for an organization called Traditional Arts of Upstate New York, and I'm going to write a travel publication for them, including the places, people, and events they want covered. This project will include interviews and the actual writing.

Giving your time away free often leads to paid work. After a young friend of mine spoke at my conference on "getting started," the editor of the local papers listened to my friend's presentation and hired him to write a weekly business feature.

If people think of you as a writer, they are likely to think of you when they want something written. A little self-promotion is good sense these days.

❑ 104

THE ALL-IMPORTANT QUERY LETTER

BY STEVE WEINBERG

ONE OF THE MOST IMPORTANT RULES FOR FREE-LANCE WRITERS TRYing to break into a magazine is too frequently violated: When trying to sell an article to an editor unfamiliar with your work, send a query letter. Do not send a complete manuscript.

A few editors buy nonfiction from writers unknown to them on the basis of a completed manuscript. But not many.

So let's discuss why it makes sense to query first, then discuss the elements of successful query letters.

Why query?

1. Time is money. Free lancers who want to make money should not invest months researching and writing a manuscript without an expression of interest from an editor. I have written successful queries after just a few hours of research. Time is precious for editors, too. They rarely want to invest in reading unsolicited manuscripts.

A query letter will help you focus your thoughts. The brevity of the form (one or two pages) will allow you to revise the letter until the phrasing is just right. When the letter reaches its destination, the editor can read it at a convenient moment, mull it over, reread it if necessary.

2. Query letters can avoid rejections based on the focus or the style, rather than the substance. The small percentage of editors who take time to read manuscripts because they like the idea frequently find they dislike the approach. Why did the writer use first person instead of omniscient third person? Why did the writer choose a question lead instead of an anecdotal opening? Rather than guide the unfamiliar writer through a major revision, the editor will just say no.

3. Editors are too distracted during their work day to hold lengthy conversations by telephone with unfamiliar writers. Trying to sell arti-

cles by telephone almost never works. Besides, editors want to see a writing sample—a query letter can serve as that sample.

The elements of successful query letters

1. Queries should be one or two single- or double-spaced pages. Brevity is mainly for the convenience of the editor, but it benefits writers, too, forcing them to distill their thoughts. A query is not the place for a writer to overwhelm an editor with mastery of the topic's detail. If editors are interested but want to know more, they will ask for more.

2. Within the brief query letter, the main idea should be described in one sentence if possible, certainly in no more than one paragraph. That description should be written compellingly, a grabber. It should not be written boringly, as in "This idea has to do with missing persons." Much better:

Murderers, thousands of them, are walking around free. That is scary enough. Even scarier is that police, prosecutors, and judges have no idea who they are. They are perpetrators of a type of homicide so common, yet so little discussed, that it lacks a commonly accepted label. Let's call it, for now, missing and presumed murdered.

When possible, it is best to write the main idea in the style of the proposed article, as in the previous paragraph from a query letter of mine. A proposed headline usually helps, too.

3. After the nutshell description, the letter should explain why readers of that magazine are likely to care. This should be subtle. Hype ("an irresistible topic") will turn off editors. So will preachiness. ("Your magazine must publish this article because of its importance to your readers.") Your query letter should make editors say, "This is irresistible" or "This is really important to my readers."

4. With the editor clued in to the "what" and "why," it is time to tell the editor the "how" of information gathering. What sources might consent to be interviewed? What documents can be consulted in libraries, government agencies or business archives? Are reference books available? If possible, work in a telling anecdote, a case history, or a statistic already in hand—and simultaneously demonstrate your passion for the topic.

5. Now that the editor knows about the process of information gathering, she or he will be curious about the proposed structure, point of view, timing and tone.

Will the article be structured chronologically? In cinematic-type scenes? An outline is often the best way to convey the structure.

As for point of view, through whose eyes will the article be told? The author's, in either first person or omniscient third person? The person who is the main subject of the article? A query proposing an article about "capital punishment" is too vague. But telling an editor the article will talk about capital punishment through the executioner's point of view might produce a "go-ahead" or assignment.

About timing: If you include the fact that the number of death-row convicts executed has doubled over the last decade, you have provided the editor with the relevance of your proposed piece.

Moving on to tone, will the article be serious or light? Or downright humorous?

6. Include something about yourself, such as prior publications, if any; and where you can be contacted by mail, telephone, fax and/or electronic mail.

Novices worry that if they cannot include previously published articles, it will mean immediate rejection. Not so. Every published writer was at some point unpublished. Furthermore, some editors put little stock in clips, because they cannot tell how much is the result of revision by an editor. For clips, aspiring authors can substitute relevant personal experience, work experience or academic training.

A caution: Some editors and experienced writers suggest placing personal information in the first paragraph. I disagree. It is the idea that should be emphasized, not the writer who will be researching the idea. Well-known writers might receive assignments on the basis of their names; beginning and intermediate writers rarely do.

7. Address your query to a specific editor. Which editor? Perhaps the editor of a particular section or department. Perhaps the managing editor, articles editor, features editor or editor-in-chief.

You may find the name of the appropriate editor in the magazine's masthead. If not, try calling the magazine. (During that call, request a copy of the magazine's guidelines for writers.)

What to leave out of query letters

Omitted from my seven-point list is something that other writers suggest including in query letters—a paragraph about what the magazine's competitors have (or have not) published on the topic. The point is apparently to convince an editor that competing magazines have not run the same story.

I disagree. Most editors do not assume their readers also buy the competitors. So if I have an idea that I want to sell to *The Atlantic Monthly,* I search a few years of its back issues to make sure I am not duplicating. If I find nothing similar, I begin drafting the query. Sure, I will also search back issues of *Harper's, Mother Jones,* and other magazines that might be considered *The Atlantic Monthly*'s competitors. But if I find an article in those publications on my topic, I will not mention it in my query. What I will do is make sure my approach is different enough from what has appeared elsewhere so that my article is advancing knowledge, not duplicating knowledge.

In your query letter, don't mention article length; payment; deadlines (unless the topic is fresh for only a short time, or seasonal); artwork (unless it is a big part of why you should get the assignment); and other contractual terms such as rights.

Editors frequently reject query letters with mistakes in grammar, incorrect punctuation or misspellings—no matter how good the idea. They are usually unimpressed by college degrees (unless directly relevant to the proposed article), friends of theirs you claim to know, or language filled with pyrotechnics at the expense of clarity. They are not interested in what you think of their magazines, and are especially offended by mini-lectures on how you would improve those magazines.

Simultaneous submission of queries?

Whether to submit the same or similar query letters simultaneously to multiple magazines is a topic without one correct answer. Debates within writers' groups and editors' forums over the decades have failed to resolve the matter.

Some free lancers say they are uncomfortable sending multiple queries. They do not want to risk having an editor remember that after making an assignment based on careful consideration, a competitor wound up with the article.

I disagree. Free lancers will starve if they wait for one editor after another to respond. Simultaneous query submissions are smart business. What if two or more editors want you to write for them? My reaction: You should be so lucky.

So now it is time to go forth and submit query letters, simultaneously.

A Sample Query Letter

Here are parts of the query letter—with brief explanations inserted—that sold my proposed article about missing persons. I addressed the query to the managing editor at the *ABA* [American Bar Association] *Journal,* based on a conversation with a writer who had already published in the magazine:

MISSING AND PRESUMED MURDERED

[The editor used the headline I suggested. He fleshed it out with this subheadline: When a young Texan vanished, he joined a phenomenon that bedevils prosecutors and police nationwide: How to find justice when they suspect homicide, but have no victim to help prove it.]

Murderers, thousands of them, are walking around free. That is scary enough. Even scarier is that police, prosecutors, and judges have no idea who they are.
[If that isn't a grabber, what is? Because I hoped it could also serve as the opening paragraph of the actual article, the editor immediately experienced the style I hoped to use.]

They are perpetrators of a type of homicide so common, yet so little discussed, that it lacks a commonly accepted label. Let's call it, for now, missing and presumed murdered.
[This paragraph expands on the grabber of a lead as well as further demonstrating my style and introducing my informal, but not flippant, tone.]

The best estimate, based on FBI statistics and anecdotal evidence, is that 21,000 children, teenagers, and adults are missing and presumed murdered. The common denominators are that their bodies remain hidden, with no conviction of perpetrators on the horizon.
[This defines an unfamiliar topic further, plus suggests some of my sources—the FBI and interviews with persons involved in such cases.]

Probably the best-known case is that of Jimmy Hoffa, who disappeared in 1975. Despite almost immediate notification of the disappearance, hundreds of law enforcement officers, including the best the FBI could offer, failed to find the Teamsters Union leader. Twenty years later, Hoffa is presumed dead. But no body has surfaced, and those responsible remain at large.
[Here I make the unfamiliar familiar by referring to a well-known case. I also further hint at the depth and breadth of my research.]

In the remainder of the query letter, I explained:
• Why readers of that particular magazine would be likely to care (because these cases frustrate the participants in the legal system and cause the citizenry at large to lose faith in that system)

• How I planned to research the article (by gathering FBI and state police statistics; interviewing family members of missing persons, police officers, prosecutors, defense attorneys and judges; reading trial transcripts; narrating the case of my brother-in-law, missing since 1981, based on notes kept and documents gathered during 14 years of investigating)

• The likely structure of the article (told in sections, beginning with a disappearance, followed by the police investigation, the decision by a prosecutor whether to move forward, the defense strategy in cases involving a specific suspect, the trial and verdict. This is largely a chronological approach, with modifications. Furthermore, each section would begin and end with my brother-in-law's case, which would serve as the connecting thread)

• The point of view (through the thoughts of the investigators, as recounted by them in hindsight and through contemporaneous reports or diaries)

I ended the query with a paragraph about my credentials. I received the assignment soon thereafter. The article appeared in the September 1995 issue of the *ABA Journal*.

❏ 105

WHAT YOU NEED TO KNOW ABOUT COPYRIGHT

BY HOWARD ZAHAROFF

"WORDS ARE JUST OUR CURRENCY, OUR MEDIUM OF EXCHANGE WITH our readers," says the writer-protagonist in Richard Ford's *The Sportswriter*. From a lawyer's perspective he's at best half-right. Although as a writer you are trading in your words, and trading on your talent, what you are selling to publishers and editors are your copyrights.

Therefore to plan your career, negotiate with publishers, even draw up your will, it is important that you understand the basics of copyright law. As a lawyer who practices in this field, I promise you that this isn't too hard. Let me prove it by answering a dozen questions that writers often ask.

Before doing so, a few comments. First, the answers I give are based on U.S. law, as it exists at the time of this writing. International issues are mostly ignored. Second, my focus is mainly on works first published or created after March 1, 1989, the last major revision of the Copyright Act (which I refer to below as the "Act"). Third, although the Copyright Office cannot provide legal advice, its Circulars and Public Information Office (call 202/707-3000) provide guidance on many of the following issues. (Start with Circular 1: "Copyright Basics.") There are also many excellent books available, such as Ellen Kozak's *Every Writer's Guide to Copyright & Publishing Law* (Owl, 1990) and *The Rights of Authors, Artists and Other Creative People: The Basic ACLU Guide to Author and Artist Rights,* by Kenneth Norwick and Jerry Chasen.

1. *What can be copyrighted?* Copyright protects nearly every original piece you write (or draw, compose, choreograph, videotape, sculpt, etc.): not just your novel, article, story or poem, but the software program you create, the advertisements and greeting cards you pub-

lished, and the love letters you wrote in college. But copyright does not protect your ideas, only the way you *express* them.

2. *What protection does copyright law provide?* A "copyright" is really a bundle of rights. The copyright owner (whom we'll call the "proprietor") controls not only the right to copy the work, but also the rights to perform or display the work publicly, to make the "first sale" of each copy of the work, and to prepare "derivative works," that is, adaptations, translations, and versions in other media, such as creating a screenplay or movie from a novel or play.

3. *How long do copyrights last and are they renewable?* For works created or first published after 1977, copyright generally lasts 50 years after the death of the author. However, for anonymous or pseudonymous works, or works made "for hire" (see below), the term expires 100 years from the creation or 75 years from publication. There are no renewals. (For works published before 1978, special rules, including rights of renewal, apply. See Circular 15: "Renewal of Copyright.") A proposal is pending to increase the term by 20 years, a change already adopted in many foreign countries.

4. *How do you obtain a copyright?* Copyright protection arises *automatically* as soon as you put your ideas into tangible form. Thus, once on paper, canvas, video, or computer disk, your creation is protected by law.

5. *Is a copyright notice required for protection?* No. Before March 1, 1989, a notice was required on all *published* copies of a work. ("Published" simply means distributed to the public; it does not require printing in a periodical or book.) However, on that day the United States joined the international copyright treaty known as the Berne Convention and removed this requirement for works published after that date.

Still, including a copyright notice alerts everyone to your claim and prevents infringers from pleading "innocence" (that is, that they had no idea your work was copyrighted). Thus, good reasons remain for including notices on all published copies of your work, and for insisting that your publisher do so.

If you are concerned that your *unpublished* work may be used or copied without permission (for example, you are circulating copies of your latest, highly marketable, piece within your newly formed writers group), you can't lose by including a notice.

6. *What should my copyright notice say?* A proper notice has three elements:

- The international copyright symbol © or the word "Copyright." Most publishers use both. (The abbreviation "Copr." is also acceptable.)
- The year in which the work is first published. (For unpublished works, you may omit a date.)
- Your name, or a recognizable abbreviation (e.g., International Business Machines Corporation may use "IBM").

In general, notices should be displayed prominently at the beginning of your work, although any reasonable location is acceptable. If your piece will appear in a magazine, anthology, or other collective work, a single notice in the publisher's name will preserve most of your rights. However, including a separate copyright notice in your own name will clarify that only you, *not* the publisher, has the right to authorize further uses of your work.

7. *Must I register my work with the Copyright Office?* Although registration is not required for copyright protection, it is a precondition to suing for infringement of the copyrights in any work first published in the U.S. (and in the unpublished works of U.S. citizens and residents), and enables you to recover both attorneys' fees and "statutory damages." (These are damages of up to $100,000, as determined by the judge, which the proprietor may elect to recover from the infringer in lieu of proving and recovering actual losses.)

You can register your copyrights at any time during the term of copyright. However, registration within three months of publication generally preserves your rights to all infringement remedies, including statutory damages, while registration within five years of publication provides special benefits in legal proceedings.

8. *How do you register a work?* Copyright Office Form TX is the basic form for nondramatic literary works. Form PA is used to register works of the performing arts, including plays and movies. These two-sided forms cost $20 to file and are fairly easy to complete (but only if you read the accompanying instructions!). Adjunct Form GR/CP

allows writers to reduce costs by making a single registration for all works published in periodicals within a 12-month period. In 1996 the Copyright Office issued new, simplified forms, including Short Form TX, a one-sided form which can now be used to register copyrights in new works of single authors. (You can order forms and circulars over the Copyright Office Hotline, 202/707-9100.)

When you apply you must submit one copy of the work, if unpublished, and two copies of the "best edition" of the work, if published. (Only one copy of the best edition is required for contributions to collective works.) The "best edition" is the published edition of highest quality, determined by paper quality, binding, and other factors listed by the Copyright Office (see Circular 7b: "'Best Edition' of Published Copyrighted Works for the Collections of Library of Congress"). For example, if the work was published in both hard and soft covers, the hard cover is normally the best edition.

9. *Should I register my work?* In most cases, no. If your work was published, your publisher may have registered it. If not, failure to register mainly loses you the option of *immediate* relief and statutory damages. Moreover, infringement is the exception and, where it occurs, often can be settled without lawsuits or registration. Besides, most writers earn too little to justify the cost of registration (certainly for articles, poems, and other short works).

10. *What is "public domain" and how can you find out what's there?* Works that are not protected by copyright are said to be in the "public domain"—that is, freely usable by the public, without the need to get permission or pay a fee. This includes works in which copyright has expired or been lost, works for which copyright is not available, and works dedicated to the public. Although there are many exceptions, in general the following are in the public domain:
- Works published more than 75 years ago.
- Works first published or copyrighted during 1920 to 1963, if the copyright was not renewed.
- Works published without a proper copyright notice before 1978.
- Works published without a prior notice between January 1, 1978 and February 28, 1989 (although the Act enables the proprietor to correct this failure).
- Works created by employees of the Federal government as part of their duties.

For a fee the Copyright Office will examine the status of a work. (See Circular 22: "How to Investigate the Copyright Status of a Work.")

11. *What is fair use?* The Act allows the limited use of others' works for research, teaching, news reporting, criticism, and similar purposes. These permitted uses are called "fair use." Although the Act never defines that term, it lists factors to consider, including the purpose and character of the use (e.g., for profit vs. teaching), the nature of the work (e.g., a science text vs. a poem), the amount and substantiality of the use, and its effect on the market for the work.

Here are some basic rules that should help you stay on the right side of the law (and help you recognize when someone's use of your work doesn't).

• Copying for noncommercial purposes, such as classroom teaching, is given a wider scope than copying for commercial use. For example, in general you may quote less of the published writings of a politician in a television docudrama than a history professor may quote in journal articles.

• Copying factual material gets more latitude than copying fiction. Fiction contains more of the "originality" protected by the Act: characters and events, sometimes even time and place, derive from the writer's imagination. Facts, on the other hand, are not "original" and cannot be copyrighted.

• Parody is a permissible use, as long as it does not appropriate too much of the original.

• Quoting or paraphrasing from unpublished works should be kept to a minimum. Until recently, copying from unpublished works without permission was almost always considered unfair. Although the latest cases, and a 1992 amendment to the Copyright Act, have made unpublished works subject to fair use, it remains difficult to prove fair use of an unpublished work.

• The Act permits certain uses of copyrighted works by libraries, archives, educators, charitable organizations, and others. See section 108–110 of the Act and Circular 21.

These rules are complex. Therefore, if you intend to copy more than a negligible amount from another person's work, write to the publisher or copyright owner, or consult a copyright lawyer. Don't take a chance.

12. *What is a "work made for hire," and who owns the rights to these works?* The creator of a work generally owns the copyrights.

There is an exception, however, for "works made for hire." Here it is the party who commissions and pays for the work, rather than the actual creator, who owns the copyrights. So when is a work "for hire"? First, unless expressly excluded by contract, all works created by employees within the scope of their employment are "for hire." (This will normally not include works created on your own time that are unrelated to your employment.) So if you are employed by a newspaper, or hired by a software publisher to write documentation, your employer owns the copyrights in the works you've been paid to create. If you use copies of these works at your next job, you are infringing your former employer's copyrights.

Second, certain specified categories of works (including translations, compilations, and parts of audiovisual works) are considered "for hire" if they have been specially commissioned and a signed writing identifies them as "for hire." Therefore, *if you are not an employee and you haven't agreed in writing that your work is "for hire" (or otherwise assigned your rights), you will generally continue to own the copyrights in your work* even if others paid you to create it (although they will have the right to use your work for the express purposes for which they paid you).

You may wonder about the division of rights when your article, story, or poem is published in a magazine (or other collective work) and there is no written agreement. The Act supplies the answer: The publisher acquires only the right to publish your piece as part of that collective work, of any revision of that work, and of any later collective work in the same series. You retain all other rights, so you are free to revise or remarket your piece.

The above is a *general* discussion of the copyright law as it applies to free lancers. Myriad qualifications and exceptions are not included here. Before making any important copyright decisions, consult a knowledgeable copyright lawyer, the Copyright Office, or a trusted publisher or agent who has an up-to-date understanding of the law.

❏ INTERVIEWS

❑ 106

A Conversation with A. S. Byatt

By Lewis Burke Frumkes

Lewis Frumkes: One of England's most distinguished writers, A. S. Byatt, won the Booker Prize for her novel *Possession,* and she has written a number of other novels, as well as criticism. Her latest work, *The Matisse Stories,* published in the United States by Random House, won high critical acclaim. Let me begin by asking A. S. Byatt to talk a little about *The Matisse Stories.* What prompted them, and what makes them different from your other stories?

A.S. Byatt: I didn't have the idea of writing a book called *The Matisse Stories.* I've come to realize that it's quite important to say that. The idea of putting these three stories together under this title actually belongs to my French translator, who said to me a couple of years ago, "I think I'll translate your three stories that have Matisse in them." So, it wasn't a commercial or technical decision for me to write three stories on this theme. It was more that I am totally obsessed with Matisse. He sort of gets into everything I do. He's my touchstone for art, the importance of art, as opposed to anything else, in its purest, most uncompromising state. The third of the three stories, "The Chinese Lobster," is one of my favorites of anything I've ever written. You know, every now and then, you do something that comes out right. I think that one goes rather deep and does come out right.

LF: You work with words the way Matisse works with tints and colors. Do you have favorite words that recur, or words you have a fondness for?

ASB: They tend to be color words. At the moment, I am very keen on vermilion and emerald, which I think are very beautiful words. I like words that go running along, like Shakespeare saying, "the multitudinous seas incarnadine/Making the green one red." I like the one thing the English can do well, setting one of those very long words next to a very short word. I like what I learned at school about putting long Latin words next to very short Anglo-Saxon words. Really, I like almost all words.

LF: You've read a lot of Iris Murdoch's work, haven't you?

ASB: Yes. When I was a post-graduate student I was really looking for a kind of novel to write that wasn't full of macho, lower-middle-class or lower-class British people beating up on girls. I discovered Iris Murdoch and felt her novels had a kind of thinking tension. They were actually trying to work out what life was about, and at the same time, they were funny. They moved fast. They were elegant and passionate. I thought, "This is it."

Then, I wrote a small book about her work. I have admired her for a long time. She believes that beauty and goodness are the same thing. She has a sort of frightening idea that all art except the very greatest is conciliation.

LF: Who were your literary heroes, heroines, and models when you were young?

ASB: Coleridge, that kind of strange world of *Kubla Khan,* and *The Ancient Mariner* . . . I read all of Jane Austen, most of Dickens, and a lot of Walter Scott, when I was a little girl, as I think children did in those days, because there was no television.

LF: And as you grew older?

ASB: George Eliot, whom I now greatly admire. Willa Cather is a very recent hero. She is my latest discovery, and she has somehow changed the way I write. *Moby Dick* is wonderful. I think Wallace Stevens is the greatest modern poet. He also has an obsession with color.

LF: When did you start writing?

ASB: Almost when I started reading. I was writing stories at about nine or ten. I had a letter from somebody in Canada who said, "I was at boarding school with you when you were writing this novel about a highwayman, and you would read it to us in the evenings in the bedroom." That is not how I remember my school days. I remember nobody speaking to me. I felt rather abashed at this kind memory this lady had sent me. I did write another whole novel, which I burned in the school furnace. I was right. Then, I wrote another novel and a half while I was a student, but it strikes me that during the whole of that time, I thought I wasn't doing anything. I thought, "Help! Help! I haven't begun. I'm nearly twenty-one, and I am a failure. I won't be a writer." I seem to need to feel that I am not getting anywhere. Then, I go even faster.

LF: Why, Antonia Susan Byatt, do you call yourself A. S. Byatt?

ASB: I think maybe it has to do with T. S. Eliot, who was another of my heroes. Also, when I grew up, there were a lot of writers who used initials. Even Dorothy Sayers wrote as D. L. Sayers. Occasionally, when I get depressed about people treating me as if I were odd or trying to change the name on the cover to Antonia, I think that P. D. James gets along fine.

LF: What writers do you read for pleasure?

ASB: I just discovered Walter Moseley. His titles all have different colors. There's one called *White Butterfly,* another called *Red Death.* His books have wonderful narrative tension. I also like reading Martin Cruz Smith, whom I have finally met. I was amazed to find that he reads my work; it didn't strike me that it would necessarily be reciprocal. I read P. D. James. These are the books I read when I need narrative and relaxation.

LF: How do you work? What are your writing habits?

ASB: I work every day if I possibly can. I write anything I regard as serious writing with a pen, slowly. I can do journalism on the word processor. I actually enjoy the word processor. I skipped the typewriter phase completely. I hate them. I still have to think with my fingers. I like to work from 9:00 a.m. to 7:00 p.m. every day. I have taken to stopping for a swim in the middle. Writing is incredibly sedentary.

LF: What advice would you give to people who would like to write?

ASB: The first is to keep reading. Read everybody. I've met a lot of people in writing groups, and one of the things they tend to say is, "I don't read other writers in case it destroys my originality." You will not be original if you do not read other authors' writing. People who do not read other people's writing are all the same. The second piece of advice is always to stop when you are in the middle of something that you know the next bit of and are excited by it. Then, you can take it up again the next morning. That keeps the continuity going, which is one of the real hassles. If you stop when you know what you are going to write next, then you do not have a blank page facing you. The third is to carry a notebook everywhere. Write down things that you see. I never write things down about myself. Play with the language. I do not have any advice about professional forms and structures. Walter Moseley is about as far from me as you can get, but I have learned things about rhythm from him. People should read very widely, and then digest what they've read.

LF: What does it feel like to be A. S. Byatt?

ASB: It feels rather good at the moment, because for a long time I went on writing all by myself and had my little audience. Suddenly, I had a very big audience. When I was talking in Boston recently, and about five people came up to me and said that I was their favorite writer. That isn't the type of thing I expect to hear. I am enjoying it, because I write as I have always written. I have another four books and about twenty stories in my head. So, I am not frightened about running out of material.

❑ 107

A CONVERSATION WITH RICHARD FORD

BY MATTHEW GILBERT

Matthew Gilbert: While you were promoting *Independence Day,* you threatened to quit writing, saying, "I don't know if I could go on being a writer if this one didn't do well." Was that for real?

Richard Ford: Writing is not an industry that I think I have to practice. It's something I choose to practice. And, for my own benefit and sense of feeling useful and encouraged, I wanted to feel like I was getting someplace, gaining a readership. I didn't want to feel like I was just being carried by my publishers. I don't think I'm worth being carried by my publishers. They carried me a long time, 20-plus years. I wanted to feel like I could do what a writer would set out to do, which is to find a large readership.

It wasn't sour grapes, it wasn't thumbing my nose, it wasn't spoilsport. I was 51 years old, young and feeling good, and I'd had the opportunity to write six good books. Maybe it was time to think about another choice of life.

The truth is, I've thought about it every time I've published a book, thought to myself, is there any need based on what I see happening here with this book to think about doing it again. And because I'm over 50, I am thinking about life with a certain kind of urgency. You think to yourself, "C'mon, c'mon, c'mon, c'mon, make this a useful life."

MG: People have a romantic view that writers have a write-or-die attitude.

RF: It's work! As I've gotten older, I seem to need to be isolated to write.

MG: Why is that?

RF: It lets me work as hard as I want to work, without distraction. I can write out in the country where it's quiet and nobody comes to visit and the phone doesn't ring. You get up and you take a walk between 12 and 2 and you don't see anybody, it's just you and the dog.

MG: You've been called an American hobo because you're constantly on the move, a writer from the South who's lived in some 12 places in 22 years. Are you still peripatetic?

RF: I've narrowed down my fields . . . to a few signal places. I go to my house up in Montana. I go to New Orleans. I've got a house in Mississippi, and if you don't count Paris, which is just an ornament on my chain, that's where I go.

MG: How do you feel about winning the Pulitzer? Is it a huge thing?

RF: I'm 52 and have been writing or trying to write books since 1968. I've written six books and every time I wrote a book I thought I'd written the best book I could possibly write. And I didn't win any awards particularly. So I got used to thinking that what I was doing was rewarding in itself. I had pretty well screwed myself down into believing that not winning awards was OK.

You can't let yourself think that you're better than you were before you got it. Because you ain't. So I'm just happy. If it encourages people to read my book, then I'm really thrilled about that. That's what I really care about.

As far as my view of myself goes, it has made me happy. It made me happy in the sense that it's like ducking a bullet. You duck the bullet of not getting it. That's the bullet I'm usually ready to receive, the bullet of not getting it. So when that bullet didn't hit me this time, I was happy. It felt freeing.

MG: Does it add a burden of expectation to what you do next?

RF: I've always had that. I've been writing pretty good books since 1982, in the sense that people have told me they were good books. Writers have written that they were good books, and people have read them and bought them, and they teach them in schools. So whatever burden I feel—which is based on the expectations of others, and I guess there's some—it's one I felt anyway.

MG: A lot of women think *Independence Day* and your other books are "guy books."

RF: That's completely wrong. There is no such thing as a guy's book. Is *Crime and Punishment* a guy's book? Is Jane Austen a gal's book? If it's a good book, it's a good book.

MG: But the hero is a man dealing with midlife issues, so maybe the book holds more for men.

RF: That's not what literature is. Literature is not a report on a specific reality. Literature is an attempt to try to make communicable—by which I mean shareable—something that is true about us all.

So I reject it completely out of hand. People who think the world is made up of women's issues and men's issues, they need to read books like mine. They need to read Jane Austen again. They need to read Charlotte Brontë again, to decide if books about women are just for women. It's those kinds of intelligences, pseudo-intelligences, that literature is actually probably most useful for.

There are lots of women in my book. They all have, in my book, strong characters. They all have lines given them which represent the fact that they absolutely control their world, or try to. The fact that the speaker of the book is a man is just one of its many formal features.

What books are trying to do is invite people to see themselves in others. Not just see themselves in the characters, but see themselves in others. But as you can tell, there's a lot of resistance to doing that, and what you just articulated was the resistance that there is out there to see oneself in others.

MG: How do you enter the process of writing a novel?

RF: It isn't as though I wander around and something pops into my head about which I say, "Oh, gee, I oughta write a novel about that." I start thinking to myself, "I'd like to write a novel now, what would I write it about?" Then I go looking through my notebooks and, depending on how long I think the book might be or what I feel I have the wherewithal for, then I try to accumulate a necessary amount of stuff. Sometimes it's lines of dialogue, sometimes it's conceptions, sometimes it's words that represent conceptions like "independence."

All of these things come out of the notebook helter-skelter. And I like that helter-skelter, because out of a seeming chaos of material, it lets me convene an order in a kind of dynamic way that's almost fun. It's a little like play. The authoritative part is there too. You're making these decisions and these will be the decisions that you will live with for the next few years. There's that sense of high authority on fate.

MG: How do you know when to stop writing?

RF: You do it until you've completely exhausted yourself. Until you really just know you couldn't generate any more lines without making it look worse. It's always the case that if you lived with the book another year, it would contain the wisdom of that year. But my belief is that whatever it would gain in that extra year would not be worth an extra year. If you keep it around long enough, you can polish that stone a little finer, but then you begin to think, "What else might I be doing, I'm a writer, what else can I learn?"

MG: Did you hesitate to write a sequel?

RF: I distrusted myself, as a person wisely should do. Ask yourself, "Am I not making a terrible mistake here?" And I thought, "Well, maybe I don't remember how hard *The Sportswriter* was to write." Or maybe these notes just represent the leavings of that other book. Which definitely is the case with notes I make now about some subsequent book about Frank. All of my notes now are the residue of the prior book and for that reason tainted.

With *Independence Day,* I kind of ran out of my own faith in it midway. Kristina [Ford's wife] had to say, "C'mon, c'mon, c'mon, c'mon, look at all this stuff." And she liked it. She had to reinflate my sense of necessity. But that happens to me. I'm such a flat-out kind of person when it comes to writing books. I kind of give it up. Sometimes I give it up and I don't get it back from the work. Somebody has to come along and tell me something encouraging, which Kristina does.

MG: The scenes between Frank and his 15-year-old son, Paul, have an intense intimacy. They seem to be the heart of *Independence Day.*

RF: They were compelling scenes to write. I would lie in bed after I'd written scenes, months after I'd written them, and think of new ways the dialogue could go. I'd get up in the middle of the night and change a word, and try to find a way for the dialogue to seem more logical. They were really where the book had to be no-nonsense and spot on. And I tried to make it spot on by brooding about it and puzzling about it.

MG: For some people, becoming a writer is a courageous move.

RF: It never seemed courageous. At no time, including now, did it ever seem like anything but a choice I made among other choices. I just happened to have made a good one, in the sense that it was one that would allow me to be useful to the lives of others, make books for them to read. I think that's great. I think that's wonderful. It's doing what great writers have done. But it doesn't require much courage. It never did.

❏ 108

A Conversation with Susan Isaacs

By Lewis Burke Frumkes

Lewis Frumkes: Susan Isaacs is one of our best-selling authors and one of our finest writers. Susan, I'll begin by asking you how your novel *Lily White,* which has received rave reviews in *The New York Times* and elsewhere, differs from your other novels.

Susan Isaacs: It is much more ambitious, because I started with a murder mystery. Lily White is a criminal defense lawyer representing a con man. The case became very fascinating: Here is this guy pulling the marriage con, accused of murdering one of his marks. Lily believes he did it, but she is a good lawyer and will defend him. Partway through it, she starts to doubt whether he actually committed the crime. Could he be covering up for somebody, and, in covering up, be performing the first decent act of his life? Or is this some other scam? So, I was really enjoying that part of it, yet I felt that somehow I needed to understand Lily better to tell about her life. Pretty soon, I realized I had to weave the two stories together—the story of the con man who betrays professionally and the story of Lily, who herself is betrayed. But, unlike the woman who dies in the book, Lily is not a victim. It is a crucial difference. I talk a lot in this book about women, about those who survive and those who do not.

LF: If you were asked to characterize this book, to place it in a genre, how would you?

SI: I wouldn't, because being the writer, my only job is to tell the best story that I possibly can. Some people say it is a mystery. Other reviewers have called it social satire, or "wildly comedic," and still others say this is my most serious book. So, I can't simply characterize it. I can either be an author, or when I review occasionally, a critic, but I can't be a critic for my own books.

LF: When you start writing, do you say, "This is going to be a funny book," or do you just write and choose at some point to make it lively or light?

SI: That happens in the telling. I don't wake up and say, "I need a snappy one-liner today." Nor, when I am writing it, do I ever think it's funny. It always amazes me when reviewers call me "the female Neil Simon," because maybe once or twice a year, I'll go, "heh, heh, heh!" Then, I move on. This is how I perceive the world, slightly bent.

LF: Sometimes when someone is telling a serious story and tries to be funny, it compromises the story. I have seen several films that I was trying to take seriously, but they tried to be funny. I thought it ruined them. They should have gone one way or the other. Your books have somehow surmounted that problem and seem at times to be hysterically funny.

SI: Well, that's it. For example, my first novel, *Shining Through,* was about a legal secretary who, by a series of very small steps, becomes a war hero. I was exploring what heroism is all about. The novel takes place against the background of the Holocaust, and yet here is essentially a cheerful, upbeat, funny woman put into a terrible situation. This happens all the time. It's not all "one-liners," and it's not all dark. It's the same with Lily White: She really has a rough time not only with the case, but in her own life; she's a survivor.

LF: *Lily White* really goes into some detail about the law. In real life, you are married to a very prominent lawyer. Did he help you with this book?

SI: Sure, he did. We've been married for 28 years. I've lived through his trials, and some of our best friends are lawyers, so I knew the technical stuff needed. But readers should never be able to see that I've done a lot of research; it has to feel authentic. If there was a phrase I needed, or if I needed a law explained to me, I would call my husband at the office, or at 11:00 at night, I'd say, "Honey, one more thing before you go to sleep." I also spoke with a lot of women lawyers, because in our culture, girls are taught to be friendly, perky, and compliant, and even feisty is O.K., but not strong. Strong makes people a little nervous. So, how does a girl go from being perky and pleasant, to fighting for a living? That's what criminal lawyers do. They earn their bread by confronting. I spoke with a lot of women litigators and cops, and I went to jail, which was an extraordinary situation. Again, I don't want all this research to show to the degree that readers see all my droplets of sweat and my hard work on the page, or I've failed as an author. I try to make it feel effortless.

LF: When did you first start writing?

SI: I started writing as a student at Queens College, for the newspaper. I really had been reading too much H. L. Mencken in those days. Everything I wrote sounded like outer-borough H. L. Mencken. From there, I got a job at *Seventeen* Magazine, writing advice to the lovelorn and doing general editorial assistant work. I stayed there for a few years and gradually rose through the ranks, really because people kept leaving, the pay was so low.

I left *Seventeen* to bring up my kids at home. I did some free-lance writing and political speechwriting. I enjoyed that, but being a political speechwriter is a full-time, late-night job. I couldn't be a mother and do that. But then I had the idea of writing a novel. I had this housewife detective, and I knew it was not a big book, or an important book, yet it was a book I had to write. It took me a year to get up the courage, and I actually bought a book called *Writing a Novel* to help me write *Compromising Positions*.

LF: As you were growing up, which writers inspired you?

SI: My mother got me a library card and said, "Here's a library," but I never had any guidance. I really didn't know about *Little Women,* for example, until I was an adult. I simply went into the library and picked whatever book I could reach. I read an awful lot about dinosaurs and a lot of historical novels about the wives of Henry VIII. The first book I really remember loving was *Auntie Mame.* It just lifted me out of Brooklyn. What a wonderful world that was! I really was not inspired by any particular writer. There were just occasional books that I liked, but on the other hand, I read everything. I never just read what people said was good for you. I lost a great deal, but I probably gained a great deal.

LF: Whom do you read now for pleasure when you are not writing?

SI: I read a lot of history and biography. As far as fiction goes, I'll read anything Anne Tyler writes and anything William Styron writes, but I like Stephen King as well.

LF: When you finish a book do you need some time off before you can begin thinking about your next project?

SI: The day after I finished *Lily White,* I knew what my next novel was going to be. The best assistant I have is my own subconscious; it does a lot of my work for me.

LF: Some people have trouble when they attempt a large work. For example, I started writing a novel and on page sixty, I realized my main character had a different name from what I'd called him in the beginning. How do you keep a complex story like *Lily White* straight?

SI: That was the hardest thing, and I was very scared. I was interweaving these two stories, and while it's a clever idea, it had to be absolutely clear to the reader who was talking. I hate books in which you do not know who is saying what. The outlines for my first six novels took me three to four weeks each; the *Lily White* outline took me one year. I mapped out exactly what was going to happen. During the writing, which took two years, the characters sometimes said, "Guess what? I am going to pull a surprise on you." I let that happen, but I had to know where I was going, especially when part of the book was a murder mystery. It had to succeed on that level. If it didn't, it wasn't going to succeed on any other level.

As for characters' names, in the beginning I draw up a list of everyone described in the outline. Naming people is very special. In fact, the name Lily White just happened. Once I saw it, I realized it was right.

LF: What advice would you give to writers starting out?

SI: I think you should get on with your life: Stay away from MFA writing programs and writing workshops. A short workshop occasionally will do, but if you are too involved with writing programs, you stop writing for yourself and begin writing for the instructor. Keep in mind that the person to write for is yourself. Tell the story that you most desperately want to read; no one will write it for you.

LF: Do you work on a word processor or write in longhand?

SI: I work on a word processor now. I wrote my first book on a typewriter, but there are only so many times you are willing to retype. With a word processor, there are no excuses. You can keep changing what you're writing until it's absolutely the way you want it, and you just print it out. I think it really makes for better writing. Having said that, I think that making chicken soup, making love, and writing are all idiosyncratic acts. No two people do it the same way; you have to follow your instincts.

❑ 109

A Conversation with Jane Yolen

By John Koch

John Koch: It's hard to imagine your having writer's block.

Jane Yolen: I don't—because I have so many projects that I'm in the middle of. Some people are pony express writers: They get on one horse and ride it until they get where they're going. Some are able to hook two matched bays together and drive them to the finish line. Some drive troikas. I'm a mule-train driver: I hook up 24 of these little suckers, and maybe one of them dies along the way, and I cut it out of the traces and keep going. So, by the time I get to the end, I've got 23!

JK: Do you really love the writing process? Many writers say they find it painful.

JY: I think they're crazy. I'm spending all day, every day—no holidays—writing. Well, I must admit, the day my granddaughter was born, 10 months ago, I didn't write. I write on the road. I write all the time. Why on earth would anyone who found the process painful do it all the time, unless they are masochists of the first order?

JK: Do you ever get entranced when you write?

JY: When I'm really *in* a book, yes. "Transportation" is really the word: You are transported in the old sense. I did a book a number of years ago called *Children of the Wolf,* which takes place in India in the 1920s, about two children who were supposedly found in a wolf's den. I had done a lot of research about India and the Sal Forest, and I remember idly writing a scene in which they're traveling through the forest, and the sound that the cart was making, and the look of a tiger and its cubs, and the sounds of the monkeys. And as I was writing it, the phone rang, and I felt as if I were swimming up out of somewhere beautiful to find . . . I wasn't even sure what it was. The phone was such a foreign and alien sound in the Sal Forest that it took me a minute to find my way back to the phone, right by my hand.

JK: Do you always know where a book you're writing is going?

JY: Rarely. I keep on writing because I want to know what's going to happen to my characters. I've had a book in which a bunch of elves walked in, and I said, "No elves in this book." And they said, "We're here." And I said, "No, you're not. Go away." And I blocked for three weeks until I figured out why they were there. So, sometimes, characters simply walk on and sort of have squatters' rights until you figure out exactly why they're there.

JK: You skillfully take readers to fantastic realms. How do you evoke them?

JY: So much of what you see now in children's books or on television, and in movies and adult books, is: "Give me everything; spell it all out. Tell me all the details, down to the last gory drop of blood." And I'm not talking just about violence. I'm really of the school of intimation and suggestion. I think, for example, that *The Turn of the Screw* and *The Haunting of Hill House,* are scarier than any of Stephen King's stuff. That's also saying to the reader: "I think you're smarter than these other people are giving you credit for. I think you can bring a lot of that to the story yourself, that you want to go to that part of you that nobody's touching anymore."

JK: In *Briar Rose,* you suggest that we need stories to survive.

JY: Human beings are animals that tell stories with a beginning, middle, and end, irony, complicated plotting, flash-forwards, and flashbacks. Within that kind of storytelling, we define ourselves, our history, our relationships among peoples. It's a way of remembering. Story really is the bedrock of civilization. If you ask me "What was the greatest story ever told?" I'd say "King Arthur—with a little more emphasis on the girls."

❑ 110

A CONVERSATION WITH DAVID BALDACCI

BY LEWIS BURKE FRUMKES

Lewis Frumkes: David Baldacci is probably best-known for his first novel, *Absolute Power,* a bestseller that was made into a hit movie starring Clint Eastwood. His second novel, *Total Control* (Warner Books), was also a bestseller.

You are a lawyer by trade. I want to begin by asking you what gave you the idea to write *Absolute Power?*

David Baldacci: I had been living in Washington and interested in the presidency for a long time. What interests me about the office is the abuse of power and what the office can turn someone into. You could be a relatively normal person running for the presidency, but it can change you. I started out in my novel with a president who's not a nice person. He'd engaged in an affair. For me, that opening was a really good start for a book because so many things can emanate from that situation. With that story in mind, I sat down to write it. I spent about two years doing it, but I had a lot of fun.

LF: When you wrote *Absolute Power* you must have had fantasies of big success. Everyone who writes does, but you really hit it with your first novel. What did you think about when you were writing it?

DB: I always wanted to write for a living, but I thought way back when that I didn't have the skills to do it. I took a long-term approach to it. I seriously began to write fiction about thirteen years ago when I started law school. First, I just tried to learn the craft. I never finished any stories for about five years. I worked on dialogue, pacing, and creating characters. I wrote short stories for about three years and got lots of rejections. Then, I wrote screenplays, which also were rejected, but eventually, they got some interest in Hollywood.

When I came up with the idea for *Absolute Power*, I thought, "Let's see if you can do a novel now. Write the book. Maybe something will happen. If it doesn't, write another one." You may write fifty books and none of them is published, but you keep going. That's what my plan was—just keep going. Things began to fall into place: I got a lot of interest from agents, and Erin Priest, a wonderful agent, ended up representing me. The book went out on Monday, Warner Books snapped it up, and I was wealthy on Tuesday. It was bizarre that it all happened so fast.

LF: I asked Dave Barry what it was like winning the Pulitzer Prize. He said it made the next column the most difficult he had ever done. Amy Tan and others have spoken about hitting a big first book and having the world watching for the second book. Now, you've come out with a very exciting second book called *Total Control*. How much pressure was on you after your success with *Absolute Power*, or did the success of the first book alleviate the pressure?

DB: I wasn't sure *Absolute Power* would really sell. While looking for an agent, I came up with the idea for *Total Control*. I started plotting it before I'd sold *Absolute Power*. So, the pressure wasn't really there at that point. I try not to worry about what other people think, or about their expectations. You cannot control that. You can control yourself and what you do. Write as good a story as you can, and the other things will fall into place.

People compare the two books, but they are very different. It is important to me not to become formulaic. I would like to write something different each time. I continue to write screenplays. That's another creative outlet for me. I am now financially secure. If I can't turn out a good book every year, so be it. I am not locked into multiple contracts. If it takes me four years to write my next one, it takes me four years. I started out writing short stories. If you sell a short story, the pay-off is you get a free copy of the magazine. I didn't start writing to make a million dollars. That is the attitude I want to keep.

LF: In *Total Control* you have done a very fascinating thing. Most people with a fear of flying are people who like to have total control, and when flying, they have to relinquish control to the pilot. Your first chapter is a thrilling and terrifying chapter, especially to those people afraid of flying. How did that first chapter come about?

DB: I like to hit the ground running with my books. I want to get the reader immediately involved with my story. With a strong opening, I am telling the reader, "This is the way it's going to be throughout this book." You're right about "total control." The airplane, technology, and finances in *Total Control* are three things that you have no control over. Other people are in control, and can be manipulated by people who have access. The story is basically about three people. Sidney Archer is a wife who has a very nice life. All of a sudden her life is turned upside down. Her husband is gone, and he's accused of all these crimes. What carries the novel for me is her fight and belief that her husband is innocent and her fight to find out the truth because she believes he could not have done these things. Somebody else did, and she's going to find out who it is. The book has the veneer of a lot of these technological issues and some other interesting subject matter, but that is all wound around this emotional trauma for this person. Without the characters, the story may be interesting, but it doesn't fly nearly as well.

LF: Some novelists plot their books meticulously; other novels are character-driven. Do you fit into either of those categories?

DB: I am very much the latter. My story evolves over time. I'll start out with a little notebook. On the first page, I plot out what I thought I wanted the story to be. After I finished *Total Control,* I went back and looked at the first page. None of it was in the book; it just evolved for me. You don't need to write every day because if you do not have anything to write about, it builds frustration. But you need to think every day. You need to sit down and think in the most precise detail possible. When you are ready to write, then you write. Then, the flow is going to come. In thrillers and mysteries, the plots are intricate. You really cannot have any glaring omissions or gaps that readers can pick up. For days at a time, I sit down and go through even the tiniest piece of information and get it all set in my head. While I'm writing I may think of something else, and I'll go completely off. I can't write from a sixty-page outline. That would blow the whole process for me.

LF: Are you afraid that there may be copycat incidences based upon what happens in your first chapter?

DB: The way I did it sounds really cool in the book, but I don't think it's plausible because it is completely unreliable. It could either happen or not happen. I've read other books where they describe how a character is going to sabotage an airliner, and it could actually work the way they describe it. I didn't want to approach a story that way.

LF: Who were some of the writers who inspired you when you were growing up?

DB: John Updike, John Irving, Mark Twain, Conan Doyle (not just Sherlock Holmes, but a lot of the other things he wrote) were the writers I admired. Mysteries with Agatha Christie, her plotting was so meticulous. I try to read a lot of different types of writers. I don't just read thrillers. I read everybody from Ludlum to Joyce Carol Oates because I feel that you can learn from good writers regardless of what they write about.

LF: Whose work among the contemporary thriller writers do you like?

DB: For the depth of her research and her authoritative tone, Patricia Cornwell is one that I admire. Ludlum is another. On the techno-thriller side, Tom Clancy, who weaves together multi-plots and a huge cast of characters. He does it very well and is a very strong writer. I admire the things he writes about and the intelligence he brings to his work.

LF: When you write, do you work on a word processor or longhand? When do you work? How do you work?

DB: I use a computer. I tend to work during the day and sometimes at night. I don't have a schedule. I work at home. I have two young kids. I'll get up and work for a few hours. Then, spend time with them and work again in the afternoon. It's whenever I feel I have something to say. I do work at it every day. If I am not thinking about it or researching it, I will actually be writing something. It is my occupation now, and I treat it seriously.

LF: You obviously enjoy language and literature. Do you have a favorite word or words that surface a lot or that you are attracted to?

DB: Some people say I use a lot of the same verbs. My verbs tend to be very active like *plunged* or *hurdled.* I like the fast pace and the action, but with total control, I try to delve more into the emotional side, more tender words trying to describe how a character is actually feeling. I guess I am a fan of most of the words I use in my books. I can't say that I have any particular favorites.

LF: Have you thought of writing in other genres?

DB: I have a dozen short stories at home that remain unpublished. A screenplay that I wrote four years ago is a character piece about a grandmother and her grandson and how their lives change. It is actually in the process of being optioned by a production company in Los Angeles. It's not a thriller. It is an emotional piece about family. One of my other screenplays deals with a historical fantasy involving a child. There are a lot of different things that I'd like to write about. I have done some opinion pieces for my old law school. My interests do not lie only in the thriller genre.

LF: What advice would you give aspiring writers?

DB: Don't say, "I should take the next two years to sit down and write a novel." Take a few years and learn how to write well. Learn the craft. Don't finish anything. Read everything you can and practice. Try to build a character to the point at which you can see the person and how he moves and acts. Practice writing dialogue until a reader would say it sounds like two people talking. Then, start with a short story, and after you've done that for a few years, try to construct a novel that is a major work. Look at it long-term. You may have raw talent as a writer. There is a big difference between having raw talent and having the skill it takes to write a book. You have to have patience and perseverance. Don't try to do too much too soon.

Where to Sell

Where to Sell

All information in these lists concerning the needs and requirements of magazines, book publishing companies, and theaters comes directly from the editors, publishers, and directors, but personnel and addresses change, as do requirements. No published listing can give as clear a picture of editorial needs and tastes as a careful study of several issues of a magazine or a book catalogue, and writers should never submit material without first thoroughly researching the prospective market. If a magazine is not available in the local library or on the newsstand, write directly to the editor for the price of a sample copy; contact the publicity department of a book publisher for an up-to-date catalogue, or a theater for a current schedule. Many companies also offer a formal set of writers guidelines, available for an SASE (self-addressed, stamped envelope) upon request.

While some of the more established markets may seem difficult to break into, especially for the beginner, there are thousands of lesser-known publications where editors will consider submissions from first-time free lancers.

All manuscripts must be typed double-space and submitted with self-addressed envelopes bearing postage sufficient for the return of the material. If a manuscript need not be returned, note this with the submission, and enclose an SASE or a self-addressed, stamped postcard for editorial reply. Use good white paper; onion skin and erasable bond are not acceptable. *Always* keep a copy of the manuscript, since occasionally material is lost in the mail. Magazines may take several weeks, or longer, to read and report on submissions. If an editor has not reported on a manuscript after a reasonable length of time, write a brief, courteous letter of inquiry.

Some publishers will accept, and may in fact prefer, work submitted on computer disk, usually noting the procedure and type of disk in their writers guidelines.

ARTICLE MARKETS

The magazines in the following list are in the market for free-lance articles in many categories. Unless listings state otherwise, a writer should submit a query first, including a brief description of the proposed article and any relevant qualifications or credits. A few editors want to see samples of published work, if available.

Submit photos or slides *only* if the editor has specifically requested them. A self-addressed envelope with postage sufficient to cover the return of the manuscript or the answer to a query should accompany all submissions.

GENERAL-INTEREST PUBLICATIONS

AIR & SPACE/SMITHSONIAN—901 D St. S.W., 10th Fl., Washington, DC 20024-2518. George Larson, Ed. General-interest articles, 1,000 to 3,500 words, on aerospace experience, past, present, and future. Pays varying rates, on acceptance. Query.

AIR FORCE TIMES—See *Times News Service.*

AMERICAN HERITAGE— 60 Fifth Ave., New York, NY 10011. Richard F. Snow, Ed. Articles, 750 to 5,000 words, on U.S. history and background of American life and culture from the beginning to recent times. No fiction. Pays $300 to $1,500, on acceptance. Query.

AMERICAN JOURNALISM REVIEW— 8701 Adelphi Rd., Adelphi, MD 20783. Rem Rieder, Ed. Articles, 500 to 5,000 words, on print and electronic journalism. Pays 20¢ a word, on publication. Query.

THE AMERICAN LEGION—Box 1055, Indianapolis, IN 46206. Joe Stuteville, Ed. Articles, 750 to 2,000 words, on current world affairs, public policy, and subjects of contemporary interest. Payment is negotiable, on acceptance. Query.

AMERICAN VISIONS, THE MAGAZINE OF AFRO-AMERICAN CULTURE—1156 15th St. N.W., Suite 615, Washington, DC 20005. Joanne Harris, Ed. Articles, 1,500 words, and columns, 750 to 2,000 words, on African-American history and culture with a focus on the arts. Pays from $100 to $1,000, after publication. Query.

AMERICAS—OAS, 19th and Constitution Ave. N.W., Washington, DC 20006. James Patrick Kiernan, Dir. & Ed. Rebecca Read Medrano, Man. Ed. Features, 2,500 to 4,000 words, on Latin America and the Caribbean. Wide focus: anthropology, the arts, travel, science, and development. "We prefer stories that can be well illustrated." No political material. Pays from $400, on publication. Query.

ARMY TIMES—See *Times News Service.*

ASIAN PAGES—P.O. Box 11932, St. Paul, MN 55111-0932. Cheryl Weiberg, Ed.-in-Chief. Bimonthly newspaper tabloid. Profiles and news events, 500 words; short stories, 500 to 750 words; poetry, 100 words; and Asianrelated fillers, 50 words. "All material must have a strong, non-offensive Asian slant." Pays $40 for articles, $25 for photos/cartoons, on publication.

THE ATLANTIC MONTHLY—77 N. Washington St., Boston, MA 02114. William Whitworth, Ed. Non-polemical, meticulously researched articles on public issues, politics, social sciences, education, business, literature, and the arts. Ideal length: 3,000 to 6,000 words, though short pieces, 1,000 to 2,000 words, are also welcome and longer text pieces will be considered. Pays excellent rates.

BON APPETIT— 6300 Wilshire Blvd., Los Angeles, CA 90048. Barbara Fairchild, Exec. Ed. Articles on fine cooking (menu format or single focus), cooking classes, and gastronomically focused travel. Pays varying rates, on acceptance; buys all rights. Query with samples of published work.

CAPPER'S—1503 S.W. 42nd St., Topeka, KS 66609-1265. Nancy Peavler, Ed. Articles, 300 to 500 words: human-interest, personal experience for family section, historical. Payment varies, on publication.

CHANGE—1319 18th St. N.W., Washington, DC 20036. Attn: Ed. Dept. Well-researched features, 2,500 to 3,500 words, on programs, people, and institutions of higher education; and columns, 700 to 2,000 words. "We can't usually pay for unsolicited articles."

THE CHRISTIAN SCIENCE MONITOR— One Norway St., Boston, MA 02115. Jane A. Lampmann, Features Ed. Articles, 800 words, on arts and entertainment, education, lifestyle, family, science and technology, sports, travel, food, profiles; essays and poetry on the"Home Forum Page"; guest columns for "Opinion Page." Pay varies, on acceptance. Original material only, exclusive rights for 90 days.

CHRONICLES—The Rockford Institute, 934 N. Main St., Rockford, IL 61103. Thomas Fleming, Ed. "A Magazine of American Culture." Articles and poetry that displays craftsmanship and a sense of form. "Read the magazine first to get a feel for what we do." No fiction, fillers or jokes. Payment varies.

COLUMBIA—1 Columbus Plaza, New Haven, CT 06510-3326. Richard McMunn, Ed. Journal of the Knights of Columbus. Articles, 500 to 1,500 words, on a wide variety of topics of interest to K. of C. members, their families, and the Catholic layman: current events, religion, education, art, etc., illustrated with color photos. Pays $250 to $500, on acceptance.

THE COMPASS—365 Washington Ave., Brooklyn, NY 11238. J.A. Randall, Ed. True stories, to 1,500 words, on the sea, sea trades, and aviation. Pays to $1,000, on acceptance. Query with SASE.

CONSUMERS DIGEST—5705 N. Lincoln Ave., Chicago, IL 60659. John Manos, Ed. Articles, 500 to 3,000 words, on subjects of interest to consumers: products and services, automobiles, health, fitness, consumer legal affairs, and personal money management. Photos. Pays from 35¢ to 50¢ a word, extra for photos, on publication. Buys all rights. Query with resumé and published clips.

COSMOPOLITAN—224 W. 57th St., New York, NY 10019. Bonnie Fuller, Ed. Guy Flatley, Man. Ed. Articles, to 3,000 words, and features, 500 to 2,000 words, on issues affecting young career women. Query.

COUNTRY JOURNAL— 4 High Ridge Park, Stamford, CT 06905. Cristin Marandino, Assoc. Ed. Articles, 500 to 1,500 words, for country and small-town residents. Helpful, authoritative pieces; how-to projects, small-scale farming, and gardening. Pays $75 to $500, on acceptance. Send SASE for guidelines. Query with SASE.

EBONY— 820 S. Michigan, Chicago, IL 60605. Lerone Bennett, Jr., Exec. Ed. No free-lance material.

THE ELKS MAGAZINE— 425 W. Diversey Parkway, Chicago, IL 60614. Judith L. Keogh, Man. Ed. Articles, 1,500 to 3,000 words, on technology, business, sports, and topics of current interest, for non-urban audience with above-average income. Pays 15¢ to 20¢ a word, on acceptance. Query with SASE.

EMERGE—BET Plaza, 1900 W. Place N.E., Washington, DC 20018. Florestine Purnell, Man. Ed. "Black America's Newsmagazine." Articles, 1,200 to 2,000 words, on current issues, ideas, or news personalities of interest to successful, well-informed African-Americans. Department pieces, 650 to 700 words, on a number of subjects. Pays 50¢ a word, on publication. Query.

ESQUIRE—250 W. 55th St., New York, NY 10019. Edward Kosner, Ed.-in-Chief. Randall Rothonborg, Ed. Dir. David Hirshey, Deputy Ed. Articles, 2,500 to 6,500 words, for intelligent adult audience. Pay varies, on acceptance. Query with published clips; complete manuscripts from unpublished writers. SASE required.

ESSENCE—1500 Broadway, New York, NY 10036. Susan L. Taylor, Ed.-in-Chief. Linda Villarosa, Exec. Ed. Provocative articles, 800 to 2,500 words, about black women in America today: self-help, how-to pieces, business and finance, work, parenting, health, celebrity profiles, and political issues. Pays varying rates, on acceptance. Query required.

EVERY WEDNESDAY—2519 N. Charles St., Baltimore, MD 21218. Avonie Brown, Ed. Illustrated feature articles, 750 to 1,000 words, on subjects covering the arts and entertainment of interests of African Americans. Pay varies, on publication. Query.

FAMILY CIRCLE—375 Lexington Ave., New York, NY 10017. Nancy Clark, Deputy Ed. Articles, to 2,000 words, on "women who have made a difference," marriage, family, and child-rearing issues; consumer affairs, health and fitness, humor and psychology. Pays top rates, on acceptance. Query required.

GLAMOUR—350 Madison Ave., New York, NY 10017. Ruth Whitney, Ed.-in-Chief. Pamela Erens, Articles Ed. Editorial approach is "how-to" for women, 18 to 35. Articles on careers, health, psychology, interpersonal relationships, etc. Fashion, health, and beauty material staff-written. Pays from $1,000 for 1,500-to 2,000-word articles, from $1,500 for longer pieces, on acceptance.

GLOBE—5401 N.W. Broken Sound Blvd., Boca Raton, FL 33487. Robert Taylor, Man. Ed. Factual articles, 500 to 1,000 words, with photos: exposés, celebrity interviews, consumer and human-interest pieces. Pays $50 to $1,500.

GOOD HOUSEKEEPING— 959 Eighth Ave., New York, NY 10019. Evelyn Renold, Articles Ed. Articles, 2,500 words, on a unique or trend-setting event; family relationships; personal medical pieces dealing with an unusual illness, treatment, and result; personal problems and how they were solved. Short essays, 750 to 1,000 words, on family life or relationships. Pays first-time writers $500 to $750 for short, essay-type articles; $1,500 to $2,000 for full-length articles, on acceptance. "Payment scale rises for writers with whom we work frequently." Buys all rights, though the writer retains the right to use material from the article as part of a book project. Queries preferred. Guidelines.

GRIT—1503 S.W. 42nd St., Topeka, KS 66609. Donna Doyle, Ed.-in-Chief. Articles, 500 to 1,200 words, on people, home, garden, lifestyle, friends and family, reminisces, grandparenting, Americana, American history and traditions, travel. Short fiction, 1,000 to 2,000 words (send to Fiction Ed.). SASE required. Pays 22¢ a word, extra for photos. Send complete manscript with photos. Send for guidelines and sample issue.

HARPER'S BAZAAR—1700 Broadway, 37th Fl., New York, NY 10019. Elizabeth Tilberis, Ed.-in-Chief. Articles for sophisticated women on current issues, books, art, film, travel, fashion and beauty. Send queries with one-to three-paragraph proposal; include clips and SASE. Rarely accepts fiction. Payment varies.

HARPER'S MAGAZINE— 666 Broadway, New York, NY 10012. Attn: Ed. Articles, 2,000 to 5,000 words. Query with SASE required. Very limited market.

HISTORIC PRESERVATION—1785 Massachusetts Ave. N.W., Washington, DC 20036. Anne Elizabeth Powell, Ed. Feature articles from published writers, 1,500 to 4,000 words, on residential restoration, preservation issues, and people involved in preserving America's heritage. Mostly staff-written. Query.

HOUSE BEAUTIFUL—1700 Broadway, New York, NY 10019. Elaine Greene, Features Ed. Articles related to the home. Pieces on architecture, design, travel, and gardening. One personal memoir each month, "Thoughts of Home," with high literary standards. Pays varying rates, on acceptance. Query with detailed outline and SASE. Guidelines.

IDEALS—P.O. Box 305300, Nashville, TN 37230. Lisa Ragan, Ed. Articles, 800 to 1,000 words; poetry, 12 to 50 lines. Light, nostalgic pieces. Payment varies. SASE for guidelines.

INQUIRER MAGAZINE—*Philadelphia Inquirer,* P.O. Box 8263, 400 N. Broad St., Philadelphia, PA 19101. Ms. Avery Rome, Ed. Local-interest features, 500 to 7,000 words. Profiles of national figures in politics, entertainment, etc. Pays varying rates, on publication. Currently overstocked; not accepting any free-lance submissions at this time.

KIWANIS—3636 Woodview Trace, Indianapolis, IN 46268. Chuck Jonak, Man. Ed. Articles, 2,500 words, on home; family; international issues; the social, health, and emotional needs of youth (especially under age 6); career and community concerns of business and professional people. No travel pieces, interviews, profiles. Pays $400 to $1,000, on acceptance. Query. Send SASE for guidelines.

LADIES' HOME JOURNAL— 125 Park Ave., New York, NY 10017. Susan Crandell, Exec. Ed. Articles on contemporary subjects of interest to women. "See masthead for specific-topic editors and address appropriate editor." Query with SASE required.

LISTEN MAGAZINE—55 W. Oak Ridge Dr., Hagerstown, MD 21740. Lincoln Steed, Ed. Articles, 1,000 to 1,200 words, on problems of alcohol and drug abuse, for teenagers; personality profiles; self-improvement articles, and drug-free activities. Photos. Pays 5¢ to 7¢ a word, extra for photos, on acceptance. Guidelines. Sample issues available. Query.

MCCALL'S—110 Fifth Ave., New York, NY 10011. Attn: Articles Ed. Articles, 1,000 to 1,800 words, on current issues, human interest, family relationships. Payment varies, on acceptance. SASE.

MADEMOISELLE—350 Madison Ave., New York, NY 10017. Faye Haun, Man. Ed. Articles, 750 to 2,500 words, on subjects of interest to single, working women in their twenties. Reporting pieces, essays, first-person accounts, and humor; how-tos on personal relationships, work, and fitness. No fiction. Pays excellent rates, on acceptance. SASE required. Query with clips.

MANGAJIN—P.O. Box 77188, Atlanta, GA 30357-1188. Articles, profiles, and book reviews, 1,000 to 1,500 words on Japanese pop culture. Query the editors. Pays $150 to $500, on publication.

METROPOLITAN HOME—1633 Broadway, New York, NY 10019. Attn: Michael Lassell, Articles Dept. Service and informational articles for residents of houses, co-ops, lofts, and condominiums, on real estate, equity, wine and spirits, collecting, etc. Interior design and home furnishing articles with emphasis on lifestyle. Pay varies. Query with clips.

THE MOTHER EARTH NEWS—49 E. 21st St., 11th Fl., New York, NY 10010. Matthew Scanlon, Ed. Articles for rural and urban readers: home improvements, how-tos, indoor and outdoor gardening, family pastimes, health, food, ecology, energy, and consumerism. Pays varying rates, on acceptance.

MOTHER JONES—731 Market St., Suite 600, San Francisco, CA 94103. Jeffrey Klein, Ed. Investigative articles, political essays, cultural analyses, multicultural issues. "OutFront" pieces, 250 to 500 words. Query with SASE.

MS.—135 W. 50th St., New York, NY 10027. Attn: Manuscript Ed. Articles relating to feminism, women's roles, and social change; reporting, essays, theory, and analysis. No poetry or fiction. Pays market rates. Query with resumé, clips, and SASE.

NATIONAL ENQUIRER—Lantana, FL 33464. Attn: C. Montgomery. Mass audience: topical news, the occult, how-to, scientific discoveries, human drama, adventure, personalities. Photos. Query (2 to 3 sentences, with source) with SASE.

NAVY TIMES—See *Times News Service.*

NEW WOMAN—2 Park Ave., 11th Fl., New York, NY 10016. Attn: Manuscripts and Proposals. Articles, 500 to 2,500 words, on relationships/sex and psychology, health news; book excerpts, essays, personal experience, and some travel. Submit seasonal material at least 5 months in advance. Simultaneous submissions. Reports in 3 months. Send #10 SASE for writer's guidelines. Pay varies.

THE NEW YORK TIMES MAGAZINE—229 W. 43rd St., New York, NY 10036. Attn: Articles Ed. Timely articles, approximately 3,000 words, on news items, forthcoming events, trends, culture, entertainment, etc. Pays to $2,500 for major articles, on acceptance. Query with clips.

THE NEW YORKER—20 W. 43rd St., New York, NY 10036. Send submissions to appropriate Editor (Fact, Fiction, or Poetry). Factual and biographical articles for "Profiles," "Reporter at Large," etc. Pays good rates, on acceptance. Query.

NEWSWEEK—251 W. 57th St., New York, NY 10019-1894. Attn: My Turn. Original opinion essays, 1,000 to 1,100 words, for "My Turn" column;

must contain verifiable facts. Submit manuscript with SASE. Pays $1,000, on publication.

PARADE—711 Third Ave., New York, NY 10017. Articles Ed. National Sunday newspaper magazine. Factual and authoritative articles, 1,200 to 1,500 words, on subjects of national interest: social issues, common health concerns, sports, community problem-solving, and extraordinary acheivements of ordinary people. "We seek unique angles on all topics." No fiction, poetry, cartoons, games, nostalgia, quotes, or puzzles. Pays from $1,000. Query with two writing samples and SASE.

PENTHOUSE—277 Park Ave., 4th Fl., New York, NY 10172-0003. Peter Bloch, Ed. Lavada B. Nahon, Sr. Ed. General-interest or controversial articles, to 5,000 words. Pays to $1 a word, on acceptance.

PEOPLE WEEKLY—Time-Life Bldg., Rockefeller Ctr., New York, NY 10020. John Saar, Asst. Man. Ed. "Vast majority of material is staff-written." Will consider article proposals, 3 to 4 paragraphs, on timely, entertaining, and topical personalities. Pays good rates, on acceptance.

PLAYBOY— 680 N. Lake Shore Dr., Chicago, IL 60611. Stephen Randall, Articles Ed. Sophisticated articles, 4,000 to 6,000 words, of interest to urban men. Humor, satire. Pays on acceptance. Query.

PLAYGIRL— 801 Second Ave., New York, NY 10017. Patrice Baldwin, Man. Ed. Articles, 1,500 to 3,500 words, on sexuality, relationships, and celebrities for women ages 18 and up. Query with clips. Fiction and nonfiction. Pays negotiable rates, after acceptance.

PSYCHOLOGY TODAY—Sussex Publishing, 49 E. 21st St., New York, NY 10010. Peter Doskoch, Exec. Ed. Bimonthly. Articles, 200 to 500 words, on general interest psychological research. No personal "memoir-style" stories, please. Pays varying rates, on publication.

QUEEN'S QUARTERLY—Queens Univ., Kingston, Ont., Canada K7L 3N6. Boris Castel, Ed. Articles, to 5,000 words, on a wide range of topics, and fiction, to 5,000 words. Poetry; send no more than 6 poems. B&W art. Pays to $400, on publication.

READER'S DIGEST—Pleasantville, NY 10570. Kenneth Tomlinson, Ed.-in-Chief. Unsolicited manuscripts will not be read or returned. General-interest articles already in print and well-developed story proposals will be considered. Send reprint or query to any editor on the masthead.

REAL PEOPLE— 450 7th Ave., Suite 1701, New York, NY 10123-0073. Alex Polner, Ed. True stories, to 500 words, on interesting people, strange occupations and hobbies, eye opening stories about people, places and odd happenings. Pays $25 to $50, on publication; send submissions to "Real Shorts," Brad Hamilton, Ed. Query for interviews, 1,000 to 1,800 words, with movie or TV actors, musicians, and other entertainment celebrities. Pays $150 to $350, on publication. SASE.

REDBOOK—224 W. 57th St., New York, NY 10019. Pamela Lister, Sr. Ed. Toni Gerber Hope, Sr. Ed. Articles, 1,000 to 2,500 words, on subjects related to relationships, marriage, sex, current social issues, crime, human interest, health, psychology, and parenting. Payment varies, on acceptance. Query with clips.

ROLLING STONE—1290 Ave. of the Americas, 2nd Fl., New York, NY 10104. Attn: Ed. Magazine of American music, culture, and politics. No fiction. "We rarely accept free-lance material." Query.

THE ROTARIAN—1560 Sherman Ave., Evanston, IL 60201-3698. Charles W. Pratt, Ed. Articles, 1,200 to 2,000 words, on international social and economic issues, business and management, human relationships, travel, sports, environment, science and technology; humor. Pays good rates, on acceptance. Query.

RUSSIAN LIFE—89 Main St., #2, Montpelier, VT 05602-2948. Mikhail Ivanov, Ed. Articles, 1,000 to 3,000 words, on Russian culture, travel, history, politics, art, business and society. "We do not want stories about personal trips to Russia, editorials on developments in Russia, or articles that promote the services of a specific company, organization, or government agency." Query. Pays 7¢ to 10¢ a word; $20 to $30 per photo, on publication.

THE SATURDAY EVENING POST—1100 Waterway Blvd., Indianapolis, IN 46202. Ted Kreiter, Exec. Ed. Family-oriented articles, 1,500 to 3,000 words: humor, preventive medicine, destination-oriented travel pieces (not personal experience), celebrity profiles, the arts, and sciences. Pays varying rates, on publication. Queries preferred.

SMITHSONIAN MAGAZINE—900 Jefferson Dr., Washington, DC 20560. Marlane A. Liddell, Articles Ed. Articles on history, art, natural history, physical science, profiles, etc. Query with clips.

SOAP OPERA DIGEST—45 W. 25th St., New York, NY 10010. Jason Bonderoff, Deputy Ed. Roberta Caploe, Carolyn Hinsey, Man. Eds. Investigative reports and profiles, to 1,500 words, about New York- or Los Angeles-based soaps. Pays from $250, on acceptance. Query with clips.

SPORTS ILLUSTRATED—1271 Ave. of the Americas, New York, NY 10020. Chris Hunt, Articles Ed. Query. Rarely uses free-lance material.

STAR—660 White Plains Rd., Tarrytown, NY 10591. Attn: Ed. Dept. Topical articles, 50 to 800 words, on show business and celebrities. Pays varying rates.

SUCCESS—733 Third Ave., 10th Fl., New York, NY 10017. Scott DeGarmo, Pub./Ed.-in-Chief. Profiles of successful executives, entrepreneurs; management science, psychology, behavior, and motivation articles, 500 to 3,500 words. Query.

TIMES NEWS SERVICE—Army Times Publishing Co., Springfield, VA 22159. Attn: R&R Ed. Articles, 500 to 750 words, that are informative, helpful, entertaining, and stimulating to a military audience for "R&R" newspaper section. Pays $75 to $100, on acceptance. Also, 1,000-to 1,200-word articles on careers after military service, travel, finance, and education for *Army Times, Navy Times,* and *Air Force Times.* Address Supplements Ed. Pays $125 to $275, on acceptance. Guidelines.

THE TOASTMASTER—P.O. Box 9052, Mission Viejo, CA 92690. Suzanne Frey, Ed. Articles, 1,500 to 2,500 words, on decision making, leadership, language, interpersonal and professional communication, humor, logical thinking, rhetorical devices, public speaking in general, profiles of great orators, speaking techniques, etc. Pays $100 to $250, on acceptance.

TOWN & COUNTRY—1700 Broadway, New York, NY 10019. Pamela Fiori, Ed.-in-Chief. Considers one-page proposals for articles. Include clips and resumé. Rarely buys unsolicited manuscripts.

TRAVEL & LEISURE—1120 Ave. of the Americas, New York, NY 10036. Nancy Novogrod, Ed.-in-Chief. Articles, 800 to 3,000 words, on destinations and travel-related activities. Regional pieces for regional editions. Pays varying rates, on acceptance. Query.

TROPIC—*The Miami Herald*, One Herald Plaza, Miami, FL 33132. Tom Shroder, Exec. Ed. Essays and articles, 1,000 to 4,000 words, on current trends and issues, light or heavy, for sophisticated audience. No short fiction (under 900 words) or poetry. Limited humor. Pays $200 to $1,000, on publication. SASE. Allow 4 to 6 weeks for response.

TV GUIDE—Radnor, PA 19088. Barry Golson, Exec. Ed. Short, light, brightly written pieces about humorous or offbeat angles of television and industry trends. (Majority of personality pieces are staff-written.) Pays on acceptance. Query.

VANITY FAIR—350 Madison Ave., New York, NY 10017. Attn: Submissions (Specify News, Arts, or Culture). Pays on acceptance. Query.

VILLAGE VOICE—36 Cooper Sq., New York, NY 10003. Doug Simmons, Man. Ed. Articles, 500 to 2,000 words, on current or controversial topics. Pays $100 to $1,500, on acceptance. Query or send manuscript with SASE.

WASHINGTON POST MAGAZINE—*The Washington Post,* 1150 15th St. N.W., Washington, DC 20071. John Cotter, Sr. Ed. Essays, profiles, and Washington-oriented general-interest pieces, to 5,000 words, on business, arts and culture, politics, science, sports, education, children, relationships, behavior, etc. Pays from $1,000, after acceptance.

WOMAN'S DAY—1633 Broadway, New York, NY 10019. Stephanie Abarbanel, Sr. Articles Ed. Articles, 500 to 2,000 words, on subjects of interest to women: marriage, education, family health, child rearing, money management, interpersonal relationships, changing lifestyles, etc. Dramatic first-person narratives about women who have experienced medical miracles or other triumphs, or have overcome common problems, such as alcoholism. SASE required. Pays top rates, on acceptance. Query; unsolicited manuscripts not accepted.

YANKEE—Yankee Publishing Co., P.O. Box 520, Dublin, NH 03444. Judson D. Hale, Ed. Articles, to 2,500 words, with New England angle. Photos. Pays $150 to $2,000 (average $800), on acceptance.

CURRENT EVENTS, POLITICS

THE AMERICAN LEGION—Box 1055, Indianapolis, IN 46206. Joe Stuteville, Ed. Articles, 750 to 2,000 words, on current world affairs, public policy, and subjects of contemporary interest. Pays $500 to $2,000, on acceptance. Query.

THE AMERICAN SCHOLAR—1811 Q St. N.W., Washington, DC 20009-9974. Joseph Epstein, Ed. Non-technical articles and essays, 3,500 to 4,000 words, on current affairs, the American cultural scene, politics, arts, religion, and science. Pays to $500, on acceptance.

THE AMICUS JOURNAL—Natural Resources Defense Council, 40 W. 20th St., New York, NY 10011. Kathrin Day Lassila, Ed. Investigative articles, profiles, book reviews, and essays, related to the environment, especially national and international environmental policy. Also poetry "rooted in nature." Pays varying rates, 30 days after publication. Queries required.

THE ATLANTIC MONTHLY—77 N. Washington St., Boston, MA 02114. William Whitworth, Ed. In-depth articles on public issues, politics, social sciences, education, business, literature, and the arts, with emphasis on information rather than opinion. Ideal length is 3,000 to 6,000 words, though short pieces, 1,000 to 2,000 words, are also welcome. Pays excellent rates, on acceptance.

BRIARPATCH—2138 McIntyre St., Regina, Saskatchewan, Canada S4P 2R7. George Manz, Man. Ed. "Saskatchewan's Independent Newsmagazine." Left-wing articles, 600 to 1,200 words, on politics, women's issues, environment, labor, international affairs for Canadian activists involved in social change issues. Pays in copies. Queries preferred.

CALIFORNIA JOURNAL—2101 K St., Sacramento, CA 95816. A.G. Block, Ed. "Independent analysis of politics and government." Balanced articles, 1,500 words, related to California government and politics. Advocacy pieces, 800 words. Pays $350 for articles, on publication. (No payment for advocacy pieces.) Query.

CAMPAIGNS & ELECTIONS—1511 K St. N.W., #1020, Washington, DC 20005. Ron Faucheaux, Ed. Feature articles, 700 to 4,000 words, related to the strategies, techniques, trends, and personalities of political campaigning. Campaign case studies, 1,500 to 3,000 words; how-to articles, 700 to 2,000 words, on specific aspects of campaigning; items, 100 to 800 words, for "Inside Politics"; and in-depth studies, 700 to 3,000 words, of public opinion, election results, and political trends that help form campaign strategy. Pays in subscriptions and free admission to certain public seminars.

CHURCH & STATE—1816 Jefferson Pl. N.W., Washington, DC 20036. Joseph L. Conn, Man. Ed. Articles, 600 to 2,600 words, on issues of religious liberty and church-state relations. Pays varying rates, on acceptance. Query.

COMMENTARY—165 E. 56th St., New York, NY 10022. Neal Kozodoy, Ed. Articles, 5,000 to 7,000 words, on contemporary issues, Jewish affairs, social sciences, community life, religious thought, culture. Serious fiction; book reviews. Pays on publication.

COMMONWEAL—15 Dutch St., New York, NY 10038. Margaret O'Brien Steinfels, Ed. Catholic. Articles, to 3,000 words, on political, social, religious, and literary subjects. Pays 3¢ a word, on acceptance.

COMMONWEALTH—55 Summer St., 9th Fl., Boston, MA 02110. Dave Denison, Ed. Articles, 2,000 to 4,500 words, on politics, government, and public policy issues affecting Massachusetts citizens. Payment varies, on acceptance. Query.

CONSERVATIVE REVIEW—1307 Dolley Madison Blvd., Rm. 203, McLean, VA 22101. Fred Smith, Ed. Articles, ideally 300 to 500 words (longer is O.K., if subject warrants), that offer information on topics, not just conservative sermons. "Writers should be intimately familiar with their subject." Pays in copies.

COUNTRY CONNECTIONS—P.O. Box 6748, Dept. TW, Pine Mountain Club, CA 93222-6748. Catherine R. Leach, Ed. Bimonthly. Articles, to 2,500 words, and fiction, to 1,500 words. Poetry. B&W photos. "Study magazine first. We serve as a forum for public discourse about ethics, politics, social justice, community, animal rights and environmental issues, and life in the country." Pays $25 for features, $15 for fiction and poetry, on publication.

CULTUREFRONT—198 Broadway, 10th Fl., New York, NY 10038. Attn: Ed. "A Magazine of the Humanities." Fiction and articles, 2,500 words, related to theme. "News and a variety of views on the production, interpretation, and politics of culture." No payment. Query for current themes.

CURRENT HISTORY—4225 Main St., Philadelphia, PA 19127. William W. Finan, Jr., Ed. Country-specific political science and current affairs articles, to 20 pages. Hard analysis written in a lively manner. "We devote each issue to a specific region or country. Writers should be experts with up-to-date knowledge of the region." Queries preferred. Pays $300, on publication.

EMERGE—BET Plaza, 1900 W. Place N.E., Washington, DC 20018. Florestine Purnell, Man. Ed. "Black America's Newsmagazine." Articles, 1,200 to 2,000 words, on current issues, ideas, or news personalities of interest to successful, well-informed African-Americans. Department pieces, 650 to 700 words, on a number of subjects. Pays 50¢ a word, on publication. Query.

ENVIRONMENT—1319 18th St. N.W., Washington, DC 20036-1802. Barbara T. Richman, Man. Ed. Articles, 2,500 to 5,000 words, on environmental, scientific, and technological policy and decision-making issues, especially on a global scale. Pays $100 to $300, on publication. Query.

FOREIGN SERVICE JOURNAL—2101 E St. N.W., Washington, DC 20037. Articles of interest to the Foreign Service and the US diplomatic community. Pays to 20¢ a word, on publication. Query.

THE FREEMAN—Foundation for Economic Education, 30 S. Broadway, Irvington-on-Hudson, NY 10533. Beth Hoffman, Man. Ed. Articles, to 3,500 words, on economic, political, and moral implications of private property, voluntary exchange, and individual choice. Pays 10¢ a word, on publication.

IN THESE TIMES—2040 N. Milwaukee Ave., Chicago, IL 60647. James Weinstein, Ed. Biweekly. Articles, 1,500 to 2,500 words, on politics, labor, women's issues, etc. "A magazine with a progressive political perspective. Please read before querying us." Payment varies, on publication. Query.

IRISH AMERICA—432 Park Ave. S., Suite 1000, New York, NY 10016. Patricia Harty, Ed. Articles, 1,500 to 2,000 words, of interest to Irish-American audience; preferred topics include history, sports, the arts, and politics. Pays 10¢ a word, after publication. Query.

LABOR'S HERITAGE—10000 New Hampshire Ave., Silver Spring, MD 20903. Stuart Kaufman, Ed. Quarterly journal of The George Meany Memorial Archives. Publishes 15- to 30-page documented articles of original research for labor scholars, labor union members, and the general public. Pays in copies.

MOMENT MAGAZINE—4710 41st St. N.W., Washington, DC 20016. Hershel Shanks, Ed. Sophisticated articles, 2,500 to 5,000 words, on Jewish culture, politics, religion, and personalities. Columns, to 1,500 words, with uncommon perspectives on contemporary issues, humor, strong anecdotes. Book reviews, 400 words. Pays $40 to $600.

MOTHER JONES—731 Market St., Suite 600, San Francisco, CA 94103. Jeffrey Klein, Ed. Investigative articles and political essays. Pays $1,000 to $3,000 for feature articles, after acceptance. Query with clips and SASE required.

THE NATION—72 Fifth Ave., New York, NY 10011. Katrina Vanden Heuvel, Ed. Articles, 1,500 to 2,500 words, on politics and culture from a liberal/left perspective. Editorials, 750 to 1,000 words. Pays $75 per published page, to $300, on publication. Query.

THE NEW YORK TIMES MAGAZINE—229 W. 43rd St., New York, NY 10036. Attn: Articles Ed. Timely articles, approximately 4,000 words, on news items, trends, culture, etc. Pays $1,000 for short pieces, from $2,500 for major articles, on acceptance. Query with clips.

THE NEW YORKER—20 W. 43rd St., New York, NY 10036. Attn: Ed., "Comment." Political/social essays, 1,000 words. Payment on acceptance. Query.

ON THE ISSUES—Choices Women's Medical Ctr., Inc., 97-77 Queens Blvd., Forest Hills, NY 11374-3317. Ronni Sandroff, Ed. "The Progressive Woman's Quarterly." Articles, up to 2,500 words, on political or social issues. Movie, music, and book reviews, 500 to 750 words. Query. Payment varies, on publication.

PEACE—2753 E. Broadway, S101-1969, Mesa, AZ 85204. Linda S. James, Ed. Quarterly. Articles and fiction, to 3,000 words, that center on the 1960s. Possible topics include life on the road; politics; interviews; and stories from those who fought in the Vietnam War and those who chose not to. Pays subscription and free extra copies (as available). Guidelines.

POLICY REVIEW—214 Massachusetts Ave. N.E., Washington, DC 20002. Attn: Articles Ed. Articles, 800 to 5,000 words, on reporting and analysis of domestic public policy issues. "We are the flagship journal of The Heritage Foundation, a conservative public policy research institute. We use articles that highlight private sector and local government alternatives to welfare state politics." Pays about $500, on publication.

THE PROGRESSIVE— 409 E. Main St., Madison, WI 53703. Matthew Rothschild, Ed. Articles, 1,000 to 3,500 words, on political and social problems. Pays $100 to $300, on publication.

REASON—3415 S. Sepulveda Blvd., Suite 400, Los Angeles, CA 90034. Brian Doherty, Ed. "Free Minds and Free Markets." Articles, 850 to 5,000 words, on politics, economics, and culture "from a dynamic libertarian's perspective." Pays varying rates, on acceptance. Query.

ROLL CALL: THE NEWSPAPER OF CAPITOL HILL— 900 2nd St. N.E., Washington, DC 20002. Susan Glasser, Ed. Factual, breezy articles with political or Congressional angle: Congressional history, human-interest subjects, political lore, etc. Political opinion or commentary on Congressional institutional issues. Pays on publication.

SATURDAY NIGHT—184 Front St. E., Suite 400, Toronto, Ont., Canada M5A 4N3. Kenneth Whyte, Ed. Canada's oldest magazine of politics, social issues, culture, and business. Features, 1,000 to 5,000 words, and columns, 800 to 1,000 words; fiction, to 3,000 words. Must have Canadian tie-in. Payment varies, on acceptance.

TIKKUN—251 W. 100th St., 5th Fl., New York, NY 10025. Michael Lerner, Ed. "A Bimonthly Jewish Critique of Politics, Culture & Society." Articles and fiction, 2,400 to 3,000 words. Poetry. "Read a copy to get a sense of what we publish. We are always interested in work pertaining to contemporary culture." Pays in copies.

VFW MAGAZINE— 406 W. 34th St., Kansas City, MO 64111. Richard K. Kolb, Ed. Articles, 1,000 words, related to current foreign policy and defense, American armed forces abroad, and international events affecting U.S. national security. Also, up-to-date articles on verteran concerns and issues affecting veterans. Pays to $500, on acceptance. Query. Guidelines.

THE WASHINGTON MONTHLY—1611 Connecticut Ave. N.W., Washington, DC 20009. Charles Peters, Ed. Helpful, informative articles, 1,000 to 4,000 words, on DC-related topics, including politics, and government and popular culture. Pays 10¢ a word, on publication.

WASHINGTON POST MAGAZINE—*The Washington Post,* 1150 15th St. N.W., Washington, DC 20071. Liza Mundy, Man. Ed. Essays, profiles, and general-interest pieces, to 5,000 words, on Washington-oriented politics and related issues. Pays from $1,000, after acceptance. SASE required.

WHO CARES: THE MAGAZINE FOR PEOPLE WHO DO—1511 K St. N.W., #412, Washington, DC 20005. Leslie Crutchfield, Heather McLeod, News and Features Eds. Rebecca Roth, Photo/Creative Ed. Articles, 1,000 words, on service programs throughout the country for "Partners in Change." Features, 1,500 to 2,500 words, on specific issues related to service and action. "Entrepreneur" pieces, 1,500 to 2,500 words, focus on the business of starting a successful nonprofit. "On Campus," 800 words, on unique service programs that involve college students. "Faith in Service," 1,000 to 1,500 words, on connections between service and spirituality. "Who's Who and What's What," 100- to 400-word news blurbs on service and action. Also, humorous essays, 800 words, and first-person narratives, related fiction, and other creative essays, 800 to 2,000 words. No payment for unsolicited articles. Payment for assigned pieces varies, on publication.

REGIONAL AND CITY PUBLICATIONS

ADIRONDACK LIFE—P.O. Box 97, Jay, NY 12941. Elizabeth Folwell, Ed. Features, to 5,000 words, on outdoor and environmental activities and issues, arts, wilderness, wildlife, profiles, history, and fiction; focus is on the Adirondack Park region of New York State. Pays to 25¢ a word, 30 days after acceptance. Query.

ALABAMA HERITAGE—The Univ. of Alabama, Box 870342, Tuscaloosa, AL 35487-0342. Suzanne Wolfe, Ed. Quarterly. Articles, to 5,000 words, on local, state, and regional history: art, literature, language, archaeology, music, religion, architecture, and natural history. Query, mentioning availability of photos and illustrations. Pays an honorarium, on publication, plus 10 copies. Guidelines.

ALASKA— 4220 B St., Suite 210, Anchorage, AK 99503. Ken Marsh, Ed. Articles, 2,000 words, on life in Alaska. Pays varying rates, on publication. Guidelines.

ALBERTA SWEETGRASS—Aboriginal Multi-Media Society of Alberta, 15001 112th Ave., Edmonton, Alberta, Canada T5M 2V6. R. John Hayes, Ed. Tabloid. Articles, 100 to 1,000 words (most often 500 to 800 words; briefs, 100 to 150 words): features, profiles, and community-based articles all with an Alberta angle.

ALOHA, THE MAGAZINE OF HAWAII AND THE PACIFIC—P.O. Box 3260, Honolulu, HI 96801. Cheryl Chee Tsutsumi, Ed. Dir. Articles, 1,500 to 2,500 words, on the lifestyle, history, arts, sports, business, music, customs, and people of Hawaii and the Pacific. Poetry. Fiction. Pays $150 to $400 for full-length features, on publication. Query.

APPELLATION—1040 Main St., Suite 102, Napa, CA 94559. Mary Chesterfield, Ed.-in-Chief. Bimonthly. Articles, 900 to 1,500 words, on the homes, gardens, food, wine, and personalities of the Napa Valley. Pays on acceptance.

APPRISE—P.O. Box 2954, 1982 Locust Ln., Harrisburg, PA 17105. Jim Connor, Ed.-in-Chief. Articles, 1,500 to 3,500 words, of regional (central Pennsylvania) interest, including profiles of notable Pennsylvanians, and broadly based articles of social interest that "enlighten and inform." Pays 10¢ a word, on publication.

ARIZONA HIGHWAYS—2039 W. Lewis Ave., Phoenix, AZ 85009. Robert J. Early, Ed. First-person experience articles, 1,600 to 1,800 words, on travel in Arizona; pieces on adventure, humor, lifestyles, nostalgia, history, archaeology, nature, etc. Departments also using personal experience pieces include "Mileposts," "Focus on Nature," "Along the Way," "Back Road Adventures," "Hiking," "Legends of the Lost," and "Arizona Humor." Pays 35¢ to 55¢ a word, on acceptance. Query required. Guidelines.

ATLANTA—1360 Peachtree St., Suite 1800, Atlanta, GA 30309. Lee Walburn, Ed. Articles, 1,500 to 5,000 words, on Atlanta subjects or personalities. Pays $300 to $2,000, on publication. Query.

ATLANTIC CITY MAGAZINE—P.O. Box 2100, Pleasantville, NJ 08232. Michael Epifanio, Ed. Lively articles, 200 to 2,000 words, on Atlantic City and the southern New Jersey shore, for locals and tourists: entertainment, casinos, business, recreation, personalities, lifestyle, local color. Pays $50 to $600, on publication. Query.

BACK HOME IN KENTUCKY—P.O. Box 681629, Franklin, TN 37068-1629. Nanci P. Gregg, Man. Ed. Articles on Kentucky history, travel, craftsmen and artisans, Kentucky cooks, and "colorful" characters; limited personal nostalgia specifically related to Kentucky. Pays $25 to $100 for articles with B&W or color photos. Queries preferred.

BALTIMORE MAGAZINE—16 S. Calvert St., Suite 1000, Baltimore, MD 21202. Ramsey Flynn, Ed. Articles, 500 to 3,000 words, on people, places, and things in the Baltimore metropolitan area. Consumer advice, investigative pieces, profiles, humor, and personal experience pieces. Payment varies, on publication. Query required.

THE BIG APPLE PARENTS' PAPER—36 E. 12th St., New York, NY 10003. Helen Rosengren Freedman, Man. Ed. Articles, 500 to 750 words, for New York City parents. Pays $35 to $50, on publication. Buys first NY-area rights.

BLUE RIDGE COUNTRY—P.O. Box 21535, Roanoke, VA 24018. Kurt Rheinheimer, Ed. Bimonthly. Regional articles, 1,200 to 2,000 words, that "explore and extol the beauty, history, and travel opportunities in the mountain regions of VA, NC, WV, TN, KY, MD, SC, and GA." Color slides or B&W prints considered. Pays $200 for photo-features, on publication. Queries preferred.

BOCA RATON—JES Publishing, Amtec Ctr., Suite 100, 6413 Congress Ave., Boca Raton, FL 33487. Marie Speed, Ed. Articles, 800 to 3,000 words, on Florida topics, personalities, and travel. Pays $50 to $500, on acceptance. Query with clips required.

THE BOSTON GLOBE MAGAZINE—*The Boston Globe*, Boston, MA 02107. Evelynne Kramer, Ed. General-interest articles on regional topics and profiles, 2,500 to 5,000 words. Query and SASE required.

BOSTON MAGAZINE—300 Massachusetts Ave., Boston, MA 02115. Lisa Gerson, Ed. Asst. Informative, entertaining features, 1,000 to 3,000 words, on Boston-area personalities, institutions, and phenomena. Query. Pays to $2,000, on publication.

BOUNDARY WATERS JOURNAL—9396 Rocky Ledge Rd., Ely, MN 55731. Stuart Osthoff, Ed. Articles, 2,000 to 3,000 words, on wilderness, recreation, nature, and conservation in Minnesota's Boundary Waters Canoe Area Wilderness and Ontario's Quetico Provincial Park. Regular features include canoe-route journals, fishing, camping, hiking, cross-country skiing, wildlife and nature, regional lifestyles, history, and events. Pays $200 to $400, on publication; $50 to $150 for photos.

BUFFALO SPREE MAGAZINE—Box 38, Buffalo, NY 14226. Johanna Van De Mark, Ed./Pub. Articles, to 1,800 words, for readers in the western New York region. Pays $75 to $125, $25 for poetry, on publication.

BUSINESS IN BROWARD—P.O. Box 7375, Ft. Lauderdale, FL 33338-7375. Sherry Friedlander, Ed. Published 8 times a year. Articles, 1,000 words, on small business in eastern Florida county. Pay varies, on acceptance.

BUZZ: THE TALK OF LOS ANGELES—11835 W. Olympic Blvd., Suite 450, Los Angeles, CA 90064. Marilyn Bethany, Ed.-in-Chief. Articles, varying lengths, of particular relevance to readers in southern California. Query. Pays $1 a word, within 45 days of acceptance.

CANADIAN GEOGRAPHIC—39 McArthur Ave., Vanier, Ont., Canada K1L 8L7. Rick Boychuk, Ed. "Making Canada Better Known to Canadians and the World." Articles on interesting places, nature and wildlife in Canada. Payment varies, on acceptance. Query.

CAPE COD LIFE—P.O. Box 1385, Pocasset, MA 02559-1385. Brian F. Shortsleeve, Pub. Articles, to 2,000 words, on current events, business, art, history, gardening, and nautical lifestyle on Cape Cod, Martha's Vineyard, and Nantucket. Pays 10¢ a word, 30 days after publication. Send queries to Laura Reckford, Man. Ed.

CARIBBEAN TRAVEL AND LIFE—P.O. Box 2456, Winter Park, FL 32790. Veronica Gould Stoddart, Ed. Articles, 500 to 3,000 words, on all aspects of travel, recreation, leisure, and culture in the Caribbean, the Bahamas, and Bermuda. Pays $75 to $750, on publication. Query with published clips.

CAROLOGUE—South Carolina Historical Society, 100 Meeting St., Charleston, SC 29401-2299. Stephen Hoffius, Ed. General-interest articles, to 10 pages, on South Carolina history. Queries preferred. Pays in copies.

CHESAPEAKE BAY MAGAZINE—1819 Bay Ridge Ave., Annapolis, MD 21403. Tim Sayles, Ed. Articles, to 3,000 words, on boating and fishing on Chesapeake Bay. No fiction or poetry. Photos. Pays $100 to $500, on acceptance. Query.

CHICAGO—500 N. Dearborn, Suite 1200, Chicago, IL 60610. Shane Tritsch, Man. Ed. Articles, 1,000 to 5,000 words, related to Chicago. Pays varying rates, on acceptance. Query.

CHICAGO HISTORY—Clark St. at North Ave., Chicago, IL 60614. Rosemary Adams, Ed. Articles, to 4,500 words, on Chicago's urban, political, social, and cultural history. Pays to $250, on publication. Query.

CINCINNATI MAGAZINE—One Centennial Plaza, 705 Central Ave., Suite 370, Cincinnati, OH 45202. Emily Foster, Ed. Articles, 500 to 3,500 words, on Cincinnati people and issues. Pays $50 to $500. Query with writing sample.

CITYLIMITS—325 N. Clippert St., Suite B, Lansing, MI 48912. Carole Eberly, Ed. Upbeat fiction, 1,500 to 2,500 words, of interest to Lansing, MI, area readers. Pays $150, on publication. Query preferred.

COLORADO BUSINESS—7009 S. Potomac, Englewood, CO 80112. Bruce Goldberg, Ed. Articles, varying lengths, on business, business personalities, and economic trends in Colorado. Preference given to Colorado residents. Pays on acceptance. Query.

COMMON GROUND MAGAZINE—P.O. Box 99, McVeytown, PA 17051-0099. Ruth Dunmire and Pam Brumbaugh, Eds. Quarterly. General-interest articles, 500 to 5,000 words, related to central Pennsylvania's Juniata River Valley and its rural lifestyle. Related fiction, 1,000 to 2,000 words. Poetry, to 12 lines. Fillers, photos, and cartoons. Pays $25 to $200 for articles, $5 to $15 for fillers, and $5 to $25 for photos, on publication. Guidelines.

COMMONWEALTH—55 Summer St., 9th Fl., Boston, MA 02110. Dave Denison, Ed. Articles, 2,000 to 4,500 words, on politics, government, and public policy issues affecting Massachusetts citizens. Payment varies, on acceptance. Query.

CONNECTICUT—789 Reservoir Ave., Bridgeport, CT 06606. Charles Monagan, Ed. Articles, 1,500 to 3,500 words, on Connecticut topics, issues, people, and lifestyles. Pays $500 to $1,200, within 30 days of acceptance.

CONNECTICUT FAMILY—See *New York Family*.

DELAWARE TODAY—P.O. Box 2087, Wilmington, DE 19899. Ted Spiker, Ed. Service articles, profiles, news, etc., on topics of local interest. Pays $75 to $125 for department pieces, $50 to $500 for features, on publication. Queries with clips required.

DETROIT MONTHLY—1400 Woodbridge, Detroit, MI 48207. Megan Swoyer, Ed. Articles on Detroit-area people, issues, lifestyles, and business. Payment varies. Query required.

EASTSIDE PARENT—Northwest Parent Publishing, 2107 Elliott Ave., #303, Seattle, WA 98121. Ann Bergman, Ed. Articles, 300 to 2,500 words, for parents of children ages 12 and under. Pays $25 to $200, on publication. Queries preferred. Also publishes *Seattle's Child, Portland Parent, Puget Sound Parent, Pierce County Parent,* and *Snohomish County Parent.*

ERIE & CHAUTAUQUA MAGAZINE—317 W. Sixth St., Erie, PA 16507. K. L. Kalvelage, Pub. Margaret Fisher Cutler, Man. Ed. Feature articles, to 2,500 words, on issues of interest to upscale readers in the Erie, Warren, and Crawford counties (PA), and Chautauqua (NY) county. Pieces with regional relevance. Pays after publication. Query preferred, with writing samples. Guidelines.

FAMILY TIMES—P.O. Box 932, Eau Claire, WI 54702. Ann Gorton, Ed. Articles, from 800 words, for parents in the Chippewa Valley, WI. Pays $35 to $50, on publication. Queries preferred. Guidelines.

FLORIDA KEYS MAGAZINE—P.O. Box 6524, Key West, FL 33041. Gibbons Cline, Ed. Articles, 800 to 2,400 words, on the Florida Keys: history, environment, personality profiles, fishing, boating, diving, etc. Fillers, humor. Photos. Pays $2 per column inch, on publication.

FLORIDA TREND—Box 611, St. Petersburg, FL 33731-0611. John F. Berry, Ed. Articles on Florida business and businesspeople. Query with SASE required.

FLORIDA WILDLIFE— 620 S. Meridian St., Tallahassee, FL 32399-1600. Attn: Ed. Bimonthly of the Florida Game and Fresh Water Fish Commission. Articles, 800 to 1,500 words, that promote native flora and fauna, hunting, fishing in Florida's fresh waters, outdoor ethics, and conservation of Florida's natural resources. Pays $50 per published page. SASE for guidelines and how-to-submit memo.

GEORGIA JOURNAL—The Indispensable Atlanta Co., Inc., P.O. Box 1604, Decatur, GA 30031-1604. David Osier, Ed./Pub. Conoly Hester, Man. Ed. Articles, 200 to 5,000 words, on Georgia's natural and human history and environment; also outdoor adventures, people, historical figures, places, events, travel in Georgia. Poetry, to 20 lines, and fiction, to 5,000 words, with Georgia settings; Georgia writers preferred. Pays $50 to $500, on publication. Query for nonfiction.

GOLDENSEAL—The Cultural Ctr., 1900 Kanawha Blvd. E., Charleston, WV 25305-0300. Ken Sullivan, Ed. Articles, 1,000 and 3,000 words, on West Virginia history, folklife, folk art and crafts, and music of a traditional nature. Pays 10¢ a word, on publication. Guidelines.

GRAND RAPIDS—549 Ottawa N.W., Grand Rapids, MI 49503. Carole R. Valade, Ed. Service articles (dining guide, travel, personal finance, humor) and issue-oriented pieces related to Grand Rapids, Michigan. Pays $35 to $200, on publication. Query.

GULF COAST GOLFER—See *North Texas Golfer*.

HAWAII—1400 Kapiolani Blvd., A25, Honolulu, HI 96814. Jim Borg, Ed. Bimonthly. Articles, 1,000 to 2,500 words, related to Hawaii. Pays 10¢ and up a word, on publication. Query.

HIGH COUNTRY NEWS—Box 1090, Paonia, CO 81428. Betsy Marston, Ed. Biweekly. Articles, 2,000 words, and roundups, 750 words, on western environmental issues, public lands management, energy, and natural resource issues; profiles of western innovators; pieces on western politics. "Writers must take regional approach." B&W photos. Pays 20¢ a word, on publication. Query.

HONOLULU—36 Merchant St., Honolulu, HI 96813. John Heckathorn, Ed. Features highlighting contemporary life in the Hawaiian islands: politics, sports, history, people, arts, events. Queries required. Pays $300 to $700, on acceptance.

ILLINOIS ENTERTAINER—124 W. Polk, Suite 103, Chicago, IL 60605. Michael C. Harris, Ed. Articles, 500 to 1,500 words, on local and national entertainment (emphasis on alternative music) in the greater Chicago area. Personality profiles; interviews; reviews. Photos. Pays varying rates, on publication. Query preferred.

INDIANAPOLIS MONTHLY—950 N. Meridian St., Suite 1200, Indianapolis, IN 46204. Sam Stall, Ed. Articles, 200 to 6,000 words, on health, sports, politics, business, interior design, personalities, controversy, and other topics. All material must have an Indianapolis/Indiana focus. Pays $50 to $500, on publication.

INQUIRER MAGAZINE—*Philadelphia Inquirer*, P.O. 8263, 400 N. Broad St., Philadelphia, PA 19101. Ms. Avery Rome, Ed. Articles, 1,500 to 2,000 words, and 3,000 to 7,000 words, on politics, science, arts and culture, business, lifestyles and entertainment, sports, health, psychology, education, religion, and humor. Pays varying rates. Query.

THE IOWAN MAGAZINE—108 Third St., Suite 350, Des Moines, IA 50309. Mark Ingebretsen, Ed. Articles, 1,000 to 3,000 words, on business, arts, people, and history of Iowa. Photos a plus. Payment varies, on acceptance. Query required.

JACKSONVILLE—White Publishing Co., 1032 Hendricks Ave., Jacksonville, FL 32207. Joseph White, Ed. Service pieces and articles, 1,500 to 2,500 words, on issues and personalities of interest to readers in the greater Jacksonville area. Department pieces, 1,200 to 1,500 words, on business, health, travel, personal finance, real estate, arts and entertainment, sports, dining out, food. Home and garden articles on local homeowners, interior designers, remodelers, gardeners, craftsmen, etc., 1,000 to 2,000 words. Pays $200 to $500, on publication. Query required. Guidelines.

JOURNAL OF THE WEST—1531 Yuma, Box 1009, Manhattan, KS 66505-1009. Robin Higham, Ed. Articles, to 20 pages, on the history and culture of the West, then and now. Pays in copies.

KANSAS!—Kansas Dept. of Commerce, 700 S.W. Harrison, Suite 1300, Topeka, KS 66603-3957. Andrea Glenn, Ed. Quarterly. Articles, 1,000 to 1,250 words, on attractions and events of Kansas. Color slides. Pays to $250, on acceptance. Query.

KENTUCKY LIVING—P.O. Box 32170, Louisville, KY 40232. Paul Wesslund, Ed. Articles, 800 to 2,000 words, with strong Kentucky angle: profiles (of people, places, events), history, biography, recreation, travel, leisure or lifestyle, and book excerpts. Pays $125 to $350, on acceptance. Queries preferred. Guidelines.

LAKE SUPERIOR MAGAZINE—P.O. Box 16417, Duluth, MN 55816-0417. Paul Hayden, Ed. Articles with emphasis on Lake Superior regional subjects: historical and topical pieces that highlight the people, places, and events that affect the Lake Superior region. Pictorial essays; humor and occasional fiction. Quality photos enhance submission. "Writers must have a thorough knowledge of the subject and how it relates to our region." Pays to $400, extra for photos, on publication. Query.

THE LOOK—P.O. Box 272, Cranford, NJ 07016-0272. John R. Hawks, Pub. Articles, 1,500 to 3,000 words, on fashion, student life, employment, relationships, and profiles of interest to local (NJ) readers ages 16 to 26. Also, beach stories and articles about the New Jersey shore. Pays $30 to $200, on publication.

LOS ANGELES MAGAZINE—11100 Santa Monica Blvd., 7th Fl., Los Angeles, CA 90025. Michael Caruso, Ed. Articles, to 3,000 words, of interest to sophisticated, affluent southern Californians, preferably with local focus on a lifestyle topic. Payment varies. Query.

LOUISVILLE—137 W. Muhammad Ali Blvd., Suite 101, Louisville, KY 40202. Ronni Lundy, Ed. Articles, 1,000 to 2,000 words, on community issues, personalities, and entertainment in the Louisville area. Photos. Pays from $50, on acceptance. Query; articles on assignment only. Limited free-lance market.

M MAGAZINE—P.O. Box 581, Hazard, KY 41702. Doug Crawford, Ed. Quarterly. "The Modern Magazine of the Mountains." Articles and stories, 2,000 to 3,000 words. Poetry, to 30 lines. Fillers and humor, 500 to 1,000 words.

"Contemporary Appalachian material needed." Artist profiles, with samples of work, also used. Pays in copies.

MARYLAND—2503 Davidsonville Rd., Gambrills, MD 21054. D. Patrick Hornberger, Ed. Dir. Articles, 800 to 2,200 words, on Maryland subjects. Pay varies, on acceptance. Query preferred. Guidelines.

MEMPHIS—Contemporary Media, Box 256, Memphis, TN 38101. Tim Sampson, Ed. Articles, 1,500 to 4,000 words, on a wide variety of topics related to Memphis and the Mid-South region: politics, education, sports, business, history, etc. Profiles; investigative pieces. Pays $50 to $500, on publication. Query. SASE for guidelines.

METROKIDS—1080 N. Delaware Ave., Suite 702, Philadelphia, PA 19125. Nancy Lisagor, Ed. Tabloid. Features and department pieces, 500 to 1,000 words, on regional family travel, dining, and entertainment in the Philadelphia metropolitan region. Pays $25 to $50, on publication.

MICHIGAN LIVING—1 Auto Club Dr., Dearborn, MI 48126-9982. Ron Garbinski, Ed. Travel articles, 75 to 1,500 words, on tourist attractions and recreational opportunities in the U.S. and Canada, with emphasis on Michigan: places to go, things to do, costs, etc. Color photos. Pays $55 to $500, (rates vary for photos).

MID-WEST OUTDOORS—111 Shore Dr., Hinsdale, IL 60521-5885. Gene Laulunen, Ed. Articles, to 1,500 words, with photos, on where, when, and how to fish and hunt, within 500 miles of Chicago. Pays $25, on publication.

MILWAUKEE MAGAZINE—312 E. Buffalo, Milwaukee, WI 53202. John Fennell, Ed. Profiles, investigative articles, and service pieces, 2,000 to 5,000 words; local tie-in a must. No fiction. Pays $400 to $900, on publication. Query preferred.

MINNESOTA MONTHLY—Lumber Exchange Bldg., 10 S. Fifth St., Suite 1000, Minneapolis, MN 55402. David Mahoney, Ed. Articles, to 4,000 words, on people, places, events, and issues in Minnesota. Pays $50 to $1,000, on acceptance. Query.

MONTANA MAGAZINE—P.O. Box 5630, Helena, MT 59604. Beverly R. Magley, Ed. Recreation, travel, general interest, regional profiles, photo-essays. Montana-oriented only. B&W prints, color slides. Pays 15¢ a word, on publication.

MPLS. ST. PAUL—220 S. 6th St., Suite 500, Minneapolis, MN 55402-4507. Brian E. Anderson, Ed. In-depth articles, features, profiles, and service pieces about the Minneapolis-St. Paul area, 300 to 4,000 words. Pays to $2,000.

NEBRASKA HISTORY—P.O. Box 82554, Lincoln, NE 68501. James E. Potter, Ed. Articles, 3,000 to 7,000 words, on the history of Nebraska and the Great Plains. B&W line drawings. Pays in copies. Cash prize awarded to one article each year.

NEVADA—1800 Hwy. 50 East, Suite 200, Carson City, NV 89710. David Moore, Ed. Articles, 500 to 700 or 1,500 to 1,800 words, on topics related to Nevada: travel, history, recreation, profiles, humor, and attractions. Special section on Nevada events and shows. Photos. Pay varies, on publication.

NEW FRONTIERS OF NEW MEXICO—P.O. Box 1299, Tijeras, NM 87059. Wally Gordon, Ed./Pub. Fiction and in-depth nonfiction, to 3,000 words, related to New Mexico and the Southwest. Humor, to 1,000 words. Poetry, to 100 lines. Pays $25 to $200, on publication.

NEW HAMPSHIRE EDITIONS—100 Main St., Nashua, NH 03060. Rick Broussard, Ed. Lifestyle, business, and history articles with a New Hampshire angle, with sources from all regions of the state, for the company's statewide magazine, and specialty publications including *New Hampshire Legacy, The World Trader* and *New Hampshire Guide to the Internet.* Query. Payment varies, on publication.

NEW HAMPSHIRE LEGACY—See *New Hampshire Editions.*

NEW JERSEY MONTHLY—P.O. Box 920, Morristown, NJ 07963-0920. Jenny DeMonte, Ed. Articles, profiles, and service pieces, 1,500 to 3,000 words; department pieces on health, business, education, travel, sports, local politics, and arts with New Jersey tie-in, 750 to 1,500 words. Pays $25 to $100 for shorts, $400 to $700 for departments, $600 to $1,750 for features, on acceptance. Query with clips. Guidelines.

NEW JERSEY REPORTER—The Ctr. for Analysis of Public Issues, 16 Vandeventer Ave., Princeton, NJ 08542. Neil Upmeyer, Ed. Bob Narus, Man. Ed. In-depth articles, 1,000 to 4,000 words, on New Jersey politics and public affairs. Pays $100 to $600, on publication. Query required.

NEW MEXICO MAGAZINE—Lew Wallace Bldg., 495 Old Santa Fe Trail, Santa Fe, NM 87503. Attn: Ed. Articles, 250 to 2,000 words, on New Mexico subjects. No poetry or fiction. Pays about 30¢ a word, on acceptance. Query.

NEW YORK FAMILY—141 Halstead Ave., Suite 3D, Mamaroneck, NY 10543. Felice Shapiro, Susan Ross, Pubs. Betsy F. Woolf, Sr. Ed. Articles related to family life in New York City. Pays $50 to $200, on publication. Same requirements for *Westchester Family* and *Connecticut Family.*

NEWPORT LIFE—174 Bellevue Ave., Suite 207, Newport, RI 02840. Lynne Tungett, Man. Ed. Quarterly. Articles, 500 to 2,500 words, on the people and places of Newport County: general-interest and historical articles, interviews, profiles, investigative pieces, and photo-features. Departments, 600 to 750 words, include "At the Helm" (on some aspect of boating), "Arts Marquee," "Food for Thought," and "Down to Business." Photos must be available for all articles. Pays 10¢ a word, on publication. Query.

NORTH DAKOTA HORIZONS—P.O. Box 2639, Bismarck, ND 58502. Lyle Halvorson, Ed. Quarterly. Articles, about 2,500 words, on people, places, and events in North Dakota. Photos. Pays $75 to $300, on publication.

NORTH GEORGIA JOURNAL—P.O. Box 127, Roswell, GA 30077. Olin Jackson, Pub./Ed. History, travel, and lifestyle features, 2,000 to 3,000 words, on north Georgia; need human-interest approach and must be written in first person. Include interviews. Photos a plus. Pays $75 to $300, on acceptance. Query.

NORTH TEXAS GOLFER—9182 Old Katy Rd., Suite 212, Houston, TX 77055. Steve Hunter, Ed. Articles, 800 to 1,500 words, involving local golfers or related directly to north Texas. Pays from $50 to $425, on publication. Query. Same requirements for *Gulf Coast Golfer* (related to south Texas).

NORTHEAST MAGAZINE—*The Hartford Courant,* 285 Broad St., Hartford, CT 06115. Lary Bloom, Ed. Submissions to Dona Prindle, Ed. Asst. Articles and short essays, 750 to 3,000 words, that reflect the concerns of Connecticut residents. Pays $250 to $1,000, on acceptance. Include manuscript size SASE for its return.

NORTHERN LIGHTS—Box 8084, Missoula, MT 59807-8084. Attn: Deborah Clow. Articles, 500 to 3,000 words, about the contemporary West. "We look for beautifully crafted personal essays that illuminate what it means to live in the Rocky Mountain West. We're looking to bust the Hollywood stereotypes." Pays 10¢ a word, on publication.

NORTHWEST PRIME TIME JOURNAL—10827 N.E. 68th St., Kirkland, WA 98033. Neil Strother, Pub./Ed. News and features on the Northwest for readers 50 and older. Pays $25 to $50, on publication. Limited market.

NORTHWEST REGIONAL MAGAZINES—P.O. Box 18000, Florence, OR 97439-0130. Attn: Jim Forst or Judy Fleagle. All submissions considered for use in *Oregon Coast, Oregon Outside* and *Northwest Travel*. Articles, 800 to 2,000 words, pertaining to travel, history, town/city profiles, events, outside activities, and nature. News releases, 200 to 500 words. Articles with photos (slides or negatives) preferred. Pays $50 to $300, after publication. Guidelines with SASE.

NORTHWEST TRAVEL—See *Northwest Regional Magazines.*

NOW & THEN—CASS/ETSU, P.O. Box 70556, Johnson City, TN 37614-0556. Jane Harris Woodside, Ed. Fiction and nonfiction, 1,500 to 3,000 words: short stories, articles, interviews, essays, memoirs, book reviews. Pieces must be related to theme of issue and have some connection to the Appalachian region. Also photos and drawings. SASE for guideline and current themes. Pays $15 to $75, on publication.

OHIO MAGAZINE—62 E. Broad St., Columbus, OH 43215. Jean Kelly, Ed. Profiles of people, cities, and towns of Ohio; pieces on historic sites, tourist attractions, little-known spots. Lengths and payment vary. Query with clips.

OKLAHOMA TODAY—Box 53384, Oklahoma City, OK 73152-9971. Jeanne M. Devlin, Ed. Articles, 1,000 to 4,000 words: travel; profiles; history; nature and outdoor recreation; and arts. All material must have regional tie-in. Pays $75 to $750, on acceptance or publication. Queries preferred. Guidelines.

ORANGE COAST—245-D Fischer Ave., Suite 8, Costa Mesa, CA 92626. Martin J. Smith, Ed. Articles, 2,000 to 3,000 words, of interest to educated Orange County residents. Pieces, 1,000 to 1,500 words, for regular departments, and 200 word pieces for "Short Cuts" (local phenomena). Query with clips. Pays $400 to $800 for features; $100 to $200 for departments; $25 to $50 for "Short Cuts," after acceptance. Write for guidelines.

OREGON COAST—See *Northwest Regional Magazines.*

OREGON OUTSIDE—See *Northwest Regional Magazines.*

ORLANDO MAGAZINE—P.O. Box 2207, Orlando, FL 32802. Brooke Lange, Ed. Locally based articles and department pieces, lengths vary, for residents of Central Florida. Query with clips.

OUR STATE: DOWN HOME IN NORTH CAROLINA—(formerly *The State: Down Home in North Carolina*) P.O. Box 4552, Greensboro, NC 27404. Mary Ellis, Ed. Articles, 750 to 1,500 words, on people, history, and places in North Carolina. Photos. Pays on publication.

OUT WEST: THE NEWSPAPER THAT ROAMS—9792 Edmonds Way, Suite 265, Edmonds, WA 98020. Chuck Woodbury, Ed./Pub. Entertaining and informative articles, 150 to 500 words, and short pieces, 30 to 75 words, on the roadside West (not the old West): interesting people, unusual places to stay, offbeat attractions. "Send for a sample of the paper before you submit." Pays about 5¢ a word, on publication. Web site is http://www.outwestnewspaper.com.

OUTDOOR TRAVELER, MID-ATLANTIC—WMS Publications, Inc., P.O. Box 2748, Charlottesville, VA 22902. Marianne Marks, Ed. Tom Gillespie, Assoc. Ed. Quarterly. Articles, 1,500 to 2,000 words, on hiking/backpacking, canoeing/kayaking/rafting, camping, mountain biking, road cycling, travel, nature, and the environment from New York state to North Carolina. Travel articles on destinations and areas that offer recreational opportunities. Departments include "Destinations," 450 to 600 words, on practical and descriptive guides to sports destinations; book and product reviews. Pays $300 to $400 for features; payment varies for departments, on publication. Guidelines.

PENNSYLVANIA HERITAGE—P.O. Box 1026, Harrisburg, PA 17108-1026. Michael J. O'Malley III, Ed. Quarterly of the Pennsylvania Historical Museum Commission. Articles, 3,000 to 4,000 words, relating to Pennsylvania fine and decorative arts, architecture, archaeology, history, industry and technology, travel, and folklore, written with an eye toward illustration. Photographic essays. Pieces should "introduce readers to the state's rich culture and historic legacy." Pays $300 to $500 for articles; up to $100 for photos and drawings, on publication.

PENNSYLVANIA MAGAZINE—Box 576, Camp Hill, PA 17001-0576. Matthew K. Holliday, Ed. General-interest features with a Pennsylvania focus. All articles must be accompanied by photocopies of possible illustrations. Guidelines.

PERSIMMON HILL—1700 N.E. 63rd St., Oklahoma City, OK 73111. M.J. Van Deventer, Ed. Published by the National Cowboy Hall of Fame. Articles, 1,500 to 2,000 words, on Western history and art, cowboys, ranching, and nature. Top-quality illustrations a must. Pays from $100 to $250, on publication. Query.

PHILADELPHIA—1818 Market St., Philadelphia, PA 19103. Eliot Kaplan, Ed. Articles, 1,000 to 5,000 words, for sophisticated audience, relating to Philadelphia area. No fiction or poetry. Pays on acceptance. Query.

PHOENIX MAGAZINE—5555 N. 7th Ave., Suite B200, Phoenix, AZ 85013. Beth Deveny, Ed. Articles, 1,000 to 3,000 words, on topics of interest to Phoenix-area residents. Pays $300 to $1,500, on publication. Query.

PIERCE COUNTY PARENT—See *Eastside Parent.*

PITTSBURGH POST GAZETTE—34 Blvd. of the Allies, Pittsburgh, PA 15230. Mark S. Murphy, Ed. Sunday magazine. Well-written, well-organized, in-depth articles of regional interest, 1,000 to 3,500 words, on issues, personalities, human interest, historical moments. No fiction, hobbies, how-tos or "timely events" pieces. Pays from $350, on publication. Query.

PORTLAND MAGAZINE—578 Congress St., Portland, ME 04101. Colin Sargent, Ed. "Maine's City Magazine." Articles on local people, legends, culture, and trends. Fiction, to 750 words. Pays on publication. Query preferred.

PORTLAND PARENT—See *Eastside Parent.*

PROVINCETOWN ARTS—650 Commercial St., Provincetown, MA 02657. Christopher Busa, Ed. Annual. Interviews, profiles, essays, 1,500 to 4,000 words. Mainstream fiction and novel excerpts, 500 to 5,000 words. Poems, submit up to 3 at a time. "We have a broad focus on the artists and writers who inhabit or visit Cape Cod." Pays from $125 for articles; $75 to $300 for fiction; $25 to $150 for poems, on publication.

PUGET SOUND PARENT—See *Eastside Parent.*

RANGE MAGAZINE—106 E. Adams, Suite 201, Carson City, NV 89706. Caroline Hadley, Ed. Quarterly. Articles, 500 to 1,200 words, on issues that threaten the West, its people, lifestyles, lands, and wildlife. "Our main purpose is to present public awareness of the positive presence of ranching operations on America's rangelands." Payment varies, on publication. Query preferred.

RECKON—Southern Culture Publications, Hill Hall, Room 301, The Univ. of Mississippi, University, MS 38677. Lynn McKnight, Ed. Quarterly. Fiction, 3,000 to 7,000 words, and articles, 1,000 to 5,000 words, on the contemporary American South. "Preference is given to prose with a distinct literary tone. Content must be informed, intelligent, and interpretive." No poetry or fillers. Pays 25¢ a word, on publication. Guidelines.

RECREATION NEWS—P.O. Box 32335, Washington, DC 20007-0635. Rebecca B. Heaton, Ed. Articles, 1,500 to 2,000 words, on recreation and travel for government workers in the Washington, DC area. "Articles should have a conversational tone that's lean and brisk." Pays $50 for reprints, to $300 for cover articles, on publication. Queries preferred. Guidelines.

RHODE ISLAND MONTHLY—95 Chestnut St., Providence, RI 02903. Paula M. Bodah, Man. Ed. Features, 1,000 to 4,000 words, ranging from investigative reporting and in-depth profiles to service pieces and visual stories, on Rhode Island and southeastern Massachusetts. Seasonal material, 1,000 to 2,000 words. Fillers, 150 to 500 words, on Rhode Island places, customs, people, events, products and services, restaurants and food. Pays $250 to $1,000 for features; $25 to $50 for shorts, on publication. Query.

RUNNER TRIATHLETE NEWS—P.O. Box 19909, Houston, TX 77224. Lance Phegley, Ed. Articles on running for road racing and multi-sport enthusiasts in TX, LA, OK, NM, and AR. Payment varies, on publication.

RURALITE—P.O. Box 558, Forest Grove, OR 97116. Attn: Ed. or Feature Ed. Articles, 800 to 2,000 words, of interest to a primarily rural and small-town audience in OR, WA, ID, WY, NV, northern CA, and AK. "Think pieces" affecting rural/urban interests, regional history and celebrations, self-help, profiles, etc. No fiction or poetry. No sentimental nostalgia. Pays $30 to $400, on acceptance. Queries required. Guidelines.

SACRAMENTO MAGAZINE— 4471 D St., Sacramento, CA 95819. Krista Hendricks Minard, Ed. Features, 2,500 words, on a broad range of topics related to the region. Department pieces, 1,200 to 1,500 words, and short pieces, 400 words, for "City Lights" column. Pays $50 to $300, on publication. Query.

SAN DIEGO MAGAZINE— 4206 W. Point Loma Blvd., P.O. Box 85409, San Diego, CA 92138. Tom Blair, Ed. Virginia Butterfield, Exec. Ed. Articles, 1,500 to 3,000 words, on local personalities, politics, lifestyles, business, history, etc., relating to San Diego area. Photos. Pays $250 to $600, on publication. Query with clips.

SAN DIEGO READER—P.O. Box 85803, San Diego, CA 92186. Jim Holman, Ed. Literate articles, 2,500 to 10,000 words, on the San Diego region. Pays $500 to $2,000, on publication.

SAN FRANCISCO EXAMINER MAGAZINE—*San Francisco Examiner*, 110 Fifth St., San Francisco, CA 94103. Attn: Ed. Articles, 1,200 to 3,000 words, on lifestyles, issues, business, history, events, and people in northern California. Query. Pays varying rates.

SAN FRANCISCO FOCUS—243 Valleja, San Francisco, CA 94111. Dale Eastman, Ed. Service features, profiles of local newsmakers, and investigative pieces of local issues, 2,500 to 3,000 words. News items, 250 to 800 words, on subjects ranging from business to arts to politics. Payment varies, on acceptance. Query required.

SASKATCHEWAN SAGE—Aboriginal Multi-Media Society of Alberta, 15001 112th Ave., Edmonton, Alberta, Canada T5M 2V6. Kenneth Williams, Ed. Tabloid. Articles, 100 to 1,000 words, most often 500 to 800 words; briefs 100 to 150 words, features, profiles, and community-based articles with a Saskatchewan angle.

SAVANNAH MAGAZINE—P.O. Box 1088, Savannah, GA 31402. Mary Beth Kerdasha, Ed. Articles, 2,500 to 3,500 words, on people and events in and around Savannah and Chatham County. Historical articles, 1,500 to 2,500 words, of local interest. Reviews, 500 to 750 words, of Savannah-based books and authors. Short pieces, 500 to 750 words, on weekend getaways near Savannah. Pays $75 to $350, after acceptance. Submit complete manuscript. Guidelines.

SEATTLE—701 Dexter Ave. N., Suite 101, Seattle, WA 98109. Giselle Smith, Ed. City, local issues, home, and lifestyle articles, 500 to 2,000 words, relating directly to the greater Seattle area. Personality profiles. Pays $100 to $700, on publication. Guidelines.

SEATTLE WEEKLY—1008 Western, Suite 300, Seattle, WA 98104. David Brewster, Ed. Articles, 250 to 4,000 words, from a Northwest perspective. Pays $25 to $800, on publication. Query. Guidelines.

SEATTLE'S CHILD—Northwest Parent Publishing, 2107 Elliott Ave., #303, Seattle, WA 98121. Ann Bergman, Ed. Articles, 400 to 2,500 words, of interest to parents, educators, and childcare providers of children under 12, and investigative reports and consumer tips on issues affecting families in the Puget Sound region. Pays $75 to $400, on publication. Query required.

SENIOR MAGAZINE—3565 S. Higuera St., San Luis Obispo, CA 93401. Attn: Ed. Articles, 600 to 900 words: personality profiles, travel pieces, articles about new things, places, business, sports, movies, television, and health; book reviews (of new or outstanding older books) of interest to seniors. Pays $1.50 per inch; $10 to $25 for B&W photos, on publication.

SILENT SPORTS—717 10th St., P.O. Box 152, Waupaca, WI 54981. Attn: Ed. Articles, 1,000 to 2,000 words, on canoeing, bicycling, cross-country skiing, running, hiking, backpacking, snowshoeing, inline skating, and other "silent" sports, in the upper Midwest region. "Articles must focus on the upper Midwest. No articles about places, people, or events outside the region." Pays $40 to $100 for features; $20 to $50 for fillers, on publication. Query.

SNOHOMISH COUNTY PARENT—See *Eastside Parent.*

SNOW COUNTRY—5520 Park Ave., Trumbull, CT 06611-0395. Kathleen Ring, Sr. Ed. Published 8 times a year. Features, 4,000 words, and articles, 1,000 to 2,000 words on skiing, mountain biking, in-line skating, camping, rafting and other year-round mountain sports as well as lifestyle issues. First-person adventure articles, travel pieces, service-oriented articles, profiles of snow country residents. "Mountain Living," 100- to 700-word pieces on people and points of view, anecdotes, trends, issues. Query with clips and resumé. Pays 80¢ a word, on acceptance.

SOUTH CAROLINA HISTORICAL MAGAZINE—South Carolina Historical Society, 100 Meeting St., Charleston, SC 29401-2299. Stephen Hoffius, Ed. Scholarly articles, to 25 pages with footnotes, on all areas of South Carolina history. Pays in copies.

SOUTH CAROLINA WILDLIFE—P.O. Box 167, Columbia, SC 29202-0167. Attn: Man. Ed. Articles, 1,000 to 2,000 words, with regional outdoors focus: conservation, natural history and wildlife, recreation. Profiles. Pays from 10¢ a word. Query.

SOUTH FLORIDA MAGAZINE— 800 Douglas Rd., Suite 500, Coral Gables, FL 33134. Nancy Moore, Ed. Features, 1,100 to 2,000 words, and department pieces, 200 to 1,300 words, on news, profiles, and hot topics related to south Florida. Short, bright items, 200 to 400 words. Pays $75 to $700, within 30 days of acceptance. Query.

SOUTHERN CULTURES— Ctr. for the Study of the American South, CB #3355, Manning Hall, UNC-CH, Chapel Hill, NC 27599-3355. Lisa Eveleigia, Man. Ed. Articles, 15 to 25 typed pages, on folk, popular, and high culture of the South. "We're interested in submissions from a wide variety of intellectual traditions that deal with ways of life, thought, belief, and expression in the United States South." Pays in copies.

SOUTHERN OUTDOORS—5845 Carmichael Rd., Montgomery, AL 36117. Larry Teague, Ed. How-to pieces, 800 to 1,200 words, and 2,000-word how-to and where-to articles on hunting and fishing, for fishermen and hunters in the Southern states. Pays 20¢ a word, on acceptance. Query.

SOUTHWEST ART—5444 Westheimer, Suite 1440, Houston, TX 77056. Susan McGarry, Ed. Articles, 1,200 to 1,800 words, on the artists, art collectors, museum exhibitions, gallery events and dealers, art history, and art trends west of the Mississippi River. Particularly interested in representational or figurative arts. Pays from $400, on acceptance. Query with at least 20 slides of artwork to be featured.

THE STATE: DOWN HOME IN NORTH CAROLINA—See *Our State: Down Home in North Carolina.*

SUNSET MAGAZINE— 80 Willow Rd., Menlo Park, CA 94025. Rosalie Muller Wright, Ed. Western regional. Limited free-lance market, but some need for western travel. Query; include clips.

SUNSHINE: THE MAGAZINE OF SOUTH FLORIDA—*The Sun-Sentinel,* 200 E. Las Olas Blvd., Ft. Lauderdale, FL 33301-2293. Mark Gauert, Ed. Articles, 1,000 to 3,000 words, on topics of interest to south Floridians. Pays $300 to $1,200, on acceptance. Query. Guidelines.

SWEAT—736 E. Loyola Dr., Tempe, AZ 85282. Joan Westlake, Ed. "South West Exercise And Training." Articles, 500 to 1,200 words, on sports, wellness, and fitness with an Arizona angle. "No personal articles or tales. We want investigative pieces. Articles must relate specifically to Arizona or Arizonans." Pays $25 to $60 for articles; $15 to $70 for photos, on publication. Queries required; no unsolicited manuscripts.

TALLAHASSEE MAGAZINE—P.O. Box 1837, Tallahassee, FL 32302-1837. Kathy Grobe, Man. Ed. Articles, 800 to 1,500 words, on the life, people, and history of the north Florida-south Georgia area. Pays on acceptance. Query.

TEXAS HIGHWAYS MAGAZINE—P.O. Box 141009, Austin, TX 78714-1009. Jack Lowry, Ed. Texas travel, history, and scenic features, 200 to 1,800 words. Pays about 40¢ to 50¢ a word, $80 to $550 per photo. Query. Guidelines.

TEXAS MONTHLY—P.O. Box 1569, Austin, TX 78767-1569. Gregory Curtis, Ed. Features, 2,500 to 5,000 words, and departments, to 2,500 words, on art, architecture, food, education, business, politics, etc. "We like solidly researched pieces that uncover issues of public concern, reveal offbeat and previously unreported topics, or use a novel approach to familiar topics." Pays varying rates, on acceptance. Queries required.

TEXAS PARKS & WILDLIFE—Fountain Park Plaza, 3000 S. Interstate Hwy. 35, Suite 120, Austin, TX 78704. Jim Cox, Sr. Ed. Articles, 800 to 1,500 words, promoting the conservation and enjoyment of Texas wildlife, parks, waters, and all outdoors. Features on hunting, fishing, birding, camping, and the environment. Department pieces, to 1,000 words, for "Parks & Places to Go," "State of Nature," and "Woods and Waters." Photos a plus. Pays to $600, on acceptance; extra for photos.

TIMELINE—1982 Velma Ave., Columbus, OH 43211-2497. Christopher S. Duckworth, Ed. Articles, 1,000 to 6,000 words, on history of Ohio (politics, economics, social, and natural history) for lay readers in the Midwest. Pays $100 to $900, on acceptance. Queries preferred.

TORONTO LIFE—59 Front St. E., Toronto, Ont., Canada M5E 1B3. John Macfarlane, Ed. Articles, 1,500 to 4,500 words, on Toronto. Pays $1,500 to $3,500, on acceptance. Query.

TROPIC—*The Miami Herald,* One Herald Plaza, Miami, FL 33132. Tom Shroder, Exec. Ed. General-interest articles, 750 to 3,000 words, for south Florida readers. Pays $200 to $1,000, on acceptance. SASE.

TUCSON LIFESTYLE—Old Pueblo Press, 7000 E. Tanque Verde, Tucson, AZ 85715. Sue Giles, Ed.-in-Chief. Local slant to all articles on businesses, lifestyles, the arts, homes, fashion, and travel in the Southwest. Payment varies, on acceptance. Query preferred.

TWIN CITIES READER—10 S. Fifth St., Minneapolis, MN 55402. Claude Peck, Ed. Articles, 1/2 page to 4 printed pages, on local public affairs and arts for readers ages 25 to 44. Pays $25 to $150, on publication.

VENTURA COUNTY & COAST REPORTER—1567 Spinnaker Dr., Suite 202, Ventura, CA 93001. Nancy Cloutier, Ed. Articles, 3 to 5 pages, on any locally slanted topic. Pays $10, on publication.

VERMONT—20 1/2 Main St., P.O. Box 800, Middlebury, VT 05753. Julie Kirgo, Man. Ed. Articles on all aspects of contemporary Vermont: its people, culture, politics, and special places. Pays $200 to $1,000, on publication. Query.

VERMONT LIFE—6 Baldwin St., Montpelier, VT 05602. Tom Slayton, Ed.-in-Chief. Articles, 500 to 3,000 words, on Vermont subjects only. Pays 20¢ a word, extra for photos. Query preferred.

VIRGINIA—The Country Publishers, Inc., P.O. Box 798, Berryville, VA 22611. Garrison Ellis, Ed. Quarterly. "Written for and about people, places, events, and activities in, around, and affecting Virginia." Features, 2,000 to 2,500 words; articles, 1,200 to 1,800 words; humor, folklore, and legend, to 2,000 words; fiction, 1,000 to 1,500 words, with regional setting or reference; related poetry, to 32 lines. Department pieces, 500 to 700 words. Photos. Pays $200 to $300, 30 days after publication.

VIRGINIA BUSINESS— 411 E. Franklin St., Suite 105, Richmond, VA 23219. James Bacon, Ed. Articles, 1,000 to 2,500 words, related to the business scene in Virginia. Pays varying rates, on acceptance. Query required.

VIRGINIA WILDLIFE—P.O. Box 11104, Richmond, VA 23230-1104. Attn: Ed. Articles, 1,000 to 1,500 words, with Virginia tie-in, on fishing, hunting, wildlife management, outdoor safety and ethics, etc. Articles may be accompanied by color photos. Pays from 15¢ a word, extra for photos, on publication. Query.

WASHINGTON POST MAGAZINE—*The Washington Post*, 1150 15th St. N.W., Washington, DC 20071. Liza Mundy, Man. Ed. Personal-experience essays, profiles, and general-interest pieces, to 6,000 words, on business, arts and culture, politics, science, sports, education, children, relationships, behavior, etc. Articles should be of interest to people living in Washington, DC, area. Pays from $750, on acceptance. Limited market.

THE WASHINGTONIAN—1828 L St. N.W., Suite 200, Washington, DC 20036. John Limpert, Ed. Helpful, informative articles, 1,000 to 4,000 words, on DC-related topics. Pays 50¢ a word, on publication.

WE ALASKANS MAGAZINE—*Anchorage Daily News*, Box 149001, Anchorage, AK 99514-9001. George Bryson, Ed. Articles, 500 to 1,000 words, and features, 3,000 to 4,000 words, mostly on Alaska topics. Profiles, narratives, essays, and humor. Pays $50 to $150 for short articles, $300 to $600 for features, on publication.

WESTCHESTER FAMILY—See *New York Family*.

WESTERN SPORTSMAN—140 Ave. F N., Saskatoon, Sask., Canada S7L 1V8. George Gruenefeld, Ed. Informative articles, to 2,500 words, on hunting, fishing, and outdoor experiences in British Columbia, Alberta, Saskatchewan, and Manitoba. How-tos, humor, cartoons. Photos. Pays $75 to $300, on acceptance.

WESTWAYS—2601 S. Figueroa St., Los Angeles, CA 90007. Attn: Ed. Articles, 1,000 to 2,500 words, on travel in California, western U.S., greater U.S., and overseas. Pays from 50¢ a word, on acceptance. Query.

WINDSPEAKER—Aboriginal Multi-Media Society of Alberta, 15001 112th Ave., Edmonton, Alberta, Canada T5M 2V6. Debora Lockyer, Ed. Tabloid. Features, news items, sports, op-ed pieces, columns, etc., 200 to 1,000 words, concerning Canada's Aboriginal peoples. Pays from $3 per published inch, after publication. Query. Guidelines.

WINDY CITY SPORTS—1450 W. Randolph, Chicago, IL 60607. Jeff Banowetz, Ed. Articles, to 1,000 words, on amateur sports in the Chicago area. Queries required. Pays $100, on publication.

WISCONSIN TRAILS—P.O. Box 5650, Madison, WI 53705. Howard Mead, Ed./Pub. Articles, 1,500 to 3,000 words, on regional topics: outdoors, lifestyle, events, history, arts, adventure, travel; profiles of artists, craftspeople, and regional personalities. Pays $150 to $500, on publication. Query.

WYOMING RURAL ELECTRIC NEWS—P.O. Box 380, Casper, WY 82606-0380. Kris Wendtland, Ed. Articles, 500 to 900 words, on issues relevant to rural Wyoming. Articles should support Wyoming's personal and economic growth, social development, and education. Wyoming writers given preference. Pays $20 to $50, on publication.

YANKEE—Yankee Publishing Co., P.O. Box 520, Dublin, NH 03444. Judson D. Hale, Ed. Articles and fiction, 500 to 2,500 words, on New England and New England people. Pays $500 to $2,500 for features, on acceptance.

TRAVEL ARTICLES

ADVENTURE WEST—P.O. Box 3210, Incline Village, NV 89451. Michael Oliver, Assoc. Ed. Bimonthly. Travel articles, 1,500 to 2,000 words, on risky wild adventures; 1,500 to 2,000 words, on shorter trips; and 1,000 to 1,500 words on short excursions with information on where to stay and what to do. Profiles and essays also used. Emphasis must be on American West, including Alaska, Hawaii, western Canada, and western Mexico. Pays 30¢ a word, on publication.

AIR FAIR: THE MAGAZINE FOR AIRLINE EMPLOYEES—1499 W. Palmetto Park Rd., #222, Boca Raton, FL 33486. Debra Fredel, Ed. Travel articles, 1,800 words, with photos, on shopping, sightseeing, dining, and nightlife for airline employees. Prices, discount information, and addresses must be included. Pays $250 to $500, after publication.

AIR FORCE TIMES—See *Times News Service.*

ARIZONA HIGHWAYS—2039 W. Lewis Ave., Phoenix, AZ 85009. Richard G. Stahl, Sr. Ed. Informal, well-researched personal-experience and travel articles, 1,600 to 1,800 words, focusing on a specific city or region in Arizona. Also articles dealing with nature, environment, flora and fauna, history, anthropology, archaeology, hiking. Departments for personal-experience pieces include "Focus on Nature," "Along the Way," "Back Road Adventures," "Hiking," and "Arizona Humor." Pays 35¢ to 55¢ a word, on acceptance. Query with published clips only. Guidelines.

ARMY TIMES—See *Times News Service.*

BIG WORLD—P.O. Box 8743-A, Lancaster, PA 17604. Jim Fortney, Ed. Bimonthly. Articles, 500 to 4,000 words, that offer advice on working and studying abroad, humorous anecdotes, first-person experiences, or other "down-to-earth" travel information. "For people who prefer to spend their traveling time responsibly discovering, exploring, and learning, in touch with locals and their traditions, and in harmony with their environment." Pays $10 to $20 for articles, $5 to $20 for photos, on publication.

BLUE RIDGE COUNTRY—P.O. Box 21535, Roanoke, VA 24018. Kurt Rheinheimer, Ed. Regional travel articles, 750 to 1,200 words, on destinations and backroads drives in the mountain regions of VA, NC, WV, TN, KY, MD, SC, and GA. Color slides and B&W prints considered. Pays to $200 for photo-features, on publication. Queries preferred.

BREW—1120 Mulberry St., Des Moines, IA 50309. Beverly Walsmith, Ed. "Traveling America's Brewpubs and Microbreweries." Bimonthly. Articles, 1,500 to 1,800 words, on new brewpubs around the country. "Our focus is on the brewpub and the community where it is located." Pays 10¢ a word, on publication. Query preferred.

CALIFORNIA HIGHWAY PATROLMAN—2030 V St., Sacramento, CA 95818-1730. Carol Perri, Ed. Travel articles, to 2,000 words, focusing on places in California. "We prefer out-of-the-way stops instead of regular tourist destinations, with a clear California Highway Patrol tie-in." Query or send complete manuscript with photos (or photo availability). SASE required. Pays 2½¢ a word, $5 for B&W photos, on publication.

CANADIAN DIVER & WATERSPORT—See *Diver Magazine.*

CAR & TRAVEL—1000 AAA Dr., Heathrow, FL 32746-5063. Douglas Damerst, Ed. Articles, 600 to 1,500 words, on consumer automotive and travel concerns. Pays $200 to $800, on acceptance. Query with writing samples required. Articles by assignment only.

CARIBBEAN TRAVEL AND LIFE—P.O. Box 2456, Winter Park, FL 32790. Veronica Gould Stoddart, Ed. Lively, informative articles, 500 to 2,500 words, on all aspects of travel, leisure, recreation, and culture in the Caribbean, Bahamas, and Bermuda, for upscale, sophisticated readers. Photos. Pays $75 to $750, on acceptance. Query.

CHILE PEPPER—1227 W. Magnolia Ave., Fort Worth, TX 76104. Joel Gregory, Pub. First-person food and travel articles, 1,000 to 1,500 words, about spicy world cuisine. Queries required. Payment varies, on publication.

CONDE NAST TRAVELER—360 Madison Ave., New York, NY 10017. Alison Humes, Features Ed. Uses very little free-lance material.

CRUISE TRAVEL—990 Grove St., Evanston, IL 60201. Robert Meyers, Ed. Charles Doherty, Man. Ed. Ship-, port-, and cruise-of-the-month features, 800 to 2,000 words; cruise guides; cruise roundups; cruise company profiles; travel suggestions for one-day port stops. "Photo-features strongly recommended." Payment varies, on acceptance. Query with sample color photos.

DIVER MAGAZINE—230-11780 Hammersmith Way, Richmond, B.C., Canada V7A 5E3. Stephanie Bold, Ed. Illustrated articles, 500 to 1,000 words, on dive destinations. Shorter pieces are also welcome. "Travel features should be brief and accompanied by excellent slides and/or prints and a map. Unsolicited articles will be reviewed only from August to October and will be considered for *Diver Magazine* and *Canadian Diver & Watersport.*" Guidelines. Limited market.

ENDLESS VACATION—Box 80260, Indianapolis, IN 46280. Laurie D. Borman, Ed. Travel features, to 1,500 words; primarily on North American destinations, some international destinations. Pays on acceptance. Query preferred. Send SASE for guidelines. Limited market.

FAMILY CIRCLE—110 Fifth Ave., New York, NY 10011. Sylvia Barsotti, Sr. Ed. Travel articles, to 1,500 words. Concept travel pieces should appeal to a national audience and focus on affordable activities for families; prefer service-filled, theme-oriented travel pieces or first-person family vacation stories. Payment varies, on acceptance. Query.

FRIENDLY EXCHANGE—P.O. Box 2120, Warren, MI 48090-2120. Dan Grantham, Ed. Articles, 700 to 1,500 words, offering readers "news you can use," on lifestyle issues, such as home, health, personal finance, and travel. Photos. Pays $400 to $1,000, extra for photos. Query required. Guidelines.

GRAND TOUR: THE JOURNAL OF TRAVEL LITERATURE—P.O. Box 66, Thorofare, NJ 08086. Jennifer Fisher, Man. Ed. Quarterly. Travel-related memoirs, essays, and articles, 1,000 to 7,000 words, that "combine the sharp eye of the reporter with the craft of the short story writer and the rhythm of the poet." Pays $50 to $200, on publication.

HISTORIC TRAVELER—6405 Flank Dr., Harrisburg, PA 17112. Tom Huntington, Ed. "The Guide to Great Historic Destinations." Bimonthly. Articles, 1,500 to 2,000 words, for upscale readers with a strong interest in history. "Accurate information on historic destinations. Possible topics: battlefields, museums, antique shows, events, hotels, inns, transportation, reenactments, preserved communities, and architectural wonders. No South Pacific Islands, Alpine skiing, or Mediterranean cruises." Guidelines. Pays $300 to $500, on acceptance. Query with SASE and clips.

INDIA CURRENTS—P.O. Box 21285, San Jose, CA 95151. Arvind Kumar, Submissions Ed. First-person accounts, 1,500 words, of trips to India or the subcontinent. Helpful tips for first-time travelers. Prefer descriptions of people-to-people interactions. Pays in subscriptions.

INTERNATIONAL LIVING—105 W. Monument St., Baltimore, MD 21201. Michael Palmer, Asst. Ed. Newsletter. Short pieces and features, 200 to 2,000 words, with useful information on investing, shopping, travel, employment, education, real estate, retirement, and lifestyles overseas. Pays $100 to $400, after publication.

ISLANDS—3886 State St., Santa Barbara, CA 93105. Joan Tapper, Ed.-in-Chief. Destination features, 2,500 to 4,000 words, on islands around the world as well as department pieces and front-of-the-book items on island-related topics. Pays from 50¢ a word, on acceptance. Query with clips required. Guidelines.

MICHIGAN LIVING—Automobile Club of Michigan, 1 Auto Club Dr., Dearborn, MI 48126. Ron Garbinski, Ed. Informative travel articles, 300 to 2,000 words, on U.S. and Canadian tourist attractions and recreational opportunities; special interest in Michigan. Pays $55 to $500 (rates vary for photos), on acceptance.

THE MIDWEST MOTORIST—12901 N. Forty Dr., St. Louis, MO 63141. Michael Right, Ed. Articles, 1,000 to 1,500 words, with color slides, on domestic and foreign travel. Pays from $150, on acceptance.

MOUNTAIN LIVING MAGAZINE—7009 S. Potomac, Englewood, CO 80112. Robyn Griggs, Ed. Travel articles, 1,200 to 1,500 words, on cities, regions, establishments in the mountainous regions of the world. Pays $200 to $300, on acceptance.

NATIONAL GEOGRAPHIC—1145 17th St. N.W., Washington, DC 20036. William L. Allen, Ed. First-person articles on geography, exploration, natural history, archaeology, and science: 40% staff-written; 60% written by published authors. Does not consider unsolicited manuscripts.

NATIONAL MOTORIST—Bayside Plaza, 188 The Embarcadero, San Francisco, CA 94105. Jane Offers, Ed. Quarterly. Illustrated articles, 500 to 1,100 words, for California motorists, on motoring in the West, domestic and international travel, car care, roads, personalities, places, etc. Color slides. Pays from 10¢ a word, on acceptance. Pays for photos on publication. SASE required.

NAVY TIMES—See *Times News Service.*

NEW YORK DAILY NEWS—450 W. 33rd St., New York, NY 10001. Gunna Bitee Dickson, Travel Ed. Articles, 700 to 900 words, on all manner of travel. Price information must be included. B&W or color photos or slides. Pays $100 to $200 (extra for photos), on publication.

THE NEW YORK TIMES—229 W. 43rd St., New York, NY 10036. Nancy Newhouse, Travel Ed. Query with SASE required; include writer's background, description of proposed article. Pays on acceptance.

NORTHWEST REGIONAL MAGAZINES—P.O. Box 18000, Florence, OR 97439. Attn: Judy Fleagle or Jim Forst. All submissions considered for use in *Oregon Coast, Oregon Outside,* and *Northwest Travel.* Articles, 800 to 2,000 words, on travel, history, town/city profiles, outdoor activities, events, and nature. News releases, 200 to 500 words. Articles with slides (or negatives) preferred. Pays $50 to $300, after publication. Guidelines with SASE.

NORTHWEST TRAVEL—See *Northwest Regional Magazines.*

OREGON COAST—See *Northwest Regional Magazines.*

OREGON OUTSIDE—See *Northwest Regional Magazines.*

OUT WEST: THE NEWSPAPER THAT ROAMS—9792 Edmonds Way, Suite 265, Edmonds, WA 98020. Chuck Woodbury, Ed./Pub. Entertaining and informative articles, 150 to 500 words, and short pieces, 30 to 75 words, on the rural West (not the old West): interesting people, unusual places to stay, offbeat attractions. "Send for a sample of the paper before you submit." Pays about 5¢ a word, on publication.

OUTDOOR TRAVELER, MID-ATLANTIC—WMS Publications, Inc., P.O. Box 2748, Charlottesville, VA 22902. Marianne Marks, Ed. Tom Gillespie, Assoc. Ed. Quarterly. Articles, 1,500 to 2,000 words, on hiking, backpacking, canoeing, kayaking, rafting, camping, mountain biking, road cycling, travel, nature, and the environment from New York state to North Carolina. Travel articles on destinations and areas that offer recreational opportunities. Departments include "Destinations," 450 to 600 words, on practical and descriptive guides to sports destinations; book and product reviews. Pays $300 to $400 for features; payment varies for departments, on publication. Guidelines.

RV WEST MAGAZINE—Vernon Publications, 3000 Northup Way, Suite 200, Bellevue, WA 98009-9643. Michelle Arab, Ed. Travel and destination articles, 750 to 1,750 words, on where to go and what to do in the 13 western states with your recreational vehicle. Color slides or B&W prints must accompany articles. Pays $1.50 per column inch, on publication. Guidelines.

SACRAMENTO MAGAZINE— 4471 D St., Sacramento, CA 95819. Krista Hendricks Minard, Ed. Articles, 1,000 to 1,500 words, on destinations within a 6-hour drive of Sacramento. Pay varies, on publication. Query.

SPECIALTY TRAVEL INDEX—305 San Anselmo Ave., #313, San Anselmo, CA 94960. C. Steen Hansen, Co-Pub./Ed. Semiannual directory of adventure vacation tour companies, destinations, and vacation packages. Articles, 1,000 to 1,200 words, with how-to travel information, humor, and opinion. Pays 20¢ per word, on publication. Slides and photos considered. Queries preferred.

TEXAS HIGHWAYS MAGAZINE—P.O. Box 141009, Austin, TX 78714-1009. Jack Lowry, Ed. Travel, historical, cultural, scenic features on Texas, 200 to 1,800 words. Pays about 40¢ to 50¢ a word; photos $80 to $400. Guidelines.

TIMES NEWS SERVICE—Army Times Publishing Co., Springfield, VA 22159. Attn: R&R Ed. Travel articles, 700 words, on places of special interest to military people for use in "R&R" newspaper section. "We like travel articles to focus on a single destination but with short sidebar covering other things to see in the area." Pays $100, on acceptance. Pays $35 for original color slides or prints. Also, travel pieces, 1,000 words, for supplements to *Army Times, Navy Times,* and *Air Force Times.* Address Supplements Ed. Pays $125 to $200, on acceptance. Guidelines.

TRANSITIONS ABROAD — 18 Hulst Rd., Box 1300, Amherst, MA 01004-1300. Jason Whitmarsh, Man. Ed. Articles for overseas travelers of all ages who seek an enriching, in-depth experience of the culture: work, study, travel, budget tips. Include practical, first-hand information. Emphasis on travel for personal enrichment. "Eager to work with inexperienced writers who want to share information not usually found in guidebooks. High percentage of material is from free-lancers. Also seeking articles from writers with special expertise on cultural travel opportunites for specific types of travelers: seniors, students, families, etc." B&W photos a plus. Pays $1.50 per column inch, after publication. SASE required. Guidelines and editorial calendar.

TRAVEL AMERICA—World Publishing Co., 990 Grove St., Evanston, IL 60201-4370. Randy Mink, Man. Ed. Robert Meyers, Ed. Features, 800 to 1,200 words, on U.S. vacation destinations. Pays up to $300, on acceptance. Top-quality color slides a must. Query.

TRAVEL & LEISURE—1120 Ave. of the Americas, New York, NY 10036. Nancy Novogrod, Ed.-in-Chief. Articles, 800 to 3,000 words, on destinations and travel-related activities. Regional pieces for regional editions. Short pieces for "Fitness & Health" and "T&L Reports." Pays on acceptance: $2,500 to $5,000 for features; $750 to $1,500 for regionals; $50 to $300 for short pieces. Query; articles on assignment.

TRAVEL SMART—Dobbs Ferry, NY 10522. Attn: Ed. Short pieces, 250 to 1,000 words, about interesting, unusual and/or economical places. Give specific details on hotels, restaurants, transportation, and costs. Pays on publication. "Send manila envelope with 2 first-class stamps for copy and guidelines."

TRAVELERS' TALES, INC. — 10 Napier Ln., San Francisco, CA 94133. Attn: Ed. Personal travel stories and anecdotes, to 20 pages, for book anthologies focused on a particular country or theme. Payment varies, on publication. Guidelines.

WESTWAYS—2601 S. Figueroa St., Los Angeles, CA 90007. Attn: Ed. Travel articles, 1,300 to 2,500 words, on southern California, the West, domestic and foreign destinations. Pays $1 a word, on acceptance.

INFLIGHT MAGAZINES

ABOARD—100 Almeria Ave., Suite 220, Coral Gables, FL 33134. Roberto Casin, Ed. Inflight magazine of 11 Latin American international airlines in Chile, Dominican Republic, Ecuador, Guatemala, El Salvador, Bolivia, Nicaragua, Honduras, Uruguay, and Paraguay. Articles, 1,200 to 1,500 words, with photos, on these countries and on science, sports, technology, adventure, wildife, fashion, business, ecology, and gastronomy. No political stories. Pays $150, on acceptance and on publication. Query required.

ALASKA AIRLINES MAGAZINE—2701 First Ave., Suite 250, Seattle, WA 98121. Paul Frichtl, Ed. Articles, 250 to 2,500 words, on business, travel, and profiles of regional personalities for West Coast business travelers. Payment varies, on publication. Query.

AMERICA WEST AIRLINES MAGAZINE—Skyword Marketing Inc., 4636 E. Elwood St., Suite 5, Phoenix, AZ 85040-1963. Michael Derr, Ed. Business articles, destination pieces, arts and culture, 500 to 2,000 words;

thoughtful but light essays. Pays from $250, on publication. Clips and SASE required. Guidelines. Very limited market.

AMERICAN WAY—P.O. Box 619640, Mail Drop 5598, DFW Airport, 4333 Amon Carter Blvd., Fort Worth, TX 76155. John Ostdick, Ed. American Airlines' inflight magazine. No unsolicited material.

EXCURSIONS—SCG, Inc., 1810 W. Northern, Suite 123, Phoenix, AZ 85018. Jennifer Wilson, Ed. Inflight magazine for Reno Air. Destination features, 600 to 1,600 words, with relevant, vibrant photos. Send SASE for current destinations and pay rates. Payment varies, on publication. Query required.

HEMISPHERES—1301 Carolina St., Greensboro, NC 27401. Ed.-in-Chief. United Airlines inflight magazine. Articles, 1,200 to 1,500 words, on business, investing, travel, sports, family, food and wine, etc., that inform and entertain sophisticated, well-traveled readers. "The magazine strives for a unique global perspective presented in a fresh, strong, and artful graphic environment." Pays good rates, on acceptance. Query. Guidelines with SASE.

HORIZON AIR MAGAZINE—2701 First Ave., #250, Seattle, WA 98121-1123. Todd Powell, Ed. Business and travel articles on the companies, people, issues, and trends that define the Northwest. News items, 200 to 500 words, and profiles for "The Region" section. Other departments pieces, 1,600 words, cover corporate and industry profiles, regional issue analysis, travel, and community profiles. Pays $100 to $600, on publication.

USAIR MAGAZINE—Pace Communications, 1301 Carolina St., Greensboro, NC 27401. Articles on travel, lifestyle trends, sports, personality profiles, food and wine, shopping, the arts and culture. Pays good rates, within 60 days of acceptance. Query with clips and SASE; no unsolicited manuscripts, faxes, or phone proposals.

WOMEN'S PUBLICATIONS

ASPIRE—107 Kenner Ave., Nashville, TN 37205. Jeanette Thomason, Ed.-in-Chief. Lifestyle magazine for Christian women. Articles, 500 to 2,000 words, on trends in health, career issues, parenting, and relationships, "inspiring and encouraging readers to incorporate faith into daily life." Pays 30¢ a word, on acceptance. Query with resumé and clips. SASE for guidelines.

BBW: BIG BEAUTIFUL WOMAN—8484 Wilshire Blvd., Suite 900, Beverly Hills, CA 90211. Janey Milstead, Ed.-in-Chief. Articles, 1,500 words, of interest to women ages 25 to 50, especially large-size women, including interviews with successful large-size women and personal accounts of how to cope with difficult situations. Tips on restaurants, airlines, stores, etc., that treat large women with respect. Payment varies, on publication. Query.

BRIDAL GUIDE—Globe Communications Corp., 3 E. 54th St., New York, NY 10022. Diane Forden, Ed.-in-Chief. Laurie Bain Wilson, Travel Ed. Bimonthly. Articles, 1,500 to 3,000 words, on wedding planning, relationships, sexuality, health and nutrition, psychology, travel, and finance. No beauty, fashion articles; no fiction, essays, poetry. Pays on acceptance. Query with SASE.

BRIDE'S—(formerly *Bride's & Your New Home*) 140 E. 45th St., New York, NY 10017. Sally Kilbridge, Man. Ed. Articles, 800 to 3,000 words, for engaged couples or newlyweds, on wedding planning, relationships, communication, sex, decorating, finances, careers, remarriage, health, birth control, religion, in-laws. Major editorial subjects: home, wedding, and honeymoon (send honeymoon queries to Travel Dept.). No fiction or poetry. Pays from 50¢ a word, on acceptance.

BRIDE'S & YOUR NEW HOME—See *Bride's*.

COMPLETE WOMAN— 875 N. Michigan Ave., Suite 3434, Chicago, IL 60611. Bonnie L. Krueger, Ed. Martha Carlson, Assoc. Ed. Articles, 1,000 to 2,000 words, with how-to sidebars, giving practical advice to women on love, sex, careers, health, personal relationships, etc. Also interested in reprints. Pays varying rates, on publication. Query with clips.

COSMOPOLITAN—224 W. 57th St., New York, NY 10019. Bonnie Fuller, Ed. Betty Nichols Kelly, Fiction and Books Ed. Articles, to 3,000 words, and features, 500 to 2,000 words, on issues affecting young career women, with emphasis on jobs and personal life. Fiction on male-female relationships: short shorts, 1,500 to 3,000 words; short stories, 3,000 to 4,000 words; condensed published novels, 25,000 words. SASE required. Payment varies.

COUNTRY WOMAN—P.O. Box 989, Greendale, WI 53129. Kathy Pohl, Man. Ed. Profiles of country women (photo-feature packages), inspirational, reflective pieces. Personal-experience, nostalgia, humor, service-oriented articles, original crafts, and how-to features, to 1,000 words, of interest to country women. Pays $25 to $75 for crafts, humor, nostalgia; pays $150 for photo-features, on acceptance.

ELLE— 1633 Broadway, New York, NY 10019. Amy Gross, Ed. Dir. Articles, varying lengths, for fashion-conscious women, ages 20 to 50. Subjects include beauty, health, fitness, travel, entertainment, and lifestyles. Pays top rates, on publication. Query required.

ESSENCE—1500 Broadway, New York, NY 10036. Susan L. Taylor, Ed.-in-Chief. Linda Villarosa, Exec. Ed. Provocative articles, 800 to 2,500 words, about black women in America today: self-help, how-to pieces, business and finance, work, parenting, health, celebrity profiles, art, travel, and political issues. Fiction, 800 to 2,500 words. Pays varying rates, on acceptance. Query for articles.

EXECUTIVE FEMALE—30 Irving Pl., New York, NY 10003. Gay Bryant, Ed.-in-Chief. Articles, 750 to 2,500 words, on managing people, time, money, companies, and careers, for women in business. Pays varying rates, on acceptance. Query.

FAMILY CIRCLE—375 Lexington Ave., New York, NY 10017. Nancy Clark, Deputy Ed. Articles, to 2,000 words, on "women who have made a difference," marriage, family, and child-care and elder-care issues; consumer affairs, psychology, humor, health, nutrition, and fitness. Pays top rates, on acceptance. Query required.

GLAMOUR—350 Madison Ave., New York, NY 10017. Ruth Whitney, Ed.-in-Chief. Laurie Sprague, Man. Ed. Articles, from 1,000 words, on careers, health, psychology, politics, current events, interpersonal relationships, etc., for women ages 18 to 35. Fashion, entertainment, travel, food, and beauty pieces staff-written. Pays from $500, on acceptance. Query Articles Ed.

GOOD HOUSEKEEPING— 959 Eighth Ave., New York, NY 10019. Evelyn Renold, Articles Ed. Lee Quarfoot, Fiction Ed. Articles, about 2,500 words, for married working women with children, 18 and under. Social issues, dramatic personal narratives, medical news, marriage, friendship, psychology, crime, finances, work, parenting, and consumer issues. Best places to break in: "Better Way" (short, advice-driven takes on health, money, safety, and consumer issues) and profiles (short takes on interesting or heroic women or families). No submissions on food, beauty, needlework, or crafts. Short stories, 2,000 to 5,000 words, with strong identification for women. Unsolicited fiction not returned; if no response in 6 weeks, assume work was unsuitable. Pays top rates, on acceptance. Guidelines. Query with SASE for nonfiction.

HARPER'S BAZAAR—1700 Broadway, 37th Fl., New York, NY 10019. Elizabeth Tilberis, Ed.-in-Chief. Articles, 1,500 to 2,500 words, for active, sophisticated women: the arts, world affairs, travel, families, education, careers, health, and sexuality. Payment varies, on acceptance. No unsolicited manuscripts; query with SASE.

IOWA WOMAN—P.O. Box 680, Iowa City, IA 52244. Joan Taylor, Ed. Fiction, poetry, creative nonfiction, book reviews, and personal essays; articles, to 6,500 words, on women in the arts and in midwestern history; interviews with prominent women; current social, economic, artistic, and environmental issues. Poems, any length (submit up to 5); photos and drawings. Pays $5 a page, $15 for illustrations, on publication. Queries preferred for articles. Guidelines.

THE JOYFUL WOMAN—P.O. Box 90028, Chattanooga, TN 37412. Joy Rice Martin, Ed. Joanna Rice, Ed. Asst. Fiction, 500 to 1,200 words, for women with a "Christian commitment." Also first-person inspirational true stories, profiles of Christian women, practical and Bible-oriented how-to articles. Pays 3¢ to 4¢ a word, on publication. Queries required.

LADIES' HOME JOURNAL—125 Park Ave., New York, NY 10017. Myrna Blyth, Pub. Dir./Ed.-in-Chief. Articles of interest to women. Send queries to: Susan Crandell, Articles Ed. (news/general interest); Elena Rover, Ed. (health/medical); Melina Gerosa, Ed. (celebrity/entertainment); Pamela Guthrie O'Brien, Features Ed. (sex/psychology); Lois Johnson, Beauty Dir. (beauty/fashion/fitness); Jan Hazard, Food Ed.; Shana Aborn, Features Ed. (personal experience); Mary Mohler, Sr. Ed. (children and families). Fiction accepted through literary agents only. True, first-person accounts, 1,000 words, "about the most intimate aspects of our lives" for anonymous "Woman to Woman": Submit typed, double-spaced manuscript with SASE to Box WW, c/o address above; pays $750. Guidelines.

MCCALL'S—110 Fifth Ave., New York, NY 10011. Attn: Articles Ed. Human-interest, self-help, social issues, and popular psychology articles, 1,200 to 2,000 words. Also publishes "Love Lessons," first person essays, 1,400 words; "Families," how-to articles, 1,400 words; "Health Sense," short newsy items; and "Medical Report," health-related items, 1,200 words. Query with SASE. Payment varies, on acceptance.

MADEMOISELLE—350 Madison Ave., New York, NY 10017. Faye Haun, Man. Ed. Articles, 1,500 to 2,500 words, on work, relationships, health, and trends of interest to single, working women in their early to mid-twenties. Reporting pieces, essays, first-person accounts, and humor. No how-to or fiction. Submit query with clips and SASE. Pays excellent rates, on acceptance.

MIRABELLA—1633 Broadway, New York, NY 10019. Amy Gross, Ed.-in-Chief. Articles, varying lengths, for fashion-conscious women, ages 20 to 50. Subjects include beauty, health, fitness, travel, entertainment, and lifestyles. Pays top rates, on publication. Query required.

MODERN BRIDE—249 W. 17th St., New York, NY 10011. Mary Ann Cavlin, Exec. Ed. Articles, 1,500 to 2,000 words, for bride and groom, on wedding planning, financial planning, juggling career and home, etc. Pays $600 to $1,200, on acceptance.

MS.—230 Park Ave., 7th Fl., New York, NY 10169. Attn: Manuscript Ed. Articles relating to feminism, women's roles, and social change; national and international news reporting, profiles, essays, theory, and analysis. No fiction or poetry accepted, acknowledged, or returned. Query with resumé and published clips.

NA'AMAT WOMAN—200 Madison Ave., Suite 2120, New York, NY 10016. Judith A. Sokoloff, Ed. Articles on Jewish culture, women's issues, social and political topics, and Israel, 1,500 to 3,000 words. Short stories with a Jewish theme. Pays 10¢ a word, on publication.

NATURAL LIVING TODAY—175 Varick St., 9th Fl., New York, NY 10014. Attn: Ed. Dept. Bimonthly. Articles, 1,000 to 2,000 words, on all aspects of a natural lifestyle for women. Pays $75 to $200, on publication. Query.

NEW WOMAN—2 Park Ave., 11th Fl., New York, NY 10016. Attn: Manuscripts and Proposals. Articles for women ages 25 to 49, on self-discovery, self-development, and self-esteem. Features: relationships, careers, health and fitness, money, fashion, beauty, food and nutrition, travel features with self-growth angle, and essays by and about women pacesetters. Pays about $1 a word, on acceptance. Query with SASE.

ON THE ISSUES—Choices Women's Medical Ctr., Inc., 97-77 Queens Blvd., Forest Hills, NY 11374-3317. Rosemary L. Bray, Ed. "The Progressive Woman's Quarterly." Articles, to 2,500 words, on political or social issues. Movie, music, and book reviews, 500 to 750 words. Payment varies, on publication. Query.

PLAYGIRL—801 Second Ave., New York, NY 10017. Judy Cole, Ed.-in-Chief. Erotic entertainment for women. Insightful articles on sexuality and romance; sizzling fiction, humor, and in-depth celebrity interviews of interest to contemporary women. Pays varying rates, after acceptance. Query with clips. Guidelines.

RADIANCE: THE MAGAZINE FOR LARGE WOMEN—P.O. Box 30246, Oakland, CA 94604. Alice Ansfield, Ed./Pub. Quarterly. "A magazine for body acceptance." Articles, 1,500 to 3,500 words, that provide information, inspiration, and resources for women all sizes of large. Features include information on health, media, fashion, and politics that relate to issues of body size. Fiction and poetry also welcome. Pays $35 to $100, on publication.

REDBOOK—224 W. 57th St., New York, NY 10019. Pamela Lister, Susan Gifford, Sr. Eds. Dawn Raffel, Fiction Ed. Toni Hope, Sr. Ed. For mothers, ages 25 to 45. Short stories, 10 to 15 typed pages; dramatic inspirational narratives, 1,000 to 2,000 words. SASE required. Pays on acceptance. Query with writing samples for articles. Guidelines.

SAGEWOMAN—P.O. Box 641, Point Arena, CA 95468-0641. Anne Newkirk Niven, Ed. Quarterly. Articles, 200 to 5,000 words, on issues of concern to pagan and spiritually minded women. Material which expresses an earth-centered spirituality: personal experience, Goddess lore, ritual material, interviews, humor, and reviews. Accepts material by women only. Pays 3¢ a word, from $10, on publication.

SELF—350 Madison Ave., New York, NY 10017. Attn: Ed. "We no longer accept unsolicited manuscripts or queries."

TODAY'S CHRISTIAN WOMAN— 465 Gundersen Dr., Carol Stream, IL 60188. Ramona Cramer Tucker, Ed. Articles, 1,500 to 1,800 words, that are "warm and personal in tone, full of real-life anecdotes that deal with marriage, parenting, friendship, spiritual life, single life, health, work, and self." Humorous anecdotes, 150 words, that have a Christian slant. Payment varies, on acceptance. Queries required. Guidelines.

VIRTUE: HELPING WOMEN BUILD CHRIST-LIKE CHARACTER— (formerly *Virtue: The Christian Magazine for Women.*) 4050 Lee Vance View, Colorado Springs, CO 80918-7102. Laura J. Barker, Ed. Articles and fiction, 1,200 to 1,400 words, on family, marriage, self-esteem, working women, humor, women's spiritual journeys, issues, relationship with family, friends and God. "Provocative, meaningful stories, especially those with bold messages shown in gracious ways." Pays 15¢ to 25¢ a word for articles; $25 to $50 for poetry, on publication. Submit up to 3 poems at a time. Query with SASE required.

VOGUE—350 Madison Ave., New York, NY 10017. Attn: Features Ed. Articles, to 1,500 words, on women, entertainment and the arts, travel, medicine, and health. General features. Pays good rates, on acceptance. Query; no unsolicited manuscripts.

WOMAN'S DAY—1633 Broadway, New York, NY 10019. Stephanie Abarbanel, Sr. Articles Ed. Human-interest or helpful articles, to 2,000 words, on marriage, child-rearing, health, careers, relationships, money management. Dramatic first-person narratives of medical miracles, rescues, women's experiences, etc. "We respond to queries promptly; unsolicited manuscripts are returned unread." SASE. Pays top rates, on acceptance.

WOMAN'S OWN—1115 Broadway, New York, NY 10010. Rachael Butler, Ed. Articles, 1,500 to 2,000 words, offering inspirational and practical advice on relationships and career and lifestyle choices for women 25 to 35. Common subjects: staying together, second marriages, working women, asserting yourself, meeting new men, "love-styles," sex, etc. Columns, 800 words, for "Suddenly Single," "Moving Up," "Round-Up," "Mindpower," "Dieter's Notes," "Fashion Advisor," and "Financial Advisor." Profiles, 250 to 500 words, of women who have overcome great odds for "Woman in the News." Fun, in-depth quizzes. Short pieces on trends and breakthroughs for "Let's Put Our Heads Together." Query. Pays $50 to $500, on acceptance.

WOMAN'S TOUCH—1445 Boonville Ave., Springfield, MO 65802-1894. Peggy Musgrove, Ed. Aleda Swartzendruber, Man. Ed. Inspirational articles, 500 to 800 words, for Christian women. Pays on publication. Allow 3 months for response. Submit complete manuscript. Guidelines and editorial calendar.

WOMAN'S WORLD—270 Sylvan Ave., Englewood Cliffs, NJ 07632. Andrea Bien, Feature Ed. Articles, 600 to 1,800 words, of interest to middle-income women between the ages of 18 and 60, on love, romance, careers, medicine, health, psychology, family life, travel; dramatic stories of adventure or crisis, investigative reports. Fast-moving short stories, about 1,900 words, with light romantic theme. (Specify "short story" on outside of envelope.) Mini-mysteries, 1,200 words, with "whodunit" or "howdunit" theme. No science fiction, fantasy, horror, ghost stories, or gratuitous violence. Pays $300 to $900 for articles; $1,000 for short stories; $500 for mini-mysteries, on acceptance. Query for articles. Guidelines.

WOMEN IN BUSINESS—American Business Women's Assn., 9100 Ward Pkwy., Box 8728, Kansas City, MO 64114-0728. Dawn J. Grubb, Assoc. Ed. How-to business features, 1,000 to 1,500 words, for working women ages 35 to 55, business trends, small-business ownership, self-improvement, and retirement issues. Profiles of ABWA members only. Pays on acceptance. Query required.

WOMEN'S CIRCLE—P.O. Box 299, Lynnfield, MA 01940. Marjorie Pearl, Ed. Success stories on home-based female entrepreneurs. How-to articles on contemporary craft and needlework projects. Unique money-saving ideas and recipes. Pays varying rates, on acceptance.

WOMEN'S SPORTS ¢ FITNESS—2025 Pearl St., Boulder, CO 80302. Dagny Scott, Ed. Articles on fitness, nutrition, outdoor sports; how-tos; profiles; adventure travel pieces; and controversial issues in women's sports, 500 to 2,000 words. Pays on acceptance.

WORKING MOTHER—MacDonald Communications, 135 W. 50th St., 16th Fl., New York, NY 10020. Attn: Ed. Dept. Articles, to 2,000 words, that help women in their task of juggling job, home, and family. "We like pieces that solve or illuminate a problem unique to our readers." Payment varies, on acceptance.

WORKING WOMAN—230 Park Ave., New York, NY 10169. Articles, 350 to 2,500 words, on business and personal aspects of the lives of executive and managerial women and entrepreneurs. Pays from $300, on acceptance.

MEN'S PUBLICATIONS

ESQUIRE—250 W. 55th St., New York, NY 10019. Edward Kosner, Ed.-in-Chief. David Hirshey, Deputy Ed. Articles, 2,500 to 4,000 words, for intelligent audience. Pays varying rates, on acceptance. Query with clips and SASE.

GALLERY— 401 Park Ave. S., New York, NY 10016-8802. Marc Medoff, Ed. Dir. Rich Friedman, Man. Ed. Articles, investigative pieces, interviews, profiles, to 2,500 words, for sophisticated men. Short humor, satire, service pieces, and fiction. Photos. Query. Guidelines.

GENRE—7080 Hollywood Blvd., Suite 1104, Hollywood, CA 90028. John Polly, Assoc. Ed. Fiction, 3,000 to 5,000 words, and articles, 750 to 3,000 words, of interest to gay men. "Feature articles should be national in scope and somehow related to the gay male experience." Pays to 50¢ a word, on publication.

GQ—350 Madison Ave., New York, NY 10017. No free-lance queries or manuscripts.

THE GREEN MAN—P.O. Box 641, Point Arena, CA 95468-0641. Diane Conn Darling, Ed. "Exploring Paths for Pagan Men." Articles, 1,500 to 5,000 words, on a theme. No payment. Query for more information and future themes.

MEN'S HEALTH—Rodale Press, 33 E. Minor St., Emmaus, PA 18098. Duane Swierczynsi, Assoc. Ed. Articles, 1,000 to 2,500 words, on fitness, diet, health, relationships, sports, and travel for men ages 25 to 55. Pays from 50¢ a word, on acceptance. Query.

MEN'S JOURNAL—1290 Ave. of the Americas, New York, NY 10104-0298. Attn: Editorial. Articles and profiles, 2,000 to 7,000 words, of interest to active men age 25 to 49. Travel, fitness, health, adventure, participatory sports. Service articles for equipment and fitness sections, 400 to 1,800 words. Pays "good rates," on acceptance. Query.

NEW MAN— 600 Rinehart Rd., Lake Mary, FL 32746. Brian Pe Ed. Articles, to 2,000 words, that help men "in their quest for godline integrity." Profiles of everyday men who are doing something extraordinary, action-packed thrill and adventure articles, trend pieces that take an in-depth look at issues facing men today. Short items, 50 to 250 words, on unusual facts, motivational quotes, perspectives on news and events. Pays 10¢ to 35¢ per word, on publication.

PENTHOUSE—277 Park Ave., 4th Fl., New York, NY 10172-0003. Peter Bloch, Ed. Lavada B. Nahon, Sr. Ed. General-interest profiles, interviews, or investigative articles, to 5,000 words. No unsolicited fiction. Pays on acceptance.

PLAYBOY— 680 N. Lake Shore Dr., Chicago, IL 60611. Stephen Randall, Ed. Articles, 3,500 to 6,000 words, and sophisticated fiction, 1,000 to 10,000 words (5,000 preferred), for urban men. (Address fiction to Attn: Fiction Ed.) Humor; satire. Science fiction. Pays to $5,000 for articles and fiction, $2,000 for short-shorts, on acceptance. SASE required.

PLAYERS— 8060 Melrose Ave., Los Angeles, CA 90046. David Jamison, Ed. Articles, 2,500 to 3,500 words, for black men: politics, economics, travel, fashion, grooming, entertainment, sports, interviews, fiction, humor, satire, health, and sex. Photos a plus. Pays on publication.

ROBB REPORT— 1 Acton Pl., Acton, MA 01720. Steven Castle, Ed. Upscale lifestyle magazine for men. Feature articles and regular columns on investment opportunities, exotic cars, classic and collectible autos, yachts, fashion, travel, investibles and collectibles, technology, profiles, etc., emphasizing luxurious lifestyles. Pays on publication. Query with SASE and clips.

SENIORS MAGAZINES

AARP BULLETIN— 601 E St. N.W., Washington, DC 20049. Elliot Carlson, Ed. Publication of the American Association of Retired Persons. Payment varies, on acceptance. Query required.

50 AND FORWARD— 160 Mayo Rd., Suite 100, Edgewater, MD 21037. Debra Asberry, Ed./Pub. Nonfiction subjects, to 1,200 words, on lifestyle before and after retirement, health and beauty, longevity, and positive attitudes."Readers are very active, 50 years old and over." Pays $25 and up, on acceptance.

FLORIDA RETIREMENT LIFESTYLES—BC Publications, 3650 N. Federal Highway, Suite 202, Lighthouse Point, FL 33064-6649. Mr. Kerry Smith, Ed. Concise and direct articles, 800 to 1,500 words, that address the issues, concerns, and humor of people contemplating a move to Florida for their retirement, and/or those currently retired or contemplating retirement who seek information for an active retirement: retirement communities, Florida inns, recreation, sports, volunteer/self-employment activities. Pays 15¢ a word, on publication.

GOOD TIMES—Senior Publications, Inc., 5148 Saint-Laurent Blvd., Montreal, Quebec, Canada H2T 1R8. Denise B. Crawford, Ed.-in-Chief. Judy Wayland, Asst. Ed. "The Canadian Magazine for Successful Retirement." Celebrity profiles as well as practical articles on health, beauty, cuisine, hobbies, fashion, leisure activities, travel, taxes, legal rights, consumer protection, etc. Canadian content only. Payment varies. Query.

GOOD TIMES—1500 Market St., 12th Fl., Centre Sq. E., Philadelphia, PA 19102. Karen Detwiler, Ed.-in-Chief. Lifestyle magazine for mature Pennsylvanians 50 years and older. Articles, 1,500 to 2,000 words, on medical issues, health, travel, finance, fashion, gardening, fitness, legal issues, celebrities, lifestyles, and relationships. Payment varies, on publication. Query. Guidelines.

GRAND TIMES— 403 Village Dr., El Cerrito, CA 94530-3355. Kira Albin, Man. Ed. Articles and fiction, 600 to 1,700 words, for active retirees in the San Francisco Bay area. "We strive to inform, inspire, and entertain. No articles that play on ageist stereotypes." Pays $10 to $35, on acceptance. SASE for guidelines. No queries.

LIFE LINES MAGAZINE—129 N. 10th St., Rm. 241, Lincoln, NE 68508-3648. Dena Rust Zimmer, Ed. Short stories, "Sports and Hobbies," "Remember When...," "Travels With...," and "Perspectives on Aging," to 450 words. Poetry, to 50 lines. Fillers and short humor, "the shorter the better." No payment.

MATURE LIFESTYLES—15951 McGregor Blvd., #2D, Ft. Myers, FL 33908. Linda Heffley, Ed. Articles, 500 to 1,200 words, for readers over 50 in Florida. No fiction or poetry. Pays $45 to $75, on publication.

MATURE LIFESTYLES—P.O. Box 44327, Madison, WI 53744. Tracy Siemion, Ed. "South Central Wisconsin's Newspaper for the Active 50-Plus Population." Syndicated national coverage and local free lance.

MATURE LIVING—127 Ninth Ave. N., Nashville, TN 37234-0140. Al Shackleford, Ed. Fiction and human-interest articles, to 1,200 words, for senior adults. Must be consistent with Christian principles. Payment varies, on acceptance.

MATURE OUTLOOK—Meredith Corp., 1912 Grand Ave., Des Moines, IA 50309-3379. Peggy Person, Ed. Bimonthly. Upbeat, contemporary articles, varying lengths, on travel and leisure topics for readers 50 and older. Regular topics include health, money, food, travel, leisure, and stories of real people, 75 to 2,000 words. Pays $50 to $1,500, on acceptance. Query required. Guidelines.

MATURE YEARS—201 Eighth Ave. S., P.O. Box 801, Nashville, TN 37202. Marvin W. Cropsey, Ed. Articles of interest to older adults: health and fitness, personal finance, hobbies and inspiration. Anecdotes, to 300 words, poems, cartoons, jokes, and puzzles for older adults. "A Christian magazine that seeks to build faith. We always show older adults in a favorable light." Include name, address, and social security number with all submissions. Allow 2 months for response.

MILESTONES—246 S. 22nd St., Philadelphia, PA 19103. Cathy Green, Ed. Robert Epp, Dir. Tabloid published 10 times a year. News articles and features, 750 to 1,000 words, on humor, personalities, political issues, etc., for readers 50 and older. Articles are written by staff and local writers only.

MODERN MATURITY— 601 E. St. N.W., Washington, DC 20049. J. Henry Fenwick, Ed. Articles, to 2,000 words, on careers, workplace, human interest, living, finance, relationships, and consumerism for readers over 50. Query. Pays $500 to $2,500, on acceptance.

NEW CHOICES: LIVING EVEN BETTER AFTER 50—28 W. 23rd St., New York, NY 10010. David A. Sendler, Ed.-in-Chief. News and service magazine for people ages 50 to 65. Articles on planning for retirement, health and fitness, financial strategies, housing options, travel, profiles/interviews (celebrities and newsmakers), relationships, leisure pursuits, etc. Payment varies, on acceptance. Query or send complete manuscript.

NEW JERSEY 50 + PLUS—1830 US Rt. 9, Toms River, NJ 08755-1210. Pat Jasin, Ed. Articles on finance, health, travel, and social issues for older readers. Pays in copies. Query required.

THE RETIRED OFFICER MAGAZINE—201 N. Washington St., Alexandria, VA 22314. Attn: Manuscripts Ed. Articles, 800 to 2,000 words, of interest to military members and their families. Current military/political affairs, recent military history (especially Vietnam and Korea), military family lifestyles, health, money, second careers. Photos a plus. Pays to $1,200, on acceptance. Queries required. Guidelines.

RX REMEDY—120 Post Rd. W., Westport, CT 06880. Val Weaver, Ed. Bimonthly. Articles, 600 to 2,500 words, on health and medication issues for readers 55 and older. Regular columns include "Housecall" and "The Nutrition Prescription." Query. Pays $1 to $1.25 a word, on acceptance.

SENIOR BEACON—P.O. Box 92467, Austin, TX 78709-2467. Carolyn Keeling, Ed. Poetry, to 100 words, and short (one-or 2-line) fillers for seniors in Texas. No payment.

SENIOR HIGHLIGHTS—26081 Merit Cir., Suite 101, Laguna Hills, CA 92653. Cindy Werelius, Asst. Ed. Articles, 800 words, on health, money, lifestyles, and travel. No payment. Queries preferred. Responds within 3 months. Guidelines.

SENIOR MAGAZINE—3565 S. Higuera St., San Luis Obispo, CA 93401. Attn: Ed. Articles, 600 to 900 words, of interest to men and women 40¢; personality profiles, travel pieces, articles about new things, places, business, sports, movies, television, and health. Reviews of new or outstanding older books. Pays $1.50 per inch; $10 to $25 for B&W photos, on publication.

SENIOR TIMES—Suite 814, 1102 Pleasant St., Worcester, MA 01602-1232. Edwin H. Gledhill, Ed. Short stories, historial or people oriented, 500 to 1,200 words. Articles, 500 to 1,200 words, on arts, travel, local interest, entertainment, and positive role models for aging. Poetry, 10 to 200 words. No payment.

SENIOR WORLD NEWSMAGAZINE—500 Feslen St., Ste. 207, El Cajon, CA 92020. Laura Impastato, Ed. Articles, 800 to 1,000 words, for active, older adults (55¢); focus is on Southern California. Articles on local, state and national news. Features about celebrities, remarkable seniors, consumer interest, finance and investment, housing, sports, hobbies, collectibles, trends, travel, etc. Health and medicine articles emphasizing wellness, preventive care, and the latest on medical treatments. Pays $75 to $100, on publication.

WESTCOAST REFLECTIONS—VP Advertising and Promotions, 2604 Quadra St., Victoria, BC, Canada V8T 4E4. Jane Kezar, Assoc. Ed. Published 10 times a year "for those 39 and holding." Upbeat, humorous, positive articles, 700 to 1,200 words, on travel, recreation, health and fitness, hobbies, home and garden, cooking, finance, and continuing education. Occasionally uses more serious pieces on housing, finances, and health. Nothing political or religious. "The articles we publish are not necessarily about people over 50, but are for them. Writing style should reflect this; use terminology understood by the mature reader." Pays 10¢ a word, on publication. Queries preferred. Guidelines.

YESTERDAY'S MAGAZETTE—P.O. Box 18566, Sarasota, FL 34276. Ned Burke, Ed. Articles and stories, 500 to 1,000 words, set in the 1920s to '70s. Photos a plus. Traditional poetry, to 24 lines. Pays $5 to $25 for articles, on publication. Pays in copies for short pieces and poetry.

HOME & GARDEN/FOOD & WINE

AFRICAN VIOLET MAGAZINE—2375 North St., Beaumont, TX 77702. Ruth Rumsey, Ed. Articles, 700 to 1,400 words, on growing methods for African violets; history and personal experience with African violets. Violet-related poetry. No payment.

THE AMERICAN COTTAGE GARDENER—P.O. Box 22232, Santa Fe, NM 87502-2232. Rand B. Lee, Ed. Quarterly. Articles, 750 to 3,000 words, for cottage gardeners: how-to; plant profiles of specific genera or cultivars; interviews with noted or experienced cottage gardeners, plant breeders, and other specialists. "Topics we're always interested in: regional and ethnic cottage gardening, unusual plants adaptable to the cottage gardening style, fruits and vegetables in the ornamental plot." Pays $25 per printed page of article plus 3 copies. Queries required.

THE AMERICAN GARDENER—(formerly *American Horticulturist*) 7931 E. Boulevard Dr., Alexandria, VA 22308-1300. Kathleen Fisher, Ed. Bimonthly. Articles, to 2,500 words, for American ornamental gardeners: profiles of prominent horticulturists, plant research and plant hunting, events and personalities in horticulture history, plant lore and literature, the politics of horticulture, etc. Humorous pieces for "Offshoots." "We run very few how-to articles." Pays $100 to $400, on publication. Query preferred.

AMERICAN HOMESTYLE & GARDENING—110 Fifth Ave., New York, NY 10011. Karen Saks, Ed.-in-Chief. Articles on interior design, remodeling, architecture, gardening, and the decorative arts. Payment varies, on acceptance. Query.

AMERICAN HORTICULTURIST—See *The American Gardener.*

AMERICAN ROSE—P.O. Box 30,000, Shreveport, LA 71130. Beth Horstman, Man. Ed. Articles on home rose gardens: varieties, products, helpful advice, rose care, etc.

APPELLATION—1040 Main St., Suite 100, Napa, CA 94559. Mary Chesterfield, Ed.-in-Chief. Bimonthly. Articles, 500 to 1,500 words, on the wine, food, destinations, gardens, people, and landscapes of the international wine country regions. Pays on acceptance.

BETTER HOMES AND GARDENS—1716 Locust St., Des Moines, IA 50309-3023. Jean LemMon, Ed. Articles, to 2,000 words, on money management, health, travel, and cars. Pays top rates, on acceptance. Query.

BIRDS & BLOOMS—5400 S. 60th St., Greendale, WI 53129. Tom Curl, Ed. Bimonthly. Articles, 700 to 1,000 words, on personal experiences with wild birds, flowers, gardening, landscaping, etc. ("No bird rescue stories, please!") Shorter pieces for "Backyard Banter." Pays $75 to $200, on publication.

BON APPETIT—6300 Wilshire Blvd., Los Angeles, CA 90048. Barbara Fairchild, Exec. Ed. Articles on fine cooking (menu format or single focus), cooking classes, and gastronomically focused travel. Query with clips. Pays varying rates, on acceptance.

BRIDE'S—(formerly *Bride's & Your New Home*) 140 E. 45th St., New York, NY 10017. Sally Kilbridge, Man. Ed. Articles, 800 to 2,000 words, for engaged couples or newlyweds on wedding planning, home and decorating, and honeymoon. No fiction or poetry. Send travel queries to Travel Dept. Pay starts at 50¢ per word, on acceptance.

BRIDE'S & YOUR NEW HOME—See *Bride's.*

CANADIAN SELECT HOMES MAGAZINE—25 Sheppard Ave. W., Suite 100, North York, Ont., Canada M2N 6S7. Barbara Dixon, Ed. How-to articles, profiles of Canadian homes, renovation, decor, and gardening features, 800 to 1,500 words. Canadian content and locations only. Pays from $400 to $900 (Canadian), on acceptance. Query with international reply coupons. Send SAE with international reply coupons for guidelines.

CANADIAN WORKSHOP MAGAZINE—130 Spy Ct., Markham, Ont., Canada L3R OW5. Hugh McBride, Ed. Articles, 1,500 to 2,800 words, on do-it-yourself home renovations, energy saving projects, etc., with photos. Pays varying rates, on acceptance.

CAROLINA GARDENER—P.O. Box 4504, Greensboro, NC 27404. L.A. Jackson, Ed. Bimonthly. Articles, 1,200 to 1,500 words, specific to southeast gardening: profiles of gardens in the southeast and of new cultivars or "good ol' southern heirlooms." Slides and illustrations should be available to accompany articles. Pays $150, on publication. Query required.

CHEF—Talcott Communications Corp., 20 N. Wacker Dr., Suite 3230, Chicago, IL 60606. Brent T. Frei, Ed.-in-Chief. "The Chef's Business Magazine." Articles, 600 to 1,000 words, that offer professionals in the foodservice business ideas for food marketing, preparation, and presentation. Pays $250, on publication.

CHILE PEPPER—1227 W. Magnolia Ave., Fort Worth, TX 76104. Joel Gregory, Pub. Eddie Lee Rider, Jr., Exec. Ed. Food and travel articles, 1,000 to 1,500 words. "No general and obvious articles, such as 'My Favorite Chile Con Carne.' We want first-person articles about spicy world cuisine." No fillers. Payment varies, on publication. Queries required.

COFFEE JOURNAL—Suite 508, 123 3rd St. N., Minneapolis, MN 55401. Susan Bonne, Ed. Quarterly. Articles on gourmet coffee and tea, product profiles, tips on brewing and enjoying, travel features, and book and music reviews. Some literary fiction, to 3,000 words. Payment varies, on publication.

COOKING LIGHT—P.O. Box 1748, Birmingham, AL 35201. Doug Crichton, Ed. Articles on fitness, exercise, health and healthful cooking, nutrition, and healthful recipes. Query.

COOK'S ILLUSTRATED—17 Station St., P.O. Box 569, Brookline, MA 02147. Keith Powers, Man. Ed. Bimonthly. Articles that emphasize techniques of home cooking with master recipes, careful testing, trial and error. Payment varies, within 60 days of acceptance. Query. Guidelines.

COUNTRY GARDENS—1716 Locust St., Des Moines, IA 50309-3023. LuAnn Brandsen, Ed. Quarterly. Garden-related how-tos and profiles of gardeners, 750 to 1,500 words. Department pieces, 500 to 700 words, on garden-related travel, food, projects, decorating, entertaining. "The gardens we feature are informal, lush, old-fashioned rather than formal and manicured." Pays $250 to $400 for columns; $350 to $800 for features, on acceptance. Query required.

COUNTRY LIVING—224 W. 57th St., New York, NY 10019. Marjorie E. Gage, Features Ed. Articles, 800 to 1,200 words, on decorating, antiques, cooking, travel, home building, crafts, and gardens. "Most material is written in-house; limited free-lance needs." Payment varies, on acceptance. Query preferred.

EATING WELL—823 A Ferry Rd., Charlotte, VT 05445. Marcelle DiFalco, Ed. Published 8 times a year. Feature articles, 2,000 to 5,000 words. Department pieces, 100 to 200 words, for "Nutrition News" and "Eating Well in America." "We look for strong journalistic voice; authoritative, timely coverage of nutrition issues; healthful recipes that emphasize good ingredients, simple preparation, and full flavor; and a sense of humor." Query. Payment varies, 45 days after acceptance.

ELLE DECOR—1633 Broadway, New York, NY 10019. Kendall Coonstrom, Features Ed. Articles, 300 to 1,000 words, on designers and craftspeople (query with photos of the designers and their work) and on houses and apartments "notable for their interior design and/or architecture." Pays $1.25 a word, on publication. Query.

FANCY FOOD—Talcott Communications Corp., 20 N. Wacker Dr., Suite 3230, Chicago, IL 60606. Carolyn Schwaar, Ed.-in-Chief. "The Business Magazine for Specialty Foods, Confections, and Upscale Housewares." Articles, 2,000 words, related to gourmet food. Pays $250, on publication.

FAST AND HEALTHY MAGAZINE—Pillsbury Co., 200 S. Sixth St., MS 28M7, Minneapolis, MN 55402. Betsy Wray, Ed. Bimonthly. Articles, 250 to 800 words, with recipes that can be prepared in 30 minutes or less. "We are open to proposals from experienced food writers or writer/recipe developers." Payment varies, on acceptance. Query.

FINE GARDENING—The Taunton Press, P.O. Box 5506, Newtown, CT 06470-5506. LeeAnne White, Ed. Bimonthly. Articles, 800 to 2,000 words, for readers with a serious interest in gardening: how-tos, garden profiles, as well as pieces on specific plants or garden equipment. "Our primary focus is on ornamental gardening and landscaping." Art-driven publication; picture possibilities are very important. Pays $150 per magazine page, part on acceptance, part on completed galley. Query. Guidelines.

FLOWER & GARDEN MAGAZINE—700 W. 47th St., Suite 310, Kansas City, MO 64112. Attn: Ed. Practical how-to articles, 500 to 1,500 words, on home gardening and landscaping. Photos a plus. Pays varying rates, on acceptance (on publication for photos). Query.

FOOD & WINE—1120 Ave. of the Americas, New York, NY 10036. Dana Cowin, Ed.-in-Chief. Mary Ellen Ward, Man. Ed. No unsolicited material.

GARDEN DESIGN—100 Ave. of the Americas, 7th Fl., New York, NY 10013. Dorothy Kalins, Ed.-in-Chief. Garden-related features, 500 to 1,000 words, on private, public, and community gardens; articles on art and history as they relate to gardens.

GOURMET: THE MAGAZINE OF GOOD LIVING—Conde Nast, 360 Madison Ave., New York, NY 10017. Attn: Ed. No unsolicited manuscripts; query.

GROWERTALKS—P.O. Box 9, 335 N. River St., Batavia, IL 60510-0009. Debbie Hamrick, Ed. Dir. Articles, 800 to 2,600 words, that help commercial greenhouse growers (not florist/retailers or home gardeners) do their jobs better: trends, successes in new types of production, marketing, business management, new crops, and issues facing the industry. Payment varies, on publication. Queries preferred.

THE HERB COMPANION—Interweave Press, 201 E. Fourth St., Loveland, CO 80537. Kathleen Halloran, Ed. Bimonthly. Articles, 1,500 to 3,000 words; fillers, 75 to 150 words. Practical horticultural information, original recipes illustrating the use of herbs, thoroughly researched historical insights, step-by-step instructions for herbal craft projects, book reviews. Pays $125 per published page, on publication.

THE HERB QUARTERLY—P. O. Box 689, San Anselmo, CA 94960. Linda Sparrowe, Ed. Articles, 2,000 to 4,000 words, on herbs: practical uses, cultivation, gourmet cooking, landscaping, herb tradition, medicinal herbs, crafts ideas, unique garden designs; profiles of herb garden experts; practical how-tos for the herb businessperson. Include garden design when possible. Pays on publication. Guidelines; send SASE.

HOME MAGAZINE—1633 Broadway, 44th Fl., New York, NY 10019. Gale Steves, Ed.-in-Chief. Linda Lentz, Articles Ed. Articles of interest to homeowners: architecture, remodeling, decorating, products, project ideas, landscaping and gardening, financial aspects of home ownership, home offices, home-related environmental and ecological topics. Pays varying rates, on acceptance. Query, with 50- to 200-word summary.

HOME MECHANIX—2 Park Ave., New York, NY 10016. Paul Spring, Ed. Articles on home improvement and home-related topics including money management, home security, home care, home environment, yard care, design and remodeling, tools, repair and maintenance, electronics, new products and appliances, building materials, lighting and electrical, home decor.

HORTICULTURE—98 N. Washington St., Boston, MA 02114. Thomas C. Cooper, Ed. Published 10 times a year. Authoritative, well-written articles, 500 to 2,500 words, on all aspects of gardening. Pays competitive rates, on publication. Query.

HOUSE BEAUTIFUL—1700 Broadway, New York, NY 10019. Elaine Greene, Features Ed. Elizabeth Hunter, Travel Ed. Service articles related to the home. Pieces on design, travel, and gardening. Query with detailed outline and photos if relevant. Guidelines.

LOG HOME LIVING—P.O. Box 220039, Chantilly, VA 20153. Janice Brewster, Exec. Ed. Articles, 1,000 to 1,500 words, on modern manufactured and handcrafted kit log homes: homeowner profiles, design and decor features. Pays $200 to $500, on acceptance.

THE MAINE ORGANIC FARMER & GARDENER—RR 2, Box 594, Lincolnville, ME 04849. Jean English, Ed. Quarterly. How-to articles and profiles, 100 to 2,500 words, for organic farmers and gardeners, consumers who care about healthful foods, and activists. Tips, 100 to 250 words. "Our readers want good solid information about farming and gardening, nothing soft." Pays about 6¢ a word, on publication. Queries preferred.

METROPOLITAN HOME—1633 Broadway, New York, NY 10019. Michael Lassell, Articles Dir. Service and informational articles for residents of houses, co-ops, lofts, and condominiums, on real estate, equity, wine and spirits, collecting, trends, etc. Interior design and home furnishing articles with emphasis on lifestyle. Payment varies. Query.

THE MOTHER EARTH NEWS— 49 E. 21st St., 11th Fl., New York, NY 10010. Matthew Scanlon, Ed. Articles on country living: home improvement and construction, how-tos, indoor and outdoor gardening, crafts and projects, etc. Also health, ecology, energy, and consumerism pieces; profiles. Pays varying rates, on acceptance.

NATIONAL GARDENING MAGAZINE—180 Flynn Ave., Burlington, VT 05401. Michael MacCaskey, Ed.-in-Chief. Feature articles, 1,200 to 2,500 words, and departments, 800 to 1,000 words, for advanced and beginning gardeners: the latest on fruits, vegetables, and flowers; profiles of edible and ornmental plants; well-tested gardening techniques; news on how to use beneficial plants and creatures; information on soil improvement; and profiles of experienced gardeners. Include photos and slides if possible. Pay starts at 25¢ per word, on acceptance. Query only. Do not send original art.

ORGANIC GARDENING—33 E. Minor St., Emmaus, PA 18098. Sandra Weida, Office Coordinator. Published 9 times a year. How-to features and profiles of expert organic gardeners, 1,000 to 2,000 words, for home gardeners; also tips, techniques, and news, 100 to 600 words. "Organic methods only! Features must include variety recommendations as well as how to grow." Pays up to 50¢ a word for features; $25 to $125 for departments. Time of payment varies. Queries preferred.

QUICK 'N EASY HOME COOKING—Long Publications, 8393 E. Holly Rd., Holly, MI 48442. Attn: Man. Ed. Family-oriented cooking articles with recipes included, 400 to 500 words and articles with a human-interest/food-related perspective. Pays to $60 for articles, on publication. "We also accept short verse, and humorous fillers, to 50 words."

ROCKY MOUNTAIN GARDENER—P.O. Box 3484, Durango, CO 81302. Susan Martineau, Pub./Ed.-in-Chief. Quarterly. How-to articles, 500 to 1,000 words, on regional techniques and varieties; profiles of regional gardeners and gardens, 500 to 1,000 words; book reviews and production reviews, 300 to 500 words. "Articles must be focused on Rocky Mountain area from New Mexico to Montana. We prefer new, novel, or specific information, not just general gardening topics." Pays 10¢ a word, on publication.

VEGGIE LIFE—1041 Shary Cir., Concord, CA 94518. Sharon Barela, Ed. Bimonthly. Features, 1,500 to 2,000 words, for "people interested in lowfat, meatless cuisine, organic gardening, natural health, nutrition, and herbal healing." Food features (include 8 to 10 recipes); department pieces, 1,000 to 1,500 words. Payment varies, on acceptance or publication. Queries preferred.

WINE SPECTATOR—387 Park Ave. S., New York, NY 10016. Jim Gordon, Man. Ed. Features, 600 to 2,000 words, preferably with photos, on news and people in the wine world, travel, food, and other lifestyle topics. Pays from $400, extra for photos, on publication. Query required.

WINES & VINES—1800 Lincoln Ave., San Rafael, CA 94901. Philip E. Hiaring, Ed. Articles, 2,000 words, on grape and wine industry, emphasizing marketing, management, and production. Pays 15¢ a word, on acceptance.

FAMILY & PARENTING MAGAZINES

ADOPTIVE FAMILIES MAGAZINE—2309 Como Ave., St. Paul, MN 55108. Linda Lynch, Ed. Bimonthly. Articles, 1,500 to 2,500 words, on living in an adoptive family and other adoption issues. Photos of families, adults, or children. Payment is negotiable. Query.

ALL ABOUT KIDS—1077 Celestial St., #101, Cincinnati, OH 1629. Tricia Mullin, Ed. Articles and fiction, to 800 words, for parents ɪɴ ᴛʜᴇ greater Cincinnati area. Fillers, to 400 words. "Our mission is to reinforce the mental health of today's families by providing information and resources that make parenting less stressful and more fun." Pays about $30 to $40, on publication. Queries preferred.

AMERICAN BABY—KIII Family & Leisure Group, 249 W. 17th St., New York, NY 10011. Judith Nolte, Ed. Articles, 1,000 to 2,000 words, for new or expectant parents on prenatal and infant care. Personal experience, 900 to 1,200 words; do not submit in diary format. Department pieces, 50 to 350 words, for "Crib Notes" (news and feature topics). No fiction, fantasy pieces, dreamy musings, or poetry. Pays $500 to $1,000 for articles, $100 for departments, on acceptance. Guidelines.

ATLANTA PARENT—Suite 506, 4330 Georgetown Sq. II, Atlanta, GA 30338. Peggy Middendorf, Ed. Articles, 800 to 2,000 words, on parenting and baby topics. Related humor, 800 to 1,500 words. Photos of parents and/or children. Pays $15 to $30 an article; $15 for photos, on publication.

BABY MAGAZINE—124 E. 40th St., Suite 1101, New York, NY 10016. Jeanne Muchnick, Ed. Bimonthly. Parenting articles, 400 to 750 words, geared toward women in the last trimester of pregnancy and the first year of baby's life. "We want how-to and personal articles designed to smooth the transitions from pregnancy to parenthood." Payment varies, on acceptance. Query.

BABY TALK—1325 Avenue of the Americas, New York, NY 10019. Trisha Thompson, Ed. Articles, 1,000 to 1,500 words, by professionals, on pregnancy, babies, baby care, etc. No poetry. Query by mail. Pays varying rates, on acceptance. SASE required.

BAY AREA BABY—See *Bay Area Parent*.

BAY AREA PARENT— 401 Alberto Way, Suite A, Los Gatos, CA 95032-5404. Mary Brence Martin, Ed. Articles, 1,200 to 1,400 words, on local parenting issues for readers in California's Santa Clara County and the South Bay area. Query. Mention availability of B&W photos. Pays 6¢ a word, $10 to $15 for photos, on publication. Also publishes *Valley Parent* for central Contra Costa County and the tri-valley area of Alameda County, *Bay Area Parent of Teens, Bay Area Baby, Preschool & Childcare Finder*, and *Education and Enrichment Guide*.

BAY AREA PARENT OF TEENS—See *Bay Area Parent*.

THE BIG APPLE PARENTS' PAPER—36 E. 12th St., New York, NY 10003. Helen Rosengren Freedman, Man. Ed. Articles, 500 to 750 words, for NYC parents. Pays $35 to $50, on publication. Buys first NYC rights.

CATHOLIC PARENT—Our Sunday Visitor, Inc., 200 Noll Plaza, Huntington, IN 46750. Woodeene Koenig-Bricker, Ed. Features, how-tos, and general-interest articles, 800 to 1,000 words, dealing with the issues of raising children "with solid values in today's changing world. Keep it anecdotal and practical with an emphasis on values and family life." Payment varies, on acceptance. Guidelines.

CENTRAL CALIFORNIA PARENT—2037 W. Bullard, #131, Fresno, CA 93711. Sally Cook, Pub. Articles, 500 to 1,500 words, of interest to parents. Payment varies, on publication.

CHILDSPLAY—P.O. Box 60744, Longmeadow, MA 01116. Barbara M. Cohen, Ed. "The Parenting Publication for New England." Articles, 1,000 to

1,500 words, for "upwardly mobile, educated parents of children under 12." Payment varies, on publication.

CHRISTIAN HOME & SCHOOL—3350 E. Paris Ave. S.E., Grand Rapids, MI 49512. Gordon L. Bordewyk, Ed. Articles for parents in Canada and the U.S. who send their children to Christian schools and are concerned about the challenges facing Christian families today. Pays $75 to $150, on publication. Send SASE for guidelines or 9"x12" SASE with 4 first-class stamps for guidelines and sample issue.

CHRISTIAN PARENTING TODAY— 4050 Lee Vance View, Colorado Springs, CO 80918. Erin Healy, Ed. Articles, 900 to 2,000 words, dealing with raising children with Christian principles. Departments: "Parent Exchange," 25 to 100 words, on problem-solving ideas that have worked for parents; "Life in our House," insightful anecdotes, 25 to 100 words, about humorous things said at home. Queries preferred for articles. Pays 15¢ to 25¢ a word, on publication. Pays $40 for "Parent Exchange," $25 for "Life in our House." Guidelines.

CONNECTICUT FAMILY—See *New York Family*.

EASTSIDE PARENT—Northwest Parent Publishing, 2107 Elliott Ave., #303, Seattle, WA 98121. Ann Bergman, Ed. Articles, 300 to 2,500 words, for parents of children under 12. Readers tend to be professional, two-career families. Queries preferred. Pays $25 to $200, on publication. Also publishes *Seattle's Child, Portland Parent, Puget Sound Parent, Snohomish County Parent,* and *Pierce County Parent*.

EDUCATION AND ENRICHMENT GUIDE—See *Bay Area Parent*.

EXCEPTIONAL PARENT—209 Harvard St., Suite 303, Brookline, MA 02146-5005. Stanley D. Klein, Ed. Articles, 1,000 to 1,500 words, for parents raising children with disabilities. Practical ideas and techniques on parenting, as well as the latest in technology, research, and rehabilitation. Query. Pays $25, on publication.

EXPECTING— 685 Third Ave., New York, NY 10017. Maija Johnson, Ed. Not buying any new material in the foreseeable future.

FAMILY—169 Lexington Ave., New York, NY 10016. Stacy P. Brassington, Ed. Articles, 1,000 to 2,000 words, of interest to women with children. Topics include: military lifestyle, home decorating, travel, moving, food, personal finances, career, relationships, family, parenting, health and fitness. Pays to $200, on publication. No recent report.

FAMILYFUN—Walt Disney Publishing Group, 244 Main St., Northampton, MA 01060. Clare Ellis, Ed. Articles, to 1,500 words, on family activities and "creative parenting." Payment varies, on acceptance.

FAMILY LIFE—1633 Broadway, New York, NY 10024. Peter Herbst, Ed.-in-Chief. Bimonthly. Articles for parents of children ages 3 to 12. Payment varies (generally $1 a word), on acceptance. Limited market. Query required.

FAMILY TIMES—P.O. Box 932, Eau Claire, WI 54702. Ann Gorton, Ed. Articles, from 800 words, on children and parenting issues: health, education, raising children, how-tos, new studies and programs for educating parents. "Information should be as specific to the Chippewa Valley, WI, as possible." Pays $35 to $50, on publication. Query preferred. Guidelines.

FULL-TIME DADS ON-LINE—(formerly *Full-Time Dads*.) P.O. Box 577, Cumberland, ME 04021. Stephen Harris, Ed. Fiction, articles, essays, and humor, 600 to 1,200 words, and short poems for fathers who are very involved with their children. "All material must relate to supportive fatherhood."

GROWING CHILD/GROWING PARENT—22 N. Second St., P.O. Box 620, Lafayette, IN 47902-0620. Nancy Kleckner, Ed. Articles, to 1,500 words, on subjects of interest to parents of children under 6. No personal experience pieces or poetry. Guidelines.

HOME LIFE—127 Ninth Ave. N., Nashville, TN 37234. Ivey Harrington, Man. Ed. Southern Baptist. Articles, to 1,500 words, on Christian marriage, parenting, and family relationships. Query with SASE required. Pays from $75 for articles, on acceptance.

JOYFUL CHILD JOURNAL—4920 E. Altadena Ave., Scottsdale, AZ 85254-4627. Quarterly. Fiction and nonfiction, 500 to 1,000 words, that "explore how society and education can more effectively nurture children (and adults) to express their fullest potential, thus releasing their inner joy. Articles on educating and parenting the whole child (body, mind, and spirit)." Some short poetry. Pays in copies. Queries preferred. Guidelines available.

L.A. BABY—See *Wingate Enterprises, Ltd.*

L.A. PARENT—See *Wingate Enterprises, Ltd.*

LIVING WITH TEENAGERS—127 Ninth Ave. N., Nashville, TN 37234. Attn: Ed. Articles from a Christian perspective for parents of teenagers. Query, resumé, and writing sample preferred.

METROKIDS—1080 N. Delaware Ave., Suite 702, Philadelphia, PA 19125. Nancy Lisagor, Ed. Tabloid for Delaware Valley families. Features and department pieces, 500 to 1,000 words, on regional family travel, dining, and entertainment. Pays $25 to $50, on publication.

MODERN DAD—7628 N. Rogers Ave., Chicago, IL 60626-1214. Elisa Kronish, Ed. Bimonthly. Articles, 200 to 3,000 words, that aid, educate, and inform fathers. "We value fathering *and* the family and explore all the possibilities of fatherhood in today's information age." Guidelines with SASE. Payment varies, on publication. Query preferred.

MOSAICA DIGEST—242 Fourth St., Lakewood, NJ 08701. Attn: Submission Dept. Joseph Ginberg, Pres. Fiction, 1,500 to 4,000 words; articles, 1,500 to 3,000 words; fillers, 100 to 300 words, of interest to Jewish families. First-person pieces, humor, travel, and history. Articles of Jewish interest are preferred (not articles about religion or religious issues). "We are a family-oriented magazine, and everything must be squeaky clean! No profanity, etc." Reprints are preferred. Pays to $50, on publication.

NEW YORK FAMILY—141 Halstead Ave., Suite 3D, Mamaroneck, NY 10543. Felice Shapiro, Susan Ross Benamram, Pubs. Betsy F. Woolf, Sr. Ed. Articles related to family life in New York City and general parenting topics. Pays $50 to $200. Same requirements for *Westchester Family* and *Connecticut Family*.

PARENTGUIDE NEWS—419 Park Ave. S., 13th Fl., New York, NY 10016. Jenine M. DeLuca, Ed.-in-Chief. Articles, 1,000 to 1,500 words, related to families and parenting issues: trends, profiles, health, education, travel, fashion, calendar of events, seasonal topics, reader's opinions, kid's page, special programs, products, etc. Humor and photos also considered.

PARENTING—See *Wingate Enterprises, Ltd.*

PARENTING—1325 Avenue of the Americas, New York, NY 10019. Attn: Articles Ed. Articles, 500 to 3,000 words, on education, health, fitness, nutrition, child development, psychology, and social issues for parents of young children. Query.

PARENTLIFE—MSN 140, 127 Ninth Ave. N., Nashville, TN 37234. Attn: Ed. Articles on Christian family issues. Resumés only.

PARENTS—685 Third Ave., New York, NY 10017. Ann Pleshette Murphy, Ed. Articles, 1,500 to 2,500 words, on parenting, family, women's and community issues, etc. Informal style with quotes from experts. Pays from $1,000, on acceptance. Query.

PARENTS EXPRESS—P.O. Box 12900, Philadelphia, PA 19108. Sharon Sexton, Ed. Articles on children and family topics for Philadelphia-area parents. Pays $120 to $250 for first rights, $25 to $35 for reprints, on publication.

PENINSULA PARENT—See *Windmill Publishing, Inc.*

PIERCE COUNTY PARENT—See *Eastside Parent.*

PORTLAND PARENT—See *Eastside Parent.*

PRESCHOOL & CHILDCARE FINDER—See *Bay Area Parent.*

PUGET SOUND PARENT—See *Eastside Parent.*

SAN DIEGO PARENT—See *Wingate Enterprises, Ltd.*

SEATTLE'S CHILD—Northwest Parent Publishing, 2107 Elliott Ave., #303, Seattle, WA 98121. Ann Bergman, Ed. Articles, 400 to 2,500 words, of interest to parents, educators, and childcare providers of children under 12, plus investigative reports and consumer tips on issues affecting families in the Puget Sound region. Pays $75 to $400, on publication. Query.

SESAME STREET PARENTS—One Lincoln Plaza, New York, NY 10023. Articles, 800 to 2,500 words, on children and violence; Susan Schneider, Exec. Ed. Articles on educational issues, health, and newsbriefs; Franny Shuker-Haines, Sr. Assoc. Ed. Articles on computer, travel, and review material; Linda Bernstein. "Covers parenting issues for families with young children (to 8 years old)." Pays $1 per word, up to 6 weeks after acceptance. SASE for guidelines.

SNOHOMISH COUNTY PARENT—See *Eastside Parent.*

STEPFAMILIES—Stepfamily Assn. of America, 215 Centennial Mall S., Suite 212, Lincoln, NE 68508-1834. Attn: Ed. Quarterly. Articles, 2 to 4 pages, relevant to stepfamily living. Fillers and poetry. No payment.

SUCCESSFUL BLACK PARENTING—P.O. Box 6359, Philadelphia, PA 19139. Marta Sanchez-Speer, Acting Ed. Bi-monthly. Features, 800 to 1,000 words; department pieces 500 to 700 words; and columns 150 to 200 words on black children and black families. Payment varies, on publication. Query.

TIDEWATER PARENT—See *Windmill Publishing, Inc.*

TOLEDO AREA PARENT NEWS—1120 Adams St., Toledo, OH 43624. Veronica Hughes, Ed. Articles on parenting, child and family health, and other family topics, 1,100 to 1,200 words. Writers must be from Northwest Ohio and Southern Michigan. Pays $75 to $100 per article, on acceptance. Query required.

TWINS—The Magazine for Parent of Multiples, 5350 S. Roslyn St., Suite 400, Englewood, CO 80111. Susan J. Alt, Ed.-in-Chief. Send submissions to

Heather White, Asst. Ed. Features, 1,100 to 1,300 words, third person. Departments, 750 to 950 words, first person. "Articles must be multiples specific and focus on every day issues parents of twins, triplets, and more face. Features should have 2 to 3 professional and/or parental experience sources." Payment is $75 to $250, on publication. Query or send complete manuscript.

VALLEY PARENT—See *Bay Area Parent.*

WESTCHESTER FAMILY—See *New York Family.*

WINDMILL PUBLISHING, INC.—Parenting Publications of America, 2753 Atwoodtown Rd., Virginia Beach, VA 23456. Peggy Sijswerda, Ed. Informational articles, 800 to 1,100 words, for regional parenting tabloids, including *Tidewater Parent* and *Peninsula Parent.* Pays $40 to $60, within 2 weeks of publication.

WINGATE ENTERPRISES, LTD.—P.O. Box 3204, 443 E. Irving Dr., Burbank, CA 91504. Attn: Eds. Publishes city-based parenting magazines with strong "service-to-parent" slant. Articles, 1,200 words, on child development, health, nutrition, and education. *San Diego Parent* covers San Diego area; *Parenting* covers the Orange County, CA, area; *L.A. Parent* is geared toward parents of children to age 10; *L.A. Baby* to expectant parents and parents of newborns. Pays $100 to $350, on acceptance. Query.

WORKING MOTHER—MacDonald Communications, 135 W. 50th St., New York, NY 10020. Attn: Ed. Dept. Articles, to 2,000 words, that help women juggle job, home, and family. Payment varies, on acceptance.

LIFESTYLE MAGAZINES

AMERICAN HEALTH FOR WOMEN—28 W. 23rd St., New York, NY 10010. Attn: Ed. Dept. Lively, authoritative articles, 1,000 to 2,000 words, on women's health and lifestyle aspects of health and fitness; 100- to 500-word news reports. Payment varies for news stories and features, on acceptance. Query with clips.

AQUARIUS: A SIGN OF THE TIMES—1028 Alpharetta St., Roswell, GA 30075. Dan Liss, Ed. Articles, 800 words (with photos or illustrations), on New Age lifestyles and positive thought, holistic health, metaphysics, spirituality, environment. No payment.

ASPIRE—107 Kenner Ave., Nashville, TN 37205. Jeanette Thomason, Ed.-in-Chief. Lifestyle magazine for Christian women. Articles, 500 to 2,000 words, on trends in health, career issues, parenting, and relationships, "inspiring and encouraging readers to incorporate faith into daily life." Pays 30¢ a word, on acceptance. Query with resumé and clips. Send SASE for guidelines.

AVATAR JOURNAL—237 N. Westmonte Dr., Altamonte Springs, FL 32714. Miken Chappell, Ed. Bimonthly. Articles, 500 to 1,000 words, on self-development, awakening consciousness, and spiritual enlightenment. "Spiritual in nature. Pieces that teach a lesson, paradigm shifts, epiphany experiences, anecdotes with theme of obtaining enlightenment, healing, inspiration, metaphysics." Pays $100 for articles; $50 for poems, on publication.

BACKHOME—P.O. Box 70, Hendersonville, NC 28793. Lorna K. Loveless, Ed. Articles, 800 to 2,500 words, on home schooling, recycling, home business, healthful cooking. "We hope to provide readers with ways to gain more control over their lives by becoming more self-sufficient: raising their own food, making their own repairs, using alternative energy, etc. We do not promote 'dropping out' of society, but ways to become better citizens and caretakers of the planet." Pays $25 per page; $20 for photos, on publication. Queries preferred.

CAPPER'S—Editorial Dept., 1503 S.W. 42nd St., Topeka, KS 66609-1265. Nancy Peavler, Ed. Human-interest, personal-experience, historical articles, 300 to 700 words. Poetry, to 15 lines, on nature, home, family. Novel-length fiction for serialization. Letters on women's interests, recipes, and hints for "Heart of the Home." Jokes. Children's writing and art section. Pays varying rates, on publication.

THE CHRISTIAN SCIENCE MONITOR—One Norway St., Boston, MA 02115. Jane A. Lampmann, Features Ed. Newspaper. Articles on lifestyle trends, women's rights, family, and parenting. Pays varying rates, on acceptance.

COMMON BOUNDARY—5272 River Rd., Suite 650, Bethesda, MD 20816. Attn: Manuscript Ed. Bimonthly. Feature articles, 3,000 to 4,000 words, exploring the connections between psychology, spirituality, and creativity. Essays, book reviews, department pieces (1,500 to 1,800 words), and 500-word news items. Readers are mental health professionals, pastoral counselors, spiritual directors, and lay readers.

COUNTRY AMERICA—1716 Locust St., Des Moines, IA 50309-3023. Bill Eftink: general inquiries. Roberta Peterson: country people, country lifestyle, almanac, travel, comedy; Neil Pond: country entertainment, entertainers' lifestyles and events; Jody Garlock: general interest, personalities, country essays, travel; Diane Yanney: foods, recipes, country crafts; Bob Ehlert: heritage and traditions, country places, country people. Articles should be light on copy with potential for several color photos. Queries preferred.

COUNTRY CONNECTIONS—14431 Ventura Blvd., #407, Sherman Oaks, CA 91423. Catherine R. Leach, Ed. Bimonthly. Articles, to 2,000 words, and fiction, to 1,000 words. Poetry. "We serve as a forum for public discourse about ethics, politics, social justice, community, city rights, animal and environmental issues." Pays in copies or subscription.

CREATION SPIRITUALITY NETWORK MAGAZINE—P.O. Box 20369, Oakland, CA 94620. Rebecca Bier, Ed. Essays, 1,500 to 2,500 words, on life and the creation spirituality movement. Payment negotiable.

CURIO—P.O. Box 522, Bronxville, NY 10708-0522. Teresa Lawrence, Ed. Quarterly. Fiction, articles, and poetry, 100 to 3,000 words, on a wide range of subjects of interest to "college educated, socially and environmentally aware readers aged 25 to 35." Read magazine for current themes. Pays $140 per page, on publication.

DIALOGUE: A WORLD OF IDEAS FOR VISUALLY IMPAIRED PEOPLE OF ALL AGES—P.O. Box 5181, Salem, OR 97304-0181. Carol McCarl, Ed. Quarterly. Articles, 800 to 1,200 words, and poetry, 20 lines, for visually impaired youth and adults. Career opportunities, educational skills, and recreational activities. "We want to give readers an opportunity to learn about interesting and successful people who are visually impaired." Payment varies, on publication. Queries are preferred. SASE.

EARTH STAR—P.O. Box 1033, Cambridge, MA 02140. Cody Bideaux, Ed. Bimonthly. Articles, 200 to 3,000 words, on health, metaphysical subjects, environment, celebrity interviews, music. Pieces on local Boston arts and entertainment. "Our readers are interested in spirituality, personal growth, social responsibility, contemporary social issues, and holistic health." Pays $50 to $200, on acceptance. Query.

FATE—P.O. Box 64383, St. Paul, MN 55164-0383. Attn: Ed. Factual fillers and true stories, to 3,000 words, on strange or psychic happenings and mystic personal experiences. Pays 10¢ a word.

FELLOWSHIP—Box 271, Nyack, NY 10960-0271. Richard Deats, Ed. Bimonthly published by the Fellowship of Reconciliation, an interfaith, pacifist organization. Features, 1,500 to 2,000 words, and articles, 750 words, "dealing with nonviolence, opposition to war, and a just and peaceful world community." Photo-essays (B&W photos, include caption information). SASE required. Pays in copies and subscription. Queries preferred.

FREE SPIRIT MAGAZINE—107 Sterling Pl., Brooklyn, NY 11217. Andrea Strudensky, Ed. Bimonthly. Articles, 4,000 words, on environmental issues, holistic health, political issues, culture/art, and general interest for readers in Manhattan. Interviews welcomed. Pays 10¢ a word, on acceptance. Query preferred.

FRIENDLY EXCHANGE—P.O. Box 2120, Warren, MI 48090-2120. Dan Grantham, Ed. Articles, 700 to 1,500 words, offering readers "news you can use," on lifestyle issues such as home, health, personal finance, and travel. Photos. Pays $400 to $1,000, extra for photos. Query required. Guidelines.

GENRE—7080 Hollywood Blvd., Suite 1104, Hollywood, CA 90028. John Polly, Assoc. Ed. Fiction, 3,000 to 5,000 words, and articles, 750 to 3,000 words, of interest to gay men. "Feature articles should be national in scope and somehow related to the gay male experience." Pays to 50¢ a word, on publication.

GERMAN LIFE—Zeitgeist Publishing, 1 Corporate Dr., Grantsville, MD 21536. Heidi Whitesell, Ed. Bimonthly. Articles, 500 to 2,500 words, on German culture, its past and present, and how America has been influenced by its German element: history, travel, people, the arts, and social and political issues. Fillers, 50 to 200 words. Pays $300 to $500 for full-length articles, to $80 for short pieces and for fillers, on publication. Queries preferred.

GOOD TIMES—1500 Market St., 12th Fl., Centre Sq. E., Philadelphia, PA 19102. Karen Detwiler, Ed.-in-Chief. Lifestyle magazine for mature Pennsylvanians 50 years and older. Articles, 1,500 to 2,000 words, on medical issues, health, travel, finance, fashion, gardening, fitness, legal issues, celebrities, lifestyles, and relationships. Guidelines. Payment varies, on publication. Query.

THE GREEN MAN—P.O. Box 641, Point Arena, CA 95468-0641. Diane Conn Darling, Ed. "Exploring Paths for Pagan Men." Articles, 1,500 to 3,000 words, exploring a theme. Pays in copies. Query for future themes.

HEALTH QUEST—200 Highpoint Dr., Suite 215, Chalfont, PA 18914. Valerie Boyd, Ed.-in-Chief. Tamara Jeffries, Man. Ed. "The Publication of Black Wellness." Articles, 500 to 1,500 words, on health issues of interest to African-American men and women. "We focus on total health, so articles cover mind, body, spirit, and cultural wellness." Payment varies, on publication. Query preferred.

HEART & SOUL—Rodale Press, Inc., 733 Third Ave., 15th Fl., New York, NY 10017. Stephanie Stokes Oliver, Ed.-in-Chief. Articles, 800 to 1,500 words, on health, beauty, fitness, nutrition, and relationships for African-

American women. "We aim to be the African-American woman's ultimate guide to a healthy lifestyle." Payment varies, on acceptance. Queries preferred.

HOW ON EARTH!—P.O. Box 339, Oxford, PA 19363-0339. Amina Chaudhri, Ed.-in-Chief. Articles, 1,000 to 2,000 words, by writers ages 13 to 24 on vegetarian living, animals, the environment, social justice, youth empowerment, and activism; essays, personal pieces, interviews, and creative writing, 400 to 800 words, on related subjects; food reviews, 300 to 700 words; music and book reviews, 200 to 500 words. "Living Vegetarian," general essays, to 800 words, about being vegetarian in a meat eating society. Adult submissions are occasionally accepted for research/information articles and general interest articles, 1,000 to 2,000 words. Pays in copies. Query. Guidelines.

ILLYRIA: THE ALBANIAN-AMERICAN NEWSPAPER—2321 Hughes Ave., Bronx, NY 10458. Joseph Finora, Man. Dir. Articles on news, politics, people, sports, history, travel, food, and culture. All articles must relate to Albania, Albanians, or Albanian-Americans. Photos. Payment negotiable, on publication.

INSIDE MAGAZINE—226 S. 16th St., Philadelphia, PA 19102-3392. Jane Biberman, Ed. Jewish lifestyle magazine. Articles, 1,500 to 3,000 words, on Jewish issues, health, finance, and the arts. Pays $75 to $600, after publication. Queries required; send clips if available.

INSIDER MAGAZINE—4124 W. Oakton, Skokie, IL 60201. David Glines, Ed. Dir. Articles, 700, 1,500, and 2,100 words, on issues, career, politics, sports, and entertainment. "We are mainly a college publication, but to appeal to college readers you must write above them." Pays 1¢ to 5¢ a word, on publication. Queries preferred.

INTERRACE—2870 Peachtree Rd., Suite 264, Atlanta, GA 30305. Candy Mills, Ed. Articles, 800 words, with an interracial, intercultural, or interethnic theme: news event, commentary, personal account, exposé, historical, interview, etc. No fiction. "Not limited to black/white issues. Interaction between blacks, whites, Asians, Latinos, Native Americans, etc., is also desired." No payment.

INTUITION—P.O. Box 460773, San Francisco, CA 94146. Colleen Mauro, Ed. Bimonthly. Articles, 750 to 6,000 words, on intuition, creativity, and spiritual development. Departments, 750 to 2,000 words, include profiles; "Frontier Science," breakthroughs pertaining to parapsychology, creativity, etc.; "Intuitive Tools," history and application of a traditional approach to accessing information. Pays $25 for book reviews to $1,200 for cover articles.

JEWISH CURRENTS—22 E. 17th St., #601, New York, NY 10003. Morris U. Schappes, Ed. Articles and book reviews, 2,400 to 3,000 words, on progressive Jewish culture or history: Holocaust resistance commemoration, Black-Jewish relations, Yiddish literature and culture, Jewish labor struggles. "We are a secular Jewish magazine." No fiction. No payment.

THE JEWISH HOMEMAKER—1372 Carroll St., Brooklyn, NY 11213. Sara Levy, Ed. Bimonthly. Articles, 1,200 to 2,000 words, for a traditional/ Orthodox Jewish audience. Humor. Payment varies, on publication. Query.

LEFTHANDER MAGAZINE—P.O. Box 8249, Topeka, KS 66608-0249. Kim Kipers, Ed. Bimonthly. Articles, 1,500 to 1,800 words, related to left-handedness: profiles of left-handed personalities; performing specific tasks or sports as a lefty; teaching left-handed children. Personal experience pieces for

"Perspective." SASE for guidelines. Pays $80 to $100, on publication. Buys all rights. Query.

LINK: THE COLLEGE MAGAZINE—The Soho Bldg., 110 Greene St., Suite 407, New York, NY 10012. Ty Wenger, Ed.-in-Chief. News, lifestyle, and issues for college students. Informational how-to and short features, 500 to 800 words, on education news, finances, academics, employment, lifestyles, and trends. Well-researched, insightful, authoritative articles. Queries preferred. Pays $100 to $500, on publication. Guidelines.

MAGICAL BLEND—133-1/2 Broadway St., Chico, CA 95928-5317. Jerry Snider, Ed. Nonfiction; positive, uplifting articles, to 3,000 words, on spiritual exploration, lifestyles, occult, white magic, New Age thought.

MEN'S JOURNAL—1290 Ave. of the Americas, New York, NY 10104-0298. Attn: Editorial. Lifestyle magazine for active men ages 25 to 49. Articles and profiles, 2,000 to 7,000 words, on travel, fitness, health, adventure, and participatory sports. Service articles, 400 to 800 words, for equipment and fitness sections. Pays "good rates," on acceptance. Query.

MOMENT MAGAZINE—4710 41st St. N.W., Washington, DC 20016. Attn: Sr. Ed. Sophisticated articles, 2,500 to 5,000 words, on Jewish culture, politics, religion, and personalities. Columns, to 1,500 words, with uncommon perspectives on contemporary issues, humor, strong anecdotes. Book reviews, 400 words. Pays $40 to $600.

MOUNTAIN LIVING MAGAZINE—7009 S. Potomac, Englewood, CO 80112. Robyn Griggs, Ed. Articles, 1,200 to 1,500 words, on topics related to the mountains of the U.S.: travel, home design, architecture, gardening, art, cuisine, sports, and people. Pays $75 to $400, on acceptance.

NATIVE PEOPLES MAGAZINE—The Arts and Lifeways 5333 N. 7th St., Suite C-224, Phoenix, AZ 85014-2804. Gary Avey, Ed. Rebecca Withers, Man. Ed. Quarterly, full-color on Native Americans. Articles, 1,800 to 2,800 words, authenticity and positive portrayals of present traditional and cultural practices necessary. Pays 25¢ a word, on publication. Query, include availability of photos. Guidelines and sample copy. SASE.

NEW AGE JOURNAL—42 Pleasant St., Watertown, MA 02172-2312. Joan Duncan Oliver, Ed. Articles for readers who take an active interest in social change, personal growth, health, and contemporary issues. Features, 2,000 to 4,000 words; columns, 750 to 1,500 words; short news items, 150 words; and first-person narratives, 750 to 1,500 words. Pays varying rates, after acceptance.

NEW CHOICES: LIVING EVEN BETTER AFTER 50—28 W. 23rd St., New York, NY 10010. David A. Sendler, Ed.-in-Chief. News and service magazine for people ages 50 to 65. Articles on retirement planning, financial strategies, housing options, as well as health and fitness, travel, leisure pursuits, etc. Payment varies, on acceptance.

NEWPORT LIFE—174 Bellevue Ave., Suite 207, Newport, RI 02840. Lynne Tungelt, Man. Ed. Quarterly. Articles, 500 to 2,500 words, on the people and places of Newport County: general-interest and historical articles, interviews, profiles, investigative pieces, and photo-features. Departments, 600 to 750 words, include "At the Helm" (on some aspect of boating), "Arts Marquee," "Food for Thought," and "Historical Newport." Photos must be available for all articles. Query. SASE.

OUT—The Soho Bldg., 110 Greene St., Suite 600, New York, NY 10012. Sarah Pettit, Ed.-in-Chief. Articles and fillers, 50 to 8,000 words, on various subjects (current affairs, culture, fitness, finance, etc.) of interest to gay and lesbian readers. "The best guide to what we publish is to read previous issues." Payment varies, on publication. Query. Guidelines.

OUT YOUR BACKDOOR— 4686 Meridian Rd., Williamston, MI 48895. Jeff Potter, Ed. Articles and fiction, 2,500 words, for thrifty, down-to-earth culture enthusiasts. "Budget travel, second-hand treasure, and homespun but high-quality culture all combine to yield an energetic, practical, folksy post-modern magazine." Study sample issue before submitting. Pays in copies.

PALM SPRINGS LIFE—Desert Publications, 303 N. Indian Canyon Dr., Palm Springs, CA 92262. Stewart Weiner, Ed. Articles, 1,000 to 3,000 words, of interest to "wealthy, upscale people who live and/or play in the desert." Pays $150 to $1,000 for features, $25 to $75 for short profiles, on publication. Query required.

PERCEPTIONS—10736 Jefferson Blvd., Suite 502, Culver City, CA 90230. Judi V. Brewer, Ed. Articles, to 2,500 words, on government, alternative health, metaphysics. Reviews, to 500 words. Cartoons. "Broad-spectrum focus crossing barriers that separate ideologies, politics, etc." Sections include Political Slant (relevant information focusing on what we have in common); Healing Spiral (little-known facts, therapies, and remedies); Concepts (a forum to broaden, awaken, and tickle the intellect). Pays in copies and $10.

THE PHOENIX—7152 Unity Ave. N., Brooklyn Ctr., MN 55429. Pat Samples, Ed. Tabloid. Articles, 800 to 1,500 words, on recovery, renewal, and growth. Department pieces for "Bodywise," "Family Skills," or "Personal Story." "Our readers are committed to physical, emotional, mental, and spiritual health and well-being. Read a sample copy to see what we publish." Pays 3¢ to 5¢ a word, on publication. Guidelines and calendar. SASE.

QUICK 'N EASY HOME COOKING—Long Publications, 8393 E. Holly Rd., Holly, MI 48442. Attn: Man. Ed. Family-oriented articles with recipes included, 400 to 500 words, on cooking, and articles with a human-interest/down-home perspective. Short verse, humorous fillers, to 50 words. Pays $20 to $60 for articles, on publication.

ROBB REPORT—1 Acton Pl., Acton, MA 01720. Steven Castle, Ed. Consumer magazine for the high-end/luxury market. Features on lifestyles, home interiors, boats, travel, investment opportunities, exotic automobiles, business, technology, etc. Payment varies, on publication. Query with SASE and published clips.

SAGEWOMAN—P.O. Box 641, Point Arena, CA 95468-0641. Anne Newkirk Niven, Ed. Quarterly. Articles, 200 to 5,000 words, on issues of concern to pagan and spiritually minded women. Material which expresses an earth-centered spirituality: personal experience, Goddess lore, ritual material, interviews, humor, and reviews. Accepts material by women only. Pays 3¢ a word, from $10, on publication.

SCIENCE OF MIND—P.O. Box 75127, Los Angeles, CA 90075. Jim Shea, Asst. Ed. Articles, 1,500 to 2,000 words, that offer a thoughtful perspective on how to experience greater self-acceptance, empowerment, and meaningful life. "Achieving wholeness through applying Science of Mind principles is the primary focus." Inspiring first-person pieces, 1,000 to 2,000 words. Interviews with notable spiritual leaders, 3,500 words. Poetry, to 28 lines. Pays $25 per page. Queries required (except for poetry).

SWING—342 Madison Ave., #1402, New York, NY 10017. Megan Liberman, Exec. Ed. Articles, 800 to 3,000 words, on issues of interest to readers in their 20s. Pays 50¢ to $1 a word, on publication. Query with clips.

T'AI CHI—P.O. Box 26156, Los Angeles, CA 90026. Marvin Smalheiser, Ed. Articles, 1,200 to 4,000 words, on T'ai Chi Ch'uan, other internal martial arts and related topics such as qigong, Chinese medicine and healing practices, Chinese philosophy and culture, health, meditation, fitness, self-improvement, as well as news about teachers and schools. Pays $75 to $500, on publication. Query required. Guidelines. SASE.

TURNING WHEEL—P.O. Box 4650, Berkeley, CA 94704. Susan Moon, Ed. Quarterly. Articles, poetry, fillers, and artwork. "Magazine is dedicated to the development of engaged Buddhism, engaged spirituality and spiritual politics." No payment.

USAIR MAGAZINE—Pace Communications, 1301 Carolina St., Greensboro, NC 27401. USAir inflight magazine. Articles on travel, lifestyle trends, sports, personality profiles, food and wine, shopping, the arts and culture. "Our goal is to provide readers with lively and colorful, yet practical articles that will make their lives and their leisure time more rewarding." Payment made within 60 days of acceptance. Query with clips; no unsolicited manuscripts.

VEGETARIAN VOICE—P.O. Box 72, Dolgeville, NY 13329. Jennie Collura, Sr. Ed. Quarterly. Informative, well-researched and/or inspiring articles, 600 to 1,800 words, on lifestyles and consumer concerns, health, nutrition, animal rights, the environment, world hunger, etc. "Our underlying philosophy is total vegetarian; all our recipes are vegan and we do not support the use of leather, wool, silk, etc." Guidelines. Pays in copies.

VENTURE INWARD—67th and Atlantic Ave., P.O. Box 595, Virginia Beach, VA 23451. A. Robert Smith, Ed. Articles, to 4,000 words, on metaphysical and spiritual development subjects. Prefer personal experience. Opinion pieces, to 800 words, for "Guest Column." "Turning Point," to 800 words, on an inspiring personal turning point experience. "The Mystical Way," to 1,500 words, on a personal paranormal experience. "Holistic Health," brief accounts of success using Edgar Cayce remedies. Book reviews, to 500 words. Pays $30 to $300, on publication. Query.

VIRTUE: HELPING WOMEN BUILD CHRIST-LIKE CHARACTER—4050 Lee Vance View, Colorado Springs, CO 80918-7102. Laura J. Barker, Ed. Articles, 1,200 to 1,400 words, on family, marriage, self-esteem, working women; women's relationships with family, friends, and God. Fiction and poetry. Pays 15¢ to 25¢ a word, $25 to $50 for poetry, on publication. Query with SASE required.

WEIGHT WATCHERS MAGAZINE—2100 Lakeshore Dr., Birmingham, AL 35209. Sr. Ed. Articles on health, nutrition, fitness, and weight-loss motivation and success. Pays on acceptance. Query with clips required. Guidelines.

WHOLE LIFE TIMES—21225 Pacific Coast Hwy., Suite B, P.O. Box 1187, Malibu, CA 90265. S.T. Alcantara, Assoc. Ed. Tabloid. Feature articles, 2,000 words, with a holistic perspective. Departments and columns, 800 words. Well-researched articles on the environment, current political issues, women's issues, and new developments in health, as well as how-to, humor, new product information, personal growth, and interviews. Pays 5¢ a word for features, 30 days after publication.

WIRED—520 Third St., San Francisco, CA 94107-1427. Ted Roberts, Ed. Asst. Lifestyle magazine for the "digital generation." Articles, essays, profiles, fiction, and other material that discusses the "meaning and context" of digital technology in today's world. Guidelines. Payment varies, on publication.

YOGA JOURNAL—2054 University Ave., Berkeley, CA 94704. Rick Fields, Ed. Articles, 1,200 to 4,000 words, on holistic health, spirituality, yoga, and transpersonal psychology; New Age profiles; interviews. Pays $100 to $1,200, on acceptance.

SPORTS & RECREATION

ADVENTURE CYCLIST—Adventure Cycling Assn., P.O. Box 8308, Missoula, MT 59807. Daniel D'Ambrosio, Ed. Articles, 1,200 to 2,500 words: accounts of bicycle tours in the U.S. and overseas, interviews, personal-experience pieces, humor, and news shorts. Pays $25 to $65 per published page.

ADVENTURE WEST—P.O. Box 3210, Incline Village, NV 89451. Michael Oliver, Assoc. Ed. Bimonthly. Recreational travel articles, 1,500 to 2,000 words, on risky wild adventures; 1,500 to 2,000 words, on shorter trips that offer a high degree of excitement; and service pieces, 1,000 to 1,500 words on short excursions. Profiles and essays also used. Emphasis must be on American West, including Alaska, Hawaii, western Canada, and western Mexico. Pays 30¢ a word, on publication.

AKC GAZETTE—(formerly *Pure-Bred Dogs/American Kennel Gazette*) 51 Madison Ave., New York, NY 10010. Mark Roland, Features Ed. "The official journal for the sport of purebred dogs." Articles, 1,000 to 2,500 words, relating to purebred dogs, for serious fanciers. Pays $200 to $450, on acceptance. Queries preferred.

THE AMERICAN FIELD—542 S. Dearborn, Chicago, IL 60605. B.J. Matthys, Man. Ed. Yarns about hunting trips, bird-shooting; articles to 1,500 words, on dogs and field trials, emphasizing conservation of game resources. Pays varying rates, on acceptance.

AMERICAN HUNTER—NRA Publications, 11250 Waples Mill Rd., Fairfax, VA 22030. Tom Fulgham, Ed. Articles, 1,400 to 2,000 words, on hunting. Photos. Pays on acceptance. Guidelines.

AMERICAN MOTORCYCLIST—American Motorcyclist Assn., 33 Collegeview Rd., Westerville, OH 43081-1484. Greg Harrison, Ed. Articles and fiction, to 3,000 words, on motorcycling: news coverage, personalities, tours. Photos. Pays varying rates, on publication. Query with SASE.

THE AMERICAN RIFLEMAN—11250 Waples Mill Rd., Fairfax, VA 22030. Mark Keefe, Man. Ed. Factual articles on use and enjoyment of sporting firearms. Pays on acceptance.

AMERICAN SQUAREDANCE MAGAZINE—661 Middlefield Rd., Salinas, CA 93906-1004. Jon Sanborn, Ed. Articles and fiction, 1,000 to 1,500 words, related to square dancing. Poetry. Fillers, to 100 words. Pays $1.50 per column inch.

ATLANTIC SALMON JOURNAL—P.O. Box 429, St. Andrews, N.B., Canada E0G 2X0. Harry Bruce, Ed. Articles, 1,500 to 3,000 words, related to Atlantic salmon: fishing, conservation, ecology, travel, politics, biology, how-tos, anecdotes. Pays $100 to $400, on publication.

BACKPACKER MAGAZINE—Rodale Press, 33 E. Minor St., Emmaus, PA 18098. John Viehman, Exec. Ed. Articles, 250 to 3,000 words, on self-propelled backcountry travel: backpacking, kayaking/canoeing, mountaineering; technique, nordic skiing, health, natural science. Photos. Pays varying rates. Query.

THE BACKSTRETCH—P.O. Box 7065, Louisville, KY 40257-0065. Barrett Shaw, Ed. United Thoroughbred Trainers of America. Feature articles, with photos, on subjects related to thoroughbred horse racing. Pays after publication. Sample issue and guidelines on request.

BACKWOODSMAN—P.O. Box 627, Westcliffe, CO 81252. Charlie Richie, Ed. Articles for the twentieth-century frontiersman: muzzleloading, primitive weapons, black powder cartridge guns, woodslore, survival, homesteading, trapping, etc. Historical and how-to articles. No payment.

BASEBALL FORECAST, BASEBALL ILLUSTRATED—See *Hockey Illustrated.*

BASKETBALL FORECAST—See *Hockey Illustrated.*

BASSIN'—NatCom, Inc., 5300 CityPlex Tower, 2448 E. 81st St., Tulsa, OK 74137-4207. Mark Chesnut, Exec. Ed. Articles, 1,200 to 1,400 words, on how and where to bass fish, for the amateur fisherman. Pays $350 to $500, on acceptance. Query.

BASSMASTER MAGAZINE—B.A.S.S. Publications, P.O. Box 17900, Montgomery, AL 36141. Dave Precht, Ed. Articles, 1,500 to 2,000 words, with photos, on freshwater black bass and striped bass. "Short Casts" pieces, 400 to 800 words, on news, views, and items of interest. Pays $200 to $400, on acceptance. Query.

BC OUTDOORS—1132 Hamilton St., #202, Vancouver, B.C., Canada V6B 2S2. Karl Bruhn, Ed. Articles, to 1,500 words, on fishing, hunting, conservation, and all forms of non-competitive outdoor recreation in British Columbia and Yukon. Photos. Pays from 20¢ to 27¢ a word, on publication.

BIRD WATCHER'S DIGEST—P.O. Box 110, Marietta, OH 45750. William H. Thompson, III, Ed. Articles, 600 to 2,500 words, for bird watchers: first-person accounts; how-tos; pieces on endangered species; profiles. Pays from $50, on publication. Submit complete manuscript. SASE for guidelines.

BLACK BELT—P.O. Box 918, Santa Clarita, CA 91380-9018. Attn: Ed. Articles related to self-defense: how-tos on fitness and technique; historical, travel, philosophical subjects. Pays $100 to $300, on publication. Guidelines.

BOUNDARY WATERS JOURNAL—9396 Rocky Ledge Rd., Ely, MN 55731. Stuart Osthoff, Ed. Articles, 2,000 to 3,000 words, on wilderness, recreation, nature, and conservation in Minnesota's Boundary Waters Canoe Area Wilderness and Ontario's Quetico Provincial Park. Regular features include canoe-route journals, fishing, camping, hiking, cross-country skiing, wildlife and nature, regional lifestyles, history, and events. Pays $200 to $400, on publication; $50 to $150 for photos.

BOW & ARROW HUNTING—Box 2429, 34249 Camino Capistrano, Capistrano Beach, CA 92624-0429. Roger Combs, Ed. Dir. Articles, 1,200 to 2,500 words, with B&W or color photos, on bowhunting; profiles and technical pieces, primarily on deer hunting. Pays $100 to $300, on acceptance. Same address and mechanical requirements for *Gun World.*

BOWHUNTER MAGAZINE—P.O. Box 8200, Harrisburg, PA 17105-8200. M.R. James, Ed. Informative, entertaining features, 500 to 2,000 words, on bow-and-arrow hunting. Fillers. Photos. "Study magazine first." Pays $100 to $400, on acceptance.

BOWLING—5301 S. 76th St., Greendale, WI 53129. Bill Vint, Ed. Articles, to 1,500 words, on all aspects of bowling, especially human interest. Profiles. "We're looking for unique, unusual stories about bowling people and places and occasionally publish business articles." Pays varying rates, on publication. Query required.

BUCKMASTERS WHITETAIL MAGAZINE—P.O. Box 244022, Montgomery, AL 36124-4022. Russell Thornberry, Exec. Ed. Semiannual. Articles and fiction, 2,500 words, for serious sportsmen. "Big Buck Adventures" articles capture the details and the adventure of the hunt of a newly discovered trophy. Fresh, new whitetail hunting how-tos; new biological information about whitetail deer that might help hunters; entertaining deer stories; and other department pieces. Photos a plus. Pays $250 to $400 for articles, on acceptance. Guidelines.

BUGLE—Rocky Mountain Elk Foundation, P.O. Box 8249, Missoula, MT 59807-8249. Jan Brocci, Asst. Ed. Quarterly. Fiction and nonfiction, 1,500 to 4,000 words, on elk and elk hunting. Department pieces, 1,000 to 3,000 words, for: "Thoughts and Theories"; "Situation Ethics"; and "Women in the Outdoors." Pays 20¢ a word, on acceptance.

CANADIAN DIVER & WATERSPORT—See *Diver Magazine.*

CANOE AND KAYAK MAGAZINE—(formerly *Canoe*) P.O. Box 3146, Kirkland, WA 98083. Paul Temple, Ed.-in-Chief. Features, 1,100 to 2,000 words; department pieces, 500 to 1,000 words. Topics include canoeing or kayaking adventures, destinations, boat and equipment reviews, techniques and how-tos, short essays, camping, environment, humor, health, history, etc. Pays 12.5¢ a word, on publication. Query preferred. Guidelines.

CAR AND DRIVER—2002 Hogback Rd., Ann Arbor, MI 48105. Csaba Csere, Ed.-in-Chief. Articles, to 2,500 words, for enthusiasts, on new cars, classic cars, industry topics. "Ninety percent staff-written. Query with clips. No unsolicited manuscripts." Pays to $2,500, on acceptance.

CASCADES EAST—716 N.E. Fourth St., P.O. Box 5784, Bend, OR 97708. Geoff Hill, Ed./Pub. Articles, 1,000 to 2,000 words, on outdoor activities (fishing, hunting, golfing, backpacking, rafting, skiing, snowmobiling, etc.), history, special events, and scenic tours in central Oregon Cascades. Photos. Pays 5¢ to 10¢ a word, extra for photos, on publication.

CHESAPEAKE BAY MAGAZINE—1819 Bay Ridge Ave., Annapolis, MD 21403. Tim Sayles, Ed. Articles, to 1,500 words, on boating, fishing, destinations and people on the Chesapeake Bay. Photos. Pays $100 to $700, on acceptance. Query.

CROSS COUNTRY SKIER—P.O. Box 50120, Minneapolis, MN 55405. Jim Chase, Ed. Published October through February. Articles, to 2,000 words, on all aspects of cross-country skiing. Departments, 1,000 to 1,500 words, on ski maintenance, skiing techniques, health and fitness. Pays $300 to $700 for features, $100 to $350 for departments, on publication. Query.

CURRENTS—212 W. Cheyenne Mountain Blvd., Colorado Springs, CO 80906. Greg Moore, Ed. Quarterly. "Voice of the National Organization for Rivers." Articles, 500 to 2,000 words, for kayakers, rafters, and river canoeists, pertaining to whitewater rivers and/or river running. Fillers. B&W action photos. Pays from $40 for articles, $30 to $50 for photos, on publication. Queries preferred.

CYCLE WORLD — 1499 Monrovia Ave., Newport Beach, CA 92663. David Edwards, Ed.-in-Chief. Technical and feature articles, 1,500 to 2,500 words, for motorcycle enthusiasts. Photos. Pays on publication. Query.

CYCLING U.S.A. — U.S. Cycling Federation, One Olympic Plaza, Colorado Springs, CO 80909. Frank Stanley, Ed. Articles, 500 to 1,000 words, on bicycle racing. Pays 10¢ a word, on publication. Query.

THE DIVER — P.O. Box 54788, St. Petersburg, FL 33739. Bob Taylor, Ed. Articles on divers, coaches, officials, springboard and platform techniques, training tips, etc. Pays $15 to $35, extra for photos ($5 to $10 for cartoons), on publication.

DIVER MAGAZINE — 230-11780 Hammersmith Way, Richmond, B.C., Canada V7A 5E3. Stephanie Bold, Ed. Illustrated articles, 500 to 1,000 words, on dive destinations. Shorter pieces are also welcome. "Travel features should be brief and accompanied by excellent slides and/or prints and a map. Unsolicited articles will be reviewed only from August to October and will be considered for *Diver Magazine* and *Canadian Diver & Watersport*." Pays $2.50 per column inch, on publication. Guidelines. Limited market.

EQUUS — Fleet Street Corp., 656 Quince Orchard Rd., Gaithersburg, MD 20878. Laurie Prinz, Exec. Ed. Articles, 1,000 to 3,000 words, on all breeds of horses, covering their health, care, the latest advances in equine medicine and research. "Attempt to speak as one horseperson to another." Pays $100 to $400, on publication.

FIELD & STREAM — 2 Park Ave., New York, NY 10016. Duncan Barnes, Ed. Articles, 1,500 to 2,000 words, with photos, on hunting, fishing. Short articles, to 1,000 words. Fillers, 75 to 500 words. Cartoons. Pays from $800 for feature articles with photos, $75 to $500 for fillers, $100 for cartoons, on acceptance. Query for articles.

FLIGHT — Air Age Publishing, 100 E. Ridge , Ridgefield, CT 06877-4606. Tom Atwood, Ed. Articles, 2,500 to 3,000 words, on "the history, the hardware, and the human heart of aviation." Send one-page outline to Dana Donia, Ed. Asst. Payment is $600.

FLY FISHERMAN — 6405 Flank Dr., Box 8200, Harrisburg, PA 17105. Philip Hanyok, Man. Ed. Query.

FLY ROD & REEL — P.O. Box 370, Camden, ME 04843. James E. Butler, Ed. Fly-fishing pieces, 2,000 to 2,500 words, and occasional fiction; articles on the culture and history of the areas being fished. Pays on acceptance. Query.

FOOTBALL DIGEST — Century Publishing Co., 990 Grove St., Evanston, IL 60201. Kenneth Leiker, Ed. William Wagner, Assoc. Ed. Articles, 1,500 to 2,500 words, for the hard-core football fan: profiles of pro and college stars, nostalgia, trends in the sport. Pays on publication. Query.

FOOTBALL FORECAST — See *Hockey Illustrated*.

FUR-FISH-GAME — 2878 E. Main St., Columbus, OH 43209. Mitch Cox, Ed. Illustrated articles, 800 to 2,500 words, preferably with how-to angle, on hunting, fishing, trapping, dogs, camping, or other outdoor topics. Some humorous or where-to articles. Pays to $150, on acceptance.

GAME AND FISH PUBLICATIONS — P.O. Box 741, Marietta, GA 30061. Attn: Ed. Dept. Publishes 30 monthly outdoor magazines for 48 states. Articles, 1,500 to 2,500 words, on hunting and fishing. How-tos, where-tos, and adventure pieces. Profiles of successful hunters and fishermen. No hiking, canoeing, camping, or backpacking pieces. Pays $125 to $175 for state-specific articles, $200 to $250 for multi-state articles, before publication. Pays $25 to $75 for photos.

GOLF DIGEST—5520 Park Ave., Trumbull, CT 06611. Jerry Tarde, Ed. Instructional articles, tournament reports, and features on players, to 2,500 words. Fiction, 1,000 to 2,000 words. Poetry, fillers, humor, photos. Pays varying rates, on acceptance. Query preferred.

GOLF FOR WOMEN—P.O. Box 951989, Lake Mary, FL 32795-1989. Pat Baldwin, Ed.-in-Chief. Golf-related articles of interest to women; fillers and humor. Instructional pieces are staff-written. Query.

GOLF JOURNAL—Golf House, P.O. Box 708, Far Hills, NJ 07931-0708. Brett Avery, Ed. Official publication of the United States Golf Association. A general-interest magazine on the game with articles on a variety of contemporary and historic topics. Pays varying rates, on publication.

GOLF TIPS—Werner Publishing Corp., 12121 Wilshire Blvd., #120, Los Angeles, CA 90025-1175. John Ledesma, Man. Ed. Articles, 500 to 1,500 words, for serious golfers: unique golf instruction, golf products, interviews with pro players. Fillers: short "shotmaking" instruction tips. Queries preferred. Pays $200 to $600, on publication.

THE GREYHOUND REVIEW—National Greyhound Assn., Box 543, Abilene, KS 67410. Tim Horan, Man. Ed. Articles, 1,000 to 10,000 words, pertaining to the greyhound racing industry: how-to, historical nostalgia, interviews. Pays $85 to $150, on publication.

GULF COAST GOLFER—See *North Texas Golfer.*

GUN DIGEST— 4092 Commercial Ave., Northbrook, IL 60062. Ken Warner, Ed. Well-researched articles, to 5,000 words, on guns and shooting, equipment, etc. Photos. Pays from 10¢ a word, on acceptance. Query.

GUN DOG—P.O. Box 35098, Des Moines, IA 50315. Rick Van Etten, Man. Ed. Features, 1,000 to 2,500 words, with photos, on bird hunting: how-tos, where-tos, dog training, canine medicine, breeding strategy. Fiction. Humor. Pays $150 to $300 for fillers and short articles, $150 to $450 for features, on acceptance.

GUN WORLD—See *Bow & Arrow Hunting.*

GUNGAMES—Box 516, Moreno Valley, CA 92556. Roni Toldanes, Ed. Bimonthly. Articles and fiction, 1,200 to 1,500 words, about "the fun side of guns and shooting. No self-defense articles." Related poetry, to 300 words. Pays $250 to $350, on publication.

HANG GLIDING—U.S. Hang Gliding Assn., P.O. Box 1330, Colorado Springs, CO 80901-1330. Gilbert Dodgen, Ed. Articles, 2 to 3 pages, on hang gliding. Pays to $50, on publication. Query.

HOCKEY ILLUSTRATED—Lexington Library, Inc., 233 Park Ave. S., New York, NY 10003. Stephen Ciacciarelli, Ed. Articles, 2,500 words, on hockey players and teams. Pays $125, on publication. Query. Same address and requirements for *Baseball Illustrated, Wrestling World, Pro Basketball Illustrated, Pro Football Illustrated, Baseball Forecast, Pro Football Preview, Football Forecast,* and *Basketball Forecast.*

HORSE & RIDER—12265 W. Bayaud Ave., Suite 300, Lakewood, CO 80228. Sue M. Copeland, Ed. Articles, 500 to 3,000 words, with photos, on western riding and general horse care geared to the performance horse: training, feeding, grooming, health, etc. Pays varying rates, on publication. Buys one-time rights. Guidelines.

HORSEMEN'S YANKEE PEDLAR—83 Leicester St., N. Oxford, MA 01537. Kelley R. Small, Pub. News and feature-length articles, about horses and horsemen in the Northeast. Photos. Pays $2 per published inch, on publication. Query.

HOT BOAT—Sport Publications, 8484 Wilshire Blvd., #900, Beverly Hills, CA 90211. Brett Bayne, Ed. Family-oriented articles, 600 to 1,000 words, on motorized water sport events and personalities: general-interest, how-to, and technical features. Pays $85 to $300, on publication. Query.

HUNTING—6420 Wilshire Blvd., Los Angeles, CA 90048-5515. Todd Smith, Ed. How-to/where-to articles on practical aspects of hunting. At least 15 photos required with articles. Query required. Guidelines. Pays $300 to $500 for articles with B&W photos, extra for color photos. Manuscripts are paid on acceptance; photos, on publication.

INSIDE SPORTS—990 Grove St., Evanston, IL 60201. Kenneth Leiker, Ed. In-depth, insightful sports articles, player profiles relating to baseball, football, basketball, hockey, auto racing, and boxing. Payment varies, on publication. Query.

INSIDE TEXAS RUNNING—9514 Bristlebrook Dr., Houston, TX 77083-6193. Joanne Schmidt, Ed. Articles and fillers on running in Texas. Pays $35 to $100 for articles; $10 for photos and short fillers, on acceptance.

KITPLANES—P.O. Box 6050, Mission Viejo, CA 92690. Dave Martin, Ed. Articles, 1,000 to 4,000 words, on all aspects of design, construction, and performance of aircraft built from kits and plans by home craftsmen. Pays $60 per page, on publication.

LAKELAND BOATING—1560 Sherman Ave., Suite 1220, Evanston, IL 60201-5047. Randall W. Hess, Ed. Articles for powerboat owners on the Great Lakes and other area waterways, on long-distance cruising, short trips, maintenance, equipment, history, regional personalities and events, and environment. Photos. Pays on publication. Query. Guidelines.

MEN'S HEALTH—Rodale Press, 33 E. Minor St., Emmaus, PA 18098. David Zinczenko, Sr. Ed. Articles, 1,000 to 2,500 words, on sports, fitness, diet, health, nutrition, relationships, and travel, for men ages 25 to 55. Pays from 50¢ a word, on acceptance. Query.

MICHIGAN OUT-OF-DOORS—P.O. Box 30235, Lansing, MI 48909. Dennis Knickerbocker, Ed. Features, 1,000 to 2,500 words, on hunting, fishing, camping, and conservation in Michigan. Pays $75 to $150, on acceptance.

MID-WEST OUTDOORS—111 Shore Dr., Hinsdale, IL 60521-5885. Gene Laulunen, Ed. Articles, 1,000 to 1,500 words, with photos, on where, when, and how to fish and hunt in the Midwest. No Canadian material. Pays $15 to $35, on publication.

MOTOR BOATING & SAILING—250 W. 55th St., 4th Fl., New York, NY 10019-5905. Peter A. Janssen, Ed./Pub. Articles, 1,500 words, on buying, maintaining, and enjoying boats. Hard-core, authoritative how-to. Query. Payment varies, on acceptance.

MOTOR TREND— 6420 Wilshire Blvd., Los Angeles, CA 90048-5515. C. Van Tune, Ed. Articles, 250 to 2,000 words, on autos, racing, events, histories, and profiles. Color photos. Pay varies, on acceptance. Query.

MOTORHOME MAGAZINE—2575 Vista Del Mar, Ventura, CA 93001. Barbara Leonard, Ed. Dir. Articles, to 2,000 words, with color slides, on motorhomes. Also travel and how-to pieces. Pays to $600, on acceptance.

MUSHING—P.O. Box 149, Ester, AK 99725-0149. Todd Hoener, Ed. Dog-driving how-tos, profiles, and features, 1,500 to 2,000 words; and department pieces, 500 to 1,000 words, for competitive and recreational dogsled drivers, weight pullers, dog packers, and skijorers. International audience. Photos. Pays $20 to $175, on publication. Queries preferred. Guidelines and sample issue on request.

NATIONAL PARKS MAGAZINE—1776 Massachusetts Ave. N.W., Washington, DC 20036. Leslie Happ, Ed.-in-Chief. Articles, 1,500 to 2,000 words, on areas in the National Park System, proposed new areas, threats to parks or park wildlife, new trends in park use, legislative issues, and endangered species of plants or animals relevant to national parks. No fiction, poetry, personal narratives, "My trip to...," or straight travel pieces to individual parks. Articles, 1,500 words, on "low-impact" travel to 4 or 5 national park sites. Pays $400 to $1,000, on acceptance. Query with clips (original slant or news hook is essential to successful query). Guidelines.

THE NEW ENGLAND SKIERS GUIDE—Box 1125, Waitsfield, VT 05673. Jill Jemison, Ed. Annual (June deadline for submissions). Articles on alpine and nordic skiing and snowboarding, equipment, and winter vacations at New England resorts. Rates vary.

NEW YORK OUTDOORS—51 Atlantic Ave., Floral Park, NY 11001. Scott Shane, Ed.-in-Chief. Features, to 1,500 words, with B&W prints or color transparencies, on any aspect of outdoor sports travel or adventure in northeast U.S. Pays to $250 for major features. Queries preferred.

NORTH TEXAS GOLFER— 9182 Old Katy Rd., Suite 212, Houston, TX 77055. Bob Gray, Ed./Pub. Articles, 800 to 1,500 words, of interest to golfers in north Texas. Pays $50 to $250, on publication. Queries required. Same requirements for *Gulf Coast Golfer* (for golfers in south Texas).

NORTHEAST OUTDOORS—Woodall Publishing Corp., 13975 W. Polo Trail Dr., Lake Forest, IL 60045-5000. Ann Emerson, Man. Ed. Articles, 500 to 1,000 words, preferably with B&W photos, on camping and recreational vehicle (RV) touring in northeast U.S.: recommended private campgrounds, camp cookery, recreational vehicle hints. Stress how-to, where-to. Cartoons. Pays $20 to $80, on publication. Guidelines.

OFFSHORE—220 Reservoir St., Needham Heights, MA 02194. Peter Serratore, Ed. Articles, 1,200 to 2,500 words, on boats, people, places, maritime history, and events along the New England, New York, and New Jersey coasts. Writers should be knowledgeable boaters. Photos a plus. Pays $250 to $500.

OPEN WHEEL— 65 Parker St., #2, Newburyport, MA 01950. Dick Berggren, Ed. Articles, to 6,000 words, on open wheel drivers, races, and vehicles. Photos. Pays to $400 on publication.

OUTDOOR AMERICA—707 Conservation Ln., Gaithersburg, MD 20878-2983. Attn: Articles Ed. Quarterly publication of the Izaak Walton League of America. Articles, 1,250 to 2,000 words, on natural resource conservation issues and outdoor recreation, with emphasis on IWLA member/chapter tie-in; especially fishing, hunting, and camping. Also, short items, 500 to 750 words. Pays 20¢ a word. Query with clips.

OUTDOOR CANADA—703 Evans Ave., Suite 202, Toronto, Ont., Canada M9C 5E9. James Little, Ed. Published 8 times yearly. Articles, 1,500 to 2,000 words, on fishing, camping, hiking, canoeing, hunting, and wildlife. Pays $400 to $600, on publication.

OUTSIDE—Outside Plaza, 400 Market St., Santa Fe, NM 87501. No unsolicited material.

PADDLER MAGAZINE—P.O. Box 775450, Steamboat Springs, CO 80477. Eugene Buchanan, Ed. Dir. Articles on canoeing, kayaking, rafting, sea kayaking. "Best way to break in is to target a specific department, i.e. 'Hotlines,' 'Paddle People,' etc." Pays $5 an inch, on publication. Query preferred. Guidelines.

PENNSYLVANIA ANGLER—Pennsylvania Fish and Boat Commission, P.O. Box 67000, Harrisburg, PA 17106-7000. Attn: Art Michaels, Ed. Articles, 500 to 3,000 words, with photos, on freshwater fishing in Pennsylvania. Pays $50 to $400, on acceptance. Must send SASE with all material. Query. Guidelines.

PENNSYLVANIA GAME NEWS—Game Commission, 2001 Elmerton Ave., Harrisburg, PA 17110-9797. Bob Mitchell, Ed. Articles, to 2,500 words, on outdoor subjects, except fishing and boating. Photos. Pays from 6¢ a word, extra for photos, on acceptance.

PETERSEN'S BOWHUNTING— 6420 Wilshire Blvd., Los Angeles, CA 90048-5515. Greg Tinsley, Ed. How-to articles, 2,000 to 2,500 words, on bowhunting. Also pieces on where to bowhunt, unusual techniques and equipment, and profiles of successful bowhunters will also be considered. Photos must accompany all manuscripts. Pays $300 to $400, on acceptance. Query.

PETERSEN'S HUNTING— 6420 Wilshire Blvd., 14th Fl., Los Angeles, CA 90048-5515. Todd Smith, Ed. How-to articles, 2,250 words, on all aspects of sport hunting. B&W photos; color slides. Pays $300 to $500, on acceptance. Query.

PLANE & PILOT—12121 Wilshire Blvd., #1200, Los Angeles, CA 90025-1175. Steve Werner, Ed. Aviation related articles, 1,500 to 3,000 words, targeted to the single engine, piston powered recreational pilot. Training, maintenance, travel, equipment, pilot reports. Occasional features on antique, classic, and kit-or home-built aircraft. Payment varies, on publication. Query preferred.

POWER AND MOTORYACHT—249 W. 17th St., New York, NY 10011. Diane M. Byrne, Man. Ed. Articles, 1,000 to 2,000 words, for owners of powerboats, 24 feet and larger. Seamanship, ship's systems, maintenance, sportfishing news, travel destinations, profiles of individuals working to improve the marine environment. "For our readers, powerboating is truly a lifestyle, not just a hobby." Pays $500 to $1,000, on acceptance. Query required.

POWERBOAT—1691 Spinnaker Dr., Suite 206, Ventura, CA 93001. Eric Colby, Ed. Articles, to 2,000 words, with photos, for high performance powerboat owners, on outstanding achievements, water-skiing, competitions; technical articles on hull and engine developments; how-to pieces. Pays $300 to $1,000, on publication. Query.

PRACTICAL HORSEMAN—Box 589, Unionville, PA 19375. Mandy Lorraine, Ed. How-to articles conveying experts' advice on English riding, training, and horse care. Pays on acceptance. Query with clips.

PRIVATE PILOT—P.O. Box 6050, Mission Viejo, CA 92690-6050. Joseph P. O'Leary, Ed. Hands-on how-to aviation articles, 1,000 to 3,000 words, for general aviation pilots, aircraft owners, and aviation enthusiasts. Photos. Pays $75 to $450, on publication. Query.

PRO BASKETBALL ILLUSTRATED—See *Hockey Illustrated.*

PRO FOOTBALL ILLUSTRATED, PRO FOOTBALL PREVIEW—See *Hockey Illustrated.*

PURE-BRED DOGS/AMERICAN KENNEL GAZETTE—See *AKC Gazette.*

RESTORATION—P.O. Box 50046, Dept. TW, Tucson, AZ 85703-1046. W.R. Haessner, Ed. Articles, 1,200 to 1,800 words, on restoration projects in general, as well as restoration of autos, trucks, planes, trains, etc., and related building (bridges and structures). Photos. Pays from $25 per page, on publication. Queries required.

RIDER—2575 Vista Del Mar, Ventura, CA 93001. Mark Tuttle Jr., Ed. Articles, to 3,000 words, with slides, on travel, touring, commuting, and camping motorcyclists. Pays $100 to $750, on publication. Query.

ROCK + ICE MAGAZINE— 603A S. Broadway, Boulder, CO 80303. Marjorie McCloy, Ed. Bimonthly. Articles, 500 to 6,000 words, and fiction, 1,500 to 4,000 words, for technical rock and ice climbers: sport climbers, mountaineers, alpinists, and other adventurers. Slides and B&W photos considered. Query. Pays $300 per published page.

RUNNER TRIATHLETE NEWS—P.O. Box 19909, Houston, TX 77224. Lance Phegley, Ed. Articles on running for road racing and multi-sport enthusiasts in TX, OK, NM, LA, and AR. Payment varies, on publication.

RUNNER'S WORLD—Rodale Press, 33 E. Minor St., Emmaus, PA 18098. Bob Wischnia, Sr. Ed. Articles for "Human Race" (submit to Eileen Shovlin), "Finish Line" (to Cristina Negron), and "Health Watch" (to Adam Bean) columns. Send feature articles or queries to Bob Wischnia. Payment varies, on acceptance. Query.

RV TRAVELER—(formerly *Trails-A-Way*) Woodall Publishing Co., P.O. Box 5000, Lake Forest, IL 60045-5000. Debbie Harmsen, Ed. RV-related travel articles, 1,000 to 1,200 words, for Midwest camping families. Pay varies, on publication.

SAFARI— 4800 W. Gates Pass Rd., Tucson, AZ 85745. William Quimby, Publications Dir. Articles, 2,000 words, on worldwide big game hunting and/or conservation projects of Safari Club International's local chapters. Pays $200, extra for photos, on publication.

SAIL—275 Washington St., Newton, MA 02158-1630. Patience Wales, Ed. Articles, 1,500 to 3,500 words, features, 1,000 to 2,500 words, with photos, on sailboats, equipment, racing, and cruising. How-tos on navigation, sail trim, etc. Pays $75 to $1,000 on publication. Guidelines.

SAILING—125 E. Main St., Port Washington, WI 53074. M. L. Hutchins, Ed. Features, 700 to 1,500 words, with photos, on cruising and racing; first-person accounts; profiles of boats and regattas. Query for technical or how-to pieces. Pays varying rates, 30 days after publication. Guidelines.

SALT WATER SPORTSMAN—77 Franklin St., Boston, MA 02110. Barry Gibson, Ed. Articles, 1,200 to 1,500 words, on how anglers can improve their skills, and on new places to fish off the coast of the U.S. and Canada, Central America, the Caribbean, and Bermuda. Photos a plus. Pays $350 to $700, on acceptance. Query.

SEA, AMERICA'S WESTERN BOATING MAGAZINE—17782 Cowan, Suite C, Irvine, CA 92614. Eston Ellis, Sr. Ed. Features, 800 to 1,500 words, and news articles, 200 to 250 words, of interest to West Coast power boaters: cruise destinations, analyses of marine environmental issues, technical pieces on navigation and seamanship, news from western harbors. No fiction, poetry, or cartoons. Pays varying rates, on publication.

SEA KAYAKER—P.O. Box 17170, Seattle, WA 98107-0870. Christopher Cunningham, Ed. Articles, 400 to 4,500 words, on ocean kayaking. Related fiction. Pays about 12¢ a word, on publication. Query with clips and international reply coupons.

SHOTGUN SPORTS—P.O. Box 6810, Auburn, CA 95604. Frank Kodl, Ed. Articles with photos, on trap and skeet shooting, sporting clays, hunting with shotguns, reloading, gun tests, and instructional shooting. Pays $25 to $200, on publication.

SILENT SPORTS—717 10th St., P.O. Box 152, Waupaca, WI 54981-9990. Attn: Ed. Articles, 1,000 to 2,000 words, on bicycling, cross country skiing, running, canoeing, hiking, backpacking, and other "silent" sports. Must have regional (upper Midwest) focus. Pays $50 to $100 for features; $20 to $50 for fillers, on publication. Query.

SKI MAGAZINE—2 Park Ave., New York, NY 10016. Andy Bigford, Ed. Articles, 1,300 to 2,000 words, for experienced skiers: profiles, and destination articles. Short, 100- to 300-word, news items for "Ski Life" column. Equipment and racing articles are staff-written. Query (with clips) for articles. Pays from $50, on acceptance.

SKI RACING INTERNATIONAL—Box 1125, Rt. 100, Waitsfield, VT 05673. Jill Jemison, Man. Ed. Articles by experts on race techniques and conditioning secrets. Coverage of World Cup, pro, collegiate, and junior ski and snowboard competition. Comprehensive results. Photos. Rates vary.

SKIN DIVER MAGAZINE— 6420 Wilshire Blvd., Los Angeles, CA 90048-5515. Bill Gleason, Pub./Ed. Illustrated articles, 500 to 2,000 words, on scuba diving activities, equipment, and dive sites. Pays $50 per published page, on publication.

SKYDIVING MAGAZINE—1725 N. Lexington Ave., DeLand, FL 32724. Michael Truffer, Ed. Timely news articles, 300 to 800 words, relating to sport and military parachuting. Fillers. Photos. Pays $25 to $200, extra for photos, on publication.

SNOW COUNTRY—5520 Park Ave., Trumbull, CT 06611-0395. Kathleen Ring, Sr. Ed. Published 8 times a year. Features, 2,500 to 4,000 words, and articles, 1,000 to 2,000 words, on skiing, mountain biking, in-line skating, camping, rafting and other year-round mountain sports as well as lifestyle issues. First-person adventure articles, travel pieces, service-oriented articles, profiles of snow country residents. "Mountain Living," 100- to 700-word pieces on people and points of view, anecdotes, trends, issues. Query with clips and resumé. Pays 80¢ a word, on acceptance.

SNOWBOARDER—P.O. Box 1028, Dana Point, CA 92629. Steve Hawk, Ed. Doug Palladini, Pub. Bimonthly. Articles, 1,000 to 1,500 words, on snowboarding personalities, techniques, and adventure; color transparencies or B&W prints. Limited fiction market, 1,000 to 1,500 words. Pays $150 to $800, on acceptance and on publication.

SNOWEST—520 Park Ave., Idaho Falls, ID 83402. Lane Lindstrom, Ed. Articles, 1,200 words, on snowmobiling in the western states. Pays to $100, on publication.

THE SNOWSHOER—Box 458, Washburn, IN 54891. Jim Radtke, Ed. Fiction and articles on snowshoeing, 1,000 to 1,500 words. Pays 5¢ a word, on publication. Queries preferred.

SOCCER JR.—27 Unquowa Rd., Fairfield, CT 06430. Joe Provey, Ed. Articles, fiction, and fillers related to soccer for readers in 5th and 6th grade. Pays $450 for features; $250 for department pieces, on acceptance. Query.

SOUTH CAROLINA WILDLIFE—P. O. Box 167, Columbia, SC 29202-0167. John E. Davis, Ed. Articles, 1,000 to 2,000 words, with state and regional outdoor focus: conservation, natural history, wildlife, and recreation. Profiles, how-tos. Pays on acceptance.

SOUTHERN OUTDOORS—5845 Carmichael Rd., Montgomery, AL 36117. Larry Teague, Ed. How-to pieces, 800 to 1,200 words, and 2,000-word how-to and where-to articles on hunting and fishing, for fishermen and hunters in the Southern states. Pays 20¢ a word, on acceptance. Query.

SPORT MAGAZINE—6420 Wilshire Blvd., Los Angeles, CA 90048. Cam Benty, Ed. Dir. No fiction, poetry, or first person. Query with clips.

SPORTS ILLUSTRATED—1271 Ave. of the Americas, New York, NY 10020. Chris Hunt, Articles Ed. Query.

SPORTS ILLUSTRATED FOR KIDS—1271 Ave. of the Americas, New York, NY 10020. Steve Malley, Asst. Man. Ed. Articles, 1,000 to 1,500 words, (submit to Amy Lennard Goehner) and short features, 500 to 600 words, (submit to Jon Scher) for 8- to 13-year-olds. "Most articles are staff-written. Department pieces are the best bet for free lancers." (Read magazine and guidelines to learn about specific departments.) Puzzles and games (submit to Erin Egan). No fiction or poetry. Pays $500 for departments, $1,000 to $1,250 for articles, on acceptance. Query required.

STOCK CAR RACING—65 Parker St., #2, Newburyport, MA 01950. Dick Berggren, Feature Ed. Articles, to 6,000 words, on stock car drivers, races, and vehicles. Photos. Pays to $400, on publication.

SURFING—P.O. Box 3010, San Clemente, CA 92674. Nick Carroll, Ed. Skip Snead, Asst. Ed. Short newsy and humorous articles, 200 to 500 words. No first-person travel articles. "Knowledge of the sport is essential." Pays varying rates, on publication.

SWEAT—736 E. Loyola Dr., Tempe, AZ 85282. Joan Westlake, Ed. Articles, 500 to 1,200 words, on sports or fitness with an Arizona angle. "No personal articles or tales. We want investigative pieces. Articles must relate specifically to Arizona or Arizonans." Pays $25 to $60 for articles; $12 to $70 for photos, on publication. Queries required; no unsolicited manuscripts.

T'AI CHI—P.O. Box 26156, Los Angeles, CA 90026. Marvin Smalheiser, Ed. Articles, 800 to 4,000 words, on T'ai Chi Ch'uan, other internal martial arts and related topics such as qigong, Chinese medicine and healing practices,

Chinese philosophy and culture, health, meditation, fitness, and self-improvement. Pays $75 to $500, on publication. Query required. Guidelines.

TENNIS—5520 Park Ave., P. O. Box 0395, Trumbull, CT 06611-0395. Donna Doherty, Ed. Instructional articles, features, profiles of tennis stars, grassroots articles, humor, 800 to 2,000 words. Photos. Payment varies, on publication. Query.

TENNIS WEEK—341 Madison Ave., #600, New York, NY 10017-3705. Eugene L. Scott, Pub. Kim Kodl, Cherry V. Masih, Merrill Chapman, Man. Eds. In-depth, researched articles, from 1,000 words, on current issues and personalities in the game. Pays $125, on publication.

TRAILER BOATS—20700 Belshaw Ave., Carson, CA 90746-3510. Randy Scott, Ed. Lifestyle, technical and how-to articles, 500 to 2,000 words, on boat, trailer, or tow vehicle maintenance and operation; skiing, fishing, and cruising. Fillers, humor. Pays $100 to $700, on acceptance.

TRAILER LIFE—2575 Vista Del Mar, Ventura, CA 93001. Barbara Leonard, Ed. Articles, to 2,000 words, with photos, on trailering, truck campers, motorhomes, hobbies, and RV lifestyles. How-to pieces. Pays to $600, on acceptance. Guidelines.

TRAILS-A-WAY—See *RV Traveler.*

TRIATHLETE—121 Second St., San Francisco, CA 94105. Lisa Y. Park, Man. Ed. Published 12 times yearly. Articles, varying lengths, pertaining to the sport of triathlon. Color slides. Pays 15¢ a word, on publication. Query.

VELONEWS—1830 N. 55th St., Boulder, CO 80301. John Wilcockson, Ed. John Rezell, Sr. Ed. Articles, 500 to 1,500 words, on competitive cycling, training, nutrition; profiles, interviews. No how-to or touring articles. "We focus on the elite of the sport." Pay varies, on publication.

THE WALKING MAGAZINE—9-11 Harcourt, Boston, MA 02116. Seth Bauer, Ed. Articles, 1,500 to 2,000 words, on fitness, health, equipment, nutrition, travel, and adventure, famous walkers, and other walking-related topics. Shorter pieces, 500 to 1,500 words, and essays for "Ramblings" page. Photos welcome. Pays $750 to $2,500 for features, $100 to $600 for department pieces, on acceptance. Guidelines.

THE WATER SKIER—799 Overlook Dr., Winter Haven, FL 33884. Jonathan Cullimore, Man. Ed. Feature articles on waterskiing. Pays varying rates, on publication.

WATERSKI—World Publications, Inc., 330 W. Canton Ave., Winter Park, FL 32789. Rob May, Ed. Features, 1,250 to 2,000 words, on boating and water skiing. Instructional features, 1,350 words, including sidebars; quick tips, 350 words. (Travel pieces and profiles are done on assignment only.) Pays $35 for fillers; $125 to $500 for columns and features, after acceptance. Guidelines. Query.

THE WESTERN HORSEMAN—P.O. Box 7980, Colorado Springs, CO 80933-7980. Pat Close, Ed. Articles, about 1,500 words, with photos, on care and training of horses; farm, ranch, and stable management; health care and veterinary medicine. Pays to $400, on acceptance.

WESTERN OUTDOORS—3197-E Airport Loop, Costa Mesa, CA 92626. Attn: Ed. Timely, factual articles on fishing, 1,200 to 1,500 words, of interest to western sportsmen. Pays $400 to $500, on acceptance. Query. Guidelines.

WESTERN SPORTSMAN—140 Ave. F N., Saskatoon, Sask., Canada S7L 1V8. George Gruenefeld, Ed. Articles, to 2,500 words, on hunting and fishing in British Columbia, Alberta, Saskatchewan, and Manitoba; how-to pieces. Photos. Pays $75 to $300, on acceptance.

WINDSURFING—P.O. Box 2456, Winter Park, FL 32790. Tom James, Ed. Features, instructional pieces, and tips, by experienced boardsailors. Fast action photos. Pays $50 to $75 for tips, $250 to $300 for features, extra for photos. SASE for guidelines.

WINDY CITY SPORTS—1450 W. Randolph, Chicago, IL 60607. Jeff Banowetz, Ed. Articles, 1,000 words, on amateur sports in Chicago. Pays $100, on publication. Query required.

WOMEN'S SPORTS + FITNESS—170 E. 61st St., 6th Fl., New York, NY 10021. Mary Duffy, Ed. Articles on fitness, nutrition, outdoor sports; how-tos; profiles; adventure travel pieces; and controversial issues in women's sports, 500 to 2,000 words. Pays on publication.

WRESTLING WORLD—See *Hockey Illustrated*.

YACHTING—20 E. Elm St., Greenwich, CT 06830. Charles Barthold, Ed. Articles, 1,500 words, on upscale recreational power and sail boating. How-to and personal-experience pieces. Photos. Pays $350 to $1,000, on acceptance. Queries preferred.

AUTOMOTIVE MAGAZINES

AMERICAN MOTORCYCLIST—American Motorcyclist Assn., 33 Collegeview Rd., Westerville, OH 43081-1484. Greg Harrison, Ed. Articles and fiction, to 3,000 words, on motorcycling: news coverage, personalities, tours. Photos. Pays varying rates, on publication. Query with SASE.

CAR AND DRIVER—2002 Hogback Rd., Ann Arbor, MI 48105. Steve Spence, Man. Ed. Articles and profiles, to 2,500 words, on unusual people or manufacturers involved in cars, racing, etc. "Ninety-five percent staff-written. Query with clips. No unsolicited manuscripts." Pays to $2,500, on acceptance.

CAR & TRAVEL—1000 AAA Dr., Heathrow, FL 32746-5063. Douglas Damerst, Ed. Automobile and travel concerns, including automotive travel, purchasing, and upkeep, 750 to 1,500 words. Pays $300 to $600, on acceptance. Query with clips; articles are by assignment only.

CYCLE WORLD—1499 Monrovia Ave., Newport Beach, CA 92663. David Edwards, Ed.-in-Chief. Technical and feature articles, 1,500 to 2,500 words, for motorcycle enthusiasts. Photos. Pays $100 to $200 per page, on publication. Query.

MOTOR TREND—6420 Wilshire Blvd., Los Angeles, CA 90048-5515. C. Van Tune, Ed. Articles, 250 to 2,000 words, on autos, auto history, racing, events, and profiles. Photos required. Pay varies, on acceptance. Query.

OPEN WHEEL—See *Stock Car Racing*.

RESTORATION—P.O. Box 50046, Dept. TW, Tucson, AZ 85703-1046. W.R. Haessner, Ed. Articles, 1,200 to 1,800 words, on restoration of autos, trucks, planes, trains, etc., and buildings (bridges, structures, etc.). Photos. Pays from $25 per page, on publication. Queries required.

RIDER—2575 Vista Del Mar Dr., Ventura, CA 93001. Mark Tuttle Jr., Ed. Articles, to 3,000 words, with color slides, on travel, touring, commuting, and camping motorcyclists. Pays $100 to $750, on publication. Query.

ROAD & TRACK—1499 Monrovia Ave., Newport Beach, CA 92663. Ellida Maki, Man. Ed. Short automotive articles, to 450 words, of a "timeless nature" for knowledgeable car enthusiasts. Pays on publication. Query.

ROAD KING—Hammock Publishing, 3322 W. End Ave., Suite 700, Nashville, TN 37203. Tom Berg, Ed. Bill Hudgins, Ed. Dir. Bimonthly. Articles, 300 to 1,500 words, on business of trucking from a driver's point of view; profiles of drivers and their rigs; technical aspects of trucking equipment; trucking history; travel destinations near major interstates; humor; fillers. No fiction. Include clips with submission. Pays negotiable rates, on acceptance.

STOCK CAR RACING—65 Parker St., #2, Newburyport, MA 01950. Dick Berggren, Ed. Features, technical automotive pieces, and profiles of interesting racing personalities, to 6,000 words, for oval track racing enthusiasts. Fillers. Pays $75 to $350, on publication. Same requirements for *Open Wheel*.

FITNESS MAGAZINES

AMERICAN FITNESS—15250 Ventura Blvd., Suite 200, Sherman Oaks, CA 91403. Peg Jordan, R.N., Ed. Rhonda Wilson, Man. Ed. Articles, 500 to 1,500 words, on exercise, health, research, trends, research, nutrition, alternative paths, etc. Illustrations, photos.

COOKING LIGHT—P.O. Box 1748, Birmingham, AL 35201. Melissa Aspell, Fitness Ed. Articles on fitness, exercise, health and healthful cooking, nutrition, and healthful recipes. Query.

FIT MAGAZINE—1700 Broadway, New York, NY 10019. Lisa Klugman, Ed. Lively, readable service-oriented articles, 800 to 1,200 words, on exercise, nutrition, lifestyle, and health for women ages 18 to 35. Writers should have some background in or knowledge of the health field. Also considers 500-word essays for "Finally Fit" column by readers who have lost weight and kept it off. Pays $100 to $300, on publication. Query.

FITNESS—Gruner & Jahr USA Publishing, 375 Lexington Ave., New York, NY 10017-5514. Sally Lee, Ed. Articles, 500 to 2,000 words, on health, exercise, sports, nutrition, diet, psychological well-being, alternative therapies, sex, and beauty for readers around 30 years old. Queries required. Pays approximately $1 per word, on acceptance.

INSIDE TEXAS RUNNING—9514 Bristlebrook Dr., Houston, TX 77083-6193. Joanne Schmidt, Ed. Articles and fillers on running in Texas. Pays $35 to $100 for articles; $10 to $25 for photos and short fillers, on acceptance.

MEN'S HEALTH—Rodale Press, 33 E. Minor St., Emmaus, PA 18098. Jeff Csatari, Sr. Ed. Articles, 1,000 to 2,500 words, on fitness, diet, health, relationships, sports, and travel, for men ages 25 to 55. Pays from 50¢ a word, on acceptance. Query.

THE PHYSICIAN AND SPORTSMEDICINE—4530 W. 77th St., Minneapolis, MN 55435. Susan Hawthorne, Exec. Ed. News and feature articles. Clinical articles must be co-authored by physicians. Sports medicine angle necessary. Pays $300 to $1,600, on acceptance. Query. Guidelines.

SWEAT—736 E. Loyola Dr., Tempe, AZ 85282. Joan Westlake, Ed. Articles, 500 to 1,200 words, on amateur sports, outdoor activities, wellness, or fitness with an Arizona angle. "No personal articles or tales. We want investigative pieces. Articles must relate specifically to Arizona or Arizonans." Pays $25 to $60 for articles; $15 to $70 for photos, on publication. Queries required; no unsolicited manuscripts.

THE WALKING MAGAZINE—9-11 Harcourt, Boston, MA 02116. Seth Bauer, Ed. Articles, 1,500 to 2,500 words, on fitness, health, equipment, nutrition, travel and adventure, and other walking-related topics. Shorter pieces, 150 to 800 words, and essays for "Ramblings" page. Photos welcome. Pays $750 to $1,800 for features, $100 to $500 for department pieces, within a week of acceptance. Guidelines.

WEIGHT WATCHERS MAGAZINE—2100 Lakeshore Dr., Birmingham, AL 35209. Articles on health, nutrition, fitness, and weight-loss motivation and success. Pays from $500, on acceptance. Query with clips required. Guidelines.

WOMEN'S SPORTS + FITNESS—170 E. 61st St., 6th Fl., New York, NY 10021. Mary Duffy, Ed. Articles on fitness, nutrition, outdoor sports; how-tos; profiles; adventure travel pieces; and controversial issues in women's sports, 500 to 2,000 words. Pays on publication.

YOGA JOURNAL—2054 University Ave., Berkeley, CA 94704. Rick Fields, Ed. Articles, 1,200 to 4,000 words, on holistic health, meditation, consciousness, spirituality, and yoga. Pays $50 to $1,200, on publication.

CONSUMER/PERSONAL FINANCE

BLACK ENTERPRISE—130 Fifth Ave., New York, NY 10011. Earl G. Graves, Ed. Articles on money management, careers, political issues, entrepreneurship, high technology, and lifestyles for black professionals. Profiles. Pays on acceptance. Query.

COMPLETE WOMAN—875 N. Michigan Ave., Suite 3434, Chicago, IL 60611. Bonnie Krueger, Ed. Lora Wintz, Assoc. Ed. Articles, 1,000 to 2,000 words, with how-to sidebars, giving advice to women. Also interested in reprints. Pays varying rates, on publication. Query with clips.

ESSENCE—1500 Broadway, New York, NY 10036. Susan L. Taylor, Ed.-in-Chief. Linda Villarosa, Ed. Articles, 800 to 2,500 words, for black women in America today, on business and finance, as well as health, art, travel, politics, and celebrity profiles, self-help pieces, how-tos. Payment varies, on acceptance. Query.

FAMILY CIRCLE—375 Lexington Ave., New York, NY 10017. Nancy Clark, Deputy Ed. Ann Matturo, Celeste Mitchells, Assoc. Eds. Enterprising, creative, and practical articles, 1,000 to 1,500 words, on investing, smart ways to save money, secrets of successful entrepreneurs, and consumer news on smart shopping. Pays $1 a word, on acceptance. Query with clips.

GOOD HOUSEKEEPING—959 Eighth Ave., New York, NY 10019. Lisa Benenson, Better Way Ed. Short advice-driven articles on money, finances, consumer issues, health, and safety for "Better Way" section. Pays good rates, on acceptance. Guidelines.

HOME MECHANIX—2 Park Ave., New York, NY 10016. Michael Chotiner, Ed. Home improvement articles, remodeling, maintenance, home finances. Time-or money-saving tips for the home, garage, or yard; seasonal reminders for homeowners. Pays $50, on acceptance.

KIPLINGER'S PERSONAL FINANCE MAGAZINE—1729 H St. N.W., Washington, DC 20006. Attn: Ed. Dept. Articles on personal finance (i.e., buying insurance, mutual funds). Pays varying rates, on acceptance. Query required.

KIWANIS—3636 Woodview Trace, Indianapolis, IN 46468. Chuck Jonak, Man. Ed. Articles, 2,500 words, on financial planning for younger families and retirement planning for older people. Pays $400 to $1,000, on acceptance. Query required.

MODERN BRIDE—249 W. 17th St., New York, NY 10011. Mary Ann Cavlin, Exec. Ed. Articles, 1,500 to 2,000 words, for bride and groom, on wedding planning, financial planning, juggling career and home, etc. Pays $600 to $1,200, on acceptance.

MODERN MATURITY— 601 E St. N.W., Washington, DC 20049. Annette Winter, Cont. Ed. Articles, 300 to 2,000 words, on a wide range of financial topics of interest to people over 50. Pays from $1 a word, on acceptance. Queries required.

THE MONEYPAPER—1010 Mamaroneck Ave., Mamaroneck, NY 10543. Vita Nelson, Ed. Financial news and money-saving ideas; particularly interested in information about companies with dividend reinvestment plans. Brief, well-researched articles on personal finance, money management: saving, earning, investing, taxes, insurance, and related subjects. Pays $75 for articles, on publication. Query with resumé and writing sample.

NEW CHOICES: LIVING EVEN BETTER AFTER 50—28 W. 23rd St., New York, NY 10010. Allen J. Sheinman, Articles Ed. David A. Sendler, Ed.-in-Chief. News and service magazine for people ages 50 to 65. Articles on retirement planning, financial strategies, housing options, as well as health and fitness, travel, leisure pursuits, etc. Payment varies, on acceptance.

ROBB REPORT—1 Acton Pl., Acton, MA 01720. Steven Castle, Ed. Features on investment opportunities for high-end/luxury market. Lifestyle articles, home interiors, boats, travel, exotic automobiles, business, technology, etc. Payment varies, on publication. Query with SASE and clips.

SENIOR HIGHLIGHTS—26081 Merit Cir., Suite 101, Laguna Hills, CA 92653. Cindy Werelius, Asst. Ed. Articles, 800 words, on money, lifestyles, health, and travel. No payment. Guidelines. Query with SASE.

SILVER CIRCLE— 4900 Rivergrade Rd., Irwindale, CA 91706. Jay Binkly, Ed. National consumer-interest quarterly. Consumer service articles, 800 to 3,000 words, on careers, money, health, home, auto, gardening, food, travel, hobbies, etc. Pays $250 to $2,000, on acceptance. Query.

WOMAN'S DAY—1633 Broadway, New York, NY 10019. Stephanie Abarbanel, Sr. Articles Ed. Articles, to 2,000 words, on financial matters of interest to a broad range of women. Pays top rates, on acceptance. Query with SASE; no unsolicited manuscripts.

WOMEN IN BUSINESS—American Business Women's Assn., 9100 Ward Pkwy., P.O. Box 8728, Kansas City, MO 64114-0728. Elaine Minter, Ed. How-to business features, 800 to 1,200 words, for working women. Business trends, small-business ownership, self-improvement, and retirement issues; all articles must include members of the American Business Women's Association. Pays on acceptance. Query.

YOUR MONEY— 8001 N. Lincoln Ave., Skokie, IL 60077. Dennis Fertig, Ed. Informative, jargon-free personal finance articles, to 2,500 words, for the general reader, on investment opportunities and personal finance. Pays 40¢ a word, on acceptance. Query with clips for assignment. (Do not send manuscripts on disks.)

BUSINESS & TRADE PUBLICATIONS

ABA JOURNAL—American Bar Assn., 750 N. Lake Shore Dr., Chicago, IL 60611. Gary A. Hengstler, Ed./Pub. Articles, to 3,000 words, on law-related topics: current events in the law and ideas that will help lawyers practice better and more efficiently. Writing should be in an informal, journalistic style. Pays from $1,000, on acceptance; buys all rights.

ACROSS THE BOARD—845 Third Ave., New York, NY 10022. Karen Gershkovich, Asst. to the Ed. Articles, 1,000 to 4,000 words, on a variety of topics of interest to business executives; straight business angle not required. Payment varies, on publication.

ALTERNATIVE ENERGY RETAILER—P.O. Box 2180, Waterbury, CT 06722. John Florian, Ed. Dir. Feature articles, 1,000 words, for retailers of hearth products, including appliances that burn wood, coal, pellets, and gas, and hearth accessories and services. Interviews with successful retailers, stressing the how-to. B&W photos. Pays $200, extra for photos, on publication. Query.

AMERICAN BANKER—One State Street Plaza, New York, NY 10004. Phil Roosevelt, Ed. Articles, 1,000 to 3,000 words, on banking and financial services, technology in banking, consumer financial services, investment products. Pays varying rates, on publication. Query preferred.

AMERICAN COIN-OP—500 N. Dearborn St., Chicago, IL 60610-9988. Paul Partika, Ed. Articles, to 2,500 words, with photos, on successful coin-operated laundries: management, promotion, decor, maintenance, etc. Pays from 8¢ a word, $8 per B&W photo, 2 weeks prior to publication. Query. Send SASE for guidelines.

AMERICAN DEMOGRAPHICS—P.O. Box 68, Ithaca, NY 14851-9989. Diane Crispell, Exec. Ed. Articles, 500 to 2,000 words, on the 4 key elements of a consumer market (its size, its needs and wants, its ability to pay, and how it can be reached), with specific examples of how companies market to consumers. Readers include marketers, advertisers, and strategic planners. Pays $100 to $500, on acceptance. Query.

AMERICAN LAUNDRY NEWS—(formerly *Laundry News*) 500 N. Dearborn St., Room 1100, Chicago, IL 60610. Larry K. Ebert Articles, 500 to 1,500 words, on the institutional laundering trade as practiced in hotels, hospitals, correctional facilities, and nursing homes. Infection control, government regulation, new technology, major projects, industrial accidents, litigation, and mergers and acquisitions. Query. Pays $100 to $300, on publication.

AMERICAN MEDICAL NEWS—515 N. State St., Chicago, IL 60610. Wayne Hearn, Topic Ed. Articles, 900 to 1,500 words, on socioeconomic developments in health care of interest to physicians across the country. No pieces on health, clinical treatments, or research. Pays $500 to $1,500, on acceptance. Query required. Guidelines.

AMERICAN SCHOOL & UNIVERSITY—P.O. Box 12901, 9800 Metcalf, Overland Park, KS 66212-2215. Joe Agron, Ed. Articles and case studies, 1,200 to 1,500 words, on design, construction, operation, and management of school and university facilities. Queries preferred.

ARCHITECTURE—1130 Connecticut Ave. N.W., Suite 625, Washington, DC 20036. Quincy Baldwin, Ed. Articles, to 3,000 words, on architecture, building technology, professional practice. Pays 50¢ a word.

AREA DEVELOPMENT MAGAZINE— 400 Post Ave., Westbury, NY 11590. Geraldine Gambale, Ed. Articles for top executives of industrial companies on sites and facility planning. Pays 25¢ per word. Query.

ART BUSINESS NEWS—270 Madison Ave., 6th Fl., New York, NY 10016. Sarah Seamark, Ed. Articles, 1,000 words, for art dealers and framers, on trends and events of national importance to the art and framing industry, and relevant business subjects. Payment varies, on publication. Query preferred.

AUTOMATED BUILDER—P.O. Box 120, Carpinteria, CA 93014. Don Carlson, Ed. Articles, 500 to 750 words, on various types of home manufacturers and dealers with slides or color prints. Pays $300, on acceptance, for articles with photos. Query required.

BARRON'S—200 Liberty St., New York, NY 10281. Edwin A. Finn, Jr., Ed. Investment-interest articles. Query.

BOATING INDUSTRY—National Trade Publications, 13 Century Hill Dr., Latham, NY 12110-2197. Anne Dantz, Man. Ed. Articles, 1,000 to 2,500 words, on recreational marine products, management, merchandising and selling, for boat dealers. Photos. Pays varying rates, on publication. Query.

BOOKPAGE—ProMotion, Inc., 2501 21st Ave. S., Suite 5, Nashville, TN 37212. Ann Meador Shayne, Ed. Book reviews, 500 words, for a consumer-oriented tabloid used by booksellers to promote new titles and authors. Query with writing samples and areas of interest; Editor will make assignments for reviews. Pays $20 per review. Guidelines.

BUILDER—Hanley-Wood, Inc., One Thomas Cir. N.W., Suite 600, Washington, DC 20005. Noreen S. Welle, Ed. Articles, to 1,500 words, on trends and news in home building: design, marketing, new products, etc. Pays negotiable rates, on acceptance. Query.

BUSINESS—P.O. Box 10010, Ogden, UT 84409. Beth McDaniel, Man. Ed. Informative articles, 1,000 words, on business concerns of the businessperson/entrepreneur in U.S. and Canada. Color photos. Pays 15¢ a word, $35 for photos, $50 for cover photos. Query. Guidelines. SASE.

BUSINESS AND COMMERCIAL AVIATION— 4 International Dr., Rye Brook, NY 10573. Attn: Ed. Articles, 2,500 words, with photos, for pilots, on use of private aircraft for business transportation. Pays $100 to $500, on acceptance. Query.

BUSINESS MARKETING—740 N. Rush St., Chicago, IL 60611. Karen Egolf, Ed. Articles on selling, advertising, and promoting products and services to business buyers. Pays competitive rates, on acceptance. Queries required.

BUSINESS TIMES—P.O. Box 580, 315 Peck St., New Haven, CT 06513. Joel MacClaren, Ed. Articles on Connecticut-based businesses and corporations. Query.

CAMPGROUND MANAGEMENT—P.O. Box 5000, Lake Forest, IL 60045-5000. Mike Byrnes, Ed. Detailed articles, 500 to 2,000 words, on managing recreational vehicle campgrounds. Photos. Pays $50 to $200, after publication.

CHEF—Talcott Communications Corp., 20 N. Wacker Dr., Suite 3230, Chicago, IL 60606. Brent T. Frei, Ed.-in-Chief. "The Chef's Business Magazine." Articles, 600 to 1,000 words, that offer professionals in the foodservice business ideas for food marketing, preparation, and presentation. Pays $250, on publication.

CHIEF EXECUTIVE—733 Third Ave., 21st Fl., New York, NY 10017. J.P. Donlon, Ed. CEO bylines. Articles, 2,500 to 3,000 words, on management, financial, or business strategies. Departments, 1,200 to 1,500 words, on investments, amenities, and travel. Features on CEOs at leisure, Q&A's with CEOs, other topics. Pays varying rates, on acceptance. Query required.

CHRISTIAN RETAILING— 600 Rinehart Rd., Lake Mary, FL 32746. Carol Chapman Stertzer, Ed. Features, 1,500 to 2,300 words, on new products, trends, or topics related to running a profitable Christian retail store. Pays $150 to $400, on publication.

CLEANING AND MAINTENANCE MANAGEMENT MAGAZINE—13 Century Hill Dr., Latham, NY 12110-2197. Dominic Tom, Ed. Articles, 500 to 1,200 words, on managing efficient cleaning and custodial/maintenance operations, profiles, photo-features, or general-interest articles directly related to the industry; also technical/mechanical how-tos. Photos encouraged. Pays to $300 for features, on publication. Query. Guidelines.

CLUB MANAGEMENT— 8730 Big Bend Blvd., St. Louis, MO 63114. Tom Finan, Pub. The official magazine of the Club Managers Assn. of America. Features, to 2,000 words, and news items from 100 words, on management, budget, cuisine, personnel, government regulations, etc., for executives who run private clubs. "Writing should be tight and conversational, with liberal use of quotes." Color photos usually required with manuscript. Query preferred. Guidelines.

COMMERCIAL CARRIER JOURNAL— Chilton Way, Radnor, PA 19089. Paul Richards, Man. Ed. Thoroughly researched articles on private fleets and for-hire trucking operations. Pays from $50, on acceptance. Queries required.

COMPUTER GRAPHICS WORLD— 10 Tara Blvd., Suite 500, Nashua, NH 03062-2801. Stephen Porter, Ed. Articles, 1,000 to 3,000 words, on computer graphics and multimedia technology and their use in science, engineering, architecture, film and broadcast, and interactive entertainment areas. Photos. Pays $600 to $1,000 per article, on acceptance. Query.

THE CONSTRUCTION SPECIFIER— Construction Specifications Institute, 601 Madison St., Alexandria, VA 22314. Anne Scott, Ed. Technical articles, 1,000 to 3,000 words, on the "nuts and bolts" of commercial construction, for architects, engineers, specifiers, contractors, and manufacturers. Pays 15¢ per word, on publication.

CONVENIENCE STORE NEWS—233 Park Ave. S., 6th Fl., New York, NY 10003. Maureen Azzato, Ed.-in-Chief. Features and news items, 750 to 1200 words, for convenience store owners and operators. Photos, with captions. Pays negotiated price for features; extra for photos, on publication. Query.

COOKING FOR PROFIT—P.O. Box 267, Fond du Lac, WI 54936-0267. Colleen Phalen, Pub./Ed.-in-Chief. Articles, of varying lengths, for foodservice professionals: profiles of successful restaurants, chains, and franchises, schools, hospitals, nursing homes, or other "institutional feeders"; also case studies on successful energy management within the foodservice environment. Business to business articles of interest to foodservice professionals. Payment varies, on publication.

CRAIN'S CHICAGO BUSINESS—740 Rush St., Chicago, IL 60611. Glenn Coleman, Man. Ed. Business articles about the Chicago metropolitan area exclusively.

DENTAL ECONOMICS—P.O. Box 3408, Tulsa, OK 74101. Dick Hale, Ed. Articles, 1,200 to 3,500 words, on business side of dental practice, patient and staff communication, personal investments, etc. Pays $100 to $400, on acceptance.

DIVIDENDS—Imagination Publishing, 820 W. Jackson, Suite 450, Chicago, IL 60607. Molly Tschida, Ed. Features, 1,000 to 1,500 words, of interest to small business owners; small-business profiles, 500 to 600 words. Pays 50¢ a word, on acceptance. Query.

DRAPERIES & WINDOW COVERINGS—450 Skokie Blvd., Suite 507, Northbrook, IL 60062-7913. Katie Sosnowchik, Ed. Articles, 1,000 to 2,000 words, for retailers, wholesalers, designers, and manufacturers of draperies and window, wall, and floor coverings. Profiles, with photos, of successful businesses in the industry; management and marketing related articles. Pays $150 to $250, after acceptance. Query.

EMERGENCY— 6300 Yarrow Dr., Carlsbad, CA 92009-1597. Doug Fiske, Ed. Articles, to 3,000 words, of interest to paramedics, emergency medical technicians, flight nurses, and other prehospital personnel; disaster management, advanced and basic life support, assessment, treatment. Pays $100 to $400 for features, $50 to $300 for departments. Photos are a plus. Guidelines and editorial calendar available.

EMPLOYEE SERVICES MANAGEMENT—NESRA, 2211 York Rd., Suite 207, Oak Brook, IL 60521-2371. Cynthia M. Helson, Ed. Articles, 1,200 to 2,500 words, for human resource and employee service professionals on work/life issues, employee services, wellness, management and personal development. Pays in copies.

THE ENGRAVERS JOURNAL—26 Summit St., P.O. Box 318, Brighton, MI 48116. Rosemary Farrell, Man. Ed. Articles, of varying lengths, on topics related to the engraving industry or small business. Pays $100 to $200, on acceptance. Query.

ENTREPRENEUR—2392 Morse Ave., Irvine, CA 92614. Rieva Lesonsky, Ed.-in-Chief. Articles for small business owners, on all aspects of running a business. Pay varies, on acceptance. Query required.

EXECUTIVE FEMALE—30 Irving Pl., New York, NY 10003. Gay Bryant, Ed.-in-Chief. Articles, 750 to 2,500 words, on managing people, time, money, companies, and careers, for women in business. Pays varying rates, on acceptance. Query.

FANCY FOOD—Talcott Communications Corp., 20 N. Wacker Dr., Suite 3230, Chicago, IL 60606. Carolyn Schwaar, Ed.-in-Chief. "The Business Magazine for Specialty Foods, Confections, and Upscale Housewares." Articles, 2,000 words, related to gourmet food. Pays $250, on publication.

FARM JOURNAL—Centre Sq. W., 1500 Market St., Philadelphia, PA 19102-2181. Sonja Hillgren, Ed. Practical business articles, 500 to 1,500 words, with photos, on growing crops and raising livestock. Pays 20¢ to 50¢ a word, on acceptance. Query required.

FINANCIAL WORLD—1328 Broadway, New York, NY 10001. Seth E. Hoyt, Pres. & Pub. Features and profiles of large companies and financial institutions and the people who run them. Pays varying rates, on publication. Query required.

FITNESS MANAGEMENT—P.O. Box 1198, Solana Beach, CA 92075. Edward H. Pitts, Ed. Authoritative features, 750 to 2,500 words, and news shorts, 100 to 750 words, for owners, managers, and program directors of fitness centers. Content must be in keeping with current medical practice; no fads. Pays 8¢ a word, on publication. Query.

FLORIST—29200 Northwestern Hwy., Southfield, MI 48034. Barbara Koch, Man. Ed. Articles, to 1,500 words, on retail florist shop management.

FLOWERS &—Teleflora Plaza, Suite 118, 12233 W. Olympic Blvd., Los Angeles, CA 90064. Joanne Jaffe, Ed.-in-Chief. Articles, 500 to 1,500 words, with how-to information for retail florists. Pays 30¢ a word, on acceptance. Query with clips.

FOOD MANAGEMENT—1100 Superior Ave., Cleveland, OH 44114. Donna Boss, Ed. Articles on food service in hospitals, nursing homes, schools, colleges, prisons, businesses, and industrial sites. Trends, legislative issues, and how-to pieces, with management tie-in. Query.

GARDEN DESIGN—100 Ave. of the Americas, 7th Fl., New York, NY 10013. Dorothy Kalins, Ed.-in-Chief. Douglas Brenner, Ed. Garden-related features, 500 to 1,000 words, on private, public, and community gardens; articles on art and history as they relate to gardens. Pays from 50¢ a word, on acceptance. Guidelines.

GENERAL AVIATION NEWS & FLYER—P.O. Box 39099, Tacoma, WA 98439-0099. Ben Sclair, Gen. Mgr. Articles, 500 to 2,500 words, of interest to "general aviation" pilots. Pays to $3 per column inch (approximately 40 words); $10 for B&W photos; to $50 for color photos; within a month of publication.

GLASS DIGEST—18 E. 41st St., New York, NY 10017-6222. Charles Cumpston, Ed. Articles, 1,200 to 1,500 words, on building projects and glass/metal dealers, distributors, storefront and glazing contractors. Pays varying rates, on publication.

GOLF COURSE NEWS—38 Lafayette St., Yarmouth, ME 04096. Hal Phillips, Ed. Features and news analyses, 500 to 1,000 words, on all aspects of golf course maintenance, design, building, and management. Pays $200, on acceptance.

GOVERNMENT EXECUTIVE—1501 M St. N.W., Washington, DC 20005. Timothy Clark, Ed. Articles, 1,500 to 3,000 words, for civilian and military government workers at the management level.

GREENHOUSE MANAGEMENT & PRODUCTION—P.O. Box 1868, Fort Worth, TX 76101-1868. David Kuack, Ed. How-to articles, innovative production and/or marketing techniques, 500 to 1,800 words, accompanied by color slides, of interest to professional greenhouse growers. Pays $50 to $300, on acceptance. Query required.

GROWERTALKS—P.O. Box 9, 335 N. River St., Batavia, IL 60510-0009. Debbie Hamrick, Ed. Dir. Articles, 800 to 2,600 words, that help commercial greenhouse growers (not florist/retailers or home gardeners) do their jobs better: trends, successes in new types of production, marketing, business management, new crops, and issues facing the industry. Payment varies, on publication. Queries preferred.

HARDWARE TRADE—10510 France Ave. S., #225, Bloomington, MN 55431. Patt Patterson, Ed. Dir. Articles, 800 to 1,000 words, on unusual hardware and home center stores and promotions in the Northwest and Midwest. Photos. Query.

HARVARD BUSINESS REVIEW—Harvard Business School Publishing Corp., 60 Harvard Way, Boston, MA 02163. Request a copy of HBR's guidelines for authors, or query editors, in writing, on new ideas about management of interest to senior executives.

HEALTH FOODS BUSINESS—2 University Plaza, Suite 204, Hackensack, NJ 07601. Gina Geslewitz, Ed. Articles, 1,200 words, with photos, profiling health food stores. Pays on publication. Query. Guidelines.

HEALTH PROGRESS— 4455 Woodson Rd., St. Louis, MO 63134-3797. Judy Cassidy, Ed. Journal of the Catholic Health Association. Features, 2,000 to 4,000 words, on hospital and nursing home management and administration, medical-moral questions, health care, public policy, technological developments in health care and their effects, nursing, financial and human resource management for health-care administrators, and innovative programs in hospitals and long-term care facilities. Payment negotiable. Query.

HEATING/PIPING/AIR CONDITIONING—2 Prudential Plaza, 180 N. Stetson Ave., Suite 2555, Chicago, IL 60601. Michael G. Ivanovich, Ed. Articles, to 5,000 words, on heating, piping, and air conditioning systems in industrial plants and large buildings; engineering information. Pays $60 per printed page, on publication. Query.

HOME OFFICE COMPUTING—Scholastic, Inc., 411 Lafayette St., New York, NY 10003. Cathy G. Brower, Exec. Ed. Articles, 3,000 words, that provide readers with practical information on how to run their businesses and use technology more effectively. Profiles of home-based entrepreneurs and small business owners. Departments, 1,200 words, on finance, legal issues, sales and marketing, communications, government. Writers must be familiar with microcomputers and software, home office products, and issues affecting small and home businesses. Payment varies, on acceptance.

HOSPITALS & HEALTH NETWORKS—737 N. Michigan Ave., Chicago, IL 60611. Mary Grayson, Ed. Articles, 800 to 900 words, for hospital administrators. Query.

HUMAN RESOURCE EXECUTIVE—LRP Publications Co., 747 Dresher Rd., Horsham, PA 19044-0980. David Shadovitz, Ed. Profiles and case stories, 1,800 to 2,200 words, of interest to people in the personnel profession. Pays varying rates, on acceptance. Queries required.

INC.—38 Commercial Wharf, Boston, MA 02110. George Gendron, Ed. No free-lance material.

INCOME OPPORTUNITIES—1500 Broadway, Suite 600, New York, NY 10036-4015. Linda Molnar, Ed.-in-Chief. Articles on marketing, financing, and managing a small or home-based business, especially on a tight budget. Profiles of entrepreneurs who started their businesses on a shoestring. Pays varying rates, on acceptance. Query; no unsolicited manuscripts.

INDEPENDENT BUSINESS—125 Auburn Ct., Suite 100, Thousand Oaks, CA 91362. Maryann Hammers, Sr. Ed. How-to articles, 1,200 to 2,000 words, of practical interest and value on all aspects of running a small business. Pays $550 to $1,500, on acceptance. Also, short fun profiles, about 400 words, on offbeat businesses; pays $50 to $100. Query. Guidelines.

INDEPENDENT LIVING PROVIDER—150 Motor Pkwy., Suite 420, Hauppauge, NY 11788-5145. Anne Kelly, Ed. Articles, 1,500 to 3,000 words, on the sales and services of home medical equipment dealers. Pays 15¢ a word, on publication. Query.

INSTANT & SMALL COMMERCIAL PRINTER—P.O. Box 7280, Libertyville, IL 60048. Anne Marie Mohan, Ed. Articles, 3 to 6 typed pages, for operators and employees of printing businesses specializing in retail printing and/or small commercial printing: case histories, how-tos, technical pieces, small-business management. Pays $150 to $250, extra for photos, on publication. Query.

INTERNATIONAL BUSINESS—9 E. 40th St., 10th Fl., New York, NY 10016. Linda Lynton, Ed.-in-Chief. Articles, 1,000 to 1,500 words, on global marketing strategies. Short pieces, 500 words, with tips on operating abroad. Profiles, 750 to 3,000 words, on individuals or companies. Pays 30¢ a word, on acceptance and on publication. Query with clips.

JEMS, JOURNAL OF EMERGENCY MEDICAL SERVICES—P.O. Box 2789, Carlsbad, CA 92018. John Becknell, Ed.-in-Chief. Articles, 1,500 to 3,000 words, of interest to emergency medical providers (EMTs, paramedics, nurses, and physicians) who work in the EMS industry worldwide.

LAUNDRY NEWS—See *American Laundry News.*

LLAMAS—P.O. Box 100, Herald, CA 95638. Cheryl Dal Porto, Ed. "The International Camelid Journal," published 7 times yearly. Articles, 300 to 3,000 words, of interest to llama and alpaca owners. Pays $25 to $300, extra for photos, on publication. Query.

LP-GAS MAGAZINE—131 W. First St., Duluth, MN 55802. Zane Chastain, Ed. Articles, 1,500 to 2,500 words, with photos, on LP-gas dealer operations: marketing, management, etc. Photos. Pays to 15¢ a word, extra for photos, on acceptance. Query.

MANAGE—2210 Arbor Blvd., Dayton, OH 45439. Doug Shaw, Ed. Articles, 800 to 1,000 words, on management and supervision for first-line and middle managers. "Please indicate word count on manuscript and enclose SASE." Pays 5¢ a word.

MANAGING OFFICE TECHNOLOGY—1100 Superior Ave., Cleveland, OH 44114. Lura Romei, Ed. Articles, 3 to 4 double-spaced, typed pages, on new concepts, management techniques, technologies, and applications for management executives. Payment varies, on acceptance. Query preferred.

MANUFACTURING SYSTEMS—191 S. Gary, Carol Stream, IL 60188. Kevin Parker, Ed. Articles, to 2,000 words, on computer and information systems for managers and executives seeking to increase productivity in manufacturing firms. Pays 10¢ to 20¢ a word, on acceptance. Query required.

MIX MAGAZINE—6400 Hollis St., Suite 12, Emeryville, CA 94608. Blair Jackson, Exec. Ed. Articles, varying lengths, for professionals, on audio, audio post-production, sound production, live sound, and music entertainment technology. Pay varies, on publication. Query.

MODERN HEALTHCARE—740 N. Rush St., Chicago, IL 60611. Clark Bell, Ed. News weekly covers management, finance, building design and construction, and new technology for hospitals, health maintenance organizations, nursing homes, and other health care institutions. Pays $200 to $400, on publication. Query; very limited free-lance market.

NATIONAL FISHERMAN—121 Free St., P.O. Box 7438, Portland, ME 04112. Clarke B. Canfield, Ed. Articles, 200 to 2,000 words, aimed at commercial fishermen and boat builders. Pays $4 to $6 per inch, extra for photos, on publication. Query preferred.

NATION'S BUSINESS—1615 H St. N.W., Washington, DC 20062-2000. Articles on small-business topics, including management advice and success stories. Pays negotiable rates, on acceptance. Guidelines.

NEPHROLOGY NEWS & ISSUES—15150 N. Hayden Rd., Suite 101, Scottsdale, AZ 85260. Mark Neumann, Ed. News articles, human-interest features, and opinion essays on dialysis, kidney transplantation, and kidney disease.

THE NETWORK JOURNAL—333 Nostrand Ave., Brooklyn, NY 11216. Njeru Waithaka, Man. Ed. Monthly newspaper. Articles, 800 to 1,500 words, on small business, personal finance, and career management of interest to African American small business owners and professionals. Profiles of entrepreneurs; how-to pieces; articles on sales and marketing, managing a small business and personal finance. Pays $35 to $75, on acceptance.

NEW CAREER WAYS NEWSLETTER— 67 Melrose Ave., Haverhill, MA 01830. William J. Bond, Ed. How-to articles, 1,500 to 2,000 words, on new ways to succeed at work in the 1990s. Pays varying rates, on publication. Query with outline and SASE. Same address and requirements for *Workskills Newsletter.*

NEW HAMPSHIRE EDITIONS— 100 Main St., Nashua, NH 03060. Rick Broussard, Ed. Lifestyle, business, and history articles with a New Hampshire angle, with sources from all regions of the state, for the company's statewide magazine and its specialty publications, *New Hampshire Legacy* and *The World Trader.* Payment varies, on publication.

NEW HAMPSHIRE LEGACY—See *New Hampshire Editions.*

THE NORTHERN LOGGER AND TIMBER PROCESSOR—Northeastern Logger's Assn., Inc., P.O. Box 69, Old Forge, NY 13420. Eric A. Johnson, Ed. Features, 1,000 to 2,000 words, of interest to the forest product industry. Photos. Pays varying rates, on publication. Query preferred.

NSGA RETAIL FOCUS—National Sporting Goods Assoc., 1699 Wall St., Suite 700, Mt. Prospect, IL 60056. Brent Heathcott, Ed. Members magazine. Articles, 1,000 to 1,500 words, on sporting goods industry news and trends, the latest in new product information, and management and store operations. Payment varies, on publication. Query.

ON THE LINE—P.O. Box 1865, Lake Havasu City, AZ 86405. Mary Lougheed, Ed. Bimonthly. "The National Publication for Payphone Industry News." Articles, 500 to 1,000 words, on regulatory and legislative issues related to telecommunications. Payment varies, on publication. Queries preferred.

OPPORTUNITY MAGAZINE— 18 E. 41st St., New York, NY 10017. Daniel Joelson, Ed. How-to articles for people who work at home, small business owners, and people interested in franchising and distributorships. Payment varies, on publication. Query.

OPTOMETRIC ECONOMICS—American Optometric Assn., 243 N. Lindbergh Blvd., St. Louis, MO 63141-7881. Gene Mitchell, Ed. Articles, 1,000 to 3,000 words, on private practice management for optometrists; direct, conversational style with how-to advice on how optometrists can build, improve, better manage, and enjoy their practices. Short humor and photos. Payment varies, on acceptance. Query.

PARTY & PAPER RETAILER—70 New Canaan Ave., Norwalk, CT 06850. Trisha McMahon Drain, Ed. Articles, 800 to 1,000 words, that offer employee, management, and retail marketing advice to the party or stationery store owner, including display ideas, success stories, financial advice, legal advice. "Articles grounded in facts and anecdotes are appreciated." Pay varies, on publication. Query with published clips.

PET BUSINESS—7-L Dundas Cir., Greensboro, NC 27407. Rita Davis, Ed. Brief, documented articles on animals and products found in pet stores; research findings; legislative/regulatory actions; business and marketing tips and trends. Pays 10¢ per word, on publication; pays $20 for photos.

PET PRODUCT NEWS—P.O. Box 6050, Mission Viejo, CA 92690. Stacy Hackett, Ed. Articles, 1,000 to 1,200 words, with photos, on pet shops, and pet and product merchandising. No fiction or news clippings. Pays $150 to $300, extra for photos. Query.

PHOTO MARKETING—3000 Picture Pl., Jackson, MI 49201. Gary Pageau, Exec. Ed. Business articles, 1,000 to 3,500 words, for owners and managers of camera/video stores or photo processing labs. Pays $150 to $500, extra for photos, on acceptance. Query; no unsolicited manuscripts.

PHYSICIAN'S MANAGEMENT—7500 Old Oak Blvd., Cleveland, OH 44130. Bob Feigenbaum, Ed. Articles, 1,500 words, on finance, investments, malpractice, and office management for primary care physicians. No clinical pieces. Pays $125 per printed page, on acceptance. Query. SASE.

PIZZA TODAY—P.O. Box 1347, New Albany, IN 47151. Bruce Allar, Ed. Articles, to 2,500 words, on pizza business management for pizza entrepreneurs. Pizza business profiles. Pays $75 to $150 per published page, on publication. Query.

P.O.B.—Business News Publishing Co., 755 W. Big Beaver Rd., Suite 100, Troy, MI 48084. Walt Walkowski, Ed. Technical and business articles, 1,000 to 4,000 words, for professionals and technicians in the surveying and mapping fields. Technical tips on field and office procedures and equipment maintenance. Pays $150 to $500, on acceptance.

POLICE MAGAZINE—6300 Yarrow Dr., Carlsbad, CA 92009-1597. Randall Resch, Ed. Articles and profiles, 1,000 to 3,000 words, on specialized groups, equipment, issues, and trends of interest to people in the law enforcement profession. Pays $100 to $400, on acceptance.

POOL & SPA NEWS—3923 W. Sixth St., Los Angeles, CA 90020. News articles for the swimming pool, spa, and hot tub industry. Pays from 10¢ to 20¢ a word, on publication. Query.

PROGRESSIVE GROCER—263 Tresser Blvd., Stamford, CT 06901. Priscilla Donegan, Man. Ed. Articles related to retail food operations; ideas for successful merchandising, promotions, and displays. Short pieces preferred. Payment varies, on acceptance.

PUBLISH—Integrated Media, Inc., 501 Second St., San Francisco, CA 94107. Jake Widman, Ed. Features, 1,500 to 2,000 words, and reviews, 400 to 800 words, on all aspects of computerized publishing. Pays $400 to $600 for reviews, $850 to $1,200 for full-length features, on acceptance.

PUBLISHERS WEEKLY—249 W. 17th St., New York, NY 10011. Daisy Maryles, Exec. Ed. Articles, 900 words, on a current issue or problem facing publishing and bookselling for "My Say" column. Articles for "Booksellers' Forum" may be somewhat longer.

QUICK PRINTING—PTN Publishing Co., 445 Broad Hollow Rd., Melville, NY 11747. Gerald Walsh, Ed. Mary Waters, Assoc. Ed. Articles, 1,500 to 2,500 words, of interest to owners and operators of quick print shops, copy shops, and small commercial printers, on how to make their businesses more profitable; include photography/figures. Also, articles on using computers in graphic arts applications. Pays from $100, on publication.

REMODELING—Hanley-Wood, Inc., One Thomas Cir. N.W., Suite 600, Washington, DC 20005. Peter Vaudevanter, Ed. Articles, 250 to 1,700 words, on remodeling and industry news for residential and light commercial remodelers. Pays on acceptance. Query.

RESEARCH MAGAZINE—2201 Third St., P.O. Box 77905, San Francisco, CA 94107. Rebecca McReynolds, Ed. Articles of interest to stockbrokers, 1,000 to 3,000 words, on financial products, selling, how-tos, and industry trends. Pays from $600 to $1,200, on publication. Query.

RESTAURANTS USA—1200 17th St. N.W., Washington, DC 20036-3097. Jennifer Batty, Ed. Publication of the National Restaurant Assn. Articles, 1,000 to 1,500 words, on the foodservice and restaurant business. Restaurant experience preferred. Pays $350 to $800, on acceptance. Query.

ROOFER MAGAZINE—12734 Kenwood Ln., Bldg. 73, Ft. Myers, FL 33907. Angela Williamson, Ed. Technical and non-technical articles, human-interest pieces, 500 to 1,000 words, on roofing-related topics: new roofing concepts, energy savings, pertinent issues, roofing contractor profiles, industry concern. Humorous items welcome. No general business or computer articles. Include photos. Pays negotiable rates, on publication. Guidelines.

THE ROTARIAN—1560 Sherman Ave., Evanston, IL 60201-3698. Willmon L. White, Ed.-in-Chief. Charles W. Pratt, Ed. Articles, 1,200 to 2,000 words, on international social and economic issues, business and management, environment, science and technology. "No political or religious subjects." Pays good rates, on acceptance. Query.

RV BUSINESS—2575 Vista Del Mar Dr., Ventura, CA 93001. Sherman Goldenberg, Ed.-in-Chief. Articles, to 1,500 words, on RV industry news and product-related features. Articles on legislative matters affecting the industry. General business features rarely used. Pays varying rates.

SAFETY COMPLIANCE LETTER—24 Rope Ferry Rd., Waterford, CT 06386. Michele Rubin, Ed. Interview-based articles, 800 to 1,250 words, for corporate safety managers, on successful compliance-based safety and health programs and issues in the workplace. Pays to 20¢ a word, on acceptance. Query.

SAFETY MANAGEMENT—24 Rope Ferry Rd., Waterford, CT 06386. Shelley Wolf, Ed. Interview-based articles, 1,000 words, for safety professionals, on improving workplace safety and health. Pays to 15¢ a word, on acceptance. Query.

SALES & MARKETING MANAGEMENT—Bill Communications, Inc., 355 Park Ave. S., New York, NY 10010. Charles Butler, Ed. Features and short articles of interest to sales and marketing executives. Looking for practical "news you can use." Pays varying rates, on acceptance. Queries preferred.

SIGN BUSINESS—P.O. Box 1416, Broomfield, CO 80038. Regan Dickinson, Ed. Articles specifically targeted to the sign business. Prefer step-by-step how-to features. Pays $150 to $300, on publication.

SMALL PRESS REVIEW—Dustbooks, P.O. Box 100, Paradise, CA 95967. Len Fulton, Ed./Pub. Reviews, 200 words, of small literary books and magazines; tracks the publishing of small publishers and small-circulation magazines. Query.

SOFTWARE MAGAZINE—One Research Dr., Westborough, MA 01581. Patrick Port, Ed. Technical features, to 1,800 words, for computer-literate MIS audience, on how various software products are used. Pays about $1,000 to $1,200, on publication. Query required. Calendar of scheduled editorial features available.

SOUTHERN LUMBERMAN—P.O. Box 681629, Franklin, TN 37068-1629. Nanci P. Gregg, Man. Ed. Articles on sawmill operations, interviews with industry leaders, how-to technical pieces with an emphasis on increasing sawmill production and efficiency and new installations. "Always looking for 'sweetheart' mill stories; we publish one per month." Pays $100 to $250 for articles with B&W photos. Queries preferred.

SOUVENIRS AND NOVELTIES—7000 Terminal Sq., Suite 210, Upper Darby, PA 19082. Attn: Ed. Articles, 1,500 words, on retailing and merchandising theme; on collectible souvenir items; and for managers at zoos, museums, hotels, airports, and souvenir stores. Pays 12¢ a word, on publication.

STONE WORLD—1 Kalisa Way, Suite 205, Paramus, NJ 07652. Michael Reis, Ed. Articles, 750 to 1,500 words, on new trends in installing and designing with stone. For architects, interior designers, design professionals, and stone fabricators and dealers. Pays $4 per column inch, on publication. Query.

TANNING TRENDS—3101 Page Ave., Jackson, MI 49203-2254. Joseph Levy, Ed. Articles on small businesses and skin care for tanning salon owners. Scientific pro-tanning articles and "smart tanning" pieces. Query for profiles. "Our aim is to boost salon owners to the 'next level' of small business ownership. Focus is on business principles with special emphasis on public relations and marketing." Payment varies, on publication.

TEA & COFFEE TRADE JOURNAL—130 W. 42nd St., New York, NY 10036. Jane P. McCabe, Ed. Articles, 3 to 5 pages, on trade issues of importance to the tea and coffee industry. Pays 20¢ per word, on publication. Query.

TEXTILE WORLD—6151 Powers Ferry Rd., Atlanta, GA 30339. Mac Isaacs, Ed. Articles, 500 to 2,000 words, with photos, on manufacturing and finishing textiles. Pays varying rates, on acceptance.

TODAY'S SURGICAL NURSE—Slack, Inc., 6900 Grove Rd., Thorofare, NJ 08086. Frances R. DeStefano, Man. Ed. Clinical or general articles, from 2,000 words, of direct interest to operating room nurses.

TOURIST ATTRACTIONS AND PARKS—7000 Terminal Sq., Suite 210, Upper Darby, PA 19082. Articles, 1,500 words, on successful management of parks and leisure attractions. News items, 250 and 500 words. Pays 10¢ a word, on publication. Query.

TRAILER/BODY BUILDERS—P.O. Box 66010, Houston, TX 77266. Paul Schenck, Ed. Articles on engineering, sales, and management ideas for truck body and truck trailer manufacturers. Pays from $100 per printed page, on acceptance.

TRAINING MAGAZINE—50 S. Ninth St., Minneapolis, MN 55402. Jack Gordon, Ed. Articles, 1,000 to 2,500 words, for managers of training and development activities in corporations, government, etc. Pays to 30¢ a word, on acceptance. Query.

TREASURY & RISK MANAGEMENT—111 W. 57th St., New York, NY 10019. Anthony Baldo, Ed. Bimonthly. Articles, 200 to 3,000 words, on treasury management for corporate treasurers, CFOs, and vice presidents of finance. Pays 50¢ to $1 a word, on acceptance. Query.

UNIQUE OPPORTUNITIES—455 S. 4th Ave., #1236, Louisville, KY 40202. Bett Coffman, Assoc. Ed. Articles, 2,000 to 3,000 words, that cover the economic, business, and career-related issues of interest to physicians who are interested in relocating or entering new practices. Doctor profiles, 500 words. "Our goal is to educate physicians about how to evaluate career opportunities, negotiate the benefits offered, plan career moves, and provide information on the legal and economic aspects of accepting a position." Pays 50¢ a word for features; $100 to $200 for profiles, on acceptance. Query.

VENDING TIMES—1375 Broadway, New York, NY 10018. Tim Sanford, Ed. Features and news articles, with photos, on vending machines. Pays varying rates, on acceptance. Query.

WINES & VINES—1800 Lincoln Ave., San Rafael, CA 94901. Philip E. Hiaring, Ed. Articles, 2,000 words, on grape and wine industry, emphasizing marketing, management, and production. Pays 15¢ a word, on acceptance.

WOODSHOP NEWS—35 Pratt St., Essex, CT 06426-1185. Ian C. Bowen, Ed. Features, one to 3 typed pages, for and about people who work with wood: business stories, profiles, news. Pays from $40 to $250 minimum, on publication. Queries preferred.

WORKING WOMAN—230 Park Ave., New York, NY 10169. Articles, 350 to 2,500 words, on business and personal aspects of working women's lives. Pays from $300, on acceptance.

WORKSKILLS NEWSLETTER—See *New Career Ways Newsletter.*

WORLD OIL—Gulf Publishing Co., P.O. Box 2608, Houston, TX 77252-2608. Robert E. Snyder, Ed. Engineering and operations articles, 3,000 to 4,000 words, on petroleum industry exploration, drilling, or production. Photos. Pays from $50 per printed page, on acceptance. Query.

WORLD SCREEN NEWS—1123 Broadway, Suite 901, New York, NY 10010. George P. Winslow, Ed. Features and short pieces on trends in the business of international television programming (network, syndication, cable, and pay). Pays to $1,000, after publication.

THE WORLD TRADER—See *New Hampshire Editions.*

IN-HOUSE/ASSOCIATION MAGAZINES

Publications circulated to company employees (sometimes called house magazines or house organs) and to members of associations and organizations are excellent, well-paying markets for writers at all levels of experience. Large corporations publish these magazines to promote good will, familiarize readers with the company's services and products, and advise them about the issues and events concerning a particular cause or industry.

AARP BULLETIN— 601 E St. N.W., Washington, DC 20049. Elliot Carlson, Ed. Publication of the American Assn. of Retired Persons. Payment varies, on acceptance. Query required.

THE AMERICAN GARDENER—(formerly *American Horticulturist*) 7931 E. Boulevard Dr., Alexandria, VA 22308-1300. Kathleen Fisher, Ed. Bimonthly publication of the American Horticulture Society. Articles, to 2,500 words, for American ornamental gardeners: profiles of prominent horticulturists, plant research and plant hunting, events and personalities in horticulture history, plant lore and literature, the politics of horticulture, etc. Humorous pieces for "Offshoots." "We run very few how-to articles." Pays $100 to $400, on publication. Query preferred.

AMERICAN HORTICULTURIST—See *The American Gardener.*

AMERICAN HOW-TO—12301 Whitewater Dr., Suite 260, Minnetonka, MN 55343. Tom Sweeney, Ed. Bimonthly magazine for members of The Handyman Club of America. Articles, 1,000 to 1,500 words, for homeowners interested in do-it-yourself projects. Carpentry, plumbing, electrical work, landscaping, masonry, tools, woodworking, and new products. Payment is 50¢ a word, on acceptance. Send SASE for editorial calendar with upcoming themes. Queries preferred.

CALIFORNIA HIGHWAY PATROLMAN—2030 V St., Sacramento, CA 95818-1730. Carol Perri, Ed. Articles on transportation safety, California history, travel, consumerism, past and present vehicles, humor, special holidays, general items, etc. Photos a plus. Buys one-time rights; pays 2 1/2¢ a word, $5 for B&W photos, on publication. Guidelines and/or sample copy with 9x11 SASE.

CATHOLIC FORESTER—355 Shuman Blvd., P.O. Box 3012, Naperville, IL 60566-7012. Dorothy Deer, Ed. Official publication of the Catholic Order of Foresters, a fraternal life insurance organization for Catholics. General-interest articles and fiction, to 1,500 words, that deal with contemporary issues; no moralizing, explicit sex or violence. Short, inspirational articles, to 500 words. "Need health and wellness, parenting, and financial articles." Pays 20¢ a word, on acceptance.

COLUMBIA—1 Columbus Plaza, New Haven, CT 06510-0901. Richard McMunn, Ed. Journal of the Knights of Columbus. Articles, 1,500 words, for Catholic families. Must be accompanied by color photos or transparencies. No fiction. Pays to $500 for articles and photos, on acceptance.

THE COMPASS—365 Washington Ave., Brooklyn, NY 11238. J.A. Randall, Ed. True stories (no first-person accounts), to 2,000 words, on the sea, sea trades, and aviation. Pays to $1,000, on acceptance. Query with SASE.

THE ELKS MAGAZINE— 425 W. Diversey Pkwy., Chicago, IL 60614. Jennifer Plants, Asst. Ed. Articles, 1,500 to 3,000 words, on technology, sports, history, and topics of current interest; for non-urban audience with above-average income. Pays 15¢ to 20¢ a word, on acceptance. Query.

FOCUS—Turnkey Publishing, P.O. Box 200549, Austin, TX 78720. J. Todd Key, Ed. Magazine of the North American Data General Users Group. Articles, 700 to 4,000 words, on Data General computers. Photos a plus. Pays to $50, on publication. Query required.

THE FURROW—Deere & Co., John Deere Rd., Moline, IL 61265. George R. Sollenberger, Exec. Ed. Specialized, illustrated articles on farming. Pays to $1,200, on acceptance.

FUTURIFIC—Foundation for Optimism, Inc., 305 Madison Ave., #10B, New York, NY 10165. Charlotte Kellar, Ed. Forecasts of what will be. "Only optimistic material will get published. Solutions, not problems. We track all developments giving evidence to our increasing life expectancy, improving international coexistence, the global tendency toward peace, and improving economic trends. We also report on all new developments, economic, political, social, scientific, technical, medical or other that are making life easier, better and more enjoyable for the greatest number of people." Pays in copies. Queries preferred.

HARVARD MAGAZINE—7 Ware St., Cambridge, MA 02138-4037. John Rosenberg, Ed. Articles, 500 to 5,000 words, with a connection to Harvard University. Pays from $100, on publication. Query required.

IDEA PERSONAL TRAINER—6190 Cornerstone Ct. E., Suite 204, San Diego, CA 92121-3773. Therese Hannon, Asst. Ed. Magazine for association of personal fitness trainers. Articles on exercise science; program design; profiles of successful trainers; business, legal, and marketing topics; tips for networking with other trainers and with allied medical professionals; client counseling; and training tips. "What's New" column includes industry news, products, and research. Payment varies, on acceptance. Query.

KIWANIS—3636 Woodview Trace, Indianapolis, IN 46268. Chuck Jonak, Man. Ed. Articles, 2,500 words (with sidebars, 250 to 350 words), on lifestyle, relationships, world view, children's issues and concerns, education, trends, small business, religion, health, etc. No travel pieces, interviews, profiles. Pays $400 to $1,000, on acceptance. Query.

THE LION—300 22nd St., Oak Brook, IL 60521. Robert Kleinfelder, Sr. Ed. Official publication of Lions Clubs International. Articles, 800 to 2,000 words, and photo-essays, on club activities. Pays from $100 to $700, including photos, on acceptance. Query.

NEW HOLLAND NEWS—New Holland, Inc., P.O. Box 1895, New Holland, PA 17557. Attn: Ed. Articles, to 1,500 words, with strong color photo support, on agriculture and rural living. Pays on acceptance. Query.

OPTIMIST MAGAZINE—4494 Lindell Blvd., St. Louis, MO 63108. Dawn Blair, Man. Ed. Articles, to 1,000 words, on activities of local Optimist Club, and techniques for personal and club success. Pays from $100, on acceptance. Query.

RESTAURANTS USA—1200 17th St. N.W., Washington, DC 20036-3097. Jennifer Batty, Ed. Publication of the National Restaurant Assn. Articles, 1,500 to 2,000 words, on the foodservice and restaurant business. Restaurant experience preferred. Pays $350 to $800, on acceptance. Query.

THE RETIRED OFFICER MAGAZINE—201 N. Washington St., Alexandria, VA 22314. Address the Manuscripts Ed. Articles, 1,800 to 2,000 words, of interest to military retirees and their families. Current military/national affairs, recent military history, health/medicine, and second-career opportunities. No fillers. Photos a plus. Pays to $1,200, on acceptance. Query. Guidelines.

THE ROTARIAN—1560 Sherman Ave., Evanston, IL 60201-3698. Willmon L. White, Ed.-in-Chief. Charles W. Pratt, Ed. Publication of Rotary International, world service organization of business and professional men and women. Articles, 1,200 to 2,000 words, on international social and economic issues, business and management, human relationships, travel, sports, environment, science and technology; humor. Pays good rates, on acceptance. Query.

SCULPTURE—International Sculpture Ctr., 1050 17th St. N.W., Suite 250, Washington, DC 20036. Glenn Harper, Ed. Magazine of the International Sculpture Center. (Also available on newsstands.) Articles on sculpture, sculptors, collections of sculpture, books on sculpture, criticism, technical processes, etc. Payment varies, on publication. Query.

VFW MAGAZINE— 406 W. 34th St., Kansas City, MO 64111. Richard K. Kolb, Ed. Articles, 1,000 words, related to current foreign policy and defense, American armed forces abroad, and international events affecting U.S. national security. Also, up-to-date articles on verteran concerns and issues affecting veterans. Pays to $500, on acceptance. Query. Guidelines.

WOMEN IN BUSINESS— 9100 Ward Pkwy., Box 8728, Kansas City, MO 64114-0728. Michelle Daniel, Man. Ed. Bimonthly publication of the American Business Women's Assn. How-to features, 1,000 to 1,500 words, for career women from 25 to 55 years old, on business trends, small-business ownership, self-improvement, and retirement issues. Profiles of ABWA members only. Guidelines. Pays 15¢ a published word, on acceptance. Query.

RELIGIOUS MAGAZINES

AMERICA—106 W. 56th St., New York, NY 10019-3893. George W. Hunt, S.J., Ed. Articles, 1,000 to 2,500 words, on current affairs, family life, literary trends. Pays $75 to $150, on acceptance.

AMERICAN JEWISH HISTORY—American Jewish Historical Society, 2 Thornton Rd., Waltham, MA 02154. Dr. Marc Lee Raphael, Ed. Academic articles, 15 to 30 typed pages, on the settlement, history, and life of Jews in North and South America. Queries preferred. No payment.

AMIT MAGAZINE— 817 Broadway, New York, NY 10003-4761. Micheline Ratzersdorfer, Rita Schwalb, Eds. Helen Teitelbaum, Managing Ed. Articles, 1,000 to 2,000 words, of interest to Jewish women: Middle East, Israel, history, holidays, travel.

ANGEL TIMES—Angelic Realms Unlimited, Inc., Suite 110, 22 Perimeter Park, Atlanta, GA 30341. Linda Whitmon Vephula, Pub. Quarterly. Articles, 1,500 words, on angels. No payment.

ANGLICAN JOURNAL— 600 Jarvis St., Toronto, Ont., Canada M4Y 2J6. Attn: Ed. National newspaper of the Anglican Church of Canada. Articles, to 1,000 words, on news of the Anglican Church across the country and around the world, including social and ethical issues and human-interest subjects in a religious context. Pays $50 to $300, on acceptance. Query required.

ANNALS OF ST. ANNE DE BEAUPRÉ—P.O. Box 1000, St. Anne de Beaupré, Quebec, Canada G0A 3C0. Roch Achard, C.Ss.R., Ed. Articles, 500 to 1,500 words, that promote devotion to St. Anne and Christian family values. "Write something inspirational, educational, objective, and uplifting." No poetry. Pays 3¢ to 4¢ a word, on acceptance.

ASPIRE—107 Kenner Ave., Nashville, TN 37205. Jeanette Thomason, Ed. Articles, 500 to 2,000 words, for Christian women on trends in health, career issues, parenting, and relationships that inspire and encourage readers to incorporate faith into daily life. Pays 30¢ a word, on acceptance. Query with resumé and clips.

BAPTIST LEADER—American Baptist Churches-USA, P.O. Box 851, Valley Forge, PA 19482-0851. D. Ng, Ed. Practical how-to or thought-provoking articles, 1,200 to 2,000 words, for local church lay leaders, pastors, and Christian education staff.

BIBLE ADVOCATE—P.O. Box 33677, Denver, CO 80233. Roy Marrs, Ed. Articles, 1,000 to 2,000 words, and fillers, 100 to 500 words, on Bible passages and Christian living. Poetry, 5 to 25 lines, on religious themes. Opinion pieces, to 700 words. "Be familiar with the doctrinal beliefs of the Church of God (Seventh Day). For example, they don't celebrate a traditional Easter or Christmas." Pays $15 per page (to $35) for articles, $10 for poetry, on publication. Guidelines.

BRIGADE LEADER—Box 150, Wheaton, IL 60189. Deborah Christensen, Man. Ed. Inspirational articles, 1,000 words, for Christian men who lead boys in Christian service brigade programs. "Most articles are written on assignment by experts; very few free lancers used. Query with clips and we'll contact you if we need you for an assignment." Pays $60 to $150.

CATECHIST—330 Progress Rd., Dayton, OH 45449. Patricia Fischer, Ed. Informational and how-to articles, 1,200 to 1,500 words, for Catholic teachers, coordinators, and administrators in religious education programs. Pays $25 to $100, on publication.

CATHOLIC DIGEST—P.O. Box 64090, St. Paul, MN 55164-0090. Attn: Articles Ed. Articles, 1,000 to 3,500 words, on Catholic and general subjects. Fillers, to 300 words, on instances of kindness rewarded, for "Hearts Are Trumps"; accounts of good deeds, for "People Are Like That." Pays from $200 for original articles, $100 for reprints, on acceptance; $4 to $50 for fillers, on publication. Guidelines.

CATHOLIC NEAR EAST MAGAZINE—1011 First Ave., New York, NY 10022-4195. Michael La Civita, Ed. Bimonthly publication of CNEWA, a papal agency for humanitarian and pastoral support. Articles, 1,500 to 2,000 words, on people of the Middle East, northeast Africa, India, and eastern Europe: their faith, heritage, culture, and present state of affairs. Special interest in Eastern Christian churches. Color photos for all articles. Pays 20¢ a word. Query.

CATHOLIC PARENT—Our Sunday Visitor, Inc., 200 Noll Plaza, Huntington, IN 46750. Woodeene Koenig-Bricker, Ed. Features, how-tos, and general-interest articles, 800 to 1,000 words, for Catholic parents. "Keep it anecdotal and practical with an emphasis on values and family life. Don't preach." Payment varies, on acceptance.

CATHOLIC TWIN CIRCLE—33 Rossotto Dr., Hamden, CT 06514. Loretta G. Seyer, Ed. Features, how-tos, and interviews, 1,000 to 2,000 words, of interest to Catholic families; include photos. Opinion or inspirational columns, 600 to 800 words. Strict attention to Catholic doctrine required. Enclose SASE. Pays from 10¢ a word for articles, $50 for columns, on publication.

CHARISMA & CHRISTIAN LIFE—600 Rinehart Rd., Lake Mary, FL 32746. Lee Grady, Ed. Dir. Charismatic/evangelical Christian articles, 1,500 to 2,500 words, for developing the spiritual life. News stories, 300 to 1,500 words. Photos. Pays varying rates, on publication.

THE CHRISTIAN CENTURY— 407 S. Dearborn St., Chicago, IL 60605. James M. Wall, Ed. Ecumenical. Articles, 1,500 to 3,000 words, with a religious angle, on political and social issues, international affairs, culture, the arts. Poetry, to 20 lines. Photos. Pays about $50 per printed page, extra for photos, on publication.

CHRISTIAN EDUCATION COUNSELOR—1445 Boonville Ave., Springfield, MO 65802-1894. Sylvia Lee, Ed. Articles, 600 to 800 words, on teaching and administrating Christian education in the local church, for local Sunday school and Christian school personnel. Pays 5¢ to 10¢ a word, on acceptance.

CHRISTIAN EDUCATION JOURNAL—Trinity Evangelical Divinity School, 2065 Half Day Rd., Deerfield, IL 60015. Dr. Perry G. Downs, Ed. Articles, 10 to 25 typed pages, on Christian education topics. Guidelines.

CHRISTIAN EDUCATION LEADERSHIP—P.O. Box 2250, Cleveland, TN 37320-2250. Lance Colkmire, Ed. Quarterly. Articles, 500 to 1,200 words, that "encourage, inform, and inspire those who teach the Bible in the local church." No fiction, poetry, fillers, or artwork. Pays $25 to $55, on acceptance.

CHRISTIAN HOME & SCHOOL—3350 E. Paris Ave. S.E., Grand Rapids, MI 49512. Gordon L. Bordewyk, Ed. Articles for parents in Canada and the U.S. who send their children to Christian schools and are concerned about the challenges facing Christian families today. Pays $75 to $150, on publication. Send SASE for guidelines.

CHRISTIAN MEDICAL & DENTAL SOCIETY JOURNAL—See *Today's Christian Doctor.*

CHRISTIAN PARENTING TODAY— 4050 Lee Vance View, Colorado Springs, CO 80918. Brad Lewis, Ed. Articles, 900 to 2,000 words, dealing with raising children with Christian principles. Departments: "Your Child Today" and "Train Them Up," 300 to 400 words, on child development (emotional, spiritual, etc.); "Healthy & Safe," 300- to 400-word how-to pieces on keeping children emotional and physically safe, home and away; "Family Room," 600 to 700 words, on parent-child activities; "The Lighter Side," humorous essays on family life, 600 to 700 words; "Parent Exchange," 25 to 100 words on problem-solving ideas that have worked for parents; "Life in Our House," insightful anecdotes, 25 to 100 words, about humorous things said at home. (Submissions for "Parent Exchange" and "Life in our House" are not acknowledged or returned.) Pays 15¢ to 25¢ a word, on publication. Pays $25 to $125 for department pieces. Guidelines; send SASE.

CHRISTIAN SINGLE—127 Ninth Ave. N., Nashville, TN 37234-0140. Stephen Felts, Ed. Articles, 600 or 1,200 words, for single adults about leisure activities, issues related to single parents, inspiring personal experiences, humor, life from a Christian perspective. Payment varies, on acceptance. Query. Guidelines.

CHRISTIAN SOCIAL ACTION—100 Maryland Ave. N.E., Washington, DC 20002. Lee Ranck, Ed. Articles, 1,500 to 2,000 words, on social issues for concerned persons of faith. Pays $75 to $125, on publication.

CHRISTIANITY TODAY— 465 Gundersen Dr., Carol Stream, IL 60188. Michael G. Maudlin, Man. Ed. Doctrinal social issues and interpretive essays, 1,500 to 3,000 words, from evangelical Protestant perspective. No fiction or poetry. Pays $200 to $500, on acceptance. Query.

CHURCH & STATE—1816 Jefferson Pl. N.W., Washington, DC 20036. Joseph L. Conn, Man. Ed. Articles, 600 to 2,600 words, on issues of religious liberty and church-state relations. Pays varying rates, on acceptance. Query.

CHURCH EDUCATOR—Educational Ministries, Inc., 165 Plaza Dr., Prescott, AZ 86303. Robert G. Davidson, Ed. How-to articles, to 1,750 words, on Christian education: activity projects, crafts, learning centers, games, bulletin boards, etc., for all church school, junior and high school programs, and adult study group ideas. Allow 3 months for response. Pays 3¢ a word, on publication.

THE CHURCH MUSICIAN—127 Ninth Ave. N., Nashville, TN 37234. Jere Adams, Ed. Articles on choral techniques, instrumental groups, worship planning, music administration, directing choirs (all ages), rehearsal planning, music equipment, new technology, drama/pageants and related subjects, hymn studies, book reviews, and music-related fillers. Pays 5 1/2¢ a word, on acceptance.

COLUMBIA—1 Columbus Plaza, New Haven, CT 06510-0901. Richard McMunn, Ed. Knights of Columbus. Articles, 1,500 words, for Catholic families. Must be accompanied by color photos or transparencies. No fiction. Pays to $500 for articles with photos, on acceptance.

COMMENTARY—165 E. 56th St., New York, NY 10022. Neal Kozodoy, Ed. Articles, 5,000 to 7,000 words, on contemporary issues, Jewish affairs, social sciences, religious thought, culture. Serious fiction; book reviews. Pays on publication.

COMMONWEAL—15 Dutch St., New York, NY 10038. Margaret O'Brien Steinfels, Ed. Catholic. Articles, to 3,000 words, on political, religious, social, and literary subjects. Pays 3¢ a word, on acceptance.

COMPASS: A JESUIT JOURNAL—Box 400, Sta. F, 50 Charles St. E., Toronto, Ont., Canada M4Y 2L8. Robert Chodos, Ed. Essays, 1,500 to 2,500 words, on current religious, political, and cultural topics. "We are ecumenical in spirit and like to provide a forum for lively debate and an ethical perspective on social and religious questions." Query preferred. Pays $100 to $500, on publication.

THE COVENANT COMPANION—5101 N. Francisco Ave., Chicago, IL 60625. John E. Phelan, Ed. Articles, 1,000 words, with Christian implications published for members and attenders of Evangelical Covenant Church, "aimed at gathering, enlightening, and stimulating devotion to Jesus Christ and the living of the Christian life." Poetry. Pays $15 to $35, on publication.

CRUSADER—P.O. Box 7259, Grand Rapids, MI 49510. G. Richard Broene, Ed. Fiction, 900 to 1,500 words, and articles, 400 to 1,000 words, for boys ages 9 to 14 that show how God is at work in their lives and in the world around them. Also, short fillers. Pays 4¢ to 6¢ a word, on acceptance.

DECISION—Billy Graham Evangelistic Assn., 1300 Harmon Pl., P.O. Box 779, Minneapolis, MN 55440-0779. Roger C. Palms, Ed. Christian testimonies and teaching articles on evangelism and Christian nurturing, 1,200 to 1,500 words. Vignettes, 400 to 1,000 words. Pays varying rates, on publication.

DISCOVERIES—WordAction Publishing Co., 6401 The Paseo, Kansas City, MO 64131. Attn: Asst. Ed. Weekly take-home paper designed to correlate with Evangelical Sunday school curriculum. Fiction, 500 to 700 words, for 8- to 10-year-olds. Stories should feature contemporary, true-to-life characters and should illustrate character building and scriptural application. No poetry. SASE required. Pays 5¢ a word, on publication. Guidelines.

DREAMS & VISIONS—Skysong Press, 35 Peter St. S., Orillia, Ont., Canada L3V 5A8. Steve Stanton, Ed. New frontiers in Christian fiction. Eclectic fiction, 2,000 to 6,000 words, that "has literary value and is unique and relevant to Christian readers today." Pays 1/2¢ per word.

ENRICHMENT: A JOURNAL FOR PENTECOSTAL MINISTRY—1445 Boonville Ave., Springfield, MO 65802. Wayde I. Goodall, Ed. Articles, 1,200 to 1,500 words, slanted to ministers, on preaching, doctrine, practice; how-to features. Pays to 10¢ a word, on acceptance.

EVANGEL—Light and Life Press, Box 535002, Indianapolis, IN 46253-5002. Julie Innes, Ed. Free Methodist. Personal experience articles, 1,000 words; short devotional items, 300 to 500 words; fiction, 1,200 words, showing personal faith in Christ to be instrumental in solving problems. Guidelines. Pays 4¢ a word for articles, $10 for poetry, on publication.

EVANGELIZING TODAY'S CHILD—Box 348, Warrenton, MO 63383-0348. Attn: Ed. Articles, 1,200 to 1,500 words, for Sunday school teachers, Christian education leaders, and children's workers. Feature articles should include teaching principles, instruction for the reader, and classroom illustrations. "Impact" articles, 700 to 900 words, show the power of the Gospel in or through the life of a child; "Resource Center," 200- to 300-word teaching tips. Also short stories, 800 to 1,000 words, of contemporary children dealing with problems; must have a scriptural solution. Pays 10¢ to 12¢ a word for articles; $15 to $25 for "Resource Center" pieces; 7¢ a word for short stories, 60 days after acceptance. Guidelines.

FAITH TODAY—M.I.P. Box 3745, Markham, Ontario, Canada L3R 5J6. Brian C. Stiller, Ed. Articles, 1,500 words, on current issues relating to the church in Canada. Pays negotiable rates, on publication. Queries required.

THE FAMILY DIGEST—P.O. Box 40137, Fort Wayne, IN 46804. Corine B. Erlandson, Ed. Articles, 750 to 1,100 words, on family life, Catholic subjects, seasonal, parish life, prayer, inspiration, how-to, spiritual life, for the Catholic reader. Also publishes short humorous anecdotes drawn from personal experience and light-hearted cartoons. Pays 5¢ a word; $10 for personal anecdotes; $20 for cartoons, 6 weeks after acceptance.

FELLOWSHIP—Box 271, Nyack, NY 10960-0271. Richard Deats, Ed. Bimonthly published by the Fellowship of Reconciliation, an interfaith, pacifist organization. Articles, 750 and 1,500 to 2,000 words; B&W photo-essays, on active nonviolence, peace and justice, opposition to war. "Articles for a just and peaceful world community." SASE required. Pays in copies and subscription. Queries preferred.

FELLOWSHIP IN PRAYER—291 Witherspoon St., Princeton, NJ 08542. Articles, to 1,500 words, relating to prayer, meditation, and the spiritual life as practiced by men and women of all faith traditions. Pays in copies. Guidelines.

FOURSQUARE WORLD ADVANCE—1910 W. Sunset Blvd., Suite 200, P.O. Box 26902, Los Angeles, CA 90026. Ronald D. Williams, Ed. Official publication of the International Church of the Foursquare Gospel. Religious fiction and nonfiction, 1,000 to 1,200 words, and religious poetry. Pays $75, on publication. Guidelines.

FRIENDS JOURNAL—1501 Cherry St., Philadelphia, PA 19102-1497. Vinton Deming, Ed. Articles, to 2,000 words, reflecting Quaker life today:

commentary on social issues, experiential articles, Quaker history, world affairs. Poetry, to 25 lines, and Quaker-related humor and crossword puzzles also considered. Pays in copies. Guidelines.

GLORY SONGS—127 Ninth Ave. N., Nashville, TN 37234. Jere V. Adams, Ed. For volunteer and part-time music directors and members of church choirs. Very easy music and accompaniments designed specifically for the small church (4 to 6 songs per issue). Includes 8-page pull-out with articles for choir members on leisure reading, music training, and choir projects. Pays 5 1/2¢ per word, on acceptance.

GROUP, THE YOUTH MINISTRY MAGAZINE—Box 481, Loveland, CO 80539. Rick Lawrence, Ed. Interdenominational magazine for leaders of junior and senior high school Christian youth groups. Articles, 500 to 1,700 words, about practical youth ministry principles, techniques, or activities. Short how-to pieces, to 300 words. Pays to $200 for articles, $35 for department pieces, on acceptance. Guidelines.

GUIDE—Review and Herald Publishing Assn., 55 W. Oak Ridge Dr., Hagerstown, MD 21740. Carolyn Rathbun, Ed. Stories, to 1,200 words, for Christian youth, ages 10 to 14. Pays 3¢ to 7¢ a word, on publication.

GUIDEPOSTS—16 E. 34th St., New York, NY 10016. Celeste McCauley, Features Ed. True first-person stories, 250 to 1,500 words, stressing how faith in God helps people cope with life. Anecdotal fillers, to 250 words. Pays $100 to $400 for full-length stories, $25 to $100 for fillers, on acceptance.

HERALD OF HOLINESS—6401 The Paseo, Kansas City, MO 64131. Attn: Man. Ed. Church of the Nazarene. Articles, 800 to 2,000 words, about distinctive Nazarenes, Christian family life and marriage, a Christian approach to social issues, seasonal material, and short devotional articles. Pays 4¢ to 5¢ a word, within 30 days of acceptance. Guidelines.

HOME LIFE—127 Ninth Ave. N., Nashville, TN 37234. Attn: Ed.-in-Chief. Leigh Neely, Man. Ed. Southern Baptist. Fiction, personal experience, and articles on Christian marriage, parenthood, and family relationships. Human-interest pieces, 200 to 1,500 words; cartoons and short verse related to family. Query with SASE required. Pays on acceptance.

INDIAN LIFE—Box 3765, RPO Redwood Centre, Winnipeg, MB, Canada R2W 3R6. Attn: Acquisitions Ed. Christian teaching articles and testimonials of Native Americans, 1,000 to 1,200 words. "Our magazine is designed to help the North American Indian Church speak to the social, cultural, and spiritual needs of Native people." Writing should be at a seventh-grade reading level. "We prefer Native writers who write from within their culture. Read the magazine before submitting." Queries preferred.

INSIDE MAGAZINE—226 S. 16th St., Philadelphia, PA 19102-3392. Jane Biberman, Ed. Jewish lifestyle magazine. Articles, 1,500 to 3,000 words, on Jewish issues, health, finance, and the arts. Pays $75 to $600, after publication. Queries required; send clips if available.

JEWISH CURRENTS—22 E. 17th St., #601, New York, NY 10003. Morris U. Schappes, Ed. Articles, 2,400 to 3,000 words, on Jewish history, Jewish secularism, progressivism, labor struggle, Holocaust and Holocaust-resistance, Black-Jewish relations, Israel, Yiddish culture. "We are pro-Israel though non-Zionist and a secular magazine; no religious articles." Overstocked with fiction and poetry. No payment.

THE JEWISH HOMEMAKER—1372 Carroll St., Brooklyn, NY 11213. Michael Lozenik, Ed. Bimonthly. Articles, 1,200 to 2,000 words, for a traditional/Orthodox Jewish audience. Humor. Payment varies, on publication. Query.

THE JEWISH MONTHLY—B'nai B'rith International, 1640 Rhode Island Ave. N.W., Washington, DC 20036. Jeff Rubin, Ed. Articles, 500 to 3,000 words, on politics, religion, history, culture, and social issues of Jewish concern with an emphasis on people. Pays 10¢ to 25¢ a word, on publication. Query with clips.

JOURNAL OF CHRISTIAN NURSING—P.O. Box 1650, Downers Grove, IL 60515. Judy Shelly, Sr. Ed. Articles, 8 to 12 double-spaced pages, that help Christian nurses view nursing practice through the eyes of faith: spiritual care, ethics, values, healing and wholeness, psychology and religion, personal and professional ethics, etc. Priority given to nurse authors, though work by non-nurses will be considered. Opinion pieces, to 4 pages, for "The Last Word" section. Pays $25 to $80. Guidelines and editorial calendar.

THE JOYFUL WOMAN—P.O. Box 90028, Chattanooga, TN 37412. Joy Rice Martin, Ed. Articles and fiction, 500 to 1,200 words, for Christian women: first-person inspirational true stories, profiles of Christian women, practical and biblically oriented how-to articles. Pays 3¢ to 4¢ a word, on publication. Queries required; no unsolicited manuscripts.

LEADERSHIP— 465 Gundersen Dr., Carol Stream, IL 60188. Kevin A. Miller, Ed. Articles, 500 to 3,000 words, on administration, finance, and/or programming of interest to ministers and church leaders. Personal stories of crisis in ministry. "We deal mainly with the how-to of running a church. We're not a theological journal but a practical one." Pays $50 to $350, on acceptance.

LIBERTY MAGAZINE—12501 Old Columbia Pike, Silver Spring, MD 20904-1608. Clifford R. Goldstein, Ed. Timely articles, to 2,500 words, and photo-essays, on religious freedom and church-state relations. Pays 6¢ to 8¢ a word, on acceptance. Query.

LIGHT AND LIFE—P.O. Box 535002, Indianapolis, IN 46253-5002. Doug Newton, Ed. Thoughtful articles about practical Christian living. Social and cultural analysis from an evangelical perspective. Pays 4¢ to 5¢ a word, on publication.

LIGUORIAN—Liguori, MO 63057-9999. Rev. Allan Weinert, Ed. Catholic. Articles and short stories, 1,500 to 2,000 words, on Christian values in modern life. Pays 10¢ to 12¢ a word, on acceptance.

THE LIVING LIGHT—U.S. Catholic Conference, Dept. of Education, Box 45, The Catholic Univ. of America, Washington, DC 20064. Berard L. Marthaler, Office of the Exec. Ed. Theoretical and practical articles, 1,500 to 4,000 words, on religious education, catechesis, and pastoral ministry.

LIVING WITH TEENAGERS—127 Ninth Ave. N., Nashville, TN 37234. Articles, 400 to 1,200 words, told from a Christian perspective for parents of teenagers; first-person approach preferred. Queries welcome; SASE required. Pay is negotiable and made on acceptance.

THE LOOKOUT— 8121 Hamilton Ave., Cincinnati, OH 45231. David Faust, Ed. Articles, 500 to 1,800 words, on spiritual growth, family issues, applying Christian faith to current issues, and people overcoming problems with Christian principles. Inspirational or humorous shorts, 500 to 800 words; fiction, to 1,800 words. Pays 6¢ to 12¢ a word, on acceptance.

THE LUTHERAN— 8765 W. Higgins Rd., Chicago, IL 60631. Edgar R. Trexler, Ed. Articles, to 1,200 words, on Christian ideology, personal religious experiences, social and ethical issues, family life, church, and community. Pays $100 to $500, on acceptance. Query required.

MARRIAGE PARTNERSHIP—Christianity Today, Inc., 465 Gundersen Dr., Carol Stream, IL 60188. Ron Lee, Ed. Articles, 500 to 2,000 words, related to marriage, for men and women who wish to fortify their relationship. Cartoons, humor, fillers. Pays $50 to $300, on acceptance. Query required.

MATURE YEARS—201 Eighth Ave. S., P.O. Box 801, Nashville, TN 37202. Marvin W. Cropsey, Ed. Nondenominational quarterly. Articles, 1,500 to 2,000 words, on retirement or related subjects, inspiration. Humorous and serious fiction, 1,500 to 1,800 words. Travel pieces for seniors or with religious slant. Poetry, to 14 lines. Include social security number with manuscript. Guidelines.

THE MENNONITE—P.O. Box 347, Newton, KS 67114. Gordon Houser, Ed. Melanie Zuercher, Asst. Ed. Articles, 1,000 words, that emphasize Christian themes. Pays 5¢ a word, on publication. Guidelines.

MESSENGER OF THE SACRED HEART— 661 Greenwood Ave., Toronto, Ont., Canada M4J 4B3. Articles and short stories, about 1,500 words, for American and Canadian Catholics. Pays from 4¢ a word, on acceptance.

MIDSTREAM—110 E. 59th St., New York, NY 10022. Joel Carmichael, Ed. Jewish/Zionist-interest articles and book reviews. Fiction, to 3,000 words, and poetry. Pays 5¢ a word, after publication. Allow 3 months for response.

THE MIRACULOUS MEDAL— 475 E. Chelten Ave., Philadelphia, PA 19144-5785. Rev. William J. O'Brien, C.M., Ed. Dir. Catholic. Fiction, to 2,400 words. Religious verse, to 20 lines. Pays from 2¢ a word for fiction, from 50¢ a line for poetry, on acceptance.

MODERN LITURGY—160 E. Virginia St., #290, San Jose, CA 95112. Nick Wagner, Ed. Practical, imaginative how-to help for Roman Catholic liturgy planners. Pays in copies and subscription. Query required.

MOMENT MAGAZINE— 4710 41st St. N.W., Washington, DC 20016. Suzanne Singer, Man. Ed. Sophisticated, issue-oriented articles, 2,000 to 4,000 words, on Jewish topics. Nonfiction only. Pays $150 to $800, on publication.

MOMENTUM—National Catholic Educational Assn., 1077 30th St. N.W., Suite 100, Washington, DC 20007-3852. Patricia Feistritzer, Ed. Articles, 500 to 1,500 words, on outstanding programs, issues, and research in education. Book reviews. Pays $25 to $75, on publication. Query.

MOODY MAGAZINE— 820 N. La Salle Blvd., Chicago, IL 60610. Andrew Scheer, Man. Ed. Anecdotal articles, 1,200 to 2,000 words, on the evangelical Christian experience in the home, the community, and the workplace. Pays 15¢ to 20¢ a word, on acceptance. Query.

THE MUSIC LEADER—Baptist Sunday School Board, 127 Ninth Ave. N., Nashville, TN 37234. Anne Trudel, Ed. Quarterly. How-to articles, to 800 words, on organizing choir rehearsals for children; also time savers and other tips for choir directors. Inspirational poetry for challenge of teaching children. True (original) short pieces about funny or touching things that happened in preschool or children's choir. "Our readers are volunteer choir directors and teachers in evangelical churches. Articles should be encouraging, not too academic, and practical." Pays 5 1/2¢ to 6 1/2¢ a word, on acceptance. Submit complete manuscript; no queries.

NEW ERA—50 E. North Temple, Salt Lake City, UT 84150. Richard M. Romney, Man. Ed. Articles, 150 to 1,500 words, and fiction, to 2,000 words, for young Mormons. Poetry; photos. Pays 5¢ to 10¢ a word, 25¢ a line for poetry, on acceptance. Query.

NEW MAN— 600 Rinehart Rd., Lake Mary, FL 32746. Brian Peterson, Ed. Articles, to 2,000 words, that help men "in their quest for godliness and integrity." Profiles of everyday men who are doing something extraordinary, action-packed thrill and adventure articles, trend pieces that take an in-depth look at issues facing men today. Short items, 50 to 250 words, on unusual facts, motivational quotes, perspectives on news and events. Pays 10¢ to 35¢ per word, on publication.

NEW WORLD OUTLOOK— 475 Riverside Dr., Rm. 1333, New York, NY 10115. Alma Graham, Ed. Articles, 500 to 2,000 words, illustrated with color photos, on United Methodist missions and Methodist-related programs and ministries. Focus on national, global, and women's and children's issues, and on men and youth in missions. Pays on publication. Query.

OBLATES—15 S. 59th St., Belleville, IL 62223-4694. Mary Mohrman, Manuscripts Ed. Christine Portell, Man. Ed. Articles, 500 to 600 words, that inspire, uplift, and motivate through positive Christian values in everyday life. Inspirational poetry, to 16 lines. Pays $80 for articles, $30 for poems, on acceptance. Send 2 first-class stamps and SASE for guidelines and sample copy.

THE OTHER SIDE—300 W. Apsley, Philadelphia, PA 19144. Doug Davidson, Nonfiction Ed. Jennifer Wilkins, Fiction Ed. Rod Jellema, Poetry Ed. Independent, ecumenical Christian magazine devoted to issues of peace, justice, and faith. Fiction, 500 to 5,000 words, that deepens readers' encounter with the mystery of God and the mystery of ourselves. Nonfiction, 500 to 4,000 words (most under 2,000 words), on contemporary social, political, economic, or racial issues in the U.S. or abroad. Poems, to 50 lines; submit up to 3 poems. Payment is 2 copies plus $20 to $350 for articles; $75 to $250 for fiction; $15 for poems, on acceptance. Guidelines.

OUR FAMILY—Box 249, Battleford, Sask., Canada S0M 0E0. Nestor Gregoire, Ed. Articles, 1,000 to 3,000 words, for Catholic families, on modern society, family, marriage, current affairs, and spiritual topics. Humor; verse. Pays 7¢ to 10¢ a word for articles, 75¢ to $1 a line for poetry, on acceptance. SAE with international reply coupons required with all submissions. Guidelines.

PARENTLIFE—MSN 140, 127 Ninth Ave. N., Nashville, TN 37234. Attn: Ed. Informative articles and personal experience pieces, 400 to 1,200 words, relating to family and the preschool child, written with a Christian perspective. Payment varies, on acceptance.

PASTORAL LIFE—Box 595, Canfield, OH 44406-0595. Anthony L. Chenevey, Ed. Articles, 2,000 to 2,500 words, addressing the problems of pastoral ministry. Pays 4¢ a word, on publication. Guidelines.

PENTECOSTAL EVANGEL—1445 Boonville Ave., Springfield, MO 65802. Hal Donaldson, Ed. Assemblies of God. Religious, personal experience, and devotional articles, 400 to 1,000 words. Pays 6¢ a word, on acceptance.

PERSPECTIVE—Pioneer Clubs, Box 788, Wheaton, IL 60189. Rebecca Powell Parat, Ed. Articles, 750 to 1,500 words, that provide growth for adult club leaders in leadership and relationship skills and offer encouragement and practical support. Readers are lay leaders of Pioneer Clubs for boys and girls (age 2 to 12th grade). "Most articles written on assignment; writers familiar with Pioneer Clubs who would be interested in working on assignment should contact us." Queries preferred. Pays $40 to $90, on acceptance. Guidelines.

PIME WORLD—17330 Quincy St., Detroit, MI 48221. Paul W. Witte, Man. Ed. Articles, 600 to 1,200 words, on Catholic missionary work in Asia, West Africa, and Latin America. Color photos. No fiction or poetry. Pays 6¢ a word, extra for photos, on publication.

POWER AND LIGHT— 6401 The Paseo, Kansas City, MO 64131. Beula J. Postlewait, Preteen Ed. Fiction, 400 to 800 words, for grades 5 and 6, defining Christian experiences and demonstrating Christian values and beliefs. Pays 5¢ a word for multi-use rights, on publication.

THE PREACHER'S MAGAZINE—10814 E. Broadway, Spokane, WA 99206. Randal E. Denny, Ed. Scholarly and practical articles, 700 to 2,500 words, on areas of interest to Christian ministers: church administration, pastoral care, professional and personal growth, church music, finance, evangelism. Pays 3 1/2¢ a word, on publication. Guidelines.

PRESBYTERIAN RECORD—50 Wynford Dr., North York, Ont., Canada M3C 1J7. John Congram, Ed. Fiction and nonfiction, 1,500 words, and poetry, any length. Short items, to 800 words, of a contemporary and often controversial nature for "Vox Populi." The purpose of the magazine is "to provide news, not only from our church but the church-at-large, and to fulfill both a pastoral and prophetic role among our people." Queries preferred. SAE with international reply coupons required. Pays about $50 (Canadian), on publication. Guidelines.

PRESBYTERIANS TODAY—100 Witherspoon, Louisville, KY 40202-1396. Catherine Cottingham, Man. Ed. Articles, 1,200 to 1,500 words, of special interest to members of the Presbyterian Church (USA). Pays to $200, before publication.

PURPOSE— 616 Walnut Ave., Scottdale, PA 15683-1999. James E. Horsch, Ed. Fiction, nonfiction, and fillers, to 750 words, on Christian discipleship and church-year related themes, with good photos; pieces of history, biography, science, hobbies, from a Christian perspective; Christian problem solving. First-person pieces preferred. Poetry, to 12 lines. "Send complete manuscript; no queries." Pays to 5¢ a word, to $2 a line for poetry, on acceptance.

QUAKER LIFE—Friends United Meeting, 101 Quaker Hill Dr., Richmond, IN 47374-1980. Johan Maurer, Ed. Ben Richmond, Man. Ed. News and analysis, devotional and study articles for members of Friends United Meeting, other Friends (Quakers), evangelical Christians, religious pacifists. Personal testimonies. Poetry. Guidelines. Pays in copies.

QUEEN OF ALL HEARTS—26 S. Saxon Ave., Bay Shore, NY 11706-8993. J. Patrick Gaffney, S.M.M., Ed. Publication of Montfort Missionaries. Articles and fiction, 1,000 to 2,000 words, related to the Virgin Mary. Poetry. Pay varies, on acceptance.

THE QUIET HOUR— 4050 Lee Vance View, Colorado Springs, CO 80919. Gary Wilde, Ed. Short devotionals. Pays $15, on acceptance. By assignment only; query.

RECONSTRUCTIONISM TODAY—30 Old Whitfield Rd., Accord, NY 12404. Lawrence Bush, Ed. Articles on contemporary Judaism and Jewish culture. No fiction or poetry. Pays in copies and subscription.

REVIEW FOR RELIGIOUS—3601 Lindell Blvd., St. Louis, MO 63108. David L. Fleming, S.J., Ed. Informative, practical, or inspirational articles, 1,500 to 5,000 words, from a Catholic theological or spiritual point of view. Pays $6 per page, on publication. Guidelines.

ST. ANTHONY MESSENGER—1615 Republic St., Cincinnati, OH 45210-1298. Norman Perry, O.F.M., Ed. Articles, 2,000 to 3,000 words, on personalities, major movements, education, family, religious and church issues, spiritual life, and social issues. Human-interest pieces. Humor; fiction, 2,000 to 3,000 words. Articles and stories should have religious implications. Query for nonfiction. Pays 14¢ a word, on acceptance.

ST. JOSEPH'S MESSENGER—P.O. Box 288, Jersey City, NJ 07303-0288. Sister Ursula Maphet, Ed. Inspirational articles, 500 to 1,000 words, and fiction, 1,000 to 1,500 words. Verse, 4 to 40 lines. Payment varies, on publication.

SEEK—8121 Hamilton Ave., Cincinnati, OH 45231. Eileen H. Wilmoth, Ed. Articles and fiction, to 1,200 words, on inspirational and controversial topics and timely religious issues. Christian testimonials. Pays 5¢ to 7¢ a word, on acceptance. SASE for guidelines.

THE SENIOR MUSICIAN—127 Ninth Ave. N., Nashville, TN 37234. Jere V. Adams, Ed. Quarterly. For music directors, pastors, organists, pianists, choir coordinators. Easy choir music for senior adult choirs to use in worship, ministry, and recreation. Also includes leisure reading, music training, fellowship suggestions, and choir projects for personal growth. Pays 5 1/2¢ a word, on acceptance.

SHARING THE VICTORY—Fellowship of Christian Athletes, 8701 Leeds Rd., Kansas City, MO 64129. John Dodderidge, Ed. Articles, interviews, and profiles, to 1,000 words, for co-ed Christian athletes and coaches in junior high, high school, college, and pros. Pays from $50, on publication. Query required.

SIGNS OF THE TIMES—P. O. Box 5353, Nampa, ID 83653-5353. Marvin Moore, Ed. Seventh-Day Adventists. Articles, 500 to 2,000 words: features on Christians who have performed community services; first-person experiences, to 1,000 words; health, home, marriage, human-interest pieces; inspirational articles. Pays to 20¢ a word, on acceptance. Send 9x12 SASE for sample and guidelines.

SISTERS TODAY—The Liturgical Press, St. John's Abbey, Collegeville, MN 56321-7500. Articles, 500 to 3,500 words, on theology, social justice issues, and religious issues for women and the Church. Poetry, to 34 lines. Pays $5 per printed page, $10 per poem, on publication; $50 for color cover photos and $25 for B&W inside photos. Send articles to: Sister Mary Anthony Wagner, O.S.B., Ed., St. Benedict's Monastery, St. Joseph, MN 56374-2099. Send poetry to: Sister Virginia Micka, C.S.J., 1884 Randolph Ave., St. Paul, MN 55105.

SOCIAL JUSTICE REVIEW—3835 Westminster Pl., St. Louis, MO 63108-3409. Rev. John H. Miller, C.S.C., Ed. Articles, 2,000 to 3,000 words, on social problems in light of Catholic teaching and current scientific studies. Pays 2¢ a word, on publication.

SPIRITUAL LIFE—2131 Lincoln Rd. N.E., Washington, DC 20002-1199. Edward O'Donnell, O.C.D., Ed. Professional religious journal. Religious essays, 3,000 to 5,000 words, on spirituality in contemporary life. Pays from $50, on acceptance. Guidelines.

STANDARD— 6401 The Paseo, Kansas City, MO 64131. Articles and fiction, 300 to 1,700 words; true experiences; poetry, to 20 lines; fiction with Christian emphasis but not overtly preachy; cartoons in good taste. Pays 3 1/2¢ a word, on acceptance.

TEACHERS INTERACTION—3558 S. Jefferson Ave., St. Louis, MO 63118. Rachael Hoyer, Ed. Practical articles, 800 to 1,200 words, for Christian teachers and how-to pieces, to 100 words, specifically for Lutheran Church-Missouri Synod volunteer church school teachers. Pays $20 to $100, on publication. Freelance submissions accepted.

THEOLOGY TODAY— Box 29, Princeton, NJ 08542. Thomas G. Long, Ed. Patrick D. Miller, Ed. Articles, 1,500 to 3,500 words, on theology, religion, and related social and philosophical issues. Literary criticism. Pays $75 to $200, on publication.

TODAY'S CHRISTIAN DOCTOR—(formerly *Christian Medical & Dental Society Journal*) P.O. Box 5, Bristol, TN 37621-0005. David B. Biebel, D. Min., Ed. Articles, 8 to 10 double-spaced pages, for Christian medical and dental professionals. Queries preferred. Guidelines.

TODAY'S CHRISTIAN WOMAN— 465 Gundersen Dr., Carol Stream, IL 60188. Ramona Cramer Tucker, Ed. Articles, 1,500 to 1,800 words, that are "warm and personal in tone, full of real-life anecdotes that deal with the following relationships: marriage, parenting, friendship, spiritual life, and self." Payment varies, on acceptance. Queries required. Guidelines.

THE UNITED CHURCH OBSERVER— 478 Huron St., Toronto, Ont., Canada M5R 2R3. Factual articles, 1,500 to 2,500 words, on religious trends, human problems, social issues. No poetry. Pays after publication. Query.

UNITED SYNAGOGUE REVIEW— 155 Fifth Ave., New York, NY 10010. Lois Goldrich, Ed. Articles, 1,000 to 1,200 words, on issues of interest to Conservative Jewish community. Query.

UNITY MAGAZINE—1901 N.W. Blue Pkwy., Unity School of Christianity, Unity Village, MO 64065. Philip White, Ed. Religious and inspirational articles, 1,000 to 1,800 words, on health and healing, Bible interpretation, and the metaphysical. Poems. Pays 20¢ a word, on acceptance.

VIRTUE: HELPING WOMEN BUILD CHRIST-LIKE CHARACTER— 4050 Lee Vance View, Colorado Springs, CO 80918. Attn: Ed. Articles and fiction for Christian women. Journalistic reports on women's issues and women's lives and their spiritual journeys. Query for articles; SASE required. Guidelines.

THE WAR CRY—The Salvation Army, P.O. Box 269, Alexandria, VA 22313. Attn: Ed.-in-Chief. Inspirational articles, to 800 words, addressing modern life and issues. Color photos. Pays 15¢ to 20¢ a word for articles, $150 to $200 for photos, on acceptance.

WITH: THE MAGAZINE FOR RADICAL CHRISTIAN YOUTH—722 Main St., Box 347, Newton, KS 67114. Eddy Hall and Carol Duerksen, Eds. Fiction, 500 to 2,000 words; nonfiction, 500 to 1,600 words; and poetry, to 50 lines for Mennonite and Brethren teenagers. "Wholesome humor always gets a close read." B&W 8x10 photos accepted. Payment is 5¢ a word, on acceptance (3¢ a word for reprints).

WOMAN'S TOUCH—1445 Boonville, Springfield, MO 65802-1894. Peggy Musgrove, Ed. Aleda Swartzendruber, Assoc. Ed. Articles, 500 to 1,000 words, that provide help and inspiration to Christian women, strengthening family life, and reaching out in witness to others. Submit complete manuscript. Allow 3 months for response. Payment varies, on publication. Guidelines and editorial calendar.

WORLD VISION MAGAZINE—P.O. Box 9716, Federal Way, WA 98063-9716. Bruce Brander, Man. Ed. Thoroughly researched articles, 1,200 to 2,000 words, on worldwide poverty, evangelism, the environment, and justice. Include reputable sources and strong anecdotes. "Turning Points," first-person articles, 450 to 700 words, about a life-changing, spiritual experience related to serving the poor. "We like articles to offer positive ways Christians can make a difference." Query required. Payment negotiable, made on acceptance.

YOUNG SALVATIONIST—The Salvation Army, 615 Slaters Ln., P.O. Box 269, Alexandria, VA 22313. Attn: Lesa Davis, Prod. Mgr. Articles, 600 to 1,200 words, that teach the Christian view of everyday living, for teenagers. Short shorts, first-person testimonies, 600 to 800 words. Pays 15¢ a word (10¢ a word for reprints), on acceptance. SASE required. Send 8 1/2x11 SASE (3 stamps) for theme list, guidelines, and sample copy.

YOUR CHURCH—465 Gundersen Dr., Carol Stream, IL 60188. Richard Doebler, Ed. Articles, to 1,000 words, about church business administration. Pays about 15¢ a word, on acceptance. Query required. Guidelines.

HEALTH

ACCENT ON LIVING—P. O. Box 700, Bloomington, IL 61702. Raymond C. Cheever, Pub. Betty Garee, Ed. Articles, 250 to 1,000 words, about physically disabled people, including their careers, recreation, sports, self-help devices, and ideas that can make daily routines easier. Good photos a plus. Pays 10¢ a word, on publication. Query.

AMERICAN BABY—KIII Family & Leisure Group, 249 W. 17th St., New York, NY 10011. Judith Nolte, Ed. Articles, 1,000 to 2,000 words, for new or expectant parents on prenatal and infant care. Personal experience, 900 to 1,200 words (do not submit in diary format). Department pieces, 50 to 350 words, for "Crib Notes" (news and feature topics) and "Medical Update" (health and medicine). No fiction, fantasy pieces, dreamy musings, or poetry. Pays $500 to $1,000 for articles, $100 for departments, on acceptance. Guidelines.

AMERICAN FITNESS—15250 Ventura Blvd., Suite 200, Sherman Oaks, CA 91403. Peg Jordan, Ed. Rhonda Wilson, Man. Ed. Articles, 500 to 1,500 words, on exercise, health, trends, research, nutrition, alternative paths, etc. Illustrations, photos.

AMERICAN HEALTH—28 W. 23rd St., New York, NY 10010. Attn: Ed. Dept. Lively, authoritative articles, 1,000 to 3,000 words, on women's health and lifestyle aspects of health and fitness; 100-to 500-word news reports. Query with clips. Pays $250 ($50 kill fee) for news stories; 75¢ to $1 per word for features (kill fee is 25% of assigned fee), on acceptance.

AMERICAN JOURNAL OF NURSING—555 W. 57th St., New York, NY 10019. Santa J. Crisall, Clinical Dir. Articles, 1,500 to 2,000 words, with photos or illustrations, on nursing or disease processes. Query.

AQUARIUS: A SIGN OF THE TIMES—984 Canton St., Roswell, GA 30075. Dan Liss, Ed. Tabloid. Articles, 800 words (plus photo or illustration) on holistic health, metaphysics, spirituality, and the environment. "We are a great way for new writers to get clips." No payment.

ARTHRITIS TODAY—The Arthritis Foundation, 1330 W. Peachtree St., Atlanta, GA 30309. Cindy McDaniel, Ed. Research, self-help, how-to, general interest, general health, and lifestyle topics, and inspirational articles, 750 to 3,000 words, and short fillers, 100 to 250 words. "The magazine is written to help people with arthritis live more productive, independent, and pain-free lives." Pays $500 to $2,000 for articles, $75 to $250 for short fillers, on acceptance.

BABY TALK—301 Howard St., San Francisco, CA 94105. Trisha Thompson, Ed. Articles, 1,000 to 1,500 words, by parents or professionals, on babies and baby care, etc. No poetry. Pay varies, on acceptance. SASE required.

COPING: LIVING WITH CANCER—P.O. Box 682268, Franklin, TN 37068. Tricia Brown, Ed. Uplifting and practical articles for people living with cancer: medical news, lifestyle issues, and inspiring personal essays. No payment.

DIABETES SELF-MANAGEMENT—150 W. 22nd St., New York, NY 10011. James Hazlett, Ed. Articles, 2,000 to 4,000 words, for people with diabetes who want to know more about controlling and managing it. Up-to-date and authoritative information on nutrition, pharmacology, exercise physiology, technological advances, self-help, and other how-to subjects. "Articles must be useful, instructive, and must have immediate application to the day-to-day life of our readers. We do not publish personal experience, profiles, exposés, or research breakthroughs." Query with one-page rationale, outline, writing samples, and SASE. Pays from $500, on publication. Buys all rights.

EATING WELL—Ferry Rd., P.O. Box 1001, Charlotte, VT 05445-1001. Marcelle DiFalco, Ed. Bimonthly. "A food book with a health perspective." Feature articles, 2,000 to 5,000 words, for readers who "know that what they eat directly affects their well-being, and believe that with the right approach, one can enjoy both good food and good health." Department pieces, 100 to 200 words, for "Nutrition News" and "Eating Well in America." "We look for strong journalistic voice; authoritative, timely coverage of nutrition issues; healthful recipes that emphasize good ingredients, simple preparation, and full flavor; and a sense of humor." Pays varying rates, 45 days after acceptance. Query.

FITNESS—Grune & Jahr USA Publishing, 110 Fifth Ave., New York, NY 10011. Sally Lee, Ed. Articles, 500 to 2,000 words, on health, exercise, sports, nutrition, diet, psychological well-being, alternative therapies, sex, and beauty. Average reader is 30 years old. Query required. Pays $1 a word, on acceptance.

HEALTH—301 Howard St., 18th Fl., San Francisco, CA 94105. Paula Motte, Ed. Asst. Articles, 1,200 words, for "Food," "Fitness," "Vanities," "Mind," and "Relationships" departments. Payment varies, on acceptance. Query with clips and SASE required.

HEALTH QUEST—200 Highpoint Dr., Suite 215, Chalfont, PA 18914. Valerie Boyd, Ed.-in-Chief. Tamara Jeffries, Man. Ed. "The Publication of

Black Wellness." Articles, 700 to 1,500 words, on health issues of interest to African-American men and women. "We focus on total health, so articles cover mind, body, spirit, and cultural wellness." Payment varies, on publication. Query preferred.

HEART & SOUL—Rodale Press, Inc., 733 Third Ave., 15th Fl., New York, NY 10017. Stephanie Stokes Oliver, Ed.-in-Chief. Articles, 800 to 2,000 words, on health, beauty, fitness, nutrition, and relationships for African-American readers. Pays varying rates, on acceptance. Queries preferred.

HERBALGRAM—P.O. Box 201660, Austin, TX 78720. Barbara Johnston, Man. Ed. Quarterly. Articles, 1,500 to 3,000 words, on herb and medicinal plant research, regulatory issues, market conditions, native plant conservation, and other aspects of herbal use. Pays in copies. Query.

IDEA TODAY—6190 Cornerstone Ct. E., Suite 204, San Diego, CA 92121-3773. Therese Hannon, Asst. Ed. Practical articles, 1,000 to 3,000 words, on new exercise programs, business management, nutrition, sports medicine, dance-exercise, and one-to-one training techniques. Articles must be geared toward the aerobics instructor, exercise studio owner or manager, or personal trainer. No consumer or general health pieces. Payment negotiable, on acceptance. Query preferred. Guidelines.

INDEPENDENT LIVING PROVIDER—150 Motor Parkway, Suite 420, Hauppauge, NY 11788-5145. Anne Kelly, Ed. Articles, 1,500 to 3,000 words, on sales and service by home medical equipment dealers. Topics: home health care business, managed care, health care reform, new products. Pays 15¢ a word, $15 per photo, on publication. Query.

LET'S LIVE—P.O. Box 74908, Los Angeles, CA 90004. Beth Salmon, Ed.-in-Chief. Articles, 1,000 to 1,500 words, on preventive medicine and nutrition, alternative medicine, diet, vitamins, herbs, exercise, recipes, and natural beauty. Pays $250, on publication. Query.

MEDIPHORS—P.O. Box 327, Bloomsburg, PA 17815. Dr. Eugene D. Radice, Ed. "A Literary Journal of the Health Professions." Short stories, essays, and commentary, 3,000 words, related to medicine and health. Poetry, to 30 lines. "We are not a technical journal of science. We do not publish research or review articles, except of a historical nature." Pays in copies. Guidelines.

NATURAL HEALTH—17 Station St., Box 1200, Brookline Village, MA 02147. Bimonthly. Features, 1,500 to 3,000 words: practical information, new discoveries, and current trends about natural health and living. Topics include: natural goods and medicines, alternative health care, nutrition, wellness, personal fitness, and modern holistic teachings. Departments and columns, 250 to 1,000 words. Pays varying rates, on acceptance.

NURSING 98—1111 Bethlehem Pike, P.O. Box 908, Springhouse, PA 19477-0908. Patricia Nornhold, Exec. Dir. Most articles are clinically oriented, and written by nurses for direct caregivers. Also covers legal, ethical, management, and career aspects of nursing; narratives about personal nursing experiences. No poetry, cartoons, or puzzles. Pays $25 to $300, on publication. Query.

NUTRITION HEALTH REVIEW—P.O. Box 406, Haverford, PA 19041. Frank Ray Rifkin, Ed. Quarterly tabloid. Articles on medical progress, information relating to nutritional therapy, genetics, psychiatry, behavior therapy, surgery, pharmacology, animal health; vignettes relating to health and nutrition. "Vegetarian-oriented; we do not deal with subjects that favor animal testing, animal foods, cruelty to animals or recipes that contain animal products." Humor, cartoons. Pays on publication. Query.

PATIENT CARE—5 Paragon Dr., Montvale, NJ 07645. Jeffrey H. Forster, Ed. Articles on medical care, for primary-care physicians; mostly staff-written. Pays varying rates, on publication. Query; all articles assigned.

PERCEPTIONS—10736 Jefferson Blvd., Suite 502, Culver City, CA 90230. Judi V. Brewer, Ed. Articles, to 2,500 words, on government, alternative health, metaphysics. Reviews, to 500 words. Cartoons. "Broad-spectrum focus crossing barriers that separate ideologies, politics, etc." Sections include Political Slant (relevant information focusing on what we have in common); Healing Spiral (little-known facts and remedies); Concepts (a forum to broaden, awaken, and tickle the intellect). Pays in copies.

THE PHOENIX—7152 Unity Ave. N., Brooklyn Ctr., MN 55429. Pat Samples, Ed. Tabloid. Articles, 800 to 1,500 words, on recovery, renewal, and growth. Department pieces for "12 Step," "Bodywise," "Family Skills," or "Personal Story." "Our readers are committed to physical, emotional, mental, and spiritual health and well-being. Read a sample copy to see what we publish." Pays 3¢ to 5¢ a word, on publication. Guidelines and calendar.

THE PHYSICIAN AND SPORTSMEDICINE—4530 W. 77th St., Minneapolis, MN 55435. Terry Monahan, Exec. Ed. News and feature articles; clinical articles coauthored with physician. Sports medicine angle necessary. Pays $150 to $1,000, on acceptance. Query. Guidelines.

PREVENTION—33 E. Minor St., Emmaus, PA 18098. Lewis Vaughn, Man. Ed. Query required. No guidelines available. Limited market.

PSYCHOLOGY TODAY—Sussex Publishing, 49 E. 21st St., New York, NY 10010. Lisa Liebman, Exec. Ed. Bimonthly. Articles, 2,000 words, on timely subjects and news. Pays varying rates, on publication.

RX REMEDY—120 Post Rd. W., Westport, CT 06880. Val Weaver, Ed. Bimonthly. Articles, 600 to 2,500 words, on health and medication issues for readers 55 and older. Regular columns include "Housecall" and "The Nutrition Prescription." Query. Pays $1 to $1.25 a word, on acceptance.

TANNING TRENDS—3101 Page Ave., Jackson, MI 49203-2254. Joseph Levy, Ed. Articles on skin care and "smart tanning" for tanning salon owners. "We promote tanning clients responsibly and professionally." Payment varies, on publication.

TODAY'S SURGICAL NURSE—Slack, Inc., 6900 Grove Rd., Thorofare, NJ 08086. Frances R. DeStefano, Man. Ed. Clinical or general articles, from 2,000 words, of direct interest to surgical nurses.

TOTAL HEALTH—165 N. 100 E. #2, St. George, UT 84770. Katherine Hurd, Ed. Articles, 1,200 to 1,400 words, on preventative health care, fitness, diet, and mental health. Color or B&W photos. Pays $50 to $75, on publication.

VEGETARIAN TIMES—P.O. Box 570, Oak Park, IL 60303. Toni Apgar, Ed. Dir. Articles, 1,200 to 2,500 words, on vegetarian cooking, nutrition, health and fitness, and profiles of prominent vegetarians. "News Items" and "In Print" (book reviews), to 500 words. "Herbalist" pieces, to 1,800 words, on medicinal uses of herbs. Queries required. Pays $75 to $1,000, on acceptance. Guidelines.

VEGETARIAN VOICE—P.O. Box 72, Dolgeville, NY 13329. Jennie Collura, Sr. Ed. Quarterly. Informative, well-researched and/or inspiring articles,

600 to 1,800 words, on health, nutrition, animal rights, the environment, world hunger, etc. Pays in copies. Guidelines.

VIBRANT LIFE—55 W. Oak Ridge Dr., Hagerstown, MD 21740. Attn: Ed. Features, 750 to 1,500 words, on total health: physical, mental, and spiritual. Upbeat articles on the family and how to live happier and healthier lives, emphasizing practical tips; Christian slant. Pays $80 to $250, on acceptance.

VIM & VIGOR—1010 E. Missouri Ave., Phoenix, AZ 85014. Jake Poinier, Ed. Positive health and fitness articles, 1,200 to 2,000 words, with accurate medical facts. By assignment only; no queries or unsolicited manuscripts. Writers with feature-or news-writing ability may submit qualifications for assignment. Pays $500, on acceptance. Guidelines.

THE WALKING MAGAZINE—9-11 Harcourt, Boston, MA 02116. Seth Bauer, Ed. Articles, 1,500 to 2,500 words, on fitness, health, equipment, nutrition, travel and adventure, famous walkers, and other walking-related topics. Shorter pieces, 150 to 800 words, and essays for "Ramblings" page. Photos welcome. Pays $750 to $1,800 for features, $100 to $500 for department pieces, on acceptance. Guidelines.

YOGA JOURNAL—2054 University Ave., Berkeley, CA 94704. Rick Fields, Ed. Articles, 1,200 to 4,000 words, on holistic health, meditation, consciousness, spirituality, and yoga. Pays $100 to $1,200, on acceptance.

YOUR HEALTH—5401 N.W. Broken Sound Blvd., Boca Raton, FL 33487. Susan Gregg, Ed.-in-Chief. Health and medical articles, 1,000 to 2,000 words, for a lay audience. Queries preferred. Pays $75 to $200, on publication.

YOUR HEALTH—1720 Washington Blvd., Box 10010, Ogden, UT 84409. Attn: Ed. Staff. Articles, 1,000 words, on individual health care needs: prevention, treatment, low-impact aerobics, fitness, nutrition, etc. Color photos required. Pays 15¢ a word, on acceptance. Guidelines.

EDUCATION

ACTIVITY RESOURCES—P.O. Box 4875, Hayward, CA 94540. Mary Laycock, Ed. Math educational material only for books geared to mathematics for grades K through 8. Submit complete book manuscript. Royalty.

AMERICAN SCHOOL & UNIVERSITY—P.O. Box 12901, 9800 Metcalf, Overland Park, KS 66212-2215. Joe Agron, Ed. Articles and case studies, 1,200 to 1,500 words, on design, construction, operation, and management of school and university facilities. Queries preferred.

THE BOOK REPORT—Linworth Publishing, 480 E. Wilson Bridge Rd., Suite L, Worthington, OH 43085-2372. Carolyn Hamilton, Ed./Pub. "The Journal for Secondary School Librarians." Articles by school librarians or other educators about practical aspects of running a school library. Write for themes and guidelines. Also publishes *Library Talk,* "The Magazine for Elementary School Librarians," and *Technology Connection,* "The Magazine for Library and Media Specialists."

CAREERS & THE DISABLED—See *Minority Engineer.*

CHANGE—1319 18th St. N.W., Washington, DC 20036. Attn: Ed. Columns, 700 to 2,000 words, and in-depth features, 2,500 to 3,500 words, on programs, people, and institutions of higher education. "We can't usually pay for unsolicited articles."

CHRISTIAN EDUCATION LEADERSHIP—P.O. Box 2250, Cleveland, TN 37320-2250. Lance Colkmire, Ed. Quarterly. Articles, 500 to 1,200 words, that "encourage, inform, and inspire those who teach the Bible in the local church." No fiction, poetry, fillers, or artwork. Pays $25 to $55, on acceptance.

THE CLEARING HOUSE—Heldref Publications, 1319 18th St. N.W., Washington, DC 20036. Judy Cusick, Man. Ed. Bimonthly for middle level and high school teachers and administrators. Articles, 2,500 words, related to education: useful teaching practices, research findings, and experiments. Some opinion pieces and satirical articles related to education. Pays in copies.

EQUAL OPPORTUNITY—See *Minority Engineer.*

GIFTED EDUCATION PRESS QUARTERLY—P.O. Box 1586, 10201 Yuma Ct., Manassas, VA 20108. Maurice Fisher, Pub. Articles, to 4,000 words, written by educators, laypersons, and parents of gifted children, on the problems of identifying and teaching gifted children and adolescents. "Interested in incisive analyses of current programs for the gifted and recommendations for improving the education of gifted students. Particularly interested in advocacy for gifted children, biographical sketches of highly gifted individuals, and the problems of teaching humanities, science, ethics, literature, and history to the gifted. Looking for highly imaginative and knowledgeable writers." Query required. Pays in subscription.

THE HISPANIC OUTLOOK IN HIGHER EDUCATION—17 Arcadian Ave., Paramus, NJ 07652. Attn: Ed. Articles, 1,500 to 2,000 words, on the issues, concerns, and potential models for furthering the academic results of Hispanics in higher education. Queries are preferred. Payment varies, on publication.

HOME EDUCATION MAGAZINE—P.O. Box 1083, Tonasket, WA 98855-1083. Helen E. Hegener, Man. Ed. Informative articles, 750 to 2,000 words, on all aspects of the growing homeschool movement. Send complete manuscript or detailed query with SASE. Pays 45¢ per column inch, on publication.

THE HORN BOOK MAGAZINE—11 Beacon St., Suite 1000, Boston, MA 02108. Roger Sutton, Ed.-in-Chief. Articles, 600 to 2,800 words, on books for young readers and related subjects for librarians, teachers, parents, etc. Payment varies, on publication. Query.

INDEPENDENT LIVING PROVIDER—See *Minority Engineer.*

INSTRUCTOR MAGAZINE—Scholastic, Inc., 555 Broadway, New York, NY 10012. Mickey Revenaugh, Ed. Articles, 300 to 1,500 words, for teachers in grades K through 8. Payment varies, on acceptance.

ITC COMMUNICATOR—International Training in Communication, P.O. Box 1809, Sutter Creek, CA 95685. JoAnn Levy, Ed. Educational articles, 200 to 800 words, on leadership, language, speech presentation, procedures for meetings, personal and professional development, written and spoken communication techniques. SASE required. Pays in copies.

LEADERSHIP PUBLISHERS, INC.—P.O. Box 8358, Des Moines, IA 50301-8358. Attn: Dr. Lois F. Roets. Educational materials for talented and gifted students, grades K to 12. Send SASE for catalogue and guidelines before submitting. Pays in royalty for books, and flat fee for booklets.

LEARNING—3515 W. Market St., Greensboro, NC 27403. Attn: Manuscript Ed. Bimonthly. Articles, 50 to 1,500 words, that help teachers deal with issues such as stress, motivation, burnout, and other self-improvement topics;

successful teaching strategies to reach today's kids; and ideas to get parents involved. SASE required. Pays $50 per published page, on acceptance. Allow 6 months for response.

LIBRARY TALK—See *The Book Report.*

MEDIA & METHODS—1429 Walnut St., Philadelphia, PA 19102. Michele Sokoloff, Ed. Dir. Articles, 800 to 1,000 words, on media, technologies, and methods used to enhance instruction and learning in K through 12th-grade classrooms. Pays $50 to $200, on publication. Query required.

MINORITY ENGINEER—1160 E. Jericho Turnpike, Suite 200, Huntington, NY 11743. James Schneider, Ed. Articles, 1,000 to 1,500 words, for college students, on career opportunities; techniques of job hunting, and role-model profiles of professional minority engineers. Interviews. Pays 10¢ a word, on publication. Query. Also publishes: *Equal Opportunity*; *Careers & the Dis-ABLED*, query James Schneider; *Woman Engineer* and *Independent Living Provider*, query Editor Anne Kelly.

MOMENTUM—National Catholic Educational Assn., 1077 30th St. N.W., Suite 100, Washington, DC 20007-3852. Patricia Feistritzer, Ed. Articles, 500 to 1,500 words, on outstanding programs, issues, and research in education. Book reviews. Query or send complete manuscript. No simultaneous submissions. Pays $25 to $75, on publication.

THE MUSIC LEADER—Baptist Sunday School Board, 127 Ninth Ave. N., Nashville, TN 37234. Anne Trudel, Ed. Quarterly. How-to articles, to 800 words, on organizing choir rehearsals for children; also time savers and other tips for choir directors. Inspirational poetry for challenge of teaching children. True (original) short pieces about funny or touching things that happened in preschool or children's choir. "Our readers are volunteer choir directors and teachers in evangelical churches. Articles should be encouraging, not too academic, and practical." Pays 5 1/2¢ to 6 1/2¢ a word, on acceptance. Send complete manuscript; no queries.

PHI DELTA KAPPAN—408 N. Union St., Box 789, Bloomington, IN 47402-0789. Pauline Gough, Ed. Articles, 1,000 to 4,000 words, on educational research, service, and leadership; issues, trends, and policy. Rarely pays for manuscripts.

REACHING TODAY'S YOUTH—National Education Service, P.O. Box 8, Bloomington, IN 47402. Alan Blankstein, Sr. Ed. Articles, 1,500 to 2,500 words, that provide an interdisciplinary perspective on positive approaches to reaching and educating youth who are troubled, angry, or disconnected from school, peers, or family. Readers are educators, parents, youth care professionals, residential treatment staff, juvenile justice professionals, police, researchers, youth advocates, child and family psychologists, community members and students. Send SASE for guidelines and current themes.

SCHOOL ARTS MAGAZINE—50 Portland St., Worcester, MA 01608. Dr. Eldon Katter, Ed. Articles, 800 to 1,000 words, on art education with special application to the classroom: successful and meaningful approaches to teaching art, innovative art projects, uncommon applications of art techniques or equipment, etc. Photos. Pays varying rates, on publication. Guidelines.

SCHOOL SAFETY—National School Safety Ctr., 4165 Thousand Oaks Blvd., Suite 290, Westlake Village, CA 91362. Ronald D. Stephens, Exec. Ed. Published 8 times during the school year. Articles, 2,000 to 3,000 words, of use to educators, law enforcers, judges, and legislators on the prevention of drugs, gangs, weapons, bullying, discipline problems, and vandalism; also on-site security and character development as they relate to students and schools. No payment.

TEACHING K-8 — 40 Richards Ave., Norwalk, CT 06854. Patricia Broderick, Ed. Dir. Articles, 1,200 words, on the profession of teaching children. Pays to $35, on publication. Queries are not necessary.

TECH DIRECTIONS — Box 8623, Ann Arbor, MI 48107. Paul J. Bamford, Man. Ed. Articles, one to 10 double-spaced typed pages, for teachers and administrators in industrial, technology, and vocational educational fields, with particular interest in classroom projects, computer uses, and legislative issues. Pays $10 to $150, on publication. Guidelines.

TECHNOLOGY CONNECTION—See *The Book Report*.

TODAY'S CATHOLIC TEACHER—330 Progress Rd., Dayton, OH 45449. Mary Noschang, Ed. Articles, 600 to 800 words, 1,000 to 1,200 words, and 1,200 to 1,500 words, on education, parent-teacher relationships, innovative teaching, teaching techniques, etc., of use to educators in Catholic schools. Pays $65 to $250, on publication. SASE required. Query. Guidelines.

WOMAN ENGINEER—See *Minority Engineer*.

FARMING & AGRICULTURE

ACRES USA—P.O. Box 8800, Metairie, LA 70011. Fred C. Walters, Ed. Articles on sustainable agriculture: technology, case reports, "hands-on" advice. "Our emphasis is on commercial production of quality food without the use of toxic chemicals." Pays 5¢ a word, on publication.

AMERICAN BEE JOURNAL—51 N. Second St., Hamilton, IL 62341. Joe M. Graham, Ed. Articles on beekeeping, for professionals. Photos. Pays 75¢ a column inch, extra for photos, on publication.

BEE CULTURE— 623 W. Liberty St., Medina, OH 44256. Mr. Kim Flottum, Ed. Basic how-to articles, 500 to 2,000 words, on keeping bees and selling bee products. Slides or B&W prints. Payment varies, on acceptance and on publication. Queries preferred.

BUCKEYE FARM NEWS—Ohio Farm Bureau Federation, 2 Nationwide Plaza, Box 479, Columbus, OH 43216-0479. Lynn Echelberger, Copy Ed. Articles, to 600 words, related to agriculture. Pays on publication. Query. Limited market.

DAIRY GOAT JOURNAL—P.O. Box 10, Lake Mills, WI 53551. Dave Thompson, Ed. Articles, to 1,500 words, on successful dairy goat owners, youths, and interesting people associated with dairy goats. "Especially interested in practical husbandry ideas." Photos. Pays $50 to $150, on publication. Query.

FARM AND RANCH LIVING—5400 S. 60th St., Greendale, WI 53129. Nick Pabst, Ed. Articles, 2,000 words, on rural people and situations; nostalgia pieces; profiles of interesting farms and farmers, ranches and ranchers. Pays $15 to $400, on acceptance and on publication.

FARM INDUSTRY NEWS—7900 International Dr., Minneapolis, MN 55425. Joe Degnan, Ed. Articles for farmers, on new products, machinery, equipment, chemicals, and seeds. Pays $350 to $500, on acceptance. Query required.

FARM JOURNAL—Centre Sq. W., 1500 Market St., Philadelphia, PA 19102-2181. Sonja Hillgren, Ed. Articles, 500 to 1,500 words, with photos, on the business of farming. Pays 20¢ to 50¢ a word, on acceptance. Query.

FARM SUPPLY RETAILING—P.O. Box 23536, Minneapolis, MN 55423-0536. Joseph Rydholm, Ed. Profiles, 1,400 words, of successful farm supply retailers and articles on running/managing a small business, preferably slanted to the farm supply retailer. Photos. Pays $150 to $200 for articles; $25 to $75 for photos, on publication.

THE FURROW—Deere & Co., John Deere Rd., Moline, IL 61265. George Sollenberger, Exec. Ed. Specialized, illustrated articles on farming. Pays to $1,200, on acceptance.

THE LAND—P.O. Box 3169, Mankato, MN 56002-3169. Randy Frahm, Ed. Articles on Minnesota agriculture and rural issues. Pays $25 to $45, on acceptance. Query required.

NEW HOLLAND NEWS—New Holland, Inc., P.O. Box 1895, New Holland, PA 17557-0903. Attn: Ed. Articles, to 1,500 words, with strong color photo support, on agriculture and rural living. Pays on acceptance. Query.

OHIO FARMER—1350 W. Fifth Ave., Columbus, OH 43212. Tim White, Ed. Technical articles on farming, rural living, etc., in Ohio. Pays $50 per column, on publication.

ONION WORLD—P.O. Box 9036, Yakima, WA 98909-9036. D. Brent Clement, Ed. Production and marketing articles, to 1,500 words (preferred length 1,200 words), for commercial onion growers and shippers. "Research oriented articles are of definite interest. No gardening articles." Pays about $125, on publication. Query preferred.

PEANUT FARMER—3000 Highwoods Blvd., Suite 300, Raleigh, NC 27604-1029. Mary Evans, Man. Ed. Articles, 500 to 2,000 words, on production and management practices in peanut farming. Pays $50 to $350, on publication.

PENNSYLVANIA FARMER—P.O. Box 4475, Gettysburg, PA 17325. John R. Vogel, Ed. Articles on farmers in PA, NJ, DE, MD, and WV; timely business-of-farming concepts and successful farm management operations. Short pieces on humorous experiences in farming. Payment varies, on publication.

PROGRESSIVE FARMER—2100 Lakeshore Dr., Birmingham, AL 35209. Toni Holifield, Ed. Asst. Articles, to 5 double-spaced pages (3 pages preferred), on farmers or new developments in agriculture; rural communities; and personal business issues concerning the farmstead, home office, relationships, worker safety, finances, taxes, and regulations. Pays $50 to $400, on publication. Query.

RURAL HERITAGE—281 Dean Ridge Ln., Gainesboro, TN 38562. Gail Damerow, Ed. How-to and feature articles, 800 to 1,200 words, related to the present-day use of work horses, mules, and oxen. Pays 5¢ a word, $10 for photos, on publication. SASE for guidelines.

SHEEP! MAGAZINE—P.O. Box 10, Lake Mills, WI 53551. Dave Thompson, Ed. Articles, to 1,500 words, on successful shepherds, woolcrafts, sheep raising, and sheep dogs. "Especially interested in people who raise sheep successfully as a sideline enterprise." Photos. Pays $80 to $150, extra for photos, on publication. Query.

SMALL FARM TODAY—3903 W. Ridge Trail Rd., Clark, MO 65243-9525. Paul Berg, Man. Ed. Agriculture articles, 800 to 1,800 words, on preserving and promoting small farming, rural living, and "agripreneurship." How-to articles on alternative crops, livestock, and direct marketing. Pays 3 1/2¢ a word, on publication. Query.

SMALL FARMER'S JOURNAL—P.O. Box 1627, Dept. 106, Sisters, OR 97759. Address the Eds. How-tos, humor, practical work horse information, livestock and produce marketing, gardening information, and articles appropriate to the independent family farm. Pays negotiable rates, on publication. Query.

TOPICS IN VETERINARY MEDICINE—Pfizer Animal Health, 812 Springdale Dr., Exton, PA 19341. Kathleen Etchison, Ed. Technical articles, 1,200 to 1,500 words, and clinical features, 500 words, on veterinary medicine. Photos. Pays $300, $150 for shorter pieces, extra for photos, on publication.

WALLACES FARMER— 6200 Aurora Ave., Suite 609E, Urbandale, IA 50322-2838. Frank Holdmeger, Ed. Features, 600 to 700 words, on farming in Iowa; methods and equipment; interviews with farmers. Query. Payment varies, on acceptance.

THE WESTERN PRODUCER—Box 2500, Saskatoon, Saskatchewan, Canada S7K 2C4. Address Man. Ed. Articles, to 800 words (prefer under 600 words), on agricultural and rural subjects, preferably with a Canadian slant. Photos. Pays from 15¢ a word; $20 to $40 for B&W photos; $35 to $100 for color photos, on acceptance.

WYOMING RURAL ELECTRIC NEWS—P.O. Box 380, Casper, WY 82606-0380. Kris Wendtland, Ed. Articles, 500 to 900 words, on issues relevant to rural Wyoming. Articles should support Wyoming's personal and economic growth, social development, and education. Wyoming writers given preference. Pays $20 to $50, on publication.

ENVIRONMENT & CONSERVATION

ALTERNATIVES JOURNAL—Faculty of Environmental Studies, Univ. of Waterloo, Waterloo, Ontario, Canada N2L 3G1. Nancy Doucet, Man. Ed. Quarterly. Feature articles, 4,000 words; notes, 200 to 500 words; and reports, 750 to 1,000 words, that focus on Canadian content in areas of environmental thought, policy, and action. No payment.

THE AMERICAN FIELD— 542 S. Dearborn, Chicago, IL 60605. B.J. Matthys, Man. Ed. Yarns about hunting trips, bird-shooting; articles, to 1,500 words, on dogs and field trials, emphasizing conservation of game resources. Pays varying rates, on acceptance.

AMERICAN FORESTS—1516 P St. N.W., Washington, DC 20005. Michelle Robbins, Ed. Looking for skilled science writers for well-documented articles on the use, enjoyment, and management of forests. Send clips. Query.

THE AMICUS JOURNAL—Natural Resources Defense Council, 40 W. 20th St., New York, NY 10011. Kathrin Day Lassila, Ed. Quarterly. Articles and book reviews on local, national, and international environmental topics. (No fiction, speeches, or product reports accepted.) Pays varying rates, 30 days after acceptance. Query with SASE required.

ANIMALS—350 S. Huntington Ave., Boston, MA 02130. Joni Praded, Dir./Ed. Informative, well-researched articles, to 2,500 words, on animal protection, national and international wildlife, pet care, conservation, and environmental issues that affect animals. No personal accounts or favorite pet stories. Pays from $350, on acceptance. Query.

ATLANTIC SALMON JOURNAL—P.O. Box 429, St. Andrews, N.B., Canada E0G 2X0. Philip Lee, Ed. Articles, 1,500 to 3,000 words, related to Atlantic salmon: fishing, conservation, ecology, travel, politics, biology, how-tos, anecdotes. Pays $100 to $400, on publication.

AUDUBON—700 Broadway, New York, NY 10003. Michael W. Robbins, Ed. Bimonthly. Articles, 300 to 4,000 words, on conservation and environmental issues, natural history, ecology, and related subjects. Payment varies, on acceptance. Query.

THE BEAR ESSENTIAL—P.O. Box 10342, Portland, OR 97296. Thomas L. Webb, Ed. Semiannual. Unique environmental articles, 750 to 2,250 words; essays, 100 to 800 words; artist profiles, 750 to 1,500 words; product watch, 250 to 1,000 words; and reviews, 100 to 1,000 words. Fiction, 750 to 4,500 words (2,500 is ideal). Poetry. Pays 5¢ a word, after publication. Query for nonfiction.

BIRD WATCHER'S DIGEST—P.O. Box 110, Marietta, OH 45750. William H. Thompson, III, Ed. Articles, 600 to 2,500 words, for bird watchers: first-person accounts; how-tos; pieces on endangered species; profiles. Pays from $50, on publication. Submit complete manuscript.

BUGLE—Rocky Mountain Elk Foundation, P.O. Box 8249, Missoula, MT 59807-8249. Jan Brocci, Asst. Ed. Quarterly. Fiction and nonfiction, 1,500 to 4,000 words, on elk and elk hunting. Department pieces, 1,000 to 3,000 words, for: "Thoughts and Theories"; "Situation Ethics"; and "Women in the Outdoors." Pays 20¢ a word, on acceptance.

CANADIAN WILDLIFE—11450 Albert Hudon, Montreal North, Quebec, Canada H1G 3J9. Martin Silverstone, Ed. Articles, 1,500 to 2,500 words, on national and international wildlife issues: wild areas, nature-related research, endangered species, wildlife management, land use issues, character profiles, and science and politics of conservation. Department pieces, 150 to 500 words, for "Backyard Habitat," "Last Call," and "Species at Risk." Pays $500 to $1,600 (Canadian) for features; $50 to $100 for departments and book reviews, on publication.

E: THE ENVIRONMENTAL MAGAZINE—Earth Action Network, Inc., P.O. Box 5098, Westport, CT 06881. Jim Motavalli, Ed. Environmental features, 4,000 words, and news for departments: 400 words for "In Brief"; and 1,000 words for "Currents." Pays 20¢ a word, on publication. Query.

FLORIDA WILDLIFE—620 S. Meridian St., Tallahassee, FL 32399-1600. Attn: Ed. Bimonthly of the Florida Game and Fresh Water Fish Commission. Articles, 800 to 1,200 words, that promote native flora and fauna, hunting, fishing in Florida's fresh waters, outdoor ethics, and conservation of Florida's natural resources. Pays $50 a page, on publication. SASE for "how to submit" memo.

HERBALGRAM—P.O. Box 201660, Austin, TX 78720. Barbara Johnston, Man. Ed. Quarterly. Articles, 1,500 to 3,000 words, on herb and medicinal plant research, regulatory issues, market conditions, native plant conservation, and other aspects of herbal use. Pays in copies. Query.

IN BUSINESS—419 State Ave., Emmaus, PA 18049-3097. Jerome Goldstein, Ed. Bimonthly. Articles, 1,500 words, for environmental entrepreneurs: reports on economically successful businesses that also demonstrate a commitment to the environment, advice on growing a "green" business, family-run businesses, home-based businesses, community ecological development, etc. Pays $100 to $250 for articles; $25 to $75 for department pieces, on publication. Query with clips.

INTERNATIONAL WILDLIFE— 8925 Leesburg Pike, Vienna, VA 22184. Jonathan Fisher, Ed. Short features, 700 words, and 1,500- to 2,500-word articles that make nature, and human use and stewardship of it, understandable and interesting. Pays $500 for one-page features, $1,800 for full-length articles, on acceptance. Writers must query with writing samples. Very limited freelance needs. Send SASE for guidelines.

NATIONAL GEOGRAPHIC— 1145 17th St. N.W., Washington, DC 20036. William Allen, Ed. First-person, general-interest, heavily illustrated articles on science, natural history, exploration, and geographical regions. Written query required.

NATIONAL PARKS MAGAZINE— 1776 Massachusetts Ave. N.W., Washington, DC 20036. Leslie Happ, Ed.-in-Chief. Articles, 1,500 to 2,000 words, on areas in the National Park System, proposed new areas, threats to parks or park wildlife, new trends in park use, legislative issues, and endangered species of plants or animals relevant to national parks. No fiction, poetry, personal narratives, "My trip to...," or straight travel pieces on individual parks. Articles, 1,500 words, on "low-impact" travel to 4 or 5 national park sites. Pays $400 to $1,000, on acceptance. Query with clips (original slant or news hook is essential to successful query). Guidelines.

NATIONAL WILDLIFE— 8925 Leesburg Pike, Vienna, VA 22184. Mark Wexler, Ed. Articles, 1,000 to 2,500 words, on wildlife, conservation, environment; outdoor how-to pieces. Photos. Pays on acceptance. Query.

OUTDOOR AMERICA— 707 Conservation Ln., Gaithersburg, MD 20878-2983. Attn: Articles Ed. Quarterly publication of the Izaak Walton League of America. Articles, 1,250 to 2,000 words, on natural resource conservation issues and outdoor recreation, with emphasis on IWLA member/chapter tie-in; especially fishing, hunting, and camping. Short items, 500 to 750 words. Pays 20¢ a word. Query with clips.

OUTDOOR TRAVELER, MID-ATLANTIC—WMS Publications, Inc., P.O. Box 2748, Charlottesville, VA 22902. Marianne Marks, Ed. Tom Gillespie, Assoc. Ed. Quarterly. Articles, 1,500 to 2,000 words, on hiking/backpacking, canoeing/kayaking/rafting, camping, mountain biking, road cycling, travel, nature, and the environment from New York state to North Carolina. Travel articles on destinations and areas that offer recreational opportunities. Departments include "Destinations," 450 to 600 words, on practical and descriptive guides to sports destinations; book and product reviews. Pays $300 to $400 for features; payment varies for departments, on publication. Guidelines.

PACIFIC DISCOVERY— California Academy of Sciences, Golden Gate Park, San Francisco, CA 94118-4599. Gordy Slack, Assoc. Ed. Quarterly. Well-researched articles, 1,500 to 3,000 words, on natural history and preservation of the environment. Pays 25¢ a word, before publication. Query.

SIERRA— 85 2nd St., San Francisco, CA 94105. Joan Hamilton, Ed.-in-Chief. Articles, 750 to 2,500 words, on environmental and conservation topics, travel, hiking, backpacking, skiing, rafting, cycling. Photos. Pays from $500 to $2,000, extra for photos, on acceptance. Query with clips.

SMITHSONIAN MAGAZINE— 900 Jefferson Dr., Washington, DC 20560. Marlane A. Liddell, Articles Ed. Articles on history, art, natural history, physical science, profiles, etc. Query with clips, SASE.

SPORTS AFIELD—250 W. 55th St., New York, NY 10019. Terry McDonell, Ed-in-Chief. Articles, 500 to 2,000 words, with quality photos, on hunting, fishing, nature, survival, conservation, ecology, personal experiences. How-to pieces; humor, fiction. Payment varies, on acceptance.

TEXAS PARKS & WILDLIFE—Fountain Park Plaza, 3000 S. Interstate Hwy. 35, Suite 120, Austin, TX 78704. Jim Cox, Sr. Ed. Articles, 800 to 1,500 words, promoting the conservation and enjoyment of Texas wildlife, parks, waters, and all outdoors. Features on hunting, fishing, birding, camping, and the environment. Department pieces, to 1,000 words, for "Parks & Places to Go," "State of Nature," and "Woods and Waters." Photos a plus. Pays to $600, on acceptance; extra for photos.

VIRGINIA WILDLIFE—P.O. Box 11104, Richmond, VA 23230-1104. Attn: Ed. Articles, 1,250 to 1,750 words, on fishing, hunting, wildlife management, outdoor safety, ethics, etc. All material must have Virginia tie-in and may be accompanied by color photos. Pays from 15¢ a word, extra for photos, on acceptance. Query.

WHOLE EARTH REVIEW— P.O. Box 38, Sausalito, CA 94966. Attn: Ed. Quarterly. Articles and book reviews. "Good article material is often found in passionate personal statements or descriptions of the writer's activities." Pays $40 for reviews; payment varies for articles, on publication.

WILDLIFE CONSERVATION—The Wildlife Conservation Society, Bronx, NY 10460. Nancy Simmons, Sr. Ed. First-person articles, 1,500 to 2,000 words, on "popular" natural history, "based on author's research and experience as opposed to textbook approach." Payment varies, on acceptance. Guidelines.

MEDIA & THE ARTS

THE AMERICAN ART JOURNAL—730 Fifth Ave., Suite 205, New York, NY 10019-4105. Jayne A. Kuchna, Ed. Scholarly articles, 2,000 to 10,000 words, on American art of the 17th through the early 20th centuries. Photos. Pays $200 to $500, on acceptance.

AMERICAN INDIAN ART MAGAZINE—7314 E. Osborn Dr., Scottsdale, AZ 85251. Roanne P. Goldfein, Ed. Detailed articles, 10 to 20 double-spaced pages, on American Indian arts: painting, carving, beadwork, basketry, textiles, ceramics, jewelry, etc. Pays varying rates, on publication. Query.

AMERICAN JOURNALISM REVIEW— 8701 Adelphi Rd., Adelphi, MD 20783. Rem Rieder, Ed. Articles, 500 to 5,000 words, on print or electronic journalism, ethics, and related issues. Pays 20¢ a word, on publication. Query.

AMERICAN VISIONS, THE MAGAZINE OF AFRO-AMERICAN CULTURE—1156 15th St. N.W., Suite 615, Washington, DC 20005. Joanne Harris, Ed. Articles, 1,500 to 2,500 words, and columns, 1,000 words, on African-American culture with a focus on the arts. Pays from $100 to $600, on publication. Query.

THE ARTIST'S MAGAZINE—1507 Dana Ave., Cincinnati, OH 45207. Sandra Carpenter, Ed. Features, 1,200 to 2,500 words, and department pieces for the working artist. Poems, to 20 lines, on art and creativity. Single-panel cartoons. Pays $150 to $350 for articles; $65 for cartoons, on acceptance. Guidelines. Query.

ARTSATLANTIC—145 Richmond St., Charlottetown, P.E.I., Canada C1A 1J1. Joseph Sherman, Ed. Articles and reviews, 600 to 3,000 words, on visual, performing, and literary arts primarily in Atlantic Canada. Also, "idea and concept" articles of universal appeal. Query.

AT THE CROSSROADS MAGAZINE—P.O. Box 317, Sta. P, Toronto, Ontario, Canada M5S 2S8. Karen Augustine, Ed.-in-Chief. Published 3 times a year. "The only real source promoting black women's art." Fiction, to 6 typed pages, and nonfiction, to 16 pages: interviews and profiles; news; reviews of black cultural events, concerts, books, dance, theatre, and music. All forms of visual arts. "We are looking for fresh, challenging articles, columns, and opinion pieces. Get as creative and controversial as you want. No anti-black or homophobic material." Pays in honorarium or subscription.

BACK STAGE WEST—5055 Wilshire Blvd., 6th Fl., Los Angeles, CA 90036. Robert Kendt, Ed. Weekly. Articles and reviews for West Coast actor's trade paper. Query required. Pays 10¢ to 15¢ a word, on publication.

BLUEGRASS UNLIMITED—Box 111, Broad Run, VA 20137-0111. Peter V. Kuykendall, Ed. Articles, to 3,500 words, on bluegrass and traditional country music. Photos. Pays 8¢ to 10¢ a word, extra for photos.

THE CHURCH MUSICIAN—127 Ninth Ave. N., Nashville, TN 37234. Jere V. Adams, Ed. Articles on choral techniques, instrumental groups, worship planning, music administration, directing choirs (all ages), rehearsal planning, music equipment, new technology, drama/pageants and related subjects, hymn studies, book reviews, and music-related fillers. Pays 5 1/2¢ a word, on acceptance.

CLASSICAL MUSIC MAGAZINE—106 Lakeshore Rd. E., Suite 212, Mississauga, Ont., Canada L5G 1E3. Derek Deroy, Ed. Feature articles, 1,500 to 3,500 words, and short pieces, to 500 words. Interviews, personality profiles, book reviews, historical articles. "All articles should pertain to the world of classical music. No academic analysis. A solidly researched historical article with source references, or an interview with a famous classical personality are your best bets." Guidelines. Pays $100 to $500 (Canadian) for articles, $35 to $75 for short pieces, on publication.

DANCE MAGAZINE—33 W. 60th St., New York, NY 10023. Richard Philp, Ed.-in-Chief. Features on dance, personalities, techniques, health issues, and trends. Photos. Query; limited free-lance market.

DANCE TEACHER NOW—3101 Poplarwood Ct., Suite 310, Raleigh, NC 27604-1010. K.C. Patrick, Ed. Articles, 1,000 to 3,000 words, for professional dance educators, senior students, and other dance professionals on practical information for the teacher and/or business owner; economic and historical issues related to the profession. Profiles of schools, methods, and people who are leaving their mark on dance. Must be thoroughly researched. Photos a plus. Pays $200 to $350, on acceptance. Query.

DECORATIVE ARTIST'S WORKBOOK—1507 Dana Ave., Cincinnati, OH 45207. Anne Hevener, Ed. How-to articles, 1,000 to 1,500 words, on decorative painting. "Painting projects only, not crafts." Profiles, 500 words, of up-and-coming painters for "The Artist of the Issue" column. Pays $150 to $250 for features; $85 for profiles, on acceptance. Query required.

DOUBLETAKE—Ctr. for Documentary Studies at Duke Univ., 1317 W. Pettigrew St., Durham, NC 27705. Attn: Manuscript Ed. Quarterly. Realistic fiction, to 5,000 words, narrative poetry (submit up to 6 poems), book excerpts, personal experience, essays, humor, and cultural criticism. Color or B&W photo-essays, works in progress, and proposals "in the broadest definition of documentary work." (Submit up to 60 slides.) "We want to be a magazine where image and word have equal weight." Payment varies, on acceptance. Guidelines. Query for nonfiction. SASE.

DRAMATICS—Educational Theatre Assoc., 3368 Central Pkwy., Cincinnati, OH 45225-2392. Don Corathers, Ed. Articles, interviews, how-tos, 750 to 4,000 words, for high school students of the performing arts with an emphasis on theater practice: acting, directing, playwriting, technical subjects. Prefer articles that "could be used by a better-than-average high school teacher to teach students something about the performing arts." Pays $25 to $300 honorarium. Complete manuscripts preferred; graphics and photos accepted.

FILM QUARTERLY—Univ. of California Press Journals, 2120 Berkeley Way, Berkeley, CA 94720. Ann Martin, Ed. Historical, analytical, and critical articles, to 6,000 words; film reviews, book reviews. Guidelines.

FLUTE TALK—Instrumentalist Publishing Co., 200 Northfield Rd., Northfield, IL 60093. Kathleen Goll-Wilson, Ed. Articles, 6 to 12 double-spaced pages, on flute performance, music, and pedagogy; fillers; photos and line drawings. Thorough knowledge of music or the instrument a must. Pays honorarium, on publication. Queries preferred.

FORBES MEDIACRITIC—P.O. Box 762, Bedminster, NJ 07921. Terry Eastland, Ed. Quarterly. "The Best and Worst of America's Journalism." Articles, 5,000 words, on any aspect of our news media. Payment varies.

GLORY SONGS—127 Ninth Ave. N., Nashville, TN 37234. Jere V. Adams, Ed. For volunteer and part-time music directors and members of church choirs. Very easy music and accompaniments designed specifically for the small church (4 to 6 songs per issue). Includes 8-page pull-out with articles for choir members on leisure reading, music training, and choir projects. Pays 5 1/2¢ per word, on acceptance.

GUITAR PLAYER MAGAZINE—411 Borel Ave., Suite 100, San Mateo, CA 94402. Attn: Ed. Articles, from 200 words, on guitars and related subjects. Pays $100 to $600, on acceptance. Buys one-time and reprint rights.

INDIA CURRENTS—P.O. Box 21285, San Jose, CA 95151. Arvind Kumar, Submissions Ed. Fiction, to 1,800 words, and articles, to 800 words, on Indian culture in the United States and Canada. Articles on Indian arts, entertainment, and dining. Also music reviews, 300 words; book reviews, 300 to 400 words; commentary on national or international events affecting the lives of Indians, 800 words. Pays in subscriptions.

INTERNATIONAL MUSICIAN—Paramount Bldg., 1501 Broadway, Suite 600, New York, NY 10036. Attn: Ed. Articles, 1,500 to 2,000 words, for professional musicians. Pays varying rates, on acceptance. Query.

KEYBOARD MAGAZINE—Suite 100, 411 Borel Ave., San Mateo, CA 94402. Tom Darter, Ed. Dir. Articles, 1,000 to 5,000 words, on keyboard instruments, MIDI and computer technology, and players. Photos. Pays $200 to $600, on acceptance. Query.

LIVING BLUES—Hill Hall, Room 301, Univ. of Mississippi, University, MS 38677. David Nelson, Ed. Articles, 1,500 to 10,000 words, about living

African-American blues artists. Interviews. Occasional retrospective/histori-
cal articles or investigative pieces. Pays $75 to $200, on publication; $25 to
$50 per photo. Query.

MODERN DRUMMER—12 Old Bridge Rd., Cedar Grove, NJ 07009. Ronald L. Spagnardi, Ed. Articles, 500 to 2,000 words, on drumming: how-tos,
interviews. Pays $50 to $500, on publication.

NEW ENGLAND ENTERTAINMENT DIGEST—P.O. Box 88, Burlington,
MA 01803. Julie Ann Charest, Ed. News and features on the arts and entertainment industry in New England. Pays $15 to $35, on publication.

PERFORMANCE—1101 University Dr., Suite 108, Fort Worth, TX 76107.
Don Waitt, Pub./Ed.-in-Chief. Reports on the touring industry: concert promoters, booking agents, concert venues and clubs, as well as support services,
such as lighting, sound, and staging companies.

PETERSEN'S PHOTOGRAPHIC—6420 Wilshire Blvd., Los Angeles, CA
90048-5515. Geoffrey B. Engel, Ed. Articles and how-to pieces, with photos,
on travel, video, and darkroom photography, for beginners, advanced ama-
teurs, and professionals. Pays $125 per printed page, on publication.

PHOTO: ELECTRONIC IMAGING MAGAZINE—57 Forsyth St. N.W.,
Suite 1600, Atlanta, GA 30303. E. Sapwater, Exec. Ed. Articles, 1,000 to 3,000
words, on electronic imaging, desktop publishing, pre-press, and multimedia.
Material must be directly related to professional imaging trends and techniques. Query required; all articles on assignment only. Payment varies, on
publication.

PLAYBILL—52 Vanderbilt Ave., New York, NY 10017. Judy Samelson,
Ed. No unsolicited manuscripts.

POPULAR PHOTOGRAPHY—1633 Broadway, New York, NY 10019. Jason Schneider, Ed.-in-Chief. How-to articles, 500 to 2,000 words, for amateur
photographers. Query with outline and photos.

ROLLING STONE—1290 Ave. of the Americas, 2nd Fl., New York, NY
10104. Attn: Ed. Magazine of American music, culture, and politics. No fiction.
Query; no unsolicited manuscripts. Rarely accepts free-lance material.

SCULPTURE—International Sculpture Ctr., 1050 17th St. N.W., Suite
250, Washington, DC 20036. Glenn Harper, Ed. Articles on sculpture, sculptors, collections of sculpture, books on sculpture, criticism, technical processes, etc. Payment varies, on publication. Query.

THE SENIOR MUSICIAN—127 Ninth Ave. N., Nashville, TN 37234. Jere
V. Adams, Ed. Quarterly music periodical. Easy choir music for senior adult
choirs to use in worship, ministry, and recreation. Also includes leisure reading, music training, fellowship suggestions, and choir projects for personal
growth. For music directors, pastors, organists, pianists, choir coordinators.
Pays 5 1/2¢ a word, on acceptance.

SOUTHWEST ART—5444 Westheimer, Suite 1440, Houston, TX 77056.
Susan McGarry, Ed. Articles, 1,200 to 1,800 words, on the artists, art collectors, museum exhibitions, gallery events and dealers, art history, and art
trends west of the Mississippi River. Particularly interested in representational
or figurative arts. Pays from $400, on acceptance. Query with at least 20 slides
of artwork to be featured.

STAGE DIRECTIONS—SMW Communications, Inc., 3101 Poplarwood
Ct., Suite 310, Raleigh, NC 27604. Stephen Peithman, Ed. Neil Offen, Man.

Ed. How-to articles, to 2,000 words, on acting, directing, costuming, makeup, lighting, set design and decoration, props, special effects, fundraising, and audience development for readers who are active in all aspects of community, regional, academic, or youth theater. Short pieces, 400 to 500 words, "are a good way to approach us first." Pays 10¢ a word, on publication. Guidelines.

STORYTELLING MAGAZINE—P.O. Box 309, Jonesborough, TN 37659. Attn: Eds. Features, 1,000 to 3,000 words, related to the oral tradition and stories, to 1,200 words, written in the oral tradition. News items, 200 to 400 words, and photos reflecting unusual storytelling events/applications. Themes for each issue; query first or send SASE to request topics. "We're looking for meaty free-lance work that reflects the ongoing dynamics of a reviving oral tradition." Pays 10¢ a word.

TCI—32 W. 18th St., New York, NY 10011. Jacqueline Tien, Pub. David Johnson, Ed. Articles, 500 to 2,500 words, on design, technical, and management aspects of theater, opera, dance, television, and film for those in performing arts and the entertainment trade. Pays on acceptance. Query.

TDR (THE DRAMA REVIEW): A JOURNAL OF PERFORMANCE STUDIES—721 Broadway, 6th Fl., New York, NY 10003. Richard Schechner, Ed. Eclectic articles on experimental performance and performance theory; cross-cultural, examining the social, political, historical, and theatrical contexts in which performance happens. Submit query or manuscript with SASE and disk. Pays $100 to $250, on publication.

U.S. ART—220 S. Sixth St., Suite 500, Minneapolis, MN 55402. Frank J. Sisser, Ed./Pub. Features and artist profiles, 2,000 words, for collectors of limited-edition art prints. Query. Pays $400 to $450, within 30 days of acceptance.

VIDEOMAKER—P.O. Box 4591, Chico, CA 95927. Stephen Muratore, Ed. Authoritative, how-to articles geared to hobbyist and professional video camera/camcorder users: instructionals, editing, desktop video, audio and video production, innovative applications, tools and tips, industry developments, new products, etc. Pays varying rates, on publication. Queries preferred.

WEST ART—P.O. Box 6868, Auburn, CA 95604-6868. Martha Garcia, Ed. Features, 350 to 700 words, on fine arts and crafts. No hobbies. Photos. Pays 50¢ per column inch, on publication. SASE required.

HOBBIES, CRAFTS, COLLECTING

AMERICAN HOW-TO—12301 Whitewater Dr., Suite 260, Minnetonka, MN 55343. Tom Sweeney, Ed. Bimonthly. Articles, 1,000 to 1,500 words, for homeowners interested in do-it-yourself projects. Carpentry, plumbing, electrical work, landscaping, masonry, tools, woodworking, and new products. Payment is 50¢ a word, on acceptance. Send SASE for editorial calendar with upcoming themes. Queries preferred.

AMERICAN WOODWORKER—Rodale Press, 33 E. Minor St., Emmaus, PA 18098. David Sloan, Ed. "A how-to bimonthly for the woodworking enthusiast." Technical or anecdotal articles, to 2,000 words, relating to woodworking or furniture design. Fillers, drawings, slides and photos considered. Pays from $150 per published page, on publication; regular contributors paid on acceptance. Queries preferred. Guidelines.

ANCESTRY—P.O. Box 476, Salt Lake City, UT 84110. Loretto Szucs, Man. Ed. Bimonthly for genealogists and hobbyists who are interested in getting the most out of their research. Articles, 1,500 to 4,000 words, that instruct (how-tos, research techniques, etc.) and inform (new research sources, new collections, etc.). No family histories, genealogies, or pedigree charts. Pays $50 to $150, on publication. Guidelines.

THE ANTIQUE TRADER WEEKLY—Box 1050, Dubuque, IA 52004. Jon Brecka, Ed. Articles, 1,000 to 2,000 words, on all types of antiques and collectors' items. Photos. Pays from $25 to $200, on publication. Query preferred. Buys all rights.

ANTIQUES & AUCTION NEWS—P.O. Box 500, Mount Joy, PA 17552. Attn: Ed. Weekly newspaper. Factual articles, 600 to 1,500 words, on antiques, collectors, collections, and places of historic interest. Photos. Query required. Pays $5 to $20, after publication.

ANTIQUEWEEK—P.O. Box 90, Knightstown, IN 46148. Tom Hoepf, Ed., Central Edition; Connie Swaim, Ed., Eastern Edition. Weekly antique, auction, and collectors' newspaper. Articles, 500 to 1,500 words, on antiques, collectibles, restorations, genealogy, auction and antique show reports. Photos. Pays from $40 to $150 for in-depth articles, on publication. Query. Guidelines.

AOPA PILOT—421 Aviation Way, Frederick, MD 21701. Thomas B. Haines, Ed. Magazine of the Aircraft Owners and Pilots Assn. Articles, to 2,500 words, with photos, on general aviation for beginning and experienced pilots. Pays to $750.

AQUARIUM FISH—P.O. Box 6050, Mission Viejo, CA 92690. Edward Bauman, Ed. Articles, 2,000 to 4,000 words, on freshwater, saltwater, and pond fish, with or without color transparencies. (No "pet fish" stories.) Payment varies, on publication.

AUTOGRAPH COLLECTOR MAGAZINE—510-A S. Corona Mall, Corona, CA 91719. Ev Phillips, Ed. Articles, 1,000 to 3,500 words, on all areas of autograph collecting: preservation, framing, and storage, specialty collections, documents and letters, collectors and dealers. Queries preferred. Payment varies.

BECKETT BASEBALL CARD MONTHLY—15850 Dallas Pkwy., Dallas, TX 75248. Tim Polzer, Ed. Articles, 500 to 2,000 words, geared to baseball card collecting, with an emphasis on the pleasures of the hobby. "We accept no stories with investment tips." Query. Pays $100 to $250, on acceptance. Guidelines.

BECKETT BASKETBALL MONTHLY—15850 Dallas Pkwy., Dallas, TX 75248. Mike McAllister, Man. Ed. Articles, 400 to 1,000 words, on the sports-card hobby, especially basketball card collecting for readers 10 to 40. Query. Pays $100 to $250, on acceptance. Also publishes *Beckett Football Card Monthly, Beckett Focus on Future Stars, Beckett Hockey Monthly,* and *Beckett Racing Monthly.* SASE for guidelines.

BIRD TALK—Box 6050, Mission Viejo, CA 92690. Kathleen Samuelson, Ed.-in-Chief. Articles for pet bird owners: care and feeding, training, safety, outstanding personal adventures, exotic birds in their native countries, profiles of celebrities' pet birds, travel to bird parks or shows. Good transparencies a plus. Pays up to 10¢ a word, after publication. Query required.

BIRD WATCHER'S DIGEST—P.O. Box 110, Marietta, OH 45750. William H. Thompson III, Ed. Articles, 600 to 3,000 words, on bird-watching experiences and expeditions: information about rare sightings; updates on endangered species; interesting backyard topics and how-tos. Pays from $50, on publication. Allow 8 weeks for response.

BIRDER'S WORLD— 44 E. 8th St., Suite 410, Holland, MI 49423. Eldon D. Greij, Ed. Bimonthly. Articles, 2,200 to 2,400 words, on all aspects of birding, especially on a particular species or the status of an endangered species. Tips on birding, attracting birds, or photographing them. Personal essays, 1,000 to 1,500 words. Book reviews, to 500 words. Pays $350 to $450, on publication. Query preferred.

BREW MAGAZINE—1120 Mulberry St., Des Moines, IA 50309. Beverly Walsmith, Ed. "Traveling America's Brewpubs and Microbreweries." Bimonthly. Articles, 1,500 to 1,800 words, on new brewpubs around the country. "Our focus is on the brewpub and the community where it is located." Pays 10¢ a word, on publication. Query preferred.

BREW YOUR OWN—Niche Publications, 216 F St., Suite 160, Davis, CA 95616. Craig Bystrynski, Ed. Practical how-to articles, 800 to 2,500 words, for homebrewers. Pays $50 to $150, on publication. Query.

CANADIAN STAMP NEWS—103 Lakeshore Rd., Suite 202, St. Catharines, Ont., Canada L2N 2T6. Ellen Rodger, Ed. Biweekly. Articles, 1,000 to 2,000 words, on stamp collecting news, rare and unusual stamps, and auction and club reports. Special issues throughout the year; send SASE for guidelines. Photos. Pays from $70, on publication.

CANADIAN WORKSHOP MAGAZINE—130 Spy Ct., Markham, Ont., Canada L3R 5H6. Doug Bennet, Ed. Articles, 1,500 to 2,800 words, on do-it-yourself home renovations, energy saving projects, etc., with photos. Pays varying rates, on acceptance.

CARD PLAYER—3140 S. Polaris #8, Las Vegas, NV 89102. Linda Johnson, Pub. "The Magazine for Those Who Play to Win." Articles on poker events, personalities, legal issues, new casinos, tournaments, and prizes. Also articles on strategies, theory and game psychology to improve poker play. Occasionally uses humor, cartoons, puzzles, or anecdotal material. Pays $35 to $100, on publication; $15 to $35 for fillers. Guidelines.

THE CAROUSEL NEWS & TRADER— 87 Park Ave. W., Suite 206, Mansfield, OH 44902. Attn: Ed. Features on carousel history and profiles of amusement park operators and carousel carvers of interest to band organ enthusiasts, carousel art collectors, preservationists, amusement park owners, artists, and restorationists. Pays $50 per published page, after publication. Guidelines.

CHESS LIFE—3054 NYS Rt. 9W, New Windsor, NY 12553-7698. Glenn Petersen, Ed. Articles, 500 to 3,000 words, for members of the U.S. Chess Federation, on news, profiles, technical aspects of chess. Features on all aspects of chess: history, humor, puzzles, etc. Fiction, 500 to 2,000 words, related to chess. Photos. Pays varying rates, on acceptance. Query; limited freelance market.

CLASSIC TOY TRAINS—21027 Crossroads Cir., Waukesha, WI 53187. Attn: Ed. Articles, with photos, on toy train layouts and collections. Also toy train manufacturing history and repair/maintenance. Pays $75 per printed page, on acceptance. Query.

COLLECTING TOYS—21027 Crossroads Cir., Waukesha, WI 53187. Tom Hammel, Ed. Bimonthly. "The premier magazine of toy collecting." Stories focus on main collector groups of post-war boys' toys: steel, tin, and especially die-cast vehicles; TV toys; model kits; action figures. Profiles of toy collectors, designers, and manufacturers; articles for toy collectors. Color photos. Pays $75 to $100 per page.

COLLECTOR EDITIONS—170 Fifth Ave., New York, NY 10010. Joan Muyskens Pursley, Ed. Articles, 750 to 1,500 words, on collectibles, mainly contemporary limited-edition figurines, plates, and prints. Pays $150 to $350, within 30 days of acceptance. Query with photos.

COLLECTORS JOURNAL—P.O. Box 601, Vinton, IA 52349. Connie Gewecke, Ed. Weekly tabloid. Features, to 2,000 words, on antiques and collectibles. Pays $10 for articles, $15 for articles with photos, on publication.

COLLECTORS NEWS—P.O. Box 156, Grundy Ctr., IA 50638. Linda Kruger, Ed. Articles, to 1,000 words, on private collections, antiques, and collectibles, especially modern limited-edition collectibles, 20th-century nostalgia, Americana, glass and china, music, furniture, transportation, timepieces, jewelry, farm-related collectibles, and lamps; include quality color or B&W photos. Pays $1 per column inch; $25 for front-page color photos, on publication.

COMBO—5 Nassau Blvd. S., Garden City S., NY 11530. Ian M. Feller, Ed. Articles, from 800 words, related to non-sports cards (comic cards, TV/movie cards, science fiction cards, etc.) and comic books; collecting and investing; fillers. Queries preferred. Pays to 10¢ a word, on publication.

COUNTRY FOLK ART MAGAZINE—8393 E. Holly Rd., Holly, MI 48442-8819. Attn: Ed. Dept. Articles on decorating, artisans, collectibles; how-to pieces, 750 to 1,000 words, with a creative slant on American folk art. Pays $150 to $300, on acceptance. Submit pieces on seasonal topics one year in advance.

COUNTRY HANDCRAFTS—See *Crafting Traditions.*

CRAFT SUPPLY—225 Gordons Corner Rd., P.O. Box 420, Manalapan, NJ 07726-0420. John Tracey, Ed. Bimonthly. Articles, 800 to 1,500 words, of interest to professional crafters; also general small business advice. Pays $75 to $200, on publication.

CRAFTING TRADITIONS—(formerly *Country Handcrafts*) 5400 S. 60th St., Greendale, WI 53129. Kathleen Zimmer, Ed. All types of craft designs (needlepoint, quilting, woodworking, etc.) with complete instructions and full-size patterns. Pays from $50 to $250, on acceptance, for all rights.

CRAFTS 'N THINGS—2400 Devon, Suite 375, Des Plaines, IL 60018-4618. Julie Stephani, Ed. How-to articles on all kinds of crafts projects, with instructions. Send manuscript with instructions and photograph of the finished item. Pays $50 to $250, on acceptance.

DOG FANCY—P.O. Box 6050, Mission Viejo, CA 92690. Julie Jordan, Ed. Articles, 900 to 1,500 words, on dog care, health, grooming, breeds, activities, events, etc. Photos. Payment varies, on publication.

DOLL WORLD—306 E. Parr Rd., Berne, IN 46711. Cary Raesner, Ed. Informational articles about dollmaking and doll collecting. Patterns for original doll and clothing designs. Original paper dolls.

FIBERARTS—50 College St., Asheville, NC 28801. Ann Batchelder, Ed. Published 5 times yearly. Articles, 400 to 2,000 words, on contemporary trends in fiber sculpture, weaving, surface design, quilting, stitchery, papermaking, felting, basketry, and wearable art. Query with photos of subject, outline, and synopsis. Pays varying rates, on publication.

FIGURINES & COLLECTIBLES—Cowles Enthusiast Media, 6405 Flank Dr., Harrisburg, PA 17112. Mindy Kinsey, Man. Ed. Articles, 1,000 to 1,500 words, for collectors of modern collectibles (Hummel, Cherished Teddies, Precious Moments, etc.): artists and manufacturer profiles, collector profiles, some travel pieces. "We do not cover plates, prints, steins, or other nonfigural pieces. No fiction or personal experience." Pays 20¢ to 25¢ a word, on publication. Query preferred.

FINE LINES—P.O. Box 718, Ingomar, PA 15127. Deborah A. Novak, Ed. Publication of the Historic Needlework Guild. Articles, 500 to 1,500 words, about historic needlework, museums, famous historic needlework, or themes revolving around stitching (samplers, needlework tools, etc.). Pays varying rates, on acceptance. Queries required.

FINE WOODWORKING—63 S. Main St., Newtown, CT 06470. Scott Gibson, Ed. Bimonthly. Articles on woodworking: basics of tool use, stock preparation and joinery, specialized techniques and finishing, shop-built tools, jigs and fixtures; or any stage of design, construction, finishing and installation of cabinetry and furniture. "We look for high-quality worksmanship, thoughtful designs, safe and proper procedures." Departments: "Methods of Work," "Q&A," "Books," "Tool Forum," and "Notes and Comments." Pays $150 per page, on publication; pays from $10 for department pieces. Query.

FINESCALE MODELER—P.O. Box 1612, Waukesha, WI 53187. Bob Hayden, Ed. How-to articles for people who make nonoperating scale models of aircraft, automobiles, boats, figures. Photos and drawings should accompany articles. One-page model-building hints and tips. Pays from $45 per published page, on acceptance. Query preferred.

FLIGHT—Air Age Publishing, 100 E. Ridge, Ridgefield, CT 06877-4606. Tom Atwood, Ed. Articles, 2,500 to 3,000 words on "the history, the hardware, and the human heart of aviation." Send one-page outline to Dana Donia, Ed. Asst. Payment is $600.

FLOWER & GARDEN CRAFTS EDITION—700 W. 47th St., Suite 310, Kansas City, MO 64112. Jessie Eisenstein, Ed. Instructions and models for original knit, crochet, tat, quilt, cross stitch and crafts. Also includes gardening features and recipes. Send photos with manuscript. Pays on acceptance; negotiable rates for instructional items.

GAMES—P.O. Box 184, Ft. Washington, PA 19034. R. Wayne Schmittberger, Ed.-in-Chief. "The magazine for creative minds at play." Features and short articles on games and playful, offbeat subjects. Visual and verbal puzzles, pop culture quizzes, brainteasers, contests, game reviews. Pays top rates, on publication. Send SASE for guidelines; specify writer's, crosswords, variety puzzles, or brainteasers.

GOLD AND TREASURE HUNTER—P.O. Box 47, Happy Camp, CA 96039. Marcie Stumpf, Man. Ed. Bimonthly. Articles, 1,500 to 2,000 words, about people discovering gold, treasure, and outdoor adventure. First-person experiences, humorous pieces, profiles, and how-to as well as fiction. "We provide family recreation opportunities and explore old sites and travel sites." Pays 3¢ a word, on publication.

HERITAGE QUEST—American Genealogical Lending Library, P.O. Box 329, Bountiful, UT 84011. Leland Meitzler, Ed. Bimonthly. Genealogy how-to articles, 2 to 4 pages; national, international, or regional in scope. Pays $30 per published page, on publication.

THE HOME SHOP MACHINIST—2779 Aero Park Dr., Box 1810, Traverse City, MI 49685. Joe D. Rice, Ed. How-to articles on precision metalworking and foundry work. Accuracy and attention to detail a must. Pays $40 per published page, extra for photos and illustrations, on publication. Guidelines.

KITPLANES—1000 Quail St., Suite 190, Newport Beach, CA 92660. Dave Martin, Ed. Articles geared to the growing market of aircraft built from kits and plans by home craftsmen, on all aspects of design, construction, and performance, 1,000 to 4,000 words. Pays $60 per page, on publication.

LOST TREASURE—P.O. Box 451589, Grove, OK 74345. Patsy Beyerl, Man. Ed. How-to articles, legends, folklore, and stories of lost treasures. Also publishes *Treasure Facts*: how-to information for treasure hunters (hunt strategies, techniques, pitfalls, how to increase finds, use equipment, locate treasure, etc.), club news, who's who in treasure hunting, tips, etc. *Treasure Cache* (annual): articles on documented treasure caches with sidebar telling how to search for cache highlighted in article. Pays 4¢ a word, $5 for photos, $100 for cover photos.

LOTTOWORLD MAGAZINE—2150 Goodlette Rd., Suite 200, Naples, FL 34102. Barry Miller, Man. Ed. Articles of interest to readers (over 18 years old) who play the lottery. Human-interest pieces on lottery winners and losers, winning systems, advice on predicting numbers and increasing your odds of winning, general information on state lotteries, etc. Payment varies, 30 days after publication.

THE MIDATLANTIC ANTIQUES MAGAZINE—P.O. Box 908, Henderson, NC 27536. Lydia Stainback, Ed. Articles, 500 to 2,000 words, on antiques, collectibles, and related subjects. "We need show and auction reporters." Queries are preferred. Payment varies, on publication.

MILITARY HISTORY—741 Miller Dr. S.E., #D2, Leesburg, VA 20175. Jon Guttman, Ed. Bimonthly. Features, 4,000 words with 500-word sidebars, on the strategy, tactics, and personalities of military history. Department pieces, 2,000 words, on intrigue, weaponry, and perspectives; book reviews. No fiction. Pays $200 to $400, on publication. Query. SASE for guidelines.

MINIATURE COLLECTOR—30595 Eight Mile Rd., Livonia, MI 48152-1761. Ruth Keessen, Pub. Articles, 800 to 1,200 words, with photos, on outstanding 1/12-scale (dollhouse) miniatures and the people who make and collect them. Original, illustrated how-to projects for making miniatures. Pays varying rates, within 30 days of acceptance. Query with photos.

MINIATURE QUILTS—See *Traditional Quiltworks*.

MODEL RAILROADER—21027 Crossroads Cir., P.O. Box 1612, Waukesha, WI 53187. Andy Sperandeo, Ed. Articles on model railroads, with photos of layout and equipment. Pays $90 per printed page, on acceptance. Query.

MOTOR BOATING & SAILING—250 W. 55th St., 4th Fl., New York, NY 10019-5905. Peter A. Janssen Ed./Pub. Articles, 1,500 words, on buying, maintaining, and enjoying boats. "Appeal to the dreams, adventures, and the lifestyles of committed boat owners." Hard-core, authoritative how-to. Query. Payment varies, on acceptance.

NEW ENGLAND ANTIQUES JOURNAL— 4 Church St., Ware, MA 01082. Jody Young, Gen. Mgr. Jamie Mercier, Man. Ed. Well-researched articles, usually by recognized authorities in their field, 1,500 to 5,000 words, on antiques of interest to dealers or collectors; auction and antiques show reviews, from 1,000 words; antiques market news, to 500 words; photos required. Pays from $100, on publication. Query or send manuscript. Reports in 2 to 4 weeks.

NUTSHELL NEWS—21027 Crossroads Cir., P.O. Box 1612, Waukesha, WI 53187. Kay Melchisedech Olson, Ed. Articles, 1,200 to 1,500 words, for dollhouse-scale miniatures enthusiasts, collectors, craftspeople, and hobbyists. Interested in artisan profiles and how-to projects. "Writers must be knowledgeable of scale miniatures." Color slides or B&W prints required. Payment varies; part on acceptance, balance on publication. Query.

PETERSEN'S PHOTOGRAPHIC— 6420 Wilshire Blvd., Los Angeles, CA 90048. Ron Leach, Ed. How-to articles on all phases of still photography of interest to the amateur and advanced photographer. Pays about $100 per printed page for article accompanied by photos, on publication.

POPULAR MECHANICS—224 W. 57th St., New York, NY 10019. Deborah Frank, Man. Ed. Articles, 300 to 1,500 words, on latest developments in mechanics, industry, science, telecommunications; features on hobbies with a mechanical slant; how-tos on home and shop projects; features on outdoor adventures, boating, and electronics. Photos and sketches a plus. Pays to $1,500; to $500 for short pieces, on acceptance. Buys all rights.

POPULAR WOODWORKING—1507 Dana Ave., Cincinnati, OH 45207. Steve Shanesy, Ed. Project articles, to 5,000 words; techniques pieces, to 1,500 words; anecdotes and essays, to 1,000 words, for the "modest production woodworker, small shop owner, wood craftsperson, intermediate hobbyist and woodcarver." Pays $500 to $1,000 for large, complicated projects; $100 to $500 for small projects and other features; pays on acceptance. Query with brief outline and photo of finished project.

QUILTING TODAY—See *Traditional Quiltworks.*

RAILROAD MODEL CRAFTSMAN—P.O. Box 700, Newton, NJ 07860-0700. William C. Schaumburg, Ed. How-to articles on scale model railroading; cars, operation, scenery, etc. Pays on publication.

RENAISSANCE MAGAZINE—Phantom Press Publications, 13 Appleton Rd., Nantucket, MA 02554. Kim Guarnaccia, Ed. Feature articles on jousting, history, costuming, Renaissance faires; interviews; and reviews of Renaissance books, music, movies, and games. Pays 3¢ a word, on publication.

RESTORATION—P.O. Box 50046, Dept. TW, Tucson, AZ 85703-1046. W.R. Haessner, Ed. Articles, 1,200 to 1,800 words, on restoring and building machines, boats, autos, trucks, planes, trains, buildings, toys, tools, etc. Photos and art required. Pays from $25 per page, on publication. Query.

REUNIONS MAGAZINE—P.O. Box 11727, Milwaukee, WI 53211-0727. Edith Wagner, Pub. Positive and instructive articles related to reunions (family, class, military reunions, searching, and some genealogy). "The magazine is reunion organizers speaking to reunion organizers. No class reunion catharsis stories." Pays honoraria and copies.

RUG HOOKING MAGAZINE—Stackpole Magazines, 500 Vaughn St., Harrisburg, PA 17110. Patrice Crowley, Ed. How-to and feature articles on rug hooking for beginners and advanced artists. Payment varies.

SCHOOL MATES—U.S. Chess Federation, 3054 NYS Rt. 9W, New Windsor, NY 12553-7698. Jay Hastings, Publications Dir. Articles and fiction, 250 to 800 words, and short fillers, related to chess for beginning chess players (primarily children, 8 to 15). "Primarily instructive material, but there's room for fun puzzles, cartoons, anecdotes, etc. All chess related. Articles on chess-playing celebrities are always of interest to us." Pays from $20, on publication. Query; limited free-lance market.

SEW NEWS—P.O. Box 1790, News Plaza, Peoria, IL 61656. Linda Turner Griepentrog, Ed. Articles, to 3,000 words, "that teach a specific technique, inspire a reader to try new sewing projects, or inform a reader about an interesting person, company, or project related to sewing, textiles, or fashion." Emphasis is on fashion (not craft) sewing. Pays $25 to $400, on acceptance. Queries required; no unsolicited manuscripts accepted.

SPORTS CARD TRADER—5 Nassau Blvd., Garden City South, NY 11530. Attn: Ed. Office. Articles, from 1,000 words, related to all sports cards, autographs, video games, phone cards, starting lineups, especially baseball, football, basketball, and hockey cards; collecting and investing. Fillers. Queries preferred. Pays 10¢ a word, on publication.

SPORTS COLLECTORS DIGEST—Krause Publications, 700 E. State St., Iola, WI 54990. Tom Mortenson, Ed. Articles, 750 to 2,000 words, on old baseball card sets and other sports memorabilia and collectibles. Pays $50 to $100, on publication.

TEDDY BEAR REVIEW—Collector Communications Corp., 170 Fifth Ave., New York, NY 10010. Stephen L. Cronk, Ed. Articles on antique and contemporary teddy bears for makers, collectors, and enthusiasts. Pays $100 to $300, within 30 days of acceptance. Query with photos.

THREADS MAGAZINE—Taunton Press, 63 S. Main St., Box 5506, Newtown, CT 06470. Attn: Ed. Bimonthly. Technical pieces on garment construction by writers who are expert sewers, quilters, embellishers, and other needle workers. Pays $150 per published page, on publication.

TRADITIONAL QUILTWORKS—Chitra Publications, 2 Public Ave., Montrose, PA 18801. Attn: Ed. Team. Specific, quilt-related how-to articles, 700 to 1,500 words. Patterns, features, and department pieces. Completed manuscripts preferred. Pays $75 per published page, on publication. Also publishes *Quilting Today* and *Miniature Quilts.*

TREASURE CACHE, TREASURE FACTS—See *Lost Treasure.*

WEST ART—Box 6868, Auburn, CA 95604-6868. Martha Garcia, Ed. Features, 350 to 700 words, on fine arts and crafts. No hobbies. Photos. Pays 50¢ per column inch, on publication. SASE required.

WESTERN & EASTERN TREASURES—P.O. Box 1598, Mercer Island, WA 98040-1598. Rosemary Anderson, Man. Ed. Illustrated articles, to 1,500 words, on treasure hunting and how-to metal-detecting tips. Pays 2¢ a word, extra for photos, on publication.

WILDFOWL CARVING AND COLLECTING—Stackpole Magazines, 500 Vaughn St., Harrisburg, PA 17110. Cathy Hart, Ed.-in-Chief. How-to and reference articles, of varying lengths, on bird carving; collecting antique and contemporary carvings. Query. Pays varying rates, on acceptance.

WOODENBOAT MAGAZINE—P.O. Box 78, Brooklin, ME 04616. Matthew Murphy, Ed. How-to and technical articles, 4,000 words, on construction, repair, and maintenance of wooden boats; design, history, and use of wooden boats; and profiles of outstanding wooden boat builders and designers. Pays $150 to $200 per 1,000 words. Query preferred.

WOODWORK— 42 Digital Dr., Suite 5, Novato, CA 94949. John McDonald, Ed. Bimonthly. Articles for woodworkers on all aspects of woodworking (simple, complex, technical, or aesthetic). Pays $150 per published page; $35 for "Techniques," on publication. Queries or outlines (with slides) preferred.

YELLOWBACK LIBRARY—P.O. Box 36172, Des Moines, IA 50315. Gil O'Gara, Ed. Articles, 300 to 2,000 words, on boys'/girls' series literature (Hardy Boys, Nancy Drew, Tom Swift, etc.) for collectors, researchers, and dealers. "Especially welcome are interviews with, or articles by past and present writers of juvenile series fiction." Pays in copies.

YESTERYEAR—P.O. Box 2, Princeton, WI 54968. Michael Jacobi, Ed. Articles on antiques and collectibles for readers in WI, IL, IA, MN, and surrounding states. Photos. Will consider regular columns on collecting or antiques. Pays from $15, on publication. Limited market.

ZYMURGY—Box 1679, Boulder, CO 80306-1679. Dena Nishek, Ed. Articles appealing to beer lovers and homebrewers. Pays after publication. Guidelines. Query.

SCIENCE & COMPUTERS

AD ASTRA—National Space Society, 922 Pennsylvania Ave. S.E., Washington, DC 20003-2140. Pat Dasch, Ed.-in-Chief. Lively, non-technical features, to 3,000 words, on all aspects of international space exploration. Particularly interested in "Living in Space" articles; space settlements; lunar and Mars bases. Pays $150 to $200, on publication. Query. Guidelines.

AMERICAN HERITAGE OF INVENTION & TECHNOLOGY— 60 Fifth Ave., New York, NY 10011. Frederick Allen, Ed. Quarterly. Articles, 2,000 to 5,000 words, on history of technology in America, for the sophisticated general reader. Pays on acceptance. Query.

THE ANNALS OF IMPROBABLE RESEARCH—AIR, P.O. Box 380853, Cambridge, MA 02238. Marc Abrahams, Ed. Science humor, science reports and analysis, one to 4 pages. Brief science-related poetry. B&W photos. "This journal is the place to find the mischievous, funny, iconoclastic side of science." Guidelines. No payment.

ARCHAEOLOGY—135 William St., New York, NY 10038. Peter A. Young, Ed.-in-Chief. Articles on archaeology by professionals or lay people with a solid knowledge of the field. Pays $250 to $500, on publication. Query required.

ASTRONOMY—P.O. Box 1612, Waukesha, WI 53187. Jeff Kanipe, Man. Ed. Articles on astronomy, astrophysics, space programs, recent discoveries. Hobby pieces on equipment and celestial events; short news items. Pays varying rates, on acceptance.

C/C¢¢ USERS JOURNAL—1601 W. 23rd St., Suite 200, Lawrence, KS 66046-4153. Marc Briand, Man. Ed. Practical, how-to articles, 2,500 words (including up to 250 lines of code) on C/C¢¢ programming. Algorithms, class designs, book reviews, tutorials. No programming "religion." Pays $110 per published page of text, $90 per published page of code, on publication. Query. Guidelines.

COMPUTERSCENE MAGAZINE—3507 Wyoming Blvd. N.E., Albuquerque, NM 87111. Greg Hansen, Man. Ed. Laine Douglas Shomaker, Asst. Ed.

Computer-related articles and fiction, 800 to 1,500 words. "We provide New Mexico computer users with entertaining and informative articles on all aspects of computers: hardware, software, technology, productivity, advice, personal experience, even computer-related fiction." Fillers, 400 to 800 words. Pays $40 to $75, on publication. Send SASE for guidelines and editorial calendar.

ELECTRONICS NOW—500 Bi-County Blvd., Farmingdale, NY 11735. Carl Laron, Ed. Technical articles, 1,500 to 3,000 words, on all areas related to electronics. Pays $50 to $500 or more, on acceptance.

ENVIRONMENT—1319 18th St. N.W., Washington, DC 20036-1802. Barbara T. Richman, Man. Ed. Factual and analytical articles, 2,500 to 5,000 words, on scientific, technological, and environmental policy and decision-making issues, especially on a global scale. Pays $100 to $300. Query.

FINAL FRONTIER—1017 S. Mountain Ave., Monrovia, CA 91016. George Hague, Ed. Articles, 1,500 to 2,500 words; columns, 800 words; and shorts, 250 words, about people, events, and new concepts of opening up the space frontier. Pays about 40¢ a word, on acceptance. Query.

FOCUS—Turnkey Publishing, Inc., P.O. Box 200549, Austin, TX 78720. J. Todd Key, Ed. Articles, 700 to 4,000 words, on Data General computers. Photos a plus. Pays to $50, on publication. Query required.

HOBSON'S CHOICE: SCIENCE FICTION AND TECHNOLOGY—The Starwind Press, P.O. Box 98, Ripley, OH 45167. Attn: Submissions Ed. Articles and literary criticism, 1,000 to 5,000 words, for readers interested in science and technology. Also science fiction and fantasy, 2,000 to 10,000 words. Pays 1¢ to 4¢ a word, on acceptance. Query for nonfiction.

HOMEPC—CMP Publications, 600 Community Dr., Manhasset, NY 11030-5772. Andrea Linne, Features Ed. Articles that help home computer users get the most out of their PCs. Payment varies, on acceptance. Query with clips and resumé required.

LINK-UP—2222 River Rd., King George, VA 22485. Loraine Page, Ed. Dir. Articles about online services, the Internet, and CD-ROM for the computer owner who uses this technology for business, home, and educational use. Pays $90 to $220 for articles, on publication. Photos a plus.

MACHOME JOURNAL—544 Second St., San Francisco, CA 94107. Sandra Anderson, Ed.-in-Chief. Jargon-free solutions to the information needs of Macintosh computer users. "Present technology in concise, factual, complete, non-condescending manner." Submissions on disk or over online services preferred; guidelines strongly recommended. Payment varies.

MACWORLD—501 Second St., Suite 500, San Francisco, CA 94107. Attn: Ed. Reviews, news, consumer, and how-to articles, of varying lengths, related to Macintosh computers. Query with clips only; no unsolicited manuscripts. Pays from $150 to $3,500, on acceptance. Guidelines.

NATURAL HISTORY—American Museum of Natural History, Central Park W. at 79th St., New York, NY 10024. Bruce Stutz, Ed.-in-Chief. Informative articles, to 3,000 words, on anthropology and natural sciences. "Strongly recommend that writers send SASE for guidelines and read our magazine." Pays from $1,000 for features, on acceptance. Query.

OMNI—General Media International, 277 Park Ave., 4th Fl., New York, NY 10172-0003. Pamela Weintraub, Ed. Monthly on-line (electrical) version.

Articles, 750 to 1,000 words, on scientific aspects of the future: space colonies, cloning, machine intelligence, ESP, origin of life, future arts, lifestyles, etc. Address fiction, 2,000 to 10,000 words, to Ellen Datlow, Fiction Ed., *OMNI Internet* at above address. Pays $800 to $3,500 for articles; $150 for shorter items, on acceptance. Query.

POPULAR ELECTRONICS—500 Bi-County Blvd., Farmingdale, NY 11735. Dan Karagiannis, Ed. Features, 1,500 to 2,500 words, for electronics hobbyists and experimenters. "Our readers are science and electronics oriented, understand computer theory and operation, and like to build electronics projects." Fillers and cartoons. Pays $25 to $500, on acceptance.

POPULAR SCIENCE—2 Park Ave., New York, NY 10016. Fred Abatemarco, Ed.-in-Chief. Articles, with photos, on developments in science and technology. Short illustrated articles on new inventions and products; photo-essays, book excerpts. Payment varies, on acceptance.

PUBLISH—Integrated Media, Inc., 501 Second St., San Francisco, CA 94107. Jake Widman, Ed. Features, 1,500 to 2,000 words, and reviews, 400 to 800 words, on all aspects of computerized publishing. Pays $400 to $600 for reviews, $850 to $1,200 for full-length features, on acceptance.

RESELLER MANAGEMENT MAGAZINE—(formerly *Reseller Magazine*) 275 Washington St., Newton, MA 02158. John Russell, Ed. Articles, 500 to 1,200 words, that emphasize profitable strategies for value-added resellers, systems, integrators, software developers, and VAR-consultants. "Magazine sections include how-tos for selling, marketing, customer, technology, business, and verticals." Payment varies. Query.

RESELLER MAGAZINE—See *Reseller Management Magazine.*

THE SCIENCES—2 E. 63rd St., New York, NY 10021. Peter G. Brown, Ed. Essays and features, 2,000 to 4,000 words, and book reviews, on all scientific disciplines. Pays honorarium, on publication. Query.

SCIENCEWORLD—Scholastic, Inc., 555 Broadway, New York, NY 10012-3999. Karen McNulty, Ed. Science articles, 750 words, and science news articles, 200 words, on life science, earth science, physical science, environmental science and/or health for readers in grades 7 to 10 (ages 12 to 15). "Articles should include current, exciting science news. Writing should be lively and show an understanding of teens' perspectives and interests." Pays $100 to $125 for news items; $200 to $650 for features. Query with a well-researched proposal, suggested sources, 2 to 3 clips of your work, and an SASE.

SKY & TELESCOPE—Sky Publishing Corp., P.O. Box 9111, Belmont, MA 02178-9111. Timothy Lyster, Man. Ed. Articles for amateur and professional astronomers worldwide. Department pieces for "Amateur Astronomers," "Astronomical Computing," "Telescope Making," "Observer's Page," and "Gallery." Also, 1,000-word opinion pieces, for "Focal Point." Mention availability of diagrams and other illustrations. Pays 10¢ to 25¢ a word, on publication. Query required.

TECHNOLOGY REVIEW—MIT, W59-200, Cambridge, MA 02139. Steven J. Marcus, Ed. General-interest articles on technology and its implications. Payment varies, on acceptance. Query.

WORDPERFECT MAGAZINES—MS 7300, 270 W. Center St., Orem, UT 84057. Attn: Ed. Features, 1,400 to 1,800 words, and columns, 1,200 to 1,400 words, on how-to subjects with easy-to-follow instructions that familiarize readers with WordPerfect software. Avoid jargon. Pays $400 to $700, on acceptance. Query. Guidelines.

ANIMALS

AKC GAZETTE—51 Madison Ave., New York, NY 10010. Mark Roland, Features Ed. "The official journal for the sport of purebred dogs." Articles, 1,000 to 2,500 words, relating to serious breeders, exhibitors, and judges of purebred dogs. Pays from $250 to $600, on acceptance. Query preferred.

ANIMAL PEOPLE—P.O. Box 960, Clinton, WA 98236-0906. Attn: Ed. "News for People Who Care About Animals." Tabloid published 10 times a year. Articles and profiles, "especially of seldom recognized individuals of unique and outstanding positive accomplishment, in any capacity that benefits animals or illustrates the intrinsic value of other species. No atrocity stories, essays on why animals have rights, or material that promotes animal abuse, including hunting, fishing, trapping, and slaughter." No fiction or poetry. Pays honorarium, on acceptance. Query.

ANIMAL PRESS—1815 Hancock St., San Diego, CA 92110. Renee Vititoe, Ed. Articles and fiction, 1,000 words. Well-written human interest, educational, or newsworthy articles about pets. No animal activist material. Pays $25 to $50, after publication.

ANIMALS—350 S. Huntington Ave., Boston, MA 02130. Joni Praded, Dir./Ed. Informative, well-researched articles, to 2,500 words, on animal protection, national and international wildlife, pet care, conservation, and environmental issues that affect animals. No personal accounts or favorite pet stories. Pays from $350, on acceptance. Query.

AQUARIUM FISH—P.O. Box 6050, Mission Viejo, CA 92690. Edward Bauman, Ed. Articles, 2,000 to 4,000 words, on freshwater, saltwater, and pond fish, with or without color transparencies. (No "pet fish" stories.) Payment varies, on publication.

BIRD TALK—Box 6050, Mission Viejo, CA 92690. Kathleen Samuelson, Ed.-in-Chief. Articles for pet bird owners: care and feeding, training, safety, outstanding personal adventures, exotic birds in their native countries, profiles of celebrities' birds, travel to bird parks or bird shows. Pays 7¢ to 10¢ a word, after publication. Query required; good transparencies a plus.

CAT FANCY—P.O. Box 6050, Mission Viejo, CA 92690. Jane Calloway, Ed. Nonfiction, to 2,500 words, on cat care, health, grooming, etc. Pays 5¢ to 10¢ a word, on publication. Query with SASE required.

DAIRY GOAT JOURNAL—P.O. Box 10, Lake Mills, WI 53551. Dave Thompson, Ed. Articles, to 1,500 words, on successful dairy goat owners, youths and interesting people associated with dairy goats. "Especially interested in practical husbandry ideas." Photos. Pays $50 to $150, on publication. Query.

DOG WORLD—PJS Publishing Inc., 29 N. Wacker Dr., Chicago, IL 60606-3298. Donna L. Marcel, Ed. Articles, to 3,000 words, for breeders, pet owners, exhibitors, kennel operators, veterinarians, handlers, and other pet professionals on all aspects of pet care and responsible ownership: health care, training, legal rights, animal welfare, etc. Allow 4 months for response. Pays $50 to $500, on acceptance. Queries required. Guidelines.

EQUUS—Fleet Street Corp., 656 Quince Orchard Rd., Gaithersburg, MD 20878. Laurie Prinz, Man. Ed. Articles, 1,000 to 3,000 words, on all breeds of horses, covering their health and care as well as the latest advances in equine medicine and research. "Attempt to speak as one horseperson to another." Pays $100 to $400, on publication.

GOOD DOG!—P.O. Box 10069, Austin, TX 78766-1069. Judi Sklar, Ed. Bimonthly. "The Consumer Magazine for Dog Owners." Articles, one to 2 pages, that are informative and fun to read. No fiction. No material "written" by the dog. Small payment, on publication.

HORSE & RIDER—12265 W. Bayaud Ave., Suite 300, Lakewood, CO 80228. Sue M. Copeland, Ed. Articles, 500 to 3,000 words, with photos, on western training and general horse care: feeding, health, grooming, etc. Pays varying rates, on publication. Guidelines.

HORSE ILLUSTRATED—P.O. Box 6050, Mission Viejo, CA 92690. Moira C. Harris, Ed. Articles, 1,500 to 2,500 words, on all aspects of owning and caring for horses. Photos. Pays $200 to $300, on publication. Query.

HORSEMEN'S YANKEE PEDLAR—83 Leicester St., N. Oxford, MA 01537. Kelley R. Small, Pub. News and feature-length articles, about horses and horsemen in the Northeast. Photos. Pays $2 per published inch, on publication. Query.

I LOVE CATS—450 7th Ave., Suite 1701, New York, NY 10123. Lisa Sheets, Ed. Fiction, preferably 500 to 700 words, about cats. Articles, to 1,000 words. No poetry, puzzles, or humor. "Read the magazine, then request guidelines with SASE." Pays $40 to $150; $20 to $25 for fillers, on publication.

LLAMAS—46 Main St., Jackson, CA 95642. Cheryl Dal Porto, Ed. "The International Camelid Journal," published 7 times yearly. Articles, 300 to 3,000 words, of interest to llama and alpaca owners. Pays $25 to $300, extra for photos, on publication. Query.

MUSHING—P.O. Box 149, Ester, AK 99725-0149. Todd Hoener, Pub. How-tos, innovations, history, profiles, interviews, and features related to sled dogs, 1,500 to 2,000 words, and department pieces, 500 to 1,000 words, for competitive and recreational dog drivers and skijorers. International audience. Photos. Pays $20 to $250, on publication. Send S.A.S.E. for guidelines.

PETLIFE: YOUR COMPANION ANIMAL MAGAZINE—1227 W. Magnolia Ave., Fort Worth, TX 76104. Jana Murphy, Man. Ed. Articles, 500 to 1,500 words, for pet owners and pet lovers; how-to and human interest pieces. "We rarely publish first-person articles." Pays $150 to $300, on acceptance.

PRACTICAL HORSEMAN—Box 589, Unionville, PA 19375. Mandy Lorraine, Ed. How-to articles on English riding, training, and horse care. Payment varies, on acceptance. Query with clips.

SHEEP! MAGAZINE—P.O. Box 10, Lake Mills, WI 53551. Dave Thompson, Ed. Articles, to 1,500 words, on successful shepherds, woolcrafts, sheep raising, and sheep dogs. "Especially interested in people who raise sheep successfully as a sideline enterprise." Photos. Pays $15 to $150, extra for photos, on acceptance. Query.

THE WESTERN HORSEMAN—P.O. Box 7980, Colorado Springs, CO 80933-7980. Pat Close, Ed. Articles, 1,500 to 2,500 words, with photos, on care and training of horses; farm, ranch, and stable management; health care and veterinary medicine. Pays to $600, on acceptance.

WILDLIFE CONSERVATION—The Wildlife Conservation Society, Bronx, NY 10460. Nancy Simmons, Sr. Ed. Articles, 1,500 to 2,000 words, that "probe conservation controversies to search for answers and help save threatened species." Payment varies, on acceptance. Guidelines.

TRUE CRIME

DETECTIVE CASES—See *Globe Communications Corp.*

DETECTIVE DRAGNET—See *Globe Communications Corp.*

DETECTIVE FILES—See *Globe Communications Corp.*

GLOBE COMMUNICATIONS CORP.—1350 Sherbrooke St. W., Suite 600, Montreal, Quebec, Canada H3G 2T4. Dominick A. Merle, Ed. Factual accounts, 3,500 to 6,000 words, of "sensational crimes, preferably sex crimes, either pre-trial or after conviction." All articles will be considered for *Startling Detective, True Police Cases, Detective Files, Headquarters Detective, Detective Dragnet,* and *Detective Cases.* Query with pertinent information, including dates, site, names, etc. Pays $250 to $350, on acceptance; buys all rights.

HEADQUARTERS DETECTIVE—See *Globe Communications Corp.*

P.I. MAGAZINE: AMERICA'S PRIVATE INVESTIGATION JOURNAL—755 Bronx Ave., Toledo, OH 43609. Bob Mackowiak, Ed. Profiles of professional investigators containing true accounts of their most difficult cases. Pays $50 to $75, plus copies, on publication.

STARTLING DETECTIVE—See *Globe Communications Corp.*

TRUE POLICE CASES—See *Globe Communications Corp.*

MILITARY

AIR FORCE TIMES—See *Times News Service.*

AMERICAN SURVIVAL GUIDE—Y-Visionary, L.P., Suite 120, 2655 Anita Dr., Orange, CA 92868-3310. Jim Benson, Ed. Articles, 1,500 to 2,000 words, with photos, on human and natural forces that pose threats to everyday life, all forms of preparedness, food production and storage, self defense and weapons, etc. All text must be accompanied by photos (and vice versa). Pays $80 per published page, on publication. Query.

AMERICA'S CIVIL WAR—Cowles History Group, 741 Miller Dr. S.E., Suite D-2, Leesburg, VA 20175. Roy Morris, Jr., Ed. Articles, 3,500 to 4,000 words, on the strategy, tactics, personalities, arms and equipment of the Civil War. Department pieces, 2,000 words. Query with illustration ideas. Pays from $150 to $300, on publication. Guidelines. SASE.

ARMY MAGAZINE—Box 1560, Arlington, VA 22210-0860. Mary B. French, Ed.-in-Chief. Features, 1,000 to 1,500 words, on military subjects. Essays, humor, history (especially World War II), news reports, first-person anecdotes. Pays 12¢ to 18¢ a word, $25 to $50 for anecdotes, on publication. Guidelines.

ARMY TIMES—See *Times News Service.*

COMMAND—P.O. Box 4017, San Luis Obispo, CA 93403. Ty Bomba, Ed. Bimonthly. Articles, 800 to 10,000 words, on any facet of military history or current military affairs. "Popular, not scholarly, analytical military history." Pays 5¢ a word, on publication. Query.

FAMILY—169 Lexington Ave., New York, NY 10016. Liz DeFranco, Ed. Articles, 1,000 to 2,000 words, of interest to military women with children. Pays to $200, on publication. Guidelines.

LEATHERNECK—Box 1775, Quantico, VA 22134-0776. William V. H. White, Ed. Articles, to 3,000 words, with photos, on U.S. Marines. Pays $50 per printed page, on acceptance. Query.

MARINE CORPS GAZETTE—Box 1775, Quantico, VA 22134. Col. John E. Greenwood, Ed. Military articles, 500 to 2,000 words and 2,500 to 5,000 words. "Our magazine serves primarily as a forum for active duty officers to exchange views on professional, Marine Corps-related topics. Opportunity for 'outside' writers is limited." Queries preferred.

MILITARY—2122 28th St., Sacramento, CA 95818. Lt. Col. Michael Mark, Ed. Articles, 600 to 2,500 words, on firsthand experience in military service: World War II, Korea, Vietnam, and all current services. "Our magazine is about military history by the people who served. They are the best historians." No payment.

MILITARY HISTORY—741 Miller Dr. S.E., Suite D-2, Leesburg, VA 20175. Jon Guttman, Ed. Bimonthly. Features, 4,000 words with 500-word sidebars, on strategy and tactics of military history. Department pieces, 2,000 words, on intrigue, personality, weaponry, perspectives, and travel. Pays $200 to $400, on publication. Query with illustration ideas. Guidelines. SASE.

NATIONAL GUARD—One Massachusetts Ave. N.W., Washington, DC 20001-1431. Pam Kane, Man. Ed. Articles on national defense. Payment varies, on publication.

NAVAL AVIATION NEWS—157-1 Washington Navy Yard, 901 M St. S.E., Washington, DC 20374-5059. Cdr. D.T. Cangelosi, Ed. Bimonthly. Articles on Naval aviation history, technology, and news. No payment.

NAVY TIMES—See *Times News Service.*

THE RETIRED OFFICER MAGAZINE—201 N. Washington St., Alexandria, VA 22314. Attn: Manuscripts Ed. Articles, 1,800 to 2,000 words, of interest to military retirees and their families. Current military/political affairs, recent military history (especially Vietnam and Korea), health, money, military family lifestyles, and second-career job opportunities. Photos a plus. Pays to $1,200, on acceptance. Queries required; no unsolicited manuscripts. Guidelines.

TIMES NEWS SERVICE—Army Times Publishing Co., Springfield, VA 22159. Attn: R&R Ed. Free-lance material for "R&R" newspaper section. Articles about military life and its problems, as well as interesting things people are doing. Travel articles, 700 words, on places of interest to military people. Profiles, 600 to 700 words, on interesting members of the military community. Personal-experience essays, 750 words. No fiction or poetry. Pays $75 to $100, on acceptance. Also articles, up to 1,200 words, for supplements to *Army Times*, *Navy Times*, and *Air Force Times*. Address Supplements Ed. Pays $125 to $350, on acceptance. Guidelines.

VFW MAGAZINE—406 W. 34th St., Kansas City, MO 64111. Richard K. Kolb, Ed. Articles, 1,000 words, related to current foreign policy and defense, American armed forces abroad, and international events affecting U.S. national security. Also, up-to-date articles on veteran concerns and issues affecting veterans. Pays to $500 on acceptance, unless specially commissioned. Query. Guidelines.

VIETNAM—Cowles History Group, 741 Miller Dr. S.E., Suite D-2, Leesburg, VA 20175. Col. Harry G. Summers, Jr., Ed. Articles, 3,500 to 4,000 words, on the strategy, tactics, personalities, arms, and equipment of the Vietnam War. Pays from $150 to $300, on publication. Query with illustration ideas. Guidelines. SASE.

WORLD WAR II—Cowles History Group, 741 Miller Dr. S.E., Leesburg, VA 20175. Michael Haskew, Ed. Articles, 3,500 to 4,000 words, on the strategy, tactics, personalities, arms, and equipment of World War II. Department pieces, 2,000 words. Pays from $100 to $200, on publication. Query with illustration ideas. Guidelines. SASE.

HISTORY

ALABAMA HERITAGE—The Univ. of Alabama, Box 870342, Tuscaloosa, AL 35487-0342. Suzanne Wolfe, Ed. Quarterly. Articles, to 5,000 words, on local, state, and regional history: art, literature, language, archaeology, music, religion, architecture, and natural history. Pays an honorarium, on publication, plus 10 copies. Query, mentioning availability of photos and illustrations. Guidelines.

AMERICAN HERITAGE—60 Fifth Ave., New York, NY 10011. Richard F. Snow, Ed. Articles, 750 to 5,000 words, on U.S. history and background of American life and culture from the beginning to recent times. No fiction. Pays from $300 to $1,500, on acceptance. Query.

AMERICAN JEWISH HISTORY—American Jewish Historical Society, 2 Thornton Rd., Waltham, MA 02154. Dr. Marc Lee Raphael, Ed. Articles, 25 to 35 typed pages, on American Jewish history. Queries preferred. No payment.

AMERICA'S CIVIL WAR—Cowles History Group, 741 Miller Dr. S.E., Suite D-2, Leesburg, VA 20175-8920. Roy Morris, Jr., Ed. Articles, 3,500 to 4,000 words, on the strategy, tactics, personalities, arms and equipment of the Civil War. Department pieces, 2,000 words. Query with illustration ideas. Pays from $150 to $300, on publication. SASE.

AVIATION HISTORY—Cowles History Group, 741 Miller Dr. S.E., Suite D-2, Leesburg, VA 20175-8920. Attn: Eds. Bimonthly. Articles, 3,500 to 4,000 words with 500-word sidebars and excellent illustrations, on aeronautical history. Department pieces, 2,000 words. Pays $150 to $300, on publication. Query.

THE BEAVER—167 Lombard Ave., #478, Winnipeg, Manitoba, Canada R3B 0T6. C. Dafoe, Ed. Articles, 500 to 3,000 words, on Canadian history, "written to appeal to general readers as well as the expert in Canadian history." Payment varies, on publication. Queries preferred.

CAROLOGUE—South Carolina Historical Society, 100 Meeting St., Charleston, SC 29401-2299. Stephen Hoffius, Ed. General-interest articles, to 10 pages, on South Carolina history. Queries preferred. Pays in copies.

CHICAGO HISTORY—Clark St. at North Ave., Chicago, IL 60614. Rosemary Adams, Ed. Articles, to 4,500 words, on political, social, and cultural history of Chicago. Pays to $250, on publication. Query.

CIVIL WAR TIMES—6405 Flank Dr., Harrisburg, PA 17112. James Kushlan, Ed. Articles, 3,000 to 4,000 words, on the Civil War. "Accurate, annotated stories with strong narrative relying heavily on primary sources and the words of eyewitnesses. We prefer gripping, top-notch accounts of battles in the Eastern Theater of the war, and Confederate eyewitness accounts (memoirs, diaries, letters) and common soldier photos." Pays $300 to $500, on acceptance. Query.

COMMAND—P.O. Box 4017, San Luis Obispo, CA 93403. Ty Bomba, Ed. Bimonthly. Articles, 800 to 10,000 words, on any facet of military history or current military affairs. "Popular, not scholarly, analytical military history." Pays 5¢ a word, on publication. Query.

EARLY AMERICAN HOMES—6405 Flank Dr., Harrisburg, PA 17112. Mimi Handler, Ed. Articles, 1,000 to 3,000 words, on early American life: arts, crafts, furnishings, history, and architecture before 1850. Pays $50 to $500, on acceptance. Query.

EIGHTEENTH-CENTURY STUDIES—Dept. of English, CB 3520, Greenlaw Hall, Univ. of North Carolina, Chapel Hill, NC 27599. Attn: Eds. Quarterly. Articles, to 6,500 words, on all aspects of the eighteenth century, especially those that are interdisciplinary or that are of general interest to scholars working in other disciplines. Blind submission policy: Submit 2 copies of manuscript; author's name and address should appear only on separate title page. No payment.

GOLDENSEAL—The Cultural Ctr., 1900 Kanawha Blvd. E., Charleston, WV 25305-0300. John Lilly, Ed. Features, 3,000 words, and shorter articles, 1,000 words, on traditional West Virginia culture and history. Oral histories, old and new B&W photos, research articles. Pays 10¢ a word, on publication. Guidelines.

THE GOLDFINCH—State Historical Society of Iowa, 402 Iowa Ave., Iowa City, IA 52240-1806. Amy Ruth, Ed. Quarterly. Articles, 200 to 800 words, and short fiction on Iowa history for young people. "All articles must correspond to an upcoming theme." Pays $25 per article, on acceptance. Query for themes.

GOOD OLD DAYS—306 E. Parr Rd., Berne, IN 46711. Ken Tate, Ed. True stories (no fiction), 500 to 1,200 words, that took place between 1900 and 1955. Departments include: "Good Old Days on Wheels," about period autos, planes, trolleys, and other transportation; "Good Old Days in the Kitchen," favorite foods, appliances, recipes; "Home Remedies," hometown doctors, herbs and poultices, harrowing kitchen table operations, etc. Pays $15 to $75, on publication.

THE HIGHLANDER—P.O. Box 22307, Kansas City, MO 64113. Crennan M. Wade, Ed. Bimonthly. Articles, 1,300 to 2,200 words, related to Scottish history. "We do not use any articles on modern Scotland or current problems in Scotland." Pays $100 to $150, on acceptance. Photos must accompany manuscripts.

HISTORIC PRESERVATION—1785 Massachusetts Ave. N.W., Washington, DC 20036. Robert Wilson, Ed. Feature articles from published writers, 1,500 to 4,000 words, on residential restoration, preservation issues, news, and people involved in preserving America's heritage. Partly staff-written. Query required.

HISTORIC TRAVELER—6405 Flank Dr., Harrisburg, PA 17112. Tom Huntington, Ed. Bimonthly. Articles, 800 to 2,500 words, for upscale readers with a strong interest in history and historic sites. "Accurate information on historic destinations. Possible topics: battlefields, museums, antique shows, events, hotels, inns, transportation, reenactments, preserved communities, and architectural wonders. No South Pacific Islands, Alpine skiing, or Mediterranean cruises." Pays $300 to $500, on acceptance. Query with SASE and clips. Guidelines.

JOURNAL OF THE WEST—1531 Yuma, Box 1009, Manhattan, KS 66505-1009. Robin Higham, Ed. Articles, to 15 pages, devoted to the history and the culture of the West, then and now. B&W photos. Pays in copies.

LABOR'S HERITAGE—10000 New Hampshire Ave., Silver Spring, MD 20903. Quarterly journal of The George Meany Memorial Archives. Articles, 80 pages, for labor scholars, labor union members, and the general public. Pays in copies.

MILITARY HISTORY—741 Miller Dr. S.E., Suite D-2, Leesburg, VA 22075. Jon Guttman, Ed. Bimonthly. Features, 4,000 words with 500-word sidebars, on the strategy, tactics, and personalities of military history. Department pieces, 2,000 words, on espionage, weaponry, personalities, perspectives, and travel. Pays $200 to $400, on publication. Query. Guidelines.

MONTANA JOURNAL—1431 S. Higgins Ave., Missoula, MT 59801. Mike Haser, Ed. Bimonthly tabloid. Human-interest articles, to 1,000 words, about the people, places, and events that helped build Montana. Pays 2¢ a word, on publication. Query preferred.

MONTANA, THE MAGAZINE OF WESTERN HISTORY—225 N. Roberts St., Box 201201, Helena, MT 59620-1201. Charles E. Rankin, Ed. Authentic articles, 3,500 to 5,500 words, on the history of the American and Canadian West; new interpretive approaches to major developments in western history. Footnotes or bibliography must accompany article. "Strict historical accuracy is essential." No fiction. Queries preferred. No payment made.

NEBRASKA HISTORY—P.O. Box 82554, Lincoln, NE 68501. James E. Potter, Ed. Articles, 3,000 to 7,000 words, relating to the history of Nebraska and the Great Plains. B&W line drawings. Allow 60 days for response. Pays in copies. Cash prize awarded to one article each year.

NOW & THEN—CASS/ETSU, P.O. Box 70556, Johnson City, TN 37614-0556. Jane Harris Woodside, Ed. Fiction and nonfiction, 1,500 to 3,000 words: short stories, articles, interviews, essays, memoirs, book reviews. Pieces must be related to theme of issue and have some connection to the Appalachian region. Also photos and drawings. SASE for guidelines and current themes. Pays $15 to $75, on publication.

OLD WEST—P.O. Box 2107, Stillwater, OK 74076. Marcus Huff, Ed. Thoroughly researched and documented articles, 1,500 to 4,500 words, on the history of the American West. B&W 5x7 photos to illustrate articles. Queries are preferred. Pays 3¢ to 6¢ a word, on acceptance.

PENNSYLVANIA HERITAGE—P.O. Box 1026, Harrisburg, PA 17108-1026. Michael J. O'Malley III, Ed. Quarterly of the Pennsylvania Historical and Museum Commission and the Pennsylvania Heritage Society. Articles, 2,500 to 3,500 words, that "introduce readers to the state's rich culture and historic legacy. Seeks unusual and fresh angle to make history come to life, including pictorial or photo essays, interviews, travel/destination pieces." Prefers to see complete manuscript. Pays to $500, up to $100 for photos or drawings, on acceptance.

PERSIMMON HILL—1700 N.E. 63rd St., Oklahoma City, OK 73111. M.J. Van Deventer, Ed. Published by the National Cowboy Hall of Fame. Articles, 1,500 words, on western history and art, cowboys, ranching, and nature. Top-quality illustrations with captions a must. Pays from $150 to $250, on publication.

PROLOGUE—National Archives, NPOL, 8601 Adelphi Rd., College Park, MD 20740-6001. Quarterly. Articles, varying lengths, based on the holdings and programs of the National Archives, its regional archives, and the presidential libraries. Query. Pays in copies.

RENAISSANCE MAGAZINE—Phantom Press Publications, 13 Appleton Rd., Nantucket, MA 02554. Kim Guarnaccia, Ed. Feature articles on Renaissance and Medieval history, costuming, jousting. Also Renaissance faires, interviews, reviews of Renaissance books, music, movies, and games. Pays 3¢ a word, on publication.

RUSSIAN LIFE— 89 Main St., #2, Montpelier, VT 05602-2948. Mikhail Ivanov, Ed. Articles, 1,000 to 3,000 words, on Russian culture, travel, history, politics, art, business, and society. "We do not want stories about personal trips to Russia, editorials on developments in Russia, or articles that promote the services of a specific company, organization, or government agency." Pays 7¢ to 10¢ a word; $20 to $30 per photo, on publication. Query.

SCOTTISH JOURNAL—P.O. Box 3165, Barrington, IL 60011. Angus J. Ray, Ed. Articles, 1,500 to 2,000 words, on Scottish history, famous Scots, clans, battles. Travel pieces on specific areas in Scotland. Queries preferred. Pays $150 to $200, on acceptance.

SOUTH CAROLINA HISTORICAL MAGAZINE—South Carolina Historical Society, 100 Meeting St., Charleston, SC 29401-2299. Stephen Hoffius, Ed. Scholarly articles, to 25 pages including footnotes, on South Carolina history. "Authors are encouraged to look at previous issues to be aware of previous scholarship." Pays in copies.

TRUE WEST—P.O. Box 2107, Stillwater, OK 74076-2107. Marcus Huff, Ed. True stories, 500 to 4,500 words, with photos, about the Old West to 1930. Some contemporary stories with historical slant. Source list required. Pays 3¢ to 6¢ a word, extra for B&W photos, on acceptance.

VIETNAM—Cowles History Group, 741 Miller Dr. S.E., Suite D-2, Leesburg, VA 20175-8920. Col. Harry G. Summers, Jr., Ed. Articles, 2,000 to 4,000 words, on the strategy, tactics, personalities, arms, and equipment of the Vietnam War. Pays $100 to $200, on publication. Query with illustration ideas. SASE.

THE WESTERN HISTORICAL QUARTERLY—Utah State Univ., Logan, UT 84322-0740. Clyde A. Milner II, Ed. Original articles about the American West, the Westward movement from the Atlantic to the Pacific, twentieth-century regional studies, Spanish borderlands, Canada, northern Mexico, Alaska, and Hawaii. No payment made.

WILD WEST—741 Miller Dr., S.E., #D-2, Leesburg, VA 20175-8920. Gregory Lalire, Ed. Bimonthly. Features, to 4,000 words, with 500-word side-bars, and department pieces, 2,000 words, on Western history from the earliest North American settlements to the end of the 19th century. Pays $150 to $300, on publication. Query with SASE.

WORLD WAR II—Cowles History Group, 741 Miller Dr. S.E., Suite D-2, Leesburg, VA 20175-8920. Michael Haskew, Ed. Articles, 3,500 to 4,000 words, on the strategy, tactics, personalities, arms, and equipment of World War II. Pays from $100, on publication. Query with illustration ideas. SASE for editorial guidelines. Web site: www.cheryls@cowles.com.

YESTERDAY'S MAGAZETTE—P.O. Box 18566, Sarasota, FL 34276. Ned Burke, Ed. Articles and fiction, to 1,000 words, on the 1920s through '70s, nostalgia and memories of people, places, and things. Traditional poetry, to 24 lines. Pays $5 to $25, on publication. Pays in copies for poetry and short pieces. Guidelines.

COLLEGE, CAREERS

THE BLACK COLLEGIAN—140 Carondelet St., New Orleans, LA 70130. James Perry, Ed. Articles, to 2,000 words, on experiences of African-American students, careers, and how-to subjects. Pays on publication. Query.

BYLINE—Box 130596, Edmond, OK 73013. Marcia Preston, Ed.-in-Chief. General fiction, 2,000 to 4,000 words. Nonfiction: 1,500- to 1,800-word features and 300- to 750-word special departments. Poetry, 10 to 30 lines preferred. Nonfiction and poetry must be about writing. Humor, 200 to 600 words, about writing. "We seek practical and motivational material that tells writers how they can succeed, not why they can't. Overdone topics: writer's block, the muse, rejection slips." Pays $5 to $10 for poetry; $15 to $35 for departments; $50 for features and $100 for short fiction, on acceptance.

CAMPUS LIFE— 465 Gundersen Dr., Carol Stream, IL 60188. Harold Smith, Exec. Ed. Fiction and humor, reflecting Christian values, 1,000 to 3,000 words, for high school and college students. Pays from $150 to $400, on acceptance. Limited free-lance market. Published writers only. Queries required. SASE.

CAREER WORLD—GLC. 900 Skokie Blvd., Northbrook, IL 60062-4028. Carole Rubenstein, Sr. Ed. Published 7 times a year, September through April/May. Gender-neutral articles about specific occupations and career development for junior and senior high school audience. Query with clips and resumé. Payment varies, on publication.

CAREERS AND THE COLLEGE GRAD—201 Broadway, Cambridge, MA 02139. Kathleen Ames, Dir. of Publishing. Annual. Career-related articles, 1,500 to 2,000 words, for junior and senior liberal arts students. Career-related fillers, 500 words and line art or color prints. Queries preferred. No payment. Same address and requirements for *Careers and the MBA* (semiannual) for first-and second-year MBA students, and *Careers and the Engineer* (semiannual) for junior and senior engineering students.

CAREERS & THE DISABLED—See *Minority Engineer.*

CAREERS AND THE ENGINEER—See *Careers and the College Grad.*

CAREERS AND THE MBA—See *Careers and the College Grad.*

CIRCLE K—3636 Woodview Trace, Indianapolis, IN 46268-3196. Nicholas K. Drake, Exec. Ed. Serious and light articles, 1,500 to 1,700 words, on careers, college issues, trends, leadership development, self-help, community service and involvement. Pays $200 to $400, on acceptance. Queries preferred.

COLLEGE BOUND MAGAZINE—2071 Clove Rd., Staten Island, NY 10304. Gina LaGuardia, Ed. Features, 600 to 1,000 words, and department pieces, 50 to 300 words, that offer high school students a view of college life.

Especially interested in personal accounts by current college students. Pays $25 to $100, on publication.

COLLEGE BROADCASTER—National Assn. of College Broadcasters, 71 George St., Providence, RI 02912-1824. Michael Russo, Ed. Quarterly. Articles, 500 to 2,000 words, on student radio and TV station operations and media careers. Pays in copies. Query.

EQUAL OPPORTUNITY—See *Minority Engineer.*

FLORIDA LEADER—c/o Oxendine Publishing, P.O. Box 14081, Gainesville, FL 32604-2081. Kay Quinn, Man. Ed. Published 3 times a year. Articles, 800 to 1,000 words, for Florida college students. "Focus on leadership, career success, profiles of growth careers in Florida and the Southeast." Pays $35 to $50, on publication.

INSIDER MAGAZINE—4124 W. Oakton, Skokie, IL 60201. David Glines, Ed. Dir. Articles, 700, 1,500, and 2,100 words, on issues, career, politics, sports, and entertainment, for primarily a college-age audience. Pays 1¢ to 5¢ a word, on publication. Queries preferred.

LINK: THE COLLEGE MAGAZINE—The Soho Building, 110 Greene St., Suite 407, New York, NY 10012. Ty Wenger, Ed.-in-Chief. News, lifestyle, and issues for college students. Informational how-to and short features, 500 to 800 words, on education news, finances, academics, employment, lifestyles, and trends. Well-researched, insightful, authoritative articles. Pays $100 to $500, on publication. Queries preferred. Guidelines.

MINORITY ENGINEER—1160 E. Jericho Turnpike, Suite 200, Huntington, NY 11743. James Schneider, Ed. Articles, 1,000 to 1,500 words, for college students, on career opportunities; techniques of job hunting; developments in and applications of new technologies. Interviews. Profiles. Pays 10¢ a word, on publication. Query. Same address and requirements for *Woman Engineer* (address Anne Kelly), and *Equal Opportunity* and *Careers & the DisABLED* (address James Schneider).

ONCE UPON A TIME—553 Winston Ct., St. Paul, MN 55118. Audrey B. Baird, Ed. "A 32-page magazine for Children's Writers and Illustrators." Quarterly. Articles, to 900 words: questions, insights, tips and experiences (no fiction) on the writing and illustrating life by published and unpublished writers. Also, short articles, 100 to 400 words. B&W artwork. No payment.

STUDENT LEADER—c/o Oxendine Publishing Inc., P.O. Box 14081, Gainesville, FL 32604-2081. Kay Quinn, Man. Ed. Semiannual. "The Magazine for America's Most Outstanding Students." Articles, 800 to 1,000 words, on leadership issues and career and college success. "Include quotes from faculty, corporate recruiters, current students, recent alumni." Pays $50 to $100, on publication.

STUDY BREAKS MAGAZINE—600 W. 28th St., #103, Austin, TX 78705. Gal Shweiki, Pub. Fillers, humor, jokes, etc., of interest to University of Texas students. No payment.

UNIQUE OPPORTUNITIES—455 S. 4th Ave., #1236, Louisville, KY 40202. Bett Coffman, Assoc. Ed. Articles, 2,000 to 3,000 words, that cover economic, business, and career-related issues of interest to physicians who are looking for their first practice or looking to make a career move. Doctor profiles, 500 words. "Our goal is to educate physicians about how to evaluate career opportunities, negotiate the benefits offered, plan career moves, and provide information on the legal and economic aspects of accepting a position." Pays 50¢ a word for features; $200 for profiles, on acceptance. Query.

WOMAN ENGINEER—See *Minority Engineer.*

OP-ED MARKETS

THE ATLANTA CONSTITUTION—P.O. Box 4689, Atlanta, GA 30302. Teresa Weaver, Op-Ed Ed. Articles related to the Southeast, Georgia, or the Atlanta metropolitan area, 200 to 800 words, on a variety of topics: law, economics, politics, science, environment, performing and manipulative arts, humor, education; religious and seasonal topics. Pays $75 to $125, on publication. Submit complete manuscript.

THE BALTIMORE SUN—P.O. Box 1377, Baltimore, MD 21278-0001. Hal Piper, Opinion-Commentary Page Ed. Articles, 600 to 1,500 words, on a wide range of topics: politics, education, foreign affairs, lifestyles, etc. Humor. Payment varies, on publication. Exclusive rights: MD and DC.

THE BOSTON GLOBE—P.O. Box 2378, Boston, MA 02107-2378. Marjorie Pritchard, Ed. Articles, to 700 words, on economics, education, environment, foreign affairs, and regional interest. Pays $100, on publication. Send complete manuscript. Exclusive rights: New England.

BOSTON HERALD—One Herald Sq., Boston, MA 02106. Attn: Editorial Page Ed. Pieces, 600 to 800 words, on economics, foreign affairs, politics, regional interest, and seasonal topics. Prefer submissions from regional writers. Payment varies, on publication. Exclusive rights: MA, RI, and NH.

THE CHARLOTTE OBSERVER—P.O. Box 30308, Charlotte, NC 28230-0308. Ed Williams, Ed. Well-written, thought-provoking articles, to 700 words. "We are only interested in articles on local (Carolinas) issues or that use local examples to illustrate other issues." Pays $50, on publication. No simultaneous submissions in NC or SC.

THE CHICAGO TRIBUNE—435 N. Michigan Ave., Chicago, IL 60611. Marcia Lythcott, Op-Ed Page Ed. Pieces, 800 to 1,000 words, on domestic and international affairs, environment, regional interest, and personal essays. SASE required.

THE CHRISTIAN SCIENCE MONITOR—One Norway St., Boston, MA 02115. Lisa Parney, Opinion Page Coordinator. Pieces, 750 to 900 words, on domestic and foreign affairs, economics, education, environment, law, media, and politics. Pays $100, on acceptance. Retains all rights for 90 days after publication.

THE CLEVELAND PLAIN DEALER—1801 Superior Ave., Cleveland, OH 44114. Gloria Millner, Assoc. Ed. Pieces, 700 to 900 words, on a wide variety of subjects. Pays $75, on publication.

DES MOINES REGISTER—P.O. Box 957, Des Moines, IA 50304. Attn: "Opinion" Page Ed. Articles, 500 to 750 words, on all topics. Prefer Iowa subjects. Pays $35 to $75, on publication. Exclusive rights: IA.

DETROIT FREE PRESS—321 W. Lafayette Blvd., Detroit, MI 48226. Attn: Op-Ed Ed. Opinion pieces, to 800 words, on domestic and foreign affairs, economics, education, environment, law, politics, and regional interest. Priority given to local writers or topics of local interest. Pays $50 to $100, on publication. Query. Exclusive rights: MI and northern OH.

THE DETROIT NEWS— 615 W. Lafayette Blvd., Detroit, MI 48226. Attn: Richard Burr. Pieces, 500 to 750 words, on a wide variety of subjects. Pays $75, on publication.

THE FLINT JOURNAL—200 E. First St., Flint, MI 48502-1925. Carlton Winfrey, Opinion Dept. Ed. Articles, 650 words, of regional interest by local writers. Non-local writers should query. No payment. Limited market.

INDIANAPOLIS STAR—P.O. Box 145, Indianapolis, IN 46206-0145. John H. Lyst, Ed. Articles, 700 to 800 words. Pays $40, on publication. Exclusive rights: IN.

LONG BEACH PRESS-TELEGRAM— 604 Pine Ave., Long Beach, CA 90844. Larry Allison, Ed. Articles, 750 to 900 words, on regional topics. Pays $75, on publication. Exclusive rights: Los Angeles area.

LOS ANGELES TIMES—Times Mirror Sq., Los Angeles, CA 90053. Bob Berger, Op-Ed Ed. Commentary pieces, 650 to 700 words, on many subjects. "Not interested in nostalgia or first-person reaction to faraway events. Pieces must be exclusive." Payment varies, on publication. Limited market. SASE required.

THE NEW YORK TIMES—229 W. 43rd St., New York, NY 10036. Attn: Op-Ed Ed. Opinion pieces, 650 to 800 words, on any topic, including public policy, science, lifestyles, and ideas, etc. Include your address, daytime phone number, and social security number with submission. "If you haven't heard from us within 2 weeks, you can assume we are not using your piece. Include SASE if you want work returned." Pays on publication. Buys first North American rights.

NEWSDAY—"Viewpoints," 235 Pinelawn Rd., Melville, NY 11747. Noel Rubinton, "Viewpoints" Ed. Pieces, 700 to 800 words, on a variety of topics. Pays $150, on publication.

THE ORANGE COUNTY REGISTER—P.O. Box 11626, Santa Ana, CA 92711. K.E. Grubbs, Jr., Ed. Articles on a wide range of local and national issues and topics. Pays $50 to $100, on publication.

THE OREGONIAN—1320 S.W. Broadway, Portland, OR 97201. Attn: Opinion & Commentary Ed. Articles, 900 to 1,000 words, of news analysis from Pacific Northwest writers or on regional topics. Pays $100 to $150, on publication. Send complete manuscript.

PITTSBURGH POST GAZETTE—34 Blvd. of the Allies, Pittsburgh, PA 15222. John Allison, Contributions Ed. Articles, to 1,000 words, on a variety of subjects. No whimsy. Pays $60 to $150, on publication. SASE required.

THE REGISTER GUARD—P.O. Box 10188, Eugene, OR 97440. Don Robinson, Editorial Page Ed. All subjects; regional angle preferred. Pays $25 to $50, on publication. Very limited use of non-local writers.

THE SACRAMENTO BEE—2100 Q St., Sacramento, CA 95852. William Kahrl, Opinion Ed. Op-ed pieces, to 750 words; state and regional topics preferred. Pays $150, on publication.

ST. LOUIS POST-DISPATCH— 900 N. Tucker Blvd., St. Louis, MO 63101. Donna Korando, Commentary Ed. Articles, 700 words, on economics, education, science, politics, foreign and domestic affairs, and the environment. Pays $70, on publication. "Goal is to have half of the articles by local writers."

ST. PAUL PIONEER PRESS—345 Cedar St., St. Paul, MN 55101. Ronald D. Clark, Ed. Articles, to 750 words, on a variety of topics. Strongly prefer authors or topics with a connection to the area. Pays $75, on publication.

ST. PETERSBURG TIMES—Box 1121, 490 First Ave. S., St. Petersburg, FL 33731. Jon East, "Perspective" Section Ed. Authoritative articles, to 2,000 words, on current political, economic, and social issues. Payment varies, on publication. Query.

SAN FRANCISCO EXAMINER—110 5th St., San Francisco, CA 94103. Attn: Op-Ed Ed. Well-written articles, 500 to 650 words, double-spaced; preference given to local and state issues and to subjects bypassed by most news media. No sports. No first-run movies. Payment varies, on publication.

SEATTLE POST-INTELLIGENCER—P.O. Box 1909, Seattle, WA 98111. Charles J. Dunsire, Editorial Page Ed. Articles, 750 to 800 words, on foreign and domestic affairs, environment, education, politics, regional interest, religion, science, and seasonal material. Prefer writers who live in the Pacific Northwest. Pays $75 to $150, on publication. SASE required. Very limited market.

USA TODAY—1000 Wilson Blvd., Arlington, VA 22229. Juan J. Walte, Ed./Columns. Articles, 600 words, on current public policy issues. Very limited market. Pays $200, on publication. Query.

THE WALL STREET JOURNAL—Editorial Page, 200 Liberty St., New York, NY 10281. David B. Brooks, Op-Ed Ed. Articles, to 1,500 words, on politics, economics, law, education, environment, humor (occasionally), and foreign and domestic affairs. Articles must be timely, heavily reported, and of national interest by writers with expertise in their field. Pays $150 to $300, on publication.

WASHINGTON TIMES—3600 New York Ave. N.E., Washington, DC 20002. Frank Perley, Articles and Opinion Page Ed. Articles, 800 to 1,000 words, on a variety of subjects. No pieces written in the first-person. "Syndicated columnists cover the 'big' issues; find an area that is off the beaten path." Pays $150, on publication. Exclusive rights: Washington, DC, and Baltimore area.

ADULT MAGAZINES

CHIC—8484 Wilshire Blvd., Suite 900, Beverly Hills, CA 90211. Scott Schalin, Lisa Jenio, Exec. Eds. Sex-related articles, interviews, erotic fiction, 2,500 words. Query for articles. Pays $150 for brief interviews, $350 for fiction, on acceptance.

D-CUP—Swank Publications, Inc., 210 Rt. 4 E., Suite 401, Paramus, NJ 07652. Bob Rosen, Ed. Erotic fiction and interviews with large-breasted models, 2,500 to 3,000 words. Pays $150 to $400, on publication.

GALLERY—401 Park Ave. S., New York, NY 10016-8802. Barry Janoff, Ed.-in-Chief. Rich Friedman, Man. Ed. Articles, investigative pieces, interviews, profiles, to 2,500 words, for sophisticated men. Short humor, satire, service pieces, and fiction. Photos. Pays varying rates, on publication. Query. Guidelines.

GENESIS—110 E. 59th St., Suite 3100, New York, NY 10022. Michael Banka, Pub. Peter Landau, Man. Ed. Articles, 2,000 words. Sexually explicit nonfiction features, 2,000 words. Photo-essays. Pays 60 days after acceptance. Query with clips.

PENTHOUSE—277 Park Ave., 4th Fl., New York, NY 10172-0003. Peter Bloch, Ed. Lavada B. Nahon, Sr. Ed. Articles, to 5,000 words: general-interest profiles, interviews (with introduction), and investigative pieces. Pays on acceptance.

PLAYBOY— 680 N. Lake Shore Dr., Chicago, IL 60611. Stephen Randall, Articles Ed. Articles, 3,500 to 6,000 words, and sophisticated fiction, 1,000 to 10,000 words (5,000 preferred), for urban men. Humor; satire. Science fiction. Pays to $5,000 for articles and fiction, $2,000 for short-shorts, on acceptance.

PLAYERS— 8060 Melrose Ave., Los Angeles, CA 90046. David Jamison, Ed. Features, 2,500 to 3,500 words, for black men: politics, economics, travel, fashion, grooming, entertainment, sports, interviews, fiction, humor, satire, health, and sex. Photos a plus. Pays on publication.

PLAYGIRL— 801 Second Ave., New York, NY 10017. Patrice Baldwin, Man. Ed. Articles, 1,500 to 4,000 words, for women 18 and older. Erotic fiction, 1,000 to 3,500 words. Pays varying rates, on acceptance.

VARIATIONS, FOR LIBERATED LOVERS—277 Park Ave., New York, NY 10172. V. K. McCarty, Ed. Dir./Assoc. Pub. First-person true narrative descriptions of "a couple's enthusiasm, secrets, and exquisitely articulated sex scenes squarely focused within one of the magazine's pleasure categories." Pays $400, on acceptance.

FICTION MARKETS

This list gives the fiction requirements of general- and special-interest magazines, including those that publish detective and mystery, science fiction and fantasy, romance and confession stories. Other good markets for short fiction are the *College, Literary, and Little Magazines* where, though payment is modest (usually in copies only), publication can bring the work of a beginning writer to the attention of editors at the larger magazines. Juvenile fiction markets are listed under *Juvenile, Teenage, and Young Adult Magazines*. Publishers of book-length fiction manuscripts are listed under *Book Publishers*.

GENERAL FICTION

ABORIGINAL SF—P.O. Box 2449, Woburn, MA 01888-0849. Charles C. Ryan, Ed. Stories, 2,500 to 7,500 words, with a unique scientific idea, human or alien character, plot, and theme of lasting value; "must be science fiction; no fantasy, horror, or sword and sorcery." Pays $200. Send SASE for guidelines.

AFRICAN VOICES—270 W. 96th St., New York, NY 10025. Carolyn A. Butts, Exec. Ed. Bimonthly. Humorous, erotic, and dramatic fiction, 500 to

2,500 words, by ethnic writers. Nonfiction, 500 to 1,500 words: investigative articles, artist profiles, essays, and first-person narratives. Poetry, to 50 lines. Pays $25 for fiction, on publication, plus 5 copies of magazine. (Payment varies for nonfiction.)

AIM MAGAZINE—P.O. Box 20554, Chicago, IL 60620. Myron Apilado, Ed. Short stories, 800 to 3,000 words, geared to proving that people from different backgrounds are more alike than they are different. Story should not moralize. Pays from $15 to $25, on publication. Annual contest.

ALFRED HITCHCOCK MYSTERY MAGAZINE—1270 Ave. of the Americas, New York, NY 10020. Cathleen Jordan, Ed. Well-plotted, plausible mystery, suspense, detection and crime stories, to 14,000 words; "ghost stories, humor, futuristic or atmospheric tales are all possible, as long as they include a crime or the suggestion of one." Pays 8¢ a word, on acceptance. Guidelines with SASE.

ALOHA, THE MAGAZINE OF HAWAII AND THE PACIFIC—P.O. Box 3260, Honolulu, HI 96801. Cheryl Tsutsumi, Ed. Fiction to 2,000 words, with a Hawaii focus. Pays $150 to $300, on publication. Query.

THE AMERICAN VOICE—332 W. Broadway, Suite 1215, Louisville, KY 40202. Frederick Smock, Ed. Avant-garde, literary fiction, nonfiction, and well-crafted poetry, any length (shorter works are preferred). "Please read our journal before attempting to submit. Interested in work from all the Americas; translations, new writers, etc." Payment varies, on publication.

ANALOG SCIENCE FICTION AND FACT—1270 Ave. of the Americas, New York, NY 10020. Stanley Schmidt, Ed. Science fiction, with strong characters in believable future or alien setting: short stories, 2,000 to 7,500 words; novelettes, 10,000 to 20,000 words; serials, to 70,000 words. Include SASE. Pays 5¢ to 8¢ a word, on acceptance. Query for novels.

ASIMOV'S SCIENCE FICTION MAGAZINE—1270 Ave. of the Americas, New York, NY 10020. Gardner Dozois, Ed. Short science fiction and fantasies, to 15,000 words. Pays 6¢ to 8¢ a word, on acceptance. Guidelines.

THE ATLANTIC MONTHLY—77 N. Washington St., Boston, MA 02114. William Whitworth, Ed. Short stories, 2,000 to 6,000 words, of highest literary quality, with "fully developed narratives, distinctive characterization, freshness in language, and a resolution of some kind." SASE. Pays $2,500, on acceptance.

THE BELLETRIST REVIEW—Marmarc Publications, P.O. Box 596, Plainville, CT 06062. Marlene Dube, Ed. Semiannual. Fiction, 1,500 to 5,000 words: adventure, contemporary, erotica, psychological horror, humor, literary, mainstream, suspense, and mystery. No fantasy, juvenile, westerns, over-blown horror, or confessional pieces. Annual fiction contest; send SASE for guidelines. Pays in copies.

THE BOSTON GLOBE MAGAZINE—*The Boston Globe*, Boston, MA 02107. Evelynne Kramer, Ed. Short stories, to 3,000 words. Include SASE. Pays on acceptance.

BOYS' LIFE—1325 W. Walnut Hill Ln., P.O. Box 152079, Irving, TX 75015-2079. Shannon Lowry, Fiction Ed. Publication of the Boy Scouts of America. Humor, mystery, science fiction, adventure, 1,200 words, for 8- to 18-year-old boys; study back issues. Pays from $750, on acceptance. Send SASE for guidelines. Send complete manuscript; no queries.

BUFFALO SPREE MAGAZINE—Box 38, Buffalo, NY 14226. Johanna Van De Mark, Ed./Pub. Fiction and humor, to 2,000 words, for readers in the western New York region. Pays $100 to $125, on publication.

BYLINE—Box 130596, Edmond, OK 73013. Marcia Preston, Ed.-in-Chief. Kathryn Fanning, Man. Ed. General fiction, 2,000 to 4,000 words. Nonfiction: 1,500- to 1,800-word features and 300- to 750-word special departments. Poetry, 10 to 30 lines preferred. Nonfiction and poetry must be about writing. Humor, 200 to 600 words, about writing. "We seek practical and motivational material that tells writers how they can succeed, not why they can't. Overdone topics: writers' block, the muse, rejection slips." Pays $5 to $10 for poetry; $15 to $35 for departments; $50 for features; and $100 for short fiction, on acceptance. SASE for guidelines or see Web page: http://www.bylinemag.com.

CAPPER'S—1503 S.W. 42nd St., Topeka, KS 66609-1265. Nancy Peavler, Ed. Fiction, 7,500 to 40,000 words (12,000 to 20,000 words preferred), for serialization. No profanity, violence, or explicit sex. Pays $75 to $400, on publication.

CATHOLIC FORESTER—355 Shuman Blvd., P.O. Box 3012, Naperville, IL 60566-7012. Dorothy Deer, Ed. Official publication of the Catholic Order of Foresters. Fiction, to 1,500 words (prefer shorter); "looking for more contemporary, meaningful stories dealing with life today." No sex or violence or "preachy" stories; religious angle not required. Pays 20¢ a word, on acceptance.

CHESS LIFE—3054 NYS Rt. 9W, New Windsor, NY 12553-7698. Glenn Petersen, Ed. Fiction, 500 to 2,000 words, related to chess for members of the U.S. Chess Federation. Also, articles, 500 to 3,000 words, on chess news, profiles, technical aspects of chess. Pays varying rates, on acceptance. Query; limited market.

COMMON GROUND MAGAZINE—P.O. Box 99, McVeytown, PA 17051-0099. Ruth Dunmire and Pam Brumbaugh, Eds. Quarterly. Fiction, 1,000 to 2,000 words, related to Central Pennsylvania's Juniata River Valley. Pays $25 to $200, on publication. Guidelines.

COSMOPOLITAN—224 W. 57th St., New York, NY 10019. Betty Kelly, Fiction Ed. Romance or mystery short stories and novel excerpts; submissions must be sent by a publisher or agent. Payment rates are negotiable. SASE.

COUNTRY WOMAN—P.O. Box 989, Greendale, WI 53129. Kathy Pohl, Man. Ed. Fiction, 750 to 1,000 words, of interest to rural women; protagonist must be a country woman. "Stories should focus on life in the country, its problems and joys, as experienced by country women; must be upbeat and positive." Pays $90 to $125, on acceptance.

CRICKET—P.O. Box 300, Peru, IL 61354-0300. Marianne Carus, Ed.-in-Chief. Fiction, 200 to 2,000 words, for 9- to 14-year-olds. Pays to 25¢ a word, on publication. SASE.

DISCOVERIES—WordAction Publishing Co., 6401 The Paseo, Kansas City, MO 64131. Attn: Asst. Ed. Weekly take-home paper designed to correlate with Evangelical Sunday school curriculum. Fiction, 500 words, for 8- to 10-year-olds. Stories should feature contemporary, true-to-life characters and should illustrate character building and scriptural application. No poetry. Pays 5¢ a word, on publication. Send SASE for guidelines and theme list.

DOGWOOD TALES MAGAZINE—P.O. Box 172068, Memphis, TN 38187. Attn: Ed. Bimonthly "for the fiction lover in all of us." Short stories,

250 to 4,500 words (prefer no more than 3,000 words), in any genre except religion or pornography. "Stories should be fresh, well-paced, and have strong endings." Contests. SASE for guidelines.

ELLERY QUEEN'S MYSTERY MAGAZINE—1270 Ave. of the Americas, 10th Fl., New York, NY 10020. Janet Hutchings, Ed. High-quality detective, crime, and mystery stories, 1,500 to 10,000 words. Also "Minute Mysteries," 250 words, short verses, limericks, and novellas, to 17,000 words. "We like a mix of classic detection and suspenseful crime." "First Stories" by unpublished writers. Pays 3¢ to 8¢ a word, occasionally higher for established authors, on acceptance.

ESQUIRE—250 W. 55th St., New York, NY 10019. Edward Kosner, Ed.-in-Chief. Send finished manuscript of short story; submit one at a time. No full-length novels. No pornography, science fiction, poetry, or "true romance" stories. Include SASE.

EVANGEL—Light and Life Communications, P.O. Box 535002, Indianapolis, IN 46253-5002. Julie Innes, Ed. Free Methodist. Fiction and nonfiction, to 1,200 words, with personal faith in Christ shown as instrumental in solving problems. Pays 4¢ a word, on publication. SASE for guidelines.

FAMILY CIRCLE—375 Lexington Ave., New York, NY 10017. Kathy Sagan, Sr. Ed. Fiction is no longer being considered.

FICTION INTERNATIONAL—English Dept., San Diego State Univ., San Diego, CA 92182-8140. Harold Jaffe, Ed. Post-modernist and politically committed fiction and theory. Query for themes. Submit between September 1st and December 15th.

FLY ROD & REEL—P.O. Box 370, Camden, ME 04843. James E. Butler, Ed. Occasional fiction, 2,000 to 2,500 words, related to fly fishing. Special annual fiction issue published in summer. Payment varies, on acceptance.

GALLERY—401 Park Ave. S., New York, NY 10016-8802. Barry Janoff, Ed. Dir. Rich Friedman, Man. Ed. Fiction, to 3,000 words, for sophisticated men. "We are not looking for science fiction, mystery, 40s-style detective, or stories involving aliens from other planets. We do look for interesting stories that enable readers to view life in an off-beat, unusual, or insightful manner: fiction with believable characters and actions. We encourage quality work from unpublished writers." Pays $500, on publication. SASE for guidelines.

GLIMMER TRAIN PRESS—710 S.W. Madison St., #504, Portland, OR 97205. Susan Burmeister-Brown, Ed. Fiction, 1,200 to 7,500 words. "Eight stories in each quarterly magazine." Pays $500, on acceptance. Submit material in January, April, July, and October; allow 3 months for response. "Send SASE for guidelines before submitting."

GOOD HOUSEKEEPING—959 Eighth Ave., New York, NY 10019. Lee Quarfoot, Fiction Ed. Short stories, 1,000 to 3,000 words, with strong identification figures for women, by published writers and "beginners with demonstrable talent." Novel condensations or excerpts from about-to-be-published books only. "Writers whose work interests us will hear from us within 8 weeks of receipt of manuscript. Please send inexpensive copies of your work; and do not enclose SASEs or postage. We can no longer return or critique manuscripts. We do accept multiple submissions, but we do not accept submissions by e-mail or fax." Pays top rates, on acceptance.

GRIT—1503 S.W. 42nd St., Topeka, KS 66609. Donna Doyle, Ed.-in-Chief. Short stories, 850 to 2,000 words. Articles, 500 to 1,200 words, on interesting people and topics; also serial fiction, 3,500 to 15,000 words. Should be upbeat, inspirational, wholesome and interesting to mature adults. No reference to drinking, smoking, drugs, sex, or violence. Also publishes true-story nostalgia. Pays 22¢ a word, extra for photos, on publication. All fiction submissions should be marked "Fiction Dept." Send for guidelines and sample copy.

GUIDEPOSTS FOR KIDS—P.O. Box 638, Chesterton, IN 46304. Mary Lou Carney, Ed. Value-centered bimonthly for 7- to 12-year-olds. Problem fiction, mysteries, historicals, 1,000 to 1,400 words, with "realistic dialogue and sharp imagery. No preachy stories about Bible-toting children." Pays $300 to $500 for all rights, on acceptance. No reprints.

HARDBOILED—Gryphon Publications, P.O. Box 209, Brooklyn, NY 11228-0209. Gary Lovisi, Ed. Hard, cutting-edge crime fiction, to 3,000 words, "with impact." "It's a good idea to read an issue before submitting a story." Payment varies, on publication. Query for articles, book and film reviews.

HARPER'S MAGAZINE— 666 Broadway, New York, NY 10012. Attn: Eds. Will consider unsolicited fiction manuscripts. Query for nonfiction (very limited market). No poetry. SASE required.

HIGHLIGHTS FOR CHILDREN— 803 Church St., Honesdale, PA 18431-1824. Christine French Clark, Man. Ed. Fiction on sports, humor, adventure, mystery, etc., 900 words, for 8- to 12-year-olds. Easy rebus form, 100 to 120 words, and easy-to-read stories, to 500 words, for beginning readers. "We are partial to stories in which the protagonist solves a dilemma through his or her own resources." Pays from 14¢ a word, on acceptance. Buys all rights.

HOMETOWN PRESS—2007 Gallatin St., Huntsville, AL 35801. Jeffrey C. Hindman, M.D., Ed.-in-Chief. Fiction, 800 to 2,500 words, well-crafted and tightly written, suitable for family reading. New and unpublished writers welcome. Guidelines.

THE JOYFUL WOMAN—P.O. Box 90028, Chattanooga, TN 37412. Joy Rice Martin, Ed. First-person inspirational true stories and sketches, 500 to 1,000 words; occasionally uses some fiction. Pays 3¢ to 4¢ a word, on publication.

LADIES' HOME JOURNAL— 125 Park Ave., New York, NY 10017. Fiction; only accepted through agents.

THE MAGAZINE OF FANTASY AND SCIENCE FICTION—Box 1806, Madison Sq. Station, New York, NY 10159. Gordon Van Gelder, Ed. Fantasy and science fiction stories, to 15,000 words. Pays 5¢ to 7¢ a word, on acceptance.

MATURE LIVING—127 Ninth Ave. N., Nashville, TN 37234. Al Shackleford, Ed. Fiction, 900 to 1,200 words, for senior adults. Must be consistent with Christian principles. Pays $75, on acceptance.

MIDSTREAM—110 E. 59th St., New York, NY 10022. Joel Carmichael, Man. Ed. Fiction with a Jewish/Zionist reference, to 3,000 words. Pays 5¢ a word, after publication. Allow one month for response.

NA'AMAT WOMAN—200 Madison Ave., 21st Fl., New York, NY 10016. Judith A. Sokoloff, Ed. Short stories, approximately 2,500 words, with Jewish theme. Pays 10¢ a word, on publication.

NEW MYSTERY MAGAZINE—The Flatiron Bldg., 175 Fifth Ave., Suite 2001, New York, NY 10010-7703. Charles Raisch, Ed. Quarterly. Mystery, crime, detection, and suspense short stories, 2,000 to 6,000 words, with "sympathetic characters in trouble and visual scenes." Book reviews, 250 to 2,000 words, of upcoming or recently published novels. Pays 3¢ to 10¢ a word, on publication. No guidelines; study back issues.

THE NEW YORKER—20 W. 43rd St., New York, NY 10036. Attn: Fiction Dept. Short stories, humor, and satire. Payment varies, on acceptance.

PLAYBOY— 680 N. Lake Shore Dr., Chicago, IL 60611. Alice K. Turner, Fiction Ed. Limited market.

PLAYGIRL— 801 Second Ave., New York, NY 10017. Judy Cole, Ed.-in-Chief. Contemporary, erotic fiction, from a female perspective, 3,000 to 4,000 words. "Fantasy Forum," 1,000 to 2,000 words. Pays from $200; $25 to $100 for "Fantasy Forum", after acceptance.

POWER AND LIGHT— 6401 The Paseo, Kansas City, MO 64131. Beula J. Postlewait, Preteen Ed. Fiction, 500 to 800 words, for grades 5 to 6, defining Christian experiences and values. Pays 5¢ a word for multiple-use rights, on publication.

PURPOSE— 616 Walnut Ave., Scottdale, PA 15683-1999. James E. Horsch, Ed. Fiction, 750 words, on problem solving from a Christian point of view. Poetry, 3 to 12 lines. Pays to 5¢ a word for fiction; to $1 per line for poetry, on acceptance.

QUEEN'S QUARTERLY—Queens Univ., Kingston, Ont., Canada K7L 3N6. Attn: Fiction Ed. Fiction, to 5,000 words, in English and French. Pays to $300, on publication.

RANGER RICK— 8925 Leesburg Pike, Vienna, VA 22184. Deborah Churchman, Fiction Ed. Action-packed nature-and conservation-related fiction, to 900 words, for 6- to 12-year-olds. No anthropomorphism. "Multicultural stories welcome." Pays to $550, on acceptance. Buys all rights. Guidelines.

REDBOOK—224 W. 57th St., New York, NY 10019. Dawn Raffel, Fiction Ed. Fresh, distinctive short stories, of interest to women. No unsolicited poetry, novellas, or novels accepted. Pays from $1,500 for short stories (to 25 pages), on acceptance. Allow 12 weeks for reply.

ST. ANTHONY MESSENGER—1615 Republic St., Cincinnati, OH 45210-1298. Norman Perry, O.F.M., Ed. Barbara Beckwith, Man. Ed. Fiction that makes readers think about issues, lifestyles, and values. Pays 15¢ a word, on acceptance. Queries or manuscripts accepted.

SCHOOL MATES—U.S. Chess Federation, 3054 NYS Rt. 9W, New Windsor, NY 12553-7698. Jay Hastings, Publications Dir. Fiction and articles, 250 to 800 words, and short fillers, related to chess for beginning chess players (primarily children, ages 6 to 16). "Instructive, but there's room for fun puzzles, anecdotes, etc. All chess related." Pays from $20, on publication. Query; limited free-lance market.

SEA KAYAKER—P.O. Box 17170, Seattle, WA 98107-0870. Christopher Cunningham, Ed. Short stories exclusively related to ocean kayaking, 1,000 to 3,000 words. Pays on publication.

SEVENTEEN— 850 Third Ave., New York, NY 10022. Ben Shrank, Fiction Ed. High-quality, literary short fiction, to 4,000 words. Pays on acceptance.

SPORTS AFIELD—250 W. 55th St., New York, NY 10019. Terry McDonell, Ed-in-Chief. Occasional fiction, 1,500 words maximum, on hunting, fishing, outdoor and nature-related topics. Humor. Payment varies, on acceptance.

STRAIGHT— 8121 Hamilton Ave., Cincinnati, OH 45231. Heather E. Wallace, Ed. Well-constructed fiction, 1,000 to 1,500 words, showing Christian teens using Bible principles in everyday life. Contemporary, realistic teen characters a must. Most interested in school, church, dating, and family life stories. Pays 5¢ to 7¢ a word, on acceptance. Guidelines.

'TEEN— 6420 Wilshire Blvd., Los Angeles, CA 90048-5515. Attn: Fiction Dept. Short stories, 2,500 to 4,000 words: mystery, teen situations, adventure, romance, humor for teens. Pays from $200, on acceptance.

TEEN LIFE—1445 Boonville Ave., Springfield, MO 65802-1894. Tammy Bicket, Ed. Fiction, to 1,200 words, for 13- to 19-year-olds. Articles, 500 to 1,000 words. Strong evangelical emphasis a must: believable characters working out their problems according to biblical principles. Buys first rights; pays on acceptance. Reprints considered.

TRUE CONFESSIONS—233 Park Ave. S., New York, NY 10003. Pat Byrdsong, Ed. Timely, emotional, first-person stories, 2,000 to 10,000 words, on romance, family life, and problems of today's young blue-collar women. Pays 5¢ a word, after publication.

VIRGINIA—The Country Publishers, Inc., P.O. Box 798, Berryville, VA 22611. Garrison Ellis, Ed. Quarterly. Fiction, 1,500 to 2,000 words, with Virginia setting or reference. Pays $200 to $300, 30 days after publication.

VIRTUE: HELPING WOMEN BUILD CHRIST-LIKE CHARACTER— (formerly *Virtue: The Christian Magazine for Women*) 4050 Lee Vance View, Colorado Springs, CO 80918-7102. Laura J. Barker, Ed. Fiction, 1,200 to 1,400 words, with a Christian slant; inspirational, women's spiritual journeys, women's perspectives. Pays 15¢ to 25¢ a word, on publication. Query with SASE for articles.

WESTERN PEOPLE—Box 2500, Saskatoon, Sask., Canada S7K 2C4. Attn: Ed. Short stories, 1,200 to 2,500 words, on subjects or themes of interest to rural readers in western Canada. Pays $100 to $200, on acceptance. Enclose international reply coupons and SAE.

WOMAN'S WORLD—270 Sylvan Ave., Englewood Cliffs, NJ 07632. Attn: Fiction Dept. Fast-moving short stories, 1,500 to 1,600 words, with light romantic theme. (Specify "short story" on outside of envelope.) Mini-mysteries, 1,000 words, with "whodunit" or "howdunit" theme. No science fiction, fantasy, or historical romance and no horror, ghost stories, or gratuitous violence. "Dialogue-driven romances help propel the story." Pays $1,000 for short stories, $500 for mini-mysteries, on acceptance. SASE for guidelines.

YANKEE—Yankee Publishing Co., P.O. Box 520, Dublin, NH 03444. Judson Hale, Ed. Edie Clark, Fiction Ed. High-quality, literary short fiction, to 3,000 words (shorter preferred), with New England setting; no sap buckets or lobster pot stereotypes. Pays $1,000, on acceptance.

DETECTIVE & MYSTERY

ALFRED HITCHCOCK MYSTERY MAGAZINE—1270 Ave. of the Americas, New York, NY 10020. Cathleen Jordan, Ed. Well-plotted, previously unpublished mystery, detective, suspense, and crime short stories, to 14,000 words. Submissions by new writers strongly encouraged. Pays 8¢ a word, on acceptance. No simultaneous submissions, please. (Submissions sent to

AHMM are not considered for, or read by, *Ellery Queen's Mystery Magazine,* and vice versa.) Guidelines with SASE.

ARMCHAIR DETECTIVE—549 Park Ave., Suite 252, Scotch Plains, NJ 07076-1705. Judi Vause, Man. Ed./Pub. Articles on mystery and detective fiction; biographical sketches, reviews, etc. No fiction. Pays $12 a printed page; reviews are unpaid.

COZY DETECTIVE MYSTERY MAGAZINE— 686 Jake Ct., McMinnville, OR 97128. David Rowell Workman, Sr. Ed. Mystery and suspense, fiction and nonfiction, to 5,000 words. Poems, to 20 lines. Pays in copies.

ELLERY QUEEN'S MYSTERY MAGAZINE—1270 Ave. of the Americas, 10th Fl., New York, NY 10020. Janet Hutchings, Ed. Detective, crime, and mystery fiction, approximately 1,500 to 10,000 words. Occasionally publishes novelettes, to 20,000 words, by established authors and humorous mystery verse. No sex, sadism, or sensationalism. Particularly interested in new writers and "first stories." Pays 3¢ to 8¢ a word, occasionally higher for established authors, on acceptance.

HARDBOILED—Gryphon Publications, P.O. Box 209, Brooklyn, NY 11228-0209. Gary Lovisi, Ed. Hard, cutting-edge crime fiction (suspense, noir, private eye) to 3,000 words. Payment varies, on publication. Query for articles, book and film reviews, and longer fiction (or novel excerpts).

MURDEROUS INTENT—P.O. Box 5947, Vancouver, WA 98668-5947. Margo Power, Ed./Pub. Quarterly. Mystery and suspense stories and mystery-related articles, 2,000 to 4,000 words; fillers, to 750 words; poems, to 30 lines. "We see way too many stories of husband and wife bumping each other off. We love humor in mysteries. Surprise us!" Pays $10, on acceptance. Query for nonfiction.

MYSTERY TIME—P.O. Box 2907, Decatur, IL 62524. Linda Hutton, Ed. Semiannual. Suspense, 1,500 words, and poems about mysteries, up to 16 lines. "We prefer female protagonists. No gore or violence." Pays $5, on acceptance.

NEW MYSTERY MAGAZINE—The Flatiron Bldg., 175 Fifth Ave., Suite 2001, New York, NY 10010-7703. Charles Raisch, Ed. Mystery, crime, detection, and suspense short stories, 2,000 to 6,000 words. No true crime. Book reviews, 250 to 2,000 words, of upcoming or recently published novels. Pays $15 to $300, on publication. No guidelines; study back issues.

OVER MY DEAD BODY!—P.O. Box 1778, Auburn, WA 98071-1778. Cherie Jung, Features Ed. Mystery, suspense, and crime fiction, to 4,000 words. Author profiles, interviews, and mystery-related travel, 750 to 1,500 words. Fillers, to 100 words. Include B&W photos. "We are entertainment for mystery fans, from cozy to hardboiled and everything in between." Pays 1¢ a word for fiction; $10 to $25 for nonfiction; $5 for fillers; $10 to $25 for illustrations, on publication.

RED HERRING MYSTERY MAGAZINE—P.O. Box 8278, Prairie Village, KS 66208. Attn: Eds. Quarterly. Mystery fiction, 2,500 to 6,000 words. Mystery-related poetry (to 30 lines), fillers, puzzles and B&W line drawings. No gratuitous sex or violence. No true crime. Pays $10 plus copy, on publication.

WHISPERING WILLOWS MYSTERY MAGAZINE—P.O. Box 890294, Oklahoma City, OK 73189-0294. Darlene Hoffman, Acquisitions Ed. Quarterly. Mystery and mystery/suspense, 500 to 5,000 words. Nonfiction, 500 to 1,250 words: mysterious personal experiences and interviews with police officers and detectives about their on-the-job experiences. "No explicit sex, gore, or extreme violence." Pays 4¢ a word, on publication.

SCIENCE FICTION & FANTASY

ABERRATIONS—P.O. Box 460430, San Francisco, CA 94146. Richard Blair, Man. Ed. Science fiction, horror, and fantasy, to 8,000 words. "Experimental, graphic, multi-genre is O.K. with science fiction/fantasy/horror tie-in." Pays 1/2¢ a word, on publication. Guidelines.

ABORIGINAL SF—P.O. Box 2449, Woburn, MA 01888-0849. Charles C. Ryan, Ed. Short stories, 2,500 to 7,500 words, and poetry, one to 2 typed pages, with strong science content, lively, unique characters, and well-designed plots. No sword and sorcery, horror, or fantasy. Pays $200 for fiction, $15 for poetry, $4 for science fiction jokes, and $20 for cartoons, on publication.

ABSOLUTE MAGNITUDE—P.O. Box 13, Greenfield, MA 01302. Warren Lapine, Ed. Quarterly. Character-driven technical science fiction, 1,000 to 25,000 words. No fantasy, horror, satire, or funny science fiction. Pays 3¢ to 5¢ a word (1¢ a word for reprints), on publication. Guidelines.

ADVENTURES OF SWORD & SORCERY—P.O. Box 285, Xenia, OH 45385. Randy Dannenfelser, Ed. Quarterly. High fantasy and heroic fantasy, 1,000 to 8,000 words. Pays 3¢ to 6¢ a word, on acceptance.

ANALOG SCIENCE FICTION AND FACT—1270 Ave. of the Americas, New York, NY 10020. Stanley Schmidt, Ed. Science fiction with strong characters in believable future or alien setting: short stories, 2,000 to 7,500 words; novelettes, 10,000 to 20,000 words; serials, to 80,000 words. Also uses future-related articles. Pays to 7¢ a word, on acceptance. Query for serials and articles.

ASIMOV'S SCIENCE FICTION MAGAZINE—1270 Ave. of the Americas, New York, NY 10020. Gardner Dozois, Ed. Short, character-oriented science fiction and fantasy, to 15,000 words. Pays 5¢ to 8¢ a word, on acceptance. Guidelines.

DRAGON MAGAZINE—201 Sheridan Springs Rd., Lake Geneva, WI 53147. Dave Gross, Ed. Articles, 1,500 to 7,500 words, on fantasy and science fiction role-playing games. Fantasy, 1,500 to 8,000 words. Pays 5¢ to 8¢ a word for fiction, on acceptance. Pays 4¢ a word for articles, on publication. All submissions must include a disclosure form. Guidelines.

FANGORIA— 475 Park Ave. S., 8th Fl., New York, NY 10016. Anthony Timpone, Ed. Published 10 times yearly. Movie, TV, and book previews, reviews, and interviews, 1,800 to 2,500 words, in connection with upcoming horror films. "A strong love of the genre and an appreciation and understanding of the magazine are essential." Pays $175 to $225, on publication.

FANTASY & TERROR—See *Fantasy Macabre.*

FANTASY MACABRE—P.O. Box 20610, Seattle, WA 98102. Jessica Salmonson, Ed. Fiction, to 3,000 words, including translations. "We look for a tale that is strong in atmosphere, with menace that is suggested and threatening rather than the result of dripping blood and gore." Pays 1¢ a word, to $30 per story, on publication. Also publishes *Fantasy & Terror* for poetry-in-prose pieces.

FORTRESS—P.O. Box 22, Fairview, PA 16415. Bryan Lindenberger, Ed. Science fiction and historical fantasy with strong and overt relationship to chess, to 10,000 words (3,500 words preferred length). Related fillers, to 100 words. Pays $20 to $30, on publication.

HAUNTS—Nightshade Publications, Box 8068, Cranston, RI 02920-0068. Joseph K. Cherkes, Ed. Horror, fantasy, and science fiction with strong character development and solid plots, 1,500 to 8,000 words. No explicit sexual scenes, famous rewrites, or pure adventure. Pays $5 to $50 for fiction; $3 per poem (submit up to 3), on publication. Manuscripts read January 1st through June 1st. SASE.

HOBSON'S CHOICE: SCIENCE FICTION AND TECHNOLOGY—The Starwind Press, P.O. Box 98, Ripley, OH 45167. Attn: Submissions Ed. Science fiction and fantasy, 2,000 to 10,000 words. Articles and literary criticism, 1,000 to 5,000 words, for readers interested in science and technology. Query for nonfiction. Pays 1¢ to 4¢ a word, on acceptance.

IN DARKNESS ETERNAL—Stygian Vortex Publications, 1085 N.E. 179th Terrace, N. Miami Beach, FL 33162-1256. Glenda Woodrum, Ed.-in-Chief. T'shai K., Fiction and Poetry Ed. Annual. Stories, articles, and artwork by and for vampire enthusiasts. "All stories must have a vampire as either the protagonist or antagonist. Stories must take place in a pre-industrial setting prior to the year 1700." No stories about serial killers, prostitutes, or anything involving people becoming vampires from the bite of a vampire; no Dracula or other media related vampire tales. Payment is 50¢ per published page; $1 to $3 for poetry. Query. Guidelines.

THE LEADING EDGE—3163 JKHB, Provo, UT 84602. David Barnett, Ed. Semiannual. Science fiction and fantasy, 3,000 to 12,000 words; poetry, to 600 lines; and articles, to 8,000 words, on science, scientific speculation, and literary criticism. No excessive profanity, overt violence, or excessive sexual situations. No simultaneous submissions. Pays $10 to $100, on publication. Guidelines.

LORDS OF ETERNAL DARKNESS—Stygian Vortex Publications, 1085 N.E. 179th Terrace, N. Miami Beach, FL 33162-1256. Glenda Woodrum, Ed.-in-Chief. T'shai K., Ed. Annual; stories for supernatural horror fiction enthusiasts. "We want tales in the style of the masters of supernatural horror." Payment is 50¢ per "our text page," $1 to $3 per poem. Query. Guidelines.

LORDS OF THE ABYSS: TALES OF HORROR—Stygian Vortex Publications, 1085 N.E. 179th Terrace, N. Miami Beach, FL 33162-1256. Glenda Woodrum, Ed.-in-Chief. Annual. Stories for horror enthusiasts. No length limits on fiction; query for stories over 9,000 words. Some book and movie reviews, to 500 words. "No serial killers, rapists, insane people, child molesters, demonically possessed vehicles, or psycho killers." Pays 50¢ per published page; $1 to $3 per poem, on publication, and one copy. Guidelines.

THE MAGAZINE OF FANTASY AND SCIENCE FICTION—Box 1806, Madison Sq. Station, New York, NY 10159-1806. Gordon Van Gelder, Ed. Fantasy and science fiction stories, to 10,000 words. Pays 5¢ to 7¢ a word, on acceptance.

MAGIC REALISM—P.O. Box 922648, Sylmar, CA 91392-2648. C. Darren Butler, Ed. Julie Thomas, Man. Ed. Quarterly. Stories, to 8,000 words (4,000 words preferred), of magic realism, exaggerated realism, some genre fantasy/dark fantasy. Occasionally publish glib fantasy like that found in folktales, fairy tales, and myths. No occult, sleight-of-hand magicians, high fantasy, or wizards/witches. Pays 1/4¢ per word for prose; $3 per page for poetry. SASE for guidelines.

MARION ZIMMER BRADLEY'S FANTASY MAGAZINE—P.O. Box 249, Berkeley, CA 94701. Marion Zimmer Bradley, Ed. Quarterly. Well-plotted stories, 3,500 to 4,000 words. Action and adventure fantasy "with no particular objection to modern settings." Send SASE for guidelines before submitting. Pays 3¢ to 10¢ a word, on acceptance.

NEURONET: STORIES FROM THE CYBERLAND—Stygian Vortex Publications, 1085 N.E. 179th Terrace, N. Miami Beach, FL 33162-1256. Glenda Woodrum, Ed.-in-Chief. Annual. Cyberpunk fiction. "All stories should be hard-hitting, gritty, and filled with the grim nature of the cyberpunk future." No length limits; query for over 8,500 words. Pays 50¢ per published page, $1 to $3 per poem, on publication, plus one copy. Guidelines.

NEXT PHASE—Phantom Press Publications, 13 Appleton Rd., Nantucket Island, MA 02554. Kim Guarnaccia, Ed. Science fiction, fantasy, experimental fiction, and commentary, to 3,000 words, and interviews with authors, poets, or artists. Poetry, any length. "We prefer upbeat, environmentally or socially conscious fiction." Pays in copies.

NIGHT TERRORS—1202 W. Market St., Orrville, OH 44667-1710. Mr. D. E. Davidson, Ed. Stories of psychological horror, the supernatural or occult, from 2,000 to 5,000 words. Pays in copies.

OMNI—General Media International, 277 Park Ave., 4th Fl., New York, NY 10172-0003. Ellen Datlow, Fiction Ed. On-line magazine. Strong, realistic science fiction, 2,000 to 10,000 words, with good characterizations. "We want to intrigue our readers with mind-broadening, thought-provoking stories that will excite their sense of wonder." Some fantasy. No horror, ghost, or sword and sorcery tales. Pays $1,300 to $2,250, on acceptance. SASE.

PIRATE WRITINGS: TALES OF FANTASY, MYSTERY & SCIENCE FICTION—P.O. Box 329, Brightwaters, NY 11718-0329. Edward J. McFadden, Pub./Ed. Tom Piccirilli, Assoc. Ed. Mystery, science fiction, fantasy, 250 to 6,000 words. Poetry, to 20 lines. Pays 1¢ to 5¢ a word, on publication.

SCAVENGER'S NEWSLETTER—519 Ellinwood, Osage City, KS 66523. Janet Fox, Ed. Fiction, 1,200 words, in the genres of science fiction, fantasy, horror, and mystery. Articles, 1,000 words, pertaining to writing and art in those genres. Poems, to 10 lines, and humor, 500 to 700 words, for writers and artists. "Most of the magazine is market information." Pays $4 for fiction, articles, and cover art; $2 for humor, poems, and inside art, on acceptance.

SCIENCE FICTION CHRONICLE—P.O. Box 022730, Brooklyn, NY 11202-0056. Andrew Porter, Ed. News items, 200 to 500 words, for science fiction and fantasy readers, professionals, and booksellers. Interviews with authors, 2,500 to 4,000 words. No fiction. Pays 3 1/2¢ to 5¢ a word, on publication. Query.

THE SCREAM FACTORY—Deadline Press, 16473 Redwood Lodge Rd., Los Gatos, CA 95030. Bob Morrish, Ed. Quarterly. Articles, 1,000 to 7,000 words, on horror fiction and film. Interviews, 750 to 4,000 words, with authors and directors; brief, analytical reviews, 100 to 400 words, of old and new books. No fiction. Query. Pays 1/2¢ a word, on publication.

SHADOW SWORD—Stygian Vortex Publications, 1085 N.E. 179th Terrace, N. Miami Beach, FL 33162-1256. Glenda J. Woodrum, Ed. Quarterly, plus 2 special issues each year. Stories, articles, and artwork for fantasy enthusiasts: heroic fantasy, sword and sorcery, high fantasy, and dark fantasy. "No 'cute' stories or fantasies set in a version of the real technological world." Pays 50¢ per published page, $1 to $3 for poetry, and one copy, on publication. Query for stories over 8,500 words. Guidelines.

SHAPESHIFTER!—Stygian Vortex Publications, 1085 N.E. 179th Terrace, N. Miami Beach, FL 33162-1256. Coyote Osborne, Ed. Annual. Stories, articles, and artwork on lycanthropes, shape-changers, and partly human creatures; some book and movie reviews. Query for stories over 9,000 words. "We prefer stories in which the shapeshifters are the heroes/protagonists, not stories in which they ravage a small town, etc." Pays one copy plus 50¢ per published page; $1 to $3 per poem, on publication. Guidelines.

TALEBONES—Fairwood Press, 10531 S.E. 250th Pl., #104, Kent, WA 98031. Patrick and Honna Swenson, Eds. Science fiction and dark fantasy, to 5,000 words. Articles, to 3,000 words, on the state of speculative fiction. Poetry. Cartoons with science fiction or fantasy themes. "I'm looking for science fiction and dark fantasy with strong characters and entertaining story lines. Fiction should be more toward the darker side, without being pure horror." Pays 1¢ a word, on acceptance.

2AM MAGAZINE—P.O. Box 6754, Rockford, IL 61125-1754. Gretta M. Anderson, Ed. Fiction, of varying lengths. "We prefer dark fantasy/horror; great science fiction and sword and sorcery stories are welcome." Profiles and intelligent commentaries. Poetry, to 50 lines. Pays from 1/2¢ a word, on acceptance. Guidelines.

THE ULTIMATE UNKNOWN—Combs Press, P.O. Box 219, Streamwood, IL 60107-0219. David D. Combs, Ed. Fiction and nonfiction on horror, science fiction, and the future, to 3,000 words. Related poetry, to 20 lines. Payment is one copy.

THE URBANITE: SURREAL & LIVELY & BIZARRE—Box 4737, Davenport, IA 52808. Mark McLaughlin, Ed. Published 3 times a year. Dark fantasy, horror (no gore), surrealism, reviews, and social commentary, to 3,000 words. Free verse poems, to 2 pages. Pays 2¢ to 3¢ a word; $10 for poetry, on acceptance. Query for nonfiction.

WORLDS OF FANTASY & HORROR—123 Crooked Ln., King of Prussia, PA 19406-2570. George Scithers, Pub. Darrell Schweitzer, Ed. Quarterly. Fantasy and horror (no science fiction), to 9,000 words. Pays about 3¢, on acceptance. Guidelines.

CONFESSION & ROMANCE

BLACK CONFESSIONS—See *Black Romance.*

BLACK ROMANCE—233 Park Ave. S., New York, NY 10003. Marcia Y. Mahan, Ed. Romance fiction, 4,500 to 5,000 words, and relationship articles. Queries preferred. Pays $100 to $125, on publication. Also publishes *Black Secrets, Bronze Thrills, Black Confessions,* and *Jive.* Guidelines.

BLACK SECRETS—See *Black Romance.*

BRONZE THRILLS—See *Black Romance.*

INTIMACY—233 Park Ave. S., 7th Fl., New York, NY 10003. Marcia Y. Mahan, Ed. Fiction, 5,000 to 5,800 words, for black women ages 18 to 45;

must have contemporary plot and contain 2 romantic and intimate love scenes. Pays $100 to $125, on publication. Guidelines.

JIVE—See *Black Romance.*

MODERN ROMANCES—233 Park Ave. S., New York, NY 10003. Colleen M. Murphy, Ed. Romantic and topical confession stories, 2,000 to 10,000 words, with reader-identification and strong emotional tone. Pays 5¢ a word, after publication. Buys all rights.

ROMANTIC HEARTS—P.O. Box 450669, Westlake, OH 44145. Debra Krauss, Ed./Pub. Short romantic fiction, 1,500 to 4,000 words; related how-to articles and essays with a romantic theme, 500 to 2,000 words; love poems, to 25 lines."We are looking for heartwarming tales of love and romance that are rich with emotion and strong characterization." Pays in copies. Guidelines.

TRUE CONFESSIONS—233 Park Ave. S., New York, NY 10003. Pat Byrdsong, Ed. Timely, emotional, first-person stories, 2,000 to 10,000 words, on romance, family life, and problems of today's young blue-collar women. Pays 5¢ a word, after publication.

TRUE EXPERIENCE—233 Park Ave. S., New York, NY 10003. Rose Bernstein, Ed. Heather Young, Assoc. Ed. Realistic first-person stories, 1,000 to 12,000 words, on family life, single life, love, romance, overcoming hardships, mysteries. Pays 3¢ a word, after publication.

TRUE LOVE—233 Park Ave. S., New York, NY 10003. Kristina M. Pappalardo, Ed. Fresh, young, true-to-life stories, on love and topics of current interest. Must be written in the past tense and first person. Pays 3¢ a word, after publication. Guidelines.

TRUE ROMANCE—233 Park Ave. S., New York, NY 10003. Pat Vitucci, Ed. True or true-to-life, dramatic and/or romantic first-person stories, 3,000 to 10,000 words. All genres: tragedy, mystery, peril, love, family struggles, etc. Topical themes. Love poems. "We enjoy working with new writers." Reports in 3 to 5 months. Pays 3¢ a word, a month after publication.

POETRY MARKETS

As the following list attests, the market for poetry in general magazines is rather limited: There aren't many general-interest magazines that use poetry, and in those that do, the competition to break into print is stiff, since editors use only a limited number of poems in each issue. In addition to the magazines listed here, writers may find their local newspapers receptive to poetry.

While poetry may be scant in general-interest magazines, it is the backbone of a majority of the college, little, and literary magazines (see page 693). Poets will also find a number of competitions offering cash awards for unpublished poems in the *Literary Prize Offers* list.

ALOHA, THE MAGAZINE OF HAWAII AND THE PACIFIC—P.O. Box 3260, Honolulu, HI 96801. Cheryl Chee Tsutsumi, Ed. Poetry relating to Hawaii. Pays $30 per poem, on publication.

AMERICA—106 W. 56th St., New York, NY 10019. Patrick Samway, S.J., Literary Ed. Serious poetry, preferably in contemporary prose idiom, 10 to 25 lines. Occasional light verse. Submit 2 or 3 poems at a time. Pays $1.40 per line, on publication. Guidelines. SASE required.

THE AMERICAN SCHOLAR—1811 Q St. N.W., Washington, DC 20009-9974. Joseph Epstein, Ed. Highly original poetry for college-educated, intellectual readers. Pays $50, on acceptance.

ASIAN PAGES—P.O. Box 11932, St. Paul, MN 55111-0932. Cheryl Weiberg, Ed.-in-Chief. Poetry, 100 words, with "a strong, non-offensive Asian slant." Pays on publication.

THE ATLANTIC MONTHLY—77 N. Washington St., Boston, MA 02114. Peter Davison, Poetry Ed. Previously unpublished poetry of highest quality. Limited market; only 2 to 3 poems an issue. Interested in new poets. Occasionally uses light verse. "No simultaneous submissions; we make prompt decisions." Pays excellent rates, on acceptance.

CAPPER'S—1503 S.W. 42nd St., Topeka, KS 66609-1265. Nancy Peavler, Ed. Free verse, light verse, traditional, nature, and inspirational poems, 4 to 16 lines, with simple everyday themes. Submit up to 6 poems at a time, with SASE. Pays $10 to $15, on acceptance.

CHILDREN'S PLAYMATE—P.O. Box 567, Indianapolis, IN 46206. Terry Harshman, Ed. Poetry for children, 6 to 8 years old, on good health, nutrition, exercise, safety, seasonal and humorous subjects. Pays from $25, on publication. Buys all rights.

THE CHRISTIAN SCIENCE MONITOR—One Norway St., Boston, MA 02115. Elizabeth Lund, Poetry Ed. Finely crafted poems that celebrate the extraordinary in the ordinary. Seasonal material always needed. No violence, sensuality, racism, death and disease, helplessness, hopelessness. Short poems preferred; submit no more than 5 poems at a time. SASE required. Pays varying rates, on publication.

COMMONWEAL—15 Dutch St., New York, NY 10038. Rosemary Deen, Poetry Ed. Catholic. Serious, witty poetry. Pays 50¢ a line, on publication. SASE required. No submissions accepted June to September.

COMPLETE WOMAN—Dept. P, 875 N. Michigan Ave., Suite 3434, Chicago, IL 60611. Attn: Poetry Ed. Send poetry with SASE. Pays in one copy.

COUNTRY WOMAN—P.O. Box 989, Greendale, WI 53129. Kathy Pohl, Man. Ed. Traditional rural poetry and light verse, 4 to 30 lines, on rural experiences and country living; also seasonal poetry. Poems must rhyme. Pays $10 to $25, on acceptance.

EVANGEL—Light and Life Communications, Box 535002, Indianapolis, IN 46253-5002. Julie Innes, Ed. Free Methodist. Devotional or nature poetry, 8 to 16 lines. Pays $10, on publication.

MATURE YEARS—201 Eighth Ave. S., P.O. Box 801, Nashville, TN 37202. Marvin W. Cropsey, Ed. United Methodist. Poetry, to 14 lines, on preretirement, retirement, Christianity, inspiration, seasonal subjects, aging. No "saccharine" poetry. Submit up to 6 poems at a time. Pays 50¢ to $1 per line.

MIDSTREAM—110 E. 59th St., New York, NY 10022. Attn: Poetry Ed. Poetry of Jewish interest. "Brevity highly recommended." Pays $25, on publication. Allow 3 months for response.

THE MIRACULOUS MEDAL— 475 E. Chelten Ave., Philadelphia, PA 19144-5785. William J. O'Brien, C.M., Ed. Catholic. Religious verse, to 20 lines. Pays 50¢ a line, on acceptance.

MODERN BRIDE—249 W. 17th St., New York, NY 10011. Mary Ann Cavlin, Exec. Ed. Short verse of interest to bride and groom. Pays $25 to $35, on acceptance.

THE NATION—72 Fifth Ave., New York, NY 10011. Grace Schulman, Poetry Ed. Poetry of high quality. Pays after publication. SASE required.

NATIONAL ENQUIRER—Lantana, FL 33463. Kathy Martin, Fillers Ed. Short poems, with traditional rhyming verse, of an amusing, philosophical, or inspirational nature. No experimental poetry. Original epigrams, humorous anecdotes, and "daffynitions." Submit seasonal/holiday material at least 2 months in advance. Pays $25, after publication. Material will not be returned; do not send SASE.

THE NEW REPUBLIC—1220 19th St. N.W., Washington, DC 20036. Attn: Mark Strand, Ed. Pays $100, after publication.

THE NEW YORKER—20 W. 43rd St., New York, NY 10036. Attn: Poetry Ed. First-rate poetry. Pays top rates, on acceptance. Include SASE.

PATHWAYS—Christian Board of Publication, Box 179, St. Louis, MO 63166. Deana L. Perdue, Ed. Short poems by 12- to 15-year-olds. Pays 30¢ a line, on publication. SASE.

PURPOSE— 616 Walnut Ave., Scottdale, PA 15683-1999. James E. Horsch, Poetry Ed. Poetry, to 8 lines, with challenging Christian discipleship angle. Pays 50¢ to $1.65 a line, on acceptance.

RADIANCE: THE MAGAZINE FOR LARGE WOMEN—P.O. Box 30246, Oakland, CA 94604. Alice Ansfield, Ed./Pub. Quarterly. Poetry, fiction, and essays for women. Payment varies, on publication.

ST. JOSEPH'S MESSENGER—P.O. Box 288, Jersey City, NJ 07303-0288. Sister Ursula Maphet, Ed. Light verse and traditional poetry, 4 to 40 lines. Pays $5 to $20, on publication.

THE SATURDAY EVENING POST—P.O. Box 567, Indianapolis, IN 46206. Steven Pettinga, Post Scripts Ed. Light verse and humor. No conventional poetry. SASE required. Pays $15, on publication.

WARRIOR POETS—P.O. Box 7616, Wantagh, NY 11793. R.J. Erbacher, Ed.-in-Chief. "The Magazine of Medieval Poetry." Poetry, any length; some stories about 2,000 words, dealing with swords and chivalry, knights and maidens, love and bravery, sorcery and dragons, warriors, and poets. "Ancient stuff that rings with clashing swords, dragon roars, damsel's screams, and wizard's incantations." Payment is in copies, on publication. Guidelines for SASE.

WESTERN PEOPLE—P.O. Box 2500, Saskatoon, Sask., Canada S7K 2C4. Michael Gillgannon, Man. Ed. Short poetry with Western Canadian themes. Pays on acceptance. Send international reply coupons.

YANKEE—Yankee Publishing Co., P.O. Box 520, Dublin, NH 03444. Jean Burden, Poetry Ed. Serious poetry of high quality, to 30 lines. Pays $50 per poem for all rights, $35 for first rights, on publication. SASE required.

YESTERDAY'S MAGAZETTE—P.O. Box 18566, Sarasota, FL 34276. Ned Burke, Ed. Traditional poetry, to 24 lines. Pays in copies for poetry and short pieces.

COLLEGE, LITERARY, & LITTLE MAGAZINES

The thousands of literary journals, little magazines, and college quarterlies published today welcome work from novices and pros alike; editors are always interested in seeing traditional and experimental fiction, poetry, essays, reviews, short articles, criticism, and satire, and as long as the material is well-written, the fact that a writer is a beginner doesn't adversely affect his or her chances for acceptance.

Most of these smaller publications have small budgets and staffs, so they may be slow in their reporting time; several months is not unusual. In addition, they usually pay only in copies of the issue in which published work appears and some (particularly college magazines) do not read manuscripts during the summer.

Publication in the literary journals can, however, lead to recognition by editors of large-circulation magazines, who read the little magazines in their search for new talent. There is also the possibility of having one's work chosen for reprinting in one of the prestigious annual collections of work from the little magazines.

Because the requirements of these journals differ widely, it is always important to study recent issues before submitting work to one of them. Large libraries may carry a variety of journals, or a writer may send a postcard to the editor and ask the price of a sample copy.

For a complete list of literary and college publications and little magazines, writers may consult such reference works as *The International Directory of Little Magazines and Small Presses*, published annually by Dustbooks (P.O. Box 100, Paradise, CA 95967).

AFRICAN AMERICAN REVIEW—Dept. of English, Indiana State Univ., Terre Haute, IN 47809. Joe Weixlmann, Ed. Essays on African American literature, theater, film, art, and culture; interviews; poems; fiction; and book reviews. Submit up to 6 poems. Pays an honorarium and copies. Query for book review assignments; send 3 copies of all other submissions. Responds in 3 months.

AFRICAN VOICES—270 W. 96th St., New York, NY 10025. Carolyn A. Butts, Exec. Ed. Quarterly. Humorous, erotic, and dramatic fiction, 500 to 2,500 words, by ethnic writers. Nonfiction, 500 to 1,500 words, including investigative articles, artist profiles, essays, and first-person narratives. Pays in copies. SASE.

AGNI—Boston Univ., Creative Writing Program, 236 Bay State Rd., Boston, MA 02215. Askold Melnyczuk, Ed. Valerie Duff, Man. Ed. Short stories, poetry, and reviews. Manuscripts read January 1 to April 30.

ALABAMA LITERARY REVIEW—Troy State Univ., Smith 253, Troy, AL 36082. Theron Montgomery, Chief Ed. Annual. Contemporary, literary fiction and nonfiction, 3,500 words, short drama, to 25 pages, and poetry, to 2 pages. Thought-provoking B&W photos. Pays in copies (honorarium when available). Responds within 3 months.

ALASKA QUARTERLY REVIEW—Univ. of Alaska Anchorage, 3211 Providence Dr., Anchorage, AK 99508. Attn: Eds. Short stories, novel excerpts, short plays, and poetry (traditional and unconventional forms). Submit manuscripts between August 15 and May 15. Pays in copies (and honorarium when funding is available).

ALBATROSS—P.O. Box 7787, North Port, FL 34287-0787. Richard Smyth, Richard Brobst, Eds. High-quality poetry; especially interested in ecological and nature poetry written in narrative form. Interviews with well-known poets. Submit 3 to 5 poems at a time with brief bio. Pays in copies.

AMELIA—329 E St., Bakersfield, CA 93304. Frederick A. Raborg, Jr., Ed. Poetry, to 100 lines; critical essays, to 2,000 words; reviews, to 500 words; belles lettres, to 1,000 words; fiction, to 4,500 words; fine pen-and-ink sketches; photos. Pays $35 for fiction; $25 for criticism; $10 to $25 for other nonfiction and artwork; $2 to $25 for poetry. Annual contest.

THE AMERICAN BOOK REVIEW—Unit for Contemporary Literature, Illinois State Univ., Campus Box 4241, Normal, IL 61790-4241. Paula Goodnight, Man. Ed. Literary book reviews, 700 to 1,200 words. Pays 2-year subscription and copies. Query with clips of published reviews.

AMERICAN LITERARY REVIEW—Univ. of North Texas, P.O. Box 13827, Denton, TX 76203-6827. Barbara Rodman, Ed. Short fiction, to 30 double-spaced pages, and poetry (submit 3 to 5 poems). Pays in copies.

THE AMERICAN POETRY REVIEW—1721 Walnut St., Philadelphia, PA 19103. Attn: Eds. Highest quality contemporary poetry. Responds in 10 weeks.

AMERICAN QUARTERLY—Dept. of English, Georgetown Univ., Washington, DC 20057. Lucy Maddox, Ed. Scholarly essays, 5,000 to 10,000 words, on any aspect of U.S. culture. Pays in copies.

THE AMERICAN SCHOLAR—1811 Q St. N.W., Washington, DC 20009-9974. Joseph Epstein, Ed. Articles, 3,500 to 4,000 words, on science, politics, literature, the arts, etc. Book reviews. Pays up to $500 for articles, $100 for reviews, on publication.

THE AMERICAN VOICE—332 W. Broadway, Suite 1215, Louisville, KY 40202. Frederick Smock, Ed. Published 3 times per year. Avant-garde, literary fiction, nonfiction, and well-crafted poetry, any length (shorter works are preferred). "Please read our journal before attempting to submit." Payment varies, on publication.

AMERICAN WRITING—4343 Manayunk Ave., Philadelphia, PA 19128. Alexandra Grilikhes, Ed. Semiannual. "We encourage experimentation, new writing that takes risks with form, point of view, language, perceptions. We're interested in the voice of the loner, states of being, and initiation." Fiction and nonfiction, to 3,500 words, and poetry. Pays in copies.

AMERICA'S BEAUTIFUL POETRY MAGAZINE—See *Feelings Poetry Journal.*

AMHERST REVIEW—Box 1811, Amherst College, P.O. Box 5000, Amherst, MA 01002-5000. Justin Snider, Ed. Fiction, to 6,000 words. Manuscripts read September through February only. Pays in copies.

ANOTHER CHICAGO MAGAZINE—3709 N. Kenmore, Chicago, IL 60613. Attn: Ed. Semiannual. Fiction, essays on literature, and poetry. "We want writing that's urgent, new, and lives in the world." Pays $5 to $50, on acceptance.

ANTHOLOGY—P.O. Box 4411, Mesa, AZ 85211-4411. Sharon Skinner, Exec. Ed. Bimonthly. Stories, 1,500 words, and nonfiction, 1,000 to 5,000 words, any genre. Poetry, any style, to 100 lines. "We also accept stories based in the fictional city of Haven, where people make their own heroes." Payment is one copy.

ANTIETAM REVIEW—7 W. Franklin St., Hagerstown, MD 21740. Susanne Kass and Ann Knox, Eds.-in-Chief. Fiction and nonfiction (interviews, essays), to 5,000 words; poetry and photography. Submissions from natives or residents of MD, PA, WV, VA, DE, or DC only. Pays from $20 to $100. Guidelines. Manuscripts read September through January.

THE ANTIGONISH REVIEW—St. Francis Xavier Univ., P.O. Box 5000, Antigonish, N.S., Canada B2G 2W5. George Sanderson, Ed. Poetry; short stories, essays, book reviews, 1,800 to 2,500 words. Pays in copies.

ANTIOCH REVIEW—P.O. Box 148, Yellow Springs, OH 45387-0148. Robert S. Fogarty, Ed. Timely articles, 2,000 to 8,000 words, on social sciences, literature, and humanities. Quality fiction. Poetry. No inspirational poetry. Pays $10 per printed page, on publication. Poetry considered from September to May; other material considered year-round.

APPALACHIA—5 Joy St., Boston, MA 02108. Parkman Howe, Poetry Ed. Semiannual publication of the Appalachian Mountain Club. Oldest mountaineering journal in the country covers nature, conservation, climbing, hiking, canoeing, and ecology. Poems, to 30 lines. Pays in copies.

ARACHNE—2363 Page Rd., Kennedy, NY 14747-9717. Susan L. Leach, Ed. Semiannual. Fiction, to 1,500 words. Poems (submit up to 7). "We are looking for rural material and would like first publication rights." No simultaneous submissions. Pays in copies. Manuscripts read in January and July.

ARIZONA QUARTERLY—Univ. of Arizona, Main Library B-541, Tucson, AZ 85721. Edgar A. Dryden, Ed. Criticism of American literature and culture from a theoretical perspective. No poetry or fiction. Pays in copies.

ART TIMES—P.O. Box 730, Mt. Marion, NY 12456. Raymond J. Steiner, Ed. Cheryl A. Rice, Poetry Ed. Fiction, to 1,500 words, and poetry, to 20 lines, for literate, art conscious readers (generally over 40 years old). Feature essays on the arts are staff-written. Pays $25 for fiction, in copies for poetry, on publication.

ARTFUL DODGE—College of Wooster, Wooster, OH 44691. Daniel Bourne, Ed. Annual. Fiction, to 20 pages. Literary essays, especially those involving personal narrative, to 15 pages. Poetry, including translations of contemporary poets; submit 3 to 6 poems at a time; long poems encouraged. Pays $5 per page, on publication, plus 2 copies. Manuscripts read year-round.

THE ASIAN PACIFIC AMERICAN JOURNAL—The Asian American Writers' Workshop, 37 St. Marks Pl., New York, NY 10003-7801. Eric Gamalinda, Eileen Tabios, Eds. Short stories, excerpts from longer fiction works, plays, and essays, 2,000 to 3,000 words, by emerging or established Asian American writers. Poetry (submit 4 to 6 poems). Pays in copies. Query required for reviews and interviews; queries preferred for other articles.

AURA LITERARY/ARTS REVIEW—P.O. Box 76, Univ. Center, UAB, Birmingham, AL 35294. Steve Mullen, Ed. Fiction and essays on literature, to 5,000 words; poetry; B&W photos. Pays in copies. Guidelines.

BANEKE—P.O. Box 2417, Gainesville, FL 32602. Jorge Ibanez, Ed. Articles, book reviews, and interviews on Latino writers and artists. Pays in copies. Query preferred.

BEACON STREET REVIEW—WLP Div., Emerson College, 100 Beacon St., Boston, MA 02116. Attn: Ed. Semiannual. Fiction, memoir, essays, to 20 pages. "Produced and edited by graduate students. We publish primarily writing by students in MFA programs." Send 3 copies of submission, short bio, and SASE. No payment.

THE BEAR ESSENTIAL—P.O. Box 10342, Portland, OR 97296. Thomas L. Webb, Ed. Semiannual. Unique environmental articles, 750 to 2,250 words; essays, 100 to 800 words; artist profiles, 750 to 1,000 words; product watch, 250 to 1,500 words; and reviews, 100 to 1,000 words. Fiction, 750 to 4,500 words (2,500 is ideal). Poetry. Pays 5¢ a word, after publication. Query for nonfiction.

BELLES LETTRES—11151 Captain's Walk Ct., N. Potomac, MD 20878-0441. Janet Mullaney, Ed. Published 3 times a year; devoted to literature by or about women. Articles, 250 to 2,000 words: reviews, interviews, rediscoveries, and retrospectives; columns on publishing news, reprints, and nonfiction titles. Query required. Pays in copies (plus honorarium if funds available).

THE BELLINGHAM REVIEW—The Signpost Press, MS 9053, Western Washington Univ., Bellingham, WA 98225. Robin Hemley, Ed. Semiannual. Fiction and nonfiction, to 10,000 words, and poetry, any length. Pays in copies and subscription. Manuscripts read from October 1 to May 1. Contests. SASE. Guidelines.

BELLOWING ARK—P.O. Box 45637, Seattle, WA 98145. Robert R. Ward, Ed. Bimonthly. Short fiction, poetry, and essays of varying lengths, that portray life as a positive, meaningful process. B&W photos; line drawings. Pays in copies. Manuscripts read year-round.

THE BELOIT FICTION JOURNAL—Box 11, Beloit College, Beloit, WI 53511. Fred Burwell, Ed. Short fiction, one to 35 pages, on all themes. No pornography, political propaganda, religious dogma. Pays in copies. Manuscripts read September to May.

BELOIT POETRY JOURNAL—RFD 2, Box 154, Ellsworth, ME 04605. Attn: Ed. Strong contemporary poetry, of any length or in any mode. Pays in copies. Guidelines. No simultaneous submissions.

BIG SKY STORIES—P.O. Box 477, Choteau, MT 59422. Happy Jack Feder, Ed. Bimonthly. Fiction, 1,000 to 5,000 words and 600 to 800 words, set in Montana or Wyoming before 1950. "Know your history. Our readers know theirs." Payment varies, on publication.

THE BITTER OLEANDER— 4983 Tall Oaks Dr., Fayetteville, NY 13066-9776. Paul B. Roth, Ed./Pub. Short stories, 2,000 to 3,000 words. Poems, one to 100 lines. Pays in copies.

BLACK BEAR REVIEW—Black Bear Publications, 1916 Lincoln St., Croydon, PA 19021-8026. Ave Jeanne, Ed. Semiannual. Book reviews and contemporary poetry. "We publish poems with social awareness, but any well-written piece is considered." Pays in one copy.

BLACK MOON: POETRY OF IMAGINATION—233 Northway Rd., Reistertown, MD 21136. Alan Britt, Ed. Imaginative poetry, long or short. Payment is one copy.

BLACK RIVER REVIEW— 855 Mildred Ave., Lorain, OH 44052-1213. Deborah Gilbert and Kaye Coller, Eds. Contemporary poetry, fiction (to 4,000 words), essays, short book reviews, B&W artwork. No greeting card verse or slick magazine prose. Submit between January 1 and May 1. Pays in copies. SASE. Guidelines.

THE BLACK WARRIOR REVIEW—The Univ. of Alabama, P.O. Box 2936, Tuscaloosa, AL 35486-2936. Mindy Wilson, Ed. Fiction; poetry; translations; reviews and essays. Pays about $100 for fiction; about $40 per poem, on publication. Annual awards. Manuscripts read year-round.

THE BLOOMSBURY REVIEW—1762 Emerson St., Denver, CO 80218. Tom Auer, Ed. Marilyn Auer, Assoc. Ed. Book reviews, publishing features, interviews, essays, poetry. Pays $5 to $25, on publication.

BLUE UNICORN—22 Avon Rd., Kensington, CA 94707. Attn: Ed. Published in October, February, and June. "We are looking for originality of image, thought, and music; we rarely use poems over a page long." Submit up to 5 poems. Artwork used occasionally. Pays in one copy. Guidelines. Contest. SASE.

BLUELINE—English Dept., SUNY, Potsdam, NY 13676. Anthony Tyler, Ed. Essays and fiction, to 3,500 words, on Adirondack region or similar areas. Poems, to 75 lines; submit no more than 5. Pays in copies. Manuscripts read September to November 30.

BORDERLANDS: TEXAS POETRY REVIEW—1501 West 5th St., Suite E-2, Austin, TX 78703. Attn: Ed. Semiannual. "Outward-looking" poetry of a political, spiritual, ecological, or social nature. Bilingual writers and writers from Texas and the Southwest given special attention. Send up to 5 poems. Essays, to 3,000 words, on contemporary poets, especially those from the Southwest. Pays one copy. Query for essays and contest.

BOSTON REVIEW—E53-407, 30 Wadsworth, MIT, Cambridge, MA 02139. Matthew Howard, Man. Ed. Reviews and essays, 800 to 3,000 words, on literature, art, music, film, photography. Original fiction, to 5,000 words. Poetry. Pays $40 to $100. Manuscripts read year-round.

BOTTOMFISH—21250 Stevens Creek Blvd., Cupertino, CA 95014. David Denny, Ed. Annual. Short stories, short-shorts, poetry, creative nonfiction, interviews, photography. Pays in copies. Manuscripts read September to February. (Decisions made in March. Magazine published in April.)

BOULEVARD— 4579 Laclede Ave., #332, St. Louis, MO 63108-2103. Richard Burgin, Ed. Published 3 times a year. High-quality fiction and articles, to 30 pages; poetry. Pays to $250, on publication.

BRIAR CLIFF REVIEW—Briar Cliff College, 3303 Rebecca St., Sioux City, IA 51104. Tricia Currans-Sheehan, Ed. Prose, to 5,000 words: fiction, humor/satire, Siouxland history, thoughtful nonfiction. Also poetry, book reviews, and art. "We're an eclectic literary and cultural magazine focusing on, but not limited to, Siouxland writers and subjects." Pays in copies. Manuscripts read August through October.

BUCKNELL REVIEW—Bucknell Univ., Lewisburg, PA 17837. Attn: Ed. Interdisciplinary journal in book form. Scholarly articles on arts, science, and letters. Pays in copies.

CALLALOO—Univ. of Virginia, Dept. of English, 322 Bryan Hall, Charlottesville, VA 22903. Charles H. Rowell, Ed. Fiction, poetry, drama, and popular essays by, and critical studies and bibliographies on Afro-American, Caribbean, and African artists and writers. Payment varies, on publication.

CALLIOPE—Creative Writing Program, Roger Williams Univ., Bristol, RI 02809-2921. Martha Christina, Ed. Poetry. Pays in copies and subscription. No submissions April through July.

CALYX, A JOURNAL OF ART & LITERATURE BY WOMEN—P.O. Box B, Corvallis, OR 97339. M. Donnelly, Man. Ed. Fiction, 5,000 words; book reviews, 1,000 words (please query about reviews); poetry, to 6 poems. Include short bio. Pays in copies and subscription. Guidelines. Submissions accepted October 1 to November 15.

THE CANDLELIGHT POETRY JOURNAL—P.O. Box 3184, St. Augustine, FL 32085-3184. Carl and Robin Heffley, Eds. Quarterly. Poetry, to 30 lines. (Submit no more than 5 poems.) Articles, 1,000 to 1,500 words, about poetry. Contests. Payment varies. Queries required for articles.

THE CAPE ROCK—Dept. of English, Southeast Missouri State Univ., Cape Girardeau, MO 63701. Harvey E. Hecht, Ed. Semiannual. Poetry, to 70 lines, and B&W photography. (One photographer per issue; pays $100.) Pays in copies and $200 for best poem in each issue. Manuscripts read August to April.

THE CARIBBEAN WRITER—Univ. of the Virgin Islands, RR 02, Box 10,000, Kingshill, St. Croix, USVI 00850. Erika J. Waters, Ed. Annual. Fiction, to 15 pages (submit no more than 2 stories at a time), poems (no more than 5), and personal essays (no more than 2); the Caribbean should be central to the work. Blind submissions policy: place title only on manuscript; name, address, and title of manuscripts on separate sheet. Pays in copies. Annual deadline is September 30.

THE CAROLINA QUARTERLY—Greenlaw Hall CB#3520, Univ. of North Carolina, Chapel Hill, NC 27599-3520. John R. Black, Ed. Fiction, to 7,000 words, by new or established writers. Poetry, to 300 lines; some nonfiction, artwork. Manuscripts read year-round.

THE CENTENNIAL REVIEW—312 Linton Hall, Michigan State Univ., East Lansing, MI 48824-1044. R.K. Meiners, Ed. Articles, 3,000 to 5,000 words, on sciences, humanities, and interdisciplinary topics. Pays in copies.

THE CHARITON REVIEW—Truman State Univ., Kirksville, MO 63501. Jim Barnes, Ed. Highest quality poetry and fiction, to 6,000 words. Modern and contemporary translations. "The only guideline is excellence in all matters."

CHELSEA—Box 773, Cooper Sta., New York, NY 10276. Richard Foerster, Ed. Alfredo de Palchi and Andrea Lockett, Assoc. Eds. Fresh, original fiction and nonfiction, to 25 manuscript pages. Poems (submit 4 to 6). Translations welcome."We are an eclectic literary magazine serving a sophisticated international audience. No racist, sexist, pornographic, or romance material." Query for book reviews. Pays $15 per page, on publication. Contests. SASE for guidelines.

CHICAGO REVIEW—5801 S. Kenwood Ave., Chicago, IL 60637. Andrew Rathmann, Ed. Essays, interviews, reviews, fiction, translations, poetry. Pays in copies plus one year's subscription. Manuscripts read year-round; replies in 2 to 3 months.

CHIRON REVIEW—522 E. South Ave., St. John, KS 67576-2212. Michael Hathaway, Ed. Contemporary fiction, to 4,000 words; articles, 500 to 1,000 words; and poetry, to 30 lines. Photos. Pays in copies. Poetry and chapbook contests.

CICADA—329 E St., Bakersfield, CA 93304. Frederick A. Raborg, Jr., Ed. Quarterly. Single haiku, sequences, or garlands; essays about the forms; haibun, tanka, renga, and fiction (one story per issue) related to haiku or Japan. Pays $10 plus copy for fiction; $10 for "best of issue" poetry.

CIMARRON REVIEW—205 Morrill Hall, Oklahoma State Univ., Stillwater, OK 74078-0135. E. P. Walkiewicz, Ed. Poetry, fiction, essays. Seeks an individual, innovative style that focuses on contemporary themes. Pays $50 for stories and essays; $15 for poems, plus one-year subscription. Manuscripts read year-round.

CLOCKWATCH REVIEW—Dept. of English, Illinois Wesleyan Univ., Bloomington, IL 61702-2900. James Plath, Ed. Semiannual. Fiction, to 4,000 words, and poetry, to 36 lines. "Our preference is for fresh language, a believable voice, a mature style, and a sense of the unusual in the subject matter." Pays $25 for fiction, $5 for poetry, on acceptance, plus copies. Manuscripts read year-round.

COLLAGES & BRICOLAGES—P.O. Box 86, Clarion, PA 16214. Marie-José Fortis, Ed. Annual. Fiction and nonfiction, plays, interviews, book reviews, and poetry. Surrealistic, feminist, and expressionistic drawings in ink. "I seek innovation and honesty. The magazine often focuses on one subject; query for themes." B&W photos; photo-collages. Pays in copies. Manuscripts read August through November.

COLORADO REVIEW—English Dept., Colorado State Univ., Fort Collins, CO 80523. David Milofsky, Ed. Short fiction and poetry on contemporary themes. Pays $5 per printed page for fiction; $10 for poetry. Manuscripts read September to April 15.

COLUMBIA: A JOURNAL OF LITERATURE & ART—(formerly *Columbia: A Magazine of Poetry & Prose*) 415 Dodge, Columbia Univ., New York, NY 10027. Attn: Ed. Semiannual. Fiction and nonfiction; poetry; essays; interviews; visual art. Pays in copies. SASE for guidelines and contest rules. Manuscripts read September to May.

THE COMICS JOURNAL—Fantagraphics, Inc., 7563 Lake City Way, Seattle, WA 98115. Attn: Man. Ed. "Looking for freelancers with working knowledge of the diversity and history of the comics medium." Reviews, 2,500 to 5,000 words; domestic and international news, 500 to 7,000 words; "Opening Shots" editorials, 500 to 1,500 words; interviews; and features, 2,500 to 5,000 words. Query for news and interviews. Pays 2¢ a word, on publication. Guidelines.

CONFLUENCE—P.O. Box 336, Belpre, OH 45714-0336. Scott Bond, Poetry Ed. Daniel Born, Fiction Ed. Published annually by Marietta College and the Ohio Valley Literary Group. Poetry and short fiction. Pays in copies. Manuscripts read September through March only.

CONFRONTATION—Dept. of English, C.W. Post of L. I. U., Brookville, NY 11548. Martin Tucker, Ed. Serious fiction, 750 to 6,000 words. Crafted poetry, 10 to 200 lines. Pays $10 to $150, on publication.

THE CONNECTICUT POETRY REVIEW—P.O. Box 818, Stonington, CT 06378. J. Claire White and Harley More, Eds. Poetry, 5 to 20 lines, and reviews, 700 words. Pays $5 per poem, $10 per review, on acceptance. Manuscripts read September to January and April to June.

CONNECTICUT RIVER REVIEW—35 Lindsley Pl., Stratford, CT 06497. Norah Christianson, Ed. Semiannual. Poetry. Submit up to 3 poems. Pays in one copy. Guidelines.

CQ/CALIFORNIA STATE POETRY QUARTERLY—California State Poetry Society, Box 7126, Orange, CA 92613. Attn: Ed. Board. Poetry, to 60 lines. All poets welcome. Payment is one copy. Responds within 2 to 4 months.

CRAZY QUILT—P.O. Box 632729, San Diego, CA 92163-2729. Attn: Eds. Fiction, to 4,000 words, poetry, one-act plays, literary criticism, and author interviews. Also B&W art, photographs. Pays in copies. Manuscripts read year-round.

CRAZYHORSE—English Dept., Univ. of Arkansas, Little Rock, AR 72204. Address Poetry Ed. or Criticism Ed. Mainstream poetry, nonfiction prose, and criticism. Pays $10, on publication.

THE CREAM CITY REVIEW—English Dept., Box 413, Univ. of Wisconsin, Milwaukee, WI 53201. Staci Leigh O'Brien, Ed. Semiannual. "We serve a national audience interested in a diversity of writing (in terms of style, subject, genre) and writers (gender, race, class, publishing history, etc.). Both well-known and newly published writers of fiction, poetry, and essays are featured, along with B&W artwork." Pays in copies. Manuscripts read September 1 to April 30.

CREATIVE NONFICTION—5501 Walnut, Suite 202, Pittsburgh, PA 15232. Lee Gutkind, Ed. "No length requirements, although we are always searching for writers who can communicate a strong idea with drama and humor in a few pages." Pays $5 and up per published page.

THE CRESCENT REVIEW—P.O. Box 15069, Chevy Chase, MD 20825. J.T. Holland, Ed. Short stories only. Pays in copies. Manuscripts read July through October and January through April.

CRITICAL INQUIRY—Univ. of Chicago Press, Wieboldt Hall, 1050 E. 59th St., Chicago, IL 60637. W. J. T. Mitchell, Ed. Critical essays that offer a theoretical perspective on literature, music, visual arts, and popular culture. No fiction, poetry, or autobiography. Pays in copies. Manuscripts read year-round.

CUMBERLAND POETRY REVIEW—P.O. Box 120128, Acklen Sta., Nashville, TN 37212. Attn: Eds. High-quality poetry and criticism; translations. Send up to 6 poems with brief bio. No restrictions on form, style, or subject matter. Pays in copies.

CUTBANK—English Dept., Univ. of Montana, Missoula, MT 59812. Attn: Eds. Semiannual. Fiction, to 40 pages (submit one story at a time), and poems (submit up to 5 poems). All manuscripts are considered for the Richard Hugo Memorial Poetry Award and the A.B. Guthrie, Jr. Short Fiction Award. Pays in copies. Guidelines. Manuscripts read August 15 to March 15.

DENVER QUARTERLY—Univ. of Denver, Denver, CO 80208. Bin Ramke, Ed. Literary, cultural essays and articles; poetry; book reviews; fiction. Pays $5 per printed page, after publication. Manuscripts read September 15 to May 15.

DESCANT—T.C.U. Box 297270, Fort Worth, TX 76129. Neil Easterbrook, Ed. Fiction, to 6,000 words. Poetry, to 60 lines. No restriction on form or subject. Pays in copies. Frank O'Connor Award ($500) is given each year for best short story published in the volume. Submit material September through May only.

THE DEVIL'S MILLHOPPER—The Devil's Millhopper Press, USC/ Aiken, 171 University Pkwy., Aiken, SC 29801-6309. Stephen Gardner, Ed. Poetry. Send SASE for guidelines and contest information. Pays in copies.

THE DISTILLERY—Motlow State Community College, P.O. Box 88100, Tullahoma, TN 37388. Stuart Bloodworth, Ed. Semiannual. Fiction, 4,000 words; poetry, 100 lines; critical essays, photos and drawings. Responds in 2 to 3 months. Pays in copies.

DOUBLE DEALER REDUX— 632 Pirate's Alley, New Orleans, LA 70116. Rosemary Jams, Ed. Quarterly. Fiction, essays, and poetry. "We showcase the work of promising writers." No payment. Query required. Contest. SASE.

DREAMS & VISIONS—Skysong Press, 35 Peter St. S., Orillia, Ontario, Canada L3V 5A8. Steve Stanton, Ed. Eclectic fiction, 2,000 to 6,000 words, that is "in some way unique and relevant to Christian readers today." Pays ½ ¢ per word.

EARTH'S DAUGHTERS—P.O. Box 41, Central Park Sta., Buffalo, NY 14215. Attn: Ed. Published 3 times a year. Fiction, to 1,000 words, poetry, to 40 lines, and B&W photos or drawings. "Finely crafted work with a feminist theme." Pays in copies. SASE for guidelines and themes.

ECLECTIC RAINBOWS—1538 Tennessee Walker Dr., Roswell, GA 30075. Linda T. Dennison, Ed./Pub. Annual. Essays (no nostalgia), articles, humor, celebrity interviews, 1,000 to 4,000 words. Poetry, to 36 lines. Limited fiction (no science fiction or horror). "New age emphasis is on personal and planetary growth and transformation." Pays to $25, on publication. Guidelines. Contests.

ELF: ECLECTIC LITERARY FORUM—P.O. Box 392, Tonawanda, NY 14150. C. K. Erbes, Ed. Fiction, 3,500 words. Essays on literary themes, 3,500 words. Poetry, to 30 lines. Allow 4 to 8 weeks for response. Pays in one copy. Guidelines. SASE.

EPOCH—251 Goldwin Smith Hall, Cornell Univ., Ithaca, NY 14853-3201. Michael Koch, Ed. Serious fiction and poetry. Pays $5 a page for fiction and poetry. No submissions between April 15 and September 21. Guidelines.

EUREKA LITERARY MAGAZINE—Eureka College, P.O. Box 280, Eureka, IL 61530. Loren Logsdon, Ed. Nancy Perkins, Fiction Ed. Semiannual. Fiction, 25 to 30 pages, and poetry, submit up to 4 poems at a time. "We seek to promote no specific political agenda or literary theory. We strive to publish the best of the fiction and poetry submitted to us." Pays in copies.

EVENT—Douglas College, Box 2503, New Westminster, BC, Canada V3L 5B2. Calvin Wharton, Ed. Short fiction, reviews, poetry. Pays $22 per printed page, on publication.

EXPRESSIONS—P.O. Box 16294, St. Paul, MN 55116. Sefra Kobrin Pitzele, Ed. Semiannual, non-profit. Literature and art by people with disabilities and ongoing illnesses. Fiction and articles, to 2,500 words. Poetry, to 64 lines. B&W artwork. "We hope to be a place where talented people who may have limited energy, finances, or physical ability can be published." Pays in copies. Guidelines. Contests.

EXQUISITE CORPSE—P.O. Box 25051, Baton Rouge, LA 70894. Andrei Codrescu, Ed. Fiction, nonfiction, and poetry for "a journal of letters and life."

B&W photos and drawings. Read the magazine before submitting. Payment is 10 copies and one-year subscription. Manuscripts read year-round.

FARMER'S MARKET—Elgin Community College, 1700 Spartan Dr., Elgin, IL 60123-7193. Attn: Ed. Short stories, to 30 pages, and poetry. Pays in copies and subscription.

FEELINGS POETRY JOURNAL—Anderie Poetry Press, P.O. Box 85, Easton, PA 18044-0085. Carole Heffley, Exec. Ed. Michael Steffen, Submissions Ed. "A Journal of Poetic Thought & Verse." Quarterly. Submit up to 3 poems, 30 lines each, "that convey an immediate sense of recognition, accessibility, and intensity of thought." Informative columns, awards, contests. Also publishes *America's Beautiful Poetry Magazine,* quarterly publication of "pleasing verse." Submit up to 3 poems, 30 lines, at same address as above.

FICTION INTERNATIONAL—English Dept., San Diego State Univ., San Diego, CA 92182-8140. Harold Jaffe, Ed. Post-modernist and politically committed fiction and theory. Query for annual themes. Pays in copies. Manuscripts read from September 1 to December 15.

THE FIDDLEHEAD—Campus House, Univ. of New Brunswick, Fredericton, N.B., Canada E3B 5A3. Attn: Ed. Serious fiction, 2,500 words. Pays about $10 per printed page, on publication. SAE with international reply coupons required. Manuscripts read year-round.

FIELD—Rice Hall, Oberlin College, Oberlin, OH 44074. Stuart Friebert, David Young, Alberta Turner, David Walker, Eds. Serious poetry, any length, by established and unknown poets; essays on poetics by poets. Translations by qualified translators. Payment varies, on publication. Manuscripts read year-round.

FIVE FINGERS REVIEW—P.O. Box 15426, San Francisco, CA 94115. Published once or twice a year. "Writing with a sense of experimentation, an awareness of tradition, and a willingness to explore artistic boundaries." Pays in copies.

THE FLORIDA REVIEW—English Dept., Univ. of Central Florida, Orlando, FL 32816. Russell Kesler, Ed. Semiannual. Mainstream and experimental fiction and nonfiction, to 7,500 words. Poetry, any style. Pays in copies.

FLYWAY—203 Ross Hall, Iowa State Univ., Ames, IA 50011-1201. Stephen Pett, Ed. Poetry, fiction, creative nonfiction, and reviews. Pays in copies. Manuscripts read September through May.

FOLIO—Dept. of Literature, American Univ., Washington, DC 20016. Attn: Ed. Semiannual. Fiction, poetry, translations, and essays. Photos and drawings. Pays in 2 copies. Submissions read September through March. Contest.

FOOTWORK, THE PATERSON LITERARY REVIEW—Poetry Ctr., Passaic County Comm. College, College Blvd., Paterson, NJ 07505-1179. Maria Mazziotti Gillan, Ed. High-quality fiction and poetry, to 10 pages. Pays in copies. Manuscripts read January through May.

THE FORMALIST—320 Hunter Dr., Evansville, IN 47711. William Baer, Ed. Metrical poetry, to 2 pages, including blank verse, couplets, and traditional forms such as sonnets, ballads, villanelles, etc. "Sound and rhythm make poetry what it is." Howard Nemerov Sonnet Award ($1,000); SASE for details.

THE FRACTAL—George Mason Univ., 4400 University Dr., MS 2D6, Fairfax, VA 22030. Christopher Elliot, Jessica Darago, Sr. Eds. Fantastic fiction, poetry, art, and nonfiction. Guidelines. Pays $25 for fiction; $50 for nonfiction; $5 for poetry, on publication. Send complete manuscript.

FREE INQUIRY—P.O. Box 664, Buffalo, NY 14226. Paul Kurtz, Ed. Tim Madigan, Exec. Ed. Articles, 500 to 5,000 words, for "literate and lively readership. Focus is on criticisms of religious belief systems, and how to lead an ethical life without a supernatural basis." Pays in copies.

FROGPOND—P.O. Box 767, Archer, FL 32618-0767. Kenneth C. Leibman, Ed. Published 3 times a year. Articles on haiku. Haiku, one to 4 lines, 17 syllables maximum. Query for articles. Pays in copies.

FUGUE—Univ. of Idaho, English Dept., Brink Hall, Room 200, Moscow, ID 83844-1102. Address Exec. Ed. Fiction, to 7,000 words. Nonfiction, to 4,000 words. Poetry, any style, 100 lines. Open to new writers. Include SASE. Pays in copies and small honorarium.

FULL-TIME DADS ON-LINE—(formerly *Full-Time Dads*) P.O. Box 577, Cumberland, ME 04021. Stephen Harris, Ed. Fiction, articles, essays, and humor, 600 to 1,200 words, and short poems for fathers who are very involved with their children. "All material must relate to supportive fatherhood."

GEORGETOWN REVIEW—P.O. Box 6309 SS, Hattiesburg, MS 39406-6309. John Fulmer, Man. Ed. Tracy Heinlen, Ed. Semiannual. Good quality fiction and essays, to 20 pages. Poetry (submit up to 5 poems). "We're not afraid of genre fiction (adventure, science fiction, etc.) if it's done well. We are looking for new, exciting voices." Also book and movie reviews. Pays in copies and "possible payment," on publication.

THE GEORGIA REVIEW—Univ. of Georgia, Athens, GA 30602-9009. Stanley W. Lindberg, Ed. Short fiction; literary, interdisciplinary, and personal essays; book reviews; poetry; artwork. Translations and novel excerpts strongly discouraged. No simultaneous submissions. Manuscripts read September through May.

THE GETTYSBURG REVIEW—Gettysburg College, Gettysburg, PA 17325. Peter Stitt, Ed. Quarterly. Poetry, fiction, essays, and essay reviews, 1,000 to 20,000 words. "Review sample copy before submitting." Pays $2 a line for poetry; $25 per printed page for fiction and nonfiction. Allow 3 to 6 months for response. No simultaneous submissions.

GLIMMER TRAIN PRESS—710 S.W. Madison St., #504, Portland, OR 97205. Susan Burmeister-Brown, Ed. Quarterly. Fiction, 1,200 to 7,500 words. Eight stories in each issue. Pays $500, on acceptance. Submit material in January, April, July, and October. Allow 3 months for response. Short story award for new writers; SASE for details.

GOTHIC JOURNAL—P.O. Box 6340, Elko, NV 89802-6340. Kristi Lyn Glass, Pub. Bimonthly. News and reviews for readers, writers, and publishers of romantic suspense, romantic mystery, and gothic, supernatural, and woman-in-jeopardy romance novels. Articles, 1,000 to 2,000 words, on gothic and romantic suspense topics; author profiles, 3,000 to 4,000 words; book reviews, 250 to 500 words. Pays $20 for articles, $30 for author profiles, on publication.

GRAHAM HOUSE REVIEW—Box 5000, Colgate Univ., Hamilton, NY 13346. Peter Balakian, Ed. Bruce Smith, Ed. Poetry, translations, and essays on modern poets. Payment depends on grants. Manuscripts read year-round; responds within 8 weeks.

GRAIN—Box 1154, Regina, Sask., Canada S4P 3B4. J. Jill Robinson, Ed. Short stories, to 30 typed pages; poems, send up to 8; visual art. Pays $30 to

$100 for stories and poems, $100 for cover art, $30 for other art. SAE with international reply coupons required. Manuscripts read year-round.

GRAND STREET—131 Varick St., #906, New York, NY 10013. Jean Stein, Ed. Quarterly. Poetry, any length. Pays $3 a line, on publication. Will not read unsolicited fiction or essays.

GRAND TOUR: THE JOURNAL OF TRAVEL LITERATURE—P.O. Box 66, Thorofare, NJ 08086. Jennifer Fisher, Man. Ed. Quarterly. Travel-related memoirs, essays, and articles, 1,000 to 7,000 words, that "combine the sharp eye of the reporter with the craft of the short story writer and the rhythm of the poet." Pays $50 to $200, on publication.

GRASSLANDS REVIEW—P.O. Box 626, Berea, OH 44017. Laura Kennelly, Ed. Semiannual. Short stories, 3,600 to 5,000 words. Poetry, any length. "We seek imagination without sloppiness, ideas without lectures, and delight in language. Our purpose is to encourage new writers." Pays in copies. Manuscripts read in March and October only.

GREEN MOUNTAIN REVIEW—Johnson State College, Johnson, VT 05656. Neil Shepard, Poetry Ed. Tony Whedon, Fiction Ed. Fiction and creative nonfiction, including literary essays, book reviews, and interviews, to 25 pages. Poetry. Manuscripts read between September 1 and May 1. Payment varies (depending on funding), on publication.

GREEN'S MAGAZINE—P.O. Box 3236, Regina, Sask., Canada S4P 3H1. David Green, Ed. Fiction for family reading, 1,500 to 4,000 words. Poetry, to 40 lines. No simultaneous submissions. Pays in copies. International reply coupons must accompany U.S. manuscripts. Manuscripts read year-round.

THE GREENSBORO REVIEW—Dept. of English, Univ. of North Carolina, Greensboro, NC 27412-5001. Jim Clark, Ed. Semiannual. Poetry and fiction. Submission deadlines: September 15 and February 15. Pays in copies. Writer's guidelines and guidelines for literary awards issue available.

GULF COAST—English Dept., Univ. of Houston, Houston, TX 77204. Attn: Ed. Semiannual. Fiction (no genre fiction), nonfiction, poetry (submit up to 5), and translations. No payment.

HALF TONES TO JUBILEE—Pensacola Junior College, English Dept., 1000 College Blvd., Pensacola, FL 32504. Walter F. Spara, Ed. Fiction, to 1,500 words, and poetry, to 60 lines. Pays in copies. Manuscripts read August 15 to May 15. Contest.

HAMMERS—1718 Sherman Ave., Suite 203, Evanston, IL 60201. Nat David, Ed. Quarterly. Poetry, "always interested in original, fresh work." Pays in copies.

HAPPY—240 E. 35th St., Suite 11A, New York, NY 10016. Bayard, Ed. Quarterly. Fiction, to 6,000 words. "No previously published work. No pornography. No racist/sexist pandering. No bourgeois boredom." Pays $5 per 1,000 words, on publication, plus one copy.

HARP-STRINGS—P.O. Box 640387, Beverly Hills, FL 34464. Madelyn Eastlund, Ed. Poems, 14 to 80 lines, on a variety of topics and in many forms. No light verse, "prose masquerading as poetry," confessions, or raw guts poems. Pays in copies.

HAUNTS—Nightshade Publications, Box 8068, Cranston, RI 02920-0068. Joseph K. Cherkes, Ed. Short stories, 1,500 to 8,000 words: horror, science-fantasy, and supernatural tales with strong characters. Pays 1/3¢ to 1¢ a word, on publication. Manuscripts read January 1 to June 1.

HAWAII REVIEW—Dept. of English, Univ. of Hawaii, 1733 Donagho Rd., Honolulu, HI 96822. Malia E. Gellert, Ed.-in-Chief. Quality fiction, poetry, interviews, and essays. Manuscripts read year-round.

HAYDEN'S FERRY REVIEW—Box 871502, Arizona State Univ., Tempe, AZ 85287-1502. Attn: Ed. Semiannual. Fiction, essays, and poetry (submit up to 6 poems). Include brief bio and SASE. Deadline for Spring/Summer issue is September 30; Fall/Winter issue, February 28. Pays in copies.

THE HEARTLANDS TODAY—Firelands Writing Ctr. of Firelands College, Huron, OH 44839. Larry Smith and Nancy Dunham, Eds. Fiction, 1,000 to 4,500 words, and nonfiction, 1,000 to 3,000 words, about the contemporary Midwest. Poetry (submit 3 to 5 poems). "Writing must be set in the Midwest, but can include a variety of themes." B&W photos. Pays $10 to $20 honorarium, plus copies. Query for current themes. Contest.

HEAVEN BONE—P.O. Box 486, Chester, NY 10918. Steve Hirsch, Ed. Annual. "The Bridge Between Muse & Mind." Fiction, to 5,000 words. Magazine and book reviews, 250 to 2,500 words. Poetry (submit no more than 10 pages at a time). "If we have a bias in subject matter, it might tend toward the so-called alternative-cultural, post-beat, surrealist, and yogic/anti-paranoiac. Read a copy before submitting." Allow 6 months for response. Pays in copies.

HEROES FROM HACKLAND—1225 Evans, Arkadelphia, AR 71923. Mike Grogan, Ed. Quarterly. Nostalgic articles, 750 to 1,500 words, on B-movies (especially westerns and serials), comic books, grade school readers, juvenile series books, cartoons, vintage autos, country music and pop music before 1956, and vintage radio and television. "We believe in heroes, especially those popular culture icons that serious critics label 'ephemera.'" Pays in copies.

THE HIGHLANDER—P.O. Box 397, Barrington, IL 60011. David Kennedy Ray, Ed. Bimonthly. Articles, 1,300 to 1,900 words, related to Scottish history. "We do not want articles on modern Scotland or current problems in Scotland." Pays $100 to $150, on acceptance.

THE HOLLINS CRITIC—P.O. Box 9538, Hollins College, Roanoke, VA 24020. R.H.W. Dillard, Ed. Published 5 times a year. Features an essay on a contemporary fiction writer or poet, cover sketch, brief biography, and book list. Also, book reviews and poetry. Pays $25 for poetry, on publication.

HOME LIFE—127 Ninth Ave. N., Nashville, TN 37234. Jon Walker, Ed.-in-Chief. Southern Baptist. Articles, 600 to 1,800 words: marriage and family, seasonal, humor and inspiration. Also uses one piece of fiction each month. Pays to $24 for poetry, from $75 for articles, on acceptance. Query.

HOME PLANET NEWS—P.O. Box 415, Stuyvesant Sta., New York, NY 10009. Enid Dame and Donald Lev, Eds. Quarterly art tabloid. Fiction, to 8 typed pages; reviews, 3 to 5 pages; and poetry, any length. "We are looking for quality poetry, fiction, and discerning literary and art reviews." Query for nonfiction. Pays in copies and subscription. Manuscripts read February 1 to May 31.

THE HUDSON REVIEW—684 Park Ave., New York, NY 10021. Frederick Morgan and Paula Deitz, Eds. Quarterly. Fiction, to 10,000 words. Essays, to 8,000 words. Poetry, submit up to 10 at a time. Payment varies, on publication. Guidelines. Reading periods: Nonfiction read January 1 through April 30. Poetry read April 1 through July 31. Fiction read June 1 through November 30.

HURRICANE ALICE: A FEMINIST QUARTERLY—Dept. of English, Rhode Island College, Providence, RI 02908. Attn: Maureen Reddy, Ed. Articles, fiction, essays, interviews, and reviews, 500 to 3,000 words, with feminist perspective. Pays in copies.

ILLYA'S HONEY— 432 Greenridge, Coppell, TX 75019. Stephen W. Brodie, Ed. Quarterly. Short fiction, any subject, any style, to 1,000 words; poetry, to 60 lines. "No forced rhyme or overly religious verse." Manuscripts read year-round.

IN THE COMPANY OF POETS—P.O. Box 10786, Oakland, CA 94610. Jacalyn Evone, Ed./Pub. Semiannual. Fiction and creative essays, to 2,500 words, for a wide multicultural range of readers. Poems of any length. Drawings and photos. Pays in 3 copies. Guidelines. Manuscripts read year-round.

INDIANA REVIEW—Ballantine 465, Indiana Univ., Bloomington, IN 47405. Geoffrey Pollock, Ed. Bob King, Assoc. Ed. Fiction with an emphasis on storytelling and sophistication of language. Poems that are well-executed and ambitious. Pays $5 per page. Manuscripts read year-round.

INTERIM—Dept. of English, Univ. of Nevada, Las Vegas, NV 89154-5034. James Hazen, Ed. Semiannual. Poetry, any form or length, and fiction, to 7,500 words (uses no more than 2 stories per issue). Pays in copies and 2-year subscription. Responds in 2 months.

INTERNATIONAL POETRY REVIEW—Dept. of Romance Languages, Univ. of North Carolina, Greensboro, NC 27412. Attn: Ed. Semiannual. Book reviews, interviews, and short essays, to 1,500 words. Original English poems and contemporary translations of poems. "We prefer material with cross-cultural or international dimension." Pays in copies.

THE IOWA REVIEW—EPB 308, Univ. of Iowa, Iowa City, IA 52242. David Hamilton, Ed. Essays, poems, stories, reviews. Pays $10 a page for fiction and nonfiction, $1 a line for poetry, on publication. Manuscripts read September 1 through April 15.

IOWA WOMAN—P.O. Box 680, Iowa City, IA 52244. Attn: Ed. Fiction, poetry, creative nonfiction, book reviews, and personal essays. Articles, to 6,500 words; interviews with prominent women; current social, economic, artistic, and environmental issues. Poems, any length (submit up to 5); photos and drawings. Queries preferred for articles. Pays $5 a page, $15 for illustrations, on publication. Guidelines.

THE JAMES WHITE REVIEW—P.O. Box 3356, Butler Quarter Sta., Minneapolis, MN 55403. Phil Willkie, Pub. "A Gay Men's Literary Quarterly." Short stories, to 9,000 words, and poetry, to 250 lines. Book reviews. Responds in 3 months.

JAPANOPHILE—Box 223, Okemos, MI 48805-0223. Earl R. Snodgrass, Ed. Fiction, to 4,000 words, with a Japanese setting. Each story should have at least one Japanese character and at least one non-Japanese. Articles, 2,000 words, that celebrate Japanese culture. "We seek to promote Japanese-American understanding. We are not about Japan-bashing or fatuous praise." Pays to $20, on publication. Annual short story contest; deadline December 31.

JOURNAL OF NEW JERSEY POETS—County College of Morris, 214 Center Grove Rd., Randolph, NJ 07869-2086. Sander Zulauf, Ed. Semiannual.

Serious contemporary poetry by current and former New Jersey residents. "Although our emphasis is on poets associated with New Jersey, we seek work that is universal in scope." Pays in copies.

JOYFUL NOISE: A JOURNAL OF CHRISTIAN POETRY—P.O. Box 401, Bowling Green, KY 42102. Jim Erskine, Ed. Christian-oriented poetry, to 30 lines. "Personal, 'small' subjects perferred over 'large' themes such as love, brotherhood, etc. No political, new age, or social issues." Pays in copies.

KALEIDOSCOPE—United Disability Services, 326 Locust St., Akron, OH 44302-1876. Darshan Perusek, Ph.D., Ed.-in-Chief. Semiannual. Fiction, essays, interviews, articles, and poetry relating to disability and the arts, to 5,000 words. Photos a plus. "We present balanced, realistic images of people with disabilities and publish pieces that challenge stereotypes." Submissions accepted from writers with or without disabilities. Pays $10 to $125. Guidelines recommended. Manuscripts read year-round; response may take up to 6 months.

KALLIOPE: A JOURNAL OF WOMEN'S ART—Florida Community College at Jacksonville, 3939 Roosevelt Blvd., Jacksonville, FL 32205. Attn: Ed. Fiction, to 2,500 words; poetry; interviews of women writers, to 2,000 words; and B&W photos of fine art. Query for interviews only. Pays $10 or in copies.

KANSAS QUARTERLY/ARKANSAS REVIEW—(formerly *Kansas Quarterly*) Dept. of English & Philosophy, P.O. Box 1890, Arkansas State Univ., State University, AR 72467. Norman Lavers, Ed. Fiction and creative nonfiction (essays, memoirs, travel to remote places, commentary on science or ecology). Limited poetry. Pays $10 per page.

KARAMU—Dept. of English, Eastern Illinois Univ., Charleston, IL 61920. Peggy Brayfield, Ed. Contemporary or experimental fiction. Creative nonfiction prose, personal essays, and memoir pieces. Poetry. Pays in copies. Manuscripts read year-round; best time to submit is January to May.

KELSEY REVIEW—Mercer County Community College, P.O. Box B, Trenton, NJ 08690. Robin Schore, Ed. Fiction and nonfiction, to 2,000 words, and poetry by writers living or working in Mercer County, NJ. Pays in copies.

THE KENYON REVIEW—Kenyon College, Gambier, OH 43022. David H. Lynn, Ed. Published 3 times a year. Fiction, poetry, essays, literary criticism, and reviews. Pays $10 a printed page for prose, $15 a printed page for poetry, on publication. Manuscripts read September through March.

KINESIS: THE LITERARY MAGAZINE FOR THE REST OF US—P.O. Box 4007, Whitefish, MT 59937. Leif Peterson, Ed./Pub. Fiction, essays, and reviews, 2,000 to 6,000 words; poetry, to 60 lines. "Make sure it moves!" Pays in copies and subscription.

KIOSK—c/o English Dept., 306 Clemens Hall, SUNY Buffalo, Buffalo, NY 14260. Tracee Howell, Ed. Jonathan Pitts, Fiction Ed. Charlotte Pressler, Poetry Ed. Fiction, to 20 pages, with a "strong sense of voice, narrative direction, and craftsmanship." Poetry "that explores boundaries, including the formally experimental." Address appropriate editor. Pays in copies. Manuscripts read September 1 to December 1.

LAMBDA BOOK REPORT—1625 Connecticut Ave. N.W., Washington, DC 20009. Kanani Kanka, Sr. Ed. Reviews and features, 500 to 1,100 words, of gay and lesbian books. Pays $15 to $75, 30 days after publication. Queries preferred.

LATINO STUFF REVIEW—P.O. Box 440195, Miami, FL 33144. Nilda Cepero-Llevada, Ed./Pub. Bilingual publication focusing on Latino topics. Short stories, 3,000 words; poetry, to one page; criticism and essays on literature, the arts, social issues. Pays in copies.

THE LEADING EDGE—3163 JKHB, Provo, UT 84602. David Burnett, Ed. Semiannual. Science fiction and fantasy, 3,000 to 12,000 words; poetry, to 600 lines; and articles, to 8,000 words, on science, scientific speculation, and literary criticism. No excessive profanity, overt violence, or excessive sexual situations. No simultaneous submissions. Pays 1/4¢ per word, on publication. Guidelines.

THE LEDGE—78-08 83rd St., Glendale, NY 11385. Timothy Monaghan, Ed. Semiannual. Poetry; submit 3 to 5 poems at a time. "We publish provocative, well-crafted poems by well-known and lesser-known poets. Excellence is our main criterion." Pays in copies.

LIGHT—Box 7500, Chicago, IL 60680. John Mella, Ed. Quarterly. Light verse. Also fiction, reviews, and essays, to 2,000 words. Fillers, humor, jokes, quips. "If it has wit, point, edge, or barb, it will find a home here." Cartoons and line drawings. Pays in copies. Query for nonfiction.

LILITH, THE INDEPENDENT JEWISH WOMEN'S MAGAZINE—250 W. 57th St., New York, NY 10107. Susan Weidman Schneider, Ed. Fiction, 1,500 to 2,000 words, on issues of interest to Jewish women.

THE LION AND THE UNICORN—Box 53, English Dept., Mankato State Univ., Mankato, MN 56002-8400. Louisa Smith, Ed. Articles, from 2,000 words, offering criticism of children's and young adult books, for teachers, scholars, artists, and parents. Query preferred. Pays in copies.

LITERAL LATTE—61 E. 8th St., Suite 240, New York, NY 10003. Jenine Gordon Bockman, Ed./Pub. Bimonthly distributed to cafés and bookstores in New York City. Fiction and personal essays, to 6,000 words; poetry, to 2,000 words; art. Pays in subscription, honorarium, and copies. Contests.

LITERARY MAGAZINE REVIEW—Dept. of English Lang. and Lit., Univ. of Northern Iowa, 1222 W. 27th St., Cedar Falls, IA 50614-0502. Grant Tracey, Ed. Reviews and articles concerning literary magazines, 1,000 to 1,500 words, for writers and readers of contemporary literature. Pays in copies. Query.

THE LITERARY REVIEW—Fairleigh Dickinson Univ., 285 Madison Ave., Madison, NJ 07940. Walter Cummins, Ed.-in-Chief. Jill Kushner, Man. Ed. Martin Green, Harry Keyishian, William Zander, Eds. Serious fiction; poetry; translations; essays and reviews on contemporary literature. Pays in copies.

THE LONG STORY—18 Eaton St., Lawrence, MA 01843. Attn: Ed. Stories, 8,000 to 20,000 words; prefer stories with a moral/thematic core, particularly about poor and working class people. Pays in copies. Manuscripts read year-round.

THE LONGNECK—P.O. Box 659, Vermillion, SD 57069. Michael Tidemann, Ed. Essays and fiction, 2,000 words. Vignettes, nostalgia. Poetry; submit no more than 5 poems. No religious material. Deadline: February 1 annually. Payment is in copies.

L'OUVERTURE: THE BLACK MARKETPLACE OF IDEAS—P.O. Box 8565, Atlanta, GA 30306. Bill Campbell, Ed. Bimonthly. Fiction, any genre. Cultural and political commentary. Poetry. "We're a multicultural publication hoping to provoke thought in our readership, to build a cacophony of dialogue." Pays in copies. Manuscripts read year-round.

LYNX EYE—c/o Scribblefest Literary Group, 1880 Hill Dr., Los Angeles, CA 90041. Pam McCully, Kathryn Morrison, Eds. Quarterly. Short stories, vignettes, novel excerpts, one-act plays, essays, belle lettres, satires, and reviews, 500 to 5,000 words; poetry, to 30 lines. Pays $10, on acceptance.

THE MACGUFFIN—Schoolcraft College, Dept. of English, 18600 Haggerty Rd., Livonia, MI 48152. Arthur J. Lindenberg, Ed. General, mainstream, and experimental fiction and nonfiction, 400 to 5,000 words. Poetry. "No religious, inspirational, confessional, romance, horror, or pornography." Pays in copies.

MAGIC REALISM—P.O. Box 922648, Sylmar, CA 91392-2648. C. Darren Butler, Ed. Quarterly. Stories, to 7,500 words (4,000 words preferred), and poetry, any length, of magic realism, exaggerated realism, some genre fantasy/dark fantasy. Occasionally publish glib fantasy like that found in folktales, fairy tales, and myths. No occult, sleight-of-hand magicians, high fantasy, or wizards/witches. Pays 1/4¢ per word, plus copy. Contest; SASE for details.

THE MALAHAT REVIEW—Univ. of Victoria, P.O. Box 1700, Victoria, BC, Canada V8W 2Y2. Derk Wynand, Ed. Fiction and poetry, including translations. Pays from $25 per page, on acceptance.

THE MANHATTAN REVIEW—440 Riverside Dr., #45, New York, NY 10027. Attn: Ed. Highest quality poetry. Pays in copies.

MANOA—English Dept., Univ. of Hawaii, Honolulu, HI 96822. Frank Stewart, Ed. Ian MacMillan, Fiction Ed. Jodi Kilcup, Book Reviews Ed. Fiction, to 30 pages; essays, to 25 pages; book reviews, 4 to 5 pages; and poetry (submit 4 to 6 poems). "Writers are encouraged to read the journal carefully before submitting." Pays $25 for poetry and book reviews; $20 to $25 per page for fiction, on publication.

MANY MOUNTAINS MOVING—420 22nd St., Boulder, CO 80302. Naomi Horii and Marilyn Krysl, Eds. Published 3 times yearly. Fiction, nonfiction, and poetry by writers of all cultures. Pays in copies.

MASSACHUSETTS REVIEW—Memorial Hall, Univ. of Massachusetts, Amherst, MA 01003. Attn: Ed. Literary criticism; articles on public affairs, scholarly disciplines. Essays. Short fiction, 15 to 25 pages. Poetry. Pays $50, on publication. Manuscripts read November through May. Guidelines.

THE MAVERICK PRESS—Rt. 2, Box 4915, Eagle Pass, TX 78852-9605. Carol Cullar, Ed. Short stories, to 1,500 words, and unrhymed poetry. Pays in copies. Query with SASE for themes.

MEDIPHORS—P.O. Box 327, Bloomsburg, PA 17815. Eugene D. Radice, MD, Ed. "A literary journal of the health professions." Short stories, essays, and commentary, 3,500 words. "Topics should have some relation to medicine and health, but may be quite broad." Poems, to 30 lines. Humor. Pays in copies. Guidelines. SASE.

MESSAGES FROM THE HEART—P.O. Box 64840, Tucson, AZ 85728. Lauren B. Smith, Ed. Quarterly. Heartfelt letters, diary excerpts, poems, or essays, to 800 words, which contain an element of hope. Drawings and B&W photos. Manuscripts read year-round. Pays in copies.

MICHIGAN HISTORICAL REVIEW—Clarke Historical Library, Central Michigan Univ., Mt. Pleasant, MI 48859. Attn: Ed. Semiannual. Scholarly articles related to Michigan's political, social, economic, and cultural history; articles on American, Canadian, and Midwestern history that directly or indirectly explore themes related to Michigan's past. Manuscripts read year-round.

MICHIGAN QUARTERLY REVIEW—3032 Rackham Bldg., Univ. of Michigan, Ann Arbor, MI 48109-1070. Laurence Goldstein, Ed. Scholarly essays on all subjects; fiction; poetry. Pays $8 a page, on publication. Annual contest for authors published in the journal.

MID-AMERICAN REVIEW—Dept. of English, Bowling Green State Univ., Bowling Green, OH 43403. George Looney, Ed. High-quality fiction, poetry, articles, translations, and reviews of contemporary writing. Fiction, to 5,000 words (query for longer work). Reviews, articles, 500 to 2,500 words. Pays to $50, on publication (pending funding). Manuscripts read September through May.

MIDWEST QUARTERLY—Pittsburg State Univ., Pittsburg, KS 66762. James B. M. Schick, Ed. Scholarly articles, 2,500 to 5,000 words, on contemporary academic and public issues; poetry. Pays in copies. Manuscripts read year-round.

THE MINNESOTA REVIEW—Dept. of English, E. Carolina Univ., Greenville, NC 27858. Attn: Ed. Politically committed fiction, 1,000 to 6,000 words; nonfiction, 5,000 to 7,500 words; and poetry, 3 pages maximum, for readers committed to social issues, including feminism, neomarxism, etc. Pays in copies. Responds in 2 to 4 months.

MISSISSIPPI MUD—1505 Drake Ave., Austin, TX 78704. Joel Weinstein, Ed. Short stories, to 50 pages, and novel excerpts, 50 to 100 pages; poetry, any length. Pays $25 for poems; $50 to $100 for fiction, on publication.

MISSISSIPPI REVIEW—Ctr. for Writers, Univ. of Southern Mississippi, Southern Sta., Box 5144, Hattiesburg, MS 39406-5144. Frederick Barthelme, Ed. Serious fiction, poetry, criticism, interviews. Pays in copies.

THE MISSOURI REVIEW—1507 Hillcrest Hall, Univ. of Missouri-Columbia, Columbia, MO 65211. Greg Michalson, Man. Ed. Speer Morgan, Ed. Evelyn Somers, Nonfiction Ed. Poems, of any length. "We do poetry features: 6 to 10 pages of poetry by 3 to 5 poets in each issue." Fiction and essays. Book reviews. Pays $20 per printed page, on contract. Manuscripts read year-round.

MODERN HAIKU—P.O. Box 1752, Madison, WI 53701-1752. Robert Spiess, Ed. Haiku and articles about haiku. Pays $1 per haiku, $5 a page for articles. Manuscripts read year-round.

MONTHLY REVIEW—122 W. 27th St., New York, NY 10001. Paul M. Sweezy, Harry Magdoff, Eds. Analytical articles, 5,000 words, on politics and economics, from independent socialist viewpoint. Pays $25 for reviews, $50 for articles, on publication.

MOOSE BOUND PRESS—P.O. Box 111781, Anchorage, AK 99511-1781. Sonia Walker, Ed. Quarterly. Short stories, to 5,000 words. Poetry, to 30 lines. Essays, to 500 words. "Wholesome, energetic, and uplifting writing. We are kind to beginning writers." Send for annual themes. No payment. SASE.

MUDDY RIVER POETRY REVIEW— 89 Longwood Ave., Brookline, MA 02146. Zvi A. Sesling, Ed. Semiannual. Poems. "While free verse is preferred, nothing will be rejected if it is quality." No previously published poems. Payment is one copy.

MYSTERY TIME—P.O. Box 2907, Decatur, IL 62524. Linda Hutton, Ed. Semiannual. Suspense, 1,500 words, and poems about mysteries, up to 16 lines. "We prefer female protagonists. No gore or violence." Pays $5, on acceptance.

THE NAPLES REVIEW— 626 Third St. N., Naples, FL 34102-5537. Mr. Leslie Waller, Ed. Quarterly. Articles, essays, short stories, novel excerpts, and plays, to 10 pages. Poetry, to 2 pages. Preference given to residents of Southwest Florida or subject matter related to the area. Pays in copies.

NEBO: A LITERARY JOURNAL—Dept. of English and Foreign Languages, Arkansas Tech. Univ., Russellville, AR 72801-2222. Attn: Ed. Poems (submit up to 5); mainstream fiction, to 3,000 words; critical essays, to 10 pages. Pays in one copy. Guidelines. Offices closed May through August. "Best time to submit is September through February."

NEGATIVE CAPABILITY— 62 Ridgelawn Dr. E., Mobile, AL 36608. Sue Walker, Ed. Poetry, any length; fiction, essays, art. Contests.

NEOLOGISMS—Box 869, 1102 Pleasant St., Worcester, MA 01602. Jim Fay, Pub. Short stories, essays, and criticism, to 10 pages. Poetry, all styles "except love-oriented mush." Submit up 5 pages of poetry. Payment is one copy.

NEW AUTHOR'S JOURNAL—1542 Tibbits Ave., Troy, NY 12180. Mario V. Farina, Ed. Fiction, to 2,000 words, and poetry. Topical nonfiction, to 1,000 words. Pays in copies. Manuscripts read year-round.

NEW DELTA REVIEW—c/o Dept. of English, Louisiana State Univ., Baton Rouge, LA 70803-5001. Attn: Eds. Semiannual. Fiction and nonfiction, to 5,000 words. Submit up to 4 poems, any length. Also essays, interviews, and reviews. "We want to see your best work." Pays in copies. Also awards prize for best annual poem and short story. Manuscripts read year-round.

NEW ENGLAND REVIEW—Middlebury College, Middlebury, VT 05753. Stephen Donadio, Ed. Jodee Stanley, Man. Ed. Fiction, nonfiction, and poetry of varying lengths. Also, speculative and interpretive essays, critical reassessments, statements by artists working in various media, interviews, testimonials, letters from abroad. "We are committed to exploration of all forms of contemporary cultural expresssion." Pays $10 per page ($20 minimum), on publication. Manuscripts read September to May.

NEW ENGLAND WRITERS' NETWORK—P.O. Box 483, Hudson, MA 01749-0483. Glenda Baker, Ed.-in-Chief. Short stories and novel excerpts, to 2,000 words. All genres except pornography. Personal and humorous essays, to 1,000 words. Upbeat, positive poetry, to 32 lines. Pays $10 for stories; pays in copies for other material. Guidelines. Submit fiction and essays June 1 to August 31 only. Poetry may be submitted year-round.

NEW LAUREL REVIEW— 828 Lesseps St., New Orleans, LA 70117. Lee Meitzen Grue, Ed. Annual. Fiction, 10 to 20 pages; nonfiction, to 10 pages; poetry, any length. Library market. No inspirational verse. International readership. Read journal before submitting. Pays in one copy.

NEW LETTERS—Univ. House, Univ. of Missouri-Kansas City, 5101 Rockhill Rd., Kansas City, MO 64110-2499. James McKinley, Ed.-in-Chief.

Fiction, 3,500 to 5,000 words. Poetry, submit 3 to 6 poems at a time. SASE for literary awards guidelines. Manuscripts read October 15 to May 15.

NEW ORLEANS REVIEW—Loyola Univ., New Orleans, LA 70118. Ralph Adamo, Ed. Serious fiction and poetry, personal essays, interviews, and B&W art.

THE NEW YORK QUARTERLY—P.O. Box 693, Old Chelsea Sta., New York, NY 10113. William Packard, Ed. Published 3 times a year. Poems of any style and persuasion, well written and well intentioned. Pays in copies. Manuscripts read year-round. SASE required.

NEXUS—Wright State Univ., W016A Student Union, Dayton, OH 45435. Mark Owens, Ed. Jos Ampleforth, Contributing Ed. Poetry, fiction, plays, essays, interviews, reviews, photography, and art. Specializes in experimental, avant-garde work, and topics that transform the world. Pays in 2 copies.

NIGHTMARES—Box 587, Rocky Hill, CT 06067-0587. Ed Kobialka, Ed. Horror fiction, to 7,000 words; preferred length, 3,000 words. Any genre, including ghost stories, science fiction/fantasy, mystery, even romance "as long as the stories are scary." Related poetry. No excessive blood and gore or explicit sex. Pays $10 for fiction, $5 per page for poetry, on acceptance. Published three times a year.

NIGHTSUN—School of Arts & Humanities, Frostburg State Univ., Frostburg, MD 21532-1099. Douglas DeMars, Ed. Annual. Short stories, about 6 pages, and poems, to 40 lines. Payment is 2 copies. Manuscripts read September 1 to May 1.

NIMROD INTERNATIONAL JOURNAL—Univ. of Tulsa, 600 S. College Ave., Tulsa, OK 74104-3189. Dr. Francine Ringold, Ed.-in-Chief. Publishes 2 issues annually, one awards and one thematic. Quality poetry and fiction, experimental and traditional. Pays $5 a page (to $25 when budget permits) and copies. Annual awards for poetry and fiction. Guidelines. SASE.

96 INC.—P.O. Box 15559, Boston, MA 02215. Attn: Ed. Semiannual. Fiction, 1,000 to 7,500 words, interviews, and poetry of varying length. Pays in subscription, 4 copies, and modest payment, provided there is available funding.

THE NORTH AMERICAN REVIEW—Univ. of Northern Iowa, Cedar Falls, IA 50614-0516. Peter Cooley, Poetry Ed. Poetry of high quality. Pays from $20 per poem, on publication. Manuscripts read year-round.

NORTH ATLANTIC REVIEW—15 Arbutus Ln., Stony Brook, NY 11790-1408. John Gill, Ed. Annual. Fiction and nonfiction, to 5,000 words; fillers, humor, photographs and illustrations. A special section on social or literary issues is a part of each issue. No unsolicited poetry. Pays in copies. Responds in 5 or 6 months.

THE NORTH DAKOTA QUARTERLY—Univ. of North Dakota, Grand Forks, ND 58202-7209. Attn: Ed. Essays in the humanities and social sciences; fiction, reviews, and poetry. Limited market. Pays in copies and subscription.

NORTHEASTARTS—Boston Arts Organization, Inc., P.O. Box 94, Kittery, ME 03904. Mr. Leigh Donaldson, Ed. Fiction and nonfiction, to 750 words; poetry, to 30 lines; and short essays and reviews. "Both published and new writers are considered. No obscene or offensive material." Payment is 2 copies.

NORTHEAST CORRIDOR—Beaver College, 450 S. Easton Rd., Glenside, PA 19038. Susan Balée, Ed. Semiannual. Literary fiction, personal essays, and interviews, 10 to 20 pages. Poetry, to 40 lines (submit 3 to 5). "We seek the work of writers and artists living in or writing about the Northeast Corridor of America." Pays $25 for stories or essays, $10 for poems, on publication.

THE NORTHERN READER—Savage Press, Box 115, Superior, WI 54880. Mike Savage, Ed. Quarterly. Fiction, to 2,000 words. Free verse and metrical poetry, essays, and fillers. Pays in copies. Guidelines.

NORTHWEST REVIEW—369 PLC, Univ. of Oregon, Eugene, OR 97403. Elizabeth Claman, Fiction Ed. Fiction, commentary, essays, and poetry. Reviews. Pays in copies. Guidelines.

NORTHWOODS JOURNAL—P.O. Box 298, Thomaston, ME 04861. Robert W. Olmsted, Ed. Articles of interest to writers and fiction, 2,500 words. Poetry, any length. "Do not submit anything until you've read guidelines." Pays $5 per page, on acceptance.

NOTRE DAME REVIEW—Creative Writing Program, English Dept., Univ. of Notre Dame, Notre Dame, IN 46556. Attn: Man. Ed. Semiannual. Fiction, 10 to 15 pages. Essays, reviews, and poetry, 3 to 5 pages. Manuscripts read September through April. Payment varies, on publication.

OASIS—P.O. Box 626, Largo, FL 33779. Neal Storrs, Ed. Short fiction and literary essays, to 7,000 words, poetry, and translations from French, German, Italian, or Spanish. Any subject. "Style is paramount." Pays $15 to $50 for prose, $5 per poem, on publication. Guidelines.

OFFERINGS—P.O. Box 1667, Lebanon, MO 65536. Velvet Fackeldey, Ed. Quarterly. Poetry, to 30 lines, traditional and free verse. No payment.

THE OHIO REVIEW—Ellis Hall, Ohio Univ., Athens, OH 45701-2979. Wayne Dodd, Ed. Short stories, poetry, essays, reviews. Pays $5 per page for prose, $1 a line for poetry, plus copies, on publication. SASE required. Submissions read September through May.

OLD CROW—FKB Press, P.O. Box 403, Easthampton, MA 01027. John Gibney, Ed. Semiannual. Fiction and nonfiction, 200 to 6,000 words. Poetry, to 500 lines. "International readership. Our purpose is to publish new and established writers who have something true to say which might raise the hairs on the backs of our readers' necks." Pays in copies. Rotating reading period.

THE OLD RED KIMONO—Humanities Div., Floyd College, Box 1864, Rome, GA 30162. Jon Hershey, Jeff Mack, and Ed Sharp, Eds. Annual. Fiction, to 1,200 words. Poetry, submit 3 to 5 poems. "Poems and stories should be concise and imagistic. Nothing sentimental or didactic." Pays in copies.

100 WORDS—473 EPB, Univ. of Iowa, Iowa City, IA 52242. Carolyn Brown, Ed. Published six times a year. Prose and poetry, no more than 100 words. Translations from all languages invited, along with original text. Each issue has a theme or "trigger" word. Send SASE for upcoming guidelines and themes.

ONIONHEAD—Arts on the Park, Inc., 115 N. Kentucky Ave., Lakeland, FL 33801-5044. Attn: Ed. Council. Short stories, to 4,000 words; essays, to 2,500 words; and poetry, to 60 lines; on provocative social, political, and cultural observations and hypotheses. Pays in copies. Send SASE for Wordart poetry contest information. Manuscripts read year-round; responds in 12 weeks.

OREGON EAST—Hoke College Ctr., EOSC, La Grande, OR 97850. Attn: Ed. Short fiction, nonfiction, to 3,000 words, one-act plays, poetry, and high-contrast graphics. Pays in copies. Manuscripts read September through March.

OSIRIS—Box 297, Deerfield, MA 01842. Andrea Moorhead, Ed. Multilingual poetry journal, publishing poetry in English, French, German, and other languages in a translation/original format. Pays in copies.

OTHER VOICES—Univ. of Illinois at Chicago, Dept. of English (M/C 162), 601 S. Morgan St., Chicago, IL 60607-7120. Lois Hauselman, Ruth Canji, Tina Peano, Eds. Semiannual. Fresh, accessible short stories, one-act plays, and novel excerpts, to 5,000 words. Pays in copies and modest honorarium. Manuscripts read October to April.

OUTERBRIDGE—College of Staten Island, English Dept. 2S-218, 2800 Victory Blvd., Staten Island, NY 10314. Charlotte Alexander, Ed. Annual. Well-crafted stories, about 20 pages, and poetry, to 4 pages, "directed to a wide audience of literate adult readers." Pays in 2 copies. Manuscripts read September to June.

THE OXFORD AMERICAN—P.O. Box 1156, Oxford, MS 38655. Marc Smirnoff, Ed. Quarterly. Short fiction and nonfiction of a Southern nature. "Our interest in good nonfiction is strong." Cartoons, photos, and drawings. Pays from $50 for poetry and art; from $100 for nonfiction, on publication.

PAINTBRUSH: A JOURNAL OF MULTICULTURAL LITERATURE—Language & Literature Div., Truman State Univ., Kirksville, MO 63501. Ben Bennani, Ed. Annual. No longer accepting freelance poetry, translations, or book reviews. Publishes special monograph issues highlighting the work of individual writers. Query.

PAINTED BRIDE QUARTERLY—230 Vine St., Philadelphia, PA 19106. Kathleen Volk-Miller, Marion Wrenn, Eds. Fiction and poetry of varying lengths. Pays $5, plus subscription.

PALO ALTO REVIEW—1400 W. Villaret, San Antonio, TX 78224-2499. Ellen Shull, Ed. Semiannual. Fiction and articles, 5,000 words. "We look for wide-ranging investigations of historical, geographical, scientific, mathematical, artistic, political, and social topics, anything that has to do with living and learning." Interviews; 200-word think pieces about almost anything for "Food for Thought"; poetry, to 50 lines (send 3 to 5 poems at a time); reviews, to 500 words, of books, films, videos, or software. "Fiction shouldn't be too experimental or excessively avant-garde." Pays in copies.

PANGOLIN PAPERS—P.O. Box 241, Nordland, WA 98358. Pat Britt, Ed. Literary fiction, 100 to 7,000 words. Pays in copies

PANHANDLER—English Dept., Univ. of West Florida, Pensacola, FL 32514-5751. Laurie O'Brien, Ed. Semiannual. Fiction, 1,500 to 3,000 words; poetry, any length. Pays in copies. Responds in one to 6 months.

PARABOLA: THE MAGAZINE OF MYTH AND TRADITION—656 Broadway, New York, NY 10012. Attn: Eds. Quarterly. Articles, to 4,000 words, and fiction, 500 words, retelling traditional stories, folk and fairy tales. "All submissions must relate to an upcoming theme. We are looking for a balance between scholarly and accessible writing devoted to the ideas of myth and tradition." Send SASE for guidelines and themes. Payment varies, on publication.

THE PARIS REVIEW—541 E. 72nd St., New York, NY 10021. Attn: Fiction and Poetry Eds. Fiction and poetry of high literary quality. Pays on publication.

PARNASSUS—205 W. 89th St., Apt. 8F, New York, NY 10024-1835. Herbert Leibowitz, Ed. Critical essays and reviews on contemporary poetry. International in scope. Pays in cash and copies. Manuscripts read year-round.

PARTING GIFTS—3413 Wilshire, Greensboro, NC 27408. Robert Bixby, Ed. Fiction, to 1,000 words, and poetry, to 100 lines. Pays in copies. Reading period is generally January to June.

PARTISAN REVIEW—Boston Univ., 236 Bay State Rd., Boston, MA 02215. William Phillips, Ed.-in-Chief. Edith Kurzweil, Ed. Serious fiction, poetry, and essays. Payment varies. No simultaneous submissions. Manuscripts read September 1 to May 30.

PASSAGER: A JOURNAL OF REMEMBRANCE AND DISCOVERY—c/o Univ. of Baltimore, 1420 N. Charles St., Baltimore, MD 21201-5779. Mary Azrael, Kendra Kopelke, Ebby Malmgren, Eds. Fiction and essays, 4,000 words, of "remembrance and discovery." Poetry, to 40 lines. "We publish writers of all ages, but with an emphasis on new older writers." Pays in copies.

PASSAGES NORTH—Northern Michigan Univ., Dept. of English, 1401 Presque Isle Ave., Marquette, MI 49855. Anne Ohman Youngs, Ed. Semiannual; published in December and June. Poetry, fiction, interviews. Pays in copies. Manuscripts read September to May.

PEARL—3030 E. Second St., Long Beach, CA 90803. Marilyn Johnson, Ed. Fiction, 500 to 1,200 words, and poetry, to 40 lines. "We are interested in accessible, humanistic poetry and fiction that communicates and is related to real life. Along with the ironic, serious, and intense, humor and wit are welcome." Pays in copies.

PEQUOD—New York Univ., English Dept., 19 University Pl., 2nd Fl., New York, NY 10003. Mark Rudman, Ed. Semiannual. Short stories, essays, and literary criticism, to 10 pages; poetry and translations, to 3 pages. Pays honorarium, on publication.

PEREGRINE: THE JOURNAL OF AMHERST WRITERS AND ARTISTS—P.O. Box 1076, Amherst, MA 01004. Pat Schneider, Ed. Annual. Fiction, personal essays, and book reviews, to 4,500 words. Poetry. "We look for heart and soul as well as technical expertise. We encourage multiple submissions because we can take a year to decide." Pays in copies. Send SASE for contest guidelines.

PERMAFROST—English Dept., Univ. of Alaska, Fairbanks, AK 99775. Poetry, up to 5 poems; short fiction and creative nonfiction, to 25 pages; B&W photos. Reading period: September 1 to March 15. SASE. Pays in copies. Contest.

PIEDMONT LITERARY REVIEW—Bluebird Ln., Rt. #1, Box 1014, Forest, VA 24551. Evelyn Miles, Man. Ed. Quarterly. Poems, any length and style (partial to rhyme and meter); submit up to 5 poems to William R. Smith, Poetry Ed., 3750 Woodside Ave., Lynchburg, VA 24503. Submit Asian verse to Dorothy McLaughlin, 10 Atlantic Rd., Somerset, NJ 08873. Submit prose, to 2,500 words, to Dr. Olga Kronmeyer, 25 W. Dale Dr., Lynchburg, VA 24501. No pornography. Acquires first North American serial rights. Pays one copy. SASE.

PIG IRON PRESS—P.O. Box 237, Youngstown, OH 44501-0237. Jim Villani, Ed. Fiction and nonfiction, to 8,000 words. Poetry, to 100 lines. Write for upcoming themes. Pays $5 per published page or poem, on publication. Manuscripts read year-round. Responds in 3 months.

PIVOT—250 Riverside Dr., #23, New York, NY 10025. Martin Mitchell, Ed. Annual. Poetry, to 75 lines. Pays 2 copies. Manuscripts read Jan. 1 to June 1.

PLEIADES—Dept. of English and Philosophy, Central Missouri State Univ., Warrensburg, MO 64093. R. M. Kinder, Exec. Ed. Traditional and experimental poetry, fiction, criticism, reviews, and occasional belles lettres. Especially welcome: cross-genre and explorations of cultural diversity. Pays $10 for prose; $3 for poetry, on publication.

PLOT MAGAZINE—Calypso Publishing, P.O. Box 1351, Sugar Land, TX 77487-1351. Christina C. Russell, Man. Ed. Fantasy, science fiction, horror, suspense, fairy tales, ghost stories, space opera, supernatural horror, sword and sorcery, and speculative fiction, to 7,500 words. "We encourage new and emerging writers." Pays $10 for stories and line drawings, on acceptance.

PLOUGHSHARES—Emerson College, 100 Beacon St., Boston, MA 02116-1596. Attn: Ed. Serious fiction, to 6,000 words. Poetry (submit up to 3 poems at a time). Pays $25 per page ($50 to $250), on publication, plus 2 copies and subscription. Manuscripts read August through March. Guidelines.

THE PLUM REVIEW—P.O. Box 1347, Philadelphia, PA 19105. Mike Hammer, Ed.-in-Chief. Semiannual. Short stories, to 5,000 words, and poems "in all styles, subjects matters, and lengths." Essays relating to poetry as well as interviews with prominent poets. Pays in copies.

POEM—c/o English Dept., U.A.H., Huntsville, AL 35899. Nancy Frey Dillard, Ed. Serious lyric poetry. Pays in copies. Manuscripts read year-round (best times to submit are December to March and June to September).

POET MAGAZINE—P.O. Box 5646, Shreveport, LA 71135. Attn: Ed. Quarterly. Broad spectrum of poetry and how-to articles. "New and experienced poets encouraged to submit." Submit copies (not originals) of up to 3 poems, any form, and articles of any length on subjects related to poetry. Include two loose first-class stamps (not SASE) for guidelines, contest information, or editorial reply; manuscripts will not be returned. Payment is one copy.

POETRY—60 W. Walton St., Chicago, IL 60610. Joseph Parisi, Ed. Poetry of highest quality. Submit 3 to 4 poems. Allow 10 to 12 weeks for response. Pays $2 a line, on publication.

POETRY EAST—DePaul Univ., English Dept., 802 W. Belden Ave., Chicago, IL 60614-3214. Richard Jones, Ed. Elizabeth Sloan, Man. Ed. Semiannual. Poetry, essays, and translations. "Please send a sampling of your best work. Do not send book-length manuscripts without querying first." Pays in copies.

THE POET'S PAGE—P.O. Box 372, Wyanet, IL 61379. Ione K. Pence, Ed./Pub. Quarterly. Poetry, any length, any style, any topic. Articles and essays on poetry and poetic forms, poets, styles, etc. Pays in copies.

POTOMAC REVIEW—P.O. Box 354, Port Tobacco, MD 20677. Eli Flam, Ed. Quarterly "with a conscience and sense of humor." Fiction, literary essays, and other tales, to 2,500 words. Poetry, to 3 pages. Pays in copies.

POTPOURRI—P.O. Box 8278, Prairie Village, KS 66208. Polly W. Swafford, Ed. Quarterly. Short stories, to 3,500 words. Literary essays, travel pieces, and humor, to 2,500 words. Poetry and haiku, to 75 lines. "We like clever themes that avoid reminiscence, depressing plots and violence." Pays in one copy.

PRAIRIE SCHOONER—201 Andrews Hall, Univ. of Nebraska, Lincoln, NE 68588-0334. Hilda Raz, Ed. Short stories, poetry, essays, book reviews, and translations. Pays in copies. SASE required. Manuscripts read September through May; responds in 3 months. Annual contests.

PRESS QUARTERLY—125 W. 72nd St., Suite 3-M, New York, NY 10023. Daniel Roberts, Ed. Short stories and poems that "deliver an invigorating dose of clear, humanized storytelling." Payment varies, on publication.

PRIMAVERA—Box 37-7547, Chicago, IL 60637. Attn: Editorial Board. Annual. Fiction and poetry that focus on the experiences of women; author need not be female. B&W photos and drawings. No simultaneous submissions; SASE. Pays in 2 copies. Responds within 3 months.

PRISM INTERNATIONAL—E462-1866 Main Mall, Creative Writing Program, Univ. of British Columbia, Vancouver, B.C., Canada V6T 1Z1. Attn: Ed. High-quality fiction, poetry, drama, creative nonfiction, and literature in translation, varying lengths. Include international reply coupons. Pays $20 per published page. Annual short fiction contest.

PROOF ROCK—P.O. Box 607, Halifax, VA 24558. Don Conner, Fiction Ed. Serena Fusek, Poetry Ed. Fiction, to 2,500 words. Poetry, to 32 lines. Reviews. Pays in copies.

THE PROSE POEM—English Dept., Providence College, Providence, RI 02198. Peter Johnson, Ed. Prose poems. Book reviews, 4 to 6 pages. Pays in copies. Query for book reviews. Manuscripts read January 1 to April 1.

PUCK—Permeable Press, 2336 Market St., #14, San Francisco, CA 94114. Brian Clark, Ed. "For Irrepressible Readers." Quarterly. Non-genre fiction, to 15,000 words; essays and "speculative" nonfiction, to 10,000 words. "Fiery editorial range. Fiction should provoke but not be dogmatic. We especially welcome un/under-published writers. Read a sample first." Pays in copies and 1/2¢ per word.

PUCKERBRUSH REVIEW—76 Main St., Orono, ME 04473-1430. Constance Hunting, Ed. Semiannual. Literary fiction, criticism, and poetry of various lengths, "to bring literary Maine news to readers." Pays in 2 copies. Manuscripts read year-round.

PUDDING MAGAZINE: THE INTERNATIONAL JOURNAL OF APPLIED POETRY—c/o Pudding House Writers Resource Ctr., Bed & Breakfast for Writers, Johnstown, OH 43031. Jennifer Bosveld, Ed. Poems on popular culture, social concerns, personal struggle; articles/essays on poetry in the schools and in human services. Manuscripts read year-round.

PUERTO DEL SOL—New Mexico State Univ., Box 3E, Las Cruces, NM 88003-0001. K. West, Kevin McIlvoy, and Antonya Nelson, Eds. Short stories and personal essays, to 30 pages; novel excerpts, to 65 pages; articles, to 45 pages, and reviews, to 15 pages. Poetry, photos. Pays in copies. Manuscripts read September 1 to March 1.

QUARTER AFTER EIGHT—Ellis Hall, Ohio Univ., Athens, OH 45701. Attn: Eds. Annual. Avant-garde short fiction, novel excerpts, essays, criticism, investigations, and interviews, to 10,000 words. Submit no more than 2 pieces. Prose poetry (submit up to 5 poems); no traditional poetry. Pays in copies. Manuscripts read September through February.

QUARTERLY WEST—317 Olpin Union, Univ. of Utah, Salt Lake City, UT 84112. Margot Schilpp and Lawrence Coates, Eds. Fiction, short-shorts, poetry, essays, translations, and reviews. Pays $25 to $50 for stories, $15 to $50 for poems. Manuscripts read year-round. Biennial novella competition in even-numbered years.

RAG MAG—P.O. Box 12, Goodhue, MN 55027-0012. Beverly Voldseth, Ed. Semiannual. Eclectic fiction and nonfiction, art, photos. Poetry, any length. Must be related to theme. No religious writing. Pays in copies. SASE for guidelines and themes.

RAMBUNCTIOUS REVIEW—1221 W. Pratt Blvd., Chicago, IL 60626. Mary Alberts, Richard Goldman, Nancy Lennon, Beth Hausler, Eds. Fiction, to 12 pages; poems, submit up to 5 at a time. Pays in copies. Manuscripts read September through May. Contests.

READER'S BREAK—Pine Grove Press, P.O. Box 40, Jamesville, NY 13078. Gertrude S. Eiler, Ed. Semiannual. Fiction, to 3,500 words. "We welcome stories about relationships, tales of action, adventure, science fiction and fantasy, romance, suspense, and mystery. Themes and plots may be historical, contemporary, or futuristic. Our emphasis is on fiction, but we will read nonfiction in story form." Poems, to 75 lines. Pays in one copy.

RED CEDAR REVIEW—Dept. of English, 17-C Morrill Hall, Michigan State Univ., E. Lansing, MI 48824-1036. Carrie Preston, Poetry Ed. David Sheridan, Fiction Ed. Fiction, to 5,000 words, and poetry (submit up to 5 poems). Pays in copies. Manuscripts read year-round.

RED ROCK REVIEW—Dept. of English, Community College of Southern Nevada, 3200 E. Cheyenne Ave., N. Las Vegas, NV 89030. Dr. Richard Logsdon, Ed. Semiannual. Short fiction, to 5,000 words; book reviews, to 1,000 words; poetry, to 2 pages. "We're geared toward publishing the work of already established writers. No taboos." Payment varies, on acceptance.

REED MAGAZINE—Dept. of English, San Jose State Univ., One Washington Sq., San Jose, CA 95192-0090. Address Man. Ed. Fiction, personal essays, and reminiscences, to 4,000 words; submit no more than 2 stories or essays at a time. Poetry, to 40 lines, on any subject; submit up to 3 at a time. "We want material of a literary nature, addressing the human condition." B&W photos. Payment is one copy. Manuscripts read August 1 to November 1.

RESPONSE: A CONTEMPORARY JEWISH REVIEW—27 W. 20th St., 9th Fl., New York, NY 10011-3707. David R. Adler, Michael Steinberg, and Charita Baumhaft, Eds. Pearl Gluck, Fiction and Poetry Ed. Fiction, to 25 double-spaced pages, in which Jewish experience is explored in an unconventional fashion. Articles, to 25 pages, with a focus on Jewish issues. Poetry, to 80 lines, and book reviews. Pays in copies.

REVIEW: LATIN AMERICAN LITERATURE AND ARTS—Americas Society, 680 Park Ave., New York, NY 10021. Alfred J. MacAdam, Ed. Semiannual. Work in English translation by and about young and established Latin American writers; essays and book reviews considered. Send queries for 1,000- to 1,500-word manuscripts, and short poem translations. Payment varies, on acceptance.

RIVER CITY—Dept. of English, Univ. of Memphis, Memphis, TN 38152. Paul Naylor, Ed. Poems, short stories, essays, and interviews. No novel excerpts. Payment varies according to grants. Manuscripts read September through April. Guidelines. Contests.

RIVER OAK REVIEW—P.O. Box 3127, Oak Park, IL 60303. Semiannual. Address Fiction, Poetry, or Nonfiction Ed. No criticism, reviews, or translations. Limit prose to 20 pages; poetry to batches of no more than 4. Pays in copies, and small honorarium, as funding permits.

RIVER STYX—3207 Washington Ave., St. Louis, MO 63103. Attn: Ed. Published 3 times a year. Poetry, fiction, personal essays, literary interviews, B&W photos, and color cover artwork. Payment is $8 per printed page plus subscription. Manuscripts read May 1 to Nov. 1; reports in 2 to 3 months.

RIVERSIDE QUARTERLY—Box 12085, San Antonio, TX 78212. Leland Sapiro, Ed. Science fiction and fantasy, to 3,500 words; reviews, criticism, any length; poetry and letters. "Read magazine before submitting." Send poetry to Sheryl Smith, 515 Saratoga, #2, Santa Clara, CA 95050. Pays in copies.

ROANOKE REVIEW—Roanoke College, Salem, VA 24153. Robert R. Walter, Ed. Quality short fiction, to 5,000 words, and poetry, to 100 lines. Pays in copies.

ROCKFORD REVIEW—P.O. Box 858, Rockford, IL 61105. David Ross, Ed.-in-Chief. Published 3 times a year. Fiction, essays, and satire, 250 to 1,300 words. Experimental and traditional poetry, to 50 lines (shorter works preferred). One-act plays and other dramatic forms, to 10 pages. "We prefer genuine or satirical human dilemmas with coping or non-coping outcomes that ring the reader's bell." Submit up to 3 works at a time. Pays in copies; two $25 Editor's Choice Prizes awarded each issue.

ROSEBUD—P.O. Box 459, Cambridge, WI 53523. Rod Clark, Ed. Quarterly. Fiction, articles, profiles, 1,200 to 1,800 words, and poems; love, alienation, travel, humor, nostalgia, and unexpected revelation. Pays $45 plus copies, on publication. Guidelines.

ROSWELL LITERARY REVIEW—P.O. Box 2412, Roswell, NM 88202-2412. Harvey Stanbrough, Ed. Quarterly. Fiction, to 6,000 words, personal essays, and poetry. Pays from 1/2¢ a word for prose, from $1 per poem.

SAN FERNANDO POETRY JOURNAL—18301 Halstead St., Northridge, CA 91325. Richard Cloke, Ed. Quality poetry, 20 to 100 lines, with social content; scientific, philosophical, and historical themes. Pays in copies.

SANSKRIT LITERARY/ART PUBLICATION—Cone Ctr., Univ. of North Carolina/Charlotte, Charlotte, NC 28223-0001. Attn: Ed. Annual. Poetry, short fiction, photos, and fine art. Pays in copies. Manuscripts read in fall only; deadline October 30.

SANTA BARBARA REVIEW—104 La Vereda Ln., Santa Barbara, CA 93108. P.S. Leddy, Ed. Short stories; occasionally plays. Biographies and essays, to 6,500 words. Poems. Translations. B&W art and photos. Pays in copies.

SCANDINAVIAN REVIEW—725 Park Ave., New York, NY 10021. Attn: Ed. Published 3 times a year. Essays on contemporary Scandinavia: arts, sciences, business, politics, and culture of Scandinavia. Fiction and poetry, translated from Nordic languages. Pays from $100, on publication.

SCRIVENER—McGill Univ., 853 Sherbrooke St. W., Montreal, Quebec, Canada H3A 2T6. Michelle LeLievre and Helen Polychronakos, Eds. Poems, submit 5 to 15; prose, to 20 pages; reviews, to 5 pages. Photography and graphics. Pays in copies.

THE SEATTLE REVIEW—Padelford Hall, Box 354330, Univ. of Washington, Seattle, WA 98195. Colleen J. McElroy, Ed. Short stories, to 20 pages, poetry, essays on the craft of writing, and interviews with northwest writers. Payment varies. Manuscripts read October 1 through May 31.

SENECA REVIEW—Hobart & William Smith Colleges, Geneva, NY 14456. Deborah Tall, Ed. Poetry, translations, and essays on contemporary poetry. Pays in copies. Manuscripts read September 1 to May 1.

SHENANDOAH—Washington and Lee Univ., Troubadour Theatre, 2nd Fl., Lexington, VA 24450-0303. R.T. Smith, Ed. Quarterly. Highest quality fiction, poetry, criticism, essays and interviews. "Please read the magazine before submitting!" Pays $25 per page for prose; $2.50 per line for poetry, on publication. Annual contests.

SHOOTING STAR REVIEW—7123 Race St., Pittsburgh, PA 15208. Sandra Gould Ford, Pub. Fiction and folktales, to 3,000 words, essays, to 2,000 words, and poetry, to 50 lines, on the African-American experience. Query for book reviews only. Pays $5 for poems; $10 for essays; $10 to $20 for fiction. Send SASE for topic deadlines. Responds to queries in 3 weeks; manuscripts in 4 months.

SING HEAVENLY MUSE! WOMEN'S POETRY & PROSE—P.O. Box 13320, Minneapolis, MN 55414. Attn: Ed. Short stories and essays, to 5,000 words. Poetry. Query for themes and reading periods. Pays in copies.

SKYLARK—2200 169th St., Hammond, IN 46323-2094. Pamela Hunter, Ed. "The Fine Arts Annual of Purdue Calumet." Fiction and articles, to 4,000 words. Poetry, to 21 lines. B&W prints and drawings. Pays in one copy. Manuscripts read November 1 through April 30 for fall publication.

THE SLATE—P.O. Box 581189, Minneapolis, MN 55458-1189. Rachel Fulkerson, Chris Dall, Patty Delaney, Eds. Published 3 times a year. Short fiction, poetry, nonfiction, and essays. "We are dedicated to reviving a cultural interest in the written word and to nourishing the relationship between writer and reader." Pays in copies. Manuscripts read year-round.

SLIPSTREAM—Box 2071, Niagara Falls, NY 14301. Attn: Ed. Contemporary poetry, any length. Pays in copies. Query for themes. Guidelines. Annual poetry chapbook contest ($500 prize) has December 1 deadline; send SASE for details. Fiction overstocked; query.

THE SMALL POND MAGAZINE—P.O. Box 664, Stratford, CT 06497-0664. Napoleon St. Cyr, Ed. Published 3 times a year. Fiction, to 2,500 words; poetry, to 100 lines. Pays in copies. Query for nonfiction. Include short bio. Manuscripts read year-round.

SMALL PRESS REVIEW—Box 100, Paradise, CA 95967. Len Fulton, Ed. Reviews, 200 words, of small literary books and magazines; tracks the publishing of small publishers and small-circulation magazines. Query.

SNAKE NATION REVIEW—Snake Nation Press, 110 #2 W. Force, Valdosta, GA 31601. Roberta George, Ed. Quarterly. Short stories, novel chapters, and informal essays, 5,000 words, and poetry, to 60 lines. Pays in copies and prizes.

SNOWY EGRET—P.O. Box 9, Bowling Green, IN 47833. Philip Repp, Ed. Poetry, fiction, and nonfiction, to 10,000 words. Natural history from artistic, literary, philosophical, and historical perspectives. Pays $2 per page for prose; $2 to $4 for poetry, on publication. Manuscripts read year-round.

SONORA REVIEW—Dept. of English, Univ. of Arizona, Tucson, AZ 85721. Attn: Fiction, Poetry, or Nonfiction Ed. (Address appropriate genre editor.) Annual contests; send for guidelines. Simultaneous submissions accepted (except for contest entries). Manuscripts read year-round.

THE SOUTH CAROLINA REVIEW—Dept. of English, Clemson Univ., Clemson, SC 29634-1503. Frank Day, Man. Ed. Semiannual. Fiction, essays, reviews, and interviews, to 4,000 words. Poems. Send complete manuscript. Pays in copies. Response time is 6 to 9 months. Manuscripts read September through May (but not in December).

SOUTH DAKOTA REVIEW—Box 111, Univ. Exchange, Vermillion, SD 57069-2390. Brian Bedard, Ed. Exceptional fiction, 3,000 to 5,000 words, and poetry, 10 to 25 lines. Critical articles, especially on American literature, Western American literature, theory and esthetics, creative nonfiction, 3,000 to 5,000 words. Pays in copies. Manuscripts read year-round; slower response time in the summer.

THE SOUTHERN CALIFORNIA ANTHOLOGY—c/o Master of Professional Writing Program, WPH 404, Univ. of Southern California, Los Angeles, CA 90089-4034. James Ragan, Ed.-in-Chief. Fiction, to 20 pages, and poetry, to 5 pages. Pays in copies. Manuscripts read September to January.

SOUTHERN EXPOSURE—P.O. Box 531, Durham, NC 27702. Pat Arnow, Ed. Quarterly forum on "Southern movements for social change." Short stories, to 3,600 words, essays, investigative journalism, and oral histories, 500 to 3,600 words. Pays $25 to $250, on publication. Query.

SOUTHERN HUMANITIES REVIEW—9088 Haley Ctr., Auburn Univ., AL 36849. Dan R. Latimer, Virginia M. Kouidis, Eds. Short stories, essays, and criticism, 3,500 to 15,000 words; poetry, to 2 pages. Responds within 3 months. No simultaneous submissions. SASE required.

SOUTHERN POETRY REVIEW—Advancement Studies, Central Piedmont Community College, Charlotte, NC 28235. Ken McLaurin, Ed. Poems. No restrictions on style, length, or content. Manuscripts read September through May.

THE SOUTHERN REVIEW— 43 Allen Hall, Louisiana State Univ., Baton Rouge, LA 70803-5005. James Olney and Dave Smith, Eds. Emphasis on contemporary literature in United States and abroad with special interest in southern culture and history. Fiction and essays, 4,000 to 8,000 words. Serious poetry of highest quality. Pays $12 a page for prose, $20 a page for poetry, on publication. No manuscripts read in the summer.

SOUTHWEST REVIEW—307 Fondren Library W., Box 750374, Southern Methodist Univ., Dallas, TX 75275-0374. Elizabeth Mills, Sr. Fiction Ed. "A quarterly that serves the interests of the region but is not bound by them." Fiction, essays, poetry, and interviews with well-known writers, 3,000 to 7,500 words. Pays varying rates. Manuscripts read September 1 through May 31.

SOU'WESTER—Southern Illinois Univ. at Edwardsville, Edwardsville, IL 62026-1438. Fred W. Robbins, Ed. Nancy Avdoian, Assoc. Ed. Steve Wilper, Poetry Ed. Susan Garrison, Fiction Ed. Allison Funk, Consulting Ed. Fiction, to 8,000 words. Poetry, any length. Pays in copies. Manuscripts not read in August.

THE SOW'S EAR POETRY REVIEW—19535 Pleasant View Dr., Abingdon, VA 24211-6827. Attn: Ed. Quarterly. Eclectic poetry and art. Submit one to 5 poems, any length, plus a brief biographical note. Interviews, essays, and articles, any length, about poets and poetry are also considered. B&W photos and drawings. Payment is one copy. Poetry and chapbook contests. SASE for guidelines.

SPARROW MAGAZINE—See *Sparrow: The Yearbook of the Sonnet.*

SPARROW: THE YEARBOOK OF THE SONNET—(formerly *Sparrow Magazine*) Sparrow Press, 103 Waldron St., W. Lafayette, IN 47906. Felix and Selma Stefanile, Eds./Pubs. Contemporary (14-line) sonnets, and occasionally formal poems in other structures. Submit up to 5 poems. Pays $3 per poem, on publication. A $25 sonnet prize is awarded to a contributor in each issue.

SPECTRUM—Univ. of California/ Santa Barbara, Box 14800, Santa Barbara, CA 93107. Attn: Ed. Annual. Short stories, experimental narrative, poetry, nonfiction essays, slides of art. Annual deadline is February 1.

SPOON RIVER POETRY REVIEW—Dept. of English, Stevenson Hall, Illinois State Univ., Normal, IL 61790-4240. Lucia Cordell Getsi, Ed. Poetry, any length. Pays in copies. Editors' Prize Contest; SASE for details.

SPRING FANTASY—Women in the Arts, P.O. Box 2907, Decatur, IL 62524-2907. Linda Hutton, Ed. Fiction for adults and children, personal essays, to 1,500 words. Poetry, to 32 lines. Payment is one copy.

SPSM&H—329 E St., Bakersfield, CA 93304. Frederick A. Raborg, Jr., Ed. Single sonnets, sequences, essays about the sonnet form, short fiction in which the sonnet plays a part, books, and anthologies. Pays $10, plus copies, for fiction and essays; "best of issue" sonnets, $14.

STAND MAGAZINE—Dept. of English, Hibbs Bldg., 900 Park Ave., Richmond, VA 23284-2005. David Latané, U.S. Ed. (179 Wingrove Rd., Newcastle upon Tyne NE4 9DA UK) British quarterly. Fiction, 2,000 to 5,000 words, and poetry to 100 lines (submit up to 6 poems). No formulaic verse.

STATE STREET REVIEW—FCCJ North Campus, 4501 Capper Rd., Jacksonville, FL 32218-4499. John Hunt, Exec. Ed. Sohrab Fracis, Michele Boyette, Howard Denson, Eds. Semiannual. Fiction, to 6,000 words. Nonfiction, 2,000 words, on writers, poets, or on writing itself. Poetry. Pays in copies.

STORY QUARTERLY—P.O. Box 1416, Northbrook, IL 60065. Anne Brashler, Diane Williams, Eds. Short stories and interviews. Pays in copies. Manuscripts read year-round.

THE STYLUS—9412 Huron Ave., Richmond, VA 23294. Roger Reus, Ed. Annual. Articles on writers ("no scholarly/heavily footnoted/dull literary theses"). Original fiction and author interviews. Pays in copies.

THE SUN—The Sun Publishing Co., 107 N. Roberson St., Chapel Hill, NC 27516. Sy Safransky, Ed. Essays, interviews, and fiction, to 7,000 words; poetry; photos, illustrations, and cartoons. "We're interested in all writing that makes sense and enriches our common space." Pays $300 to $500 for fiction, $300 to $750 for nonfiction, $50 to $200 for poetry, on publication.

SUN AND SHADE—4205 Quail Ranch Rd., New Smyrna Beach, FL 32168. Kim M. Nicastro, Ed. Semiannual. Fiction, 500 to 2,000 words. Preference given to Florida writers. Pays $15 to $35, on publication.

SYCAMORE REVIEW—Purdue Univ., Dept. of English, West Lafayette, IN 47907. Rob Davidson, Ed.-in-Chief. Semiannual. Poetry, short fiction (no genre fiction), personal essays, drama, and translations. Pays in copies. Manuscripts read September to April.

TALE SPINNER—P.O. Box 336, Bedford, IN 47421. Joe Glasgow, Ed. Semiannual. Commercial fiction, 800 to 4,000 words, and poems, to 20 lines. No erotic material.

TALKING RIVER REVIEW—Lewis-Clark State College, 8th Ave. & 6th St., Lewiston, ID 83501. Attn: Eds. Semiannual. Short stories, novel excerpts, and essays, to 5,000 words. Poetry, any length or style; submit up to 5 poems. "We publish emerging writers alongside established writers." Pays in copies and subscription. Manuscripts read September through April.

TALUS AND SCREE—P.O. Box 851, Waldport, OR 97394. Carla Perry, Ed. Semiannual. Poetry (no length limit), short fiction (including novel excerpts), memoir vignettes, interviews, reviews, line drawings, photos, and cartoons. Pays in copies.

TAR RIVER POETRY—Dept. of English, East Carolina Univ., Greenville, NC 27858-4353. Peter Makuck, Ed. Poetry and reviews. "We prefer poems with strong imagery and figurative language. We are not interested in poems featuring trite, worn-out phrases, vague abstractions, or cliché situations." Pays in copies. Submit from September through April.

THE TEXAS REVIEW—English Dept., Sam Houston State Univ., Huntsville, TX 77341. Paul Ruffin, Ed. Fiction, poetry, articles, to 20 typed pages. Reviews. Pays in copies and subscription.

THEMA—Box 74109, Metairie, LA 70033-4109. Virginia Howard, Ed. Theme-related fiction, to 20 pages, and poetry, to 2 pages. Pays $25 per story; $10 per short-short; $10 per poem; $10 for B&W art/photo, on acceptance. Send SASE for themes and guidelines.

32 PAGES—Rain Crow Publishing, 101-308 Andrew Pl., W. Lafayette, IN 47906-3932. Michael S. Manley, Pub. Bimonthly. Poetry, short fiction, creative nonfiction, drama, and graphical narrative, to 8,000 words. Pays $5 per published page, on publication. Guidelines.

360 DEGREES: ART & LITERARY REVIEW—980 Bush St., Suite 404, San Francisco, CA 94109. Karen Kinnison, Ed. Quarterly art and literary review, featuring fiction and poetry (any length), artwork, graphic imagery, and "art-text," words mixed with images. Send photocopies and photographs only. Pays in copies.

THE THREEPENNY REVIEW—P.O. Box 9131, Berkeley, CA 94709. Wendy Lesser, Ed. Fiction, to 5,000 words. Poetry, to 100 lines. Essays, 1,500 to 3,000 words, on books, theater, film, dance, music, art, television, and politics. Pays to $200, on acceptance. Limited market. Guidelines. Manuscripts read September through May.

TIGHTROPE—323 Pelham Rd., Amherst, MA 01002. Ed Rayher, Ed. Limited-edition, letterpress semiannual. Poetry, any length. Pays in copies. Manuscripts read year-round.

TOMORROW MAGAZINE—P.O. Box 148486, Chicago, IL 60614-8486. Tim W. Brown, Ed. Poetry with an underground sensibility. "Our goal is to publish tomorrow's writing today." Pays in copies.

TOMORROW SPECULATIVE FICTION—P.O. Box 6038, Evanston, IL 60204. Algis Budrys, Ed. Bimonthly. Fiction, any length, science fiction, fantasy, and horror. No poetry, cartoons, or nonfiction. Pays 4¢ to 7¢ a word, on publication.

TOUCHSTONE—P.O. Box 8308, Spring, TX 77387. Bill Laufer, Pub. Annual. Fiction, 750 to 2,000 words: mainstream, experimental. Interviews, essays, reviews. Poetry, to 40 lines. Pays in copies. Manuscripts read year-round. Query with SASE.

TREASURE HOUSE—See *Verb.*

TRIQUARTERLY—Northwestern Univ., 625 Colfax Ave., Evanston, IL 60208-4210. Attn: Ed. Serious, aesthetically informed and inventive poetry and prose, for an international and literate audience. Pays $5 per page for prose, 50¢ per line for poetry. Manuscripts read October through March. Allow 10 to 12 weeks for reply.

2AM MAGAZINE—P.O. Box 6754, Rockford, IL 61125-1754. Gretta Anderson, Ed. Poetry, articles, reviews, and personality profiles, 500 to 2,000 words, as well as fantasy, horror, and some science fiction/sword-and-sorcery short stories, 500 to 5,000 words. Pays 1/2¢ a word, on acceptance. Manuscripts read year-round.

THE URBANITE: SURREAL & LIVELY & BIZARRE—Box 4737, Davenport, IA 52808. Mark McLaughlin, Ed. Published 3 times a year. Dark fantasy, horror (no gore), surrealism, reviews, and social commentary, to 3,000 words. Free verse poems, to 2 pages. Pays 2¢ to 3¢ a word; $10 for poetry, on acceptance. Query for nonfiction.

URBANUS MAGAZINE—P.O. Box 192921, San Francisco, CA 94119. P. Drizhal, Ed. Semiannual. Fiction and nonfiction, 1,000 to 6,000 words, and poetry, to 40 lines, that reflect contemporary and urban influences for a "readership generally impatient with the mainstream approach." B&W photos and drawings. Pays 1¢ to 2¢ a word; $10 a page plus 5 copies for poetry, on acceptance. Query for guidelines and reading periods.

VERB (formerly *Treasure House*)—Treasure House Publishing, P.O. Box 4167, Hagerstown, MD 21741-4167. Attn: Ed.-in-Chief. Fiction, 1,500 to 3,000 words. "We are also interested in offbeat essays tied to literature and writing for our website." Payment varies, often in copies/subscriptions. Guidelines.

VERMONT INK—P.O. Box 3297, Burlington, VT 05401-3297. Donna Leach, Ed. Quarterly. Short stories, 2,000 words, that are well-written, entertaining, and "basically G-rated": adventure, historical, humor, mainstream, mystery and suspense, regional interest, romance, science fiction, and westerns. Poetry, to 25 lines, should be upbeat or humorous. Pays to $25 for stories; to $10 for poetry, on acceptance. Send complete manuscript with short bio and SASE.

VERSE UNTO US—907 Oak Lane Dr., Joshua, TX 76058. Alan Steele, Ed. Quarterly. Fiction, 500 to 2,750 words, any subject. Poetry, to 30 lines, any style or subject. Pays $5 for fiction; $5 for best poem in magazine, on publication.

VERVE—P.O. Box 3205, Simi Valley, CA 93093. Ron Reichick, Ed. Contemporary fiction and nonfiction, to 1,000 words, that fit the theme of the issue. Poetry, to 2 pages; submit up to 5 poems. Pays in one copy. Query for themes.

VIGNETTE—P.O. Box 109, Hollywood, CA 90078-0109. Dawn Baillie, Ed. Fiction, to 5,000 words, based on one-word concepts. Send SASE for current themes. Pays $100 to $300, on publication.

THE VILLAGER—135 Midland Ave., Bronxville, NY 10708. Amy Murphy, Ed. Mary Hazzah, Fiction/Articles Ed. Mrs. Joseph Aiello, Poetry Ed. Fiction, 900 to 1,500 words, "in good taste": mystery, adventure, humor, romance. Short, preferably seasonal poetry. Pays in copies.

VINCENT BROTHERS REVIEW— 4566 Northern Cir., Riverside, OH 45424-5733. Kimberly Willardson, Ed. Published 3 times a year. Fiction, nonfiction, poetry, fillers, and B&W art. "Read sample copies/back issues before submitting." Pays from $10 for fiction and nonfiction; $10 for poetry used in "Page Left" feature. Guidelines. SASE.

VIRGINIA QUARTERLY REVIEW— One W. Range, Charlottesville, VA 22903. Attn: Ed. Quality fiction and poetry. Serious essays and articles, 3,000 to 6,000 words, on literature, science, politics, economics, etc. Pays $10 per page for prose, $1 per line for poetry, on publication.

VISIONS INTERNATIONAL—Black Buzzard Press, 1007 Ficklen Rd., Fredericksburg, VA 22405. Bradley R. Strahan, Ed. Published 3 times a year. Poetry, to 50 lines, and B&W drawings. (Query first for art.) "Nothing amateur or previously published. Read magazine before submitting." Pays in copies (or honorarium when funds available). Manuscripts read year-round.

WASCANA REVIEW— c/o Dept. of English, Univ. of Regina, Regina, Sask., Canada S4S 0A2. Kathleen Wall, Ed. Short stories, 2,000 to 6,000 words; critical articles on short fiction and poetry; poetry. Pays $3 per page for prose, $10 for poetry, after publication.

WASHINGTON REVIEW—P.O. Box 50132, Washington, DC 20091-0132. Clarissa Wittenberg, Ed. Poetry; articles on literary, performing and fine arts in the Washington, D.C., area. Fiction, 1,000 to 2,500 words. Area writers preferred. Pays in copies. Responds in 3 months.

WEST BRANCH—Bucknell Hall, Bucknell Univ., Lewisburg, PA 17837. Karl Patten, Robert Taylor, Eds. Poetry and fiction. Pays in copies and subscriptions.

WHETSTONE—P.O. Box 1266, Barrington, IL 60011. Attn: Eds. Fiction and creative nonfiction, to 20 pages. Poems, submit up to 7. Payment varies, on publication.

THE WILLIAM AND MARY REVIEW—P.O. Box 8795, College of William and Mary, Williamsburg, VA 23187-8795. Erica Weitzman, Ed. Annual. Fiction, critical essays, and interviews, 2,500 to 7,500 words; poetry, all genres (submit 4 to 6 poems); and art, all media. Pays in copies. Manuscripts read September through April. Responds in 3 months.

WILLOW SPRINGS—MS-1, Eastern Washington Univ., Cheney, WA 99004-2496. Attn: Ed. Fiction, poetry, translation, and art. Length and subject matter are open. No payment. Manuscripts read September 15 to May 15.

WIND MAGAZINE—P.O. Box 24548, Lexington, KY 40524. Charlie Hughes and Leatha Kendrick, Eds. Semiannual. Short stories, poems, and essays. Reviews of books from small presses and news of interest to the literary community. Pays in copies. Contests. Manuscripts read year-round.

THE WINDLESS ORCHARD—Dept. of English, Indiana-Purdue Univ., Ft. Wayne, IN 46805. Robert Novak, Ed. Contemporary poetry; submit up to 3 poems. Pays in copies. SASE required. Manuscripts read year-round.

WINDSOR REVIEW—Dept. of English, Univ. of Windsor, Windsor, Ont., Canada N9B 3P4. Attn: Ed. Short stories, poetry, and original art. Pays $15 for poetry; $50 for fiction, on publication. Responds in one to 3 months.

WITNESS—Oakland Community College, 27055 Orchard Lake Rd., Farmington Hills, MI 48334. Peter Stine, Ed. Thematic journal. Fiction and essays, 5 to 20 pages, and poems (submit up to 3). Pays $6 per page for prose, $10 per page for poetry, on publication.

THE WORCESTER REVIEW—6 Chatham St., Worcester, MA 01609. Rodger Martin, Ed. Poetry (submit up to 5 poems at a time), fiction, critical articles about poetry, and articles and reviews with a New England connection. Pays in copies. Responds within 6 months.

WORDWRIGHTS—The Argonne Hotel Press, 1620 Argonne Pl. N.W., Washington, DC 20009. R.D. Baker, Pub. Quarterly. Fiction and nonfiction, to 10 pages. Poetry, to 50 lines. "Allow at least 3 months for reply. Manuscripts may remain under consideration for 6 months or more." Pays in copies.

THE WORMWOOD REVIEW—P.O. Box 4698, Stockton, CA 95204-0698. Marvin Malone, Ed. Quarterly. Poetry and prose-poetry, 4 to 400 lines. "We encourage wit and conciseness." Pays 3 to 20 copies or cash equivalent.

WRITERS' FORUM—Univ. of Colorado, 1420 Austin Bluffs Pkwy., Colorado Springs, CO 80933-7150. C. Kenneth Pellow, Ed. Annual. Mainstream and experimental fiction, 1,000 to 8,000 words. Poetry (one to 5 poems per submission). Emphasis on western themes and writers. Pays in copies. Manuscripts read year-round, but best time to submit is July through November.

WRITERS' INTERNATIONAL FORUM—P.O. Box 516, Tracyton, WA 98393-0516. Sandra Haven, Ed. Dir. Fiction, 500 to 2,000 words, all genres except horror. "We help writers improve skills and marketability through the exchange of ideas and responses to our published stories by our readers." *Special Fiction for Children*: Stories, to 2,000 words, written by and for children 8 to 16 years old. Pays from $5, on acceptance. Write for guidelines and contest information.

WRITERS ON THE RIVER—P.O. Box 40828, Memphis, TN 38174. Miss Demaris C. Smith, Ed. Russell H. Strauss, Prose Ed. Dr. Wanda A. Rider, Poetry Ed. Fiction (adventure, fantasy, historical, humor, mainstream, mystery/suspense), and nonfiction (profiles, scholarly essays, regional history), to 2,500 words. All types of poetry considered; submit up to 6. "We try to promote good writing and act as a sounding board for Southern writers." Submit 2 copies of manuscripts. Submissions accepted from: AR, AL, MS, LA, TN, KY, and MO only. Pays in copies. Manuscripts read year-round.

XANADU—Box 773, Huntington, NY 11743-0773. Mildred Jeffrey, Weslea Sidon, Lois V. Walker, Sue Kain, Eds. Poetry on a variety of topics; no length restrictions. Prose poems. Pays in copies. Manuscripts read September through June.

YALE REVIEW—Yale Univ., P.O. Box 208243, New Haven, CT 06520-8243. J.D. McClatchy, Ed. Susan Bianconi, Man. Ed. Serious poetry, to 200 lines, and fiction, 3,000 to 5,000 words. Pays average of $400.

THE YALOBUSHA REVIEW—P.O. Box 186, University, MS 38677-0186. Attn: Ed. Annual. Short stories, to 35 pages. Creative essays, to 20 pages. Poetry, any length. "We seek a balance of local, regional, and national writers. We publish new as well as established writers." Pays in copies.

YARROW—English Dept., Lytle Hall, Kutztown State Univ., Kutztown, PA 19530. Harry Humes, Ed. Semiannual. Poetry. "Just good, solid, clear writing. We don't have room for long poems." Pays in copies. Manuscripts read year-round.

ZYZZYVA— 41 Sutter, Suite 1400, San Francisco, CA 94104. Howard Junker, Ed. Publishes work of West Coast writers only: fiction, essays, and poetry. Pays $50, on acceptance. Manuscripts read year-round.

GREETING CARDS & NOVELTY ITEMS

Companies selling greeting cards and novelty items (T-shirts, coffee mugs, buttons, etc.) often have their own specific requirements for the submission of ideas, verse, and artwork. In general, however, each verse or message should be typed double-space on a 3x5 or 4x6 card. Use only one side of the card, and be sure to put your name and address in the upper left-hand corner. Keep a copy of every verse or idea you send. (It's also advisable to keep a record of what you've submitted to each publisher.) Always enclose an SASE, and do not send out more than ten verses or ideas in a group to any one publisher. Never send original artwork unless a publisher indicates a definite interest in using your work.

AMBERLEY GREETING CARD COMPANY—11510 Goldcoast Dr., Cincinnati, OH 45249-1695. Dave McPeek, Ed. Humorous ideas for cards: birthday, illness, friendship, anniversary, congratulations, "miss you," etc. Send SASE for market letter before submitting ideas. Pays $150. Buys all rights.

AMERICAN GREETINGS—One American Rd., Cleveland, OH 44144. Kathleen McKay, Ed. Recruitment. Study current offerings and query before submitting.

BLUE MOUNTAIN ARTS, INC.—P.O. Box 1007, Boulder, CO 80306. Attn: Editorial, Dept. TW. Poetry and prose about love, friendship, family, philosophies, etc. Also material for special occasions and holidays: birthdays, get well, Christmas, Valentine's Day, Easter, etc. Submit seasonal material 5 months in advance of holiday. No artwork or rhymed verse. Include SASE. Pays $200 per poem.

BRILLIANT ENTERPRISES—117 W. Valerio St., Santa Barbara, CA 93101-2927. Ashleigh Brilliant, Ed. Illustrated epigrams. Send SASE for the price of a catalogue and samples. Pays $40, on acceptance.

COMSTOCK CARDS—600 S. Rock, Suite 15, Reno, NV 89502-4115. David Delacroix, Ed. Adult humor, outrageous or sexual, for greeting cards. SASE for guidelines. Payment varies, on publication.

DAYSPRING GREETING CARDS—P.O. Box 1010, Siloam Springs, AR 72761. Ann Woodruff, Ed. Religious/Christian cards. Uses unrhymed (preferred) and rhymed messages, traditional and light verse (various lengths) for humorous, inspirational, juvenile, and religious cards: anniversary, birthday, holidays, congratulations, friendship, get well, graduation, keep in touch, love, miss you, new baby, please write, sympathy, thank you, wedding, etc. Submit holiday/seasonal material one year ahead. Pays $35 to $50, on acceptance. SASE for guidelines. E-mail: annw@dayspring.com

DESIGN DESIGN, INC.—P.O. Box 2266, Grand Rapids, MI 49501-2266. Tom Vituj, Creative Dir. Short verses for both humorous and sentimental concepts for greeting cards. Everyday (birthday, get well, just for fun, etc.) and seasonal (Christmas, Valentine's Day, Easter, Mother's Day, Father's Day, Graduation, Halloween, Thanksgiving) material. Flat fee payment on publication.

DUCK & COVER—P.O. Box 21640, Oakland, CA 94620. Jim Buser, Ed. Outrageous, off the wall, original one-liners for buttons and magnets. SASE for guidelines. Pays $25, on publication.

EPHEMERA, INC.—P.O. Box 490, Phoenix, OR 97535. Attn: Ed. Provocative, irreverent, and outrageously funny slogans for novelty buttons and magnets. Submit typed list of slogans with SASE. Pays $35 per slogan, on publication. SASE for guidelines; also available from website: http// www.mind.net/ephemera

FREEDOM GREETING CARD COMPANY—P.O. Box 715, Bristol, PA 19007. Jay Levitt, Ed. Dept. Traditional and humorous verse and love messages. Inspirational poetry for all occasions. Pays negotiable rates, on acceptance. Query with SASE.

HALLMARK CARDS, INC.—Box 419580, Mail Drop 216, Kansas City, MO 64141. No unsolicited submissions.

KATE HARPER DESIGNS—P.O. Box 2112, Berkeley, CA 94703. Attn: Guidelines TW. Calligraphic greeting card line; only accepting submissions for new line of "How-To" cards. Cards have a theme and a list of tips; something you are expert at, from how to be a CEO to how to raise a child; humor is a must. Send SASE for very specific guidelines. Responds in 3 to 5 weeks. Payment is $50.

OATMEAL STUDIOS—Box 138 TW, Rochester, VT 05767. Attn: Ed. Humorous, clever, and new ideas needed for all occasions. Send legal-size SASE for guidelines.

PANDA INK—P.O. Box 5129, West Hills, CA 91308-5129. Ruth Ann Epstein, Ed. Judaica, metaphysical, cute, whimsical, or beautiful sentiment for greeting cards, bookmarks, clocks, and pins. Submit ideas typed on 8 1/2 x 11 paper, include SASE. "Best time to submit is beginning of the year; decisions are made in January." Payment varies, on acceptance.

PARAMOUNT CARDS—P.O. Box 6546, Providence, RI 02940-6546. Attn: Editorial Freelance. Humorous and traditional card ideas for birthday, relative's birthday, friendship, romance, get well, Christmas, Valentine's Day, Easter, Mother's Day, Father's Day, and Graduation. Submit each idea (5 to 10 per submission) on 3x5 card with name and address on each. Payment varies, on acceptance.

PLUM GRAPHICS—P.O. Box 136, Prince Station, New York, NY 10012. Yvette Cohen, Ed. Editorial needs change frequently; write for guidelines (new guidelines 3 to 4 times per year). Queries required. Pays $40 per card, on publication.

RED FARM STUDIO—1135 Roosevelt Ave., P.O. Box 347, Pawtucket, RI 02862. Attn: Production Coord. Traditional cards for birthday, get well, wedding, anniversary, friendship, new baby, sympathy, congrats, and Christmas; also light humor. Pays $4 a line.

ROCKSHOTS, INC.— 632 Broadway, New York, NY 10012. Bob Vesce, Ed. Adult, provocative, humorous gag lines for greeting cards. Submit on 4x5 cards with SASE. Pays $50 per line, on acceptance. SASE for guidelines.

SUNRISE PUBLICATIONS, INC.—P.O. Box 4699, Bloomington, IN 47402-4699. Attn: Text Ed. Original copy for holiday and everyday cards. "Submit up to 15 verses, one to 4 lines, on 3x5 cards; simple, to-the-point ideas that could be serious, humorous, or light-hearted, but sincere, without being overly sentimental. Rhymed verse not generally used." Allow 2 months for response. SASE for guidelines and for return of your submission. Pays standard rates.

VAGABOND CREATIONS, INC.—2560 Lance Dr., Dayton, OH 45409. George F. Stanley, Jr., Ed. Greeting cards with graphics only on cover (no copy) and short punch line inside: birthday, everyday, Valentine's Day, Christmas, and graduation. Mildly risqué humor with double entendre acceptable. Ideas for illustrated theme stationery. Pays $15, on acceptance.

WEST GRAPHICS PUBLISHING—1117 California Dr., Burlingame, CA 94010. Attn: Production Dept. Outrageous humor concepts, all occasions (especially birthday) and holidays, for photo and illustrated card lines. Submit on 3x5 cards: concept on one side; name, address, and phone number on other. Pays $100, 30 days after publication.

HUMOR, FILLERS, & SHORT ITEMS

Magazines noted for their filler departments, plus a cross-section of publications using humor, short items, jokes, quizzes, and cartoons, follow. However, almost all magazines use some type of filler material from time to time, and writers can find dozens of markets by studying copies of magazines at a library or newsstand.

THE AMERICAN FIELD—542 S. Dearborn, Chicago, IL 60605. B.J. Matthys, Man. Ed. Short fact items and anecdotes on hunting dogs and field trials for bird dogs. Pays varying rates, on acceptance.

AMERICAN SPEAKER—Attn: Current Comedy, 1101 30th St. N.W., Washington, DC 20007. Aram Bakshian, Ed.-in-Chief. Original, funny, performable jokes on news, fads, topical subjects, business, etc., for "Current Comedy" section of *American Speaker* Magazine. Jokes for roasts, retirement dinners, and for speaking engagements. Humorous material specifically geared for public speaking situations such as microphone feedback, introductions, long events, etc. Also interested in longer original jokes and anecdotes that can be used by public speakers. No poems, puns, ethnic jokes, or sexist material. Pays $12, on publication. Guidelines.

AMERICAN WOODWORKER—Rodale Press, 33 E. Minor St., Emmaus, PA 18098. David Sloan, Ed. Fillers relating to woodworking or furniture design. Guidelines.

THE ANNALS OF IMPROBABLE RESEARCH—AIR, P.O. Box 380853, Cambridge, MA 02238. Marc Abrahams, Ed. Science humor, science reports and analysis, one to 4 pages. B&W photos. "This journal is the place to find the mischievous, funny, iconoclastic side of science. An insider's journal that lets anyone sneak into the company of wonderfully mad scientists." Guidelines. No payment.

ARMY MAGAZINE—2425 Wilson Blvd., Arlington, VA 22210-0860. Mary B. French, Ed.-in-Chief. True anecdotes on military subjects. Pays $25 to $50, on publication.

ASIAN PAGES—P.O. Box 11932, St. Paul, MN 55111-0932. Cheryl Weiberg, Ed.-in-Chief. Profiles and news events, 500 words; short stories, 500 to 750 words; poetry, 100 words; and Asian-related fillers, 50 words. "All material must have a strong, non-offensive Asian slant." Pays $40 for articles, $25 for photos/cartoons, on publication.

THE ATLANTIC MONTHLY—77 N. Washington St., Boston, MA 02114. Attn: Ed. Sophisticated humorous or satirical pieces, 1,000 to 3,000 words. Some light poetry. Pays from $500 for prose, on acceptance.

ATLANTIC SALMON JOURNAL—P.O. Box 429, St. Andrews, N.B., Canada E0G 2X0. Philip Lee, Ed. Fillers, 50 to 100 words, on salmon politics, conservation, and nature. Pays $25 for fillers, on publication.

BYLINE—Box 130596, Edmond, OK 73013. Marcia Preston, Ed.-in-Chief. Humor, 200 to 400 words, about writing. Pays $15 to $20 for humor, on acceptance.

CAPPER'S—1503 S.W. 42nd St., Topeka, KS 66609-1265. Nancy Peavler, Ed. Letters, to 300 words, sharing heartwarming experiences, nostalgic accounts, household hints, poems, and recipes, for "Heart of the Home." Pieces, to 600 words, on people or groups who are making a difference, for "Community Heartbeat." Jokes, submit up to 6 at a time. Pays varying rates (and in gift certificates), on publication.

CASCADES EAST—716 N. E. 4th St., P. O. Box 5784, Bend, OR 97708. Kim Hogue, Ed. Fillers related to travel, history, and recreation in central Oregon. Pays 5¢ to 10¢ a word, extra for photos, on publication.

CATHOLIC DIGEST—P.O. Box 64090, St. Paul, MN 55164-0090. Attn: Filler Ed. Articles, 200 to 500 words, on instances of kindness, for "Hearts Are Trumps." Stories about conversions, for "Open Door." Reports of tactful remarks or actions, for "The Perfect Assist." Accounts of good deeds, for "People Are Like That." Humorous pieces, 50 to 300 words, on parish life, for "In Our Parish." Amusing signs, for "Signs of the Times." Jokes; fillers. No fiction. Pays $2 per line, on publication.

CHICKADEE—179 John St., Suite 500, Toronto, Ont., Canada M5T 3G5. Susan Berg, Ed. Juvenile poetry, 10 to 15 lines. Fiction, 800 words. Pays on acceptance. Enclose $2.00 money order and SASE for reply.

CHILDREN'S PLAYMATE—1100 Waterway Blvd., P.O. Box 567, Indianapolis, IN 46206. Terry Harshman, Ed. Articles and fiction, puzzles, games, mazes, poetry, crafts, and recipes for 6- to 8-year-olds, emphasizing health, fitness, sports, safety, and nutrition. Pays to 17¢ a word (varies on puzzles), on publication.

COLUMBIA JOURNALISM REVIEW—Columbia Univ., 700 Journalism Bldg., New York, NY 10027. Gloria Cooper, Man. Ed. Amusing mistakes in news stories, headlines, photos, etc. (original clippings required), for "Lower Case." Pays $25, on publication.

COMBO—5 Nassau Blvd. S., Garden City South, NY 11530. Ian M. Feller, Ed. Fillers related to non-sports cards (comic cards, TV/movie cards, science fiction cards, etc.) and comic books. Pays 10¢ a word, on publication.

COUNTRY WOMAN—P. O. Box 989, Greendale, WI 53129. Kathy Pohl, Man. Ed. Short rhymed verse, 4 to 20 lines, seasonal and country-related. All material must be positive and upbeat. Pays $10 to $15, on acceptance.

CRACKED—Globe Communications, Inc., 3 E. 54th St., 15 Fl., New York, NY 10022-3108. Lou Silverstone, Andy Simmons, Eds. Cartoon humor, one to 5 pages, for 10- to 15-year-old readers. "Queries are not necessary, but read the magazine before submitting material!" Pays from $100 per page, on acceptance.

CYCLE WORLD—1499 Monrovia Ave., Newport Beach, CA 92663. David Edwards, Ed.-in-Chief. News items on motorcycle industry, legislation, trends. Pays on publication.

FACES—Cobblestone Publishing, 7 School St., Peterborough, NH 03458-1454. Lynn L. Sloneker, Ed. Puzzles, mazes, crosswords, and picture puzzles for children. Send SASE for list of monthly themes before submitting.

FAMILY CIRCLE—375 Lexington Ave., New York, NY 10017. Uses some short humor, 750 words. No fiction. Payment varies, on acceptance.

THE FAMILY DIGEST—P.O. Box 40137, Fort Wayne, IN 46804. Corine B. Erlandson, Ed. Family- or Catholic parish-oriented anecdotes, 10 to 125 words, of funny or unusual real-life parish and family experiences. Pays $20, one month after acceptance.

FARM AND RANCH LIVING—5400 S. 60th St., Greendale, WI 53129. Nick Pabst, Ed. Fillers on rural people and living, 200 words. Pays from $15, on acceptance and publication.

FATE—P.O. Box 64383, St. Paul, MN 55164-0383. Attn: Ed. Factual fillers, to 300 words, on strange, psychic, or paranormal happenings. True personal stories, to 500 words, on proof of mystic experiences. Pays 10¢ a word for fillers, $25 for personal accounts. SASE for guidelines.

FIELD & STREAM—2 Park Ave., New York, NY 10016. Duncan Barnes, Ed. Fillers on hunting, fishing, camping, etc., to 500 words. Cartoons. Pays $75 to $250, sometimes more, for fillers; $100 for cartoons, on acceptance.

FINESCALE MODELER—P.O. Box 1612, Waukesha, WI 53187. Bob Hayden, Ed. One-page hints and tips on building nonoperating, scale models. Payment varies, on acceptance.

GAMES—P.O. Box 184, Ft. Washington, PA 19034. R. Wayne Schmittberger, Ed.-in-Chief. Pencil puzzles, visual brainteasers, and pop culture tests. Humor and playfulness a plus; quality a must. Pays top rates, on publication.

GERMAN LIFE—Zeitgeist Publishing, 1 Corporate Dr., Grantsville, MD 21536. Heidi Whitesell, Ed. Fillers, 50 to 200 words, on German culture, its past and present, and how America has been influenced by its German element: history, travel, people, the arts, and social and political issues; also humor and cartoons. Articles, 500 to 2,000 words. Pays to $80 for fillers; $300 to $500 for articles, on publication. Queries preferred for articles.

GLAMOUR—350 Madison Ave., New York, NY 10017. Attn: Viewpoint Ed. Articles, 1,000 words, for "Viewpoint" section: opinion pieces for women. Pays $500, on acceptance.

GUIDEPOSTS—16 E. 34th St., New York, NY 10016. Celeste McCauley, Features Ed. Inspirational anecdotes, to 250 words. Pays $10 to $50, on acceptance.

THE HERB COMPANION—Interweave Press, 201 E. Fourth St., Loveland, CO 80537. Kathleen Halloran, Ed. Bimonthly. Fillers, 75 to 150 words, for herb enthusiasts: practical horticultural tips, original recipes using herbs, etc. Payment varies, on publication.

THE JEWISH HOMEMAKER—1372 Carroll St., Brooklyn, NY 11213. Mayer Bendet, Ed. Humor and fillers for traditional/Orthodox Jewish audience. Payment varies, on publication.

MAD MAGAZINE—1700 Broadway, 5th Fl., New York, NY 10019. Attn: Eds. Humorous pieces on a wide variety of topics. Two- to 8-panel cartoons (not necessary to include sketches with submission). Pays top rates, on acceptance. Guidelines strongly recommended.

MATURE LIVING—127 Ninth Ave. N., MSN 140, Nashville, TN 37234. Attn: Ed. Brief, humorous, original items. "Grandparents Brag Board" items; Christian inspirational pieces for senior adults, 125 words. Pays $10 to $20.

MATURE YEARS—201 Eighth Ave. S., P.O. Box 801, Nashville, TN 37202. Marvin W. Cropsey, Ed. Poems, cartoons, puzzles, jokes, anecdotes, to 300 words, for older adults. Allow 2 months for manuscript evaluation. "A Christian magazine that seeks to build faith. We always show older adults in a favorable light." Include name, address, social security number with all submissions.

MID-WEST OUTDOORS—111 Shore Dr., Hinsdale, IL 60521-5885. Gene Laulunen, Man. Ed. Where to and how to fish and hunt in the Midwest, 700 to 1,500 words, with 2 photos. Pays $15 to $30, on publication.

MODERN BRIDE—249 W. 17th St., New York, NY 10011. Mary Ann Cavlin, Exec. Ed. Humorous pieces, 500 to 1,000 words, for brides. Pays on acceptance.

NATIONAL ENQUIRER—Lantana, FL 33463. Kathy Martin, Fillers Ed. Short, humorous or philosophical fillers, witticisms, anecdotes, jokes, tart comments. Original items only. Short poetry with traditional rhyming verse, amusing, philosophical, or inspirational in nature. No obscure or artsy poetry. Submit seasonal/holiday material at least 3 months in advance. Pays $25, after publication.

THE NEW YORKER—20 W. 43rd St., New York, NY 10036. Attn: Newsbreaks Dept. Amusing mistakes in newspapers, books, magazines, etc. Pays $10, on acceptance.

OPTOMETRIC ECONOMICS—American Optometric Assn., 243 N. Lindbergh Blvd., St. Louis, MO 63141. Gene Mitchell, Man. Ed. Short humor for optometrists; writers should have some knowledge of optometry. Payment varies, on acceptance.

OUTDOOR LIFE—2 Park Ave., New York, NY 10016. Todd W. Smith, Ed. Short instructive items, 900 to 1,100 words, on hunting, fishing, boating, and outdoor equipment; regional pieces on lakes, rivers, specific geographic areas of special interest to hunters and fishermen. Photos. No fiction or poetry. Pays $300 to $350, on acceptance.

PLAYBOY— 680 N. Lake Shore Dr., Chicago, IL 60611. Attn: Party Jokes Ed. or After Hours Ed. Jokes; short original material on new trends, lifestyles, personalities; humorous news items. Pays $100 for jokes; $50 to $350 for "After Hours" items, on publication.

PLAYGIRL— 801 Second Ave., New York, NY 10017. Attn: Man. Ed. Humorous pieces, 800 to 1,500 words, on romance and relationships with a sexual twist, from male or female perspective, 800 to 1,000 words, for "Playgirl Punchline." Pays varying rates, after acceptance. Query.

READER'S DIGEST—Pleasantville, NY 10570. Consult "Contributor's Corner" page for guidelines. No submissions acknowledged or returned.

REAL PEOPLE— 450 7th Ave., Suite 1701, New York, NY 10123-0073. Brad Hamilton, Ed. True stories, to 500 words, about interesting people for "Real Shorts" section: strange occurrences, everyday weirdness, etc.; may be funny, sad, or hair-raising. Also humorous items, to 75 words, taken from small-circulation magazines, newspapers, etc. Pays $25 to $50, on publication.

RHODE ISLAND MONTHLY— 95 Chestnut St., Providence, RI 02903. Paula M. Bodah, Ed. Short pieces, to 500 words, on Rhode Island and southeastern Massachusetts: places, customs, people and events. Pays $50 to $150. Query.

ROAD KING—Hammock Publishing, 3322 W. End Ave., Suite 700, Nashville, TN 37203. Attn: Fillers Ed. Trucking-related cartoons and fillers. Payment is negotiable, on publication.

THE ROTARIAN—1560 Sherman Ave., Evanston, IL 60201-3698. Charles W. Pratt, Ed. Occasional humor articles. Payment varies, on acceptance. No payment for fillers, anecdotes, or jokes.

SACRAMENTO MAGAZINE— 4471 D St., Sacramento, CA 95819. Krista Minard, Ed. "City Lights," interesting and unusual people, places, and behind-the-scenes news items, to 400 words. All material must have Sacramento tie-in. Payment varies, on publication.

SKI MAGAZINE— 929 Pearl St., Suite 200, Boulder, CO 80302. Andrew Bigford, Ed.-in-Chief. Short, 100- to 300-word items on news, events, and people in skiing for "Ski Life" department. Pays on acceptance.

SLICK TIMES—P.O. Box 1710, Valley Center, CA 92082. Michael Johnson, Ed. Political humor, 1,000 to 2,000 words, "poking fun at the Clintons." Pays $250 to $375, on publication.

SOAP OPERA UPDATE—270 Sylvan Ave., Englewood Cliffs, NJ 07632. Dawn Mazzurco, Exec. Ed. Soap opera-oriented fillers, to 500 words. Payment varies, on publication.

SPORTS AFIELD—250 W. 55th St., New York, NY 10019. Attn: Almanac Ed. Unusual, useful tips, anecdotes, 100 to 300 words, for "Almanac" section: hunting, fishing, camping, and boating. Photos. Pays on publication.

STAR— 660 White Plains Rd., Tarrytown, NY 10591. Attn: Ed. Topical articles, 50 to 800 words, on show business and celebrities. Pays varying rates.

STITCHES, THE JOURNAL OF MEDICAL HUMOUR—16787 Warden Ave., R.R. #3, Newmarket, Ont., Canada L3Y 4W1. Simon Hally, Ed. Humorous pieces, 250 to 2,000 words, for physicians. "Most articles have something to do with medicine." Short humorous verse and original jokes. Pays 30¢ to 40¢ (Canadian) a word; $50 (Canadian) for cartoons, on publication.

TECH DIRECTIONS—Box 8623, Ann Arbor, MI 48107. Paul J. Bamford, Man. Ed. Cartoons, puzzles, brainteasers, and humorous anecdotes of interest to technology and industrial education teachers and administrators. Pays $20 for cartoons; $25 for puzzles, brainteasers, and other short classroom activities; $5 for humorous anecdotes, on publication.

THOUGHTS FOR ALL SEASONS: THE MAGAZINE OF EPIGRAMS—478 N.E. 56th St., Miami, FL 33137. Michel P. Richard, Ed. Epigrams and puns, one to 4 lines, and poetry, to one page. "Writers are advised not to submit material until they have examined a copy of the magazine." Payment is one copy.

TOUCH—Box 7259, Grand Rapids, MI 49510. Carol Smith, Man. Ed. Puzzles based on the NIV Bible, for Christian girls ages 8 to 14. Pays $10 to $15 per puzzle, on publication. Send SASE for theme update.

TRAVEL SMART—Dobbs Ferry, NY 10522. Attn: Ed. Interesting and useful travel-related tips. Practical information for vacation or business travel. Fresh, original material. Pays $5 to $150. Query for over 250 words.

WISCONSIN TRAILS—P.O. Box 5650, Madison, WI 53705. Attn: Ed. Short fillers, 300 words, about Wisconsin: places to go, things to do, etc.

JUVENILE & YOUNG ADULT MAGAZINES

JUVENILE MAGAZINES

AMERICAN GIRL—8400 Fairway Pl., P.O. Box 998, Middleton, WI 53562-0998. Attn: Magazine Dept. Asst. Bimonthly. Articles, to 800 words, and contemporary or historical fiction, to 3,000 words, for girls ages 8 to 12. "We do not want 'teenage' material, i.e. articles on romance, make-up, dating, etc." Payment varies, on acceptance. Query for articles; include photo leads with historical queries.

BABYBUG—P.O. Box 300, Peru, IL 61354. Marianne Carus, Ed.-in-Chief. Stories, to 4 sentences; poems, and action rhymes, to 8 lines, for infants and toddlers, 6 months to 2 years. Pays from $25, on publication. Guidelines.

BOYS' QUEST—P.O. Box 227, Bluffton, OH 45817-4610. Attn: Ed. Bimonthly. Fiction and nonfiction, 500 words, for boys ages 6 to 12. "We are looking for articles, stories, and poetry that deal with timeless topics such as pets, nature, hobbies, science, games, sports, careers, simple cooking, etc." B&W photos a plus. Pays 5¢ a word, on publication. Send SASE for guidelines.

CALLIOPE: WORLD HISTORY FOR YOUNG PEOPLE—Cobblestone Publishing, Inc., 7 School St., Peterborough, NH 03458. Rosalie Baker and Charles Baker, Eds. Theme-based magazine, published 9 times yearly. Articles,

750 words, with lively, original approach to world history (East/West) through the Renaissance. Shorts, 200 to 750 words, on little-known information related to issue's theme. Fiction, to 1,200 words: historical, biographical, adventure, or retold legends. Activities for children, to 800 words. Poetry, to 100 lines. Puzzles and games. Pays 20¢ to 25¢ a word, on publication. Guidelines and themes.

CHICKADEE—Owl Communications, 179 John St., Suite 500, Toronto, Ont., Canada M5T 3G5. Susan Berg, Ed. Adventure, folktale, and humorous stories and poems for 6- to 9-year-olds. Also puzzles, activities, and observation games. No religious material. Pays varying rates, on acceptance. Submit complete manuscript with $2.00 check or money order for return postage. Send $4.28 (Canadian dollars) for guidelines.

CHILD LIFE—1100 Waterway Blvd., P.O. Box 567, Indianapolis, IN 46206. Lise Hoffman, Ed. Nostalgia and some health-related material, the latter generated in-house or assigned, for 9- to 11-year-olds. Currently not accepting manuscripts for publication.

CHILDREN'S DIGEST—1100 Waterway Blvd., P.O. Box 567, Indianapolis, IN 46206. Layne Cameron, Ed. Health and general-interest publication for preteens. Informative articles, 500 to 1,200 words, and fiction (especially realistic, adventure, mystery, and humorous), 500 to 1,500 words. Historical and biographical articles. Poetry and activities. Pays from 12 1/2¢ a word, from $15 for poems, on publication.

CHILDREN'S PLAYMATE—1100 Waterway Blvd., P.O. Box 567, Indianapolis, IN 46206. Terry Harshman, Ed. General-interest and health-related short stories (health, fitness, nutrition, safety, and exercise), 500 to 600 words, for 6- to 8-year-olds. Simple science articles and how-to crafts pieces with brief instructions. Poems, puzzles, easy recipes, dot-to-dots, mazes, hidden pictures. Pays to 17¢ a word, from $25 for poetry, on publication. Buys all rights.

CLUBHOUSE—Box 15, Berrien Springs, MI 49103. Krista Phillips, Ed. Action-oriented Christian stories, 800 to 1,200 words. Children in stories should be wise, brave, funny, kind, etc. Pays $25 to $35 for stories.

COBBLESTONE: THE AMERICAN HISTORY MAGAZINE FOR YOUNG PEOPLE—7 School St., Peterborough, NH 03458-1454. Meg Chorlian, Ed. Theme-related articles, biographies, plays, and short accounts of historical events, 700 to 800 words, for 8- to 15-year-olds; also supplemental nonfiction, 300 to 600 words. Fiction, 700 to 800 words. Activities (crafts, recipes, etc.) that can be done either by children alone or with adult supervision. Poetry, to 100 lines. Crossword and other word puzzles using the vocabulary of the issue's theme. Pays 20¢ to 25¢ a word, on publication. (Payment varies for activities and poetry.) Send SASE for guidelines and themes.

CRAYOLA KIDS—Meredith Custom Publishing, 1912 Grand Ave., Des Moines, IA 50309-3379. Mary L. Heaton, Ed. Bimonthly for families with children, 3 to 8 years old. Hands-on crafts and seasonal activities, one to 4 pages. Puzzle ideas related to issue themes. Pays $100 to $250, on acceptance. Send for theme list. Query with resumé and work samples.

CRICKET—P.O. Box 300, Peru, IL 61354-0300. Marianne Carus, Ed.-in-Chief. Articles and fiction, 200 to 2,000 words, for 9- to 14-year-olds. (Include bibliography with nonfiction.) Poetry, to 30 lines. Pays to 25¢ a word, to $3 a line for poetry, on publication. Guidelines.

DISCOVERIES—WordAction Publishing Co., 6401 The Paseo, Kansas City, MO 64131. Attn: Asst. Ed. Weekly designed to correlate with Evangelical

Sunday school curriculum. Fiction, 500 to 700 words, for 8- to 10-year-olds should feature contemporary, true-to-life characters and illustrate character building and scriptural application. No poetry. Pays 5¢ a word, on publication. Guidelines.

THE DOLPHIN LOG—The Cousteau Society, 777 United Nations Plaza, New York, NY 10017. Lisa Rao, Ed. Articles, 400 to 600 words, on a variety of topics related to our global water system: marine biology, ecology, natural history, and water-related subjects, for 7- to 13-year-olds. No fiction. Pays $50 to $200, on publication. Query.

FACES—Cobblestone Publishing, 7 School St., Peterborough, NH 03458-1454. Lynn Slonecker, Ed. In-depth feature articles, 800 words, with an anthropology theme. Shorts, 300 to 600 words, related to themes. Fiction, to 800 words, on legends, folktales, stories from around the world, etc., related to theme. Activities, to 700 words, including recipes, crafts, games, etc., for children. Published monthly, September through May. Pays 20¢ to 25¢ a word. Write for guidelines and themes.

THE FLICKER MAGAZINE—P.O. Box 660544, Vestavia Hills, AL 35266-0544. Lynn Christmas, Submissions Ed. Bimonthly. Features, maximum of 1,000 words; articles, 600 to 800 words; and short pieces, to 300 words, for elementary-age children. Positive fiction, articles on real-life role models, and activities that provide hands-on fun. "Avoid magic, ghosts, space fantasies, and supernatural happenings not involving God." Pays 8¢ to 12¢ a word, on acceptance.

THE FRIEND—50 E. North Temple, 23rd Fl., Salt Lake City, UT 84150. Vivian Paulsen, Man. Ed. Stories and articles, 1,000 to 1,200 words. Stories, to 250 words, for younger readers and preschool children. Pays from 9¢ a word, from $25 per poem, on acceptance. Prefers completed manuscripts. Guidelines.

GIRLS' LIFE—Monarch Avalon, Inc., 4517 Harford Rd., Baltimore, MD 21214. Kelly White, Sr. Ed. Features of various lengths and one-page fillers that entertain and educate girls ages 7 to 14. Payment varies, on publication. Query with resumé and clips. Send SASE for guidelines.

THE GOLDFINCH—State Historical Society of Iowa, 402 Iowa Ave., Iowa City, IA 52240-1806. Amy Ruth, Ed. Quarterly. Articles, 200 to 800 words, and short fiction on Iowa history for young people. "All articles must correspond to an upcoming theme." Pays $25 per article, on acceptance. Query for themes.

GUIDEPOSTS FOR KIDS—P.O. Box 638, Chesterton, IN 46304. Mary Lou Carney, Ed. Issue-oriented, thought-provoking articles, 1,000 to 1,500 words. "Things kids not only need to know, but want to know." Fiction: historicals and mysteries, 700 to 1,300 words, and contemporary stories, 1,000 words. "Not preachy. Dialogue-filled and value-driven." Pays competitive rates, on acceptance. Query for articles.

HIGHLIGHTS FOR CHILDREN— 803 Church St., Honesdale, PA 18431-1824. Beth Troop, Manuscript Coord. Easy-to-read stories, to 500 words for 6- to 8-year olds: humor, adventure, mystery, fantasy, folk tales, and talking animal stories. "We'd also like to see stories that don't fit in any of those categories, but are good, meaningful stories for children. Pays from 14¢ a word, on acceptance. SASE for guidelines.

HOPSCOTCH, THE MAGAZINE FOR GIRLS—P.O. Box 164, Bluffton, OH 45817-0164. Marilyn Edwards, Ed. Bimonthly. Articles and fiction, 600 to

1,000 words, and short poetry for girls ages 6 to 12. Special interest in articles, with photos, about girls involved in worthwhile activities. "We believe young girls deserve the right to enjoy a season of childhood before they become young adults; we are not interested in such topics as sex, romance, cosmetics, hairstyles, etc." Pays 5¢ a word, on publication. Send SASE for guidelines.

HUMPTY DUMPTY'S MAGAZINE—1100 Waterway Blvd., P.O. Box 567, Indianapolis, IN 46206. Sandy Grieshop, Ed. General-interest publication with an emphasis on health and fitness for 4- to 6-year-olds. Easy-to-read fiction, to 500 words, some with health and nutrition, safety, exercise, or hygiene as theme; humor and light approach preferred. Creative nonfiction, including photo stories. Crafts with clear, brief instructions. No-cook recipes using healthful ingredients. Short verse, narrative poems. Pays to 22¢ a word, from $25 for poems, on publication. Buys all rights.

JACK AND JILL—1100 Waterway Blvd., P.O. Box 567, Indianapolis, IN 46206. Daniel Lee, Ed. Articles, 500 to 800 words, for 7- to 10-year-olds, on sports, fitness, health, nutrition, safety, exercise. Features, 500 to 700 words, on history, biography, life in other countries, etc. Fiction, to 700 words. Short poems, games, puzzles, projects, recipes. Photos. Pays 10¢ to 20¢ a word, extra for photos, on publication.

JUNIOR TRAILS—1445 Boonville Ave., Springfield, MO 65802-1894. Sinda Zinn, Ed. Fiction, 1,000 to 1,500 words, with a Christian focus, believable characters, and moral emphasis. Articles, 300 to 500 words, on science, nature, biography. Pays 3¢ to 5¢ a word, on acceptance.

KID CITY—Children's Television Workshop, 1 Lincoln Plaza, New York, NY 10023. "We do not accept any free-lance work."

KIDS WORLD MAGAZINE—108-93 Lombard Ave., Winnipeg, Manitoba, Canada R3B 3B1. Stuart Slayen and Leslie Malkin, Eds. Bimonthly. Humorous, empowering fiction, 650 to 750 words; and contemporary, educational nonfiction, 750 to 1,200 words, for readers aged 9 to 12. (Magazine is distributed in elementary schools.) Pays $75 to $400 (Canadian), on publication. Queries preferred.

LADYBUG—P.O. Box 300, Peru, IL 61354-0300. Marianne Carus, Ed.-in-Chief. Paula Morrow, Ed. Picture stories and read-aloud stories, 300 to 750 words, for 2- to 6-year-olds; poetry, to 20 lines; songs and action rhymes; crafts, activities, and games. Pays 25¢ a word for stories; $3 a line for poetry, on publication. Guidelines.

MUSE—The Cricket Magazine Group, 332 S. Michigan Ave., Suite 2000, Chicago, IL 60604. *Muse* Submissions Ed. Bimonthly. Articles, 1,000 to 2,500 words, "on problems connected with a discipline or area of practical knowledge," for children ages 6 to 14. Query with resumé, writing samples, list of possible topics, and SASE. Payment is 50¢ per word, within 60 days of acceptance.

MY FRIEND—Pauline Books & Media, Daughters of St. Paul, 50 St. Pauls Ave., Boston, MA 02130. Sister Kathryn James Hermes, Ed. "The Catholic Magazine for Kids." Readers are 6 to 12 years old. Fiction, Catholic-focused articles, media literacy, lives of saints, etc., 150 to 600 words. Buys first rights. Pays $35 to $100 for articles, $5 for fillers. Query for artwork. Guidelines.

NATIONAL GEOGRAPHIC WORLD—1145 17th St. N.W., Washington, DC 20036-4688. Susan Tejada, Ed. Picture magazine for young readers, ages

8 and older. Natural history, adventure, archaeology, geography, science, the environment, and human interest. Proposals for picture stories only. No unsolicited manuscripts.

NEW MOON, THE MAGAZINE FOR GIRLS AND THEIR DREAMS— P.O. Box 3620, Duluth, MN 55803-3620. Barbara Stretchberry and Tya Ward, Man. Eds. "Our goal is to celebrate girls and support their efforts to hang on to their voices, strengths, and dreams as they move from being girls to becoming women." Profiles of girls and women, 300 to 1,000 words. Science and math experiments, 300 to 600 words. Submissions from both girls and adults. Queries preferred. Pays 5¢ to 8¢ a word, on publication. Also publishes companion letter, *New Moon Network: For Adults Who Care About Girls.*

ODYSSEY: SCIENCE THAT'S OUT OF THIS WORLD— Cobblestone Publishing, 7 School St., Peterborough, NH 03458-1454. Elizabeth Lindstrom, Ed. Features, 750 words, on astronomy, space science, and other related physical sciences for 8- to 14-year-olds. Science-related fiction, myths, legends, and science fiction stories. Experiments and games. Pays 20¢ to 25¢ a word, on publication. Guidelines and themes.

ON THE LINE— 616 Walnut, Scottdale, PA 15683-1999. Mary Clemens Meyer, Ed. Monthly magazine for 9- to 14-year-olds. Nature, general nonfiction, and how-to articles, 350 to 500 words; fiction, 1,000 to 1,800 words; poetry, puzzles, cartoons. Pays to 5¢ a word, on acceptance.

OWL— Owl Communications, 179 John St., Suite 500, Toronto, Ont., Canada M5T 3G5. Nyla Ahmad, Ed.-in-Chief. Articles, 500 to 1,000 words, for 8- to 12-year-olds, about animals, science, people, technology, new discoveries, activities. Pays varying rates, on acceptance. Enclose $2.00 money order and SASE for reply. Guidelines.

PLAYS, THE DRAMA MAGAZINE FOR YOUNG PEOPLE— 120 Boylston St., Boston, MA 02116-4615. Elizabeth Preston, Man. Ed. Wholesome one-act comedies, dramas, skits, satires, farces, and creative dramatic material suitable for school productions at junior high, middle, and lower grade levels. Plays with modern settings preferred. Also uses dramatized classics, folktales and fairy tales, puppet plays. No religious plays or musicals. Pays good rates, on acceptance. Buys all rights. Query for classics, folk and fairy tales. Guidelines.

POCKETS— 1908 Grand Ave., Box 189, Nashville, TN 37202-0189. Janet Knight, Ed. Ecumenical magazine for 6- to 12-year-olds. Fiction and scripture stories, 600 to 1,500 words; short poems; games and family communication activities; role model stories; and stories about children involved in justice and environmental projects. Pays from 12¢ a word, $2 per line for poetry, on acceptance. Guidelines and themes. Annual fiction contest; send SASE for details.

POWER AND LIGHT— 6401 The Paseo, Kansas City, MO 64131. Beula J. Postlewait, Preteen Ed. Fiction, 500 to 800 words, for grades 5 and 6, with Christian emphasis. Cartoons and puzzles. Pays 5¢ a word for multi-use rights, 1 3/4¢ a word for reprints. Pays $15 for cartoons and puzzles.

R-A-D-A-R— Standard Publishing, 8121 Hamilton Ave., Cincinnati, OH 45231. Elaina Meyers, Ed. Weekly Sunday school take-home paper. Articles, 400 to 500 words, on nature, hobbies, crafts. Short stories, 900 to 1,000 words: mystery, sports, school, family, with 10-year-old as main character; serials, 2,000 words. Christian emphasis. Poems. Pays to 7¢ a word, to 50¢ a line for poetry, on acceptance.

RANGER RICK—National Wildlife Federation, 8925 Leesburg Pike, Vienna, VA 22184. Gerald Bishop, Ed. Articles, to 900 words, on wildlife, conservation, natural sciences, and kids in the outdoors, for 6- to 9-year-olds. Nature-related fiction, mysteries, fantasies, and science fiction welcome. Games (no crosswords or word-finds), crafts, humorous poems, outdoor activities, and puzzles. For nonfiction, query with sample lead, list of references, and names of experts you plan to contact. SASE. Guidelines. Pays to $550, on acceptance.

REAL KIDS—Kids With Character Publications, Inc., P.O. Box 14491, Huntsville, AL 35815. Joe Leahy, Ed. Bimonthly. Character-building stories, to 800 words, for 7- to 13-year-old readers. Fiction: adventure, humor, inspiration, and sports stories. Nonfiction: how-to, historical, personal experience, profiles, and humor. Kid-tested crafts pieces, to 500 words. Crosswords, mazes, word finds, and other activities. Pays from 5¢ a word; from $10 for fillers, crafts, and puzzles, on publication.

SCIENCEWORLD—Scholastic, Inc., 555 Broadway, New York, NY 10012-3999. Karen McNulty, Ed. Science articles, 750 words, and science news articles, 200 words, on life science, earth science, physical science, technology, environmental science and/or health for readers in grades 7 to 10 (ages 12 to 15). "Articles should include current, exciting science news. Writing should be lively and show an understanding of teens' perspectives and interests." Pays $100 to $125 for news items; $200 to $650 for features. Query with a well-researched proposal, suggested sources, 2 to 3 clips of your work, and an SASE.

SESAME STREET MAGAZINE—One Lincoln Plaza, New York, NY 10023. Anne Heller, Exec. Ed. Articles on children and violence: Susan Schneider, Articles Ed. Articles on educational issues: Nadia Zonis, Medical/Health Ed. Articles, 800 to 2,500 words, on medical, psychological, and educational issues for families with young children (up to 8 years old). Pays 50¢ to $1 per word, up to 6 weeks after acceptance.

SHOFAR— 43 Northcote Dr., Melville, NY 11747. Gerald H. Grayson, Ed. Short stories, 500 to 1,000 words; articles, 500 to 1,000 words; poetry, to 50 lines; short fillers, games, puzzles, and cartoons for Jewish children, 8 to 13. All material must have a Jewish theme. Pays 10¢ a word, on publication. Submit holiday pieces at least 6 months in advance.

SKIPPING STONES—P.O. Box 3939, Eugene, OR 97403. Arun N. Toké, Exec. Ed. "A Multicultural Children's Magazine." Articles, approximately 500 to 750 words, relating to "Living in the Inner City," "My Name," community and family, religions, culture, nature, traditions, and cultural celebrations in other countries, for 7- to 15-year-olds. "Especially invited to submit are children from cultural backgrounds other than European-American and/or those with physical challenges. We print art, poetry, songs, games, stories, and photographs from around the world and include many different languages (with English translation)." Payment is one copy, on publication. Annual contest; send SASE for guidelines.

SOCCER JR.—27 Unquowa Rd., Fairfield, CT 06430. Joe Provey, Ed. Fiction and fillers about soccer for readers ages 8 and up. Pays $450 for a feature or story; $250 for department pieces, on acceptance. Query.

SPIDER—P.O. Box 300, Peru, IL 61354. Attn: Submissions Ed. Fiction, 300 to 1,000 words, for 6- to 9-year-olds: realistic, easy-to-read stories, fantasy, folk and fairy tales, science fiction, fables, myths. Articles, 300 to 800 words, on nature, animals, science, technology, environment, foreign culture, history (include short bibliography with articles). Serious, humorous, or nonsense poetry, to 20 lines. Puzzles, activities, and games, to 4 pages, also considered. Pays 25¢ a word, $3 per line for poetry, on publication.

SPORTS ILLUSTRATED FOR KIDS—Time & Life Bldg., 1271 Ave. of the Americas, New York, NY 10020. Stephen Malley, Sr. Ed. Articles, 1,000 to 1,500 words (submit to Amy Lennard Goehner), and short features, 500 to 600 words (submit to Jon Scher), for 8- to 13-year-olds. "Most articles are staff-written. Department pieces are the best bet for free lancers." (Read magazine and guidelines to learn about specific departments.) Puzzles and games (submit to Erin Egan). No fiction or poetry. Pays $500 for departments, $1,000 to $1,250 for articles, on acceptance. Query required.

STONE SOUP, THE MAGAZINE BY YOUNG WRITERS AND ARTISTS—Box 83, Santa Cruz, CA 95063-0083. Gerry Mandel, Ed. Stories, free-verse poems, plays, book reviews by children under 14. "Preference given to writing based on real-life experiences." Pays $10.

STORY FRIENDS—Mennonite Publishing House, Scottdale, PA 15683. Rose Stutzman, Ed. Stories, 350 to 800 words, for 4- to 9-year-olds, on Christian faith and values in everyday experiences. Poetry. Pays to 5¢ a word, to $10 per poem, on acceptance.

SUPERSCIENCE BLUE—Scholastic, Inc., 555 Broadway, New York, NY 10012. Attn: Ed. Science news and hands-on experiments for grades 4 through 6. Article topics are staff-generated and assigned to writers. For consideration, send children's and science writing clips to Editor. Include large SASE for editorial calendar and sample issue. Pays $50 to $500, on acceptance.

3-2-1 CONTACT—Children's Television Workshop, 1 Lincoln Plaza, New York, NY 10023. Curtis Slepian, Ed. Entertaining and informative articles, 600 to 1,000 words, for 8- to 14-year-olds, on all aspects of science, computers, scientists, and children who are learning about or practicing science. Pays $75 to $500, on acceptance. No fiction. Query.

TOUCH—Box 7259, Grand Rapids, MI 49510. Carol Smith, Man. Ed. Upbeat fiction and features, 500 to 1,000 words, for Christian girls ages 8 to 14; personal life, nature, crafts. Poetry, puzzles. Pays 2 1/2¢ a word, extra for photos, on publication. Query with SASE for theme update.

TURTLE MAGAZINE FOR PRESCHOOL KIDS—1100 Waterway Blvd., Box 567, Indianapolis, IN 46206. Nancy S. Axelrad, Ed. Heavily illustrated articles with an emphasis on health and nutrition for 2- to 5-year-olds. Humorous, entertaining fiction. Also, crafts, pencil activities, and simple science experiments. Simple poems. Action rhymes and read-aloud stories, to 300 words. Pays to 22¢ a word for stories; from $15 for poems; payment varies for activities, on publication. Buys all rights. Send SASE for guidelines.

U.S. KIDS—1100 Waterway Blvd., P.O. Box 567, Indianapolis, IN 46206. Jeff Ayers, Health/Fitness Ed. Articles, to 1,000 words, on issues related to kids ages 5 to 10, fiction, true-life adventures, science and nature topics. Special emphasis on health and fitness. Fiction with real-world focus; no fantasy.

WONDER TIME— 6401 The Paseo, Kansas City, MO 64131. Lois Perrigo, Ed. Stories, 250 to 350 words, for 6- to 8-year-olds, with Christian emphasis to correlate with Sunday school curriculum. Pays $25 for stories, on production. Send SASE for guidelines, themes, and sample issue.

YOUNG JUDEAN—50 W. 58th St., New York, NY 10019. Deborah Neufeld, Ed. Quarterly. Articles, 500 to 1,000 words, with photos, for 9- to 12-

year-olds, on Israel, Jewish holidays, Jewish-American life, Jewish history. Fiction, 800 to 1,000 words, on Jewish themes. Fillers, humor, reviews. No payment.

YOUTH UPDATE—*St. Anthony Messenger Press,* 1615 Republic St., Cincinnati, OH 45210. Attn: Ed. "Articles for Catholic teens that address timely topics. Avoid cuteness, glib phrases and clichés, academic or erudite approaches, preachiness." Pays on acceptance, 14¢ a word. Query with outline and SASE.

ZILLIONS—Consumers Union of the United States, 101 Truman Ave., Yonkers, NY 10703-9925. Moye Thompson, Man. Ed. Bimonthly. Articles, 1,000 to 1,500 words, on consumer education (money, product testing, health, etc.), for kids ages 9 to 14. "We are the *Consumer Reports* for kids." Pays $500 to $2,000, on publication. Guidelines.

YOUNG ADULT MAGAZINES

ALL ABOUT YOU— 6420 Wilshire Blvd., Los Angeles, CA 90048-5515. Roxanne Camron, Ed. Dir. Beth Mayall, Sr. Ed. Articles, 1,000 to 1,500 words, on issues of interest to young women. Payment varies, on acceptance. Queries.

BLUE JEAN MAGAZINE—P.O. Box 90856, Rochester, NY 14609. Sherry S. Handel, Pub./Ed.-in-Chief. Profiles, 1,000 to 3,000 words, on women business owners. Articles on nonprofit groups, environmental action, teen adventurers, careers, college information. Fiction and poetry. "About 75% of magazine is written by teen writers. You won't find supermodels, tips on dieting, or fashion spreads in our magazine." Pays $25 to $100, on publication.

BOYS' LIFE—1325 W. Walnut Hill Ln., P.O. Box 152079, Irving, TX 75015-2079. Monthly publication of the Boy Scouts of America. Articles and fiction, 500 to 1,500 words, for 8- to 18-year-old boys. Pays from $350 for major articles, $750 for fiction, on acceptance. Query for articles; send complete manuscript for fiction. SASE.

BRIO—Focus on Family, 8605 Explorer Dr., Colorado Springs, CO 80920. Susie Shellenberger, Ed. Articles of interest to Christian teen girls: profiles, how-to pieces, adventures that show the fun Christian teens can have together. Fiction, to 2,000 words, with realistic character development, good dialogue, and a plot that teen girls will be drawn to. Stories may contain a spiritual slant but should not be preachy. Short humorous pieces. Pays 8¢ to 12¢ a word, on acceptance.

CAMPUS LIFE— 465 Gundersen Dr., Carol Stream, IL 60188. Harold Smith, V.P./Ed. Articles reflecting Christian values and world view, for high school and college students. Humor, general fiction, and true, first-person experiences. "If we have a choice of fiction, how-to, and a strong first-person story, we'll go with the true story every time." Photo-essays, cartoons. Pays 15¢ to 20¢ a word, on acceptance. Query.

CHALLENGE—1548 Poplar Ave., Memphis, TN 38104-2493. Jeno Smith, Ed. Southern Baptist. Articles, to 800 words, for 12- to 18-year-old boys, on teen issues, current events. Photo-essays on Christian sports personalities. Pays 5¢ a word, extra for photos, on acceptance.

CRACKED—Globe Communications, Inc., 3 E. 54th St., 15 Fl., New York, NY 10022-3108. Lou Silverstone, Andy Simmons, Eds. Humor, one to 5 pages, for 10- to 15-year-old readers. Cartoons/comic book style work; no short stories or poetry. "Read magazine before submitting." Pays $100 per page, on acceptance.

EDGE, THE HIGH PERFORMANCE ELECTRONIC MAGAZINE FOR STUDENTS— 4905 Pine Cone Dr., Suite 2, Durham, NC 27707. Greg Sanders, Ed. Magazine for bright high school students, available only on the World Wide Web at http://www.jayi.com/Fishnet/Edge. Features, 1,200 to 1,500 words. Departments include "News to Use," 400 to 500 words; "Performance," 750 words; "Mindstuff," 500-word reviews of older books; "What's Hot Now," 250 to 400 words, on interesting, worthwhile products. "The magazine is not about school; it's about teenagers living the learning lifestyle. Our readers are sophisticated. Don't write anything elementary, preachy, or thoughtless. Especially interested in literary journalism/creative nonfiction." Pays $400 to $500 for features, $25 to $300 for department pieces, on acceptance. Queries preferred. Guidelines available on Web site.

EXPLORING—P.O. Box 152079, 1325 W. Walnut Hill Ln., Irving, TX 75015-2079. Scott Daniels, Exec. Ed. Publication of Boy Scouts of America. Articles, 500 to 1,500 words, for 14- to 21-year-old boys and girls, on teenage trends, college, computer games, music, education, careers, "Explorer" activities (hiking, canoeing, camping), and program ideas for meetings. No controversial subjects. Pays $250 to $1,000, on acceptance. Query. Guidelines.

HOW ON EARTH!—P.O. Box 339, Oxford, PA 19363-0339. Amina Chaudhri, Ed.-in-Chief. Articles, 1,000 to 2,000 words, by writers ages 13 to 24 on vegetarian living, animals, the environment, social justice, youth empowerment, and activism; essays, personal pieces, interviews, and creative writing, 400 to 800 words, on related subjects; food reviews, 300 to 700 words; music and book reviews, 200 to 500 words. "Living Vegetarian," general essays, to 800 words, about being vegetarian in a meat-eating society. Adult submissions are occasionally accepted for research/information articles and general interest articles, 1,000 to 2,000 words. Pays in copies. Query. Guidelines.

KEYNOTER—3636 Woodview Trace, Indianapolis, IN 46268. Julie A. Carson, Exec. Ed. Articles, 1,500 to 1,800 words, for high school leaders: general-interest features; self-help; contemporary teenage problems. No fillers, poetry, first-person accounts, or fiction. Pays $150 to $350, on acceptance. Query preferred.

LISTEN MAGAZINE—55 W. Oak Ridge Dr., Hagerstown, MD 21740. Lincoln Steed, Ed. Articles, 1,200 to 1,500 words, providing teens with "a vigorous, positive, educational approach to the problems arising from the use of tobacco, alcohol, and other drugs." Pays 5¢ to 7¢ a word, on acceptance.

MERLYN'S PEN: THE NATIONAL MAGAZINES OF STUDENT WRITING—P.O. Box 1058, Dept. WR, East Greenwich, RI 02818. R. James Stahl, Ed. *Intermediate Edition*: writing by students in grades 6 through 9. Short stories and essays, to 3,500 words; reviews; travel pieces; and poetry, to 100 lines. *Senior Edition*: for writers in grades 9 through 12. Fiction and essays, 3,500 words. Poetry, to 200 lines. Responds with a brief critique in 10 weeks. Pays $5 to $50, plus copies. Guidelines.

NEW ERA—50 E. North Temple, Salt Lake City, UT 84150. Richard M. Romney, Ed. Articles, 150 to 1,500 words, and fiction, to 2,000 words, for young Mormons. Poetry. Photos. Pays 5¢ to 20¢ a word, 25¢ a line for poetry, on acceptance. Query.

REACT—Parade Publications, 711 Third Ave., New York, NY 10017. Attn: Man. Ed. Weekly. Articles, to 800 words, on national and international news, entertainment, sports, social issues related to teenagers, and profiles of notable young people for readers 11 to 17. Fillers, to 250 words, on news, sports, and entertainment. Payment varies, on acceptance. Query.

SCHOLASTIC UPDATE—555 Broadway, New York, NY 10012-3999. Steve Manning and Herbert Buchsbaum, Eds. Biweekly. News articles, 500 words or 1,000 to 1,500 words, for teenagers. Pays $150 to $1,000, on acceptance. Send SASE for guidelines before querying.

SCIENCE WORLD—Scholastic, Inc., 555 Broadway, New York, NY 10012-3999. Attn: Eds. Articles, 750 words, on life science, earth science, physical science, environmental science, or health science for 7th to 10th graders (ages 12 to 15). Science news pieces, 200 words. Submit well-researched proposal, including suggested sources, 2 to 3 clips of your work, and SASE. Pays $100 to $125 for news items; $200 to $650 for features.

SEVENTEEN— 850 Third Ave., New York, NY 10022. Susan Brenna, Features Ed. Articles, to 2,500 words, on subjects of interest to teenagers. Sophisticated, well-written fiction, 1,000 to 4,000 words, for young adults. Personal essays, to 1,200 words, by writers 23 and younger for "Voice." Pays varying rates, on acceptance.

SISTERS IN STYLE—233 Park Ave. S., 5th Fl., New York, NY 10003. Cynthia Marie Horner, Ed. Dir. Bimonthly. "For Today's Young Black Woman." Articles. No fiction or poetry. Beauty, fashion, quizzes, and advice for African-American teens. Payment varies, on publication. Query.

STRAIGHT— 8121 Hamilton Ave., Cincinnati, OH 45231. Heather E. Wallace, Ed. Articles on current situations and issues for Christian teens. Humor. Well-constructed fiction, 1,000 to 1,500 words, showing teens using Christian principles. Poetry by teenagers. Photos. Pays about 5¢ to 7¢ a word, on acceptance. Guidelines.

'TEEN— 6420 Wilshire Blvd., Los Angeles, CA 90048-5515. Attn: Ed. Short stories, 2,500 to 4,000 words: mystery, teen situations, adventure, romance, humor for teens. Pays from $200 to $600, on acceptance. Buys all rights.

TEEN LIFE—1445 Boonville Ave., Springfield, MO 65802-1894. Tammy Bicket, Ed. Articles, 500 to 1,000 words, and fiction, to 1,200 words, for 13- to 19-year-olds; strong evangelical emphasis. Interviews with Christian athletes and other well-known Christians; true stories; up-to-date factual articles. Send SASE for current topics. Pays on acceptance.

TEEN POWER—Box 632, Glen Ellyn, IL 60138. Sarah M. Peterson, Ed. Take-home Sunday school paper. True-to-life fiction or first-person (as told to), true teen experience stories with Christian insights and conclusion, 700 to 1,000 words. Pays 8¢ to 12¢ a word, extra for photos, on acceptance.

TEEN VOICES—P.O. Box 116, Boston, MA 02123. Alison Amoroso, Ed.-in-Chief. Quarterly. Fiction, 200 to 400 words; nonfiction, 200 to 400 words; and poetry, any length. Submissions by teenage girls only. Pays in copies.

TIGER BEAT—Sterling/MacFadden Partnership, 233 Park Ave. S., New York, NY 10003. Louise Barile, Ed. Articles, to 4 pages, on young people in show business and the music industry. Pays varying rates, on acceptance. Query.

WHAT! A MAGAZINE—108-93 Lombard Ave., Winnipeg, Manitoba, Canada R3B 3B1. Stuart Slayen and Leslie Malkin, Eds. Published 5 times a year. Articles, 650 to 2,000 words, on contemporary issues for teenaged readers. (Magazine is distributed in high schools.) Pays $100 to $500 (Canadian), on publication. Queries preferred.

YM—685 Third Ave., New York, NY 10017. Maria Baugh, Man. Ed. Articles, to 2,500 words, on entertainment, lifestyle, fashion, beauty, relationships, health, for women ages 14 to 19. Payment varies, on acceptance. Query with clips.

YOUNG AND ALIVE—4444 S. 52nd St., Lincoln, NE 68506. Richard J. Kaiser, Man. Ed. M. Marilyn Brown, Ed. Quarterly. Feature articles, 800 to 1,400 words, for blind and visually impaired young adults on adventure, biography, camping, careers, health, history, hobbies, holidays, marriage, nature, practical Christianity, sports, and travel. Photos. Pays 3¢ to 5¢ a word, $5 to $20 for photos, on acceptance. Guidelines.

YOUNG SALVATIONIST—The Salvation Army, 615 Slaters Ln., P.O. Box 269, Alexandria, VA 22313. Attn: Lesa Davis, Production Mgr. Articles for teens, 800 to 1,200 words, with Christian perspective; fiction, 800 to 1,200 words; short fillers. Pays 10¢ to 15¢ a word, on acceptance.

ZELOS—Box 632, Glen Ellyn, IL 60138. Sarah M. Peterson, Ed. First-person true stories, personal experience, how-tos, humor, fiction, to 1,000 words, for 15- to 20-year-olds. Send photos, if available. Must have Christian emphasis. Pays 8¢ to 20¢ a word.

THE DRAMA MARKET

Community, regional, and civic theaters and college dramatic groups offer the best opportunities today for playwrights to see their work produced, whether on the stage or in dramatic readings. Indeed, aspiring playwrights will be encouraged to hear that many well-known playwrights received their first recognition in the regional theaters. Payment is generally nominal, but regional and university theaters usually buy only the right to produce a play, and all further rights revert to the author. Since most directors like to work closely with authors on any revisions necessary, theaters will often pay the playwright's expenses while in residence during rehearsals. The thrill of seeing your play come to life on the stage is one of the pleasures of being on hand for rehearsals and performances. In addition to producing plays and giving dramatic readings, many theaters also sponsor competitions or new play festivals.

Aspiring playwrights should query college and community theaters in their region to find out which ones are interested in seeing original scripts. Dramatic associations of interest to playwrights include the Dramatists Guild (1501 Broadway, Suite 701, New York, NY 10036), and Theatre

Communications Group, Inc. (355 Lexington Ave., New York, NY 10017), which publishes the annual *Dramatists Sourcebook*. *The Playwright's Companion*, published by Feedback Theatrebooks (305 Madison Ave., Suite 1146, New York, NY 10165), is an annual directory of theaters, play publishers, and prize contests seeking scripts. See the *Organizations for Writers* list for details on dramatists' associations.

Some of the theaters on this list require that playwrights submit all or some of the following with scripts—cast list, synopsis, resumé, recommendations, return postcard—and with scripts and queries, SASEs must always be enclosed.

While the almost unlimited television offerings on commercial, educational, and cable TV stations, in addition to the hundreds of films released yearly, may lead free-lance writers to believe that opportunities to sell movie and television scripts are infinite, unfortunately, this is not true. With few exceptions, TV and film producers and programmers will read scripts and queries submitted only through recognized agents. (For a list of agents, see page 858.) Writers who want to try their hand at writing directly for this very limited market should be prepared to learn the special techniques and acceptable format of scriptwriting, either by taking a workshop through a university or at a writers conference, or by reading one or more of the many books that have been written on this subject. Also, experience in playwriting and a knowledge of dramatic structure gained through working in amateur, community, or professional theaters can be helpful.

REGIONAL & UNIVERSITY THEATERS

ACTORS THEATRE OF LOUISVILLE—316 W. Main St., Louisville, KY 40202. Michael Bigelow Dixon, Lit. Mgr. Ten-minute comedies and dramas, to 10 pages. Longer one-act and full-length plays accepted from literary agents, and from playwrights with letter of recommendation from another professional theatre. SASE. Annual contest. Guidelines.

A. D. PLAYERS—2710 W. Alabama, Houston, TX 77098. Attn: Lit. Mgr. Jeannette Clift George, Artistic Dir. Full-length or one-act comedies, dramas, musicals, children's plays, and adaptations with Christian world view. Submit synopsis and cast list with SASE. Readings. Pays negotiable rates.

ALABAMA SHAKESPEARE FESTIVAL—The State Theatre, #1 Festival Dr., Montgomery, AL 36117-4605. Eric Schmiedl, Lit. Assoc. Full-length scripts with southern and/or African-American themes, issues, or history; and scripts with southern and/or African-American authors. One work per author; query.

ALLEY THEATRE—615 Texas Ave., Houston, TX 77002. Travis Mader, Dramaturg. Full-length plays, including translations and adaptations. No unsolicited scripts; agent submissions or professional recommendations only.

ALLIANCE THEATRE COMPANY—1280 Peachtree St. N.E., Atlanta, GA 30309. Attn: Lit. Dept. Full-length comedies and dramas, especially those that "deal with moral/spiritual questions of life in multicultural America." Also, new musicals and children's plays. Query with synopsis and up to ten pages of sample dialogue; no unsolicited scripts. Pay varies.

AMERICAN LITERATURE THEATRE PROJECT—Fountain Theatre, 5060 Fountain Ave., Los Angeles, CA 90029. Simon Levy, Prod. Dramaturg. One-act and full-length stage adaptations of classic and contemporary American literature. Sets and cast size are unrestricted. Send synopsis and SAS postcard. Rate of payment is standard, as set by the Dramatists Guild.

AMERICAN LIVING HISTORY THEATER—P.O. Box 752, Greybull, WY 82426. Dorene Ludwig, Artistic Dir. One-act (one or 2 characters preferred), historically accurate (primary source materials only) dramas dealing with marketable or known American historical and literary characters and events. Submit treatment and letter with SASE. Responds within 6 months. Pays varying rates.

AMERICAN PLACE THEATRE—111 W. 46th St., New York, NY 10036. Martin Blank, Artistic Assoc. "No unsolicited manuscripts accepted. Writers may send a synopsis and the first 20 pages with SASE. We seek challenging, innovative works and do not favor obviously commercial material."

AMERICAN THEATRE OF ACTORS—314 W. 54th St., New York, NY 10019. James Jennings, Artistic Dir. Full-length dramas for a cast of 2 to 6. Submit complete play and SASE. Reports in one to 2 months.

MAXWELL ANDERSON PLAYWRIGHTS SERIES, INC.—Box 671, W. Redding, CT 06896. Bruce Post, Exec. Dir. Robert Decina, Artistic Dir. Produces 6 professional staged readings of new plays each year in Greenwich, CT. Send complete script with SASE.

ARENA STAGE—Sixth and Maine Ave. S.W., Washington, DC 20024. Cathy Madison, Lit. Mgr. No unsolicited manuscripts; send synopsis, first 10 pages of dialogue, and bio.

ARKANSAS REPERTORY THEATRE COMPANY—601 S. Main, P.O. Box 110, Little Rock, AR 72203-0110. Brad Mooy, Lit. Mgr. Full-length comedies, dramas, and musicals; prefer up to 8 characters. Send synopsis, cast list, resumé, and return postage; do not send complete manuscript. Reports in 3 months.

ARTREACH TOURING THEATRE—3074 Madison Rd., Cincinnati, OH 45209. Kathryn Schultz Miller, Artistic Dir. One-act dramas and adaptations for touring family theater; up to 3 cast members, simple sets. Submit script with synopsis, cast list, resumé, recommendations, and SASE. Payment varies.

BARTER THEATER—P.O. Box 867, Abingdon, VA 24212-0867. Richard Rose, Artistic Dir. Full-length dramas, comedies, adaptations, and children's plays. Submit synopsis, dialogue sample, and SASE. Allow 6 to 8 months for report. Payment rates negotiable.

BERKSHIRE THEATRE FESTIVAL—Box 797, Stockbridge, MA 01262. Arthur Storch, Artistic Dir. Full-length comedies, musicals, and dramas; cast to 8. Submit through agent only.

BOARSHEAD THEATER—425 S. Grand Ave., Lansing, MI 48933. John Peakes, Artistic Dir. Full-length comedies and dramas with simple sets and cast of up to 10. Send précis, 5 to 10 pages of dialogue, cast list with descriptions. SAS postcard for reply.

BRISTOL RIVERSIDE THEATRE—Box 1250, Bristol, PA 19007. Susan D. Atkinson, Producing/Artistic Dir. Full-length plays with up to 15 actors and a simple set.

CALIFORNIA UNIVERSITY THEATRE—California, PA 15419. Dr. Richard J. Helldobler, Chairman. Unusual, avant-garde, and experimental one-act and full-length comedies and dramas, children's plays, and adaptations. Cast size varies. Submit synopsis with short, sample scene(s). Payment available.

CENTER STAGE—700 N. Calvert St., Baltimore, MD 21202. James Magruder, Resident Dramaturg. Full-length comedies, dramas, translations, adaptations. No unsolicited manuscripts. Send synopsis, a few sample pages, resumé, cast list, and production history. Allow 8 to 10 weeks for reply.

CHILDSPLAY, INC.—Box 517, Tempe, AZ 85280. David Saar, Artistic Dir. Multigenerational plays running 45 to 120 minutes: dramas, musicals, and adaptations for family audiences. Productions may need to travel. Submissions accepted July through December. Send synopsis and 10-page dialogue sample. Reports in 2 to 6 months.

CIRCLE IN THE SQUARE/UPTOWN—1633 Broadway, New York, NY 10019-6795. Michael Breault, Artistic Assoc. Accepts agented material only. SASE.

CITY THEATRE COMPANY—57 S. 13th St., Pittsburgh, PA 15203. Literary Dept. Full-length cutting-edge comedies and dramas; especially interested in women and minorities. Cast to 10; simple sets. Query September to May. Royalty.

CLASSIC STAGE COMPANY—136 E. 13th St., New York, NY 10003. Mary Esbjornson, Exec. Dir. David Esbjornson, Artistic Dir. Full-length adaptations and translations of existing classic literature. Submit synopsis with cast list and 12 pages of sample dialogue, September to May. Offers readings. Pays on royalty basis.

THE CONSERVATORY THEATRE ENSEMBLE—c/o Tamalpais High School, 700 Miller Ave., Mill Valley, CA 94941. Daniel Caldwell, Artistic Dir. Comedies, dramas, children's plays, adaptations, and scripts addressing high school issues for largely female cast (about 3 women per man). "One-act plays of approximately 30 minutes are especially needed, as we produce 40 short plays each season using teenage actors." Send synopsis and resumé.

CROSSROADS THEATRE CO.—7 Livingston Ave., New Brunswick, NJ 08901. Ricardo Khan, Artistic Dir. Full-length and one-act dramas, comedies, musicals, and adaptations; issue-oriented experimental plays that offer honest, imaginative, and insightful examinations of the African-American experience. Also interested in African and Caribbean plays and plays exploring cross-cultural issues. No unsolicited scripts; queries only, with synopsis, cast list, resumé, and SASE.

DELAWARE THEATRE COMPANY—200 Water St., Wilmington, DE 19801-5030. Cleveland Morris, Artistic Dir. Full-length comedies, dramas, and musicals. Prefer cast of no more than 10. Send synopsis or complete script; SASE required. Reports in 6 months. Write for competition details (new plays dealing with interracial dynamics in America, any genre, using historical or contemporary settings).

DETROIT REPERTORY THEATRE—13103 Woodrow Wilson Ave., Detroit, MI 48238. Barbara Busby, Lit. Mgr. Full-length comedies and dramas. Scripts accepted October to April. Enclose SASE. Pays royalty.

STEVE DOBBINS PRODUCTIONS—650 Geary Blvd., San Francisco, CA 94102. Alan Ramos, Lit. Dir. Full-length comedies, dramas, and musicals.

Cast of up to 12. Query with synopsis and resumé. No unsolicited manuscripts. Reports in 6 months. Offers workshops and readings. Pays 4% to 6% of gross.

DORSET THEATRE FESTIVAL—Box 519, Dorset, VT 05251. Jill Charles, Artistic Dir. Full-length comedies, musicals, dramas, and adaptations for up to 8 cast members; simple set preferred. Query with synopsis, cast size, and SAS postcard. Pays varying rates. Residencies at Dorset Colony House for Writers available September to November, March to May; inquire. E-mail: theatre@sover.net. Web site http://www.genghis.com/theatre.htm

EAST WEST PLAYERS— 4424 Santa Monica Blvd., Los Angeles, CA 90029. Tim Dang, Artistic Dir. Ken Narasaki, Lit. Mgr. Produces 4 to 5 new plays annually. Original plays, translations, adaptations, musicals, and youth theater, "all of which must illuminate the Asian or Asian-American experience, or resonate in a significant fashion if cast with Asian-American actors." Readings. Prefer to see query letter with synopsis and 10 pages of dialogue; complete scripts also considered. Reports in 5 to 6 weeks for query; 6 months for complete script.

FLORIDA STUDIO THEATRE—1241 N. Palm Ave., Sarasota, FL 33577. Chris Angermann, New Play Development. Innovative plays with universal themes. Query with synopsis and SASE. Also accepting musicals and musical revues.

WILL GEER THEATRICUM BOTANICUM—Box 1222, Topanga, CA 90290. Attn: Lit. Dir. All types of scripts for outdoor theater, with large playing area. Submit synopsis with SASE. Pays varying rates.

THE GOODMAN THEATRE—200 S. Columbus Dr., Chicago, IL 60603. Susan V. Booth, Lit. Mgr. Queries from recognized literary agents or producing organizations required for full-length comedies or dramas. No unsolicited scripts.

THE GUTHRIE THEATER—725 Vineland Pl., Minneapolis, MN 55403. Attn: Lit. Dept. Full-length dramas and adaptations of world literature, classic masterworks, oral traditions, and folktales. No unsolicited scripts; professional recommendation or letter of inquiry from playwright/agent. SASE. Reports in 3 to 4 months.

HIPPODROME STATE THEATRE—25 S.E. Second Pl., Gainesville, FL 32601. Tamerin Corn, Dramaturg. Full-length plays with unit sets and casts of up to 8. Agent submissions and professional recommendations only; no unsolicited material.

HOLLYWOOD THESPIAN COMPANY—12838 Kling St., Studio City, CA 91604-1127. Rai Tasco, Artistic Dir. Full-length comedies and dramas for integrated cast. Include cast list and SAS postcard with submission.

HORIZON THEATRE COMPANY—P. O. Box 5376, Station E, Atlanta, GA 31107. Jeff and Lisa Adler, Artistic Dirs. Full-length comedies, dramas, and satires. Encourages submissions by women writers. Cast of no more than 10. Submit synopsis with cast list, resumé, and recommendations. Pays percentage. Readings. Reports in 6 months.

HUNTINGTON THEATRE COMPANY—252 Huntington Ave., Boston, MA 02115. Scott Edmiston, Lit. Assoc. Full-length comedies and dramas. Query with synopsis, cast list, and resumé.

ILLINOIS THEATRE CENTER— 400 Lakewood Blvd., Park Forest, IL 60466. Attn: Producing Dir. Full-length comedies, dramas, musicals, and adaptations, for unit/fragmentary sets, and up to 8 cast members. Send summary and SAS postcard. No unsolicited manuscripts. Pays negotiable rates. Workshops and readings offered.

ILLUSTRATED STAGE COMPANY—Box 640063, San Francisco, CA 94164-0063. Steve Dobbins, Artistic Dir. Full-length comedies, dramas, and musicals for a cast of up to 18. Query with synopsis and SASE. No unsolicited manuscripts. Offers workshops and readings.

JEWISH REPERTORY THEATRE—1395 Lexington Ave., New York, NY 10128. Ran Avni, Artistic Dir. Full-length comedies, dramas, musicals, and adaptations, with up to 10 cast members, relating to the Jewish experience. Pays varying rates. Enclose SASE.

KUMU KAHUA THEATRE, INC.— 46 Merchant St., Honolulu, HI 96813. Harry Wong III, Artistic Dir. Full-length plays especially relevant to life in Hawaii. Prefer simple sets for arena and in-the-round productions. Submit resumé and synopsis January through April. Pays $50 per performance. Readings. Contests.

LIVE OAK THEATRE—200 Colorado, Austin, TX 78701. Michael Hankin, Lit. Mgr. Full-length plays and adaptations. "Special interest in producing works of Texan and southern topics and new American plays." No musicals. Send letter of inquiry with SASE. Contest; send SASE for details. Guidelines.

LOS ANGELES DESIGNERS' THEATRE—P.O. Box 1883, Studio City, CA 91614-0883. Richard Niederberg, Artistic Dir. Full-length comedies, dramas, musicals, fantasies, or adaptations. Religious, political, social, and controversial themes encouraged. Nudity, "adult" language, etc., O.K. "Please detail in the cover letter what the writer's proposed involvement with the production would be beyond the usual. Do not submit material that needs to be returned." Send proposals or complete scripts. Payment varies.

THE MAGIC THEATRE—Fort Mason Ctr., Bldg. D, San Francisco, CA 94123. Kent Nicholson, Lit. Mgr. Comedies and dramas. "Special interest in poetic, non-linear, and multicultural work for mainstage productions." Query with synopsis, resumé, first 10 to 20 pages of script, and SASE; no unsolicited manuscripts. Pays varying rates.

MANHATTAN THEATRE CLUB—311 W. 43rd St., New York, NY 10036. Attn: Kate Loewald. Full-length and one-act comedies, dramas, and musicals. No unsolicited manuscripts or queries; agent submissions only.

METROSTAGE—P.O. Box 329, Alexandria, VA 22313. Carolyn Griffin, Prod. Dir. Full-length comedies, dramas, and children's plays; casts of no more than 8. Send synopsis, 10 page dialogue sample, resumé, and return post card. Responds in one month.

MILL MOUNTAIN THEATRE—One Market Sq., Second Fl., Roanoke, VA 24011-1437. Jo Weinstein, Lit. Mgr. One-act comedies and dramas, 25 to 35 minutes. For full-length plays, send letter, resumé, and synopsis. Send SASE for guidelines for new play competition. Payment varies.

MISSOURI REPERTORY THEATRE— 4949 Cherry St., Kansas City, MO 64110. Felicia Londré, Dramaturg. Full-length comedies and dramas. Query with synopsis, cast list, resumé, and SAS postcard. Royalty. Allow 6 months for response.

MUSICAL THEATRE WORKS— 440 Lafayette St., New York, NY 10003. Andrew Barrett, Lit. Mgr. Full-length musicals, for a cast of up to 15. Submit manuscript and cassette score with SASE. Responds in 4 to 6 months.

NATIONAL BLACK THEATRE—2033 Fifth Ave., Harlem, NY 10035. Attn: Tunde Samuel. Drama, musicals, and children's plays. "Scripts should reflect African and African-American lifestyle. Historical, inspirational, and ritualistic forms appreciated." Workshops and readings.

NATIONAL PLAYWRIGHTS CONFERENCE, EUGENE O'NEILL THEATRE CENTER—234 W. 44th St., Suite 901, New York, NY 10036. Mary F. McCabe, Man. Dir. Annual competition to select new stage plays and teleplays/screenplays for development during the summer at organization's Waterford, CT, location. Submission deadline: December 1. Send #10-size SASE in the fall for guidelines. Pays stipend, plus travel/living expenses during conference.

NEW THEATRE, INC.—P.O. Box 173, Boston, MA 02117-0173. Attn: NEWorks Submissions Program. New full-length scripts for readings, workshop, and main stage productions. Include SASE.

NEW TUNERS/THE THEATRE BUILDING—1225 W. Belmont Ave., Chicago, IL 60657. Warner Crocker, Artistic Dir. Full-length musicals only, for cast to 15; no wing/fly space. Send query with brief synopsis, cassette tape of score, cast list, resumé, SASE, and SAS postcard. Pays on royalty basis.

NEW YORK SHAKESPEARE FESTIVAL/JOSEPH PAPP PUBLIC THEATER— 425 Lafayette St., New York, NY 10003. Shirley Fishman, Mervin P. Antonio, Lit. Mgrs. Plays and musical works for the theater, translations, and adaptations. Submit sample dialogue with synopsis, cassette (for musicals), and SASE. Allow 4 to 6 months for response.

NEW YORK STATE THEATRE INSTITUTE—155 River St., Troy, NY 12180. Attn: Patricia Di Benedetto Snyder, Producing Artistic Dir. Emphasis on new, full-length plays and musicals for family audiences. Query with synopsis and cast list. Payment varies.

ODYSSEY THEATRE ENSEMBLE—2055 S. Sepulveda Blvd., Los Angeles, CA 90025. Ron Sossi, Artistic Dir. Full-length comedies, dramas, musicals, and adaptations: provocative subject matter, or plays that stretch and explore the possibilities of theater. Query Jan Lewis, Lit. Mgr., with synopsis, 8 to 10 pages of sample dialogue, and resumé. Pays variable rates. Allow 2 to 6 months for reply to script; 2 to 4 weeks for queries. Workshops and readings.

OLDCASTLE THEATRE COMPANY—Bennington Center for the Arts, P.O. Box 1555, Bennington, VT 05201. Eric Peterson, Dir. Full-length comedies, dramas, and musicals for a small cast (up to 10). Submit synopsis and cast list in the winter. Reports in 6 months. Offers workshops and readings. Pays expenses for playwright to attend rehearsals. Royalty.

OMAHA THEATER COMPANY FOR YOUNG PEOPLE—2001 Center St., Omaha, NE 68102. James Larson, Artistic Dir. Theatre for young audiences. Referrals only.

PENGUIN REPERTORY COMPANY—Box 91, Stony Point, Rockland County, NY 10980. Joe Brancato, Artistic Dir. Full-length comedies and dramas with cast size to 5. Submit script, resumé, and SASE. Payment varies.

PEOPLE'S LIGHT AND THEATRE COMPANY—39 Conestoga Rd., Malvern, PA 19355. Alda Cortese, Lit. Mgr. Full-length comedies, dramas, adaptations. No unsolicited manuscripts; query with synopsis, 10 pages of script required. Reports in 6 months. Payment negotiable.

PIER ONE THEATRE—Box 894, Homer, AK 99603. Lance Petersen, Lit. Dir. Full-length and one-act comedies, dramas, musicals, children's plays, and adaptations. Submit complete script; include piano score with musicals. "We are now concentrating on plays by Alaskan playwrights or of special significance to the Alaskan experience." Pays 8% of ticket sales for mainstage musicals; other payment varies.

PLAYHOUSE ON THE SQUARE—51 S. Cooper in Overton Sq., Memphis, TN 38104. Jackie Nichols, Artistic Dir. Full-length comedies, dramas; cast of up to 15. Contest deadline is April for fall production. Pays $500.

PLAYWRIGHTS HORIZONS— 416 W. 42nd St., New York, NY 10036. Address Literary Dept. Full-length, original comedies, dramas, and musicals by American authors. No one-acts or screenplays. Synopses discouraged; send script, resumé and SASE, include tape for musicals. Off Broadway contract.

PLAYWRIGHTS' PLATFORM— 164 Brayton Rd., Boston, MA 02135. Attn: Lit. Dir. Script development workshops and public readings for New England playwrights only. Full-length and one-act plays of all kinds. No sexist or racist material. Residents of New England send scripts with short synopsis, resumé, SAS postcard, and SASE. Readings conducted at Massachusetts College of Art (Boston).

POPLAR PIKE PLAYHOUSE—7653 Old Poplar Pike, Germantown, TN 38138. Frank Bluestein, Artistic Dir. Full-length and one-act comedies, dramas, musicals, and children's plays. Submit synopsis with SAS postcard and resumé. Pays $300.

PORTLAND STAGE COMPANY—Box 1458, Portland, ME 04104. Attn: Lit. Dir. Not accepting unsolicited material at this time.

PRINCETON REPERTORY COMPANY— 44 Nassau St., Suite 350, Princeton, NJ 08542. Victoria Liberatori, Artistic Dir. One-act and full-length comedies and dramas for a cast of up to 10. "We are dedicated to the production of unusual plays, new and reinterpreted, which promote a greater awareness of contemporary issues, especially those focusing on women." Submit synopsis with resumé, cast list, and 3-page dialogue sample. Consideration for reading and/or production. Responds within one year.

THE PUERTO RICAN TRAVELING THEATRE—141 W. 94th St., New York, NY 10025. Miriam Colon Valle, Artistic Dir. Full-length and one-act comedies, dramas, and musicals; cast of up to 8; simple sets. "We prefer plays based on the contemporary Hispanic experience, material with social, cultural, or psychological content." Payment negotiable.

THE REPERTORY THEATRE OF ST. LOUIS—Box 191730, St. Louis, MO 63119. Attn: Lit. Dir. Query with brief synopsis, technical requirements, and cast size. Unsolicited manuscripts will be returned unread.

ROUND HOUSE THEATRE—12210 Bushey Dr., Silver Spring, MD 20902. Attn: Production Office Mgr. Full-length comedies, dramas, and adaptations; cast of up to 10; prefer simple set. Send one-page synopsis with 3 or 4 sample pages, cast list, and technical requirements. No unsolicited manuscripts.

SALT AND PEPPER MIME COMPANY/NEW ENSEMBLE ACTORS THEATRE PROJECT—320 E. 90th St., #1B, New York, NY 10128. Ms. Scottie Davis, Dir. One-acts, all genres, conducive to "nontraditional" casting, surreal sets with mimetic concepts. One-or 4-person cast. Send resumé to 250 W. 65th St., New York, NY 10023. Scripts reviewed from May to December.

Works also considered for readings, critiques, storyplayers, and experimental development.

SEATTLE REPERTORY THEATRE—155 Mercer St., Seattle, WA 98109. Sharon Ott, Artistic Dir. Full-length comedies, dramas, and adaptations. Submit synopsis, 10-page sample, SAS postcard, and resumé to Kurt Beattie, Artistic Assoc. New plays series with workshops each spring.

SOCIETY HILL PLAYHOUSE—507 S. 8th St., Philadelphia, PA 19147. Walter Vail, Dramaturg. Full-length dramas, comedies, and musicals with up to 6 cast members and simple set. Submit synopsis and SASE. Reports in 6 months. Nominal payment.

SOUTH COAST REPERTORY—P. O. Box 2197, Costa Mesa, CA 92628. John Glore, Lit. Mgr. Full-length comedies, dramas, musicals, juveniles. Query with synopsis and resumé. Payment varies.

SOUTHERN APPALACHIAN REPERTORY THEATRE—P.O. Box 1720, Mars Hill, NC 28754. James W. Thomas, Artistic Dir. Full-length comedies, dramas, musicals, and plays including (but not limited to) scripts with Appalachian theme. Submit resumé, recommendations, full script, and SASE. Send SASE for information on Southern Appalachian Playwright's Conference (held in April each year). Pays $500 royalty if play is selected for production during the summer season. Deadline for submissions is October 1 each year.

THE SPUYTEN DUYVIL THEATRE CO.—P.O. Box 1024, New York, NY 10024. Attn: Lit. Dir. Full-length comedies and dramas with single set and cast size to 10. "Good women's roles needed." SASE required.

STAGE ONE: PROFESSIONAL THEATRE FOR YOUNG AUDIENCES— (formerly *Stage One: The Louisville Children's Theatre*) 5 Riverfront Plaza, Louisville, KY 40202. J. Daniel Herring, Assoc. Dir. Adaptations of classics and original plays for young audiences ages 4 to 18. Submit script with resumé and SASE. Reports in 4 to 5 months.

STAGE ONE: THE LOUISVILLE CHILDREN'S THEATRE—See *Stage One: Professional Theatre for Young Audiences.*

STAGES REPERTORY THEATRE—3201 Allen Pkwy., #101, Houston, TX 77019. Rob Bundy, Artistic Dir. Unproduced new works by women for Women's Repertory Project; accepts plays October 1 through December 31; full-length dramas, comedies, translations, and adaptations. Submit synopsis; no unsolicited scripts. Send for guidelines for Texas playwrights' festival held in the spring.

MARK TAPER FORUM—135 N. Grand Ave., Los Angeles, CA 90012. Pier Carlo Talenti, Lit. Assoc. Full-length comedies, dramas, musicals, juveniles, adaptations. Query.

THE TEN MINUTE MUSICALS PROJECT—Box 461194, W. Hollywood, CA 90046. Michael Koppy, Prod. One-act musicals. Include audio cassette, libretto, and lead sheets with submission. "We are looking for complete short musicals." Pays $250.

THEATER MU—3010 Hennepin Ave. S., #290, Minneapolis, MN 55408. Rick Shiomi, Artistic Dir. Zaraawar Mistry, Assoc. Artistic Dir. Full-length and one-act comedies and dramas for primarily Asian-American cast. Submit synopsis with cast list, return post card, resumé, recommendations, and SASE. Allow 6 months for response. Also sponsors New Eyes Festival with staged readings for selected scripts. No payment.

THEATRE AMERICANA—Box 245, Altadena, CA 91003. Attn: Lit. Dir. Full-length comedies and dramas, preferably with American theme. No children's plays. Language and subject matter should be suitable for a community audience. Send bound manuscript with cast list, resumé, and SASE, by February 1. No payment. Allow 3 to 6 months for reply. Submit no more than 2 entries per season.

THEATRE OF THE FIRST AMENDMENT—George Mason University, Institute of the Arts, Fairfax, VA 22030. Rick Davis, Artistic Dir. Full-length and one-act comedies, drama, and adaptations. Send synopsis and resumé with return post card.

THEATRE/TEATRO—Bilingual Foundation of the Arts, 421 N. Ave., #19, Los Angeles, CA 90031. Agustin Coppola, Lit. Mgr. Margarita Galban, Artistic Dir. Full-length plays about the Hispanic experience; small casts. Submit manuscript with SASE. Pays negotiable rates.

THEATREWORKS/USA— 890 Broadway, 7th Fl., New York, NY 10003. Barbara Pasternack, Lit. Mgr. One-hour children's musicals and plays with music for 5-person cast. Playwrights must be within commutable distance to New York City. Submit outline or treatment, sample scenes, and music in spring, summer. Pays royalty and commission.

WALNUT STREET THEATRE COMPANY— 825 Walnut St., Philadelphia, PA 19107. Beverly Elliott, Lit. Mgr. Mainstage: Full-length comedies, dramas, musicals, and popular, upbeat adaptations; also, one- to 4-character plays for studio stage. Submit 10 to 20 sample pages with SAS postcard, character breakdown, and synopsis. Musical submissions must include an audio cassette. Reports in 6 months. Payment varies.

THE WESTERN STAGE—156 Homestead Ave., Salinas, CA 93901. Joyce Lower, Dramaturg. Harvey Landa, Exec. Dir. The Salinas River Playwriting Festival, September through October in even-numbered years. Presentations in theater, dance, music, the visual arts, film, poetry. Also workshops, classes, displays, etc. Write for guidelines and required application.

WOOLLY MAMMOTH THEATRE COMPANY—1401 Church St. N.W., Washington, DC 20005. Jim Byrnes, Lit. Mgr. Looking for offbeat material, unusual writing. Unsolicited scripts accepted. Payment varies.

GARY YOUNG MIME THEATRE—23724 Park Madrid, Calabasas, CA 91302. Gary Young, Artistic Dir. Comedy monologues and vignettes, for children and adults. Currently overstocked; not seeking new material.

PLAY PUBLISHERS

ALABAMA LITERARY REVIEW—Troy State Univ., 253 Smith Hall, Troy, AL 36082. Theron Montgomery, Ed. Full-length and one-act comedies and dramas, to 50 pages. Query preferred. Responds to queries in 2 weeks; 2 to 3 months for complete manuscripts. Do not submit material in August. Payment is in copies; honorarium when available.

AMELIA—329 E St., Bakersfield, CA 93304. Frederick A. Raborg, Jr., Ed. One-act comedies and dramas; no longer than 45 minutes running time. Responds in 2 to 3 months. Payment is $35, on acceptance.

ANCHORAGE PRESS—Box 8067, New Orleans, LA 70182. Attn: Ed. Plays and musicals that have been proven in multiple production, for children ages 6 to 18. "We publish 8 to 10 new playbooks and one to 3 new hardcover books each year." Royalty.

ART CRAFT PUBLISHING COMPANY—P.O. Box 1058, Cedar Rapids, IA 52406. Attn: Geri Stonebraker. Two- and 3-act comedies, mysteries, farces, and musicals and one-act comedies or dramas, with one interior setting and a large cast, for production by middle, junior, and senior high school students. Pays royalty or flat fee. E-mail: geri@hitplays.com

BAKER'S PLAYS—100 Chauncy St., Boston, MA 02111. Raymond Pape, Assoc. Ed. Scripts for amateur production: full-length plays, one-act plays, children's plays, musicals, religious dramas; plays for high school, community theatre, and regional theatre production. Allow 4 months for response.

BLIZZARD PUBLISHING—73 Furby St., Winnipeg, Manitoba, Canada R3C 2A2. Peter Atwood, Man. Ed. One-act and full-length dramas, children's plays, and adaptations. Queries preferred. Responds in 3 to 4 months. Royalty.

CALLALOO—Dept. of English, Univ. of Virginia, Charlottesville, VA 22903. Charles H. Rowell, Ed. One-act dramas by and about African-American, Caribbean, and African writers. Scripts read September through May. Responds in 3 to 6 months. Payment varies, on publication.

I. E. CLARK PUBLICATIONS— P.O. Box 246, Schulenburg, TX 78956. Donna Cozzaglio, Ed. One-act and full-length plays and musicals for children, young adults, and adults. Serious drama, comedies, classics, fairytales, melodramas, and holiday plays. "We seldom publish a play that has not been produced." Responds in 2 to 6 months. Royalty.

COLLAGES & BRICOLAGES—P.O. Box 86, Clarion, PA 16214. Marie-José Fortis, Ed. One-act avant-garde comedies and dramas. Manuscripts read August through November; responds in one to 3 months. Payment is in copies.

CONFRONTATION—Dept. of English, C.W. Post of L.I.U., Greenvale, NY 11548. Martin Tucker, Ed. One-act comedies, dramas, and adaptations. Manuscripts read September through May. Responds in 6 to 8 weeks. Pays $25 to $100, on publication.

CONTEMPORARY DRAMA SERVICE—Meriwether Publishing Co., Box 7710, 885 Elkton Dr., Colorado Springs, CO 80903. Arthur Zapel, Ed. Easy-to-stage comedies, skits, one-acts, musicals, and full-length comedy plays for schools and churches. (Junior high through college level; no elementary level material.) Adaptations of classics and improvised material for classroom use. Character education plays and comedy monologues and duets. Chancel drama for Christmas and Easter church use. Enclose synopsis. Books on theater arts subjects, scene books, and anthologies. Textbooks for speech and drama. Pays by fee arrangement or royalty.

DRAMATIC PUBLISHING —311 Washington St., Woodstock, IL 60098. Linda Habjan, Ed. Full-length and one-act plays and musicals for the professional, stock, amateur, and children's theater market. Send SASE. Royalty. Responds within 16 weeks. E-mail: 75712.3621@compuserve.com

DRAMATICS—Educational Theatre Assoc., 3368 Central Pkwy., Cincinnati, OH 45225-2392. Don Corathers, Ed. One-act and full-length plays for high school production. Pays $100 to $400 for one-time, non-exclusive publication rights, on acceptance.

ELDRIDGE PUBLISHING COMPANY—P. O. Box 1595, Venice, FL 34284. Nancy Vorhis, Ed. Dept. One-act and full-length plays and musicals suitable for performance by schools, churches, and community theatre groups. Comedies, tragedies, dramas, skits, spoofs, and religious plays (all holidays). Submit complete manuscript with cover letter, biography, and SASE. Responds in 2 months. Flat fee for one-act and religious plays, paid on publication; royalties for full-length plays. E-mail: info@histage.com. Web site: http.// www.histage.com

SAMUEL FRENCH, INC.— 45 W. 25th St., New York, NY 10010. Lawrence Harbison, William Talbot, Eds. Full-length plays and musicals for dinner, community, stock, college, and high school theaters. One-act plays, 20 to 45 minutes. Children's plays, 45 to 60 minutes. Royalty.

HEUER PUBLISHING COMPANY—Drawer 248, Cedar Rapids, IA 52406. C. Emmett McMullen, Ed. One-act comedies and dramas for contest work; two-and three-act comedies, mysteries, or farces, and musicals, with one interior setting, for middle school and high school production. Pays royalty or flat fee. E-mail: editor@hitplays.com. Web site: www.hitplays.com

LYNX EYE— c/o Scribblefest Literary Group, 1880 Hill Dr., Los Angeles, CA 90041. Pam McCully, Kathryn Morrison, Co-Eds. One-act plays, 500 to 5,000 words, for thoughtful adults who enjoy interesting reading and writing. Also, short stories, vignettes, novel excerpts, essays, belle lettres, satires, and reviews; poetry, to 30 lines. Pays $10, on acceptance.

NATIONAL DRAMA SERVICE—MSN 170, 127 Ninth Ave. N., Nashville, TN 37234. Attn: Ed. Scripts, 2 to 7 minutes long: drama in worship, puppets, clowns, Christian comedy, mime, movement, readers theater, creative worship services, and monologues. "We publish dramatic material that communicates the message of Christ. We want scripts that will give even the smallest church the opportunity to enhance their ministry with drama." Payment varies, on acceptance. Guidelines.

PIONEER DRAMA SERVICE—P. O. Box 4267, Englewood, CO 80155. Attn: Ed. Full-length and one-act plays as well as musicals, melodramas, and children's theatre. No unproduced plays or plays with largely male casts or multiple sets. Query preferred. Royalty. Web site: www.pioneerdrama.com

PLAYERS PRESS, INC.—P.O. Box 1132, Studio City, CA 91614-0132. Robert W. Gordon, Ed. One-act and full-length comedies, dramas, and musicals. "No manuscript will be considered unless it has been produced." Query with manuscript-size SASE and 2 #10 SASEs for correspondence. Include resumé and/or biography. Responds in 3 to 12 months. Royalty.

PLAYS, THE DRAMA MAGAZINE FOR YOUNG PEOPLE— 120 Boylston St., Boston, MA 02116-4615. Elizabeth Preston, Man. Ed. One-act plays, with simple contemporary sets, for production by young people, 7 to 17: comedies, dramas, farces, skits, holiday plays. Also adaptations of classics, biography plays, puppet plays, and creative dramatics. No musicals or plays with religious themes. Maximum lengths: lower grades and skits, 10 double-spaced pages; middle grades, 15 pages; junior and senior high, 20 pages. Guidelines. Pays good rates, on acceptance. Query for adaptations of folk tales and classics. Buys all rights.

THE RADIO PLAY—The Public Media Foundation, 100 Boylston St., Suite 230, Boston, MA 02116. Valerie Henderson, Exec. Prod. Original radio plays and radio dramatizations of American classics in the public domain, 28 to 29 pages, to fit a 30-minute program format. Query for dramatizations only. Send SASE for style sheet.

RAG MAG—P.O. Box 12, Goodhue, MN 55027. Beverly Voldseth, Ed. Semiannual. Full-length and one-act comedies and dramas. SASE for guidelines and themes. Query with 3 to 7 pages of play. Pays in copies.

ROCKFORD REVIEW—P.O. Box 858, Rockford, IL 61105. David Ross, Ed. One-act comedies, dramas, and satires, to 1,300 words. "We prefer genuine or satirical human dilemmas with coping or non-coping outcomes that illuminate the human condition." Publishes one to 2 plays per issue. Pays in copies (plus invitation to attend reading-reception in the summer). Two $25 Editor's Choice Prizes awarded each issue.

SINISTER WISDOM—P.O. Box 3252, Berkeley, CA 94703. Akiba Onada-Sikwoia, Ed. Quarterly. One-act (no longer than 15 pages) lesbian drama. "We are particularly interested in work that reflects the diversity of our experiences: as lesbians of color, ethnic lesbians, Jewish, old, young, working class, poor, disabled, fat. Only material by born-woman lesbians is considered." Responds in 3 to 9 months; write for upcoming themes. Payment is in 2 copies, on publication. SASE.

SMITH AND KRAUS, INC.—P.O. Box 127, Main St., Lyme, NH 03768. Marisa Smith, Pres. Original plays and teaching texts for the K-to-12 market only. Does not accept full-length and one-act plays unless the play in question has been produced within the year and is therefore eligible for the "Best Scene and Monologue Series for the Year." Does not return manuscripts. Response time is 3 months. Pays on publication.

BOOK PUBLISHERS

The following list includes the major book publishers for adult and juvenile fiction and nonfiction and a representative number of small publishers from across the country, as well as a number of university presses.

Before submitting a complete manuscript to an editor, it is advisable to send a brief query letter describing the proposed book, and an SASE. The letter should also include information about the author's special qualifications for dealing with a particular topic and any previous publication credits. An outline of the book (or a synopsis for fiction) and a sample chapter may also be included.

While it is common practice to submit a book manuscript to only one publisher at a time, it is becoming more and more acceptable to submit the same query or proposal to more than one editor simultaneously. When sending multiple queries, *always* make note of it in each submission.

Book manuscripts may be packaged in typing paper boxes (available from a stationery store) and sent by first-class mail, or, more common and less expensive, by "Special Fourth Class Rate—Manuscript." For rates, details of insurance, and so forth, inquire at your local post office. With any submission to a publisher, be sure to enclose sufficient postage for the manuscript's return.

Royalty rates for hardcover books usually start at 10% of the retail price of the book and increase after a certain number of copies have been sold. Paperbacks generally have a somewhat lower rate, about 5% to 8%. It is customary for the publishing company to pay the author a cash advance against royalties when the book contract is signed or when the finished manuscript is received. Some publishers pay on a flat-fee basis.

While most of the publishers on this list consider either unsolicited manuscripts or queries, an increasing number now read only agented submissions. Since finding an agent is not an easy task, especially for newcomers, writers are advised to try to sell their manuscripts directly to the publisher first.

Writers seeking publication of their book-length poetry manuscripts are encouraged to enter contests that offer publication as the prize (see *Literary Prize Offers,* page 803); many presses that once considered unsolicited poetry manuscripts by emerging or unpublished writers now limit their reading of such manuscripts to those entered in their contests for new writers.

ABBEVILLE PRESS— 488 Madison Ave., New York, NY 10022. Attn: Meredith Wolf, Submissions Ed. Illustrated adult nonfiction books on art, architecture, gardening, fashion, interior design, decorative arts, cooking, and travel. Submit outline, sample illustrations, and sample chapters. Art-related juvenile books or those with an educational component. For juveniles, submit complete manuscript to Thomas Sand. Do not send original art or transparencies. Royalty.

ABBEY PRESS—St. Meinrad, IN 47577. Lisa Engelhardt, Books Ed. Not considering any new material at this time.

ABINGDON PRESS—P.O. Box 801, Nashville, TN 37202. Sally Sharpe, Ed. General-interest books: mainline, social issues, marriage/family, self-help, exceptional people. Query with outline and one or 2 sample chapters. Guidelines.

ACADEMIC PRESS—Harcourt Brace, 525 B St., Suite 1900, San Diego, CA 92101. Attn: Ed. Dept. Scientific and technical books and journals for research-level scientists, students, and professionals; upper-level undergraduate and graduate science texts. Query.

ACADEMY CHICAGO PUBLISHERS—363 W. Erie St., Chicago, IL 60610. Anita Miller, Ed. General adult fiction; classic mysteries with emphasis on character and/or puzzle. History; biographies; travel; books by and about women; no explicit sex. Also interested in reprinting books dropped by other houses, including academic titles and anthologies. No electronic submissions accepted. Query with 4 sample chapters. SASE required. Royalty.

ACCENT PUBLICATIONS—Box 36640, 4050 Lee Vance View, Colorado Springs, CO 80936. Nonfiction church resources facilitating Christian education curriculum programs for the local church; evangelical Christian perspective; no trade books. "Request guidelines before querying." Royalty. Paperback only.

ACE BOOKS—200 Madison Ave., New York, NY 10016. Susan Allison, V.P., Ed.-in-Chief. Science fiction and fantasy. Query with first 3 chapters and outline to Anne Sowards, Ed. Royalty.

ACTIVITY RESOURCES—P.O. Box 4875, Hayward, CA 94540. Mary Laycock. Math educational material only. "Our main focus is on grades K through 8." Submit complete manuscript. Royalty.

ADAMS-BLAKE PUBLISHING— 8041 Sierra St., Fair Oaks, CA 95628. Monica Blane, Ed. Books on business, careers, and technology. Query or send complete manuscript. Multiple submissions accepted. Royalty.

ADAMS-HALL PUBLISHING—11661 San Vicente Blvd., Suite 210, Los Angeles, CA 90049. Sue Ann Bacon, Marketing Dir. Business and personal finance books with wide market appeal. Query with proposed book idea, a listing of current competitive books, author qualifications, and the reason that the book is unique. Royalty.

ADDISON WESLEY—See *Scott Foresman/Addison Wesley.*

ALASKA NORTHWEST BOOKS—2208 N.W. Market St., Suite 300, Seattle, WA 98107. Marlene Blessing, Ed.-in-Chief. Nonfiction, 50,000 to 100,000 words, with an emphasis on natural world and history of Alaska and the Pacific Northwest: travel books; cookbooks; field guides; children's books; outdoor recreation; natural history; native culture; lifestyle. Send query or sample chapters with outline. Guidelines.

ALGONQUIN BOOKS OF CHAPEL HILL—Box 2225, Chapel Hill, NC 27515. Shannon Ravenel, Ed. Dir. Trade books, literary fiction and nonfiction, for adults.

ALPINE PUBLICATIONS—225 S. Madison Ave., Loveland, CO 80537. B.J. McKinney, Pub. Nonfiction books, 35,000 to 60,000 words, on dogs, horses, cats, and companion animals. Submit outline and sample chapters or complete manuscript. Royalty.

ALYSON PUBLICATIONS—P.O. Box 4371, Los Angeles, CA 90078. Attn: Ed. Gay and lesbian adult fiction and nonfiction books, from 65,000 words. *Alyson Wonderland* imprint: Children's picture books with gay and lesbian themes; young adult titles, from 65,000 words. Query with outline only. Royalty.

ALYSON WONDERLAND—See *Alyson Publications.*

AMERICAN EDUCATION PUBLISHING—c/o Landoll, Inc., 425 Orange St., Ashland, OH 44805. Attn: Ed. Dir. Children's books, 32 to 64 pages. Submit complete manuscript. Royalty.

AMERICAN PARADISE PUBLISHING—P.O. Box 37, St. John, USVI 00831. Gary M. Goodlander, Ed. "We are interested in 'hopelessly local' books, between 80 and 300 pages. We need useful, practical books that help our Virgin Island readers lead better and more enjoyable lives." Guidebooks, cookbooks, how-to books, books on sailing, yacht cruising, hiking, snorkeling, sportfishing, local history, and West Indian culture, specifically aimed at Caribbean readers/tourists. Query with outline and sample chapters. Royalty.

THE AMERICAN PSYCHIATRIC PRESS—1400 K St. N.W., Washington, DC 20005. Carol C. Nadelson, M.D., Ed.-in-Chief. Books that interpret scientific and medical aspects of psychiatry for a lay audience and that address specific psychiatric problems. Authors must have appropriate credentials to write on medical topics. Query required. Royalty.

ANCHOR BOOKS—Imprint of Doubleday and Co., 1540 Broadway, New York, NY 10036. Martha K. Levin, Pub. Adult trade paperbacks and hardcovers. Nonfiction, multicultural, sociology, psychology, philosophy, women's interest, etc. No unsolicited manuscripts.

ANCHORAGE PRESS—Box 8067, New Orleans, LA 70182. Attn: Acquisitions Ed. Dramatic publishers. Plays for children ages 4 to 18. "We publish 8 to 10 new playbooks and one to 3 new hardcover books each year." Royalty.

AND BOOKS—702 S. Michigan, South Bend, IN 46601. Janos Szebedinsky, Ed. Adult nonfiction. Topics include computers, fine arts, health, philosophy, regional subjects, and social justice.

ANHINGA PRESS—P.O. Box 10595, Tallahassee, FL 32302-0595. Rick Campbell, Ed. Poetry books. (Publishes 3 books a year.) Query or send complete manuscripts. Flat fee. Annual poetry prize of $2,000 plus publication; send #10 SASE for details.

ANTIQUE TRADER BOOKS—P.O. Box 1050, Dubuque, IA 52004-1050. Allan W. Miller, Man. Ed. Collector guides and reference books, 200 pages, on antiques and collectibles. Query with outline and sample chapter. Royalty.

APPALACHIAN MOUNTAIN CLUB BOOKS—5 Joy St., Boston, MA 02108. Attn: Ed. Dept. Regional (New England) and national nonfiction titles, 250 to 400 pages, for adult audience; juvenile and young adult nonfiction. Topics include guidebooks on non-motorized backcountry recreation, nature, mountain history/biography, search and rescue, conservation, and environmental management. Query with outline and sample chapters. Multiple queries considered. Royalty.

ARCADE PUBLISHING—141 Fifth Ave., New York, NY 10010. Richard Seaver, Pub./Ed., Jeannette Seaver, Assoc. Pub., Timothy Bent, Sean McDonald, David Martyn, Eds. Fiction and nonfiction. No unsolicited manuscripts. Query.

ARCHWAY/MINSTREL BOOKS—Pocket Books, 1230 Ave. of the Americas, New York, NY 10020. Patricia MacDonald,V.P./ Ed. Dir. Young adult contemporary fiction (suspense thrillers, romances) and nonfiction (popular current topics), for ages 12 to 16. *Minstrel Books*: young reader fiction including thrillers, adventure, fantasy, humor, animal stories, for ages 6 to 11. Send query, outline, sample chapters to Attn: Manuscript Proposals.

ASTARTE SHELL PRESS—P.O. Box 3648, Portland, ME 04104. Sapphire, Ed. Books on theology, politics, and social issues from a feminist/woman's/multicultural perspective. No poetry. "We are no longer accepting unsolicited manuscripts." Royalty.

AUGUST HOUSE—P.O. Box 3223, Little Rock, AR 72203. Liz Parkhurst, Ed.-in-Chief. Adult books pertaining to folklore, folktales, and storytelling. Illustrated children's books featuring traditional folktales are published under the *August House LittleFolk* imprint. Submit proposal with sample chapters (at least 40 pages) and a descriptive outline or table of contents with an SASE. Royalty.

AVALON BOOKS— 401 Lafayette St., New York, NY 10003. Wilhelm H. Mickelsen, Pres. Marcia Markland, V.P./Pub. Hardcover books, 40,000 to 50,000 words: romances, mysteries, and westerns. No explicit sex. Query with first 3 chapters and outline; nonreturnable. SASE for guidelines.

AVERY PUBLISHING GROUP—120 Old Broadway, Garden City Park, NY 11040. Attn: Man. Ed. Nonfiction, from 40,000 words, on health, childbirth, child care, healthful cooking. Query. Royalty.

AVISSON PRESS, INC.—3007 Taliaferro Rd., Greensboro, NC 27408. Martin L. Hester, Exec. Ed. Helpful nonfiction books on health, lifestyle, finance, etc., for older Americans; books on teenage issues, teen problems, and parenting; young adult biography (for readers 10 to 18). Query with outline or sample chapter, bio and SASE. Royalty.

AVON BOOKS—1350 Ave. of the Americas, New York, NY 10019. Robert Mecoy, Ed.-in-Chief. Genre fiction, general nonfiction, historical romance, 60,000 to 200,000 words. *Avon Hardcover*: Adult commercial fiction and nonfiction. Send one-or 2-page query letter describing book (including its length) with SASE. *AvoNova*: science fiction, 75,000 to 100,000 words. Query with synopsis and sample chapters. Ellen Edwards, Historical Romance; John Douglas, Science Fiction; Chris Miller, Fantasy. *Camelot Books*: Ellen Krieger, Ed. Fiction and nonfiction for 7-to 10-year-olds. Query. *Flare Books*: Ellen Krieger, Ed. Fiction and nonfiction for 12-year-olds and up. Query. Royalty. Paperback only.

AVONOVA—See *Avon Books.*

BAEN BOOKS—Baen Publishing Enterprises, P.O. Box 1403, Riverdale, NY 10471-1403. Jim Baen, Pres./Ed.-in-Chief. Strongly plotted science fiction; innovative fantasy. Query with synopsis and manuscript. Advance and royalty. Guidelines available for letter-sized SASE.

BAKER BOOK HOUSE—P. O. Box 6287, Grand Rapids, MI 49516-6287. Jane Schrier, Asst. to the Dir. of Pub. Religious nonfiction: books for trade, clergy, seminarians, collegians. Religious fiction. Royalty.

BALBOA—See *Tiare Publications.*

BALLANTINE BOOKS—201 E. 50th St., New York, NY 10022. Attn: Ed.-in-Chief. General fiction and nonfiction. Query.

BALSAM PRESS—36 E. 22nd St., 9th Fl., New York, NY 10010. Barbara Krohn, Exec. Ed. General and illustrated adult nonfiction. Query. Royalty.

BANKS CHANNEL BOOKS—P.O. Box 4446, Wilmington, NC 28406. Attn: Book Ed. Books of regional interest by North Carolina writers only. "Currently overstocked; not accepting any new material."

BANTAM BOOKS—1540 Broadway, New York, NY 10036. Irwyn Applebaum, Pres./Pub. Adult fiction and nonfiction. Mass-market titles, submit queries to the following imprints: *Crime Line*, crime and mystery fiction; *Domain*, frontier fiction, historical sagas, traditional westerns; *Spectra*, science fiction and fantasy; *Bantam Nonfiction*, wide variety of commercial nonfiction, including true crime, health and nutrition, sports, reference. Agented queries and manuscripts only.

BANTAM, DOUBLEDAY, DELL—See *Bantam Books, Doubleday and Co.* and *Dell Books.*

BANTAM SPECTRA BOOKS—1540 Broadway, New York, NY 10036. Anne Lesley Groell, Ed. Patrick LoBrutto, Sr. Ed. Science fiction and fantasy, with emphasis on storytelling and characterization. First 3 chapters and synopsis with SASE; no unsolicited manuscripts. Royalty.

BARRICADE BOOKS—150 Fifth Ave., New York, NY 10011. Lyle Stuart, Pub. General nonfiction, celebrity biographies, controversial subjects. No fiction. Send synopsis only with SASE. Modest advances against royalties.

BARRON'S EDUCATIONAL SERIES, INC.—250 Wireless Blvd., Hauppauge, NY 11788. Grace Freedson, Acquisitions Dir. Juvenile nonfiction (science, nature, history, hobbies, and how-to) and picture books for ages 3 to 6.

Adult nonfiction (business, pet care, childcare, sports, test preparation, cookbooks, foreign language instruction). Query with SASE. Guidelines.

BAUHAN, PUBLISHER, WILLIAM L.—Box 443, Dublin, NH 03444. William L. Bauhan, Ed. Biographies, fine arts, gardening, architecture, and history books with an emphasis on New England. Submit query with outline and sample chapter.

BAYLOR UNIVERSITY PRESS—P.O. Box 97363, Baylor Univ., Waco, TX 76798-7363. Janet L. Burton, Academic Publications Coordinator. Scholarly nonfiction, especially oral history and church-state issues. Query with outline. Royalty.

BEACON PRESS—25 Beacon St., Boston, MA 02108. Attn: Camille Andrews. General nonfiction: world affairs, women's studies, anthropology, history, philosophy, religion, gay and lesbian studies, environment, nature writing, African-American studies, Asian-American studies, Native-American studies. Series: "Concord Library" (nature writing); "Barnard New Women Poets"; "Black Women Writers" (fiction); "Men and Masculinity" (nonfiction). Query. Agented manuscripts only.

BEHRMAN HOUSE—235 Watchung Ave., W. Orange, NJ 07052. Adam Siegel, Projects Ed. Adult and juvenile nonfiction, varying lengths, in English and in Hebrew, on Jewish subject matter. Query with outline and sample chapters. Flat fee or royalty.

BENCHMARK BOOKS—99 White Plains Rd., Tarrytown, NY 10591-9001. Judith Whipple, Ed. Dir. Books, 3,000 to 30,000 words, for young readers (grades 3 up) on science, sports, the arts, wildlife, math, and health. Series include: "Cultures of the World," "Cultures of the Past," "Biomes of the World," "Life Issues," "Discovering Math," and others. Query with outline. Royalty or flat fee. No single title submissions.

BERKLEY PUBLISHING GROUP —200 Madison Ave., New York, NY 10016. General-interest fiction and nonfiction; science fiction, suspense, and mystery novels; romance. Submit through agent only. Publishes both reprints and originals. Paperback books, except for some hardcover mysteries and science fiction. Young adult books: Laura Anne Gilman, Ed. Horror, suspense, adventure, and romance. Query required.

THE BESS PRESS—3565 Harding Ave., Honolulu, HI 96816. Revé Shapard, Ed. Nonfiction books about Hawaii, Asia, and the Pacific for adults, children, and young adults. Submit outline with sample chapters or complete manuscript. Royalty.

BETHANY HOUSE PUBLISHERS—11300 Hampshire Ave. S., Minneapolis, MN 55438. Attn: Ed. Dept. Religious fiction and nonfiction. Query with sample chapters. Royalty.

BETTER HOMES AND GARDENS BOOKS—See *Meredith Corp. Book Publishing.*

BICK PUBLISHING HOUSE—307 Neck Rd., Madison, CT 06443. Dale Carlson, Ed. Books, 64 to 250 pages, on wildlife rehabilitation, special needs/disabilities, psychology. Submit outline and sample chapters. Royalty.

BINFORD & MORT PUBLISHING—1202 N.W. 17th Ave., Portland, OR 97209. P.L. Gardenier, Ed. Books on subjects related to the Pacific Coast and the Northwest. Lengths vary. Query. Royalty.

BIRCH LANE PRESS—See *Carol Publishing Group.*

BLACK BELT PRESS—Black Belt Communications Group, Inc., P.O. Box 551, Montgomery, AL 36101. Randall Williams, Ed.-in-Chief. Southern fiction, biography, history, and folklore. Query with cover letter, synopsis or outline, author bio, and SASE for reply. Royalty varies.

BLACK BUTTERFLY CHILDREN'S BOOKS—Writers and Readers Publishing, 625 Broadway, New York, NY 10012. Deborah Dyson, Ed. Titles featuring black children and other children of color, ages 9 to 13, for Young Beginners series. Picture books for children up to 11; board books for toddlers; juvenile fiction for all ages. Query. Royalty.

BLACK BUZZARD PRESS—Vias, Visions-International, 1007 Ficklen Rd., Fredericksburg, VA 22405. Bradley R. Strahan, Ed. Poetry manuscripts, to 30 pages. Query. Royalty.

BLAIR, PUBLISHER, JOHN F.—1406 Plaza Dr., Winston-Salem, NC 27103. Carolyn Sakowski, Pres. Books from 50,000 words: biography, history, folklore, and guidebooks, with southeastern tie-in. Query. Royalty.

BLUE DOLPHIN PUBLISHING, INC.—P.O. Box 8, Nevada City, CA 95959. Paul M. Clemens, Ed. Books, 200 to 300 pages, on comparative spiritual traditions, lay and transpersonal psychology, self-help, health, healing, and "whatever helps people grow in their social awareness and conscious evolution." Query with outline, sample chapters, and SASE. Royalty.

BLUE HERON PUBLISHING—24450 N.W. Hansen Rd., Hillsboro, OR 97124. Dennis Stovall, Ed. Adult nonfiction for series on writing/publishing. Also literary nonfiction relevant to education relating to the Northwest. Query. Royalty.

BLUE MOON BOOKS, INC.—61 Fourth Ave., New York, NY 10003. Barney Rosset, Pub. Erotic fiction and nonfiction on a variety of topics. Send synopsis and sample chapters; SASE.

BOB JONES UNIVERSITY PRESS—1700 Wade Hampton Blvd., Greenville, SC 29614. Gloria Repp, Ed. Books for young readers, ages 6 to 12, that reflect "the highest Christian standards of thought, feeling, and action." Fiction, 8,000 to 40,000 words. Nonfiction, 10,000 to 30,000 words. Young adult books, 40,000 to 60,000 words. Read guidelines, then submit sample chapters. Pays on royalty or flat fee basis.

BONUS BOOKS—160 E. Illinois St., Chicago, IL 60611. Rachel Drzewicki, Man. Ed. Nonfiction; topics vary widely. Query with sample chapters and SASE. Royalty.

BOTTOM DOG PRESS, INC.—c/o Firelands College, Huron, OH 44839. Larry Smith, Dir. Collections of personal essays, stories, 50 to 200 pages, and poetry for combined chapbook publication (30 to 50 poems). Subjects should be midwestern in focus. "Interested writers should query." Royalty.

BOYDS MILLS PRESS—815 Church St., Honesdale, PA 18431. Beth Troop, Manuscript Coord. Hardcover trade books for children. Fiction: picture books; middle-grade fiction with fresh ideas and involving story; young adult novels of literary merit. Nonfiction should be "fun, entertaining, and informative." Send outline and sample chapters for young adult novels and nonfiction, complete manuscripts for all other categories. Royalty.

BRANDEN PUBLISHING COMPANY—17 Station St., Box 843, Brookline Village, MA 02147. Attn: Ed. Dept. Novels, biographies, and autobiographies. Especially books by or about women, 250 to 350 pages. Also considers queries on history, computers, business, performance arts, and translations. Query only with SASE. Royalty.

BRASSEY'S, INC.—1331 Dolley Madison Blvd., Suite 401, McLean, VA 22101-3926. Don McKeon, Ed. Dir. Nonfiction books, 75,000 to 130,000 words: national and international affairs, history, foreign policy, defense, military and political biography, sports. No fiction. Query with synopsis, author bio, outline, and sample chapters. Royalty.

BRAZILLER PUBLISHERS, GEORGE—171 Madison Ave., Suite 1103, New York, NY 10016. Attn: Ed. Dept. Fiction and nonfiction. Mostly art, art history; some profiles of writers, collections of essays and short stories, anthologies. Send art history manuscripts to Adrienne Baxter, Ed.; others to Fiction Editor. Send outline with sample chapters. Payment varies.

BREAKAWAY BOOKS—336 W. 84th St., #4, New York, NY 10024. Garth Battista, Pub. Literary sports novels and single stories and poems, any length, for anthology series. "Our goal is to bring to light literary writing on the athletic experience." Royalty.

BRETT BOOKS, INC.—P.O. Box 290-637, Brooklyn, NY 11229-0637. Barbara J. Brett, Pres./Pub. Nonfiction for adult trade market. "Submit a query letter of no more than 2 pages, stating your professional background and summarizing your book proposal in 2 to 4 paragraphs." SASE. Royalty.

BRIDGE WORKS—Box 1798, Bridgehampton, NY 11932. Barbara Phillips, Pres./Ed. Dir. Mainstream adult literary fiction and nonfiction, 50,000 to 75,000 words. Royalty.

BRISTOL PUBLISHING ENTERPRISES—P.O. Box 1737, San Leandro, CA 94577. Jennifer L. Newens, Ed. Cookbooks. Query with outline, sample chapters, resumé, and SASE. Royalty.

BROADMAN AND HOLMAN PUBLISHERS—127 Ninth Ave. N., Nashville, TN 37234. Richard P. Rosenbaum, Jr., Ed. Dir. Religious and inspirational nonfiction. Query with SASE. Royalty. Guidelines.

BROADWAY BOOKS—A Div. of Bantam, Doubleday, Dell, 1540 Broadway, New York, NY 10036. John Sterling, Ed.-in-Chief. Adult nonfiction; small and very selective fiction list. Query with outline, sample chapters, and SASE. Royalty.

BROWNDEER PRESS—Imprint of Harcourt Brace & Co. Children's Books, 9 Monroe Pkwy., Suite 240, Lake Oswego, OR 97035-1487. Linda Zuckerman, Ed. Dir. Picture books, humorous middle-grade fiction, and young adult material written from an unusual perspective or about an unusual subject. Considers submissions from agents, published authors, or members of SCBWI only. Query for nonfiction with cover letter, resumé, and sample chapter; send complete manuscript for picture books (avoid rhyming text). For longer fiction, send first 3 chapters, synopsis, and short cover letter including list of published works. SASE required for all correspondence.

BUCKNELL UNIVERSITY PRESS—Bucknell Univ., Lewisburg, PA 17837. Greg Clingham, Dir. Scholarly nonfiction. Query. Royalty.

BULFINCH PRESS—34 Beacon St., Boston, MA 02108. Attn: Ed. Dept. Books on fine arts and photography. Query with outline or proposal and vita.

BYRON PREISS VISUAL PUBLICATIONS—24 W. 25th St., New York, NY 10010. Attn: Ed. Dept. Book packager. "We are primarily interested in seeing samples from established authors willing to work to specifications on firm deadlines." Genres: science fiction, fantasy, horror, juvenile, young adult, nonfiction. Pays competitive advance against royalties for commissioned work.

C&T PUBLISHING—P.O. Box 1456, Lafayette, CA 94549. Todd Hensley, Pub. Quilting books, 64 to 200 finished pages. "Our focus is how-to, although we will consider picture, inspirational, or history books on quilting." Send query, outline, or sample chapters. Multiple queries considered. Royalty.

CALYX BOOKS—P.O. Box B, Corvallis, OR 97339. Margarita Donnelly, Micki Reaman, Eds. Feminist publisher. Novels, short stories, poetry, nonfiction, translations, and anthologies by women. Currently overstocked; query for anthologies and creative nonfiction. Send SASE for guidelines before submitting. Limited market.

CAMELOT BOOKS—See *Avon Books*.

CANDLEWICK PRESS—2067 Massachusetts Ave., Cambridge, MA 02140. Elizabeth Bicknell, Ed.-in-Chief. No unsolicited material.

CAPSTONE PRESS, INC.—P.O. Box 669, Mankato, MN 56001-0669. Attn: Ed. Dept. High-interest/low-reading level and early reader nonfiction for children, specifically reluctant and new readers. Send SASE for catalogue of series themes. Query required; no complete manuscripts. Flat fee.

CAROL PUBLISHING GROUP—600 Madison Ave., New York, NY 10022. Allan J. Wilson, Ed. General nonfiction. *Citadel Press*: biography (celebrity preferred), autobiography, film, history, and self-help, 70,000 words. *Birch Lane Press*: adult nonfiction, 75,000 words. *Lyle Stuart*: adult nonfiction, 75,000 words, of a controversial nature, gaming, etc.; address Hillel Black, Ed. Also *University Books*. Query with SASE required. Royalty.

CAROLRHODA BOOKS—241 First Ave. N., Minneapolis, MN 55401. Rebecca Poole, Ed. Complete manuscripts for ages 4 to 12: biography, science, nature, history, photo-essays; historical fiction. Guidelines. Hardcover.

CAROUSEL PRESS—P.O. Box 6061, Albany, CA 94706-0061. Stephanie Dillon, Ed. Travel guides, especially family-oriented. Send letter, table of contents, and sample chapter. "We publish one or 2 new books each year and will consider out-of-print books that the author wants to update." Modest advance and royalty.

CARROLL AND GRAF PUBLISHERS, INC.—260 Fifth Ave., New York, NY 10001. Kent E. Carroll, Exec. Ed. General fiction and nonfiction. No unagented submissions.

CARTWHEEL BOOKS—Scholastic, Inc., 555 Broadway, New York, NY 10012. Picture, novelty, and easy-to-read books, to about 1,000 words, for children, preschool to third grade. No novels or chapter books. Royalty or flat fee. Query; no unsolicited manuscripts.

CASSANDRA PRESS—P.O. Box 150868, San Rafael, CA 94915. Attn: Ed. Dept. New age, holistic health, metaphysical, and psychological books. Query with outline and sample chapters, or complete manuscript. Include SASE. Royalty (no advance).

THE CATHOLIC UNIVERSITY OF AMERICA PRESS—620 Michigan Ave. N.E., Washington, DC 20064. David J. McGonagle, Dir. Scholarly nonfiction: American and European history (both ecclesiastical and secular); Irish studies; American and European literature; philosophy; political theory; theology. Query with prospectus, annotated table of contents, or introduction and resumé. Royalty.

CELESTIAL ARTS—See *Ten Speed Press.*

CHARLESBRIDGE — 85 Main St., Watertown, MA 02172. Juliana McIntyre, Ed. 32-page books, especially on nature or science themes, as well as board books for younger readers. Send complete manuscript. Pays royalty or flat fee.

CHATHAM PRESS—P. O. Box A, Old Greenwich, CT 06870. Roger H. Lourie, Man. Dir. Books on the Northeast coast, gardening, New England maritime subjects, and the ocean. Large photography volumes. Query with outline, sample chapters, illustrations, and SASE. Royalty.

CHELSEA GREEN PUBLISHING CO.—P.O. Box 428, White River Junction, VT 05001. Jim Schley, Ed. Nonfiction: natural history, environmental issues, energy and shelter, organic agriculture, and ecological lifestyle books with strong backlist potential. Query with outline and SASE. Not considering any unsolicited manuscripts at this time. Royalty.

CHELSEA HOUSE PUBLISHERS—1974 Sproul Rd., Broomall, PA 19008. Attn: Acquisitions Ed. Juvenile books (for ages 8 up) for publication in a series format. Series include: "Black Americans of Achievement"; "Indians of North America"; "Life in America 100 Years Ago"; "Lives of Notable Gay Men and Lesbians"; and "Great Achievers: Lives of the Physically Challenged," among others. No unsolicited manuscripts. Query with writing sample for consideration of assignments. SASE required. Flat fee.

CHICAGO REVIEW PRESS— 814 N. Franklin St., Chicago, IL 60610. Cynthia Sherry, Ed. Nonfiction: activity books for young children, project books for ages 10 to 18, general nonfiction, architecture, pregnancy, how-to, popular science, and regional gardening and other regional topics. Query with outline and sample chapters.

CHILDREN'S BOOK PRESS—246 First St., Suite 101, San Francisco, CA 94105. Submissions Ed. Bilingual and multicultural picture books, 750 to 1,500 words, for children in grades K through 6. "We publish folktales and contemporary stories reflecting the traditions and culture of the emerging majority in the U.S. and worldwide. Ultimately, we want to help encourage a more international, multicultural perspective on the part of all young people." Query. Pays advance on royalties.

CHILDREN'S LIBRARY PRESS—P.O. Box 1919, Joshua Tree, CA 92252. Attn: Acquisitions Ed. Texts for picture books. Submit complete manuscript. Royalty.

CHILDREN'S PRESS—Sherman Turnpike, Danbury, CT 06813. Attn: Ed. Dir. Juvenile nonfiction: science, biography, 10,000 to 25,000 words, for supplementary use in classrooms. Picture books, 50 to 1,000 words. Royalty or outright purchase. Currently overstocked; not accepting unsolicited manuscripts.

CHINA BOOKS—2929 24th St., San Francisco, CA 94110. Wendy K. Lee, Sr. Ed. Books relating to China or Chinese culture. Adult nonfiction, varying lengths. Juvenile picture books, fiction, nonfiction, and young adult books. Query. Royalty. Manuscript guidelines available on the web at www.chinabooks.com.

CHRONICLE BOOKS— 85 Second St., San Francisco, CA 94105. Attn: Ed. Dept. Fiction, art, photography, architecture, design, nature, food, giftbooks, regional topics. Children's books. Send proposal or complete manuscript for fiction with SASE.

CITADEL PRESS—See *Carol Publishing Group.*

CLARION BOOKS—215 Park Ave. S., New York, NY 10003. Dorothy Briley, Ed.-in-Chief/Pub. Fiction, nonfiction, and picture books: short novels and lively stories for ages 6 to 10 and 8 to 12, historical fiction, humor; picture books for infants and children to age 7; biography, natural history, social studies, American and world history for readers 5 to 8, and 9 up. Royalty. Hardcover. Currently overstocked; no unsolicited manuscripts.

CLEIS PRESS—P.O. Box 8933, Pittsburgh, PA 15221. Frédérique Delacoste, Ed. Fiction and nonfiction, 200 pages, by women. No poetry. Send SASE with 2 first-class stamps for catalogue before querying. Royalty.

CLOVER PARK PRESS—P.O. Box 5067-T, Santa Monica, CA 90409-5067. Martha Grant, Acquisitions Ed. Nonfiction adult books on California (history, natural history, travel, culture, or the arts), biography of extraordinary women, nature, travel, exploration, scientific/medical discovery. Query with outline, sample chapter, author bio, and SASE.

COBBLEHILL BOOKS—375 Hudson St., New York, NY 10014. Joe Ann Daly, Ed. Dir. Rosanne Lauer, Exec. Ed. Fiction and nonfiction for preschoolers through junior high school. Query for manuscripts longer than picture books; send complete manuscript with SASE for picture books. Royalty.

COFFEE HOUSE PRESS—27 N. 4th St., Suite 400, Minneapolis, MN 55401. Attn: Chris Fischbach. Literary fiction (no genres). Query with SASE.

COLLIER BOOKS—See *Macmillan Reference USA.*

CONARI PRESS—2550 Ninth St., Suite 101, Berkeley, CA 94710. Claudia Schaab, Ed. Assoc. Adult nonfiction: women's issues, personal growth, parenting, and spirituality. Submit outline, sample chapters, and 6-1/2" x 9-1/2" SASE. Royalty.

CONCORDIA PUBLISHING HOUSE—3558 S. Jefferson Ave., St. Louis, MO 63118. Attn: Book Development. Practical family books and devotionals. Children's fiction with explicit Christian content. No poetry. Query. Royalty.

CONFLUENCE PRESS—Lewis Clark State College, 500 8th Ave., Lewiston, ID 83502-2698. James Hepworth, Dir. Fiction, nonfiction, and poetry, of varying lengths, "to promote and nourish emerging writers, in particular, to achieve literary and artistic excellence." Send query, outline, and sample chapters. Flat fee or royalty.

CONSUMER REPORTS BOOKS—101 Truman Ave., Yonkers, NY 10703. Mark Hoffman, Ed. Medicine/health, food/nutrition, personal finance, retirement planning, automotive, home maintenance. No unsolicited manuscripts.

CONTEMPORARY BOOKS, INC.—See *NTC/Contemporary Publishing Co.*

COPPER BEECH BOOKS—See *The Millbrook Press.*

COPPER CANYON PRESS—P.O. Box 271, Port Townsend, WA 98368. Sam Hamill, Ed. Poetry books only. No multiple submissions. Query with SASE. Royalty.

CORNELL UNIVERSITY PRESS—Box 250, Sage House, 512 E. State St., Ithaca, NY 14851. Frances Benson, Ed.-in-Chief. Scholarly nonfiction, 80,000 to 120,000 words. Query with outline. Royalty.

COTLER BOOKS, JOANNA—See *HarperCollins Children's Books.*

COUNTERPOINT—1627 I St. N.W. , Suite 850, Washington, DC 20006. Jack Shoemaker, Ed.-in-Chief. Adult literary nonfiction, including art, religion, history, biography, science, and current affairs; some literary fiction. Submit sample chapters and synopsis. Royalty.

CRAFTSMAN BOOK COMPANY— 6058 Corte del Cedro, P.O. Box 6500, Carlsbad, CA 92018. Laurence D. Jacobs, Ed. How-to construction and estimating manuals and software for professional builders, 450 pages. Query. Royalty. Paperback.

CREATIVE ARTS BOOK CO.— 833 Bancroft Way, Berkeley, CA 94710. Donald S. Ellis, Pub. Adult nonfiction and fiction: women's issues, music, African-American and Asian, and California topics. Query with outline, sample chapters, SASE. Royalty.

CRIME LINE—See *Bantam Books.*

THE CROSSING PRESS—P.O. Box 1048, Freedom, CA 95019. Elaine Goldman Gill, Pub. Health and nutrition, holistic health, women's interests, spiritual growth, alternative parenting, cookbooks, pets. Royalty.

CROWN BOOKS FOR YOUNG READERS—201 E. 50th St., New York, NY 10022. Simon Boughton, Pub. Dir. Children's nonfiction (science, sports, nature, music, and history) and picture books for ages 3 and up. Query for nonfiction. Send complete manuscript for picture books to Submissions Ed. Guidelines.

CUMBERLAND HOUSE PUBLISHING—2200 Abbott Martin Rd., Suite 102, Nashville, TN 37215. Leslie Peterson, Ed. Adult nonfiction, to 100,000 words and mysteries. Query with outline and sample chapters. Royalty.

CURBSTONE PRESS—321 Jackson St., Willimantic, CT 06226. Alexander Taylor, Pub./Ed. Fiction, nonfiction, poetry books, and picture books that reflect a commitment to social change, with an emphasis on contemporary writing from Latin America and Latino communities in the U.S. Agented material only. Royalty.

DANIEL AND COMPANY, JOHN—P.O. Box 21922, Santa Barbara, CA 93121. John Daniel, Pub. Books, to 200 pages, in the field of belles lettres and literary memoirs; stylish and elegant writing; essays and short fiction dealing with social issues; one poetry title per year. Send synopsis or outline with no more than 50 sample pages and SASE. Allow 8 weeks for response. Royalty.

DAVIES-BLACK PUBLISHING—3803 E. Bayshore Rd., Palo Alto, CA 94303. Melinda Adams Merino, Acquisitions Ed. Books, 250 to 400 manuscript pages. Professional and trade titles on business and careers.

DAVIS PUBLICATIONS, INC.—50 Portland St., Worcester, MA 01608. Books, 100 to 300 manuscript pages, for the art education market; mainly for teachers of art, grades K through 12. Must have an educational component. Grades K through 8, address Claire M. Golding; grades 9 through 12, address Helen Ronan. Query with outline and sample chapters. Royalty.

DAW BOOKS, INC.—375 Hudson St., 3rd Fl., New York, NY 10014-3658. Elizabeth R. Wollheim, Ed.-in-Chief. Sheila E. Gilbert, Sr. Ed. Peter Stampfel, Submissions Ed. Science fiction and fantasy, 80,000 words and up. No short stories, collections, or anthologies. Royalty.

DAWN PUBLICATIONS— 14618 Tyler Foote Rd., Nevada City, CA 95959. Glenn J. Hovemann, Ed. Dept. Nature awareness books for children. Children's picture books with a positive, uplifting message to awaken a sense of appreciation and kinship with nature. For children's works, submit complete manuscript and specify intended age. SASE for guidelines. Royalty.

DEARBORN FINANCIAL PUBLISHING, INC.—155 N. Wacker Dr., Chicago, IL 60606-1719. Carol Luitjens, V.P. Books on financial services, real estate, banking, small business, etc. Query with outline and sample chapters. Royalty and flat fee.

DEE PUBLISHER, INC., IVAN R.—1332 N. Halsted St., Chicago, IL 60622-2637. Ivan R. Dee, Pres. Nonfiction books on history, politics, biography, literature, and theater. Query with outline and sample chapters. Royalty.

DEL REY BOOKS—201 E. 50th St., New York, NY 10022. Shelly Shapiro, Exec. Ed. Veronica Chapman, Sr. Ed. Science fiction and fantasy, 60,000 to 120,000 words; first novelists welcome. Fantasy with magic basic to plotline. Query with outline and 3 sample chapters. Include manuscript-size SASE. Royalty.

DELACORTE PRESS—1540 Broadway, New York, NY 10036. Leslie Schnur, Jackie Farber, Maureen O'Neal, Jackie Cantor, Eds. Adult fiction and nonfiction. Accepts fiction (mystery, young adult, romance, fantasy, etc.) from agents only.

DELL BOOKS—1540 Broadway, New York, NY 10036. Attn: Editorial Dept., Book Proposal. Commercial fiction and nonfiction, family sagas, historical romances, war action, general fiction, occult/horror/psychological suspense, true crime, men's adventure. Send narrative synopsis for fiction (to 4 pages) or outline (also to 4 pages) for nonfiction. Enclose SASE. No poetry. Allow 2 to 3 months for response.

DELTA BOOKS—1540 Broadway, New York, NY 10036. Attn: Ed. Dept., Book Proposal. General-interest nonfiction: submit detailed chapter outline with sample chapters. Fiction: submit full manuscript with narrative synopsis (no more than 10 pages). Poetry not considered. Allow 3 months for reply. SASE.

DEVIN-ADAIR PUBLISHERS, INC.—P.O. Box A, Old Greenwich, CT 06870. J. Andrassi, Ed. Books on conservative affairs, Irish topics, photography, Americana, self-help, health, gardening, cooking, and ecology. Send outline, sample chapters, and SASE. Royalty.

DI CAPUA BOOKS, MICHAEL—See *HarperCollins Children's Books.*

DIAL PRESS—1540 Broadway, New York, NY 10036. Susan Kamil, Ed. Dir. Quality fiction and nonfiction. No unsolicited material.

DIMI PRESS—3820 Oak Hollow Ln. S.E., Salem, OR 97302-4774. Dick Lutz, Pres. How-to books, 35,000 words. "Books that help people live better lives." Query. Royalty.

DOMAIN—See *Bantam Books.*

DOUBLEDAY AND CO.—1540 Broadway, New York, NY 10036. Arlene Friedman, Pub./Pres. Proposals from literary agents only. No unsolicited material.

DUNNE BOOKS, THOMAS—175 Fifth Ave., New York, NY 10010. Thomas L. Dunne, Ed. Adult fiction (mysteries, trade, etc.) and nonfiction (history, biographies, science, politics, humor, etc.). Query with outline, sample chapters, and SASE. Royalty.

DUQUESNE UNIVERSITY PRESS—600 Forbes Ave., Pittsburgh, PA 15282-0101. Attn: Ed. Dept. Scholarly publications in the humanities and social sciences; creative nonfiction (book-length only) by emerging writers. Guidelines.

DUTTON ADULT—375 Hudson St., New York, NY 10014. Arnold Dolin, Sr. V.P./Assoc. Pub. Fiction and nonfiction books. Manuscripts accepted only from agents or on personal recommendation.

DUTTON CHILDREN'S BOOKS—375 Hudson St., New York, NY 10014. Lucia Monfried, Ed.-in-Chief. Picture books, easy-to-read books; fiction and nonfiction for preschoolers to young adults. Submit outline and first 3 chapters with query for fiction and nonfiction, complete manuscripts for picture books and easy-to-read books. Manuscripts should be well written with fresh ideas and child appeal. Include SASE.

EAKIN PRESS—P.O. Drawer 90159, Austin, TX 78709-0159. Melissa Roberts, Sr. Ed. Adult nonfiction, 60,000 to 80,000 words: Texana, regional cookbooks, Mexico and the Southwest, WWII, military. Children's books: history, culture, geography, etc., of Texas and the Southwest. Juvenile picture books, 5,000 to 10,000 words; fiction, 20,000 to 30,000 words; young adult fiction, 25,000 to 40,000 words. Currently overstocked; query. Royalty.

EASTERN WASHINGTON UNIVERSITY PRESS—Mail Stop 14, Eastern Washington Univ., 526 5th St., Cheney, WA 99004-2431. Attn: Eds. Literary essays, history, social commentary, and other academic subjects. Limited fiction and well-researched historical novels (one title every 2 years or so). One or 2 books of poetry, 60 to 150 pages, each year. "We are a small regional university press, publishing titles that reflect our regional service, our international contacts, our strong creative writing program, and research and interests of our exceptional faculty." Send complete manuscript, query with outline, or Mac-compatible diskette. Royalty.

THE ECCO PRESS—100 W. Broad St., Hopewell, NJ 08525. Daniel Halpern, Ed-in-Chief. Literary fiction, general nonfiction, poetry, travel, cooking. No unsolicited manuscripts. Queries only.

EERDMANS PUBLISHING COMPANY, INC., WM. B.—255 Jefferson Ave. S.E., Grand Rapids, MI 49503. Jon Pott, Ed.-in-Chief. Protestant, Roman Catholic, and Orthodox theological nonfiction; American religious history; ethics; philosophy; history; spiritual growth. For children's religious books, query Amy De Vries, Children's Book Ed. Royalty.

ELEMENT BOOKS—P.O. Box 830, 21 Broadway, Rockport, MA 01966. Roberta Scimone, Acquisitions Ed. Books on world religions, ancient wisdom, astrology, meditation, women's studies, and alternative health and healing. Study recent catalogue. Query with outline and sample chapters. Royalty.

ELLIOTT & CLARK—Black Belt Communications Group, Inc., P.O. Box 551, Montgomery, AL 36101. Attn: Submissions Ed. Illustrated books on history, photography, gardening, health, music. Query with cover letter, synopsis or outline, author bio, and SASE for reply. Royalty varies.

ENSLOW PUBLISHERS, INC.—P.O. Box 605, 44 Fadem Rd., Springfield, NJ 07081. Brian D. Enslow, Ed./Pub. No fiction; nonfiction books for young people only. Areas of emphasis are children's and young adult books for ages 10 to 18 in the fields of social studies, science, and biography. Also reference books for all ages and easy reading books for teenagers.

EPICENTER PRESS—P.O. Box 82368, Kenmore, WA 98028. Kent Sturgis, Pub. Quality nonfiction trade books, contemporary western art and photography titles, and destination travel guides emphasizing Alaska and the West

Coast. "We are a regional press whose interests include but are not limited to the arts, history, environment, and diverse cultures and lifestyles of the North Pacific and high latitudes." Flat fee.

ERIKSSON, PUBLISHER, PAUL S.—P.O. Box 62, Forest Dale, VT 05745. Attn: Ed. Dept. General nonfiction (send outline and cover letter); some fiction (send 3 chapters with query). Royalty.

EVANS & CO., INC., M.—216 E. 49th St., New York, NY 10017. Attn: Ed. Dept. Books on health, self-help, popular psychology, and cookbooks. Limited list of commercial fiction. Query with outline, sample chapter, and SASE. Royalty.

EVENT HORIZON PRESS—P.O. Box 867, Desert Hot Springs, CA 92240. Joseph Cowles, Pub. Adult fiction and nonfiction. Poetry books, from 50 pages. Currently overstocked; no unsolicited manuscripts.

EXCALIBUR PUBLICATIONS—Box 36, Latham, NY 12110-0036. Alan M. Petrillo, Ed. Books on military history, firearms history, antique arms and accessories, military personalities, tactics and strategy, history of battles. Query with outline and 3 sample chapters. SASE. Royalty or flat fee.

FABER AND FABER—53 Shore Dr., Winchester, MA 01890. Attn: Ed. Dept. Novels, anthologies, and nonfiction books on topics of popular culture and general interest. Query (no more than 2 pages); publisher will contact author if interested; no calls, please. Royalty.

FACTS ON FILE, INC.—11 Penn Plaza, New York, NY 10001. Reference and trade books on science, health, literature, language, history, the performing arts, ethnic studies, popular culture, sports, etc. (No fiction, poetry, computer books, technical books or cookbooks.) Query with outline, sample chapter, and SASE. Royalty. Hardcover.

FAIRVIEW PRESS—2450 Riverside Ave. S., Minneapolis, MN 55454. Lane Stiles, Sr. Ed. (Adult). Jessica Thoreson, Children's Book Ed. Adult books, 80,000 words, that offer advice and support on relationships, parenting, domestic violence, divorce, family activities, aging, health, self-esteem, social issues, addictions, etc. Children's picture books, about 1,000 words, for readers 4 to 9, on related subjects. Query with outline and sample chapters for adult books. Submit complete manuscript for picture books. Royalty.

FANFARE—1540 Broadway, New York, NY 10036. Beth de Guzman, Wendy McCurdy, Sr. Eds. Cassie Goddard, Stephanie Rip, Assoc. Eds. Historical and contemporary adult women's fiction, about 90,000 to 150,000 words. Study field before submitting. Query. Paperback and hardcover.

FARRAR, STRAUS & GIROUX—19 Union Sq. W., New York, NY 10003. Adult and juvenile literary fiction and nonfiction.

FAWCETT/IVY BOOKS—201 E. 50th St., New York, NY 10022. Barbara Dicks, Exec. Ed. Adult mysteries, regencies, and historical romances, 75,000 to 120,000 words. "In the last year, all our acquisitions have been through agents." Query with outline and sample chapters. Average response time is 3 to 6 months. Royalty.

THE FEMINIST PRESS AT THE CITY UNIVERSITY OF NEW YORK—311 E. 94th St., New York, NY 10128. Florence Howe, Pub. Reprints of significant "lost" fiction, original memoirs, autobiographies, biographies; multicultural anthologies; handbooks; bibliographies. "We are especially interested in international literature, women and peace, women and music, and women of color." Royalty.

FINE, BOOKS, DONALD I.—Penguin U.S.A., Inc., 375 Hudson, New York, NY 10014. Attn: Ed. Dept. Literary and commercial fiction. General nonfiction. No queries or unsolicited manuscripts. Submit through agent only.

FIREBRAND BOOKS—141 The Commons, Ithaca, NY 14850. Nancy K. Bereano, Ed. Feminist and lesbian fiction and nonfiction. Royalty. Paperback and library edition cloth.

FIRESIDE BOOKS—1230 Ave. of the Americas, New York, NY 10020. No unsolicited manuscripts.

FLARE BOOKS—See *Avon Books.*

FODOR'S TRAVEL GUIDES—201 E. 50th St., New York, NY 10022. Karen Cure, Ed. Dir. Travel guides for both foreign and U.S. destinations. "We generally hire writers who live in the area they will write about or who have a very intimate knowledge of the area they will cover." Books follow established format; send writing sample and details about your familiarity with a given area.

FONT & CENTER PRESS—P.O. Box 95, Weston, MA 02193. Ilene Horowitz, Ed./Pub. Cookbooks. How-to books. Alternative history for adults and young adults. Send proposal, outline, and sample chapter(s). Responds in 3 months. SASE required. Royalty.

FORGE—Tom Doherty Associates, 175 Fifth Ave., 14th Fl., New York, NY 10010. Melissa Ann Singer, Sr. Ed. General fiction; limited nonfiction, from 80,000 words. Query with complete synopsis and first 3 chapters to Jennifer Hogan, Asst. Ed. Advance and royalty.

FORTRESS PRESS—426 S. Fifth St., Box 1209, Minneapolis, MN 55440. Dr. Marshall D. Johnson, Dir. Books in the areas of biblical studies, theology, ethics, professional ministry, and church history for academic and professional markets, including libraries. Query.

FORUM—c/o Prima Publishing, 3875 Atherton Rd., Rocklin, CA 95765. Steven Martin, Ed. Serious nonfiction books on current affairs, public policy, libertarian/conservative thought, high-level management, individual empowerment, and historical biography. Submit outline and sample chapters. Royalty.

THE FREE PRESS—See *Macmillan Reference USA.*

FREE SPIRIT PUBLISHING—400 First Ave. N., Suite 616, Minneapolis, MN 55401-1730. Elizabeth H. Verdick, Acquisitions Ed. Nonfiction self-help for kids, with an emphasis on school success, self-awareness, self-esteem, creativity, social action, lifeskills, and special needs. Creative classroom activities for teachers; adult books on raising, counseling, or educating children. Queries, sample chapters, or complete manuscripts. "Request free catalogue and guidelines." Royalty.

FULCRUM PUBLISHING—350 Indiana St., Suite 350, Golden, CO 80401. Attn: Submissions Dept. Adult trade nonfiction: travel and gardening. No fiction. Send cover letter, sample chapters, table of contents, author credentials, and market analysis. Royalty.

GENESIS PUBLISHING CO., INC.—1547 Great Pond Rd., N. Andover, MA 01845-1216. Gerard M. Verschuuren, Ed. Adult fiction and nonfiction, especially religion and philosophy books. Query. Royalty.

GERINGER BOOKS, LAURA—See *HarperCollins Children's Books.*

GIBBS SMITH, JUNIOR—(formerly *Peregrine Smith Books*) P.O. Box 667, Layton, UT 84041. Theresa Desmond, Ed. Juvenile books: western/cowboy; activity; how-to; nature/environment; and humor. Fiction picture books, to 2,000 words; nonfiction books, to 10,000 words, for readers 4 to 12. Royalty.

GIBBS SMITH PUBLISHER—P.O. Box 667, Layton, UT 84401. Madge Baird, Ed. Dir. Adult nonfiction. Query. Royalty.

GINIGER CO. INC., THE K.S.—250 W. 57th St., Suite 519, New York, NY 10107. Attn: Ed. Dept. General nonfiction. Query with SASE; no unsolicited manuscripts. Royalty.

GLENBRIDGE PUBLISHING LTD.— 6010 W. Jewell Ave., Lakewood, CO 80232. James A. Keene, Ed. Nonfiction books on a variety of topics, including business, history, and psychology. Query with sample chapter. Royalty.

GLOBE PEQUOT PRESS, THE— 6 Business Park Rd., Box 833, Old Saybrook, CT 06475. Laura Strom, Acquisitions Ed. Nonfiction with national and regional focus; travel; outdoor recreation; home-based business. Query with sample chapter, contents, and one-page synopsis. SASE required. Royalty or flat fee.

GODINE PUBLISHER, DAVID R.—P.O. 9103, 9 Lewis St., Lincoln, MA 01773. Attn: Ed. Dept. Query; no unsolicited manuscripts. "Please familiarize yourself with our list before querying." Royalty.

GOLD EAGLE—See *Worldwide Library.*

GOLD 'N' HONEY—See *Questar Publishers.*

GOLDEN BOOKS FAMILY ENTERTAINMENT—(formerly *Western Publishing Co., Inc.*) 850 Third Ave., New York, NY 10022. Patty Sullivan, Exec. V.P./Pub., children's publishing group. Children's fiction and nonfiction: picture books, storybooks, concept books, novelty books. Adult nonfiction. No unsolicited manuscripts. Royalty or flat fee.

GOLDEN WEST PUBLISHERS— 4113 N. Longview, Phoenix, AZ 85014. Hal Mitchell, Ed. Cookbooks and nonfiction Western history and travel books. Currently seeking writers for state and regional cookbooks. Query. Royalty or flat fee.

GOODFELLOW PRESS—16625 Redmond Way, Suite M20, Redmond, WA 98053-4499. Pamela R. Goodfellow, Pub. Character-based novels, 90,000 to 150,000 words. Send for guidelines. Royalty.

GRAYWOLF PRESS—2402 University Ave., Suite 203, St. Paul, MN 55114. Attn: Ed. Dept. Literary fiction (short story collections and novels), poetry, and essays.

GREAT QUOTATIONS—1967 Quincy Ct., Glendale Heights, IL 60139. Patrick Caton, Ed. General adult titles, 80 to 365 pages, with strong, clever, descriptive titles and brief, upbeat text. "We publish small, quick-read gift books." Query with outline and sample chapters or send complete manuscript. Royalty.

GREENWILLOW BOOKS—1350 Ave. of the Americas, New York, NY 10019. Susan Hirschman, Ed.-in-Chief. Children's books for all ages. Picture books.

GROSSET AND DUNLAP, INC.—200 Madison Ave., New York, NY 10016. Jane O'Connor, Pub. Mass-market children's books. Currently not accepting unsolicited manuscripts. Royalty.

GROVE/ATLANTIC MONTHLY PRESS— 841 Broadway, 4th Fl., New York, NY 10003-4793. Morgan Entrekin, Pub. Distinguished fiction and non-fiction. Query; no unsolicited manuscripts. Royalty.

GRYPHON HOUSE, INC.—P.O. Box 207, Beltsville, MD 20705. Kathy Charner, Ed.-in-Chief. Resource books, 150 to 500 pages, for parents and teachers of young children from birth to 8 years old. Query with outline and sample chapters. Royalty.

GULLIVER BOOKS—See *Harcourt Brace & Co. Children's Book Div.*

HACHAI PUBLISHING—156 Chester Ave., Brooklyn, NY 11218. Dina Rosenfeld, Ed. Full-color children's picture books, 32 pages, for readers ages 2 to 8; Judaica, Bible tales. Query or send complete manuscript. Flat fee.

HANCOCK HOUSE PUBLISHERS, LTD.—1431 Harrison Ave., Blaine, WA 98230. Attn: Ed. Dept. Adult nonfiction: guidebooks, biographies, natural history, popular science, conservation, animal husbandry, falconry, and sports. Some juvenile nonfiction. Query with outline and sample chapters or send complete manuscript. Multiple queries considered. Royalty.

HARCOURT BRACE & CO.—525 B St., Suite 1900, San Diego, CA 92101. Attn: Ed. Dept. Adult trade nonfiction and fiction. No unsolicited manuscripts. Queries accepted with SASE.

HARCOURT BRACE & CO. CHILDREN'S BOOK DIV.—525 B St., Suite 1900, San Diego, CA 92101-4495. Attn: Manuscript Submissions. Juvenile fiction and nonfiction for beginning readers through young adults under the following imprints: *HB Children's Books, Browndeer Press, Gulliver Books, Red Wagon Books, Odyssey Paperbacks,* and *Voyager Paperbacks.* Query with SASE; manuscripts accepted from agents.

HARCOURT BRACE PROFESSIONAL PUBLISHING—525 B St., Suite 1900, San Diego, CA 92101-4495. Attn: Ed. Dept. Professional books for practitioners in accounting, auditing, tax and financial planning. Query. Royalty and work-for-hire.

HARDSCRABBLE BOOKS—See *University Press of New England.*

HARLEQUIN BOOKS/CANADA—225 Duncan Mill Rd., Don Mills, Ont., Canada M3B 3K9. Randall Toye, Ed. Dir. *Mira Books*: Dianne Moggy, Sr. Ed. Contemporary women's fiction, 100,000 words. Query. *Harlequin Superromance*: Paula Eykelhof, Sr. Ed. Contemporary romance, 85,000 words, with a mainstream edge. Query. *Harlequin Temptation*: Birgit Davis-Todd, Sr. Ed. Sensuous, humorous contemporary romances, 60,000 words. *Love and Laughter*: Malle Vallik, Assoc. Sr. Ed. The lighter side of love, 55,000 words. Query.

HARLEQUIN BOOKS/U.S.—300 E. 42nd St., 6th Fl., New York, NY 10017. Debra Matteucci, Sr. Ed. Contemporary romances, 70,000 to 75,000 words. Send for tip sheets. *Harlequin American Romances*: bold, exciting romantic adventures, "where anything is possible and dreams come true." *Harlequin Intrigue*: set against a backdrop of mystery and suspense, worldwide locales. Query. Paperback.

HARPERCOLLINS CHILDREN'S BOOKS—10 E. 53rd St., New York, NY 10022-5299. Picture books, chapter books, and fiction and nonfiction for middle-grade and young adult readers. "Our imprints (*HarperTrophy* paperbacks, *Joanna Cotler Books, Michael di Capua Books*, and *Laura Geringer Books*) are committed to producing imaginative and responsible children's books. All publish from preschool to young adult titles." Guidelines. Royalty.

HARPERCOLLINS PUBLISHERS—10 E. 53rd St., New York, NY 10022-5299. Adult Trade Department: Address Man. Ed. Fiction, nonfiction (biography, history, etc.), reference. Submissions from agents only. College texts: Address College Dept. No unsolicited manuscripts; query only.

HARPERCOLLINS SAN FRANCISCO—1160 Battery St., San Francisco, CA 94111-1213. Attn: Acquisitions Ed. Books on spirituality and religion. No unsolicited manuscripts; query required.

HARPERPAPERBACKS—HarperCollins, 10 E. 53rd St., New York, NY 10022. Carolyn Marino, Ed. Dir. John Silbersack, Science Fiction/Fantasy Ed.-in-Chief. John Douglas, Exec. Ed. Jessica Lichtenstein, Sr. Ed. Abigail Kamen-Holland, Caitlin Blasdell, Eds.

HARPERPRISM—10 E. 53rd St., New York, NY 10022-5299. John Silbersack, Sr. V.P./Pub. Dir. John Douglas, Exec. Ed. Caitlin Blasdell, Ed. Science fiction/fantasy. No unsolicited manuscripts; query.

HARPERTROPHY—See *HarperCollins Children's Books.*

HARVARD COMMON PRESS—535 Albany St., Boston, MA 02118. Bruce Shaw, Ed. Adult nonfiction: cookbooks, travel guides, books on family matters, health, small business, etc. Send outline and sample chapters or complete manuscript. SASE. Royalty.

HARVEST HOUSE PUBLISHERS—1075 Arrowsmith, Eugene, OR 97402. LaRae Weikert, Ed. Mgr. Nonfiction with evangelical theme: how-tos, marriage, women, contemporary issues. Fiction. No biographies, autobiographies, history, music books, or poetry. Query with SASE.

HAWORTH PRESS, INC.—10 Alice St., Binghamton, NY 13904-1580. Bill Palmer, Ed. Scholarly press interested in research-based adult nonfiction: psychology, social work, gay and lesbian studies, women's studies, family and marriage; some recreation and entertainment. Send outline with sample chapters or complete manuscript. Royalty.

HAY HOUSE—P.O. Box 5100, Carlsbad, CA 92018-5100. Attn: Ed. Dir. Self-help books on health, self-awareness, spiritual growth, astrology, psychology, philosophy, metaphysics, and the environment. Query with outline, a few sample chapters, and SASE. Royalties.

HAZELDEN EDUCATIONAL MATERIALS—Box 176, Center City, MN 55012. Kate Kjorlien, Trade Asst. Self-help books, 100 to 400 pages, relating to addiction, recovery, spirituality, and wholeness. Query with outline and sample chapters. Multiple queries considered. Royalty.

HB CHILDREN'S BOOKS—See *Harcourt Brace & Co. Children's Book Div.*

HEALTH COMMUNICATIONS, INC.—3201 S.W. 15th St., Deerfield Beach, FL 33442. Christine Belleris, Ed. Dir. Books, 250 pages, on self-help, recovery, inspiration, and personal growth for adults. Query with outline and 2 sample chapters and SASE. Royalty.

HEALTH INFORMATION PRESS—4727 Wilshire Blvd., #300, Los Angeles, CA 90010. Kathryn Swanson, Ed. Books, 250 pages, that "simplify complicated health and medical issues so that consumers can make informed decisions about their health and medical care." Query with outline and sample chapters. Royalty.

HEALTH PRESS—P.O. Box 1388, Santa Fe, NM 87504. K. Schwartz, Ed. Health-related adult and children's books, 100 to 300 pages. "We're seeking cutting-edge, original manuscripts that will excite, educate, and help readers." Author must have credentials, or preface/intro must be written by M.D., Ph.D., etc. Controversial topics are desired; must be well researched and documented. Submit outline, table of contents, and first chapter with SASE. Royalty.

HEARST BOOKS —See *William Morrow and Co., Inc.*

HEARTSONG PRESENTS—P.O. Box 719, Uhrichsville, OH 44683. Rebecca Germany, Man. Ed. Contemporary and historical romances, 50,000 to 55,000 words, that present a conservative, evangelical Christian world view. Pays flat fee.

HEBREW UNION COLLEGE PRESS—3101 Clifton Ave., Cincinnati, OH 45220. Barbara Selya, Ed. Scholarly books, 200 pages, on very specific topics in Judaic studies. "Our usual print run is 500 books, and our target audience is mainly rabbis and professors." Query with outline and sample chapters. No payment.

HEINEMANN—361 Hanover St., Portsmouth, NH 03801. Attn: Ed. Dept. Practical theatre, world literature, and literacy education. Query.

HEMINGWAY WESTERN STUDIES SERIES—Boise State University, 1910 University Dr., Boise, ID 83725. Tom Trusky, Ed. Artists' and eccentric format books (multiple editions) relating to Rocky Mountain environment, race, religion, gender, and other public issues. Guidelines.

HIGGINSON BOOK COMPANY—148 Washington St., Salem, MA 01970. Attn: Ed. Dept. Nonfiction genealogy and local history only, 20 to 1,000 pages. Specializes in reprints. Query. Royalty.

HIGHSMITH PRESS—P.O. Box 800, Fort Atkinson, WI 53538-0800. Donald Sager, Pub. Adult books, 80 to 360 pages, on professional library science, education, and reference. Teacher activity and curriculum resource books, 48 to 240 pages, for pre-K through 12. Query with outline and sample chapters. Royalty.

HIPPOCRENE BOOKS—171 Madison Ave., New York, NY 10016. George Blagowidow, Ed. Dir. Language instruction books and foreign language dictionaries, travel guides, and military history of Polish interest. Send outline and sample chapters with SASE for reply. Multiple queries considered. Royalty.

HMR PUBLICATIONS—1 Union Sq. W., New York, NY 10003. Tony Harold, Pub. All types of fiction (except science fiction, fantasy, and children's books); some nonfiction, about 50,000 to 250,000 words. Send one to 3 sample chapters (neither the first nor the last chapter). Royalty.

HOLIDAY HOUSE, INC.— 425 Madison Ave., New York, NY 10017. Regina Griffin, V. P. Allison Cunningham, Assoc. Ed. General juvenile fiction and nonfiction. Submit complete manuscript for picture book or 3 sample chapters and summary for novel; enclose SASE. Royalty. Hardcover only.

HOLT AND CO., HENRY—115 W. 18th St., New York, NY 10011. Michael Naumann, Pub. Distinguished works of biography, history, fiction, and natural history; humor; child activity books; parenting books; books for the entrepreneurial business person; and health books. "Virtually all submissions come from literary agents or from writers whom we publish."

HOME BUILDER PRESS—National Assoc. of Home Builders, 1201 15th St. N.W., Washington, DC 20005-2800. Doris M. Tennyson, Sr. Ed. How-to and business management books, 150 to 200 manuscript pages, for builders, remodelers, and developers. Writers should be experts in homebuilding, remodeling, land development, sales, marketing, and related aspects of the building industry. Query with outline and sample chapter. Royalty. For author's packet TW, call John Tuttle (800) 368-5242, ext. 222.

HOUGHTON MIFFLIN COMPANY—222 Berkeley St., Boston, MA 02116-3764. Attn: Ed. Dept. Fiction: literary, historical. Nonfiction: history, biography, psychology. No unsolicited submissions. Children's books: picture books, fiction, and nonfiction for all ages. Address Children's Trade Books. Query. Royalty.

HOWARD UNIVERSITY PRESS—1240 Randolph St. N.E., Washington, DC 20017. Ed Gordon, Dir. Nonfiction books, 300 to 500 manuscript pages, on African diaspora, history, political science, literary criticism, biography, women's studies. Query with outline and sample chapters. Royalty.

HP BOOKS—200 Madison Ave., New York, NY 10016. Attn: Ed. Dept. Illustrated how-tos on cooking, automotive topics. Query with SASE.

HUMANICS PUBLISHING GROUP—P.O. Box 7400, Atlanta, GA 30357. W. Arthur Bligh, Acquisitions Ed. Inspiring trade books, 100 to 300 pages: self-help, spiritual, instructional, philosophy, and health for body, mind, and soul. Also, children's educational books/teacher resource guides for grades K through 6. "We are interested in books that people go to for help, guidance, and inspiration." Query with outline and SASE required. Royalty.

HUNGRY MIND PRESS—1648 Grand Ave., St. Paul, MN 55105. David Unowsky, Ed. Pearl Kilbride, Ed. Biographies and memoirs; contemporary affairs; cultural criticism; nature writing; spiritual reflection; travel essays; nonfiction. "Books that examine the human experience, encourage reflection, and enrich everyday life. We want to involve writers in the planning and marketing of their books and build a strong relationship with booksellers." Query with outline. Royalty.

HUNTER PUBLISHING, INC.—130 Campus Dr., Edison, NJ 08818. Kim André, Acquisitions Dept. Travel guides to the U.S., South America, and the Caribbean.

HYPERION—114 Fifth Ave., New York, NY 10011. Material accepted from agents only. No unsolicited manuscripts or queries considered.

IMPACT PUBLISHERS, INC.—P.O. Box 1094, San Luis Obispo, CA 93406. Attn: Acquisitions Ed. Popular psychology books, from 200 pages, on personal growth, relationships, families, communities, and health for adults. Children's books for "Little Imp" series on issues of self-esteem. "Writers must have advanced degrees and professional experience in human-service fields." Query with outline and sample chapters. Royalty.

INDIANA UNIVERSITY PRESS—601 N. Morton St., Bloomington, IN 47404-3797. Attn: Ed. Dept. Scholarly nonfiction, especially cultural studies, literary criticism, music, history, women's studies, African-American studies, science, philosophy, African studies, Middle East studies, Russian studies, anthropology, regional, etc. Query with outline and sample chapters. Royalty.

INNER TRADITIONS INTERNATIONAL, INC.—One Park St., Rochester, VT 05767. Jon Graham, Acquisitions Ed. Books representing the spiritual, cultural, and mythic traditions of the world, focusing on inner wisdom and the perennial philosophies. Query. Royalty.

INSTRUCTOR BOOKS—See *Scholastic Professional Books.*

INTERNATIONAL MARINE—A Div. of McGraw-Hill, Box 220, Camden, ME 04843. Jonathan Eaton, Ed. Dir. Books on boating (sailing and power).

INTIMATE MOMENTS—See *Silhouette Books.*

IRON CASTLE PRODUCTIONS—See *Wordware Publishing.*

ISLAND PRESS—1718 Connecticut Ave. N.W., Suite 300, Washington, DC 20009. James Jordan, V.P./Pub. Nonfiction focusing on natural history, literary science, the environment, and natural resource management. "We want solution-oriented material to solve environmental problems. For our imprint, *Shearwater Books,* we want books that express new insights about nature and the environment." Query or send manuscript. SASE required.

ITHACA BOOKS, INC.—246 Mero, La Canada, CA 91011. Christopher J. Husa, Man. Dir. Books, 10,000 to 12,000 words, for children ages 8 to 13, based on true stories of adventure, exploration, and discovery. "Accuracy is critical; research is essential." Royalty.

JAI PRESS, INC.—55 Old Post Rd., #2, P.O. Box 1678, Greenwich, CT 06836. Herbert Johnson, Ed. Research and technical reference books on such subjects as business, economics, management, sociology, political science, computer science, life sciences, and chemistry. Query or send complete manuscript. Royalty.

JALMAR PRESS—24426 S. Main St., Suite 702, Carson, CA 90745. Dr. Bradley L. Winch, Pub. Nonfiction books for parents, teachers, and caregivers. "Our emphasis is on helping children and adults live from the inside/out so that they become personally and socially responsible." Special interest in peaceful conflict resolution and whole brain learning. Multiple queries considered. Submit outline. Royalty.

JAMES BOOKS, ALICE—Univ. of Maine at Farmington, 98 Main St., Farmington, ME 04938. Jean Amaral, Program Dir. "Shared-work cooperative" publishes books of poetry (72 to 80 pages) by writers living in New England and New York. Manuscripts read in September and January. "We emphasize the publication of poetry by women and poets of color, but also welcome and publish manuscripts by men." Authors paid with 100 copies of their books. Write for guidelines. Holds national competition for Beatrice Hawley Award.

JESUIT WAY—See *Loyola Press.*

JOHNSON BOOKS, INC.—1880 S. 57th Ct., Boulder, CO 80301. Stephen Topping, Ed. Dir. Nonfiction: environmental subjects, archaeology, geology, natural history, astronomy, travel guides, outdoor guidebooks, fly fishing, regional. Query. Royalty.

JONA BOOKS—P.O. Box 336, Bedford, IN 47421. Joe Glasgow, Ed. Nonfiction: biographies, Native American history, old west, and military history. Fiction: action adventure, alternative history, historical fiction, mysteries, and military science fiction. Contracts negotiated; no advances.

JONATHAN DAVID PUBLISHERS, INC.—68-22 Eliot Ave., Middle Village, NY 11379. Alfred J. Kolatch, Ed.-in-Chief. General nonfiction (how-to, sports, cooking and food, self-help, etc.) and books on Judaica. Query with outline, sample chapter, resumé, and SASE. Royalty or outright purchase.

JOVE BOOKS—200 Madison Ave., New York, NY 10016. Fiction and nonfiction. No unsolicited manuscripts.

KALMBACH BOOKS—21027 Crossroads Cir., Waukesha, WI 53187. Terry Spohn, Sr. Acquisitions Ed. Adult nonfiction, 18,000 to 50,000 words, on scale modeling, railroading, model railroading, miniatures, and amateur astronomy. Send outline with sample chapters. Accepts multiple queries. Royalty.

KAR-BEN COPIES— 6800 Tildenwood Ln., Rockville, MD 20852. Judye Groner, Ed. Books on Jewish themes for preschool and elementary children (to age 9): picture books, fiction, and nonfiction. Complete manuscript preferred; SASE. Royalty. Website: http://www.karben.com

KEATS PUBLISHING, INC.—27 Pine St., Box 876, New Canaan, CT 06840. Norman Goldfind, Pub. Health, nutrition, alternative and complimentary medicine, and preventive health care. Royalty.

KENSINGTON PUBLISHING CORP.— 850 Third Ave., New York, NY 10022. Paul Dinas, Ed.-in-Chief. Ann LaFarge, Exec. Ed. Popular fiction; historical and contemporary romance; *Lovegram Romances* (110,000 words); Arabesque (African American) romances; regencies (80,000 words); westerns; nonfiction. Agented material only.

KENT STATE UNIVERSITY PRESS—Kent State Univ., Kent, OH 44242. John T. Hubbell, Dir. Julia Morton, Ed.-in-Chief. Interested in scholarly works in history and literary criticism of high quality, any titles of regional (Ohio) interest, scholarly biographies, archaeological research, the arts, and general nonfiction.

KNOPF BOOKS FOR YOUNG READERS, ALFRED A.—201 E. 50th St., New York, NY 10022. Distinguished juvenile fiction and nonfiction. Query; no unsolicited manuscripts. Royalty. Guidelines.

KNOPF, INC., ALFRED A.—201 E. 50th St., New York, NY 10022. Attn: Sr. Ed. Distinguished adult fiction and general nonfiction. Query for nonfiction. Royalty.

KODANSHA AMERICA, INC.—114 Fifth Ave., New York, NY 10011. Attn: Ed. Dept. Nonfiction books, 50,000 to 200,000 words, on cross-cultural, Asian and other international subjects. Query with outline, sample chapters, and SASE. Royalty.

KRAUSE PUBLICATIONS, INC.—700 E. State St., Iola, WI 54990-0001. Patricia Klug, Man. Antiques and collectibles, sewing and crafts, antique automotive topics, numismatics, sports, philatelics, outdoors, guns and knives, toys, records and comics.

LADYBIRD BOOKS, INC.—Imprint of Penguin USA, 375 Hudson St., New York, NY 10014-3657. Attn: Ed. Dept. Books for toddlers, preschoolers, and older children. Fairy tales, classics, science and nature, and novelty items. Rarely accepts unsolicited manuscripts. Query required.

LAREDO PUBLISHING— 8907 Wilshire Blvd., Beverly Hills, CA 90211. Sam Laredo, Ed. Bilingual and ESL (English as a second language) titles in Spanish and English. Children's fiction and young adult titles. Query with outline. Royalty.

LARK BOOKS—50 College St., Asheville, NC 28801. Rob Pulleyn, Pub. Distinctive books for creative people in crafts, how-to, leisure activities, and "coffee table" categories. Query with outline. Royalty.

LAUREL-LEAF—1540 Broadway, New York, NY 10036. Attn: Ed. Dept. Unsolicited young adult manuscripts are accepted only for the Delacorte Press

Prize for a first young adult novel. This must be a work of fiction written for ages 12 to 18, by a previously unpublished author. Send SASE for rules and guidelines.

LEADERSHIP PUBLISHERS, INC.—P.O. Box 8358, Des Moines, IA 50301-8358. Dr. Lois F. Roets, Ed. Educational materials for talented and gifted students, grades K to 12, and teacher reference books. No fiction or poetry. Send SASE for catalogue and writer's guidelines before submitting. Query or send complete manuscript. Royalty for books; flat fee for booklets.

LEE & LOW BOOKS—95 Madison Ave., New York, NY 10016. Philip Lee, Pub. Elizabeth Szabla, Ed.-in-Chief. Focus is on fiction and nonfiction picture books for children ages 4 to 10. "Our goal is to meet the growing need for books that address children of color and to provide subjects and stories they can identify with. Of special interest are stories set in contemporary America. Folklore and animal stories not considered." Include SASE. Royalty.

LIFETIME BOOKS, INC.—2131 Hollywood Blvd., Hollywood, FL 33020. Brian Feinblum, Sr. Ed. Nonfiction (200 to 300 pages): general interest, how-to, self-help, cooking, hobby, business, health, and inspiration. Query with letter or outline and sample chapter, SASE. Royalty. Send 9x12 SASE with 5 first-class stamps for catalogue.

LIMELIGHT BOOKS—See *Tiare Publications*.

LINCOLN-HERNDON PRESS, INC.— 818 S. Dirksen Pkwy., Springfield, IL 62703. Shirley A. Buscher, Asst. Pub. American humor that reveals American history. Humor collections. Query.

LITTLE, BROWN & CO.—1271 Ave. of the Americas, New York, NY 10020. Attn: Ed. Dept. Fiction, general nonfiction, sports books; divisions for law and medical texts. Query only.

LITTLE, BROWN & CO. CHILDREN'S BOOK DEPT.—34 Beacon St., Boston, MA 02108. Attn: Ed. Dept. Juvenile fiction and nonfiction and picture books. No unsolicited manuscripts. Accepts agented material only.

LITTLE TIGER PRESS—N16 W 23390 Stoneridge Dr., Waukesha, WI 53188. Acquisitions Ed. Picture books, 500 to 1,500 words, for the preschool to 8-year-old range. Send complete manuscript with cover letter and SASE. Do not send original artwork.

LLEWELLYN PUBLICATIONS—P.O. Box 64383, St. Paul, MN 55164-0383. Nancy J. Mostad, Acquisitions Mgr. Books, from 75,000 words, on subjects of self-help, how-to, alternative health, astrology, metaphysics, new age, and the occult. Metaphysical/occult fiction. "We're interested in any kind of story (mystery, historical, gothic, occult, metaphysical adventure), just as long as the theme is authentic occultism, and the work is both entertaining and educational." Query with sample chapters. Multiple queries considered. Royalty.

LODESTAR—375 Hudson St., New York, NY 10014. Virginia Buckley, Ed. Dir. Fiction (picture books to young adult, mystery, western) and nonfiction (science, contemporary issues, nature, history) considered for ages 9 to 11, 10 to 14, and 12 up. Also fiction picture books for ages 4 to 8. "We are not accepting submissions at this time, but writers may query."

LOTHROP, LEE & SHEPARD BOOKS—1350 Ave. of the Americas, New York, NY 10019. Susan Pearson, Ed.-in-Chief. Juvenile fiction and nonfiction, picture books. No unsolicited material. Royalty.

LOUISIANA STATE UNIVERSITY PRESS—P.O. Box 25053, Baton Rouge, LA 70894-5053. Attn: Ed. Dir. Scholarly adult nonfiction, dealing with the U.S. South, its history and its culture. Query with outline and sample chapters. Royalty.

LOVE AND LAUGHTER—See *Harlequin Books/Canada.*

LOVEGRAM ROMANCES—See *Kensington Publishing Corp.*

LOVESWEPT—1540 Broadway, New York, NY 10036. Susann Brailey, Sr. Ed. Joy Abella, Administrative Ed. Adult contemporary romances, approximately 55,000 to 60,000 words. Study field before submitting. Query required. Paperback only.

LOYOLA PRESS—3441 N. Ashland Ave., Chicago, IL 60657-1397. Austin Tighe, Ed. Dir. Jeremy Langford, Man. Ed. Religious and ethics-related material for college-educated Christian readers. "Loyola Press Series": art, literature, and religion; contemporary Christian concerns. Imprints include *Jesuit Way*: Ignatian spiritual exercises and commentaries, related biographies; *Wild Onion Books*: Chicago-area interests and personalities, including churches, art, history. Nonfiction, 200 to 400 pages. Query with outline. Royalty.

LUCENT BOOKS—P.O. Box 289011, San Diego, CA 92198-9011. Bonnie Szumski, Man. Ed. David Haugen, Ed. Books, 18,000 to 25,000 words, for junior high/middle school students. "Overview" series: current issues (political, social, historical, environmental topics). Other series include "World History," "Importance Of" (biography), "The Way People Live" (exploring daily life and culture of communities worldwide, past and present). No unsolicited material; work is by assignment only. Flat fee. Query for guidelines and catalogue.

LYLE STUART—See *Carol Publishing Group.*

LYONS & BURFORD, PUBLISHERS—31 W. 21st St., New York, NY 10010. Peter Burford, Ed. Books, 100 to 300 pages, related to the outdoors (camping, gardening, natural history, etc.) or sports. Query with outline. Royalty.

MCCLANAHAN BOOK CO.—23 W. 26th St., New York, NY 10010. Elise Donner, Ed. Dir. Mass-market books for children, preschool to third grade. "Most books published as part of a series." Submit complete manuscript. Flat fee.

MCELDERRY BOOKS, MARGARET K.—1230 6th Ave., New York, NY 10020. Margaret K. McElderry, V.P./Pub. Emma Dryden, Ed. Children's and young adult books, including picture books; quality fiction; fantasy; beginning chapter books; humor; realism; and nonfiction. Request guidelines before querying.

MCFARLAND & COMPANY, INC., PUBLISHERS—Box 611, Jefferson, NC 28640. Robert Franklin, Pres./Ed.-in-Chief. Scholarly and reference books, from 225 manuscript pages, in many fields, except mathematical sciences. No new age, inspirational, children's, poetry, fiction, or exposés. Submit complete manuscripts or query with outline and sample chapters. Royalty.

MCGREGOR PUBLISHING—118 S. Westshore Blvd., Suite 233, Tampa, FL 33609. Lonnie Herman, Pub. Fiction and nonfiction, especially biography, sports, self-help. Query with outline and sample chapters or send complete manuscript. Royalty.

MACMILLAN REFERENCE USA—1633 Broadway, New York, NY 10019. Attn: Ed. Dept. General Book Division: Religious, sports, science, travel, and reference books. No fiction. Paperbacks: *Collier Books*. History, psychology, contemporary issues, sports, popular information, childcare, health. *The Free Press:* College texts and professional books in social sciences, humanities. Query. Royalty.

MACMURRAY & BECK, INC.—1649 Downing St., Denver, CO 80218. Frederick Ramey, Exec. Dir. Quality fiction and narrative nonfiction. Royalty. No unsolicited manuscripts; query.

MADISON BOOKS— 4720 Boston Way, Lanham, MD 20706. James E. Lyons, Pub. Full-length nonfiction: history, biography, contemporary affairs, trade reference. Query required. Royalty.

MADLIBS—See *Price Stern Sloan, Inc.*

MAGIC ATTIC PRESS— 866 Spring St., P.O. Box 9722, Portland, ME 04104-5022. Robin Haywood, Man. Ed. Series fiction for young girls, ages 7 to 12. Submit writing samples only: a portion of a work in progress or a chapter from a finished book (to 10 pages); include resumé and SASE.

MARKOWSKI INTERNATIONAL PUBLISHERS—See *Success Publishing*.

MEADOWBROOK PRESS—5451 Smetana Dr., Minnetonka, MN 55343. Attn: Submissions Ed. Upbeat, useful books, 60,000 words, on pregnancy, childbirth, and parenting; shorter works of humor, party planning, and children's activities; fiction anthologies and humorous poetry for children. Send for guidelines. Royalty or flat fee.

MEGA-BOOKS, INC.—240 E. 60th St., New York, NY 10022. Toni Ann Scaramuzzo, Man. Ed. Book packager. Young adult books, 150 pages, children's books. Query for guidelines. Flat fee.

MEREDITH CORP. BOOK PUBLISHING—(*Better Homes and Gardens Books*) 1716 Locust St., Des Moines, IA 50309-3023. James D. Blume, Ed.-in-Chief. Books on gardening, crafts, decorating, do-it-yourself, cooking, health; mostly staff-written. "Interested in free-lance writers with expertise in these areas." Limited market. Query with SASE.

THE MICHIGAN STATE UNIVERSITY PRESS—1405 S. Harrison Rd., Suite 25, E. Lansing, MI 48823-5202. Scholarly nonfiction, with concentrations in history, regional history, women's studies, business, social philosophy, and Civil War; also Native American Series, Rhetoric Series, and Lotus Poetry Series. Submit prospectus, table of contents, and sample chapters to Acquisitions Ed. Authors should refer to *The Chicago Manual of Style, 14th Edition*, for formats and styles.

MIDDLE PASSAGE PRESS—5517 Secrest Dr., Los Angeles, CA 90043-2029. Barbara Bramwell, Ed. Small press. Nonfiction that focuses on African-American experience in the historical, social, and political context of American life. Query with sample chapters. Royalty.

MILKWEED EDITIONS— 430 First Ave. N., Suite 400, Minneapolis, MN 55401-1743. Emilie Buchwald, Ed. "We publish excellent award-winning fiction, poetry, essays, and nonfiction, the kind of writing that makes for good reading." Publishes about 15 books a year. Send SASE for guidelines before submitting manuscript. Royalty. Also publishes *Milkweeds for Young Readers*: high quality novels for middle grades.

THE MILLBROOK PRESS—2 Old New Milford Rd., Brookfield, CT 06804. Dottie Carlson, Manuscript Coord. Nonfiction for early elementary grades through grades 7 and up, appropriate for the school and public library or trade market, encompassing curriculum-related topics and extracurricular interests. Some picture books. Imprint: *Copper Beech Books*. Query with outline and sample chapter. Royalty.

MILLS & SANDERSON, PUBLISHERS—P.O. Box 833, Bedford, MA 01730-0833. Jan H. Anthony, Pub. Books. Not considering any new material at this time.

MINSTREL BOOKS—See *Archway Paperbacks*.

MIRA BOOKS—See *Harlequin Books/Canada*.

THE MIT PRESS—5 Cambridge Center, Cambridge, MA 02142. Larry Cohen, Ed.-in-Chief. Books on computer science/artificial intelligence; cognitive sciences; economics; architecture; aesthetic and social theory; linguistics; technology studies; environmental studies; and neuroscience.

MONDO PUBLISHING—One Plaza Rd., Greenvale, NY 11548. Attn: Submissions Ed. Picture books, nonfiction, and early chapter books for readers ages 4 to 10. "We want to create beautiful books that children can read on their own and find so enjoyable that they'll want to come back to them time and time again." Query. Royalty.

MONTANA HISTORICAL SOCIETY—225 N. Roberts, Helena, MT 59620. Martha Kohl, Ed. Books on Montana history. Query. Royalty.

MOON HANDBOOKS—Moon Publications, Inc., P.O. Box 3040, Chico, CA 95927-3040. Taran March, Exec. Ed. Travel guides, 400 to 500 pages. Will consider multiple submissions. Query. Royalty.

MOREHOUSE PUBLISHING— 871 Ethan Allen Hwy., Suite 204, Ridgefield, CT 06877. Deborah Grahame, Ed. E. Allen Kelley, Pub. Theology, pastoral care, church administration, spirituality, Anglican studies, history of religion, books for children, youth, elders, etc. Query with outline, contents, and sample chapter. SASE required. Royalty.

MORROW AND CO., INC., WILLIAM—1350 Ave. of the Americas, New York, NY 10019. Attn: Eds. Adult fiction and nonfiction: no unsolicited manuscripts. *Mulberry Books* (children's paperbacks), Amy Cohn, Ed. Dir.; *Hearst Books* (general nonfiction).

MOUNTAIN PRESS PUBLISHING—1301 S. 3rd W., P.O. Box 2399, Missoula, MT 59806. Attn: John Rimel. Nonfiction, 300 pages: natural history, field guides, geology, horses, Western history, Americana, outdoor guides, and fur trade lore. Query with outline and sample chapters; multiple queries considered. Royalty.

THE MOUNTAINEERS BOOKS—1001 S.W. Klickitat Way, Suite 201, Seattle, WA 98134. Margaret Foster, Ed.-in-Chief. Nonfiction books on noncompetitive aspects of outdoor sports such as mountaineering, backpacking, walking, trekking, canoeing, kayaking, bicycling, skiing; independent adventure travel. Field guides, how-to and where-to guidebooks, biographies of outdoor people; accounts of expeditions. Natural history and conservation. Submit sample chapters and outline. Royalty.

MUIR PUBLICATIONS, JOHN—P.O. Box 613, Santa Fe, NM 87504-0613. Cassandra Conyers, Acquisitions Ed. Travel guidebooks for adults and travel-related books for children, 6 to 12. Alternative health topics for adults and children. Send manuscript or query with sample chapters. No fiction. Royalty or work for hire.

MULBERRY BOOKS—See *William Morrow and Co., Inc.*

MULTNOMAH BOOKS—See *Questar Publishers.*

MUSTANG PUBLISHING CO., INC.—Box 3004, Memphis, TN 38173. Rollin A. Riggs, Ed. Nonfiction for 18- to 40-year-olds, specializing in travel, humor, and how-to. Send queries for 100- to 300-page books, with outlines and sample chapters. Royalty. SASE required.

THE MYSTERIOUS PRESS—Time and Life Bldg., 1271 Ave. of the Americas, New York, NY 10020. William Malloy, Ed.-in-Chief. Mystery/suspense novels. Agented manuscripts only.

NAIAD PRESS, INC.—Box 10543, Tallahassee, FL 32302. Barbara Grier, Ed. Adult fiction, 48,000 to 50,000 words, with lesbian themes and characters: mysteries, romances, gothics, ghost stories, westerns, regencies, spy novels, etc. Query with letter and one-page précis only. Royalty.

NATUREGRAPH PUBLISHERS—P.O. Box 1075, Happy Camp, CA 96039. Barbara Brown, Ed. Nonfiction: Native-American culture, natural history, outdoor living, land, gardening, Indian lore, and how-to. Query. Royalty.

THE NAVAL INSTITUTE PRESS—Annapolis, MD 21402. Attn: Acquisitions Dept. Nonfiction, 60,000 to 100,000 words: military histories; biographies; ship guides; how-tos on boating and navigation. Occasional fiction, 75,000 to 110,000 words. Query with outline and sample chapters. Royalty.

NEW CANAAN PUBLISHING COMPANY—P.O. Box 752, New Canaan, CT 06840. Kathy Mittelstadt, Ed. Juvenile fiction, to 40,000 words, for readers ages 5 to 16. "We want children's books with strong educational and moral content." Submit complete manuscript. No multiple queries. Royalty.

NEW HORIZON PRESS—P.O. Box 669, Far Hills, NJ 07931. Joan Dunphy, Ed.-in-Chief. True stories, 96,000 words, dealing with contemporary issues, especially true crime, that revolve around a hero or heroine. Royalty. Query.

NEW LEAF PRESS, INC.—P.O. Box 726, Green Forest, AR 72638. Jim Fletcher, Acquisitions Ed. Nonfiction, 100 to 400 pages, for Christian readers: how to live the Christian life, devotionals, gift books. Query with outline and sample chapters, or submit complete manuscript. Royalty.

THE NEW PRESS— 450 W. 41st St., New York, NY 10036. Andre Schiffrin, Dir. Serious nonfiction: history, economics, education, politics. Fiction in translation. Query required.

NEW RIVERS PRESS— 420 N. 5th St., Suite 910, Minneapolis, MN 55401. C.W. Truesdale, Ed./Pub. Collections of short stories, essays, and poems from emerging writers in upper Midwest. "Most of our books are published through the Minnesota Voices Project competition. SASE for guidelines." Query.

NEW VICTORIA PUBLISHERS—P.O. Box 27, Norwich, VT 05055. Re-Becca Béguin, Ed. Lesbian feminist fiction and nonfiction, including mystery, biography, history, fantasy; some humor and education. Guidelines. Query with outline and sample chapters; SASE. Royalty.

NEW WORLD LIBRARY—14 Pamaron Way, Novato, CA 94949. Attn: Submissions Ed. Inspirational and practical nonfiction books and audio cassettes on spirituality, personal growth, health and wellness, business and prosperity, religion, recovery, multicultural studies, and women's studies.

"Dedicated to awakening individual and global potential." Query with outline, sample chapter, and SASE. Multiple queries accepted. Royalty.

NEW YORK UNIVERSITY PRESS—70 Washington Sq. S., New York, NY 10012. Niko Pfund, Ed.-in-Chief. Scholarly nonfiction. Submit manuscript and/or proposal with sample chapters and curriculum vitae.

NEWCASTLE PUBLISHING—13419 Saticoy St., N. Hollywood, CA 91605. Al Saunders, Pub. Nonfiction manuscripts, 200 to 250 pages, for older adults on personal health, health care issues, and relationships. "We are not looking for fads or trends. We want books with a long shelf life." Multiple queries considered. Royalty.

NEWMARKET PRESS—18 E. 48th St., New York, NY 10017. Esther Margolis, Pub. Nonfiction on health, psychology, self-help, child care, parenting, music, and film. Query required. Royalty.

NORTH COUNTRY PRESS—RR 1, Box 1395, Unity, ME 04988. Patricia Newell, Mary Kenney, Eds. Nonfiction with a Maine and/or New England tie-in with emphasis on the outdoors; also limited fiction (Maine-based mystery). "Our goal is to publish high-quality books for people who love New England." Query with SASE, outline, and sample chapters. No unsolicited manuscripts. Royalty.

NORTHEASTERN UNIVERSITY PRESS—360 Huntington Ave., 416 CP, Boston, MA 02115. Scott Brassart, Ed. Nonfiction, 50,000 to 200,000 words: trade and scholarly titles in music, criminal justice, women's studies, ethnic studies, law, sociology, environmental studies, American history, and literary criticism. Submit query with outline and sample chapter or complete manuscript. Royalty.

NORTHERN ILLINOIS UNIVERSITY PRESS—DeKalb, IL 60115. Mary L. Lincoln, Dir. Books, 250 to 450 pages, for scholars and informed general readers. Submit history and Russian studies topics to Mary Lincoln; politics, philosophy, anthropology, economics, and literature to Robert Anthony. "Regional topics are our special interest." Query with outline. Royalty.

NORTHLAND PUBLISHING—P.O. Box 1389, Flagstaff, AZ 86002. Erin Murphy, Ed.-in-Chief. Nonfiction books on natural history; fine arts; Native American culture, myth, art, and crafts; and cookbooks. Unique children's picture books, 350 to 1,500 words, and middle reader chapter books, approximately 20,000 words, with American West/Southwest regional themes. Potential market for proposed adult and middle reader books. Query with outline, sample chapters. For children's books, send complete manuscript. "Include SASE with all submissions and queries. No queries by phone or fax." Royalty.

NORTHWORD PRESS, INC.—Box 1360, Minocqua, WI 54548. Barbara K. Harold, Man. Ed. Nonfiction nature and wildlife books for children and adults. Send SASE with 7 first-class stamps for catalogue and SASE for guidelines. Royalty or flat fee.

NORTON AND CO., INC., W.W.—500 Fifth Ave., New York, NY 10110. Attn: Ed. High-quality literary fiction and nonfiction. No occult, paranormal, religious, genre fiction (formula romance, science fiction, westerns), cookbooks, arts and crafts, young adult, or children's books. No unsolicited manuscripts.

NTC/CONTEMPORARY PUBLISHING CO.—(formerly *Contemporary Books, Inc.*) 4255 W. Touhy Ave., Lincolnwood, IL 60646. John T. Nolan, Ed. Dir. Trade nonfiction, 100 to 400 pages, on health, fitness, sports, cooking, humor, business, popular culture, biography, real estate, finance, women's issues, quilting, and crafts. Query with outline, sample chapters, and SASE. Royalty.

ODYSSEY PAPERBACKS—See *Harcourt Brace & Co. Children's Book Div.*

OHIO UNIVERSITY PRESS/SWALLOW PRESS—Scott Quadrangle, Athens, OH 45701. David Sanders, Dir. Scholarly nonfiction, 350 to 450 manuscript pages, especially literary criticism, regional studies, African studies. *Swallow Press*: general interest and western Americana. Query with outline and sample chapters. Royalty.

THE OLIVER PRESS—Charlotte Square, 5707 W. 36th St., Minneapolis, MN 55416. Teresa Faden, Assoc. Ed. Collective biographies for young adults. Submit proposals for books, 20,000 to 25,000 words, on people who have made an impact in such areas as history, politics, crime, science, and business. Flat fee (approximately $1,000).

OPEN COURT PUBLISHING CO.—332 S. Michigan Ave., Suite 2000, Chicago, IL 60604. Attn: Acquisitions Dept. Scholarly books on philosophy, Jungian psychology, psychology, personal stories of development, religion, eastern thought, history, public policy, feminist thought, education, science, social issues, contemporary culture, and related topics. Send sample chapters with outline and resumé. Royalty.

OPEN HAND PUBLISHING—P.O. Box 22048, Seattle, WA 98122. Pat Andrus, Acquisitions Ed. Books that reflect the diverse cultures within the United States, with emphasis on the African American. "Our mission is to publish books which will promote positive social change as well as better understanding among all people." Query. Royalty.

ORCHARD BOOKS—95 Madison Ave., New York, NY 10016. No unsolicited manuscripts.

ORCHISES PRESS—P.O. Box 20602, Alexandria, VA 22320. Roger Lathbury, Ed. Nonfiction books, 128 to 500 pages; and intellectually sophisticated, technically expert poetry books, 48 to 128 pages. No fiction. Query with sample chapters. Royalty.

OREGON STATE UNIVERSITY PRESS—101 Waldo Hall, Corvallis, OR 97331. Attn: Ed. Dept. Scholarly books in a limited range of disciplines and books of particular importance to the Pacific Northwest, especially dealing with the history, natural history, culture, and literature of the region or with natural resource issues. Query with summary of manuscript.

OSBORNE/MCGRAW HILL—2600 Tenth St., Berkeley, CA 94710. Scott Rogers, Ed.-in-Chief. Computer books for general and technical audience. Query. Royalty.

OUR SUNDAY VISITOR PUBLISHING—200 Noll Plaza, Huntington, IN 46750. Jacquelyn M. Lindsey, Jim Manney, Acquisitions Eds. Catholic-oriented books of various lengths. No fiction. Query with outline and sample chapters. Royalty.

THE OVERLOOK PRESS—386 W. Broadway, 4th Fl., New York, NY 10012. Tracy Carns, Ed. Dir. Literary fiction, some fantasy/science fiction, foreign literature in translation, general nonfiction, including art, architecture, design, film, history, biography, crafts/lifestyle, martial arts, Hudson Valley regional interest, and children's books. Query with outline, sample chapters and SASE. Royalty.

OWEN PUBLISHERS, INC., RICHARD C.—Dept. TW, P.O. Box 585, Katonah, NY 10536. Janice Boland, Ed. Fiction and nonfiction. Brief storybooks, approximately 45 to 100 words, suitable for 5-, 6-, and 7-year-old beginning readers for the "Books for Young Learners" collection. Also, short stories that interest, inform, inspire, fascinate, and entertain, for 8-, 9-, and 10-year olds for "Books for Fluent Readers" collection. Royalties for writers. Flat fee for illustrators. Writers must send SASE for guidelines before submitting.

OXFORD UNIVERSITY PRESS—198 Madison Ave., New York, NY 10016. Attn: Ed. Dept. Authoritative books on literature, history, philosophy, etc.; college textbooks, medical, scientific, technical and reference books. Query. Royalty.

PALISADES—See *Questar Publishers.*

PANTHEON BOOKS—201 E. 50th St., New York, NY 10022. Attn: Ed. Dept. Quality fiction and nonfiction. Query required. Royalty.

PAPIER-MACHE PRESS— 627 Walker St., Watsonville, CA 95076. Sandra Martz, Ed. Fiction, poetry, and nonfiction books; 6 to 8 books annually. "We emphasize, but are not limited to, the publication of books and related items for midlife and older women." Write for guidelines. Query. Royalty.

PARA PUBLISHING—P.O. Box 8206-238, Santa Barbara, CA 93118-8206. Dan Poynter, Ed. Adult nonfiction books on parachutes and skydiving only. Author must present evidence of having made at least 1,000 jumps. Query. Royalty.

PARAGON HOUSE—2700 University Ave. W., Suite 47, St. Paul, MN 55114-1016. Gordon Anderson, Pub. Serious nonfiction, including philosophy, religion, and current affairs. Query. Royalty.

PASSPORT BOOKS— 4255 W. Touhy Ave., Lincolnwood, IL 60646-1975. Linda Gray, Ed. Adult nonfiction, 200 to 400 pages; picture books up to 120 pages; and juvenile nonfiction. Send outline and sample chapters for books on foreign language, travel, and culture. Multiple queries considered. Royalty and flat fee.

PAULIST PRESS—997 Macarthur Blvd., Mahwah, NJ 07430. Donald Brophy, Man. Ed. Adult nonfiction, 100 to 400 pages; and picture books, 8 to 10 pages, for readers 5 to 7 or 8 to 10. For adult books, query with outline and sample chapters. For juvenile books, submit complete manuscript to Karen Scialabba, Ed. Royalty.

PEACHPIT PRESS—2414 Sixth St., Berkeley, CA 94710. Roslyn Bullas, Ed. Books on computer and graphic-design topics. Query with outline and sample chapters for manuscripts 100 to 1,100 words. E-mail address is roslyn-@peachpit.com. Web site is http://www.peachpit.com.

PEACHTREE PUBLISHERS, LTD.— 494 Armour Cir. N.E., Atlanta, GA 30324. Attn: Ed. Dept. Wide variety of children's books, fiction, and nonfiction. No religious material, science fiction/fantasy, romance, mystery/detective, historical fiction; no business, scientific, or technical books. Send outline and sample chapters. SASE required. Royalty.

PELICAN PUBLISHING CO., INC.—P.O. Box 3110, Gretna, LA 70054. Nina Kooij, Ed.-in-Chief. General nonfiction: Americana, regional, architecture, travel, cookbooks. Royalty.

PENGUIN BOOKS—375 Hudson St., New York, NY 10014. Attn: Ed. Dept. Adult fiction and nonfiction paperbacks. Royalty.

PEREGRINE SMITH BOOKS—See *Gibbs Smith, Junior.*

THE PERMANENT PRESS—Noyac Rd., Sag Harbor, NY 11963. Judith Shepard, Ed. Original and arresting novels. Query. Royalty.

PERSPECTIVES PRESS—P.O. Box 90318, Indianapolis, IN 46290-0318. Pat Johnston, Pub. Nonfiction books on infertility, adoption, closely related reproductive health and child welfare issues (foster care, etc.). "Writers must read our guidelines before submitting." Query. Royalty.

PHILOMEL BOOKS—200 Madison Ave., New York, NY 10016. Patricia Lee Gauch, Ed. Dir. Juvenile picture books, young adult fiction, and some biographies. Fresh, original work with compelling characters and "a truly childlike spirit." Query required.

PINEAPPLE PRESS—P.O. Box 3899, Sarasota, FL 34230. June Cussen, Ed. Serious fiction and nonfiction, Florida-oriented, 60,000 to 125,000 words. Query with outline, sample chapters, and SASE. Royalty.

PINNACLE BOOKS— 850 Third Ave., New York, NY 10022. Paul Dinas, Ed.-in-Chief. Nonfiction books: true crime, celebrity biographies, and humor. No unsolicited material.

PIPPIN PRESS—229 E. 85th St., Gracie Sta., Box 1347, New York, NY 10028. Barbara Francis, Pub. Small chapter books for children ages 7 to 10, emphasizing humor and fantasy, humorous mysteries; imaginative nonfiction for children of all ages. Query with SASE only; no unsolicited manuscripts. Royalty.

PLANET DEXTER—Addison-Wesley Publishing Co., One Jacob Way, Reading, MA 01867-3999. Beth Wolfensberger, Ed. Nonfiction educational books for children ages 5 to 12. "Our goal is to create book-based products with an accompanying toy, electronic gadget, craft item, or learning tool." No fiction or poetry. No textbook-style academic writing. SASE required.

PLAYERS PRESS, INC.—P.O. Box 1132, Studio City, CA 91614. Robert Gordon, Ed. Plays and musicals for children and adults; juvenile and adult nonfiction related to theatre, film, television, and the performing arts. Lengths vary. Query. Royalty.

PLENUM PUBLISHING CORP.—233 Spring St., New York, NY 10013. Linda Greenspan Regan, Exec. Ed. Trade nonfiction, approximately 300 pages, on popular science, criminology, psychology, social science, anthropology, and health. Query required. Royalty. Hardcover.

PLUME BOOKS—375 Hudson St., New York, NY 10014. Attn: Ed. Dept. Nonfiction: hobbies, business, health, cooking, child care, psychology, history, popular culture, biography, and politics. Fiction: serious literary and gay. Query.

POCKET BOOKS—1230 Ave. of the Americas, New York, NY 10020. Adult and young adult fiction and nonfiction. Mystery line: police procedurals, private eye, and amateur sleuth novels, 60,000 to 70,000 words. Royalty.

POPULAR PRESS—Bowling Green State Univ., Bowling Green, OH 43403. Ms. Pat Browne, Ed. Nonfiction, 250 to 400 pages, examining some aspect of popular culture. Query with outline. Flat fee or royalty.

POTTER, CLARKSON —201 E. 50th St., New York, NY 10022. Lauren Shakely, Ed. Dir. General trade books. Submissions accepted through agents only.

PRAEGER PUBLISHERS— 88 Post Rd. W., Westport, CT 06880-4232. Attn: Pub. General nonfiction; scholarly and textbooks. Query with outline. Royalty.

PRESIDIO PRESS—505B San Marin Dr., Suite 300, Novato, CA 94945-1340. Attn: Ed. Dept. Nonfiction: military history and military affairs, from 90,000 words. Fiction: selected military and action-adventure works and mysteries, from 100,000 words. Query. Royalty.

PRICE STERN SLOAN, INC.—200 Madison Ave., New York, NY 10016. Attn: Submissions Ed. Witty or edgy middle-grade fiction and nonfiction, calendars, and novelty juvenile titles. Imprints include *Troubador Press, Wee Sing, MadLibs*. Query with SASE required. Royalty.

PRIMA PUBLISHING—3875 Atherton Rd., Rocklin, CA 95765. Ben Dominitz, Pub. Paula Munier Lee, Assoc. Pub. Jennifer Basye, Ed. Nonfiction on variety of subjects, including business, health, self-help, entertainment, computers, inspiration, and cookbooks. "We want books with originality, written by highly qualified individuals." Advance against royalty.

PROMPT PUBLICATIONS—2647 Waterfront Pkwy. E. Dr., Indianapolis, IN 46214-2041. Attn: Acquisitions Ed. Nonfiction softcover technical books on electronics, how-to, troubleshooting and repair, electrical engineering, video and sound equipment, cellular technology, etc., for all levels of technical experience. Query with outline, sample chapters, author bio, and SASE. Royalty.

PRUETT PUBLISHING COMPANY—2928 Pearl St., Boulder, CO 80301. Jim Pruett, Pub. Nonfiction: outdoors and recreation, western U.S. history, travel, natural history and the environment, fly fishing. Query. Royalty.

PUTNAM'S SONS, G.P.—200 Madison Ave., New York, NY 10016. Attn: Children's Ed. Dept. General trade nonfiction, fiction. Query Nancy Paulsen, Pres. and Pub., for children's books. No unsolicited manuscripts. Royalty.

QED PRESS—155 Cypress St., Fort Bragg, CA 95437. Cynthia Frank, Ed. Health, gerontology, and psychology books. Query with outline and sample chapters. Royalty.

QUEST BOOKS—Theosophical Publishing House, 306 W. Geneva Rd., P.O. Box 270, Wheaton, IL 60189-0270. Brenda Rosen, Exec. Ed. Nonfiction books on Eastern and Western religion and philosophy, holism, healing, transpersonal psychology, men's and women's spirituality, creativity, meditation, yoga, ancient wisdom. Query. Royalty.

QUESTAR PUBLISHERS—204 W. Adams Ave., P.O. Box 1720, Sisters, OR 97759. Attn: Ed. Evangelical, Christian publishing house with 3 imprints: *Multnomah Books*, message-driven, clean, moral, uplifting fiction (not necessarily religious); address Ed. Dept. *Palisades*, contemporary romance that upholds strong Christian values; address Karen Ball, Ed. *Gold 'n' Honey*, developmentally appropriate stories for children; address Melody Carlson, Ed. Submit 2 or 3 sample chapters with outline, cover letter, and SASE. Royalty.

QUIXOTE PRESS—3544 Blakeslee St., Wever, IA 52658. Bruce Carlson, Pres. Adult fiction and nonfiction including humor, folklore, and regional cookbooks; some juvenile fiction. Query with sample chapters and outline. Royalty.

RAGGED MOUNTAIN PRESS—A Div. of McGraw-Hill, Box 220, Camden, ME 04843. Jonathan Eaton, Ed. Dir. Jeff Serena, Acquisitions Ed. Books on outdoor recreation.

RAINTREE STECK-VAUGHN PUBLISHERS—National Education Corp., 466 Southern Blvd., Chatham, NJ 07928. Walter Kossmann, Frank Sloan, Eds. Nonfiction books, 5,000 to 30,000 words, for school and library market: biographies for grades 3 and up; and science, social studies, and history books for primary grades through high school. Query with outline and sample chapters; SASE required. Flat fee or royalty.

RANDOM HOUSE, INC.—201 E. 50th St., New York, NY 10022. Attn: Ed. Dept. General fiction and nonfiction. Agented material only.

RANDOM HOUSE JUVENILE DIV.—201 E. 50th St., New York, NY 10022. Kate Klimo, Pub. Dir. Fiction and nonfiction for beginning readers; paperback fiction line for 7- to 9-year-olds. No unsolicited manuscripts. Agented material only.

RED CRANE BOOKS—2008 Rosina St., Suite B, Santa Fe, NM 87505. Marianne O'Shaughnessy, Ed. Art and folk art, bilingual material with Spanish and English, cookbooks, essays, gardening, herbal guides, how-to books for arts and crafts, natural history, novels, social and political issues and social history. No children's books. Send a short synopsis, 2 sample chapters, resumé, and SASE.

RED SAGE PUBLISHING, INC.—P.O. Box 4844, Seminole, FL 33775. Alexandria Kendall, Acquisitions Ed. Novella submissions for anthologies. Sensual romantic fiction, 15,000 to 30,000 words. "Love scenes should be sophisticated, erotic, and emotional. Push the envelope beyond the normal romance novel." Query with sample chapters. Royalty.

THE RED SEA PRESS—11-D Princess Rd., Suites D, E, F, Lawrenceville, NJ 08648. Kassahun Checole, Pub. Adult nonfiction, 360 double-spaced manuscript pages. "We focus on nonfiction material with a specialty on the Horn of Africa." Query. Royalty.

RED WAGON BOOKS—Harcourt, Brace & Co. Children's Books, 525 B St., Suite 1900, San Diego, CA 92101-4495. Attn: Acquisitions Ed. No unsolicited material. Query letter only with SASE.

REGNERY PUBLISHING, INC.—422 First St. S.E., Washington, DC 20003. Attn: Ed. Dept. Nonfiction books. Query. Royalty.

RENAISSANCE HOUSE—541 Oak St., P. O. Box 177, Frederick, CO 80530. Eleanor H. Ayer, Ed. Regional guidebooks. Guidebooks on CO, AZ, CA, and the Southwest. "We use only manuscripts written to our specifications for new or ongoing series." Essay contest; send for guidelines.

REPUBLIC OF TEXAS PRESS—See *Wordware Publishing*.

RISING TIDE PRESS—5 Kivy St., Huntington Sta., New York, NY 11746. Lee Boojamra, Ed. Books for, by, and about lesbians. Fiction, 60,000 to 80,000 words: romance, mystery, and science fiction/fantasy. Nonfiction, 40,000 to 60,000 words. Royalty. Reports in 3 months. SASE for guidelines.

RIZZOLI INTERNATIONAL PUBLICATIONS, INC.—300 Park Ave. S., New York, NY 10010. Manuela Soares, Children's Book Ed. Original manuscripts that introduce children to fine art, folk art, and architecture of all cultures for a small list. Nonfiction and fiction for all ages. Query with SASE or response card. Royalty.

ROC—375 Hudson St., New York, NY 10014. Laura Anne Gilman, Exec. Ed. Jennifer Smith, Assoc. Ed. Science fiction, fantasy. Agented manuscripts only.

ROCKBRIDGE PUBLISHING—P.O. Box 351, Berryville, VA 22611. Katherine Tennery, Ed. Book-length nonfiction on the Civil War, Virginia history, and travel guides to Virginia. Query. Royalty.

RODALE PRESS—33 E. Minor St., Emmaus, PA 18098. Pat Corpora, Pub. Books on men's health, women's health, gardening, cookbooks, inspirational/spiritual, sewing, quilting, woodworking. Query with outline and sample chapter. Royalty and outright purchase. "We're always looking for truly competent free lancers to write chapters for books conceived and developed in-house." Payment on a work-for-hire basis; address Lois Hazel, Asst. Acquisitions Ed.

ROYAL FIREWORKS PRESS—Box 399, First Ave., Unionville, NY 10988. Charles Morgan, Ed. Adult science fiction and mysteries. Juvenile and young adult fiction, biography, and educational nonfiction. Submit complete manuscripts with a brief plot overview. No multiple queries. Royalty.

RUNNING PRESS—125 S. 22nd St., Philadelphia, PA 19103. Attn: Exec. Ed. Trade nonfiction: art, craft, how-to, self-help, science, lifestyles. Young adult books and interactive packages. Query. Royalty.

RUTGERS UNIVERSITY PRESS—P.O. Box 5062, New Brunswick, NJ 08903. Paula Kantenwein, Editorial Asst. Nonfiction, 70,000 to 120,000 words. Query with outline and sample chapters. Royalty.

RUTLEDGE HILL PRESS—211 Seventh Ave. N., Nashville, TN 37219. Mike Towle, Ed. Market-specific nonfiction. Query with outline and sample chapters. Royalty.

ST. ANTHONY MESSENGER PRESS—1615 Republic St., Cincinnati, OH 45210-1298. Lisa Biedenbach, Man. Ed. Inspirational nonfiction for Catholics, supporting a Christian lifestyle in our culture; prayer aids, scripture, church history, education, practical spirituality, parish ministry, liturgy resources. Query with 500-word summary. Royalty.

ST. MARTIN'S PRESS—175 Fifth Ave., New York, NY 10010. Attn: Ed. Dept. General adult fiction and nonfiction. Query. Royalty.

SAINT MARY'S PRESS—702 Terrace Heights, Winona, MN 55987-1320. Stephan Nagel, Ed.-in-Chief. Progressive Catholic publisher. Fiction, to 40,000 words, for young adults ages 14 to 17, "that gives insight into the struggle of teens to become healthy, hopeful adults and also sheds light on Catholic experience, history, or cultures." Query with outline and sample chapter. Royalty.

SANDLAPPER PUBLISHING, INC.—P.O. Drawer 730, Orangeburg, SC 29116-0730. Amanda Gallman, Book Ed. Nonfiction books on South Carolina history, culture, cuisine. Query with outline, sample chapters, and SASE.

SASQUATCH BOOKS— 615 2nd Ave., Suite 260, Seattle, WA 98104. Attn: Ed. Dept. Regional books on a wide range of nonfiction topics: travel, natural history, gardening, cooking, history, and public affairs. Books should have a Pacific Northwest and/or West Coast subject or theme. Query with SASE. Royalty.

SCARECROW PRESS— 4720 Boston Way, Lanham, MD 20706. Shirley Lambert, Ed. Dir. Reference works and bibliographies, from 150 pages, especially in the areas of cinema, TV, radio, and theater, mainly for use by libraries. Query or send complete manuscript; multiple queries considered. Royalty.

SCHOCKEN BOOKS—201 E. 50th St., New York, NY 10022. Attn: Ed. Dept. General nonfiction: Judaica, women's studies, education, history, religion, psychology, cultural studies. Query with outline and sample chapter. Royalty.

SCHOLASTIC, INC.—555 Broadway, New York, NY 10012. No unsolicited manuscripts.

SCHOLASTIC PROFESSIONAL BOOKS—411 Lafayette St., New York, NY 10003. Attn: Shawn Richardson. Books by and for teachers of kindergarten through eighth grade. *Instructor Books*: practical, activity/resource books on teaching reading and writing, science, math, etc. *Teaching Strategies Books*: 64 to 96 pages on new ideas, practices, and approaches to teaching. Query with outline, sample chapters or activities, contents page, and resumé. Flat fee or royalty. Multiple queries considered. 8 1/2" x 11" SASE for guidelines.

SCHWARTZ BOOKS, ANNE—1230 Ave. of the Americas, New York, NY 10020. Anne Schwartz, Ed. Picture books through juvenile fiction and nonfiction as well as illustrated collections. Query; no unsolicited manuscripts.

SCOTT FORESMAN/ADDISON WESLEY—1900 E. Lake Ave., Glenview, IL 60025. Pat Donaghy, Pres. Elementary and secondary textbooks. Royalty or flat fee.

SCRIBNER—1230 Ave. of the Americas, New York, NY 10020. Attn: Ed. Dept. No unsolicited manuscripts.

SEAL PRESS—3131 Western Ave., Suite 410, Seattle, WA 98121-1041. Holly Morris, Ed. Dir. Feminist/women's studies books: popular culture and lesbian studies; parenting; domestic violence; health and recovery; sports and outdoors. Query. Royalty.

SEASIDE PRESS—See *Wordware Publishing*.

SEVEN STORIES PRESS—632 Broadway, 7th Fl., New York, NY 10012. Dan Simon, Pub. Small press. Fiction and nonfiction. Query with SASE. Royalty.

SHAW PUBLISHERS, HAROLD—388 Gunderson Dr., Box 567, Wheaton, IL 60189. Joan L. Guest, Dir. Ed. Nonfiction, 120 to 320 pages, with an evangelical Christian perspective. Some fiction and literary books. Query. Flat fee or royalty.

SHEARWATER BOOKS—See *Island Press*.

SIERRA CLUB BOOKS—85 Second St., San Francisco, CA 94105. Attn: Ed. Dept. Nonfiction: environment, natural history, the sciences, outdoors and regional guidebooks, nature photography; children's fiction and nonfiction. Query with SASE. Royalty.

SIGNAL HILL PUBLICATIONS—1320 Jamesville Ave., Box 131, Syracuse, NY 13210. Jennifer Lashley, Ed. Fiction and nonfiction, 5,000 to 9,000 words, and poetry for adults who read at low levels, for use in adult basic education programs, volunteer literacy organizations, and job training programs "No unsolicited manuscripts." Royalty or flat fee.

SIGNATURE BOOKS, INC.—564 W. 400 North, Salt Lake City, UT 84116-3411. Attn: Board of Dirs. Adult fiction and nonfiction, from 100 pages. Adult poetry from 80 pages. Royalty.

SILHOUETTE BOOKS—300 E. 42nd St., New York, NY 10017. Isabel Swift, Ed. Dir. *Silhouette Romances*: Melissa Senate, Sr. Ed. Contemporary romances, 53,000 to 58,000 words. *Special Edition*: Tara Gavin, Sr. Ed. Sophisticated contemporary romances, 75,000 to 80,000 words. *Silhouette Desire*:

Lucia Macro, Sr. Ed. Sensuous contemporary romances, 53,000 to 60,000 words. *Intimate Moments*: Leslie Wainger, Sr. Ed./Ed. Coord. Sensuous, exciting contemporary romances, 80,000 to 85,000 words. *Silhouette Yours Truly*: Leslie Wainger, Ed. Contemporary, fun romances with written word hook. Historical romance: 95,000 to 105,000 words, and more; query with synopsis and 3 sample chapters to Tracy Farrell, Sr. Ed. Query with synopsis and SASE to appropriate editor. Tipsheets available.

SILVER MOON PRESS—160 Fifth Ave., Suite 622, New York, NY 10010. No unsolicited manuscripts.

SIMON & SCHUSTER—1230 Ave. of the Americas, New York, NY 10020. Adult books. No unsolicited material; manuscripts must be submitted by an agent.

SIMON & SCHUSTER BOOKS FOR YOUNG READERS—1230 Ave. of the Americas, New York, NY 10020. Stephanie Owens Lurie, V.P./Ed. Dir. Books for ages preschool through high school: picture books to young adult; nonfiction for all age levels. Hardcover only. Request guidelines before querying. SASE required for reply.

SINGER MEDIA CORP.—Seaview Business Park, 1030 Calle Cordillera, #106, San Clemente, CA 92673. Helen J. Lee, Acquisitions Dir. International literary agency and syndicate specializing in licensing foreign rights to books in the fields of business, management, celebrity biographies, self-help, occult, and fiction in all genres. No poetry. Query first with SASE.

SKYLARK BOOKS—See *Yearling Books*.

THE SMITH— 69 Joralemon St., Brooklyn, NY 11201-4003. Harry Smith, Pub./Ed. Michael McGrinder, Assoc Ed. Fiction, send up to 2 chapters (no synopsis); literary nonfiction, send outline and up to 2 chapters; and poetry, no more than 7 poems. "While publishing at a high level of craftsmanship, we have pursued the increasingly difficult, expensive, and now relatively rare policy of keeping our titles in print over the decades." Query; no complete manuscripts. Royalty. SASE.

SMITH AND KRAUS, INC.—P.O. Box 127, Main St., Lyme, NH 03768. Marisa Smith, Pres. Original plays, teaching texts for the K through 12 market only. Does not accept full-length and one-act plays unless the play in question has been produced within the year and is therefore eligible for the "Best Scene and Monologue Series of the Year." Does not return manuscripts. Response time is 3 months. Pays on publication.

SOHO PRESS— 853 Broadway, New York, NY 10003. Juris Jurjevics, Pub. Mysteries, thrillers, and contemporary fiction and nonfiction, from 60,000 words. Send SASE and complete manuscript. Royalty.

SOUNDPRINTS—353 Main Ave., Norwalk, CT 06851. Dierdre Langeland, Ed. Asst. Factual children's books, 800 to 2,000 words, about oceanic and backyard animals and history for young readers in preschool through fifth grade. No anthropomorphism. "Read one of our current stories in the relevant series before submitting." Pays flat fee.

SOUTHERN ILLINOIS UNIVERSITY PRESS—P.O. Box 3697, Carbondale, IL 62902-3697. James Simmons, Ed. Dir. Nonfiction in the humanities, 200 to 300 pages. Query with outline and sample chapters. Royalty.

SOUTHERN METHODIST UNIVERSITY PRESS—Box 415, Dallas, TX 75275. Kathryn Lang, Sr. Ed. Literary fiction. Nonfiction: scholarly studies in religion, medical ethics (death and dying); film, theater; scholarly works on Texas or Southwest. No juvenile material, science fiction, or poetry. Query. Royalty.

SPECIAL EDITION—See *Silhouette Books*.

SPECTACLE LANE PRESS—Box 1237, Mt. Pleasant, SC 29465-1237. Attn: Ed. Dept. Humor books, 500 to 5,000 words, on subjects of strong, current interest, illustrated with cartoons. Buys text or text/cartoon packages. Occasional nonfiction, non-humor books on provocative subjects of wide concern. Royalty.

SPECTRA—See *Bantam Books*.

SPINSTERS INK—32 E. First St., #330, Duluth, MN 55802. Nancy Walker, Acquisitions Ed. Adult fiction and nonfiction books, 200-plus pages, that deal with significant issues in women's lives from a feminist perspective and encourage change and growth. Main characters and/or narrators must be women. Query with synopsis. Royalty.

STACKPOLE BOOKS—5067 Ritter Rd., Mechanicsburg, PA 17055. Judith Schnell, Ed. Dir. Books on the outdoors, nature, fishing, carving, woodworking, sports, sporting literature, cooking, gardening, history, and military reference. Query. Royalty; advance. Unsolicited materials will not be returned.

STA-KRIS, INC.—P.O. Box 1131, Marshalltown, IA 50158. Kathy Wagoner, Pres. Fiction and nonfiction adult-level gift books that portray universal feelings, truths, and values; or have a special-occasion theme. Query with bio, list of credits, complete manuscript, and SASE.

STANDARD PUBLISHING— 8121 Hamilton Ave., Cincinnati, OH 45231. Attn: Acquisitions Coord. Christian education resources and children's books. No unsolicited material except for Program books, which include material for special days such as Easter, Mother's Day, Father's Day, Thanksgiving, and Christmas. Guidelines.

STANFORD UNIVERSITY PRESS—Stanford Univ., Stanford, CA 94305-2235. Norris Pope, Dir. "For the most part, we publish academic scholarship." No original fiction or poetry. Query with outline and sample chapters. Royalty.

STARBURST PUBLISHERS—Box 4123, Lancaster, PA 17604. Ellen Hake, Ed. Dir. Health, inspiration, Christian, and self-help books. Query with outline for nonfiction book, synopsis for fiction book, and 3 sample chapters. Royalty. SASE.

STARRHILL PRESS—Black Belt Communications Group, Inc., P.O. Box 551, Montgomery, AL 36101. Attn: Submission Ed. Affordable, succinct titles on American arts and letters. Query with cover letter, outline, author bio, and SASE for reply. Royalty varies.

STEERFORTH PRESS—105-106 Chelsea St., Box 70, S. Royalton, VT 05068. Michael Moore, Ed. Adult nonfiction and some literary fiction. Fifteen books a year: novels; serious works of history, biography, politics, current affairs. Query with SASE. Royalty.

STEMMER HOUSE PUBLISHERS, INC.—2627 Caves Rd., Owings Mills, MD 21117. Barbara Holdridge, Ed. Juvenile picture books and adult nonfiction. Specializes in art, design, cookbooks, children's, and horticultural titles. Query with SASE. Royalty.

STERLING PUBLISHING CO., INC.—387 Park Ave. S., New York, NY 10016. Sheila Anne Barry, Acquisitions Dir. How-to, hobby, woodworking, alternative health and healing, fiber arts, crafts, dolls and puppets, ghosts, wine, nature, oddities, new consciousness, puzzles, juvenile humor and activities, juvenile nature and science, medieval history, Celtic topics, gardening, alternative lifestyle, business, pets, recreation, sports and games books, reference, and home decorating. Query with outline, sample chapter, and sample illustrations. Royalty.

STONEYDALE PRESS—523 Main St., Box 188, Stevensville, MT 59870. Dale A. Burk, Ed. Adult nonfiction, primarily how-to, on outdoor recreation with emphasis on big game hunting. "We're a very specialized market. Query with outline and sample chapters essential." Royalty.

STOREY COMMUNICATIONS—Schoolhouse Rd., Pownal, VT 05261. Gwen Steege, Ed. Dir. How-to books for country living. Adult books, 100 to 350 pages, on gardening, animals, crafts, building, cooking, beer, and how-to. Juvenile nonfiction, 64 to 160 pages, on gardening, crafts, and cooking. Royalty or flat fee.

STORY LINE PRESS—Three Oaks Farm, Brownsville, OR 97327-9718. Robert McDowell, Ed. Fiction, nonfiction, and poetry of varying lengths. Query. Royalty.

STRAWBERRY HILL PRESS—3848 S.E. Division St., Portland, OR 97202-1641. Carolyn Soto, Ed. Nonfiction: biography, autobiography, history, cooking, health, how-to, philosophy, performance arts, and Third World. Query with sample chapters, outline, and SASE. Royalty.

SUCCESS PUBLISHERS—(formerly *Markowski International Publishers*) One Oakglade Cir., Hummelstown, PA 17036. Marjorie L. Markowski, Ed. Nonfiction, from 30,000 words: personal development, self-help, sales and marketing, leadership training, network marketing, motivation, and success topics. "We are interested in how-to, motivational, and instructional books of short to medium length that will serve recognized and emerging needs of society." Query with outline and 3 sample chapters. Royalty.

SUNDANCE PUBLISHING—P.O. Box 1326, Taylor Rd., Littleton, MA 01460. M. Elizabeth Strauss, Pub. Curriculum materials to accompany quality children's, young adult, and adult literature. Flat fee only.

SWALLOW PRESS—See *Ohio University Press/Swallow Press.*

TAYLOR PUBLISHING CO.—1550 W. Mockingbird Ln., Dallas, TX 75235. Attn: Ed. Dept. Adult nonfiction: gardening, sports, health, popular culture, celebrity biographies, parenting, home improvement. Query with outline, sample chapter, author bio, and SASE. Royalty.

TEACHING STRATEGIES BOOKS—See *Scholastic Professional Books.*

TEMPLE UNIVERSITY PRESS—1601 N. Broad St., USB 306, Philadelphia, PA 19122-6099. Michael Ames, Ed. Adult nonfiction. Query with outline and sample chapters. Royalty.

TEN SPEED PRESS—P.O. Box 7123, Berkeley, CA 94707. Attn: Ed. Dept. Self-help and how-to on careers, recreation, etc.; natural science, history, cookbooks. Imprints include: *Tricycle Press* and *Celestial Arts.* Query with outline, sample chapters, and SASE. Paperback. Royalty.

THIRD WORLD PRESS—P.O. Box 19730, Chicago, IL 60619. Attn: Ed. Board. "Progressive Black Publishing." Adult fiction, nonfiction, and poetry, as well juvenile fiction and young adult books. Query with outline. Royalty.

796

THUNDER'S MOUTH PRESS— 632 Broadway, 7th, 10012. Neil Ortenberg, Ed. Mainly nonfiction: current aff memoirs, and biography, to 300 pages. Royalty.

TIARE PUBLICATIONS—P.O. Box 493, Lake Ger L. Dexter, Ed. General fiction, *Limelight* imprint; jazz disc mentaries, *Balboa* imprint. Query with outline and sample chapters.

TILBURY HOUSE—132 Water St., Gardiner, ME 04345. Attn: Acquisitions Ed. Children's books that deal with cultural diversity or the environment; appeal to children and parents as well as the educational market; and offer possibilities for developing a separate teacher's guide. Adult books: nonfiction books about Maine or the Northeast. Query with outline and sample chapters.

TIME-LIFE FOR CHILDREN—777 Duke St., Alexandria, VA 22314. Mary Saxton, Submissions Coord. Juvenile books. Publishes series of 12 to 36 volumes (no single titles), so author must have a series concept. No unsolicited work.

TIMES BOOKS—201 E. 50th St., New York, NY 10022. Peter Bernstein, Pub. No unsolicited manuscripts or queries accepted.

TOPAZ—375 Hudson St., New York, NY 10014. Constance Martin, Ed. Historical romance. Query.

TOR BOOKS—Tom Doherty Associates, 175 Fifth Ave., 14th Fl., New York, NY 10010. Patrick Nielsen Hayden, Sr. Ed. Science fiction and fantasy, from 80,000 words. Query with complete synopsis and first 3 chapters. Advance and royalty.

TOUCHSTONE—1230 Ave. of the Americas, New York, NY 10020. Attn: Ed. No unsolicited manuscripts.

TRICYCLE PRESS—Ten Speed Press, P.O. Box 7123, Berkeley, CA 94707. Nicole Geiger, Ed. Children's books: Picture books, submit complete manuscripts. Activity books, submit about 20 pages and complete outline. "Real life" books that help children cope with issues. SASE required. Do not send original artwork. Responds in 10 weeks. Royalty.

TROUBADOR PRESS—See *Price Stern Sloan, Inc.*

TSR, INC.—201 Sheridan Springs Rd., Lake Geneva, WI 53147. Attn: Manuscript Ed. Epic high fantasy, gritty, action-oriented fantasy, Gothic horror, some science fiction, about 100,000 words. Query. Advance royalty.

TUDOR PUBLISHERS, INC.—P.O. Box 38366, Greensboro, NC 27438. Pam Cox, Ed. Helpful nonfiction books for senior citizens, teenagers, and minorities. Young adult biographies and occasional young adult novels. Reference library titles. Occasional high-quality adult fiction. Send proposal or query with sample chapters. Royalty.

TWENTY-FIRST CENTURY BOOKS—115 W. 18th St., New York, NY 10011. Attn: Submissions Ed. Juvenile nonfiction, 20,000 to 30,000 words, for use in school and public libraries. Science, history, health, and social studies books for grades 5 and up. No fiction, workbooks, or picture books. Also accepts single titles for middle-grade and young adult readers. "Books are published primarily in series of 4 or more; not all titles in a series are necessarily by the same author." Submit outline and sample chapters. Royalty.

TYNDALE HOUSE—351 Executive Dr., Box 80, Wheaton, IL 60189. Ron Beers, V.P. Adult fiction and nonfiction on subjects of concern to Christians. Picture books with religious focus for preschool and early readers. No unsolic-

.ted manuscripts. Send 9 x 12 SASE with 9 first-class stamps for catalogue and guidelines.

UAHC PRESS—838 Fifth Ave., New York, NY 10021. Greg Sanders, Man. Ed. Religious educational titles on or related to Judaism. Adult nonfiction; juvenile picture books, fiction, nonfiction, and young adult titles. Query with outline. Royalty.

UNIVERSE PUBLISHING—300 Park Ave. S., New York, NY 10010. Bonnie Eldon, Man. Ed. Fine arts, photography, popular culture. Query with SASE. Royalty.

UNIVERSITY BOOKS—See *Carol Publishing Group.*

UNIVERSITY OF ALABAMA PRESS—P.O. Box 870380, Tuscaloosa, AL 35487-0380. Attn: Ed. Dept. Scholarly and general regional nonfiction. Submit to appropriate editor: Nicole Mitchell, Ed. (history, public administration, political science, women's studies); Curtis Clark, Ed. (English, rhetoric and communication, Judaic studies); Judith Knight, Ed. (archaeology, anthropology). Send complete manuscript or proposal. Royalty.

UNIVERSITY OF ARIZONA PRESS—1230 N. Park Ave., Suite 102, Tucson, AZ 85719-4140. Stephen Cox, Dir. Joanne O'Hare, Sr. Ed. Christine R. Szuter, Martha Moutray, Acquiring Eds. Scholarly and popular nonfiction: Arizona, American West, anthropology, archaeology, behavioral sciences, environmental science, geography, Latin America, Native Americans, natural history, space sciences, women's studies. Query with outline, sample chapters, and current curriculum vitae or resume. Royalty.

UNIVERSITY OF ARKANSAS PRESS—Div. of The Univ. of Arkansas, McIlroy House, 201 Ozark Ave., Fayetteville, AR 72701. John Coghlan, Dir. Short stories, nonfiction, and poetry. Query. Royalty.

UNIVERSITY OF CALIFORNIA PRESS—2120 Berkeley Way, Berkeley, CA 94720. Attn: Acquisitions Dept. Scholarly nonfiction. Query with cover letter, outline, sample chapters, curriculum vitae, and SASE.

UNIVERSITY OF GEORGIA PRESS—330 Research Dr., Athens, GA 30602-4901. Karen Orchard, Dir. Short story collections and poetry, scholarly nonfiction and literary criticism, Southern and American history, regional studies, biography and autobiography. For nonfiction, query with outline and sample chapters. Poetry collections considered in September and January only; short fiction in June and July only. A $10 fee is required for all poetry and fiction submissions. Royalty. SASE for competition guidelines.

UNIVERSITY OF HAWAII PRESS—2840 Kolowalu St., Honolulu, HI 96822. Patricia Crosby, Pam Kelley, and Sharon Yamamoto, Eds. Scholarly books on Asian, Asian American, and Pacific studies from disciplines as diverse as the arts, history, language, literature, natural science, philosophy, religion, and the social sciences. Query with outline and sample chapters. Royalty.

UNIVERSITY OF ILLINOIS PRESS—1325 S. Oak St., Champaign, IL 61820. Richard L. Wentworth, Ed.-in-Chief. Short story collections, 140 to 180 pages; nonfiction; and poetry, 70 to 100 pages. Rarely considers multiple submissions. Query. Royalty. No unsolicited manuscripts at this time.

UNIVERSITY OF MINNESOTA PRESS—111 Third Ave. S., Suite 290, Minneapolis, MN 55401-2520. Nonfiction: literary and cultural theory, social and political theory; communications/media; anthropology; geography; international relations; Native American studies; regional titles, 50,000 to 225,000 words. Query with detailed prospectus or introduction, table of contents, sample chapter, and resumé. Royalty.

UNIVERSITY OF MISSOURI PRESS—2910 LeMone Blvd., Columbia, MO 65201-8227. Beverly Jarrett, Dir./Ed.in-Chief. Mr. Clair Wilcox, Acquisitions Ed. Scholarly books on American and European history; American, British, and Latin American literary criticism; political philosophy; intellectual history; regional studies; and short fiction.

UNIVERSITY OF NEBRASKA PRESS—312 N. 14th St., Lincoln, NE 68588-0484. Attn: Ed.-in-Chief. Specializes in the history of the American West, Native-American studies, literary and cultural nonfiction, fiction in translation, music, and sports history. Send proposals with summary, a sample chapter, and resumé. Write for guidelines for annual North American Indian Prose Award.

UNIVERSITY OF NEW MEXICO PRESS—Univ. of New Mexico, Albuquerque, NM 87131. Elizabeth C. Hadas, Ed. Dir. David V. Holtby, Larry Ball, Dana Asbury, and Barbara Guth, Eds. Scholarly nonfiction on social and cultural anthropology, archaeology, Western history, art, and photography. Query. Royalty.

UNIVERSITY OF NORTH CAROLINA PRESS—P.O. Box 2288, Chapel Hill, NC 27515-2288. David Perry, Ed.-in-Chief. General-interest books (75,000 to 125,000 words) on the lore, crafts, cooking, gardening, travel, and natural history of the Southeast. No fiction or poetry. Query preferred. Royalty.

UNIVERSITY OF NORTH TEXAS PRESS—P.O. Box 13856, Denton, TX 76203-6586. Frances B. Vick, Dir. Charlotte M. Wright, Assoc. Dir. Books on Western Americana, Texan culture, history (including regional), women's studies, multicultural studies, and folklore. Series include: "War and the Southwest" (perspectives, histories, and memories of war from authors living in the Southwest); "Western Life Series"; "Philosophy and the Environment Series"; and "Texas Writers" (critical biographies of Texas writers). Send manuscript or query with sample chapters; no multiple queries. Royalty.

UNIVERSITY OF OKLAHOMA PRESS—1005 Asp Ave., Norman, OK 73019-0445. John Drayton, Asst. Dir. Books, to 300 pages, on the history of the American West, Indians of the Americas, congressional studies, classical studies, literary criticism, natural history, and women's studies. Query. Royalty.

UNIVERSITY OF PITTSBURGH PRESS—3347 Forbes Ave., Pittsburgh, PA 15261. Attn: Eds. Scholarly nonfiction; poetry, for poets who have previously published full-length collections of poetry. Send manuscripts in September and October only; responds by late Spring. Send for rules.

UNIVERSITY OF SOUTH CAROLINA PRESS—205 Pickens St., Columbia, SC 29208. Fred Kameny, Ed.-in-Chief. Books on art and architecture, international relations, African-American studies, gardening and nature, business, history, cookbooks and culinary history, among other subjects. Submit outline with sample chapters. Royalty.

UNIVERSITY OF TENNESSEE PRESS—293 Communications Bldg., Knoxville, TN 37996-0325. Attn: Acquisitions. Nonfiction, regional trade, and regional fiction, 200 to 300 manuscript pages. No poetry. Query with outline and sample chapters. Royalty.

UNIVERSITY OF TEXAS PRESS—Div. of Univ. of Texas, Box 7819, Austin, TX 78713-7819. Joanna Hitchcock, Dir. Nonfiction books, 75,000 to 100,000 words. "Our press is located in the heart of Texas, but our books know no regional or even national boundaries." Query with outline. Royalty.

UNIVERSITY OF WISCONSIN PRESS—114 N. Murray St., Madison, WI 53715-1199. Attn: Acquisitions Ed. Scholarly nonfiction and regional books. Offers Brittingham Prize in Poetry and Pollak Prize in Poetry; query for details.

UNIVERSITY PRESS OF COLORADO—P.O. Box 849, Niwot, CO 80544. Attn: Ed. Dept. Scholarly books in the humanities, social sciences, and applied sciences. Fiction for new series.

THE UNIVERSITY PRESS OF KENTUCKY— 663 S. Limestone St., Lexington, KY 40508-4008. Nancy Grayson Holmes, Ed.-in-Chief. Scholarly books in the major fields. Serious nonfiction of general interest. Books related to Kentucky and the Ohio Valley, the Appalachians, and the South. No fiction, drama, or poetry. Query.

UNIVERSITY PRESS OF MISSISSIPPI— 3825 Ridgewood Rd., Jackson, MS 39211-6492. Seetha Srinivasan, Ed.-in-Chief. Scholarly and trade titles in American literature, history, and culture; southern studies; African-American, women's and American studies; social sciences; popular culture; folklife; art and architecture; natural sciences; and other liberal arts.

UNIVERSITY PRESS OF NEW ENGLAND—23 S. Main St., Hanover, NH 03755-2048. Attn: Ed. Dept. General and scholarly nonfiction. American history, literature, and cultural studies. Jewish studies, women's studies, studies of the New England region, and environmental studies, and performance studies. *Hardscrabble Books* imprint: fiction of New England, University Poetry Series.

VAN NOSTRAND REINHOLD—115 Fifth Ave., New York, NY 10003. Marianne Russell, CEO. Business, professional, scientific, and technical publishers of applied reference works. Hospitality, culinary, architecture, graphic and interior design, industrial and environmental health and safety, computer science, engineering, and technical management.

VANDAMERE PRESS—P.O. Box 5243, Arlington, VA 22205. Jerry Frank, Assoc. Acquisitions Ed. General trade, fiction and nonfiction, including history, military, parenting, healthcare/disability studies, and travel. Also books about the nation's capital for a national audience. Prefer to see outline with sample chapter for nonfiction; for fiction send 4 or 5 sample chapters. Multiple queries considered. Royalty. SASE required.

VIKING—375 Hudson St., New York, NY 10014. Barbara Grossman, Pub. Fiction and nonfiction. Nonfiction: psychology, sociology, child-rearing and development, cookbooks, sports, and popular culture. Query. Royalty.

VIKING CHILDREN'S BOOKS—375 Hudson St., New York, NY 10014. Attn: Ed. Dept. Fiction and nonfiction, including biography, history, and sports, for ages 7 to 14. Humor and picture books for ages 2 to 6. Query Children's Book Dept. with outline and sample chapter. For picture books, please send entire manuscript. SASE required. Royalty.

VILLARD BOOKS—201 E. 50th St., New York, NY 10022. Jennifer Webb, Assoc. Ed. Inspiration, how-to, biography, humor, etc. "We look for authors who are promotable and books we feel we can market well." Royalty.

VINTAGE BOOKS—201 E. 50th St., New York, NY 10022. Attn: Ed. Dept. Quality fiction and serious nonfiction. Query with sample chapters for fiction; query for nonfiction.

VOYAGER PAPERBACKS—See *Harcourt Brace & Co. Children's Book Div.*

VOYAGEUR PRESS—123 N. Second St., Stillwater, MN 55082. Todd R. Berger, Editorial Assoc. Books, 15,000 to 100,000 words, on wildlife, travel, Americana, collectibles, natural history, hunting and fishing, regional topics; and Native American fiction, any length. "Photography is very important for most of our books." Guidelines. Query with outline and sample chapters. Royalty.

WALKER AND COMPANY—435 Hudson St., New York, NY 10014. Attn: Ed. Dept. Adult fiction: mysteries. Adult nonfiction: Americana, biography, history, science, natural history, health, psychology, parenting, sports, popular science, self-help, business, and music. Juvenile nonfiction, including biography, science, history, music, and nature. Juvenile fiction: Middle grade and young adult novels. Query with synopsis and SASE. Guidelines. Royalty.

WARNER BOOKS—1271 Ave. of the Americas, New York, NY 10020. No unsolicited manuscripts or proposals.

WASHINGTON SQUARE PRESS—1230 Ave. of the Americas, New York, NY 10020. Nancy Miller, Dir. Agented work only.

WASHINGTON STATE UNIVERSITY PRESS—Cooper Publications Bldg., P.O. Box 645910, Pullman, WA 99164-5910. Keith Petersen, Acquisitions Ed. Glen Lindeman, Ed. Books on northwest history, prehistory, and culture, 200 to 350 pages. Query. Royalty.

WATTS, FRANKLIN—Sherman Turnpike, Danbury, CT 06813. Curriculum-oriented nonfiction for grades K to 12, including science, history, social studies, and biography. No unsolicited submissions.

WEE SING—See *Price Stern Sloan, Inc.*

WEISS ASSOCIATES, DANIEL—33 W. 17th St., New York, NY 10011. Kieran Scott, Ed. Asst. Book packager. Young adult books, 45,000 words; middle grade books, 33,000 words; elementary books, 10,000 to 12,000 words. Query with outline and 2 sample chapters. Royalty and flat fee.

WESLEYAN UNIVERSITY PRESS—110 Mt. Vernon St., Middletown, CT 06459-0433. Tom Radko, Dir. Wesleyan Poetry series: 64 to 80 pages. Query. Royalty.

WESTERN PUBLISHING CO., INC.—See *Golden Books Family Entertainment.*

WESTMINSTER JOHN KNOX PRESS—100 Witherspoon St., Louisville, KY 40202. Richard Brown, Dir. Stephanie Egnotovich, Man. Ed. Books that inform, interpret, challenge, and encourage Christian faith and living. Royalty. Send SASE for guidelines.

WHISPERING COYOTE PRESS—300 Crescent Ct., Suite 860, Dallas, TX 75201. Ms. Lou Alpert, Ed. Picture books, 32 pages, for readers ages 4 to 12. Submit complete manuscript with SASE. Royalty.

WHITE PINE PRESS—10 Village Sq., Fredonia, NY 14063. Elaine LaMattina, Ed. Novels, books of short stories, and essay collections, 250 to 350 pages. Query with outline and sample chapters. Royalty.

WHITECAP BOOKS—351 Lynn Ave., N. Vancouver, BC, Canada V7J 2C4. Colleen MacMillan, Pub. Juvenile books, 72 to 84 pages, and adult books, varying lengths, on such topics as natural history, gardening, cookery, parenting, history and regional subjects. Query with table of contents, synopsis, and one sample chapter. Royalty, occasionally flat fee.

WHITMAN, ALBERT— 6340 Oakton, Morton Grove, IL 60053. Kathleen Tucker, Ed. Picture books for preschool children; novels, biographies, mysteries, and nonfiction for middle-grade readers. Send complete manuscript for picture books, 3 chapters and outline for longer fiction; query for nonfiction. Royalty.

WILD ONION BOOKS—See *Loyola Press.*

WILDERNESS PRESS—2440 Bancroft Way, Berkeley, CA 94704. Caroline Winnett, Ed. Nonfiction: outdoor sports, recreation, and travel in the western U.S. Royalty.

WILEY & SONS, JOHN— 605 Third Ave., New York, NY 10158-0012. Attn: Ed. Dept. Nonfiction: science/technology; business/management; real estate; travel; cooking; biography; psychology; computers; language; history; current affairs; health; finance. Send proposals with outline, author vita, market information, and sample chapter. Royalty.

WILEY CHILDREN'S BOOKS— 605 Third Ave., New York, NY 10158-0012. Kate Bradford, Ed. Nonfiction books, 96 to 128 pages, for 8- to 12-year-old children. Query. Royalty.

WILLIAMSON PUBLISHING CO.—P.O. Box 185, Charlotte, VT 05445. Attn: Nonfiction Ed. Active learning books for children and teachers. No children's picture books. Writers must send annotated table of contents, 2 sample chapters, and SASE.

WILLOW CREEK PRESS— 9931 Hwy. 70 W., P.O. Box 147, Minocqua, WI 54548. Tom Petrie, Ed. Books, 25,000 to 50,000 words, on nature, wildlife, and outdoor sports. Query with sample chapters. No fiction. Royalty.

WILSHIRE BOOK COMPANY—12015 Sherman Rd., N. Hollywood, CA 91605-3781. Melvin Powers, Pub. Nonfiction: self-help, motivation/inspiration/spiritual, psychology, recovery, how-to, entrepreneurship, mail order, horsemanship, and how to make money on the Internet; minimum, 60,000 words. Fiction: allegories that teach principles of psychological/spiritual growth. Send synopsis/detailed chapter outline, 3 chapters, and SASE. Royalty.

WINDSWEPT HOUSE PUBLISHERS—Mt. Desert, ME 04660. Jane Weinberger, Pub. Children's picture books; young adult novels; adult fiction and nonfiction. Query.

WOODBINE HOUSE— 6510 Bells Mill Rd., Bethesda, MD 20817. Susan Stokes, Ed. Books for or about people with disabilities only. No personal accounts, poetry, or novels. Query or submit complete manuscript with SASE. Guidelines. Royalty.

WORDWARE PUBLISHING—1506 Capital Ave., Plano, TX 75074. James S. Hill, Ed., *Wordware Computer Books.* Mary Goldman, Ed., *Republic of Texas Press*: Texana, Southwest regional, historical nonfiction including tales and legends of the old west and "legendary" characters, military history, women of the west and country humor. Mary Goldman, Ed., *Seaside Press*: Cities uncovered history/guidebooks, pet care, humor. George Baxter, Ed., *Iron Castle Productions*: Game books and games. Query with sample chapters, manuscript completion date, and author experience. Royalty.

WORKMAN PUBLISHING CO., INC.—708 Broadway, New York, NY 10003. Attn: Ed. Dept. General nonfiction. Normal contractual terms based on agreement.

WORLDWIDE LIBRARY—225 Duncan Mill Rd., Don Mills, Ont., Canada M3B 3K9. Randall Toye, Ed. Dir. Feroze Mohammed, Sr. Ed. Action adventure series for *Gold Eagle* imprint; mystery fiction reprints only. No unsolicited manuscripts.

WYNDHAM HALL PRESS—52857 C.R. 21, Bristol, IN 46507. Milton L. Clayton, Pub. Academic nonfiction. Submit complete manuscript. Royalty.

YALE UNIVERSITY PRESS—Box 209040, New Haven, CT 06520-9040. Adult nonfiction, 400 manuscript pages. Query. Royalty.

YEARLING BOOKS—1540 Broadway, New York, NY 10036. Attn: Ed. Dept. Books for K through 6. Manuscripts accepted from agents only. Same address and requirements for *Skylark Books*.

ZONDERVAN PUBLISHING HOUSE—5300 Patterson S.E., Grand Rapids, MI 49530. Attn: Manuscript Review. Christian titles. General fiction and nonfiction; academic and professional books. Query with outline, sample chapter, and SASE. Royalty. Guidelines.

SYNDICATES

Syndicates buy material from writers and artists to sell to newspapers all over the country and the world. Authors are paid either a percentage of the gross proceeds or an outright fee. Of course, features by people well known in their fields have the best chance of being syndicated. In general, syndicates want columns that have been popular in a local newspaper or magazine. Since most syndicated fiction has been published previously in magazines or books, beginning fiction writers should try to sell their stories to magazines before submitting them to syndicates.

Always query syndicates before sending manuscripts, since their needs change frequently, and be sure to enclose SASEs with queries and manuscripts.

ARKIN MAGAZINE SYNDICATE—500 Bayview Dr., Suite F, N. Miami Beach, FL 33160. Joseph Arkin, Ed. Dir. Articles, 750 to 2,200 words, for trade and professional magazines. Must have small-business slant, be written in layman's language, and offer solutions to business problems. Articles should apply to many businesses, not just a specific industry. No columns. Pays 3¢ to 10¢ a word, on acceptance. SASE required; query not necessary.

CONTEMPORARY FEATURES SYNDICATE—P. O. Box 1258, Jackson, TN 38302-1258. Lloyd Russell, Ed. Articles, 1,000 to 10,000 words: how-to, money savers, business, etc. Self-help pieces for small business. Pays from $25, on acceptance. Query.

HARRIS & ASSOCIATES FEATURES—15915 Caminito Aire Puro, San Diego, CA 92128. Dick Harris, Ed. Sports- and family-oriented features, to 1,200 words; fillers and short humor, 500 to 800 words. Queries preferred. Pays varying rates.

THE HOLLYWOOD INSIDE SYNDICATE—Box 49957, Los Angeles, CA 90049-0957. John Austin, Dir. Feature articles, 750 to 2,500 words, on TV and film personalities with B&W photo(s). Article suggestions for 3-part series. Pieces on unusual medical and scientific breakthroughs. Pays on percentage basis for features, negotiated rates for ideas, on publication.

KING FEATURES SYNDICATE—235 E. 45th St., New York, NY 10017. Paul Eberhart, Exec. Ed. Columns, comics. "We do not consider or buy individual articles. We are interested in ideas for nationally syndicated columns." Submit cover letter, six sample columns of 650 words each, bio sheet and any additional clips, and SASE. No simultaneous submissions. Query with SASE for guidelines.

LOS ANGELES TIMES SYNDICATE—Times Mirror Sq., Los Angeles, CA 90053. Commentary, features, columns, editorial cartoons, comics, puzzles and games; news services and online products. Send SASE for submission guidelines.

NEW YORK TIMES SYNDICATION SALES—122 E. 42nd St., New York, NY 10168. Gloria Brown Anderson, Pres. Nanette Varian, Sr. Ed. Carolee Morrison, International Ed. Previously published health, lifestyle, and entertainment articles only, to 1,500 words. Query with published article or tear sheet and SASE. No calls please. Pays 50% royalty on collected sales.

NEWSPAPER ENTERPRISE ASSOCIATION—200 Madison Ave., 4th Fl., New York, NY 10016. Robert Levy, Exec. Ed. Ideas for new concepts in syndicated columns. No single stories or stringers. Payment by contractual arrangement.

SINGER MEDIA CORP.—#106, 1030 Calle Cordillera, San Clemente, CA 92673. Helen J. Lee, V.P. International syndication, some domestic. Subjects must be of global interest. Features: celebrity interviews and profiles, women's, health, fitness, self-help, business, computer, etc., all lengths; psychological quizzes; puzzles (no word puzzles) and games for children or adults. Pays 50%.

UNITED FEATURE SYNDICATE—200 Madison Ave., 4th Fl., New York, NY 10016-3903. Diana Loevy, V.P./Ed. Dir. No one-shots or series. Payment by contractual arrangement. Send samples with SASE.

UNITED PRESS INTERNATIONAL—1510 H St. N.W., Suite 600, Washington, DC 20005. Tobin Beck, Man. Ed., domestic; Howard Dicus, Gen. Mgr. No free-lance material.

LITERARY PRIZE OFFERS

Writers seeking the thrill of competition should review the extensive list of literary prize offers, many of them designed to promote the as yet unpublished author. All of the competitions listed here are for unpublished manuscripts and usually offer publication in addition to a cash prize. The prestige that comes with winning some of the more established awards can do much to further a writer's career, as editors, publishers, and agents are likely to consider the future work of the prizewinner more closely.

There are hundreds of literary contests open to writers in all genres, and the following list covers a representative number of them. The summaries given below are intended merely as guides; since submission requirements are more detailed than space allows, writers should send an SASE for complete guidelines before entering any contest. Writers are also advised to check the monthly "Prize Offers" column of *The Writer* Magazine (120 Boylston St., Boston, MA 02116-4615) for additional contest listings and up-to-date contest requirements. Deadlines are annual unless otherwise noted.

✔**ACADEMY OF AMERICAN POETS**—Walt Whitman Award, 584 Broadway, Suite 1208, New York, NY 10012-3250. An award of $5,000 plus publication and a one-month residency at the Vermont Studio Center is offered for a book-length poetry manuscript by a poet who has not yet published a volume of poetry. Deadline: November 15. Entry fee.

ACADEMY OF MOTION PICTURE ARTS AND SCIENCES—The Nicholl Fellowships, Dept. WR, 8949 Wilshire Blvd., Beverly Hills, CA 90211-1972. Up to five fellowships of $25,000 each are awarded for original screenplays that display exceptional craft and engaging storytelling. Deadline: May 1. Entry fee.

ACTORS' PLAYHOUSE—National Children's Theatre Festival, Miracle Theatre, 280 Miracle Mile, Coral Gables, FL 33134. Attn: Thomas Pender, Education Dir. First prize of $1,000 plus production and a second prize of $300 is awarded for a musical, 45 to 60 minutes running time, for 5- to 12-year olds. Prizes of $500 plus production and two $100 prizes are awarded for plays 40 to 50 minutes long, for ages 12 to 17. Deadline: April 30. Entry fee.

ACTORS THEATRE OF LOUISVILLE—Ten-Minute Play Contest, 316 W. Main St., Louisville, KY 40202-4218. A prize of $1,000 is offered for a previously unproduced ten-page script. Deadline: December 1.

AMERICAN ACADEMY OF ARTS AND LETTERS—Richard Rogers Awards, 633 W. 155th St., New York, NY 10032. Offers subsidized productions or staged readings in New York City by a nonprofit theater for a musical, play with music, thematic review, or any comparable work. Deadline: November 1.

AMERICAN ANTIQUARIAN SOCIETY—Fellowships for Historical Research, 185 Salisbury St., Worcester, MA 01609-1634. Attn: John B. Hench. At least three fellowships are awarded to creative and performing artists, writers, filmmakers, and journalists for research on pre-20th century American history. Residencies are four- to eight-weeks; travel expenses and stipends of $1,200 per month are offered. Deadline: October 1.

THE AMERICAN-SCANDINAVIAN FOUNDATION—Translation Prize, 725 Park Ave., New York, NY 10021. A prize of $2,000 is awarded for an outstanding English translation of poetry, fiction, drama, or literary prose originally written in Danish, Finnish, Icelandic, Norwegian, or Swedish. Second prize is $500. Deadline: June 1.

ANHINGA PRESS—Anhinga Prize for Poetry, P.O. Box 10595, Tallahassee, FL 32302-0595. A $2,000 prize will be awarded for an unpublished full-length collection of poetry, 48 to 72 pages, by a poet who has published no more than one full-length collection. Deadline: March 15. Entry fee.

ARMY MAGAZINE—Essay Contest, Box 1560, Arlington, VA 22210. Prizes of $1,000, $500, and $250 plus publication are awarded for essays on a given theme. Deadline: May 31.

THE ASSOCIATED WRITING PROGRAMS—Awards Series, Tallwood House, Mail Stop 1E3, George Mason Univ., Fairfax, VA 22030. In the categories of poetry, short fiction, the novel, and nonfiction, the prize is book publication and a $2,000 honorarium. Deadline: February 29. Entry fee.

ASSOCIATION OF JEWISH LIBRARIES—Sydney Taylor Manuscript Competition, 1327 Wyntercreek Ln., Dunwoody, GA 30338. Attn: Paula Sandfelder, Coordinator. Offers $1,000 for the best fiction manuscript, 64 to 200 pages, by an unpublished book author, writing for readers 8 to 11. Stories must have a positive Jewish focus. Deadline: January 15.

BAKER'S PLAYS—High School Playwriting Contest, 100 Chauncy St., Boston, MA 02111. Plays about the high school experience, written by high school students, are eligible for awards of $500, $250, and $100. Deadline: January 31.

BANTAM DOUBLEDAY DELL BOOKS FOR YOUNG READERS—Marguerite de Angeli Prize, Dept. BFYR, 1540 Broadway, New York, NY 10036. A prize of $1,500 and a $3,500 advance against royalties is awarded for a middle-grade fiction manuscript that explores the diversity of the American experience. Open to U.S. and Canadian writers who have not previously published a novel for middle-grade readers. Deadline: June 30.

✔ **BARNARD COLLEGE**—New Women Poets Prize, Women Poets at Barnard, Columbia Univ., 3009 Broadway, New York, NY 10027-6598. Attn: Directors. A prize of $1,500 and publication by Beacon Press is offered for an unpublished poetry manuscript, 50 to 100 pages, by a female poet who has never published a book of poetry. Deadline: October 15.

THE BELLETRIST REVIEW—Fiction Contest, Marmarc Publications, P.O. Box 596, Plainville, CT 06062-0596. Prize of $200 plus publication is awarded for an unpublished short story, 2,500 to 5,000 words. Deadline: July 15. Entry fee.

THE BELLINGHAM REVIEW—Tobias Wolff Award in Fiction/49th Parallel Poetry Award, MS-9053, Western Washington Univ., Bellingham, WA 98225. Tobias Wolff Award in Fiction: Offers prizes of $500 plus publication, $250, and $100 for a short story or novel excerpt. Deadline: March 1. Annie Dillard Award in Nonfiction: Offers prizes of $500 plus publication, $250, and $100 for previously unpublished essays. Deadline: March 1. 49th Parallel Poetry Award: Offers publication and prizes of $500, $250, and $100 for individual poems. Deadline: November 30. Entry fees.

BEVERLY HILLS THEATRE GUILD/JULIE HARRIS PLAYWRIGHT AWARD—2815 N. Beachwood Dr., Los Angeles, CA 90068. Attn: Marcella Meharg. Offers prize of $5,000, plus possible $2,000 for productions in Los Angeles area, for previously unproduced and unpublished full-length play. A

$2,000 second prize and $1,000 third prize are also offered. Deadline: November 1.

✔**BIRMINGHAM-SOUTHERN COLLEGE**—Hackney Literary Awards, Box 549003, Birmingham, AL 35254. A prize of $2,000 is awarded for an unpublished novel, any length. Deadline: September 30. Also, a $2,000 prize is shared for the winning short story, to 5,000 words, and poem of up to 50 lines. Deadline: December 31. Entry fees.

BLUE MOUNTAIN CENTER—Richard J. Margolis Award, 294 Washington St., Suite 610, Boston, MA 02108. A prize of $1,000 is awarded annually to a promising journalist or essayist whose work combines warmth, humor, wisdom, and a concern with social issues. Applications should include up to 30 pages of published or unpublished work. Deadline: June 1.

BOISE STATE UNIVERSITY—The Rocky Mountain Artists' Book Competition, Hemingway Western Studies Center, Boise, ID 83725. Tom Trusky, Ed. A prize of $500 and publication is awarded for up to 3 books; manuscripts (text and/or visual content) and proposals are considered for the short-run printing of books on public issues, especially the Inter-Mountain West. Deadline: year-round.

BOSTON REVIEW—Short Story Contest, E53-407, MIT, Cambridge, MA 02139. A prize of $300 plus publication is awarded for the best previously unpublished story of up to 4,000 words. Deadline: October 1. Entry fee.

ARCH AND BRUCE BROWN FOUNDATION—P.O. Box 45231, Phoenix, AZ 85064. Offers $1,000 grants for positive gay and lesbian fiction. Deadline: May 31.

BUCKNELL UNIVERSITY—The Philip Roth Residence in Creative Writing, Stadler Center for Poetry, Bucknell Univ., Lewisburg, PA 17837. Attn: Cynthia Hogue, Dir. The fall residency, which includes studio, lodging, meals, and a $1,000 stipend, may be used by a writer, over 21, not currently enrolled in a university, to work on a first or second book. The residency is awarded in odd-numbered years to a fiction writer, and in even-numbered years to a poet. Deadline: March 1.

CENTER FOR BOOK ARTS—Poetry Chapbook Prize, Center for Book Arts, 626 Broadway, 5th Floor, New York, NY 10012. Offers $1,000, publication and a public reading for poetry manuscript, to 500 lines. Deadline: December 31. Entry fee.

CHELSEA AWARD COMPETITION—P.O. Box 1040, York Beach, ME 03910. Attn: Ed. Prizes of $750 plus publication are awarded for the best unpublished short fiction and poetry. Deadlines: June 15 (fiction); December 15 (poetry). Entry fees.

THE CHICAGO TRIBUNE—Nelson Algren Awards, 435 N. Michigan Ave., Chicago, IL 60611. A first prize of $5,000 and three runner-up prizes of $1,000 are awarded for outstanding unpublished short stories, 2,500 to 10,000 words, by American writers. Deadline: February 1.

✔**CLAREMONT GRADUATE SCHOOL**—Kingsley Tufts Poetry Awards, 160 E. 10th St., Claremont, CA 91711. An award of $50,000 is given to an American poet whose work is judged most worthy. An award of $5,000 is given to an emerging poet whose work displays extraordinary promise. Books of poetry published or manuscripts completed in the calendar year are considered. Deadline: September 15.

CLAUDER COMPETITION—P.O. Box 383259, Cambridge, MA 02238-3259. Awards $2,500 plus professional production for a full-length play by a New England writer. Runner-up prizes of $500 and a staged reading also awarded. Deadline: June 30 (of odd-numbered years).

✔ **CLEVELAND STATE UNIVERSITY POETRY CENTER**—Poetry Center Prize, Dept. of English, Rhodes Tower, Rm. 1815, 1983 E. 24th St., Cleveland, OH 44115-2440. Publication and $1,000 are awarded for a previously unpublished book-length volume of poetry. Deadline: March 1. Entry fee.

COALITION FOR THE ADVANCEMENT OF JEWISH EDUCATION—David Dornstein Memorial Creative Writing Contest, 261 W. 35th St., Floor 12A, New York, NY 10001. Publication and prizes of $700, $200, and $100 are awarded for the three best original, previously unpublished short stories, to 5,000 words, on a Jewish theme or topic, by writers age 18 to 35. Deadline: December 31.

COLONIAL PLAYERS, INC.—Promising Playwright Award, 98 Tower Dr., Stevensville, MD 21666. Attn: Fran Marchano. A prize of $750 plus possible production will be awarded for the best full-length play by a resident of MD, DC, VA, WV, DE, or PA. Deadline: December 31 (of even-numbered years).

COLORADO STATE UNIVERSITY—Colorado Prize for Poetry, Colorado Review, Dept. of English, Fort Collins, CO 80523. Attn: David Milofsky, Ed. Offers $1,000 plus publication for collection of original poems. Deadline: January 15. Entry fee.

COMMUNITY CHILDREN'S THEATRE OF KANSAS CITY—8021 E. 129th Terrace, Grandview, MO 64030. Attn: Mrs. Blanche Sellens, Dir. A prize of $500, plus production, is awarded for the best play, up to one hour long, to be performed by adults for elementary school audiences. Deadline: January 31.

COMMUNITY WRITERS ASSOCIATION—CWA Writing Contest, P.O. Box 312, Providence, RI 02901. A prize of $250 plus free conference tuition is offered for short stories, to 2,000 words, and poetry, any length. Deadline: June 1. Entry fee.

EUGENE V. DEBS FOUNDATION—Bryant Spann Memorial Prize, Dept. of History, Indiana State Univ., Terre Haute, IN 47809. Offers a prize of $1,000 for a published or unpublished article or essay on themes relating to social protest or human equality. Deadline: April 30.

DEEP SOUTH WRITERS CONFERENCE—Contest Clerk, Drawer 44691, Univ. of Southwestern Louisiana, Lafayette, LA 70504-4691. Prizes ranging from $50 to $300 are offered for unpublished manuscripts in the following categories: Fiction (including science fiction); Novel; Nonfiction; Poetry; Drama; and French literature. Deadline: July 15. Miller Award: offers $500 for a play dealing with some aspect of the life of Edward de Vere (1550-1604), the 17th Earl of Oxford. Deadline: July 15 (of odd-numbered years). Entry fee.

DELACORTE PRESS—Prize for First Young Adult Novel, Bantam Doubleday Dell BFYR, 1540 Broadway, New York, NY 10036. A writer who has not previously published a young adult novel may submit a book-length manuscript with a contemporary setting suitable for readers ages 12 to 18. The prize is $1,500, a $6,000 advance, and hardcover and paperback publication. Deadline: December 31.

DRURY COLLEGE—Playwriting Contest, 900 N. Benton Ave., Springfield, MO 65802. Attn: Sandy Asher, Writer-in-Residence. Prizes of $300 and two $150 honorable mentions, plus possible production, are awarded for original, previously unproduced one-act plays. Deadline: December 1 (of even-numbered years).

DUBUQUE FINE ARTS PLAYERS—One-Act Playwriting Contest, 1321 Tomahawk Dr., Dubuque, IA 52003. Attn: Jennifer G. Stabenow, Coordinator. Prizes of $600, $300 and $200 plus possible production are awarded for unproduced, original one-act plays of up to 40 minutes. Deadline: January 31. Entry fee.

DUKE UNIVERSITY—Dorothea Lange-Paul Taylor Prize, Prize Committee, Center for Documentary Studies, Box 90802, Duke Univ., Durham, NC 27708-0802. A grant of up to $10,000 is awarded to a writer and photographer working together in the formative stages of a documentary project that will ultimately result in a publishable work. Deadline: January 31. Entry fee.

ELF: ECLECTIC LITERARY FORUM—Ruth Cable Memorial Prize, P.O. Box 392, Tonawanda, NY 14150. Awards of $500 and three $50 prizes are given for poems up to 50 lines. Short Fiction Prize awards $500 plus publication and two $50 prizes for stories, to 3,500 words. Deadline: March 31. Fiction deadline: August 31. Entry fee.

EMPORIA STATE UNIVERSITY—Bluestem Award, English Dept., Emporia State Univ., Emporia, KS 66801-5087. A prize of $1,000 plus publication is awarded for a previously unpublished book of poems by a U.S. author. Deadline: March 1. Entry fee.

THE FLORIDA REVIEW—The Editors Awards (specify Fiction, Nonfiction, or Poetry), Dept. of English, Univ. of Central Florida, Orlando, FL 32816-0001. Attn: Russell Kesler, Ed. Prizes of $500 plus publication are offered for short stories, essays, and creative nonfiction to 7,500 words, as well as groups of 3 to 5 poems, to 25 lines. Deadline: March 15. Entry fee.

FLORIDA STUDIO THEATRE—Shorts Contest, 1241 N. Palm Ave., Sarasota, FL 34236. Attn: Christian Angermann. Short scripts, songs, and other performance pieces on a given theme are eligible for a prize of $500. Deadline: February 15.

THE FORMALIST—Howard Nemerov Sonnet Award, 320 Hunter Dr., Evansville, IN 47711. A prize of $1,000 plus publication is offered for a previously unpublished, original sonnet. Deadline: June 15. Entry fee.

FOUR WAY BOOKS—The Levis Poetry Prize, P.O. Box 535, Village Sta., New York, NY 10014. Attn: M. Barrett. Awards $2,000 plus publication for a book-length collection of poems by a U.S. poet. Deadline: April 30. Entry fee.

GEORGE MASON UNIVERSITY—Greg Grummer Award in Poetry, *Phoebe: A Journal of Literary Arts*, 4400 Univ. Dr., Fairfax, VA 22030. A prize of $500 plus publication is offered for an outstanding previously unpublished poem. Deadline: December 15. Entry fee.

GEORGE WASHINGTON UNIVERSITY—Jenny McKean Moore Writer-in-Washington, Dept. of English, Washington, DC 20052. Attn: Prof. Christopher Sten. A salaried teaching position for two semesters is offered to a creative writer (of various mediums in alternate years) having "significant publications and a demonstrated commitment to teaching. The writer need not have conventional academic credentials." Deadline: November 15.

GLIMMER TRAIN PRESS—Semiannual Short Story Award for New Writers, 710 S.W. Madison St., #504, Portland, OR 97205. Writers whose fiction has never appeared in a nationally distributed publication are eligible to enter their stories of 1,200 to 7,500 words. Prizes are $1,200 plus publication, $500, and $300. Deadlines: March 31; September 30. Entry fee.

GREENFIELD REVIEW LITERARY CENTER—North American Native Authors First Book Awards, P.O. Box 308, 2 Middle Grove Rd., Greenfield Center, NY 12833. Attn: Joseph Bruchac, Dir. Native Americans of American Indian, Aleut, Inuit, or Metis ancestry who have not yet published a book are eligible to enter poetry, 64 to 100 pages, and prose, 200 to 300 pages (fiction or nonfiction) for $500 prizes plus publication. Deadline: March 15.

GROLIER POETRY PRIZE—6 Plympton St., Cambridge, MA 02138. Two $150 honorariums are awarded for poetry manuscripts of up to 10 double-spaced pages, including no more than five previously unpublished poems, by writers who have not yet published a book of poems. Deadline: May 1. Entry fee.

HEEKIN GROUP FOUNDATION—Fiction Fellowships Competition, Box 1534, Sisters, OR 97759. Awards the following fellowships to beginning career writers: two $1,500 Tara Fellowships in Short Fiction; two $3,000 James Fellowships for a Novel in Progress; one $2,000 Mary Molloy Fellowship for a Juvenile Novel in Progress (address H.G.F., P.O. Box 209, Middlebury, VT 05753; and one $2,000 Siobhan Fellowhip for a Nonfiction Essay (address H.G.F., P.O. Box 3385, Stamford, CT 06905). Writers who have never published a novel, a children's novel, more than five short stories in national publication, or an essay are eligible to enter. Deadline: December 1. Entry fee.

✔ **HELICON NINE EDITIONS**—Literary Prizes, 3607 Pennsylvania, Kansas City, MO 64111. Marianne Moore Poetry Prize: offers $1,000 for an original unpublished poetry manuscript of at least 48 pages. Willa Cather Fiction Prize: offers $1,000 for an original novella or short story collection, from 150 to 300 pages. Deadline: May 1. Entry fee.

✔ **LORIAN HEMINGWAY SHORT STORY COMPETITION**—P.O. Box 993, Key West, FL 33041. Awards a $1,000 prize to an original, unpublished short story, to 3,000 words by a writer whose fiction has never appeared in a nationally distributed publication. Deadline: June 1. Entry fee.

HIGHLIGHTS FOR CHILDREN—Fiction Contest, 803 Church St., Honesdale, PA 18431. Three $1,000 prizes plus publication are offered for stories on a given subject, up to 900 words. Deadline: February 28.

RUTH HINDMAN FOUNDATION—H.E. Francis Award, Dept. of English, Univ. of Alabama, Huntsville, AL 35899. A prize of $1,000 plus publication is awarded for a short story of up to 5,000 words. Deadline: December 31. Entry fee.

L. RON HUBBARD'S WRITERS OF THE FUTURE CONTEST—P.O. Box 1630, Los Angeles, CA 90078. Unpublished fiction writers are eligible to enter science fiction or fantasy short stories under 10,000 words, or novellas under 17,000 words. Quarterly prizes: $1,000, $750, and $500. Annual prize: $4,000. Deadlines: March 31; June 30; September 30; December 31.

IUPUI CHILDREN'S THEATRE—Playwriting Competition, Indiana University-Purdue University at Indianapolis, 525 N. Blackford St., Indianapolis, IN 46202-3120. Offers four $1,000 prizes plus staged readings for plays for young people. Deadline: September 1 (of even-numbered years).

ALICE JAMES BOOKS—Beatrice Hawley Award, Univ. of Maine at Farmington, 98 Main St., Farmington, ME 04938. A prize of publication plus

100 free copies is offered for the best poetry manuscript, 60 to 70 pages. Deadline: January 15. Entry fee.

JOE JEFFERSON PLAYERS ORIGINAL PLAY COMPETITION—P.O. Box 66065, Mobile, AL 36660. A prize of $1,000 plus production is offered for an original, previously unproduced play. Deadline: March 1.

JEWISH COMMUNITY CENTER THEATRE—Dorothy Silver Playwriting Competition, 3505 Mayfield Rd., Cleveland Heights, OH 44118. Attn: Elaine Rembrandt, Dir. Offers $1,000 and a staged reading for an original, previously unproduced full-length play, on some aspect of the Jewish experience. Deadline: December 15.

CHESTER H. JONES FOUNDATION—National Poetry Competition, P. O. Box 498, Chardon, OH 44024. Prizes of $1,000, $750, $500, $250, and $100, as well as several $50 and $10 prizes are awarded for original, unpublished poems of up to 32 lines. Deadline: March 31. Entry fee.

JAMES JONES SOCIETY—First Novel Fellowship, c/o Dept. of English, Wilkes Univ., Wilkes-Barre, PA 18766. An award of $2,500 is offered for a first novel-in-progress by an American. Deadline: March 1. Entry fee.

THE JOURNAL: THE LITERARY MAGAZINE OF O.S.U.—The Ohio State Univ. Press, 180 Pressey Hall, 1070 Carmack Rd., Columbus, OH 43210-1002. Attn: David Citino, Poetry Ed. Awards $1,000 plus publication for at least 48 pages of original, unpublished poetry. Deadline: September 30. Entry fee.

KALLIOPE: A JOURNAL OF WOMEN'S ART—Sue Saniel Elkind Poetry Contest, Florida Community College at Jacksonville, 3939 Roosevelt Blvd., Jacksonville, FL 32205. Publication and $1,000 are awarded for the best poem, under 50 lines, written by a woman. Deadline: October 30. Entry fee.

KEATS/KERLAN MEMORIAL FELLOWSHIP—The Ezra Jack Keats Memorial Fellowship Committee, 109 Walter Library, 117 Pleasant St. S.E., Univ. of Minnesota, Minneapolis, MN 55455. A $1,500 fellowship is awarded to a talented writer and/or illustrator of children's books who wishes to use the Kerlan Collection for furtherance of his or her artistic development. Deadline: May 1.

KENT STATE UNIVERSITY PRESS—Stan and Tom Wick Poetry Prize, P.O. Box 5190, Kent, OH 44242-0001. Publication and $1,000 are offered for a book of poems, 48 to 68 pages, by a writer who has not previously published a collection of poetry. Deadline: May 1. Entry fee.

LIVE OAK THEATRE—New Play Award, 200 Colorado St., Austin, TX 78701. Attn: Michael Hankin. Offers $1,000 plus possible production for the best full-length, unproduced, unpublished play. Deadline: April 1.

LODI ARTS COMMISSION—Drama Festival, 125 S. Hutchins St., Suite D, Lodi, CA 95240. A prize of $1,000 plus production is awarded for a full-length play; a prize of $500 plus production is awarded for a children's play. Deadline: April 1 (of odd-numbered years).

LOVE CREEK PRODUCTIONS—One-Ace Play Festivals, 79 Liberty Pl., Weehawken, NJ 07087-7014. One-act plays and theme-based plays are awarded production or staged readings. Deadlines vary.

AMY LOWELL POETRY TRAVELLING SCHOLARSHIP—Choate, Hall & Stewart, Exchange Pl., 53 State St., Boston, MA 02109-2891. Attn: F. Davis Dassori. A scholarship of approximately $29,000 is awarded for a poet to spend the year abroad to advance the art of poetry. Deadline: October 15.

THE MADISON REVIEW—Dept. of English, 600 N. Park St., Helen C. White Hall, Univ. of Wisconsin-Madison, Madison, WI 53706. Phyllis Smart Young Prize in Poetry: awards $500 plus publication for a group of three unpublished poems. Chris O'Malley Prize in Fiction: awards $500 plus publication for an unpublished short story. Deadline: September 30. Entry fees.

MIDDLEBURY COLLEGE—Katharine Bakeless Nason Prizes, c/o Bread Loaf Writers' Conference, Middlebury College, Middlebury, VT 05753. Attn: Carol Knauss. Publication and fellowships to the Bread Loaf Writers' Conference are offered for previously unpublished first books of poetry, fiction, and nonfiction. Deadline: March 1. Entry fee.

MID-LIST PRESS—First Series Awards, 4324 12th Ave. S., Minneapolis, MN 55407-3218. Publication and an advance against royalties are awarded for first books in the following categories: a novel in any genre, from 50,000 words; poetry, from 65 pages; short fiction, from 50,000 words; creative nonfiction, from 50,000 words. Deadline: February 1 (novel and poetry); July 1 (short fiction and creative nonfiction). Entry fees.

MIDWEST RADIO THEATRE WORKSHOP—MRTW Script Contests, 915 E. Broadway, Columbia, MO 65201. Workshop Script Contest: offers $800 in prizes, to be divided among two to four winners, and free workshop participation for contemporary radio scripts, 25 to 30 minutes long. Deadline: November 15. Entry fee.

MIDWEST THEATRE NETWORK—Biennial Rochester Playwright Festival, 5031 Tongen Ave. N.W., Rochester, MN 55901. Five to eight scripts of various lengths and types are chosen for festival production. Deadline: November 30 (of odd-numbered years).

MILL MOUNTAIN THEATRE—New Play Competition, 2nd Floor, One Market Square, Roanoke, VA 24011-1437. Attn: Jo Weinstein. Offers a $1,000 prize and staged reading, with possible full production, for an unpublished, unproduced, full-length or one-act play or musical. Cast size to ten. Deadline: January 1.

MISSISSIPPI REVIEW—Prize for Short Fiction and Poetry, The Center for Writers, Univ. of Southern Mississippi, Box 5144, Hattiesburg, MS 39406-5144. Attn: R. Fortenberry. Publication and $1,000 are offered for the best short story; $500 plus publication for the best poem. Deadline: May 31. Entry fee.

THE MISSOURI REVIEW—Editors' Prize, 1507 Hillcrest Hall, UMC, Columbia, MO 65211. Publication plus $1,500 is awarded for a short fiction manuscript (25 pages); $1,000 for an essay (25 pages); and $1,500 for poetry (10 pages). Deadline: October 15. Entry fee.

THE MOUNTAINEERS BOOKS—The Barbara Savage/"Miles from Nowhere" Memorial Award, 1001 S. W. Klickitat Way, Suite 201, Seattle, WA 98134. Offers a $3,000 cash award, plus publication and a $12,000 guaranteed advance against royalties for an outstanding unpublished, book-length manuscript of a nonfiction, personal-adventure narrative. Deadline: October 1 (of even-numbered years).

NATIONAL ENDOWMENT FOR THE ARTS—Nancy Hanks Center, 1100 Pennsylvania Ave. N.W., Room 720, Washington, DC 20506. Attn: Dir., Literature Program. Offers fellowships to writers and translators of poetry, fiction, plays, and creative nonfiction. Deadline: varies.

NATIONAL FEDERATION OF STATE POETRY SOCIETIES—Poetry Manuscript Contest, 3520 St. Rd. 56, Mechanicsburg, OH 43044. Attn: Amy Zook, Chairman. A prize of $1,000 is awarded for the best manuscript of poetry, 35 to 60 pages. Deadline: October 15. Entry fee.

NATIONAL POETRY SERIES—P.O. Box G, Hopewell, NJ 08525. Attn: Emily Wylie, Coordinator. Sponsors Annual Open Competition for unpublished book-length poetry manuscripts. Five manuscripts are selected for publication, and each winner receives a $1,000 award. Deadline: February 15. Entry fee.

NEW ENGLAND POETRY CLUB—Annual Contests, 11 Puritan Rd., Arlington, MA 02172. Attn: Virginia Thayer. Prizes range from $100 to $500 in various contests for members, nonmembers, and students. Deadline: April 15. Entry fee.

NEW ENGLAND THEATRE CONFERENCE—John Gassner Memorial Playwriting Award, c/o Dept. of Theatre, Northeastern Univ., 360 Huntington Ave., Boston, MA 02115. A $1,000 first prize and a $500 second prize are offered for unpublished, unproduced full-length plays written by New England residents or members of the NETC. Deadline: April 15. Entry fee.

NEW ISSUES PRESS/WESTERN MICHIGAN UNIVERSITY—New Issues Poetry Prize, Western Michigan Univ., Kalamazoo, MI 49008-5092. Attn: Herbert Scott, Ed. Awards $1,000 plus publication for a book-length collection of poetry by a poet who has never before published a full-length collection. Deadline: November 30. Entry fee.

NEW LETTERS—University of Missouri-Kansas City, 5100 Rockhill Rd., Kansas City, MO 64110-2499. Offers $750 for the best short story, to 5,000 words; $750 for the best group of three to six poems; $500 for the best essay, to 5,000 words. The work of each winner and first runner-up will be published. Deadline: May 15. Entry fee.

NEW YORK UNIVERSITY PRESS—New York University Press Prizes, 70 Washington Sq. S., 2nd Fl., New York, NY 10012-1091. Awards $1,000 plus publication to a book-length poetry manuscript and a book-length fiction manuscript. Deadline: May 1.

NIMROD/HARDMAN AWARDS—*Nimrod International Journal*, 600 S. College Ave., Tulsa, OK 74104-3189. Katherine Anne Porter Prize: offers prizes of $2,000 and $1,000 for fiction, to 7,500 words. Pablo Neruda Prize: offers prizes of $2,000 and $1,000 for one long poem or a selection of poems. Deadline: April 15. Entry fees.

NORTH CAROLINA WRITERS' NETWORK—International Literature Prizes, 3501 Hwy. 54 West, Studio C, Chapel Hill, NC 27516. Thomas Wolfe Fiction Prize: offers $500 for a previously unpublished short story or novel excerpt. Deadline: August 31. Paul Green Playwrights Prize: offers $500 for a previously unproduced, unpublished play. Deadline: September 30. Randall Jarrell Poetry Prize: offers $500 for a previously unpublished poem. Deadline: November 1. Entry fees.

NORTHEASTERN UNIVERSITY PRESS—Samuel French Morse Poetry Prize, English Dept., 406 Holmes, Northeastern Univ., Boston, MA 02115. Attn: Prof. Guy Rotella, Chairman. Offers $500 plus publication for a full-length poetry manuscript by a U.S. poet who has published no more than one book of poems. Deadline: August 1 (for inquiries); September 15 (for entries). Entry fee.

NORTHERN KENTUCKY UNIVERSITY—Y.E.S. New Play Festival, Dept. of Theatre, FA 227, Nunn Dr., Highland Hts., KY 41099-1007. Attn: Mike King, Project Dir. Awards three $400 prizes plus production for previously unproduced full-length plays and musicals. Deadline: October 15 (of even-numbered years).

NORTHERN MICHIGAN UNIVERSITY—Mildred & Albert Panowski Playwriting Competition, Forest Roberts Theatre, Northern Michigan Univ., 1401 Presque Isle Ave., Marquette, MI 49855-5364. Awards $2,000, plus production for an original, full-length, previously unproduced and unpublished play. Deadline: November 15.

OFF CENTER THEATER—Women Playwright's Festival, Tampa Bay Performing Arts Center, P.O. Box 518, Tampa, FL 33601. A $1,000 prize, production, and travel are offered for the best play about women, written by a woman; runner up receives staged reading. Deadline: September 15. Entry fee.

OLD DOMINION UNIVERSITY—Vassar Miller Prize in Poetry, c/o English Dept., Old Dominion University, Norfolk, VA 23529. Attn: Scott Cairns, Series Ed. Awards $500 plus publication by the University of North Texas Press for an original, unpublished poetry manuscript, 50 to 80 pages. Deadline: October 31. Entry fee.

O'NEILL THEATER CENTER—National Playwrights Conference, 234 W. 44th St., Suite 901, New York, NY 10036. Attn: Mary F. McCabe. Offers stipend, staged readings, and room and board at the conference, for new stage and television plays. Deadline: December 1. Entry fee.

PASSAGES NORTH—Elinor Benedict Poetry Prize, Dept. of English, Northern Michigan Univ., 1401 Presque Isle Ave., Marquette, MI 49855. Offers $500 prize for unpublished poem. Deadline: December 1. Entry fee.

PEN CENTER USA WEST—International Imitation Hemingway Contest, 672 S. Lafayette Park Pl., #41, Los Angeles, CA 90057. Offers round-trip airline tickets and dinner for two at Harry's Bar & American Grill in Florence, Italy, plus publication in *The Paris Review* of the winning one-page Hemingway imitation. Deadline: March 15.

PEN CENTER USA WEST—Grants for Writers with HIV/AIDS, 672 S. Lafayette Park Pl., #41, Los Angeles, CA 90057. Grants of $1,000 are awarded to writers with HIV/AIDS to continue and/or finish a current literary project. Writers living in the western U.S. who have been actively involved in creating literary work during the past three years are eligible to apply. Deadline: October 1.

PEN/JERARD FUND AWARD—PEN American Center, 568 Broadway, New York, NY 10012. Attn: John Morrone, Programs & Publications. Offers $4,000 to beginning female writers for a work-in-progress of general nonfiction. Applicants must have published at least one article in a national magazine or major literary magazine, but not more than one book of any kind. Deadline: January 1 (of odd-numbered years).

PEN WRITERS FUND—PEN American Center, 568 Broadway, New York, NY 10012. Attn: India Amos, Writers Fund Coordinator. Grants and interest-free loans of up to $500 are available to published writers or produced playwrights facing unanticipated financial emergencies. If the emergency is due to HIV- and AIDS-related illness, professional writers and editors qualify through the Fund for Writers and Editors with AIDS; all decisions are confidential. Deadline: year-round.

PEN WRITING AWARDS FOR PRISONERS—PEN American Center, 568 Broadway, New York, NY 10012. County, state, and federal prisoners are eligible to enter one unpublished manuscript, to 5,000 words, in each of these categories: fiction, drama, and nonfiction. Prisoners may submit up to 10 poems (any form) in the poetry category (to 20 pages total). Prizes of $100, $50, and $25 are awarded in each category. Deadline: September 1.

PEREGRINE SMITH POETRY SERIES—Gibbs Smith, Publisher, P.O. Box 667, Layton, UT 84041. Offers a $500 prize plus publication for a previously unpublished 64-page poetry manuscript. Deadline: April 30. Entry fee.

PETERLOO POETS—Open Competition, 2 Kelly Gardens, Calstock, Cornwall PL18 9SA, U.K. Prizes totalling 5,100 British pounds, including a grand prize of #4,000 plus publication, are awarded for poems of up to 40 lines. Deadline: March 1. Entry fee.

PHILADELPHIA FESTIVAL OF WORLD CINEMA—"Set in Philadelphia" Screenwriting Competition, 3701 Chestnut St., Philadelphia, PA 19104-3195. A $5,000 prize is awarded for the best screenplay, 85 to 130 pages, set primarily in the greater Philadelphia area. Deadline: January 1. Entry fee.

PIG IRON PRESS—Kenneth Patchen Competition, P.O. Box 237, Youngstown, OH 44501. Awards paperback publication, $100, and 50 copies of the winning manuscript of fiction (in even-numbered years) and poetry (in odd-numbered years). Deadline: December 31. Entry fee.

PIONEER DRAMA SERVICE—Shubert Fendrich Memorial Playwriting Contest, P.O. Box 4267, Englewood, CO 80155-4267. A prize of publication plus a $1,000 advance is offered for a previously produced, though unpublished, full-length play suitable for community theater. Deadline: March 1.

PIRATE'S ALLEY FAULKNER SOCIETY—William Faulkner Creative Writing Competition, 632 Pirate's Alley, New Orleans, LA 70116. Prizes are $7,500 for an unpublished novel of over 50,000 words; $2,500 for a novella of under 50,000 words; $1,500 for a short story of under 15,000 words; and $1,500 for a personal essay under 2,500 words. All awards include additional prize money to be used as an advance against royalties to encourage publisher interest. Deadline: April 1. Entry fees.

PLAYBOY—College Fiction Contest, 680 N. Lakeshore Dr., Chicago, IL 60611. Prizes of $3,000 plus publication, and $500, are offered for a short story, up to 25 pages, by a college student. Deadline: January 1.

PLAYHOUSE-ON-THE-SQUARE—New Play Competition, 51 S. Cooper, Memphis, TN 38104. Attn: Mr. Jackie Nichols, Exec. Dir. A stipend plus production is awarded for a full-length, previously unproduced play or musical. Deadline: April 1.

THE PLAYWRIGHTS' CENTER—Jerome Fellowships, 2301 Franklin Ave. E., Minneapolis, MN 55406. Five emerging playwrights are offered a $7,000 stipend and 12-month residency; housing and travel are not provided. Deadline: September 15.

THE PLUM REVIEW—Poetry and Fiction Contests, P.O. Box 1347, Philadelphia, PA 19105-1347. Publication and $500 are awarded for previously unpublished poems in any form or style. Deadline: February 28. Publication and $500 are awarded for fiction of any length, style, and subject matter. Deadline: November 30.

POCKETS—Fiction Contest, c/o Lynn W. Gilliam, Assoc. Ed., P.O. Box 189, Nashville, TN 37202-0189. A $1,000 prize goes to the author of the winning 1,000- to 1,600-word story for children in grades 1 to 6. Deadline: August 15.

POETS AND PATRONS OF CHICAGO— 6565 W. Belmont, 202 N, Chicago, IL 60634. Attn: Agnes Wathall Tatera. Prizes are $75 and $25 for original, unpublished poems of up to 40 lines. Deadline: September 1.

POETS CLUB OF CHICAGO—130 Windsor Park Dr., C-323, Carol Stream, IL 60188. Attn: LaVone Holt. Shakespearean/Petrarchan Sonnet Contest, with prizes of $50, $35, and $15. Deadline: September 1.

PRISM INTERNATIONAL—Short Fiction Contest, Creative Writing Dept., Univ. of B.C., E462-1866 Main Mall, Vancouver, B.C., Canada V6T 1Z1. Publication, a $2,000 first prize, and five $200 prizes are awarded for stories of up to 25 pages. Deadline: December 1. Entry fee.

✔**PURDUE UNIVERSITY PRESS**—Verna Emery Poetry Award, 1532 S. Campus Courts-E, W. Lafayette, IN 47907-1532. Unpublished collections of original poetry, 60 to 90 pages, are considered for an award of publication plus royalties. Deadline: April 15. Entry fee.

RANDOM HOUSE JUVENILE BOOKS—Dr. Seuss Picturebook Award Contest, 201 E. 50th St., New York, NY 10022. A prize of $25,000 plus publication is awarded for a picturebook manuscript by an author/illustrator who has not published more than one book. Deadline: December 1 (of even-numbered years).

✔**RIVER CITY**—Writing Awards in Fiction, Dept. of English, Univ. of Memphis, Memphis, TN 38152. Awards of $2,000 plus publication, $500, and $300 are offered for previously unpublished short stories, to 7,500 words. Deadline: December 1. Entry fee.

ROME ART & COMMUNITY CENTER—Milton Dorfman Poetry Prize, 308 W. Bloomfield St., Rome, NY 13440. Offers prizes of $500, $200, and $100 plus publication for the best original, unpublished poems. Deadline: November 1. Entry fee.

IAN ST JAMES AWARDS—P.O. Box 60, Cranbrook, Kent TN17 2ZR, England. Attn: Merric Davidson. Offers 20 prizes of 200 to 2,000 British pounds plus publication for short stories. Deadline: April 30. Entry fee.

✔**ST. MARTIN'S PRESS/MALICE DOMESTIC CONTEST**—Thomas Dunne Books, 175 Fifth Ave., New York, NY 10010. Offers publication plus a $10,000 advance against royalties, for a best first traditional mystery novel. Deadline: October 15.

ST. MARTIN'S PRESS/PRIVATE EYE NOVEL CONTEST—PWA Contest, 175 Fifth Ave., New York, NY 10010. Co-sponsored by Private Eye Writers of America. The writer of the best first private eye novel, from 60,000 words, receives publication plus $10,000 against royalties. Deadline: August 1.

✔ **SARABANDE BOOKS**—Poetry and Short Fiction Prizes, P.O. Box 4999, Louisville, KY 40204. Prizes are $2,000, publication, and a standard royalty contract in the competition for the Kathryn A. Morton Prize in Poetry (for a collection of poems, from 48 pages) and the Mary McCarthy Prize in Short Fiction (for a collection of short stories or novellas, 150 to 300 pages). Deadline: February 15. Entry fee.

SHENANARTS—Shenandoah International Playwrights Retreat, Rt. 5, Box 167-F, Staunton, VA 24401. Full fellowships are offered to playwrights to attend the four-week retreat held each August. Each year the retreat focuses on plays having to do with a specific region of the world. Deadline: February 1.

SIENA COLLEGE—International Playwrights' Competition, Siena College, 515 Loudon Rd., Loudonville, NY 12211-1462. Offers $2,000 plus campus residency expenses for the winning full-length script; no musicals. Deadline: June 30 (of even-numbered years).

SIERRA REPERTORY THEATRE—Taylor Playwriting Award, P. O. Box 3030, Sonora, CA 95370. Attn: Dennis Jones, Producing Dir. Offers $500, plus possible production, for a full-length play or musical that has received no more than two productions or staged readings. Deadline: August 31.

SNAKE NATION PRESS—Fiction and Poetry Contests, 110 #2 W. Force St., Valdosta, GA 31601. Attn: Nancy Phillips. Violet Reed Haas Prize: Offers publication plus $500 for a previously unpublished book of poetry, 50 to 75 pages. Deadline: January 15. *Snake Nation Review* Contest Issues: Prizes are publication plus $300, $200, and $100 for short stories; $100, $75, and $50 for poems. Deadlines: April 1; September 1. Entry fee.

SONORA REVIEW—Contests, Univ. of Arizona, Dept. of English, Tucson, AZ 85721. Poetry Contest: offers $500 plus publication for the best poem. Deadline: July 1. Short Story Contest: offers $500 plus publication for the best short story. Deadline: December 1. Entry fees.

SONS OF THE REPUBLIC OF TEXAS—Summerfield G. Roberts Award, 1717 8th St., Bay City, TX 77414. A prize of $2,500 is awarded for published or unpublished creative writing on the Republic of Texas, 1836-1846. Deadline: January 15.

THE SOUTHERN ANTHOLOGY—The Southern Prize, 2851 Johnston St., #123, Lafayette, LA 70503. A prize of $600 and publication are awarded for the best original, previously unpublished short story or novel excerpt, up to 7,500 words, or poem. Deadline: May 30. Entry fee.

SOUTHERN APPALACHIAN REPERTORY THEATRE—Playwrights' Conference, P.O. Box 1720, Mars Hill, NC 28754-0620. Attn: Dianne J. Chapman. Unproduced, unpublished scripts will be considered; up to 5 playwrights are selected to attend the conference and hear their plays read by professional actors; full production is possible. Deadline: October 31.

SOUTHERN POETRY REVIEW—Guy Owen Poetry Prize, Southern Poetry Review, Advancement Studies Dept., Central Piedmont Community College, Charlotte, NC 28235. Attn: Ken McLaurin, Ed. A prize of publication plus $500 is awarded for the best original, previously unpublished poem. Deadline: April 30. Entry fee.

THE SOW'S EAR PRESS—19535 Pleasant View Dr., Abingdon, VA 24211-6827. Chapbook Competition: offers a prize of $500 plus 50 published copies for the best poetry manuscript, as well as two $100 prizes. Deadline: April 30. Poetry Competition: offers prizes of $500, $100, and $50 for a previously unpublished poem of any length. Deadline: October 31. Entry fees.

SPOON RIVER POETRY REVIEW—Editors' Prize, 4240 Dept. of English, Illinois State Univ., Normal, IL 61790-4240. Publication and a $500 prize, as well as two $100 prizes, are awarded for single poems. Deadline: May 1. Entry fee.

STAND MAGAZINE—Short Story Competition, 179 Wingrove Rd., Newcastle upon Tyne, NE4 9DA, U.K. Prizes totalling 2,500 British pounds, including a #1,500 first prize, are awarded for previously unpublished stories under 6,000 words. Winning stories are published in *Stand Magazine*. Deadline: June 30 (of odd-numbered years). Entry fee.

STATE UNIVERSITY OF NEW YORK AT STONY BROOK—Short Fiction Prize, Dept. of English, Humanities Bldg., State Univ., Stony Brook, NY 11794-5350. Attn: Carolyn McGrath. A prize of $1,000 is offered for the best short story, up to 5,000 words, written by an undergraduate currently enrolled full-time in an American or Canadian college. Deadline: February 28.

STORY LINE PRESS—Nicholas Roerich Prize, Three Oaks Farm, Brownsville, OR 97327-9718. A prize of $1,000 plus publication is awarded for an original book of poetry by a poet who has never before published a book of poetry. Deadline: October 15. Entry fee.

SUNY FARMINGDALE—Paumanok Poetry Award, Visiting Writers Program, Knapp Hall, SUNY Farmingdale, Farmingdale, NY 11735. Prizes of $1,000 and two $500 prizes are offered for entries of three to five poems. Deadline: September 15. Entry fee.

SYRACUSE UNIVERSITY PRESS—John Ben Snow Prize, 1600 Jamesville Ave., Syracuse, NY 13244-5160. Attn: Dir. Awards a $1,500 advance, plus publication, for an unpublished book-length nonfiction manuscript about New York State, especially upstate or central New York. Deadline: December 31.

TEN MINUTE MUSICALS PROJECT—Box 461194, W. Hollywood, CA 90046. Attn: Michael Koppy, Prod. Musicals of 7 to 20 minutes are eligible for a $250 advance against royalties and musical anthology productions at theaters in the U.S. and Canada. Deadline: August 31.

TENNESSEE MOUNTAIN WRITERS—The Tennessee Literary Awards, P.O. Box 4895, Oak Ridge, TN 37831-4895. Offers $250, $150, and $75 in two categories: Fiction and Poetry. Deadline: September 30. Entry fee.

DAVID THOMAS CHARITABLE TRUST—Open Competitions, P.O. Box 4, Nairn IV12 4HU, Scotland, U.K. The trust sponsors a number of theme-based poetry and short story contests open to beginning writers, with prizes ranging from #25 to #1,200. Deadline: varies. Entry fee.

THE THURBER HOUSE—Thurber House Residencies, 77 Jefferson Ave., Columbus, OH 43215. Attn: Michael J. Rosen, Lit. Dir. Three-month residencies and stipends of $5,000 each are awarded in the categories of writing, playwriting, and journalism. Winners have limited teaching responsibilities with The Ohio State University. Deadline: December 15.

TRITON COLLEGE—Salute to the Arts Poetry Contest, 2000 Fifth Ave., River Grove, IL 60171. Winning original, unpublished poems, to 60 lines, on designated themes, are published by Triton College. Deadline: April 1.

UNICO NATIONAL—Ella T. Grasso Literary Award Contest, 72 Burroughs Pl., Bloomfield, NJ 07003. A prize of $1,000 is awarded for the best essay or short story, 1,500 to 2,000 words, on the Italian-American experience; two $250 prizes also awarded. Deadline: April 1.

U.S. NAVAL INSTITUTE—Arleigh Burke Essay Contest, *Proceedings Magazine*, 118 Maryland Ave., Annapolis, MD 21402-5035. Attn: Bert Hu-

binger. Awards prizes of $3,000, $2,000, and $1,000 plus publication, for
on the advancement of professional, literary, or scientific knowledge in the
naval or maritime services, and the advancement of the knowledge of sea
power. Deadline: December 1. Also sponsors several smaller contests; deadlines vary.

UNIVERSITIES WEST PRESS—Emily Dickinson Award in Poetry, P.O.
Box 697, Williams, AZ 86046-0697. A prize of $500 plus publication is awarded
for an unpublished poem. Deadline: July 31. Entry fee.

UNIVERSITY OF AKRON PRESS—The Akron Poetry Prize, 374B Bierce
Library, Akron, OH 44325-1703. Publication and $500 are offered for a previ-
ously unpublished collection of poems. Deadline: June 30. Entry fee.

UNIVERSITY OF CALIFORNIA IRVINE—Chicano/Latino Literary
Contest, Dept. of Spanish and Portuguese, UCI, Irvine, CA 92697-5275. Attn:
Alejandro Morales, Dir. A first prize of $1,000 plus publication, and prizes of
$500 and $250 are awarded in alternating years for poetry, drama, novels, and
short stories. Deadline: April 30.

UNIVERSITY OF COLORADO—Nilon Award for Excellence in Minority
Fiction, Fiction Collective Two, English Dept. Publications Ctr., Campus Box
494, Boulder, CO 80309-0494. Awards $1,000 plus joint publication for original,
unpublished, book-length fiction, in English, by a U.S. citizen. Open to writers
of the following ethnic minorities: African American, Hispanic, Asian, Native
American or Alaskan Native, and Pacific Islander. Deadline: November 30.

UNIVERSITY OF GEORGIA PRESS—Flannery O'Connor Award for
Short Fiction, Univ. of Georgia Press, 330 Research Dr., Athens, GA 30602-
4901. Two prizes of $1,000 plus publication are awarded for book-length collec-
tions of short fiction. Deadline: July 31. Entry fees.

**UNIVERSITY OF GEORGIA PRESS CONTEMPORARY POETRY SE-
RIES**—Athens, GA 30602-4901. Offers publication of manuscripts from poets
who have published at least one volume of poetry. Deadline: January 31. Publication of book-length poetry manuscripts is offered to poets who have never
had a book of poems published. Deadline: September 30. Entry fee.

UNIVERSITY OF HAWAII AT MANOA—Kumu Kahua Playwriting Contest, Dept. of Drama and Theatre, 1770 East-West Rd., Honolulu, HI 96822.
Awards $500 for a full-length play, and $200 for a one-act, set in Hawaii and
dealing with some aspect of the Hawaiian experience. Also conducts contest
for plays written by Hawaiian residents. Deadline: January 1.

UNIVERSITY OF IOWA—Iowa Publication Awards for Short Fiction,
Dept. of English, 308 English Philosophy Bldg., Iowa City, IA 52242-1492. The
John Simmons Short Fiction Award and the Iowa Short Fiction Award, both
for unpublished full-length collections of short stories, offer publication under
a standard contract. Deadline: September 30.

UNIVERSITY OF MASSACHUSETTS PRESS—Juniper Prize, Amherst,
MA 01003. Offers a prize of $1,000 plus publication for a book-length manu-
script of poetry; awarded in odd-numbered years to writers who have never
published a book of poetry, and in even-numbered years to writers who have
published a book or chapbook of poetry. Deadline: September 30. Entry fee.

UNIVERSITY OF NEBRASKA-OMAHA—Awards in Poetry and Fiction,
The Nebraska Review, Univ. of Nebraska-Omaha, Omaha, NE 68182-0324.

Offers $500 each plus publication to the winning short story (to 5,000 words) and the winning poem (or group of poems). Deadline: November 30. Entry fee.

UNIVERSITY OF NEBRASKA PRESS—North American Indian Prose Award, 312 N. 14th St., Lincoln, NE 68588-0484. Previously unpublished book-length manuscripts of biography, autobiography, history, literary criticism, and essays will be judged for originality, literary merit, and familiarity with North American Indian life. A $1,000 advance and publication are offered. Deadline: July 1.

√ **UNIVERSITY OF PITTSBURGH PRESS**—3347 Forbes Ave., Pittsburgh, PA 15261. Agnes Lynch Starrett Poetry Prize: offers $3,000 plus publication in the Pitt Poetry Series for a book-length collection of poems by a poet who has not yet published a volume of poetry. Deadline: April 30. Entry fee. Drue Heinz Literature Prize: offers $10,000 plus publication and royalty contract for an unpublished collection of short stories or novellas, 150 to 300 pages, by a writer who has previously published a book-length collection of fiction or at least three short stories or novellas in nationally distributed magazines. Deadline: August 31.

UNIVERSITY OF SOUTHERN CALIFORNIA—Ann Stanford Poetry Prize, Master of Professional Writing Program, WPH 404, Univ. of Southern California, Los Angeles, CA 90089-4034. Publication plus prizes of $750, $250, and $100 are awarded; submit up to five poems. Deadline: April 15. Entry fee.

UNIVERSITY OF WISCONSIN PRESS POETRY SERIES—114 N. Murray St., Madison, WI 53715. Attn: Ronald Wallace, Ed. Previously unpublished manuscripts, 50 to 80 pages, are considered for the Brittingham Prize in Poetry and the Felix Pollak Prize in Poetry, each offering $1,000 plus publication. Deadline: October 1. Entry fee.

THE UNTERBERG POETRY CENTER OF THE 92ND STREET Y— "Discovery"/*The Nation*, 1395 Lexington Ave., New York, NY 10128. Four prizes of $300, publication, and a reading are awarded for original 10-page manuscripts by writers who have not yet published a book of poetry. Deadline: February 1. Entry fee.

VETERANS OF FOREIGN WARS—Voice of Democracy Audio Essay Competition, VFW National Headquarters, 406 W. 34th St., Kansas City, MO 64111. Several national scholarships totalling over $125,000 are awarded to high school students for short, tape-recorded essays. Themes change annually. Deadline: November 1.

VILLA MONTALVO—Biennial Poetry Competition, P.O. Box 158, Saratoga, CA 95071. Residents of CA, NV, OR, and WA are eligible to enter poems in any style for prizes of: $1,000 plus an artist residency at Villa Montalvo, $500, and $300, as well as eight prizes of $25. Deadline: October 1 (of odd-numbered years). Entry fee.

WAGNER COLLEGE—Stanley Drama Award, Dept. of Humanities, 631 Howard Ave., Staten Island, NY 10301. Awards $2,000 for an original, previously unpublished and unproduced full-length play or musical or thematically related one-acts. Deadline: September 1.

TENNESSEE WILLIAMS/NEW ORLEANS LITERARY FESTIVAL— University of New Orleans, Lakefront, New Orleans, LA 70148. A $1,000 prize plus a staged reading and full production are offered for an original, unpublished one-act play. Deadline: December 1.

WRITERS AT WORK—Fellowship Competition, P.O. Box 1146, Centerville, UT 84014-5146. Prizes of $1,500 plus publication, and $500, in fiction and poetry categories, are awarded for excerpts of unpublished short stories, novels, essays, or poetry. Open to any writer who has not yet published a book-length volume of original work. Deadline: March 15. Entry fee.

THE WRITER'S VOICE—Annual Writing Awards, 5 W. 63rd St., New York, NY 10023. Capricorn Awards for writers over 40: $1,000 for a 48- to 68-page manuscript of poetry, and for the first 150 pages of a novel. Open Voice Awards: $500 each for published or unpublished writers of up to 10 pages of fiction or poetry. Deadline: December 31.

YALE UNIVERSITY PRESS—Yale Series of Younger Poets Prize, Box 209040, Yale Sta., New Haven, CT 06520-9040. Attn: Ed. Series publication is awarded for a book-length manuscript of poetry written by a poet under 40 who has not previously published a volume of poems. Deadline: February 29. Entry fee.

YOUNG PLAYWRIGHTS, INC.—Young Playwrights Festival, Dept. T, 321 W. 44th St., Suite 906, New York, NY 10036. Festival productions and readings are awarded for the best plays by writers 18 or younger. Deadline: October 15.

WRITERS COLONIES

Writers colonies offer solitude and freedom from everyday distractions so that writers can concentrate on their work. Though some colonies are quite small, with space for just three or four writers at a time, others can provide accommodations for as many as thirty or forty. The length of a residency may vary, too, from a couple of weeks to five or six months. These programs have strict admissions policies, and writers must submit a formal application or letter of intent, a resumé, writing samples, and letters of recommendation. As an alternative to the traditional writers colony, a few of the organizations listed offer writing rooms for writers who live nearby. Write for application information first, enclosing a stamped, self-addressed envelope. Residency fees are subject to change.

THE EDWARD F. ALBEE FOUNDATION, INC.
14 Harrison St.
New York, NY 10013
(212) 266-2020
David Briggs, *Foundation Secretary*
Located on Long Island, "The Barn," or the William Flanagan Memorial Creative Persons Center, is maintained by the Albee Foundation.

"The standards for admission are, simply, talent and need." Ten to 12 writers are accepted each season for one-month residencies, available from June 1 to October 1; applications, including writing samples, project description, and resumé, are accepted from January 1 to April 1. There is no fee, though residents are responsible for their own food and travel expenses.

ALTOS DE CHAVÒN
c/o Parsons School of Design
2 W. 13th St., Rm. 707
New York, NY 10011
(212) 229-5370
Stephen D. Kaplan, *Arts/Education Director*

Altos de Chavòn is a nonprofit center for the arts in the Dominican Republic committed to education, design innovation, international creative exchange, and the promotion of Dominican culture. Residencies average 12 weeks and provide the emerging or established artist an opportunity to live and work in a setting of architectural and natural beauty. All artists are welcome to apply, though writers should note there are no typewriters; the library is oriented more toward the design profession, and the apartments housing writers also accommodate university students. Two to three writers are chosen each year for the program. The fee is $300 per month for an apartment with kitchenette; linen and cleaning services are available at an extra cost. Applications include a letter of interest, writing sample, and resumé; artists are chosen in July.

MARY ANDERSON CENTER FOR THE ARTS
101 St. Francis Dr.
Mount St. Francis, IN 47146
(812) 923-8602
Sarah Roberson Yates, *Executive Director*

Founded in 1989, the artists' residency and retreat is situated on the grounds of a Franciscan friary. Space is available for seven residents at a time, including private rooms, working space, and a visual artists' studio; meals are provided. Two-week to three-month residencies are available and are granted based on project proposal and the artist's body of work; applications are accepted year-round. Fees are $30 per day, plus $15 to apply.

ATLANTIC CENTER FOR THE ARTS
1414 Art Center Ave.
New Smyrna Beach, FL 32168
(904) 427-6975
Nicholas Conroy, *Program Director*

The center is located on the east coast of central Florida, with 67 acres of pristine hammockland on a tidal estuary. All buildings, connected by raised wooden walkways, are handicapped accessible and air conditioned. The center provides a unique environment for sharing ideas, learning, and collaborating on interdisciplinary projects. Master artists meet with talented artists for readings and critiques, with time out for individual work. Residencies are three weeks. Fees are $100 a week for tuition and $25 a day for housing; off-site, tuition-only plans are available; financial aid is limited. Application deadlines vary.

BERLINER KÜNSTLERPROGRAM
Artists-in-Berlin Program
950 Third Ave.
New York, NY 10022
(212) 758-3223
Dr. Rolf Hoffmann, *Director*
   One-year residencies are offered to well-known and emerging writers, sculptors, painters, filmmakers, and composers to promote cultural exchange. Up to 20 residencies are offered for periods beginning between January 1 and June 30. Room, board, travel, and living expenses are awarded. Application, project description, and copies of publications are due by January 1 of the year preceding the residency.

BLUE MOUNTAIN CENTER
Blue Mountain Lake, NY 12812-0109
(518) 352-7391
Harriet Barlow, *Director*
   The Center hosts month-long residencies for artists and writers from mid-June to late October. Established fiction and nonfiction writers, poets, and playwrights whose work evinces social and ecological concern are eligible; 14 residents are accepted per session. Residents are not charged for their stay, although all visitors are invited to contribute to the studio construction fund. There is no application form; apply by sending a brief biographical sketch, a plan for work at Blue Mountain, five to 10 slides or a writing sample of any length, an indication of preference for an early summer, late summer, or fall residence, and a $20 application fee, attention: *Admissions Committee*. Applications are due February 1.

BYRDCLIFFE ARTS COLONY
Artists' Residency Program
Woodstock Guild
34 Tinker St.
Woodstock, NY 12498
(914) 679-2079
Attn: *Director*
   The Villetta Inn, located on the 400-acre arts colony, offers private studios and separate bedrooms, a communal kitchen, and a peaceful environment for fiction writers, poets, playwrights, and visual artists. One-month residencies are offered from June to September. Fee is $500 per month. Submit application, resumé, writing sample, and two letters of recommendation; the deadline is in mid-March.

THE CAMARGO FOUNDATION
125 Park Square Ct.
400 Sibley St.
St. Paul, MN 55101-1982
Ricardo Bloch, *Administrative Assistant*
   The Camargo Foundation maintains a center of studies in France for the benefit of nine scholars and graduate students each semester who wish to pursue projects in the humanities and social sciences relative to France and Francophone culture. In addition, one artist, one composer, and one writer are accepted each semester. The foundation offers furnished apartments and a reference library in the city of Cassis. Research should be at an advanced stage and not require resources unavailable in the Marseilles-

Aix-Cassis region. Fellows must be in residence at the foundation; the award is exclusively a residential grant. Application materials include: application form, curriculum vitae, three letters of recommendation, and project description. Writers, artists, and composers are required to send work samples. Applications are due February 1.

CENTRUM
P.O. Box 1158
Port Townsend, WA 98368
(360) 385-3102
Marlene Bennett, *Program Facilitator*

Writers are awarded one-month residencies between September and May. Applicants selected by a peer jury receive free housing and a $300 stipend. Previous residents may return on a space-available basis for a monthly fee. Applications are due October 1. The application fee is $15.

CHATEAU DE LESVAULT
Writers Retreat Program
Onlay
58370 Villapouriòn
France
(33)-3-86-84-32-91; fax: (33)-3-86-84-35-78
Bibbi Lee, *Director*

This French country residence is located in western Burgundy, in the national park of Le Morvan. Five large rooms, fully equipped for living and working, are available October through April, for one month or longer. Residents in this small artists' community have access to the entire chateau, including the salon, library, and grounds. The fee is 4,500 francs (approximately $900) per month, or 2,500 francs for two weeks, and includes room, board, and utilities. Apply by writing to the selection committee, including project description, two references, writing samples, and publications list, if available. Applications are handled on a first-come basis.

DJERASSI RESIDENT ARTISTS PROGRAM
2325 Bear Gulch Rd.
Woodside, CA 94062-4405
(415) 747-1250; fax: (415) 747-0105; e-mail: residency@djerassi.org
Judy Freeland, *Residency Coordinator*

The Djerassi Program offers living and work spaces in a rural, isolated setting to playwrights, screenwriters, poets, translators, composers, librettists, and lyricists seeking undisturbed time for creative work. Residencies are four or six weeks; 60 artists are accepted each year. There are no fees other than the $25 application fee. Applications, with resumé and documentation of recent creative work, are due February 15. SASE for application.

DORLAND MOUNTAIN ARTS COLONY
Box 6
Temecula, CA 92593
(909) 676-5039
e-mail: dorland@ez2.net; internet: http://www.ez2.net/dorland/
Attn: *Admissions Committee*

Dorland is a nature preserve and "primitive retreat for creative people" located in the Palomar Mountains of Southern California. "Without electricity, residents find a new, natural rhythm for their work." Novelists, playwrights, poets, nonfiction writers, composers, and visual artists are encouraged to apply for residencies of one to two months. The fee of $300 a month includes cottage, fuel, and firewood. Send SASE for application; deadlines are March 1 and September 1.

DORSET COLONY HOUSE
Box 510
Dorset, VT 05251
(802) 867-2223
John Nassivera, *Director*
　　Writers and playwrights are offered low-cost room with kitchen facilities at the historic Colony House in Dorset, Vermont. Residencies are one week to one month, and are available in the fall and spring. Applications are accepted year-round, and up to eight writers stay at a time. The fee is $95 per week; financial aid is limited. For more information, send SASE.

FINE ARTS WORK CENTER IN PROVINCETOWN
24 Pearl St.
Provincetown, MA 02657
Hunter O'Hanian, *Executive Director*
　　Fellowships, including living and studio space and monthly stipends, are available at the Fine Arts Work Center on Cape Cod, for fiction writers and poets to work independently. Residencies are for seven months, October through May; apply before February 1 deadline. Five poets and five fiction writers are accepted. Send SASE for details; indicate that you are a writer in the request.

GLENESSENCE WRITERS COLONY
1447 W. Ward Ave.
Ridgecrest, CA 93555
(619) 446-5894
Allison Swift, *Director*
　　Glenessence is a luxury villa located in the Upper Mojave Desert, offering private rooms with bath, pool, spa, courtyard, shared kitchen, fitness center, and library. Children, pets, and smoking are prohibited. Residencies are offered at $565 per month; meals are not provided. Reservations are made on a first-come basis.

THE TYRONE GUTHRIE CENTRE
Annaghmakerrig, Newbliss
County Monaghan
Ireland
(353) 47-54003; fax: (353) 47-54380
Bernard Loughlin, *Director*
　　Set on a 450-acre country estate, the center offers peace and seclusion to writers and other artists to enable them to get on with their work. All art forms are represented. One- to three-month residencies are offered throughout the year, at the rate of 2,000 pounds per month; financial assistance is available to Irish citizens only. A number of longer term self-catering houses in the old farmyard are also available at #300 per week. Writers chosen on the basis of c.v., samples of published work, and outline of intended project. Writers may apply for acceptance year-round.

THE HAMBIDGE CENTER
P.O. Box 339
Rabun Gap, GA 30568
(706) 746-5718; fax: (706) 746-9933
Judy Barber, *Director*
　　The Hambidge Center for Creative Arts and Sciences is located on 600 pristine acres of quiet woods in the north Georgia mountains. Eight private cottages are available for fellows. All fellowships are partially underwritten, residents are asked to contribute $125 per week. Two-week to six-week residencies, from March through December are offered to serious artists from all disciplines. Send SASE for application form. Application deadlines: November 1 and May 1.

HEADLANDS CENTER FOR THE ARTS
944 Fort Barry
Sausalito, CA 94965
(415) 331-2787
　　Programs at the Headlands Center, located on 13,000 acres of open coastal space, are available to residents of Ohio, North Carolina, and California. Application requirements vary by state. Decisions are announced in October for residencies beginning in February. There are no residency or application fees. Send SASE for more information.

HEDGEBROOK
2197 E. Millman Rd.
Langley, WA 98260
(360) 321-4786
Attn: *Director*
　　Hedgebrook provides women writers, published or not, of all ages and from all cultural backgrounds, with a natural place to work. Established in 1988, the retreat is located on 30 acres of farmland and woods on Whidbey Island in Washington State. Each writer has her own cottage, equipped with electricity and woodstove. A bathhouse serves all six cottages. Writers gather for dinner in the farmhouse every evening and frequently read in the living room/library afterwards. Limited travel scholarships are available. Residencies range from one week to two months. April 1 is the application deadline for residencies from mid-June to mid-December; October 1 for mid-January to late May. Applicants are chosen by a selection committee composed of writers. There is a $15 fee to apply; send SASE for application.

KALANI ECO-RESORT, INSTITUTE FOR CULTURE AND WELLNESS
Artist-in-Residence Program
RR2, Box 4500
Pahoa-Beach Road, HI 96778
(808) 965-7828; (800) 800-6886; fax: (808) 965-9613
e-mail: kh@ILHawaii.net; internet: http://randm.com/kh.html
Richard Koob, *Program Coordinator*
　　Located in a rural coastal setting of 113 botanical acres, Kalani Eco-Resort hosts and sponsors educational programs "with the aloha experience that is its namesake: harmony of heaven and earth." Residencies range from two weeks to two months and are available throughout the

year. Fees range from $30 to $43 per day, meals available at additional fee. Applications accepted year-round.

LEIGHTON STUDIOS FOR INDEPENDENT RESIDENCIES
Office of the Registrar
The Banff Centre for the Arts
Box 1020, Station 28
107 Tunnel Mountain Dr.
Banff, Alberta T0L 0C0
Canada
(403) 762-6180; (800) 565-9989; fax: (403) 762-6345
e-mail: arts_info@banffcentre.ab.ca
internet: http://www.banffcentre.ab.ca/Leighton_studios/
Registrar

The Leighton Studios are open year-round, providing time and space for artists to produce new work. Established writers, composers, musicians, and visual artists of all nationalities are encouraged to apply. Artists working in other mediums at the conceptual state of a project will also be considered. Weekly fees (Canadian dollars): $315 studio; $263 single room; $98.00 meals (optional). Reductions in the studio fee are available to applicants demonstrating financial need. Applications are accepted at any time. Space is limited; apply at least six months prior to preferred starting date. Write for application form or apply online.

THE MACDOWELL COLONY
100 High St.
Peterborough, NH 03458
(603) 924-3886; Internet: http://www.macdowellcolony.org
Pat Dodge, *Admissions Coordinator*

Studios, room, and board are available for writers to work without interruption in a woodland setting. Selection is competitive. Apply by January 15 for stays May through August; April 15 for September through December; and September 15 for January through April. Residencies last up to eight weeks, and 80 to 90 writers are accepted each year. Send SASE for application.

THE MILLAY COLONY FOR THE ARTS
444 East Hill Rd.
P.O. Box 3
Austerlitz, NY 12017-0003
(518) 392-3103
Gail Giles, *Assistant Director*

At Steepletop, the former home of Edna St. Vincent Millay, writers are provided studios, living quarters, and meals at no cost. Residencies last one month. Application deadlines are February 1, May 1, and September 1. Send SASE for more information and application. Applications can also be accessed by e-mail (application@millaycolony.org).

MILLETT FARM: AN ART COLONY FOR WOMEN
295 Bowery
New York, NY 10003
Kate Millett, *Director*

Summer residencies are offered to women writers and visual artists at a picturesque tree farm in rural New York. In return for housing, all residents contribute five hours of work each weekday morning and contribute $70 a week toward meals. Preference is given to writers who can stay all summer or at least six weeks. For more information send an SASE.

MOLASSES POND WRITERS' RETREAT AND WORKSHOP
RR 1, Box 85C
Milbridge, ME 04658
(207) 546-2506
Martha Barron Barrett and Sue Wheeler, *Coordinators*
Led by published authors who teach writing at the University of New Hampshire. The one-week workshop is held in June and includes time set aside for writing, as well as manuscript critique and writing classes. Up to 10 writers participate, staying in a colonial farmhouse with private bed/work rooms for each participant and common areas for meals and classes. The $400 fee covers lodging, meals, and tuition. Applicants must be serious about their work. No children's literature or poetry. Submit statement of purpose and 15 to 20 pages of fiction or nonfiction between February 15 and March 1.

MONTANA ARTISTS REFUGE
Box 8
Basin, MT 59631
(406) 225-3525
Writers are offered low-cost apartment and studio space in a relaxed and unpretentious atmosphere, where they can work with other artists or in solitude. Residencies range from three months to one year, and rents range from $200 to $400 per month. Limited financial aid is available. Send SASE for information.

JENNY McKEAN MOORE WRITER-IN-WASHINGTON
Dept. of English
The George Washington University
Washington, DC 20052
Attn: Prof. Christopher Sten
The fellowship allows for a writer to teach two paid semesters (salary: $48,000) at The George Washington University. Teaching duties include a workshop each semester for students from the metropolitan community who may have had little formal education; and one class each semester for university students. Fiction and poetry alternate years. Applications include letter, indicating publications and other projects, extent of teaching experience, and other qualifications. The application must also include a resumé and a ten- to fifteen-page sample of your work. The application deadline is November 15.

THE N.A.L.L. ASSOCIATION
232, Boulevard de Lattre
06140 Vence
France
(33) 93-58-13-26; fax: (33) 93-58-09-00
Attn: *Director*
This international center for writers and artists is located on eight acres of the Mediterranean village of Vence. Residents stay in cottages equipped with kitchen, bath, and private garden. One afternoon a week is set aside for residents to discuss their work with local artists over

tea. Six-month residencies are encouraged. Cottages are rented at various rates, to members of the N.A.L.L. (Nature, Art, and Life League); membership is 500 francs (about $100) per year. Meals are not included. Submit resumé, writing sample, and project description. Applications are accepted year-round.

NEW YORK MILLS ARTS RETREAT AND REGIONAL CULTURAL CENTER
24 N. Main Ave.
P.O. Box 246
New York Mills, MN 56567
(218) 385-3339
Kent Scheer, *Retreat Coordinator*

The Cultural Center, housed in a restored 1895 general store, is an innovative non-profit organization offering gallery exhibits, musical performances, theater, literary events, educational programs, the Great American Think-Off philosophy competition, and the Continental Divide Film and Music Festival. The Arts Retreat provides housing at the Whistle Stop Inn, a bed and breakfast located in an old, Victorian style home. Each artist receives financial assistance through a stipend, ranging from $750 for a two-week residency to $1,500 for four weeks, provided by the Jerome Foundation. Five to seven emerging artists, writers, filmmakers, or musicians are accepted throughout the year. There is a review process twice a year; the deadlines are April 1 and October 1.

THE NORTHWOOD UNIVERSITY
Alden B. Dow Creativity Center
3225 Cook Rd.
Midland, MI 48640-2398
(517) 837-4478; fax: (517) 837-4468
Carol B. Coppage, *Director*

The Fellowship Program allows individuals time away from their ongoing daily routines to pursue their project ideas without interruption. A project idea should be innovative, creative, and have potential for impact in its field. Four ten-week residencies, lasting from early-June to early-August, are awarded yearly. There is a $10 application fee. A $750 stipend plus room and board are provided. No spouses or families. Applications are due December 31.

OX-BOW
37 S. Wabash Ave., Rm. 707
Chicago, IL 60603
(312) 899-7455

One-week residencies are available mid-June to mid-August for writers who wish to reside and work in a secluded, natural environment. Recipients are required to pay room and board. The mission of the Ox-Bow program is to nurture the creative process through instruction, example, and community. Resident writers are encouraged to present a reading of their work and to participate in the community life at Ox-Bow. For application form write or call. Application deadline is May 15.

RAGDALE FOUNDATION
1260 N. Green Bay Rd.
Lake Forest, IL 60045
(847) 234-1063
Sonja Carlborg, *Director*

Uninterrupted time and peaceful space allow writers a chance to finish works in progress, to begin new works, to solve thorny creative problems, and to experiment in new genres. The foundation is located 30 miles north of Chicago, on 55 acres of prairie. Residencies of two weeks to two months are available for writers, artists, and composers. The fee is $15 a day; some full and partial fee waivers available, based solely on financial need. Send SASE for deadline information. Application fee: $20.

SASKATCHEWAN WRITERS GUILD
Writers/Artists Colonies and Individual Retreats
P.O. Box 3986
Regina, Saskatchewan S4P 3R9
Canada
(306) 757-6310
Attn: *Director*

The Saskatchewan Colonies are at two locations: St. Peter's Abbey, near Humboldt, provides a six-week summer colony (July-August) and a two-week winter colony in February, for up to eight writers and artists at a time; applicant stays vary. Individual retreats of up to a month are offered year-round at St. Peter's, for up to three residents at a time. Emma Lake, near Prince Albert, is the site of a two-week residency in August. A fee of $125 (Saskatchewan Writers Guild members) or $175 (nonmembers) per week includes room and board. Submit application form, resumé, project description, two references, and a 10-page writing sample. Saskatchewan residents are given preference. Apply two to three months in advance.

THE JOHN STEINBECK ROOM
Long Island University
Southampton College Library
Southampton, NY 11968
(516) 287-8382
Robert Gerbereux, *Library Director*

The John Steinbeck Room at Long Island University provides a basic research facility to writers who have either a current contract with a book publisher or a confirmed assignment from a magazine editor. The room is available for a period of six months with one six-month renewal permissible. Send SASE for application.

THE THURBER HOUSE RESIDENCIES
c/o Thurber House
77 Jefferson Ave.
Columbus, OH 43215
(614) 464-1032; fax: (614) 228-7445
Michael J. Rosen, *Literary Director*

Residencies in the restored home of James Thurber are awarded to journalists, poets, and playwrights. Residents work on their own writing projects, and in addition to other duties, teach one class at the Ohio State University. A stipend of $5,000 per quarter is provided. A letter of interest and curriculum vitae must be received by December 15, at which time applications are reviewed for the upcoming academic year.

UCROSS FOUNDATION
Residency Program
2836 U.S. Hwy. 14-16 East
Clearmont, WY 82835
(307) 737-2291; fax: (307) 737-2322
Sharon Dynak, *Executive Director*

Residencies, two to eight weeks, in the foothills of the Big Horn Mountains in Wyoming, allow writers, artists, and scholars to concentrate on their work without interruption. Two residency sessions are scheduled annually: February to June and August to December. There is no charge for room, board, or studio space. Application deadlines are March 1 for the fall session and October 1 for the spring session. Send SASE for more information.

VILLA MONTALVO ARTIST RESIDENCY PROGRAM
P.O. Box 158
Saratoga, CA 95071
(408) 961-5818
Judy Moran, *Artist Residency Program Director*
Villa Montalvo, in the foothills of the Santa Cruz Mountains south of San Francisco, offers one- to three-month residencies free of charge to writers working on a specific project. Several merit-based fellowships are available. The application deadlines are September 1 and March 1; call for brochure and application form. Application fee is $20.

VIRGINIA CENTER FOR THE CREATIVE ARTS
Sweet Briar, VA 24595
(804) 946-7236
Craig Pleasants, *Acting Director*
A working retreat for writers, composers, and visual artists in Virginia's Blue Ridge Mountains. Residencies from two weeks to two months are available year-round. Application deadlines are the 15th of January, May, and September; about 300 residents are accepted each year. A limited amount of financial assistance is available. Send SASE for more information.

WEYMOUTH CENTER FOR THE ARTS & HUMANITIES
555 East Connecticut Ave.
Southern Pines, NC 28388
(910) 692-6261; fax (910) 692-1815
The Writers-in-Residence program offers writers and composers stays of up to two weeks to pursue their work, free of charge. There is space for six writers, though generally three writers are in residence at a time. To be eligible, writers must have a connection with North Carolina (whether as a native, having gone to school there, etc.). For more information, send an SASE.

THE WRITERS ROOM
10 Astor Pl., 6th Fl.
New York, NY 10003
(212) 254-6995; fax: (212) 533-6059
Donna Brodie, *Executive Director*
Located in the East Village, The Writers Room provides subsidized work space to all types of writers at all stages of their careers. "We offer urban writers a quiet place to escape from noisy neighbors, children, roommates, and other distractions of city life." The room holds 30 desks separated by partitions, a typing room with five desks, a kitchen, and a library. Open 24 hours a day, 365 days a year. There is a $50 initiation fee; fees for the three-month period include $175 for "floater" desk. Call, fax or write for application (no visits without appointment).

THE WRITERS STUDIO
The Mercantile Library Association
17 E. 47th St.
New York, NY 10017
(212) 755-6710
Harold Augenbraum, *Director*
   The Writers Studio is a quiet place in which writers can rent space conducive to the production of good work. A carrel, locker, small reference collection, electrical outlets, and membership in the Mercantile Library of New York are available at the cost of $200 per three-month residency. Submit application, resumé, and writing samples; applications are considered year-round.

HELENE WURLITZER FOUNDATION OF NEW MEXICO
Box 545
Taos, NM 87571
(505) 758-2413
   Rent-free and utility-free studios in Taos are offered to writers and creative artists in all media. "All artists are given the opportunity to be free of the shackles of a 9- to-5 routine." Length of residency varies from three to six months. The foundation is open from April 1 through September 30 and on a limited basis October through March. Residencies are assigned into the year 2000, but cancellations do occur.

YADDO
Box 395
Saratoga Springs, NY 12866-0395
(518) 584-0746; fax: (518) 584-1312
e-mail: CHWAIT@aol.com
Candace Wait, *Program Coordinator*
   Visual artists, writers, choreographers, film/video artists, performance artists, composers, and collaborators are invited for stays from two weeks to two months. Room, board, and studio space are provided. No stipends. Deadlines are January 15 and August 1. There is a $20 application fee; send SASE for form.

WRITERS CONFERENCES

   Each year, hundreds of writers conferences are held across the country. The following list, arranged by state, represents a sampling of conferences. Each listing includes the location of the conference, the month during which it is usually held, and the name and address of the person to contact for full details. Always enclose an SASE. Additional conferences are listed annually in the May issue of *The Writer* Magazine (120 Boylston St., Boston, MA 02116-4615).

ALABAMA

WRITING A NOVEL THAT SELLS—Various locations & dates. Michael Garrett, Dir., P.O. Box 100031, Birmingham, AL 35210.

WRITING TODAY—Birmingham, AL. March 20-21. Martha Andrews, Dir., Office of Special Events, Birmingham-Southern College, Box 549003, Birmingham, AL 35254.

SOUTHERN CHRISTIAN WRITERS CONFERENCE—Birmingham, AL. June. Joanne Sloan, Dir., SCWC, P.O. Box 1106, Northport, AL 35476.

SCBWI "WRITING AND ILLUSTRATING FOR KIDS"—Birmingham, AL. October 17. Joan Broerman, Reg. Advisor, SCBWI, 1616 Kestwick Dr., Birmingham, AL 35226.

ALASKA

SITKA SYMPOSIUM ON HUMAN VALUES & THE WRITTEN WORD—Sitka, AK. June. Carolyn Servid, Dir., The Island Institute, P.O. Box 2420, Sitka, AK 99835.

ARIZONA

PIMA WRITERS' WORKSHOP—Tucson, AZ. May 29-31. Meg Files, Dir., Pima College, 2202 W. Anklam Rd., Tucson, AZ 85709-0295.

ARKANSAS

WHITE RIVER WRITERS' WORKSHOP—Batesville, AR. June. Andrea Hollander Budy, Dir., White River Writers' Workshop, Lyon College, P.O. Box 2317, Batesville, AR 72503

CALIFORNIA

MICHAEL HAUGE'S SCREENWRITING FOR HOLLYWOOD SEMINARS—Various locations & dates. Michael Hauge, Dir., P.O. Box 55728, Sherman Oaks, CA 91413.

SAN DIEGO STATE UNIVERSITY WRITERS' CONFERENCE—San Diego, CA. Jan. 17-18. Jan Wahl, Dir., SDSU College of Extended Studies, 5250 Campanile Dr., San Diego, CA 92182-1920.

SOUTHERN CALIFORNIA WRITERS' CONFERENCE—San Diego, CA. March 13-15. Barbara Hartner Sack, Dir., 2596 Escondido Ave., San Diego, CA 92123.

JACK LONDON WRITERS' CONFERENCE—San Francisco, CA. March 14. Mario Faulkner, 135 Clark Dr., San Mateo, CA 94402-1002.

WRITERS' FORUM—Pasadena, CA. March 14. Meredith Brucker, Dir., Community Education, C-117, Pasadena City College, 1570 E. Colorado Blvd., Pasadena, CA 91106-2003.

AMERICAN CHRISTIAN WRITERS CONFERENCE—Fullerton, CA. March 27-28. Reg A. Forder, Dir., American Christian Writers, P.O. Box 110390, Nashville, TN 37222.

MOUNT HERMON CHRISTIAN WRITERS CONFERENCE—Mount Hermon, CA. April 3-7. David R. Talbott, Dir., Mount Hermon Assn., Inc., P.O. Box 413, Mount Hermon, CA 95041.

PALM SPRINGS WRITERS' CONFERENCE—Palm Springs, CA. April 15-18. Mary Valentine, Dir., PSWC, 26700 N. Cahvenga Blvd., #4204, Los Angeles, CA 96008.

SANTA BARBARA WRITERS CONFERENCE—Santa Barbara, CA. June. Barnaby Conrad, Dir., SBWC, Box 304, Carpinteria, CA 93014.

MENDOCINO COAST WRITERS CONFERENCE—Fort Bragg, CA. June 13-14. Marlis Broadhead, Dir., 1211 Del Mar Dr., Fort Bragg, CA 95437.

OUTDOOR WRITERS ASSOCIATION OF AMERICA 71ST ANNUAL CONFERENCE—Redding, CA. June 14-18. Eileen N. King, Dir., 2017 Cato Ave., Suite 101, State College, PA 16801-2768.

FOOTHILL COLLEGE WRITERS' CONFERENCE—Los Altos Hills, CA. June 25-30. Kim Wolterbeek, Dir., Foothill College, 12345 El Monte Rd., Los Altos Hills, CA 94022.

BOOK PASSAGE MYSTERY WRITERS' CONFERENCE—Corte Madera, CA. July. Cecilia McGuire, Dir., 51 Tamal Vista Blvd., Corte Madera, CA 94925.

ROUND TABLE COMEDY WRITERS CONVENTION—Palm Springs, CA. July. Linda Perret, Dir., Box 786, Agoura Hills, CA 91376-0786.

INTERNATIONAL BLACK WRITERS & ARTISTS LOS ANGELES ANNUAL JULY CONFERENCE—Los Angeles, CA. July 17-19. Linda A. Hughes, Dir., IBWA-LA Conference, P.O. Box 43576, Los Angeles, CA 90043.

SQUAW VALLEY COMMUNITY OF WRITERS—Squaw Valley, CA. July-August. Brett Hall Jones, Dir., Squaw Valley Community of Writers, 10626 Banner Lava Cap, Nevada City, CA 95959.

ROMANCE WRITERS OF AMERICA 18TH ANNUAL NATIONAL CONFERENCE—Anaheim, CA. July 29-August 2. Allison Kelley, Dir., Romance Writers of America, 13700 Veterans Memorial, #315, Houston, TX 77014.

WRITERS AND ILLUSTRATORS CONFERENCE IN CHILDREN'S LITERATURE—Los Angeles, CA. August. Lin Oliver, Dir., SCBWI, 345 N. Maple Dr., Beverly Hills, CA 90210.

BOOK PASSAGE TRAVEL WRITERS' CONFERENCE—Corte Madera, CA. August 20-23. Mary Lou Miller, Dir., 51 Tamal Vista Blvd., Corte Madera, CA 94925.

UCI EXTENSION'S FIFTH ANNUAL WRITING CONFERENCE—Irvine, CA. Fall. Nancy Warzer-Brady, UCI Extension, Arts & Humanities, P.O. Box 6050, Irvine, CA 92616-6050.

CUESTA COLLEGE WRITERS' CONFERENCE—San Luis Obispo, CA. Sept. David Congalton, Dir., Cuesta College, San Luis Obispo, CA 93403.

COLORADO

1998 NATIONAL WRITERS ASSOCIATION SUMMER CONFERENCE—Aurora, CO. June. Sandy Whelchel, Dir., National Writers Assn., 1450 S. Havana, Suite 424, Aurora, CO 80012.

ASPEN WRITERS' CONFERENCE—Aspen, CO. June 7-13. Jeanne McGovern Small, Dir., Box 7726, Aspen, CO 81612.

STEAMBOAT SPRINGS WRITERS CONFERENCE—Steamboat Springs, CO. July 11. Harriet Freiberger, Dir., P.O. Box 774284, Steamboat Springs, CO 80477.

CONNECTICUT

WESLEYAN WRITERS CONFERENCE—Middletown, CT. June 22-27. Anne Greene, Dir., Wesleyan Univ., Middletown, CT 06459.

FLORIDA

SOUTHWEST FLORIDA WRITERS' CONFERENCE—Ft. Myers, FL. January. Joanne Hartke, Dir., Edison Comm. College, Division of Cont. Ed., P.O. Box 60210, Ft. Myers, FL 33906-6210.

16TH ANNUAL KEY WEST LITERARY SEMINAR, "ONCE UPON A TIME: CHILDREN'S LITERATURE IN THE LATE 20TH CENTURY"—Key West, FL. January 5-11. Miles Frieden, Dir., 9 Sixth St., Plum Island, MA 01951.

KEYS WRITING SEMINAR—Key West, FL. January 7-14. David Axelrod, Dir., Box 698, Centereach, NY 11720.

FLORIDA SUNCOAST WRITERS' CONFERENCE—St. Petersburg, FL. February 5-7. Steve Rubin, Dir., Dept. of English, Univ. of South Florida, Tampa, FL 33620.

FLORIDA ROMANCE WRITERS FUN IN THE SUN CONFERENCE—Ft. Lauderdale, FL. February 20-22. Barry I. Glusky, 9630 N.W. 25th St., Sunrise, FL 33322.

SLEUTHFEST '98—Fort Lauderdale, FL. April. Stuart McIver, Dir., 2201 N.E. 32nd Ct., Lighthouse Point, FL 33064.

FLORIDA REGION SCBWI CONFERENCE—Palm Springs, FL. September 13. Barbara Casey, Dir., 2158 Portland Ave., Wellington, FL 33414.

AMERICAN CHRISTIAN WRITERS CONFERENCE—Ft. Lauderdale, FL. November 14. Reg A. Forder, Dir., American Christian Writers, P.O. Box 110390, Nashville, TN 37222.

GEORGIA

AMERICAN CHRISTIAN WRITERS CONFERENCE—Atlanta, GA. May 1-2. Reg A. Forder, Dir., American Christian Writers, P.O. Box 110390, Nashville, TN 37222.

SANDHILLS WRITERS CONFERENCE—Augusta, GA. May 14-16. Anthony Kellman, Dir., Dept. of Lang., Lit., & Comm., Augusta State Univ., 2500 Walton Way, Augusta, GA 30904.

SOUTHEASTERN WRITER'S CONFERENCE—St. Simons Island, GA. June. Pat Laye, Secretary, Rt. 1, Box 102, Cuthbert, GA 31740.

MOONLIGHT AND MAGNOLIAS CONFERENCE—Atlanta, GA. September. Lillian Richey, Dir., Georgia Romance Writers, 4605 Settles Point Rd., Suwanee, GA 30174-1988.

HAWAII

THE FIRE WITHIN: WRITING AT THE VOLCANO—Volcano, HI. June. Pamela Frierson, Dir., Volcano Art Center, P.O. Box 104, Hawaii National Park, Volcano, HI 96718.

NINTH BIENNIAL CONFERENCE ON LITERATURE AND HAWAII'S CHILDREN—Honolulu, HI. June 11-13. Conf. Dir., Children's Literature Hawaii, Dept. of English, Univ. of Hawaii, Honolulu, HI 96822.

IDAHO

IDAHO WRITERS CONFERENCE—Coeur d'Alene, ID. September. Betty Rohrscheib, Dir., 6952 N. Davenport, Coeur d'Alene, ID 83814-9535.

ILLINOIS

WRITE-TO-PUBLISH CONFERENCE—Wheaton, IL. June. Lin Johnson, Dir., 9731 N. Fox Glen Dr., #6F, Niles, IL 60714-5861.

"OF DARK AND STORMY NIGHTS" WRITERS CONFERENCE—Rolling Meadows, IL. June 6. W.W. Spurgeon Jr., Dir., P.O. Box 1944, Muncie, IN 47308-1944.

MISSISSIPPI VALLEY WRITERS CONFERENCE—Rock Island, IL. June 7-12. David R. Collins, Dir., 3403 45th St., Moline, IL 61265.

MIDWEST MYSTERY WRITERS' CONFERENCE—Normal, IL. July. Mary Adams, Dir., Lincoln College, 715 W. Raab Rd., Normal, IL 61761.

AMERICAN CHRISTIAN WRITERS CONFERENCE—Chicago, IL. August 21-22. Reg A. Forder, Dir., American Christian Writers, P.O. Box 110390, Nashville, TN 37222.

INDIANA

BUTLER UNIVERSITY CHILDREN'S LITERATURE CONFERENCE—Indianapolis, IN. January 31. Valiska Gregory, Dir., Butler Univ., Writers' Studio, 4600 Sunset Dr., Indianapolis, IN 46208.

INDIANA UNIVERSITY WRITERS' CONFERENCE—Bloomington, IN. June 21-26. Maura Stanton, Dir., Indiana Univ. Writers' Conference, Ballantine 458, Bloomington, IN 47405.

MIDWEST WRITERS WORKSHOP—Muncie, IN. July 29-August 1. Earl Conn, Dir., Ball State Univ., Muncie, IN 47306.

IOWA

SINIPEE WRITERS' WORKSHOP—Dubuque, IA. April 18. John Tigges, Dir., Box 902, Dubuque, IA 52004-0902.

IOWA SUMMER WRITING FESTIVAL—Iowa City, IA. June, July. Peggy Houston, Dir., Univ. of Iowa, Iowa City, IA 52242.

KANSAS

WRITERS WORKSHOP IN SCIENCE FICTION—Lawrence, KS. June 29-July 12. James Gunn, Dir., English Dept., Univ. of Kansas, Lawrence, KS 66045.

KENTUCKY

OAKBROOK FARM WRITERS WORKSHOPS—Glendale, KY. Various dates. Bill Thomas, Dir., Box 59, Glendale, KY 42740.

GREEN RIVER WRITERS NOVELS-IN-PROGRESS WORKSHOP—Louisville, KY. March 15-23. Mary E. O'Dell, Dir., Green River Writers, Inc., 11906 Locust Rd., Middletown, KY 40243.

BLUEGRASS SPRING WRITERS' WORKSHOP—Lexington, KY. April 12-18. Karl Garson, Dir., Box 3098, Princeton, NJ 08543-3098.

EKU CREATIVE WRITING CONFERENCE—Richmond, KY. June. Dorothy M. Sutton, Dir., English Dept., Case Annex 467, Eastern Kentucky Univ., 40475-3140.

GREEN RIVER WRITERS RETREAT—Louisville, KY. July. Mary E. O'Dell, Dir., Green River Writers, Inc., 11906 Locust Rd., Middletown, KY 40243.

ANNUAL APPALACHIAN WRITERS WORKSHOP—Hindman, KY. Summer. Mike Mullins, Dir., Box 844, Hindman, KY 41822.

LOUISIANA

NOLA ROMANCE & MORE: TREASURES OF THE HEART—Shreveport, LA. March 6-8. Deborah A. McMartin, Dir., 2110 Surrey La., Bossier City, LA 71111.

LET'S WRITE!—Lafayette, LA. April 3-4. Rosalind Foley, Dir., Writers' Guild of Acadiana, P.O. Box 51532, Lafayette, LA 70505-1532.

INVESTIGATIVE REPORTERS & EDITORS NATIONAL CONFERENCE—New Orleans, LA. June 3-7. Brant Houston, Executive Dir., 138 Neff Annex, Columbia, MO 65211.

MAINE

WELLS WRITERS' WORKSHOP 1998—Wells, ME. May, July, September. V.A. Levine, Dir., 69 Broadway, Concord, NH 03301-2736.

STONECOAST WRITERS' CONFERENCE—Freeport, ME. July. Conf. Dir., Summer Session Office, Univ. of Southern Maine, 37 College Ave., Gorham, ME 04038.

DOWNEAST MAINE WRITER'S WORKSHOPS—Stockton Springs, ME. July, August, October. Janet J. Barron, Dir., P.O. Box 446, Stockton Springs, ME 04981.

58TH ANNUAL STATE OF MAINE WRITERS' CONFERENCE—Ocean Park, ME. August 25-28. Richard F. Burns, Dir., P.O. Box 7146, Ocean Park, ME 04063-7146.

MARYLAND

SANDY COVE CHRISTIAN WRITERS CONFERENCE—North East, MD. October 4-8. Gayle Roper, Dir., P.O. Box B, North East, MD 21901.

MASSACHUSETTS

TRURO CENTER FOR THE ARTS AT CASTLE HILL WRITERS WORKSHOPS—Truro, MA. Various dates. Marge Piercy, Dir., P.O. Box 756, Truro, MA 02666.

OUTWRITE CONFERENCE—Boston, MA. February 20-22. Ann Holder, Dir., 29 Stanhope St., Boston, MA 02116.

EASTERN WRITER'S CONFERENCE—Salem, MA. June 12-13. Rod Kessler, Dir., Salem State College, 352 Lafayette St., Salem, MA 01970.

AMERICAN CHRISTIAN WRITERS CONFERENCE—Boston, MA. June 19-20. Reg A. Forder, Dir., American Christian Writers, P.O. Box 110390, Nashville, TN 37222.

HARVARD SUMMER SCHOOL WRITING PROGRAM—Cambridge, MA. June 23-August 14. David Gewanter, Dir., Harvard Summer School, 51 Brattle St., Cambridge, MA 02138.

CAPE COD WRITERS' SUMMER CONFERENCE—Craigville, MA. August 16-21. Don Ellis, Dir., Cape Cod Writers' Center, Inc., P.O. Box 186, Barnstable, MA 02630.

MICHIGAN

MIDLAND WRITER'S CONFERENCE—Midland, MI. June. Katherine T. Redwine, Dir., 1710 W. St. Andrews, Midland, MI 48640.

MARANATHA CHRISTIAN WRITERS SEMINAR—Muskegon, MI. August 17-21. Leona Hertel, Dir., 4759 Lake Harbor Rd., Muskegon, MI 49441-5299.

37TH ANNUAL WRITERS' CONFERENCE CO-SPONSORED BY OAKLAND UNIVERSITY AND DETROIT WOMEN WRITERS—Rochester, MI. October 17-18. Gloria J. Boddy, Dir., Writers' Conference, 231 Varner Hall, Oakland Univ., Rochester, NY 48309-4401.

MINNESOTA

NORCROFT: A WRITING RETREAT FOR WOMEN—Lutsen, MN. May-October. Jean Sramek, Dir., 32 East First St., #330, Duluth, MN 55802.

YOUNG PLAYWRIGHTS' SUMMER CONFERENCE—St. Paul, MN. July 12-25. Buffy Sedlachek, Dir., The Playwrights' Center, 2301 Franklin Ave. E., Minneapolis, MN 55406-1099.

SPLIT ROCK ARTS PROGRAM-UNIVERSITY OF MINNESOTA—Duluth, MN. July-August. Andrea Gilats, Dir., 306 Wesbrook Hall, Univ. of Minnesota, 77 Pleasant St. S.E., Minneapolis, MN 55455.

"WRITING TO SELL"—Minneapolis, MN. August 8. Minneapolis Writers' Workshop, P.O. Box 24356, Minneapolis, MN 55424.

AMERICAN CHRISTIAN WRITERS CONFERENCE—Minneapolis, MN. August 14-15. Reg A. Forder, Dir., American Christian Writers, P.O. Box 110390, Nashville, TN 37222.

MISSISSIPPI

SPRINGMINGLE '98!—Hattiesburg, MI. March. Joan Broerman, Reg. Advisor, SCBWI, 1616 Kestwick Dr., Birmingham, AL 35226.

MISSOURI

NEW LETTERS WEEKEND WRITERS CONFERENCE—Kansas City, MO. June. James McKinley, Dir., Arts & Sciences Cont. Ed., UMKC, 215 SSB, Kansas City, MO 64110.

THE WRITING CAMP TEENAGERS—Springfield, MO. June. Sandy Asher, Dir., Drury College, 900 N. Benton Ave., Springfield, MO 65802.

HEARTLAND WRITERS CONFERENCE—Sikeston, MO. June 4-6. Boni Heck, Dir., P.O. Box 5, Cape Girardeau, MO 63701.

AMERICAN CHRISTIAN WRITERS CONFERENCE—St. Louis, MO. September 11-12. Reg A. Forder, Dir., American Christian Writers, P.O. Box 110390, Nashville, TN 37222.

SENIOR WRITERS RETREAT—Springfield, MO. October. Sandy Asher, Dir., Drury College, 900 N. Benton Ave., Springfield, MO 65802.

CAT WRITERS' ASSN. ANNUAL WRITERS' CONFERENCE—Kansas City, MO. November 20-22. Amy D. Shojai, Pres., P.O. Box 1904, Sherman, TX 75091-1904.

MONTANA

SAGEBRUSH WRITERS WORKSHOP—Big Timber, MT. Spring. Gwen Petersen, Dir., Sagebrush Writers, Box 1255, Big Timber, MT 59011-4227.

ENVIRONMENTAL WRITING INSTITUTE—Corvallis, MT. May. Hank Harrington, Dir., Environmental Studies Program, Univ. of Montana, Missoula, MT 59812.

YELLOW BAY WRITERS' WORKSHOP—Flathead Lake, MT. August 9-15. Annick Smith, Dir., Ctr. for Cont. Ed., Univ. of Montana, Missoula, MT 59812.

NEVADA

READING AND WRITING THE WEST—Reno, NV. July 12-24. Stephen Tchudi, Dir., Dept. of English (098), Univ. of Nevada, Reno, NV 89557-0031.

NEW HAMPSHIRE

ODYSSEY: THE SUMMER FANTASY WRITING WORKSHOP—Manchester, NH. June-July. Jeanne Cavelos, Dir., Odyssey, 20 Levesque La., Mont Vernon, NH 03057.

20TH ANNUAL FESTIVAL OF POETRY—Franconia, NH. August 2-8. Donald Sheehan, Dir., The Frost Place, Box 74, Franconia, NH 03580.

SEACOAST WRITERS ASSOCIATION FALL CONFERENCE—Chester, NH. October. Paula Flanders, Dir., Seacoast Writers Assoc., P.O. Box 6553, Portsmouth, NH 03802-6553.

NEW JERSEY

THE COLLEGE OF NEW JERSEY—Trenton, NJ. April. Jean Hollander, Dir., The Writers Conference, Dept. of English, The College of New Jersey, Hillwood Lakes 4700, Trenton, NJ 08650-4700.

NEW MEXICO

WRITING RETREAT CANOE TRIP WITH SHARON OLDS—Heron Lake State Park, NM. May 16-23. Beverly Antaeus, Dir., Hawk, I'm Your Sister, P.O. Box 9109, Santa Fe, NM 87504-9109.

TAOS SCHOOL OF WRITING—Taos Ski Valley, NM. July. Norman Zollinger, Dir., P.O. Box 20496, Albuquerque, NM 87154.

SOUTHWEST WRITERS WORKSHOP 16TH ANNUAL CONFERENCE—Albuquerque, NM. September 17-19. Carol Bruce-Fritz, Dir., Southwest Writers Workshop, 1338-B Wyoming Blvd. N.E., Albuquerque, NM 87112.

NEW YORK

"MEET THE AGENTS/BIG APPLE WRITING WORKSHOPS"—New York, NY. April 18-19. Hannelore Hahn, Dir., International Women's Writing Guild, P.O. Box 810, Gracie Station, New York, NY 10028.

HOFSTRA UNIVERSITY/SCBWI CHILDREN'S LITERATURE CONFERENCE—Hempstead, NY. April 25. Lewis Shena, Dir., Hofstra Univ., Hempstead, NY 11550-1090.

ASJA ANNUAL WRITER'S CONFERENCE—New York, NY. May 9-10. Alexandra Cantor Owens, Dir., ASJA, 1501 Broadway, #302, New York, NY 10036.

VASSAR COLLEGE INSTITUTE OF PUBLISHING AND WRITING: CHILDREN'S BOOKS IN THE MARKETPLACE—Poughkeepsie, NY. June. Maryann Bruno, Assoc. Dir. of College Relations, Vassar College, Box 300, 124 Raymond Ave., Poughkeepsie, NY 12604.

WRITER'S CONFERENCE '98 SIXTH ANNUAL—New York, NY. June. Lewis Burke Frumkes, Dir., Marymount Manhattan College, 221 E. 71st St., New York, NY 10021.

THE COLGATE UNIVERSITY CHENANGO VALLEY WRITERS' CONFERENCE—Hamilton, NY. June 28-July 4. Frederick Busch, Dir., CVWC, Colgate Univ., Hamilton, NY 13346.

MANHATTANVILLE'S SUMMER WRITERS' WEEK—Purchase, NY. June 29-July 3. Ruth Dowd, RSCJ, Manhattanville College, 2900 Purchase St., Purchase, NY 10577.

HOFSTRA UNIVERSITY SUMMER WRITERS' CONFERENCE—Hempstead, NY. July. Lewis Shena, Dir., UCCE, Hofstra Univ., Hempstead, NY 11550-1090.

FEMINIST WOMEN'S WRITING WORKSHOPS—Geneva, NY. July. Kit Wainer, Dir., P.O. Box 6583, Ithaca, NY 14851.

NEW YORK STATE SUMMER WRITERS INSTITUTE—Saratoga Springs, NY. July 6-31. Robert Boyers, Dir., NYS Summer Writers Institute, Skidmore College, Saratoga Springs, NY 12866.

ROBERT QUACKENBUSH'S CHILDREN'S BOOK WRITING AND ILLUSTRATING WORKSHOPS—New York, NY. July 13-17. Robert Quackenbush, Dir., Quackenbush Studios, 460 E. 79th St., New York, NY 10021.

"REMEMBER THE MAGIC" 21ST ANNUAL SUMMER CONFERENCE—Saratoga Springs, NY. August 14-21. Hannelore Hahn, Dir., International Women's Writing Guild, P.O. Box 810, Gracie Station, New York, NY 10028.

North Carolina

NORTH CAROLINA WRITERS' NETWORK ANNUAL SPRING GATHERING—Chapel Hill, NC. June 6. Bobbie Collins-Perry, Program Dir., 1998 Spring Gathering, NC Writers' Network, P.O. Box 954, Carrboro, NC 27510.

THE ASHEVILLE POETRY FESTIVAL—Asheville, NC. July 10-12. Allan Wolf, Dir., Poetry Alive!, 20 Battery Park, Suite 505, Asheville, NC 28801.

DUKE UNIVERSITY WRITERS' WORKSHOPS—Durham, NC. June-September. Georgann Eubanks, Dir., Box 90700, Durham, NC 27708.

NORTH CAROLINA WRITERS' NETWORK'S FIFTEENTH ANNUAL FALL CONFERENCE—Winston-Salem, NC. November 20-22. Bobbie Collins-Perry, Program Dir., NCWN 1998 Fall Conference, NC Writers' Network, P.O. Box 954, Carrboro, NC 27510.

Ohio

LEA LEEVER OLDHAM'S WRITERS CONFERENCES—Various locations & dates. Lea Leever Oldham, Dir., 34200 Ridge Rd., #110, Willoughby, OH 44094.

READING, WRITING & ROMANCE—Cincinnati, OH. April 17-18. Lisa Anne Howell, Dir., 20 Maple Valley La., Alexandria, KY 41001.

THE HEIGHTS WRITER'S CONFERENCE—Beachwood, OH. May 2. Lavern Hall, Dir., Writer's World Press, P.O. Box 24684, Cleveland, OH 44124-0684.

SECOND ANNUAL MAUMEE VALLEY FREELANCE WRITER'S CONFERENCE—Sylvania, OH. May 16. Gloria Burke, Dir., Lourdes College, 6832 Convent Blvd., Sylvania, OH 43560.

ANTIOCH WRITERS' WORKSHOP—Yellow Springs, OH. Summer. Gilah Rittenhouse, Dir., Antioch Writers' Workshop, P.O. Box 494, Yellow Springs, OH 45387.

IMAGINATION—Cleveland, OH. July. Neal Chandler, Dir., English Dept., Cleveland State Univ., Cleveland, OH 44115.

SKYLINE WRITERS CONFERENCE—North Royalton, OH. August. Mildred Claus, Dir., Skyline Writers Club, P.O. Box 33343, North Royalton, OH 44133.

THE COLUMBUS WRITERS CONFERENCE—Columbus, OH. September. Angela Palazzolo, Dir., The Columbus Writers Conference, P.O. Box 20548, Columbus, OH 43220.

30TH ANNUAL MIDWEST WRITERS' CONFERENCE—Canton, OH. October 2-3. Debbie Ruhe, Dir., Midwest Writers' Conference, Kent State Univ., Stark Campus, 6000 Frank Ave. N.W., Canton, OH 44720.

Oklahoma

OPPORTUNITY '98 WRITERS AND ARTISTS WORKSHOP—Norman, OK. March. Polly G. Blanton, Dir., Rt. 2, Box 104, Noble, OK 73068.

NORTHWEST OKLAHOMA WRITER'S WORKSHOP—Enid, OK. Spring. Dr. Earl Mabry, Dir., P.O. Box 1308, Enid, OK 73702.

SHORT COURSE ON PROFESSIONAL WRITING—Norman, OK. June. J. Madison Davis, Dir., Univ. of Oklahoma, 226 Copeland Hall, Norman, OK 73019.

THE OKLAHOMA FALL ARTS INSTITUTE'S WRITING WORK-SHOP—Stillwater, OK. October 22-25. Mary Gordon Taft, Dir., Oklahoma Arts Institute, P.O. Box 18154, Oklahoma City, OK 73154.

THIRD ANNUAL FALL WRITER'S CONFERENCE—Ada, OK. October 24-25. Pamela Bailey, Dir., East Central Univ., Ctr. for Cont. Ed., Box E-3, Ada, OK 74820.

OREGON

FISHTRAP WINTER & SUMMER GATHERING—Wallowa Lake, OR. February, July. Rich Wandschneider, Dir., Fishtrap, P.O. Box 38, Enterprise, OR 97828.

COOS BAY WRITERS CONFERENCE—Coos Bay, OR. Summer. Mary Scheirman, Dir., Box 4022, Coos Bay, OR 97420.

THE FLIGHT OF THE MIND, SUMMER WRITING WORKSHOP FOR WOMEN—McKenzie Bridge, OR. June 19-26. June 28-July 5. Judith Barrington, Dir., Flight of the Mind, 622 S.E. 29th Ave., Portland, OR 97214.

PENNSYLVANIA

PENNWRITERS ANNUAL CONFERENCE—Grantville, PA. May. C.J. Houghtaling, Dir., R.R. 2, Box 241, Middlebury Center, PA 16935.

PHILADELPHIA WRITER'S CONFERENCE—Philadelphia, PA. June. Dina Leacock, Dir., 11 Colleen Ct., Medford, NJ 08055.

ST. DAVID'S CHRISTIAN WRITERS CONFERENCE—Beaver Falls, PA. June. Audrey Stallsmith, Registrar, 87 Pines Rd. E., Hadley, PA 16130.

MONTROSE CHRISTIAN WRITERS' CONFERENCE—Montrose, PA. July 6-10. Patti Souder, Dir., 5 Locust St., Montrose, PA 18801.

12TH ANNUAL LIGONIER VALLEY WRITERS CONFERENCE—Ligonier, PA. July 10-12. Tina Thoburn, Dir., Box B, Ligonier, PA 15658.

BOUCHERCON 29, THE WORLD MYSTERY CONVENTION—Philadelphia, PA. October 1-4. Deen Kogan, Dir., 507 S. Eighth St., Philadelphia, PA 19147.

RHODE ISLAND

PROVIDENCE WRITERS CONFERENCE—Providence, RI. October. Eleyne Austen Sharp, Dir., Community Writers Assoc., P.O. Box 312, Providence, RI 02901.

SOUTH CAROLINA

5TH ANNUAL SOUTH CAROLINA PLAYWRIGHT'S CONFERENCE—Beaufort, SC. June. Nancy Andrepont, Secretary, SCPC, 1003 Charles St., Beaufort, SC 29902.

SOUTH CAROLINA CHRISTIAN WRITERS CONFERENCE—Conestee, SC. September 26. Betty Robertson, Dir., P.O. Box 12624, Roanoke, VA 24027.

SOUTH CAROLINA WRITERS WORKSHOP—Myrtle Beach, SC. October 10-12. Elizabeth Leopard, Dir., 79 Suffolk Dr., Aiken, SC 29803-7825.

TENNESSEE

RHODES WRITING CAMP—Memphis, TN. June 14-26. Dr. Beth Kamhi, Dir., Dept. of English, Rhodes College, 2000 North Pkwy., Memphis, TN 38112.

SEWANEE WRITERS' CONFERENCE—Sewanee, TN. July 14-26. Wyatt Prunty, Dir., 310 St. Luke's Hall, 735 University Ave., Sewanee, TN 37383-1000.

AMERICAN CHRISTIAN WRITERS RETREAT—Nashville, TN. September 4-7. Reg A. Forder, Dir., American Christian Writers, P.O. Box 110390, Nashville, TN 37222.

TEXAS

AUSTIN WRITERS' LEAGUE SPRING & FALL CONFERENCES—Austin, TX. Ongoing. Angela Smith, Dir., Austin Writers' League, 1501 W. 5th St., Suite E-2, Austin, TX 78703.

AMERICAN CHRISTIAN WRITERS CONFERENCE—Dallas, TX. May 15-16. Reg Forder, Dir., American Christian Writers, P.O. Box 110390, Nashville, TN 37222.

AGENTS! AGENTS! AGENTS!—Austin, TX. July. Angela Smith, Dir., Austin Writers' League, 1501 W. Fifth St., Suite E-2, Austin, TX 78703.

VERMONT

WILDBRANCH WORKSHOP IN OUTDOOR NATURAL HISTORY & ENVIRONMENTAL WRITING—Craftsbury Common, VT. June. David W. Brown, Dir., Wildbranch, Sterling College, Craftsbury Common, VT 05827.

BREAD LOAF WRITERS' CONFERENCE—Ripton, VT. August 11-23. Michael Collier, Dir., BLWC, Middlebury College, Middlebury, VT 05753.

THE OLDERS' CHILDREN'S WRITING WORKSHOP—Albany, VT. Fall. Effin & Jules Older, Dirs., 3 New St., Albany, VT 05820.

VIRGINIA

NORTHERN VIRGINIA CHRISTIAN WRITERS' CONFERENCE—Fairfax, VA. March 14. Jennifer Ferranti, Dir., NOVA Christian Writers, Box 629, Dunn Loring, VA 22027.

CHRISTOPHER NEWPORT UNIVERSITY WRITERS' CONFERENCE—Newport News, VA. April. Terry Cox-Joseph, Dir., Office of Cont. Education, Christopher Newport Univ., 50 Shoe La., Newport News, VA 23606.

VIRGINIA CHRISTIAN WRITERS CONFERENCE—Hampton, VA. April 4. Betty Robertson, CCM Publishing, Box 12624, Roanoke, VA 24027.

HIGHLAND SUMMER CONFERENCE—Radford, VA. June. Grace Toney Edwards, Dir., Appalachian Regional Studies Ctr., P.O. Box 7014, Radford Univ., Radford, VA 24142.

ED PRESS CONFERENCE—Alexandria, VA. June. Charlene F. Gaynor, Rowan Univ./ Ed Press, 201 Mullia Hill Rd., Glassboro, NJ 08028.

SHENANDOAH INTERNATIONAL PLAYWRIGHTS RETREAT—Staunton, VA. August. Robert Graham Small, Dir., Pennyroyal Farm, Rt. 5, Box 167-F, Staunton, VA 24401.

WASHINGTON

WRITER'S WEEKEND AT THE BEACH—Ocean Park, WA. February. Birdie Etchison, Dir., P.O. Box 877, Ocean Park, WA 98640.

CLARION WEST SCIENCE FICTION & FANTASY WRITERS WORKSHOP—Seattle, WA. June 21-July 31. Leslie Howle, Dir., 340 15th Ave. E., Suite 350, Seattle, WA 98112.

PORT TOWNSEND WRITERS' CONFERENCE—Port Townsend, WA. July. Sam Hamill, Dir., Centrum-Writers' Conference, Box 1158, Port Townsend, WA 98368.

AMERICAN CHRISTIAN WRITERS CONFERENCE—Seattle, WA. October 2-3. Reg Forder, Dir., American Christian Writers, P.O. Box 110390, Nashville, TN 37222.

WISCONSIN

UW-MADISON SCHOOL OF THE ARTS AT RHINELANDER CONFERENCE—Rhinelander, WI. July. Harv Thompson, Dir., 715 Lowell Hall, 610 Langdon St., Madison, WI 53703.

GREEN LAKE WRITERS CONFERENCE—Green Lake, WI. July 4-11. Jan DeWitt, Program V.P., Green Lake Conference Ctr., W2511 State Hwy. 23, Green Lake, WI 54941-9300.

WISCONSIN SCBWI FALL RETREAT—Madison, WI. October. Patricia Pfitsch, Dir., Rt. 1, Box 136, Gays Mills, WI 54631.

INTERNATIONAL

BERMUDA NATURE & SCIENCE WRITING—Biological Station, Bermuda. March. Bill Sargent, Dir., 7 Lawnwood Pl., Charlestown, MA 02129.

SIMON FRASER UNIVERSITY SUMMER PUBLISHING WORKSHOPS—Vancouver, BC, Canada. July-August. Ron Woodward, Dir., Simon Fraser Univ. at Harbour Centre, 515 W. Hastings St., Vancouver, BC, Canada V6B 5K3.

VICTORIA SCHOOL OF WRITING—Victoria, BC, Canada. July 14-17. Margaret Dyment, Dir., 607 Linden Ave., Victoria, BC, Canada V8V 4G6.

PRAGUE SUMMER WRITERS WORKSHOP—Prague, Czech Republic. July 5-August 2. Trevor Top, Dir., UNO, Box 1171, New Orleans, LA 70148.

EIGHTEENTH ANNUAL WRITERS' CONFERENCE—Winchester, Hampshire, England. June 28-30. Barbara Large, Dir., Chinook Southdown Rd., Shawford, Hampshire, England SO21 2BY.

WRITER'S WORKSHOPS IN GUATEMALA—La Antigua, Guatemala. Various dates. Liza Fourré, Dir., Art Workshops in La Antigua, Guatemala, 4758 Lyndale Ave. S., Minneapolis, MN 55409-2304.

JERUSALEM INTERNATIONAL WRITERS' WORKSHOP—Jerusalem, Israel. August. Trevor Top, Dir., UNO, Box 1171, New Orleans, LA 70148.

LATIN AMERICA WRITERS' WORKSHOP—Taxco, Mexico. January, March. Trevor Top, Dir., UNO, Box 1171, New Orleans, LA 70148.

ST. PETERSBURG WRITERS' WORKSHOP—St. Petersburg, Russia. June. Trevor Top, Dir., UNO, Box 1171, New Orleans, LA 70148.

STATE ARTS COUNCILS

State arts councils sponsor grants, fellowships, and other programs for writers. To be eligible for funding, a writer *must* be a resident of the state in which he is applying. Write or call for more information; 1-800 numbers are toll free for in-state calls only; numbers preceded by TDD indicate Telecommunications Device for the Deaf; TTY indicates Teletypewriter.

ALABAMA STATE COUNCIL ON THE ARTS
201 Monroe St., Suite 110
Montgomery, AL 36130
(334) 242-4076; fax: (334) 240-3269
Albert B. Head, *Executive Director*

ALASKA STATE COUNCIL ON THE ARTS
411 W. 4th Ave., Suite 1E
Anchorage, AK 99501-2343
(907) 269-6610; fax: (907) 269-6601
Shannon Planchon, *Grants Officer*
Kathy Fisher, *Contact Person*

ARIZONA COMMISSION ON THE ARTS
417 W. Roosevelt
Phoenix, AZ 85003
(602) 255-5882; fax: (602) 256-0282
Attn: Jill Bernstein, *Presenting/Touring/Literature Director*

ARKANSAS ARTS COUNCIL
1500 Tower Bldg.
323 Center St.
Little Rock, AR 72201
(501) 324-9766; fax: (501) 324-9154
James E. Mitchell, *Executive Director*

CALIFORNIA ARTS COUNCIL
1300 I St., Suite 930
Sacramento, CA 95814
(916) 322-6555; fax: (916) 322-6575; TDD: (916) 322-6569; e-mail:
cac@cwo.com; internet: http://www.cac.ca.gov
Gay Carroll, *Public Information Officer*

COLORADO COUNCIL ON THE ARTS
750 Pennsylvania St.
Denver, CO 80203-3699
(303) 894-2617; fax: (303) 894-2615
Fran Holden, *Executive Director*

CONNECTICUT COMMISSION ON THE ARTS
1 Financial Plaza
Hartford, CT 06103
(860) 566-4770; fax: (860) 566-6462
John Ostrout, *Executive Director*

DELAWARE DIVISION OF THE ARTS
Carvel State Building
820 N. French St.
Wilmington, DE 19801
(302) 577-8278; fax: (302) 577-6561
Barbara King, *Artist Services Coordinator*

FLORIDA ARTS COUNCIL
Dept. of State
Div. of Cultural Affairs
The Capitol
Tallahassee, FL 32399-0250
(904) 487-2980; fax: (904) 922-5259; TTY: (904) 488-5779
internet: www.dos.state.fl.us
Attn: Ms. Peyton Fearington

GEORGIA COUNCIL FOR THE ARTS
530 Means St. N.W., Suite 115
Atlanta, GA 30318
(404) 651-7920; fax: (404) 651-7922
Caroline Ballard Leake, *Executive Director*
Ann R. Davis, *Grants Manager, Literature*

HAWAII STATE FOUNDATION ON CULTURE AND THE ARTS
44 Merchant St.
Honolulu, HI 96813
(808) 586-0300; fax: (808) 586-0308
Holly Richards, *Executive Director*

IDAHO COMMISSION ON THE ARTS
Box 83720
Boise, ID 83720-0008
(208) 334-2119; fax (208) 334-2488
Attn: Diane Josephy Peavey

ILLINOIS ARTS COUNCIL
James R. Thompson Center
100 W. Randolph, Suite 10-500
Chicago, IL 60601
(312) 814-4990; (800) 237-6994; fax: (312) 814-1471
Richard Gage, *Director of Communication Arts*

INDIANA ARTS COMMISSION
402 W. Washington St., Rm. 072
Indianapolis, IN 46204-2741
(317) 232-1268; TDD: (317) 233-3001; fax: (317) 232-5595
Dorothy Ilgen, *Executive Director*

IOWA ARTS COUNCIL
600 E. Locust
Des Moines, IA 50319-0290
(515) 282-6500; fax: (515) 242-6498
Attn: Stephen Poole

KANSAS ARTS COMMISSION
Jayhawk Tower
700 S.W. Jackson, Suite 1004
Topeka, KS 66603-3758
(913) 296-3335; fax: (913) 296-4989; TTY: (800) 766-3777
Robert T. Burtch, *Editor*

KENTUCKY ARTS COUNCIL
31 Fountain Pl.
Frankfort, KY 40601
(502) 564-3757; fax: (502) 564-2839; TDD: (502) 564-3757
Attn: Gerri Combs, *Executive Director*

LOUISIANA STATE ARTS COUNCIL
Box 44247
Baton Rouge, LA 70804
(504) 342-8180; fax: (504) 342-8173
James Borders, *Executive Director*

MAINE ARTS COMMISSION
25 State House Station
Augusta, ME 04333-0025
(207) 287-2724; fax: (207) 287-2335; TDD: (207) 287-6740
Alden C. Wilson, *Director*

MARYLAND STATE ARTS COUNCIL
Arts-in-Education Program
601 N. Howard St.
Baltimore, MD 21201
(410) 333-8232; fax: (410) 333-1062
Linda Vlasak, *Program Director*
Pamela Dunne, *Artists-in-Education Program Coordinator*

MASSACHUSETTS CULTURAL COUNCIL
120 Boylston St., 2nd Floor
Boston, MA 02116-4802
(617) 727-3668; (800) 232-0960; TTY: (617) 338-9153
Attn: Robert Ayres

MICHIGAN COUNCIL FOR ARTS AND CULTURAL AFFAIRS
1200 Sixth St., Suite 1180
Detroit, MI 48226-2461
(313) 256-3731; fax: (313) 256-3781
Betty Boone, *Executive Director*

MINNESOTA STATE ARTS BOARD
Park Square Court
400 Sibley St., Suite 200
St. Paul, MN 55101-1928
(612) 215-1600; (800) 8MN-ARTS; fax: (612) 215-1600
Karen Mueller, *Artist Assistance Program Associate*

COMPAS: WRITERS & ARTISTS IN THE SCHOOLS
304 Landmark Center
75 W. Fifth St.
St. Paul, MN 55102
(612) 292-3254; fax: (612) 292-3258
Daniel Gabriel, *Director*

MISSISSIPPI ARTS COMMISSION
239 N. Lamar St., Suite 207
Jackson, MS 39201
(601) 359-6030; fax: (601) 359-6008
Betsy Bradley, *Executive Director*

MISSOURI ARTS COUNCIL
Wainwright Office Complex
111 N. 7th St., Suite 105
St. Louis, MO 63101-2188
(314) 340-6845; fax: (314) 340-7215
Michael Hunt, *Program Administrator for Literature*

MONTANA ARTS COUNCIL
316 N. Park Ave., Suite 252
Helena, MT 59620-2201
(406) 444-6430; fax: (406) 444-6548
Fran Morrow, *Director of Artists Services*

NEBRASKA ARTS COUNCIL
3838 Davenport St.
Omaha, NE 68131-2329
(402) 595-2122; fax: (402) 595-2334
Jennifer Severin, *Executive Director*

NEVADA STATE COUNCIL ON THE ARTS
602 N. Curry St.
Carson City, NV 89703
(702) 687-6680; fax: (702) 687-6688
Susan Boskoff, *Executive Director*

NEW HAMPSHIRE STATE COUNCIL ON THE ARTS
Phenix Hall
40 N. Main St.
Concord, NH 03301-4974
(603) 271-2789; fax: (603) 271-3584; TDD: (800) 735-2964
Audrey Sylvester, *Artist Services Coordinator*

NEW JERSEY STATE COUNCIL ON THE ARTS
Artist Services
CN 306
Trenton, NJ 08625
(609) 292-6130; fax: (609) 989-1440
Beth Vogel, *Manager Arts Education & Artists Services*

NEW MEXICO ARTS
228 E. Palace Ave.
Santa Fe, NM 87501
(505) 827-6490; fax: (505) 827-6043
Randy Forrester, *Local Arts Coordinator*

NEW YORK STATE COUNCIL ON THE ARTS
915 Broadway
New York, NY 10010
(212) 387-7022; fax: (212) 387-7164
Kathleen Masterson, *Director, Literature Program*

NORTH CAROLINA ARTS COUNCIL
Dept. of Cultural Resources
Raleigh, NC 27601-2807
(919) 733-2111 ext. 22; fax: (919) 733-4834; e-mail:
dmcgill@ncacmail.dcr.state.nc.us
Deborah McGill, *Literature Director*

NORTH DAKOTA COUNCIL ON THE ARTS
418 E. Broadway, Suite 70
Bismarck, ND 58501-4086
(701) 328-3954; fax: (701) 328-3963
Patsy Thompson, *Executive Director*

OHIO ARTS COUNCIL
727 E. Main St.
Columbus, OH 43205-1796
(614) 466-2613; fax: (614) 466-4494
Bob Fox, *Literature Program Coordinator*

OKLAHOMA ARTS COUNCIL
P.O. Box 52001-2001
Oklahoma City, OK 73152-2001
(405) 521-2931; fax: (405) 521-6418
Betty Price, *Executive Director*

OREGON ARTS COMMISSION
775 Summer St. N.E.
Salem, OR 97310
(503) 986-0084; fax: (503) 986-0260; e-mail:
oregon.artscomm@state.or.us; internet: http://www.das.state.or.us/oac/
Attn: *Assistant Director*

PENNSYLVANIA COUNCIL ON THE ARTS
Room 216, Finance Bldg.
Harrisburg, PA 17120
(717) 787-6883; fax (717) 783-2538
James Woland, *Literature Program*
Attn: *Director Education Program*

RHODE ISLAND STATE COUNCIL ON THE ARTS
95 Cedar St., Suite 103
Providence, RI 02903
(401) 277-3880; fax: (401) 521-1351
Randall Rosenbaum, *Executive Director*

SOUTH CAROLINA ARTS COMMISSION
1800 Gervais St.
Columbia, SC 29201
(803) 734-8696; fax: (803) 734-8526
Sara June Goldstein, *Director, Literary Arts Program*

SOUTH DAKOTA ARTS COUNCIL
800 Governors Dr.
Pierre, SD 57501-2294
(605) 773-3131; fax: (605) 773-6962
Attn: Dennis Holub, *Executive Director*

TENNESSEE ARTS COMMISSION
401 Charlotte Ave.
Nashville, TN 37243-0780
(615) 741-1701; fax: (615) 741-8559; e-mail: aswanson@mail.state.tn.us
Attn: Alice Swanson

TEXAS COMMISSION ON THE ARTS
P.O. Box 13406
Austin, TX 78711-3406
(512) 463-5535; fax: (512) 475-2699

UTAH ARTS COUNCIL
617 E. South Temple
Salt Lake City, UT 84102-1177
(801) 533-5895; fax: (801) 533-6196
Guy Lebeda, *Literary Coordinator*

VERMONT ARTS COUNCIL
136 State St., Drawer 33
Montpelier, VT 05633-6001
(802) 828-3291; fax: (802) 828-3363
Michele Bailey, *Artist Grants Coordinator*

VIRGINIA COMMISSION FOR THE ARTS
223 Governor St.
Richmond, VA 23219
(804) 225-3132; fax: (804) 225-4327
Peggy J. Baggett, *Executive Director*

WASHINGTON STATE ARTS COMMISSION
234 E. 8th Ave.
P.O. Box 42675
Olympia, WA 98504-2675
(360) 753-3860 or (360)586-2421
Bitsy Bidwell, *Community Arts Development Manager*

WEST VIRGINIA DIVISION OF CULTURE & HISTORY
WV Commission on the Arts
Culture and History Division
The Cultural Center, Capitol Complex
1900 Kanawha Blvd. E.
Charleston, WV 25305-0300
(304) 558-0220; fax: (304) 558-2779
Lakin Ray Cook, *Executive Director*

WISCONSIN ARTS BOARD
101 E. Wilson St., 1st Floor
Madison, WI 53702
(608) 266-0190; fax: (608) 267-0380
George Tzougros, *Executive Director*

WYOMING ARTS COUNCIL
2320 Capitol Ave.
Cheyenne, WY 82002
(307) 777-7742; fax: (307) 777-5499; e-mail: mshay@missc.state.wy.us
Michael Shay, *Literature Program Manager*

ORGANIZATIONS FOR WRITERS

ACADEMY OF AMERICAN POETS
584 Broadway, Suite 1208
New York, NY 10012
(212) 274-0343; fax: (212) 274-9427
Jonathan Galassi, *President*
    The Academy was founded in 1934 to support American poets at all stages of their careers and to foster the appreciation of contemporary poetry. The largest organization in the country dedicated specifically to the art of poetry, the academy sponsors a number of prizes and programs: an annual fellowship for distinguished poetic achievement; the Tanning prize, the largest annual literary award in the U.S.; the Lenore Marshall Poetry Prize; the James Laughlin Award; the Walt Whitman Award; the Harold Morton Landon Translation Award; poetry prizes at colleges and universities; and the American Poets Fund and the Atlas Fund, which provide financial assistance to poets and publishers of poetry. Readings, lectures, and regional symposia take place in New York City and throughout the United States. Membership is open to all. Annual dues: $25 and up.

AMERICAN SOCIETY OF JOURNALISTS AND AUTHORS, INC.
1501 Broadway, Suite 302
New York, NY 10036
(212) 997-0947
e-mail: ASJA@compuserve.com; web site: http://www.asja.org
Alexandra Owens, *Executive Director*
    A nationwide organization of independent writers of nonfiction dedicated to promoting high standards of nonfiction writing through monthly

meetings, annual writers' conferences, etc. The ASJA produces a free electronic bulletin board for freelance writers on contract issues in the new-media age, and the organization offers extensive benefits and services including referral services, numerous discount services, and the opportunity to explore professional issues and concerns with other writers. Members also receive a monthly newsletter with confidential market information. Membership is open to professional free-lance writers of nonfiction; qualifications are judged by the membership committee. Call or write for application details.

THE ASSOCIATED WRITING PROGRAMS
Tallwood House, Mail Stop 1E3
George Mason University
Fairfax, VA 22030
(703) 993-4301; fax: (703) 993-4302
Attn: *Membership*

The AWP seeks to serve writers and teachers in need of community, support, information, inspiration, contacts, and ideas. Provides publishing opportunities, job listings, and an active exchange of ideas on writing and teaching, including an annual conference. Members receive six issues of *AWP Chronicle* and seven issues of *AWP Job List*. Publications include *The AWP Official Guide to Creative Writing Programs*. Annual dues: $50, *individual*; $30, *student*.

THE AUTHORS GUILD, INC.
330 W. 42nd St., 29th Fl.
New York, NY 10036-6902
(212) 563-5904; fax: (212) 564-5363
e-mail: staff@authorsguild.org
Attn: *Membership Committee*

As the largest organization of published writers in America, membership offers writers of all genres legal advice, reviews of publishing and agency contracts, and access to seminars around the country on subjects of concern to authors. The Authors Guild also lobbies on behalf of all authors on issues such as copyright, taxation, and freedom of expression. A writer who has published a book in the last seven years with an established publisher, or has published three articles in periodicals of general circulation within the last eighteen months is eligible for active voting membership. An unpublished writer who has received a contract offer may be eligible for associate membership. All members of the Authors Guild automatically become members of its parent organization, the Authors League of America. First year annual dues: $90.

THE DRAMATISTS GUILD
1501 Broadway, Suite 701
New York, NY 10036-3909
(212) 398-9366
Peter Stone, *President*; Richard Garmise, *Executive Director*

The national professional association of playwrights, composers, and lyricists, the guild was established to protect dramatists' rights and to improve working conditions. Services include use of the guild's contracts; a toll-free number for members in need of business counseling; a discount ticket service; access to two health insurance programs and a group term life insurance plan; and numerous seminars. The Frederick Lowe room is available to members for readings and rehearsals at a nominal fee. Publications include *The Dramatists Guild Quarterly*, *The Dramatists Guild Resource Directory*, and *The Dramatists Guild Newsletter*. All playwrights, produced or not, are eligible for membership. Annual dues: $125, *active*; $75, *associate*; $35, *student*.

THE GENRE WRITER'S ASSOCIATION
P.O. Box 6301
Concord, CA 94524
(510) 254-7053
Bobbi Sinha-Morey, *Editor*

An international service organization, GWA is dedicated to the promotion of excellence in the fields of science fiction, fantasy, mystery, western, and horror writing. Members receive *The Genre Writer's News* plus market supplements, *Horror: The News Magazine of the Horror & Fantasy Field*, a membership roster, and discounts on certain products. The association also sponsors awards. Membership is open to any writer, poet, artist, editor, publisher, or calligrapher who participates in these literary genres. Annual dues are $25 for U.S. members; $30 for others.

INTERNATIONAL ASSOCIATION OF CRIME WRITERS
(NORTH AMERICAN BRANCH)
P.O. Box 8674
New York, NY 10116-8674
(212) 243-8966
J. Madison Davis, *President*

This international association was founded in 1987 to promote communications among crime writers worldwide, encourage translation of crime writing into other languages, and defend authors against censorship and other forms of tyranny. The IACW sponsors a number of conferences, publishes a quarterly newsletter, *Border Patrol*, and annually awards the Hammett prize for literary excellence in crime writing to a work of fiction by a U.S. or Canadian author. Membership is open to published authors of crime fiction, nonfiction, and screenplays. Agents, editors, and booksellers in the mystery field are also eligible to apply. Annual dues: $50.

INTERNATIONAL ASSOCIATION OF THEATRE FOR CHILDREN
AND YOUNG PEOPLE
Box 22365
Seattle, WA 98122-0365
(206) 392-2147; fax: (206) 443-0442
e-mail: ASSITEJ@aol.com
Dana Childs, *Office Manager*

The development of professional theater for young audiences and international exchange are the organization's primary mandates. Provides a link between professional theaters, artists, directors, training institutions, and arts agencies; sponsors festivals and forums for interchange among theaters and theater artists. Annual dues: $50, *individual*; $25, *student and retiree*.

THE INTERNATIONAL WOMEN'S WRITING GUILD
Box 810, Gracie Station
New York, NY 10028-0082
(212) 737-7536; fax: (212) 737-9469
e-mail: http://www.iwwg.com
Hannelore Hahn, *Executive Director & Founder*

Founded in 1976, serving as a network for the personal and professional empowerment of women through writing. Services include six issues of a 32-page newsletter, a list of literary agents and publishing services, access to health insurance plans at group rates, access to writing conferences and related events throughout the U.S., including the annual "Remember the Magic" summer conference at Skidmore College in Saratoga Springs, NY, regional writing clusters, and year-round supportive networking. Any woman may join regardless of portfolio. Annual dues: $35; $45 *international.*

MYSTERIES FOR MINORS—(See *Sisters in Crime*)

MYSTERY WRITERS OF AMERICA, INC.
17 E. 47th St., 6th Fl.
New York, NY 10017
(212) 888-8171; fax: (212) 888-8107
Priscilla Ridgway, *Executive Director*
   The MWA exists for the purpose of raising the prestige of mystery and detective writing, and of defending the rights and increasing the income of all writers in the field of mystery, detection, and fact crime writing. Each year, the MWA presents the Edgar Allan Poe Awards for the best mystery writing in a variety of fields. The four classifications of membership are: *active,* open to any writer who has made a sale in the field of mystery, suspense, or crime writing; *associate,* for professionals in allied fields; *corresponding,* for writers living outside the U.S.; *affiliate,* for unpublished writers. Annual dues: $65; $32.50 *corresponding members.*

NATIONAL ASSOCIATION OF SCIENCE WRITERS, INC.
P.O. Box 294
Greenlawn, NY 11740
(516) 757-5664
Diane McGurgan, *Administrative Secretary*
   The NASW promotes the dissemination of accurate information regarding science through all media, and conducts a varied program to increase the flow of news from scientists, to improve the quality of its presentation, and to communicate its meaning to the reading public. Anyone who has been actively engaged in the dissemination of science information is eligible to apply for membership. Active members must be principally involved in reporting on science through newspapers, magazines, TV, or other media that reach the public directly. Associate members report on science through limited-circulation publications and other media. Annual dues: $60.

NATIONAL CONFERENCE OF EDITORIAL WRITERS
6223 Executive Blvd.
Rockville, MD 20852
(301) 984-3015
   A nonprofit professional organization established in 1947, NCEW exists to improve the quality of editorial pages and broadcast editorials, and to promote high standards among opinion writers and editors in North America. The association offers members networking opportunities, regional meetings, page exchanges, foreign tours, educational opportunities and seminars, an annual convention, and a subscription to the quarterly journal *The Masthead.* Membership is open to opinion writers and editors for general-circulation newspapers, radio or television stations, and syndicated columnists; teachers and students of journalism; others who deter-

mine editorial policy. Annual dues are based on circulation or broadcast audience and range from $85 to $150 (journalism educators: $75; students: $50).

THE NATIONAL LEAGUE OF AMERICAN PEN WOMEN, INC.
The Pen Arts Building
1300 17th St. N.W.
Washington, DC 20036-1973
(202) 785-1997
Elaine Waidelich, *National President*

Founded in 1897, the league promotes development of the creative talents of professional women in the arts. Membership is through local branches, available by invitation from current members in the categories of Art, Letters, and Music.

THE NATIONAL WRITERS ASSOCIATION
1450 S. Havana, Suite 424
Aurora, CO 80012
(303) 751-7844
Sandy Whelchel, *Executive Director*

New and established writers, poets, and playwrights throughout the U.S. and Canada may become members of the NWA, a full-time, customer-service-oriented association founded in 1937. Members receive a bimonthly newsletter, *Authorship*, and may attend the annual June conference. Annual dues: $60, *professional*; $50, *regular*; add $25 outside the U.S., Canada, and Mexico.

NATIONAL WRITERS UNION
113 University Place, 6th Fl.
New York, NY 10003
(212) 254-0279
Jonathan Tasini, *President*

Dedicated to bringing about equitable payment and fair treatment of free-lance writers through collective action. Membership is over 4,500 and includes book authors, poets, cartoonists, journalists, and technical writers in 14 chapters nationwide. The union offers its members contract and agent information, group health insurance, press credentials, grievance handling, a quarterly magazine, and sample contracts and resource materials. It sponsors workshops and seminars across the country. Membership is open to writers who have published a book, play, three articles, five poems, one short story or an equivalent amount of newsletter, publicity, technical, commercial, government, or institutional copy, or have written an equivalent amount of unpublished material and are actively seeking publication. Annual dues: $80 to $180.

NORTHWEST PLAYWRIGHTS GUILD
408 S.W. Second Ave., Suite 427
Portland, OR 97204
(503) 222-7010
e-mail: bjscript@teleport.com
Bill Johnson, *Office Manager*

The guild supports and promotes playwrights living in the Northwest through play development, staged readings, and networking for play competitions and production opportunities. Members receive monthly and quarterly newsletters. Annual dues: $25.

OUTDOOR WRITERS ASSOCIATION OF AMERICA, INC.
2155 E. College Ave.
State College, PA 16801
(814) 234-1011
James W. Rainey, *Executive Director*

A non-profit, international organization representing professional communicators who report and reflect upon America's diverse interests in the outdoors. Membership, by nomination only, includes a monthly publication, *Outdoors Unlimited*; annual conference; annual membership directory; contests. The association also provides scholarships to qualified students.

PEN AMERICAN CENTER
568 Broadway
New York, NY 10012
(212) 334-1660
Karen Kennerly, *Executive Director*

PEN American Center is one of more than 120 centers worldwide that compose International PEN. The 2,800 members of the American Center are poets, playwrights, essayists, editors, and novelists, as well as literary translators and those agents who have made a substantial contribution to the literary community. PEN American headquarters is in New York City, and branches are located in Boston, Chicago, New Orleans, Portland, Oregon, and San Francisco. Among the activities, programs, and services sponsored are literary events and awards, outreach projects to encourage reading, assistance to writers in financial need, and international and domestic human rights campaigns on behalf of many writers, editors, and journalists censored or imprisoned because of their writing. Membership is open to writers who have published two books of literary merit, as well as editors, agents, playwrights, and translators who meet specific standards; apply to membership committee.

THE PLAYWRIGHTS' CENTER
2301 Franklin Ave. E.
Minneapolis, MN 55406
(612) 332-7481
Carlo Cuesta, *Executive Director*

The Playwrights' Center fuels the theater by providing services that support playwrights and playwriting. Members receive applications for all programs, a calendar of events, eligibility to participate in special activities, including classes, outreach programs, and PlayLabs. For membership information, contact Jennifer Kane, Development and Communications Director. Annual dues: $40.

POETRY SOCIETY OF AMERICA
15 Gramercy Park
New York, NY 10003
(212) 254-9628; fax: (212) 673-2352
e-mail: poetrysocy@aol.com; web site: www.poetrysociety.org
Elise Paschen, *Executive Director*

Founded in 1910, the PSA seeks to raise the awareness of poetry, to deepen the understanding of it, and to encourage more people to read, listen to, and write poetry. To this end, the PSA presents national series of readings including "Tributes in Libraries" and "Poetry in Public Places," mounts poetry posters on mass transit vehicles through "Poetry in Motion," and broadcasts an educational poetry series on cable television. The PSA also offers annual contests for poetry, seminars, poetry festivals, and publishes a newsletter. Annual dues: from $40 ($25 for students).

POETS AND WRITERS, INC.
72 Spring St.
New York, NY 10012
(212) 226-3586; fax: (212) 226-3963
web site: http://www.pw.org
Elliot Figman, *Executive Director*
Poets & Writers, Inc., was founded in 1970 to foster the development of poets and fiction writers and to promote communication throughout the literary community. A non-membership organization, it offers a nationwide information center for writers; *Poets & Writers Magazine* and other publications; as well as support for readings and workshops at a wide range of venues.

PUBLICATION RIGHTS CLEARINGHOUSE
National Writers Union/National Office West
337 17th St., Suite 101
Oakland, CA 94612
(510) 839-0110; fax: (510) 839-6097
e-mail: nwu@nwu.org
Irvin Muchnick, *Director of Licensing*
Publication Rights Clearinghouse, the collective-licensing agency of the National Writers Union, was created in 1996 to help writers license and collect royalties for the reuse of their works in electronic databases and other new digital media. It is modeled after similar organizations that have long existed in the music industry. Enrollment is open to both NWU members and non-members. One-time enrollment fee is $20 for NWU members, or members of other writers' organizations that are associate sponsors of PRC; $40 for others.

ROMANCE WRITERS OF AMERICA
13700 Veterans Memorial Dr., Suite 315
Houston, TX 77014
(713) 440-6885; fax: (713) 440-7510
Allison Kelley, *Executive Manager*
An international organization with over 150 local chapters across the U.S., Canada, Europe, and Australia; membership is open to any writer, published or unpublished, interested in the field of romantic fiction. Annual dues of $60, plus $10 application fee for new members; benefits include annual conference, contest, market information, and monthly professional journal, *Romance Writers' Report*.

SCIENCE-FICTION AND FANTASY WRITERS OF AMERICA, INC.
532 La Guardia Pl., #632
New York, NY 10012-1428
Michael Capobianco, Pres.
An organization whose purpose it is to foster and further the professional interests of science fiction and fantasy writers. Presents the annual Nebula Award for excellence in the field and publishes the *Bulletin* and *SFWA Handbook* for its members (also available to non-members).

Any writer who has sold a work of science fiction or fantasy is eligible for membership. Annual dues: $50, *active* ; $35, *affiliate*; plus $10 installation fee; send for application and information.

SISTERS IN CRIME
P.O. Box 442124
Lawrence, KS 66044-8933
e-mail: sistersincrime@juno.com
Sue Henry, *President*

Sisters in Crime was founded in 1986 to combat discrimination against women in the mystery field, educate publishers and the general public as to inequalities in the treatment of female authors, and raise the level of awareness of their contribution to the field. Membership is open to all and includes writers, readers, editors, agents, booksellers, and librarians. Publications include a quarterly newsletter and membership directory. Annual dues: $35, U.S.; $40, foreign. Members interested in mysteries for young readers may join Mysteries for Minors (Elizabeth James, Chair, P.O. Box 442124, Lawrence, KS 66044-8933) with no additional dues.

SOCIETY FOR TECHNICAL COMMUNICATION
901 N. Stuart St., #904
Arlington, VA 22203-1854
(703) 522-4114
web site: http://www.stc-va.org.
William C. Stolgitis, *Executive Director*

A professional organization dedicated to the advancement of the theory and practice of technical communication in all media. The 21,000 members in the U.S. and other countries include technical writers and editors, publishers, artists and draftsmen, researchers, educators, and audiovisual specialists. Annual dues: $95.

SOCIETY OF AMERICAN TRAVEL WRITERS
4101 Lake Boone Trail, Suite 201
Raleigh, NC 27607
(919) 787-5181; fax: (919) 787-4916
e-mail: msoomg@aol.com
Michael S. Olson, CAE, *Executive Director*

The Society of American Travel Writers represents writers and other professionals who strive to provide travelers with accurate reports on destinations, facilities, and services. Membership is by invitation. Active membership is limited to travel writers and free lancers who have a steady volume of published or distributed work about travel. Application fees: $250, *active*; $500, *associate*. Annual dues: $120, *active*; $240, *associate*.

SOCIETY OF CHILDREN'S BOOK WRITERS & ILLUSTRATORS
345 N. Maple Dr., #296
Beverly Hills, CA 90210
web site: www.scbwi.org
Lin Oliver, *Executive Director*

A national organization of authors, editors, publishers, illustrators, librarians, and educators, the SCBWI offers a variety of services to people who write, illustrate, or share an interest in children's literature. Full memberships are open to those who have had at least one children's book or story published. Associate memberships are open to all those with an interest in children's literature. Annual dues: $50.

SOCIETY OF ENVIRONMENTAL JOURNALISTS
P.O. Box 27280
Philadelphia, PA 19118
(215) 836-9970; fax: (215) 836-9972
e-mail: SEJOffice@aol.com
web site: http://www.SEJ.org
Beth Parke, *Executive Director*

Dedicated to improving the quality, accuracy, and visibility of environmental reporting, the society serves 1,200 members with a quarterly newsletter, the *SEJournal*, national and regional conferences, computer online services on AOL, Compuserve, and the World Wide Web, and an annual directory. Annual dues: $35; $30, *student.*

SOCIETY OF PROFESSIONAL JOURNALISTS
16 S. Jackson St.
Greencastle, IN 46135-0077
(765) 653-3333; fax: (765) 653-4631
web site: http://spj.org
Greg Christopher, *Executive Director*

With 13,500 members and 300 chapters, the Society seeks to serve the interests of print, broadcast, and wire journalists. Services include legal counsel on journalism issues, jobs-for-journalists career search newsletter, professional development seminars, and awards that encourage journalism. Members receive *Quill*, a monthly magazine that explores current issues in the field. SPJ promotes ethics and freedom of information programs. Annual dues: $68, *professional*; $34, *student.*

THEATRE COMMUNICATIONS GROUP
355 Lexington Ave.
New York, NY 10017
(212) 697-5230
John Sullivan, *Executive Director*

TCG, a national organization for the American theater, provides services to facilitate the work of playwrights, literary managers, and other theater professionals. Publications include the annual *Dramatists Sourcebook* and a line of theater books including plays. Individual members receive *American Theatre* magazine. Annual dues: $35, *individual.*

WESTERN WRITERS OF AMERICA, INC.
1012 Fair St.
Franklin, TN 37064
(615) 791-1444
James A. Crutchfield, *Secretary/Treasurer*

Membership is open to qualified professional writers of fiction and nonfiction related to the history and literature of the American West. Its chief purpose is to promote a more widespread distribution, readership, and appreciation of the West and its literature. Holds annual convention in the last week of June. Sponsors annual Spur Awards, Owen Wister Award, and Medicine Pipe Bearer's Award for published work and produced screenplays. Annual dues: $75.

WRITERS GUILD OF AMERICA, EAST, INC.
555 W. 57th St.
New York, NY 10019
(212) 767-7800; fax: (212) 582-1909
web site: http://www.wgaeast.org
Mona Mangan, *Executive Director*

WRITERS GUILD OF AMERICA, WEST, INC.
7000 W. 3rd St.
Los Angeles, CA 90048
(213) 951-4000
Brian Walton, Executive Director
The Writers Guild of America (East and West) represents writers in motion pictures, broadcast, cable and new media industries, including news and entertainment. In order to qualify for membership, a writer must fulfill current requirements for employment or sale of material in one of these fields.
The basic dues are $25 per quarter for both organizations. In addition, there are quarterly dues based on percentage of the member's earnings in any one of the fields over which the guild has jurisdiction. The initiation fee is $1,500 for WGAE, for writers living east of the Mississippi, and $2,500 for WGAW, for those living west of the Mississippi.

WRITERS INFORMATION NETWORK
P.O. Box 11337
Bainbridge Island, WA 98110
(206) 842-9103; fax: (206) 842-0536
e-mail: WritersInfoNetwork@juno.com
web site: http://www.bluejaypub.com/win/
Elaine Wright Colvin, *Director*
W.I.N. was founded in 1983 to provide a link between Christian writers and the religious publishing industry. Offered are a bimonthly newsletter, market news, editorial services, advocacy and grievance procedures, referral services, and conferences. Annual dues: $29.95; $35, *foreign.*

LITERARY AGENTS

As the number of book publishers that will consider only agented submissions grows, more writers are turning to agents to sell their manuscripts. The agents in the following list handle both literary and dramatic material. Included in each listing are such important details as type of material represented, submission procedure, and commission. Since agents derive their income from the sales of their clients' work, they must represent writers who are selling fairly regularly to good markets. Nonetheless, many of the agents listed here note they will consider unpublished writers. Always query an agent first, and enclose a self-addressed, stamped envelope; most agents will not respond without it. Do not send any manuscripts until the agent has asked you to do so; and be wary of agents who charge fees for reading manuscripts. All of the following agents have indicated they do *not* charge reading fees, and those who pass on postage, phone, or photocopying fees to their clients have indicated such.

To learn more about agents and their role in publishing, the Association of Authors' Representatives, Inc., publishes a canon of ethics as well as an up-to-date list of AAR members, available for $7 (check or money order) and a 55¢ legal-size SASE. Write to: Association of Authors' Representatives, Inc., 10 Astor Pl., 3rd Floor, New York, NY 10003.

Another good source that lists agents and their policies is *Literary Market Place*, a directory found in most libraries.

BRET ADAMS LTD.— 448 W. 44th St., New York, NY 10036. Attn: Bruce Ostler or Bret Adams. Screenplays, teleplays, stage plays, and musicals. Unproduced writers considered. Query with synopsis, bio, resumé, and SASE. Commission: 10%. Fees: none.

LEE ALLAN AGENCY—7464 N. 107 St., Milwaukee, WI 53224-3706. Attn: Mr. Lee A. Matthias. Adult genre fiction, nonfiction. Screenplays. Unpublished writers considered. Query with SASE. Commission: 15% books; 10% scripts. Fees: photocopying, overnight shipping, telephone. "Go to a bookstore and locate the exact place in the store where your book would be displayed. If it realistically fits a popular market niche, is not derivative or imitative, meets the size constraints, and you can't make it any better yourself, you are ready to find an agent."

JAMES ALLEN LITERARY AGENT—538 East Harford St., P.O. Box 909, Milford, PA 18337. Attn: James Allen. Adult fiction. Query with 2- to 3-page synopsis; no multiple queries, requires exclusive. Commission: 10% domestic; 20% foreign. "My list is quite full these days; I'm mainly interested in taking on only people with previous booklength fiction publishing credits."

MICHAEL AMATO AGENCY— 1650 Broadway, Rm. 307, New York, NY 10019. Attn: Michael Amato. Screenplays. Send query or complete manuscript. Commission: 10%. Fees: none.

MARCIA AMSTERDAM AGENCY— 41 W. 82nd St., #9A, New York, NY 10024. Attn: Marcia Amsterdam. Adult and young adult fiction; mainstream nonfiction. Screenplays and teleplays: comedy, romance, psychological suspense. Query with resumé; multiple queries O.K.; three-week exclusive for requested submissions. Commission: 15% books; 10% scripts. Fees: photocopying and shipping.

AVATAR LITERARY AGENCY, INC.— 4611 S. University Dr., Suite 438, Davie, FL 33328. K. Lisa Brodsky, Agent. Fiction and nonfiction in all categories and genres, including collections of short stories and young adult novels. No other children's material; no poetry. Submit an e-mail query (avatar@reps.net); send hard copy with SASE; or send entire manuscript on diskette with SASE. Commission: 10% domestic; 15% foreign.

THE AXELROD AGENCY—54 Church St., Lenox, MA 01240. Adult fiction and nonfiction. Unpublished writers considered. Query; multiple queries O.K. Commission: 10% domestic; 20% foreign. Fees: photocopying.

MALAGA BALDI LITERARY AGENCY, INC.—2112 Broadway, Suite #403, New York, NY 10023. Attn: Malaga Baldi. Adult fiction and nonfiction. Unpublished writers considered. Query first; "if I am interested, I ask for proposal, outline, and sample pages for nonfiction, complete manuscript for fiction." Multiple queries O.K. Commission: 15%. Fees: none. Response time: 10 weeks minimum.

THE BALKIN AGENCY—P.O. Box 222, Amherst, MA 01004. Attn: Rick Balkin. Adult nonfiction. Unpublished writers considered. Query with outline; no multiple queries. Commission: 15% domestic; 20% foreign. Fees: none. "Most interested in serious nonfiction."

VIRGINIA BARBER AGENCY—101 Fifth Ave., New York, NY 10003. Adult fiction and nonfiction. No unsolicited manuscripts. Query with outline, sample pages, bio/resumé and SASE. No multiple queries. Commission: 15% domestic; 20% foreign. Fees: photocopying.

LORETTA BARRETT BOOKS—101 Fifth Ave., New York, NY 10003. Attn: Loretta Barrett. Adult fiction and nonfiction. Unpublished writers considered. Query with outline, bio/resumé, and SASE; no multiple queries. Commission: 15%. Response time: 4 weeks; "Please do not call before then."

REID BOATES LITERARY AGENCY—Box 328, 69 Cooks Crossroad, Pittstown, NJ 08867-0328. Attn: Reid Boates. Adult mainstream fiction and nonfiction. Unpublished writers considered. Query; no multiple queries. Commission: 15%. Fees: none.

BOOK DEALS, INC.—Civic Opera Bldg., 20 N. Wacker Dr., Suite 1928, Chicago, IL 60606. Caroline Carney, President. General-interest adult fiction and nonfiction. Query with lead, 2 sample chapters, and SASE. Commission: 15% domestic; 20% foreign. Fees: Professional expenses.

GEORGES BORCHARDT, INC.—136 E. 57th St., New York, NY 10022. Adult fiction and nonfiction. Unpublished writers considered by recommendation only. No unsolicited queries or submissions. Commission: 15%. Fees: photocopying, shipping.

BRANDT & BRANDT LITERARY AGENTS—1501 Broadway, New York, NY 10036. Adult fiction and nonfiction. Unpublished writers considered occasionally. Unsolicited query by letter only; no multiple queries. Commission: 15%. Fees: photocopying.

THE HELEN BRANN AGENCY—94 Curtis Rd., Bridgewater, CT 06752. Attn: Carol White. Adult fiction and nonfiction. Unpublished writers considered. Commission: 15%. Fees: none.

ANDREA BROWN LITERARY AGENCY—P.O. Box 429, El Granada, CA 94018. Attn: Andrea Brown. Juvenile fiction and nonfiction only. Unpublished writers considered with a reference or from a writers conference. Query with outline, sample pages, bio and resumé, and SASE; no faxes. Commission: 15% domestic; 20% foreign. Fees: none.

KNOX BURGER ASSOCIATES, LTD.—39½ Washington Square S., New York, NY 10012. Adult fiction and nonfiction. No science fiction, fantasy, or romance. Highly selective. Query with SASE; no multiple queries. Commission: 15%. Fees: photocopying.

SHEREE BYKOFSKY ASSOCIATES, INC.—11 East 47th St., New York, NY 10017. Adult nonfiction and fiction. Unpublished writers considered. Query with outline, up to 3 sample pages or proposal, and SASE. Multiple queries O.K. if indicated as such. Commission: 15%. Fees: none.

MARTHA CASSELMAN—P.O. Box 342, Calistoga, CA 94515-0342. Martha Casselman, Agent. Darlene Dozier, Associate. Nonfiction, especially interested in cookbooks. Unpublished writers considered. Query with outline, sample pages, bio/resumé, and SASE for return. Multiple queries O.K. if noted as such. Commission: 15%. Fees: photocopying, overnight and overseas mail, phone, fax.

JULIE CASTIGLIA AGENCY—1155 Camino del Mar, Suite 510, Del Mar, CA 92014. Attn: Julie Castiglia. Fiction: mainstream, ethnic and literary. Nonfiction: psychology, health, finance, women's issues, science, biography, business, outdoors, and niche books. Query letter; no unsolicited manuscripts. No multiple queries. Commission: 15%. No reading fees. "Please do not query on the phone. Attend workshops and writers' conferences before approaching an agent."

HY COHEN LITERARY AGENCY, LTD.—P.O. Box 43770, Upper Montclair, NJ 07043. Attn: Hy Cohen. Adult fiction, nonfiction, and juvenile. Unpublished writers considered. Unsolicited queries and manuscripts O.K., "with SASE, please!" Multiple submissions considered. Commission: 10% domestic; 20% foreign. Fees: phone, photocopying, postage.

RUTH COHEN, INC.—P.O. Box 7626, Menlo Park, CA 94025. Attn: Ruth Cohen. Adult mysteries and women's fiction; quality juvenile fiction and nonfiction. Unpublished writers seriously considered. Query with first 10 pages, synopsis, bio and resumé, and SASE. Commission: 15%. Fees: some shipping, photocopying, and foreign agents.

DON CONGDON ASSOCIATES, INC.—156 Fifth Ave., Suite 625, New York, NY 10010. Adult fiction and nonfiction. Query with outline; no multiple queries. Commission: 10% domestic. Fees: photocopying.

THE DOE COOVER AGENCY—P.O. Box 668, Winchester, MA 01890. Attn: Doe Coover, Colleen Mohyde. Adult fiction and general nonfiction. Unpublished writers considered. Query with outline, sample pages, bio/resumé, and SASE; multiple queries O.K. Commission: 15%. Fees: photocopying.

RICHARD CURTIS ASSOCIATES, INC.—171 E. 74th St., New York, NY 10021. Adult nonfiction. Unpublished writers considered. Query with bio/resumé and SASE; no multiple queries. Commission: 15% domestic; 20% foreign. Fees: photocopying, shipping, purchase of author copies, Federal Express.

CURTIS BROWN LTD.—10 Astor Pl., New York, NY 10003. General trade fiction and nonfiction; also juvenile. Unpublished writers considered. Query; no multiple queries. Commission: unspecified. Fees: photocopying; express mail.

ANITA DIAMANT AGENCY, INC.—310 Madison Ave., # 1105, New York, NY 10017. Attn: R. Rue. Adult fiction: literary, mystery, romance. Also nonfiction "anything not technical." Query with outline or sample pages, and bio/resumé. No multiple queries. Commission: 15%. Fees: none.

SANDRA DIJKSTRA LITERARY AGENCY—1155 Camino del Mar, Suite 515C, Del Mar, CA 92014. Attn: Sandra Zane. Adult and children's fiction and nonfiction. Query with outline and bio/resumé. For fiction, submit first 50 pages and synopsis; for nonfiction, submit proposal. Commission: 15% domestic, 20% foreign. Fees: none. SASE.

THE JONATHAN DOLGER AGENCY—49 E. 96th St., 9B, New York, NY 10128. Attn: Tom Wilson. Adult trade fiction and nonfiction. Considers unpublished writers. Query with outline and SASE. Commission: 15%. Fees: photocopying, shipping. "No category mysteries, romance, or science fiction."

DOUGLAS, GORMAN, ROTHACKER & WILHELM, INC.—1501 Broadway, Suite 703, New York, NY 10036. Attn: Literary Office. Screenplays and full-length teleplays. Query with 10-page synopsis, bio/resumé. Commission: 10%. Fees: none.

DWYER & O'GRADY, INC.—P.O. Box 239, East Lempster, NH 03605. Attn: Elizabeth O'Grady. Branch office: P.O. Box 790, Cedar Key, FL 32625. Specialize in children's picture books for ages 6 to 12. Require strong story line, dialogue, and character development. Unpublished writers considered. Query with bio/resumé; no multiple queries. Commission: 15%. Fees: photocopying, shipping. "Our primary focus is the representation of illustrators who also write their own stories; however, we represent authors who write for the children's market."

JANE DYSTEL LITERARY MANAGEMENT—One Union Square W., Suite 904, New York, NY 10003. Attn: Jane Dystel, Miriam Goderich. Adult fiction and nonfiction. Unpublished writers considered. Query with bio/resumé; no multiple queries. Commission: 15%. Fees: shipping.

EDUCATIONAL DESIGN SERVICES—P.O. Box 253, Wantaugh, NY 11793. Attn: Bertram L. Linder. Educational texts only. Unpublished writers considered. Query with outline, sample pages or complete manuscript, bio/resumé, and SASE. No multiple queries. Commission: 15%. Fees: none.

ETHAN ELLENBERG LITERARY AGENCY—548 Broadway, Suite 5E, New York, NY 10012. Ethan Ellenberg, Agent. Commercial and literary fiction and nonfiction. Specialize in first novels, thrillers, children's books, romance, science fiction, and fantasy. Nonfiction: health, new age/spirituality, pop-science, biography. No poetry or short stories. Query with first 3 chapters, synopsis, and SASE. "We respond within 2 weeks if interested." Commission: 15% domestic; 20% foreign. Fees: photocopying, shipping.

ANN ELMO AGENCY—60 E. 42nd St., New York, NY 10165. Attn: Lettie Lee, Andree Abecassis, or Mari Cronin. Adult fiction, nonfiction, and plays. Juvenile for middle grades and up. No picture books. Unpublished writers considered. Please query first with outline, sample pages, and bio/resumé. No multiple queries. Commission: 15%. Fees: none.

FELICIA ETH—555 Bryant St., Suite 350, Palo Alto, CA 94301. Attn: Felicia Eth. Small list of adult fiction, "highly selective, mostly contemporary." Also issue-oriented, provocative nonfiction. Unpublished writers considered. Query with outline, sample pages, and bio/resumé. Multiple queries O.K. if noted. Commission: 15% domestic; 20% foreign. Fees: photocopying. "I am a small, highly personal agency, not right for everyone but very committed to those I work with. I tend to work with writers based either on the West Coast or at least west of the Mississippi."

FARBER LITERARY AGENCY—14 E. 75th St., New York, NY 10021. Attn: Ann Farber. Adult fiction, nonfiction, and stage plays; juvenile books. Considers unpublished writers. Query with outline, sample pages, and SASE. Commission: 15% "with services of attorney." Fees: photocopying.

JOYCE FLAHERTY—816 Lynda Ct., St. Louis, MO 63122. Attn: Joyce Flaherty. "We accept only the work of currently published authors of book-length manuscripts, who continue to write in their specialties." Adult fiction and nonfiction. Query with outline, sample chapter (first chapter for nonfiction), and bio. Commission: 15% domestic; 30% foreign. Fees: none.

FLANNERY LITERARY—34-36 28th St., #5, Long Island City, NY 11106-3516. Attn: Jennifer Flannery. Fiction and nonfiction; juvenile. Unpublished writers considered. Query by letter only (no phone or fax queries); multiple queries O.K. Commission: 15%. Fees: none.

FOGELMAN LITERARY AGENCY—7515 Greenville Ave., Suite 712, Dallas, TX 75231. Attn: Linda M. Kruger. Adult romance. Commerical books of pop-culture. Query with SASE. Commission: 15% domestic; 10% foreign. Fees: none.

ROBERT A. FREEDMAN DRAMATIC AGENCY, INC.—1501 Broadway, Suite 2310, New York, NY 10036. Attn: Robert A. Freedman or Selma Luttinger. Screenplays, teleplays, and stage plays. Send query only; multiple queries O.K. Commission: standard. Fees: photocopying.

SAMUEL FRENCH, INC.— 45 W. 25th St., New York, NY 10010. Attn: Lawrence Harbison. Stage plays. Unpublished writers considered. Query with complete manuscript; unsolicited and multiple queries O.K. Fees: none.

GELFMAN SCHNEIDER—250 W. 57th St., Suite 2515, New York, NY 10107. Attn: Jane Gelfman. Adult fiction and nonfiction. Unpublished writers only considered if recommended by other writers or teachers. Query with outline, sample pages, and bio; no multiple queries. Commission: 15% domestic; 20% foreign. Fees: none.

GOLDFARB & GRAYBILL— 918 16th St. N.W., Suite 400, Washington, DC 20006. Attn: Nina Graybill. Adult fiction and nonfiction. No poetry, romance, science fiction, or children's books. Query with bio/resume; for fiction, include a synopsis, sample chapter. Multiple queries O.K. Commission: 15%. Fees: photocopying, shipping. "We appreciate succinct, grammatical query letters and samples."

GOODMAN ASSOCIATES—500 West End Ave., New York, NY 10024. Attn: Elise Simon Goodman. Adult fiction and nonfiction. Unpublished writers considered. Query with outline, sample pages, and bio/resume. Multiple queries O.K. Commission: 15% domestic; 20% foreign. Fees: photocopying, long-distance telephone, overseas postage.

SANFORD J. GREENBURGER—55 Fifth Ave., 15th Fl., New York, NY 10003. Attn: Faith Hornby Hamlin. Nonfiction, including sports books, health, business, psychology, parenting, science, biography, gay; juvenile books. Unpublished writers with strong credentials considered. Query with outline, sample pages, bio, and SASE; multiple queries O.K. Commission: 15% domestic; 20% foreign. Fees: photocopying.

MAIA GREGORY ASSOCIATES— 311 E. 72nd St., New York, NY 10021. Adult nonfiction only. Query with sample pages and bio/resume. No multiple queries. Commission: 15%. Fees: none.

THE CHARLOTTE GUSAY LITERARY AGENCY—10532 Blythe, Los Angeles, CA 90064. Screenplays. Query only, bio/resume, and SASE; multiple queries discouraged. Commission: 10%.

HARDEN CURTIS ASSOCIATES— 850 Seventh Ave., Suite 405, New York, NY 10019. Attn: Mary Harden. Stage plays. Query with bio and resume, SASE; no multiple queries. Commission: 10%. Fees: none.

JOY HARRIS LITERARY AGENCY, INC.—156 Fifth Ave., Suite 617, New York, NY 10010. Adult fiction and nonfiction. Unpublished writers considered. Query with outline, sample pages, and bio/resumé. No multiple queries. Commission: 15%. Fees: photocopying, shipping.

HEACOCK LITERARY AGENCY, INC.—1523 Sixth St., Suite 14, Santa Monica, CA 90401. Attn: Rosalie Heacock, Pres. Adult fiction and nonfiction. Published and unpublished writers welcome to query with outline, bio/resumé, and SASE. No multiple queries. Commission: 15%. Fees: out-of-pocket expenses. "The agency offers thoughtful representation and provides sounding board for new book ideas for established clientele. Please write your query letter as well as you write your original manuscript, for it is the first sample of your writing that the agent will see and evaluate. Good luck!"

FREDERICK HILL ASSOCIATES—1842 Union St., San Francisco, CA 94123. Attn: Irene Moore. Branch office: 8446½ Melrose Pl., Los Angeles, CA 90069. Adult fiction and nonfiction. Unpublished writers considered. Query with outline and bio/resumé; multiple queries O.K. Commission: 15%. Fees: photocopying, postage.

JOHN L. HOCHMANN BOOKS—320 E. 58th St., New York, NY 10022. Attn: John L. Hochmann. Nonfiction only: biography, social history, health and food, college textbooks. Unpublished writers considered, "provided they present evidence of substantial expertise in the field they are writing about." Query with outline, sample pages, bio/resumé, and SASE. No multiple queries. Commission: 15% for domestic/Canadian; plus 15% foreign language and U.K. Fees: photocopying. "Do not submit jacket copy. Submit detailed outlines and proposals that include evaluations of competing books."

BARBARA HOGENSON AGENCY—165 West End Ave., Suite 19-C, New York, NY 10023. Attn: Barbara Hogenson. Adult fiction, nonfiction. Screenplays, teleplays, and stage plays. Query with bio and synopsis, SASE; multiple queries O.K. Commission: 10% scripts; 15% books. Fees: none.

HULL HOUSE LITERARY AGENCY—240 E. 82nd St., New York, NY 10028. Attn: David Stewart Hull, Pres. New writers contact Lydia Mortimer, associate. Nonfiction: true crime, biography, military, general history. Fiction, especially crime fiction. Query with outline and bio/resumé; include sample pages with nonfiction queries only. Multiple queries O.K. Commission: 15% domestic; 10% foreign. Fees: photocopying, overseas fax and postage.

IMG BACH LITERARY AGENCY—22 E. 71st St., New York, NY 10021. Attn: Julian Bach, Carolyn Krupp. Adult fiction and nonfiction. Unpublished writers considered. Query with outline, sample pages, and bio/resumé. No multiple queries. Commission: 15%. Fees: photocopying.

INTERNATIONAL PUBLISHER ASSOCIATES, INC.—304 Guido Ave., Lady Lake, FL 32159. Attn: J. DeRogatis, Exec. Vice Pres. Adult fiction and nonfiction: current events, politics, business, biography, the arts, cooking, diet, health, sports, women, gardening, history, self-help, true crime, etc. No children's books. Unpublished writers considered. Query with outline, sample pages, and SASE; multiple queries O.K. Commission: 15% domestic, 20% foreign. Fees: photocopying, shipping.

SHARON JARVIS & CO.—Toad Hall, Inc., RR2, Box 16B, Laceyville, PA 18623. Adult fiction and nonfiction. Unpublished writers considered. Query with bio or resumé, and outline or synopsis. No unsolicited manuscripts. Commission: 15%. Fees: photocopying. "Pay attention to what's selling and what's commercial."

JCA LITERARY AGENCY, INC.—27 W. 20th St., Suite 1103, New York, NY 10011. Adult fiction and nonfiction. Unpublished writers considered.

Query with sample pages; multiple queries O.K. Commission: 15% domestic, 20% foreign. Fees: photocopying, shipping. "Be as straightforward and to-the-point as possible. Don't try to hype us or bury us in detail."

NATASHA KERN LITERARY AGENCY, INC.—P.O. Box 2908, Portland, OR 97208-2908. Attn: Natasha Kern. Adult fiction and nonfiction. Query. Commission: 15% domestic; 10% foreign. Fees: none.

LOUISE B. KETZ AGENCY—1485 First Ave., Suite 4B, New York, NY 10021. Attn: Louise B. Ketz. Adult nonfiction on science, business, sports, history, and reference. Considers unpublished writers "with proper credentials." Query with outline and bio/resumé; multiple queries occasionally considered. Commission: 10% to 15%. Fees: photocopying, shipping.

KIDDE, HOYT & PICARD—335 E. 51st St., New York, NY 10022. Attn: Katharine Kidde, Laura Langlie. General interest/trade nonfiction on current affairs, social sciences, and the arts. Adult mainstream fiction; literary, mysteries, romances, historical. No science fiction, horror, or poetry. Unpublished writers not considered, "but we'll consider writers who have published short fiction or nonfiction—a published book is not necessary." Query with 2 or 3 chapters and synopsis; also include past writing experience. Multiple queries O.K. Commission: 15%. Fees: photocopying, postage.

KIRCHOFF/WOHLBERG, INC.—866 United Nations Plaza, Suite 525, New York, NY 10017. Attn: Liza Voges. Juvenile fiction and nonfiction only. Unpublished writers considered. Query; multiple submissions O.K. Commission: 15%. Fees: none.

HARVEY KLINGER, INC.—301 W. 53rd St., New York, NY 10019. Attn: Harvey Klinger. Adult fiction and nonfiction. Unpublished writers considered. Query with outline, sample pages, and bio/resumé. No multiple queries. Commission: 15% domestic; 25% foreign. Fees: photocopying, shipping.

BARBARA S. KOUTS—P.O. Box 560, Bellport, NY 11713. Attn: Barbara S. Kouts. Adult fiction, nonfiction, and juvenile. Unpublished writers considered. Query with bio/resumé. Multiple queries O.K. Commission: 10%. Fees: photocopying. "Send your best work always!"

PETER LAMPACK AGENCY, INC.—551 Fifth Ave., Suite 1613, New York, NY 10176. Attn: Sandra Blanton, Agent. Loren Soeiro, Assoc. Agent. Literary and commercial fiction; "We like contemporary relationship and historical fiction in addition to thrillers, psychological suspense, mystery, action-adventure. We do not handle romance, science fiction, or horror." Also handle biography/autobiography, nonfiction on politics, finance, and law written by experts in the fields. Unpublished writers considered. Query with synopsis/outline and bio/resumé. Sample pages will be solicited after queries. Multiple queries O.K. Commission: 15% domestic; 20% foreign. Fees: photocopying.

MICHAEL LARSEN/ELIZABETH POMADA—1029 Jones St., San Francisco, CA 94109. Attn: M. Larsen, nonfiction; E. Pomada, fiction. Fiction: literary, commercial, and genre. Nonfiction: general, including biography, business, nature, health, history, arts, travel. Unpublished writers welcome. Query for fiction with first 30 pages, synopsis, SASE, and phone number; send #10 SASE for brochure. For nonfiction, query by phone: (415) 673-0939. Multiple queries O.K., "as long as we're told." Commission: 15%. Fees: none.

THE MAUREEN LASHER AGENCY—P.O. Box 888, Pacific Palisades, CA 90272. Attn: Ann Cashman. Adult fiction and nonfiction. Unpublished writers considered. Query with outline, sample pages, and bio/resumé. No multiple queries. Commission: 15%. Fees: none.

LEVANT & WALES, INC.—108 Hayes St., Seattle, WA 98109. Attn: Elizabeth Wales, Adrienne Reed. Adult fiction and nonfiction. Unpublished writers considered. Query with outline, sample pages, and bio/resumé. Multiple queries O.K. Commission: 15%. Fees: photocopying.

ELLEN LEVINE LITERARY AGENCY, INC.—15 E. 26th St., Suite 1801, New York, NY 10010. Adult fiction and nonfiction; juvenile material. Unpublished writers considered. Query with SASE. Commission: 15% domestic; 20% foreign. Fees: photocopying, shipping.

LICHTMAN, TRISTER, SINGER & ROSS—1666 Connecticut Ave. N.W., Suite 500, Washington, DC 20009. Attn: Gail Ross, Howard Yoon. Adult nonfiction. Unpublished writers considered. Query with outline, sample pages, resumé, and SASE. Multiple queries O.K. Commission: 15%. Fees: none.

NANCY LOVE LITERARY AGENCY—250 E. 65th St., New York, NY 10021. Mostly nonfiction, including medical, alternative health care, parenting, spiritual and inspirational books, social issues, current affairs, crime, self-help; some fiction, but no genre except mysteries and thrillers. Unpublished writers considered. Query; no multiple submissions on novels. Commission: 15%. Fees: photocopying.

DONALD MAASS LITERARY AGENCY—157 W. 57th St., Suite 703, New York, NY 10019. Attn: Donald Maass, Pres. Jennifer Jackson, Associate. Adult fiction: science fiction, fantasy, mystery, suspense, historical, romance, mainstream, literary. Unpublished writers considered. Query with SASE; multiple queries O.K. if noted as such. Commission: 15% domestic; 20% foreign. Fees: none.

GINA MACCOBY LITERARY AGENCY—P.O. Box 60, Chappaqua, NY 10514. Adult fiction and nonfiction; juvenile for all ages. Unpublished writers considered. Query; multiple queries O.K. Commission: 15%. Fees: photocopying, overseas postage, bank charges for converting foreign currencies. No unsolicited manuscripts.

CAROL MANN LITERARY AGENCY—55 Fifth Ave., New York, NY 10003. Attn: Carol Mann. Christy Fletcher, subs rights. 30% fiction; 70% nonfiction. Query; multiple queries O.K. Commission: 15%. Fees: photocopying, shipping.

MANUS ASSOCIATES, INC.— 417 E. 57th St., Suite 5D, New York, NY 10022. Attn: Janet Manus. Branch office: 430 Cowper St., Palo Alto, CA 94301. Adult fiction and nonfiction. No science fiction, category romance, or military books. Unpublished writers considered. Query with outline, sample pages, and bio/resumé. Multiple queries O.K. "on occasion." Commission: 15%. Fees: photocopying, shipping.

ELISABETH MARTON AGENCY— One Union Square W., Rm. 612, New York, NY 10003-3303. Attn: Tonda Marton. Plays only. Not considering new work at this time. Commission: 10%. Fees: none.

JED MATTES, INC.—2095 Broadway, #302, New York, NY 10023-2895. Adult fiction and nonfiction. Unpublished writers considered. Query; multiple queries O.K. Commission: 15% domestic; 20% foreign. Fees: none.

HELMUT MEYER LITERARY AGENCY—330 E. 79th St., New York, NY 10021. Attn: Helmut Meyer, Literary Agent. Adult fiction and nonfiction.

Telephone queries preferred: (212) 288-2421. For letter queries, include outline, sample pages, and bio/resumé. No multiple queries. Commission: 15%. Fees: none.

HENRY MORRISON, INC.—Box 235, Bedford Hills, NY 10507. Adult fiction and nonfiction; book-length only. Unpublished writers considered. Query with outline; multiple queries O.K. Commission: 15% domestic; 20% foreign. Fees: photocopying, shipping. "We are concentrating on a relatively small list of clients, and work toward building them in the U.S. and international marketplaces. We tend to avoid autobiographical novels and extremely literary novels, but always seek good nonfiction on major political and historical subjects."

MULTIMEDIA PRODUCT DEVELOPMENT— 410 S. Michigan Ave., Suite 724, Chicago, IL 60605. Jane Jordan Browne, Pres. Adult fiction and nonfiction, as well as juvenile fiction and nonfiction. "We are interested in commercial, overnight sellers in the areas of mainstream fiction and nonfiction." No short stories, poems, screenplays, articles, or software. Query with bio and SASE. Commission: 15% domestic; 20% foreign. Fees: photocopying, foreign postage.

JEAN V. NAGGAR LITERARY AGENCY—216 E. 75th St., New York, NY 10021. Attn: Jean Naggar, Frances Kuffel, or Anne Engel (nonfiction). Adult mainstream fiction and nonfiction; no romance or formula science fiction. Signs on "hardly any" new writers. Query with outline, SASE, bio, and resumé; query for completed novels only; no multiple queries. Commission: 15%. Fees: long-distance calls, galleys, etc.; no reading fee.

RUTH NATHAN AGENCY—53 E. 34th St., Suite 207, New York, NY 10016. Decorative arts, show business, biography. Selected historical fiction, pre-1500. No unsolicited queries. Commission: 15%. Fees: photocopying, shipping. "To writers seeking an agent: Please note what my specialties are. Do not send science fiction, fantasy, children's books, or business books."

NEW ENGLAND PUBLISHING ASSOCIATES—P.O. Box 5, Chester, CT 06412. Attn: Elizabeth Frost Knappman, Edward W. Knappman. Adult nonfiction, especially women's studies, minority issues, literature, business, and reference. Unpublished writers considered. Query; "send a carefully thought-out proposal with concept statement, market analysis, competitive survey, author bio, annotated chapter outline, and 50 to 70 pages of sample chapters. Write a thorough proposal and never give up." Commission: 15% domestic; 20% foreign. Fees: none.

BETSY NOLAN LITERARY AGENCY—224 W. 29th St., 15th Fl., New York, NY 10001. Attn: Betsy Nolan. Adult nonfiction, especially popular psychology, child care, cookbooks, gardening, music books, African-American and Jewish issues. Query. Commission: 15%. Fees: none.

THE RICHARD PARKS AGENCY—138 E. 16th St., 5B, New York, NY 10003. Adult nonfiction; fiction by referral only. Unpublished writers considered. Query with SASE; multiple queries O.K. if noted as such. Commission: 15% domestic; 20% foreign. Fees: photocopying. "No phone calls or faxed queries, please."

L. PERKINS ASSOCIATES—5800 Arlington Ave., Suite 18J, Riverdale, NY 10471. Attn: Lori Perkins or Peter Rubie. Adult fiction and nonfiction. No romance or children's books. Unpublished writers considered. Query with outline, sample pages, bio, and resumé; multiple queries O.K. Commission:

15% U.S.; 20% foreign. Fees: photocopying, shipping. "No unprofessional presentation or behavior; keep queries simple, direct, and to the point."

JAMES PETER ASSOCIATES, INC.—P.O. Box 772, Tenafly, NJ 07670. Attn: Bert Holtje. Adult nonfiction. Unpublished writers considered. Query with outline, sample pages, and bio/resumé. No multiple queries. Commission: 15%. Fees: none.

ALISON PICARD, LITERARY AGENT—P.O. Box 2000, Cotuit, MA 02635. Attn: Alison Picard. Adult fiction, nonfiction, and juvenile. Unpublished writers considered. Query; multiple queries O.K. Commission: 15%. Fees: none.

PINDER LANE & GARON-BROOKE ASSOCIATES, LTD.—159 W. 53rd St., Suite 14-E, New York, NY 10019. Attn: Dick Duane, Robert Thixton, or Nancy Coffey. Adult fiction and nonfiction. Unpublished writers considered. Query with outline, bio/resumé, and SASE; no multiple queries. Commission: 15% domestic; 30% foreign. Fees: photocopying.

SUSAN ANN PROTTER—110 W. 40th St., Suite 1408, New York, NY 10018. Adult fiction and nonfiction only, specializing in mysteries, contemporary thrillers and science fiction, health, psychology, true crime, self-help, popular science, medicine, and parenting. Query by mail only, with description, bio/resumé, synopsis, and SASE. Commission: unspecified. Fees: $10 handling fee for requested manuscripts to cover cost of return.

ROBERTA PRYOR, INC.—288 Titicus Rd., North Salem, NY 10560. Attn: Roberta Pryor. Adult fiction, nonfiction, current affairs, biographies, ecology. Unpublished writers considered. Query with outline, sample pages, and bio/resumé. Multiple queries O.K. Commission: 10% domestic; 10% foreign and film. Fees: photocopying, Federal Express. "When submitting book proposals, taboo is the coy refusal to give away any plot resolution. How do we know the author can resolve his plot, take care of loose ends? Some applicants feel a copywriter's approach, i.e. jacket copy come-on, will tickle our fancy. Not so."

RAINES & RAINES—71 Park Ave., Suite 4A, New York, NY 10016. Attn: Keith Korman, Joan Raines, Theron Raines. Adult fiction, nonfiction, and juvenile for all ages. Query; no multiple queries. Commission: 15% domestic; 20% foreign. Fees: photocopying and copies of books. "Keep query to one page."

HELEN REES LITERARY AGENCY—308 Commonwealth Ave., Boston, MA 02115. Literary fiction and nonfiction. No short stories, science fiction, or poetry. Unpublished writers considered. Query with outline, bio/resumé, and sample, to 50 pages. No multiple queries. Commission: 15%. Fees: none.

NAOMI REICHSTEIN LITERARY AGENCY—5031 Foothills Rd., Room G, Lake Oswego, OR 97034. Attn: Naomi Reichstein, Agent. Adult fiction and nonfiction: novels, history, cultural studies and issues, travel, geography, the environment, science, music, the arts, architecture, memoirs, literature, psychology, how-to, and humor. Commission: 15% domestic; 20% foreign.

JODY REIN BOOKS, INC.—7741 S. Ash Ct., Littleton, CO 80122. Attn: Sandra Bond. Literary and mainstream adult nonfiction by writers who have genuine expertise and solid writing skills. Query with SASE. Commission: 15%. Fees: shipping.

RENAISSANCE/H.N. SWANSON, INC.—8523 Sunset Blvd., Los Angeles, CA 90069. Attn: Steven Fisher or Brian Lipson, Agents. Screenplays and teleplays. Unpublished, unproduced writers sometimes considered. Query first; no multiple queries. Commission: 10%. Fees: none.

JANE ROTROSEN AGENCY—318 E. 51st St., New York, NY 10022. Attn: Ruth Kagle, Andrea Cirillo, Meg Ruley, or Stephanie Tade. Adult fiction and nonfiction. Unpublished writers considered. Query; multiple queries O.K. Commission: 15% U.S. and Canada; 20% foreign and film/TV. Fees: none.

PESHA RUBINSTEIN LITERARY AGENCY—1392 Rugby Rd., Teaneck, NJ 07666. Attn: Pesha Rubinstein. Commercial fiction and nonfiction. Contemporary women's fiction. Juvenile books. No poetry or short stories. Unpublished writers considered. Query with first 10 pages; multiple queries O.K. Commission: 15% domestic, 20% foreign. Fees: photocopying. "Don't tell me you'll make me rich. Do tell me the ending of the story in the synopsis."

RUSSELL & VOLKENING, INC.—50 W. 29th St., New York, NY 10001. Adult and juvenile fiction and nonfiction; specializing in literary fiction and narrative nonfiction. Queries for juvenile books should be addressed to Jennie Dunham. No screenplays, horror, romance, science fiction, or poetry. Unpublished writers considered. Query with letter and SASE. Commission: 10%. Fees: none.

RUSSELL-SIMENAUER LITERARY AGENCY, INC.— See *Jacqueline Simenauer Literary Agency, Inc.*

SANDUM & ASSOCIATES—144 E. 84th St., New York, NY 10028. Attn: Howard E. Sandum. Primarily nonfiction. Query with sample pages and bio/resumé. Multiple queries O.K. Commission: 15% domestic; 10% when foreign or TV/film subagents are used. "We do not consider manuscripts in genres such as science fiction, romance, or horror unless surpassing literary qualities are present."

SEBASTIAN AGENCY—333 Kearny St., Suite 708, San Francisco, CA 94108. Attn: Laurie Harper. Adult nonfiction only. "We have a full and active client list, so we must be very selective. We continue to look at proposals, mainly in the areas of psychology, consumer reference, health and beauty, or business books." Query with outline and bio. Commission: 15% domestic; 20% to 25% foreign. Fees: $100 annual administrative fee to all clients.

THE SHUKAT COMPANY, LTD.—340 W. 55th St., Suite 1A, New York, NY 10019. Attn: Scott Shukat, Pat McLaughlin, or Maribel Rivas. Screenplays and stage plays. Unpublished, unproduced writers occasionally considered. Query with outline, sample pages, and bio; no multiple queries. Commission: 15%. Fees: none. "Since this is a small office, we will reply only if we are interested in the material. SASE not necessary."

BOBBE SIEGEL, RIGHTS LITERARY AGENT— 41 W. 83rd St., New York, NY 10024. Attn: Bobbe Siegel. Adult fiction and nonfiction. Unpublished writers considered. Query; multiple queries O.K. SASE required. Commission: 15%. Fees: photocopying and faxes. "Keep query short, to the point, and literate. Don't sing your own praises; manuscript should speak for itself."

JACQUELINE SIMENAUER LITERARY AGENCY, INC.—(formerly *Russell-Simenauer Literary Agency*) P.O. Box 43267, Upper Montclair, NJ 07043. Attn: Jacqueline Simenauer. Nonfiction: medical, pop psych, how-to/self-help, women's issues, health, alternative health concepts, fitness, diet, nutrition, current issues, true crime, business, celebrities, reference. Fiction: literary, commercial, mysteries, historical novels, first novels. Query with outline, SASE. Multiple queries O.K. Commission: 15% domestic; 25% foreign. Fees: phone, photocopying.

F. JOSEPH SPIELER LITERARY AGENCY—154 W. 57th St., Rm. 135, New York, NY 10019. Attn: F. Joseph Spieler, Lisa M. Ross, John F. Thornton, Literary Agents. Branch office: Victoria Shoemaker, Agent, The Spieler Agency West, 1760 Solano Ave., Suite 300, Berkeley, CA 94707. Adult fiction and nonfiction; also juvenile for all ages. Unpublished writers considered. Query with outline; no multiple queries. Commission: 15%. Fees: third-party charges (e.g., messengers, photocopying) will be billed back at discretion, regardless of sale of project. No material will be returned if no SASE.

PHILIP G. SPITZER LITERARY AGENCY—50 Talmage Farm Ln., East Hampton, NY 11937. Attn: Philip Spitzer. Adult fiction and nonfiction. Query. Commission: 15% domestic; 20% foreign. Fees: photocopying.

GLORIA STERN AGENCY—2929 Buffalo Speedway, #2111, Houston, TX 77098. Attn: Gloria Stern. Adult nonfiction, literary fiction. Query with short outline, bio/resume, one chapter, and SASE. Multiple queries O.K. Commission: 15%. Fees: photocopying.

GUNTHER STUHLMANN, AUTHOR'S REPRESENTATIVE—P.O. Box 276, Becket, MA 01223. Attn: Barbara Ward. Literary fiction and nonfiction, especially biography, letters, and history. No mysteries, romance, science fiction, or adventure. Unpublished writers sometimes considered. Query with letter and SASE; no multiple queries. Commission: 10% North America; 15% Britain and Commonwealth; 20% foreign. "We take on few new clients at this time."

THE TANTLEFF OFFICE—375 Greenwich St., Suite 700, New York, NY 10013. Attn: Charmaine Ferenczi, stage plays. Jill Bock, film and television. Stage plays, screenplays, teleplays. Unpublished writers considered. Query with synopsis, up to 10 sample pages, bio/resumé; multiple queries O.K. Commission: 10% scripts. Fees: none.

JOHN A. WARE LITERARY AGENCY—392 Central Park W., New York, NY 10025. Attn: John Ware. Adult fiction and nonfiction. "Literate, accessible, noncategory fiction, plus thrillers and mysteries." Nonfiction: biography, history, current affairs, investigative journalism, social criticism, Americana and folklore, science, medicine, sports, memoir. Unpublished writers considered. Query letter only, with SASE; multiple queries O.K. Commission: 15% domestic; 20% foreign. Fees: photocopying. "No telephone queries, please, without referral."

WATKINS/LOOMIS AGENCY—133 E. 35th St., Suite One, New York, NY 10016. Attn: Tracy Smith. Adult fiction and nonfiction. Unpublished writers considered. Query with SASE; no multiple queries. Commission: 15%. Fees: none.

SANDRA WATT & ASSOCIATES—8033 Sunset Blvd., Suite 4053, Los Angeles, CA 90046. Attn: Sandra Watt. Adult fiction and nonfiction. Unpublished writers considered. Query with bio/resumé; multiple submissions O.K. Commission: 15%. Fees: marketing fees for shipping, telephone, faxes, for new writers only. "We're old fashioned. We love good writing."

WIESER & WIESER, INC.—118 E. 25th St.,7th Fl., New York, NY 10010. Attn: Olga Wieser. Adult fiction and nonfiction. Unpublished writers considered. Query with outline and bio/resumé. No multiple queries. Commission: 15%. Fees: photocopying, shipping.

WITHERSPOON ASSOCIATES—235 E. 31st St., New York, NY 10016. Adult fiction and nonfiction. Unpublished writers considered. Query with sample pages; no multiple queries. Commission: 15%. Fees: none.

RUTH WRESCHNER, AUTHORS' REPRESENTATIVE—10 W. 74th St., New York, NY 10023. Attn: Ruth Wreschner. Adult fiction (mainstream novels, genre books, mysteries, romance) and nonfiction (by experts in a particular field); also young adult. No pornography, incest, or sexual abuse. Unpublished writers considered. Query with outline, sample pages, and bio/resumé. Multiple queries O.K. Commission: 15% domestic; 20% foreign. Fees: photocopying and postage.

ANN WRIGHT REPRESENTATIVES—165 W. 46th St., Suite 1105, New York, NY 10036-2501. Attn: Dan Wright. Adult fiction must have strong film potential. Unpublished writers considered. Screenplays and teleplays. Query with bio/resumé and SASE. No multiple queries. Commission: 10% to 20%. Fees: photocopying, shipping.

WRITERS HOUSE—21 W. 26th St., New York, NY 10010. Attn: Simon Lipskar, fiction. John Hodgeman, nonfiction; Alexa Lichtenstein, juvenile and young adult. Liza Landsman, multimedia. Adult fiction and nonfiction; juvenile for all ages; and young adult. Unpublished writers considered. "Query with one-page letter on why your project is excellent, what it's about, and why you're the wonderful author to write it." No multiple queries. Commission: 15% domestic; 20% foreign. Fees: out-of-pocket expenses only.

WRITERS' PRODUCTIONS—P.O. Box 630, Westport, CT 06881. Attn: David L. Meth. Adult fiction and nonfiction, both of literary quality. Children's books that fit into multimedia fantasies. Unpublished writers considered. Query with SASE. Multiple queries considered, but not preferred. Commission: 15% domestic; 25% foreign, dramatic, multimedia, software sales, licensing, and merchandising. Fees: photocopying, shipping. "Send your best, most professional written work. Research your market, know your field."

ZACHARY SHUSTER LITERARY AGENCY—375 Riverside Dr., New York, NY 10025. Attn: Lane Zachary or Todd Shuster. Branch office: 45 Newbury St., Boston, MA 02116. Adult fiction and nonfiction. Juvenile fiction and nonfiction. Screenplays. Query with sample pages or submit complete manuscript. Commission: 15% domestic; 20% foreign. Fees: none.

SUSAN ZECKENDORF ASSOCIATES, INC.—171 W. 57th St., New York, NY 10019. Attn: Susan Zeckendorf. Fiction: literary fiction; mysteries; thrillers; women's commercial fiction. Nonfiction: science; music; biography; social history. Unpublished writers considered. Query with outline and bio/resumé. Commission: 15% domestic; 20% foreign. Fees: photocopying. "Keep your description of the work brief."

Glossary

Advance—The amount a publisher pays a writer before a book is published; it is deducted from the royalties earned from sales of the finished book.

Agented material—Submissions from literary or dramatic agents to a publisher. Some publishing companies accept agented material only.

All rights—Some magazines purchase all rights to the material they publish, which means that they can use it as they wish, as many times as they wish. They cannot purchase all rights unless the writer gives them written permission to do so.

Assignment—A contract, written or oral, between an editor and writer, confirming that the writer will complete a specific project by a certain date, and for a certain fee.

B&W—Abbreviation for black-and-white photographs.

Book outline—Chapter-by-chapter summary of a book, frequently in paragraph form, allowing an editor to evaluate the book's content, tone, and pacing, and determine whether he or she wants to see the entire manuscript for possible publication.

Book packager—Company that puts together all the elements of a book, from initial concept to writing, publishing, and marketing it. Also called **book producer** or **book developer.**

Byline—Author's name as it appears on a published piece.

Clips—Copies of a writer's published work, often used by editors to evaluate the writer's talent.

Column inch—One inch of a typeset column; often serves as a basis for payment.

Contributor's copies—Copies of a publication sent to a writer whose work is included in it.

Copy editing—Line-by-line editing to correct errors in spelling, grammar, and punctuation, and inconsistencies in style. Differs from **content editing,** which evaluates flow, logic, and overall message.

Copy —Manuscript pages before they are set into type.

Copyright —Legal protection of creative works from unauthorized use. Under the law, copyright is secured automatically when the work is set down for the first time in written or recorded form.

Cover letter—A brief letter that accompanies a manuscript or book proposal. A cover letter is *not* a query letter (see definition, page 875).

Deadline —The date on which a written work is due at the editor's office, agreed to by author and editor.

Draft —A complete version of an article, story, or book. **First drafts** are often called **rough drafts.**

Fair use—A provision of the copyright law allowing brief passages of copyrighted material to be quoted without infringing on the owner's rights.

Feature —An article that is generally longer than a news story and whose main focus is an issue, trend, or person.

Filler—Brief item used to fill out a newspaper or magazine column; could be a news item, joke, anecdote, or puzzle.

First serial rights—The right of a magazine or newspaper to publish a work for the first time in any periodical. After that, all rights revert to the writer.

Galleys—The first typeset proofs of a manuscript, before they are divided into pages.

Ghostwriter—Author of books, articles, and speeches that are credited to someone else.

Glossy—Black-and-white photo with a shiny, rather than a matte, finish.

Hard copy—The printed copy of material written on a computer.

Honorarium—A modest, token fee paid by a publication to an author in gratitude for a submission.

International reply coupon (IRC) —Included with any correspondence or submission to a foreign publication; allows the editor to reply by mail without incurring cost.

Kill fee—Fee paid for an article that was assigned but subsequently not published; usually a percentage of the amount that would have been paid if the work had been published.

Lead time—Time between the planning of a magazine or book and its publication date.

Libel—A false accusation or published statement that causes a person embarrassment, loss of income, or damage to reputation.

Little magazines—Publications with limited circulation whose content often deals with literature or politics.

Mass market—Books appealing to a very large segment of the reading public and often sold in such outlets as drugstores, supermarkets, etc.

Masthead—A listing of the names and titles of a publication's staff members.

Ms—Abbreviation for manuscript; mss is the plural abbreviation.

Multiple submissions—Also called **simultaneous submissions.** Complete manuscripts sent simultaneously to different publications. Once universally discouraged by editors, the practice is gaining more acceptance, though some still frown on it. **Multiple queries** are generally accepted, however, since reading them requires less of an investment in time on the editor's part.

On speculation—Editor agrees to consider a work for publication "on speculation," without any guarantee that he or she will ultimately buy the work.

One-time rights—Editor buys manuscript from writer and agrees to publish it one time, after which the rights revert to the author for subsequent sales.

Op-ed—A newspaper piece, usually printed opposite the editorial page, that expresses a personal viewpoint on a timely news item.

Over-the-transom—Describes the submission of unsolicited material by a free-lance writer; the term harks back to the time when mail was delivered through the open window above an office door.

Payment on acceptance—Payment to writer when manuscript is submitted.

Payment on publication—Payment to writer when manuscript is published.

Pen name —A name other than his or her legal name that an author uses on written work.

Public domain—Published material that is available for use without permission, either because it was never copyrighted or because its copyright term is expired. Works published at least 75 years ago are considered in the public domain.

Q-and-A format—One type of presentation for an interview article, in which questions are printed, followed by the interviewee's answers.

Query letter—A letter—usually no longer than one page—in which a writer proposes an article idea to an editor.

Rejection slip—A printed note in which a publication indicates that it is not interested in a submission.

Reporting time—The weeks or months it takes for an editor to evaluate a submission.

Reprint rights—The legal right of a magazine or newspaper to print an article, story, or poem after it has already appeared elsewhere.

Royalty—A percentage of the amount received from retail sales of a book, paid to the author by the publisher. For hardcovers, the royalty is generally 10% on the first 5,000 copies sold; 12 ½% on the next 5,000 sold; 15% thereafter. Paperback royalties range from 4% to 8%, depending on whether it's a trade or mass-market book.

SASE—Self-addressed, stamped envelope, required with all submissions that the author wishes returned— either for return of material or (if you don't need material returned) for editor's reply.

Slush pile—The stack of unsolicited manuscripts in an editor's office.

Tear sheet—The pages of a magazine or newspaper on which an author's work is published.

Unsolicited submission—A manuscript that an editor did not specifically ask to see.

Vanity publisher—Also called **subsidy publisher.** A publishing company that charges author all costs of printing a book. No reputable book publisher operates on this subsidy basis.

Work for hire—When a work is written on a "for hire" basis, all rights in it become the property of the publisher. Though the work-for-hire clause applies mostly to work done by regular employees of a company, some editors offer work-for-hire agreements to free lancers. Think carefully before signing such agreements, however, since by doing so you will essentially be signing away your rights and will not be able to try to resell your work on your own.

Writers guidelines—A formal statement of a publication's editorial needs, payment schedule, deadlines, and other essential information.

INDEX TO MARKETS